W9-AAN-192

THE ROUGH GUIDE TO

The Pyrenees

WITHDRAWN

There are more than two hundred Rough Guide titles
covering destinations from Alaska to Zimbabwe
and subjects from Acoustic Guitar to Travel Health

Forthcoming travel guides include
Devon & Cornwall • Malta • Tenerife
Thai Beaches and Islands • US Rockies • Vancouver

Forthcoming reference guides include
Cuban Music • 100 Essential Latin CDs • Personal Computers
Pregnancy & Birth • Trumpet & Trombone

Rough Guides Online
www.roughguides.com

ROUGH GUIDE CREDITS

Text editor: David Glen
Series editor: Mark Ellingham
Editorial: Martin Dunford, Jonathan Buckley, Jo Mead, Kate Berens, Amanda Tomlin, Ann-Marie Shaw, Paul Gray, Helena Smith, Judith Bamber, Orla Duane, Olivia Eccleshall, Ruth Blackmore, Geoff Howard, Claire Saunders, Gavin Thomas, Alexander Mark Rogers, Polly Thomas, Joe Staines, Andrew Tomičić, Richard Lim, Duncan Clark, Peter Buckley, Sam Thorne, Lucy Ratcliffe, Clifton Wilkinson (UK); Andrew Rosenberg, Mary Beth Maioli, Stephen Timblin, Yuki Takagaki (US)
Production: Susanne Hillen, Andy Hilliard, Link Hall, Helen Ostick, Julia Bovis, Michelle Draycott, Katie Pringle, Robert Evers, Mike Hancock, Zoë Nobes

Cartography: Melissa Baker, Maxine Repath, Ed Wright, Katie Lloyd-Jones
Picture research: Louise Boulton, Sharon Martins
Online: Kelly Cross, Anja Mutić-Blessing, Jennifer Gold, Audra Epstein, Suzanne Welles (US)
Finance: John Fisher, Gary Singh, Edward Downey, Mark Hall, Tim Bill
Marketing & Publicity: Richard Trillo, Niki Smith, David Wearn, Chloë Roberts, Birgit Hartmann, Claire Southern (UK); Simon Carloss, David Wechsler, Kathleen Rushforth (US)
Administration: Tania Hummel, Demelza Dallow, Julie Sanderson

ACKNOWLEDGEMENTS

The editor would like to thank: Link Hall for typesetting; Maxine Repath and Sam Kirby for cartography; Louise Boulton for cover design; Sharon Martins for picture editing; and Jo Mead for editorial guidance.

Marc Dubin would like to thank Air Aventure Pyrénées for introducing me to parapente; Andrea and Philip in Barèges for hospitality and (again) info; Peter Derbyshire and Jude Lock, also in Barèges, and Richard and Sandra Loder at Casa Guilla for more of the same; Marta and Ramon at Can Fabrica for restaurant tips; Michael and Rosi Peters at La Miana for hospitality and still more recommendations; fellow guide author Jordi Bastart for sharing his knowledge of Catalunya; Ana at Casa del Arco; the entire Bardaji family and Xep in Taüll; Niki & Richard in the Valle de Echo for hospitality and once more reviewing critical bits of the manuscript; and finally Pamela, for sharing the last week of research and again tolerating my prolonged absences.

The author would also like to acknowledge the contributions of the updaters for the Rough Guides to France and Spain, to Paul Jenner and Christine Smith for their input on winter mountaineering on the long-ago first edition (1990) of this guide, to David Price for proofreading, to Sam Kirby for massively revised cartography, and last but not least to David Glen for being tolerant of an ever-expanding text, and for catching numerous undefined foreign words which have eluded us all up to now but which are now safely in the Glossary.

Brian Catlos would like to thank Núria Silleras Fernández, Elena Aznar, Peter Catlos, Gîtes de France, Valérie Crouineau (CDT Ariège-Pyrénées) and Myriam Journet-Fillaquier (CDT Aude).

PUBLISHING INFORMATION

This fourth edition published May 2001 by
Rough Guides Ltd, 62–70 Shorts Gardens,
London WC2H 9AH.
Distributed by the Penguin Group:
Penguin Books Ltd, 27 Wrights Lane, London W8 5TZ
Penguin Putnam, Inc. 375 Hudson Street, NY 10014, USA
Penguin Books Australia Ltd, 487 Maroondah Highway, PO Box 257, Ringwood, Victoria 3134, Australia
Penguin Books Canada Ltd, 10 Alcorn Avenue, Toronto, Ontario, Canada M4V 1E4
Penguin Books (NZ) Ltd, 182–190 Wairau Road, Auckland 10, New Zealand
Typeset in Linotron Univers and Century Old Style to an original design by Andrew Oliver.
Printed in England by Clays Ltd, St Ives PLC
Illustrations in Part One and Part Three by Edward Briant.

Illustrations on p.1 by Tommy Yamaha and on p.509 by Simon Fell
© Marc Dubin 2001
No part of this book may be reproduced in any form without permission from the publisher except for the quotation of brief passages in reviews.
592pp – Includes index
A catalogue record for this book is available from the British Library
ISBN 1-85828-701-4

The publishers and authors have done their best to ensure the accuracy and currency of all the information in *The Rough Guide to The Pyrenees*, however, they can accept no responsibility for any loss, injury, or inconvenience sustained by any traveller as a result of information or advice contained in the guide.

THE ROUGH GUIDE TO

The Pyrenees

written and researched by

Marc Dubin

with additional contributions by

Brian Catlos and Lance Chilton

ROUGH
GUIDES

We set out to do something different when the first Rough Guide was published in 1982. Mark Ellingham, just out of university, was travelling in Greece. He brought along the popular guides of the day, but found they were all lacking in some way. They were either strong on ruins and museums but went on for pages without mentioning a beach or taverna. Or they were so conscious of the need to save money that they lost sight of Greece's cultural and historical significance. Also, none of the books told him anything about Greece's contemporary life – its politics, its culture, its people, and how they lived.

So with no job in prospect, Mark decided to write his own guidebook, one which aimed to provide practical information that was second to none, detailing the best beaches and the hottest clubs and restaurants, while also giving hard-hitting accounts of every sight, both famous and obscure, and providing up-to-the-minute information on contemporary culture. It was a guide that encouraged independent travellers to find the best of Greece, and was a great success, getting shortlisted for the Thomas Cook travel guide award,

and encouraging Mark, along with three friends, to expand the series.

The Rough Guide list grew rapidly and the letters flooded in, indicating a much broader readership than had been anticipated, but one which uniformly appreciated the Rough Guide mix of practical detail and humour, irreverence and enthusiasm. Things haven't changed. The same four friends who began the series are still the caretakers of the Rough Guide mission today: to provide the most reliable, up-to-date and entertaining information to independent-minded travellers of all ages, on all budgets.

We now publish more than 150 titles and have offices in London and New York. The travel guides are written and researched by a dedicated team of more than 100 authors, based in Britain, Europe, the USA and Australia. We have also created a unique series of phrasebooks to accompany the travel series, along with an acclaimed series of music guides, and a best-selling pocket guide to the Internet and World Wide Web. We also publish comprehensive travel information on our Web site:

www.roughguides.com

HELP US UPDATE

We've gone to a lot of effort to ensure that the fourth edition of *The Rough Guide to The Pyrenees* is accurate and up to date. However, things change — places get "discovered", opening hours are notoriously fickle, restaurants and rooms raise prices or lower standards. If you feel we've got it wrong or left something out, we'd like to know, and if you can remember the address, the price, the time, the phone number, so much the better.

We'll credit all contributions, and send a copy of the next edition (or any other Rough Guide if you prefer) for the best letters. Please mark letters: "Rough Guide Pyrenees Update" and send to:
Rough Guides, 62–70 Shorts Gardens, London WC2H 9AH, or Rough Guides, 4th Floor, 345 Hudson St, New York, NY 10014.
Or send email to: mail@roughguides.co.uk
Online updates about this book can be found on Rough Guides' Web site at **www.roughguides.com**

THE AUTHORS

Marc Dubin first went to the Pyrenees in 1986 – and thigh-deep in snowmelt, discovered why most facilities are shut in May. Since then he has returned numerous times to both sides of the range, on one occasion toting a 23-kilo pack through the mountains in the course of researching a hiking guide to Spain. He is now thoroughly hooked, not least on Pyrenean cuisine. Prior to researching this edition he finally learned to downhill ski, and can now descend any blue run (and the easier reds) with more determination than finesse.

READERS' LETTERS

Thanks to all readers who wrote in with helpful comments since the last edition was published. The roll of honour, in alphabetical order, follows. Apologies to anyone whose signature couldn't be correctly deciphered.

George Banks, Claire Boardman, Vincent Bron, Paul Brookes, Vivienne & John Brucker, John Clayton, Iain Dryden, Alistair Elliot, Jackie Gartledge, Dany Geiling, Professor Andor Gomme, Michael Gotz, Jenny Harris, Phil Hayward, Anthony Henshaw, Anne Instone, Doug & Laura Johnston, Bernard M. Jones, Michael Kennedy, Beatriz Lacasa, David E. Lloyd, Nigel Malcolm-Smith, Rachel Manson, Ken & Sue Napier, Stacey Nicholson, Sandra Oakins, Kevin O'Dowd, Carol & Jon Parly, D. Quadling, Chris Sholl, Jörg Sendele, Crispin Truman, Pierre Willems, Professor Tom J. Winnifrith.

CONTENTS

Introduction ix

● CHAPTER 4: AROUND THE NATIONAL PARKS 327–436

● CHAPTER 5: THE WESTERN PYRENEES 437–507

PART THREE CONTEXTS   509

LIST OF MAPS

The Pyrenees x–xi
Chapter divisions map 87

The Eastern Pyrenees 90–91
Perpignan 96
The Aude and the Lower Têt 102–103
The Upper Tet, the Tech and Canigou 116–117
The Mediterranean Coast 129
Figueres 147
Girona 153
Olot 164
The Garrotxa and El Ripollès 168
Ripoll 174

Andorra and around 186–187

The Cadí-Moixeró Park 190–191
La Seu d'Urgell 203
Andorra 206
Puigcerdà 220
Carlit Massif and the Cerdagne 224
The Ariège and Pays de Sault 230–231

The Val D'Aran Region 250–251
Aigüestortes and Sant Maurici 276–277
Maladeta, Posets and the Parque Natural 287
The Couserans, The Comminges and Montcalm/Estats 304–305

Around the National parks 328–329
Northern Approaches 332–333
Tarbes 351
Lourdes 353
Pau 377
Southern Approaches 396–397
Jaca 421
Sierra de Guara 429

The Western Pyrenees 438–439
The Karst Country 444
Camino de Santiago and Basque Coast 464–465
Bayonne 479
Central Biarritz 484
San Sebastián 498–499

MAP SYMBOLS

─── Railway	▲ Mountain peak
═══ Road	⁄⁄ Mountain pass
= = = Track	⸾⸾ Gorge
– – – Footpath	∩ Historic bridge
─── Waterway	⌒ Cave
─•─ Chapter division boundary	♨ Spa or spring
─••─ International borders	𝕀 Waterfall
✈ Airport	─ Wall
P Parking	🎿 Downhill ski area
★ Bus stop	🎿 Cross country ski area
▣ Restaurant	ⓘ Tourist office
◉ Hotel	✉ Post office
Ⓐ Campsite	▰ Building
♙ Refuge	✚ Church or cathedral (town maps)
♖ Castle	Park
⌂ Abbey or monastery (regional maps)	National park
✝ Church, chapel or shrine (regional maps)	

INTRODUCTION

Anyone could find their perfect retreat in the **Pyrenees**, a range that encompasses in its four-hundred-kilometre length a diversity of landscapes rarely equalled in Europe. Between the balmy beaches of the Mediterranean and the more turbulent Atlantic coast lie regions of lush meadowland, peaks permanently clad in ice, sun-beaten canyons of sinuously sculpted rock, swathes of dense broadleaf forest, weirdly eroded limestone pinnacles and valleys so sheer and overgrown that scarcely a ray of light penetrates them.

These mountains challenge and invite rather than intimidate. Generally rounded and crumbling, most of their peaks are attainable even to people with little experience of such terrain. **Aneto**, at 3404 metres the highest summit of the Pyrenees, stands within reach of any determined and properly equipped walker, as do all the next ranking peaks – **Posets**, **Monte Perdido** and **Vignemale**. Other natural wonders of the range are also available to the averagely fit. The **Valle de Ordesa**, the most spectacular of many canyons, can be traversed on nearly level footpaths, as can the great glaciated amphitheatre of the **Cirque de Gavarnie**, just to the north. The stalactite-draped cavern of **Lombrives** is the largest cave in western Europe to which there's unrestricted public access, while a visit to the **Sala de la Verna**, the largest chamber in one of the world's deepest cave systems – the Gouffre Pierre-Saint-Martin – requires no great physical effort. If you join an organized group, there are any number of lively rivers to raft down on both sides of the range, including the **Noguera Pallaresa** in Catalunya and the **Gállego** in Aragón, as well as several tamer ones on the French side. **Canyoners** of all ability levels are similarly well catered to in the "pre-Pyrenean" **Sierra de Guara**, also in Spanish Aragón.

Walking the entire range from end to end has become a classic endeavour, and thousands of people have followed the **Haute Randonnée Pyrénéenne** (HRP) just to either side of the watershed, or the more circuitous, but less demanding, **Grande Randonnée 10** (GR10) entirely within France. These long-established footpaths were supplemented during the 1980s by the equally spectacular Spanish **Gran Recorrido 11** (GR11); maps for every part of the Pyrenees show numerous other, briefer itineraries, suitable for hikers at all levels.

The **wildlife** of the Pyrenees is exceptionally rich, despite the devastating impact of human activity on many of its most engaging species. Populations of deer and wild boar hide in the forests, and in certain dense woodlands a dwindling number of **brown bear** still manage to survive despite the depredations of hunters. In contrast, the ubiquitous **isard** – or Pyrenean chamois – is on the increase, as are shy **wildcats**; **marmots** are plentiful (and audible); while majestic **birds of prey** circle in the skies. The **capercaillie**, a game bird now extinct in the French Alps, still thrives in the Pyrenees, and the tiny **desman**, a sort of aquatic mole, is unknown anywhere else in western Europe, except the Picos de Europa.

Traces of **human habitation** in the Pyrenees predate recorded history by thousands of years, with artefacts found (and often displayed) at a half-dozen caves in the Ariège, the Couserans and the Comminges regions. The prehistoric **painted caves** around **Tarascon-sur-Ariège** are rivalled only by those of the Dordogne and the Spanish province of Cantabria, with the paintings in the **Grotte de Niaux** rated as the best examples open to public view anywhere in the world.

Architectural highlights of the Pyrenees are its extraordinary **Romanesque churches and monasteries**, of which there are literally hundreds, including such renowned examples as Saint-Martin-du-Canigou, Serrabone, Santa Maria de Ripoll,

Sant Climent de Taüll and a host of others in the Vall de Boí, Saint-Bertrand-de-Comminges, Saint-Lizier, San Juan de la Peña, and Saint-Engrâce in the Haute-Soule. So-called "Roman" **bridges** still linking isolated villages are even older, though not necessarily pre-Christian. Towards the western half of the range, numerous monuments bear testimony to the thousands of pilgrims who during the Middle Ages followed the **pilgrimage trail** to Santiago de Compostela in Galicia via the fabled Puerto de Ibañeta near Roncesvalles, or the nearby Col du Somport. At the eastern end, from the Mediterranean to the Ariège, the strength of the heretical **Cathar** religion is reflected in many immensely evocative ruined **castles**, notably the crag-top citadel of Montségur, site of the faith's effective extinction.

The **people** of the Pyrenees are as disparate as the landscape. The east and west ends of the range are the respective homelands of the Catalans and the Basques, each with a tenaciously preserved cultural vitality, as embodied in the sombre sardana, the Catalan communal dance, or the lightning-quick and potentially lethal Basque game of *pelota/pelote*. As you traverse the Pyrenees you'll certainly hear Catalan, Aranese, Aragonese and Euskera (the Basque tongue), not to mention a few others – notably Occitan – not officially accorded the status of a distinct language. For centuries before the final unifications of France and Spain, every valley effectively constituted a mini-republic with its own argot and traditions, jealously guarding customary privileges against encroachment from distant central governments, and defying them further with a thriving trade in **smuggling**. Remoteness and neglect long made the mountains a refuge for political as well as religious dissidents, most recently during the Spanish

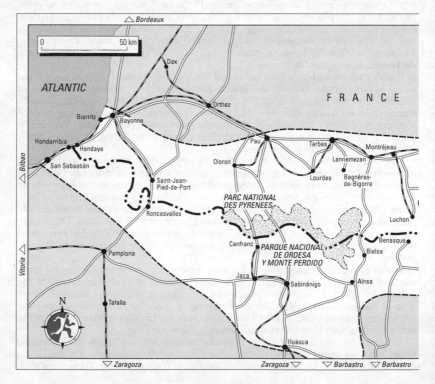

Civil War and World War II when thousands of **refugees** took advantage of the shepherds' and smugglers' knowledge to evade capture. After 1968, hundreds of disillusioned French protesters and "alternative" types again took up residence in the back country, swelling the traditional local vote for the political Left – and adopting the longstanding local habit of self-sufficiency. Indeed the Pyreneans' historical disregard for the often-altered boundaries between France and Spain has been vindicated and accentuated by the post-1993 European single market, as old border posts lie abandoned and a strong regional identity bridging the watershed seems set to reassert itself.

After decades of playing second fiddle to the Alps, the Pyrenees have finally come into their own as a **travellers' destination**. Infrastructure and amenities improve by the year, as exemplified by increasing numbers of quality lodgings (especially on the Spanish side), ever-multiplying adventure-sport outfitters and a plethora of no-frills airlines offering service into hitherto sleepy regional airports. It has never been easier to visit these mountains.

When and where to go
There's something to do in the Pyrenees at all times of the year. Snowfall permitting, the **downhill/cross-country ski season** gets seriously under way in January, while spring sees high-level ski touring. With the spring thaw, **rafting** and **canoeing** become practicable, and then the long summer **walking** season begins in early June – also a good time for riding, cycling, and the more extreme pursuits of **canyoning** and **parapente**, the latter essentially a cross between hang-gliding and parachuting. In autumn

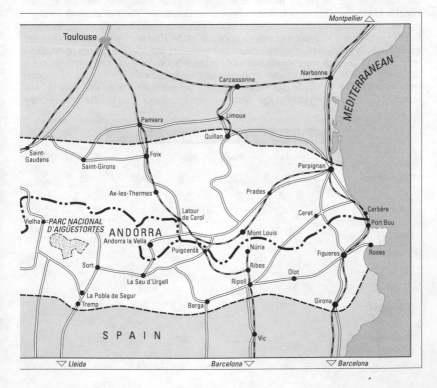

the crowds depart and the mountain trails are left to solitary walkers not afraid of the odd snow flurry.

The optimum time to visit obviously depends on what you want to do, but if possible you should **avoid the French and Spanish national summer holidays**, which run from mid-July to the end of August. It's preferable to come after this lemming stampede rather than before: spring and autumn offer equal solitude, but high passes may still be blocked until July, and in September you'll have the freedom of all the mountains. Besides the crowds, **thunderstorms** cause problems in high summer: the Pyrenees are very prone to them and during July and August several storms a week can be guaranteed. If you are out on the high peaks during summer you should always aim to be well down by early afternoon, when the storms tend to break.

The **weather** in the Pyrenees resists generalization, as temperatures can be erratic owing to marine influences, and microclimates abound. In summer, the cooling action of the sea can give each coastal strip a temperature several degrees lower than a few miles inland, while for every 100–200m of ascent, the temperature often falls by as much as one degree Celsius. Thus a summer train-ride up from Barcelona to Núria in Catalunya might take you through a drop of more than ten degrees. Conversely, there's the common phenomenon of temperature inversion (especially on the French slopes), when the valleys become colder than the peaks, which protrude like islands from a white sea of cloud. The Barèges valley, for example, has particularly idiosyncratic weather, where a warm May can be followed by snowstorms in June.

If you've only got two weeks at your disposal, the Pyrenees are too vast to tour in their entirety, but in places **public transport** is good enough to explore a region roughly corresponding to one of the chapters in this book. The rail networks will get you within striking distance of the most interesting areas, and buses are often available to take you deeper into the mountains. A circuit of the Eastern Pyrenees, for example, could begin at Perpignan, continue south by train along the Mediterranean coast, move west by road through the verdant Garrotxa to the Ripollès valleys; then north by rail to the sunny plain of the Cerdanya/Cerdagne, and finally return to Perpignan by another train through the dramatic Têt valley. Circular itineraries such as this can be constructed in many other parts of the range – around Andorra or in the Basque country,

AVERAGE TEMPERATURES (°C)						
	Jan	Mar	May	July	Sept	Nov
Perpignan (Mediterranean coast)	12.4	12.5	20.1	28.4	26.1	15.8
Olot (Inland Catalunya)	4.4	9	14.3	20.7	17.7	7.7
Ransol (Andorra)	-2.1	1.4	7.3	13.6	10.9	2
Tarbes (Midi-Pyrénées)	10	12.3	19.1	27.6	25	15.5
Panticosa (Alto Aragón)	0.1	2.6	8.2	15.5	12.3	4.1
Bayonne (Atlantic coast)	10	12.2	18	27.2	24.2	15.4

for example – and even isolated, underpopulated zones such as the central Maladeta and Posets massifs lend themselves to loops on foot from trailhead villages served by buses. With a **car** or **bicycle**, you could probably see the best of two consecutive chapters in two to three weeks.

If you want to concentrate on one area, the **Ariège** will suit most tastes with its fabulous scenery, cave art, ruined castles and almost every form of outdoor activity. Over the border in Catalunya, the **Parc Nacional de Aigüestortes i Sant Maurici**, easily accessible from the Val d'Aran, makes an excellent introduction to the glacial glories of the higher peaks. Gavarnie, Barèges or Cauterets in France, and Torla or Bielsa in Spain, are comfortable gateways for the best of the French **Parc National des Pyrénées** and the Spanish **Parque Nacional de Ordesa y Monte Perdido**, the great, contiguous national parks in the heart of the range. For walks and climbs on the highest summits further east, make the all-purpose resorts of **Benasque** or **Bagnères-de-Luchon** your bases, while the westernmost high peaks – before the range dips below 2500m elevation – can also be easily explored from developed villages such as **Lescun** or **Sallent de Gállego**. During winter, most of these settlements are conveniently close to many of the best **ski resorts**, which include Candanchú-Astún, Barèges-La Mongie, Piau-Engaly, Peyragudes, Baqueira-Beret and Boí-Taüll, many of them the equal of the better-known winter sports centres in commercialized **Andorra**.

Towards the west end of the range, **Pau** is the largest and most cosmopolitan city of the Pyrenees, on a main transport route to **Jaca**, historic county town of the Aragonese mountains. They are the most logical and congenial gateways to the surreal karst country extending between the French **Vallée d'Aspe** and the Spanish valleys of **Echo** and **Ansó**. Southeast of Jaca, beyond the sleepy provincial capital of Huesca, the **Sierra de Guara** is available for visits most of the year owing to lower altitude.

Inland from the surf-pounded Atlantic coast, with its elegant resorts of **San Sebastián** and **Biarritz**, the seductively green horizons and sumptuous domestic architecture of the **Basque country** beckon, with graceful **Bayonne** and atmospheric **Saint-Jean-Pied-de-Port** as focuses. The Mediterranean beaches are more varied and – at least at the picturesque port-resorts of **Collioure** or **Cadaqués** – more beautiful, and the climate reliably sunny. From here there are also opportunites for forays inland to the mysterious, volcanic **Garrotxa basin** in Catalunya or to the gorge-slashed foothills of the **Canigou massif** in Roussillon. Whichever part of the range you decide to visit, take the opportunity to sample both sides of the border if at all possible – the north-to-south change of landscape, climate and culture is one of the delights of the Pyrenees.

PART ONE

THE

BASICS

GETTING THERE FROM BRITAIN

The most convenient and economical way of getting to the Pyrenees is to fly – flights from London take just under two hours to Barcelona, less to Biarritz, Toulouse, Carcassone and Perpignan. Reaching the Pyrenees overland has been simplified since the opening of the Channel Tunnel and Eurotunnel services. There are also two ferry services direct to northern Spain, bypassing France.

BY AIR

Air travel to Pyrenean foothill airports has been revolutionized since the late 1990s with the provi-sion of year-round direct flights by a number of no-frills, short-haul airlines. It's no longer neces-sary to put up with the severe limitations of char-ters or the exorbitant fares of national flag carri-ers; you can even purchase advantageous one-way tickets. Several formerly useful ski-season charters have been cut following the withdrawal of most major package operators from Pyrenean winter resorts, so scheduled routes remain your most reliable option year-round.

SCHEDULED FLIGHTS: SHORT-HAUL AIRLINES

The **short-haul airlines** profiled here typically offer **no frills** – remote London airports, no meal or drink, occasionally restricted baggage allowances – and usually a slight discount off their already cheap fares for booking on the Web rather than phone. They also don't issue actual tickets, but fax or email you a booking reference number which you must carefully retain. If some-thing goes awry with their passenger list, it may be the only way you can prove that you've booked and paid for the flight. The earlier you book, the better the result – fares are "load sen-sitive", ie the cheapest seats fill first; with easyJet in particular, you can end up paying as much as with a major airline if you leave it to the last minute.

Ryanair has the widest variety of services to the Pyrenean foothills, with daily year-round flights

---

AIRLINES

Air France ☎0845/0845 111, *www.airfrance.fr*
Daily from London Heathrow to Barcelona, Toulouse, Perpignan, Lourdes-Tarbes and Biarritz-Bayonne via Paris.

British Airways ☎0845/722 2111, *www.britishairways.com*
Daily London Gatwick to Toulouse direct, summer only; also Manchester/Birmingham/London Gatwick to Barcelona, and London Gatwick to Bilbao.

Buzz ☎0870/240 7070, *www.buzzaway.com*
London Stansted to Girona, all year, and to Toulouse, winter only.

easyJet ☎0870/600 0000, *www.easyjet.com*
Daily from Liverpool and London Luton to Barcelona.

Go ☎0845/6054321, *www.go-fly.com*
Daily from London Stansted to Barcelona and Bilbao.

Iberia ☎0990/341341, *www.iberia.com*
London Heathrow or Gatwick to Barcelona and Bilbao; also Manchester direct to Barcelona.

Lufthansa ☎0845/773 7747, *www.lufthansa.co.uk*
London Heathrow to Toulouse or Barcelona, both via Frankfurt/Munich.

Ryanair ☎0870/3331250, *www.ryanair.com*
Daily, year-round service from London Stansted to Perpignan, Carcassone and Biarritz-Bayonne.

from **London Stansted** (cheap connection from **Glasgow**) to **Perpignan** and nearby **Carcassone** in the east of the range, and to **Biarritz-Bayonne** in the west. Round-trip low-season fares vary £40–60, though watch their Web site and adverts in newspaper travel supplements for amazing specials. Cheap high-season fares for a three-week holiday are consistent at about £105 to the three destinations. They fly all year to Girona

Go offers a daily service to **Barcelona** and **Bilbao** from **London Stansted**; Bilbao is two to three hours' overland travel from the mountains, but it's a fairly easy initial journey by rail to San Sebastián. Fares for a three-week holiday period vary from £70 in low season to £110 in peak season, with reasonable add-on flights from Belfast, Glasgow and Edinburgh.

EasyJet flies one to three times daily from **London Luton**, and once daily from **Liverpool**, to **Barcelona**, with add-ons with easyJet from

Belfast and most Scottish airports. Barcelona fares start at £115 return for a few weeks away, while Liverpool-based itineraries cost £135 and up. At present, flights from **London Stansted** to **Toulouse** on **Buzz** are Sundays only from Christmas to April, but they may resume in future during summer; allow £80 return during ski season.

SCHEDULED FLIGHTS: NATIONAL CARRIERS

Scheduled, usually indirect flights on **national carriers** like Air France, British Airways and Lufthansa are unlikely to prove attractive. The least expensive tickets go by different names throughout the year, but they're usually valid for seven to thirty days, require you to stay at least one Saturday night, and don't allow for change or cancellation. Slightly higher fares are valid up to ninety days, but again carry heavy restrictions.

DISCOUNT FLIGHT AGENTS

AVRO plc, Vantage House, 1 Weir Rd, Wimbledon, London SW19 (☎020/8715 4440, *www.avro-flights.co.uk*). One- or two-week charters to Girona only.

Eclipse Reservations, Astral Towers, Bettsway, London Rd, Crawley, West Sussex (☎0293/554444). Charter flights, for 1–2 weeks only, to Girona.

Mancunia Travel ☎0161/228 2840 Twice-weekly summer charter flights from Manchester to Lourdes.

North South Travel, Moulsham Mill Centre, Parkway, Chelmsford, Essex CM2 7PX (☎01245/608 291, *www.northsouthtravel.co.uk*). Friendly, competitive travel agency, offering discounted fares worldwide – profits are used to support projects in the developing world, especially the promotion of sustainable tourism.

Spanish Travel Services, 138 Eversholt St, London NW1 (☎020/7387 5337). Spanish flight-only specialists.

STA Travel ☎0870/160 6070, *www.statravel.co.uk*

86 Old Brompton Rd, London SW7; 117 Euston Rd, London NW1; 85 Shaftesbury Av, London W1; 40 Bernard St, Russell Square, WC1N; 25 Queen's Rd, Bristol BS8 1QE; 38 Sidney St, Cambridge CB2 3HX; 36 George St, Oxford OX1 2OJ; 75 Deansgate, Manchester M3 2BW; 6

Civic Centre Rd, Southampton SO14. Independent travel specialists; discounted flights.

Trailfinders, *www.trailfinders.com* 215 Kensington High St, London W6 (☎020/7937 5400); 22–24 The Priory, Queensway, Birmingham B4 6BS (☎0121/236 1234); 48 Corn St, Bristol BS1 1HQ (☎0117/929 9000); 254–284 Sauchiehall St, Glasgow G2 3EH (☎0141/353 2224); 58 Deansgate, Manchester M3 2FF (☎0161/839 6969). One of the best-informed and most efficient scheduled flight and car-rental agencies for independent travellers; all branches open daily long hours.

Usit CAMPUS *www.usitcampus.com*

52 Grosvenor Gardens, London SW1 (☎020/7730 3402); 541 Bristol Rd, Selly Oak, Birmingham (☎021/414 1848); 37–39 Queen's Rd, Clifton, Bristol (☎0117/929 2494); 5 Emmanuel St, Cambridge (☎01223/324 283); 53 Forest Rd, Edinburgh (☎0131/225 6111); 166 Deansgate, Manchester (☎0161/833 2046); 13 High St, Oxford (☎01865/242 067). Also at YHA shops and university campuses throughout Britain. Youth/student specialist.

Wildwings, First Floor, 577–579 Fishponds Rd, Bristol BS16 3AF (☎0117/965 8333). Heavily discounted fares to Bilbao, Pamplona and Barcelona with Iberia, but these must be used in conjunction with a minimum of three nights' hotel accommodation (booked with whomever you like).

More flexible tickets are valid 180 days, can be date-changed and are variably refundable, though you'll pay much more for such privileges. Fares bought directly from the airlines are considerably more expensive, though it is worth checking their Web sites for special offers. It's also worth looking at UK **travel Web sites** such as *www.expedia.co.uk*, *www.travelocity.com* and *www.travelselect.com*. Bear in mind, though, that such sites typically only offer 'M' or 'H' economy fares; for the really cheap 'Q' or 'V' fares you're often better off dealing with a staffed specialist agent.

Spain's national airline, Iberia, and British Airways together have the widest range of scheduled flights to destinations **south of the Pyrenees**, the nearest airports being **Bilbao** and **Barcelona**. Iberia also flies direct from Manchester into Barcelona, with BA offering flights from Manchester and Birmingham to Barcelona. Fares from London to Barcelona booked through a specialist or discount agent range £145–250 depending on season and day of the week, while to Bilbao, west of the range, ticket prices are comparable at £140–230. From Manchester or Birmingham, you're looking at £165–250 to Barcelona, and much the same to Bilbao. High-season Web site flights for London Heathrow to Barcelona are £185–200 on Air France or Lufthansa, and £195 from Gatwick on British Airways; from Gatwick to Bilbao, budget on £200 for one of British Airways' daily flights.

North of the Pyrenees, Air France, British Airways and (sometimes) Lufthansa have the best offerings to **Toulouse** and **Biarritz-Bayonne**; Pau no longer has through fares quoted to it, and those for Perpignan and Lourdes-Tarbes are absurdly expensive. All Air France services are from **London Heathrow via Paris**, where you may change terminals from De Gaulle to Orly, or vice versa (free shuttle bus). A quick survey of agencies and travel Web sites can turn up some occasionally bizarre routings in exchange for a discounted fare. Heathrow–Toulouse is the best served route, for which a high-season one-month fare might be £145 on Lufthansa (via Frankfurt or Munich), or £155 on Air France (via Paris). The only direct service to Toulouse is British Airways' summer-only service three times daily from London Gatwick; allow £185–215 with the airline or a Web booking, £20 less through a specialist agency. Air France is the sole carrier serving Biarritz–Bayonne, with minimum fares of £170 via Paris.

YOUTH FARES

Students and anyone under 26 can take advantage of special discount flights on the major national airlines, most commonly into Barcelona, Toulouse or Bilbao. The best agencies for these are independent travel specialists STA Travel and Campus Travel (see box for addresses). Student or youth tickets tend to be quite flexible: they are often valid for up to a year, and the return date – while you must specify one upon purchase – is changeable for little or no penalty. You can expect to pay around £120 return to Toulouse; £165–180 to Barcelona; and £150–180 to Bilbao – figures comparing poorly, in the latter two cases, with the short-haul airlines.

CHARTER FLIGHTS

The number of charter flights from Britain into the Pyrenean region is limited, and getting more so all the time, given successful competition from the budget, Web-based airlines. **From mid-April to late October**, you can buy a cheap-and-cheerful, seat-only package to Girona in Catalunya for under £100, but they have severe time restrictions – two weeks maximum, sometimes only one week. You may find a few summer pilgrims' charters into Lourdes from London Gatwick or Manchester, but these are at least £150. **Ski-season** charters to Lourdes have been suspended as of writing; a few still survive into Toulouse or Barcelona, but these will typically be booked out by Andorran operators.

The major disadvantage of any charter flight is its fixed return date – unlike certain scheduled fares, which can be changed on payment of a variable penalty fee.

PACKAGES

Package holiday deals can be worth looking at, especially if you book early, late, or off-peak season. While the cheaper, mass-market packages which restrict you to the tackier parts of the Costa Brava might still be the most common on offer, there are an increasing number of **high-quality, specialist** hiking, skiing or rural-accommodation-based packages available on both sides of the range. Fly-Drive deals are well worth considering, too, as a combined air ticket and car rental arrangement can be excellent value. For recommended companies, see the box oveleaf.

TOUR AND PACKAGE OPERATORS

Allez France ☎01903/745793, www.greatescapes.co.uk Fly-drive accommodation packages (no flight-only) from London to Toulouse with Air France; for example, £345 for a week's cottage stay in July, plus £200 per person for the car and flight.

Alto Aragón ☎01869/337339, www.altoaragon.co.uk
The best and most varied offerings for the Spanish Pyrenees: horse riding in the Sierra de Guara, cross-country skiing near Ansó, and well-planned 8- or 15-day treks, including supported traverses of selected sections of the GR11 and HRP. Also self-guiding holidays from selected high-end hotels. Prices from £515 for 8 days, land only.

La Balaguère ☎0033/5.62.97.20.21, www.balaguere.com Well-respected adventure travel outfit based at a *gîte* in Arrens-Marsous, France; they offer a wide variety of treks and expeditions in the Pyrenees, though English-language guiding cannot be guaranteed.

Blue Bear Travels, ☎0131/660 1331, www.bluebeartravels.com Eight-day walking holidays between Berguedà and the Núria area of Catalunya; add-on stays at high-quality rural accommodation in the same area.

Borderline Holidays ☎0033/5.62.92.68.95, www.borderlinehols.com British-run but Barèges-based small company offering guided walking holidays in summer (May–Sept) and affordable quality skiing packages in winter (Dec–March) for about £500 for one week, based in a small pension. Flights to French foothill airports arrangeable on request.

Chambres d'Hôtes/Gîtes de France Ltd, c/o Sally Lines (☎0990/360360). Houses and cottages in the Pyrenean foothills; ferry crossings priced separately.

Exodus Expeditions ☎0181/675 5550, www.exodustravels.co.uk Eight-day trekking and multi-activity packages to the central Pyrenees, beginning at Luchon but mostly on the Spanish side.

Igloo ☎0870/870 5787, www.iglu.com General marketers of skiing holidays; Pyrenean resorts typically featured include Arcalis, Arinsal and Soldeu–

El Tarter in Andorra, Barèges in France, and Boí-Taüll and Baqueira-Beret in Spain.

Inntravel ☎01653/628862, www.inntravel.co.uk Upmarket summer programme includes supported, 7-to-10-day hikes along the Catalan coast, from Camprodon to the Núria area, or through the French Cerdagne (latter two can be combined into longer loop). They've also cross-country skiing holidays based at Valcebollère in the Cerdagne.

Panorama Holidays ☎01273/427070, www.panoramaholidays.co.uk Andorra ski-package specialists, featuring all the major resorts, with prices from £199 for self-catering apartments or £285–335 in two-to-four-star hotels, for a week (skiing costs excluded). Flights, which are included, on Ryanair or charter carriers from a wide variety of British airports to Toulouse or Carcassone.

Pyrenean Mountain Tours ☎01635/297209, www.pyrenees.co.uk. Extensive summer hiking programme, ranging from 1-to-2-day walks out of Luz -Saint-Sauveur to the HRP between Pic du Midi and Vignemale, by way of treks around Monte Perdido from Gavarnie. Also downhill skiing packages based in Barèges, or ski-touring from and in the Parc National, Posets/Maladeta, Aigüestortes/Sant Maurici.

Pyrenees Adventures ☎01433/621498, ☎07802/770701, www.pyradv.demon.co.uk Guided mountain walks in the French Basque Pyrenees, based in a restored eighteenth-century farmhouse near St-Jean-Pied-de-Port.

Sherpa Expeditions ☎020/8577 2717, www.sherpa-walking-holidays.co.uk Trekking in the Pyrenees, in particular a spectacular high-level traverse during summer, plus lower-altitude jaunts for spring and autumn.

Ski Miquel Holidays ☎01457/821200 One- or 2-week packages, with English-speaking instructor, at Baqueira-Beret in the Val d'Aran.

Waymark Holidays ☎01753/516477, fax 01753/517016 Pyrenean summer hiking programme, including easy walks in the Aigüestortes park (Spain), the Garrotxa region (Spain), the Baronnies and Vallée de Campan near Bagnerres de Bigorre (France), the Cerdagne highlands (France), and the Cathar country (France).

BY TRAIN

From London to the extreme west or east of the Pyrenees takes just under 24 hours by train and ferry, though by using services from London to Paris through the Channel Tunnel (see below) you can shave a good six hours off this total. Either option involves changing trains (and stations, from Nord to Austerlitz on Metro Line 5) in Paris. **Hendaye** on the Atlantic coast and **Cerbère** on the Mediterranean coast are the last French stations on the main runs; there's a change of train at Spanish Irún and Port Bou.

In addition to these routes, there are a couple of other slightly more exciting (and expensive) ones. Rail Europe will sell you a train ticket (about £160 return) to **Oloron-Sainte-Marie** in France, where you then buy a rail-bus ticket on to the Spanish railhead at **Canfranc**. If you want to visit the Aspe/Ossau region of the French Pyrenees or the Aragonese Pyrenees, this route makes some sense. A second alternative, a fraction cheaper, is via Foix to **Bourg-Madame** in the French Cerdagne; again Rail Europe fares are quoted only up to there, where you must change trains and buy another ticket for the Spanish network, entering Spain at Puigcerdà. This is the closest you can get to Andorra (which has no trains) and also gives handy direct access to the Ariège and the Carlit massif.

EUROSTAR

High-speed **Eurostar** trains from Waterloo International in London serve Paris via Ashford in Kent and the Channel Tunnel in just over three hours, cutting a good six hours off travel time to the Pyrenees. Frequencies and **prices** change regularly and must be checked seasonally; economy class return fares to Paris range £110–200, with slight discounts for Interail pass-holders. Besides special offers and day-trips, the cheapest regular ticket is the "Excursion", a return ticket

---

TRAIN INFORMATION

Eurostar, Waterloo station, London SE1 (☎0870/160 6600, *www.eurostar.com*)

Rail Europe, 179 Piccadilly, London W1V, or Victoria station, London SW1 (☎0870/584 8848, *www.raileurope.co.uk*). Extremely limited booking capability of Web site; best to ring them.

BUS INFORMATION

Eurolines/National Express, 164 Buckingham Palace Rd, London SW1 (☎0870/580 8080, *www.GoByCoach.com*). Web site relatively clear and easy to use for bookings and info.

---

which can be purchased up to 30min before departure and must include a Saturday night, with fixed outward and return dates and no refunds. You can get through-ticketing – including the tube to Waterloo International – from mainline train stations in Britain; typical add-on price for a return ticket to Paris from Edinburgh or Glasgow is £30, from Manchester £20 and Birmingham £13.50. There is still no sign of the promised direct high-speed Eurostar services from the north of England, Scotland and the Midlands.

TICKETS AND PASSES

A **standard rail/boat ticket** currently costs (for example) £125 return from London to Girona, is valid for two months and allows you to stop anywhere along the way. There is a slight discount for students. If you're travelling by **Eurostar**, it's £230–430 for a return to Girona (depending on age, season, day of week and time of day). Reservation charges from Paris are £3–4 for a seat or £10–15 for a couchette (included in the price if you're taking the Eurostar).

Tickets are bookable through some travel agents, London's Victoria Station, and Usit CAMPUS; note that Rail Europe will only sell tickets using the Eurostar. It's also currently cheaper – especially if you're under 26 or a student – to buy your Eurostar tickets from an agent.

If you plan to travel extensively in France or Spain by train, there's a better-value option than simply buying a return ticket to a Pyrenean gateway city. You can invest in an **InterRail pass** from Rail Europe or a travel agent; the only restriction is that you must have been resident in Europe for at least six months. This comes in two forms: either an InterRail Global pass, valid for one month's unlimited travel in 26 European countries including France and Spain (£309, or £219 for under-26s), or an InterRail zonal pass, whereby the 26 countries are split into seven zones and you choose which countries you want the pass to be valid for. A 22-day pass for any one zone costs £179/129; any two zones (which would get you Spain and France), valid for one month, costs £235/169. In addition all InterRail passes offer discounts on rail travel in the UK and on cross-Channel ferries. Since both France and Spain have extensive rail networks this is basically a bargain, though be prepared (see "Getting Around") to pay various and unpredictable supplements on some of the Spanish services; there are also one or two private rail lines (Núria, La Rhune) on which passes are not valid.

You can save £10 on all the above fares by booking on the InterRail Web site, *www.inter-rail.co.uk*

BY BUS

There are two regular **direct bus routes** from Britain to either end of the Pyrenees: London–Perpignan–Girona (18/21hr) and London–Bordeaux–San Sebastián (21hr). Both of these routes are operated by Eurolines in Britain and by Iberbus/Linebus and Julia in Spain. In both Britain and Spain tickets are bookable through most major travel agents and at *www.gobycoach.com*; Eurolines also sells tickets and through-transport to London at all British National Express bus terminals. In summer there are three weekly departures to the Atlantic coast, and five weekly departures to the Mediterranean, falling out of season to two a week to San Sebastián and three weekly to Girona. Fares start at around £101 return to Perpignan or San Sebastián, £111 to Girona.

The sole advantage of a bus ticket is that you can arrange an **open return** at a slight extra cost. Among several obvious disadvantages are the facts that it's slow and tiring, and that most of the time flying on one of the no-frills airlines costs rather less. To San Sebastián or Girona the journey is long enough but quite bearable – just make sure you take along enough to eat, drink and read, and a small amount of French and Spanish currency for meal breaks. There are stops for around twenty minutes every four to five hours and the routine is also broken by the Dover–Calais/Boulogne ferry (which is included in the cost of a ticket).

BY CAR: FERRY OR TUNNEL

The bus routes follow the most direct road routes from London to the Pyrenees: if you plan to drive yourself, unless you're into nonstop rally motoring, you'll need to roughly double the times. In addition to the time-honoured French services, there are two direct ferry sailings to Bilbao and Santander from Britain. See the box below for ferry company addresses, or contact your local travel agent for the latest ticket and departure details.

EUROTUNNEL AND CROSS-CHANNEL SERVICES

Eurotunnel service through the Channel Tunnel hasn't reduced travel times to the Pyrenees for drivers as much as for rail passengers, though it does of course speed up the cross-Channel section of the journey. **Eurotunnel** operates trains 24 hours a day, carrying cars, motorcycles, buses and their passengers, and taking 35 minutes between Folkestone and Calais. At peak times, services operate every fifteen to twenty minutes; during the night, services are once or twice hourly. Advance booking is advisable, especially if you have a motorcycle, caravan or motor caravan. Rates depend on the time of year, time of day and length of stay; it's cheaper to travel between 10pm and 6am, while the highest fares are reserved for weekend departures and returns during July and August. Caravans and other large vehicles can cost more than twice as much as a car. For a small saloon with two passengers going away for a month in summer, count on close to £200 return.

Traditional cross-Channel options are the **ferry** links between Dover and Calais or Boulogne, or, if you're headed for the western portion of the mountains, ferries to Le Havre (from Portsmouth), Cherbourg (from Portsmouth and Weymouth), St Malo (from Portsmouth) or even Roscoff (from Plymouth). Any of these latter routes cuts out the

---

FERRY COMPANIES AND EUROTUNNEL

Brittany Ferries Millbay Docks, Plymouth; Wharf Rd, Portsmouth; New Harbour Rd, Poole (☎0870/901 1500, *www.brittany-ferries.com*). To Santander, St Malo, Roscoff, Cherbourg and Caen.

Eurotunnel Customer Services Centre (☎0870/535 3535, *www.eurotunnel.com*).

P&O European Ferries Continental Ferry Port, Peninsular House, Wharf Rd, Portsmouth PO2 8TA (☎0870/242 4999,

www.poef.com/portsmouth/). To Cherbourg, Le Havre and Bilbao.

P&O Stena Line Ferries Channel House, Channel View Rd, Dover (info ☎0870/980 980, reservations ☎0870/600 0600, *www.posl.com*). To Calais and Bilbao.

SeaFrance Eastern Docks, Dover, Kent CT16 1JA (☎0870/571 1711, *www.seafrance.co.uk*). To Calais

trek around or through Paris, and opens up some interesting detours around Brittany and the French Atlantic coast.

Ferry **prices** vary according to the time of year and, for motorists, the size of your car. The Dover–Calais/Boulogne runs, for example, start at about £100–165 one-way (£245–340 open return) for a car, two adults and two kids, but these figures can nearly double in high season. Foot passengers should be able to cross for about £15 one-way, or £20–30 open return. For both ferries and tunnel, fares are lower if you travel during off-peak (10pm–6am).

TO SANTANDER AND BILBAO

Direct car and passenger ferry services from England to Spain are convenient but expensive. The ferry from **Plymouth to Santander** (four hours' drive from the west end of the Pyrenees) is operated by Brittany Ferries, takes 24 hours and runs on Mondays and Wednesdays during the summer (April to mid-Sept) and Wednesdays and Sundays for the rest of the year. Ticket prices vary enormously according to the season, the number of passengers carried and the length of time you want the ticket valid; for example, a return ticket for a car and two adults can cost anything from £128 (valid for 5 days in low-season) to £710 (for an open ticket in high-season). Foot passengers pay around £50–80 one-way (depending on season), and everyone has to book some form of accommodation; a pullman seat is cheapest at £4–6, a berth costs £20–25, and two- and four-berth cabins are available for £57–77 and £80–100 respectively. Tickets are best booked in advance, through any major travel agent.

P&O provides a twice-weekly ferry service from **Portsmouth to Bilbao**, two hours closer to the mountains than Santander. The journey takes approximately 35 hours and leaves Portsmouth on Saturdays and Tuesdays. Return fares for a car and two people work out at between £310–720 (according to season), with foot passengers paying £260–400. Cabin berths are included in these prices. This sailing is significantly cheaper for motorcyclists than for cars, especially if you can find one of the frequent discounts offered by motorcycling publications.

GETTING THERE FROM IRELAND

There are no direct flights of any sort to the French Pyrenees from Dublin or Belfast, except some rather expensive, summer pilgrimage charters into Lourdes. However, using the Irish Republic's very own Ryanair, scheduled alternatives via London Stansted are keenly priced and well worth considering, with speedy connections on to Biarritz or Perpignan at opposite ends of the range. Quite pricey year-round scheduled air services operate from the Republic of Ireland to Barcelona, and there are a few summer charters to Girona.

If you're intent on flying to the Pyrenees in the cheapest possible way, you'll find that a **Ryanair** flight **from Dublin, Kerry, Cork or Knock to London Stansted** – count on IR£41 in peak season, but wildly cheap, single-figure specials at other times – is your best option, followed by their connecting daily services **to Biarritz or Perpignan**. For a three- or four-week non-changeable return flight in June or July, budget £105, with civilized flying times and afternoon arrivals; again, in off-season, there are often some fairly unbelievable deals (£30 or so return plus tax).

AIRLINES

Aer Lingus, www.aerlingus.ie
Northern Ireland reservations ☎0645/737 747;
40–41 O'Connell St, Dublin 1; 13 St Stephen's
Green, Dublin 2; 12 Upper St George's St, Dun
Laoghaire (centralized reservations at Dublin airport ☎01/705 3333/☎8444777); 2 Academy St,
Cork (☎021/327 155); 136 O'Connell St, Limerick
(☎061/474 239); Minicom/Text telephone
(☎01/705 3994).

British Airways, www.britishairways.com
1 Fountain Centre, College St, Belfast BT1 6ET
(☎0345/222 111, travel agency services

☎0345/326 566). BA doesn't have a Dublin
office, for reservations from Eire, call
☎0044/141/2222345.

British Midland, www.iflybritishmidland.com
Belfast airport ☎0345/554 554; Dublin airport
☎01/283 8833.

Iberia, 54 Dawson St, Dublin 2 (☎01/677 9846,
www.iberia.com).

Ryanair Phoenix House, Conyngham Rd, Dublin
8 (☎01/609 7800, www.ryanair.com).

AGENTS IN IRELAND

Aran Travel, 58 Dominick St, Galway (☎091/562
595, arantvl@iol.ie).

CIE Tours International, 35 Abbey St Lower,
Dublin 1 (☎01/703 1888).

Co-op Travel Care, 35 Belmont Rd, Belfast 4
(☎028/9047 1717).

Fahy Travel, 3 Bridge St, Galway (☎091/56 30
55).

Joe Walsh Tours, 69 Upper O'Connell St,
Dublin 2 (☎01/872 2555); 8–11 Baggot St, Dublin
2 (☎01/676 3053); 117 St Patrick St, Cork (☎021/
277 959). General budget fares agent.

Lee Travel, 24 Princes St, Cork (☎021/277 111).

Liffey Travel, 12 Upper O'Connell St, Dublin 1
(☎01/878 8322 or 878 8063). Package tour
specialists.

McCarthy Travel, 56 Patrick St, Cork (☎021/270
127).

Student & Group Travel, First Floor, 71 Dame
St, Dublin 2 (☎01/677 7834). Student and group
specialists, mostly to Europe.

Thomas Cook, 11 Donegall Place, Belfast
(☎028/9055 0232 or 9055 4455); 118 Grafton St,
Dublin 2 (☎01/677 0469). Package holiday and
flight agent, with occasional discount offers.

Trailfinders, 4–5 Dawson St, Dublin 2 (☎01/677
7888, www.trailfinders.com/dublin.htm).
Competitive fares out of all Irish airports, as well
as deals on hotels, insurance, tours and car
rental worldwide.

Travel Machine, 39 Dame Street, Dublin
(☎01/679 9020).

USIT Now, www.usitnow.ie
Fountain Centre, College St, Belfast BT1 6ET
(☎028/9032 4073); 10–11 Market Parade, Patrick
St, Cork (☎021/270 900); 33 Ferryquay St, Derry
(☎01504/371 888); 19 Aston Quay, Dublin 2
(☎01/602 1777 or 677 8117, Europe and UK
☎01/602 1600 or 679 8833, long-haul ☎01/602
1700); Victoria Place, Eyre Square, Galway
(☎091/565 177); Central Buildings,O'Connell St,
Limerick (☎061/415 064); 36–37 Georges St,
Waterford (☎051/872 601). Student and youth
specialists for flights and trains.

Iberia has nonstop **scheduled flights** from
Dublin to Barcelona costing from IR£223/€283
return in the low season (Jan–Feb) to
IR£265/€336 in July and August. These cheapest fares have several restrictions: you must
stay at least one Saturday night but no more
than one month, and no changes or refunds are
allowed. For non-direct flights via London
Heathrow, **fares** on Aer Lingus, BA and Iberia
are basically the same. Students, and anyone
under the age of 31, should contact USIT, which

generally has the best discount deals on flights
such as these.

There are also once-weekly summer (late June
to early Sept) **charter flights** to the Costa Brava
from Belfast (around £270–300 return), and from
Dublin to Barcelona (IR£190–210/€241–266),
with prices highest during August and dropping a
little in the months either side. If you're prepared
to book at the last minute, you'll often get much
better flight-only deals than this (as little as £99
from Belfast).

GETTING THERE FROM NORTH AMERICA

Being mountainous and remote, the Pyrenean region isn't a major air destination, though there are several secondary airports either side of the range, including relatively busy Barcelona. Whether you fly straight into one of these airports, or to Paris or Madrid and travel overland from there, will depend on your budget and your schedule.

If you don't mind spending a few days in a city first, or if you were planning to visit other parts of Europe anyway, it might not be worth flying all the way into the Pyrenees. Instead, consider buying a cheap transatlantic flight to a major gateway, and arranging onward travel when you get there.

If you're looking to regroup somewhere in Europe before continuing to the Pyrenees, and particularly starting from Canada, **London** is a good place to aim for: there are plenty of flights and overland options from there. If you plan to do the cross-Europe journey **by train** with a Eurail pass, see "Rail Passes" on p.14; for advice on getting from London to the Pyrenees, see "Getting There from Britain," pp.3–9.

SHOPPING FOR TICKETS

On high-traffic routes, discount outlets – advertised in Sunday newspaper travel sections such as the *New York Times* – are usually your best bet for cheap tickets, which come in several forms. **Consolidators** buy up large blocks of tickets that airlines don't think they can sell at their published fares, and unload them at a discount. Many advertise fares on a one-way or open-jaw basis,

enabling you to fly into one city and out from another without penalty. Consolidators normally don't impose advance purchase requirements (although in busy times you'll want to book ahead just to be sure of getting a ticket), but they do often charge very stiff fees for date changes. Also, these companies' profit margins are pretty tiny, so they make their money by dealing in volume – don't expect them to entertain lots of questions. **Discount agents** also deal in blocks of tickets offloaded by the airlines, but they typically offer a range of other travel-related services like travel insurance, rail passes, youth and student ID cards, car rentals and tours. These agencies tend to be most worthwhile to students and under-26s, who can often benefit from special fares and deals. **Travel clubs** are another option for those frequently on the move; most charge an annual membership fee, which may be worth it for their discounts on air tickets and car rental. You should also check the travel section in your major local newspaper for current bargains, and consult a good travel agent. Some agencies specialize in **charter flights**, which may be even cheaper than anything available on a scheduled flight, but again there's a trade-off: departure dates are fixed, and change/cancellation penalties are high (check the refund policy).

For destinations not handled by discounters – which applies to most of the Pyrenean airports – you'll have to deal with airlines' published fares. A good first stop for checking these are **travel Web sites** such as *www.travelselect.com*, *www.travelocity.com* or *www.expedia.com* The main problem is that these sites often list only the 'M' and 'H' full economy fares, and less reliably the really cheap 'Q' and 'V' tickets.

The cheapest way to go is with an **APEX** (Advance Purchase Excursion) ticket, though these carry certain restrictions. You usually have to book – and pay – at least 21 days before departure and spend at least seven days abroad (maximum stay three months), and you're liable to penalties if you change your schedule. Some airlines also issue **Special APEX** tickets to youth/student travellers, often with fewer restrictions on length of stay.

Regardless of who sells you your ticket, transatlantic fares are heavily dependent on **season**. As a rule, they're highest from early June to

DISCOUNT AGENTS, CONSOLIDATORS AND TRAVEL CLUBS

Airtech, 588 Broadway, Suite 204, New York, NY 10017 (☎1-800/575-8324 or 212/219-7000, *www.airtech.com*). Standby seat broker; also deals in consolidator fares and courier flights.

Council Travel, *www.counciltravel.com*
Head Office, 205 E 42nd St, New York, NY 10017 (☎1-800/226-8624 or 1-888/COUNCIL or 212/822-2700); 530 Bush St, Suite 700, San Francisco, CA 94108 (☎415/421-3473); 10904 Lindbrook Drive, Los Angeles 90024 (☎310/208-3551); 3300 M St NW, 2nd Floor, Washington, DC 20007 (☎202/337-6464); 1153 N Dearborn St, Chicago, IL 60610 (☎312/951-0585); 273 Newbury St, Boston, MA 02116 (☎617/266-1926). Nationwide specialists in student travel.

Moment's Notice, 7301 New Utrecht Ave, Brooklyn, NY 11204 (☎718/234-6295, *www.moments-notice.com*). Discount travel club.

New Frontiers/Nouvelles Frontières 12 E 33rd St, New York, NY 10016 (☎1-800/366-6387); 1221 Rue St Hubert, Suite 100, Montréal H2L3Y8 (☎514/288-4800). French discount travel firm. Other branches in LA, San Francisco and Québec City.

STA Travel, *www.sta-travel.com*
10 Downing St, New York, NY 10014 (☎1-800/777-0112 or 212/627-3111); 7202 Melrose Ave, Los Angeles, CA 90046 (☎323/934-8722); 51 Grant Ave, San Francisco, CA 94108 (☎415/391-8407); 297 Newbury St, Boston, MA 02115 (☎617/266-6014); 429 S Dearborn St,

Chicago, IL 60605 (☎312/786-9050); 3730 Walnut St, Philadelphia, PA 19104 (☎215/382-2928); 317 14th Ave SE, Minneapolis, MN 55414 (☎612/615-1800). Worldwide specialists in independent travel.

TFI Tours International, 34 W 32nd St, 12th Floor, New York, NY 10001 (☎1-800/745-8000 or 212/736-1140). Consolidator.

Travac, 989 6th Ave, New York NY 10018 (☎1-800/872-8800, *www.thetravelsite.com*). Consolidator and charter broker mostly to Europe; has another office in Orlando.

Travel Avenue, 10 S Riverside, Suite 1404, Chicago, IL 60606 (☎1-800/333-3335 or 1-312/876-6866, *www.travelavenue.com*). Discount travel company.

Travel CUTS, *www.travelcuts.com*
187 College St, Toronto, ON M5T 1P7 (☎1-800/667-2887 or 416/979-2406); 180 MacEwan Student Centre, University of Calgary, Calgary, AB T2N 1N4 (☎403/282-7687); 12304 Jasper Av, Edmonton, AB T5N 3K5 (☎403/488-8487); 1613 Rue St Denis, Montréal, PQ H2X 3K3 (☎514/843-8511); 555 W 8th Ave, Vancouver, BC V5Z 1C6 (☎1-888/FLY CUTS; 604/822-6890); University Centre, University of Manitoba, Winnipeg MB R3T 2N2 (☎204/269-9530). Canadian student travel organization.

Unitravel, 11737 Administration Drive, St Louis, MO 63146 (☎1-800/325-2222 or 314/569-2501, *www.flightsforless.com*). General consolidator.

the end of August, when everyone wants to travel; they drop during the "shoulder" seasons, September–October and April–May, and you'll get the best deals during the low season, November through March (excluding Christmas/New Year's). Note that flying on weekends ordinarily adds US$50/CDN$75 to the round-trip fare; **price ranges quoted in the following sections assume midweek travel and exclude** taxes (around US$50 or CDN$40–55).

PYRENEAN AIR CONNECTIONS

Flying into the Pyrenean region, your choices are Perpignan, Toulouse or Biarritz (in France) and Barcelona or Bilbao (in Spain). Of these, **Barcelona** is by far the biggest place, and therefore the most economical choice – Iberia has the

widest selection of transatlantic routes into Barcelona, and discount agencies or travel Web sites can put you on any of a dozen other airlines that fly there via Madrid or other European capitals (see box opposite). But through fares to Toulouse and Bilbao can be surprisingly attractive, and shouldn't be overlooked – though Bilbao is a good three hours' land journey from the mountains.

Fares **to Barcelona from the US** are very much in line with those to Madrid: figure around $570 **from New York** in low season, $920 in high season, direct on Iberia or via London Heathrow on British Airways. **From Miami**, budget $600/990, on British Airways via London or Iberia via Madrid; **from LA**, $700/1130, again on Iberia via New York or Chicago/Madrid. For Bilbao, some creative routings may be necessary – eg, from New York to Paris on Air France, and then to Bilbao on Iberia, for $975 in peak season. **Canadian fares** are broadly comparable; count on CDN$955 **from Toronto to Barcelona** in high season on either Air Canada or Lufthansa via Munich or Montreal, or CDN$1395 **to Bilbao** on a three-stop marathon with different airlines.

For the French side of the Pyrenees, there's a fair selection of flights into Paris from most points in the US, and the strong links between France and Canada's Francophone community keep those fares reasonable as well. For air fares **to Paris**, figure on $425 in the low season, $545 in the high season **from New York**, for example on British Airways via Manchester or Heathrow; **from LA or San Francisco**, $600/$1000, perhaps on US Air and BA via Pittsburgh and Heathrow; and **from Chicago**,

$500/$920 on United or American via Montreal, thence on Air France. From **Montreal**, expect to pay CDN$1375 direct to Paris on Air France or Air Canada, while flights **from Vancouver** may exceed CDN$2000 in high season.

Closer to the mountains, **Toulouse** may prove a worthwhile target for a through fare in high season: $545 **from New York** on British Airways via London Gatwick, $1035 from **Los Angeles** on Air France via Paris, and a surprising $740 **from Chicago**, though you may be routed via Madrid outbound on Iberia, back via London on Air France or British Airways. **Montreal** also has fairly competitive fares to Toulouse: CDN$1440 on KLM via Amsterdam or on Sabena via Brussels. **Biarritz** comes out poorly in comparison, and it's probably not worth insisting on this destination: $980 **from New York** on Air France, $1090 **from Los**

AIRLINES

Only gateway cities are listed for each airline; other routings are always possible using connecting flights.

Air Canada Canada ☎1-800/263-0882, US 1-800/776-3000, *www.aircanada.ca* Regular flights from Montreal, Toronto and Vancouver to Paris.

Air Europa ☎1-800/327-1225, *www.air-europa.com*

Flights from New York to Madrid five times a week.

Air France US ☎1-800/237-2747, Canada ☎1-800/667-2747, *www.airfrance.com* From New York, Chicago, Atlanta, Miami, San Francisco, Los Angeles, Washington DC, Toronto and Montreal to Paris, with onward connections to Toulouse and Biarritz.

American Airlines ☎1-800/433-7300, *www.americanair.com* Regular nonstop flights from Chicago to Madrid and to Paris.

British Airways US ☎1-800/247-9297, Canada ☎1-800/668-1059, *www.britishairways.com* From Montreal, Toronto and Vancouver plus 21 gateway cities in the US to Toulouse and Barcelona, all via London.

Canadian Airlines Canada ☎1-800/665-1177, US ☎1-800/426-7000, *www.cdnair.ca* Montreal, Toronto and Vancouver to Paris.

Delta Airlines ☎1-800/241-4141, *www.delta-air.com* Daily nonstop flights from New York and Atlanta to Barcelona with connections from most

other major North American cities; also regular links Boston and Cincinnati to Paris.

Iberia ☎1-800/772-4642, *www.iberia.com* From New York, Los Angeles, Miami and Chicago nonstop to Madrid with connections to Bilbao and Pamplona; direct New York to Barcelona.

Lufthansa US ☎1-800/645-3880, Canada ☎1-800/563-5954, *www.lufthansa-usa.com* From major US cities to Barcelona and Bilbao via Frankfurt; from Toronto via Munich.

Northwest/KLM US ☎1-800/447-4747, Canada ☎1-800/361-5073, *www.klm.com* From major US and Canadian cities to Barcelona or Toulouse via Amsterdam.

Sabena ☎1-800/955-2000, *www.sabena.com* Select East Coast and Midwest cities to Barcelona, Toulouse and Bilbao, via Brussels.

TAP Air Portugal ☎1-800/221-7370, *www.tap-airportugal.pt* Flights to Madrid and Barcelona via Lisbon; daily from New York and from Boston on Tuesday, Thursday & Saturday.

TWA ☎1-800/892-4141, *www.twa.com* Several weekly New York, Boston and St Louis to Paris and Barcelona.

United ☎1-800/241-6522, *www.ual.com* Daily nonstop flights from Washington DC to Madrid; from Chicago, San Francisco and Washington to Paris.

TOUR OPERATORS IN NORTH AMERICA

Backroads ☎1-800/462-2848,
www.backroads.com Eight-day walking tours,
spring and autumn, in the French Pays-Basques,
based around St-Jean-Pied-de-Port.

BCT Scenic Walking ☎1-800/473-1210,
www.bctwalk.com Offers an 8-day jaunt through
the Spanish and French Basque foothills, with
mild walking.

Camino Tours ☎1-800/938-9311,
www.caminotours.com Fairly leisurely and
sybaritic week from the Catalan coast up to La
Seu d'Urgell.

Mountain Travel/Sobek ☎1-888/MTSOBEK,
www.mtsobek.com Hiking in the Basque
Pyrenees.

Saranjan Tours ☎1-800/858-9594,
www.saranjan.com Spain specialists doing an
ambitious, 9-day tour from La Seu to San
Sebastián, with moderate walking.

Wilderness Travel ☎1-800/368-2794,
www.wildernesstravel.com Hiking in the
Pyrenees or Basque country.

Angeles using Delta via Cincinnati to Paris, $985
from Chicago via Montreal and Paris, though
Montreal to Biarritz isn't too bad at CDN$1445,
on a multi-stop itinerary with Sabena and Air
France.

PACKAGE TOURS

Package tours may not sound like your kind of
travel, but don't dismiss the idea out of hand. If
you really want to get up into the Pyrenees, you
might find it worthwhile to have a company make
the arrangements for you – especially if your time
is limited. A package trip can also be great for
your peace of mind, if only to ensure a worry-free
first week while you're finding your feet on a
longer tour.

That said, not many North American companies go to the Pyrenees. Most of those that do
specialize in vehicle-supported **hiking** trips,
which can cost around $2000 per week.

RAIL PASSES

A Eurail Pass is not likely to pay for itself if you're
planning to stick to the Pyrenees, or even Spain
and/or France. You stand a better chance of getting
your money's worth out of a Eurail **Flexipass**,
which is good for a certain number of travel days in
a two-month period. This comes in under-26 and
first-class versions: 10 days cost $458/654; and 15
days, $599/862. A further alternative is to attempt
to buy an InterRail pass in Europe (see "Getting
There from Britain") – most agents don't check residential qualifications, but once you're in Europe it'll
be too late to buy a Eurail Pass if you have problems.

North Americans are also eligible to purchase
more specific passes valid for travel in France or
Spain only (see "Getting Around," p.32 and p.36).
All these passes can be reserved through Rail
Europe (☎1-800/848-7245) – with a half-dozen
branches across North America – or youth-oriented travel agents.

GETTING THERE FROM AUSTRALIA AND NEW ZEALAND

There are no direct flights to the Pyrenees from Australia or New Zealand, so you'll have to aim initially for Paris, Barcelona or Madrid. Layovers mean a journey of around 24 hours' flying time via Asia, or 30 hours via North America – not counting time spent waiting for connections – with flights via Asia typically cheaper. Air France's services to Paris from Sydney or Auckland are the most direct, though fares are among the most expensive going. The lowest return fares to Paris, Barcelona and Madrid tend to be with carriers such as JAL, MAS, Thai International and Singapore Airlines. Before consulting an in-the-flesh travel agency, have a look at the useful travel Web sites *www.travelshop.com.au*, *www.sydneytravel.com* and *www.travel.com.au* – these give you an idea of the sometimes bizarre routings to France or Spain, and what you can expect to pay.

Regular return **fares** vary according to the season. Low season is from mid-January to the end of February and October–November; high season is mid-May to August and December–January; the remainder of the year is made up of a variety of shoulder seasons. Most regular return economy fares to Madrid, Barcelona or Paris cost between A$1800 in the low season and A$2800 in the high season from eastern Australian gateways, and NZ$2000–3000 from Auckland, with fares climbing by A$300/NZ$300 increments in the intermediate shoulder seasons. A survey of the Australian Internet travel sites will often turn up high-season

quotes of (for example) A$1835 from Sydney to Paris, or A$1945 from Sydney to Barcelona or Madrid, for tickets valid six months. New Zealanders tend to be slightly worse off choice-wise – though NZ$2540 as a high-season fare to Paris via Sydney, or NZ$2900 to Madrid via London, aren't too bad as samples of what you can get on a major airline.

Alternatively, you can find a **rock-bottom** return fare to Amsterdam, London or another European hub city with Garuda or SriLankan Air for around A$1400/NZ$1700 low season, and then either pick up a cheap flight (see pp.3–4) or travel overland by road (see p.8) or rail (see "Tickets and passes" on p.7). However, with the high living and transport costs in northwestern Europe, this rarely works out any cheaper in practice, unless you specifically intend to see the intervening territory.

If you're planning to visit the Pyrenees as part of a wider world trip, then **Round-the-World** tickets (valid for a year) offer greater flexibility (though they typically exclude South America) and are better value than a straightforward return flight. These are put together by code-sharing airlines – marketing groups such as Star Alliance and Oneworld – and are usually priced according to either the number of stopovers you make, or the distance you cover. For example, a RTW ticket from Sydney or Auckland to Singapore or Bangkok, then on to Delhi, Frankfurt, Madrid, New York, LA, Honolulu or Papeete and back home again starts at around A$2399/NZ$2899.

Tickets purchased direct from the airlines tend to be expensive, those from Web sites slightly less so. **Travel agents** generally offer much better deals, and have the latest information on limited special offers and stopovers. Some of the best discounts are offered by companies such as Flight Centre, STA and Trailfinders (see box on p.17); these can also help with visas, travel insurance and tours. Students and under-26s are usually able to get at least ten percent off published prices.

RAIL PASSES

Only if you're planning to visit the Pyrenees as part of a longer European trip is it worth buying a **Eurail** pass, but it wouldn't pay for itself if you're flying into Paris or Madrid and just intent on get-

AIRLINES

Air France Australia ☎02/9244 2100, New Zealand ☎09/308 3352; *www.airfrance.fr*
Daily direct flights to Paris from major Australian gateway cities, continues to Madrid and Barcelona; first leg of journey may be with code-sharing Qantas.

Air New Zealand ☎09/336 2364, *www.ansett.com.au*
Code-shares with United Airlines and Air Canada, among others in Star Alliance, to provide onward connections/fares from its initial destinations of Los Angeles and London, including RTW fares.

British Airways Australia ☎02/8904 8800; New Zealand ☎09/356 8690
Daily services to London from Sydney, with good add-ons to Barcelona and Toulouse in particular; code-shares with Qantas to provide a RTW fare.

Garuda Australia ☎1300/365 330; New Zealand ☎09/366 1855 or 1800/128 510
Several flights weekly from major cities in Australia and New Zealand to Paris, with either a transfer or an overnight stop in Denpasar or Jakarta; onward connection to Spain on a different airline.

Japan Airlines Australia ☎02/9272 1111; New Zealand ☎09/379 9906; *www.japanair.com*
Daily flights to Madrid or Paris from Brisbane and Sydney, and several flights a week from Cairns and Auckland, all involving a transfer or overnight stop in Tokyo or Osaka. Code-shares with Iberia and Air New Zealand.

Lauda Air Australia ☎02/9251 6155 or 1800/642 438; *www.lauda-air.com*
Four flights weekly to Barcelona from Sydney with transfers in Kuala Lumpur or Vienna.

Malaysia Airlines Australia ☎13 2627; New Zealand ☎09/373 2741 or 008/657 472

Twice weekly, to Madrid via Kuala Lumpur and Istanbul, and to Paris via Kuala Lumpur and Munich, from Brisbane, Sydney, Melbourne, Perth and Auckland.

Qantas Australia ☎13/1313; NZ ☎09/357 8900 or 0800/808 767; *www.qantas.com.au*
Daily flights to Madrid, Barcelona and Paris from major cities in Australia and New Zealand with a transfer in Singapore or Bangkok, and London. May code-share with British Airways for last leg of trip.

Royal Jordanian Airlines Australia ☎02/9244 2701; NZ agent ☎03/365 3910
Twice weekly to Madrid via Amman.

Singapore Airlines Australia ☎02/9350 0262 or 13 1011; New Zealand ☎09/303 2129 or 0800/808 909; *www.singaporeair.com*
Daily flights to Madrid and Paris from Brisbane, Sydney, Melbourne, Perth and Auckland with either a transfer or overnight stop in Singapore.

SriLankan Airlines Australia ☎02/9244 2234; New Zealand ☎09/308 3353
Three flights a week to London, Paris and Rome from Sydney with a transfer or overnight stop in Colombo; onward connections to Barcelona.

Thai Airways Australia ☎1300/651 960; New Zealand ☎09/377 3886; *www.thaiair.com*
Several flights weekly to Madrid and Paris from Sydney, Melbourne, Brisbane and Auckland via Bangkok, and possible transfers in Rome or Frankfurt.

United Airlines Australia ☎13 1777; New Zealand ☎09/379 3800; *www.ual.com*
Several flights a week to Madrid from Sydney, Melbourne and Auckland with transfers in LA and Washington, DC. Code-shares with Spanair from Washington. Also several weekly to Paris from Auckland via LA, code-sharing with Air New Zealand.

---

ting to the mountains. Such passes need to be bought in your home country before you leave; terms and conditions for Australian and New Zealand travellers are much the same as for Americans and Canadians (see p.14).

The **Eurail Flexipass** is good for a certain number of travel days in a two-month period and also comes in youth/first-class versions: 10 days cost A$725/1040 (NZ$891/1279); and 15 days, A$950/1370 (NZ$1168/1685). A scaled-down version of the Flexipass, the Europass allows travel in France,

Germany, Italy, Spain and Switzerland for (youth/first-class) A$370/550 (NZ$455/676) for five days in two months, on up to A$815/1155 (NZ$1002/1420) for 15 days in two months; there's also the option of adding adjacent "associate" countries (Austria, Hungary, Benelux, Portugal and Greece).

Passes are available through **Rail Plus** (in Australia ☎1300/555 003 or 03/9642 8644, *info@railplus.com.au*; in New Zealand ☎09/303 2484) or **CIT World Travel** (☎02/9267 1255, *www.cittravel.com.au*).

DISCOUNT TRAVEL AGENTS IN AUSTRALIA/NEW ZEALAND

Anywhere Travel, 345 Anzac Parade, Kingsford, Sydney (☎02/9663 0411 or 018 401 014, *anywhere@ozemail.com.au*).

Budget Travel, 16 Fort St, Auckland, plus branches around the city (☎09/366 0061 or 0800/808 040).

Destinations Unlimited, 220 Queen St, Auckland (☎09/373 4033).

Flight Centre Australia, *www.flightcentre.com.au* 82 Elizabeth St, Sydney, plus branches nationwide (☎02/9235 3522, nearest branch ☎13 1600). New Zealand: 350 Queen St, Auckland (☎09/358 4310), plus branches nationwide.

Northern Gateway, 22 Cavenagh St, Darwin (☎08/8941 1394, *oztravel@norgate.com.au*).

STA Travel, *www.statravel.com.au* Australia: 855 George St, Sydney; 256 Flinders St, Melbourne; other offices in state capitals and major universities (nearest branch ☎13 1776, fastfare telesales ☎1300/360 960). New Zealand: 10 High St, Auckland (☎09/309 0458, fastfare telesales ☎09/366 6673), plus branches in Wellington, Christchurch, Dunedin, Palmerston North, Hamilton and at major universities.

Student Uni Travel, 92 Pitt St, Sydney (☎02/9232 8444, *sydney@backpackers.net*) plus branches in Brisbane, Cairns, Darwin, Melbourne and Perth.

Thomas Cook, *www.thomascook.com.au* Australia: 175 Pitt St, Sydney (☎02/9231 2877); 257 Collins St, Melbourne; plus branches in other state capitals (local branch ☎13 1771, Thomas Cook Direct telesales ☎1800/801 002); New Zealand: 191 Queen St, Auckland (☎09/379 3920).

Trailfinders, 8 Spring St, Sydney (☎02/9247 7666); 91 Elizabeth St, Brisbane (☎07/3229 0887); Hides corner, Shield St, Cairns (☎07/4041 1199).

Travel.com.au, 76–80 Clarence St, Sydney (☎02/9249 5444 or 1800 000 447, *www.travel.com.au*).

Usit Beyond, cnr Shortland St and Jean Batten Place, Auckland (☎09/379 4224 or ☎0800/788 336, *www.usitbeyond.co.nz*) plus branches in Christchurch, Dunedin, Palmerston North, Hamilton and Wellington.

SPECIALIST AGENTS AND OPERATORS

The Adventure Travel Company, 164 Parnell Rd, Parnell, Auckland (☎09/379 9755, *advakl@hot.co.nz*). NZ agent for Peregrine (see below).

Adventure Specialists, 1/69 Liverpool St, Sydney (☎02/9261 2927). A good selection of adventure holidays in the Pyrenees.

Adventure World, *www.adventureworld.com.au* 73 Walker St, North Sydney (☎02/9956 7766 or 1300/363 055), plus branches in Adelaide, Brisbane, Melbourne and Perth; 101 Great South Rd, Remuera, Auckland (☎09/524 5118). Agents for a vast array of international adventure travel companies that operate trips to the Pyrenees.

France Unlimited 16 Goldsmith St, Elwood,

Melbourne (☎03/9531 8787). All French travel arrangements, including cycling tours.

Peregrine Adventures, 258 Lonsdale St, Melbourne (☎03/9662 2700 or 1300 655 433, *www.peregrine.net.au*), plus offices in Brisbane, Sydney, Adelaide and Perth. Guided walking and biking holidays in the Pyrenees.

Snow Bookings Only, 1141 Toorak Rd, Camberwell, Melbourne (☎03/9809 2699 or 1800/623 266). Arranges skiing and snow-boarding holidays.

Walkabout Gourmet Adventures, PO Box 52, Dinner Plain, Victoria 3898 (☎03/51 596556, *www.reho.com/walkabout*). All-inclusive 14-day food-and-wine walking trip through the Pyrenees (from $3200/NZ$3800 land-only).

RED TAPE AND VISAS

For EU citizens there is no problem moving around in the Pyrenees, since the range straddles two member nations, and for most other nationals life has been made easier by the relaxation of various tourism restrictions. If you're making a brief excursion across the border in the mountains, it is still advisable to carry a passport or other ID, since hotels and refuges often demand identification – in particular Spain, where non-EU citizens must fill out a registration card at every lodging.

Australia and Norway, do not need any visa to enter France, and can stay for up to ninety days. All other passport holders (including British Travel Document holders) must obtain a visa before arrival in France. Obtaining one from your nearest French consulate is fairly automatic, but check their hours before turning up, and leave plenty of time, since there are often queues (particularly in London during summer).

Three types of visa are currently issued: a transit visa, valid for two months; a short-stay (*court séjour*) visa, valid for ninety days after date of issue and good for multiple entries; and a long-stay visa (*long séjour*), which allows for multiple stays of ninety days over three years, but only issued after examination of individual circumstances.

EU citizens (and other non-visa nationals) who **stay longer than three months** are officially supposed to apply for a *Carte de Séjour*, for which you'll have to show proof of income at least equal to the minimum wage. However, EU passports are no longer stamped, so there is no evidence of how long you've been in the country. If your non-EU passport is stamped, cross the border – a highly likely event anyway if you're in the Pyrenees – and re-enter for another ninety days legitimately.

FRANCE

Citizens of **EU countries**, and thirty other nations including **Canada**, the **USA**, **New Zealand**,

SPAIN

Citizens of most **EU countries** (and of Norway and Iceland) need only a valid national identity

FRENCH EMBASSIES AND CONSULATES

Australia 31 Market St, Sydney, NSW 2000 (☎02/9261 5779); 492 St Kilda Rd, Melbourne, VIC 3001 (☎03/9820 0921).

Britain Consulate General (Visa Section), 6a Cromwell Place, London SW7, Mon–Fri 9–10am &1.30–2.30pm only (☎020/7838 2051); 7–11 Randolph Crescent, Edinburgh, Mon–Fri 9.30am–1pm (☎0131/220 6324).

Canada 42 Promenade Sussex, Ottawa ONT K1M 2C9 (☎613/789 1795). There are consulates in Montreal, Québec, Toronto, Moncton and Vancouver.

Ireland 36 Ailesbury Rd, Dublin 4 (☎01/260 1666).

New Zealand 34–42 Manners St, PO Box 11-343, Wellington (☎04/384 2555)

USA Embassy: 4101 Reservoir Rd NW, Washington DC 20007 (☎202/944-6000). Consulates: Prominence in Buckhead, Suite 1840, 3475 Piedmont Rd NE, Atlanta, GA 30305 (☎404/495 1660); Park Square Building, Suite 750, 31 St James Ave, Boston MA 02116 (☎617/542 7374); 737 North Michigan Ave, Olympia Centre, Suite 2020, Chicago, IL 60611 (☎312/787 5360); 10990 Wilshire Blvd, Suite 300, Los Angeles CA 90024 (☎310/235 3200); 934 Fifth Ave, New York NY 10021 (☎212/606 3688); 2 South Biscayne Blvd, One Biscayne Tower, Suite 1710, Miami FL 33131 (☎305/372-9799); 340 Poydras St, Amoco Building, Suite 1718, New Orleans LA (☎504/523-5772); 540 Bush St, San Francisco, CA 94108 (☎415/397 4330).

SPANISH EMBASSIES AND CONSULATES

Australia 15 Arkana St, Yarralumla, ACT 2600 (☎02/6273 3555); 24th Floor, St Martin Tower, 3131 Market St, Sydney, NSW 2000 (☎02/9261 2433); 4th Floor, 540 Elizabeth St, Melbourne, VIC 3000 (☎03/9347 1966).

Britain 20 Draycott Place, London SW3 2RZ (☎020/7589 8989); Suite 1a, Brook House, 70 Spring Gardens, Manchester M22 2BQ (☎0161/236 1262).

Canada 74 Stanley Ave, Ottawa, Ontario K1M 1P4 (☎613/747-2252); 1 Westmount Sq #1456, Ave Wood, Montréal, Quebec H3Z 2P9 (☎514/935-5235); Simcoe Place, 200 Front St, #2401, Toronto, Ontario M5V 3K2 (☎416/977-1661).

Ireland 17a Merlyn Park, Ballsbridge, Dublin 4 (☎01/269 1640).

New Zealand contact the consulate in Sydney.

USA 2375 Pennsylvania Ave NW, Washington DC 20009 (☎202/728-2330); 150 E 58th St, New York, NY 10155 (☎212/355-4090); 545 Boylston St #803, Boston, MA 02116 (☎617/536-2506); 180 N Michigan Ave #1500, Chicago, IL 60601 (☎312/782-4588); 1800 Bering Dr #660, Houston, TX 77057 (☎713/783-6200); 5055 Wilshire Blvd #960, Los Angeles, CA 90036 (☎323/938-0158); 2655 Le Jeune Rd #203, Coral Gables, Miami, FL 33134 (☎305/446-5511); 2102 World Trade Center, 2 Canal St, New Orleans, LA 70130 (☎504/525-4951); 1405 Sutter St, San Francisco, CA 94109 (☎415/922-2995).

card to enter Spain for up to ninety days. Since Britain has no identity-card system, however, British citizens do have to take a passport. **US, other European, Canadian, Australian and New Zealand citizens** also only require a passport and can stay for up to ninety days. Under the Schengen agreement a visa valid for France will also do for Spain under the same ninety-day period, and vice versa.

To **stay longer**, EU nationals (and citizens of Norway and Iceland) can apply for a *permiso de residencia* (residence permit) once in Spain. A temporary residency permit is valid for up to a year, and you'll need an extension after that (valid for up to five years). Applications need to be made at the *Oficina de Extranjeros* in the main cities or at the police station nearest to where you'll be taking up residency. You'll either have to produce proof that you have sufficient funds (officially 5000ptas/€30 a day) to be able to support yourself without working – easiest done by keeping bank exchange forms every time you change money – or you'll have to have a contract of employment (*contrato de trabajo*) or become self-employed (for example as a teacher), which involves registering at the tax office. US citizens can apply – usually at any police station – for one ninety-day extension, showing proof of funds. Other nationalities will need to get a special visa from a Spanish consulate before departure (see above for addresses).

COSTS, MONEY AND BANKS

Prices in the Pyrenees don't differ greatly from those in towns and cities away from the mountains. If you do spend less than you budget on a Pyrenean holiday, it will be because there isn't much scope to go financially wild once you're off the beaten track.

There are a couple of things to bear in mind if you're really determined to keep costs down. Transport is likely to be a major expense in both countries, but with the limited rail network in the mountains, any rail pass is unlikely to pay for itself unless you travel in the flatlands as well. However, if you're entitled to one, be sure to carry an ISIC (International Student Identity Card) – it will get you free or reduced entry to many museums and sites as well as other occasional discounts. As always, if you're travelling alone you'll end up spending much more than you would in a

group of two or more – sharing rooms saves greatly.

FRANCE

Because of the relatively low cost of accommodation and eating out, at least by northern European standards, France is not an outrageously expensive place to visit. **On average**, staying exclusively at *gîtes* or refuges, or camping, and being strong-willed about denying yourself cups of coffee and culture, you could just about survive on £24/US$35 per person per day, including an inexpensive restaurant meal. For a more comfortable existence, including a basic, shared hotel room and restaurant or café stops, you need to budget about £35–40/$55–65 per person per day. If you're planning to stay in fancier lodgings, and eat and drink to your heart's content, £55/$80 per day per head wouldn't be an unreasonable estimate.

Two or more people will find that sharing **hotel accommodation** can occasionally be as cheap as staying at refuges or at a *gîte d'étape*, – certainly the case with relatively basic hotels in our category ② (see p.41) – though a more usual estimate for a double room would be £15–20/$23–30), corresponding to category ③. There are large numbers of good **restaurants** with three- or even four-course menus for £7–12/$11–19). **Picnic fare**, obviously, is much less costly, while more sophisticated, but reasonably priced, **takeaway** meals – salads and ready-to-reheat dishes – can be put together at *charcuteries* (delis) and the equivalent

THE EURO

Spain and France are two of twelve European Union countries who have changed over to a single currency, the **euro** (€). The transition period, which began on January 1, 1999, is however lengthy: euro notes and coins are not scheduled to be issued until January 1, 2002, with Spanish pesetas and French francs remaining in place for cash transactions, at a fixed rate of 166.386 pesetas to 1 euro, and 6.55957 francs to 1 euro, until they are scrapped entirely at the end of February, 2002.

Even before euro cash appears in 2002, you can opt to pay in euros by credit card and you can get travellers' cheques in euros – you should not be charged commission for changing them in any of the twelve countries in the euro zone (also known as "Euroland"), nor for changing from any of the old Euroland currencies to any other (pesetas to francs, for example).

All restaurant, accommodation and admission **prices in this book** are given in pesetas or francs, and the euro equivalent, with the euro price rounded up to the nearest decimal unit.

Euro notes will be issued in **denominations** of 5, 10, 20, 50, 100, 200 and 500 euros, and coins in denominations of 1, 2, 5, 10, 20 and 50 cents and 1 and 2 euros.

counters of many supermarkets. Note that **museums, theme parks and monuments**, at 10–75F/€1.50–11.50 per entrance, can make substantial inroads into a daily budget.

Transport will inevitably be a large item of expenditure if you're not strictly on a walking tour. The standard tariff for trains is about 70 centimes per kilometre (sample fare: Bayonne to Perpignan, over 500km, 330F). Buses are less expensive though prices vary enormously from one operator to another. Rental bikes cost about £10/$15 per day. For fuel prices, see "Getting Around", p.34.

CURRENCY AND THE EXCHANGE RATE

While it endures, the **French currency** is the **franc**, abbreviated as F or sometimes FF, divided into 100 centimes. It comes in notes of 500, 200, 100, 50 and 20F, and coins of 10, 5, 2 and 1F, and 50, 20, 10 and 5 centimes. The current exchange rate for the franc is just under 11F to the pound sterling, and just under 8F to the US dollar – as weak as it's been for years against these currencies, and likely to firm up a bit in the future. The fixed rate against the euro is €=6.5597F. For the most up-to-date exchange rates, consult the very useful currency speculators' Web site, *www.oanda.com*

TRAVELLER'S AND GIRO CHEQUES

Traveller's cheques are one of the safest ways of carrying your money, available from almost any major bank (whether you have an account there or not), usually for a service charge of one to two percent of the amount purchased. Your own bank may offer cheques free of charge provided you meet certain conditions – it's always worth asking first. Thomas Cook, Visa and American Express are the most widely recognized brands in France. Obtaining **French franc traveller's cheques** at the outset could be very worthwhile: they can often be used as cash, and French banks are supposed to give you the face value of the cheques when you change them, so commission is only paid on purchase. Also worth considering are post office International **Giro Cheques**, which work like ordinary bank cheques except that you can cash them at post offices, which are more common and have longer opening hours than banks. The Eurocheque scheme was discontinued on January 1, 2001.

The latest way of carrying your money abroad is with a **Visa TravelMoney** Card, a sort of electronic traveller's cheque. This disposable debit card is "loaded up" with a prepaid amount, and it can then be used in any Visa-compatible ATM, with a PIN which you select yourself. UK commissions are two percent per transaction. Once your funds are depleted, you simply throw the card away. It's recommended you buy at least a second card as a back-up in case your first is lost, stolen or damaged, though like paper cheques, the cards can be replaced if mishaps occur. Up to nine cards can be bought to access the same funds – useful for couples/families travelling together. In the UK, the cards are sold by Thomas Cook, through their offices, or by phone on ☎01733/381900. In the US, call ☎1-800/444-1244, (*www.visa.com*).

CREDIT/DEBIT CARDS

Credit/debit cards are widely accepted; it's always worth asking beforehand, however, in smaller hotels and restaurants. Transactions are debited with immediate effect, the waiter or desk clerk running your card through an online swipe reader without use of the PIN number. Visa – known as the *Carte Bleue* in France – is almost universally recognized; American Express and Mastercard – sometimes called Eurocard – rank considerably lower, with only Crédit Agricole and the Crédit Mutuel providing facilities for the latter. Retailers in particular hate American Express, so you should not expect to find much acceptance for it in France. Cash advances on credit cards can be obtained at most bank counters, but with a PIN number you can take advantage of the numerous electronic autotellers (**ATM**s) dotted across the Pyrenean foothills. The words for 'ATM' **in French** are *guichet automatique*, or *distributeur de billets*. Many of these – in particular ATMs attached to post offices (*La Poste*) – also accept debit cards of the Cirrus and/or Plus systems, but the machines have been known to eat or refuse incompatible cards. Debit cards are considerably cheaper to use in this manner, with commissions of two percent versus nearly four percent for credit cards, but there is a minimum charge of about £1.50/$2, so don't be constantly withdrawing small sums. Lost or stolen cards should be reported either to your own-country emergency number, or one of the following French hotlines: Carte Bleue (Visa) ☎01.42.77.11.90; American Express ☎01.47.77.72.00; Mastercard (Eurocard) ☎01.45.67.53.53.

CHANGING MONEY

Standard banking hours are Monday to Friday 9am–4 or 5pm, many closing at midday (noon–2pm or 12.30–2.30pm). A few are open Saturday 9am–noon, but all close on Sundays and holidays. Rates of exchange and commissions vary from bank to bank. The Crédit Mutuel usually offers the best rates and takes the least commission; it also keeps Saturday-morning hours.

There are **money-exchange counters** at the train stations of all big cities, and usually a few in the town centre as well. You'll also find **automatic bill-changer machines** at airports and train stations, accepting notes in dollar, sterling and major non-euro currencies such as Swiss francs. However, rates for both these facilities tend to be poor and the commission high, so it would be a sensible precaution to buy some French francs before arriving in France.

SPAIN

Although people still think of Spain as a budget destination, hotel prices have increased considerably since the late 1980s, and in the more popular parts of the Catalan Pyrenees especially, you can easily spend more than in neighbouring France. Overall, though, there are still few places in Europe where you'll get a better deal on the cost of simple meals and drink, and sharp devaluations of the peseta since 1995 have cushioned the impact of rising prices – for outsiders, anyway.

On average, if you're prepared to buy your own picnic lunch, stay in inexpensive *pensiones* and hotels, and stick to the most basic restaurants and bars, you could get by on £20–25/US$29–36 per person per day. If you intend to upgrade your accommodation, experience town nightlife and eat fancier meals then you'll need more like £40/$58 a day. On £50–60/$73–87 a day and upwards you'll only be limited by your energy reserves – though of course if you're planning to stay in four- and five-star hotels, this figure won't even cover your room.

Room prices vary considerably according to season, but in the Pyrenees you'll find little below 2200ptas (£8/$11) single, 3500ptas (£13/$19) double – 3200ptas single (£12/$17), 4800ptas double (£18/$26) might be a more realistic average. Campsites start at around 400ptas (£1.50/$2.50) a night per person (up to 700ptas in some of the major resorts), plus a similar charge for a tent.

The cost of **eating** can vary wildly, but in most Pyrenean towns there'll be restaurants offering a basic three-course meal for somewhere between 1200 and 2100ptas (£4.50–7.75/$6.50–11.25). As often as not, though, you'll end up wandering from one bar to the next sampling *tapas* without getting round to a real sit-down meal – though this is rarely any cheaper. Drink, and wine in particular, costs ridiculously little: £3/$5 will see you through a night's very substantial intake of the local vintage.

Long-distance **transport**, if used extensively, may prove a major expense. Although per-kilometre prices compare well with the rest of Europe, Spain is a very large country. Even rural Pyrenean journeys between nearby places tend to be long because of the tortuous routings. Urban transport almost always operates on a flat fare of 150–250ptas/60–90p/$0.90–1.30.

All of the above, inevitably, are affected by **where you are and when**. The big towns and tourist resorts are invariably more expensive than remoter areas, and certain regions tend also to have higher prices – notably the industrialized lowlands of Euskadi and Catalunya. Prices are hiked up, too, to take advantage of special events.

One thing to look out for on prices generally is the addition of sales tax – **IVA** – which may come as an unexpected extra when you pay the bill for food or accommodation. The magic words, often in small print at the bottom of the menu, are *IVA (no) incluido* in Castilian or *IVA (no) inclós* in Catalan. Even fairly modest restaurants and hotels often add seven percent IVA to the total after the fact.

CURRENCY AND THE EXCHANGE RATE

Until supplanted by the euro (see box p.20), the **Spanish currency** is the **peseta**, indicated in this book as "ptas". Coins come in denominations of 5, 10, 25, 50, 100, 200 and 500 pesetas; notes as 1000, 2000, 5000 and 10,000 pesetas. The only oddity is that in a shop when paying for something, you'll often be asked for a *duro* (5ptas) or *veinte duros* (100ptas). A widespread colloquial word for pesetas, while they last, is *pelas* (literally, "peels").

The exchange rate for the Spanish peseta is currently around 275 to the pound sterling, 195 to the US dollar; as with French francs, see *www.oanda.com* for up-to-the-minute rates. The exchange rate with the euro has been fixed at €=166.386ptas. You can take in as much money as you want (in any form), although amounts over a million pesetas must be declared, and you can only take up to 500,000 pesetas out unless you can prove that you brought more with you in the first place. Not, perhaps, a major holiday worry.

CHEQUES AND CREDIT/DEBIT CARDS

In Spain, too, the easiest way for non-European nationals to carry funds is in **traveller's cheques** (see "France" section above), though you should watch out for occasionally outrageous commissions; 500–600ptas per transaction for non-euro currencies isn't unusual. Any Visa or Mastercard credit card, as well as any **debit card** that is part of the Cirrus or Plus systems, can be used for **withdrawing cash** from the numerous ATMs in the Pyrenean foothills and resorts. The Castilian for 'ATM' is *cajero automatico*. As in France, Spanish "holes in the wall" are highly sophisticated and will give instructions in a variety of languages. Check your bank's literature for surcharges on such transactions, which usually vary from about two percent (for debit cards) to nearly four percent (credit cards).

Leading **credit cards** are also recognized by major retailers, car rental firms, petrol stations and expensive hotels. American Express, and Visa, which has an arrangement with the Banco Bilbao Vizcaya, are the most useful; Mastercard is less widely accepted.

CHANGING MONEY

Spanish **bancos** (banks) and **cajas de ahorro** (savings banks) have branches in all but the smallest towns, and many of them are prepared to change traveller's cheques – though stick to major brands like Amex, Visa and Thomas Cook to avoid refusal. The Banco Central Hispano and Banco Bilbao Vizcaya are two of the most efficient and widespread; elsewhere you may have to queue up at two or three windows, a twenty-to-thirty-minute process. Both these banks change most brands of traveller's cheques, and give cash advances on credit cards; commissions at the Banco Central Hispano are generally the lowest around.

Banking hours are Mon–Fri 9am–2pm, Sat 9am–1pm (except June–Sept when banks close on Sat). Outside these times, it's usually possible to change cash at larger hotels (generally bad rates, low commission) or with travel agents, who may initially grumble but will eventually concede a rate with the commission built in – useful for small amounts in a hurry.

In tourist areas you'll also find specialist **casas de cambio**, with more convenient hours (though exchange rates vary – "no commission charged" often means a poor rate). Most branches of El Corte Inglés, a major department store found throughout Spain, have efficient exchange facilities open throughout store hours and offering competitive rates and generally a much lower commission for cheques than the banks (though they're worse for cash).

INSURANCE

Some form of travel insurance is highly recommended for the Pyrenees. Besides covering medical emergencies and the cost of any drugs prescribed by pharmacies (see p.25–26), policies also cover loss or theft of luggage, tickets, money and other property. Note that claims for theft can only be dealt with if a report is made to the local police within 24 hours and a copy of the report sent with the claim. Also very few insurers will arrange on-the-spot payments in the event of a major expense or loss; you will usually be reimbursed only after going home.

A typical travel insurance policy usually provides cover for the loss of baggage, tickets and – up to a certain limit – cash or cheques, as well as cancellation or curtailment of your journey and/or bankruptcy of air carriers. Most of them exclude so-called dangerous sports unless an extra premium is paid. Read the small print and benefits tables of prospective policies carefully; coverage can vary wildly for roughly similar premiums. Many policies can be chopped and changed to exclude coverage you don't need – for example, sickness and accident benefits can often be excluded or included at will. If you do take medical coverage, ascertain whether benefits will be paid as treatment proceeds or only after return home, and whether there is a 24-hour medical emergency number. When securing baggage cover, make sure that the per-article limit – typically under £500 equivalent – will cover your most valuable possession. If you need to make a claim, you should keep receipts for medicines and medical treatment, and in the event you have anything stolen, you must obtain an official statement from the police.

British credit cards often have certain levels of medical or other insurance included – though typically only for death or loss of limbs – and you may automatically get some sort of coverage if you use a major credit card to pay for your trip. If you have a good all-risks home insurance policy, it *may* cover your possessions against loss or theft even when overseas (again, conditions vary). Many private medical schemes such as BUPA or PPP also offer coverage plans for abroad, including baggage loss, cancellation or curtailment and cash replacement as well as sickness or accident.

ROUGH GUIDES TRAVEL INSURANCE

Rough Guides now offers its own **travel insurance**, customized for our readers by a leading UK broker and backed by a Lloyds underwriter. It's available for anyone, of any nationality and age, travelling anywhere in the world.

There are two main Rough Guide insurance plans: **Essential**, for basic, no-frills cover; and **Premier** – with more generous and extensive benefits. Alternatively, you can take out annual **multi-trip insurance**, which covers you for any number of trips throughout the year (with a maximum of 60 days for any one trip). Unlike many policies, the Rough Guides schemes are calculated by the day, so if you're travelling for 27 days rather than a month, that's all you pay for. If you intend to be away for the whole year, the **Adventurer** policy will cover you for 365 days. Each plan can be supplemented with a "Hazardous Activities Premium" if you plan to indulge in sports considered dangerous, such as skiing, scuba-diving or trekking. Rough Guides also does good deals for older travellers, and will insure you up to any age, at prices comparable to SAGAs.

For a **policy quote**, call the Rough Guides Insurance Line on UK freefone 0800015 0906, or, from the US, call ☎1-866/220 5588. If you're calling from outside Britain dial (+44) 1243/621 046. Alternatively, get an online quote, or buy your policy online, at *www.roughguides.com/insurance*

Americans and Canadians should also check that they're not already covered. Canadian provincial health plans usually provide partial cover for medical mishaps overseas. Holders of official student/teacher/youth cards are entitled to accident coverage and hospital in-patient benefits. Students will often find that their student health coverage extends during the vacations and for one term beyond the date of last enrolment. Homeowners' or renters' insurance often covers theft or loss of documents, money and valuables while overseas. In **Australia and New Zealand**, travel insurance is available from most travel agents (see p.17) or direct from insurance companies, for periods ranging from a few days to a year or even longer.

EXTRA COVER

You should bear in mind that ordinary travel insurance policies are rarely valid for sporting activities such as skiing, trekking, climbing or horse-riding and certainly not for parapente, canyoning or caving. For these two latter categories you'll have to take out extra cover such as that supplied by the French Carte Neige, which can be obtained in sports centres, equipment shops and clubs. It's inexpensive, valid Europe-wide and lasts a year, but basically meets just the cost of recovery, offering only limited medical expenses and no property protection. Spanish ski resorts tend to offer recovery insurance as a top-up to lift-pass prices. Members of diving clubs or other comparable organizations might be covered by their ordinary annual policy. In Britain, Snowcard Insurance Services (☎01327/262805) specializes in mountaineering and activity holiday travel insurance.

Otherwise inform your travel insurer of your intentions, who will then attach a "dangerous sports" rider to the basic policy and probably charge you an extra premium – up to thirty to fifty percent more. If you are taking a package holiday that might involve participating in some hazardous recreation, be sure to inform the travel agent at the time of booking, so that enquiries can be made on the spot.

HEALTH MATTERS

Citizens of all EU countries are entitled to take advantage of each other's health services under the same terms as the residents of the country, provided they have the correct documentation. So British or Irish citizens in France and Spain may expect to receive medical attention on the same terms as a French or Spanish national, if they have form E111 with them. To apply for this, you must first fill in form SA30, which you get over the counter at any main post office; they will then issue you an E111.

Only citizens of EU member states are covered under the scheme; anyone else is strongly advised to take out travel insurance with medical cover (see above), and supplementary health insurance for EU nationals is highly advisable in any case.

FRANCE

General health care in France is of the highest standard, and no vaccinations are required when entering the country. A peculiarity of the French social security system is that every hospital visit, doctor's consultation and prescribed medicine incurs a **charge** (though not up front in an emergency). While all employed French people are entitled to a refund of 75–80 percent of medical expenses, this can still leave a hefty shortfall, especially after a stay in hospital (accident victims even have to pay for the ambulance that takes them there).

PHARMACIES, DOCTORS AND HOSPITALS

To find a **doctor** stop at any *pharmacie* and ask for an address. Consultation fees for a visit should be 150–180F/€23–27 and in any case you'll be given a *Feuille de Soins* (Statement of Treatment) for later documentation of private or social insurance claims. Prescriptions should be taken to a *pharmacie* which is also equipped – and obliged – to give first aid (for a fee). For minor illnesses pharmacists will dispense free advice and a wide range of medication. The medicines you buy will have little stickers (*vignettes*) attached to them, which you must remove and stick to your *Feuille de Soins* together with the prescription itself. In serious emergencies in France you will always be admitted to the nearest **hospital** (*hôpital*) – an ambulance can be summoned by dialling ☎18. Another useful phone number is ☎15, the national medical emergency service.

Since complicated bureaucracy is involved in getting a refund through your social security department back home, it's better to have ordinary travel insurance, which usually allows almost full reimbursement (less the first few pounds or dollars of the excess), and covers the cost of repatriation. If you're travelling in your own vehicle, you may want to have breakdown cover which includes return of the vehicle if you're incapacitated.

SPAIN

No inoculations are required for Spain; the worst that's likely to happen to you is that you might fall victim to an upset stomach. Wash fruit and avoid *tapas* that look like they were cooked last week.

PHARMACIES, DOCTORS AND HOSPITALS

For minor complaints, go to a **farmacia** – they're listed in the phone book in major towns and you'll also find one in virtually every village. Pharmacists are highly trained, willing to give advice (often in English) and able to dispense many drugs which would be available only on prescription in most other countries. They keep usual shop hours (Mon–Fri 9am–1pm & 4–8pm), but some open late and at weekends, while a rota system keeps at least one open 24 hours. The rota is displayed in the window of every pharmacy, or check in one of the local newspapers under *Farmacias de guardia*.

In more serious cases you can get the address of an English-speaking **doctor** from the nearest relevant consulate, or with luck from a *farmacia*, the local police or tourist office. In emergencies dial ☎091 for the *Servicios de Urgencia*, or look up the *Cruz Roja Española* (Red Cross) which runs a national ambulance service. Treatment at public hospitals for EU citizens in possession of form E111 is free; otherwise you'll be charged at private hospital rates, which can be expensive. Accordingly, it's essential to have some kind of comprehensive travel insurance.

SPAS

On both sides of the Pyrenees, but especially in France, you'll come across **thermal spas**. They were the original, eighteenth- or nineteenth-century impetus for tourism in these parts, and while many have been remodelled in brutalist style, a few others retain their Belle Époque decor. They used to be the exclusive preserve of the elderly and/or the unwell – the **curistes**, in French – who would stay for weeks on end, with the French social security system footing the bill. Recently, however, the authorities have made it clear that they will no longer subsidize indefinite stays at the waters, and in order to survive economically the spas have had to reinvent themselves. **Remis en Forme** (Get in Shape) programmes, with gyms, yoga classes and similar trappings, are now the rule, designed to attract a younger, more active clientele. Spas are typically open only during summer, with morning hours reserved for the dwindling numbers of *curistes*, and late afternoons for casual trade. But increasing numbers of thermal stations near ski resorts – Barèges, Luchon, St-Lary-Soulan, Cauterets, for example – have a late-afternoon session in winter, aimed at chilled and muscle-sore skiers. Take advantage, when available.

INFORMATION AND MAPS

away large quantities of maps and glossy brochures for every region of France, including useful lists of hotels and campsites and festival programmes.

In the French Pyrenees you'll find a tourist information centre – **Office du Tourisme**, as it's usually called – in practically every town and many villages. From these you can get specific local information – including, most importantly, the **météo** or daily weather report, posted in the window – and you should always ask for the free town plan. Many bureaux also publish hotel and restaurant listings, bus and train timetables and local car and walking itineraries. In mountain regions they are often right next door to local trekking and climbing organizers.

The national tourist organizations of both France and Spain have numerous overseas outlets, well stocked with literature, and are also conspicuously represented in towns at home. Both sides of the Pyrenean range itself are also meticulously mapped, though so far French products often have a slight edge over Spanish in terms of quality.

FRENCH INFORMATION OFFICES

Branches of the **French Government Tourist Office** (*www.franceguide.com*) overseas give

SPANISH INFORMATION OFFICES

The **Spanish National Tourist Office** (SNTO; *www.tourspain.es*) similarly produces and gives away an impressive variety of maps, pamphlets and special interest leaflets. Visit one of their offices before you leave home and stock up, especially on city plans, as well as province-by-province lists of hotels, *hostales* and campsites. However, be aware that overseas staff can be less than helpful, palming you off with obsolete pamphlets which only vaguely have to do with your query.

FRENCH GOVERNMENT TOURIST OFFICES ABROAD

Australia Level 22, 25 Blight St, Sydney NSW 2000 (☎02/9231 5244, fax 9221 8682).

Britain 178 Piccadilly, London W1V 0AL (☎0891/244123, fax 020/7493 6594).

Canada 1981 av McGill College, Suite 490, Montréal, QC H3A 2W9 (☎514/288 4264, fax 514/845 4868).

Ireland 10 Suffolk St, Dublin 1 (☎01/679 0813, fax 01/679 0814).

USA 444 Madison Ave, 16th Floor, New York, NY 10020 (☎212/838-7800, fax 212/838-7855); 676 North Michigan Ave, Chicago, IL 60611 (☎312/751-7800, fax 312/337-6339); 9454 Wilshire Blvd, Suite 715, Beverly Hills, CA 90212 (☎310/271-6665, fax 276-2835).

REGIONAL AND DEPARTMENTAL TOURIST OFFICES

Comité Départemental du Tourisme Pyrénées-Orientales, 7 quai de Lattre-de-Tassigny, BP 540, 66005 Perpignan (☎04.68.66.61.11, fax 04.68.67.06.10, *www.pyrenees-orientales.com*).

Comité Départemental du Tourisme Ariège-Pyrénées, 31bis av de Général-de-Gaulle, BP 143, 09004 Foix (☎04.61.02.30.70, fax 04.61.65.17.34, *www.ariege.pyrenees.com*).

SNTO OFFICES ABROAD

Australia 1st Floor, 178 Collins St, Melbourne, VIC 3000 (☎03/9650 7377 or toll free ☎1/800 817 855).

Britain 22–23 Manchester Square, London W1M 5AP (☎020/7486 8077).

Canada 2 Bloor St West, 34th Floor, Toronto, Ontario M4W 3E2 (☎416/961-3131).

New Zealand contact the office in Australia.

USA www.okspain.org 666 Fifth Ave, 35th Floor, New York, NY 10103 (☎212/265-8822; San Vincente Plaza Bldg, 8383 Wilshire Blvd, Suite 956, Beverly Hills, CA 90211 (☎323/658-7188); 845 North Michigan Ave, Suite 915-E, Chicago, IL 60611 (☎312/642-1992); 1221 Brickell Ave, Suite 1850, Miami, FL 33131 (☎305/358-1992).

In Spain itself you'll find SNTO offices in virtually every major town (addresses are detailed in the guide) and from these you can usually get more specific local information. In many towns, the SNTO office is supplemented or replaced by a separately administered provincial or municipal **Turismo** (*Turisme* in Catalan). These vary enormously in quality – those of the Basque country and Catalunya are usually excellent – but while they are generally extremely useful for regional information and local maps, they cannot be relied on to know anything about what goes on outside their patch. Like their French counterparts, they post **weather reports**, often for three days at a time, on their windows.

Spanish tourist office **hours** are usually Mon–Fri 9am–1pm and 3.30–6pm, Sat 9am–1pm; but you can't always rely on the official hours, especially in the more out-of-the-way places, where hours of Mon–Fri 9am–2.30pm are more representative.

PYRENEAN TREKKING MAPS

Maps specifically dedicated to the Pyrenees are a problem if you want to trek through the entire range. A scale of at least 1:50,000 is essential, and the **1:25,000 TOP 25** series published by the French **Institut Géographique National** (IGN) would be better for the northern slopes. Apart from the enormous expense of thirty-odd sheets at that scale, they're tedious to carry. In principle, it would be better to buy maps as you go, because of the stiff mark-up overseas; in practice, however, you would be wise to buy the most indispensable maps before arrival, as they're often sold out in their area of use.

A compromise for the GR10/HRP traverse **on the French side** would be the eleven **1:50,000 Cartes de Randonnées** published jointly by the IGN and Randonnées Pyrénéennes (Rando Éditions), numbered from 1 to 11 going from west to east. They cover the entire range from coast to coast, with *gîtes d'étape*, refuges and recommended GR and Tour routes highlighted (the 1:25,000 series also includes locally marked trails featuring in tourist-board-recommended walks). These maps are generally excellent, though not perfect – a number of paths are shown incorrectly, partly owing to last revision dates for most of 1990–93, though the all-important Béarn (no. 3) and Bigorre (no. 4) titles date from 1998–99. At 57–60F apiece (£8.95 in the UK) though, the complete set of 1:50,000 sheets still represents a substantial investment in money and pack weight. For both IGN and Cartes de Randonnées maps, relevant titles are quoted throughout the text.

The most widely available Spanish productions for the **Spanish side** of the range are the maps of Catalunya-based **Editorial Alpina** – some 1:25,000 and 1:40,000, one at 1:30,000 – covering the most popular walking areas between the Catalan coast and Navarra (relevant titles are quoted throughout the text). The accompanying booklets (Castilian or Catalan, rarely in English) supply useful information about accommodation, walking routes, winter mountaineering and caves, but the maps themselves don't cover the Basque country, and trail tracings are often woefully inaccurate, scarcely changed since the maps first appeared in the late 1940s. You should preferably buy Editorial Alpina titles in Spain: not only are they much cheaper there (675–750ptas/€4–4.50 versus £6–7), but you'll want the most current

---

When using a **compass** in the Pyrenees, the magnetic declination from true north is about 3° west.

MAP OUTLETS

Most of the outlets listed here offer a mail order service.

BRITAIN

Aberdeen Aberdeen Map Shop, 74 Skene St, AB10 1QE (☎01224/637999).

Bristol Stanfords, 29 Corn Street, BS1 1HT (☎0117/929 9966).

Cambridge Heffers Map and Travel, 19 Sidney St, CB2 3HL (☎01223/568467, *www.heffers.co.uk*).

Glasgow John Smith and Sons, 57–61 St Vincent St, G2 5TB (☎0141/221 7472).

Inverness James Thin Melven's Bookshop, 29 Union St, Inverness, IV1 1QA (☎01463/233500, *www.jthin.co.uk*).

Keswick Call of the Wild, 21 Station St, Cumbria CA12 5HH (☎01768/771014).

Leeds Austick's City Bookshop, 91 The Headrow, LS1 6OJ (☎0113/243 3099).

Leicester The Map Shop, 30a Belvoir St, LE1 6QH (☎0116/247 1400).

London National Map Centre, 22–24 Caxton St, SW1H 0QH (☎020/7222 2466, *www.mapsworld.com*); Stanfords, 12–14 Long Acre, WC2E 9LP (☎020/7836 1321, *sales@stanfords.co.uk*), The Travel Bookshop, 13–15 Blenheim Crescent, W11 2EE (☎020/7229 5260, *www.thetravelbookshop.co.uk*).

Manchester Waterstone's, 91 Deansgate, M3 2BW (☎0161/837 3000, *www.waterstones -manchester-deansgate.co.uk*).

Newcastle upon Tyne Newcastle Map Centre, 55 Grey St, NE1 6EF (☎0191/261 5622, *www.newtraveller.com*).

Oxford Blackwell's Map and Travel Shop, 53 Broad St, OX1 3BQ (☎01865/792792, *bookshop.blackwell.co.uk*).

Upton-upon-Severn The Map Shop, 15 High St, Worcestershire WR8 0HJ (☎01684/593146).

IRELAND

Belfast Waterstone's, Queens Bldg, 8 Royal Ave, BT1 1DA (☎028/9024 7355).

Dublin Easons Bookshop, 40 O'Connell St (☎01/873 3811, *www.eason.ie*); Fred Hanna's

Bookshop, 27–29 Nassau St (☎01/677 1255); Hodges Figgis Bookshop, 56–58 Dawson St (☎01/677 4754, *www.hodgesfiggis.com*); Waterstone's, 7 Dawson St (☎01/679 1415).

USA

Burlington Adventurous Traveler Bookstore, PO Box 64769, Burlington, VT 05406 (☎1-800/282-3963; *www.AdventurousTraveler.com*).

Chicago Rand McNally, 444 N Michigan Ave, Chicago, IL 60611 (☎312/321-1751). Note: Rand McNally now has more than twenty stores across the US; call ☎1-800/234-0679 or visit *www.randmcnally.com* for the address of your nearest store, or for direct mail plans.

Corte Madera Book Passage, 51 Tamal Vista Blvd, Corte Madera, CA 94925 (☎415/927-0960, *www.bookpassage.com*).

New York The Complete Traveler Bookstore, 199 Madison Ave, New York, NY 10016 (☎212/685-9007, *www.completetraveller.com*); Traveler's Choice Bookstore, 22 W 52nd St, New York, NY (☎212/941-1535, *tvlchoice@aol.com*).

Palo Alto Phileas Fogg's Books & Maps, #87 Stanford Shopping Center, Palo Alto, CA 94304 (☎1-800/533-FOGG, *www.foggs.com*).

Pasadena Distant Lands, 56 S Raymond Ave, Pasadena, CA 91105 (☎626/449-3220, *www.distantlands.com*).

San Francisco The Complete Traveler Bookstore, 3207 Fillmore St, San Francisco, CA 94123 (☎415/923-1511, *www.completetraveller.com*); Sierra Club Bookstore, 730 Polk St, San Francisco, CA 94110 (☎415/977-5653, *www.sierraclubbookstore.com*).

Santa Barbara Map Link, 30 S La Patera Lane, Unit #5, Santa Barbara, CA 93117 (☎805/692-6777, *www.maplink.com*).

Seattle Elliot Bay Book Company, 101 S Main St, Seattle, WA 98104 (☎206/624-6600, *www.elliottbaybook.com*).

Washington, DC ADC Map and Travel Center, 1636 I St NW, Washington DC 20006 (☎202/628 2608); Travel Books & Language Center, 4437 Wisconsin Ave NW, Washington, DC 20016 (☎1-800/220-2665).

continues overleaf...

MAP OUTLETS contd.

CANADA

Montreal Ulysses Travel Bookshop, 4176 St-Denis, Montréal (☎514/843-9447, www.ulysses.ca).

Ottawa World of Maps, 1235 Wellington St, Ottawa, ON K1Y 3A3 (☎613/724-6776, www.worldofmaps.com).

Toronto Open Air Books and Maps, 25 Toronto St, Toronto, ON M5R 2C1 (☎416/363-0719).

Vancouver World Wide Books and Maps, 552 Seymour St, Vancouver, BC V6B 3J5 (☎604/687-3320, www.itmb.com).

AUSTRALIA

Adelaide The Map Shop, 6 Peel St (☎08/8231 2033)

Brisbane Worldwide Maps and Guides, 187 George St (☎07/3221 4330)

Melbourne Mapland, 372 Little Bourke St (☎03/9670 4383)

Perth Map Centre, 1/884 Hay St (☎08/9322 5733)

Sydney Travel Bookshop, Shop 3, 175 Liverpool St (☎02/9261 8200)

NEW ZEALAND

Auckland Specialty Maps, 46 Albert St (☎09/307 2217).

Christchurch Mapworld, 173 Gloucester St, Christchurch (☎03/374 5399, fax 03/374 5633, www.mapworld.co.nz)

cartography, which does improve with painful slowness over time – overseas stocks are often out of date. New editions since 1998 have predominantly green jackets (older ones are plain red or plain orange), with a booklet format of 21cm x 11cm, waterproof maps and improved detail on the French side of the border (where applicable).

The only serious alternative to Editorial Alpina are the 1:50,000 **Mapas Excursionistas**, produced since 1999 by the Institut Cartografic de Catalunya and modelled exactly on the French *Cartes des Randonées*. They're numbered 1 to 20 from east to west – so far they've only reached as far as the Ordesa area – and retail for 1300–1400ptas/€7.80–8.40 in Spain.

Where necessary, either of the above series can be supplemented by the full range of **topographical maps** issued by two Spanish government agencies: the Instituto Geográfico Nacional (IGN) and the Servicio Geográfico del Ejército (SGE). They are available at scales of 1:100,000, 1:50,000 and occasionally 1:25,000. Though neither series is yet up to the standard of French products, the IGN's has recently taken a quantum leap in quality, replacing Castilian with local place names, indicating magnetic declination from true north and including useful regional language vocabularies in the margins. Moreover, a plain-blue-jacketed folding series, analogous to the French Série Bleue and produced together by IGN and MOPU (the ministry of public works), has recently appeared for many areas at scales of 1:50,000 and occasionally 1:25,000. Many bookshops in Spain, and a few specialist overseas stores, stock these more convenient maps, though as with the Editorial Alpina products, you'll find them much cheaper on arrival – typically 330ptas/€2 – and again less accurate than their French equivalents.

PYRENEAN ROAD MAPS

In terms of **road maps**, only the Spanish-produced Firestone "Pireneos" 1:200,000 map covers the entire range, showing both sides of the border at the same level of detail and even indicating parts of the French GR10 and Spanish GR11. Although two-sided, it's very easy to unfold and use, but available only in Spain (about 750ptas/€4.50) – look for the blue-fringed red cover. Despite not having been updated since about 1990, it remains remarkably accurate – nothing else sold overseas is anywhere near as useful. If you want to try and special-order it from a map retailer abroad, the product number is T-33, and the ISBN is 84-86907-16-0.

For the **French side** only, two one-sided IGN "TOP 250" *Série Rouge* 1:250,000 maps document the entire range: no. 113, "Pyrénées Languedoc Roussillon", and no. 114, "Pyrénées Occidentales". A better French production, and perhaps a good compromise – especially for **cyclists** – between such a vague road map and a bulky stack of *randonnée* maps, is the IGN 1:100,000 Série Verte. This shows contours and the GR10, covering the whole French side (and some of Spain) in four one-sided sheets: no. 69 "Pau Bayonne", no. 70 "Tarbes Bagnères-de-Luchon", no. 71 "Saint-Gaudens Andorre" and no. 72 "Perpignan Béziers".

A useful **free map** for drivers, obtainable from petrol stations and traffic information kiosks in France, is the *Bison Futé* (Crafty Buffalo) map, showing alternative secondary routes to the congested main highways; it's keyed to special green *Bison Futé* road signs.

Road maps for the **Spanish side** of the range are best bought in bookshops (*librerías*), street kiosks or service stations in Spain itself. Among the best are those published by Editorial Almax, which also produces reliable indexed street plans for the main cities. A passably accurate second choice, especially if you're shopping before arrival – though cumbersome and almost impossible to use effectively in a car – is the double-sided 1:300,000 "Costa Brava/Pyrenees/Basque Country, Aragón, Navarra, Catalonia, Andorra" map published by Euro-Map and distributed through GeoCenter International in both the UK and the US.

GETTING AROUND

If you're not driving, cycling or walking, getting around in the Pyrenees takes a bit of organization and attention to detail. There are surprisingly good bus services (and sometimes trains) along the main valley floors and between major centres, but timings are often geared to school and work hours. Approximate journey times and frequencies can be found in the "Travel Details" at the end of each chapter, and local peculiarities are also pointed out in the text of the guide.

If you intend to hitch in the Pyrenees, it's always safest to try and arrange a lift in advance by asking at your hotel, *gîte* or refuge. However, this guide **does not recommend hitching** as a reliable means of transport; in peak season you can wait for hours for a ride, as scores of crammed-full vehicles pass you by. The same risks apply as for hitching anywhere else.

FRANCE

France has the most extensive rail network in **western Europe**, although rural services have been severely cut back since the 1980s. Trains are an excellent way of travelling parallel to the line of the mountains and along the coasts, but the lines tend to give out as the gradients increase and the populations dwindle. However, where the train stops an **SNCF** (the French rail company) **bus** often continues the route. Private bus services are confusing, uncoordinated and often poorly publicized – where possible, it is much simpler to use the SNCF. If you have the time and the vehicle, **driving** or **cycling** are both excellent ways of seeing the Pyrenean foothills.

TRAINS

SNCF **trains** are by and large clean, fast and frequent, and their staff usually courteous and helpful. All but the smallest stations have an information desk and *consignes automatiques* – coin-operated lockers big enough to take a rucksack. Many rent out bicycles, sometimes of rather doubtful reliability. **Fares** are reasonable, at an average – off peak – of about 70 centimes per kilometre. The ultra-fast TGVs (*Trains à Grande Vitesse*) require a supplement at peak times and a compulsory reservation costing 20F/€3 and up. Slower trains, stopping at most stations, are often marked with a bicycle symbol in the timetable – on these you can travel with a bike as free accompanied luggage (see below for details).

Regional **rail maps** and complete **timetables** are on sale at tobacconist shops, though you will find them for free at the biggest tourist offices. Leaflet timetables for a particular line are available free at stations, and again many tourist offices. *Car* at the top of a column means it's an SNCF bus service, on which train tickets and passes are valid.

All **tickets** – though not passes – must be **date-stamped** in the orange machines at station platform entrances or foyers. It is an offence if you don't "*compostez votre billet*", and people caught riding without tickets are liable to a 150-franc spot fine. Train journeys may be broken any time, anywhere, but after a break of 24 hours you must date-stamp your ticket again upon resuming your journey.

While **InterRail** (p.7) and Eurail (p.14) passes are valid on all trains, and worth investigating before you leave home, the SNCF itself offers a whole range of **discount fares** on *Période Bleue* (Blue Period) days – in effect, most of the year. A leaflet showing the blue, white (smaller discount) and red (peak) periods is given out at train stations.

One of the most valuable passes is the **EuroDomino pass**, which for use in France has to be purchased outside the country. It offers unlimited rail travel on any three, four, five, seven or eight days within a calendar month; respective prices, for under26s/full second class, are £79/£99, £95/£119, £111/£139, £127/£159, £143/£178 and £159/£198. The pass also entitles you to a reduction on Eurostar (ask for details at time of booking). Note, however, that you probably won't get full value out of it unless you're planning to reach the Pyrenees by train from the UK, as well as travelling a few days along the foothills.

Other SNCF discount cards are available only in France, from travel agents or mainline stations.

Couples or groups of up to four are entitled to a 25 percent discount on return fares if they travel together and start their journey on a blue-period day. If you're **over 60**, you can get a *Carte Senior* for 285F/€43.50, a one-year discount scheme which gets you up to half off on most journeys starting in a blue period, including TGVs, a 25 percent reduction on white-period fares, and 30 percent off on most international journeys from western Europe – for example, Britain to the Pyrenees. The same percentage reductions are available for under-26s with the **Carte 12–25**, which costs 270F/€41.20, and is also valid for a year. **Families** of up to five can use a **Enfant Plus Carte** (350F/€53.40) for which one child under 12 is the holder, securing the above-cited discounts for the rest of the family.

BUSES

With the exception of SNCF services, **buses** play a generally minor role, even in the Pyrenees. The most frustrating thing about them is that they rarely serve the regions outside the SNCF network – which is precisely where you need them. Where they do exist (mostly in the foothills) timetables are constructed to suit working, school and market hours – it will be a real stroke of luck if one is going where and when you want. Buses are, generally speaking, cheaper and slower than trains.

Larger towns usually have a **gare routière** (bus station), often next to the train station. However, this is not always the case, as the private bus companies have difficulty coordinating their efforts and tend to leave from an array of different points. Their locations, as well as schedule booklets, are often available from tourist offices, or at the very least there will be a timetable posted at the stop.

DRIVING AND VEHICLE RENTAL

Using a car gives you enormous advantages of access to remote areas. If you're camping or trekking, the ability to carry extra equipment can make driving an attractive proposition, but you will only save money – especially with a rented vehicle – if there are several of you to share the cost. Breakdown liability, the complication of point-to-point treks, and insulation from the feel of the country and its people are other minuses.

Car rental arranged on the spot costs upwards of 2000F/€305 per week; you need to be at least 21 (or 23, depending on which category of car you want to rent). It's normal to leave an indemnity of about 2000F/€305 against any damage to the car not covered by the CDW premium; this is usually done on a credit-card slip which should be destroyed upon safe return of the vehicle. Cars are delivered with a full tank of fuel and must be returned full. Most travel agents can arrange Fly-Drive packages, which often let you pick the car up on arrival at one airport and leave it at another at the end of your holiday – though you'll pay an extra fee for this facility. Among the UK rental agencies listed in the box on p.34, Transhire, Global Leisure and Autos Abroad usually have the best rates for the French Pyrenees – typically £120–140 per week depending on agency and season. Renault Clio diesel saloons are often available as a roomy Group B car, and their fuel economy easily offsets their slightly bumped up rental price compared to the typical Group A buggy.

Any EU (including British) **drivers' licence** is valid in France, but North Americans technically require an International Driving Permit (available from the AAA for a small fee). The vehicle registration document and the insurance papers must be carried; if it's a rental car, agency staff should point them out to you. If you bring your own car with right-hand drive, have your headlight dip adjusted to the right before you go – it's a legal requirement, as is a GB sticker – and, as a courtesy, change or paint them yellow or stick on black glare deflectors. All the major car manufacturers have service stations in France – get a list of addresses from the manufacturers before you go. If you have an accident or break-in, make a report to the local police (and keep a copy) in order to make an insurance claim. If you need to be towed, look in the *Pages Jaunes* (Yellow Pages) under *Dépannages* (Breakdowns).

The main **rule of the road** to remember in France is the law of *priorité à droite*, which means that you must often give way to traffic coming from your right, even when it is coming from a minor road. Because it has been a major cause of accidents, it is being phased out, and so only applies in built-up areas, where you have to be vigilant – watch the roadside for signs with a **yellow diamond** on a white background, which means that you have the right of way; such a diamond with an oblique black line through it means you must yield to right-hand traffic. Signs saying *STOP* or *CEDEZ LE PASSAGE* also mean you must give way. **Roundabouts**, of which there are many

> For information on road conditions call the multilingual Autoroutel (☎08.36.68.10.77) or consult their Web site at *www.autoroutes.fr*

in Pyrenean towns, work just like those in Britain, except in the opposite direction: signs always warn you *VOUS N'AVEZ PAS LA PRIORITÉ*. Other common warning signs are *DÉVIATION* (diversion), *GRAVILLONS* (loose chippings), *NIDS DE POULES* (potholes) and *CHAUSSÉE DÉFORMÉE* (uneven surface).

Fines for driving violations are paid on the spot in cash or French-franc traveller's cheques; if you don't have the funds, you and the vehicle can be locked up immediately. The main N-numbered highways swarm with *gendarmes* (see p.72) manning checkpoints and speed traps; failure to wear a seatbelt (required) nets you a spot fine of 150F. The minimum fine for speeding is 1000F/€150, going up to 5000F/€760 for really blatant violations. Speed limits are as follows: 130kph/80mph on toll *autoroutes*; 110kph/68mph on dual carriageways; 90kph/56mph on other roads; 50kph/37mph in towns. For all drivers in bad weather, and those with less than two years' experience, the out-of-town limits are 110kph, 100kph and 80kph. All this notwithstanding, bear in mind that driving in France can be a stressful experience. The country has the dubious honour of being tied with Spain for third place amongst EU states for level of **unsafe driving** and accident fatalities (Portugal and Greece are first and second, respectively). If you're not doing at least 20kph over the posted speed limit, you can be guaranteed of having someone crawling up your rear bumper, except on the remotest and narrowest roads.

Motorway – **autoroute** – driving, though fast, is very boring when it's not hair-raising, and the tolls are expensive: Paris to Perpignan, for example, costs almost 400F/€60. On the whole, it's best not to waste your money on the toll routes, of which there are few in this book anyway; a French N (*nationale*) or RN (*route nationale*) **road** is the equal of a good UK "A" road, or a well-maintained state highway in the US. Use the Bison Futé map (see p.31) to avoid the endless traffic jams that build up over the weekends between July 15 and August 15. In the Pyrenees, you will become acquainted of necessity with the D (*départmentale*) roads: many quite good, with

INTERNATIONAL CAR RENTAL AGENCIES

UK
Autos Abroad ☎08700/667788,
www.autosabroad.co.uk
Avis ☎0870/60 60 100, *www.avis.com*
Budget ☎0541/565656,
www.budgetrentacar.com
easyRentacar *www.easyRentacar.com*
Europcar ☎9870/607 5000, *www.europcar.com*
Global Leisure/Suncars ☎0870/ 500 5566
Hertz ☎0870/844 8844, *www.hertz.com*
Holiday Autos ☎0870/400 4453,
www.kemwel.com
National Car Rental ☎0870/400 4502,
www.nationalcar-europe.com
Thrifty ☎01494/751600, *www.thrifty.co.uk*
Transhire ☎0870/789 8000, *www.transhire.com*

Ireland
Avis
Northern Ireland ☎0990/900 500; Eire ☎01/874 5844.

Budget
Northern Ireland ☎0800/181 181; Eire ☎0800/973 159.

Europcar
Northern Ireland ☎0345/222 525; Eire ☎01/874 5844.

Hertz
Northern Ireland ☎0990/996 699; Eire ☎01/676 7476.

Holiday Autos
Northern Ireland ☎0990/300 400; Eire ☎01/872 9366, freefax 1800/729 366,
info@holidayautos.ie

North America
Alamo ☎1-800/522-9696, *www.goalamo.com*
Auto Europe ☎1-800/223-5555, *www.autoeurope.com*
Avis ☎1-800/331-1084, *www.avis.com*
Budget ☎1-800/527-0700, *www.budget.com*
Dollar ☎1-800/800-6000, *www.dollar.com*,
www.europcar.com
Europe by Car ☎1-800/223-1516 or ☎212/245-1713, *www.europebycar.com*
Hertz ☎1-800/654-3001, *www.hertz.com*
Kemwel Holiday Autos ☎1-800/422-7737,
www.kemwel.com
National ☎1-800/CAR-RENT,
www.nationalcar.com
Thrifty ☎1-800/367-2277, *www.thrifty.com*
US Rent-a-Car ☎1-800/777-9377, *www.us-rentacar.com*

Australia
Avis ☎1800/225 533
Budget ☎1300/362 848
Dollar ☎02/9223 1444
Hertz ☎1800/550 067
National ☎13/1908
Thrifty ☎1300/367 227

New Zealand
Apex ☎1800/121 029
Avis ☎09/526 2800
Budget ☎0800/ 652 227 or 09/375 2270
Hertz ☎0800/ 655 955 or 09/309 0989
National ☎09/537 2582
Thrifty ☎09/309 0111

two lanes (but no verge), others one-lane and barely paved. Some have been constructed over high passes or along corniches with spectacular views in mind; minor roads over the passes are typically **snowed up** between November and May, though giant signboards may advise you of opened, snowploughed corridors and chain requirements, especially near ski resorts.

Fuel (*essence*) prices are fairly standard for continental Europe at just under 7F/€1.10 a litre for four-star "super", just over 6F/€0.90 for 95–98 octane "normal", and something over 4F/€0.62 a litre for diesel (*gasoil*) – though it's often cheaper if you buy it at out-of-town supermarkets. All fuel is now lead-free (*sans plomb*).

Mopeds and **scooters** are relatively easy to find and although they're not built for any kind of long-distance touring, they're ideal for exploring the environs of foothill towns. Places which rent out bicycles (see below) usually have motorized vehicles, too; expect to pay 160F/€25 per day for a 50cc Suzuki, or 200F/€30 per day for an 80cc scooter. **Crash helmets** are now compulsory when using any motorized two-wheelers.

CYCLING

Bicycles (*vélos*) have high status in France. All the car ferries from Britain carry them for little or nothing; SNCF makes minimal charges; and individual French people respect cyclists, both as traffic and potential customers. Restaurants and hotels along the way are nearly always obliging about looking after your bike, even to the point of allowing it into your room. Local motorists normally give you plenty of room – it's the lumbering foreign camper van you have to watch out for.

You can normally load your bike straight onto the train at your **ferry port of disembarkation**, but remember that you must first go to the ticket office of the station – don't just try to climb on the train with it. In addition to the ferries, British Airways and Air France both take bikes free within the normal baggage weight allowance. You may have to box them, though, and you should contact the airlines for details. Eurostar allows you to take your bicycle within your normal baggage allowance, provided it's dismantled and stored in a special bike bag, whose flat dimensions don't exceed 120cm x 90cm. However we've had a reader complaint that Eurostar can be awkward on this point, insisting that it be brought to the station 24 hours beforehand. More likely, it will be sent on unaccompanied, with guaranteed arrival within 24 hours (register it up to 10 days in advance – book through Esprit Europe on ☎0800/186186); the fee is £20 each way.

The **SNCF** runs various schemes for cyclists, all detailed in the free leaflet *Train et Vélo*, available from most train stations. Trains marked with a bicycle in the timetable are usually the only ones on which you can travel with a bike as free accompanied luggage. Otherwise, you have to send your bike bundled up as registered luggage for a fee of 150F/€23. Although it may well arrive in less time, the SNCF won't guarantee delivery in under five days, and very occasionally bicycles disappear altogether.

At most French train stations, **rental bikes** are also available. For around 70F/€10.70 per day, you can expect to get an averagely well-maintained Peugeot, and this can be returned to any other station (as long as you specify which when renting). The SNCF does not ask for a deposit, but does require a guarantee such as a credit-card number. For a bit more, you can also rent better bikes from campsites, youth hostels and *gîtes d'étape*, as well as from some tourist offices and a fair number of bike shops (which are more likely to have mountain bikes, see below). Most rental bikes are **not insured**, however, and you will be presented with the bill for its replacement or repair if it's stolen or damaged. Check in advance whether your travel insurance policy covers these contingencies.

Lately more and more cyclists are using **mountain bikes** (*VTT* or *Vélo Touts Terrains* in French) for touring holidays. However, it's actually less strenuous, and much quicker, to cycle long distances on asphalt and carry luggage on a traditional touring or racing model.

Most sizeable foothill towns have well-stocked **retail and repair shops**, where parts are normally cheaper than in Britain or the US. However, with a foreign-made bike it's wise to carry spare tyres, as French sizes differ. It's still not that easy, either, to find parts for mountain bikes, with French enthusiasm mainly directed towards highly geared road racers. Inner tubes are not a problem, as they adapt to either tyre size, though make sure you have the right valves.

SPAIN

Despite their relative remoteness, the Spanish Pyrenees are often as well (or as poorly) served by public transport as the French. However, there are no trains into the central Pyrenees; the rail lines consist, on the whole, of a chain of services connecting the towns of the Atlantic and Mediterranean coasts. On shorter or less obvious routes buses tend to be quicker anyway, and will also normally take you closer to your destination; some train stations are several kilometres from the town or village they serve, with no guarantee of a connecting bus. Car rental may also be worth considering, with costs among the lowest in Europe (if prearranged).

TRAINS

RENFE, the Spanish rail company, operates a horrendously complicated variety of train services, few of which will be of use to readers of this guide. Of the three main categories, the cheapest are *regionales*, equivalent to buses in speed and cost; *regional exprés* and *Delta trens* tend to cover longer distances. **Largo recorrido** (long-distance) express trains have a bewildering number of names: in ascending order of speed and luxury, they are known as *Diurno, Intercity* (IC), *Estrella* (often just signified by a star *), *Talgo, Talgo Pendular, Talgo 200* (T200), and *Trenhotel*. Anything above Intercity can cost upwards of twice as much as standard second class. Be aware that the different train types produce their own separate timetables; looking at just one can give the false impression that the overall service is dramatically less than it is. If you're daunted by conflicting or missing schedules, you can ring the centralized RENFE information and reservation number on ☎91 – though you'll need to speak Spanish – or look at *www.renfe.es* (English version available). The Spanish tend to use *largo recorrido* trains in much the same way as aeroplanes, with **advance booking** essential for both the outward and return journey.

Since the 1980s, many bona fide train services have been phased out in favour of buses operated jointly by RENFE and a private bus company. This is particularly the case when the connection is either indirect or the daily train or trains leave(s) at inconvenient times. On some routes the **rail buses** outnumber the conventional departures by a ratio of four to one. Prices are the same as on the trains, and these services usually leave and arrive from the bus stations/stops of the towns concerned.

RENFE offers a whole range of **fares**, discounted 25–40 percent for those over 60, the disabled, children aged 4 to 11 years and groups of more than ten. Return fares are also discounted by ten percent on *regionales* (valid 15 days) and twenty percent on *largo recorridos* (valid 60 days) – you can buy a single, and so long as you show it when you buy the return, you'll still get the discount.

Tickets can be bought at the stations between sixty days and fifteen minutes before the train leaves, from the *venta anticipada* window, or in the final two hours from the *venta inmediata* window. Don't leave it to the last minute, as there are usually long queues. There may also be separate windows for *largo recorrido* (long-distance) trains and *regionales* or *cercanías* (locals). If you board the train without a ticket the conductor may charge you up to double the normal fare; if you don't have the cash, they'll call the police. If you do get on a train without a ticket it's always best to find the conductor first and explain, rather than wait to have them find you.

A good way to avoid the queues is to buy tickets at **travel agents** which display the RENFE sign – they have a sophisticated computer system which can also make seat reservations (500ptas/€3), obligatory on *largo recorrido* trains; the cost is the same as at the station. Most larger towns also have a **RENFE office** in the centre, or you can use the centralized 24-hour **telephone reservation service** – ☎902 240 202. You can **change** the departure date of an electronically issued, reserved-seat, *largo recorrido* ticket up to one hour before your originally scheduled departure, for a token 200ptas/€1.20 charge. A full **cancellation** of the same class of ticket entails losing fifteen percent of the purchase price, provided it's done at least half an hour before scheduled departure.

InterRail (see p.7) and **Eurail** (p.14) passes are valid on all RENFE trains (though not on private lines such as the Núria *cremallera*), but there's a supplement payable for travelling on the fastest trains. The apparently random nature of these **surcharges** – which seem to depend on the individual train guard – can be a source of considerable irritation. It's better to know what you're letting yourself in for by reserving a seat in advance, something you'll be obliged to do in any case on some trains. For 600ptas/€3.60 you'll get a large, computer-printed ticket which will satisfy even the most unreasonable of guards.

If you're using the trains extensively in Spain, but not outside the country, you might consider a **RENFE Tarjeta Explorerail**, accepted on most trains – and currently the only pass available within Spain itself. You can buy passes for seven, fifteen- or thirty-day periods; a second-class seven-day pass costs 19,000ptas/€114; a fifteen-day pass costs 23,000ptas/€138; and a thirty-day pass costs 30,000ptas/€180. Passes are available from RENFE offices and many local travel agencies.

British and Irish residents might alternatively consider purchasing a Spanish **EuroDomino pass** from Rail Europe (see p.7), Usit or certain other travel agents before arrival. These allow three, five or ten days' travel in one calendar month within Spain, though you're unlikely to get much value out of them travelling, say, between a trek trailhead and Bilbao/Barcelona airport. Prices for those under/over 26 are three days for £69/89, five days for £106/132, and ten days (£182/227). North Americans and Australasians will get even less joy out of the expensive Spain Flexipass schemes available in their home countries.

BUSES

Buses will probably meet most of your public transport needs; most small Pyrenean villages are accessible only by bus, almost always originating in the capital of their province. Service varies in quality, but on the whole the buses are reliable enough, with prices pretty standard at around 950ptas/€5.70 per 100 kilometres. The only real problem is that many towns still have no main bus station, and buses may leave from a variety of places (even if they're heading in the same direction, since some destinations are served by more than one company). Where a new terminal has been built, it's often on the outer fringes of town. As far as possible, departure points are detailed in the text.

One important point to remember is that all public transport, and the bus service especially, is drastically reduced **on Sundays and holidays** – it's best not even to consider travelling to out-of-the-way places on these days. The Castilian words to look out for on timetables are *diario* (daily), *laborables* (workdays, including Saturday) and *domingos y festivos* (Sundays and holidays). On Catalan timetables, the equivalent expressions are *diari* (daily), *feiners* (workdays), *festius* (holidays), *dissabtes* (Saturdays) and *diumenges* (Sundays).

DRIVING

While getting around on public transport is easy enough, you'll obviously have a great deal more freedom with your own car. Major river-valley roads are generally good, the mountain corniches more than serviceable, and traffic, while a little hectic in the cities, is moderately well behaved – though see the note above on Spanish and French accident rates. But you'll be spending a bit more (even with a full car): fuel prices, though half that of current British ones, are still almost double North American prices, and in the big cities at least you'll probably want to pay extra for a hotel with parking, or be forced to stay on the outskirts. Also, vehicle crime is rampant – never leave anything of value visible in the car.

All EU **driver's licences** are honoured in Spain – but North American or Australasian drivers should get hold of an an International Driving Permit (available in North America from the AAA), which is technically now an EU-required backup for non-European licences. If you're bringing your own car, you no longer require a Green Card from your insurers, or the infamous bail bond or extra coverage for legal costs, since a 1996 EU directive stipulates that insurance contracted in any EU member state is valid in any other state. However, you are automatically entitled only to statutory minimum coverage – that is, third-party **insurance**. To make sure that you are fully protected, you may have to pay a top-up premium to get comprehensive pan-European coverage.

Away from main roads you yield to vehicles approaching from the right, but rules are not too strictly observed anywhere. **Speed limits** are posted – the maximum on urban roads is 60kph, other roads 90kph, motorways 120kph – and (on the main highways at least) speed traps are common, especially in the morning. If you're stopped for any violation, the Spanish police can and usually will levy a stiff **on-the-spot fine** before letting you go on your way, especially since as a foreigner you're unlikely to want, or be able, to appear in court. Motorcycle-borne polica or Guardia Civil Trafica are also on the lookout for non-belt-wearers, though unlike in France you may get off with just a warning to buckle up. **Parking laws** are rigorously enforced in large towns, and any illegally parked vehicle will be removed promptly – with a sticker left on the road telling you where to pay the hefty fine to retrieve it.

Spanish mechanics are most familiar with what the locals drive – small Fords, Renaults, Opels, Citroëns, Peugeots, Fiats/Seats – so with a larger or more unusual model you may have some problems should you **break down.**

Fuel currently costs about 141ptas/€0.85 per litre for Super 98, 132ptas/€0.80 for *Sin Plomo* (Lead-Free) 95. The latter is hard to come by in villages off the main routes, where limited pump space is dedicated instead to diesel (*gasoleo*). **Credit cards** are accepted at almost all stations on main highways. They are also always taken at the motorway toll gates either side of Girona, though the amount is often trivial; stick the card in the reader and the bar opens. Otherwise you must have exact change for the coin slots, or go to the few attended gates. The **tolls** themselves add up – well over 1000ptas/€6 from Figueres to Barcelona airport – so these motorways are best avoided unless you're in a hurry.

VEHICLE RENTAL

You'll find a choice of car rental companies in the largest towns and coastal resorts, with the biggest ones – Hertz, Avis, Budget and Europcar –

Road infrastructure around Barcelona airport has improved since the late 1990s, when first-time arrivals piloting a rental car were almost guaranteed to get lost, but it is still not foolproof. To **head north** towards Girona and France, you simply follow signage for the A7 motorway.

Returning south to the airport isn't as straightforward. Using the A7 to the A17, and next the A12 to the A161, will get you there but is fiddly; however, staying with the A17 to the airport ring road cuts through Barcelona at relatively low speed by a series of tunnels.

represented at most airports. You'll need to be 21 (and have been driving for at least a year), and you're looking at from 6000ptas/€36 per day for a small car (less by the week, special rates over weekends) as a rack rate. **Fly-Drive** deals with Iberia and other operators can be good value if you know in advance that you'll want to rent a car. The big companies all offer schemes, but you'll often get a better deal through someone who deals with local agents. As in France, Autos Abroad, Global Leisure and Transhire (see box on p.34) are among the best, substantially undercutting the large companies – rates work out less than in France, at £100–130 a week depending on vendor and season. Strictly on the Internet, easyRentacar (*www.easyRentacar.com*) offers car rental from Barcelona from (in theory) as little as £9 (2340ptas/€14) per day. If you're going in high season, it's best to try and reserve well in advance. And if you have any choice in the matter of a Group A car, avoid the Seat Arosa – though it's easy to park, it has a dinky 800cc engine, an apparent top speed of about 85km/hr, and scarcely room for two adults with luggage.

Renting **motorcycles** (from 3000–4000ptas/€18–24 per day, cheaper by the week) is also possible. You have to be 14 to ride a machine under 75cc, 18 for one over 75cc and production of a driving licence is extremely useful. Crash helmets, incidentally, have been obligatory since 1982, though they're often of the "derby" type usually worn by cyclists in Britain. Note that mopeds and motorcycles are often rented out with insurance that doesn't include theft – always check with the company first. You will

generally be asked to produce a driving licence as a deposit.

CYCLING

Taking your own **bicycle** can be an inexpensive and flexible way of getting around, and of seeing a great deal of the country that would otherwise pass you by. Do remember, though, that even just the foothills of the Pyrenees are often horrifically steep – and torrid in summer. In the wake of Miguel Indurain's multiple Tour de France triumphs, the Spanish are keen cycle fans – which means that you'll be well received and find reasonable facilities.

There are bike shops in the larger towns and parts can often be found at auto repair shops or garages – look for Michelin signs. Cars tend to toot horns before they pass, which can be alarming at first but is useful once you're used to it. Cycle-touring guides to most of the Pyrenees can be found in good bookshops – written in Spanish, Catalan or Euskera, of course.

Getting your bike there should present few problems. Most **airlines** are happy to take them as ordinary baggage provided they come within your allowance (though it's sensible to check first; crowded charters may be less obliging). Deflate the tyres to avoid explosions in the unpressurized hold. Spanish **trains** are also reasonably accessible, though bikes can only go on a train with a guard's van (*furgón*) and must be registered – go to the *Equipajes* or *Paquexpres* desk at the station. If you are not travelling with the bike you can either send it as a package or buy an undated ticket and use the method above. Most *hostales* seem able to find somewhere safe for overnight storage.

ACCOMMODATION

This book details where to find accommodation throughout the Pyrenees, and gives a price range for each establishment, from the most basic rooms to luxury hotels.

FRANCE

During spring or autumn it's possible to turn up in any Pyrenean town and find a room, or a place in a campsite. However, reserving a couple of nights in advance can be reassuring; it saves the effort of trudging around and ensures that you know what you'll be paying. Many hoteliers and campsite managers – and almost all youth hostel managers – will speak some English. In most towns you'll be able to find a double for 160–210F/€24–32, or a single for 130–180F/€20–27.

Problems arise in the mountains mainly during the **February** half-term skiing rush and **between July 15 and August 15**, when the French take their own vacations en masse. The first weekend of August is the busiest time of all. During this period, hotel and hostel accommodation can be hard to come by – particularly in the coastal resorts – and you may find yourself falling back on local tourist offices for help and ideas. With campsites, you can be more relaxed, unless you're touring with a caravan or camper van.

Full **accommodation lists** for each province are available from any French Government Tourist Office (see p.27) or from local tourist offices. If you're travelling in peak season, especially, it is worth getting hold of these, together with a handbook for the *Logis et Auberges de France* – independent hotels, renowned for their consistently

salubrious – if not always innovative – food and good-value rooms (each one is surveyed annually); they're recognizable on the spot by a green-and-yellow logo of a hearth. See also *www.logis -de-france.fr*

HOTELS AND CHAMBRES D'HÔTE

All French Pyrenean **hotels** are graded from zero to three stars. Prices more or less correspond to the number of stars, though the system is a little haphazard, having more to do with ratios of bathrooms-per-guest, and the presence or absence of lobbies, than with genuine quality; renovated single-star hotels are often very good. However, unless you patronize fairly expensive, modernized hotels, you will have to contend with traditional French **pillows**, which are best described as sausages or long sacks of cement, often inextricably worked into the bedding; if your neck is fussy, consider bringing a small inflatable or orthopedic pillow. At the budget level, what makes a difference in cost is whether a room contains a shower: if it does not have one, the final bill will be around 30–50F more, since an extra charge of about 10F is often made each time you use the shower down the hall. A **taxe de séjour** of 1–4F/€0.15–0.60 per person per day, according to the star rating, may be added to the final bill.

Breakfast, too, can add 26–38F/€4.00–5.80 per person to a bill – though there is no obligation to take it and you will nearly always do better at a café. Officially it is illegal for hotels to insist on your taking **meals** – but they often do, and in busy resorts you may not find a room unless you agree to *demi-pension* (half-board). This often works in your favour, however, as *demi-pension* rates (often not available for stays of less than three days) will often save you twenty percent of the cost of room and board taken separately. **Single rooms** – or more properly, rooms considered most suitable for a lone person, with single prices quoted – are only marginally less expensive than more generously proportioned quarters, so sharing always slashes costs. Most hotels willingly provide rooms with extra beds, for three or more people, at good discounts.

Many Pyrenean hotels take a **month or so off** per year – usually sometime between November and May, unless they're in a major skiing area. You may also find that their restaurants – often the reception too – may close one night, plus one day, a week. We've given days and months of closure where known, but it's always best to phone ahead to check.

In country areas, in addition to standard hotels, you will come across **chambres d'hôte**, bed-and-breakfast accommodation in someone's house or farm. These vary in standard but are certainly affordable, falling mostly into the ④ category; in many instances they are good sources of traditional home-cooking. Leaflets available in tourist offices list most of them.

HOSTELS, GÎTES D'ÉTAPE AND REFUGES

At 60–90F/€9.20–13.70 per night for a dormitory bunk, *Auberges de Jeunesse* – **youth hostels** – are invaluable for single budget travellers. For couples, however, and certainly for groups of three or more people, they'll not necessarily be cheaper than hotels – though many of the newer hostels offer double rooms. Stays are usually limited to three consecutive nights maximum, though you may be able to negotiate longer stays in off-peak times. Another drawback is that, especially in the Pyrenees, you often have to share the place with large, raucous school parties. However, many hostels are beautifully sited, and they allow you to cut costs by preparing your own food in their kitchens, or eating in inexpensive canteens. In the more popular regions, advance reservations may be necessary. All that said, you can count the number of French youth hostels in this book on two hands, so they're unlikely to be your accommodation of choice. To use them, you are supposed to be a member of the International Youth Hostel Federation, but you can often join on the spot. There are two rival French youth hostel associations: the Fédération Unie des Auberges de Jeunesse (FUAJ), whose hostels are detailed in the *International Handbook*, and the Ligue Française pour les Auberges de Jeunesse (LFAJ). IYHF membership covers both associations.

Another hostel-type alternative – the **gîte d'é-tape** – is more popular and useful in the countryside, especially in trekking or cycling areas. In the Pyrenees, *gîtes* are administered under the umbrella of the publishing and outdoors activities organization Randonnées Pyrénéennes, which was originally established to create a chain of medium-category hostelries for trekkers, cyclists and horse-riders. All *gîtes* must have self-catering kitchen facilities, some form of heating, supposedly a minimum of fifteen bunks in dormitories or

private rooms (bedding is generally not provided), laundry, shower and toilet facilities, and may or may not be open year-round. Hot evening meals are often provided, and re-provisioning might be possible. A bed will be 50–85F/€7.60–13.00, and a meal will rarely cost more than 80F – thus all *gîtes* in the *Guide* are rated as ①. Description of a *gîte* as a **Rando'Plume** means either that rooms are of extraordinarily high standard – typically with some en-suite facilities, and a low number of beds, with proper linen – and/or that the *gîte* is affiliated to some top-rated activity centre in the area (a trekking or winter sports outfitter, horse-riding, parapente, etc), whose devotees make up the main clientele.

Although *gîtes* must give priority to long-distance travellers on a traverse, it is sometimes possible to use one as a base for several nights; if you do this, the manager will almost certainly be able to share an intimate knowledge of the region. The large-scale IGN walkers' maps show the location of *gîtes*, and they are noted in the individual GR *topo-guides* or guide booklets to local Tours.

Most **mountain refuge huts** are open only in summer, though in winter there is nearly always at least a simple annexe with sleeping platforms and perhaps a fireplace or stove. A few refuges are still extremely basic and antiquated, while most others are passably comfortable and modern – with hot showers in a few cases. Almost all of them have cooking facilities and offer meals, though these are often not the best value (60–85F/€9–13 for an emphasis on wine and carbohydrates), the price reflecting the fact that foodstuffs usually have to be brought in by mule or helicopter. Especially in or around the Parc National des Pyrénées, refuges are often packed to the seams in summer, and there have been reports of trekkers having to sleep on and under tables – for the normal fee. Costs range 55–75F/€8.40–11.40 for the night, less if you're a member of a climbing organization affiliated to the Club Alpin Français; either a membership card or your passport will be held as security against payment.

Éditions Lacadole publishes a complete guide, *Gîtes d'étape et Refuges*, available in French bookshops for 110F/€16.75. Failing this, look for the free folding pamphlet, available in many Pyrenean tourist offices, detailing the 140–odd certified *gîtes d'étape* in the Pyrenees and foothills.

RENTED ACCOMMODATION

If you are planning to stay a week or more in any one place it might be worth considering **renting a rural house**, known as *gîte rural* or *gîte de séjour*. You can do this through one of the holiday firms in Britain which market accommodation/travel packages (see p.6); or use the official French government service, the **Gîtes de France** (59 rue St-Lazare, 75009 Paris ☎01.49.70.75.75, *www.gites -de-france.fr*, or in the UK through Brittany Ferries ☎0990/360360). A small membership fee gets you a copy of their handbook which features proper-ties all over France, listed by *département*. The houses vary in size and comfort, but all are basically acceptable holiday homes. There is a photograph and description of each one and the computerized booking service means that you can instantly reserve one for any number of full weeks. The cost varies with the season, and may include concessionary ferry rates.

CAMPING

Practically every village and town in the Pyrenees has at least one **campsite** to cater for the thou-

---

ACCOMMODATION PRICE CODES

All the accommodation establishments listed in this book, on both sides of the Pyrenees, have been **price-graded** according to the following scale. The range in **euros**, which is supposed to be sole legal tender in France and Spain after February 2002, is given first, followed by bands in **pesetas** and **francs**. Spanish prices include seven-percent IVA (VAT) where applied. Youth hostels, mountain refuges, *albergues* and *gîtes d'étape* are all graded as ①, which is a per-person rate. Other categories indicate the **cheapest available double room** in each hotel during high season. Remember, though, that many of the budget places will also have more expensive rooms including en-suite facilities, and that in France the cheaper rooms are often the first to fill. Sometimes the categories are further qualified by 'B&B' (bed and breakfast) or 'HB' (half-board). In the case of **apartments** intended for 4–6 persons, the current raw prices are given, with euro equivalents.

In Spain, rooms in the ② band correspond to the **most basic** *pensiones* and *fondas* without private bath, as well as the older non-en-suite *turismos rurales*; there will, however, often be a washbasin in the room, along with the minimum of furniture besides a decently firm bed. In France, ② means the most basic hotel rooms, which may be unmodernized: exposed, retrofitted wiring, saggy beds, interwar wallpaper, musty carpets, and – enthroned in one corner – a so-called *cabinette de toilette*, a sink side by side with a bidet. In Spain, ③ rooms, whether in a *hostal* or a better class of *turismo rural*, will be bigger and probably have a **private bathroom**, with a so-called *medio baño* or very short bathtub meant to be used primarily as a shower; there will also be a modicum of extra furniture, possibly a balcony, maybe a telephone. In France, ③ will almost certainly have a partitioned area – possibly even a proper separate room – with a sink, shower and bidet, but the toilet will still be down the hall, and maybe up or down a flight of stairs. Spanish ④ and ⑤ rooms will be **impeccably furnished**, with telephones, full bathtubs, TV, built-in closets, and heating plus double glazing guaranteed for the winter; at ④, **on-site restaurants** (as opposed to just breakfast provision) are pretty certain, while at ⑤ **sizeable common areas** and swimming pools make their appearance. Spanish ⑥ will get you all these goodies (except perhaps the pool), plus **swish accoutrements** like spot lighting, parquet floors, original artwork, designer fixtures and maybe key-cards to work the electric switch. At French ④, **full en-suite facilities** with a toilet are just about guaranteed, as are sizeable gardens and common areas, but you won't see bathtubs – or proper pillows, as opposed to the dreaded "cement sacks" (see p.39) – until ⑤, which should also get you such benefits as the first swimming pools and off-street parking, and sometimes situation in a building of outstanding **architectural interest**. For ⑥, French facilities will be completely **modernized** – possibly a bit bland and sterile – while ⑦ in both countries guarantees most creature comforts and distractions. You don't get much extra for your money once far beyond ⑦'s lower limits, and except for a few unusual spots in the Central Pyrenees or San Sebastián, this book does not include many such.

① Under €13/2200ptas/85F	⑤ €40–52/6600–8600ptas/260–340F
② €15–24/2500–4000ptas/100–160F	⑥ €52–65/8600–10,800ptas/340–430F
③ €24–32/4000–5400ptas/160–210F	⑦ Over €65/10,800ptas/430F
④ €32–40/5400–6600ptas/210–260F	

sands of French people who spend their holiday under canvas – or in a caravan. The cheapest – at 25–30F/€3.80–4.60 per person per night – is usually the **camping municipal**, run by the local municipality. When officially open, they are always clean, and often situated in prime locations, though hot water can be unreliable. Out of season, many of them don't even bother to collect the overnight charge.

On the coast especially, there are **superior categories** of campsite, where you'll pay prices similar to those of a *gîte d'étape* or hostel for the facilities: bars, restaurants, sometimes swimming pools. These have rather more permanent status than the *campings municipals*, with people often spending a whole holiday in one place. If you plan to do the same, and particularly if you have a caravan or camper, or a substantial tent, it's wise to reserve in advance. Count on 35F/€5.30 a head all-in with a tent, 40F/€6.10 with a camper van.

Inland, **camping à la ferme** – on somebody's farm – is another possibility, though facilities often leave much to be desired. Lists of sites are detailed in the *Accueil à la Campagne* booklet, sold by the French Government Tourist Office. With these you should make sure of what you'll be charged before you pitch up – it's easy to get stung the following morning.

Lastly, a **word of caution**: never camp rough (*camping sauvage*, as the French call it) on anyone's land without first asking permission. If the dogs don't get you, guns might – farmers have been known to shoot before asking any questions. In many parts of the Pyrenees *camping sauvage* on public land – including the beaches – is not tolerated, or is subject (as in the Parc National des Pyrénées) to severe restrictions.

SPAIN

Simple, reasonably priced rooms are still very widely available in Spain, and in almost any inland Pyrenean town you'll be able to find a double room for as little as 3500ptas/€21, or a single for 2200ptas/€13.20 and up. Only in major coastal resorts, particularly in San Sebastián or some of the Costa Brava ports, might you have to pay more. Festivals tend to result more in accommodation filling quickly rather than outrageous rate hikes.

In Spain, unlike most countries, you don't seem to pay any more for a central location, though you do tend to get a comparatively bad deal if you're

travelling on your own as there are relatively few **single rooms** – though certainly more than in France. Where present, they're about sixty to seventy percent of double rates; otherwise you'll have to negotiate a reduction from the price of a double. In Catalunya particularly, **half-board** at *hostals* with restaurants is often encouraged or obligatory, and usually very good value.

Otherwise, there seems little scope for genuine **bargaining** over room prices in the Pyrenees. High season is construed as August 1–23 and Easter week (Wednesday to the following Monday), when peak prices are adhered to; during the rest of the year, official rates (always posted in the entry hall) may be half to two-thirds as much, and that's your "bargain". If there are more than two of you, most places have rooms with three or four beds at not a great deal more than the double-room price – a good deal, especially if you are travelling with children. Remember always to establish whether quoted rates include seven-percent IVA (Value Added Tax) or not; usually they don't, but proprietors may waive it as a small concession.

FONDAS, PENSIONES, HOSTALES AND HOTELES

Travellers need to be familiar with the various categories of places to stay. Least expensive, though just about extinct in the Pyrenees, are **fondas** (identifiable by a square blue sign with a white "**F**" on it, and often positioned above a bar), closely followed up the price scale by **pensiones** (*pensió* in Catalan singular; "**P**"). Since the 1980s, most surviving *fondas* have reinvented themselves as one- or two-star *pensiones*; the original meaning of *fonda*, now being reverted to, is a roadside taverna in an isolated area (not offering beds). *Pensiones* usually serve food, and an increasing number may offer rooms only on a meals-inclusive basis.

Slightly more expensive but more common are **hostales** (*hostals* in Catalan; marked "**Hs**") and **hostal-residencias** ("**HsR**"). These are categorized from one to three stars, but prices vary enormously according to location and facilities – a place in a slightly down-at-heel medieval quarter with no car-parking facilities is bound to cost less than new premises on a suburban street or the town's access road. Most *hostales* offer good, if functional rooms, often with private shower, and, for doubles at least, they can be excellent value. The *residencia* designation means that no meals other than perhaps breakfast are served. Faced, however, with competition from *turismo rural* (see below), many town-centre **hostales** in the budget range have folded in recent years, as they were perceived as poor value in comparison.

Moving up the scale you finally reach fully-fledged **hoteles** ("H"), again star-graded (from one to five) by the authorities. One-star hotels cost no more than three-star *hostales* – sometimes they're actually less expensive, and remain officially graded as *hostales* – but at three stars you pay a lot more, and at four or five you're in luxury facilities with prices to match. Near the top end of this scale there are also state-run **paradores**: occasionally beautiful places converted from castles, monasteries and other minor Spanish monuments (though the few purpose-built ones are hideous). Even if you can't afford to stay, the older buildings are often worth a look in their own right, and usually have pleasantly classy bars. People over 65 may find that they can in fact afford them; most *paradores* are discounted thirty percent to OAPs except on peak days.

Outside all these categories you will sometimes find **habitaciones** (rooms) advertised in private houses or above bars. If you're travelling on a very tight budget these can be worth looking out for – particularly if you're offered one at a bus station and the owner is prepared to bargain.

TURISMO RURAL

Each of the autonomous communities featured in this book – Catalunya, Aragón, Navarra and Gipuzkoa – give official support to "**agroturismo**" programmes, akin to the French *chambres d'hôte* or *gîtes de France*, but by no means equivalent. *Turismos rurales*, as they're better known, are either a private residence where extra rooms are rented out; self-contained, self-catering flats or cottages; or, at their best, a bed-and-breakfast or half-board inn occupying a medieval farmhouse. They have gone from strength to strength in Spain since the early 1990s, booked months in advance for peak times. The fad for them – especially among big-city yuppies – shows no sign of abating, and deservedly so: top-drawer *turismos rurales* comprise some of the best accommodation the Spanish Pyrenees have to offer.

In Catalunya they are termed **cases de pagès**, or belong to a **turisme rural** scheme. In Aragón and Navarra they are called **casas de payés**, **casas rurales** or **viviendas de turismo rural**, while in Gipuzkoa they are identified by a red-and-green circular sign with the word **nekazalturismoa**. Each autonomous region publishes comprehensive guide-booklets or lists to all their *agroturismo* outfits, available overseas or from the better-stocked local tourist offices. To have been included in this book, they satisfy certain criteria: they are attended most of the year (too many proprietors just throw up an unstaffed modern villa, call it an *agroturismo*, and post the keys to advert-answerers); possess some architectural merit; are near points of interest or along a major trail; welcome walk-in, short-term trade; and offer breakfast if not half-board, providing regional and/or vegetarian specialities.

YOUTH HOSTELS, MOUNTAIN REFUGES AND MONASTERIES

Spanish **albergues juveniles** (youth hostels) are rarely of much use except for solo, short-term travellers who may not find any other kind of vacancy during the Pyrenean summer. The handful of useful ones are detailed in the guide, or you can get a complete list (with opening times and phone numbers) from your home hostelling association. Be warned that most of the hostels tend to have curfews, are often block-reserved by school groups for weeks on end, and demand production of a membership card (though this is generally available on the spot if you haven't already bought one from your national organization). At 1000–1700ptas/€6–10.20 a person, too, you can quite easily pay as much as for sharing an inexpensive double room in a *fonda* or *pensión*.

There are, however, a number of privately run, similarly priced but less institutional **albergues** conforming fairly exactly to the notion of a French *gîte d'étape*, strategically sited in select mountain villages. These are often aimed more specifically at trekkers or those pursuing a particular local activity (skiing, canyoning, etc).

Additionally, in the high Pyrenees the Federación Aragonesa de Montañismo the Federación Navarra de Montaña, plus three Catalunyan clubs – the FEEC, the CEC and the UEC – and a handful of private individuals all run a number of **refugios** (refuges; *refugis* in Catalan). Like their French counterparts, these are simple, inexpensive dormitory huts for climbers and trekkers, generally equipped with bunk-beds, a common room and cooking space (except in the CEC huts where self-catering is forbidden). As in France, some sort of emergency adjacent shelter is occasionally open all year, and the most popular refuges are generally staffed from mid-June to late September, plus selected snowy weeks and holidays (Christmas, Easter) during the colder months.

As on the French side, quite a number of elderly Spanish *refugios* have been renovated and/or enlarged since 1990, often with little regard for the immediate environment. Critics of the trend note that many such new facilities resemble roadhouses rather than alpine huts, and just encourage what's disparagingly called **dominguismo** in Castilian – "Sunday-tripping" by those with little true knowledge of, or affection for, the mountains. At the same time, many eight-to-twenty place, unstaffed huts in strategic high-altitude locales go to wrack and ruin for lack of maintenance.

The cost of **accommodation** in the wardened refuges is 1100ptas/€6.60 (the cheaper private refuges) to 1500ptas/€9 (the fanciest Catalan ones), unless you are a member of a reciprocally recognized alpine club, in which case you'll get half off at the club-affiliated refuges. At about 1700ptas/€10.20, **meals** can cost a bit less than in French refuges, and have improved in quality since the early 1990s; word has gone out from Spanish alpine club headquarters that they must consist of at least three courses – soup and/or salad, a meat dish, dessert or fruit, and wine.

Again off the beaten track, it is sometimes possible to stay at wonderfully sited **monasterios** or **conventos** in Aragón and Catalunya. Often severely underpopulated, these may let empty cells for a small charge; in many other cases, wings have been renovated expressly as *hostales*, with prices to match, whether or not the monastery or convent is still functioning as a religious community. You can just turn up and ask – many will take visitors regardless of sex – but if you want to be sure of a good reception it's best to approach the local tourist office first, and phone ahead. Those following the **Camino de Santiago** can also take advantage of monastic accommodation specifically reserved for pilgrims along the route; the best places are detailed in the text.

Monasteries and youth hostels aside, if you have any **problems** with Spanish rooms – overcharging, most obviously – you can usually encourage an immediate resolution by asking for an *hoja de reclamaciones* (complaints sheet). By law all establishments must stock these and provide them on demand to an unhappy customer. Once filled out, you send it off to the government of the province or autonomous region – not as futile an exercise as it may sound, as we know of at least one hotel in Aragón which was prosecuted in response to a foreigner's complaint.

CAMPING

There are about 150 authorized **campsites** in the Spanish Pyrenees, including coastal areas. If you plan to camp extensively then pick up the free *Mapa de Campings* from the Spanish tourist board, which marks and names virtually all of them. A complete *Guía de Campings* (1000ptas/€6) listing full prices, facilities and exact locations, is available at most Spanish bookshops. They usually charge about 400–500ptas/€2.40–3.00 plus as much again for a tent and a similar amount for car or caravan; only a few of the best-sited or most popular sites are significantly more expensive.

However, mountain trekkers will find the majority of Pyrenean sites **biased towards use by caravans**, and equipped with amenities (electric power hookup, sewage purge tanks, etc) that they don't really need or want. Many sites, even some of the newer ones, are fairly squalid, shadeless and packed out at peak times. Many others are effectively closed to casual trade because they house long-term residents. Tent-friendly and attractive deviations from this norm are singled out in the text. Also of potential interest for trekkers are the various *áreas de acampada libre* or "free camping zones" dotted about the Catalan and Aragonese Pyrenees. Some of them are not financially "free", with a token charge, but all are fairly basic, at or below the level of the most modest *camping à la ferme* or *camping municipal* in France. But you do always get toilets and cold running water, possibly picnic furniture and a tiny drinks bar.

Camping outside campsites is legal – but with certain restrictions. There must be fewer than ten people in your group, and you're not allowed to camp "in urban areas, areas prohibited for military or touristic reasons, or within 1km of an official campsite". What this means in practice is that you can't camp on tourist beaches (though you can, discreetly, nearby) but with a little sensitivity you can set up a tent for a short period almost anywhere in the mountains. (Conspicuous exceptions are the Ordesa/Monte Perdido, Posets-Maladeta and Aigüestortes national/natural parks, where camping is prohibited outside designated areas.) Whenever possible ask locally first.

EATING AND DRINKING

Not surprisingly, the best Pyrenean restaurant food tends to be based on what's available locally, which means a preponderance of river (or sometimes farmed) trout, salmon, fresh chestnuts, wild mushrooms or berries, goat meat, and game such as wild boar, rabbit, grouse and pigeon. In the mountains, ordinary restaurants often rely on a small fixed menu, with little in the way of à la carte dishes, though special requests for vegetarian meals should produce some response. Self-catering is a splendid (and if you're trekking a lot, necessary) alternative, with a vast choice of seasonal specialities.

FRANCE

Mountain restaurants within easy reach of major centres can be very popular and consequently expensive, but elsewhere, except in peak holiday season, most restaurants are low-key, informal and very reasonable. If you've just arrived and are looking for a good place to eat, go wherever the largest numbers of locals go – the favourites will be particularly easy to locate on a Sunday lunchtime, when whole families turn out for the traditional weekly get-together. Except in the major towns, which often have at least one Chinese/Vietnamese and Moroccan eatery apiece, you'll find little in the way of non-European food.

BREAKFAST, SNACKS AND PICNICS

A croissant, *pain au chocolat* or a sandwich in a bar or café, with a hot chocolate or coffee, is gen-erally the best way to eat **breakfast** – at a fraction of the price charged by most hotels, where all you'll often get for 28F/€4.30 and up is a pile of stale if toasted bread and foil-sealed jam, plus a pot of tea or coffee. *Brasseries* – which serve full meals (see below) – are also possibilities for a coffee and a quick bite. If you're standing at the counter, which is cheaper than sitting down, you may see a basket of croissants or some hard-boiled eggs (usually gone by 9.30 or 10am). Help yourself – the waiter will keep an eye on how many you've eaten and bill you accordingly.

At **midday** you may find cafés offering a *plat du jour* (chef's daily special) for between 45F/€6.85 and 80F/€12.20, or *formules*, a limited or no-choice menu. *Croque-Monsieurs* or *Croque-Madames* (variations on the grilled-cheese sandwich) are on sale at cafés, brasseries and many street stalls, along with *frites*, *crêpes*, *galettes* (wholewheat pancakes), *gaufres* (waffles), *glaces* (ice creams) and all sorts of sand-wiches.

Crêpes or filled pancakes, which have spread all over France from their original home in Brittany, are also popular for light meals, at 15–40F/€2.25–6.10 each. The more expensive savoury buckwheat variety (*galettes*) are served as a main course; the sweet light-flour ones are for dessert. Pizzerias, often *au feu du bois* (wood-fired oven), are also common and somewhat better value in that you can fill up for 50–75F/€7.60–11.50, though quality varies widely – check for surplus empty seats before nosing your way in the door.

For **picnics**, the local *halle* (covered produce market) or supermarket will provide anything you want in the way of cheese, pâté and salad ingredients. For more elaborate **takeaway food**, there's nothing to beat the *charcuteries* (delicatessens) which you'll find everywhere, even in small villages. Such shops sell meat dishes (mostly pork-based), salads and fully prepared main courses; these are also available less expensively at supermarket *charcuterie* counters. You buy by weight, or you can ask for *une tranche* (a slice), *une barquette* (a carton), or *une part* (a portion). *Boulangeries* or **bakeries** often sell not just bread but an array of baked snacks with meat or cheese in them, such as *quiche*, eminently suitable for a lunch on the hoof.

MEALS AND RESTAURANTS

There's little difference between **restaurants** (or *auberges* or *relais* as they sometimes call themselves) and **brasseries** in terms of quality or price range. The distinction is that *brasseries*, which resemble cafés, serve quicker meals at most hours of the day, while restaurants tend to stick to the traditional meal times of noon–2pm (or 2.30pm in the larger towns) and 7–9pm (or 10pm in towns). After 9pm or so, restaurants may serve only à la carte meals – invariably more expensive than the set *menu*. **Serving hours** tend to be extremely inflexible, to the sorrow of many unsuspecting visitors; even if a place is still packed at its 10pm closing time, you won't be seated or served if you arrive at 10.01, or at 9.50 for that matter. Even if you're staying in a particular hotel-restaurant, they will be loath to reopen their kitchen, and will demand to know from 6pm onwards whether you're planning to dine there that night. Following the introduction of the 35-hour work week, this tendency has become more pronounced; at slow times, the help will simply be sent home early to avoid their going over the statutory limit, and no amount of pleading with the proprietor will persuade them to serve you a hot meal, even if you've arrived well within the stated hours. To be on the safe side, assume that you're guaranteed a feed only between 12.15–1.30pm and 8.15–9pm, though the Guide makes a point of highlighting establishments whose kitchen functions later than usual. In small towns it will be impossible to get anything other than a bar sandwich after 9.30pm; in major cities or busy resorts like Biarritz, town-centre *brasseries* will serve until 11pm or midnight and one or two may stay open all night.

For the more upmarket places it's wise to make reservations – easily done on the same day. Don't forget that hotel restaurants are open to nonresidents, and often very good value; in many small Pyrenean villages, the sole hotel may also have the only restaurant. As noted in the "Accommodation" section, *Logis de France* establishments are always safe and salubrious, if somewhat bland in the menu. Otherwise, when hunting for a restaurant, avoid places that are half-full at peak time, be suspicious of overlong menus (whose ingredients will rarely be kept fresh) and use your instinct; asking locals for recommendations – the French equivalent of commenting on the weather – will usually net strong views and sound advice.

Prices and menus are almost always posted outside. Normally there is a choice between one to four **menus** – where the number of courses has already been determined and the choice is limited. At the bottom of the price range, *menus* revolve around standard dishes such as steak (*steak*) and chicken (*poulet*) served with fried potatoes (*frites*), or various concoctions involving innards. Look for the *plat du jour*, which may be a regional dish and also more appealing. Increasingly, however, restaurants are offering a range of *menus*, the more expensive of which offer quite a wide choice, and run to four or five courses. For 115F/€17.50 and up, you should expect an array of regional dishes, or at least generic *haute cuisine* that will have you leafing through the menu master (see pp.48–53) for translations.

Going **à la carte** is always more expensive but does, however, offer greater flexibility and, in the better restaurants, unlimited access to the chef's specialities. A simple and perfectly legitimate tactic is to have just two courses instead of the expected three or four. You can share dishes or just have several starters – a useful strategy for vegetarians (see opposite for more on this). There's usually no minimum charge, except sometimes at peak hours/days.

In the French **sequence of courses**, any salad – sometimes vegetables, too – arrives separately from the main dish, and cheese precedes – or is the alternative to – dessert. You will be offered coffee, which always costs extra, to finish off the meal. The waiter/waitress will approach with the words *Ça-y-était?* to take finished plates away, which inevitably throws some people as the expression isn't in most phrasebooks. Incidentally, you address staff as *monsieur* or *madame, mademoiselle* if a young woman, not by the school-French *garçon*.

On menus or bills, *TTC* means that all local taxes and sales tax (IVA) is included (the rule); *service compris* or *s.c.* means the service charge is included (less common). *Service non compris*, *s.n.c.* or *servis en sus* means that it isn't and you need to calculate an additional fifteen percent. Wine (*vin*) or a drink (*boisson*) may be included, though rarely on menus under 150F/€22.90. When ordering wine, ask for *un quart* or *un pichet* (250ml), *un demi-litre* (half a litre) or *une carafe* (a litre). You'll normally be given the house wine unless you specify otherwise; if you're concerned about costs ask for *vin ordinaire* or *vin de pays*.

The French are well-disposed towards **children** in restaurants, not just in the ubiquitous offering of cut-price *menu enfants*, but by fostering an atmosphere – even in otherwise fairly snooty establishments – that positively welcomes kids. It is regarded as self-evident that large family groups should be able to eat together. More difficult to accept may be the idea of **dogs** in the dining room, considered quite normal (though increasing numbers of places have signs up forbidding the practice). The French are absolutely besotted with their pooches, and it may come as a shock in provincial (and urban) restaurants to realize that a significant number of your fellow diners are concealing pets under the table.

VEGETARIANS AND VEGANS

Vegetarians should expect a somewhat lean time in the French Pyrenees. *Crêperies* and pizzerias can be good standbys; elsewhere you'll either have to hope for a sympathetic proprietor willing to replace a meat dish on a *menu* with an omelette, resign yourself to combing the *carte* for something acceptable, or (literally) swallow your principles and eat fish or shellfish.

Vegans should probably forget altogether about eating in French restaurants – since "no animal products" means it's still considered okay to douse everything in butter – and resort to self-catering. Many French health shops stock vegan margarine, plus the usual instant meals and supplements; the La Vie Claire health chain has branches all over France, but be prepared to pay over the odds.

> The magic words are *je suis végétarien(ne); est-ce qu'il y a des plats sans viande ou poisson?* (I'm a vegetarian; are there any dishes without meat or fish?)

ALCOHOLIC DRINKS

Where you can eat you can invariably drink, and to a certain extent the reverse is true. **Drinking** is done at a leisurely pace whether it's a prelude to food (*apéritif*), a sequel (*digestif*), or the accompaniment, and **cafés** are the standard places to do it. Every bar or café has to display its full price list (usually without a fifteen-percent service charge added), with the cheapest drinks at the bar (*au comptoir*), and progressively increasing prices for sitting at a table inside (*la salle*), or on the terrace

(*la terrasse*). You pay when you leave, and it's quite acceptable to sit for an hour over one cup of a coffee.

Wine – *vin* – is drunk at just about every meal or social occasion. Red is *rouge*, white *blanc*, or there's *rosé*. *Vin de table* or *vin ordinaire* – table wine – is generally drinkable and always cheap; it may be disguised and marked up as the house wine, or *cuvée*. In wine-producing areas the local *vin de pays* can be very good indeed. In bars you normally buy wine by the glass – just ask for *un rouge* or *un blanc* – though as in restaurants you can also get *un pichet*: a 250-ml, 500-ml or 1-litre jug.

A.O.C. (*Appellation d'Origine Contrôlée*) wines are another matter. They can be excellent value at the lower end of the quality scale, where lenient French taxes keep prices down to 20–30F/€3–4.60 or so a bottle retail, but move up and you're soon paying serious prices; restaurant mark-ups of A.O.C. wines can be well over 100 percent. Popular A.O.C. wines found on most restaurant lists include Côtes du Rhône (from the Rhône valley), St-Emilion and Médoc (from Bordeaux), Beaujolais and very upmarket Burgundy. Peculiar to the central Pyrenees is Madiran, a high-tannin, full-bodied red used also in cooking. From the environs of Pau comes Jurançon, a dry, almost vinegary white, also used at the stove. Irouléguy, from the *domaine* of the namesake village in the Pays Basque, is excellent, and available as rosé, red or even white. At the opposite end of the range, Banyuls is found in both Spain and France near the namesake town, as either a dry or sweet dessert wine. The basic terms are *brut*, very dry; *sec*, dry; *demi-sec*, sweet; *doux*, very sweet; *mousseux* or *pétillant*, sparkling; *méthode champenoise*, mature and sparkling.

Alsatian brands such as Kanterbrau, Karlsbrau and Kronenbourg account for virtually all of the **beer** served in the Pyrenees. Draught (*à la pression*) is the cheapest drink you can have next to coffee and wine – although the smallest glass, *un demi* (250ml) rarely costs less than 10F/€1.50. **Cider** (*cidre*) is fairly common in the Pyrenees, and also comes as *brut* or *doux* – six percent is the usual strength.

Stronger alcohol is consumed from as early as 5am as a pre-work fortifier, and right through the day according to inclination. **Cognac** or **Armagnac** brandies and the dozens of *eaux de vie* (brandies distilled from fruit) and **liqueurs** are

FRENCH FOOD AND DISHES

Basics

Pain	Bread	*Huile*	Oil	*Vinaigre*	Vinegar	*Couteau*	Knife
Beurre	Butter	*Poivre*	Pepper	*Bouteille*	Bottle	*Cuillère*	Spoon
Oeufs	Eggs	*Sel*	Salt	*Verre*	Glass	*Table*	Table
Lait	Milk	*Sucre*	Sugar	*Fourchette*	Fork	*L'addition*	The bill

Typical French snacks

Un sandwich/une baguette au ...	A sandwich with ...	*Omelette ...*	Omelette ...
jambon	ham	*nature*	plain
fromage	cheese	*aux fines herbes*	with herbs
saucisson	sausage	*au fromage*	with cheese
à l'ail	garlic	*Salade de ...*	Salad of ...
poivre	pepper	*tomates*	tomatoes
pâté (de campagne)	with pâté (country-style)	*betteraves*	beets
Croque-monsieur	Grilled cheese and ham sandwich	*concombres*	cucumber
		carottes rapées	grated carrots
Croque-madame	Grilled cheese and bacon, sausage, chicken or an egg	*Crêpe*	Pancake
		au sucre	with sugar
		au citron	with lemon
Oeufs	Eggs	*au miel*	with honey
au plat	fried	*à la confiture*	with jam
à la coque	boiled	*aux oeufs*	with eggs
durs	hard-boiled	*à la crème de marrons*	with chestnut purée
brouillés	scrambled		

Other fillings/salads:

Anchois	Anchovy	*Fonds d'artichauts*	Artichoke hearts
Andouillette	Tripe sausage	*Hareng*	Herring
Boudin	Black pudding	*Langue*	Tongue
Coeurs de palmiers	Hearts of palm	*Poulet*	Chicken
Epis de maïs	Corn on the cob	*Thon*	Tuna fish

And Some Terms:

Chauffé	Heated	*Emballé*	Wrapped	*Salé*	Salted/spicy
Cuit	Cooked	*À emporter*	Takeaway	*Sucré*	Sweet
Cru	Raw	*Fumé*	Smoked		

Soups (*Soupes*)

Bisque	Shellfish soup	*Potage*	Thick soup, usually vegetable
Bouillabaisse	Fish soup	*Rouille*	Red pepper, garlic and saffron mayonnaise served with fish soup
Bouillon	Broth or stock		
Bourride	Thick fish soup		
Consommé	Clear soup	*Velouté*	Thick soup, usually fish or poultry
Pistou	Parmesan, basil and garlic paste, sometimes added to soup		

Starters (*Hors d'oeuvres*)

Assiette anglaise	Plate of cold meats or *de charcuterie*	*Hors d'oeuvres variés*	Combination of the previous two plus smoked or marinated fish
Crudités	Raw vegetables with dressings		

Fish (*Poisson*), Seafood (*Fruits de mer*) and Shellfish (*Crustacés* or *Coquillages*)

Anchois	Anchovies	*Ecrevisse*	Freshwater crayfish	*Louvine*	Similar to sea bass
Anguilles	Eels				
Baudroie	Monkfish, anglerfish	*Éperlan*	Smelt or whitebait	*Maquereau*	Mackerel
				Merlan	Whiting
Bar (Pays Basque)	Sea bass	*Escargots*	Snails	*Morue*	Salt cod
		Espadon	Swordfish	*Moules (marinière)*	Mussels (with shallots in white wine sauce)
Brème	Bream	*Favou(ille)*	Tiny crab		
Bulot	Whelk	*Flétan*	Halibut		
Cabillaud	Cod, unsalted	*Gambas*	King prawns		
Calmar	Squid	*Grenouilles (cuisses de)*	Frogs (legs)	*Palourdes*	Clams
Carrelet	Plaice			*Poulpe*	Octopus
Claire	Type of oyster	*Hareng*	Herring	*Praires*	Small clams
Colin	Hake	*Homard*	Lobster	*Raie*	Skate
Congre	Conger eel	*Huîtres*	Oysters	*Rouget*	Red mullet
Coques	Cockles	*Langouste*	Spiny lobster	*Saumon*	Salmon
Coquilles Saint-Jacques	Scallops	*Langoustines*	Saltwater crayfish	*Saint-Pierre*	John Dory
				Sole	Sole
Crabe	Crab	*Limande*	Lemon sole	*Thon*	Tuna
Crevettes grises	Shrimps	*Lotte de mer*	Monkfish	*Truite*	Trout
Crevettes roses	Prawns	*Loup de mer*	Sea bass	*Turbot*	Turbot
Dorade, daurade	Sea bream				

Terms (Fish)

Aïoli	Garlic mayonnaise served with salt cod and other fish	*Fumet*	Fish stock
		Gigot de mer	Large fish baked whole
Béarnaise	Sauce made with egg yolks, white wine, shallots and vinegar	*Grillé*	Grilled
		Hollandaise	Butter and vinegar sauce
		À la meunière	In a butter, lemon and parsley sauce
Colbert	Fried in egg and breadcrumbs		
Darne	Fillet or steak	*Mousse*	Mousse
La douzaine	A dozen	*/mousseline*	
Frit	Fried	*Pané*	Breaded
Friture	Assorted deep-fried small fish	*Quenelles*	Light dumplings
Fumé	Smoked	*Tourte*	Tart or pie

Meat (*Viande*) and Poultry (*Volaille*)

Agneau	Lamb	*Entrecôte*	Ribsteak
Andouille, andouillette	Tripe sausage	*Faux filet*	Sirloin steak
		Foie	Liver
Bavette d'échalote	Cheap steak fried with shallots	*Foie gras*	Fattened liver of duck or goose
		Fraises de veau	Veal testicles
Boeuf	Beef	*Cervelle*	Brains
Bifteck	Steak	*Châteaubriand*	Porterhouse steak
Boudin blanc	Sausage of white meats	*Cheval*	Horse meat
Boudin noir	Black pudding	*Fricadelles*	Meatballs
Caille	Quail	*Gibier*	Game
Canard	Duck	*Gigot (d'agneau)*	Leg of lamb
Caneton	Duckling		
Chevreau	Kid goat	*Gigot de . . .*	Leg of another meat
Contrefilet	Sirloin roast	*Graisse*	Fat
Coquelet	Cockerel	*Grillade*	Grilled meat
Dinde, dindon, dindonneau	Turkey of different ages and genders	*Hâchis*	Chopped meat or hamburger
		Langue	Tongue

continues overleaf...

FRENCH FOOD AND DISHES contd.

Meat (*Viande*) and Poultry (*Volaille*) contd.

Lapin, lapereau	Rabbit, young rabbit	*Poussin*	Baby chicken
Lard, lardons	Bacon, diced bacon	*Ris*	Sweetbreads
Lièvre	Hare	*Rognons*	Kidneys
Marcassin	Young wild boar	*Rognons blancs*	Testicles
Merguez	Spicy, red sausage	*Sanglier*	Wild boar
Mouton	Mutton	*Steak*	Steak
Museau de veau	Muzzle of veal	*Tête de veau*	Calf's head in jelly
		Toro	Bull meat
Oie	Goose	*Tortue*	Turtle
Os	Bone	*Tournedos*	Thick slices of fillet
Porc, pieds de porc	Pork, pig's trotters	*Travers de porc*	Spare ribs
		Tripes	Tripe
Poulet	Chicken	*Veau*	Veal
Poulette	Young chicken	*Venaison*	Venison

Dishes and terms (meat and poultry)

Boeuf bourguignon	Beef Stew with burgundy, onions and mushrooms	*Carré*	Best end of neck, chop or cutlet
		Civet	Game stew
Canard à l'orange	Roast duck with an orange-and-wine sauce	*Confit*	Meat preserve, often served baked or roasted
Cassoulet	A casserole of beans, carrots and meat, usually sausage	*Côte*	Chop, cutlet or rib
		Cou	Neck
		Cuisse	Thigh-and-leg portion
Choucroute	Pickled cabbage with peppercorns, sausages, bacon and salami	*Epaule*	Shoulder
		Médaillon	Round piece
		Pavé	Thick slice
Coq au vin	Chicken cooked until it falls off the bone with wine, onions and mushrooms	*En croûte*	In pastry
		Farci	Stuffed
		Au feu de bois	Cooked over wood fire
		Au four	Baked
Croustillant	In a pastry crust	*Galantine*	Cold dish of meat in aspic
Steak au poivre (vert/rouge)	Steak in a black peppercorn sauce (green/red)	*Garni*	With vegetables
		Gésier	Gizzard
Steak tartare	Raw chopped beef usually accompanied by a raw egg yolk	*Grillé*	Grilled
		Jarret	Knuckle
		Magret de canard	Cured duck breast slices
Blanquette, daube, estouffade, hochepôt, navarin, ragoût	Regional types of stews	*Marmite*	Casserole
		Mijoté	Stewed
		Museau	Muzzle
Aile	Wing	*À la Périgordine*	In a truffle and foie gras sauce
Blanc	Breast or white meat		
Bordelaise	In a red wine, shallots and bone marrow sauce	*Persillade*	Cooked in parsley and oil
		Poêlée	Pan-fried, sautéed
		Rillade	Coarse pork-and-goose paté
À la boulangère	Baked with potatoes and onions	*Rôti*	Roast
À la bourgeoise	With carrots, onions, celery, bacon and braised lettuce	*Sauté*	Lightly cooked in butter
		Terrine	Solid loaf of finely puréed substance (duck liver, raspberry, etc)
À la broche	Spit-roasted		

Terms for steaks

Bleu	Almost raw	*A point*	Medium	*Très bien cuit*	Very well cooked
Saignant	Rare	*Bien cuit*	Well done	*Brochette*	Kebab

Garnishes and sauces

Beurre blanc	Sauce of white wine and shallots, with butter	*Mornay*	Cheese sauce
		Pays d'Auge	Cream and cider
Chasseur	White wine, mushrooms and shallots	*Piquante*	Gherkins or capers, vinegar and shallots
Diable	Strong mustard seasoning	*Provençale*	Tomatoes, garlic, olive oil and herbs
Forestière	With bacon and mushroom		
Fricassée	Rich, creamy sauce		

Vegetables (*Légumes*)

Algue	Seaweed	*Laitue*	Lettuce
Artichaut	Artichoke	*Lentilles*	Lentils
Asperges	Asparagus	*Maïs*	Corn
Avocat	Avocado	*Navet*	Turnip
Betterave	Beetroot	*Oignon*	Onion
Carotte	Carrot	*Oseille*	Sorrel
Céleri	Celery	*Panais*	Parsnip
Champignons	Mushrooms; types include: *de bois, de Paris, cèpes, chanterelles, girolles, grisets, mousserons*	*Pâte*	Pasta or pastry
		Petits pois	Peas
		Pignons	Pine nuts
		Pissenlits	Dandelion leaves
Chicorée frisée	Curly chicory	*Poireau*	Leek
chou (rouge)	(red) cabbage	*Pois chiche*	Chickpeas
Choufleur	Cauliflower	*Pois mange-tout*	Snow peas
Citrouille	Pumpkin		
Concombre	Cucumber	*Poivron (vert, rouge)*	Sweet pepper (green, red)
Cornichon	Gherkin		
Cresson	Watercress	*Pommes (de terre)*	Potatoes
Échalotes	Shallots		
Endive	Chicory	*Primeurs*	Spring greens
Épinards	Spinach	*Radis*	Radishes
Epis de maïs	Corn on the cob	*Riz*	Rice
Fenouil	Fennel	*Salade verte*	Green salad
Fèves	Broad beans	*Sarrasin/ sarrazin*	Buckwheat
Flageolet	White beans		
Haricots (verts/ rouges/blancs/ beurres	Beans (string (French)/ kidney/white/ butter)	*Seigle*	Rye
		Tomates	Tomatoes
		Truffes	Truffles

Herbs (*Herbes*) and Spices (*Épices*)

Ail	Garlic	*Gingembre*	Ginger	*Piment*	Pimento
Anis	Aniseed	*Girofle*	Clove	*Pistou*	Ground basil, olive oil and garlic
Basilic	Basil	*Laurier*	Bay leaf		
Cannelle	Cinnamon	*Marjolaine*	Marjoram	*Raifort*	Horseradish
Ciboulettes	Chives	*Menthe*	Mint	*Romarin*	Rosemary
Estragon	Tarragon	*Moutarde*	Mustard	*Safran*	Saffron
Genièvre	Juniper	*Persil*	Parsley	*Serpolet*	Wild thyme

continues overleaf...

FRENCH FOOD AND DISHES contd.

Some vegetable dishes and terms

Biologique	Organic	Rémoulade	Mustard mayonnaise and herb dressing
Farci	Stuffed		
Gratin dauphinois	Potatoes baked in cream and garlic	Salade niçoise	Salad of tomatoes, radishes, cucumber, hard-boiled eggs, anchovies, onion, artichokes, green peppers, beans, basil and garlic (rarely so comprehensive, even in Nice)
Gratiné	Browned with cheese or butter		
Jardinière	With mixed diced vegetables		
A la parisienne	Sautéed in butter (potatoes); with white wine sauce, and shallots		
Parmentier	With potatoes	Sauté	Lightly fried in butter
Pommes château fondantes	Quartered potatoes sautéed in butter	A la vapeur	steamed
		Je suis végétarien(ne).	I'm a vegetarian. Are there any non-meat dishes?
Pommes lyonnaise	Fried onions and potatoes	Il y a quelques plats sans viande?	
Ratatouille	Mixture of aubergine, courgette, tomatoes, and garlic		

Fruits (*Fruits*) and Nuts (*Noix*)

Abricot	Apricot	Framboises	Raspberries	Pistache	Pistachio
Amandes	Almonds	Grenade	Pomegranate	Poire	Pear
Ananas	Pineapple	Groseilles	Redcurrants or gooseberries	Pomme	Apple
Banane	Banana			Prune	Plum
Brugnon, nectarine	Nectarine	Marrons	Chestnuts	Pruneau	Prune
		Melon	Melon	Raisins	Grapes
Cacahouètes	Peanuts	Mirabelles	Greengages (type of plum)	Rhubarbe	Rhubarb
Cassis	Blackcurrants				
Cérises	Cherries			**Terms:**	
Citron	Lemon	Myrtilles	Blueberries	Beignet	Fritter
Citron vert	Lime	Noisette	Hazelnut	Compôte de . . .	Stewed . . .
Coing	Quince	Noix	Nuts	Coulis	Sauce
Dattes	Dates	Orange	Orange	Flambé	Set aflame in alcohol
Figues	Figs	Pamplemousse	Grapefruit		
Fraises	Strawberries	Pastèque	Watermelon	Frappé	Iced
Fraises de bois	Wild strawberries	Pêche (blanche)	(White) peach		

Desserts (*Desserts* or *Entremets*) and Pastries (*Pâtisserie*)

Bombe	An ice cream dessert made in a round or conical mould	Gateaux	Fruit pies, usually apple, peach or pear
Bonbons	Sweets	Glace	Ice cream
Brioche	Sweet, yeasty breakfast roll	Îles flottantes/ oeufs à la neige	Soft meringues floating on custard
Charlotte	Custard and fruit in lining of almond fingers		
Clafoutis	Fruit tart, usually with berries	Lait caillé	Cream-based dessert, like Italian *panna cotta*
Crème Chantilly	Vanilla flavoured and sweetened whipped cream	Madeleine	Small, scalloped-edge sponge cake
Crème fraîche	Sour cream	Marrons Mont Blanc	Chestnut purée and cream on a rum-soaked sponge cake
Crème pâtissière	Thick pastry-filling made with eggs	Palmiers	Caramelized puff pastries
Crêpes suzettes	Thin pancakes with orange juice and liqueur	Parfait	Frozen mousse, sometimes ice cream
Flan caramel	Caramelized pudding	Petit Suisse	A smooth mixture of cream and curds
Fromage blanc	Cream cheese, more like strained yoghurt	Petits fours	Bite-sized cakes or pastries

Poires Belle Hélène	Pears and ice cream in chocolate sauce	Coupe	A serving of ice cream
Religieuse	Coffee or chocolate-coated pastry puffs, supposedly in the shape of a nun	Crêpes	filled pancakes
		Gênoise	Rich sponge cake
		Sablé	Shortbread biscuit
Yaourt, yogourt	Yoghurt	Savarin	A filled, ring-shaped cake
		Tarte	Tart
Terms:		Tartelette	Small tart
Barquette	Small boat-shaped flan	Truffes	Truffles, the chocolate or liqueur variety
Bavarois	Refers to the mould, could be a mousse or custard		

Cheese (*Fromage*)

There are over four hundred types of French cheese, most of them named after their place of origin. *Chèvre* is goat's cheese, *brebis* is ewe's cheese. *Le plateau de fromages* is the cheeseboard, and bread, but not butter, is served with it. Some useful phrases: *une petite tranche de celui-ci* (a small piece of this one); *puis-je le goûter?* (may I taste it?)

REGIONAL FOOD

Catalonia:

Bouillinade	Fish stew flavoured with dry Banyuls wine
Perdreau à la Català	Partridge cooked with bitter oranges
Cargolade	Small grilled snails
Palombe	Pigeon
Bolet	Wood mushroom, often fried in olive oil, to accompany game dishes
Louillade	A stew of mixed vegetables and *charcuterie*, a popular winter dish in the Cerdagne
Bunyetes	Custard doughnuts
Rosquillas	Almond cake

Béarn:

Tourin	Onion, garlic and tomato soup
Cousinette	Mixed soup that often includes beet, sorrel or chicory
Garbure	A very thick soup using carrots, turnips, cabbage, parsley, and beans in poultry, lamb or pork stock
Poule au pot	Boiled chicken with vegetables
Tourtière	Puff pastry flavoured with rum or plums soaked in Armagnac

Pays Basque:

Axea	Veal-based dish, typical of Espelette
Gasna	Type of sheep's cheese
Piperade	Omelette with peppers and tomatoes, served as a main dish but often just the vegetables served as an accompaniment
Ttoro	Fish stew, usually with tuna
Chipirones/ txiporomes	Small squid, either casseroled or stuffed and baked
Piballes	Baby eels
Tripotcha	Veal tripe cooked with spices
Loukinkas	Small garlic sausages
Jambon de Bayonne	Ham from Bayonne, eaten cold and thinly sliced
Gâteau Basque	Almond-custardy pie in a crumb crust, usually topped with cherry conserve
Touron	Marzipan garnished with pistachio nuts
Macarons	Macaroons, especially good from Saint-Jean-de-Luz
Mamia	Same as *cuajada* (see Spanish foods)

favourite sips. In the centre and west of the range, **sweet dessert** wines such as Murançon are popular. A Pay Basque speciality is the green or yellow **Izarra** liqueurs, strong and bitterly herbal. Measures are generous, but they don't come cheap; the same applies for imported spirits like whisky, always called *Scotch*. *Pastis*, an aniseed-flavoured drink branded as Pernod or Ricard, is served diluted with water and ice (*glaçons*) – very refreshing and not expensive.

Two drinks designed to stimulate the appetite are **pineau**, cognac and grape juice, and **kir**, white wine with a dash of blackcurrant syrup, or with champagne for a *kir royal*.

SOFT DRINKS AND HOT DRINKS

You can buy cartons of unsweetened **fruit juice** in supermarkets, but in cafés bottled (sweetened) nectars such as apricot (*jus d'abricot*) and blackcurrant (*cassis*) still prevail. You can also get fresh orange and lemon juice (*orange/citron pressé*) at a price; otherwise it's just the standard fizzy canned stuff, such as Rio (based on blood-orange juice), or Fun Tea, essentially Lipton's peach- or lemon-flavoured iced tea. Rather better are **siropes** – concentrated pure-fruit essences dissolved in water, served at many mountain refuges and cafés. Bottles of **mineral water** (*eau minérale*) and spring water (*eau de source*) – either sparkling (*pétillante*) or still (*eau plate*) – abound, but there's usually nothing wrong with tap water (*l'eau du robinet*).

Coffee is invariably espresso, in small cups and very strong. *Un café* or *un express* is black; *un crème* is with milk; *un grand café* or *un grand crème* is a large cup. In the morning you can also ask for *un café au lait* – espresso in a large cup or bowl filled up with hot milk. *Un déca* is decaf, widely available but only as powdered in a sachet. Ordinary **tea** (*thé*) is Lipton's ninety percent of the time; to have it served with milk, ask for *un peu de lait frais* (a bit of fresh milk).

The most common varieties of **herbal teas** (*infusions* or *tisanes*) are *verveine* (verbena), *tilleul* (linden blossom), *menthe* (mint) and *camomille* (chamomile). *Chocolat chaud* – **hot chocolate** – unlike tea, lives up to the high standards of French food and drink and can be had in any café.

SPAIN

There are two ways to eat out in Spain: you can go to a *restaurante* or *comedor* (dining room; *menjador* in Catalunya) and have a full meal, or you can have a succession of *tapas* (small snacks) or *raciones* (larger ones) at one or more bars. Bars tend to work out pricier but are sometimes more interesting, allowing you to do the rounds and sample different local or house specialities.

BREAKFAST, SNACKS AND SANDWICHES

For **breakfast** you're best off in a bar or café, though some *hostales* and *fondas* will serve the "Continental" basics, and in Catalunya you may be offered the choice of a heartier **savoury breakfast** (*esmorzar de forquilla* in Catalan, *desayuno salado* in Castilian) – instead of coffee and pastry, you'll be given a spread of ham, salami, cheese and wine, sometimes with omelettes and sausages too, at roughly the same price.

Another typical Catalan snack or breakfast dish is **pa amb tomaquet**, "bread with tomato" –

LIVING OFF THE LAND

In season, **fresh produce** throughout the Pyrenees is both inexpensive and excellent. In Roussillon, for instance, crates of peaches, cherries, nectarines and, later in the year, apples, pears and kiwi fruit can be had for a song. You can buy local fresh eggs, honey and goat's cheese almost everywhere. Fresh produce in Spain is nearly as good; melons, olives, figs, plums, nectarines and asparagus are reliable treats there.

Pick-your-own is a possibility when you're on the road. Obviously nothing should be gathered in national parks, and nothing taken which you know to be endangered. As a rule, selective picking is probably not too damaging. Hedgerow fruits and nuts – blackberries, rowanberries, raspberries, hazelnuts, chestnuts – can be taken as long as there aren't signs to the contrary. Ask permission where appropriate. If you know your wild mushrooms, the woods and fields provide delicious and plentiful harvesting in the early autumn – check what the locals are selecting, and beware in Spain of signs reading "Cota Municipal de Setas", which means that harvesting is restricted to local residents. Common varieties include chanterelle (pale yellow and trumpet-shaped), *Lactarius deliciosus* (orange with ghastly green patches, but a pleasantly firm texture) and the large *cèp de bordeaux*, the french favourite.

If you're trekking long distances, you'll have to rely on basic stocks; many refuges and mountain villages have very little in the way of victuals. Remember that food stores tend to close at lunchtime (noon–2pm in France; 2–4 or 5pm in Spain). Most mountain villages also have clean fountains, though if collecting from a stream check your map for upstream villages – they will almost certainly discharge everything into the watercourse.

the ingredients, including also garlic cloves, are supplied for you to make it yourself. Cut the garlic cloves crossways (not lengthwise) and rub this furiously into the bread slices; then halve the preferably mushy tomatoes, and mash this next onto the surface. You're not expected to eat the bruised remains of the vegetables.

The traditional Spanish breakfast is *churros con chocolate* – greasy, tubular doughnuts (not for the weak of stomach) dunked in thick drinking chocolate. But most places also serve *tostadas* (toasted rolls) with oil (*con aceite*) or butter and jam (*con mantequilla y mermelada*), or more substantial dishes such as fried eggs (*huevos fritos*). *Tortilla* (potato omelette) also makes an excellent breakfast, perhaps along with *magdalenas* (little cupcakes).

Coffee and pastries (*pastas*) or doughnuts (*donuts*) are available at most cafés, too, though for a wider selection of cakes you should head for one of the many excellent *pastelerías* or *confiterías*. In larger towns, especially in Catalunya, there will often be a *panadería* or *croissantería* serving quite an array of appetizing (and healthier, whole-grain) baked goods besides the obvious bread, croissants and pizza.

Some bars specialize in **sandwiches** (*bocadillos*), and as they're usually outsize affairs in French bread, they'll do for breakfast or a light lunch. In a bar with *tapas* (see below), you can have most of what's on offer put in a sandwich, and you can often get them prepared (or buy the materials to do so) at grocery stores. Incidentally, a *sandwich* is a toasted cheese and ham sandwich, usually on rather sad processed bread.

TAPAS

One of the advantages of eating in **bars** is that you can experiment. Many places have food laid out on the counter, so you can see what's available and order by pointing without necessarily knowing the names; others have blackboards (see the lists of snacks in the box on p.56). **Tapas** are small portions – three or four small chunks of fish or meat, or a dollop of salad – which traditionally used to be served up free with a drink. These days you have to pay for anything more than a few olives (where you do get free food now, it will often be called a *pincho*), but a single helping rarely costs more than 250–450ptas/€1.50–2.70 unless you're somewhere very flash. In much of the Pyrenees, alas, *tapas* more often than not are apt to consist of just a cube of cheese or some tinned shellfish.

Raciones, literally "portions", are simply bigger plates of the same, and can be enough in themselves for a light meal; be sure you make it clear whether you want a *ración* or just a *tapa*. The more people you're with, of course, the better; half a dozen *tapas* or *pinchos* and three *raciones* can make a varied and quite filling meal for three or four diners.

Tascas, **bodegas**, **cervecerías** and **tabernas** are all types of bar where you'll find *tapas* and *raciones*. Most of them have different sets of prices depending on whether you stand at the bar to eat (the basic charge) or sit at tables (up to fifty percent more expensive – and even more if you sit out on a terrace).

Wherever you have *tapas*, it is important to find out what is the local "**special**" and to order it. Spaniards will commonly move from bar to bar, having just the one dish that they consider each bar does best. Other dishes, these days, can all too often be microwaved – not a good way to reheat fried squid.

MEALS AND RESTAURANTS

Once again, there are numerous distinctions. You can sit down and have a full meal in a *comedor*, a *cafetería*, a *restaurante* or a *marisquería* – all in addition to the more food-oriented bars.

Comedores (called **menjadors** in Catalunya) are the places to seek out if your main criteria are price and quantity. Sometimes you will see them attached to a bar (often in a room behind), or as the dining room of a *pensión* or *hostal*, but as often as not they're virtually unmarked and discovered only if you pass an open door. You'll pay 1200–1800ptas/ €7.20–10.80 for a **menú del día**, a complete meal of several courses, usually with house wine; many *pensiones* and *hostales* offer only this, and no **a la carta**. At the upper end of this price range, you should expect four courses – a salad, then usually a soup, a main course and a dessert, and unlimited access to a soup tureen and wine bottle. You'll be gently pushed to take coffee after the *postre* or dessert, and it will almost always be charged extra.

Incidentally, the *comedores* of the **fancier hostales** share only the name with their humbler cousins; they can be very fancy indeed, with table linen, uniformed waiting staff and fare – and bills – to match. Incidentally, off the beaten tourist track, menus in Catalunya are often **in Catalan only** – thus the thorough translation list in the box.

Replacing *comedores* to some extent are **cafeterías**, which the local authorities now grade

SPANISH FOOD AND DISHES

Basics

Pan	Bread	Sal	Salt	Tenedor	Fork
Mantequilla	Butter	Azúcar	Sugar	Cuchillo	Knife
Huevos	Eggs	Vinagre	Vinegar	Cuchara	Spoon
Ajo	Garlic	Miel	Honey	Mesa	Table
Aceite	Oil	Botella	Bottle	La cuenta	The bill
Pimienta	Pepper (Black)	Vaso	Glass		

Typical Spanish snacks

The most usual **fillings for bocadillos** are *lomo* (loin of pork), *tortilla* and *calamares* (all of which may be served hot), *jamón* (york or, much better, *serrano*), *chorizo*, *salchichón* (and various other regional sausages – like the small, spicy Catalan *botifarras*), *queso* (cheese) and *atún* (probably canned).

Standard tapas and raciones might include:

Aceitunas	Olives	Ensaladilla	Russian salad	Patatas	Potato stew
Albondigas	Meatballs	Escalibada	Aubergine/egg-	riojanas	with flecks of
Anchoas	Anchovies		plant and		vegetable and
Arroz a la	Rice topped		pepper salad		chorizo
cubana	with fried egg	Gambas	Shrimps	Pimientos	Peppers
	and red sauce	Habas	Beans	Pincho (pintxo)	Kebab
Berberechos	Cockles	Habas con	Beans with ham	moruno	
Boquerones	Fresh anchovies	jamón		Pulpo	Octopus
Calamares	Squid	Hígado	Liver	Riñones al	Kidneys in
Callos	Tripe	Huevo cocido	Hard-boiled egg	Jerez	sherry
Caracoles	Snails	Jamón serrano	Dried ham	Salchichon	Salami
Carne en salsa	Meat in tomato	Jamón york	Ordinary ham	Sepia	Cuttlefish
	sauce	Mejillones	Mussels	Tortilla	Potato omelette
Champiñones	Mushrooms	Morcillo	Blood pudding	española	
Chorizo	Spicy sausage	Navajas	Razor clams	Tortilla	Plain omelette
Cocido	Stew	Patatas alli olli	Potatoes in	francesa	
Empanadilla	Fish/meat		mayonnaise		
	turnover	Patatas bravas	Spicy potatoes		

Soups (*Sopas*)

Sopa de mariscos	Seafood soup	Gazpacho	Cold tomato and
Caldo de gallina	Chicken soup		cucumber soup with
Sopa de pescado	Fish soup		garlic and other spices
Caldo verde or gallego	Thick cabbage-based broth	Sopa de cocido	Meat soup
Caldillo	Clear fish soup	sopa de pasta (fideos)	Noodle soup

Seafood (*Mariscos*)

Almejas	Clams	Vieiras	Scallops
Calamares	Squid	Arroz con mariscos	Rice topped with
Centolla	Spider-crab		assorted seafood
Cigalas	King prawns	Arroz a la banda	Similar to paella but with
Conchas finas	Large scallops		no chicken
Gambas	Shrimps	Chipirones en su tinta	Squid in ink
Langosta	Lobster	Merluza/calamares	Hake/squid (or just about
Langostinos	Giant king prawns	a la romana	anything else) fried in
Mejillones	Mussels		batter
Nécora	Sea-crab	Paella	Classic Valencian dish
Percebes	Goose-barnacles		with saffron rice,
Pulpo	Octopus		chicken, seafood etc
Sepia	Cuttlefish	Zarzuela de mariscos	Seafood casserole

Fish (*Pescados*)

Anguila	Eel	*Chanquetes*	Whitebait	*Rape*	Monkfish
Angulas	Elvers (baby eel)	*Jurelas*	Similar to anchovies	*Raya*	Ray, skate
Atún	Tuna	*Lenguado*	Sole	*Rodaballo*	Turbot
Bacalao	Cod (often salt)	*Merluza*	Hake	*Salmonete*	Mullet
Bonito	Tuna	*Mero*	Perch	*Sardinas*	Sardines
Boquerones	Anchovies (fresh)	*Pez espada*	Swordfish	*Trucha*	Trout

Meat (*Carne*) and Poultry (*Aves*)

Butifarra	Bratwurst	*Criadillas*	Testicles	*Lengua*	Tongue
Callos	Tripe	*Escalope* or	Breaded schnitzel	*Lomo*	Loin (of pork)
Carne de vaca	Beef	*Milanesa*		*Pato*	Duck
Cerdo	Pork	*Fabada*	Hotpot with butter	*Pavo*	Turkey
Chuletas	Chops	*asturiana*	beans, black	*Perdiz*	Partridge
Ciervo	Venison		pudding, etc	*Pollo*	Chicken
Cochinillo	Suckling pig	*Habas con*	Ham and beans	*Rebeco*	Chamois
Codorniz	Quail	*jamón*		*Riñones*	Kidneys
Conejo	Rabbit	*Hígado*	Liver	*Solomillo*	Pork flank steak
Cordero	Lamb	*Jabalí*	Wild boar	*Ternera*	Veal

Vegetables (*Verduras y Legumes*)

Ac(i)elga	Chard	*Grelos*	Turnips	*Trigueros*	Green asparagus
Alcachofas	Artichokes	*Guisantes*	Peas	*Zanahorias*	Carrots
Arroz	Rice	*Habas*	Broad beans	*Arroz a la*	Rice with banana
Berenjena	Aubergine	*Judías*	Haricot beans	*Cubana*	and egg
Calabacín	Courgette/	*blancas*		*Pimientos*	Stuffed peppers
	zucchini	*Judías verdes,*	Green, red,	*rellenos*	
Cardo, cardón	cardoon thistle	*rojas, negras*	black beans	*Ensalada*	(Mixed/green)
	stems	*Lechuga*	Lettuce	*(mixta/verde)*	salad
Cebollas	Onions	*Lentejas*	Lentils	*Menestra/*	Vegetable
Champiñones/	Mushrooms	*Patatas (fritas)*	Potatoes (fried)	*Panache de*	medley
Setas		*Pepino*	Cucumber	*verduras*	
Cogollos	Lettuce hearts	*Pimientos*	Peppers	*Pisto*	Ratatouille
Coliflor	Cauliflower	*Puerros*	Leeks	*manchego*	
Espinacas	Spinach	*Repollo*	Cabbage	*Verduras con*	Boiled potatoes
Garbanzos	Chickpeas	*Tomate*	Tomatoes	*patatas*	with greens

Fruits (*Frutas*)

Albaricoques	Apricots	*Higos*	Figs	*Peras*	Pears
Chirimoyas	Custard apples	*Limón*	Lemons	*Piña*	Pineapple
Cerezas	Cherries	*Manzanas*	Apples	*Plátanos*	Bananas
Ciruelas	Plums, prunes	*Melocotónes*	Peaches	*Sandía*	Watermelon
Datiles	Dates	*Melón*	Melon	*Toronja*	Grapefruit
Frambuesas	Raspberries	*Naranjas*	Oranges	*Uvas*	Grapes
Fresas	Strawberries	*Pavías*	Nectarines		

Sweets (*Postres*)

Arroz con leche	Rice pudding	*Helados*	Ice cream	*Requesón*	Whipped or
Cuajada	Cream-based	*Melocotón*	Peaches in syrup		beaten sweet-
	dessert, like	*en almíbar*			whey dessert,
	Italian *panna*	*Membrillo*	Quince paste		served with
	cotta, served	*Nata*	Whipped cream		honey
	with honey	*Natillas*	Custard	*Yogur*	Yogurt
Flan (de huevo)	Crème caramel	*Pasta/Tarta*	Cheesecake		
	(egg-based)	*de queso*			

continues overleaf...

SPANISH FOOD AND DISHES contd.

Cheese

Cheeses (*quesos, formatges* in Catalan) are on the whole local, though you'll get the hard, slightly salty *Queso manchego* everywhere. The best variety is *roncalés*, a sheep-milk product from the Valle de Roncal.

Some common terms

al ajillo	in garlic	*cazuela* or *cocido*	stew
asado	roast	*chilindrón*	tomato, olive-oil and
a la Navarra	stuffed with ham		pepper sauce served
a la parilla/plancha	grilled		on poultry and meat
a la Romana/rebozado	fried in egg batter	*en salsa*	in (usually tomato) sauce
al horno	baked	*frito*	fried
ali olli	with garlic mayonnaise	*guisado*	casserole
¡Bon Profit! (Catalan)/	bon appétit!	*jarrete*	joint (of meat)
¡Buen provecho! or		*rehogado*	baked
¡Aproveche! (Castilian)		*salteado*	stir-fried

REGIONAL FOOD
Catalunya: recipes and dishes

Amanida (catalana)	Salad (with salami)	*Faves estofades*	Pork and broad beans
Bacallá	Salt cod, served *a l'all* (with garlic) or *a l'all cremat* (creamed garlic)	*Fideuà*	Paella made with noodles, not rice
Calçots	Grilled baby spring onions	*Mongets (amb ventresca)*	White beans (with pancetta)
Carn d'olla	Thick meat soup	*Pa amb tomaquet*	Tomato-ed and garlic-ed
Escalivada	Baked or fried mixture of aubergines, tomatoes and peppers, often on toasted bread		bread, usually taken as a late breakfast, though available all day
Escudella	Thick soup based on ham or veal stock	*Peus de porc*	Pigs' feet
Espinacs a la Catalana	Spinach, pine nuts and raisins	*Samfaina*	Ratatouille
		Suquet de peix	Fish soup
Esqueixada	Salt-cod and tomato salad	*Trinxat*	Cerdanyan hot-pot made from bacon, winter cabbage, and potatoes or turnips
Faves a la catalana	Catalan version of *fabada asturiana*		

Catalunya: desserts

Crema Catalana	Scorched-top custard	*Menjar blanc*	Almond pastry
Mel i mató	Same as Castilian *requesón*		

Catalunya: basic ingredients
Meat, game, fowl

Ànec	Duck	*Conill*	Rabbit	*Senglar*	Boar
Botifarra	Bratwurst-like sausage	*Guatlles*	Quails	*Vedella*	Veal
		Llebre	Hare	*Xai*	Lamb
Cansalada	Bacon	*Pernil*	Ham		
Carn	Meat	*Pollastre*	Chicken		

Seafood

Anxoves	Anchovies	*Sèpia*	Cuttlefish	*Xipirons*	Baby squid
Musclos	Mussels	*Truita*	Trout, or omelette		

Produce

Albergenia	Eggplant/ aubergine	*Codony*	Quince	*Pebrot*	Peppers
Cigrons	Garbanzos	*Llentics*	Lentils	*Pèsols*	Peas
		Maduixas	Strawberries		

General terms

A la brasa	Grilled	*Esmorzar de*	Breakfast of	*Graellada*	Barbecued
Barrejat	Mixed, assortment	*forquilla*	meats, cheese,	*Pastis*	Tureen, pâté
Civet	Any rich game stew		omelette and	*Pastisso*	Cake, torte
Confit	Tender roast poultry thigh-leg, usually		perhaps wine	*Suc*	Fruit juice
	de ànec	*Farcit*	Stuffed		

Aragón:

Boliches	Bean and sausage hot-pot	*Salmorej*	Egg concoction like a potato and rice omelette, eaten with lots of garlic or an unusual poached-egg stew
Chireta	Haggis made with rice and blood pudding		
Guiso	Bony pork stewed in a sweet sauce	*Sopa de cana*	Christmas mix of milk, bread, cinnamon and turkey fat
Migas	Fry-up of breadcrumbs, bacon and spices	*Ternasco*	Lamb back, stewed or baked; quality varies; also Catalunya
Magras	Wind-dried raw ham, served thinly sliced		
Menestra de Tudela	Vegetable stew, using artichokes, beans, asparagus and anything else in season	*Guirlache*	Almond and toffee dessert

Basque Country:

Ajoarriero	Salted cod, served with potatoes, red peppers, tomatoes, garlic	*Merluza a la Vasca*	Hake in sauce
Angulas	Baby eels, often with garlic and hot peppers	*Pimientos de piquillo*	Red, sweet-hot peppers stuffed with cod
Calderete	Potato stew with sausage	*Ttoro*	Mixed fish stew
Idiazábal	A smoked cheese, identifiable by its yellow rind	*Txangurro*	Spider crab
		Txipirones en su tinto	Tiny squid cooked in their own ink
Marmitako	Fish, potato, pepper and tomato stew	*Txistorra*	A spicy sausage

from one to three cups (the ratings, as with restaurants, seem to be based on facilities offered rather than the quality of the food). These can be good value, too, especially the self-service places, but their emphasis is more on northern European food, and the light meals served tend to be dull. Food here often comes in the form of a **plato combinado** – literally a "combined plate", *plats combinats* in Catalan – which will be something like egg and chips or *calamares* and salad (or occasionally a weird combination like steak and a piece of fish), often with bread and a drink included. This will generally cost in the region of 700–1000ptas/€4.20–6. *Cafeterías* often serve some kind of *menú del día* as well. You may prefer to get your *plato combinado* at a bar, which in small towns with no *comedores* may be the only way to eat inexpensively.

Moving up the scale, there are **restaurantes** (designated by one to five forks) and **marisquerías**, the latter specializing in fish and seafood. *Restaurantes* at the bottom of the scale are often not much different in price to *comedores*, and will also generally have *platos combinados* available. A fixed-price *cubierto*, *menú del día* or *menú de la casa* (all of which mean the same thing) is often better value, though: two or three courses plus wine and bread for 1300–2500ptas/€7.80–15. Move above two forks, however, or find yourself in one of the fancier *marisquerías* (as opposed to a basic seafront fish-fry place), and prices can escalate rapidly.

In addition, in all but the most rock-bottom establishments it is customary to leave a small **tip**: the amount is up to you, though ten percent of the bill is quite sufficient. Service is normally included in a *menú del día*. The other thing to take account of in mid-range and top-end restaurants is the addition of **IVA**, a seven-percent sales tax on your bill. It should say on the menu (thus, *IVA no incluido*; in Catalan, *IVA no inclòs*) if you have to pay this. *Menús* formerly included this as a rule, but increasingly they don't; *a la carta* meals never do.

Spaniards eat very late by Anglo-Saxon or French standards, so many places serve food from around 1 until 4pm and from 8pm to midnight. However, as in France, increasingly strict labour laws and the phasing out of exclusively family-staffed businesses mean that 1–3.30pm and 8.30–11pm are currently more realistic schedules. Many restaurants **close on Sunday evening and Monday all day**.

DISHES

It's possible to make a few generalizations about Spanish food. If you like **fish and seafood**, you'll be in heaven in Spain, since this forms the basis of a vast variety of *tapas* and is fresh and excellent even hundreds of kilometres from the sea. It's not cheap, so rarely forms part of the lowest priced *menús* (though you may get the most common fish: cod, hake or squid) but you really should make the most of what's on offer. Fish stews (*zarzuelas*) and rice-based *paellas* (which also contain meat, usually rabbit or chicken) are often memorable in seafood restaurants. *Paella* comes originally from Valencia, but you'll find versions of it all over the Pyrenees – regrettably much of it prepackaged and microwaved.

Meat is most often grilled and served with a few fried potatoes and a couple of salad leaves, or cured or dried and served as a starter or in sandwiches. *Jamón serrano*, the Spanish version of Parma ham, is superb, though the best varieties, hailing from Extremadura and Andalucía, are extremely expensive. **Game** is quite common in the hills – typically venison, rabbit or boar – and almost always freshly hunted.

Vegetables seldom amount to more than a few fries or boiled potatoes with the main dish, though you can often order a side dish, too, and at the better restaurants there will often be a few more elaborate vegetable-based recipes offered. It's more usual to start your meal with a **salad**, or you may get hearty vegetable soups or a plate of boiled potatoes and greens as a starter. **Dessert** in the less expensive places is nearly always fresh fruit or *flan*, the Spanish *crème caramel*.

There are also various varieties of *pudín* – rice pudding or assorted blancmange mixtures. Even in fancy restaurants you'll seldom find much better – stick to fruit and cheese, or make a separate foray to a *pastelería* (cake-shop). Worth a mention, if only for their grotesqueness, are certain **dessert oddities**: frozen citrus fruit (*limon* and *naranja*) stuffed with sherbet of the corresponding flavour; *músic* (nuts in muscatel); and various other decadent ice cream concoctions, mostly made by Camy and Menorquina, the two main factories. Indeed, if offered ice cream it's best to go up to the glass-front chiller and point to your choice; descriptions and ingredients are complicated, and the trade names not too informative. If you encounter a genuine *heladería* (ice cream parlour) that whips up its own, count your blessings.

VEGETARIANS AND VEGANS

Vegetarians have a fairly hard time of it in Spain: there's always something to eat, but you may get weary of eggs and omelettes (*tortilla francesa* is a plain omelette, *con champiñones* with mushrooms) offered in place of meat as a *segundo* on *menús* – and charged the same. In the larger Pyrenean foothill towns you'll find a bare handful of vegetarian and non-European restaurants, which serve vegetable dishes. Otherwise, superb fresh produce is always available in the markets and shops, while cheese, fruit and eggs are found everywhere. In restaurants you're faced with the extra problem that pieces of meat – especially ham, which the Spanish don't seem to regard as real meat – are often added to vegetable dishes to "spice them up". For example, *ensalada ilustrada* consists of lettuce, eggs, olives, asparagus spears, tomato wedges – plus a few chunks of ham that you'll have to flick aside.

If you're a **vegan**, you're either going to have to be not too fussy or accept weight loss if you're away for any length of time. Some salads and vegetable dishes are strictly vegan, but they're few and far between. Fruit and nuts are widely available, though, nuts being sold by street vendors everywhere.

> The phrase to learn is *Soy vegetariano. Hay algo sin carne?* (I'm a vegetarian. Is there anything without meat?); you may have to add *y sin mariscos* (and without seafood) *y sin jamón* (and without ham) to be really safe.

ALCOHOLIC DRINKS

Vino (wine), either *tinto* (red) – *ví negre* in Catalunya – *blanco* (white, *ví blanc* in Catalan) or *rosado/clarete* or *rosat* (rosé), is the invariable accompaniment to every meal and is, as a rule, extremely inexpensive. The most common bottled variety is Valdepeñas, a good standard wine from the central plains of New Castile; Rioja, from the area around Logroño, is better but a lot more expensive. Both are found all over the country. There are also scores of local wines – some of the best in Catalunya (Bach, Sangre de Toro) and Aragón (Somontano Viñas del Vero and Montesierra), the latter four often offered as the house wine.

Otherwise it's whatever comes out of the barrel, or the house-bottled or special-ordered vintage (ask for *de cubo* or *de la casa*). This can be great – especially the very light rosé or red wines from around Tremp – or it can be lousy, but at least it will be distinctively local. In a bar, a small glass of wine will generally cost around 100–150ptas/€0.60–0.90; in a restaurant, if wine is not included in the *menú*, prices start at around 550ptas/€3.30 a bottle. If it is included you'll usually get a whole bottle for two people, a *media botella* (a third to a half of a litre) of red or rose – never white – for one. Often wine will appear in a *porrón* (*porró* in Catalan), a glass vessel which looks like a salad-dressing cruet in meltdown. Uncork the larger opening on top, brandish it aloft, and potentially make a mess (and a fool of yourself) by aiming a stream of wine into your waiting mouth. Or take the easy way out by filling glasses through the top hole. In Catalunya, **cavas** are the generic term for sparkling wines and champagnes (*champaña*) trading in disguise; Freixenet will be familiar to Britons, Reimat Brut less so.

Cerveza, lager-type beer, is generally pretty good, though more expensive than wine. It comes in 300- to 330-ml bottles (*botellines*) or, for about the same price, on tap – a *caña* of draught beer is a small, 125-ml glass, a *caña doble* 250 ml. Many bartenders will assume you want a *doble*, so if you don't, say so. You get a *tubo* (tall narrow glass) or a *jarra media* (squat stein); 500-ml measures – a full *jarra* – are available as well. Locally brewed brands, such as Estrella Damm in Catalunya, or Ambar in Aragón, tend to be more exciting than nationally available ones like Águila.

Equally refreshing, though often deceptively strong, is **sangría**, a wine-and-fruit punch which you'll come across at fiestas and in tourist bars; *tinto de verano* is basically the same red-wine-and-soda or lemonade combination.

In mid-afternoon – or even at breakfast – many Spaniards take a *copa* of **liqueur** with their coffee. The best are *aguardiente de orujo*, distilled from grape pressings like Italian *grappa*, and 45 percent alcohol; or *coñac*, excellent local brandy with a distinct vanilla flavour (try Magno, Soberano, or 103 to get an idea of the variety). In the Western Pyrenees, *pacharan* (often spelled *patxaran*) is a brandy made from rowanberries, not to be confused with the French wine Pacherenc. If you're in the Garrotxa, try *ratafia*, a nut-and-spice-based apéritif.

Most **spirits** are ordered by brand name, since there are generally less expensive Spanish equivalents for standard imports. Larios Gin from Málaga, for instance, is about half the price of Gordon's Gin. Specify *nacional* to avoid getting an expensive foreign brand. Spirits can be very expensive at the trendier bars; however, wherever they are served, they tend to be staggeringly generous – the bar staff pouring from the bottle until you suggest they stop.

Mixed drinks are universally known as *Cuba Libre* or *Cubata*, though strictly speaking this is rum and Coke. Juice is *zumo*; orange, *naranja*; lemon, *limón*; tonic is *tónica*.

SOFT DRINKS AND HOT DRINKS

Try in particular *granizado* (fruit-syrup-flavoured slush), the ubiquitous Bitter Kas (like a nonalcoholic Campari, very refreshing) or *horchata* (a milky drink made from *chufa* or tiger nuts, a semitropical tuber grown near Valencia) from one of the street stalls that spring up everywhere in summer. You can also get these drinks from *horchaterías* and from *heladerías* (ice cream parlours), or in Catalunya from the wonderful milk bars known as *granjas*. Fruit juices, typically orange, are called *zumos*. In the Pyrenees you can drink the **water** almost everywhere, and a *jarrón* or carafe of tap water (*agua de grifa*) is proudly provided at table – unless there is something wrong with the local spring, in which case bottled water will be offered, often on the house. Such *agua mineral* comes either as sparkling (*con gas*) or still (*sin gas*).

Café (coffee) – served in cafés, *heladerías* and bars – is invariably espresso, slightly bitter and, unless you specify otherwise, served black (*café solo*). If you want it white ask for *café cortado* (small cup with a drop of milk) or *café con leche* (made with lots of hot milk). For a large cup ask for a *doble* or *grande*; decaff is *descafeinado*. Coffee is also frequently mixed with brandy or cognac (much less often with red wine), such concoctions being called *carajillo*. Spanish **hot chocolate** (*chocolate caliente*) can be very good

indeed as long as you avoid Cola Cao brand – an insipid formula aimed at small children.

Té (tea) is also available at most bars, although Spaniards usually drink it black. If you want milk it's safest to ask afterwards, since ordering *té con leche* might well get you a glass of warm milk with a teabag floating on top.

COMMUNICATIONS: POST, PHONES AND MEDIA

Both the French and Spanish postal and telecommunications systems work reasonably well, and with a smattering of secondary-school or university language study, you can derive enjoyment – or at least information – from the respective French and Spanish newspapers and magazines.

FRANCE

French **post offices** are signed as *La Poste* in bright yellow. Pyrenean post offices are generally open 9am to noon and 2pm to 5pm, Monday to Saturday morning, though in the smaller villages lunch hours and closing times can vary. You can have letters sent to any post office; they should be addressed (preferably with the surname underlined and in capitals) **Poste Restante**, Poste Centrale, followed by the name of the town. To collect your mail you need a passport and there may be a small charge. Ask for all your names to be checked, as filing systems tend to be idiosyncratic.

For **sending** letters remember that you can buy **stamps** (*timbres*) with less queuing from tobacconists (*tabacs*). Large letters or small packets are best sent at a main *poste*, where they'll probably be more conversant with overseas rates. Ordinary postcards and letters within the EU cost 3F/€0.45, to North America 4.40F/€0.70 and to the Antipodes 5.20F/€0.80. If you need to send something quickly within the EU, a special, self-seal cardboard envelope – 10F postage included – is sold which can hold several documents or a very small object, with two-day delivery time the rule. The postal service in the mountains is extremely efficient, though a little more relaxed than elsewhere in France. If there's snow blocking the road the post might not get collected, for instance, but delays are on the whole no more common than down in the lowlands.

TELEPHONES

You can make **domestic and international phone calls** from any phone box (*cabine*) and can receive calls where there's a blue logo of a ringing bell – the number is usually on a metal plaque overhead. **Phone cards**, obtainable from PTT branches, train stations and some *tabacs*, have now mostly replaced coin phones; the cheapest cards cost 40.60F/€6.20 for 50 units or 97.50F/€14.90 for 120 units. At the dwindling number of coin-only phone boxes, still found in cafés, bar basements and rural districts, put the money in first (0.5F, 1F, 2F, 5F, 10F pieces, minimum charge 1F) after lifting the receiver but before dialling; you can add more once you're connected. There are also a number of "Point Phone" telephones in bars, restaurants, hotels and even shops, but these tend to be expensive, as the tariff is set by the proprietor.

For all calls within France, dial all ten digits of **the number**, even within the same region indicated by the first two digits. Numbers beginning with ☎08.00 are toll-free; those beginning with ☎08.36 are premium rate, while those beginning with ☎06 are mobiles and also expensive to ring. For international calls, dial ☎00, wait for a tone, and then dial the country code and subscriber number.

Cheap rates are in effect from 7pm to 8am Monday to Friday, from midnight to 8am and noon to midnight on Saturday, and all day Sunday. Calls from a public phone to the UK will cost 2.17–2.57F/€0.35–0.40 per minute, to North America 2.85–3.52F/€0.45–0.55 per minute, and to Australasia 8–10.16F/€1.20–1.55 per minute – less from a private phone, obviously much more from a hotel – but costs are dropping continually due to fierce competition from private carriers. **Calling-cards**, either pre-loaded or billed to a credit card, are far more expensive, plus you need to remember their free access number for France

and your own account number when dialling – and the access numbers are often engaged. The best strategy is probably to secure a locally produced calling card – for example the **Intercall Carte Téléphone**, available through the Tati chain of stores, which for 50F/€7.60 allows 15 minutes of chat to the Antipodes, 32 minutes to North America, and 49 minutes to the UK – far cheaper than from any call box or private line. You can avoid payment altogether with a **reverse-charge** or **collect call**, known in French as *téléphoner en PCV*. To do this for Britain through a UK operator, dial ☎08.00.89.00.33; for North America's AT&T operator, dial ☎00.00.11.

Coverage for roaming dual-band **mobile phones** can be poor to nonexistent in the higher Pyrenees – especially in the depopulated Ariège where there seem to be very few base stations – but is adequate in the foothills. There are two or three local networks which your UK-based handset will automatically select; experience has shown that ITINERIS is a much cheaper one to

---

FRANCE: USEFUL PHONE NUMBERS

Speaking clock ☎36.99

PCV/Reverse charge/collect call operators:
For the UK: Home Direct, ☎08.00.89.00.33
For North America: ☎00.00.11

Mountain weather

Météo France – the national meteorological service – operates a 24-hour weather forecast hotline, with special extensions for snow conditions, avalanche risk, etc (see p.81). For the basic *prévision*, dial ☎08.36.68.02.xx – the last two variable digits are uniquely assigned to each *département*. For example ☎08.36.68.02.65 for Midi-Pyrénées (basically the central Pyrenees), ☎08.36.68.02.64 for Pyrénées-Atlantiques (the west of the range, including the Pays-Basques), ☎08.36.68.02.66 for Pyrénées-Orientales (the east around Perpignan) and ☎08.36.68.02.09 for the Ariège.

Phoning abroad from France

to Australia: dial ☎00, wait for the international tone, then dial 61 + area code minus first 0 + number.

to Britain: dial ☎00, wait for the international tone, then dial 44 + area code minus first 0 + number.

to Ireland: dial ☎00, wait for the international tone, then dial 353 + area code minus first 0 + number.

to New Zealand: dial ☎00, wait for the international tone, then dial 64 + area code minus first 0 + number.

to North America: dial ☎00, wait for the international tone, then dial 1 + area code + number.

Phoning France

France no longer has area codes per se; the first two digits of the ten-digit number indicate the region of the country (eg, '04' covers the southeast, '05' means the southwest) or the type of service. When dialling from overseas, however, omit the first '0'.

from Australia: dial ☎011 + 33 + nine-digit number (omitting first 0).

from Britain & Ireland: dial ☎00 + 33 + nine-digit number (omitting first 0).

from New Zealand: dial ☎0044 + 33 + nine-digit number (omitting first 0).

from North America: dial ☎011 + 33 + nine-digit number (omitting first 0).

piggyback onto than SFR-France. North Americans currently need a triband rig to enjoy any service in Europe.

Partly owing to a low rate of personal computer ownership, and partly to the lingering presence of France's own, 1980s-vintage, clunky Minitel system, **Internet** use has been slow to catch on – though this guide furnishes all Web site and email addresses where applicable. This is doubly so in the Pyrenees, where the low population density means that there are almost no Internet cafés. If you can't live without your email (forget about surfing the Net), one possible strategy is to carry a laptop with you, and a length of RJ11-compatible phone cable (plus necessary adaptors), plugging in whenever you find a hotel with a suitable wall socket, and dialling your UK service provider long distance. As WAP technology for mobile phones becomes more advanced and widespread, however, this shouldn't be strictly necessary.

THE MEDIA

A reasonable selection of **foreign newspapers** is on sale in selected resorts and larger towns such as Pau or Perpignan. Among **French national dailies**, *Le Monde* is the most intellectual, using a mainstream-style French that is easiest to understand, but austerely photo-less. *Libération* (*Libé* for short), is moderately left-wing, independent and colloquial, with good, selective, mostly feature coverage and colour format; it tends to sell out quickly. *L'Humanité* is the far-left, Communist-affiliated paper. Among the right-of-centre papers, *Le Figaro* is the most respected and readable.

Weeklies, in the *Time/Newsweek* mould, include left-leaning *Le Nouvel Observateur*, its conservative counterpart *L'Express*, the boringly centrist *L'Événement de Jeudi* and relative-newcomer-with-a-bite, *Marianne*. **Satirical investigative journals** include the weekly *Canard Enchaîné*, best of the lot, while *Charlie-Hebdo* fits the mould of the UK *Private Eye* or *Spy* in the US.

Nationwide **monthlies** include the young, trendy and cheap *Nova*, with excellent listings for cultural events, and *Actuel*, which is good for news analysis. The bimonthly **Pyrénées** (widely available, 40F/€6) is well worth a browse for destination features, news snippets and suggestions for obscure trekking or touring routes; twice a year or so, there are *hors série* special issues

(50F/€7.60), devoted to distinct topics (eg the Basque country, Cathar castles, family day-walks).

If you've got a **radio**, you can catch the BBC World Service on 648kHz or 198kHz longwave from midnight to 5am, and Radio 4 during the day; BBC Radio 5 Live can be picked up on 693kHz. For radio news in French, there's the state-run France Inter (87.8FM), Europe 1 (104.7FM) or round-the-clock news on France Infos (105.5FM). The Voice of America transmits on 90.5, 98.8 and 102.4FM.

French **TV** has six terrestrial channels, three public – FR2, Arte/La Cinquième and FR3 – one subscription – Canal Plus, with some unencrypted programmes – and two commercial open broadcasts – TF1 and M6. Arte/La Cinquième is a joint Franco-German endeavour devoted to high-brow fare including opera, films and critics' panels. Canal Plus is the main movie channel (and funder of the French film industry), though FR3 screens a fair selection of serious films, especially (undubbed) late Sunday night on its *Cinéma de Minuit* programme. The main news broadcasts are at 8.30pm on Arte, and at 8pm on FR2 and TF1.

Additionally, there are the **cable** networks, available in better hotels, which include BBC World Service, BBC Prime, MTV, Planète, Paris Première and Canal Jimmy.

SPAIN

Post offices in Spain – marked *Correos* in Castilian, *Correus* in Catalan – are generally open Monday to Friday from 8am to noon and again from 5 to 7.30pm, though you will encounter differing schedules throughout the country. Big branches in large cities may have considerably longer hours, without midday closure; except in the largest cities there's only one post office in each town.

You can have letters sent **poste restante** (*Lista de Correos*) to any Spanish post office: they should be addressed (preferably with the surname underlined and in capitals) to *Lista de Correos* followed by the name of the town and province. To collect, take along your passport and, if you're expecting mail, ask the clerk to check under all of your names – letters are often found filed under first or middle names.

Outbound mail is reasonably reliable, with letters or cards taking around five days to a week to the UK, a week to ten days to North America.

TELEPHONES

Spanish public **phone boxes** work well, though no number is posted so you can't phone them back. If you can't find one, many bars also have pay phones you can use. Boxes take both coins (5, 25-, 50-, 100- 250- or sometimes 500-peseta coins), or you can buy 1000-peseta or 2000-peseta **phonecards** at tobacconists, or use the most common **credit cards** (200ptas minimum, but you'll have no trouble exceeding that on overseas calls). With credit cards, the swipe readers are rather temperamental; you'll know you've succeeded when the LCD display says "processing" in the local language. Spanish provincial (and some overseas) dialling codes are displayed in most cabins, as well as dialling – and credit card – instructions in English. The local **ringing tone** is long, **engaged** is shorter and rapid; the standard Spanish response is *dígame* (speak to me).

For **international calls,** you can use any phone box marked *teléfono internacional,* or go to one of the dwindling number of public **Telefónica** offices, where you pay afterwards. International and domestic rates historically among the priciest in the EU, but now much reduced owing to competition from mobiles – are slightly cheaper after 10pm, and after 2pm on Saturday and all day

> ### ANDORRA
>
> Andorra has its own phone code, ☎376. UK-based mobiles enjoy good reception in the principality, despite its extreme topography. For more details, see p.207

Sunday. If you're using a phone box to call abroad, you're best off using a phone card or a credit card; failing that, insert at least 200ptas initially to ensure a connection, and make sure you have a tall stack of 100-peseta pieces ready.

If you want to make a **reverse-charge** or **collect call** (*cobro revertido*), you'll have to go to a Telefónica, where you can expect queues at cheap-rate times. Some hotels will arrange reverse-charge calls for you, but as with all phone calls from hotels you'll often be stung with an outrageous surcharge.

Dual-band **mobile phones** from the UK are much better catered to in Spain than in France; the Spanish are obsessed with them and coverage, especially in Catalunya, is respectable. In terms of local networks, Airtel is less widely available for logging onto than Movistar (run by Telefónica), but considerably cheaper to use.

SPAIN: USEFUL PHONE NUMBERS

Directory Enquiries ☎1003
International Operator (Europe) ☎1008
International Operator (rest of world) ☎1005

Mountain weather

Catalan Pyrenees (general) ☎933 256 391

Girona province ☎906 365 317

Lleida province ☎906 365 325

Huesca province (Aragón) ☎906 365 322

Navarra province (western Pyrenees) ☎906 365 331

You can also check snow and weather conditions online at *www.inm.es* (Spain) and *www.icc.es/allausb* (Catalunya).

Phoning abroad from Spain

to Australia: dial ☎00, then 61 + area code minus first 0 + number.

to Britain: dial ☎00, then 44 + area code minus first 0 + number.

to Eire: dial ☎00, then 353 + area code minus first 0 + number.

to New Zealand: dial ☎00, then 64 + area code minus first 0 + number.

to North America: dial ☎00, then 1 + area code + number.

Phoning Spain

Like France, Spain no longer has area codes per se, but nine-digit unitary numbers. The first three digits are particular to each province or type of service.

from Australia: dial ☎011 + 34 + nine-digit number.

from Britain, France & Ireland: dial ☎00 + 34 + nine-digit number.

from New Zealand: dial ☎0044 + 34 + nine-digit number.

from North America: dial ☎011 + 34 + nine-digit number.

Again, North Americans will require triband handsets for any joy.

As for the **Internet**, cafés are as lacking in the Spanish Pyrenees as on the French side, but for different reasons: personal computer ownership is very high, especially in the wealthier parts of Catalunya and the Basque country. If you're addicted to your email, see the advice under France, above; RJ11 phone sockets are standard in Spain, with hard-wiring of phones into walls less common.

THE MEDIA

British newspapers and the *International Herald Tribune* are on sale during the summer season in most large foothill towns, particularly Girona, Pamplona and San Sebastián.

Of the **Spanish newspapers** the best are currently Madrid's *El Mundo* and Barcelona's *La Vanguardia*, both of which are fairly liberal in outlook and have good arts and foreign news coverage, including comprehensive regional "what's on" listings and supplements each weekend. Madrid's *El País*, formerly the top-ranked quality daily, has declined to a timid, boring read, though it still employs exceptional (and independent) columnists such as Miguel García Posada.

The regional press is generally run by local magnates and is predominantly right-wing, though often supporting local autonomy movements. Nationalist dailies include *Avui* in Catalunya, printed largely in Catalan, and the Basque papers *El Diario Vasco*, *Deia* and *Egin* – the last a supporter of ETA, and partly in Euskera.

One of Spain's more interesting **magazines** is *Ajo Blanco*, a monthly from Barcelona, providing a generally stimulating mix of politics, culture and style. And of course, Spain is the home of chatty *Holá* – the parent of Britain's *Hello*.

If you can read Spanish, glossy bimonthly **El Mundo de los Pireneos** (750ptas/32F/€4.50) should be your first stop for excellent news analyses, hiking or skiing tips and features on Pyrenean personalities, festivals and impending ecological/development crises on both sides of the border. Issued by outdoor publishers SUA Edizoak in Bilbao, it's a newish (started 1998) publication that deserves support; back issues available (☎944 169 430, fax 944 166 976, *sua@jalgi.com*). Also worth a look is the Spanish travel magazine *Altaïr* (published in Barcelona; 550ptas/€3.30), which has a regular "Aire Libre" section on walking, biking or canyoning excursions to some of the more obscure corners of the country, as well as occasional main features.

Even up in the mountains, you'll inadvertently catch more **TV** than you expect (or want to) sitting in bars and restaurants; Spaniards are reckoned to be the continent's champion tube-heads in terms of annual hours per person spent in front of the box. Soaps – known as *culebrones* in Castilian – are a particular speciality, either South American *telenovas*, which take up most of the daytime programming, or well-travelled British or American exports. Sports fans are well catered for, with regular live coverage of **football/soccer** and basketball matches, mainly on Canal 5. In Catalunya, channels 3 and 4 broadcast exclusively in Catalan.

If you have a **radio** which picks up short wave you can tune in to the BBC World Service, broadcasting in English for most of the day on frequencies between 12MHz (24m) and 4MHz (75m). The FM dial is often rewarding, particularly Catalunya's **classical station**, which can even be picked up in the high-altitude wilds of the Cerdanya or Aigüestortes.

OPENING HOURS AND PUBLIC HOLIDAYS

Almost everything in both France and Spain – shops, museums, churches, tourist offices, most banks – closes for a siesta of at least two hours in the hottest part of the day. There's a lot of variation but basic summer working hours are 9.30am to 1.30pm and 4.30 to 8pm in Spain, and 8am to noon or 1pm and 2 or 3pm to 6.30 or 7.30pm in France. In both countries certain shops do now stay open all day, and since the implementation of the 35-hour week in France there has been a move towards shorter, "normal" working hours. Nevertheless, you'll get far less aggravated if you accept that the early afternoon is best spent asleep, or in a restaurant, or both.

FRANCE

Food shops in France often don't reopen until halfway through the afternoon, closing between 7.30 and 8pm or just before the evening meal. So if you're intent on buying a picnic lunch, you'll need to do so before you're ready to think about eating. Sunday and Monday are the standard French **closing days**, though you'll always find at least one *boulangerie* (baker's) open. Street markets tend to operate in the mornings only.

Museums open between 9 and 10am, close for lunch at noon until 2pm or 3pm, with an afternoon shift only until 5pm or 6pm. Summer times may differ from winter times; if they do, both are indicated in the listings. **Summer hours** usually extend from early June to mid-September, but sometimes they apply only during July and August, occasionally even from Palm Sunday to All Saints' Day. Don't forget **closing days** – usually Monday or Tuesday, sometimes both. Admission charges can be very off-putting, though most state-owned museums have one or two days of the week when they're free and you can get a significant reduction at most places by showing a student card (or passport if you're under 26 or over 60).

Cathedrals are almost always open all day, with charges only for the crypt, treasuries or cloister, and little fuss about how you're dressed. Small village **churches**, however, can be usually closed, so you may have to go during Mass to take a look, on Sunday morning or at other times which you'll see posted up on the door. In small towns and villages, however, getting the key is not difficult – ask anyone nearby or hunt out the priest, whose house is known as the *presbytère*.

SPAIN

Most **museums** observe the siesta with a break between 1 and 4 in the afternoon. Their summer schedules are listed in the Guide; watch out for Sundays (most open mornings only) and Mondays (most close all day). Admission charges vary, but there's usually free entrance or a reduction if you show an ISIC card. Anywhere run by the Patrimonio Nacional, the national organization which preserves monuments, is free to EU citizens on Wednesday – take your passport to prove your nationality.

FRENCH NATIONAL HOLIDAYS

There are thirteen **French national holidays** (*jours fériés*), when most shops and businesses, some museums, though not (usually) restaurants, are closed. They are:

January 1 New Year's Day

Easter Sunday

Easter Monday

Ascension Day (forty days after Easter)

Pentecost (seventh Sunday after Easter, plus the Monday)

May 1 May Day/Labour Day

May 8 Victory in Europe Day

July 14 Bastille Day

August 15 Assumption of the Virgin Mary

November 1 All Saints' Day

November 11 1918 Armistice Day

December 25 Christmas Day

SPANISH NATIONAL HOLIDAYS

January 1 *Año Nuevo* (New Year's Day)

January 6 *Tres Reyes* (Three Kings; Epiphany)

Maundy Thursday *Jueves Santo*, not in Catalunya

Good Friday *Viernes Santo*

Easter Sunday *Pascua, Domingo de la Resurección*

Easter Monday *Lunes de Pascua*

May 1 *Fiesta de Trabajo* (May Day/Labour Day)

Corpus Christi (early or mid-June)

June 24 *Día de San Juan* (St John's Day), the king's name-saint

July 25 *Día de Santiago* (St James of Compostella)

August 15 *Assunción de la Virgen* (Assumption of the Virgin)

October 12 *Virgen del Pilar* (National Day)

November 1 *Todos Santos* (All Saints' Day)

December 6 *Día de la Constitución* (Constitution Day)

December 8 *Día de la Concepción Inmaculada* (Immaculate Conception)

December 25 *Navidad* (Christmas Day)

Getting into **churches** can present more of a problem. The really important ones, including most cathedrals, operate in much the same way as museums and almost always have some entry charge to see their most valued treasures and paintings, or their cloisters. Other churches, though, are usually kept locked, opening only for worship in the early morning and/or the evening (between around 6 to 9pm). So you'll either have to try at these times, or find someone with a key. This is time-consuming but rarely difficult, since a sacristan or custodian almost always lives nearby and most people will know where to direct you. You're expected to give a small tip, or donation. For all churches "decorous" dress is required, ie no shorts, bare shoulders, etc.

Public holidays can (and will) disrupt your plans at some stage. Besides the Spanish national holidays listed in the box above, there are scores of **local festivals** (different in every town and village, usually marking the local saint's day); any of them will mean that everything except bars (and *hostales*, etc) locks its doors.

In addition, **August** is Spain's own holiday month, when the big cities are semi-deserted, and many of the shops and restaurants, even museums, close. In contrast, it can prove nearly impossible to find a room in the more popular coastal and mountain resorts at these times; similarly, seats on planes, trains and buses at this time should be booked well in advance. **Easter**, incidentally, is worse; whereas people's summer breaks are slightly staggered – and indeed July is becoming nearly as busy as August – at Eastertime the entire population is on the move, and every desirable (and most unattractive) accommodation is booked literally months ahead.

FESTIVALS

Especially in July and August, it's practically impossible not to stumble on some sort of
festival during your stay: either a tourist-
board-organized concert series, often in a
wonderful medieval venue, or just a brass
band and drinks in a pennant-hung village
square. On both sides of the Pyrenees religion and folk history are the main launching
platforms for a party, but apart from the
occasional Mass to ensure everybody is
spiritually insured, the festivities rarely
dwell on solemn matters. Even pilgrimages
are often celebrated with great gusto and,
like many of the town and village celebrations, involve a colourful and photogenic
procession. Festivals in major resorts tend
to be more tourist-oriented, though, featuring music, art and theatre programmes.

The list of festivals is potentially endless, and
although you'll find the major events detailed in
features at the beginning of each chapter, we don't
pretend that it's exhaustive. Local tourist offices
should have more information about what's going
on in their area at any given time. Outsiders are
always welcome at festivals, the main problem
being that during any of the most popular ones
you'll find it difficult and expensive to find a bed. If
you're planning to coincide with a festival, try to
reserve your accommodation well in advance.

FRANCE

Catholicism is still deeply ingrained in the culture
of the French Pyrenees; thus saints' days still
bring people out in all their finery, ready to
indulge before or after Mass has been said. Such
occasions, along with the celebrations focused on
wine and food production, are usually very genuine affairs intended for a local audience. Other
festivals, based on historical events, folklore or
literature, are more obviously money-spinners
and forums for municipal prestige. Finally, there
are the cultural seasons of the larger towns and
resorts, centred on film, music or drama, which
while enjoyable enough have few pretensions to
religious significance.

Some **harvest** celebrations are highly public,
with charges levied for sampling; others – in the
smaller vineyards and cooperatives – are more a
private celebration for the pickers and packers,
though here again there are often open days for
public tastings of previous years' produce. From
early September the **Roussillon** wine region is
particularly active, and later in the month there
are *Fêtes des Pommes* all over the place (especially the **Têt valley**), with plenty of opportunity
to sample and buy local produce from apple jelly
to potent cider. An unusual variation on the harvest *fête* is the late October celebration of the
pepper crop at **Espelette**, in the Western
Pyrenees.

Easter Week is normally marked by special
church services, processions and associated parties. One of the most striking is the *Procession de
la Sanch* at **Perpignan**, where penitents parade
around in red robes, tall pointed hats and masks
reminiscent of Ku Klux Klan garb. Many small
towns and villages have their own processions,
often venerating an image from the parish church
– a popular example is the *Procession de la
Vierge* at **Font-Romeu** in September. A good
example of the often more boisterous **folklore**
festivals is the *Fête de l'Ours* at **Arles-sur-Tech**
in February, which involves a lot of men chasing
another lot of men dressed in bear costumes.

Most local carnivals are held in midsummer,
and usually involve several days of eating, drinking and merrymaking; as a rule, they do not
prompt the increased hotel prices of some of the
better-known events. Throughout the French
Pyrenees, **Bastille Day** (July 14) is commemorated by marvellous firework displays. Innumerable
other **historical events**, of varying degrees of
importance, are celebrated all over the region. For

instance, at Montségur in June there are *Son et Lumière* shows and fireworks commemorating the Cathars, while the next month at Foix there is a week-long festival celebrating the life of Gaston Fébus, including jousting and a medieval fair.

Sports events are great crowd-pullers, none more so than the **Tour de France** bike race, which visits the Pyrenees in July – even the police relax and enjoy themselves, loosening collars and accepting cool drinks. *Boules* tournaments and – in Basque areas – *pelote* championships are also guaranteed to stop normal business.

SPAIN

It's hard to beat the experience of arriving in some small Spanish village, expecting no more than a bed for the night, to discover the streets festooned with flags and streamers, a band playing in the plaza and the entire population out celebrating the local *fiesta*. Everywhere in the country, from the tiniest hamlet to the great cities, will take at least one day off a year – not always during tourist "season" – to devote to partying. Usually it's the local saint's day, but there are celebrations, too, of harvests, of deliverance from the Moors, of safe return from the sea – any excuse will do. It's often the obscure and unexpected event which proves to be most fun; there is always music, dancing, traditional costume and an immense spirit of enjoyment. The main event of most *fiestas* is a parade, either a solemn one behind a revered holy image, or a more lighthearted affair with fancy costumes and *gigantones*, grotesque giant carnival figures which trundle down the streets terrorizing children.

Easter, perhaps the major national religious feast, is observed in a particularly poignant manner in Catalunya, where several municipalities have elaborate and vivid Good Friday eve processions. In particular, several towns enact Passion plays, involving a Via Crucis (Stations of the Cross), culminating in a mock Crucifixion with local volunteers as Christ and the Two Thieves.

As in France, **harvest** time is also a big excuse for boozy celebrations, especially in the **Alt Empordà** region. Many of the festivals in the Spanish Pyrenees are more conspicuously **religious** than on the French side, with more weight given to the procession of the revered holy image before the partying begins. Amongst betterknown Catalan events are *Carnival* at various villages along the Noguera Pallaresa, the festival of *Sant Marc* at the shrine of Queralt on April 25 and – all over Catalunya – bonfires as the centrepiece of *Dia de Sant Joan* (June 21–24, variable) observances. The Corpus Christi *Festa de Patum* at **Berga** is the biggest late-spring bash in Catalunya, renowned for its high spirits and outrageous *gigantones*.

Folkloric and **rural** festivals are celebrated enthusiastically, often including demonstrations of dwindling skills in addition to the normal shenanigans: examples are the leather fair at Sort in January, Rialp's sheep-shearing contest in June and the traditional log-rafting at La Pobla de Segur on the first Sunday in July. An unusual **historical** event is the battle of the women, fought on the first Friday in May at **Jaca**, celebrating the role played by townswomen in a defeat of the Muslim enemy in 795.

Spain too has its succession of **local cultural programmes** in **July** and **August**, particularly at **San Sebastián**, interpolated with the two festivals of the **Virgin**: her ascension into heaven (*Assunción*) on August 14–15, and her birth on September 8.

BULLFIGHTS

Bullfights are an integral part of many Pyrenean festivals, on both sides of the frontier; the larger foothill towns often stage a three- or four-day season during summer. **Los Toros**, as Spaniards refer to bullfighting, are big business. Each year an estimated 24,000 bulls are killed in Spain before ringside audiences of over thirty million, and many more on televison. The Interior Ministry

SAINTS' DAYS

Note that saints' day festivals can **vary in date**, often being observed over the weekend closest to the dates given in our "Festivals" listings at the start of each chapter. In other cases the fun occurs on the **evening before** the date given, with only a Mass taking place on the morning concerned. Our listings often try to indicate this by giving a range of dates – the earlier you show up, the more likely the chance of coinciding with the actual party.

If you want to know more about the international **opposition to bullfighting**, contact the World Society for the Protection of Animals, 89 Albert Embankment, London SE1 7OP (☎020/7793 0540, *www.wspa.org.uk*); PO Box 190, Boston, MA 02130 (☎617/522-7000); 44 Victoria Street, Suite 1310, Toronto, ON M5C 1Y2 (☎416/369-0044, *wspacanada@compserve.com*); 46 Nicholson St, St Leonards, Australia (☎02/9901 5277). Spain's main opposition to bullfighting is organized by ADDA (Association para la Defensar de los Derechos de Animal), c/Bailén 164, Local 2 Interior E08037, Barcelona (*www.intercom.es/adda/*). They coordinate the International Bullfight Campaign and also produce a bi-annual newsletter in Spanish and English.

estimates that 200,000 people are involved in some way in the Spanish industry, and the top performers, the **matadores**, have incomes on a par with the country's biggest pop stars. There is some opposition to the activity from Spanish animal-welfare groups, rather more from the French, but neither is widespread: if Spaniards tell you that bullfighting is controversial, they are probably referring to practices in the trade. In recent years, bullfighting critics (whom you will find on the arts pages of the newspapers) have been expressing their perennial outrage at the routine but illegal shaving of bulls' horns prior to the *corrida*. Bulls' horns are as sensitive as fingernails a few millimetres in, and raw horns deter the animal from charging; they affect the creature's gauging of distance, too, reducing the danger for the *matador* still further.

Notwithstanding such abuses (and there are plenty of others), *Los Toros* keep their **aficionados** engaged across Spain. Indeed, their number is on the rise, with the elaborate argot of the *corrida* attaining cult status among the young as the days of Franco's patronage of bullfighting are forgotten, and TV stations paying big money for major events. A surprising number of devotees are women and teenage girls – who have been known to shower heart-throb-handsome *matadores* with knickers and bras in the ring as tokens of appreciation. For the more serious *aficionados* (a word that implies more knowledge and appreciation than the English "fan"), "the bulls" are a culture and a ritual in which the emphasis is on the way man and bull "perform" together, with art the issue rather than cruelty.

In France, the resurgence of *Les Taureaux*, as it's called there, has been attended by fierce debate over whether *corridas* are really a traditional folkloric manifestation of the regions concerned – Languedoc-Roussillon and the Basque country, precisely those areas with a large population descended from Spanish immigrants settled there since the turn of the twentieth century.

Thus advocates have been at pains to demonstrate evidence of bullfighting from before 1900; it appears that spectacles will be allowed to proceed south of a line approximately joining Bayonne, Toulouse and Nîmes.

Whether you attend a *corrida*, obviously, is down to your own feelings and ethics. If you spend any time at all in the Pyrenees during the season (which runs March–Oct), you will encounter bullfights, at least on a bar TV, and that will as likely as not make up your mind. If you decide to go, try to see the biggest and most prestigious event available, where star performers are likely to despatch the bulls with "art" and a successful, "clean" kill. There are few sights worse than a *matador* making a prolonged and messy kill, while the audience whistles – unfortunately more likely in France, where there's not as yet significant homegrown talent in man or beast, and often second-rate bullfighters (and bulls) have to be imported. Established and popular **matadores** include Enrique Ponce, Cesar Rincón, Victor Mendes, Joselito, Litri, David "El Rey" Silveti and José María Manzanares. Two newer stars currently in the headlines are Seville's golden boy, Antonio Bareas, and the 17-year-old prodigy Julián "El Juli" López. Cristina Sanchez, the first woman to make it into the top flight for many decades, retired in May 1999 after a decade in the ring, tired of sexist organizers, audiences and fellow matadores. The most exciting and skilful performances of all are by **mounted matadores**, or *rejoneadores*; this is the oldest form of *corrida*, developed in Andalucía during the seventeenth century.

Tickets for *corridas* in Spain are 2000ptas/€12 and up – as much as 14,000ptas/€84 for the prime seats and prestigious fights. The cheapest seats are *gradas*, the highest rows at the back, from where you can see everything that happens without too much of the detail; the front rows are known as the *barreras*. Seats are also divided into *sol* (sun), *sombra* (shade) and *sol y sombra* (shaded after a while), though these distinctions have become less relevant as more and more bullfights start later in the day, at 6pm or 7pm, rather than the traditional 5pm. The *sombra* seats are more expensive, not so much for the spectators' comfort as the fact that most of the action takes place in the shade. On the way in, you can rent **cushions** – two hours sitting on concrete is not much fun. Beer and soft drinks are sold inside.

TROUBLE, POLICE AND SEXUAL HARASSMENT

In general both sides of the Pyrenees are remarkably safe, with weather and terrain often posing the most threat. In the foothill towns and busy ski resorts, take normal precautions: keep your wallet in your front pocket and your handbag under your elbow, and you won't have much to worry about. If you should get confronted – only likely in the two or three largest cities described – hand over the money and start dialling the cancellation numbers for your travellers' cheques and credit cards.

FRANCE

All the comments about leaving cars unattended under "Spain", p.73, apply to France as well, with an extra need for vigilance in such larger towns as Perpignan, Pau and Bayonne. Foreign cars with their distinctive number plates are easy to spot, rental vehicles much less so. Good insurance is the only answer, but even so do not tempt fate by leaving vehicles unlocked or valuables in plain sight, either lapse probably invalidating the best of policies.

OFFENCES

• If you have an **accident** while driving, you are required to fill in and sign a *constat à l'aimable* (jointly agreed statement); car insurers are supposed to give you this with a policy, as are car rental agencies, though in practice few seem to have heard of it.

For non-criminal **driving violations** such as speeding or not wearing seat belts, the police will impose an on-the-spot fine; if you can't pay in cash or traveller's cheques, you and the vehicle may be locked up. You can be stopped anywhere in France and asked to produce ID – a far more likely proposition if you're black or Asian. If it happens, it's not worth being difficult or facetious.

• Should you be arrested on any charge, you have the right to contact your consulate or embassy.

• People caught smuggling or possessing **drugs**, even a few grams of marijuana, are liable to find themselves in jail, and consulates will not be sympathetic. This is not to say that hard-drug consumption isn't a visible activity: there are scores of kids dealing in *poudre* (heroin) in the big French cities and the authorities seem unable to do much about it. As a rule, people are no more nor less paranoid about marijuana busts than they are in the UK or USA.

POLICE

There are two main types of French police (popularly known as *les flics*): the **Police Nationale** and the **Gendarmeries Nationale**. For all practical purposes, they are indistinguishable; if you need to report a theft, or other incident, you can go to either. Although the police are not always as cooperative as they might be, it *is* their duty to assist you – likewise in the case of losing your passport or all your money.

A different proposition are the **CRS** (*Compagnies Républicaines de Sécurité*), a mobile force of heavies, sporadically dressed in green combat gear and armed with riot equipment, whose brutality in the May 1968 battles turned public opinion to the side of the students. But in the Pyrenees you may come across specialized **mountaineering sections** of the CRS; unlike their urban brethren, these are unfailingly helpful, friendly and approachable, providing rescue services and guidance.

SEXUAL AND RACIAL HARASSMENT

There's no need for women to feel any less safe in France than at home. Unlike further south in the Mediterranean, machismo is not overt, and young men don't, on the whole, feel honour-bound to pester any unaccompanied young female. In trains and on the trail alike, passers-by are prone to look you up and down and possibly make comment, but this is something women do as much as men.

Problems can arise, however, from misjudging situations without familiar linguistic and cultural clues. An unelicited "Bonjour" or "Bonsoir" on the street is almost always a pick-up line. If you so much as return the greeting, you let yourself in for a persistent monologue and a difficult brush-off job. On the other hand, it's not unusual to be offered a drink in a rural bar if you're on your own and not to be pestered even if you accept, so not every overture is necessarily a come-on.

You may, as a woman, be warned about "*les Arabes*" – routine French **racism**. If you are Arab, Asian or black your chances of completely avoiding unpleasantness are slim. Empty hotels claiming to be full, police demanding your papers and abusive treatment from both immigration officials and ordinary people are depressingly commonplace. The recent clampdown on illegal immigration and much tougher public order laws have resulted in a significant increase in police stop-and-search operations, so carrying your passport at all times is a good idea.

In the Pyrenees specifically, locals are slowly getting used seeing to school outings including members of racial minorities, or the odd person of colour out on the trail or the ski slopes. But French nationals of Arab or black African descent are not yet present in the numbers that their proportion of the population would lead you to expect.

SPAIN

While you're unlikely to encounter any trouble during the course of a normal visit to the Spanish

Pyrenees, it's worth remembering that the Spanish police, polite enough in the usual course of events, can be extremely unpleasant if you get on the wrong side of them.

If you have a **car**, and especially if you're doing loop treks with the vehicle left at a trailhead, leave as little as possible in view, or indeed in the car at all. At the very least take the tape deck with you, or stash it out of sight. In the lonelier valleys organized gangs rifle parked cars, and they're not too picky about what they steal: tools, clothing, the registration papers in particular. The vehicles themselves are rarely stolen, if that's any consolation. **Cars with French numberplates** are more likely to be vandalized in the Spanish Basque country – this is usually ascribed to retaliation by ETA sympathizers for the French crackdown on their brethren. Rental vehicles, fortunately, are not conspicuously labelled as such.

The American Embassy in Madrid says it frequently receives reports of **roadside thieves** posing as "good Samaritans" to persons experiencing engine or tyre defects. The thieves typically attempt to divert the driver's attention by pointing out a mechanical problem and then steal items from the vehicle while the driver is looking elsewhere. Be cautious about accepting help from anyone other than a uniformed Spanish police officer, and, if you do break down, keep your valuables in sight or lock them in the vehicle.

Looking for hotel rooms, don't leave any bags unattended anywhere. This applies especially to buildings where the hotel or *hostal* is on the higher floors and you're tempted to leave baggage in the hallway or ground-floor lobby.

Catalunya now has a special tourist/consumer protection troubleshooting hotline: dial ☎900 300 303 (it's free), and an English-speaking operator will help you with misrepresented hotels, problems with air tickets, etc. It's designed more for package-tour patrons, but could be worth a try for other situations.

If your car or room is burgled, you need to **go to the police** to report it, not least because your insurance company will require a police report. Don't expect a great deal of concern if your loss is relatively small – and expect the process of completing forms and formalities to take ages. In the unlikely event that you're **mugged**, or otherwise threatened, *never* resist; hand over what's wanted and go straight to the police, who on these occasions will be more sympathetic.

OFFENCES

There are a few **offences** you might commit unwittingly that it's as well to be aware of.

• In theory you're supposed to carry some kind of **identification** at all times, and the police can stop you in the streets and demand it. In practice they're rarely bothered if you're clearly a (white) foreigner routinely trekking back and forth across the border ridge, but it's still a good idea to have passports or ID handy, since mountain refuges often require them as security against payment.

• **Nude bathing** or **unauthorized camping** are activities more likely to bring you into contact with officialdom, though a warning to cover up or move on is more likely than any real confrontation. In the Pyrenees, pitching a tent in any possible suitable place – except right in view of a *refugio* or in a protected national park – is the norm. **Topless** tanning is commonplace at all the trendier coastal resorts, but by Pyrenean streams and lakes, where attitudes are rather more traditional, you should take care not to upset local sensibilities.

• Spanish **drug laws** are in a somewhat ambiguous state at present. After the PSOE came to power in 1983, cannabis use (possession of up to 8g of hashish, *chocolate* in Castilian) was decriminalized. Subsequent pressures, and an influx of harder drugs, have changed that policy and – in theory at least – any drug use is now forbidden. You'll see signs in some bars saying "*porros no*" (no joints), which you should heed. However, the police are in practice little worried about personal use. Larger quantities (and any other drugs) are a very different matter.

• Should you be **arrested** you have the right to contact your **consulate**, and although they're notoriously reluctant to get involved they are required to assist you to some degree if you have your passport stolen or lose all your money. If you've been detained for a drugs offence, don't expect any sympathy or help from your consulate.

• If you have an **accident** while **driving**, try not to make a statement to anyone who doesn't speak English. Car rental agencies will provide you, in the glove box, with a bilingual statement to be filled in by both drivers if another car is involved. The SNTO in your home country can provide a detailed list of the driving rules for Spain.

THE POLICE

There are three basic types of Spanish **police**: the *Guardia Civil*, the *Policía Municipal* and the *Policía Nacional*, all of them armed.

The **Guardia Civil,** in green uniforms, are the most officious and the ones to avoid. Though their role has been drastically cut back since they operated as Franco's right hand – you'll see many of their barracks abandoned in the Pyrenees – they remain a reactionary force (it was a *Guardia Civil* colonel, Tejero, who held the parliament hostage in the February 1981 failed coup).

If you do need the police – and above all if you're reporting a serious crime such as rape – always go to the more sympathetic **Policía Municipal,** who wear blue-and-white uniforms with red trim. In the countryside there may be only the *Guardia Civil*; though they're usually helpful, they are inclined to resent the suggestion that any crime exists on their turf and you may end up feeling as if you are the one who stands accused.

The brown-uniformed **Policía Nacional** are mainly seen in cities, armed with submachine guns and guarding key installations such as embassies, stations, post offices and their own barracks. They are also the force used to control crowds and demonstrations. In Euskadi there exists an additional autonomous Basque police force, distinguished by their red *boinas* or berets.

SEXUAL AND RACIAL HARASSMENT

Spain's macho image has faded dramatically in the post-Franco years and these days there are relatively few parts of the country where foreign women, travelling alone, are likely to feel threatened, intimidated or noteworthy.

Inevitably, the **larger towns** – like any others in Europe – have their no-go areas, where street crime and especially drug-related hassles are on the rise, but there is little of the pestering and propositions that you have to contend with in, say, the larger Italian or Greek cities. The outdoor culture of *terrazas* (terrace bars) and the tendency of Spaniards to move around in large, mixed crowds, filling central bars, clubs and streets late into the night, help to make you feel less exposed. If you are in any doubt, there are always taxis – plentiful and reasonably priced.

Predictably, it is in **more isolated regions,** separated by less than a generation from desperate poverty (or still starkly poor), that most serious problems can occur. In some areas you can walk for hours without reaching an inhabited farm or house, or anyone other than a shepherd working alone most of the summer for minimal returns. It's rare that this poses a threat – help and hospitality are much more the norm – but you are certainly more vulnerable. That said, **back-country trekking** is becoming more popular in Spain as a whole and many women happily tramp the Pyrenees from one end to the other alone and without incident.

Despite – or more probably because of – having been at the receiving end of prejudice during their several decades of emigration to northern Europe, Spaniards are beginning to display some of the same **racist attitudes** long espoused by their French neighbours. These have been aggravated by continual, large-scale illegal immigration

of "boat people" across the Straits of Gibralter, and violent, racially based riots in Tarrassa (Catalunya) in summer 1999, and in El Ejido (Almería) during spring 2000. In both cases Moroccans were the main instigators or victims, but anyone darker than expected for "tourists" should keep their papers handy at all times – and perhaps expect some raised eyebrows in the Pyrenees, where the only people of colour seen thus far tend to be Arab or black African immigrants in menial jobs across foothill Catalunya.

THE GREAT OUTDOORS

Although high-rise resort apartments and wide pistes make skiing the most conspicuous outdoor pursuit of the Pyrenees, walking is a more widely practised Pyrenean recreation, and much of the range is crossed with well-maintained footpaths. In addition to these, the mountains and their coastal fringes offer a great range of variously energetic diversions, whether gentle cross-country rides on horseback, scuba plunges into the Mediterranean, or the pulse-racing thrills of parapente.

WALKING

Not many people would argue with the proposition that the Pyrenees is the finest walking area in Europe. Unlike the Alps, where the high peaks are beyond the skills of the average person, any fit walker with a little determination can reach most of the major summits. All over the Pyrenees, paths and trails of varying length are marked and (variably) maintained, some by activity clubs and mountaineering federations, others by local government. Many tourist offices will have details of shorter itineraries, and at least some information on the major walking routes.

LONG-DISTANCE WALKS

The principal **long-distance walks** are listed below; summaries of their routes are given where applicable throughout the Guide.

• **Haute Randonnée Pyrénéenne** (HRP) is the shortest and toughest traverse from Atlantic to

Mediterranean, sticking close to the frontier, mainly in France but crossing into Spain when the terrain dictates, with many variants entirely in Spain. It's planned as a 45-day hike covering nearly 500km, staying in mountain refuges and unstaffed shelters. Not all of it is difficult but some sections do call for map-reading skills, a head for heights and the use of crampons and ice-axe early in the season. Often the HRP is not waymarked, but in places it merges with the well-marked GR10 – which can also make a good alternative to the hardest parts of the HRP. Georges Véron has written a detailed if slightly dated description – see "Books", in *Contexts*.

• **Grande Randonnée 10** (GR10) is a lower-level traverse, entirely in France, that adds about 300km on the distance. Most nights can be spent in *gîtes d'étape*, huts or village accommodation, but there are sections where a tent or bivouac are necessary. The GR10 is marked in its entirety with red-and-white paint bars, and described in detail by the French Topoguide series; for an English-language text, the best guide is Douglas Streatfeild-James' *Trekking in the Pyrenees* (Trailblazer, UK) – see "Books" in *Contexts*.

• **Gran Recorrido 11** (GR11) is the Spanish equivalent of the GR10, a well-marked itinerary – again with red-and-white bars – which mostly uses well-established footpaths. Much of this route – which includes some of the wildest, most spectacular scenery in the Pyrenees, and a good compromise between the HRP and GR10 – is served by a mix of attended refuges and unstaffed huts, though again a tent or the willingness to bivouac is occasionally required. The Basque-country section of the trail west of Isaba has, alas, been reported to be less than brilliantly marked and maintained in recent years.

Thorough documentation of this *Senda Pirenaica*, as it's often called in Castilian, exists mainly in Spanish or Catalan, with the Catalunyan, Aragonese and Navarran alpine clubs each publishing a convenient paperback *topoguía* detailing the portion of the GR11 falling within their autonomous region. Alternatively, there's the mammoth, non-portable ring-binder edition combining all three regions, published jointly by Prames, FEDME and the Federación Aragonesa de Montaña – the loose pages are meant to be replaced periodically with updates. In English, there's only a single summary pocket guide, Paul Lucia's *Through the Spanish Pyrenees: GR11* (see "Books" in *Contexts*).

•**GR12** shares much of the GR11's course within Navarra, but diverges at either edge of the region to trace the watershed between Navarra to the south and Gipuzkoa and Lapurdi to the north.

•**GR15**, the *Sendero Prepirenaico*, runs parallel to the GR11 at a much lower altitude, and can thus be followed when the higher elevations are inaccessible due to snow; in this guide it is described only at the southern fringes of the Ordesa region, and in the Valle de Gistau.

•**GR19** is a short trail confined to Alto Aragón, which crosses the GR15 and is most useful as a pleasant way between Viadós, the Valle de Gistau and Ordesa.

•**GR36/GR4** is one of several major north–south traverses of the Pyrenees, from Albi in France to Montserrat in Spain, via Canigou and the Cerdagne/Cerdanya. GR36 is the French designation, GR4 the Spanish.

•**GR7** is the second major north–south traverse, reaching the Pyrenees in the Pays de Sault, curving through Andorra and into Spain as far as Barcelona. It is described in both a French *topoguide* and a Catalan-produced *topoguía*.

•**GR107**, from Montségur to the Sierra del Cadí, is also called the *Chemin des Bonshommes* or *Camí de les Bons Hommes*, and claims to follow the route of fleeing Cathars. A *topoguide/topoguía* should now be available.

•**GR65**, the modern version of the medieval *Camino de Santiago/Chemin de Saint Jacques* pilgrimage route, crosses the Pyrenees from Saint-Jean-Pied-de-Port in the French Basque Country, via the Ibañeta pass and Roncesvalles to Pamplona and then across northern Spain to Santiago de Compostela. The entire route is covered in detail by various guides, published by Cicerone Press or the confraternity of St James. The traditional Aragonese spur of the main route is now marked as the **GR65.3**, which enters Spain from the Vallée d'Aspe at the Somport pass, then descends to Jaca where it turns ninety degrees west, joining the GR65 southwest of Pamplona at Puenta la Reina. The Aragonese mountain club (FAM) describes this route in a *topoguía* available in English. You should expect slight changes in the route between Jaca and Pamplona in the near future, as the proposed Yesa reservoir enlargement will inundate some portions of the existing trail.

•**Le Sentier Cathare** is a partial traverse, linking all the sites from the Mediterranean to Foix that were significant to the Cathar religion. You pass through some fantastic scenery in Corbières and the Pays de Sault and visit great ruined fortresses such as Quéribus, Peyrepertuse, Puylaurens and Montségur. Well marked and well equipped with *gîtes d'étape*, it is described in French in *Le Sentier Cathare* by Louis Salavy and J.L. Sarret (Randonnées Pyrénéennes).

Mention must be made of **variants** (*variantes* in both French and Castilian), which are exactly what they sound like: alternative routings diverging briefly from the main GR, often of greater difficulty or providing necessary side links to villages just off the principal trail. Both the GR11 and GR10 have been substantially rerouted in spots during recent years, in response to requests from both walkers and farmers, who no longer want people traipsing through or past their land. Old sectors, if not altogether abandoned, tend to be demoted to *variante* status. One problem arising from the re-marking, or fresh plotting of **new trails**, is that the marking committee volunteers tend to do their work with little fanfare, leaving local villagers none the wiser; when asked, the locals will thus often deny that any path has been (re-)marked in their neighbourhood.

On both sides of the frontier there exist PR trails (**pequeño recorrido** in Castilian, **petit randonnée** in French), usually marked in yellow and white (in Spain), in yellow and red (France), or sometimes blue and yellow or even green and blue; these are itineraries designed to be completed within a day by persons with limited experience of high-mountain walking. Nonetheless, they are also of use to long-haul trekkers, often sparing you some fairly miserable road-tramping, and frequently sharing, or running parallel to, the course of a GR route. They are found in greatest numbers around Benasque and Ansó/Hecho in Spain, and Ax-les-Thermes, Luchon or Cauterets in France, though any tourist board worth its salt seems to be devising these for every resort or valley. Locally produced guidelets describe most of them.

In the French Pyrenees, there are also more than twenty **local circuits** called Tours, lasting from three to seven days. These are all indicated with varying precision on the 1:50,000 maps published by Rando Éditions (Randonnées Pyrénéennes) and some of the IGN ones, and most are also described in guidebooks from the same publisher. The best of these loops are summarized in the relevant chapters of this guide. On the Spanish side, you'll have to devise your own itineraries, using the Editorial Alpina maps and booklets, plus the other publications listed in *Contexts*.

WALKING SKILLS AND EQUIPMENT

Gauging the **distance** that can be covered in a day obviously depends on many variables, the most significant being level of fitness, type of terrain and load being carried. As rough estimates, most people can walk at about 4.5km per hour over flat country with a fairly light load, and climb at most 450m/1500ft per hour off-road; with a full (15- to 20-kilo) pack, they rarely exceed a climb of 350m/1150ft per hour off-road. You should knock off 50m per hour from these climbing figures for bad trail surface or extraordinarily heavy loads, and always assume that going downhill is no quicker than ascending – if you love your knees, it won't be. If you're not used to it, 1000m of ascent in a single day, with a full pack, is pretty exhausting. You should reckon on **10km horizontally and 1000m of ascent as a sustainable daily average** at first. If you are reasonably fit you could doubtless manage 20km and/or 2000m of climb, but you probably won't feel much like walking the next day. As an idea of what really experienced individuals can achieve, the participants of the Cauterets-to-Vignemale race, involving 52km horizontally and 2700m of ascent, take between four and a half and eight hours. **Trailhead signs** on the Spanish side of the range often predict

wildly optimistic times for the hikes ahead – take them with a grain of salt; by contrast, French estimates are often rather slower than reality.

Plenty of people attempt a Pyrenean traverse without having done any serious walking before. There's no reason why you shouldn't, but you must follow a few basic guidelines. As a rule of thumb you can carry a quarter of your own body weight comfortably in a **backpack**. A frame pack takes its load more easily but one of the hi-tech soft packs with internal struts is more versatile, closer fitting and with nothing to get caught on rocks when scrambling.

You shouldn't skimp on **boots**; if you're on the HRP or walking anywhere in winter you're going to need proper ones. Although serious mountain footwear weighs at least one kilo each side, you don't notice it so much when they're on your feet. High-tech, synthetic boots not only tend to be much hotter than old-fashioned leather ones, but fail to provide vital ankle support – as do trainers, which should never be worn on anything other than an hour-long, level stroll from car park to a nearby lake, without a full pack. As a compromise between flimsy trainers and rigid, expensive monsters intended to accommodate crampons, there are numerous all- or partly-leather designs with Vibram-type tread, moisture-wicking liner material and some degree of stiffening around the ankle. In wetter regions where heat is not a big issue, as in the Western Pyrenees, many walkers favour rubber boots, while in the warm, arid Eastern Pyrenees canvas boots are popular.

You'll also need a **walking stick** or some other self-arrest device, if you don't want your knees to be in dreadful condition by the end of a multi-day trek. If you're following the GR10 or GR11 from west to east, simple sticks or the more elaborate pilgrim's *makila* are easy to buy in the Basque country. In the central part of the range, hi-tech telescoping poles with snow tips are widely sold in the busier trailhead resorts. Alternatively, you could find some deadfall or abandoned cuttings in a beech grove, and fashion your own stick with the saw attachment of a pocket knife. It will take about fifteen minutes to strip the bark and sharp nubbins down to the pale yellow wood, but the result – if free of bends – is a superbly strong device, even where tiny cracks develop as the stick dries out. You judge the length as you would a ski pole – the grip should be comfortable with your forearm extended at a right angle.

Unless you're going up above 2500m or are camping in winter, there's no need for a specialist **tent**, though you should always pick one that's self-supporting and has a sewn-in groundsheet. The most up-to-date two-person tents can weigh in at less than four kilos, if optimistically rated in terms of capacity: two people will fit snugly, with no room for gear inside. Six or seven kilos is a more realistic allowance. Many long walks can be done without a tent, and hard cases can manage any of the traverses with a good poncho or cagoule and the use of caves, huts, refuges and *gîtes d'étape*. A big army-type poncho keeps you and your pack dry when you're on the trail, and at night you can roll it around your sleeping bag, or (with strips sewn on in strategic places) rig it as a canopy. It's not too comfortable, but many consider the saving on weight and bulk worthwhile.

As far as **clothing** is concerned, follow the **layer** principle. When you're ascending on a hot day you'll want only shorts and a T-shirt – silk ski tops are excellent, as they wick sweat out and dry quickly – but in colder conditions you'll need a long-sleeved shirt and trousers or breeches with long socks. There are all kinds of part-synthetic **pile/fleece** garments nowadays, warm and easy to wash. A pile top over a wool shirt, with long underwear as the lowest layer, should be as much warmth as you need. If it's raining, wear overtrousers and cagoule.

For the HRP or **winter** walking you're going to need **gaiters** to stop snow going down your boots, **crampons** (which fit only stiff mountaineering boots) and an ice-axe – plus the skill to use it effectively.

A good **sleeping bag** is essential. Down gives the best insulation relative to weight and bulk, but its efficiency falls drastically when it gets damp, which it's bound to do unless you have a proper tent, and a poncho to protect your pack from showers. An artificial filling is better, though much heavier and less compressible. Underneath either sort of bag you'll need a foam **mat** to protect it. Also get a sleeping-bag **liner** – cotton or thermal – which you can wash and dry easily en route, leaving the cleaning of your bag for back home.

Your personal gear will be complete with a **hat** (maybe two) for warmth and/or protection from the sun, **gloves**, **sunglasses**, **sunscreen**, including **lip-balm** with a sun-protection factor, and some sort of **insect repellant** – Pyrenean biting flies can be fierce. For navigation a **com-pass** and **pocket altimeter** are both vital, together with the appropriate **maps**.

WATER AND FOOD

On a non-strenuous day the average person needs two litres of **water** from liquids and from food. Hiking you need at least **twice** that, and ski touring **three times** as much. In the mountains you can usually get fresh water along the way. Check your map for habitation upstream, as plenty of mountain villages still discharge untreated sewage into rivers; if there's nothing upstream a vigorous flow will be safe. If in doubt – ie, if there are signs of livestock – add water purification tablets (available from all outdoor shops) or boil for four minutes.

On an easy walk you'll need forty calories minimum per day per kilo of body weight – fifty for a tough hike and as much as sixty for ski touring. Fats provide the most energy for their weight, at around 7500 calories per kilo; dehydrated main-meal foods can give you 5000 calories per kilo; nuts and chocolate work out at around 4500 calories per kilo. Picking up **supplies** on the GR10, GR7 or GR65 is easy, as they're designed to pass through plenty of villages. On the HRP or the GR11 you'll probably have to make diversions. It is possible to pick wild food along the way – in season you'll find edible mushrooms plus things like wild spinach, wild strawberries, hazelnuts and herbs – but these have low caloric value and should be regarded only as supplements to the trekking diet.

For long trips in the wild you will need a **stove**. The best is the multi-fuel or MSR type, which is light, versatile, powerful – and expensive. Next best are French-made Bleuet 206 or English-made Coleman 3001 HPX butane-cartridge stoves, as their fuel is clean, light and almost universally available – the Coleman cartridges somewhat less so, though they are self-sealing and can therefore be safely removed if necessary. However, this type of stove doesn't burn well at low temperatures or when the cartridge is running down. For the evening meal, packet soups, dried potatoes, couscous or thin pasta, supplemented with dry cheese or cured meat, are quick, high-calorie, light to carry and fuel-efficient. Although there's often little else suitable to buy in high villages, try to avoid canned goods, as they're not only heavy to carry but aggravate existing Pyrenean litter problems no matter where you dispose of them. For short excursions from civilization, a vacuum flask can carry enough hot water to rehydrate dried foods.

CLIMBING

Although the principal summits of the Pyrenees can be reached with only rudimentary climbing skills, the range has technical routes as demanding as any elsewhere. There are few places in the Pyrenees where you can't climb, but particularly good areas include Aigüestortes, Maladeta and the entire Ordesa country in Spain, and the Haute-Garonne, Vallée d'Aure, Cirque de Gavarnie and the tops of the Aspe and Ossau valleys in France.

The traditional climbing grades 1 to 6 were long ago surpassed with the arrival of new techniques and equipment – routes at level 8 are now routinely tackled (especially on the Troubat cliffs near Montréjeau) and the rock gymnasts have been setting new parameters at level 9 throughout the early 1990s. Some climbers find artificial walls worthwhile. Indeed, the current French attitude – exemplified by the multicoloured tights and other high-fashion gear – is the closer to an appreciative audience, the better. Tarbes has one of the biggest climbing walls, with routes up to 7b, but plenty of mountain villages have now installed them, including Luz-Saint-Sauveur. In 1993 Spain inaugurated a climbing wall at its mountaineering school at Benasque, though it's intended for Spanish or select overseas guides. There's a public wall in Sallent de Gallego, plus a few other villages on the Spanish side.

There are plenty of climbing courses on offer to summer visitors throughout the Pyrenees, most of them charging in the region of €70 for four to six hours' tuition.

CAVING

The northern and southern foothills of the Pyrenees are largely Cretaceous or Jurassic **limestone**, and some of the high peaks are too, for example Monte Perdido, Europe's highest limestone mountain. Although limestone is soluble, it's also nonporous, which means it dissolves only at tiny cracks where water can penetrate. Over millennia, this dissolving action produces vertical potholes and vast caverns. Thus, below the bizarrely eroded limestone around Pic d'Anie lurks the deepest cave system yet discovered in the Pyrenees, and one of the deepest in the world: the **Gouffre Pierre-Saint-Martin**. The Pyrenees also boasts the world's highest **ice caves** (caves

hung with frozen waterfalls), at the top of the Cirque de Gavarnie.

If you've never done any caving, are not in the least athletic, but would still like to experience it, there are several managed caves open to the public, such as **Grandes Canalettes** near Villefranche-de-Conflent or the **prehistoric** painted caves like **Niaux** and **Bédeilhac** in the Ariège. The next stage of difficulty would be a cave like **L'Aguzou** in the Aude, where small pre-booked, fully equipped parties are guided around an unilluminated system.

But if you're intent on caving as a sport, then you need to make arrangements through your own caving club or by signing up with a commercial school. It is possible to head off with your own gear if you know what you're doing, but many of the best caverns have now been locked, and only approved people can get the key. Rewarding areas include the karst country around **Pic d'Anie**, the entire **Cirque de Gavarnie/Monte Perdido** region, the **Comminges** and northern **Couserans**, the **Pays de Sault**, the **Ariège**, the **Aude**, the **Serra del Cadí**, the **Alta Garrotxa** region and the **Têt valley** around Villefranche-de-Conflent.

SKIING

The comparatively gentle slopes of the Pyrenees are the perfect place to savour the delights of **ski mountaineering** and **cross-country** skiing for the first time. Compared with the Alps, the risk of avalanche is much less, and the chance of falling into a crevasse or having a similar accident is minimal. There is no better way of getting real solitude than ski-traversing in the Pyrenees in winter. To learn, sign on with a guide in a resort like Barèges or Gavarnie, both spots giving access to marvellous itineraries ranging from one day to several. If you're already a mountain walker and a competent downhill skier, you're well on the way.

In terms of **downhill skiing**, snow quality on prepared runs seldom approaches the powder standard more often found in the Alps – late in the season things get downright mushy and/or thin near the bottom. As a general rule, resorts in the eastern half of the range have these problems compounded by low precipitation and strong sun (also a problem on much of the Spanish side of the border), and by wind, which either packs the snow hard or scours it away. In the west there is a tendency to mist – also a great snow-eater –

and rain, brought in by the Atlantic weather systems. Don't set out specially for a week's holiday without checking conditions at your chosen resort first.

Snowboarding – *surfismo* in Castilian, *surfisme* in French/Catalan – is now a Big Thing in the Pyrenees, and boarders – *surfistas*/*surfistes* respectively – are well catered to in virtually every resort. **Snow-blading** is somewhat less widespread, as is **carving**; the latter are adapted skis some 10cm shorter than conventional ones – much more manoeuvrable, confidence-building and forgiving of minor mistakes.

EASTERN RESORTS

Proximity to the Mediterranean means that snow can be unreliable at the **eastern resorts** of **Vallter 2000** and **Núria** in Spain, and **Cambre d'Aze**, or **Puigmal 2600** in France. For ski mountaineering and cross-country skiing, on the other hand, the higher reaches of this region are a delight, with little risk of either avalanche or exposure.

Pas de la Casa offers the most reliable snow immediately around **Andorra**, but the development itself is a monstrosity. Best all-rounders within Andorra are **Ordino-Arcalis**, set amongst magnificent high-mountain wilderness, or **Soldeu El Tarter**. Andorra in general is trying to reinvent itself as a family skiing destination, and shed its enduring reputation as a downmarket, wintertime Club 18–30.

Back in France, Ax-les-Thermes has its own ski station of **Ax-Bonascre**, another blot on the landscape – but when you get up the lifts the scenery is sublime. Just south, in the contiguous Capcir and Cerdagne regions, the most famous resort is **Font-Romeu**, though **Porté-Puymorens**, **Les Angles**, **Formigueres** and **Puyvalador** are all superior. For **cross-country skiing** (*ski de fondo* in Castilian, *ski de fond* in French and Catalan), the whole of the Cerdagne/Cerdanya and much of the Serra del Cadí are a playground of trails, during spring bathed in sunshine. **Ski-mountaineering** can be as easy or as tough as you want; the fearless can tackle the Ariège uplands, nicknamed the *Terre Courage*.

CENTRAL AND WESTERN RESORTS

Spain has several serious resorts relatively near the Val d'Aran; the best of these **Masella**, overlooking the Spanish Cerdanya, **Port-Ainé**, in the Noguera Pallaresa valley, **Boï-Taüll**, beside the

Aigüestortes park, and **Baqueira-Beret**, at the head of the valley and the only one with an international reputation. There are more ski resorts in **Aragón**'s stretch of the Pyrenees and most of them – following massive investment in the 1990s, plus a current bid to host the 2010 Winter Olympics – are well equipped, particularly **Cerler**, **Formigal**, and **Candanchú-Astún**. When all is said and done, however, the **north slope** of the **central French Pyrenees** provides the most reliable conditions: **Barèges-La Mongie** comes first for its size and recent infrastructure improvements. Other normally dependable destinations in this area include **Piau-Engaly**, **Cauterets** and **Gavarnie-Gèdre**.

Every significant surviving resort in the Pyrenees is described in the *Guide*, with details of top-point elevation and the number and type of pistes. The system for **grading pistes** is based on a universal **colour code**: green for beginners, blue for easy, red for intermediate and black for advanced skiers. It's not a completely dependable system – a red run in one resort might rate only as blue in another – but it should give a fair idea of what to expect. The most important thing is that a run should be long enough. Unlike in the Alps, **beginners** are well looked after – Gavarnie, Soldeu and Port-Ainé, for example, all have green runs from their top lifts.

COSTS AND PACKAGES

Pyrenean skiing tends to **cost less** than the Alps because the range lacks international cachet (and really convenient airports – Barcelona, Lourdes-Tarbes, Perpignan and Toulouse are the closest choices), and the **clientele** is almost totally local and family-oriented. There's little of the snootiness or nocturnal excess occasionally met with in the Alps, and as a foreigner (particularly in Spain) you'll be the object of benign curiosity or outright friendliness – though again in Spain you may have trouble finding English-speaking **instruction**. In France, the local École du Ski Français will have at least one multilingual instructor per resort; rates begin at 175F/€26.70 for one or two persons per lesson at a less popular spot. **Infrastructure** is adequate to quite good, best wherever sums have been spent on snow cannons, new lifts or piste extension. But especially in Spain and Andorra, *pistes*/*pistas* are often **poorly marked** by Alps standards; the margin lollipops (*espiolettes*/*espiolets*) are not colour-keyed, so it's fairly easy to stray onto the wrong run.

AVALANCHE SAFETY

Ideally, anyone embarking on a long high-level traverse should learn the requisite safety skills on a course or from an experienced person, or read a specialist book on the subject. If you are undertaking a mountain walk early in the summer season, a winter climb or a ski tour, it is absolutely essential that you know the basics of avalanche safety.

Firstly, **always take local advice**: a shepherd or high-mountain guide will tell you which slopes avalanche regularly, which sometimes avalanche and which have never avalanched in living memory. Secondly, there are very few occasions when the crossing of a potential avalanche slope cannot be avoided; if there is even the remotest chance of avalanche, **don't do it**. Nobody is going to be impressed because, by good luck, you happened to cross a dangerous slope without mishap – certainly not the mountain rescue teams who might have to risk their lives to dig you out (see below). Good route-finding is the key. **The safest routes** are along broad ridges, the bottoms of slopes beyond the estimated run-out zone of a possible avalanche, and areas with dense tree cover. Certain climatological conditions make avalanches more likely: heavy snowfall in the preceding 24 hours; a strong wind in the same period; and a rapid rise in temperature. In such conditions, **avoid** the following:

- gullies and bowls
- convex slopes showing signs of bulge or stress
- leeward concave slopes and any slopes overhung by cornices
- slopes with an incline greater than 25 degrees

- south-facing slopes in strong sun with conditions above freezing
- canyons and gorges with dangerous slopes above
- sparsely treed or open slopes.

If you're forced to **cross a potential avalanche slope**, do so one at a time or spaced at 100-metre intervals if it's wide. Do up zips, buttons and hoods, take your hands out of ski pole straps, release ski-retaining straps and tie a scarf around your mouth and nose. Some items of **safety equipment** are good investments if you'll be spending some time in open country – shovels, probes and rescue beacons or (second-best) avalanche cords for every member of the party. Read Tony Daffern's *Avalanche Safety for Skiers and Climbers* (published by Diadem in the UK).

If you're **caught in an avalanche**, you should jettison poles, skis and pack if there's time, and grab hold of a tree or rock, or swim or roll to the side of the avalanche path – and keep your mouth closed. If buried, try to hollow out a breathing space, relax and wait for rescue. Those spared the avalanche **should not go for help** unless it is not more than half an hour away and there is no way of freeing the victims quickly. Avalanche victims can soon suffocate, and it's therefore essential to begin excavation immediately.

If worst comes to worst, and you're near a staffed refuge, **mountain rescue squads** can be summoned from various spots on both sides of the range (see below). They should only be called on in real need, as these helicopter-equipped teams must be paid for and are extremely expensive if you're not insured for them.

MOUNTAIN RESCUE PHONE NUMBERS

There's an ongoing debate about the true utility of **mobile phones** as a mountain safety device. They do have reception in surprisingly remote places, particularly on the top of ridges. But you cannot count on them to be working exactly when and where you need them – especially if they've been damaged in an accident – and they should never encourage you to take chances which you otherwise wouldn't. Do take them along by all means, but they are only an aid to safety, not a guarantee of it.

SPAIN

Navarra ☎112

Aragón ☎112

Catalunya ☎085 (also for forest fires)

Roncal ☎948 893 248

Jaca ☎974 311 350

Stations also at Panticosa, Boltaña, Benasque and Vielha.

ANDORRA ☎112

FRANCE

Western Pyrenees (general) ☎112

Oloron-Sainte-Marie ☎05.59.39.86.22

Gavarnie valley ☎05.62.92.41.41

Luchon ☎05.61.79.28.36 or 05.61.79.83.79

Perpignan ☎04.68.61.79.20

General alpine conditions (Dec–April) ☎08.36.68.04.04

Snowpack and avalanche risk (Dec–April) ☎08.36.68.10.20

Package holidays are often the cheapest way of skiing – you may well find a UK-based deal offering tuition, equipment rental, accommodation and insurance at under £700 for two weeks. In such cases be sure to check the piste diagram in the resort brochure carefully – if a run ends below 1800m it's unlikely that you'll get snow, whether natural or artificial, all the way down. The main destination promoted in Britain is Andorra, though some agents (and ski Web sites, see p.6) offer Núria, Baqueira-Beret, Barèges-La Mongie and Piau-Engaly as well. Whether you arrive on a package or under your own steam (see below), you should take advantage of the slower midweek periods and thus avoid the weekends and major holiday breaks when all accommodation is booked months in advance.

Arranging matters **on the spot**, expect to pay (in Spain) 3000–4600ptas/€18–27.65 for a peak-day **lift pass**, in Andorra 3700–4200ptas/€22.25–25.25 and in France 110–150F/€16.80–22.90 depending on the complexity and quality of the lift and piste scheme – some of the mickey-mouse French resorts can accordingly be very cheap indeed (under 100F/€15.25). Skis, boots and poles typically **rent** for 1700–2000ptas/€10.20–12.00 per peak day in Spain, 65F/€9.90 in France or Andorra. Slope **insurance** tends to be pushed in Spain; at 200ptas/€1.20/day it's probably a good idea if your general travel policy is lacking in this respect. Obviously 6-day passes or long-term rental are more advantageous. In Spain at least, an increasing number of resorts are offering the possibility of arranging on-the-spot **"mini-packages"**. The local tourist office will usually keep literature detailing valley hotels which offer all-in deals of half-board and lift pass which save a good 25 percent compared to doing it "à la carte", even more if you restrict yourself to weekdays.

Cross-country skiing is altogether less costly; for example, at a good Spanish Cerdanyan resort, expect peak-day access to run about 950ptas/€5.70, while in France it's typically 30–43F/€4.60–6.55. Gear rental is also about a third less compared to downhill.

CYCLING

Cyclists shouldn't be daunted by the Pyrenees. You can find plenty of rolling hills and even some almost flat terrain – the Cerdanya/Cerdagne, for example. There are numerous recognized circuits on the French side and recommended routes are marked in yellow on the Randonnées Éditions maps. In the east there are relatively easy tours such as the Circuit des Aspres (85km) and Circuit des Donjons Cathares (105km); in the central zone the going gets tougher, but you can still find fairly undemanding routes through the Baronnies or in the Pays de Sault. On the other hand, if you want to emulate the heroics of the Tour de France riders, there are limitless opportunities, especially within a short radius of the Col de Tourmalet.

On the Spanish side you don't have the same extent of planned routes as in France – though more and more Spanish guides to bike-touring are being published – and the hotter weather discourages all but the hardiest from cycling inland, though you should find company as you get nearer to the sea, particularly on the Santiago de Compostela route.

If you're planning to cover long distances each day, a proper **touring bike** is the best machine, and you should always carry a basic kit of spanners, Allen keys, inner tube, lubricant and puncture repair set. Spare parts are not a problem on the French side – where many large villages will at least have a shop that can carry out temporary repairs – nor are they scarce on the Spanish side in Catalunya, or the more populated parts of Navarra and Gipuzkoa.

A **mountain bike** (abbreviated VTT or *Vélo Touts Terrains* in French, BTT or *Bici Todo Terreno* in Spanish) of course allows you to go hurtling around off-road, but whereas a touring bike's curled handlebars lets you shift riding position occasionally, the straight bars of a mountain bike force you to stay in the same stance, which after a few hours becomes exhausting. Should you want to get off the asphalt, either plan on covering relatively short distances (if you're out of condition mountain-biking will feel scarcely easier than tour-biking over the same slope), lash your mountain bike to your car's roof-rack, or rent one when you get there – the latter an option at plenty of resorts.

Rental rates on the Spanish side currently run to 1700–2300ptas/€10.20–13.80 per day, though the number of rental outlets – plus the quality of machines on offer – seems to be on the wane as more and more Spaniards are buying their own. Most French train stations also rent out bikes, though you'll find better maintained and more current models from specialist outlets (from 80F/€12.20 per day). The best **maps** for cyclists are recommended in "Information and Maps" (see p.27).

If you want to make contact with cycling clubs ask at a **tourist office** or get hold of the *Randonnées dans les Pyrénées* information pack from Randonnées Pyrénéennes, listing all those on the French side.

HORSE-RIDING

As recently as the 1980s there were only a few riding stables in the Pyrenees but nowadays riding is available throughout the range, mostly in the foothills. The classic mount of the high mountains is the native Mérenguais breed – the Ariège is the place to ride these stocky horses, especially the village of **Mérens-les-Vals** south of Ax-les-Thermes or at **Aulus-les-Bains** in the Couserans. There's also a prominent stable at **L'Estanguet** in the Vallée d'Aspe. On the Spanish side, there are particularly renowned stables at **La Miana** in the Garrotxa, as well as two near **Puigcerda** in the Cerdanya. If you're only looking for a day or two's riding, you'll have plenty of opportunities as you tour around. A full day in the saddle should cost around 400F/€61 on the French side, slightly less on the Spanish side, where part-day rates of 2000ptas/€12 per hour are about standard.

RIVER SPORTS

The Pyrenees have plenty of rivers suitable for **canyoning**, **hydrospeed**, **kayaking** and **rafting**, especially in the east of the range and in Aragón around the Ordesa park and the Sierra de Guara.

Canyoning basically involves jumping into a suitably smooth watercourse and letting it take you along, sometimes whooshing down waterfalls, sometimes abseiling down vertical drops, sometimes merely wading through near-freezing water. For the easier rivers you don't need any special abilities or equipment other than a wet suit and knowing how to swim, but tougher sections require helmets, inflatables, ropes and abseiling skills. Obviously it can be dangerous, so unless you know what you're doing, it's best to go in a group led by a professional, who can give guidance and supply the gear (see the box on p.000 for more on this). The undisputed canyoning centre for the Pyrenees, if not all of Europe, is the **Sierra de Guara** though it's also practised in the **Garganta de Escuaín** (both in Spain).

Hydrospeed is the same principle applied to really violent water: you cling to a sort of floating toboggan, wearing a wet suit, padding, helmet and Day-Glo coloured buoyancy jacket. You look stupid, but once you've launched yourself into the waterfalls and whirlpools you don't really care. It's great fun, but can be dangerous, despite the armour. Sample prices in Spain are 6500ptas/€39 for a seven-kilometre beginner's session of hydrospeed.

The Spanish **Noguera Pallaresa** is the most celebrated **rafting and kayaking** river of the whole range, but there are plenty of others, nearly or just as good and scarcely as crowded, where tuition and equipment are also available. These include the drainages of the **Têt**, **Aude**, **Ariège**, **Salat**, **Adour**, **Aure**, **Louron**, **Gave d'Oloron**, **Gave de Pau**, **Ossau**, **Aspe**, and **Nive** in France, and the **Veral**, **Aragón**, **Ara**, **Gállego**, **Ésera**, **Noguera Ribagorçana** and **Segre** in Spain. To help you find every stretch of worthwhile white water, look no further than Patrick Santal's specialist guide *White Water Pyrénées* (see p.544 in "Books").

SCUBA DIVING

While there is a centre or two in Biarritz on the French Atlantic, most Pyrenean **scuba facilities** line the Catalan coast, between Collioure and Roses. These take advantage of the clearer Mediterranean, and in particular the marine reserve off Cap de Creus. There are nine centres on the Spanish side between Roses and Llança, most of them both CMAS and PADI certified and many (in theory) operating year-round on demand. Although many centres only quote rates as part of an all-inclusive package with an affiliated hotel, where available per-dive prices for qualified divers run about 140F/3500ptas/€21, while a full PADI Open Water Diver course will typically set you back 49,000ptas/2000F/€295.

PARAPENTING

The relatively new sport of **parapente** is a blend of hang-gliding and parachuting, the arc-shaped parapente steering something like a hang-glider but having no rigid parts. You take off by running or skiing down a slope until you get enough lift; in 1000m of descent you might cover a distance of 4–6km. In the early days there were frequent accidents but improvements in design and teaching now make it relatively safe, if a bit expensive. You can get a single-flight "baptism" for about 250F–400F€38–61, but a week's course can cost ten times as much and a full two-week course, taking you to a stage where you should be able to go off on your own, costs around 4500F/€685.

Major venues in the central Pyrenees include **Accous**, **Barèges**, **Saint-Lary-Soulan**, **Val Louron**, **Luchon** and **Guzet-Neige** in France,

and **Ager** and **Castejón de Sos** in Spain. Areas near the coast tend to be unsuitable because of the unpredictability of the winds, but **Baigura**, near Saint-Jean-Pied-de-Port in the French Pays-Basques, is beginnning to make a name for itself.

DIRECTORY

FRANCE

ADDRESSES are written as: 18 bis rue Henri-Foucault 1er, which means an annexe or sub-premises of no.18 Henri-Foucault Street, on the first (*premier*) floor. Common abbreviations – used in this book – are pl for *place*, rte for *route*, av for *avenue* and bd for *boulevard*.

BEACHES are public property within five metres of the high-tide mark, so you can kick sand past private villas and land boats on islands but – under a different law – you can't camp on shorelines.

CHILDREN/BABIES are allowed in all bars and restaurants, most of which will offer children's menus or cook simpler food if you ask. Hotels charge by the room – there's a small supplement for an additional bed or cot – and family-run places will usually baby-sit while you go out. You'll have no difficulty finding disposable nappies (*couches à jeter*), baby foods and milk powders, though the latter two tend to be sweetened

and/or very rich. The SNCF charges half-fare on trains and buses for kids aged 4 to 11, nothing for under-4s. As far as entertainment goes, most local tourist offices detail specific children's activities, and wherever you go there's generally a good reception.

CONTRACEPTIVES Condoms (*préservatifs*) have always been available at pharmacies, as well as from many bar or street dispensers (typically 10F for 3–4 condoms), though contraception was only legalized in 1967. You can also purchase (with a prescription) the pill (*la pillule*).

DISABLED TRAVELLERS France has no special reputation for ease of access and facilities, but at least information is available. The tourist offices in most big towns have a free booklet *Touristes Quand Même!* covering accommodation, transport, accessibility of public places and particular aids such as buzzer signals on pedestrian crossings, ramps and trains adapted for wheelchairs.

ELECTRICITY is 220V out of double, round-pin wall sockets. Travellers from Britain and Australasia will therefore need the appropriate three-to-two adaptors for appliances, and North Americans will additionally require a step-down transformer.

EQUIPMENT for skiing, climbing and other mountain activities is more expensive in France than in the USA, but often much less than in the UK, with a wider range available – and you'll find some bargains in Andorran supermarkets.

FISHING You need to become a member of a fishing club to get rights – this is not difficult, any tourist office will give you a local address.

GAY AND LESBIAN LIFE France is more liberal than most other European countries on homosexuality. The legal age of consent is 16 and there are thriving gay communities in many of the southern towns. Lesbian life is rather less upfront. Try to get hold of the annually published country-wide *Gai Pied Guide* (79F/€12 from newsagents or book-shops, or consult *www.gaipied.fr*).

LAUNDRIES have multiplied over the last few years in the bigger towns but are still not the commonest sight along French main streets – have a look in the Yellow Pages under *Laveries Automatiques*. It's a good idea to carry travel soap or cold-water washing liquid so that you can wash your own. If you're staying in hotels, keep quantities small as often it's expressly forbidden to wash clothes in rooms.

LEFT LUGGAGE There are various-sized lockers at all train stations and *consignes* for bigger items or longer periods.

SWIMMING POOLS are well signposted in most French Pyrenean towns and reasonably priced (typically about 16F/€2.45 for a swim). Both men and women may be required to wear a bathing cap – be prepared.

TIME France is always one hour ahead of Britain since the institution of uniform EU Daylight Savings. Except for a few weeks in April and October, French time is six hours ahead of US Eastern Standard Time, nine ahead of US Pacific Standard Time.

TOILETS are called *les toilets* or WC (pronounced "vay say"); *lavabo* means wash basin, not lavatory. Toilets are usually found downstairs in bars or restaurants, along with the phone, but they're often hole-in-the-ground squat-type, and paper is rare. Bar-restaurant and museum toilets are usually free, though ones in rail stations often have attendants or coin-operated locks, so keep a few coins handy.

ADDRESSES are written as: c/Picasso 2, 4° izda. – which means Carrer or Calle Picasso no. 2, 4th floor, left- (*izquierda*) hand flat or office (dcha. – *derecha* – is right; cto. *centro* or centre). Other confusions in Spanish addresses result from the different spellings, and sometimes words, used in Catalan, Aragonese and Euskera – all of which are to some extent replacing their Castilian counter-parts – and from the removal of Franco and other

Falangist heroes from the main *avenidas* and *plazas*. On this latter front, Avenidas del Generalísimo have pretty much vanished all over the country (often changing to "Libertad" or "España"); so too are José Antonios, General Molas, Primo de Riveras, Falanges, and Caudillos. Note that a dwindling number of maps – including some official ones – haven't yet caught up with either local-language or anti-Falangist renaming. In some towns dual numbering systems are also in effect, and looking at the house plates it's difficult to tell which is the old and which the new scheme.

CHILDREN/BABIES don't pose great travel problems. *Hostales*, *pensiones* and *restaurantes* generally welcome them and offer rooms with three or four beds; RENFE allows children under four to travel free on trains, with 40 percent dis-count for those aged four to twelve; and some cities and resorts have special pamphlets on kids' attractions. As far as babies go, food seems to work out quite well (*hostales* often prepare food specially – or will let you use the kitchen to do so). If you're travelling in the winter, however, bear in mind that most Pyrenean *hostales* (as opposed to more expensive hotels) don't have any heating systems – and it can get cold. Disposable nappies and other standard needs are very wide-ly available. Many *hostales* will be prepared to baby-sit, or at least to listen out for trouble. This is obviously more likely if you're staying in an old-fashioned family-run place than in the fancier hotels.

CONSULATES Closest UK consulates to the Pyrenees are in Bilbao and Barcelona; the US is represented only in Barcelona.

CONTRACEPTIVES Condoms (*condones*) and the pill (prescription only; *la píldora*) are available from most *farmacías* and increasingly from vend-ing machines in the trendier bars – Spain has one of the higher European incidences of AIDS (*SIDA*).

ELECTRICITY The current in most of Spain is 220 volts AC; all European appliances should work as long as you have an adaptor for European-style two-pin plugs. North Americans will need this plus a step-down transformer.

EQUIPMENT for the outdoors is easily available in the largest foothill towns, well priced by European standards and in a profusion not always matched in Britain; addresses of the better shops are given in the *Guide*.

FILM Movie-going remains a remarkably cheap and popular entertainment, with crowded cinemas in larger foothill and coastal towns. The majority of what's screened is Hollywood mainstream poorly dubbed into Spanish, but in the biggest cities you'll find some films in their original language with subtitles. Look for *voz* or *versión original* (*subtitulada*), abbreviated "v.o.", in the listings; "v.e." means *versión español*.

FISHING Fortnightly permits are easily and cheaply obtained from any ICONA office – there's one in every big town (addresses from the local tourist office).

GAY AND LESBIAN LIFE Attitudes in the resorts are fairly relaxed, but the nearest thriving gay scene to the Pyrenees is in Barcelona. The age of consent is 18.

LAUNDRIES You'll find a few self-service launderettes (*lavanderías automáticas*) in medium-sized towns like Jaca, Pamplona or Olot, but otherwise they're absent – you normally have to leave your clothes for the full (and somewhat expensive) works. Remember that you're not allowed officially to leave laundry hanging out of windows over a street, though this law is increasingly ignored. A dry cleaner is a *tintorería*.

LEFT LUGGAGE At most important Spanish train stations, you'll find lockers large enough to hold most backpacks, plus a smaller bag, which cost about 300–600ptas/€1.80–3.60 a day. Put the coins in to free the key or key-card. These are not a viable alternative for long-term storage, however, as they're periodically emptied out by station staff. Bus terminals have staffed *consignas* where you present a claim stub to get your gear back; cost is about the same.

SWIMMING POOLS Most Spanish Pyrenean foothill towns – even quite small places – have a public swimming pool, or *piscina municipal* – a lifesaver in the summer and an excellent way to get the kinks out of muscles fatigued from trekking. Admission prices vary, but count on 400–500ptas/€2.40–3.00; remember that the water is almost never heated.

TIME Spain is one hour ahead of the UK all year now that Daylight Savings in the EU (clocks forward end March, back end September) is uniform. Spain is six hours ahead of US Eastern Standard Time and nine hours ahead of US Pacific Standard Time, except for brief periods during April and October.

TOILETS Public ones are averagely clean, and occasionally still squat-style, but very rarely have any paper (best to carry your own). They are most commonly referred to and labelled as *los servicios* (*servei* in Catalan), though signs may point you to *baños*, *aseos*, *retretes*, or *sanitarios*. Damas (Ladies) and Caballeros (Gentlemen) are the usual distinguishing signs for gender, though you may also see the confusing *Señoras* (Women) and *Señores* (Men).

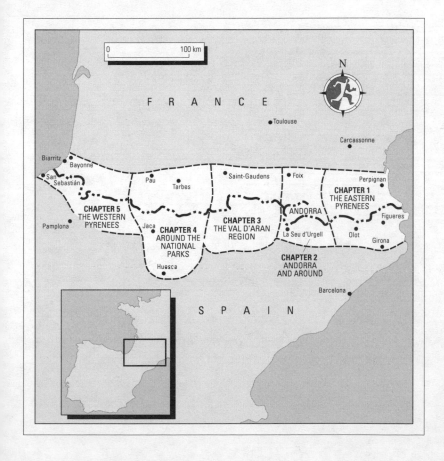

CHAPTER ONE

THE EASTERN PYRENEES

The **Eastern Pyrenees**, despite their comparatively modest height, are among the best-loved and most visited parts of the range. In part, this is due to ease of access – there are busy international airports at Perpignan in France and Barcelona or Girona in Spain – although visitors are also drawn by the ocean-tempered climate and sparkling scenery. The nearby Mediterranean intensifies the light, while the contrast in landscapes – between coastal wetlands and rainless scrub, or low-altitude deciduous groves and orchards and alpine forests – is immense. Given the terrain, there's a correspondingly wide variety of wildlife: waterfowl and upland birds of prey stipple the skies, while the land supports a surprising number of mammals, small and large, not yet eradicated by avid local hunters.

Running along the crest of the Albères section of the Pyrenees, the **border** is breached by just three road passes: the coastal **Col dels Balistres**, the **Col de Perthus** in the middle of the chain – supposedly used by Hannibal, and today the route of the main highway – and the **Col d'Ares** in the west. However, off-road vehicles and hikers can cross east of the Col de Perthus at the **Col de Banyuls**, rather isolated despite its close proximity to the resort-speckled Mediterranean. There are, of course, numerous other footpaths and tracks across the mountains, used by smugglers for centuries and by refugees escaping north during the Spanish Civil War, and south in World War II.

For the **Catalan people** in both Spain and France, the national border is a fiction – even more so since the European Union did away with Customs controls in 1993. Locals regularly cross back and forth on foot or by vehicle, as they always have done with their flocks and contraband. But while the Catalan language (*Català*) is the official language of Spanish Catalonia (*Catalunya*), it's no more than an option in the schools of Roussillon or French Catalonia; there is scarcely any interest in a politically unified, cross-border Catalan state, the universal presence of *els quatre barres* (the red-and-yellow Catalan pennant) notwithstanding. The whole of Catalonia was last under one ruler in the mid-seventeenth century, and the glories of the early medieval Catalan–Aragonese kingdoms are an even more distant memory.

Artificial though the border may be, it's convenient to consider the Eastern Pyrenees as three distinct parts: the **French valleys**, flowing in every direction between the Cerdagne and the sea from the main Pyrenean crest; the **Mediterranean coast**, shared between the two parts of Catalonia; and the more uniformly south-facing **Spanish valleys**.

Perpignan is the only substantial town on the French side and the inevitable transport hub for the French valleys; most visitors head southwest up the parallel valleys of the **Tech** and **Têt**, where congenial towns like **Céret**, **Arles-sur-Tech**, **Prats-de-Molló** and **Prades** serve as handy forward bases. Monumental interest is lent by the medieval fortifications at **Mont-Louis** and **Villefranche-de-Conflent**, defending the Têt approaches to Perpignan, and by such compelling Romanesque foothill monasteries as the **Prieuré de Serrabone**, **Saint-Michel-de-Cuxa** and **Saint-Martin-du-Canigou**. The peak of **Canigou** itself, beacon and virtual logo of the region, offers several approaches and a variety of walking routes.

Because of the precipitous descent of the Pyrenean foothills, the Mediterranean coast is predominantly rocky, the shore road and rail line forging along as corniche

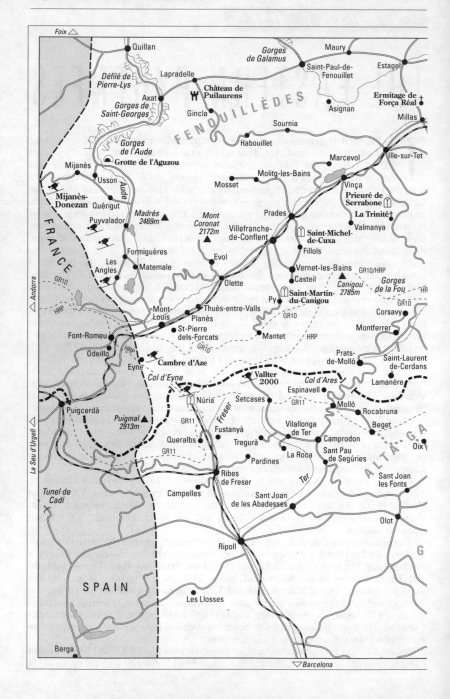

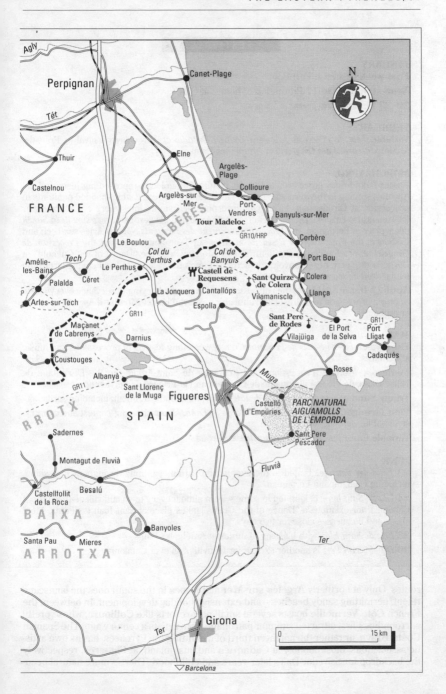

FESTIVALS

JANUARY
First week Festival at Port Bou.
Nearest Sunday to 17 Procession of horses at Olot.
20–22 *Festa de Sant Vicent* at Llança.

FEBRUARY
Variable *Fête de l'Ours* at Arles-sur-Tech; *L'Encadanat*, three-day carnival at Prats-de-Molló; *Mascarade des Grégoires* at Amélie-les Bains.

MARCH/APRIL
Easter Palm Friday procession at Besalú, culminating in locals representing Jesus and the Apostles singing in the town square. On Good Friday, there are white-hooded penitents in procession at Girona, and darker-coloured ones at Camprodon, where a *Via Crucis* or Passion is also enacted. On the French side, the red-and-black-robed *Procession de la Sanch* takes place at Perpignan; the *Procession Nocturne des Pénitents Noirs* at Arles-sur-Tech and Collioure; the *Procession du Réssucité* at Arles-sur-Tech and Céret; and the *Procession de l'Angelet* at Villefranche-de-Conflent. Easter Monday sees the "Dance of the Cuckold" at Cornellà de Terri, near Banyoles, which celebrates the release of local couples from the feudal *droit de seigneur*.
April 23 *Dia de Sant Jordi*, the patron saint of Catalunya. Varying observance everywhere (if only a procession to nearest rural church); observed Easter Monday if April 23 is before or on Easter.

MAY
Third week *Fires i Festes de la Santa Creu*, a week-long festival of processions and music at Figueres.
Pentecost Monday Processions at L'Ermitage de Saint-Antoine in the L'Ermitage de Nôtre-Dame-de-Vie at Villefranche-de-Conflent and at Prieuré de Serrabonne.
Trinity Sunday *Fête de l'Ermitage de lat Trinité*, near Boule d'Amont, including sardanas.
First fortnight, variable Sunday *Festa de la Lana*, sheep-shearing contest and country-style public wedding at Ripoll.
Variable *Curso International de Música* at Girona.

JUNE
23 *Fêtes des Feux* celebrated in the evening on various summits throughout Roussillon, including Canigou and Perpignan.
24 *Dia de Sant Joan*, celebrated in some way in almost every town and village throughout Catalonia; for example, a "Dance of the Giants" takes place at Sant Joan les Fonts. Most shops and businesses close for two days.
25 *Fête de Sant Eloi*, with blessing of mules at Amélie-les-Bains.
29 *Dia de Sant Pere* is another excuse for festivities all over Catalonia.

routes. Only at northerly **Argelès-sur-Mer** and **Roses** in the south does the landscape relent, permitting sandy beaches – and extensive holiday development. In between, the French **Côte Vermeille** boasts several small port-resorts like **Collioure**, whose pretty surroundings first attracted summer patronage from artists a century ago. The Spanish **Costa Brava**, or rather the northern third of it abutting the Pyrenees, has its own artistic associations, most tangibly at **Cadaqués** and, just inland, at **Figueres**, respectively the backdrop for Salvador Dalí's later years and childhood. There's more natural beau-

JULY
Sunday closest to 10 *Sant Cristobal* in Olot, with traditional dances and processions.

Nearest weekend to 14 Taurine sports, sardanas, street bands in Céret.

25 *Festa de Sant Jaume* at Port Bou.

Variable Sardanas at Ripoll and Camprodon; *Salon des Arts* at Quillan.

JULY/AUGUST
Music festivals at Besalú, Cadaqués, Castellfollit de la Roca, Girona, Llança, Prades, Ripoll and Roses.

Regattas of *llaguts* (six-man catboats) and lateen-riggers at Cadaqués.

AUGUST
First fortnight Amateur village violinists and accordionists play strictly by ear at Camprodon.

1–10 *Festa Major*, including the *Chasse à l'Ours*, at Saint-Laurent-de-Cerdans.

6 Annual festival at El Port de la Selva.

10–12 Annual festival at Castelló d'Empuries.

14–15 Festivals at Santa Pau, Darnius, Ribes de Freser and Collioure (where there are fireworks on the water).

23–25 *Fête de Saint-Louis* at Le Perthus.

29 *Fête Folklorique* at Banyuls-sur-Mer.

SEPTEMBER
1 Shepherds' *Festa de Sant Gil*, at the Núria meadows.

First week, especially 5–6 Generalized festivites at Cadaqués.

First Sunday Sheepdog trials at Ribes de Freser.

7–8 Celebrations at Olot, in particular a "Dance of the Giants", and also at Núria.

10 Dance of the *Pabordes* at Sant Joan de les Abadesses.

11 *La Diada*, National day celebrations with sardanas all over Catalunya (Spain).

24 Annual festival at Besalú.

29 Annual festival at Colera.

OCTOBER
7 *Grand Fête Patronale* in Thuir and Amélie-les-Bains.

Second fortnight *Tria de Mulats*, selection of mares and foals by livestock dealers, at Espinavell.

Last week *Fires de Sant Narcis* in Girona; also *Festa de Sant Martiriano* in Banyoles.

NOVEMBER
11 *Foire de la Saint-Martin* in Perpignan.

ty on this part of the coast, too, ranging from the relatively uncrowded coves around low-key holiday centres like **Port Bou** and **Llançà**, to the bird-haunted marshes of the **Parc Natural dels Aiguamolls de l'Empordà**.

Poised just below the Spanish foothills, **Girona** – like Perpignan on the other side of the border – is the staging-post for the nearby valleys; unlike Perpignan, you may well stay longer than planned in what is a charming, manageable city. Following the Fluvià river inland from here – first north, then west – takes you past medieval **Besalú** and

> ### ACCOMMODATION PRICE CODES
>
> Each place to stay in this book has been given a code which corresponds to one of the
> following price categories.
>
> ① Under €13/2200ptas/85F   ② €15–24/2500–4000ptas/100–160F
> ③ €24–32/4000–5400ptas/160–210F   ④ €32–40/5400–6600ptas/210–260F
> ⑤ €40–52/6600–8600ptas/260–340F   ⑥ €52–65/8600–10,800ptas/340–430F
>   ⑦ Over €65/10,800ptas/430F
>
> Category ① refers to the price *per person* of a bed; the other categories correspond
> to the **cheapest available double room in high season**. B&B and HB denote, respec-
> tively, when the price includes breakfast, and when it includes half-board. For more
> details, see p.41.

Santa Pau, and through the volanic **Garrotxa** country, en route to the lively county
town of **Olot**. Climbing higher, medieval religious monuments are integrated into the
very fabric of the small towns, as demonstrated by superb monasteries at **Ripoll** and
Sant Joan de les Abadesses. However, the heads of the valleys seem less densely
inhabited than in France, with only **Camprodon** and **Núria** conspicuous as (pre-)
alpine hill stations.

Most of the Eastern Pyrenees is served well by **public transport**. The international
train line links Perpignan and Barcelona, running along the Côte Vermeille and the
northern Costa Brava before turning inland to Figueres and Girona. There are also trains
along the Têt valley, and from Barcelona to Ripoll and Ribes de Freser – with an extension from the latter to Núria along the incredible *cremallera* rack-and-pinion rail line (see
p.181). **Buses** serve the Têt and Tech valleys, the resorts of the Côte Vermeille, parts of
the Costa Brava and much of the Albères and Garrotxa, though – as ever – services tend
to dwindle near the tops of the valleys on either side of the watershed.

THE FRENCH VALLEYS

Good international and local transport connections make **Perpignan**, 30km north of
the border, the main gateway for the **French valleys** of the Eastern Pyrenees. Once
the seat of a medieval kingdom that straddled the mountains, modern Perpignan is one
of the most vital and multicultural cities of the Pyrenees, thanks to the influence of substantial immigrant communities from Spain and North Africa and a growing university
population.

The favourite routes inland from Perpignan lie along the **Têt** and **Tech** valleys,
respectively northwest and southeast of the Canigou massif. **Prades**, famous for its
summer music held in the medieval monastery of Saint-Michel-de-Cuxa, serves
effectively as the "capital" of the Têt, whose other principal attractions are the fortified
towns of **Villefranche-de-Conflent** and **Mont-Louis**, linked by the touristic **Train
Jaune** – a narrow-gauge, electrically powered train service which spectacularly negotiates the river valley. **Céret**, with its modern art collection, forms an attractive introduction to the Tech watershed, while the spa town of **Amélie-les-Bains** and medieval
Arles-sur-Tech beckon up-valley.

On the tops, an ascent of **Canigou** is essential to any exploration of the Eastern
Pyrenees. It's virtually the sacred mountain of Catalonia, and though it's far from the
highest, the beauty of the approaches to the peak are impeccable as are the views
towards Marseille and Andorra from the top.

Perpignan

PERPIGNAN, the capital of Roussillon or French Catalonia, is the most ethnically diverse city in the Pyrenees. A substantial part of its population is descended from Spanish Catalans who fled Franco's regime at its inception; there is a sizeable Romany contingent; some of the suburbs are settled by French Moroccans and Algerians who fled the independence upheavals of the 1950s and 1960s; and a run-down zone in the centre has become the quarter for native Moroccans and Algerians who moved here in search of a brighter economic future.

Perpignan's medieval walls were demolished in the early 1900s to allow for expansion, and replaced by wide boulevards. This, in fact, maintained the separation of the city's older districts from the new, and it's still easy and enjoyable to get around the compact medieval areas on foot, where a number of interesting monuments and museums will keep you busy. The overriding impression is favourable: the Mediterranean is perceptible to the east, the River Têt skirts the town to the north, while the narrow River La Basse threads through the centre, dispensing welcome greenery along its banks. Between place de la Loge and place Rigaud, where the old streets are now a maze of chic boutiques, you could be on the Left Bank in Paris.

The city has had a surprisingly quiet history. Too far from the sea to serve as a port, Perpignan was a sizeable if unremarkable town until the thirteenth century, when it began to boom as a textile centre. This prosperity was enhanced in 1276, when Jaume II of Mallorca and Roussillon made it his alternate, mainland capital. When that kingdom evaporated the city was absorbed by the Catalan-Aragonese Crown until finally being absorbed by France in 1659.

The City

The marble-paved **place de la Loge** has been the city's forum for eight hundred years, and now lies at the heart of the pedestrianized zone, graced with the most upscale shopping streets in Perpignan. However, the square itself is so small and narrow that you may not realize you've reached it until spotting the voluptuous statue of Venus by Aristide Maillol (see box p.136). Its principal landmark, the 1397-built Gothic **Loge de Mer**, was once the city's stock exchange and headquarters for maritime trade (symbolized by the weathervane in the shape of a medieval sailing ship); the ground floor has now been taken over by a fast-food restaurant, which sits incongruously with the lacy balustrades and gargoyles adorning the upper storeys. The adjoining building is the sixteenth-century **Hôtel de Ville** (with a second Maillol bronze, *La Méditerranée*, in the courtyard) and next door again is the fifteenth-century **Palais de la Députation**, once home to the Roussillon parliament. The square long served as the scene of grisly executions, notably during a Catalan revolt of 1670 against recently imposed French rule. During World War II, place de la Loge's busy pavement cafés were the place to meet *passeurs*, the men – and sometimes women – who guided refugees across the Pyrenees into Spain.

To the north of place de la Loge rises the fourteenth-century, red-brick **Le Castillet**, the emblem of the city, a surviving fragment of the medieval walls and later used as a prison. The adjoining **Porte Notre-Dame** was added in 1478 by Louis XI as the main entrance to the town through its now mostly vanished walls. The whole building, with its massive nail-studded doors and spiral stone staircase, is now home to the **Casa Païral** (daily except Tues summer 9.30am–7pm; winter 9am–6pm; 25F/€3.80), a fascinating and beautifully designed museum of Catalan arts, crafts and traditional culture, with a great view from the roof of the town and distant mountains. The place de Verdun, on the south side of Le Castillet, is the setting for summer evening performances of the

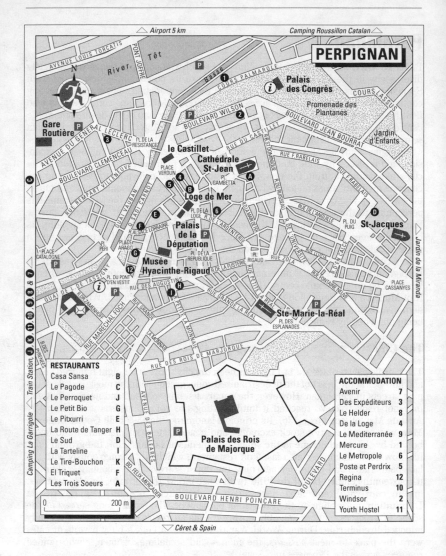

sardana, the solemn and passionate Catalan folk dance (see feature on p.146). Nearby, at 1 boulevard Wilson, is the battered but splendidly ornate **Cinéma Castillet**, the oldest cinema in France, now converted into an eight-screen complex.

A couple of minutes' walk to the southeast of place de la Loge is the **place Rigaud**. Hyacinthe Rigaud – commemorated by a statue in the square – was born in Perpignan in 1659 and went on to become court painter to Louis XIV. The **Musée Hyacinthe-Rigaud** at 16 rue de l'Ange, between place Arago and place des Poilus (Wed–Sun noon–7pm; 25F/€3.80), is dedicated to his work and that of early Catalan masters, but also has a collection of predominantly Fauvist and Cubist paintings by Maillol, Dufy, Picasso and others.

East of place de la Loge, along rue Saint-Jean and across place Gambetta, stands the **Cathédrale Saint-Jean** (Mon & Wed–Sat 10am–noon & 2–5pm, Tues & Sun 2–5pm; free), commissioned in 1324 by Sancho, king of Mallorca (see below), and elevated to cathedral status in 1602, displacing Elne. Adjacent stands the Romanesque St-Jean le Vieux (closed for renovations), the two churches joined by mammoth buttresses. The cathedral exterior sports bands of river stones sandwiched by brick. The interior is most interesting for its elaborate if dimly lit altarpieces and, in the south transept (entry via a separate door), for the polychrome crucifix called the *Dévot Christ*, dating from the early fifteenth century and probably of Rhenish origin.

From the back of the cathedral, rue François Rabelais curves round to **place du Puig** (pronounced "Pooch"), at the core of Perpignan's poor Romany quarter. The area around neighbouring **place Cassanyes** is inhabited almost exclusively by recent arrivals from North Africa, with spoken and written Arabic (plus men in *jalabbiyas* or kaftans) much in evidence. These cramped quarters, littered with refuse and hung with washing, are both cause and effect for the recent xenophobic tilt in French (and local) politics, symbolized by Le Pen's National Front and its allies. Between the two squares, the medieval **church of Saint-Jacques** (Mon & Sun 2–6pm, Tues–Sat 10am–noon & 2–6pm) is the starting point for the Good Friday *Procession de la Sanch* (*sanch* meaning "blood"), a sinister-looking parade of penitents in red or black hoods and robes, bearing images of Christ's Passion. Behind the church lies the secluded and quiet **Jardin de la Miranda** (July & Aug 8am–noon & 2.30–6.30, Sept–June 8am–noon & 2.30–5.30; free), occupying a section of the city's old fortifications and providing an airy respite for the inhabitants of this quarter.

The Palais des Rois de Majorque

Perpignan's most famous sight, and the kernel around which it grew, is the massive **Palais des Rois de Majorque** (daily: June–Sept 10am–6pm; Oct–May 9am–5pm; closed Jan 1, May 1, Nov 1, Dec 25; 20F/€3) on the southern fringe of the old city. The entrance is in rue des Archers, around fifteen minutes' walk from place de la Loge.

The history of Perpignan is more or less synonymous with that of the palace, originally built in the late thirteenth century as a residence for Jaume I of Mallorca, son of Jaume I of Aragón (The Conqueror), who conquered Muslim Mallorca. At his death the king divided his kingdom between his two sons: to the elder, Pere II, went the titles of Count of Barcelona and King of Aragón and Valencia, along with the greater portion of the realm; the remainder, including Roussillon and Mallorca, went to the younger Jaume. The two branches of the family were immediately at each other's throats, and stayed that way until Roussillon was reunited with Aragón and Catalonia during the fourteenth century by the powerful Pere III. Having passed to the French in 1475, then back to the Catalans in 1493, Perpignan changed hands for the last time in 1642, a couple of years after France had occupied Roussillon in the wake of the revolt of the Catalans against the Habsburg rulers of Madrid. In September of that year, after a siege that was at times commanded personally by Louis XIII and Cardinal Richelieu, Perpignan fell. Vauban, military engineer to Louis XIV, constructed the imposing outer walls in the fit of over-enthusiastic fortification that followed the confirmation of French sovereignty by the 1659 Treaty of the Pyrenees.

Perhaps the best aspects of a visit are the Romany buskers in the tunnel entrance, and a view of Canigou from the gardens, which you can enter free of charge. Neither is a ticket needed for a look at the splendid **courtyard**, highlight of the palace, with its two storeys of dissimilar, now-Gothic, now-Moorish arches. The lower of the adjacent piggy-back **chapels** – one for the queen's worship, one for the king's – has elegant marble tracery on its porch. The interior apartments, though, with the exception of the majestic **great hall**, are barely furnished and less engaging: the king's quarters are now occupied by a wine shop, the queen's retaining good period ceilings and windows.

Practicalities

The small **airport**, Aéroport International Perpignan-Rivesaltes (☎04.68.52.60.70), 6km north of town, handles daily flights to and from Paris, as well as daily services from London. The airport **shuttle bus** (*la navette*; 28F/€4.30) makes the twenty-minute trip up to eight times daily, stopping at the bus station (see below), the train station, and the Place de Catalogne; a taxi into the centre will cost around three times the bus fare.

Perpignan's **train station** (☎08.36.35.35.35), at the west end of av Général-de-Gaulle, was once dubbed "the centre of the world" by Salvador Dalí – hence the milestone atop an arch near the entrance announcing "Centre du Monde: 0.0km"; all **long-distance buses** stop outside the station. To get into the heart of the city from here, walk along the avenue, through place de Catalogne, and cross the River Basse at **place Arago**, close by the *quartier de piétonnes* (pedestrian zone) – a twenty-minute hike. The other three key squares, **place de la Loge**, **place Rigaud** and **place Cassanyes** zigzag east-wards, five to ten minutes' walk from each other.

If you arrive by local bus or airport shuttle, you'll be dropped at the **gare routière** (☎04.68.35.29.02), just off av du Général-Leclerc near Pont Arago, a short distance north-west of place de la Résistance. For **city buses**, including frequent buses to Canet-Plage, the CTP kiosk in place Peri (near the *Palmarium* café) supplies information and tickets.

Driving in or around Perpignan is a nuisance, the bypass involving a maddening series of roundabouts. For the old town, drive straight in along the "Route National" and follow signs for the "Centre". There are some enclosed fee-garages, but also free and metered street **parking** on most roads outside of the pedestrian area. The car park of the Palais des Rois is a good option; avoid leaving your car in the seedier areas of the old town.

The **municipal tourist office** (15 June–15 Sept Mon–Sat 9am–7pm, Sun 10am–noon & 2–5pm, otherwise Mon–Fri 9am–6pm, Sat 9am–noon & 2–6pm; ☎04.68.66.30.30, *www.little-france.com/perpignan*) is in the Palais des Congrès, the ren-ovated white building at the end of the leafy Promenade des Platanes which runs par-allel to bd Wilson. There's also a well-stocked **regional tourist office** (Mon 2–6pm, Tues–Fri 9am–12.30pm & 2–6pm; ☎04.68.34.29.94, *www.cg66.fr*) on the quai de Lattre-de-Tassigny, near the main **post office**. There are numerous **banks**, especially between quai Vauban and bd Clémenceau; you can also change money at the main post office, and the *bureau de change* in the train station. If you need a **laundry**, look no fur-ther than Laverie Foch at 23 rue Maréchal Foch (daily 9am–7pm).

Accommodation

For full **accommodation** lists, ask at the tourist office in the Palais des Congrès, or at the information bureau in the train station. Accommodation is quite plentiful in Perpignan, and given its relative distance from the beaches means that even in summer there are vacancies. For a full list of **hotels**, ask at the central tourist office, or at the information bureau in the train station. Cheaper places tend to cluster along noisy

---

INTERSITE CARD

If you are planning to visit more than a few of the castles and museums of the Pyrénées-Orientales, you should consider purchasing an 'Intersite' discount card. For 25F/€3.80, this pass, valid for one month and available at museums and tourist offices, gives you 15–50 percent discounts to 23 museums and monuments in the *département*, including museums in Perpignan, Elne and the most important fortresses and churches of the Tech and Conflent Valleys. If you visited every sight, the total saving would be 177F/€27.

avenue Général-de-Gaulle by the train station, but they're a long way from the sights – central lodgings are more convenient and comfortable.

The well-run **youth hostel** (☎04.68.34.63.32; closed Dec 20–Jan 20; curfews 11am–4pm & 11pm–7.30am; ①) is between the train and bus stations in Parc de la Pépinière, behind the police station on av de Grande-Bretagne; it's clean and friendly but overlooks a noisy main road to the rear. There are two reasonable **campsites**, both with a swimming pool, well signposted from the city centre: the well-amenitied *Roussillon Catalan* on route de Bompas north of town (☎04.68.63.16.92; open March–Oct) and the smaller, more basic *La Garrigole*, west of town at 2 rue Maurice-Lévy (☎04.68.54.66.10; open all year).

NEAR THE STATION

Avenir, 11 rue de l'Avenir (☎04.68.34.20.30, fax 04.68.34.15.63). Unpretentious, simple comfort on a relatively quiet side street. Wide range from singles to family rooms; also has secure parking. ②.

Des Expéditeurs, 19 av du Général-Leclerc (☎04.68.35.15.80). On a rather desolate stretch near the bus terminal, this small place is the absolute cheapest in town, but has a good restaurant. ①.

Le Helder, 4 av Général-de-Gaulle (☎04.68.34.38.05, fax 04.68.34.31.09). Slightly seedy yet two-star, this has a lift and laundry service, plus some of the staff speak English. ③.

Le Mediterranée, 62-bis av Général-de-Gaulle (☎04.68.34.87.48, fax 04.68.34.51.12; *www.hotel -mediterranee.com*). Newish bar/hotel/cyber-café very popular with the backpack set. The building is not stellar and service is laid back. ③.

Terminus, 2 av Général-de-Gaulle (☎04.68.34.32.54, fax 04.68.35.48.16). Old but well kept, this has rooms with and without bath. ③.

IN THE OLD TOWN

De la Loge, 1 rue Fabriques-Nabot (☎04.68.34.41.02, fax 04.68.34.25.13). Beautifully renovated medieval mansion with a central fountain courtyard, on a quiet alley in the old town. Good value for three-star price; air-con in some rooms. ⑤.

Mercure, 5-bis cours Palmarole, edge of old town (☎04.68.35.67.66, fax 04.68.35.58.13). Ideal for families, this has five suites in addition to well-equipped doubles. ④.

Le Metropole, 3 rue des Cardeurs (☎04.68.34.43.34). Basic, backpackers' favourite in a narrow, bistro-lined street not far from the Loge. ②

Poste et Perdrix, 6 rue Fabriques-Nabot (☎04.68.34.42.53, fax 04.68.34.58.20). Nineteenth-century hotel with gorgeous period details, including balconies. One of the better central deals. Closed Feb & March. ③.

Regina, 4 place Arago (☎04.68.34.28.80, fax 04.68.34.92.61). Warm, old-fashioned hotel on Perpignan's best square. The rooms are simple but comfortable, some with TV. ③.

Windsor, 8 bd Wilson (☎04.68.51.18.65, fax 04.68.51.01.00, *www.inter-hotel.com*). Large, modern building with balconied rooms and all mod cons; well located between the Castillet and the tourist office. ⑥.

Restaurants, cafés and markets

Don't dally when pondering **dinner**: most of Perpignan's restaurant shutters seem to roll down at 10pm sharp, though you can get served later at several brasseries which stay open till midnight, including the popular *Arago* and *Café Vienne* in the palm-shaded place Arago, or the Art Deco *Brasserie le Vauban* at 29 Quai Vauban. For a fix of Asian or North African food, head for the eastern side of the old town, particularly rue Llucia, where modest establishments serve up stir-fries and couscous/tajine dishes – you'll find food like this in very few other places along the Pyrenees.

Café life is centred on place de la Loge – call in at *Brasserie de la Loge* or *Grande Café de la Bourse* – and place de Verdun, where the *Grande Café de la Poste*, shaded by huge plane trees, is the best. *Café la Paix* in place Arago is another popular choice but best of all is the huge, airy *Palmarium*, on the opposite side overlooking the River Basse, a downbeat, self-service place, very popular with the locals, where you can linger for hours over a coffee. The *Espi* is the largest of several ice-cream parlours and teashops along quai Vauban.

The daily **markets** in place Rigaud and place de la République offer mainly fruit and vegetables, but the most colourful market takes place on Saturday and Sunday mornings in the tree-shaded place Cassanyes, with a mixture of French, Arab and African traders selling cheap clothes, crafts and all sorts of local produce.

RESTAURANTS

Casa Sansa, 3 rue Fabriques-Nadal. Catalan cuisine served up in this comfortable establishment, popular with students and travellers. Closed Sun. Menus from 49F/€7.50; à la carte 100F/€15.30 and up.

Les Expéditeurs, 19 av Général Leclerc, in eponymous hotel. Cheap if unsophisticated (tripe and other offal) local cuisine, from only 65F/€9.90. Closed Sat evening & Sun.

Le Pagode, 6 cours Lazare Escarguel (☎04.68.33.40.38). Worth the walk past place de Catalogne, this superb Vietnamese restaurant has savoury menus from 98F/€15.

Le Perroquet, 1 av Charles-de-Gaulle (☎04.68.34.34.36). By the station on the north side of the street, with a good choice of Catalan specialities. Closed Wed Sept–April; menus from 55F/€8.40.

Le Petit Bio, 1 rue d'Iéna (☎04.68.51.11.00). The city's only organic food stop, open lunch only (11am–3pm). Menus from 40F/€6.

La Pitxurri, 7 rue de la Poissonerie. Basque specialities here, heavy on the seafood (lots of cod), and elaborate Euskadi-style *tapas*. Menu from 80F/€12.20.

La Route de Tanger, 1 rue du Four St-Jean (☎04.68.51.07.57). Welcoming Moroccan restaurant with the usual *tajines* and couscous as well as more adventurous hybrid recipes. Closed Sun & Mon lunch. Menu 79F/€12.

MOVING ON FROM PERPIGNAN

Perpignan serves as an important transport junction for the entire region. It's also the best place to rent transport if you haven't already done so. For **car rental**, contact Citer, 22 av Général-de-Gaulle (☎04.68.51.09.09); Europcar, 28 av Général-de-Gaulle (☎04.68.34.65.03); or Avis, 13 bd du Conflent (☎04.68.34.26.71). **Bicycles** can be rented at Cycles Mercier, 1 rue de Président-Doumer.

Buses

Several local bus companies (including Car Inter 66 and Car Verts du Roussillon) operate from the *gare routière*; the bus station's information office (daily 6.45am–7.15pm; ☎04.68.35.29.02) supplies timetables and can issue a **Tourist Pass** (150F/€22.90) for eight days' unlimited bus travel around the Pyrenees–Roussillon (bring a photo and your passport). Regular services run south to Argelès and Collioure on the **Côte Vermeille**, where you can pick up the Interplages bus service in summer (linking coastal resorts from Le Barcarès in the north to Cerbère in the south). Along the **Tech valley** there are more or less two-hourly services along the D115 via Le Boulou, Céret, Amélie-les-Bains and Arles-sur-Tech; from Arles there are two connections daily to Saint-Laurent-de-Cerdans, and three daily to the valley's end at Prats-de-Molló. Along the **Têt valley**, there are half a dozen daily buses along the N116 to Villefranche-de-Conflent (where you can pick up the *Train Jaune*); three buses continue as far as Latour-de-Latour-de-Carol, with one detouring to Font-Romeu. Four services a day (except Sun) travel the D612 to **Thuir**, while four daily buses (except Sun) run south on the N9 to the border at **Le Perthus**; from here, a Spanish minibus goes south to **Figueres**.

Trains

Trains run south from Perpignan station to the coast at **Argelès-sur-Mer**, **Collioure** and onwards to the French–Spanish border at **Cerbère/Port-Bou**, where you change for trains to Figueres, Girona and Barcelona. Inland, the train service along the **Têt valley** ends at **Villefranche-de-Conflent** where you have to continue by the *Train Jaune* (see p.115), which terminates at Latour-de-Carol. Northwards, there are services to **Rivesaltes** and **Narbonne**, with connections for Toulouse, Montpellier and Paris.

Le Sud, 12 rue Bausil (☎04.68.34.55.71). Eclectic and delicious Mediterranean cuisine served up in the heart of Perpignan's Romany quarter. No menu, à la carte about 160F/€24.40.

La Tarteline, 10 rue Petite la Monnaie. Delicious home-made quiches and tarts, to eat in or take away. Open midday only Mon–Fri (except hols). Menu at 50F/€7.60.

Le Tire-Bouchon, 20 av Général-de-Gaulle (☎04.68.34.31.91). Small family-run brasserie, best of the lot in the vicinity of the station. Continuous service 7am–9pm; closed Sun. Menu at 70F/€10.70.

El Triquet, 9 rue Lazare (☎04.68.35.19.18). Friendly Spanish-run eatery specializing in Catalan cuisine as well as *tapas*. Menus from 70F/€10.70.

Les Trois Soeurs, 2 rue Fontfroide (☎04.68.51.22.33). Elaborate seafood creations at this cheerful establishment near the cathedral. Lunch menu from 80F/€12.20; otherwise 125–160F.

Entertainment and nightlife

The monthly *Perpignan Mag*, available for free at the tourist office and around town will keep you abreast of cultural events. Perpignan is not a great city for **nightlife**, but during July & August, the town comes alive on Thursday nights with a street festival featuring markets and music. Otherwise there are **"bars-musicals"** scattered across town. Try *Casa Nova*, 8 rue de la Fusterie, for Afro-Cuban music; *La Movida*, 45 avenue Général-Leclerc, for Spanish sounds; or *O'Shannon* at 3 rue de l'Incindie, local headquarters for stout.

The Aude valley

The dramatic, short-lived **Aude** is one of the great rivers of the French Pyrenees, matched in the east of the range only by the Ariège. Rising on the east side of the Carlit Massif, it is restrained for a time by the dams of Matemale and Puyvalador, then let loose to hurtle through gorges by **Quillan**. Just upstream from the gorges, around **Quérigut**, sprawl vast forests of beech and pine interspersed with lush meadows. This is the **Donezan**, a scenic – but poor and neglected – corner of the Ariège. From Quillan, the Aude flows north across the plain to Carcassonne and into the sea between Narbonne and Béziers.

Quillan is linked to Perpignan by a regular **bus** service through Axat and Saint-Paul-de-Fenouillet, and to Carcassonne by both **train** and SNCF bus.

Quillan

Clustered on the west bank of the Aude about halfway along its course, **QUILLAN** makes a handy stopover on the way to the high Pyrenees. The main attraction of this semi-industrialized place is the river itself, a sturdy torrent running right past the town. Canoeing and rafting are organized by the Centre de Séjour Sports Nature de la Forge (☎04.68.20.23.79, fax 04.68.20.13.64) at the south edge of Quillan en route to Axat, which also runs climbing and canyoning trips, and functions as a **gîte d'étape** (①). The only monument of interest is the ruined **castle** on the east bank of the Aude just across the Pont Vieux. Built on the site of a Visigothic fortress, it was burned by Huguenots in 1575 and partly dismantled in the eighteenth century, but the remnants are still worth a scramble.

Train and bus **terminals** are central, opposite the least expensive **hotel** in town – *Le Terminus*, at 45 bd Charles-de-Gaulle (☎ & fax 04.68.20.93.33; ④). All other accommodation is on this same, noisy street, which doubles as the D117. You won't get peace and quiet, but will get comfort for scarcely more money at the *Cartier*, no. 31 (☎04.68.20.05.14, fax 04.68.20.22.57; ④) or the *Canal* at no. 36 (☎04.68.20.08.62, fax 04.68.20.08.27.96; ③). All have attached **restaurants**, though the *Canal*'s closes

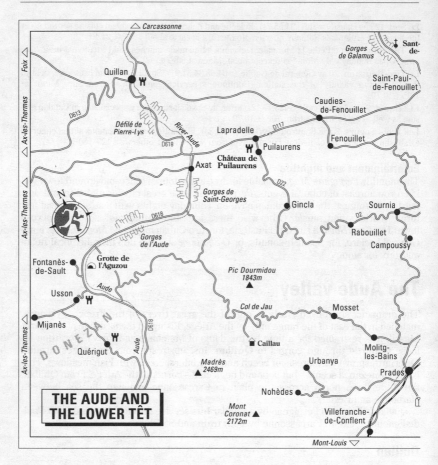

Sunday. *La Sapinette* at 21 rue René-Delpech, off bd Jean Bourrel, is the closest **camp-site**. The **tourist office** occupies a prominent kiosk beside the station (summer Mon–Sat 8am–noon & 2–7pm, Sun 9am–noon; ☎04.68.20.07.78), and can help with Grotte de l'Aguzou reservations (see opposite) among other things.

South from Quillan: gorges and caves

The road **south from Quillan** is a fabulous approach to the eastern peaks of the Pyrenees. Coursing down from the Capcir plateau, the Aude has cut successively through granite, gneiss and schist, and finally soft limestone, carving spectacular cave systems and ever-deeper gorges. Public transport is limited to just a thrice-weekly summer **bus** service to Quérigut, 44km south of Quillan.

Défilé de Pierre-Lys and Axat

Gorge country begins almost immediately after you leave Quillan heading south, with rock overhangs blasted to allow passage. The narrowest bit is the **Défilé de Pierre-**

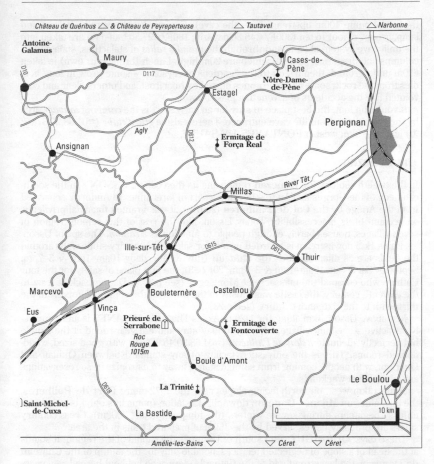

Lys, 8km south, where climbers can be seen swinging above the road. Four kilometres beyond the defile, there's a campsite, *Le Moulin du Pont d'Aliès* (☎04.68.20.53.27; April–Nov; canteen), at the junction where the D117 peels east towards the Fenouillèdes. Just adjacent, Sud Rafting (☎04.68.20.53.73) offers canyoning through the Gorges de Galamus and rafting or hydrospeed through the closer Aude gorges.

Continuing south one kilometre beyond the junction on the D618 brings you to **AXAT**, where an old bridge, under which rafters enter, links the through-road district with the east-bank quarter. There's just one **hotel** here, the *Hôtel de la Poste* (☎04.68.20.59.20; closed part Sept; ④), at 16 route National, the main street.

Grotte de l'Aguzou

If you have sufficient time in this region, try to visit the **Grotte de l'Aguzou**, 15km southwest of Axat towards the upstream end of the Gorges de l'Aude. The guided tour of this magnificent complex is your opportunity to enter the kind of place which normally only speleologists get to see (booking essential, usually several days' notice; contact Philippe Moreno, ☎04.68.20.45.38, *grotte.aguzou@wanadoo.fr*, or at the booth near the petrol pump 400m upstream from the cave). Equipped with overalls, helmet and lamp, groups of four to ten (300F/€45.80 day-trip, 180F/€27.50 half-day) are taken into the unlit cave system at 9am, and through the *grandes salles* of stalactites, stalagmites, columns and draperies, some of which are 20m high. Lunch (bring your own) is taken 600m underground, then it's on to the "gardens of crystals" – some grow in long needles from the rock, some like pine cones dusted by hoarfrost, and others clear and convoluted like the accidents of a Venetian glass-blower.

If you're on foot, the best place to **stay** for an early start is the *camping sauvage* area by the river, 300m from the cave entrance. There's also a *gîte d'étape* (☎04.68.20.37.07; ①) just over 3km west at **FONTANÈS-DE-SAULT**.

The Donezan

In the twelfth century the **Donezan** region and its then capital **USSON** – in the southern neck of the Gorges de l'Aude – became a sort of forerunner to Andorra: separated from the Ariège by the **Col de Pailhères** (2001m), it was granted financial privileges on account of its inaccessibility. Today Usson, like the rest of this remote region of seven villages, houses barely enough people to function as a *canton*. The spa of Usson-les-Bains 1km downstream is boarded up and for sale, while the dry-stone walls around the fields are as dilapidated as the **château** (July & Aug daily 10am–1pm & 3–7pm; Sept–Nov Sat & Sun 10am–1pm & 3–7pm; 20F/€3), the first place of safety for the four Cathars who escaped the massacre at Montségur (see p.243). Dating back at least to the eleventh century, the castle was mostly in the hands of the counts of Foix from the thirteenth to the sixteenth century (see p.239).

Just above Usson, 3km along the D25 to Ax-les-Thermes, **MIJANÈS** is an immensely attractive stone-built village, where you may **stay** and **eat** year-round at the simple but perfectly adequate *Relais de Pailhères* (☎04.68.20.46.97; ③), with good-sized, wood-floored rooms. This is the only such facility of any standard between Quillan and Quérigut, with people coming from some distance away to patronize it, so reservations are advisable at weekends.

Some 13km west, on north-facing slopes near the 1972-metre **Port de Pailherès**, the tiny, nine-run **Mijanès-Donezan** downhill ski station (poma lifts only) is strictly for unfussy beginners during severe winters (the top point is just 2000m). Cross-country skiers are probably better served by the 36km of prepared trails in the area.

These days, **QUÉRIGUT**, 7km south of Usson, is the capital of the region. It stands at the head of a slope of neglected terraces, notable only for the stump of the **Château de Donezan**, the last stronghold of the Cathar leaders, who held out here eleven years after the fall of Montségur. Quérigut makes a good walking base for jaunts southwest through the forest; **accommodation** is at the *Hôtel du Donezan* (☎04.68.20.42.40, fax 04.68.20.47.06; ③), uphill from the church opposite the fountain (also with the only **restaurant**), and the **campsite**, *Le Bousquet*, down by the stream below the village. Usson and Quérigut can be reached on Monday, Wednesday and Friday afternoons by Petit Charles **bus** from Quillan, about an hour's ride in total.

The lower Têt

From Perpignan the **Têt valley** (also known as the Conflent), provides a fast if initially not very scenic route southwest into the Pyrenees. The upper Têt is covered on p.114; the most interesting parts of the **lower Têt** are in foothills north of the valley, and in the region of **Les Aspres** to the east. Nevertheless, there are some pleasant small towns along the N116: **Millas**, **Ille-sur-Têt** and **Prades**, the latter the most attractive and one of the gateways to Canigou.

Buses from Perpignan serve the lower Têt along the N116 roughly every two hours, while **trains** run about six times a day, taking fifteen minutes to reach Millas, 25 minutes to Ille-sur-Têt and 45 minutes to Prades.

Upstream towards Prades

MILLAS, 17km west of Perpignan, appeared in prehistoric times, developed under Roman rule and flourished during the Middle Ages. Unfortunately, the only vestige of this long history is the fourteenth-century village church, with its intricately carved interior. Surrounded by orchards and market gardens with windbreaks of cypress or poplar, Millas is a good place to buy fruit and vegetables, and that's about all that can be said for it.

It's a pleasant stroll out of town to the **Ermitage de Força Réal**, along a footpath which starts about 1500m on the road north to the Col de la Bataille. The hermitage is 4km further, standing atop a low ridge next to the remains of a twelfth-century Aragonese fort. The fort now functions as a radio relay station, and the hermitage as a café, with a huge stone terrace from which to enjoy the view. To the north you'll see the parched Fenouillèdes hills; to the south the equally arid Aspres; to the east the coastal plain; and to the west the steadily rising line of the Pyrenees, with the scrubby Mediterranean vegetation giving way to forests of pine.

Thuir and Castelnou

THUIR, 9km southeast of Millas on the D612, is the main producer of the red apéritif wine called **Byrrh** (pronounced "beer"), stored in what is claimed to be the biggest oak vat in the world. The free 45-minute visit to the winery, located at 6 bd Violet (July–Aug daily 10–11.45am & 2–6.45pm; April–June & Sept Mon–Sat 9–11.45am & 2.30–5.45pm; Oct same hours but closed Sat; Nov–March by appointment only; ☎04.68.53.05.42), includes a tasting – it's rather like sweet vermouth. You can reach Thuir directly by **bus** from Perpignan (4 daily, except Sun), but to continue west to Ille-sur-Têt in the main valley you'll have to drive or hitch. The direct way to Ille is 13km on the D615 (via Corbère-les-Cabane), but it's more interesting to divert southwest first, via Castelnou, 4km from Thuir.

CASTELNOU is a lovely stone village with a tenth-century **château** above, restored after a fire in 1981 and now a museum (daily: Jan, Feb, Nov & Dec 11am–6pm; Mar to mid-June & mid-Sept to Nov 11am–7pm; mid-June to mid-Sept 10am–8pm; 28F/€4.30). Its exterior and view up top are more compelling than the empty rooms within. Just up the street from the town's old gate, *Le Patio* (☎04.68.53.23.30; closed part-Oct & part-Jan), offers Catalan-flavoured cuisine in a relaxed, personal atmosphere at 98–130F/€15–19.80.

The route beyond the village curves through the exquisite low hills of the eastern Aspres, past the picturesque **Ermitage de Fontcouverte**, before dropping down to Ille-sur-Têt, a 25-kilometre journey.

Ille-sur-Têt, Vinça and Eus

Seven kilometres up-valley from Millas, the picturesque medieval quarter of **ILLE-SUR-TÊT** has streets so narrow you have to flatten yourself against the houses if a car comes by. The town's **Centre d'Art Sacré** in the seventeenth-century Hospice d'Illà (mid-June to Sept daily 10am–noon & 2–7pm; Nov to mid-June, Tues–Fri 10am–noon & 3–6pm, Sat & Sun 3–6pm; 20F/€3), has changing exhibitions to show the rich variety of paintings, sculptures, wood carving and precious objects from churches in the region. More remarkable are the clay cliffs just across the River Têt on the road north towards Sournia, which the elements have eroded into extraordinary figures known as Les Orgues, or the Demoiselles d'Ille (March to mid-June Sat & Sun 10am–5pm; second half of June & Sept daily 9.30am–7.30pm; July & Aug daily 9.30am–9.30pm;

20F/€3). Two kilometres south of Ille, at St Michel de Llotes, is the **Musée de l'Agriculture Catalane** (mid-June to Sept daily 10am–noon & 3–7pm; Oct to mid-June daily except Tues 10am–noon & 2–6pm; 20F/€3), an interesting collection of old farming implements and techniques, from beekeeping to winemaking. If you decide that Ille calls for an overnight **stay**, there are *chambres d'hôtes* in rue Pierre Forché – better than the noisy and uninviting *Hôtel du Midi* on the main av Pasteur (☎ & fax 04.68.84.19.60; ⑥). In addition to being a stop on the Têt bus routes, Ille is also visited by a daily bus (not Sun) from Perpignan into the Fenouillèdes.

Eight kilometres upstream, beyond the fortified village of Bouleternère, lies **VINÇA**, a place with few attractions other than **eating** at *Al Cargole*, which features *cargolade* (a mixed grill of snails, lamb and sausage), or *La Petite Auberge*, at 64 av Général de Gaulle, which specializes in trout and *canards gras*. The nearby reservoir provides good swimming, windsurfing and canoeing. If you'd like to have a go at canoeing, contact Base de Canoë-Kayak UDSIS (☎04.68.96.20.33) at **EUS**, the expensively renovated medieval village perched above the Têt, just beyond the reservoir. For a brief but pleasant outing, a one-hour stroll north along an old mule path from beside Eus's church takes you to the derelict hamlet of Comes.

Les Aspres

The gentle hills of **Les Aspres** are best entered by turning south at Bouleternère and continuing through the gorge of the River Boulès; however, there's no public transport. About 8km along, the steeply winding D84 leads 4km west up to the most celebrated Romanesque monument in Roussillon, the **Prieuré de Serrabone** (daily except public holidays 10am–6pm; 10F/€1.50), whose exterior blends with the surrounding rocky landscape. Walkers can get there by following a ten-kilometre route that starts as track just outside Bouleternère, then continues as footpath under the ridge of Roque Rouge. The setting is impressive, and the surrounding flora so lush and diverse that a *jardin botanique* has been created around the priory.

Small slabs of local schist cover most of the plain exterior, and only the short paired columns of the cloister gallery – topped by ornate and amazingly well-preserved capitals – anticipate the richness inside. Halfway along the nave, against the bare walls, stands a fastidiously decorated tribune of rose marble with motifs of flowers and animals mythic and real, which symbolize various aspects of the beliefs and history of the Christian Church. Excavated columns found here suggest that much of the original priory – founded in the twelfth century – was as elaborate as the tribune.

Continuing south for 5km along the D618 through the village of Boule d'Amont brings you to the chapel of **La Trinité**, just before the Col Xatard (752m); it can also be reached in a three-hour walk by footpath from the priory. Superb ironwork adorns the outside of the door, and inside there's a *Christ en Majesté*, a figure of the same type as the *Majestat* at Beget (see p.172).

From Col Xatard, the D618 drops south into the Tech valley at Amélie-les-Bains, 20km away. An attractive option for drivers is to complete a loop back to the Têt valley at Vinça. The road goes through the tiny village of **LA BASTIDE**, which has a *gîte d'étape* (☎04.68.39.41.56; ①), then takes in Valmanya and Baillestavy (see "The Canigou Massif", p.109).

Prades

PRADES, a giant of a town compared with others in the Têt valley, has several singular distinctions. Aside from its pink-marble masonry and pavements, and its status as the birthplace in 1915 of the American Catholic mystic Thomas Merton, Prades also attracts thousands of visitors each July and August for a **music festival** first staged in

1950 by the Catalan cellist **Pablo Casals** (Pau Casals in Catalan; 1876–1973). Casals spent much of his life playing and composing here in exile from Franco's Spain; his works include the oratorio *The Crib* and the popular *Song of the Birds*, after which he named his house. The **Casals Museum** (summer Mon–Sat 9am–noon & 2–6pm; winter Mon–Fri 9am–noon & 2–5pm; free), in the same building as the municipal tourist office (see below), is currently restricted to one large room, filled with photographs and memorabilia, though plans are afoot to move the museum and tourist office to larger premises.

The festival performances take place at the monastery of **Saint-Michel-de-Cuxa**, whose single square tower suddenly appears above a copse of poplars 3km south of town, on the orchard-lined road to Taurinya. Founded by a ninth-century Benedictine community which had abandoned a flooded monastery on the Têt, Saint-Michel reached its peak in the eleventh century, then went into slow decline. In 1790 the foundation was closed, having suffered vandalism during the Revolution, and by the early part of this century more bits and pieces of the monastery were being bought up from nearby villages and shipped to the Cloisters Museum in New York – like many other Romanesque fragments from the region. Restoration began in the 1950s, using original materials wherever possible, and it's now open to visit (daily, except mornings on Sun & hols: May–Sept 9.30–11.50am & 2–6pm; Oct–April 9.30–11.50am & 2–5pm; 20F/€3). Some of the arches now incorporated into the gallery abutting the church were recovered from buildings in Prades, whereas the far side is composed of modern materials, except for the carved capitals.

Back in Prades itself, the church of **Saint-Pierre**, in the main place de la République, contains a huge and sumptuous seventeenth-century retable, a masterpiece by the Catalan sculptor Josep Sunyer. Prades is conspicuously Catalan in feel, hosting a summertime Catalan university (☎04.68.96.10.84) and having established the first Catalan-language primary school in France. On Tuesdays there is an excellent market in the square and surrounding streets.

Practicalities

The **train station** is at the southern edge of Prades, about ten minutes' walk from the centre; **buses** set you down on the RN116 (av Général de Gaulle), which is the main road through the centre. The **tourist office** (July & Aug Mon–Sat 9am–12.30pm & 2–7pm, Sun 9am–noon; Sept–June Mon–Fri 9am–noon & 2–5pm; ☎04.68.05.41.02, fax 04.68.05.21.79, *www.prades.com*), at 4 rue Victor-Hugo, is a mine of information about everything from *chambres d'hôtes* and changing money to walking trails, biking trails and climbing the Canigou. The **music festival office** is next door (☎04.68.96.33.07, fax 04.68.96.50.95). You can rent touring and mountain **bikes** at Cycles Cerda, 114 av Général de Gaulle, or Michel Flament, 8 rue Arago.

For cheap and reasonable **accommodation**, you can't beat the faded elegance of the white-painted, simply furnished *Hostalrich*, at 156 av Général de Gaulle (☎04.68.96.05.38, fax 04.68.96.00.73; ②), still run by a family who were friends of Casals; its spacious restaurant, with a *menu* at 70F/€10.70, also offers the best value in town. The best alternative is *Les Glycines* at 129 av Général de Gaulle (☎04.68.96.51.65, fax 04.68.96.45.57; ⑤), more expensive and rather more bourgeois but spotlessly clean and friendly. The beautifully sited and well-managed municipal campsite (☎04.68.96.29.83; April–Oct), in the valley just east of the town centre off chemin du Gaz, has eighteen well-equipped and reasonably priced chalets for rent by the week or weekend (up to five people), and a great view of Canigou; the nearby *plan d'eau* is stocked for trout fishing, with rods for hire (35F/€5.30 for up to four trout).

If you have a car, you could try **MOLITG-LES-BAINS**, the spa which lies 7km away on the north bank of the river, for **accommodation**. It has plenty of one-star hotels, of which the best are *Hôtel Saint Joseph* (☎04.68.05.00.92, fax 04.68.05.01.62; April–Oct;

⑨), with a good restaurant, and *L'Oasis* (☎04.68.05.00.92, fax 04.68.05.01.62; April to mid-Nov; ⑨), both in the spa sector, and, fifteen minutes away in the village proper, the two-star *Col de Jau* (☎04.68.05.03.20, fax 04.68.05.04.38; ⑨).

Eating out in Prades presents slightly better choices than accommodation: apart from the reliable *Hostalrich* (see above), you could try *El Patio*, at 19 place de la République (closed Wed except school holidays), which serves both traditional and Andalusian-style food for about 120F/€18.30, or *L'Hostal de Nougarols* at Codalet on the road to Saint-Michel-de-Cuxa (closed Tues evening & Wed), serving Catalan specialities at similar prices. Café life is centred on the place de la République, where the *Café de France* has a reputation for the best *plats du jour*.

West from Prades

The D14, through Molitg and beyond, is a quiet and beautiful way of travelling **west to the Aude valley**. The road climbs 5km to **MOSSET**, where you'll find the *Ferme-Auberge Mas Lluganas* (☎04.68.05.00.37; ③ B&B) with rustic accommodation in the farmhouse, or *chambres d'hôtes* in the nearby *La Forge* (③ B&B) and home-cooked meals using their own produce. It then goes over the **Col de Jau** (1504m) where a track leads 5km south to the **Refuge Caillau** (☎04.68.05.00.06; ①), close to the route of the **Tour du Coronat**, a very easy four-day walking circuit in the forests and open hillsides around Mont Coronat. Northwest of the Col de Jau, the road drops 23km through forests of fir to join the Aude at the Gorges de Saint-Georges.

Villefranche-de-Conflent

Beyond Prades the Têt valley narrows dramatically into a gorge 6km further on, where the high walls of **VILLEFRANCHE-DE-CONFLENT** almost block the way. As there's almost no construction outside the walls, the town looks much as it did three hundred years ago: an elongated, two-street place squeezed between the palisade just to the south and the river. Within the ramparts, though, it's something of a let-down; entering through the Porte de France, at the eastern end, or the opposite Porte d'Espagne, you'll be confronted by over-restored houses and shops selling the sort of stuff you regret buying as soon as you're home. The atmosphere of the past is strongest on the bank of the Têt, by the thirteenth-century **Saint-Pierre**; the best view is from the far side, where the weathered red-tiled roofs and the tower of the twelfth-century church of **Saint-Jacques** peer over the ramparts. But more satisfying, perhaps, than any man-made constructions are the vast cave complexes (see below) which riddle the strata below and around the town.

Villefranche dates from 1092, when – the Muslim threat having receded – Guillaume Raymond, count of Cerdagne, granted the charter for the foundation of Villa Libéra, soon called Villafranca and finally Villefranche. His seat was at Corneilla, just up the valley of the Cady, and as the principal menace was now the count of Roussillon, the logical site for a stronghold was here, at the confluence of the Cady and the Têt. Some remnants from that period still stand, notably the **Tour d'en Solenell** on the little square known as the **Placette**. In 1654 Villefranche – then controlled by Spain – was besieged by Louis XIV's troops, and fell after eight days' fighting. After the Treaty of the Pyrenees annexed Roussillon, the French rebuilt the Spanish fortifications, according to plans drawn up by Vauban.

As you walk the **ramparts** (daily: Feb, March, Nov & Dec 2–5pm; April, May, Sept & Oct 10am–noon & 2–6pm; June & Sept 10am–7pm, July & Aug 10am–8pm; 20F/€3), their vulnerability to attack from the surrounding heights is obvious – a defensive weakness that Vauban remedied by adding various bastions and building the upper château now known as **Fort Liberia** (daily: June–Sept 9am–8pm; Oct–May 10am–6pm; 30F/€4.60). Reached by a 734-step underground staircase or a much gentler trail (or by minibus from outside Porte de France, near the Prades–Vernet road – look for signs for *Navette Liberia*), the château has seen more service as a prison than as a fortress, and during World War I it held German POWs.

The caves

The most celebrated incident in Villefranche's history was the 1674 revolt against French rule, which culminated in the betrayal of **Charles de Llar** and his co-conspirators by Llar's daughter Inès. The tale was turned into melodrama by Louis Bertrand in his novel *L'Infante*, published in 1930 and still in print. Llar's hiding place was the **Cova Bastéra**, a cave with an exit inside the walls of the town (daily: July & Aug 10am–8pm; Sept–June 10am–noon & 2–6pm; 30F/€4.60).

A double ticket gains admission to the Cova Bastéra and the limestone formations of **Grottes les Canalettes** (daily 10am–6pm; guided visit 45min; 35F/€5.30), 1km along the road south towards Vernet-les-Bains; the most spectacular caves, however, are the adjoining **Grottes des Grandes Canalettes** which require a separate ticket (April to mid-June & mid-Sept to Nov daily 10am–noon & 2–5.30pm; mid-June to mid-Sept daily 10am–6pm; Dec–Feb Sun 2–5pm or by appointment ☎04.68.96.23.11; guided visit approx 1hr; 30F/€5.30). Entry is via a 160-metre passageway, hollowed out by water over four hundred million years; the water dripping down the sides is now directed over moulds to create limestone images for sale at the shop. Beyond a door you enter a succession of huge chambers (*Blanche, Balcon, Angkor, Dôme Rouge*) crammed with stalactites, stalagmites, pillars and tiny feathery formations. Beyond the *Dôme Rouge* lies the *Gouffre sans Fond* (The Bottomless Pit), stretching for several kilometres and the domain of speleologists only. If you have some caving experience, you can see caves that have not been rigged up with coloured illumination by contacting the Spéléo Club de Villefranche-de-Conflent, in town at 18 rue Saint-Jacques (☎04.68.96.40.35).

Practicalities

The **tourist office** (Feb–Dec daily 10am–12.30pm & 2–5.30pm; ☎04.68.96.22.96) is in place de l'Église; in addition to the usual services, it sells copies of Bertrand's *L'Infante*. There are two **hotels**, *Le Vauban* in place de l'Église (☎04.68.96.18.03; closed Oct–Mar; ③) in the town, and the magnificent old *Auberge du Cédre* (☎04.68.96.05.05; closed Nov–April; ④) situated just east of the old walls. There is also *gîte* accommodation (contact the *mairie*, ☎04.68.96.10.78). There are several more **restaurants** and **crêperies**, most interesting the *Calypso*, also serving vegetarian food, in rue Saint-Pierre, the alley leading down to the Pont Saint-Pierre (and to one of the sets of stairs leading up to Fort Liberia).

To continue along the Têt, simply change platforms at the Villefranche train station to catch the yellow-and-red tourist train known as the **Train Jaune** (see box p.115), which continues to Mont-Louis, Font-Romeu, Bourg-Madame and Latour-de-Carol. **Buses** run south to Vernet-les-Bains (Mon–Sat 7 daily, Sun 3 daily) from outside the train station or from the route Nationale stop just outside the town walls at Porte de France.

The Canigou Massif

Rising to a height of 2785m between the Tech and Têt valleys, **Canigou** (*Canigó* in Catalan) is the great landmark of Catalonia, visible across the Empordà plain from the beaches of the Costa Brava and across the Roussillon lowlands from the Côte Radieuse. However, Canigou is not the highest mountain in Catalonia, nor even in the immediate area: a little to the west there's a whole group of greater peaks, including Pic de Prats de Bassibès (2845m) and Pic du Géant (2882m). Although situated well inside France, it symbolizes a Catalan unity endorsed by the small Catalan flags and other patriotic paraphernalia festooned from its summit cross.

There are essentially only two ways of reaching the top of Canigou – via the **Chalet Cortalets** (2150m) on the northern slopes, or via the **Refuge Mariailles** (1718m) to the southwest. The various bases from which to approach these shelters are detailed below. Routes from the Tech valley to the south are longer and therefore not specifically recommended for climbing Canigou – although you might use them to move from the Tech to the Têt, taking in Canigou along the way. If you're serious about exploring the massif – which is a partly protected natural reserve, good for several days' trekking – either the 1:50,000 "Canigou/Vallespir/Fenouillèdes" *carte de randonnée* published by IGN, or the TOP 25 1:25,000 **map** no. 2349ET "Massif du Canigou", is a mandatory investment, available at shops and souvenir stalls in most of the surrounding villages.

Northern approaches to Canigou

The northeastern route up Canigou is the quiet and impressively steep (but not difficult) approach from **Valmanya**. To its northwest, a 4WD track from near **Prades** is the scenic but busy alternative.

The Valmanya route

From Vinça in the Têt valley (see p.106) the D13 follows the River Lentilla south along the eastern flanks of Canigou, past Finestret (4km), your last chance to stock up at an *épicerie* for a while. From here the **GR36** cuts through the wooded slopes and fields of the valley, rejoining the road at **BAILLESTAVY** (12km from Vinça), where there is a twelve-berth *gîte d'étape* (☎04.68.05.82.03; ①). As the russet streaks on nearby rocks suggest, the Canigou massif is rich in iron ore; there's a mine above the village and traces of a first-century forge by the river.

The Resistance stronghold of **VALMANYA**, another 5km by road or GR trail, was destroyed by the Germans in 1944 – some of the houses were reduced to rubble, others set ablaze. Despite rebuilding and the magnificent setting at 900m, there's a lingering sadness to the place; it has no hotel and just one seasonal bar. For the ascent of Canigou, it's best to **camp** rough beside the river just beyond the hamlet of Los Masos, 2km past Valmanya (don't confuse this with the Los Masos near Prades).

From Los Masos, the **GR36** climbs sharply through woods more used by isards than walkers, to the awesome drop at **Ras del Prat Cabrera** (1739m), where it joins the track from Villerach, near Prades, and more attractively the **GR10**, which traverses a bit higher via la Tartère to the *Chalet des Cortalets*. Alternatively you can head south from Valmanya on a minor trail to pick up the GR10 at the forestry hut at **Estagnole**. You could just about make the return trip from Valmanya to Canigou's summit in a day but it's more manageable with a night at or near the refuge.

The Prades route

The gentlest ascent to *Chalet des Cortalets* is the one used by the 4WD-taxis (roughly 150F/€22.90 per person) from Prades; booking offices in Prades include Amalric Sports Shop (☎04.68.96.26.47) and La Bohec (☎04.68.05.20.48). If you're driving, take the D35 out the south side of Prades to Villerach (8km; signposted as "Clara-Villerach"), where a dirt track rises to the chalet 20km away – an hour's drive. (If you're on foot, there are much better hiking approaches – for which read on.) This is a superb approach, often running close to the River Llech, each turn revealing a new arrangement of rock, water, sky and forest. An ordinary car can easily get as far as the ruined hut at Prat Cabrera (1650m), an hour's walk from the *Chalet des Cortalets*, and – with extra care and ideal conditions – all the way to Cortalets.

Northwestern approaches: Vernet-les-Bains and around

More direct footpaths from the northwestern side begin from Fillols and Casteil, both above Vernet-les-Bains, the closest proper town to the massif. Seven buses a day come from Perpignan through Villefranche to **VERNET-LES-BAINS**, the most pleasant of the spas around Canigou, though it's still somewhat stuffy. English visitors like Rudyard Kipling made the place fashionable during the last century and a waterfall, 3km out of town on a well-marked track, is even called the **Cascade des Anglais**. Along with the thermal plunge-pools and adjoining therapy wings – first installed in 1377 – a range of more contemporary pastimes are now offered (mountain biking, canyoning, hydrospeed and caving), though the baths are still the focus of activity. Visitors intent on these and nothing else often overlook the old quarter's warren of alleys, capped by the ninth-century but much-restored double church of **Nôtre-Dame-del-Puig/Saint-Saturnin**, which incorporates remaining bits of a castle. You can also visit the town's geological museum (April, May & Oct Wed–Sun 10am–noon & 2–6pm; June–Sept 10am–12.30pm & 2.30–6.30pm; 20F/€3), which has a collection of local *silex* and other fossils.

Vernet has a *gîte d'étape* (☎04.68.05.53.25; ①) in chemin St-Saturnin, on the left bank of the Cady next to the municipal pool. The town's three two-star **hotels** each offer a range of amenities such as television and parking but are basically indistinguishable apart from the *Eden*, 2 promenade du Cady (☎04.68.05.54.09, fax 04.58.05.60.50; ⑤), which is the cheapest. The *Moderne*, 7 av des Thermes (☎04.68.05.52.17, fax 04.68.05.66.64; ⑤), and the *Princesse*, rue de Lavandiers (☎04.68.05.56.22, fax 04.58.05.62.45; ⑤) offer essentially the same comfortable, if not unexceptional, accommodation. There are plenty of **campsites** too: nearest are *Les Cerisiers* (☎04.68.05.60.38; June–Sept), on the same side of the river as the *gîte*, and *Dels Bosc*, 1km north on the Villefranche road (☎04.68.05.51.62; March to mid-Oct). **Eating out**, you can easily spend a fortune dining on wood-roasted meats and tasty home-made desserts in the elegant surroundings of *Le Cortal* (closed Mon and Oct & Nov), up in the old quarter behind the church at rue de Château. Down in the modern town, best value of about five restaurants is *L'Escapade* on av des Thermes.

The **tourist office** is quite central, on place de la Mairie, near the corner of bd Lambert-Violet and rue du Canigou (Mon–Fri 9am–noon & 2–6pm; ☎04.68.05.55.35, fax 04.68.05.60.33). **4WD-taxis** up Canigou (same price as from Prades) can be arranged just 50m from the *d'Angleterre*, or through Taurigna (☎04.68.05.54.39).

The Fillols routes

The standard **walking ascent** from Vernet is by a footpath that begins 1km northeast along the D27, towards the tiny village of **FILLOLS**. Climbing 1km within three hours to the **Refuge de Bonneaigue** (Bonaigua; 1741m), the path joins the **GR10** to the *Chalet des Cortalets* after another two hours; the eight-person Bonneaigue hut is very primitive, and the adjacent spring often dries up.

For those with a 4WD or a very sturdy car, a track begins some 5km from Vernet, just past Fillols; this route is also used by taxis from the two villages – you can book one at the *Café de l'Union* in Fillols (☎04.68.05.63.06), as well as arrange a meal. The track rises gradually at first, past the *Les Sauterelles* **campsite** (☎04.68.05.63.72; open June–Sept), then with dramatic steepness in a series of tight hairpins to the large **Refuge de Balatg** (1610m), the derelict *Cabane des Cortalets* (1975m), and finally the chalet itself. This isn't as pretty a route as that from Prades – and the poorer surface makes it inadvisable for much-loved cars – but a more open topography on the north face of the massif produces awesome views.

Casteil – and Saint-Martin-du-Canigou

From Vernet-les-Bains the paved road leads 2500m south to **CASTEIL**, where you can eat and stay at either *Relais St-Martin* (☎04.68.05.56.76; ③), or the more picturesque two-star *Molière* (☎04.68.05.50.97, fax 04.68.05.55.11; ⑤), with a delightful summer restaurant in the apple orchard. There's also a *gîte d'étape* (☎04.68.05.51.30; ①) and a campsite, *Camping St-Martin*, (☎04.98.05.52.09; April–Sept) with a swimming pool. If you're lucky, you'll coincide with one of the four daily buses from Perpignan, via Villefranche-de-Conflent (Mon–Sat). Casteil is an appealing, quiet hamlet, well placed for Canigou and the GR10, the latter less than an hour away on the **Col de Jou**, accessible by a delightful short trail designated "Itinéraire 1" which shortcuts the road. On the ridge just east stands the restored twelfth century **Tour de Goa**, reached by another path from the *col* which eventually drops to the spa at Vernet.

But you're more likely to visit Casteil for the nearby monastery of **Saint-Martin-du-Canigou**, whose image is ubiquitous, celebrated on local book covers, postcards and posters. Access is only by a thirty-minute climb up the path, or 4WD from Casteil on a steep, narrow road, which helps protect the place from the worst tour-bus excesses – as does its continued use by an active religious community.

Built from tan stone and roofed with grey slates, the monastery ranks as one of the most gorgeous monuments in the Eastern Pyrenees, and the surrounding woods of sweet chestnut, beech and aspen form a perfect backdrop to the pinnacle of rock on which it stands. The foundation stone of the building was laid in 1001 by Count Guifred de Cerdagne, who retired with his second wife Elisabeth to the monastery in 1035; you can see their purported **sarcophagi** at the base of the tower. Severely damaged by an earthquake in the fifteenth century – the tower lost a storey – and thoroughly pillaged after abandonment in 1782, Saint-Martin was restored in two phases (1902–32 and 1952–82), initially through the efforts of the bishop of Perpignan. The glory of the place resides in its **cloister capitals**, retrieved by the good cleric from a particularly wide dispersal.

The monastery is now occupied by an unusual mixed order of monks and nuns, called the "Beatitudes", with a sprinkling of lay workers. Ordinarily, visitors are allowed only on silent, **guided tours** (departures every 60min: June to mid-Sept 10am–noon & 2–5pm; mid-Sept to May 10am–noon & 2.30–4.30pm; 20F/€3). The "Beatitudes" sponsor extended retreats by individuals (write to the abbey at 66820 Casteil, or phone ☎04.68.05.50.03), but your Christian beliefs had better be genuine – before 1988, the order styled itself as that of the "Lion of Judah and the Immolated Lamb".

Descending from the rear of the complex, you can take an alternative marked footpath for half an hour back to Casteil via the entrance to the **Gorges du Cady**, where the river falls 500m over a distance of 3km, making this a popular spot for canyoning.

Saint-Martin to Mariailles or Cortalets

At the rear of the monastery grounds another path leads up to a signposted viewpoint. You can continue on the path, an excruciatingly steep but shady, beautiful and well-marked route, for four hours to the **Col de Segalès** (2040m) on the GR10. Despite the grade, this provides the most direct all-trail access from the Vernet area to the staffed *Refuge Mariailles* (see opposite), another two hours of up-and-down trekking, south of the *col* by a roundabout route. The two-and-a-half-hour traverse north to the *Bonneaigue* shelter and then to *Cortalets* is quite scenic and a bit more direct, but again there is a fair bit of roller-coastering and a short stretch of track-walking. Many people prefer to do the Saint-Martin-to-Cortalets leg in reverse, as part of an east–west traverse of the massif, beginning from Valmanya or Batère (for which see pp.110 & 126).

Cortalets to the summit

A *maquisard* hideout in the last war, and consequently heavily shelled by occupation forces, the restored **Chalet des Cortalets** (☎04.68.96.36.19; open May–Oct; other times emergency shelter only; ①) is now run by the Club Alpin Français. There are double rooms as well as beds in the **dormitories**; **meals** in the bar-restaurant cost about 70F/€10.80. The smaller shelter adjacent, with no bunk linen provided, costs half as much as the dorms. Be warned that the main lodge can get overcrowded, and the tracks bring up cars full of revellers – as opposed to walkers – at weekends to picnic at the tables around the little lake, ten minutes' walk west of the refuge. **Tents** are tolerated on the lake shore, and next to another smaller pond closer to *Cortalets*.

The summit

The normal, well-marked approach **to the summit** goes past the larger lake, with its fine view up into the summit cirque, then climbs south along the ridge connecting with the **Pic Joffre**, which often teems with isards at sunset. It takes about ninety minutes and provides only a slight sense of exposure as you reach the wrought-iron summit cross and *table d'orientation*. Even though it's the getting to the top – rather than standing on the peak – that makes Canigou so memorable, the views taking in everything from Andorra to the sea are wonderful.

At midsummer (observed in Catalonia on the eve of June 23–24, the *Festa de Sant Joan*), the refuge and the peak are spots to avoid or gravitate towards depending on your temperament: seemingly half the population of Barcelona descends for merrymaking and the lighting of the traditional bonfire, a flame of which is then relayed to ignite numerous others in Catalan villages on both sides of the frontier. Even at other times, a patriotic Catalan or two is prepared to bivouac the night beside the peak's highest cairn.

There is an alternative, less frequented and even more dramatic route, climbing south from the *Cortalets* chalet along the **Crête de Barbet** to the **Porteille de Valmanya** (2591m), a beautiful ridge walk that becomes nerve-wracking beyond the *porteille*, where the route drops along a narrow cleft, leaving you to clamber over boulders to the summit (2hr 30min). The Pic Joffre and Barbet routes can, of course, be combined to make a circuit.

Southwestern approaches: the Rotja valley

To tackle ascents of Canigou **from the southwest**, take a bus from Prades or Villefranche (Mon–Sat 1–2 daily) along the **Rotja valley** to Sahorre.

PY, 6km upstream, remains a traditional mountain village – certainly compared to more-visited Casteil or Mantet (see below) – but even here there are plenty of houses for sale, and signs of seasonal occupation. So far the only concessions to tourism are a horse-riding stable, one *gîte d'étape* (☎04.68.05.66.28; ①) and a combination café-restaurant-*épicerie* with a few rooms to rent.

The usual approach to Canigou from Py is to follow the **GR10** northeast to the **Col de Jou** (1125m), then take the track (recently made suitable for saloon cars, somewhat shortcut by the onward GR path) to the large and comfortable **Refuge Mariailles** (☎04.68.96.22.90; 1718m), four hours on foot from Py. After a night at *Mariailles*, take the GR10 south then east into the forest, climbing to the **Col Vert**, then dropping to the Cady valley. Shortly afterwards the footpath heads west, then north, roller-coastering to the *Chalet des Cortalets* – an attractive route covered on the preceding page.

The direct way to the **summit** from this side, though, is to continue east along the Cady valley, past the simple, unstaffed *Refuge Arago*. From there the route climbs north to the **Porteille de Valmanya** (2591m), then along the line of the ridge (keep below it – the view over the other side is frightening) and up an easy gully to the summit.

Mantet

From Py the paved road climbs steeply southwest through countless hairpins, many of which can be bypassed on the GR10, though generally it's a dull, steep hike. When you reach the **Col de Mantet** (1761m), three hours' walking from Py, a glorious wilderness unfolds before you: the village of Mantet is invisible, clinging to the hill 200m below the *col*, while further south spreads the beautiful Alemany valley, its eastern flank covered in pines. The far end of the valley, where the **Porteille de Mantet** (2419m) leads into Spain, is the preserve of isards; currently protected by *réserve naturelle* status, it is threatened by development from the local Caisse d'Epargne.

The inhabitants of **MANTET** were expelled by the Nazis towards the end of World War II, and it wasn't until the 1960s that the village was resettled. It's since been expensively restored for holiday homes, and despite having only twenty or so permanent inhabitants, Mantet supports an *auberge*, *Chez Richard* (☎04.68.05.60.99; ⑤ HB), and a *gîte* run by the owner of the stable *La Cavale* (☎04.68.05.57.59; dorm ①, rooms ④). There are also two **hotels**, the *Bouf'tic* (☎04.68.05.51.76; ④ HB), with the liveliest bar in the village, and *La Girada* (☎04.68.05.68.69; ③), specializing in adventure sports.

Walks around Mantet

From Mantet the most spectacular **route up Canigou** involves climbing through the woods southeast from the Col de Mantet to the **Pla Segala** (2200m), and then along the ridge to **Roc Colom**. From there you can pick up the **HRP** and follow it along the line of rock teeth known as the *Esquerdes de Rotja* to **Collade des Roques Blanches** and then **Pla Guillem** (2277m), where there is a simple, unstaffed refuge. It's already a long day but if you still have daylight and strength, the *Refuge Mariailles* – a ninety-minute descent further – is a lot more congenial.

Canigou aside, this is a great walking and riding area. Especially worthwhile treks are south along the **Ressec valley** (east of the main Alemany valley) to the source of the Mantet stream (4hr), and along the **Caret valley** (west of the Alemany), with its groups of ruined stone cottages and shady riverside path. The **GR10** climbs from the Alemany valley west over the **Col del Pal** (2294m) into the **Carança gorge** (5hr from Mantet; staffed summer refuge about halfway along). From here, if you don't stick with the GR10 until Mont-Louis, you can head north down the valley for Thuès (see p.116) or south into Spain at Núria (see p.181).

The upper Têt

The lower Têt finishes at Villefranche-de-Conflent, above which the shaggy flanks of the **upper Têt** close dramatically around the *Train Jaune* line and the N116, which forge separately along the river to Mont-Louis, at the top of the Têt. En route there are a number of small villages, on the valley floor or perched just above, which make serviceable bases for excursions into the hills. Of these, the hot springs and no-nonsense **Carança gorge** near **Thuès**, and the **Mont Coronat** area north of **Olette**, are the most rewarding.

Many of the **abandoned villages** on the upper and lower slopes of the Têt valley have become home to colonies of ageing hippies and "travellers" (the modern, punkified version). The presence of these mainly non-French interlopers in this isolated and conservative mountain society still causes some tension, but most locals have grown accustomed to their flamboyant appearance and accepted them in the quiet spirit of rural *convivencia*. At any rate, these settlers, frequently seen operating market stalls in lower-altitude centres, are here to stay – after more than twenty years of continuous habitation they have acquired legally binding "squatter's rights" to their properties and cannot be removed from the hamlets, many of which still lack utilities or any other municipal services.

Excursions around the valley

Most of the villages along the Têt valley aren't really worth leaving the train for, but they do give access to a number of marvellous hikes. Alighting at Serdinya, for instance, you could hitch the 7km south to **ESCARO** with its *gîte d'étape*

(☎04.68.97.01.77; ③) for the three-stage **Tour des Tres Esteles**; accommodation for the other overnight stops is available in Py and Mantet (see pp.113–114).

At **OLETTE**, the next stop, you can stay comfortably at *La Fontaine* (☎04.68.97.03.67; ③), on the main street. Incidentally, Olette is also home to the only grocery stores until Mont-Louis. From Olette it's a two-hour hike northeast to **JUJOLS**, where you can start the four-stage **Tour du Coronat**, a waymarked trip around the **Mont Coronat** massif. You could use the *gîte d'étape* (☎04.68.97.02.40; ①) in Jujols overnight, but the *gîte* at Urbanya (☎04.68.96.29.92; ①) can only be booked for stays of a week or more, so unless you plan on staying that long, you'll have to camp out for three nights.

An alternative from Olette is to hitch or walk a couple of kilometres north to **EVOL**, where the church of **Saint André** contains a splendid painted retable by the so-called Maître du Roussillon, dating from 1428. The massive ruined **château**, just above the village on the pot-holed road to the Col de Portus, was built in 1260, at a time when security from potential Muslim raids was still considered necessary. At the *col* (1736m) you can join the Tour du Coronat or climb northwest to the lakes known as the **Gorg Estelat** and **Gorg Nègre**, situated at the foot of the gentle **Pic Madrès** (2470m). The lakes are served by the basic *Refuge de Nohèdes*, beyond which rises **Roc Nègre**, a tough but not technically difficult approach to the summit.

Between Olette and Evol the D4 peels off into the tranquil **Cabrils valley**, a longer but more attractive road to Mont-Louis and the Capcir than the Têt route. The going is fairly tough for cyclists – the **Col de la Llose** rises to almost 1800m – and chances of a lift aren't good, so it's better left to those with transport.

The Carança gorge area

A few minutes past Olette on the *Train Jaune* at **NYER** (*Camping La Catalane*; ☎04.68.97.07.63; open all year), the road south from the station to the village climbs into

---

THE TRAIN JAUNE

The best way to move up the Têt valley towards the Cerdagne is on the **Train Jaune**, once an essential local service, but now more of a fun ride – during summer some carriages are open-air. Built in the early twentieth century, the railway climbs 63km from Villefranche (427m) to Latour-de-Carol (1231m), where it connects with the Transpyrenean railway (Toulouse–Barcelona). Tourism saved the scenic narrow-gauge line from closure in the early 1970s, but a yearly repertory melodrama still features threats of funding cutbacks, counter-protests and a general air of future uncertainty. As it is, return tickets are valid for only 24 hours, with **fares** double those of French main-line services; as an example, Villefranche to Mont-Louis and back (the most popular stretch) will cost at least 98F/€15.

From late May to September there are four to six daily **departures** in each direction; the first leaves Latour-de-Carol soon after 8am, and takes two and a half hours to reach Villefranche. For the rest of the year service is cut to two round-trips. Since most of the line is single track, there are often delays caused by long halts at Mont-Louis or Font-Romeu to allow the uphill train to pass, the first of these leaving Villefranche well before 8am. The train is scheduled to stop only at certain stations, designated in capital letters on the timetables and train maps; if you want to alight at one of the smaller, unstaffed stations (designated *arrêts facultatifs* on carriage placards) you have to notify the driver, otherwise the train will chug on past. Similarly, to get on at such stations, you have to flag the train down.

For information on timetables and prices, contact the following stations: Villefranche-Vernet-Fuilla (☎04.68.96.56.62); Mont-Louis (☎04.68.04.23.27); Font-Romeu (☎04.68.30.03.12); Bourg-Madame (☎04.68.04.53.29); or Latour-de-Carol (☎04.68.04.80.62). You can also call the main information number (☎04.68.96.56.62) or consult *www.ter.sncf.fr/trjaune*.

the impressive Gorges de Nyer. You can eat in Nyer at *Castel Val*, installed, as the name implies, in a small château; the gourmet restaurant features trout and quail for 90–120F/€13.70–18.30.

However, you're probably better off staying on the train until Thuès-Carança station, four minutes above the small spa of Thuès-les-Bains and gateway for the even more spectacular Gorges de Carança. The nearby village of **THUÈS-ENTRE-VALLS** is home to a delightful **gîte-campsite**, *Mas de Bordes* (☎04.68.97.05.00, fax 04.68.97.11.51; ①), next to the church – follow signs up the path from the train stop or the main road (N116). This restored farm is part of a 300-hectare property which includes its own outdoor hot springs, a remote log cabin and a meadow for pitching tents. The place is always mobbed during July and August, when you must ring ahead, but it's worth trying to fit it into your plans for a night or two. Good *table d'hôte* dinners are provided for about 80F/€12.20, a blessing since the village itself is not up to much.

The **Gorges de Carança** is clearly signposted from the train station and from Thuès village, and more notices at its mouth (over which the Train Jaune clatters on a bridge) advise you to enter at your own risk. After a short walk from the car park, the path divides: the left-hand path (signposted for Roc Madrieu) climbs steeply up the wooded side of the valley, while the right-hand path (over a small bridge) follows the more spectacular cor-

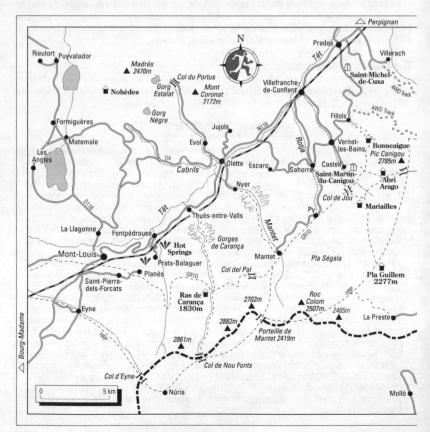

niche route; the two converge at the *pont des singes* (suspension bridge). The first ninety minutes of corniche walkway are the most amazing, poised over sheer four-hundred-metre drops – not for the vertigo-prone. Next are a series of nerve-wracking catwalks, ladders and wobbly metal suspension bridges, the latter not advisable for heavily laden walkers.

Yet the overall climb towards the border is the gentlest around, so the canyon makes a popular outing: start off early to beat the crowds and the heat. Beyond the narrows, the route becomes a shady, streamside trail on the west bank; the countryside opens out, and you reach **Ras de Carança** (1830m), with its summer-staffed refuge, in about three-and-a-half hours. The twelve-bunk refuge offers very simple food, and there's plenty of camping space nearby. To reach the first of a series of lakes – the easternmost along the main Pyrenees crest – requires another ninety minutes, while the border at Col de Nou Fonts, opening towards Núria, is four hours distant and thus beyond the scope of a day-trip from Thuès.

On to Planés

If you're a fan of hot springs, you can leave the train at **Fontpédrouse** station, the stop above Thuès-Carança, and follow the twisty road up towards the village of **PRATS-BALAGUER** on the south slope. From the second hairpin, you'll find a path that leads

THE UPPER TET, THE TECH AND CANIGOU

east down to a trio of open and undeveloped **thermal pools** on the far side of the valley. Alternatively, head for the large, beautifully renovated, open-air thermal baths at **SAINT-THOMAS-LES-BAINS** (daily 10am–8pm, July & Aug until 9pm; 20F/€3), 3km from Fontpédrouse station, open all year round for a hot sulphurous dip and jacuzzi after skiing or hiking.

Just before Planès, the *Train Jaune* passes over the 150-metre-long **Pont Gisclard** suspension bridge, which carries the track 80m above the river. It was designed early this century by mathematician and engineer Albert Gisclard, who was tragically killed by a runaway train on the very day of the official bridge trial in 1909. The peculiar triangular church at **PLANÈS** was once thought to be an adapted Muslim structure, but the belltower is typical of the Cerdagne, and the dome surrounded by three semicircular half-domed apses has close parallels throughout the region. Near Planès, there's a *gîte d'étape* (☎04.68.04.21.40; ①) at *La Cassagne* farm – to go directly there, get off the train at Planès station and follow the GR10 footpath north towards Mont-Louis for about twenty minutes.

Mont-Louis and around

The next *Train Jaune* station – **La Cabanasse** – serves the garrison town of **MONT-LOUIS**, at 1600m the highest town of the Têt, lying 14km southeast of the river's source, the Lac des Bouillouses. Known as the gateway to the Cerdagne, Mont-Louis (about ten minutes' walk up from the station) is the quintessential work of **Vauban**, Louis XIV's military engineer, and has something of the ruthless chill of a missile silo. Vauban designed Mont-Louis for his royal client between 1679 and 1682, and reputedly selected the site not only on logistical grounds, but also because he was impressed by the longevity, the white teeth and sparkling eyes of the villagers.

In contrast to the high, fragile walls of Villefranche, the moated **ramparts** of Mont-Louis are massive, built low to maximize resistance to artillery fire. Also unlike Villefranche, even Vauban admitted that the finished product might fail in its intended function: and indeed, throughout the eighteenth century hostile armies entered France through the Cerdagne along roads unguarded by the citadel. Though promoted as a resort, Mont-Louis is still essentially a military town, with French commandos occupying its citadel and training on surrounding slopes. Apart from the walls, Mont-Louis' only other attraction is the world's first **solar oven** (*four solaire*), built in 1949 and now open for guided tours (daily: summer 10am–6.30pm; winter 10am–12.30pm & 2–6pm; 1hr 30F/€4.60); the huge mirror for the oven stands in the moat, just to the left of the main gate (Porte de France). There's another *four solaire* in nearby Odeillo (see p.224).

There is a **tourist office** in rue du Marché (July & Aug 9.30am–noon & 2–7pm; Sept–June Tues–Sat 10am–noon & 2–6pm; ☎04.68.04.21.97). The best deal for accommodation at Mont-Louis is the attractively furnished *La Taverne*, in rue Victor Hugo (☎04.68.04.23.67, fax 04.68.04.13.35; ⑤), which has comfortable rooms, outfitted with such luxuries as TV, and whose restaurant serves excellent-value menus from 68F/€10.40 and delicious wood-fired pizzas. If this is full, try the *Bernagie*, 10 rue Victor (☎04.68.04.23.67, fax 04.68.04.13.35; *www.bernagie.fr*; ③) whose restaurant does Catalan cuisine. *Lou Roubaillou*, near the barracks in rue des Ecoles Laïque, no longer offers rooms, but maintains its celebrated restaurant offering mushrooms, boar and duck among other local delicacies (menus 125–195F/€19.10–29.70). The closest campsite, *Pla de Barres* (☎04.68.04.21.18; mid-June to mid-Sept), lies 3km west along the road towards Lac des Bouillouses; though a bit squalid in high summer when the uncollected rubbish accumulates, it is inexpensive and beautifully set under the pines by a stream.

The Eyne area: skiing and walking

The road from Mont-Louis to Planès passes through **SAINT-PIERRE-DELS-FOR-CATS**, one of the base villages for the amalgamated ski zones known as the **ESPACE**

CAMBRE D'AZE, after the eponymous peak overhead (2711m), cloven by a quarry-like cirque. Heading right at the fork above Saint-Pierre takes you to EYNE, the other base village (the *Train Jaune* stop is Bolquère-Eyne); a joint ski pass covers both zones. The 28 runs, served almost entirely by drag lifts, are biased towards beginners and intermediates, though some are quite long and end scenically amidst the pines. Espace Cambre d'Aze is north-facing, with respectable top points of 2400m/2300m for the two sectors (where the few advanced pistes start), but snow can be unreliable this close to the Mediterranean – 162 snow canons try to make up for any deficit.

Saint-Pierre no longer has accommodation, but at Eyne you can stay at the two-star *Le Roc Blanc* (☎04.68.04.72.72; ⑤), or at the **gîte/chambres d'hôtes** *Cai Pai* (☎04.68.04.06.96; ③), each of which serve up excellent country-style meals for under 100F/€15.30. Half- or full-day horse-riding and botanical outings are available through *Le Licol Vert* (☎04.68.04.72.48).

Above Eyne to the southeast is the **Col d'Eyne** (or **Col de Núria**), the second most important bird migration corridor in the Pyrenees, after the Col Organbidexka in Basque country; autumn migration produces the greatest variety, including honey buzzards, kites and falcons, as well as the bee-eater and other rarities. A signposted path about 300m west of Eyne village, part of the HRP, runs up to the *col* through the forested river valley, which is blessed with a peculiar microclimate and thus boasts a wealth of flowers and herbs in its meadows. After four hours the HRP attains the *col*, drops to Núria in Spain on the far side (see p.181), and loops back up to the Col de Nou Fonts at the head of the Carança valley.

The Capcir

Between the upper Têt valley and the gorges of the upper Aude spreads the sedimentary plateau called the **Capcir**. Bare and extremely flat in the centre – traits accentuated by the large artificial lakes of Matemale and Puyvalador – it is cradled by densely wooded slopes that sweep up to Pic Madrès and the Carlit Massif, with only the **ski-resort** pistes interrupting the trees. One of the harshest winter climates in southern France makes this excellent cross-country ski terrain, while summer promises wonderful, easy walking, with several refuges or *gîtes d'étape*, plus hotels in three of its eight villages. In July and August, and during ski season, all the main Capcir villages and resorts are served by a twice-daily taxi-bus, which departs from the Mont-Louis/La Cabanasse rail station.

Capcir ski resorts

All of the Capcir **ski resorts** lie on, or just off, the D118 road served by the taxi-bus. Nearest to Mont-Louis, northeast-facing **LES ANGLES** is also the area's largest and most advanced centre, with 32 pistes, more than half of them red-rated, totalling over 40km. Two *télécabines* and a chair-lift get you up from the base station and village (1650m) to a plateau at 1900–2000m, from where there's another chair-lift to the secondary top point, 2325-metre **Roc d'Aude**, where two poma lifts give access to the true summit at **Mont Llaret** (2377m). Numerous poma lifts and 255 snow canons fill any gaps in coverage. Chalets rather than high-rises predominate, but the old village has still been almost completely swamped. **Accommodation** is in five hotels and about twenty *résidences*, least expensive being *Le Coq d'Or* hotel, place du Coq d'Or (☎04.68.04.42.17, fax 04.68.04.44.84; ⑥). The Bureau Montagne (☎04.68.04.34.30) is a multidisciplinary sports outfitter for summertime activities such as horse-riding, mountain-biking and canyoning.

Formiguères

FORMIGUÈRES, 6km further north, is far more attractive with its shops (some selling outdoor gear), cafés and crêperies giving it the feel of a county town. Its church of Sainte-Marie features an unusual triangular facade culminating in the belfry; inside is a masterful, seventeenth-century *majestat*, typical of the Catalan region. The seventeen downhill runs (total 20km), through the conifers between 2350m and 1700m, are pitched at strong intermediates, but more interestingly perhaps are the over 100km of local **cross-country skiing** trails. A good-value seasonal pass is available through the local tourist office (see below).

On the southeast corner of the church square there's a helpful **tourist office** (July & Aug 8.30am–12.30pm & 2.30–6.30pm; Sept–June 9am–noon & 3–6pm; ☎04.68.04.47.35) which, among other things, rents keys for the municipal tennis courts. Horse-riding is offered through Balade à Cheval, 1km out on the Les Angles road (☎04.68.04.48.44). Formiguères has two **hotels**: the one-star *Picheyre* behind the church (☎04.68.04.40.07, fax 04.68.30.99.03, *hotel-picheyre@wanadoo.fr*; ④; closed late April, May & Nov) and the fancier *Auberge de la Tutte*, on the road out of town by the junction for Les Angles (☎04.68.04.40.21; ⑥). There's a *gîte d'étape* in an old barn, with a few doubles and meals offered, at *Espousouille* (☎04.68.04.45.37; ①), a kilometre or so up through the trees by footpath – but 6km by road. The **restaurant** in the *Picheyre* is resolutely old-fashioned, good value at 75F/€11.40 (no à la carte) but dull of menu, like lunching at your gran's and with a clientele to match.

Matemale, Puyvalador and Rieutort

If that doesn't suit, the *Auberge de la Belle Aude* in **MATEMALE**, a deceptively large village tucked in a hollow by the Aude 4km south, has more comfortable accommodation and traditional Catalan menus, which include typical dishes such as *boules de picoulat*, as well as roast meats and fish, starting at 95F/€14.50 (☎04.68.04.40.11, fax 04.68.04.39.89; ⑤); they've even managed to squeeze in a tiny pool under a conservatory for rare *capcinoise* hot days. More serious outdoor pursuits here include mountain biking through Fugues VTT (☎04.68.04.42.06), down by the Matemale reservoir, as well as watersports.

The ski station at **PUYVALADOR**, at the north end of the Capcir plateau, is 5km west of its namesake reservoir and village (which has no amenities). It's the smallest of the Cerdagne resorts, with just sixteen east- or north-facing runs between 2382m (the **Pic du Ginèvre**) and 1700m, with more here for beginners or weak intermediates than at Formiguères. The only tourist facilities at this end of the plateau, outside the ski station, are at **RIEUTORT**, 2km west of Puyvalador village. Here Vagabond'ane (☎04.68.04.41.22) on the main square rents mules and organizes donkey safaris; in winter snowshoeing is offered instead. Some fifty paces above the square you can feast on trout and crayfish straight from a tank at the excellent *Al Cortal* (open supper only during ski season; lunch and dinner in summer; weekends only otherwise), with slightly pricey four-course menus for 140F/€21.50.

Hiking: La Tour du Capcir

The Capcir woodlands are eminently suitable hiking territory, well within the capabilities of a novice walker. The Randonnées Pyrénéennes organization issues maps and booklets describing **La Tour du Capcir**, a four-day circuit (easy to pick up at Espousouille, Puyvalador or Matemale) that runs along both sides of the valley as well as taking in **Pic Madrès** (2469m) to the east. You can make use of the *gîtes d'étape* at Espousouille, the hotel at Matemale plus the staffed refuges at Bouillouses (see p.228) and Camporells, with one night either camping out or staying in the unstaffed *Refuge de Nohèdes*, a little to the southeast of Madrès summit. The *Refuge de Camporells*

(☎04.68.04.49.86; open mid-June to mid-Sept; ③), by the cluster of eponymous lakes on the western leg of the Tour, is wonderfully set in an area rich in wildlife, also partly accessible by the chair lift which operates even in summer at Formiguères (45-min walk from the top of the lift to the refuge).

The portion of the route between Camporells and Bouillouses passes close to the **Carlit Massif**, so you could improve the circuit with an ascent of the peak (add a day); alternatively you could hike on westwards to follow part of the Tour du Carlit, emerging at Porté-Puymorens (see "The Carlit Massif", p.227) or in the Ariège valley (see p.229). Moving **eastwards** out of the Capcir, you could link up with the Tour du Coronat after the Madrès ascent (see "The upper Têt", p.114).

The Tech valley and the Albères

The **Tech valley** (or Vallespir) is the southernmost in France, and its exceptional sunshine (300 days a year) and relatively low rainfall nurture a flora that includes oranges, cacti and bougainvillea – as well as dense forest on the higher, wetter slopes. Proximity to the border made the Tech a tense place during World War II, when it was a major escape route from occupied France. The easiest mid-elevation pass into Spain, the **Col d'Ares**, was so heavily patrolled that the *passeurs* had to use more remote routes along the main **Albères** ridge, whose enduring loneliness still appeals to casual walkers. Escapers making contact at **Céret** or **Le Boulou** would be led out over one of two *cols*, either Lly (south of Céret) or Llosa. From **Amélie-les-Bains** – today a busy spa – there was a tough ascent over the 1450-metre Roc de France. From **Arles-sur-Tech**, further up the valley, the route led to **Saint-Laurent-de-Cerdans** and **Coustouges**, then either over Col des Massanes or along the Riou Majou into Alta Garrotxa. From the tiny spa of **La Preste** and the small walled town of **Prats-de-Molló**, refugees fled along the ancient paths of the *contrabandiers*, through the Col del Pal or the Collade de Prats. The solitude of this central part of the Albères – which extends from Saint-Laurent-de-Cerdans and Coustouges in the west to the Mediterranean at Banyuls-sur-Mer – is broken only on the east side of the Tech at **Le Perthus**, little better than a border shopping town and truck-stop.

Today, there is no border control and crossing from France into Spain is easy. Besides the crossing at Le Perthus, the D115 road up the Tech valley slips into Spain at the Col d'Ares, a scenic and almost equally popular route.

From Le Boulou to the border

LE BOULOU, a traffic-clogged little town situated just off the autoroute 20km south of Perpignan (12 buses daily), is the **cork** capital of France. At the beginning of the century there were 140 square kilometres under cork oak cultivation in this area, planted as a substitute for grapevines destroyed by phylloxera. Cultivated primarily to produce stoppers for the champagne industry, the plantations shrank to around 50 square kilometres in the face of competition from less expensive Portuguese cork, but a recent revival has been spurred by chronic local brush fires, as cork oak is very flame-resistant and therefore a better bet than more combustible crops. You can find out more at the **Musée de Liège** in Maureillas, 5km south of Le Boulou (mid-June to mid-Sept daily 10.30am–noon & 3.30–7pm; rest of year daily except Tues 2–5pm; 15F/€2.30).

At least eight buses a day continue from Le Boulou along the Tech valley to Céret and Arles-sur-Tech, and four buses a day (except Sun) to the border at Le Perthus, and back; it's also a possible changing-point for buses east to the Côte Vermeille at Argelès-sur-Mer (Cars Verts du Roussillon, 1 daily, via Saint-Genis-des-Fontaines and Sorède).

A few minutes' ride south of Le Boulou, just beyond Bains du Boulou, stands the remarkable chapel of **Saint-Martin-de-Fenollar** (mid-June to mid-Sept daily 10.30am–noon & 3.30–7pm; rest of year daily except Tues 2–5pm; 15F/€2.30), signposted to the west of the N9. Its twelfth-century frescoes are the best Romanesque wall paintings in Roussillon, and their clarity and simplicity of line may well have influenced Picasso, who sometimes stayed in nearby Céret.

A stretch of the old, non-toll N9 follows the line of the Roman Via Domitia, and there's evidence of the antiquity of the route 4km south of Saint-Martin, where a pair of ruined Roman forts cap the steep outcrops flanking the road. The one to the west, known as the **Château des Maures**, can be reached only by fording a stream. The other requires a thirty-minute climb up the D71B from **L'ÉCLUSE** – a village whose name is derived from the Latin *clausura*, indicating the closure or control point on a road. The crumbling structure will fascinate none but ardent classicists, but the adjacent church of Saint-Nazaire contains frescoes reminiscent of those at Saint-Martin, and possibly by the same painter (key available from the *mairie* in L'Écluse).

Le Perthus and the frontier

On the night of February 5, 1939, a column of twenty thousand Spanish Republicans arrived at the border post of **LE PERTHUS** (El Pertus or Els Límits, in Spain), 4km beyond L'Écluse, to seek sanctuary in France. Nowadays a consumer army descends here every day, disgorging from coaches to spend their money on foodstuffs, booze and perfume that is in fact not much cheaper than in Spain. If you're on a GR10 traverse and looking for a place to stay, your only choice is *Chez Grand-Mère* at the summit of the main road (☎04.68.83.60.96; ④ HB).

In Roman times the Via Domitia crossed the Albères 2km west at the **Col de Panissars**, which is probably the way Hannibal came in 218 BC. When Pompey returned victorious from Spain a century and a half later, he ordered a triumphal monument to be built at the *col*, and the excavated base of this edifice is now visible through barbed wire. On a nearby mound, overlooking Panissars and Le Perthus, rises the **Fort de Bellegarde** (July–Sept daily 10.30am–12.30pm & 2.30–6.30pm; rest of the year, phone for details ☎04.68.83.60.15; 15F/€2.30). Built in the sixteenth century and later reinforced by Vauban, it comprises two rows of dilapidated buildings and the deepest well in Europe (63m) within an enclosure of mighty walls, and gives superb views south into Spain and north across Roussillon. Both fort and monumental base are reached by taking the signposted road west out of Le Perthus, from near the high point of the main road. After fifteen minutes you're among cork oaks, as the road curves behind a hill and the noise of cash registers fades away; the fort is about fifteen minutes further, while the monument is five minutes beyond that.

If you want to move on **into Spain** on foot you could simply pick your way from Col de Panissars down through the scrub, but it's so close to the road that anyone crossing here might arouse suspicion of cannabis smuggling – it's better to return to Le Perthus and take the minibus to Figueres (3 daily Mon–Sat, 2 on Sun), or hitch. Both the **GR10** and the **HRP**, here combined, pass through Le Perthus/Panissars on their east–west route along the summits of the Albères.

Banyuls-sur-Mer, on the Côte Vermeille (see p.134), lies two easy days' walking east of Le Perthus along the GR10, split by a night at the simple *Refuge de la Tagnarède*, just beyond **Pic Néulos**. You may prefer, at least for lunch, the *Chalet de l'Albère* (☎04.68.83.62.20; ③), three hours distant at the **Col de l'Ouillat**. This clean, sixty-person *gîte d'étape* has a good **restaurant**, and is accessible in considerably less time by the D71 secondary road from Le Perthus through Saint-Jean and Saint-Martin hamlets. Heading west on the GR10/HRP, the nearest *gîte* is at **LAS ILLAS** (☎04.68.83.23.93; ③), just under half a day away but the only spot to divide the long stage to Arles-sur-Tech.

Céret

The cherry orchards of **CÉRET** are the basis of its prosperity, yielding around 4000 tonnes of fruit towards the end of April. It's a friendly and bustling town, with a shady old quarter of narrow and winding streets that open onto small squares like **place des Neuf-Jets**, named after the fountain at its centre. Of the medieval fortifications, only parts of the two medieval gates remain, though many houses are incorporated integrally into the walls themselves.

According to legend the single-arched **Pont du Diable** – one of three bridges that span the Tech at Céret – was built by the Devil in 1321 in return for the soul of the first Céretian to cross. The engineer who made the bargain duly sent a cat over first, but the trick backfired as none of the locals would then risk the Devil's vengeance by using the bridge themselves. Other sights include the **war memorial** by Aristide Maillol and the **monument** to the composer Déodat de Séverac by the Catalan sculptor Manolo (who was the first artist to settle here), in av Clemenceau, just around the corner from bd Maréchal Joffre, up at the edge of the old quarter.

What brings most visitors to Céret is the **Musée d'Art Moderne** at 8 bd Maréchal Joffre (mid-June to mid-Sept daily 10am–7pm; May to mid-June & mid-Sept to Oct daily 10am–6pm; Nov–Mar daily except Tues 10am–6pm; 35F/€5.30). Established largely through the efforts of the artist Pierre Brune, who arrived here in 1916 when the town was already something of a creative colony, the collection evokes splendidly the milieu of the Fauves, Cubists and Surrealists, and the building has recently been expanded and renovated by architects Jaume Freixa and Philippe Pous. Much of the collection was donated by artists who came to stay: the extensive Picasso section includes a fine series of ceramic bowls depicting bullfights, plus a sketch of a local sardana, which he gave to the local branch of the Communist Party, who in turn donated it to the museum. There are a couple of slapdash Dalís, a pair of typical Chagalls, and some pieces by Matisse and Maillol, but the best come from Juan Gris and lesser-known artists represented by their major works – such as Pignon's nudes.

Practicalities

The easiest way of reaching Céret is by **bus** from Perpignan (12 daily, first 8am, last 8pm), which stops about 250m north of the old quarter at the bottom of av Clemenceau; most buses continue along the Tech to Arles, and three or four go right to the head of the valley at Prats-de-Molló.

The **tourist office** (July & Aug Mon–Sat 9am–12.30pm & 2–7pm, Sun 10am–12.30pm; Sept–May Mon–Fri 10am–noon & 2–5pm, Sat 10am–noon; ☎04.68.87.00.53, *www.ot-ceret.fr*) is at the top of av Clemenceau, on the corner of bd Maréchal Joffre. If you need to **rent a car**, try Rey Autocar (☎04.68.87.10.70) in bd Maréchal Joffre. The most central and best **accommodation** is provided by the cheerfully decorated one-star *Vidal*, housed in the old bishop's palace, off place Soutine (☎04.68.87.00.85, fax 04.68.87,62.33; ⑤). Opposite stands the two-star *Arcades* (☎04.68.87.12.30, fax 04.68.87.49.44; ⑤), and you might also try the *Pyrénées*, an old house hidden down rue de la République (☎04.68.87.11.02, fax 04.68.87.31.66; ②). All these places have a variety of rooms available, with and without bath. There are several local **campsites**, two of them on route de Maureillas: *Les Cerisiers* (☎04.68.87.00.08; open all year) and *Les Deux Rivières*.

When it's time to **eat out**, you should perhaps forgo the hotel kitchens in favour of the good bistro-*crêperie*, *Le Pied dans le Plat* (closed Sun), and an adjacent pizzeria, both on place des Neuf-Jets, with outdoor seating. Social life at the *Grand Café* in bd Maréchal Joffre is perhaps not what it was when the *barde* Picasso hung out there, but it's still a good place to sit outside with a glass of wine and a plate of *frites*; there are more **cafés** around the corner by the Porte de France. Saturdays see a morning farmers' **market** on place Pablo-Picasso and av d'Espagne, the street stalls groaning with local produce.

Festivals

Céret is very Catalan – extending to such details as bilingual street-signs – and the arena in the north of the town holds regular bullfights and sardanas in summer. To get to the arena, go down rue Joseph Parayre until you reach rue des Arènes on your right. The biggest local bash takes place in July, over the weekend closest to Bastille Day, when the street on the perimeter of the old town fills with booths selling sausages, seafood and drink; after dark, *coblas* (traditional folk music groups) give place to more riotous conventional dance bands. There's also a Languedocian-style **running of bulls** (*abrivado* or *encierro*), in which half a dozen horsemen surround each beast as it is driven through the streets. This is followed by a Spanish-style **bullfight** (*corrida*) with ticket prices comparable to those south of the border (160–400F/€24–60).

Every August the **Festival International de la Sardane** provides a more generally appealing spectacle at the arena, the seats crowded and the ring packed with concentric circles of dancers. On the other hand, if you are looking for something more contemporary and up-tempo, try the massive Méditeranéennes de Céret music festival (☎01.44.79.0036, fax 01.44.79.00.34, *Azimuthprod@wanadoo.fr*). For three days (around Sept 30), up to 12,000 people party to Latin and Mediterranean bands.

Amélie-les-Bains and Palalda

The next stop, 8km up the valley, is the spa town of **AMÉLIE-LES-BAINS**, which tends to attract the elderly and rheumatic. Unless you are taking a cure (*balneotherapie, drainage lymphatique* or other such dire treatments), there's nothing much to see or do here. Attempts have been made to inject a bit of youth interest by promoting mountain biking, horse-riding and hiking, without much success. Nor is it worth pausing to see the claimed tourist attractions of the much-restored Roman baths and the Gorges du Mondony, poor relation of the nearby Gorges de la Fou (see below), while Fort les Bains (part of Vauban's defences), perched high above the town, is not open to visit. Two kilometres downstream, on the opposite bank, is the sister town of **PALALDA**, whose medieval centre might delay you a little longer. Afterwards it's a choice between moving along the valley, striking north into the Aspres foothills between the Tech and the Têt (see "The lower Têt", p.104) or picking up the GR10 west into Canigou.

It's unlikely you'll want to stay in either place, but Amélie does have a glut of **accommodation**. The **tourist office** (July & Aug Mon–Sat 9am–7pm, Sept–June Mon–Fri 9am–noon & 2–6pm Sat 9am–noon; ☎04.68.39.01.38, *www.amelie-les-bains.com*), near the bus stop on quai du Huit Mai (between the river and place de la République), can help you track it down. There's plenty of choice along the av du Vallespir, running through the centre of town, including the attractive one-star *La Chaumière* at no. 2 (☎04.68.39.05.35; closed Dec–Mar; ②), and the two-star *La Pergola* at no. 60, with a choice between rooms and studios (☎04.68.39.05.71, fax 04.68.39.81.15; ③); alternatively try the kitsch but friendly one-star *Jeanne d'Arc* (☎04.68.87.96.96; closed Dec–Jan; ②) in place de la République, which overlooks the river on one side. The municipal **campsite** (☎04.68.39.22.37; Feb–Nov) is by the river, just off av Beau Soleil, the main road into town; *Camping du Gaou* (☎04.68.39.19.19; June–Sept) is nearby, on the south side of the road.

For **eating out**, try the attractive *Au Poivre Vert* in place de la République, which offers Catalan specialities (closed Mon & mid-Dec to Jan; menus 68–130F/€1.40–19.80); for an extra treat, head for the excellent patisserie and teashop *Pi-Roue*, at 6 av du Vallespir.

Arles-sur-Tech

ARLES-SUR-TECH, 4km further along the valley, is quieter and more atmospheric than Amélie, with a medieval quarter focused on the **abbey of Sainte-Marie**. The first abbey, built late in the eighth century, was soon destroyed by Viking raiders and the present church (daily: March–June, Sept & Nov 10am–noon & 2–6pm; July & Aug Mon–Fri 8am–noon & 2–7pm, Sat 2–7pm, Dec–Feb by appointment; 20F/€3) was consecrated in 1046 and modified two centuries later. The abbey's most renowned feature is the tranquil **cloister**, an elegant addition from the end of the thirteenth century, with pointed double-columned arches surrounding an attractive garden of box and cypress. In the middle stands the **La Tomb Sainte**, formerly a reliquary for the bones of two obscure early saints, and now focus of a phenomenon which has resisted scientific explanation. Since the bones were removed, this sacrophagus has produced hundreds of litres of water annually, periodically drawn off and distributed to the faithful. The cloister also houses a museum of iron forgery (daily except Tues: April–June & Sept–Nov 10am–noon & 3–6pm, July & Aug 10am–noon & 3–6pm; 10F/€1.50).

Arles is a close-knit community with an award-winning folk-dance group and rugby team; it is most famous, however, for its February **Fête de l'Ours**, a pagan holdover claimed to be among the oldest observances in Europe. Traditionally, bears were said to interrupt their hibernation at the February new moon, terrorizing the villagers, who hit on the ploy of luring the boldest animal with a local girl, before chaining the bear and then shaving it. There being a contemporary shortage of bears, these days a young man is dressed in a bear skin, hunted down by the crowds, captured and stripped, after which a communal meal is served.

The **tourist office** (Mon–Sat 9am–noon & 2–6pm; ☎04.68.39.11.99), in rue Barjou at the top of the town, has suggestions for walks and trails around Arles, plus a map for 25F/€3.80 (the GR10, which passes through the town, is not well signposted locally); it also stocks a list of *chambres d'hôtes*, invaluable in hotel-poor Arles. The only hotel is the comfortable two-star *Les Glycines*, 7 rue du Jeu-de-Paume (☎04.68.39.10.09, fax 04.68.3.83.02; ⑥), which also has the best **restaurant** in town, with a shaded terrace and Catalan specialities (*menus* 105–165F/€16–26). The alternatives for eating out are *La Treille* (☎04.68.39.89.59; Sept–May closed Mon) at the beginning of bd Riuferrer, with a pleasant vine-shaded terrace (70F/€10.70 *menu*); the grill-bar at the Musée Jean Cordomi (March–Dec 10am–10pm), opposite the *mairie*; or the *Bar Central*, for a very reasonable omelette-and-*frites*. For homemade pâtés and takeaway savoury dishes, there's the exceptional *Frères Coll*, at 7 rue Jean-Vilar.

Among **campsites**, the scenic *Riuferrer* (☎04.68.39.11.06; open all year), is on the west side of town, near the mouth of the Freixe stream; *Le Vallespir* (☎04.68.39.90.00; closed Nov–March) lies on the road to Amélie-les-Bains; or there's the naturist camp *Le Ventous* (☎04.68.87.83.38, *www.perso.club-internet.fr/le vento*; June to mid-Sept) on the road to Prats-de-Molló.

The Gorges de la Fou

A couple of kilometres up the main valley road from Arles are the **Gorges de la Fou** (Easter–end Oct 10am–6pm, closed during bad weather; ☎04.68.39.16.21; 30F/€4.60), one of the great – if touristy – spectacles of the Eastern Pyrenees. You need at least an hour to cover the 1500m of metal walkway to the end and back, squeezing between 200-metre-high walls, so close together that they have trapped falling rocks. In places, water erosion has made the walls as smooth as plaster, and the force of the torrent during storms in 1988 was sufficient to sweep part of the walk away. If you don't think you'll make it to the Gorges de Kakouetta in the French Basque country (see p.457), these are a more than respectable consolation prize. However, if the weather looks doubtful, phone to check that the gorge is open before visiting.

Walking out of Arles: to the Albères or Canigou

The GR10 climbs **southeast** from the town through the Arles forest to Montalba (no facilities), at the head of the Mondony gorge, and onto the summit ridge of the Albères, just below Roc de France (1450m). There's little habitation between Arles and the *gîte* at Las Illas (see "Le Perthus and the frontier", p.122), a long day's trek away.

Heading **northwest**, the **Arles-to-Cortalets** approach could be done in a single day, given an early enough start, but it's an arduous walk, beyond the capabilities of most walkers. From Arles, it's wisest to forego the first, unsightly section of the GR10 in favour of the blue-dot-marked "Dolmen 1hr 30min" path, which leaves the road towards the campsite, just above the town pool. You can break the trek five hours along at the *gîte d'étape* (☎04.68.39.12.01; April–Oct; 80F/€12.20) installed in the old miners' hostel at **BATÈRE**, which has a good bistro. The ironworks are evident as an ugly scar resulting from open-cast extraction between the twelfth and seventeenth centuries; some galleries are still worked today. If you're in a group, you're advised to save yourself some rather tedious trekking by taking a **taxi** up to the *gîte*, along the paved D43 sideroad, which begins just beyond Arles. After 7km you'll pass the stone-built village of **CORSAVY** (7km), with its Romanesque chapel of Saint-Martin-de-Corsavy and three places to eat.

North of the mine and *gîte* the road turns to track, climbing on past the ruined **Tour de Batère** before dropping to the road for Valmanya (see "The Canigou Massif", p.109).

Alpine Canigou truly begins just west of the *gîte* at the **Col de le Cirère** (1730m), beyond which unfurls the section of corniche trail dubbed the **Balcon du Canigou** for its sweeping views northeast. Two hours beyond Batère, the eight-bunk forestry hut at **Estagnole** has a good spring and an adjacent terrace suitable for camping; it's also easily reached from Valmanya, visible below, in less time. The *Chalet des Cortalets* (p.112) is still a good four-and-a-half hours away along the GR10.

The upper Tech

Accessible both along the D44 from Corsavy, and the D54 from the main valley floor, **MONTFERRER**, 6km from Arles by the shortest route, is – with its ruined castle and Romanesque church – one of the most attractive settlements in the upper Tech. Set amongst dense forest and crags, with sweeping views east to the opposite side of the valley, it enjoys its status as the truffle capital of Roussillon – the village can also muster a good campsite with a swimming pool.

Some 7km beyond Arles-sur-Tech, the D3 sideroad ascends south from the main D115 through forests of sweet chestnut to the village of **SAINT-LAURENT-DE-CER-DANS** (9km from the junction). Three workday buses serve the village from Perpignan (2 on Sun). During World War II the local clergy oversaw the passage of refugees southwest towards Mont Nègre, crossing the frontier by the Col des Massanes (1126m), or up to Coustouges for the Riou Majou trail. Nowadays, marked footpaths – variants of the HRP – run east and west along the border from both Saint-Laurent and Coustouges.

Passeurs normally asked their clients to wear *espadrilles*, which are quieter than ordinary shoes and – some claim – better suited to rock climbing. Saint-Laurent was once a major producer of *bigatanes*, the special Catalan espadrille that has a double rope sole and ankle-laces. You can see how *espadrilles* were made, and discover other rural crafts such as weaving and beekeeping, in the local history museum, **Musée d'Arts et Traditions Populaire** (May, June & Sept 10am–noon & 3–6pm, July & Aug 10am–noon & 3–7pm; 10F/€1.50), near the tourist office on the main road through town. Beside the Laurent stream are a pair of **campsites** (one just before you enter the village and another just beyond it), while the nearest **hotel** is the very comfortable but pricey *Domaine de Falgos*, converted from an old barn about 5km from Saint-Laurent in the direction of Coustouges (☎04.68.39.51.42, fax 04.68.39.52.30, *www.silencehotel.com*; ⑦; closed Jan & Feb).

From Saint-Laurent the road climbs 5km further east to the tiny hamlet of **COUS-TOUGES** (1 bus daily Mon–Sat), from where the spine of the Albères rises northeast to the highest point of the chain at **Roc de France** (1450m). The large church, built in unusual pink sandstone and granite, and with a richly carved portal, would have also served the villages over the present frontier at the time of its construction in the twelfth century.

Returning by road to the Tech valley, you can cut off along the D64, from which a short detour brings you to Serralongue, which has a **campsite**. An alternative is to take the high-level *variante* footpath west from Coustouges, which leads to the delightfully secluded **LAMANÈRE**, the most southerly village in France; path and track continue from here to the frontier at Col d'Ares, or the paved D44 descends north to the main valley.

Prats-de-Molló

From Arles, the D115 climbs 19km to the medieval city of **PRATS-DE-MOLLÓ**. The present road follows the path of a former railway (the old station houses can be seen along the way), since the old road, with houses and bridges, was washed away by disastrous floods during October 1940.

In the seventeenth century, when the Treaty of the Pyrenees subjected this area to the outrageous tax policies of Louis XIV, Prats-de-Molló and a number of other towns and villages revolted against the French Crown. Living at the far end of what was then a densely wooded valley, the rebels probably felt they could act with impunity when they murdered the king's tax collectors. And indeed they held off two battalions before the forces of Maréchal de Noailles made a surprise attack over the western flanks of Canigou to put down the insurrection. **Fort Lagarde** (daily: April–June 2–6pm; July & Aug 10am–7pm; Sept–Feb 2–5pm; 20F/€3), which dominates the town from above, was built in 1680 under the direction of Vauban, as much to subdue the local population as to keep the Spanish at bay; the town walls, raised on fourteenth-century foundations, are another Vauban relic from this period. To climb up to the fort (about 25min), head for Porte de la Fabrique, then either follow the footpath which winds up the hill from behind the church or take the 170-metre covered walk leading steeply upwards to a square tower, followed by a dark 100-metre underground tunnel (the entrance to the covered walk is in a ruined building to the right of the cemetery entrance). The fort itself has been beautifully restored, and there are superb views all round from the ramparts. An extra attraction here is the **Visite-Spectacle** on summer afternoons, when horsemen dressed as cavaliers re-create eighteenth-century cavalry exercises, with trick riding, sword fights and the firing of muskets and cannons (daily except Sat: June 3.30pm; July & Aug 2.30pm & 4pm; 42F/€6.40).

With Canigou at its back and the River Tech in front, picturesque Prats-de-Molló has become a tourist attraction but is still surprisingly unspoilt – particularly the old *ville haute* within the city wall, with its steep, cobbled streets and ancient fortified church. In summer, the pedestrianized streets buzz with activity; the rest of the year the hotels are locked up, and locals pass the time playing *boules* under the plane trees of El Firal, the huge square outside the walls, where markets and fairs have been held since 1308.

The **tourist office** in place le Firal (Jan–Mar & Nov–Dec Mon–Fri 9am–noon & 2–6pm; April–May & Sept–Oct Mon–Sat 9am–noon & 2–6pm; July & Aug daily 9am–12.30pm & 1.30–6.30pm; ☎04.68.39.70.83, *www.pratsdemollolapreste.com*) has a wealth of information, including maps and advice for walking in the Haut-Vallespir. The only one-star **hotel** is the chintzy *Ausseil*, place Joseph Trinxeria (☎04.68.39.70.36; ③); among the two-star hotels, the family-oriented *Le Relais*, 3 place Joseph Trinxeria (☎04.68.39.71.30, *www.lerelais.aol.com*; ③), and the friendly *Bellevue* overlooking place le Firal (☎04.68.39.72.48, fax 04.68.39.78.04; closed Nov–March; ④), serve reasonable **meals**, *Le Relais* at tables outside in the square. There's plenty of local **camping**, too. The two sites with the longest seasons are *St Martin* (☎04.68.39.77.40; open all year) and *Can Nadal* (☎04.68.39.77.89; March–Nov) about 1km along the road towards La Preste.

Onward routes: into Spain

Transport from Prats-de-Molló is a problem: there are three or four **buses** a day back down the Tech, but none **into Spain**. From Prats the road climbs 14km to the Spanish border at **Col d'Ares**, dropping on the other side to Camprodon (see p.177). Roughly halfway to the border, just beyond the Col de la Seille on the left, you'll find the *Ferme-Auberge La Coste d'Adalt* (☎04.68.39.74.40; ④), a working farm with spotless rooms and good food, near the terminus of the path and track coming west from Lamanère. Four kilometres along the path towards Lamanère is a *gîte d'étape* at Ermitage Notre Dame du Coral (☎04.68.39.75.00; ①–②), with half-board rates available.

The easiest of the former escape trails is the one to the **Collade de Prats** (1596m) from the south side of the Tech, a short way along the N115. The route passes the ruined **Tour de Mir**, one of the series of signal towers built by Jaume of Mallorca in the late thirteenth century, like the Tour Madeloc above Banyuls-sur-Mer (see p.134); allow three hours to the pass (and two-plus back if you're not continuing into Spain).

From the nearby spa of **LA PRESTE** (8km west) there was a higher and more difficult route through the **Coll del Pal** (2319m) over towards Setcases, between Pic de Costabona (2465m) and the smoothly rounded Roc Colom (2507m), on whose eastern flanks the Tech has its source. A good base for walking in the area above La Preste is the small refuge of *Chalet les Conques* (☎04.68.39.76.52, fax 04.68.39.23.49; daily May–Oct; group bookings out of season on ☎04.68.39.23.49; ①).

Canigou from the south

Another possibility at Prats-de-Molló is to ascend Canigou from the south and descend on the Têt side. Take the road to La Preste (1130m), then the track up to the **Collade des Roques Blanches**, at the end of the long ridge of tooth-like rocks known as the **Esquerdes de Rotja**. From there you turn east to **Pla Guillem** (2277m) – where there's a simple refuge – and then continue to *Refuge Mariailles*. Alternatively, at the *collade*, you can veer west, either along the Esquerdes or on a forest track, towards Mantet. For a complete description of Pla Guillem, *Mariailles* and Mantet, see pp.113–114, and consult the maps recommended in the introduction to "The Canigou Massif".

THE MEDITERRANEAN COAST

The Pyrenees meet the sea with a magnificent abruptness. Approaching from the north, **Argelès-sur-Mer** marks the point at which the flat strands of the Côte Radieuse give way to the rocky coves and scented foothills of the Albères, the most easterly limb of the Pyrenean range. This colourful clash of land and water has long attracted artists, most notably the group of early twentieth-century French painters known as the **Fauves** (Wild Beasts) for their vividly emotional use of colour and form, who passed their summers at **Collioure**, immediately south of Argelès.

Continuing south, the corniche road traces an ever more tortuous line along the **Côte Vermeille** to the easternmost point of the French Pyrenees, where the mountains plummet into the Mediterranean at **Cap Cerbère**. Here the sea floor drops precipitously to a depth of 40m, creating a habitat that has been protected since 1974 by the *réserve marine* between **Banyuls-sur-Mer** and **Cerbère**. Once the most elegant resort of the Côte Vermeille, Banyuls was the home of Aristide Maillol, sculptor of robust

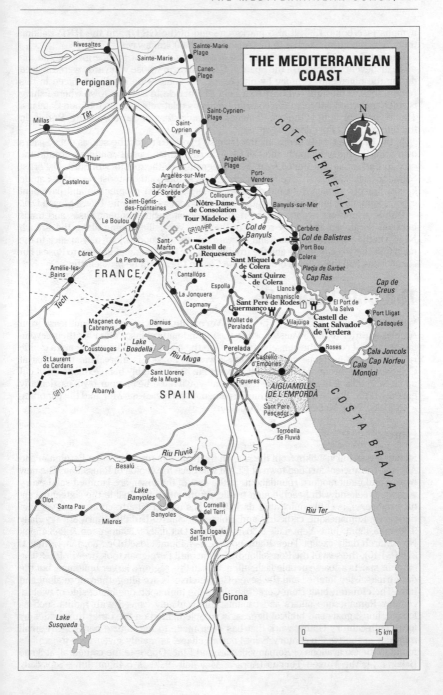

nymphs (see box p.136); it also marks one end of the **GR10** and the **HRP** walking trails, which both run across to the Atlantic coast, 400km away.

Beyond the border at **Port Bou**, the orderly vineyards of France give way to the more dishevelled terraces of the Spanish **Costa Brava**, whose vineyards were ravaged during the nineteenth century by phylloxera. Yet some wine is still produced in this region, such as the light red Garnatxa from **El Port de la Selva**, a town where fishing is still a major industry and the coastline remains relatively unknown to non-Catalans. The major local sight is the pre-Romanesque monastery of **Sant Pere de Rodes**, in the hills above El Port de la Selva.

At the **Cap de Creus** peninsula the Spanish Pyrenees reach the sea, as does Spain's own trans-Pyrenean footpath, the **GR11**. The rugged landscape continues around the cape to **Cadaqués** and **Port Lligat**, both pregnant with the memory of Surrealist artist Salvador Dalí, who lived here for decades. **Roses**, the southernmost resort of Cap de Creus, brashly mimics the Côte d'Azur with its palm-lined promenade and pavement cafés; inland, the county town of **Figueres** is most remarkable for its Teatre-Museu Dalí.

Public transport is generally more than adequate, with frequent buses and trains between Perpignan and every resort of the Côte Vermeille, strung along the French N114. On the Spanish side trains and buses are nearly as good as long as you stick to the main C252 between Figueres and the frontier and the C260 linking Figueres to Roses, but connections into the Albères or around the Cap de Creus can be problematic.

The Côte Vermeille

When the Fauves discovered the **Côte Vermeille**, which extends southeast from Argelès-sur-Mer to the Spanish border, they found natural inspiration for their revolutionary use of colour: the sunsets (from which the coast earned its name) are a gentle red, the sea is turquoise and, as Matisse wrote, "no sky is more blue than that at Collioure". The beauty of this stretch of coastline has inevitably been exploited, but cut up into the hills at the back of the resorts and you'll often be on your own: particularly enticing is the Balcon du Côte Vermeille path, out of Argèles-sur-Mer, and the panoramic trail past Tour Madeloc, south of Collioure.

Elne

Standing on a hill just 6km from the sea, on the main bus route between Perpignan and Argelès, the ancient fortified town of **ELNE** was once the capital of Roussillon. The new bypass and giant modern roundabout, to the east of the town, are jammed solid every summer weekend with beach-bound traffic but the old town, inside the sixteenth-century ramparts, is eerily quiet after dark. Elne has one great attraction worth visiting, the partly Romanesque cathedral and cloister of **Sainte-Eulalie** (April & May daily 9.30am–5.45pm; June–Sept daily 9.30am–6.45pm; Oct daily 9.30am–noon & 2–5.45pm; Nov–March daily except Tues 10am–noon & 2–4.45pm; closed Dec 25, Jan 1, May 1, 27F/€4.10), the seat of the Roussillon bishopric until Perpignan took over in 1602. The exterior sports a coarse pebbledash, often seen in this region's larger buildings, but the dark triple-aisled interior and the seven Gothic chapels are altogether more aloof and holy. The **cloister**, built from Céret marble, is the high spot: one intact side of twelfth-century Romanesque pillars and capitals, immaculately carved with motifs such as foliage, lions, goats and biblical figures, is complemented on the other three sides by fourteenth-century Gothic work that has been made to harmonize perfectly. A small museum in the twelfth-century Saint-Laurent chapel is mainly given over to exhibits found in the excavations of Roman villas around Elne. Opposite the cathedral, at 3 rue Balaguer, is the **Musée Terrus** (April & May daily 9.30am–5.45pm; June–Sept daily

9.30am–6.45pm; Oct daily 9.30am–noon & 2–5.45pm; Nov–March daily except Tues 10am–noon & 2–4.45pm; entry with same ticket as cloister), dedicated to the landscape painter Etienne Terrus (1857–1922), a contemporary of the Fauves and friend of Maillol (whose bust of Terrus stands on the Plateau des Garaffes, nearby); the *salon de thé*, on the first floor, has a panoramic view.

Practicalities

The **train station**, on the main line from Perpignan to the Côte Vermeille, lies about ten minutes' walk west of the old town; **buses** stop at the parking place in the centre of the old town, near the cathedral. The **tourist office** is at 2 rue du Docteur Bolte (June & Sept Mon–Fri 9.30am–noon & 2–5pm Sat 9.30am–noon; July & Aug Mon–Fri 9.30am–noon & 2–6pm Sun 9.30am–noon; Oct–May Mon–Fri 9.30am–noon & 2–5pm; ☎04.68.22.05.07, *www.ot-elne.fr*), between the **post office** and *Hôtel de Ville*. Of the three **hotels**, the modest *Cara Sol* (☎04.68.22.10.42; ②), in bd Illibéris on the edge of the old town offers by far the best value and the best setting, with great views from the front rooms over the Tech valley, the Albères and Canigou and whose owners will make you feel at home. More upmarket is the cosily renovated farm house, the two-star *Le Weekend*, 31 av Paul Reig (☎04.68.22.06.68, fax 04.68.22.17.16; ⑤), just off centre on the Argelès road, with a celebrated garden **restaurant** (*menus* 90–120F/€13.70–18.30); less well situated is *Le Carrefour*, 1 av Paul Reig (☎04.68.22.06.08; ③), at a small but busy crossroads. There are two municipal **campsites**: *Les Padraguets* (☎04.68.22.21.59; June–Sept) on the Argelès road and *Al Mouly* (☎04.68.22.08.46; June–Sept) on bd d'Archimède, in the direction of St-Cyprien.

Argelès-sur-Mer

More properly belonging to the Côte Radieuse than the Côte Vermeille, **ARGELÈS-SUR-MER** has the last wide, sandy beach until Roses, well into Spain. At the end of the Spanish Civil War thousands of refugees lived in camps here, including the Republican poet Antonio Machado, who failed to survive the first harsh winter. When the war against Germany began in 1939, the desperation of camp life, civic and monetary incentives from the French government and a further opportunity to combat fascism led nearly ten thousand refugees to volunteer to serve in the French army.

Nowadays, more than any other resort on this section of coast, this is a mass-tourist town, wooing visitors with holiday essentials like mini-golf, gambling tables and beauty contests. This is also where the **Balcon de la Côte Vermeille** begins, a tough 25-kilometre walk to Banyuls, just feasible in a single long day. Set mostly on high ground with wide views over the coastline and its villages, it also gives glimpses south into the lonely landscape of Spain's Alt Empordà.

The town itself is divided in two: the old **Argelès-Ville**, a little inland, and the new **Argelès-Plage**, which annually receives up to three hundred thousand French, Belgian, Dutch and English visitors. Plage Nord and Plage des Pins are smooth, sandy and potentially windblown, whereas **Le Racou** – the first bay of the Côte Vermeille – is more intimate and offers a taste of mountain coastline. The only cultural attraction is the old town's **Casa de les Albères** (June–Sept Mon–Fri 9am–noon & 3–6pm, Sat 9am–noon; 10F/€1.50), in place des Castellans, a small museum of local art and traditions, mostly agricultural tools and implements

Practicalities

The **train station** is a few minutes' walk west of the centre of the old town, while **buses** stop opposite the *Hôtel de Ville*. An hourly bus service (10F/€1.50) runs in summer between the station, the old town and the beach (Plage Nord). There is a summer **tourist office** in the old town (July & Aug Mon–Sat 9.30am–12.30pm & 2.30–6.30pm;

☎04.68.95.81.55), by the *Hôtel de Ville* on allée Ferdinand-Buisson; Argelès-Plage has its own office (summer daily 8.30am–8pm; out of season Mon–Fri 9am–noon & 2–6pm, Sat 9am–noon; ☎04.68.81.15.85, *www.argeles-sur-mer.com*), in place de l'Europe, on the corner of av des Platanes and av des Mimosas.

Rooms can be difficult to find in midsummer, especially for a short stay. If you're looking for a hotel in Argelès-Ville, try the long-established and beautifully decorated one-star *Le Soubirana*, 58 route Nationale (☎04.68.81.01.44; ②), or the two-star *Clair Logis*, 78 route de Collioure (☎04.68.81.03.27, fax 04.68.95.93.01; ⑤). Among dozens of hotels in Argelès-Plage, the two-star *Les Mimosas*, 51 av des Mimosas (☎04.68.81.14.77, fax 04.68.81.50.96; ⑤), and *Al Pescadou*, rue des Aloes (☎04.68.81.31.12; ⑤), are small, basic and nondescript, but reasonably priced and well situated. There should never be a problem finding a spot for your tent, as there are more than fifty **campsites** in the neighbourhood: *Calanque de l'Ouille* (☎04.68.81.12.79; April–Sept) and *Mini Camping* (☎04.68.81.08.72; April–Sept) are two desirable seafront establishments in the direction of Collioure.

Southwest: Saint-André and Saint-Genis

The Cars Verts du Roussillon **bus** service from Argelès-sur-Mer runs southwest along the D618 road through the Albères foothills to Le Boulou, right by the highway on the northern flank of the Albères range.

Some of the buses call at **SAINT-ANDRÉ-DE-SORÈDE**, 5km away, some at **SAINT-GENIS-DES-FONTAINES**, a similar distance beyond, and some at both. Most of the **Benedictine** abbey at Saint-Génis, founded in the ninth century, has disappeared (the cloister to the Philadelphia Museum), but the two-metre lintel over the doorway of the church, dating from 1020, is one of the earliest examples of Romanesque sculpture in France (June–Sept Mon–Fri 10am–noon & 3–7pm, Sat & Sun 9am–noon & 3–7pm; Oct–May daily 9.30am–noon & 2–5pm; 10F/€1.50). The similar lintel at Saint-André – showing Christ surrounded by angels and apostles – is probably a slightly later copy, though the contemporary church that it adorns is in better condition than Saint-Genis.

Collioure

A short bus or train ride down the coast from Argelès-sur-Mer is **COLLIOURE**, a true Côte Vermeille town, which to a certain extent still banks on its maritime and artistic past. Established as a trading port by the Phoenicians and ancient Greeks, Collioure was later occupied by the Romans (who stayed for five centuries), the Visigoths and Arabs. Altogether, the place has been the focus of nearly a dozen territorial squabbles, including four invasions by the French and two by the Spanish. The sixteenth-century **Fort St Elme** overlooking the town from the south (now privately owned), and the seventeenth-century **Fort Miradou** to the north (still used by the military), are reminders of this turbulent past.

In the early 1900s, invaders of a different sort came, saw and stayed. The group of painters – including Matisse and Derain – known as **Les Fauves** made Collioure their summer base. Some of their original work adorns the bar at *Les Templiers* (see below), but for a comprehensive showing you must visit the art museum in Céret (see p.123). You can also follow the *Chemin du Fauvisme* around the town, a trail of twenty reproductions of paintings by Matisse and Derain placed on the sites at which they were painted (map available from the tourist office). Among other personalities drawn to the town, the poet Antonio Machado arrived with his family in January 1939, but died of pneumonia fifteen days later; after an appeal initiated by Pablo Casals, André Malraux and Albert Camus, he was reburied in a tomb in Collioure's cemetery in 1956. A Picasso poster, *Hommage à Antonio Machado*, is on display in Collioure's **Musée d'Art**

Moderne (July & Aug daily 10am–noon & 2–6pm; rest of year closed Tues; 12F/€1.80), housed in the beautiful Villa Pams on the edge of the town in route de Port-Vendres, with a small permanent collection and temporary exhibitions by artists associated with the region. The historical novelist Patrick O'Brian lived as a recluse just outside of town from 1949 almost until his death in 2000.

The artistic tradition of Collioure survives today, albeit with less distinction; Collioure is tame and middle-class, and none of the art is wild. The forest of easels that occupies the promenade in summer produces mainly tourist souvenirs, but there are also a few serious commercial galleries and, if you're inclined to try your own hand, plenty of studios for rent. Many of these are in the old quarter of the town, the **Mouré**, whose steep, narrow streets are lined by pastel-tinted houses and assorted shops and cafés. Lateen-rigged fishing boats might be moored in the **harbour** itself, or drawn up on the palm-lined beach; those no longer used by fishermen are now beautifully restored and sailed as pleasure vessels by their new owners. The working fleet – distinguished by bow-lamps – brings in the local catch of anchovies (cured in salt, an ancient technique for which Collioure is famous) and sardines (grilled fresh).

Château-Royal (daily: July & Aug 10am–6pm; Sept–June 9am–5pm; closed Dec 25 & Jan 1–5 ; 20F/€3), the imposing fortress which dominates the harbour, was founded by the Templars in the twelfth century, rebuilt and used as a summer residence by the kings of Mallorca and Aragón two hundred years later, and modernized by Vauban after the Treaty of the Pyrenees. The impressive ramparts and some of the well-restored rooms provide terrific settings for exhibitions of sculptures and paintings, and displays relating to local subjects like quilting and cork production, with great views over the harbour, town and vine-covered hills beyond; the beautiful courtyard at the heart of the castle is used for summer concerts.

At the opposite end of the harbour, the **Église Nôtre-Dame-des-Anges** was erected in the seventeenth century, replacing the ancient Sainte-Marie, razed on the orders of Vauban. The distinctive round bell-tower – once doubling as the lighthouse – onto which it was grafted has been damaged many times by storm and war: the base dates from the thirteenth century, the middle from the fourteenth to seventeenth centuries, and the bell-chamber from the nineteenth. It's worth taking a look inside the church (daily 8am–noon & 2–5.30pm) to see the magnificent gilt retable, carved and painted in three tiers, by seventeenth-century Catalan sculptor Joseph Sunyer. Beyond the church, the tiny **Chapelle-St-Vincent** stands above the sea on a rocky peninsula, with the south-facing St Vincent beach on one side and the Plage Nord on the other.

Practicalities

Collioure's **train station** is less than ten minutes' walk west of the centre, along av Aristide Maillol; **buses** stop at the central car park, off av Général de Gaulle. The very helpful **tourist office** is just behind the harbour in place du 18 Juin (July & Aug daily 9am–8pm; Sept–Jun Mon–Sat 9am–noon & 2–6.30pm; ☎04.68.82.15.47, *www.little -france.com/collioure*), with information on everything from accommodation and eating to walking tours, diving and sailing schools, and cruises around the bay. There is also an information kiosk (July–Sept Mon–Sat 9am–5pm) in the small tower by the beach on the other side of the castle. For **eating out**, there's a great choice of very reasonable *crêperies*, sandwich bars and pizza-pasta places around the old Mouré quarter, but it's worth the premium to sit at a table on the fashionable rue Camille Pelletan, by the harbour, to watch the world go by – the most atmospheric being *Les Templiers*, a café-bar well known to the Fauves, and now filled with drawings and paintings donated by Matisse, Maillol, Picasso and Dufy, among many other artists. **Markets** (Wed & Sun morning) are held in place du Général Leclerc.

The quieter Plage Boutigue, southeast of the harbour, has some desirable seaview **hotels** including the attractively furnished *Le Boramar* (☎04.68.82.07.06; closed

Nov–April; ⑤) and the nearby, year-round *Triton*, 1 rue Jean-Bart (☎04.68.98.39.39, fax 04.68.82.11.32; ④). The most unusual accommodation is *Hostellerie des Templiers*, 12 quai de l'Amirauté (reservations essential on ☎04.68.98.31.10, fax 04.68.98.01.24; ⑥), in which the individually decorated rooms, staircases and dining rooms are filled with original artworks. There's some low-cost accommodation as well, though it's difficult to find in high season. One-star hotels include *Bona Casa* on the busy av de la République (☎04.68.82.06.62; ③), with a fish restaurant attached (menus from 89F/€13.60). There are three summer-only **campsites** to the north of the town, near the coast: the *Criques de Porteils* (☎04.68.81.12.73), on the Argelès road; *Les Amandiers* (☎04.68.81.14.69), in the sheltered bay known as L'Ouille; and, best of the bunch, *La Girelle*, plage d'Ouille (☎04.68.81.25.56).

Walks south from Collioure

For an easy walk out of Collioure, take rue de la République from the harbour, cross the main road and follow signs for **Nôtre-Dame-de-Consolation**, reached by track, then path, within ninety minutes. This is an old hermitage, now in ruins but much loved locally for its barbecue and *boules* area; strangely for such an out-of-the-way place, there's also a *chambre d'hôtes* (☎04.68.82.17.66; ③). If you're really serious about hiking and happy to progress south, continue on the trail to **Tour Madeloc** on the crest of a ridge (650m), descending on Banyuls-sur-Mer after about six hours; the last section uses the long-distance GR10 and HRP footpaths. The tower, also accessible by road from Banyuls, was built by Jaume I of Mallorca at the end of the thirteenth century as one of a chain of such signal stations.

Port-Vendres

The next settlement southeast, **PORT-VENDRES** (a 5min bus or train ride from Collioure), is marred by the busy main road, but for a genuine, unsophisticated fishing port, this is your best (indeed only) choice on the Côte Vermeille. You probably won't want to stay longer than it takes to look around the port and tuck into a fish lunch, or to watch the fish auctions held at the far end of the port every weekday evening (usually 5–7pm). A huge fish-processing factory dominates one side of the harbour, while sardine- and tuna-fishing boats are moored under the Maillol-designed war memorial opposite, with nets and other paraphernalia piled along the harbour wall. Salt has taken its toll on Maillol's work, and the uncharacteristically draped figures have lost limbs, noses and various other features.

To the Romans the town was *Portus Veneris* (Port of Venus), a place of strategic trading importance. By the Middle Ages its significance was diminishing in direct relation to the rising star of neighbouring Collioure, but by the eighteenth century it had recovered somewhat through the business of shipping Roussillon wines. In 1830 it became the primary port for dispatching soldiers and supplies to the French colony in Algeria, a link that lasted for more than a century.

Banyuls-sur-Mer to the frontier

As the road crosses the Col du Père Carnère and drops towards the Plage des Elmes, the once-elegant wine town of **BANYULS-SUR-MER** comes into view, with dry-stone walls and orderly rows of vines stretching into hills behind it. You could keep going for days on free samplings of the **Banyuls** dessert wine, which the French tend to drink as an aperitif (but the Spanish Catalans after meals). Try a guided tour of one of the larger cellars, such as the Cellier des Templiers in route du Mas-Reig (April–Oct daily 9am–7pm; rest of year Mon–Sat 9am–noon & 2–6pm).

Less fashionable than Collioure, Banyuls is still a lively and popular seaside resort. It's marred by a busy road which runs along the seafront, and the wide, stony main beach is less attractive than some smaller bays to the north and south, but the whole town comes alive in the evenings when everyone gets together to promenade along the seafront, play *boules* or eat out at one of the many beach cafés and seafood restaurants.

Don't leave Banyuls without visiting the **Laboratoire Arago**, the large white building overlooking the port. Run by the marine biology and land ecology department of the Sorbonne, its **aquarium** (daily: July & Aug 9am–noon & 2–10pm; rest of year 9am–noon & 2–6.30pm; 24F/€3.70) comprises over forty tanks of fascinating local specimens, including seahorses, bright red starfish and wicked-looking eels, along with a comprehensive display of local birds. The coastal waters of this area, rich in marine life due to the Pyrenees' steep underwater descent, were the first *réserve marine* declared in France, indeed the Mediterranean; more than 530 species of invertebrates have been identified within the zone. Those with requisite qualifications (PADI Open Water rating or BSAC equivalent) can **dive** within the reserve area by contacting Plongez Rederis Club, operating from the port (☎04.68.88.31.66 or 04.68.92.02.01).

Practicalities

The **train station** lies at the western edge of town, while **buses** stop on the coastal boulevard. The **tourist office** is on the seafront, opposite the *mairie* (July & Aug daily 9.30am–12.30pm & 2.30–7pm; Sept–June Tues–Sat 9.30am–12.30pm & 2–6.30pm; ☎04.68.88.31.58). Recommended one-star **hotels**, open all year, include the quaint and unpretentious *Canal*, 9 rue Dugommier (☎04.68.88.00.75; ②), the slightly smarter *Le Manoir*, 20 rue de Maréchal-Joffre (☎04.68.88.32.98; closed Nov & Dec; ⑤), and its neighbour *Sant Sebastien* (☎04.68.88.34.90, fax 04.68.88.11.71; ②), all in the quieter back streets. For a reasonably priced hotel on the seafront, try *La Pergola*, 5 av du Fontaulé (☎04.68.88.02.10, fax 04.68.88.55.45; closed Nov & Dec; ⑤), near the port, where most of the rooms have a balcony and seaview; they also have a good restaurant (*menus* from 90F/€13.70). **Camping** is at the *Camping du Stade*, rue Jean Boin (☎04.68.88.31.70; open all year), or the cheaper *Camping Municipal La Pinède* nearby, on route du Mas-Reig (☎04.68.88.32.13; March–Nov).

Banyuls has a good choice of **restaurants** specializing in fresh seafood. The most expensive, with starched tablecloths and live lobster tanks – among which *Le Sardinal*, 4 bis place Paul Reig, is reckoned the best – are lined up opposite the sea front, but there are several less expensive choices. Of these, the best is *Les Canadells*, just off the main boulevard at 4 av du Général de Gaulle, with excellent menus (from 78F/€11.90) and specializing in *zarzuela*. Nearby rue St-Pierre is home to a number of restaurants, including *Chez Rosa*, at number 22; *Casa Miguel*, with Spanish and Catalan specialties at number 3; and the livelier and more exotic *La Paillotte*.

Walks from Banyuls: Maillol's tomb and Col de Banyuls

The four-kilometre hike from Banyuls to **Maillol's tomb** and country house makes a pleasant excursion up into the vine-clad Albères. Walk the length of avenue Général de Gaulle, past the PTT, and under a bridge. Shortly afterwards, where the road curves to the right, take the left-hand road, following the line of a river: signs from here point to the "Musée et Tombeau de Maillol". The round trip takes about two and a half hours.

Keen hikers could continue to the **Col de Banyuls** (2hr) and into Spain (consult the Rando Éditions' *Carte de Randonnées* 1:50,000 "Roussillon" map, or the Editorial Alpina 1:80,000 "Cadaqués" map). In 1793 the *col* was the scene of a brave but doomed stand by a small French force, which held back the Spaniards long enough for their army to regroup; this was also the route followed by many refugees from the Spanish Civil War and from Nazism. Once over the pass you can walk to Espolla or follow the GR11 to

ARSTIDE MAILLOL (1861–1944)

Sculptor **Aristide Maillol**, the local Banyuls boy made good, began his professional life as a painter and tapestry designer; recognition came only in his forties, after he had devoted himself to sculpture and returned to Banyuls-sur-Mer from Paris.

In 1904, his Parisian admirers brought him to the attention of **Count Harry Kessler**, who became Maillol's patron and confidant over the next forty years. The two men could hardly have been more different: Kessler, son of a wealthy Prussian industrialist, known as the "Red Count" for his political leanings, the passion of his repressed homosexuality directed towards art collecting and generous sponsorship; Maillol, a Catalan peasant through and through, never picking up the tab for anything, apolitical at best, accused of pro-Falange or pro-Nazi sympathies at the worst of times. Yet the collaboration between them endured almost until 1937, when Kessler, driven into exile from Germany four years previously, died impoverished in Paris.

Unlike Rodin, Maillol initially had no taste for the **male nude**, and later found it difficult to find local peasants willing to pose; Kessler, with his contacts among handsome athletes, dancers and labourers, solved the problem. In 1922, Kessler attempted to complete Maillol's "classical" education – that was how many saw his work, in embryo – by taking him on a surprisingly productive trip to Greece. There was not, after all, that great a distance between Maillol's vision and the ancient masterpieces, nor between Kessler's tastes and the Greek youths.

In the best tradition of bohemian artisits, Maillol's long and unhappy marriage to the suitably jealous Clotilde Maillol was punctuated by dalliances with female models in his old age; Clotilde nearly wrecked his studio when she caught him *in flagrante* with Lucile Passavant, in 1930. But it was his next and last model-mistress, **Dina Vierny**, who really eclipsed Clotilde. Maillol was introduced to Vierny in 1935, and by 1938, aged just 19, she was living next door to him in Banyuls, and spending most days with the sculptor up in the hills at his retreat. After the Nazi occupation of northern France, Vierny – of Russian Jewish background, and a Communist sympathizer – joined the Comité de Secours Américain pour Intellectuels Antifascistes, and helped to smuggle a number of Jews, dissidents and other anti-Nazis over the border. Apparently Maillol, whatever his political views, taught her the best route into Spain.

When the Vichy regime got wind of her activities, Vierny was confined to house arrest in Banyuls, and then picked up by the Gestapo when she escaped to Paris in early 1943. Maillol appealed to his old acquaintance **Arno Breker**, the official Third Reich sculptor then resident in Paris, to help secure her release. A little flattery of Breker and the Nazi elite's reciprocal artistic admiration of Maillol – thus the accusations of collaboration – did the trick. Vierny was saved from deportation to a concentration camp in October 1943, and warned to stay out of trouble, but after a brief period at Banyuls, she drifted back to Paris and never saw Maillol again. The latter died of injuries sustained in a car crash in September 1944 – but not before he had made Vierny, and his son Lucien by Clotilde, his joint heirs and executors.

Upon Clotilde's death in 1952, Lucien – never much of a businessman – made Vierny sole executor, and between 1964 and 1996 she honoured Maillol's memory by founding three French **museums** dedicated to his work: two in Paris, and one at Maillol's country retreat, **La Métairie** (for directions, see "Walks from Banyuls"), where he is buried in a tomb topped by his *La Pensée*. The farmhouse museum (daily except Tues: May–Sept 10am–noon & 4–7pm; Oct, Nov & Jan–April 10am–noon & 2–5pm; closed public holidays; 20F), installed in the rooms where he lived and worked, displays over thirty bronze statues, with supporting photographs.

Elsewhere nearby, major works by the sculptor include, in Banyuls proper, a half-relief war memorial on the **Ile Grosse**, the islet at the end of the jetty; a sculpture in the garden of the *mairie* (access via the back gate from av Général-de-Gaulle); and another, *La Jeune Fille*, on the raised promenade above the harbour. Maillol's birthplace, now a Catalan crafts shop, is at 6 rue du Puig del Mas.

Llança via Sant Quirze de Colera (see, p.151). Either of these options requires a fairly long day.

Cerbère

The Côte Vermeille comes to an end at **CERBÈRE**. The harbour is quite pretty and the mountain backdrop impressive, but the beach negligible. Depending on the service, train passengers change either here or on the Spanish side at the much nicer Port Bou (see below), where the rail line changes track size in a deliberate manoeuvre by the Spaniards during the late nineteenth century to hamper any possible invasion from Europe. In Cerbère, you can **stay** and **eat** at *La Dorade* on the harbour (☎04.68.88.41.93; ⑤) or tent down at the palm- and cactus-fringed *Camping del Sorell* (☎04.68.88.41.64; June–Sept).

The Costa Brava

The **Costa Brava** extends some 200km from the border to just north of Barcelona, a realm synonymous with the first – and some of the worst – stirrings of postwar package tourism. Yet despite the commercialized tower-block fleshpots, it is still possible to encounter stretches of relatively unsullied shoreline, graced by the dramatic cliffs, pine-fringed coves and beaches that prompted all the development in the first place. This is far more likely in the northern reaches of the Costa Brava, near the Mediterranean terminus of the Spanish GR11 at Cap de Creus, and accordingly coverage here is restricted to the smaller, more human-scale resorts north of the Golfo de Roses, where tired hill-walkers will appreciate the chance of a few days by the sea.

One thing you'll notice upon crossing the border at the **Col dels Balistres** (Col des Balitres in French) is an abrupt change from the tidy viniculture of the French hillsides to the shaggier Spanish slopes. The effects of the phylloxera plague during the nineteenth century, as devastating here as on the French side, were compounded by a killing frost in 1956 which finished off commercial olive production. There have been continual brush- and forest-fires ever since, whose only beneficial result is the production of honey flavoured by the aromatic heather, lavender and myrtle which colonize the ashes.

Such deterioration of the agricultural economy has of course been accelerated by migration to Barcelona and further afield, and by the exponential growth of tourism. The most northerly resorts of the *costa* – **Port Bou, Colera, Llançà** and **El Port de la Selva** – are still very much for Catalans and passing French motorists, with little of the internationally pitched development that has created the blight further down the coast. In season, **Cadaqués** is more cosmopolitan and, thanks to Dalí, has a self-consciously arty feel. Large-scale holiday developments start at **Roses**, where the terrain becomes easier for building. You'll never find complete tranquillity nearby in summer, but if you're willing to walk a bit you can still discover some near-empty beaches on the fire-ravaged **Cap de Creus** peninsula, as well as some worthwhile inland sites, like the heavy-handedly restored Benedictine monastery of **Sant Pere de Rodes** or the wildlife reserve at **Aiguamolls de l'Empordà**.

Port Bou

PORT BOU, just 3km below the Spanish border, is the most northerly settlement of the Costa Brava, its isolation and good anchorage formerly making it a haven for smugglers. The village is built around a superbly protected bay in the green foothills of the Albères, surrounded by the sort of scenery that moved the Spanish poet Fernando Agulló to bestow the epithet *brava* (rugged) on what was then known simply as the *Costa de*

Llevant (East Coast). Besides the main stony harbour-beach, still used by fishermen to mend their nets, small, clean coves flank the harbour on either side, accessible by paths threading over the rocks. The road in from the south climbs vertiginously up to the 202-metre **Col de Frere**, which affords tremendous views before dropping into town.

Port Bou's main claim to fame is as a terminus of the Barcelona rail line; if you arrive by train, the **massive station** with its souvenir stalls and shunting sidings, built in 1929 and nearly as large as the town, creates a poor impression. The railway has transformed the place from small port to obligatory stop on the dash in and out of Spain, getting much of its trade from French tourists who come to stock up on booze and souvenirs before crossing straight back into France. Other visitors include those killing the afternoon hours before the night train from Cerbère to Paris, certainly a better way to pass the time than sitting in the Cerbère station bar.

But the most illustrious – and ill-fated – visitor was German-Jewish Marxist philosopher **Walter Benjamin**, who arrived here on September 27, 1940, as a refugee from the Nazis. When it appeared as though the Spanish were going to deny him entry and deport him back to certain death – he was near the top of the Gestapo's "wanted" list – he committed suicide by ingesting an overdose of morphine. Today he is honoured locally up at the *mirador* by a plaque on the wall of the cemetery, where he was interred for five years; and, down in the town hall, a semi-permanent propaganda-art exhibit entitled "L'Ultima Frontera de Walter Benjamin".

Practicalities

There's a **tourist information booth** (May–Sept daily 9am–8pm; ☎972 390 284) right at the harbour on Passeig de la Sardana, which has a map and list of hotels to give away; staff here are friendly and more than willing to help with recommendations. Out of season, you're on your own, with little if any choice in **accommodation**, as many establishments have closed recently or are clearly on their last legs. About as basic as you'd want is the *Hostal Juventus*, Avda de Barcelona 3 (☎972 390 241; ③) a block in from the water, which only opens summer if at all; next notch up is the *Hostal Costa Brava* at c/Alcalde Benjamí Cervera 20 (☎972 390 386; ④–⑤), with some sea views and en-suite rooms, but again only open June to October.

Food options are a bit more wide-ranging; there are some respectable **restaurants**, both inland and lining the quay, where you can get an excellent meal for 1300ptas/€7.80 and up. On Passeig de la Sardana, *L'Ancora* offers an excellent seafood paella and also serves beer in virtual buckets if you're set for an afternoon's chat with the barman; the adjacent *Espanya* might also be worth trying, as well as the *Tauro* (summer only), on Avinguda de Barcelona (the Colera road). For sandwiches, or just a drink, *Casa David* in the main Plaça del Mercat has popular outdoor seating, and over the road is the little **market** hall itself, open in the mornings for picnic fixings.

Colera and around

Some 10km from the border, **COLERA** – signposted as "Sant Miquel", its official name – is the first halt for slow trains on the Port Bou–Barcelona run. It's a shabby, down-at-heel place, with numerous high-rise blocks crammed into the narrow gulch leading down to the coarse-pebble bay, and blighted further by the rail viaduct which splits Colera in two. Not surprisingly then, it's used mainly by Spanish holidaymakers, who splash about in water rather cleaner than the town's off-putting name implies. As at Port Bou, short-term **accommodation** is in short supply, limited pretty much to the two-star *Hotel Gambina* on the harbour front (☎972 389 172; ⑦), slightly less expensive out of peak season. There are a couple of pricey **restaurants** overlooking the water, or some more reasonable, equally congenial, alternatives inland on the village square, Plaça Pi i Margall.

There's also a **campsite**, *Sant Miquel* (☎972 389 018; April–Sept), set well back from the beach, just off the main road, but for a better beach and cheaper lodging head south 2km to **Platja de Garbet**, where the eponymous campsite (☎972 389 001; April–Oct) is poor and caravan-crammed but the affiliated *Pensió Garbet* (③) with en-suite rooms is perfectly adequate. Two adjacent **restaurants** face the scenic, gravel-and-sand bay: one rough-and-ready, the other with table nappery and bow-tied waiters.

From Colera you can follow the Molinars valley 8km west by road to the ruined eponymous settlement around the twelfth-century church of **Sant Miquel de Colera**, which now stands as semi-restored testimony to the fears and hardships of the coastal populations who fled inland from pirates. There's an annual *aplec* here on the Sunday closest to May 8.

Llançà

The rail line leaves the coast at **LLANÇÀ**, also set back from its port to preclude the attentions of pirates. The place historically bred rugged fishermen, on account of its relatively exposed, north-facing harbour, but has been opened up to the passing tourist trade by the road and rail route to France – and is cheerfully brazen in its attempts to cash in. Unlike many such towns, however, it does have compensatory attractions, and is pitched slightly more upmarket than Colera.

The beach is a good 2km from the **train station** (buses stop outside), but the (not very) old town is much closer, just off to the right as you emerge. Once prosperous thanks to its marble industry, Llançà does not have a great deal to commend it, except for its attractive, café-ringed **Plaça Major**. This is flanked by an outsize fifteenth-century episcopal palace attached to an eighteenth-century parish church, as well as the renovated remains of a fourteenth-century defensive tower, which houses an exhibition (summer daily 10am–1pm & 6–9pm; winter Sat & Sun 4–6pm) of photographs of bygone Llança.

The road down to the **port** is lined with restaurants, souvenir shops and miniature golf courses. At first glance the harbour seems dominated by pleasure craft, its coarse-sand beach backed by a concrete esplanade and car park; the fish depot and commercial anchorage lie around the corner, under the landmark headland which everyone seems to climb to get sweeping views.

For better, more secluded **beaches**, you'll need to head 2–3km north to **Cap Ras**, a promontory covered by a forested nature reserve criss-crossed by trails. First you'll pass the strand of **Grifeu** with its hotel (see below), but best continue to the cape itself, where north-facing **Borró** is the main sandy bay near the parking area. Beyond Borró, accessible by path only, lie more protected coves popular with nudists.

Practicalities
The **Turisme** is on Avda d'Europa (July & Aug Mon–Sat 9.30am–9pm, Sun 10am–1pm; Sept–June Mon–Fri 9.30am–2pm & 4.30–8pm, Sat 10am–1pm & 5–7pm, Sun 10am–1pm; ☎972 380 855, *www.llanca.net*), the road into town. For **accommodation**, there are a few *habitacions,* hostals and hotels in the old town: *Habitaciones Can Pau,* c/Puig d'Esquer 4 (☎972 380 271; ③); *Hostal La Florida Blanca* (☎972 120 161; ③ May–Sept), with its own car park; or *Hotel Carbonell* around the corner on c/Major 19 (☎972 380 209; ④). Alternatively, you can stay down by the water, either at *Hostal Miramar*, Passeig Maritim 7 (☎972 380 132; ④), which overlooks the quieter side of the pedestrianized beach esplanade or out at the pink, slightly kitsch *Hotel Grifeu* (☎972 380 050; Easter–Sept; ⑤), at the namesake beach. There is also a **campsite**, signposted on the way in from the station: *L'Ombra* (☎972 380 335; open all year).

Reliable **restaurants** include the somewhat pricey *La Brasa*, two blocks inland at Plaça de Catalunya 6 (closed Dec–Feb), specializing in grilled meat, and *Can Manel* (closed Thurs in winter), just behind the harbourside car park, where reasonable seafood (especially *paella*) compensates for unpredictably brusque staff. For less outlay and more pleasant service at the southeast end of the esplanade, go for *La Finestra*, a snack-bar good for crêpes, salads and roast chicken: open through the afternoon and an unrivalled people-watching spot.

El Port de la Selva and inland

From Llançà, it's 8km along the coastal road (9 daily buses in summer, 2 otherwise) to El Port de la Selva; hikers can get there indirectly via the **GR11**, which climbs up through vineyards and aromatic scrub to the monastery of **Sant Pere de Rodes** (see below) before dropping down to the sea again.

Sitting on the eastern side of a large bay formed by the promontory of Cap de Creus, **EL PORT DE LA SELVA** is again a locals' family resort, but also the first place, heading south, that you'll see other foreigners (mostly Germans) in any numbers. It's not especially picturesque (though rather more so than Llança), and rather dull by night, but makes a good base for cape-walking. **Fishing** constitutes the lifeblood of the place: unless the *tramontana* is blowing, the boats venture forth most days to set their *bous* (nets pulled between two boats) or *teranyines* (long nets pulled by a single vessel). Weekend flats and villas for Catalans, especially on the west shore of the bay, are a Big Thing, and accordingly short-term **accommodation** choices are extremely limited. The en-suite *Pensió Sol y Sombra*, one block inland from the water at c/Nou 8, a quiet lane (☎972 387 060; ⑤), seems the least expensive option, though half-board may be mandatory; the nearest alternative is *Hostal La Tina* at c/Major 15 (☎972 387 149, fax 972 126 013, *www.gna.es/hostallatina/*; ④–⑤), which also has half-board rates. You may as well take up any offers of half-board, as there are few recommendable independent eateries here. El Port de la Selva's top-end choice is *Hotel Porto Cristo*, c/Major 59 (☎972 387 062, fax 972 387 529, *http://personalz.iddeo.es/portocristo*; ⑦), but priority may be given to clients of the in-house **scuba diving centre** (March–Dec), one of the more active on the Costa Brava. There is another independent one in town, the French-run Centre d'Immersió Port de la Selva, at c/Playa 9 (☎972 126 584, *cips.trossel@mx3.redestb.es*). If these are full, the run-down and vastly overpriced *Hostal Amberes* at the southwest edge of town (☎972 387 030; ⑥) will likely have a vacancy and does at least have parking in the municipal lot next door. There are two surviving local **campsites**: shady *Port de la Selva*,1km up the road to Cadaqués (☎972 387 287; June to mid-Sept) and the gigantic *Port de la Vall*, 5km along the road towards Llança, (☎972 387 186; April to mid-Sept), sloping down to its own patch of beach.

Sant Pere de Rodes

Just below the 670-metre-high summit of the Serra de Roda stands the Benedictine monastery of **Sant Pere de Rodes** (daily except Tues: June–Sept 10am–7pm; Oct–May 10am–1pm & 3–5pm; 600ptas/€3.60, plus 200ptas/€1.20 per car). It's 8km up the paved **road** from El Port, via Selva de Mar; signs at the parking area of La Pallera warn of an epidemic of car break-ins. Approaching **by foot**, rather than follow the GR11 – which is forced repeatedly onto the access road – use the marked trail through the Vall de Santa Creu, beginning at Molí de la Vall, just past the *Port de la Vall* campsite; count on ninety minutes from Port de la Selva, emerging just below the monastery at the plane-tree-shaded Font de los Monjos, which possibly prompted founding of the monastery in the first place.

Set on the seaward side of the mountain with views of a magnificent stretch of coast from Colera south, this was one of many religious institutions established in this area after the departure of the Moors. According to legend, when Rome was threatened by barbarians, Pope Boniface IV ordered the Church's most powerful relics – including

the head of St Peter – to be hidden, and dispatched three monks to find a safe refuge. The monks eventually dropped anchor at the port of Armen Rodes (now El Port de la Selva), where they hid their treasures in a cave on the remote cape. Subsequently unable to remember the exact hiding place, they founded the monastery rather than return to face the wrath of the pope. Legend or not, the monastery was probably built over a pagan temple dedicated to the Pyrenean Venus, Afrodita Pyrene – a theory based on a second- or first-century BC Egyptian map, written narratives from the third and fourth centuries AD, and the discovery of fragments of pagan sculptures and Corinthian capitals in the area.

The first reference to Sant Pere dates from 879, but it must have existed earlier. In 934 it became independent, answerable only to Rome; by the late tenth century it was the most powerful monastery in the region, commanding vast financial resources and administrating huge territories. Inevitably it aroused local jealousy, with disputes early on between the monastery and feudal lords of the surrounding country. As Sant Pere was enlarged it was also fortified against attack, starting a period of splendour that lasted four hundred years before its decline set in. Already by the late thirteenth century the monks were being condemned for spending time in the fleshpots of Selva de la Mar, and by 1789 the last discredited monks had departed and the buildings were abandoned to the elements and to plunderers, especially the French during the Peninsular War, though some rescued silver can be seen in Girona's Museu d'Art.

Whatever its origins, Sant Pere *used* to be one of the most romantic ruins in Catalonia, its central church universally recognized as the precursor of the Catalan Romanesque style. But following a brutal 1996–99 restoration with lots of civil engineering and concrete (and not much sensitivity in evidence), the monastery now unhappily ranks as a tourist trap of the first order; the sole thing missing to complete the "experience" is a canned sound track of Benedictine chants. No original columns or capitals remain in the cloister, and only the lofty, well-lit **cathedral** retains its mystery and original stonework from the tenth to fourteenth centuries, including eleventh-century column capitals carved with wolves' and dogs' heads. The crypt also remains as it was, while a steep spiral staircase leads up to tiny Sant Miquel chapel, then to the *girolla* or ambulatory above the apse, which retains a few Romanesque fresco fragments. Features are labelled only in Spanish, French or Catalan, though to the renovators' credit their steps and metal catwalks do get you to most corners of the building.

Castell de Sant Salvador de Verdera and Santa Elena

From the monastery a steep, narrow path climbs twenty minutes more to the top of the mountain and the severely ruined **Castell de Sant Salvador de Verdera**, contemporary of Sant Pere and another possible original site of the temple of Venus. Its views south across the bay of Roses and the now-drained marshlands of the Empordà plain made it the perfect lookout for the frequent invasions (French or Moorish), normally from the sea. In the event of attack, fires were lit on the hill to warn the whole surrounding area. Following the paved road 1km away from the monastery brings you to the pre-Romanesque church of **Santa Elena**, all that remains of the small rural community which grew up around the monastery. Though locked, you can glimpse its cavernous, three-aisled interior through a grating. Even on peak visitor days – when Sant Pere itself is absolutely to be avoided, at least from 11am to 4pm – you'll likely have only the birdsong of the Serra de Roda for company.

Dolmens – and Vilajuïga

A possible continuation from Sant Pere involves following the nine-kilometre road to Vilajuïga, a village on the Barcelona–Port Bou train line and connected by bus to Cadaqués, Roses and Figueres. Small signs along the way indicate paths to **dolmens** at **Vinyes Mortes** dating from 4000 BC. Particularly impressive is a pair of tombs off to the left of the road, under 3km from the monastery car park (near where there are more signposted dolmens). Walkers will find that the marked path down to Vilajuïga shortcuts a considerable amount of the curvy road.

VILAJUÏGA itself can offer the ruined Visigothic **Castell de Quermançó** just north and an eleventh/twelfth-century **synagogue** in the centre. Cool, damp and barrel-vaulted, this now serves as the antechamber to the hideous late-medieval church of **Sant Feliu**. Getting to the castle involves a ten-minute walk across the fields followed by a scramble up a steep outcrop, whose rocks blend into the crumbling walls. If you want to **stay**, there's just the en-suite *Hostal Xavi* on the main road near the train station (☎972 530 003; ③), adequate if a bit beset by traffic; there are several **restaurants** to choose from on the same road or in the village proper.

Cadaqués and Port Lligat

CADAQUÉS is the most pleasant base on the Pyrenean Costa Brava, reached only by a single, winding road over the hills behind Port de la Selva or Roses, and consequently retaining an air of isolation. With box-like, whitewashed houses lining narrow, hilly streets, a tree-lined promenade and craggy headlands to either side of a harbour that is still a working fishing port, it's genuinely picturesque.

Already by the 1920s and 1930s the place had begun to attract the likes of Utrillo, Picasso, Man Ray, García Lorca, Buñuel, Thomas Mann and Einstein. But Cadaqués really "arrived" as an **artistic-literary colony** after World War II when Surrealist painter Salvador Dalí and his wife Gala settled at nearby Port Lligat, attracting for some years a floating bohemian community. Cadaqués no longer gets the sort of hippie crowd that once flocked here in the 1960s and 1970s, and is now a bit too hedonistic and trendy for its own good. Nonetheless, Cadaqués remains (just) accessible. There are beautiful people around and more than a few Mercedes, but the current scene falls far short of Côte d'Azur snobbery. Out of season Cadaqués can be great and even in midsummer – if you can bear the dense crowds and the high prices – you'll probably have fun.

The extravagantly large **church** – conspicuous whether you approach by sea or from inland – is a landmark that has guided generations of seafarers past the rocks and reefs at the harbour entrance. It might have been better off less visible: the village suffered numerous pirate raids, one of the worst being at the hands of the Ottoman "admiral" Barbarossa, who in 1543 sacked the town and burned the original church. The present edifice was built in the seventeenth century and has a remarkable Baroque altarpiece carved by Pedro Costa.

Local **beaches** are all tiny and pebbly, but there are some enjoyable walks around the harbour and nearby coves, while the town itself makes for an interesting stroll, clambering around the streets below the church. The number of private art galleries here has mushroomed since the moneyed set began stopping by, and a couple of good museums soak up browsers, too. Close to the church, the **Museu d'Art Municipal** on c/Narcis Monturiol (April–Oct Mon–Sat 11am–1pm & 4–8.30pm, Sun 11am–1pm; 600ptas/€3.60) features changing exhibits of local artists inspired mostly by the nearby coastline, juxtaposing almost every modern style. The **Museu Perrot-Moore** in the middle of town at c/Vigilant 1 (Easter–Dec daily 10.30am–1.30pm & 4.30–8.30pm; 700ptas/€4.20) now contains only Dalí prints plus a few Picassos, other works having been dispersed to various museums worldwide.

Practicalities

Buses (several a day from Figueres/Roses, one a day from El Port de la Selva) arrive at the little SARFA bus office on c/Sant Vicens, on the edge of town, from where it's less than ten minutes' walk, following c/Unió and c/Vigilant, to the central beachside

Plaça Frederic Rahola. Having a **car** is a distinct liability here – you're virtually forced to use the large fee car park near the bus stop. The **Turisme** is adjacent to the beach-side square at c/des Cotxes 2 (July–Sept Mon–Sat 9.30am–2pm & 4–9pm, Sun 10am–1pm; Oct–June Mon–Sat 10.30am–1pm & 5–7pm; ☎972 258 315).

ACCOMMODATION
A town plan posted at the bus stop will indicate all **accommodation** possibilities, which dwindle to nil at peak season. Least expensive rooms are at either the *Fonda Cala d'Or* at c/Tórtola 2, left and then 100m inland as you face the water (☎972 258 149; ②), with just four rooms, or *Pensío Vehí* (☎972 258 470; open Easter–Sept; ③), better situated, below the church at Plaça de l'Església 5. Moving one notch up in comfort, *Hostal Marina* (☎972 258 199; ④), and *Hostal Cristina*, with limited parking (☎972 258 138; ④), are both just behind the waterfront *plaça*, offering pricier rooms with bath and off-season discounts. *Hostal Ubaldo*, on the way into town from the bus stop at c/Unió 13 (☎972 258 125; ⑤), represents good value with all rooms en suite. The area's eight **hotels** predictably trade on the arty reputation, charging well over the odds; a good-value exception is the low-rise *Aparthotel Calina*, on the scrappy beach at Port Lligat (☎ & fax 972 258 851), with a large pool, parking, variable views and a variety of units ranging from simple doubles (④) to self-catering studios (9500ptas/€57). For **camping** – plus some cabins (5000ptas/€30 with shower) – there's the noisy *Camping Cadaqués* (☎972 258 126; April–Sept), 1km along the road to Port Lligat.

EATING AND DRINKING
The harbourside esplanade is chock-a-block with fairly indistinguishable pizzerias and **restaurants**. If you're not sick of it yet, Cadaqués is a good spot to sit outside and dive into a *paella*, which most places offer as part of a *menú del día*. Elsewhere, standouts (working up the price ladder) include the *menjador* of *Fonda Cala d'Or* (closed Sun out of season), a smoky, kitsch-decor holdover from the hippie days, where the service is friendly, the food basic (*paella, gambas, aroz negre*), and prices (1000–2000ptas/€6–12 for three courses) equally so; or the restaurant attached to the *Pensió Vehí*, with seafood *menús* at 1400–1600ptas/€8.40–9.60 and a seaview terrace. *El Pescador*, 150m off to the right as you face the water, has an elegant two-storeyed dining room and seats outside, an authentic Catalan *paella* (with seafood, sausage and spare ribs), plus *menús* at 2100ptas/€12.60; and last but not least is *Casa Anita* on c/Miquel Rosells, a long-running, obligatorily sociable institution where diners are seated together at long tables, the food's excellent and queues form early in the evening during high season. Miquell Rosells, one block inland from the esplanade and perpendicular to c/Unió-Vigilant, is also home to most of Cadaqués' **nightlife** – virtually every other address is a *tapas* bar, music club or full-on restaurant. Otherwise, on the front near *El Pescador* is a barn-like café-bar open long hours, founded and run municipally, as in so many Catalan villages, and enduringly popular.

Port Lligat and the Casa-Museu Salvador Dalí
There's no public transport to the smaller harbour of **PORT LLIGAT**, 2km north, but there is a choice of cross-country routes for walkers, none taking over twenty minutes. As the road north from Cadaqués descends, the landscape opens out to a scene of hotels and well-spaced villas. For decades Salvador Dalí lived here with his wife and muse, Gala, having gradually converted a series of waterside fishermen's cottages into a sumptuous home that has all the quirks you would expect of the couple, such as speckled rooftop eggs and a giant fish painted on the ground outside. The house is now open to the public as the **Casa-Museu Salvador Dalí** (mid-March to mid-June Tues–Sun 10.30am–6pm; mid-June to mid-Sept daily 10.30am–9pm; mid-Sept to early Jan Tues–Sun 10.30am–6pm; 1300ptas/€7.80), and while there's not much in the way

of artwork, and visitor numbers are strictly controlled (maximum 8 people at a time; you're given an entry time on your ticket), it's worth the wait to see first-hand how the bizarre couple lived until Gala's death in 1982, after which Dalí moved to Figueres.

Tours take in most of the house, and include Dalí's studio, the exotically draped model's room, the couple's master bedroom and bathroom, and, perhaps best of all, the oval-shaped sitting-room that Dalí designed for Gala, which, apparently by accident, boasts stunning acoustics. Upstairs you can see the garden and swimming pool where the couple entertained guests – they didn't like too many strangers trooping through their living quarters. The phallic swimming pool and its various decorative features, including a giant snake and a stuffed lion, are a treat.

Roses

Several daily buses run from Cadaqués west to **ROSES** along the steep road threading through umbrella pine forest and terraced hillsides. The town is easily accessible, too, from Figueres, with even more frequent bus connections throughout the day. This area has been inhabited since at least 3000 BC, as evidenced by the dolmens hereabouts. Greeks from Asia Minor established the trading port of Rhoda here in about 1000 BC, and by the eleventh century AD the town's fine natural harbour had effectively supplanted that of nearby Castelló d'Empúries, by then silting up. In 1543, Carlos I of Spain built the now-ruined, star-shaped fortress of **La Ciudadela**, dismantled by the French during the Peninsular War.

Roses is big for these parts, and getting larger every year. Four kilometres of beach on the wide sweep of the **Golfo de Roses** have been emphatically discovered by the package-holiday industry, while the Narbonne–Barcelona motorway has accelerated the resort's growth; the massive new development of Empuriabrava (sandwiched between the two halves of the Aiguamolls de l'Empordà nature reserve, see below) bills itself as "the biggest residential marina in the world". Outside high season, Roses has a palm-fringed elegance of sorts, but by summer it has all gone to pieces, the general tone set by the water park and go-kart track on the outskirts. The beach is good, though, the setting photogenic, and advertised **boat excursions** around the cape to Cadaqués or out to the Illes Medes worthwhile.

Practicalities

Buses stop at the corner of c/Gran Via Pau Casals and c/Riera Ginjolas, and on the seafront promenade there's a **Turisme** (daily: June–Sept 9am–9pm; Oct–May 9am–1pm & 4–8pm; ☎972 257 331, *otroses@ddgi.es*) – whose aid will have to be enlisted if you show up mid-season without an **accommodation** reservation. At slower times you might sample *Pensió Cal Catalá*, c/Francesc Macía 14 (☎972 256 336; ④) or the *Pensió Sant Jordi*, Platja del Rastrell (☎972 256 321; ⑥). There are also several huge **campsites** on the road between Roses and Figueres. Recommendations for **eating out** seem fairly pointless, given Roses' full-blown status as a resort, with a predictable rash of cafés and restaurants, not to mention "supermarkets", discos and "English breakfasts".

Parc Natural dels Aiguamolls de l'Empordà

Inland and mainly to the south of Roses extends the **Parc Natural dels Aiguamolls de l'Empordà** (daily; free), an important wetland reserve created by the Catalan government in 1983 to save what remained of the Empordà marshland, which once covered the entire plain here but has gradually disappeared over the centuries as a result of agricultural developments and cattle-raising. Relying heavily on natural history students from Barcelona University and volunteers, the park looks a little raw in places – especially after severe fires in August 2000 – but attracts a wonderful selection of birds to both its coastal terrain and the paddy fields typical of the area. There are several easy **paths** around lagoons and marshes, some passing within yards of the beach, and **hides** have been created along the way; morning and early evening are the best times for bird-watching in the marshes and you'll witness the largest number of species during the migration periods (March–May & Aug–Oct). You'll almost certainly see marsh harri-ers and various waterfowl, and might spot bee-eaters, kingfishers and the rare glossy ibis. A lesser-known hide stands 5km from Castelló d'Empúries, on the road to Palau-Saverdera; you have to walk or hitch, watching out for the tiny signpost by an electric-ity pylon on the left.

Without your own transport, access is by one of the numerous daily **buses** of the SARFA company (which provides most buses on the Costa Brava) plying the Figueres–Roses road. To reach the heart of the park, get off the bus at Castelló d'Empúries and take the turning south towards Sant Pere Pescador. After about 4km, you'll see a sign on the left for the **visitors' centre** at El Cortalet (daily: March–Sept 9.30am–2pm & 4.30–7pm; Oct–Feb 9.30am–2pm & 3.30–6pm; ☎972 454 222), where you can pick up a brochure of recommended routes, and see an exhibition on local birds and migrant species. You can cut out the walk to the centre by using the twice-daily Roses–Girona bus (via Sant Pere Pescador); buses en route from Figueres (see overleaf) to Palafrugell also stop at the slightly shabby resort of Sant Pere Pescador, about 3km south of the centre. To get the most out of the park, take a pair of binocu-lars – and in summer and autumn you'll need mosquito repellent.

The only **camping** allowed within the park is at the massive "first-class" *Nàutic Almatà* (☎972 454 477; mid-May to Sept), and, closer to Castelló d'Empúries, at the smaller *La Laguna* (☎972 450 553; April–Oct).

Castelló d'Empúries

The delightful small town of **CASTELLÓ D'EMPÚRIES**, halfway between Roses and Figueres, makes by far the most attractive base for the park – and indeed is worth a stop in passing anyway. A five-minute walk from the outskirts where the **bus** halts (and where **cars** should be parked) brings you into a little medieval cluster poised above the Riu Muga, that's lost little of its genteel charm despite being so close to the beach-bound hordes. Formerly the capital of the Counts of Empúries, the town's narrow alleys and streets conceal some fine preserved buildings, a medieval bridge, and a thirteenth-century battlemented church, Santa María, whose ornate doorway alone is reward enough for the trip.

There are several places to **stay**, and while rates can be surprisingly high, it's a price worth paying for the peace and quiet when the day-trippers have all gone home. There are two places next to each other south of the centre at the corner of Avgda Generalitat and c/Santa Clara, near where the bus stops, which are much nicer than their position suggests. The *Hostal Ca L'Anton* (☎972 250 509; ④) has an attached restaurant with a fine *menú* and plenty of local cuisine, while the adjacent *Pensió Serratosa* (☎972 250 508; ③) is better appointed and better value, with off-street parking and again its own *men-jador*. At the heart of the old quarter, the two-star *Hotel Canet* (☎972 250 340, fax 972 250 607, *www.hotelcanet.com*; ⑤) enjoys a fine position at Plaça Joc de la Pilota 2, with a recommendable terrace restaurant and limited parking.

Finally, connoisseurs of **cases rurals** will want to consider two local offerings. The first is *La Caputxeta*, just across the river from Castelló and past the roundabout (☎972 250 310 or 250 646; ④ B&B), whose spotless, tiled-floor rooms belie the somewhat scruffy exterior. It's run by a French-speaking sculptor couple who present art semi-nars; there's a self-catering kitchen and a choice of continental or traditional Catalan breakfast. The other, in the remoter village of **SIURANA D'EMPORDÀ** between

---

THE SARDANA

The great difference between the **sardana** – the traditional dance of Catalonia – and many other folk dances is that it is not performed solely by specialists, but is instead the inheritance of the entire community. However, this doesn't mean that you can simply barge in and have a go. It is a very complex dance, and etiquette demands that you join a circle of dancers of your own standard. Following the movements of the arms isn't too challenging, as every dancer holds hands with his or her neighbours in the circle – consequently, your limbs will be hauled up and down at the appropriate moments. But the footwork is fiendishly difficult, with the step changing mid-bar and the beat changing mid-step. The haunting musical accompaniment is provided by a band known as a **cobla**, comprising ten wind instruments plus a double bass, a brass section and percussion. The dignity and intensity of the event, the linking of the hands and the upright posture all suggest Classical Greek images of dancers, and indeed the sardana may have originated with the ancient Greek settlers who established the port of Roses (though cynics claim it was artificially resuscitated during the nineteenth century as part of the resurgence in Catalan national feeling).

On summer Sundays and festival days the sardana is danced all along the Costa Brava (and on the Côte Vermeille too), as well as at plenty of inland towns and villages – a particularly big occasion being *La Diada* (National Day) on September 11. Dates for other major sardanas are given in the "Festivals" feature on pp.92–93.

Figueres and Sant Pere Pescador, is *El Molí* (☎972 525 139; ⑤ B&B), an award-winning premises set amongst vast gardens, overlooked by balconied, en-suite rooms, with half-board available.

Figueres and around

FIGUERES is the capital of Alt Empordà county – the upper part of the massive alluvial plain formed by the rivers Muga and Fluvià – but its sole claim on most tourists, excepting its role as transport hub, is that **Salvador Dalí** (1904–89) was born here, began his career here and died here. Yet if you linger after touring the museum devoted to his work, you'll discover a pleasant provincial town with some 30,000 inhabitants, a lively central *rambla* and adequate food and lodging.

From Figueres, most travellers head either to the coast or the high Pyrenees, ignoring the **Albères hills** immediately north of town. From **Maçanet de Cabrenys** in the west to **Espolla** in the east stretches this virtually unknown region of semi-ruined villages hidden among resin-scented hills, dotted with occasional vineyards, olive groves and shady cork-oak plantations.

The Town

Figueres' **Teatre-Museu Dalí** (July–Sept daily 9am–7.15pm, plus 10.30pm–12.30am in Aug; Oct–June Tues–Sun 10.30am–6pm; July–Sept 1200ptas/€7.20, Oct–June 1000ptas/€6; *www.dali-estate.org*) is the most visited museum in Spain after Madrid's Prado and the Guggenheim in Bilbao, but it's more a theatrical fantasy, appealing to everyone's innate love of absurdity and participation, than a conventional art collection. Appropriately enough, the building was once the municipal theatre, the venue for Dalí's first exhibition of paintings in 1919 (when he was 14) but destroyed at the end of the Spanish Civil War. Upon its reconstruction in 1974, the artist inaugurated a museum within, which he then set about fashioning into an inspired repository for some of his most bizarre works. Having moved back to Figueres at the end of his life (see box p.148), Dalí died here on January 23, 1989; his body now lies behind a simple granite slab inside the museum.

The **building** (signposted from just about everywhere, on Plaça Gala i Salvador Dalí, a couple of minutes' walk off the Rambla) was designed as an exhibit in itself. Three-cornered bread rolls stud the exterior walls, one of which is painted terra-cotta pink; topped by a huge metallic-glass dome, the roof line is studded with luminous giant eggs and stylized figures preparing to dive from the heights. It gets even crazier **inside**: every part of the theatre, from the circular central atrium and stage to the crypt, foyer and staircases, has been transformed by Dalí's unique designs and artworks. You can water the snail-infested occupants of a steamy Cadillac by feeding it with coins, view the face of Mae West constructed as a living room with a shiny red sofa as the lips, use telescopes and coin-operated machines to see paintings and constructions move and change, and gaze at a soaring totem pole of car tyres topped with a boat and an umbrella. Other galleries on various levels contain a complete life-sized orchestra, skeletal figures, adapted furniture (a bed with fish tails), sculpture and ranks of surreal paintings. Although many of Dalí's paintings and sculptures (and some by other artists) are on display, this is not a collection of Dalí's "greatest hits"; nonetheless, the thematically arranged assembly beggars description and is not to be missed.

The nearby **Museu de l'Empordà** at Rambla 1 (July–Sept Tues–Sat 11am–1pm & 4–9pm, Sun & public holidays 5–9pm; Oct–June Tues–Sat 11am–7pm, Sun & public holidays 10am–2pm; 300ptas/€1.80), a serious collection of local Roman finds, paintings by regional artists and works borrowed from the Prado in Madrid, remains largely unvisited. Figueres also has a toy museum with over three thousand exhibits from all over Catalunya, the **Museu dels Joguets** (Mon–Sat 10am–1pm & 4–7pm, Sun 11am–1.30pm & 5–7.30pm; winter closed Tues & Sun pm; 650ptas/€3.90), housed in a beautiful but crumbling old hotel in the Rambla, above *Cafe Emporium*. The statue at the bottom of the **Rambla** is a monument to Narcis Monturiol, a local who distin-

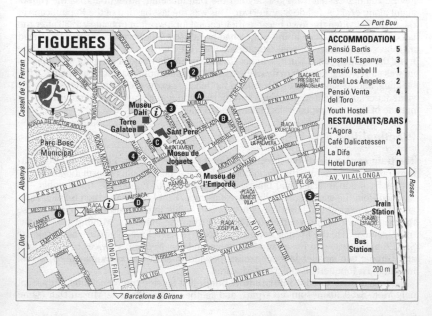

ACCOMMODATION
Pensió Bartis — 5
Hostel L'Espanya — 3
Pensió Isabel II — 1
Hotel Los Ángeles — 2
Pensió Venta del Toro — 4
Youth Hostel — 6

RESTAURANTS/BARS
L'Agora — B
Café Dalicatessen — C
La Difa — A
Hotel Duran — D

DALÍ: WHOSE LIFE IS IT ANYWAY?

Controversy surrounds **Salvador Dalí's final years**, with some observers believing that he didn't so much choose to live as a recluse as find himself imprisoned by his three guardians, who controlled all his artistic and financial dealings. Dalí suffered severe burns in a fire at his house in Púbol in 1984, after which he moved into the Torre Galatea, the tower adjacent to the museum. Fitted with a pacemaker and suffering psychological problems, Dalí became increasingly depressed, and several Spanish government officals and friends fear that, in his senile condition, he was manipulated. In particular, it's alleged that he was made to sign blank canvases – which has inevitably led to the questioning of the authenticity of some later works. From the mid-1980s onwards, there were a series of trials in the US based on charges that various individuals exploited bogus prints and lithographs. In 1990, two Americans, William Mett and Marvin Wiseman, were found guilty of art fraud – in particular of promoting spurious Dalí reproductions – fined nearly US$2 million and sentenced to three years' prison.

The divison of his legacy of paintings (genuine or otherwise) is made yet more complicated by the fact that Dalí, under the terms of his final will in 1982, left his entire estate, valued at US$130 million, to the Spanish state, with the works of art to be divided between Madrid and Figueres. The Catalan art world was outraged, and battled successfully to keep any canvases from being carted off to Madrid – plans are under way to exhibit over a hundred of the paintings in an as-yet undecided location in Catalunya.

guished himself by inventing the submarine. Pavement cafés line the Rambla, and you can browse around the art galleries and gift shops in the streets and squares surrounding the church of Sant Pere.

The only other sight is the huge eighteenth-century **Castell de Sant Ferran** (daily: June–Sept 10.30am–8pm; Oct–May 10.30am–2pm; free), 1km northwest of town – follow Pujada del Castell from just beyond the Dalí museum, straight across the roundabout along c/al Castell de Sant Ferran. This was the last bastion of the Republicans in the Civil War, when the town became their capital for a week in February 1939 after the fall of Barcelona. Earlier in the war, it had been used as a barracks for newly arrived members of the International Brigades before they moved on to Barcelona and the front: the sculptor Jason Gurney, in his *Crusade in Spain*, wrote of sleeping in dungeons he was still excited enough to describe as the "most beautiful barracks in Spain . . . the building, and its setting in the Pyrenean foothills . . . exquisite". The castle is open for visits (afternoons winter, mornings summer); if you find it shut, the circuit around the outside of the star-shaped walls makes a good walk.

Practicalities

The **train station** lies 500m directly east of the centre, in Plaça Estació; the **bus station**, opposite and across the *plaça*, has left-luggage lockers, plus information and tickets for local and international buses. The focal point of Figueres – the Rambla – is reached from the stations by walking west along c/Sant Llàtzer and then turning right at c/Nou. **Parking** your own car is nearly impossible in the centre; either pay to use the car parks or resign yourself to a walk in from the outskirts. **Moving on**, regular trains run north to the French frontier and south to Barcelona. There are fairly regular SARFA bus services to Roses and Cadaqués, and less frequent services to Palafrugell and Girona; two smaller bus companies provide weekday services into the Albères, including La Jonquera, Espolla and Maçanet.

There's a small **tourist information booth** just outside the bus station (July–Sept only Mon–Sat 9.30am–1pm & 4–7pm), and another on the Plaça de Museu Dalí (same hours). The central **Turisme** is at Plaça del Sol opposite the post office (Easter–June & Oct Mon–Fri 8.30am–3pm & 4.30–8pm, Sat 9.30am–1.30pm & 3.30–6.30pm; July–Sept Mon–Sat 8.30am–8.30pm, Sun 9am–3pm; Nov–Easter Mon–Fri 8.30am–3pm; ☎972 503 155, *www.figueres.org*), reached by leaving the Rambla by its southwest corner along c/Lasauca. Both services should provide a town map, handy hotel lists, and timetables for onward transport. There's also an **Internet café**, *Pizz@fono*, near the bus station at c/Antonio 27 (June–Aug daily 9.30am–1pm & 4–11pm; Sept–May Tues–Sun 4–11pm; 500ptas/€3 per hour, first 10min free).

Accommodation

Accommodation options range from the most basic to upmarket, though many of the better hotels and *hostales* lie on main roads out of town. The least expensive place to stay, though perfectly acceptable, is *Pensió Bartis*, c/Mendez Nunyez 2 (☎972 501 473; ②), near the bus and train stations. Moving up in price, halfway between the central tourist office and the Museu Dalí, is the friendly *Pensió Venta del Toro* on c/Pep Ventura (☎972 510 510; ③), with a bar downstairs. For a very reasonable *hostal* right in the centre of town, try *Hostal L'Espanya* (☎972 500 869; ③) at c/Jonquera 26, corner c/Muralla, very close to the Museu Dalí, or the cheaper but less attractive *Pensió Isabel II*, c/Isabel II 16 (☎972 504 735; ③). Another comfortable lodging in the city centre is the slightly overpriced *Hotel Los Ángeles* (☎972 510 661, fax 972 510 700, *hangeles@olemail.com*; ④), where the bathrooms are as big as the smallish bedrooms, done up in vulgar-Spanish-Modern, and off-street parking costs extra.

There's a good **youth hostel** (☎972/50 12 13; closed Sept; ①), at c/Anicet Pagès 2, off Plaça del Sol, immediately behind the tourist office. Figueres also has a **campsite** about 2km out on the main N11 northwest towards France, the smallish, shady *Pous* (☎972 675 496; April–Oct).

Eating and drinking

A gaggle of tourist **restaurants** cram the narrow streets around the Dalí museum, particularly along c/Jonquera; they offer low-price menus of variable quality but usually charge extra for wine, water and coffee, which can double the bill. More stylish, but still reasonably priced, is *L'Agora* in the old casino building, on the corner of c/Ample and c/Peralada, a spacious, modern bar-restaurant with excellent *menús* (1350–2700ptas/€8.10–16.20) including Catalan specialities. *La Difa*, c/Muralla 17 (closed Sun, Mon night & Sat lunch) is slightly pricier but has vegetarian main courses. If money's no object, head for the *Hotel Duran*, c/Lasauca 5, where they serve generous regional dishes with a modern touch.

The Rambla has several popular pavement **cafés**, though ones on Plaça Ajuntament and Plaça Pius XII, near the Dalí museum, are quieter and less cramped. For something better than the usual hostal breakfast, *Café Dalicatessen* at c/Sant Pere 17–19 offers good juices, pots of Earl Grey tea and fresh croissants. Eating aside, Figueres is generally fairly comatose **at night**: on weekend evenings there are traffic jams on the road to Roses as everyone heads out to the coast.

West and north of Figueres

The most interesting inland outings **west from Figueres** visit large villages either side of the forest-fringed **Pantà (Reservoir) de Boadella**, less impressive than it seems on the map, especially after dry winters, but still a focus for local water-sports enthusiasts. During World War II the region **north of Figueres** was so deserted that there were no Guardia Civil stationed between the Castell de Requesens and Port Bou, which made the eastern Albères a favoured escape route from France. Of late, numbers of foreigners – mainly Dutch and German – have moved in to convert the crumbling farms, and Catalan daytrippers scour the countryside at weekends, replenishing their cellars at the many wineries that dot the area, especially around Capmany.

Sant Llorenç de la Muga and Albanyà

There's a single midday bus to these settlements; driving yourself, follow signs out of town for the N11 to La Jonquera, and keep an eye peeled for the poorly marked turning for Llers, and then to **SANT LLORENÇ DE LA MUGA**, about 17km west of the town. Without there being much specific to see, this large, fortified village, nestled in greenery along the Riu Muga, makes an excellent destination; it's linked to Macenet de Cabrenys (see below) by a marked but rough track (hikers or 4WDs only) skirting wetlands on the reservoir's west shore. The medieval stone houses form much of the defensive perimeter, but there are two portcullised thirteenth-century gates – one on the west, the other south opening onto the old *camí* to Girona – and stout towers at scattered points, for example behind the twelfth-century parish church. If you enter Sant Llorenç from the north, you pass an old bridge and a millrace leading down to a dilapidated mill, doubtless soon to be gentrified as a restaurant; for now the sole **eatery** is *Sa Muga* on the central Rambla, while you can drink outside in fine weather at either *El Lluro* on Plaça Baixa, or the municipally run *Societat La Fraternitat* on the Rambla. As yet there's no place to **stay** in the old quarter, though you'll find a small-scale, tent-friendly **camping**, *La Fradera* (☎972 542 054; Easter–Oct), 1.5km west, and a **casa rural** about 4km along: *Can Carreras* (☎972 569 199; ⑤ B&B), set by itself overlooking the river, with half-board available.

By contrast, **ALBANYÀ**, 7km upstream from Sant Llorenç and officially within Alta Garrotxa, is nothing special architecturally, though here too there's a minuscule medieval core with an arched gate giving onto the old *camí* to Sant Llorenç. If you're on a **GR11** traverse you'll necessarily pass through, as Albanyà lies between the **Col de Bassegoda**, 11km west and the true district boundary, and Macenet de Cabrenys (20km or five walking hours north). The asphalt gives out 1.5km west at the caravan-dominated and rather off-putting *Camping Bassegoda* (☎972 542 020, open all year); trekkers might prefer to beg a *habitació* in town, upstairs from the **restaurant** by the ancient church, and top up supplies at the single shop.

Darnius and Maçanet de Cabrenys

North of the Pantà de Boadella – accessible from the Muga valley by a link road below the dam, or directly off the N11 – lies **DARNIUS**, which has regular bus links to Figueres with the company David i Manel. It's not exactly a thriving place – its plight symbolized by the smashed, abandoned hotel on the central village street, and an uninspiring *hostal* up on the main bypass road. If you're going to **stay** nearby, far better to do so at *La Central* (☎972 535 053, fax 972 550 431, *www.lacentral.com*; ③–⑥), 6km southwest along a well-marked and -graded side track. A *modernista* chalet formerly owned by the power-generating company (thus the name), this has idyllic surroundings, superb common areas and three grades of rooms for which reservations are mandatory: ordinary, "rustic" and deluxe suites. The in-house **restaurant** is renowned for seafood caught from its own boat at Roses, served in the tropical-kitsch dining room (giant fish tank, a waterfall-wall out the window) – you can get away with 3000ptas/€18 per head, but best budget 4000ptas/€24.

Culture buffs may prefer to stay on the bus or make their own way to the livelier and more atmospheric **MAÇANET (MASSANET) DE CABRENYS** 26km from Figueres. Cars (and the **bus**) stop south of this densely packed, oval-shaped medieval ensemble, next to a **Turisme** which should open in 2001. There are two recommendable places to **stay** and **eat**. *Hostal La Quadra* at the northwest edge of town (☎972 544 032; ③) has a vaulted cellar restaurant with regional specialties (closed Tues except July–Sept). The

Hotel Pirineos (☎972 544 000; ⑤) in the centre occupies a four-hundred-year-old baronial mansion, in the same family for much of that time, and converted by the present, gracious descendant. Here a meal of homemade soup, jugged partridge, dessert and good house red wine will run about 2500ptas/€15. The only other specific "sight" in Maçanet is the **Menhir O Pedra Dreta**, dating from around 3000 BC and standing 2m high on the western fringe of the village, just beyond Mas Pitxo. It's also worth knowing that there's a cross-border road (paved but narrow) to Coustouges in France, via the Santuari de Salines.

The Espolla region

The environs of Espolla, northeast of Figueres and served by just one daily bus from Figueres, is even more fruitful for prehistorians, with at least ten known sites in the immediate area. Easiest to find is the **Dolmen de la Cabana Arqueta**, nearly five thousand years old; from Espolla take the Sant Climent road, and at the rising bend 1km beyond the village take the farm track to the right – the dolmen is ten minutes' walk on. The most important, however, is **Dolmen del Barranc**, the only carved tomb yet found in the area: it lies 3km from the village off the track leading north to the Col de Banyuls (see p.135).

ESPOLLA itself is a typical Alt Empordà village, its shuttered houses crammed in a labyrinth of streets that come to life each year during the flurry of the grape harvest. The only **accommodation** here is the friendly, family-run *Hostal Manela*, Plaça del Carmé 7 (☎972 563 065; ②), which also serves sustaining, inexpensive meals, though their *menjador* is tiny and must be reserved most weekends.

Showing up on spec, you're probably better off **eating** hearty country fare at *Ca La Maria* (closed Sun night, Mon night, Tues all day) in the very centre of **MOLLET DE PERALADA**, 4km south. No seating problems at this big barn of a place (it was a wine warehouse), where well under 4000ptas/€24 nets you generous starters of salami and olives, *bacalla amb xamfaina* (cod in tomato sauce), stir-fried artichoke hearts and pear tart washed down with a *porró* of *Banyuls* dessert wine. Despite uneven service, it's an Alt Empordà institution and highly recommended.

Walking routes north

If you continue along the Col de Banyuls path to the goat-overrun farmstead of Jaça de l'Home, and then turn onto the waymarked GR11, you can reach the ruined, tenth-century monastery of **Sant Quirze de Colera** in around four hours: it's startlingly impressive in its wilderness location, and camping is possible as there's a spring. From here, bear southeast to the village of **VILAMANISCLE**, where you can spend the night (ask for private rooms), and pick up the Figueres-bound bus early in the morning. The walk from the monastery to the coast at Colera or Llançà will take about five hours more.

Alternatively, from Espolla it's possible to walk northwest for a very long day to the **Col du Perthus** via Cantallóps, where there are more dolmens – enquire locally before setting out, though, as the route goes through army territory, and shooting is common on weekdays. **CANTALLÓPS** is also the start of a well-marked path to the **Castell de Requesens**, an easy walk that becomes increasingly worthwhile as the views over Alt Empordà grow ever wider and the castle looms ahead. Standing amidst marvellous cork forest, the dilapidated castle is usually closed, but keys can be obtained at the nearby farm.

THE SPANISH VALLEYS

The higher valleys on the Spanish side of the Eastern Pyrenees don't really begin until well away from the Mediterranean coast. The easiest access to the mountains goes via **Girona**, 40km south of Figueres, an ancient capital with ample cultural appeal; it also has Catalunya's largest airport outside Barcelona, handling April-to-November charter flights from Britain. From Girona, the most attractive route involves heading northwest through lakeside **Banyoles** to the exquisite medieval town of **Besalú**, then west into the heart of the volcanic **Garrotxa** region, centred on the town of **Olot**. Continuing in the same direction brings you to **Ripoll** and its famous monastery, or to **Sant Joan de les Abadesses**, with another monastic cathedral. Just northeast of here, **Camprodon** is the first town truly enclosed by the foothills, but for a more dramatic introduction to the Spanish Catalan Pyrenees, the upper **Freser valley** awaits just north of Ripoll, with its popular narrow-gauge train and grandiose Marian shrine at **Núria**.

Public transport connections from Girona towards the hills are excellent, with numerous daily bus departures as far as Olot, via Banyoles and Besalú; a few services continue on to Ripoll. Heading northeast from Girona, there are frequent train services towards Figueres and the northerly Costa Brava resorts.

Girona and around

The obvious way-station on any eastern approach to the Spanish Pyrenees is **GIRONA** (formerly Gerona), which sits on a fortified hill above the occasionally stagnant but carp-clogged Riu Onyar, just before it joins the Ter. Like Perpignan – the equivalent gateway city on the French side – it has a distinctly Arab flavour, but here the influence dates from the Moorish conquest, retained in the architecture and narrow streets of its old quarter. Full of historical and cultural interest, it's a fine place to relax before or after tackling the mountains, where you're likely to spend more time than planned. At least two nights are recommended: although the town now gets plenty of attention from passing French motorists and day-tripping tour groups from nearby Costa Brava resorts, calm returns to the old town after dark, when Girona's abiding character reasserts itself.

The "City of a Thousand Sieges", Girona has been fought over in almost every century since it was the Roman fortress of Gerunda on the Via Augusta. In the eighth century it suffered seven sieges and became the seat of an earldom within Charlemagne's empire. The Muslims stayed for over two hundred years, a fact apparent in the web of narrow central lanes, and there was also a continuous Jewish presence through six centuries. By the eighteenth century Girona had been besieged on 21 occasions, and in the next century it earned the nickname "Immortal" by surviving five attacks, of which the longest was a seven-month assault by the French. Each occupier left a mark on the architecture of the town, and connoisseurs can identify a succession of styles in various buildings from Roman Classicism to *modernisme*. The overall impression, though, is of an overwhelmingly beautiful medieval city, augmented by its river setting and adorned by multistoreyed pastel houses leaning over the banks.

Arrival and information

Girona's **airport**, 13km south of the city, is used mainly by Costa Brava package charters whose clientele transfer to their resorts in special buses; accordingly there's no public airport bus, so you'll have to take a taxi (2000–2500ptas/€12–15) into town. The **train station** is at Plaça d'Espanya, southwest of the centre; the **bus station** – also serving international arrivals – is at the rear of the same building. Both are a mere twenty-minute walk from the old quarter, where you'll probably spend most of your time. Public urban buses serve Girona, but you're more likely to use a **taxi** – the handiest ranks are at the train station, Plaça Catalunya and the old-town end of the Pont de Pedra.

If you **drive** in, you'll find **parking** nightmarish to say the least. The old town is a controlled-access zone for residents only, so you'll be fined or towed unless your lodgings

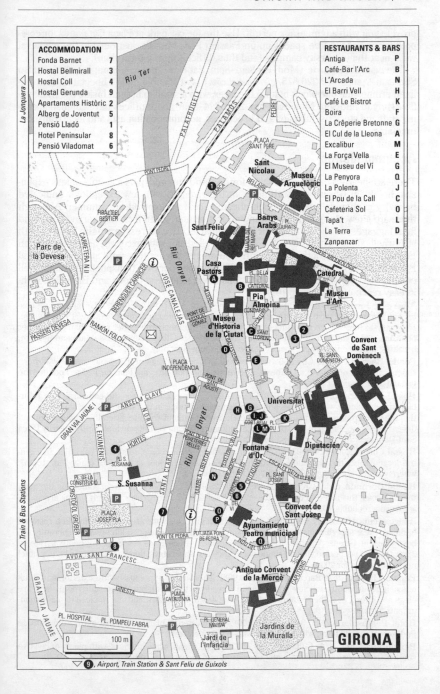

ACCOMMODATION

Fonda Barnet	7
Hostal Bellmirall	3
Hostal Coll	4
Hostal Gerunda	9
Apartaments Històric	2
Alberg de Joventut	5
Pensió Lladó	1
Hotel Peninsular	8
Pensió Viladomat	6

RESTAURANTS & BARS

Antiga	P
Café-Bar l'Arc	B
L'Arcada	N
El Barri Vell	H
Café Le Bistrot	K
Boira	F
La Crêperie Bretonne	G
El Cul de la Lleona	A
Excalibur	M
La Força Vella	E
El Museu del Ví	G
La Penyora	Q
La Polenta	J
El Pou de la Call	C
Cafeteria Sol	O
Tapa't	D
La Terra	L
Zanpanzar	I

GIRONA

⬁ La Jonquera

⬁ Train & Bus Stations

0   100 m

▽ 9, Airport, Train Station & Sant Feliu de Guíxols

provide you with a temporary permit. Use the fee car park at Plaça Catalunya, or compete for one of the free spaces up on Passeig Fora Muralla, just outside the medieval walls near the university campus (and thus difficult during term time).

The central **Turisme** (Mon–Fri 8am–8pm, Sat 8am–2pm & 4–8pm; July & Aug also Sun 9am–2pm; ☎972 226 575, *girona-net.com*) is at Rambla de la Llibertat 1, the tree-lined promenade one block behind the river, with a satellite branch inside the train station (July to mid-Sept Mon–Sat 9am–2pm & 4–8pm); both offices have English-speaking staff and stock useful maps and brochures, accommodation lists and local transport timetables.

Accommodation

There are nearly a dozen reasonable **fondas and hostals**, plus a couple of less expensive hotels, in Girona, on both sides of the river, so with few exceptions (indicated below) you shouldn't need to book ahead, except perhaps during summer. Although there are a few places near the train and bus station, given a civilized arrival time and light luggage, you should make for the old quarter. The nearest **campsite** is 8km south at Fornells de la Selva (☎972 476 117; open all year), with excellent amenities and an English-speaking proprietor, though you might prefer to camp at more pastoral Banyoles, 27km northwest (see p.159). If you have your own transport, you might well consider a couple of *turisme rural* establishments between Girona and Banyoles, within easy reach of both (see p.160).

Alberg de Joventut, c/dels Ciutadans 9, near the Plaça del Vi (☎972 218 003). Girona's youth hostel has a central old-town location and smart modern facilities, including laundry, TV and video. However, it's mostly used as a student residence in term time, hardly better value than the cheaper pensions, and if you're over 25 it's actually more expensive. Reception open 8–11am and 6–10pm; breakfast included in price, supper available. Open July–Sept only. ①–②.

Fonda Barnet, c/Santa Clara 16 (☎972 200 033). Cheapest digs near the old town – well-worn rooms with sink only – but an unbeatable riverside location near the Pont de Pedra. Look for the ground-floor *menjador*. ②.

Hostal Bellmirall, c/Bellmirall 3 (☎972 204 009). Prime location near the cathedral, in a refurbished old building with antiques and artily exposed pointing in the stone walls. Main problem is that the seven rooms are small (nos. 1–4 best); several without en suite. Friendly management and decent breakfast, served in the courtyard in summer; parking permit provided for the nearby Plaça Sant Domènec. All that said, it's still overpriced. ⑤.

Hostal Coll, c/Hortes 24 (☎972 203 086). Inexpensive, clean rooms, some with balconies, in a central location near the Plaza de la Constitució. Enquire next door at *Bar Coll* (daily 7am–10pm), where you can also get a 950ptas/€5.70 midday *menú*. ③.

Hostal Gerunda, c/de Barcelona 34 (☎972 202 285). Just in front of the train station, on the main through road, this makes a reasonable en-suite fallback for late arrivals, though rooms are somewhat claustrophobic. ③.

Apartaments Històric, c/Bellmirall 4/A (☎972 223 583, *www.meridian.es/historic*). In a restored building, these superb two-, four- or six-person flats with fully equipped kitchens are currently the best value in Girona. Voluble, friendly management (Xavier speaks English) quote a rate of 3500ptas/€21 per person, and do single occupancy and short stays; they're preparing a luxury hotel next door, ready for 2002.

Pensió Lladó, c/de la Barca 31 (☎972 210 998). Thoroughly unprepossessing exterior, and dubious neighbourhood (see below – you'll need three keys to get in), but the en-suite rooms here are clean and cheap, as is the restaurant of the *Bar Girona* downstairs, and you're close to many monuments and museums. ③.

Hotel Peninsular, c/Nou 3 (☎972 203 800). Well-located, if bland, hotel just across the Pont de Pedra from the old town, with all rooms converted to en suite. ⑤.

Pensió Viladomat, c/de Ciutadans 5 (☎972 203 176). Clean, white interiors, with plenty of cell-like singles, in this central building; a mix of en suite and not which fill quickly in summer. ③–④.

The City

Although most of the modern city sprawls southwest of the Riu Onyar, all points of interest are concentrated in the compact medieval quarter, or **Casc Antic**, spilling down the north hillside to the east bank. As it only takes twenty minutes to walk from end to end, this fascinating zone of parapeted walls, stepped streets and secluded courtyards is easy to explore thoroughly. Recent restoration and inevitable gentrification have not yet managed to completely banish the everyday life of local shops and bars. Girona is also home to a small university, its student contingent providing a healthy balance to chi-chi galleries and high-end outlets for designer clothing and furniture, which reflect the fact that Girona and its province have the highest per capita income in Spain.

The Catedral and the Museu d'Art

Balanced on a steep slope and reached by a majestic Baroque staircase, the **Catedral** (summer Tues–Sat 10am–2pm & 4–7pm, Sun 10am–2pm; winter opening hours vary), is the focus of the *Casc Antic* and, with its emphasis on width and height, an outstanding example of "Catalan Gothic". There has been a place of worship here since a temple was built in Roman times, and a mosque stood on the site before the foundation of the cathedral in 1038. Most of the building dates from the fifteenth century, though parts are four hundred years older, notably the five-storey **Torre de Carlemany** and the Romanesque **cloisters** with their exquisite sculpted capitals.

The main **façade**, remodelled in the eighteenth century, writhes with exuberant ornamentation: figures, coats-of-arms, and saints Peter and Paul flanking the door. Inside, the cathedral is awesome – no aisles, just a single **nave** with a span of 22m, the widest Gothic vault in the world. Contemporary sceptics deemed the proposed design unsafe, and the vault was only raised after an appeal by the architect, Guillermo Bofill, to an independent panel of architects. The walls rise to stained-glass windows, the single object interrupting the sweep of space being an enormous organ installed late in the nineteenth century.

Admission to the cloisters is by the same ticket that gets you into the **Museu Capitular** (summer Tues–Sat 10am–2pm & 4–6pm, Sun 10am–2pm, winter hours vary; 500ptas/€3), a small but first-rate collection of religious art that includes a copy of Beatus's *Commentary on the Apocalypse* made in 975 by Mozarabic miniaturists, and a magnificent tapestry of *The Creation* dating from around 1100, the finest surviving specimen of Romanesque textile, depicting in strong colours the seasons and elements of the earth. The irregularly shaped cloisters themselves (1180–1210) boast minutely carved figures and scenes on double columns, while steps lead up to a chamber above full of ecclesiastical garb and adornments.

Girona's **Museu d'Art** (March–Sept Tues–Sat 10am–7pm, Sun 10am–2pm; Oct–Feb Tues–Sat 10am–6pm, Sun 10am–2pm; 300ptas/€1.80), in the well-restored episcopal palace next door, has galleries arranged chronologically as you climb through five floors. Early wings highlight Romanesque art, particularly rare manuscripts, such as an eleventh-century copy of Bede and an amazing martyrology from the monastery of Poblet, and impressive *Majestats* (wooden images of Christ garbed in a tunic). The top two floors progress through Renaissance works to the collection of nineteenth- and twentieth-century Catalan art. Noteworthy here is a selection of pieces by the "Olot School" (better represented in the Olot museum, see p.163), depictions of the French siege and some entertaining pieces of *modernista* sculpture in the highest hall.

Sant Feliu and around

One of Girona's best-known landmarks is the blunt tower of **Sant Feliu**, best viewed as you descend the cathedral steps. Shortened by a lightning strike in 1581 and never repaired, the belfry tops a hemmed-in church that happily combines Romanesque,

Gothic and Baroque styles. Massive restoration works are under way at present, as well as some "urban clearance" on the river side of the church.

The narrow streets northwest of Sant Feliu towards the river, especially c/de la Barca, are a bit shabbier than is normal in Girona, with their bare bars and corner groceries. This has historically been a rather tame red-light district, but the area is being steadily gentrified, so many premises are bricked up with "for sale" signs. Doubtless this little warren will soon receive the sort of attention visited on c/de la Barca's southern continuations, c/Calderers and c/Ballesteries, now lined with lively bars and exclusive shops.

The Banys Arabs

Very near the cathedral, reached by going through the twin-towered **Portal de Sobreportas**, and then turning right, stand the so-called **Banys Arabs** or "Arab Baths" (April–Sept Tues–Sat 10am–7pm, Sun 10am–2pm; Oct–March Tues–Sun 10am–2pm; 200ptas/€1.20), probably built by Moorish craftsmen during the thirteenth century, some two hundred years after the Moorish occupation of Girona had ended. The finest of their type in Spain apart from those at Granada, they have the usual under floor heating system and the Roman-derived layout of three principal rooms. The *apodyterium* (changing room) is the most interesting, despite the installation of some unfortunate modern art; there are niches for one's clothes and a stone bench for relaxation after bathing, while the room is unusually lit by a central vaulted skylight supported by an octagon of columns.

The Museu Arqueològic and the city walls

From the Banys Arabs it's a short downhill stroll, over the usually dry Riu Galligants, to the **Museu Provincial Arqueològic** (summer Tues–Sat 10.30am–1.30pm & 4–7pm, Sun 10am–2pm; winter Tues–Sat 10am–2pm & 4–6pm, Sun 10am–2pm; 300ptas/€1.80), housed in the former church of Sant Pere Galligants. The church itself contains Roman artefacts, while the fine **cloisters** shelter medieval relics, including nearly a dozen inscribed stones from the former Jewish cemetery. The Romanesque architecture is perhaps the most memorable feature of a visit, reinforced by the inclusion of a full-size replica of the west rose window in the transept. Extensive galleries above the cloisters methodically outline the region's history from Paleolithic to Roman times, but unless you read Catalan or Spanish you'll get little out of these exhibits.

Near the museum you can gain access to the nearby Passeig Arqueològic, with steps through landscaped grounds beside the Banys Arabs leading up onto the **city walls**, from where there are fine views over Girona and the Ter valley. Once onto the ramparts (daily 8am–10pm), walkways lead completely around their perimeter, with intermediate exits behind the Sant Domènec convent and at the gate of the university, before the final descent to Plaça Catalunya, at the south end of the old town.

The Call

Heading back south instead of north through the Portal de Sobreportas, c/de la Força leads past the **Call**, reached via the intersecting c/Sant Llorenç and considered the best-preserved Jewish quarter in western Europe. A **Jewish community** was well established in Girona by the late ninth century – probably earlier – with an initial settlement near the cathedral shifting up to **Carrer de la Força**, which follows the course of a Roman road. With a population of almost a thousand at its peak, the new quarter became known as the *Call*, forming a semi-autonomous town within Girona, under royal protection in exchange for payment of a tribute. But from the eleventh century onwards, Jews here suffered systematic and escalating persecution, conditions only improving temporarily under Alfons II and Alfons III of Aragón. In 1391 a mob stormed the *Call* and killed forty of its residents, after which the neighbourhood became a restrictive ghetto like those of northern Europe, until the expulsion of the Jews from Spain a century later.

For an idea of the layout of this sector of tall narrow houses and maze-like interconnecting passages, visit the **Centre Bonastruc Ça Porta** (May–Oct Mon–Sat 10am–8pm, Sun 10am–3pm; Nov–April Tues–Sat 10am–6pm, Sun 10am–3pm; 200ptas/€1.20), signposted as "Call Jueu" at the top of c/Sant Llorenç. Opened to the public in 1975, this multi-level complex of rooms, stairways and a courtyard was the site of the synagogue, the kosher slaughterhouse and community baths. Excavations are ongoing, with nearby alleys sealed off pending investigation; at the main site there's an information and ticket office, temporary exhibitions in the lower levels, a café and a small library (Mon–Fri 10am–3pm & 5–8pm, Sun 10am–2pm; books in English available). A new museum charting the history of the Jews in Catalunya, the Museu de los Judeos en Catalunya, is also due to open here in 2001.

The Museu d'Historia de la Ciutat

Not part of the *Call* proper but housed in the eighteenth-century convent of Sant Antoni just across c/de la Força, the **Museu d'Historia de la Ciutat** (Tues–Sat 10am–2pm & 5–7pm, Sun 10am–2pm; 200ptas/€1.20) completes Girona's complement of museums, and despite being labelled only in Catalan, is likely to prove the most rewarding one – and certainly the most eclectic. A portion of the convent's cemetery is visible on the right as you enter, with niches for the (vanished) deceased. The entire ground floor is given over to the development of local industry and technology, with an antique dealer's bonanza (salvaged from around the province) of ancient phones, printing presses, dynamos and even an arc-lamp cine projector. The first floor covers the evolution of the sardana, the history of broadcasting in Catalunya – complete with some magnificent old radio sets – and Roman Gerunda, featuring a rather crude mosaic from a villa on the surrounding plain. On the top floor you'll find a modern art exhibition, including a few works by Dalí and Miró.

Eating, drinking and nightlife

Most of Girona's more adventurous **restaurants** and **bars** are grouped along and just off c/de la Força, or on c/Ballesteries, while outdoor daytime **cafés** cluster on and around the Rambla de la Llibertat, and on the parallel Plaça del Vi. Formal **nightlife** in Girona is a bit ropey, with a host of designer bars and discos strung out along c/de Barcelona, but very few options in the old town. After 3am your only choice here is *Platea*, a tacky disco housed in an old theatre near the post office.

Restaurants

El Barri Vell, c/Cort-Reial 17. Cheap and cheerful competition for *La Força Vella* (see below); a full if not very elegant feed for about 1300ptas/€7.80. Open lunch and dinner.

Café Le Bistrot, Pujada de Sant Domènec 4. Despite the name, really a full-on restaurant-bar that's packed at meal times with the *beau monde* of Girona, for good reason: excellent gourmet-minceur *menú* (eggplant terrine, cod in sauce, homemade chocolate cake, bottled house wine) for the amazing sum of 1400ptas/€8.40. Stylish, Belle-Époque tile-floor surroundings inside, with jazz soundtrack, or live classical music Tues & Weds. Limited seating on the steps outside in summer.

Boira, Plaça de la Independencia 17. The best food on the square, with two menus (1200ptas/€7.20 lunch only, 2000ptas/€12). Outdoor seating, or upstairs in the river-view salon; there's also a street-level bar, good for breakfast, with river windows.

El Cul de la Lleona, c/Calderers 8. Cosy if pricey bistro specializing in Moroccan dishes; three courses (including house wine and lovely Catalan or North African sweets) will run about 3200ptas/€19.25. Also a much cheaper "local" *menú* at lunchtime.

La Força Vella (aka Los Jara), c/de la Força 4. *Menus* (1300ptas/€7.80) served in the stone-clad area in front of the bar; bog-standard *comedor/menjador* fare (*tortilla, calamares a la romana*), of average portion size and quality. Open 1–4pm & 7–11pm.

El Museu del Ví, c/Cort-Reial 14. Conspicuously Catalan bar-restaurant serving up typical dishes in its pebble-dashed *comedor.* Plenty of filling *plats combinats* (700ptas/€4.20), a *menú* (1150ptas/€6.90) and excellent *torradas* (toasts). Closed Mon.

La Penyora, c/Nou del Teatre 3. Catalan *nouvelle cuisine* in suitably minimalist surroundings; achingly slow service (count on two hours for dinner), painfully high bills. Only really worth it at lunchtime, when there's a 1500-pta/€9 *menú*. Closed Tues.

La Polenta, c/Cort-Reial l6. This tiny vegetarian restaurant serves delicious organic grub – the *menú* is 1300ptas/€9 – and is generally busy. Open Mon–Fri: lunchtimes only; closed Sat, Sun and Aug.

El Pou de la Call, c/de la Força 14. More elaborate than usual recipes and ingredients such as game in exceptionally pleasant surroundings right next to the *Call*; *menú* (1350ptas/€8.10) usually available, otherwise count on about 3500ptas/€21 per head.

Bars and cafés

Antiga, Plaça del Vi 8. A nice line in cakes, puddings, *orxata* in summer and other sweet delights at this *xocalateria* under the arches.

Café-Bar l'Arc, Plaça de la Catedral 9. The only café in Girona with a cathedral on the terrace. During the day it's a pleasant spot for coffee, while at night it becomes a bit of a secluded hideaway, with fine alternative tunes. Closed mid-Jan to mid-Feb.

L'Arcada, Rambla de la Llibertat 38. Bar-café tucked under the arcades, with designer-minimalist interior and sought-after outdoor tables, serving good breakfast pastries and enviable pizzas.

La Crêperie Bretonne, c/Cort-Reial 14. Savoury or sweet crêpes 375–900ptas/€2.30–5.40, prepared by a French ex-pat. Vast interior belies narrow street frontage, which is dominated by a converted minibus (part of the pantry). Closed Mon, & Wed lunchtime in winter.

Excalibur, Plaça de l'Oli 1. Friendly bar, frequented by both ex-pats and locals, decorated according to Spanish notions of Ye Olde English (there's even a bell to call "time"). Guinness plus bitter on tap, and a fine selection of international bottled beers. Open daily until 3am.

Cafeteria Sol, Plaça del Vi. No-nonsense bar, right by *Antiga*, that's good for breakfast under the arcade.

Tapa't, c/Cort-Reial 1. A decent *tapas* bar with generous portions, where you can assemble a small meal for about 1200ptas/€7.20.

La Terra, c/Ballesteries 23 (no sign). The main student hangout, open from 6pm until late: a wonderfully cavernous space, with glazed tiles everywhere and river-view windows. Juices, foreign beers, coffees, sandwiches.

Zanpanzar, c/Cort-Reial, near *La Polenta*. Opened early 2000, and already reckoned the best of Girona's *tapas* bars, serving delicious and reasonably priced Basque *pintxos* as well as a superb 1400ptas/€8.40 lunchtime *menú*.

Listings

Airport ☎972 186 600 for flight information.

Banks and exchange There's an exchange bureau in the train station, and you'll find several banks with ATMs on Rambla de la Llibertat.

Books and maps Ulyssus, c/Ballesteries 29, is an excellent travel-book specialist with lots of Spanish- and Catalan-language guides to Catalunya, all Editorial Alpina and many SGE and IGN maps, plus a few Rough Guides.

Buses Teisa (☎972 200 275) runs services northeast through the Garrotxa to Olot, with connections from there into the *comarques* of Ripoll and Cerdanya. Barcelona Bus (☎972 202 432) offers express departures to Figueres.

Car rental Most agencies are found on c/de Barcelona, near the train station; for example, Avis (☎972 206 933) and Hertz (☎972 210 108). Local operators such as Cabeza, c/Barcelona 30 (☎972 218 208), will work out cheaper, but you'll have to return the vehicle to Girona.

Emergencies Dial ☎092 or contact the Creu Roja (☎972 222 222).

Hospitals Dr Josep Trueta, Avda França 60 (☎972 202 700), at the northern outskirts of town.

Internet Teranyina, c/Bonaventura Carreras Peralta 2, near c/Força, is a computer shop with Internet facilities (800ptas/€4.80 per hour) and friendly, knowledgeable staff.

Music recordings Harmonia Mundi at Cort-Reial 21 is the designated retail outlet for classical and world music CDs on that label, as well as Network and Chant du Monde – at prices a third less than in Britain.

Newspapers English-language papers are available at the kiosks on Plaça de Independencia and along Rambla de la Llibertat.

Police Policia Municipal at c/Bacià 4 (☎972 419 090 or 972 419 092); Mossos d'Esquadra (Catalan police; ☎972 213 450).

Train information RENFE is on ☎972 207 093.

The Fluvià valley and the Garrotxa

Northwest of Girona lies the beautiful Garrotxa region, bisected by the Río Fluvià, which for much of its course is more or less paralleled by the main C150 road up towards Andorra. Lush and humid, the landscape of the Garrotxa fosters an extraordinary diffuse light, which can make this old-fashioned rural area nostalgically resemble an early photograph.

South of the Fluvià extends the volcanic **Baixa Garrotxa**, where ten thousand years of erosion have moulded dormant cinder cones into rounded and fertile hills. The northern part, the **Alta Garrotxa**, is an area of deserted farms set amidst low chunky limestone mountains, the highest of which – the 1558-metre Puig de Comanegra – straddles the frontier.

Any route traced straight through the area will miss something special. The easiest option on public transport is to take the regular bus from Girona along the C150, which is often spectacular, especially as it approaches resolutely medieval **Besalú**, or **Castellfollit de la Roca**, whose houses peer over a sheer basalt cliff. But along this road you see little of back-country Garrotxa. A more rewarding approach with your own vehicle is the tiny C524 from **Banyoles** to **Olot**, capital of the Garrotxa region, via Santa Pau (a much less frequent bus route). Here, there's some easy, scenic walking in the **Parc Natural de la Zona Volcanica**, set aside to protect the best of the Garrotxa's landscapes, including remnants of the great beech wood known as **La Fageda d'en Jordà**.

Banyoles

The Pyrenees are only on the horizon at **BANYOLES**, just 17km north of Girona, but it's a moderately pleasant place to pass a few hours, or the night, on the way to Besalú or Santa Pau. What makes Banyoles special, however, is the **Estany** (lake), 75m at its deepest point just offshore from the swimming club. Although under state protection since 1951, it's no longer the wilderness it once was: cruises, rowing boats and pedaloes are on offer, and private waterside gazebos, lakeside hotels and restaurants have transformed the lake, a process completed by its hosting of the 1992 Olympic rowing events. Non-boaters can have an enjoyable picnic on the shore, throwing any leftovers to the famous giant carp. The eight-kilometre walking circuit of the lake passes through the tiny hamlet of **Porqueres**, whose barrel-vaulted church of **Santa Maria** was consecrated in 1182 and has unusual capitals with plant and animal designs.

Back in town, the arcaded **Plaça Major**, studded with plane trees, has hosted a Wednesday market since the eleventh century. From here, it's 200m northeast to the nearby **Museu Arqueològic Comarcal** (July & Aug Tues–Sat 11am–1.30pm & 4–8pm, Sun 10.30am–2pm; Sept–June Tues–Sat 10.30am–1.30pm & 4–6.30pm, Sun

10.30am–2pm; 300ptas/€1.80; Catalan labelling only but English crib sheet provided). Installed in a thirteenth-century almshouse on Plaça de la Font, the collection used to contain the famous jawbone of a pre-Neanderthal woman found in the nearby Serinya caves, but nowadays you have to make do with a replica; authentic specimens include Paleolithic tools and Pleiocene/Pleistocene bison, rhino and elephant bones, all found in local quarry works. Galleries of historical eras feature three bronze figures of the Roman deities Lar, Fortuna and Mercury, remounted in a *lararium* or household shrine that would have graced local villas from the first to seventh centuries, as well as medieval painted plates, found in a dry well in the almshouse. The **Museu Darder d'Història Natural** (more accurately, the "Museum of Moth-Eaten Taxidermy") in nearby Plaça dels Estudis (same hours, same admission ticket), is eminently missable, being merely the obsessive collection of preserved, mostly non-native specimens gathered by a zookeeper and Barcelona zoology professor of the early 1900s. Further northeast of the two museums stands the ninth-century Benedictine **Monestir de Sant Esteve**, easily the most imposing structure in the old quarter and the kernel around which the town later grew. It's closed to the public, who miss seeing a sumptuous fifteenth-century *retablo* (altarpiece) by Joan Antigo, and an eighteenth-century cloister. Between the monastery and the museums stands the **Llotja del Tint**, the medieval dye market.

Practicalities

All **buses** stop on Passeig de la Industria, with the ticket office nearby at the intersection with c/Alvarez de Castro. The Plaça Major lies two minutes' walk northeast from here, while the **tourist office** is in the opposite direction at Passeig de la Industria 25 (Mon–Fri 10am–2pm & 5–7pm, Sat 10am–1pm; June & Aug also open Sat pm & Sun; ☎972 575 573), selling a town plan. The Centre Excursionista de Banyoles at c/del Puig 6, near Sant Esteve (Mon, Wed & Fri 7–9pm), has a range of maps and information available for local treks and hikes.

With Girona (and some attractive *turismes rurals* so near, there's little point in staying in Banyoles itself, where most **accommodation** is overpriced anyway – the two-star *Hotel l'Ast* (☎ & fax 972 570 414; ⑥) on Passeig Dalmau 63 is representative of the lakeside establishments. An exception is the immaculate *Fonda Comas*, c/de la Canal 19 (☎972 570 127; ③), west of Plaça dels Estudis, a modern but unobtrusive building built around a courtyard, with its own restaurant. **Camping** by the lake takes better advantage of the town's setting; there are four sites, including the large *El Llac* (☎972 570 305), on the way to Porqueres, just below and before the church.

If you've a car or bike, two good local **turismes rurals** best solve accommodation problems. *Can Ribes*, 6km south of Banyoles beyond the hamlet of Camós (☎972 573 211, fax 972 581 073, *can.ribes@retemail.es*; ⑤ B&B), popular with special-interest groups, has simple, tile-floor rooms, a roof terrace and meal service. Even better (and almost equidistant –14km – to Girona or the coast) is *Can Fabrica* (☎ & fax 972 594 629; closed Jan 7–Palm Sunday; ⑤ B&B), another restored seventeenth-century farmhouse on a hilltop 1km beyond the hamlet of Santa Llogaia del Terri, run by kindly English-speaking proprietors Ramon Caralt and Marta Casanovas. Their antique-furnished rooms are spacious and delightfully different, while decent three-course dinners feature homemade desserts, with Marta's jams and vinegar for sale. There's also a swimming pool, and mountain bikes for rent.

There are a very limited number of places to **eat** in Banyoles' old quarter, just enough perhaps to make Banyoles a feasible lunch stop. Top honours for imaginative, salubrious fare goes to *El Rebost d'en Pere* at c/Ángel Guimerà 14, just off Plaça Major, a tiny (six-table) spot run by a young couple. Otherwise *Fonda Comas* offers a basic 1100-peseta/€6.60 *menu*, while *Can Banal*, just off Plaça dels Turers at c/del Doctor Hysern 2, is probably the town's most elaborate restaurant, with *menus* at 1000ptas/€6 and 1400ptas/€8.40. Eating at the hotel restaurants overlooking the lake is more expensive, though the *Mirallac* at Passeig Darder 50 won't break the bank as long as you eat meat rather than fish.

If you have transport, better bets in the surrounding countryside include *Can Xapac* in Cornellà del Terri, or *La Barretina* in the centre of Orfes, 19km north of *Can Fabrica* by meandering back roads, or a similar distance northeast of Banyoles.

Besalú

From the road, the imposing eleventh-century fortified bridge by the confluence of the Fluvià and Capellada rivers is the only sign that there is anything remarkable about **BESALÚ**, 14km from Banyoles. But pass under the portcullis in the bridge's central gatehouse and you'll enter a medieval settlement that arguably provides the most interesting half-day outing from Girona. Steep narrow streets, sunbaked squares and cave-like arcaded shops bear silent witness to an illustrious history out of proportion to its current humble status. Besalú was an important town before the medieval period – Roman, Visigothic, Frankish and Muslim despots came and went – but all the surviving monuments date from the eleventh century and after, when it briefly became the seat of a small, independent principality.

Christian rather than Muslim intolerance drove the Jews out of Besalú, and their **Miqvé** (ritual bathhouse) was later turned into a dyeworks. Originally attached to a synagogue, the Miqvé (key from tourist office; 100ptas/€0.60 per person) hides inconspicuously down by the river, at the end of signposted Baixada de Mikwè, underneath the bridge-viewing platform. It proves to be a high, single-vaulted chamber, with steps leading down into the former plunge pool.

Continuing in the same direction, you'll reach the porticoed **Plaça Llibertat**, enveloped by medieval buildings such as the thirteenth-century Casa de la Vila, now home to the *Ajuntament* and the tourist office. The weekly market takes place here on Tuesday, under the arches. Majestically arcaded c/Tallaferro leads uphill to the ruined shell of Santa Maria (no admission), which for just two years was the cathedral of the bishopric of Besalú; political union with Barcelona brought an end to its short-lived episcopal independence.

Further west, you'll emerge onto a vast, fan-shaped square, the Prat de Sant Pere, dominated by the twelfth-century Benedictine monastery church of **Sant Pere**. The barrel-vaulted interior is impressive enough, with a fine colonnaded ambulatory preserving some carved column capitals, but the church's most eye-catching feature is the arched Gothic window of the main facade, flanked by a pair of grotesque stone lions; it's best admired from a pair of cafés immediately opposite. Also on the square is the **Casa Cornellà**, a rare example of Romanesque domestic architecture which houses a museum of antique household and agricultural implements.

Working your way up towards the main road brings you to **Sant Vicenç**, whose east entrance arches are decorated with mythical monsters; it, too, has a Gothic window, high up on its southwest facade, while the little landscaped square around it, Plaça Sant Vicenç, is far more intimate than Prat de Sant Pere.

Practicalities

Buses stop on the main road, from where it's a short walk south to the central Plaça de la Llibertat. The **tourist office** here (daily 10am–2pm & 4–7pm; ☎972 591 240) keeps the usual stock of brochures, as well as keys to locked monuments, and can help sort out vacancies in the surrounding area when accommodation in Besalú is full (often the case in summer).

If you can manage it, **staying** is recommended, since Besalú's character changes completely for the better once the daily quota of trippers has departed, and the *turístic* train has ceased its to-ings and fro-ings. Of the three accommodation outfits, the pin-neat, en-suite *Fonda Venència* at c/Major 6 (☎972 591 257; ③) represents the best value; *Habitacions-Residència Marià*, Plaça Llibertat 7 (☎972 590 106; ③) is a more atmos-pheric, rambling old building, also with heated en-suite rooms; while *Fonda Siqués* at Avda Lluis Companys 6 (☎972 590 110; ④), just east of the bus stop on the main through highway, proves the noisiest of the three, but comfortable enough and used by self-guided walking tours.

Parking in Besalú is difficult most of the year; those with transport may be happier staying at two well-regarded **casas rurals** about 10km northeast, between the hamlets of **Beuda** and **Maià de Montcal**. Take the minor road north to Beuda, then swing east to meet first *Mas Salvanera* (☎972 590 975, fax 972 590 863, *www.girona-soft.com /salvanera*; ⑦ B&B), generally reckoned the most expensive – and most exquisitely appointed – of Girona province's *turisme rural* specimens. Continue a kilometre or so more to **Noguer de Segueró**, where the more reasonable *Can Felicià* (☎972 590 523; *www.beuda.com/canfelicia*; ⑦ HB) occupies the old Segueró schoolhouse, completely refurbished in 2000, and has quickly established a reputation for excellent cooking. The closest recommended **campsite** to Besalú is also here: *Masia Can Coromines* at Maià de Montcal (☎972 591 108, *coromines@grn.es*), centred on an ancient farmhouse dou-bling as a restaurant, and far more characterful than the standard Spanish campings.

The best-value **food** in Besalú is at *Can Quei* (closed Weds), Plaça Sant Vicenç 4, with well-selected *menus* at 1400ptas/€8.40 and 2000ptas/€12 served in the smart *comedor*, while Fonda Siqués' restaurant (closed Sun pm & Mon) has a 2500-peseta/€15 *menu*. For 4000ptas/€24 you've free choice of the *carta* at Pont Vell, c/Pont Vell 28, which has tables more or less under the bridge, and is considered rather better value for the same price than *Curia Reial* at Plaça Llibertat 14, which gets large coach parties.

Castellfollit de la Roca and Sant Joan les Fonts

CASTELLFOLLIT DE LA ROCA, 14km west of Besalú, promises great things as it perches atop a sixty-metre precipice overlooking the Riu Fluvià, with the church crowd-ed by houses onto the very edge of the cliff. Arrival is most impressive by night, when spotlights play on the natural basalt columns. But as the road curls around and up, Castellfollit proves a disappointment, with a traffic-plagued main street whose tightly packed rows of grubby brown buildings give no hint of the extraordinary palisade. You might leave your vehicle, however, to sample the view from the cliff: head south from the prominent clocktower to the church and the banistered viewing platform behind. On the through road, 100m downhill from the clocktower, Castellfollit's **Museum of Sausages** (Mon–Sat 9.30am–1.30pm & 4–8pm, Sun 9.30am–2pm & 4.30–8pm), run by the Sala family to celebrate a century and a half in the skin-stuffing business, is almost certainly unique – as claimed. Pungent with the smell of sausages, it's mainly an excuse to sell them (counter on the premises); the exhibits consist mostly of antique produc-tion machinery.

There's absolutely no need to **stay** the night, but if you get stuck, try the two-star *Pensió Cala Paula*, next to the clocktower at Plaça de Sant Roc 3 (☎972 294 015; ③), which has a decent and popular ground-floor bar-restaurant.

SANT JOAN LES FONTS lies 3km west of Castellfollit, along the alternate route to Olot. You'll soon glimpse its enormous monastery-church in the distance, high above the river, though this vies for prominence with the idle smokestacks of obsolete indus-tries, plus a modern paper mill. From the lower end of the village, cross the restored medieval bridge, which spreads beneath the massive but much-battered twelfth-centu-ry walls of Romanesque **Sant Esteve**, and take the path (signposted as "Ruta de les Tres Colades") which passes below and to the right of the church. This, also Route 16 amongst Garrotxa short walks keyed on the national park brochure, leads within 250m to the so-called **Molí Fondo**, actually massive waterfalls spilling from a dam on the Fluvià, next to which is the mill (*molí*) of the name. You might have a dip in the pool above or splash about under the falls – no guarantees about water quality – or continue along the numbered route another 250m to **Boscarró**, basalt columns twisted into a variety of shapes. Afterwards, you can drive, pedal, walk or take public transport the remaining 4km to Olot – all buses coming from Besalú go through Sant Joan, which has no reliable places to eat or stay.

Olot

Unlike Castellfollit, **OLOT** – capital of the Garrotxa region – is far more rewarding than its sprawling, anonymous outskirts suggest. Follow any of the narrow lanes north into the *barri antic* from the through road, and the scene quickly changes to one of intimate squares, elegant shops, a pleasant *rambla* and convivial bars. Except for the church of Sant Esteve with its landmark belfry just behind the *rambla*, most of the centre consists of eighteenth- and nineteenth-century buildings, a consequence of devastating fifteenth-century earthquakes which levelled the medieval town. Olot lies between three (dormant) volcanic cones easily accessible without long treks or drives; the bare-topped **Montsacopa volcano** in particular is worth the walk, with its summit chapel of Sant Francesc affording good views. Moreover, frequent bus connections and a fair choice in food and lodging (some of this just out of town) make Olot the best base for touring the Garrotxa.

The town's enduring prosperity is based on its crafts tradition. A religious-images business was established here in 1880 and remained a major industry until the 1950s. Cotton-milling also flourished during the late eighteenth century, alongside workshops printing the textiles with coloured patterns; the latter were instrumental in the formation of the Escola Pública de Dibuix (Public School of Drawing) in 1783. Joaquim Vayreda i Vila (1843–94), a founder of the Olot School of painters which included Josep Berga i Boix and Modest Urgell, was a pupil at the drawing school, but an 1871 trip to Paris brought him under the spell of Millet's rural painting, and exposed him to the Impressionists. From these influences, and the strange Garrotxa scenery, sprang the distinctive style of the Olot artists.

The Town

Some of the best work produced by the Olot School can be seen in the **Museu Comarcal de la Garrotxa** (Mon, Wed–Sat 11am–2pm & 6–8pm; Sun 11am–2pm; 300ptas/€1.80, same ticket to Casal dels Volcans), installed in a converted eighteenth-century hospital at c/Hospici 8. Of the works in the collection, Joaquim Vayreda's *Les Falgueres* is typical in its rendering of the Garrotxa light, but not all the collection's pieces are landscapes. Ramon Casas' famous *La Càrrega*, for example, long thought to depict the violent suppression of a 1902 Barcelona demonstration but actually painted in 1899, evokes Goya's great protest paintings, while the "Paris Cigarettes" poster series consists of local entries for a contest sponsored by an Argentine manufacturer. Sculpture is also strongly represented, notably in the work of Miquel Blay i Fabrega and Josep Clarà i Ayals; other pieces by this pair can be seen around town in the eponymous Plaça Clarà and Passeig d'en Blay.

There are also extensive exhibits devoted to rural and town crafts. Besides the saints' images from religious workshops, the secular figures of Ramon Amadeu are outstandingly vivid, fluid and, on occasion, humorous. Olot's specialization in textiles meant, among other activities, a large number of turn-of-the-century workshops for production of *barretinas* or *gores* – the typical Catalan men's cap.

A well-signposted half-hour walk from the centre brings you to the landscaped **Jardí Botànic** (April–Sept 9am–9pm; Oct–March 9am–7pm), where – especially if you read

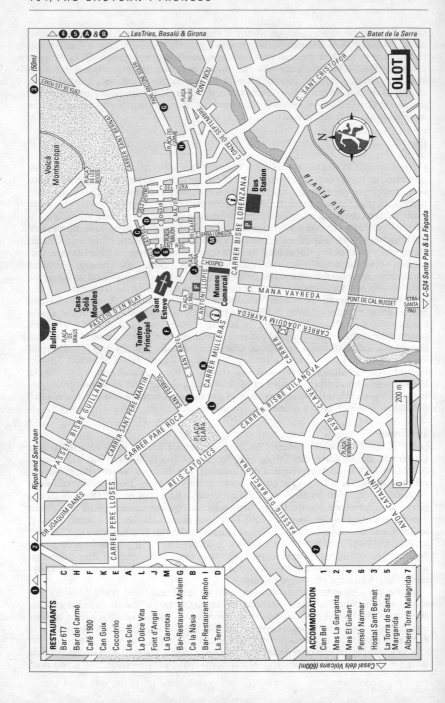

△ ❹, ❺, Ⓐ & Ⓑ   △ Les Tries, Besalú & Girona   △ Batet de la Serra

OLOT

C. SANT CRISTOFOR

❸ △ (50m)

CTRA DE LES FEIXES

PARE ANTON SOLER

CARRER SANT BERNAT

Volcà
Montsacopa

PLAÇA DE LES FEIXES

PONT NOU

PLAÇA PALAU

Ⓖ

CONXE DE SEPTEMBRE

CARRER BISBE LORENZANA

PLAÇA DEL CARME

Ⓗ

C. DEL TURA

C. DELS SASTRES

CARRER BISBE LORENZANA

Ⓟ Bus Station

Ⓘ

C. BOMARE

C. MAJOR

C. BELLAIRE

Ⓒ

PLAÇA MAJOR

Ⓔ

Ⓢ

SANT ROC

PLAÇA CLARA

C. SERRA I GINESTA

Ⓜ

C. BELTAIRE

CARRER DELS SASTRES

Riu Fluvià

△ C-524 Santa Pau & La Fageda

Casa Solà Morales

PASSEIG D'EN BLAY

Sant Esteve

C.HOSPICI

Ⓙ

Ⓟ

PLAÇA DEL MIG

C. ANTONI LLOPIS

Museu Comarcal

C. MANA VAYREDA

PONT DE CAL RUSSET

▷ CTRA-SANTA PAU

Bullring

PLAÇA DE BRAUS

Teatre Principal

Ⓕ

Ⓘ

CARRER JOAQUIM VAYREDA

CARRER JOAQUIM VAYREDA

PASSEIG BISBE GUILLAMET

CARRER SANT PERE MARTIR

C. SANT RAFEL

Ⓚ

CARRER MULLERAS

CARRER BISBE VILANOVA

AVDA. CLAVE

PLAÇA ESPANYA

△ Ripoll and Sant Joan

Ⓛ

SANT FERRIOL

CARRER PARE ROCA

PLAÇA CLARA

PASSEIG DE BARCELONA

AVDA. CATALUNYA

200 m

CARRER PERE LLOSES

REIS CATOLICS

0

DR JOAQUIM DANES

❷ △

N

Casal dels Volcans (600m) ▷

❶ △

Catalan or Castilian – you'll learn a lot about the Garrotxa volcanic region from the displays, photographs, diagrams and rock samples in the **Casal dels Volcans** (daily except Tues, & Sun pm: July–Sept 10am–2pm & 5–7pm; Oct–June 10am–2pm & 4–6pm; same ticket as Museu Comarcal), housed within the gardens. The building also houses an information centre for activities throughout the Garrotxa.

Practicalities

Olot is easily accessible by **bus**: from Barcelona and Girona through Banyoles and Besalú, direct from Figueres, from Ripoll and Sant Joan de les Abadesses, and (less frequently) from Banyoles via Mieres and Santa Pau. Arriving by **car**, you can usually find **parking** spaces, both fee and free, near the post office; otherwise use the central enclosed car parks shown on the map.

   The county **tourist office** (Mon–Fri 9am–3pm & 5–7pm, Sat 10am–2pm & 5–7pm, Sun 11am–2pm; ☎972 260 141) is right opposite the bus station on c/Bisbe Lorenzana; there's also a helpful, municipally funded **information office** at no. 33 of the street's westerly continuation, c/Mulleras (Mon–Fri 9am–1pm & 4–7pm, Sat 10am–1pm & 5–7pm; ☎972 270 242, *www.futrnet.es/citolot/*), in the central market building. One or the other should stock all-important schematic maps (inside the "Parc Natural" folding brochure) of the designated walking routes through the Garrotxa. Next to the whimsical Teatre Principal on Passeig d'en Blay, the irregularly open Centro Excursionista de Olot is another potential source of information on hiking and the great outdoors. At the southeast end of the same *passeig*, on the ground floor of a *modernista* building, the Drac **bookstore** keeps commercial maps and guides (in Spanish or Catalan) for the area.

ACCOMMODATION

Since the closure of two marginal *hostals* in the centre, in-town lodgings (including a somewhat inconvenient youth hostel) are very limited, and especially if you've transport you're well advised to cast your net a bit wider to the *turismes rurals* in neighbouring hamlets. Closest **campsites** are the riverside *Les Tries* (☎972 262 405; May–Oct), 2km east of town on the main Girona road – shady and offering discounted tickets to the swimming pool next door – and *La Fageda* (☎972 271 239; open all year), 4km out on the minor road to Santa Pau, well laid out and with its own pool. Olot's **youth hostel**, the *Alberg Torre Malagrida*, Passeig de Barcelona 15 (☎972 264 200 or 934 838 363, *www.gencat.es/catalunyajove*; ①), lies southwest of the centre, in an adapted 1920s villa overlooking the river, about halfway to the Casal dels Volcans. Reception hours are 8–10am and 1pm–midnight; it's closed September, and Sunday and Monday October to May, when about half of its rooms (4–10 bed) are given over to long-term student residence.

   Pick of the surviving conventional **accommodation** is the 1998-renovated *Hostal Sant Bernat*, Ctra de les Feixes s/n (☎972 261 919, fax 972 268 844; *bernat@agtat.es*; ②), whose secure garage makes it the best urban choice if you have a car or bike. It's slightly out-of-the-way towards the northeastern end of the town, but quiet, excellent value and very friendly, offering singles, doubles and triples with bath, heating and TV. The clean, modern rooms at *Pensió Narmar*, c/Sant Roc 1, on the corner of Plaça Major (☎972 269 807; ③), including a few cheaper singles with sinks, aren't nearly as good value, though there's a decent restaurant on the ground floor.

   If you do have a car or bike, however, you may as well continue to one of the four excellent **cases de pagès** which lie within 5km or so of Olot. First choice is Inès Puigdevall's *Mas La Garganta*, at the edge of La Pinya hamlet (follow signs west out of Olot towards Riudaura; ☎972 271 289; *garganta@agtat.es*; ⑦ HB). This rambling hillside farmhouse looks southwest over the very flat, fertile Vall d'en Bas towards Collsecabra volcano, with breakfast served on a view balcony. The seven minimally restored rooms are tasteful and en suite, with double beds or quads suitable for families, and strategic fireplaces guaranteeing year-round operation. The cooking's excellent, drawing on the family's sausage shop in town, though vegetarian/macrobiotic options are available, plus a kitchen for self-catering. If it's full (possible, as *Mas La Garganta* has been profiled in Spanish *Vogue*), there's also *Can Bel* (☎972 267 586; *bel@agtat.es*; ⑤ B&B), in the hamlet of Riudaura, 3km further, with just three rooms.

Over the next ridge, in the Vall de Bianya about 5km along the road to Camprodon, is another pair of establishments, close to each other on the hillside above **Sant Andreu de Socarrats** village. *Mas El Guitart* (☎972 292 140, *guitart@agtat.es*; min stay 2 days; ④) perches just above the Romanesque *ermita* of Santa Margarida, with mock-antique-furnished wood-floor rooms. There are also self-catering apartments, a duck-pond and a plunge pool. More old-fashioned and homy, but still en suite, is *La Torra de Santa Margarida* just east (☎972 291 321; ⑤ HB), a working cattle farm where at least two roaring fires heat common areas during colder months (vital on this north-facing slope).

EATING AND DRINKING

The centre of Olot offers a number of **bars** and **restaurants**, where you'll find the grilled meat specialities of the region, as well as a surprisingly wide range of non-regional dishes. With transport and a fuller wallet, there are also some worthy possibilities on the outskirts, or just out of town.

If you want to try some of the region's outstanding local produce, there's a farmers' market every morning along c/del Rengle. Finally, *ratafia* is the local liqueur produced from walnuts and herbs; if you acquire a taste for it, get your own bottle at Ratafia Russet, at the start of the road to Santa Pau.

Ca la Nàsia, 1km west of La Canya suburb in Llocalou hamlet. Fancy spot specializing in *faisà a la terra* (pheasant cooked with raisins in a clay pot), game and wild mushrooms. Closed Mon; reserve on ☎972 290 200.

Can Guix, c/Mulleras 3. Cheerful bar-restaurant where queues form outside for down-to-earth Catalan food. Eat heartily for 1400ptas/€8.40. The local wine comes by the *porró*, but you get a glass to decant it into if you chicken out. Closed Sun.

Les Cols, at the northern outskirts of town on Crta de la Canya, towards the Camprodon road. Currently reckoned the best food (just) within Olot city limits; they do *cuina de mercado* (seasonal ingredients as found in the market) and, since it's the sort of place that caters for big dos, reservations are suggested (☎972 269 209; closed Sun & 20 July–15 Aug).

La Dolce Vita, Passeig de Barcelona 2. Smart and trendy pizzeria serving the best pizza in town for around 1500ptas/€9 a head.

Font de l'Àngel, Plaça Móra 3. Snack-bar/café with garden seating and inexpensive *menús* and *plats combinats*. Closes Sundays after characteristically lively Saturday nights.

La Garrotxa, c/Serra i Ginesta 14. Don't turn your nose up at the institutional decor of this self-service restaurant near the museum. A changing list of specials that you'd never see in a typical bar for the price (1100ptas/€6.60 *menú* or *a la carta*) – fish soup, grilled quails, potatoes stuffed with sardines – represents excellent value. Open daily.

Bar-Restaurant Ramón, Plaça Clara 11. Bar serving mid-priced Catalan *tapas* plus an economical *menú*; its under-arcade seating also makes a good vantage point if you just want a drink.

La Terra, c/Bonaire 22 (☎972 274 151). Macrobiotic veggie restaurant that serves a very tasty lunchtime *menú* for 1300ptas/€7.80. Closed evenings and weekends, though open by arrangement for groups of six or more.

NIGHTLIFE AND ENTERTAINMENT

More than a dozen **bars** and **cafés** between the bullring and Plaça Carmé at the eastern end of the *barri antic* cater to most tastes. Aside from some obvious ones on the Passeig d'en Blay (itself the best place for an outdoor drink), two to pick out are the arty, genteel *Cocodrilo* on c/Sant Roc, and *Café 1900* on c/San Rafel, offering herb teas or stronger stuff, plus snacks, on two level premises. More youthful alternative choices include *Bar 6T7* at c/dels Sastres 35; the Senegalese-run *Bar-Restaurant Malem*, c/Pare Antoni Soler 6, a spacious converted clothing factory decorated with original artwork that also serves a good Catalan *menú*, and the raucous *Bar del Carmé*, Plaça del Carmé 3, which plays all sorts of music and hosts impromptu jam sessions.

There are even two **cinemas** screening first-run fare, the Colom on the Passeig d'en Blay and the Núria at Verge del Carmé 8, near Plaça Verge del Carmé. Most concerts and other events in the **summer festival** take place in Plaça del Mig, behind the museum. If you hear **music** you'd like to get hold of **on disc**, well-stocked Gong Music at Baixa del Tura 3 near Plaça del Carmé is part of a small chain of CD stores across northern Spain, and one of the biggest you'll find in the Spanish Pyrenees.

The Baixa Garrotxa Volcanic Zone

In 1985 the Catalan parliament decreed that much of the **Baixa Garrotxa**, a vast area extending southeast of Olot, would become the **Parc Natural de la Zona Volcànica de la Garrotxa**. This designation means less than one might think. The volcanic cones, and the **Fageda d'en Jordà** beech wood lying between the cones and Olot, gained some necessary protection, but cinder-quarrying (for building materials) and large-scale rubbish dumping had already spoiled some of the proposed park.

The Baixa Garrotxa is not a zone of belching steam and boiling mud. It's been nearly twelve thousand years since the last eruption, during which time the ash and lava have weathered into a fertile soil whose luxuriant vegetation – including extensive fields of corn, beans (the tiny local white *fegolets* are especially esteemed) and various grains – masks the contours of the dormant volcanoes. There are thirty cones in all, the largest of them around 160m high and 1500m wide.

FLORA AND FAUNA OF THE GARROTXA REGION

The lower slopes of the Garrotxa region's distinctive hills are clothed with **forests** of evergreen oak (*Quercus mediterraneo-montanum*) yielding higher up to deciduous oak and beech woods, with subalpine meadows and pastures at higher altitudes. More than 1500 species of **vascular plant** have been recorded within the park, ranging from typical forest-floor dwellers like snowdrops, yellow wood anemones and rue-leaved isopyrum to high-altitude specialities like ramonda and Pyrenean saxifrage. In addition, the Garrotxa contains a number of Iberian rarities, several of which are found nowhere else in the world: the white-flowered *Allium pyrenaicum*, typical of rocky limestone cliffs; Pyrenean milkwort (*Polygala vayredae*), a woody species with large pinkish-purple flowers; and shrubby gromwell (*Aithodora oleifolia*), a scrambling plant with pale pink flowers that turn blue with age.

A phenomenal 143 species of **bird** have been observed in the region. Since three-quarters of the park is covered with forest, goshawks, tawny owls, short-toed treecreepers, great spotted woodpeckers and nuthatches are common. Flocks of bramblings and hawfinches take refuge in the beech woods during winter, while the more barren volcanic summits support alpine choughs and alpine accentors. Summer visitors include short-toed eagles, hobbies, wrynecks, red-backed shrikes and Bonelli's warblers, along with Mediterranean species such as subalpine warblers, golden orioles and bee-eaters.

Forest-dwelling **mammals** include beech martens, wildcats, genets, badgers and acorn-loving wild boar, as well as a number of small insectivores – common, pygmy and Etruscan shrews – and the nocturnal oak dormouse, characterized by its "Lone Ranger" mask and long, black-tufted tail. Otters are also sighted along the rivers from time to time.

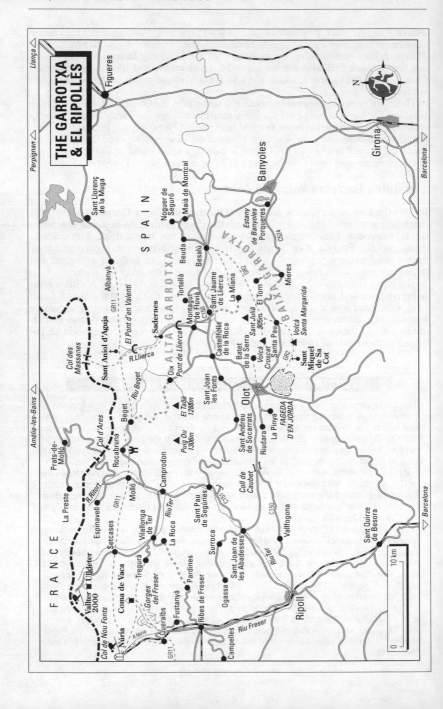

THE GARROTXA
& EL RIPOLLÈS

Santa Pau

The central village of the volcanic zone, medieval **SANTA PAU**, 9km southeast of Olot, presents to the outside world a defensive perimeter of continuous and almost window-less house walls. Slightly less discovered than Besalú, it's even more atmospheric, though verging on the twee. At the very least, it's a mandatory meal stop, and would be a good base for exploring the park's ever-increasing network of signposted paths and tracks. Without your own vehicle, it's a three-to-four-hour trail-walk from Olot (a route covered below), or you can catch one of the thrice-weekly buses on the Olot–Mieres–Banyoles route.

Santa Pau's outer archways open onto dark, ancient buildings, many of them sympa-thetically converted into business premises and homes. At the core of the village is the thirteenth-century **Firal dels Bous** (also known as Plaça Major), with its pair of archway shops, the Can Vayreda information centre (summer Mon–Sat 10.30am–2pm & 4.30–7pm, Sun 10.30am–2pm), and Romanesque church of **Santa Maria** with its fine inte-rior groin vaulting (though it's crumbling, and donations are requested towards restora-tion). In the adjacent Plaçeta dels Balls, overlooked by the three-storeyed tower of the Balls family, you'll find pricey but tasty **meals** at *Cal Sastre* (closed Sun night & Mon, open Fri–Sat only in winter), though several more average restaurants have lately sprung up on the approaches to the old quarter. The management of *Cal Sastre*, despairing of their cramped upstairs rooms as **accommodation**, have expanded into a renovated old building at the edge of town, c/de les Cases Noves 1 (☎972 680 049, fax 972 680 481, *sastre@agtat.es*; ⑥), a highly regarded hotel with antique furnishings and beamed ceil-ings, used as a stopover by self-guided walking clients. Two kilometres up the road towards Olot, at the foot of the Volcà Santa Margarida (see below) and within 1km of the GR2, *Mas Collelldemunt* (☎972 680 523, fax 972 270 101, *www.turismerural.net/collellde-munt*; ④ B&B or ⑤ HB) is a less expensive *casa rural* co-run by Gonzalo, the only offi-cially certified guide for the park (organized hikes offered); facilities are basic, but there's wheelchair access and it's open all year except Dec 24–Jan 7. Another kilometre back towards Olot there's *Lava* (☎972 68 03 58; open all year), a large, well-positioned camp-site in the shadow of two cones.

A loop walk

An excellent way to get acquainted with the Baixa Garrotxa is to take a loop walk out of Olot, which almost completely avoids paved roads and can easily be completed in a single day. Note that this route does not exactly correspond to any of the numbered and signposted itineraries – often just point-to-point – prepared by the park authorities, but combines the virtues of several.

From Olot, follow the signposts across the Riu Fluvià, from where it's an hour south along surfaced country lanes – equally suited to horse-riding or mountain-biking (as is most of this circuit) – to the **Fageda d'en Jordà**. Although much reduced, this beech forest is still a treat in the autumn when the leaves are turning; it takes about half an hour more to emerge on the far side of the spooky, maze-like groves, deserted except for the tourist *carruatges* (horsecarts) visiting from Santa Pau.

Turn left when you meet the helpfully marked **GR2** long-distance trail, then right twice in succession when you encounter the track to Sa Cot. Follow the signposts to stay on the GR2, which soon becomes a proper path as it heads east for thirty minutes to the medieval chapel of **Sant Miquel de Sa Cot**, a popular weekend picnic spot.

The **Volcà Santa Margarida** is visible just behind the chapel, and within forty min-utes you should be up on its rim and then down in its grassy caldera, where another tiny *ermita* (country chapel) sits at the bottom; allow at least an extra hour for this side trip. From the turn-off to Santa Margarida – just fifteen minutes from Sant Miquel – you resume the main route, and descend to the **Font de Can Roure**, source of the only water en route, before skirting Roca Negra with its disused quarry and entering Santa

Pau: 45 minutes from the shoulder of Santa Margarida, and some three hours from Olot (not counting the detour to the caldera).

Rather than follow the onward GR2 (see below), which would inconveniently lengthen the circuit for dayhikers, bear west at **Can Mascou** and approach Volcà Croscat via the *Lava* campsite (see above). You skirt the northeast flank of Croscat, badly scarred by quarrying; from the campsite it's another hour, along a progressively narrowing track – unsignposted except for "BATET" painted on hunting-zone signs – to the high (720m) plateau of **Batet de la Serra**, scattered with handsome farms.

Here you meet a marked path-and-track coming west from the Serra de Sant Julià del Mont, turning west yourself to follow the road briefly before taking the well-marked *camí*, beautiful and partly cobbled in basalt, which passes the hamlet of **Santa Maria de Batet** on its way down to Olot. It takes just under another hour of downhill progress, or a total of something less than seven hours on the day, to emerge at the top of c/Sant Cristòfor, which runs right down to the main boulevard through Olot.

La Miana

From Santa Pau the GR2 continues briefly north towards the scenic Serra de Sant Julià del Mont, then veers east away from park itinerary no. 6 down a valley to Besalú. East of the summit and accessible by a 45-minute spur trail from the streamside hamlet of **EL TORN** (bar and shop in summer) are a group of excellent *turismes rurals* at **La Miana**, which can also be reached by a signposted, six-kilometre dirt track from Sant Jaume de Llierca on the Besalú–Olot road. The proprietors have indicated the side path in from El Torn, as well as down from the summit of Sant Julià, itself already reachable by using itineraries 6 and 8. They have also signposted onward, non-GR trails to Sant Ferriol and Besalú (3hr).

Can Jou (☎972 190 263, fax 972 190 444, *canjou@turismerural.net*; ⑤ or ⑦ HB), co-managed by the helpful Michael Peters, has capacity for fifteen in modernized, en-suite rooms and sits right on the Coll de Jou with views south and west, especially from the medium-sized pool just above the *masia*. Michael, his wife Rosina and assistants also run the area's best **horse-riding** programme, with half-day rides around the mountain, full-day excursions to Santa Pau, and longer trips to the coast on request. Just 300m east is the amazing *Rectoria de la Miana* (☎972 190 190 or 972 223 059; ⑥ HB only, vegetarian on request), run by Dutchman Franz Engelhard, a medieval manor house complete with crumbling twelfth-century Romanesque chapel. Although the room-to-bathroom ratio is not as good as at *Can Jou*, every room is unique and antique-furnished, with meals served in the arcaded ground-floor hall. Both places enjoy incredible tranquillity in the middle of forested nowhere and are thus massively popular – best to reserve rather than showing up on spec, as they've been well publicized.

If you come up empty here, there's one more *casa rural* in the immediate vicinity: *El Turrós* (☎972 687 350, fax 972 687 733, *turros@agtat.es*; ⑥ HB), just under 4km north down the dirt track towards Sant Jaume de Llierca, and then another very rough kilometre down a steep drive. This rambling country manor has a maximum capacity of fourteen in four rooms and is particularly good for families, though it's not nearly so convenient for walkers as *Can Jou* or *Rectoria de la Miana*. While cited in literature as being in Argelaguer, the nearest village on the main highway, note that there's no road access from there – this is the *only* way in.

The Alta Garrotxa

The Alta Garrotxa stretches north from the main Besalú–Olot road as far as the frontier summits. Unlike the lower Garrotxa, the rock strata here are mostly limestone, and thus for speleologists the region is almost inexhaustible, with more than a hundred catalogued caves. For walkers or mountain-bikers it's a rewarding area as well, especially in spring or late autumn when the highest Pyrenees are inaccessible. Whichever of the following routes you go for – all begin outside Castellfollit de la Roca – the Editorial Alpina "Garrotxa" 1:40,000 map is a useful, though as ever far from infallible, aid.

North to France: the Llierca Valley

It's 8km from Castellfollit up the Llierca valley (served by a one-lane paved road) past Montagut de Fluvià to Sadernes. At Montagut another minor road is signposted west to the most attractive and least regimented of three local **campsites**, the unfortunately named *Can Banal* (☎972 687 681; March–Oct), close to the GR1 and astride a minor path (and road) on to Oix. Dutch-run and centred on an old farmhouse, it has shady, well-separated parcels intended for tenters; an apartment in the old house is also available by the week. Continuing on the main Llierca valley route brings you after 2km to the much-promoted *Camping Montagut* (☎972 287 202), equipped with all mod cons but hopelessly sterile, packed and shadeless, but of a style tourist authorities seem keen to encourage. However, nearby stands the wonderful photogenic **Pont de Llierca**, a Roman bridge which today carries the **GR1** over it, on its way to Besalú (3hr distant).

The asphalt gives out just below **SADERNES**, which notwithstanding its depiction on maps, is barely a hamlet, let alone a village. This has as a focus the sparely handsome tenth-century church of **Santa Cecília**, sacked by the Republicans in 1936, subsequently restored and now usually locked; surviving interior treasures, including a carved Crucifixion, apsidal frescoes and an image of the saint, have been whisked away to museums in Girona and Barcelona. One of the few other buildings here is the popular *Hostal de Sadernes*, which despite its name offers just **meals** and only operates Friday evening to Sunday evening (plus holidays), but the food is hearty country fare – 2200ptas/€13.20 for three courses, such as *mongetes amb ventresca*, mixed grill, sweet, house wine and coffee – served on the arcaded ground floor of an old farmhouse. This gives its name to the less-than-inspired adjacent **campsite**, *Masia de Sadernes*, hopelessly crowded and staked out by semi-permanent caravans.

Upstream from Sadernes, the dirt track steadily worsens as you begin to thread the scenic gorge of the Llierca; after 2.5km you reach the short side path to **El Pont d'en Valentí**, a medieval bridge much used by smugglers of old, with a ruined mill on the far side. Beyond this point vehicles are banned – there's a barrier, and parking proves nearly impossible anyway along this stretch. From the bridge it's ninety minutes on foot, first on the track and then on a trail veering off to the ninth-century **Ermita de Sant Aniol d'Aguja**, a landmark, rather squat chapel astride the GR11.

Dedicated to an obscure third-century local saint, this has a charming legend attached to it; Aniol, fleeing Roman persecutions in Gaul, slept on this spot but was roused by two persistent oxen. Taking this as a sign from God (the ox being the Evangelist Matthew's symbol for the self-sacrifice of Christ), Aniol returned to his homeland and was promptly martyred in 208 AD. Yearly on Ascension Day there occurs here the **Aplec dels Francesas**, a pilgrimage festival attended by various Alta Garrotxa folk and the inhabitants of Sant Llorenç (Sant Laurent) de Cerdans, the closest large village on the French side of the border (see "The upper Tech", pp.126–127). This, or slightly higher, smaller Coustouges can be reached by continuing northeast on the footpath from the refuge towards the much-used **Col des Massanes** (1126m) on the frontier.

Northwest to El Ripollès: Oix, Beget and Rocabruna

Staying in Spain, a more populated route heads **northwest** into the Ripoll region, covered in the next section. From Castellfollit de la Roca, take the paved but one-lane road 9km northwest to **OIX**, which dominates a bowl-shaped, intensely cultivated valley. The attractive village, surrounded by huge modern barns, features the Romanesque church of Sant Llorenç and a small but graceful Roman bridge. Right opposite the church on

Plaça Major, you can **stay** at the *Hostal de la Rovira* (☎ & fax 972 294 347; ⑤ B&B) in a restored mansion, which has tastefully done rooms with all mod cons, plus a ground-floor **restaurant** offering gourmet menus with bumped-up prices at weekends. Otherwise, there are two **campsites** 1km west, on opposite sides of the valley: *Els Alous*, in a plantation of trees (☎972 294 173), and the smaller *Masia Can Vila*, on the grounds of an old farm (☎972 294 232). Both have swimming pools, and the latter a restaurant.

To continue, leave the village passing under the "castle" (a fortified manor house), ignoring private roads, and then bear left at the signposted fork 500m outside Oix. This wide, comfortable dirt road leads northwest 12km, passing little other than the high hamlet of Sant Miquel de Pera and ambling cattle, to the showcase village of **BEGET** (510m), done up by lowlanders as a weekend retreat verging on twee. Two slender bridges link three neighbourhoods separated by the confluence of two streams, and the graceful twelfth-century church of **Sant Cristòfor**, standing at the entrance to the village, is celebrated for its particularly solemn and serene *Majestat*. All but a dozen or so of these Catalan wooden images of a fully dressed Christ were destroyed in 1936; this example, perhaps as old as the church itself, is one of the very few that can be seen in its intended context (keys available from the souvenir shop at no. 15 when the church is closed). Beget has three **restaurants**, two with **accommodation**: *Can Joanic*, by the church (☎972 741 241; ④), which has rooms sharing bathrooms above a fair-value *menjador* with a riverside terrace, and the pricier *El Forn* (☎972 741 230; ⑦ HB) near the top of the village, where the en-suite, heated rooms and the outdoor terrace of the restaurant have commanding views. The food here is slightly more ambitious – rabbit with figs and such, though still affordable – the results sustaining rather than elegant. The GR11 passes through Beget, and these are the only places to stay on this stretch of the trail.

Some 7km west on either the GR11 or the now-paved road, **ROCABRUNA**, with its ruined castle and stubby but handsome Romanesque church, stands just below the watershed dividing the Garrotxa from El Ripollès, the county of Ripoll. The unnervingly narrow (though paved) onward road, among other reasons, means there's no bus service along the 7km separating Rocabruna from the Camprodon–Molló highway. The only place to **stay**, 2km west on the main road and then 1km down a dirt track, but right astride the GR11, is the friendly, English-speaking *turisme rural Exalde* (☎972 130 317; ⑤), a working dairy farm where you can watch sheep's cheese being made in the basement. No meals are served, and some of the large rooms are without en suite, but self-catering kitchens on each of two floors make it ideal for trekkers or cyclists. Surprisingly for such a tiny place, Rocabruna has two **restaurants** good enough to draw crowds on weekend nights from far off. Particularly noteworthy is *Can Po* (☎972 741 045), reckoned one of the best eateries in the Alta Garrotxa, where a meal of cold lentil-and-smoked-fish salad, duck *confit*, prunes in armagnac and house wine runs to 3000ptas/€18, but you can easily spend 5000ptas/€30 a head by sampling the premium wine list.

El Ripollès

Moving towards Cerdanya and Andorra along the main roads from the Costa Brava, you truly begin to feel among high mountains in the *comarque* (county) of **El Ripollès**. The C150 climbs west from Olot through densely tree-clad foothills to the Coll de Caubet, where a vista of receding peaks opens up, then drops to the county town of **Ripoll**, along the scenic Vallfogona valley. Motorists, and the occasional bus, can also use the C153 from Olot to Sant Pau de Seguries, a route shortened some twenty minutes by tunnels under the Coll de Capsacosta. By train the approach is different, entering El Ripollès from the south via Sant Quirze de Besora.

From Ripoll an important "Romanesque Route" of beautiful churches and monasteries – most notably at **Sant Joan de les Abadesses** and **Camprodon** – may be followed northeast towards the high ridges. Above Camprodon, isolated valleys lead up to the frontier and road crossing at the Col d'Ares/Aras (1513m); winter sport enthusiasts can patronize the ski station of **Vallter 2000**.

Due north of Ripoll, road and rail climb gently to **Ribes de Freser** and then more sharply west out of the *comarque* via the Collada de Toses. From Ribes, there's the option of riding the dramatic, narrow-gauge *cremallera* railway up the gorge to **Queralbs** and **Núria**, the combined pilgrimage shrine and all-year resort below the summit of 2910-metre **Puigmal**. Walkers can link the valleys of Ter and Núria by hiking between Setcases and Queralbs, along the marvellous Riu Freser trail.

Ripoll is the hub of **public transport**, with trains continuing north to Puigcerdà and the French border, while the most regular bus lines head east to Olot and northeast to Sant Joan and Camprodon.

Ripoll

RIPOLL occupies so prominent a place in Catalunya's history that it's impossible not to be initially disappointed by this rather shabby place, buzzed by traffic and divided by the manifestly polluted Riu Ter. The inhabitants seem to agree, resigned to working here but deserting it in droves at weekends when Ripoll assumes the air of a ghost town. But just ten minutes' walk from the southeast corner of town – where trains and buses stop – lies a small, relatively peaceful old quarter, with one of the most remarkable monuments in the Catalan Pyrenees, the Monestir de Santa Maria, founded in 888 to spur Christian resettlement of the surrounding valleys following the expulsion of the Muslims.

The chief monastic centre of medieval Catalonia, Ripoll later became a major producer of weapons, a development foreshadowed by the career of the monastery's founder, **Guifré el Pilós** (Wilfred the Hairy). He was the archetypal "fighting Christian", first of the powerful counts of Barcelona who, in the mid-ninth century, ruled not only that city, but also the counties of Cerdagne, Urgell and Osona, and ultimately Girona and Besalú as well. He was killed in 898, struck by a Muslim chief's lance during a raid.

The Town

Following an 1835 fire, the Benedictine **Monestir de Santa Maria** lay in ruins; today's barrel-vaulted nave (daily 8am–1pm & 3–8pm) is a copy of the original structure erected over Guifré's tomb by Abbot Oliba in the early eleventh century. (Oliba and his twelfth-century successors created an important library here and – in contrast with Guifré – were instrumental in the preservation of Islamic scholarship.) The magnificent Romanesque **west portal**, however, survived the fire, and is now protected by a glass conservatory against the elements. Erected in the twelfth century, and now the main entrance, this portal squirms with carvings of religious and astrological subjects: the Apocalypse (across the top), the Book of Kings (to the left), Exodus (to the right), scenes from the lives of David, St Peter and St Paul (at the bottom), and the months of the year (around the inner side of the pillars).

The double-columned **cloisters** (daily 10am–1pm & 3–7pm; 100ptas/€0.60), far less damaged in the succession of earthquakes, sackings and fires visited on the monastery, are particularly beautiful. The **capitals**, dating from the twelfth-century Romanesque "Golden Age", portray monks and nuns, beasts mundane and mythical, plus secular characters of the period. They completely overshadow the nominal **Museu Lapidari** here, which displays assorted stonework, sarcophagi and funerary art along the walls.

Adjacent to the monastery stands the fourteenth-century church of **Sant Pere**, part of which houses the **Museu dels Pirineus** (Tues–Sun: late June–late Sept

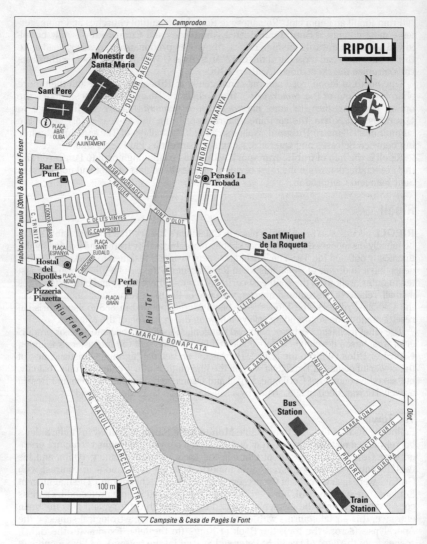

Campsite & Casa de Pagès la Font

9.30am–7pm; late Sept–late June 9.30am–1.30pm & 3.30–6pm; 400ptas/€2.40), with a diverse collection of folk, craft and archeological exhibits, particularly relating to the seventeenth-century local arms and metal-smelting industry. You're only likely to get inside the church when it serves as a venue for Ripoll's **music festival**, staged on successive weekends during July and August.

Besides the monastery and museum there's little to detain you, though it's worth climbing around the back of Sant Pere to a **terrace** from where you can overlook Santa Maria. A nearby bar has tables here, too, certainly the nicest seats in town. Down in the modern district, two *modernista* buildings may claim your attention: the spouting stone flourishes of **Can Bonada**, c/del Progés 14, on the way to the bus and train stations, and the tiny church of **Sant Miquel de la Roqueta** (1912), a couple of blocks up the hill, looking like a pixie's house with a witch's cap on top.

Practicalities

The **train and bus stations** stand within sight of each other, just a ten-minute walk from the heart of town, over the Pont d'Olot. On Plaça d'Abat Oliba, the tourist office (daily 9.30am–1.30pm & 4–7pm, Sun 10am–1pm; ☎972 702 351) stands near the Museu dels Pirineus, under the sundial, stocking plenty of maps, pamphlets and local transport timetables.

Aside from this helpful spot, conventional tourism in Ripoll marches resolutely backwards; places to stay are sharply limited, and there are many bars but very few places for a sit-down meal. This makes it highly advisable to base yourself somewhere nearby and make a flying visit. Surviving **accommodation** choices, all in or near the old town, can be overpriced, noisy and uninspiring. Least expensive is the *Habitacions Paula*, Plaça de l'Abat Arnulf 6 (☎972 700 011; ③), thirty seconds' walk left from the tourist office as you face it. It was renovated in 2000 to provide proper plumbing arrangements for the rooms, so expect a rise in both price and comfort. Next niche up is occupied by the *Hostal del Ripollès* on Plaça Nova (☎972 700 215; ③), entered through its ground-floor pizzeria. *Pensió La Trobada*, Passeig Honorat Vilamanyà 4 (☎972 714 353; ⑤), across the river, represents the highest standard in town but is overpriced. There's also a large **campsite**, the *Solana de Ter* (☎972 701 062; open all year), 2km south of town on the Barcelona road, with the usual preponderance of caravans.

If you have transport, it's worth foregoing all of the preceding in favour of a **casa de pagès** adhering to the *turisme rural* programme, in the hamlet of **Les Llosses**, 18km distant on the road to Berga. The large rooms at *La Font* (☎972 198 087; ④ B&B) are particularly well suited for families or groups; dinner is also served in the fine upstairs common area, with views over the adjacent wooded hillside.

Eating and **drinking** options, too, are far from plentiful. *Restaurant Perla*, Plaça Gran 4, features rather expensive *a la carta* food along with humdrum *menús*, though the *Pizzeria Piazetta* on the ground floor of the *Hostal del Ripollès* is more reasonable and appetizing. These are the only full-service restaurants in the centre; for excellent *tapas* and crêpes, head for *Bar El Punt* at Plaça Ajuntament 10, which has tables both outside and in the air-conditioned premises.

Sant Joan de les Abadesses

The small town of **SANT JOAN DE LES ABADESSES**, 11km northeast of Ripoll, owes its existence to the eponymous **monastery** (July–Aug daily 10am–7pm; May–June & Sept daily 10am–2pm & 4–7pm; March–April & Oct daily 10am–2pm & 4–6pm; mid-June to mid-Sept daily 10am–2pm & 4–7pm; Nov–Feb daily 10am–2pm, also 4–6pm weekends; 200ptas/€1.20) founded in 887 by Guifré el Pilós, apparently for the benefit of his daughter Emma, the first abbess. Within two centuries, however, the institution was closed temporarily in 1017 by Pope Benedict III as a result of politically motivated accusations of immorality (see box overleaf) by Comte (Count) Bernat Tallaferro, to whom devolved – not coincidentally – all the prior feudal privileges of the convent. The present church, consecrated in 1150, is a single-nave structure of impressive austerity, built to a Latin-cross plan with five apses, and housing a curious thirteenth-century wooden sculpture, the *Santíssim Misteri*, in its main chapel. This moving work, depicting Christ's deposition, retains on His forehead "a piece of Holy Bread . . . preserved untouched for seven hundred years", according to the monastery's literature. Admission to the monastery also includes entry to the Gothic **cloisters** and the

---

THE LEGEND OF COMTE ARNAU

The monastery at Sant Joan des Abadesses is inextricably linked with numerous durable legends concerning one **Comte (Count) Arnau**, a quasi-historical feudal lord of the eleventh century, notorious for parsimony towards his serfs. More sensationally, he is immortalized in local folk-song and poetry as a Ripollès Don-Juan equivalent, renowned for his lust and fecklessness in numerous amorous adventures. Arnau even managed to secure the affections of Sant Joan's incumbent abbess, Engelberga, whom he visited at night on horseback by means of an enormous, long tunnel from his lands between Gombrèn and Campdevànol, some 15km west. Her death hardly curtailed his ardour or his appearances, as in the meantime he had managed to seduce a fair number of the lower-ranking nuns; the new abbess attempted to secure all the orifices of the convent, so to speak, but Arnau had concluded a pact with the Devil and used his new-found satanic powers to filter through the very walls.

However, unlike Don Juan, the count eventually fell genuinely and abjectly in love with a young local lass, who understandably failed to return such sentiments given his rather chequered history. To escape his continued advances, she enrolled as a novice at the nunnery; after a humbling vigil at the gates, Arnau managed to gain entrance by conventional methods, only to find the object of his affections recently dead. As he approached the bier, she returned to life just long enough to denounce his various misdemeanours in an other-worldly voice. Filled with terror and remorse, Comte Arnau fled back to his feudal estates, condemned both before and after death to eternally wander the hills above. On stormy nights he has also been seen as a mournful ghost in the cloister of the monastery itself, but the favoured venue for his hauntings remains the vicinity of Gombrèn, where the count supposedly appears as a baleful apparition on horseback, accompanied by spectral packs of hunting dogs in full howl.

Museu del Monestir, whose well-presented exhibits include ornate chalices, curiosities such as a crucifix in rock crystal, and a fine series of late medieval altarpieces.

Other than the monastery, there are few specific sights in Sant Joan, but the old quarter boasts a fair-sized grid of ancient houses along streets almost shorter than their names, all leading to a small but appealingly arcaded **Plaça Major**. The slender twelfth-century bridge down in the well-tilled valley was only restored in the 1970s, after being destroyed in fierce fighting of February 1939, during the final Republican retreat of the Civil War. Having strolled around and scared the pigeons from the abandoned shell of Sant Pol church in the centre, you've pretty much exhausted the potential of the town.

Practicalities

Buses arrive at a shelter behind the monastery church apse; the **tourist office** (Mon–Sat 10am–2pm & 4–7pm, Sun 10am–2pm; ☎972 720 599), well stocked with both free literature and booklets for sale, occupies the cloistered, fifteenth-century **Palau de Abadia** or episcopal palace, just fifty paces left from the Museu del Monestir's entrance.

In theory Sant Joan would make a far more pleasant base than Ripoll, with frequent bus links in each direction; in practice this may prove difficult, given the same process of attrition in lodging. Sole surviving **accommodation** consists, in the new district near the bus stop, of *Hostal Casa Nati* at c/Pere Rovira 3 (☎972 720 114; ②), with large rooms, and *Hostal Fonda Can Janpere*, around the corner at c/del Mestre Josep Andreu 3 (☎972 720 077; ④), offering comfortable en-suite rooms with heating and TV.

Preferable to either, if you have a car, is the **turisme rural** member *Mas Mitjavila*, 11km northwest of Sant Joan at the hamlet of **OGASSA** (☎972 722 020; ⑤ B&B). From the north side of the new bridge, follow the asphalt road 4km to Surroca village, and then continue the remaining distance on a cement driveway. With the adjacent tenth-century church of Sant Martí de Ogassa, *Mas Mitjavila* was once a dependency of the monastery of Sant Joan, and enjoys a superb eyrie-like setting 1300m up, overlooking the valleys of Ripoll. Half board and farm produce are both available, as are easy hikes in the surrounding mountains.

Back in town, *Can Janpere* has an attached **restaurant**, with economical *menús* and a more adventurous *carta*; otherwise you can sit outside at the pleasant cafés on the main *rambla*, Passeig Comte Guifré, one of which (*Cafeteria La Rambla*) does a *menú* and *plats combinats*.

Camprodon

Approaching from points south, the first place that feels like a real mountain town is **CAMPRODON** (950m), a fact exploited last century by the Catalan gentry who arrived by a (now defunct) rail line to spend summer in the hills. The town, 14km from Sant Joan, still retains the prosperous air of those times, with shops full of leather goods, outdoor gear, cheese and sausages. Ornate villas front a *rambla* clogged with towering trees, and other town houses are occasionally embellished with *modernista* flourishes.

Like Ripoll, Camprodon straddles the confluence of two rivers, here the Ter and the Ritort, and is knit together by little bridges. The principal one, the sixteenth-century **Pont Nou**, still has a defensive tower. From here you can follow the narrow main commercial street, pedestrianized c/València, to the restored Romanesque monastic church of **Sant Pere** (consecrated in 904, not to be confused with the larger parish church of Santa Maria adjacent), near the northeast end of town. There is also a small castle overhead, but no apparent way up.

Camprodon was the birthplace of the composer **Isaac Albéniz** (1860–1909), a fact which neither the town nor the region made much of until recently – probably because there is little distinctively Catalan in the music he produced during his wanderings through Spain. (His most celebrated work, for piano or guitar, is entitled *Iberia*.) However, the great man now has a street, and a **café** on c/València (recommended for croissants and coffee) named after him, a bust near Sant Pere, a summer **music festival** in his honour, and a less worthwhile **museum** near the bridge commemorating his life and times (daily 11am–2pm & 4–7pm, 400ptas/€2.40).

Practicalities

Buses from Ripoll stop at the TEISA depot, well south of the main Plaça d'Espanya, where you'll find the **tourist office** (July–Sept Mon–Sat 10am–1.30pm & 4.30–8pm, Sun 10am–2pm; Oct–June Mon–Fri 10am–2pm & 4–7pm, Sat 10am–2pm & 4–8pm, Sun 10am–2pm; ☎972 740 010) in the *Ajuntament* building. Two doors down from the TEISA terminal, Ski 2000 is the main in-town outlet for **equipment rental** during winter.

Accommodation tends to be expensive, given the town's role as a minor ski resort, with advance reservations advisable throughout the year. Working roughly up the price-and-comfort ladder, on often noisy c/Josep Morer there's *Can Ganasi* at no. 9 (☎972 740 134; ④) and *Hostal Sayola* at no. 4 (☎972 740 142; ④), both en suite. The blatantly overpriced *Hostal Sant Roc* (☎972 740 119; ⑦) and the better-value *Hostal La Placeta* (☎972 740 807; ③) overlook Plaça del Carmé, just east of c/Josep Morer and the first square you reach as you come into town from Sant Joan. The elegance of the dead-central *Hotel Güell*, Plaça d'Espanya 8 (☎972 740 011; ⑤), justifies a mild splurge. Some 3km up the road to Molló there's a less-than-brilliant **campsite**, *Els Solans* (☎972 740 012), occupied by permanently anchored caravans.

Can Ganasi's **restaurant** offers several different *menús* plus local dishes such as duck and trout, while *Hotel La Placeta* also has a salubrious attached *menjador* (dinner only). Otherwise *Bar-Restaurant Núria*, at Plaça d'Espanya 11, is a characterful place and features a good-value lunch *menú* (*a la carta* only at night, including such delights as "prog legs"). Local specialities, besides the ubiquitous *ànec amb peras* (duck with pears), include *pinyes*, extremely rich and dense pine-nut sweets, which you can find on sale at bakeries throughout the town.

Beyond Camprodon: the Ter and Ritort valleys

Beyond Camprodon you're increasingly dependent on your own transport and ultimately your own legs. The majority of people who venture this way are either hikers, or skiers driving northwest up the **Ter valley** to the runs of Vallter 2000, with comparatively little traffic moving northeast up the **Ritort** that isn't bound for France. The construction of holiday flats for lowlanders, and of more short-term tourist facilities, now reigns supreme, but you still catch a glimpse of the area's former agricultural economy in the herds of grazing horses, and cattle ambling home at dusk.

The first settlement that might tempt you to stop is the rather ordinary **VILALLONGA DE TER**, 5km from Camprodon. Opposite the standard-issue Romanesque church of **San Martín** on the main *plaça* are two **accommodation** possibilities: *Hostal Pastoret* (☎972 740 319; ⑦ HB) at c/Constitució 10, and the unstaffed *Habitacions Cal Mestre* around the corner at c/del Pou 1 (but info at c/Major 3; ☎972 740 407; ④). There are also two independent **restaurants** in town, as well as a **campsite**, *Conca de Ter* (☎972 740 629; open all year) at the outskirts, better equipped than Camprodon's but still pitched mainly at well-anchored caravanners. Just one bus daily from Camprodon passes through here on its way to Setcases (see below).

Immediately south of Vilallonga, on the far side of the valley, the hamlet of **LA ROCA** huddles strikingly under the unmissable namesake monolith; there's no accommodation but three **restaurants**, including the popular *Can Fortià*, are much resorted to by visitors. A rough vehicle track leads from here west to Pardines (see p.180).

Alternatively, you can bear left 1km past Vilallonga for the steep detour to **TREGURÀ**, 4km from the main road; perched on a sunny hillside at 1400m, with sweeping views east over the valley, the upper part of this double village has a church dating from about 980. There are also two places to **stay**: the welcoming *Fonda Rigà* (☎972 136 000; ⑤ B&B or ⑥ HB), with its massively popular and reasonable **restaurant**, and the rather more institutional *Hotel El Serrat* (☎972 136 019; ⑦ HB).

From Tregurà, it's possible to **hike west** in a day to Queralbs, where you can pick up the rack-and-pinion railway down to Ribes or up to Núria. This route provides a lower-altitude, far more scenic alternative to the GR11, which crosses the Ter valley much higher up. The lower path, now designated the **GR11.7**, climbs towards Puig Castell (2125m) and then through the Coll dels Tres Pics (2hr) to the 1999-built **Refugi Coma de Vaca** (4hr, 2000m) at the top of the Gorges del Freser. This FEEC refuge, run by Xavier and Yolanda (42 places, staffed Easter, May Day, mid-June to late Sept & Oct hols; ☎972 198 082, or off-season by arrangement on ☎936 824 237; ①), offers above-average evening meals, hot showers and a full activities programme, including rock-climbing at marked routes five minutes away.

From just before the refuge, on the south bank of the Freser, a distinct and beautiful trail – the onward GR11.7 – drops westwards through a stunning gorge to Queralbs (7hr from Tregurà). Another path connects Coma de Vaca with the **Refugi Ulldeter** (2220m elevation; 75 places; open July–Sept and weekends all year; snack bar; ①) on the slopes of the Vallter ski resort. In summer, hikers can also follow the ski-mountaineering itineraries described opposite.

Setcases and Vallter 2000

Back in the Ter valley, **SETCASES**, 6km northwest of Vilallonga, has been completely gentrified from its former decrepitude. Once an important agricultural village, it was almost totally abandoned until the nearby ski station began to attract hoteliers, chalet developers and second-home owners. The ski trade ensures that some short-term beds and food are relatively pricey, with some fairly gruff characters amongst local proprietors – a shame, as Setcases straddles the GR11, a half-day's march west from Molló (see below). If you need to **stay**, the most affordable accommodation stands adjacent on the riverbank road: the *Hostal Ter* (☎972 136 096; ④) or the *Nueva Can Tiranda* (☎972 136 037; ③), though you may be required to take half–board – as you definitely are in the village centre at *Hostal El Molí* (☎972 136 049; ⑥ HB). At those rates, the relative luxury of *Hotel La Coma* (☎972 136 073; ⑤ B&B), at the very entrance to the village, might be worth considering. Local trippers flock here to **eat** at weekends, most notably at the independent restaurant *Can Jepet* (reserve on ☎972 136 104). Prices are bumped up (no *menú* at weekends), but so are portion sizes, making the food – well-presented salads, slightly oily grilled quail with artichoke and roast peppers, genuinely homemade *flan* – excellent value at under 3000ptas/€18 a head.

Situated at the head of the valley, below the frontier summits of Bastiments (2874m) and Pic de la Dona (2702m), compact **VALLTER 2000** is the most easterly downhill ski resort in the Pyrenees. While south-facing, the glacial bowl here has a chilly microclimate that lets snow linger into April most years – though the runs remain heavily dependent on canons. Even beginners get bored with the two nursery runs, though weak intermediates will find plenty of challenge in the two-kilometre blue (Jordi Pujol) or easy red (El Clot) runs from the top point of 2535m (served by chair lift busy days, otherwise poma). Only strong intermediates should attempt the five-kilometre Riu-Xalet joint *piste*, nominally blue but ending in a narrow, strongly red drop to the low point at 1910m, from where another chair lift returns you to the resort centre at 2200m. Here you'll find a better-than-average restaurant and equipment rental. In short, enough to keep you interested for the duration of a weekend, when Barcelonans flood the place; certain Camprodon and Ter valley hotels offer all-in packages of half-board and lift pass which save a good twenty-five percent compared to doing it piecemeal.

Ski mountaineers can work their way **westwards** to Núria, either via the 2826-metre Pic de la Vaca (about 10hr) or above the Riu Freser (8hr), a route that's more advisable in windy conditions. Going **eastwards** via the 2507-metre (but gently rounded) Roc Colom to the French *Refuge Mariailles* (see p.113) is not technically difficult, but the distance of 25km means it's for the hardy only — and a pre-dawn start is necessary. The unstaffed *Refuge Jean Dasilva* in the Rotja valley provides a bailing-out point from the Collade des Roques Blanches, about two-thirds of the way along – allow about an hour to drop down to the hut from the pass. Less ambitious off-piste skiers can traverse from the top lift of Vallter **northwards** to the Portella de Mantet (2415m), and then drop down to the French village of Mantet (see p.113): you'll need about three hours to get there, twice that to get back again next day.

Along the Ritort

From Camprodon, the road up to the **Col d'Ares** (1513m) and down into France initially follows the relatively treeless **Ritort valley**. The main, slight attraction of **MOLLÓ**, 8km from Camprodon, is the Romanesque church of Santa Cecília, with its four-storey bell-tower; one daily bus (not Sun) makes the trip up here from Camprodon. But especially if you're on a GR11 traverse, give its two overpriced conventional accommodation options a miss in favour of an excellent, French-speaking **casa de pagès** 3km north in Ginestosa district, *Can Illa* (☎972 740 512; ⑥ HB only), accessible by road or a half-hour, yellow-and-white-marked spur path. A working cattle ranch with sweeping views just above a filling station, *Can Illa* has a bath for almost every room, double beds, self-catering kitchen, a common room with wood stove, and a refuge-type dorm for groups. Your final chance of food and a place to stay before the border is in the attractive hillside hamlet of **ESPINAVELL**, 2km northeast of the main road, turning off before Ginestosa; here the *Habitacions El Quintà* (☎972 741 374; ⑤ B&B) also offers half-board through the adjacent affiliated *Restaurant Les Planes*.

The upper Freser valley

From Ripoll, the Freser valley rises to Ribes de Freser (912m) and then climbs steeply to Queralbs, where it swings eastwards through a gorge of remarkable beauty. Just above Queralbs, to the north, the Riu Núria has scoured out a second gorge, beyond which lie the ski station and valley sanctuary of Núria itself (1967m), the usual point of access to Puigmal (2913m) and other frontier peaks.

Ribes de Freser

Generally bypassed in the rush up to Núria, dull but unobjectionable **RIBES DE FRESER** offers little to the traveller except hotels – more plentiful and better value than anything in Ripoll – and, out of season, its integrity as a real town. Local shops sell sacks of grain, seeds, oils and other agricultural and domestic paraphernalia – often in astonishingly random juxtapositions – and there's a lively weekly market. More organized diversions consist of a much-used *petanca* court in the centre, and an annual sheepdog contest every September.

You won't necessarily see any of this if you're merely intent on getting up to Núria. Regular **trains** on the Barcelona–Puigcerdà line serve Ribes in either direction. Alight at "Ribes de Freser-RENFE" for the ten-minute walk into town, or just cross the platform to "Ribes-Enllaç" and take the *cremallera* train (see box opposite), which makes a stop in the centre of town (Ribes-Vila) to pick up more passengers before trundling off into the mountains.

If the idea of **staying** appeals, pick of the bunch is *Mas Ventaiola* (booking essential on ☎972 727 948; ③), a *casa de pagès* 1km from the centre, reached via the cemetery track taking off from the Pardines road. Perched on the hillside and completely over-hauled during 1999–2000 in the best taste, this offers en-suite rooms and several 4-bed apartments (10,000ptas/€60); no meals provided but there are fully equipped kitchens and common areas. Otherwise, in the town itself, very close to the *cremallera* station, quietest choices are *Hotel Caçadors,* c/Balandrau 24–26 (☎972 727 006, fax 972 728 001; ④–⑥), offering en-suite rooms of three grades in two separate premises, or the *Hostal Porta de Núria* just around the corner at c/de N. S. de Gràcia 3 (☎972 727 137; ③). If you're still stuck, there's a helpful **tourist office** on Plaça de l'Ajuntament (Tues–Sat 10am–2pm & 5–8pm, Sun 11am–1pm) by the church of Santa Maria, mostly destroyed like so many in 1936 and rebuilt a decade later. **Eating** out, the ground-floor restaurant at the *Caçadors* is pleasant if slightly overpriced – no *menú*, count on 2500ptas/€15 for three courses – while the restaurant in the *Hotel Prats* out on the main through road works out rather less and generally features a number of fish dishes of the day.

Pardines and Campelles

If you still come up empty – a possibility in midsummer, or during ski season – two adjacent villages, each 6km from Ribes in opposite directions, have more **accommodation** and **eating** possibilities. **PARDINES** (1250m), reached via a two-lane road east, enjoys a wonderful hilltop setting only slightly marred by sprouting apartments; the medieval core, whose Romanesque church of **Sant Esteve** sports a round, thirteenth-century fortified belfry, remains atmospheric and reassuringly livestock-patrolled. Both options here are on the main square with its vaulted fountain: the *Hostal Casa Serra* (☎972 728 078; ③), also serving meals, or the more comfortable *Ca la Pepa* (☎972 201 226 or call at *Bar Can Manel*; ③), a *turisme rural* property. **CAMPELLES**, to the southwest at a similar altitude, seems more open in layout and gentrified, and has the year-round *Fonda Costa* (☎972 727 274; ⑤ HB), also with a country-style *menjador*.

Queralbs and Fustanyà

The only intermediate stop on the *cremallera*, **QUERALBS** (1220m) is an attractive stone-built village, though now being dwarfed by apartment complexes on its outskirts, and suffering from the attentions of too many tourists in peak season. Near the highest point, beside the GR11 which passes through here, stands the tenth-century church of **Sant Jaume**, adorned with fine colonnaded porch. Reasonable en-suite **accommodation** is provided by the co-managed *Fonda Sierco/Hostal L'Avet*, on the main street 70m in from the car park (☎972 727 377; weekends only low season; ⑦ HB), much cheaper room-only rates outside summer. The *hostal* rooms are small and wood-trimmed, with a cosy lounge on the ground floor, while the refurbished *fonda* units are directly over the restaurant *Ca La Mary*, which has all keys. Unaffiliated **restaurants** here include the recommended *Masia Constans*, 1km north of the village on the Fontalba road, perched right above the *cremallera* tracks; they too serve country fare daily in summer but only weekends/holidays otherwise.

For more reliable, year-round board and lodging, head 3km out of Queralbs to the well-signposted *Mas La Casanova* on the opposite side of the valley (☎972 198 077; ④ B&B), in **FUSTANYÀ** hamlet. This 1999-inaugurated, en-suite *casa de pagès* is a superbly restored manor house with a bit of a literary pedigree: a classic Catalan play, *Terra Baixa*, had as main characters the former tenants of this farm. The current, outgoing proprietress provides reasonable *table d'hôte* evening meals, and there are also large family suites.

Núria

Beyond Queralbs, the *cremallera* railway hauls itself up the precipitous valley to **NÚRIA**, twenty minutes further on. Once the train passes the entrance to the Gorges del Freser, seen tantalizingly to the right, and enters the Gorges de Núria, the views are dramatic and your exposure sometimes terrifying – the impact enhanced by a sequence of tunnels.

Having passed through a final tunnel, you emerge into a south-facing bowl, with a small, dam-augmented lake at the bottom and – at the far end – the hideously monolithic, coffee-coloured **Santuari de Nuestra Senyora de Núria**, founded in the eleventh century on the spot where an image of the Virgin was miraculously found. Local shepherds actually revere **Sant Gil**, an eighth-century Benedictine abbot who

---

THE CREMALLERA RAILWAY

The **cremallera** ("Zipper" in Catalan) railway, built in 1931, is the last rack-and-pinion line operating in Catalunya, a miniature – though rather more daring – version of the *Train Jaune* just over the border. After a leisurely start through the lower valley, the tiny, three-car train lurches up into the mountains relying on its third rail, following the river between great crags before starting to climb high above both river and forests. Occasionally it slows down, leaving you poised between a sheer drop into the valley and an equally precipitous rock-face soaring overhead.

Services **depart** Ribes-Enllaç daily with some frequency year-round except November. "Low season" (defined as weekdays Dec–June except Christmas, New Year's and Easter, plus mid-Sept/Oct) sees 6 daily departures between 7.30am and 5.30pm; there's an additional, final departure around 8.55pm Fridays and Saturdays, plus an extra train daily at 10.35am whenever the ski station is functioning. "High season" (winter holidays, and July to mid-Sept) features a minimum of 9 daily trains from about 7.30am until 5.30pm, plus up to four extra departures on holidays. Trains pass through Ribes-Vila, where there's a weather report posted, eight minutes later, though note that the day's first train often starts at Ribes-Vila, *not* Ribes-Enllaç. The **journey time** up or down is 45 minutes; return **tickets** to Núria from Ribes cost around 2200ptas/€13.20 (one-ways available at about 60 percent of prevailing price). Children's tickets are 1200ptas/€7.20, but rail passes of any kind are not valid.

crossed over from France, set up shop in this valley, and attempted to proselytize the then-pagan herdsmen. The Virgin of Núria, of more general appeal, is believed to bestow fertility on female pilgrims, and many Catalan girls – presumably the result of successful supernatural intervention – are named after her.

The sanctuary building combines a dull church, tourist office (which posts weather reports), bar, restaurants, ski centre and **hotel** all in one. The **restaurant** at *Hotel Vall de Núria* (☎972 732 000, fax 972 732 001; ⑦) opens for lunch and supper, and offers some cheap *menús*. The only indoor budget lodging is the youth hostel *Pic de L'Àliga* (☎972 732 048; ①), marvellously poised at the top of the ski centre's cable-car line (free ride up with return train ticket). **Camping** is permitted only at a designated area behind the sanctuary complex.

Besides the hotel, **eating** options include *La Cabana dels Pastors*, a separate building behind the complex offering expensive bistro fare at lunchtime only; the *Bar Finestrelles*, downstairs in the sanctuary building, offering typical bar snacks; and, best value of all, the lunchtime-only *Autoservei* self-service restaurant in the west wing, where you can eat reasonably well for 1800–2200ptas/€10.80–3.20. Above *Bar Finestrelles*, a shop, La Botica, sells souvenir-type food, though it's not a really serious option for stocking up to go trekking.

Activities laid on in the valley include an archery range, horse-riding programme (high summer only) and boating on the lake. The entire resort has a dedicated **Web site** (*www.valldenuria.com*).

Skiing and winter mountaineering

Downhill **skiing** at Núria is surprisingly popular – given that the lift system is very limited, the chair lift only reaches 2262m, and the maximum altitude difference is a paltry 288m. The longest run, the blue Les Creus piste from the top of the cable car, is just 1750m, while the red-rated Mulleres traces just over a kilometre down from Point 2262, so Núria is best for beginners and weak intermediates. Lift passes are cheap by Pyrenean standards though equipment hire is much the same as elsewhere.

Off-piste, the summits of **Pic/Puig de Finestrelles** (2829m) and **Puigmal** (2913m) are fairly easy to conquer. Finestrelles is more or less northwest of the sanctuary, reached by following the namesake valley and then bearing away a little to the west before curving back towards the top. The approach to Puigmal begins in the same way but soon turns southwest along the route known as the **Coma de l'Embut**; at the rain gauge swing southeast for the Collada de l'Embut and, once through, make straight for the summit. Each ascent takes three to five hours, depending on conditions and skill; crampons may be required. It's possible to take in both peaks as a full day's outing, passing between them along the frontier ridge.

Ascending northeast of Núria to the Col de Nou Fonts you can continue to the **Carança lakes** in France, returning the same day, or continue east to Vallter 2000, a full day away. Many of these routes are detailed on the Editorial Alpina 1:25,000 "Puigmal-Núria" map and accompanying booklet.

Walking

Walkers in summer can follow the same routes, with slight variations that are clear from the trodden paths; for example, hikes east along the **GR11**, which follows the frontier ridge and the HRP for a few hours – a risky stretch in poor visibility – end up in Setcases rather than Vallter 2000. Hikes northeast are especially recommended; once over the Col de Nou Fonts (visited by the GR11) you have a choice between the various itineraries described under "The Carança gorge area" on p.115.

A **return to Queralbs** on foot along the river gorge is perhaps the most popular hike out of Núria. The GR11 threads the gorge on a high-quality, well-marked path, but you'll still want good, over-the-ankle shoes and a water bottle (there are a few drinkable torrents and springs en route). You'll need two to two and a half hours descending, depending on load and stops, three to three and a half hours going up. The trail generally adopts the opposite side of the gorge to the *cremallera* tracks, giving you the opportunity to watch the little train at work; the valley begins to open out below Sallent del Sastre, and after crossing back to the west bank for good at the Pont de Cremal, you'll see the Freser gorge yawning to the east.

A more challenging, six-hour descent, traced more or less correctly on the "Catalunya Valle de Núria" tourist brochure, gives you the best of both gorges. Start by initially climbing southeast along the east bank of Núria gorge, beginning under the cable-car lines, on the so-called "Engineers' Trail". This soon swings east and drops into the Gorges del Freser, where the precipices are unforgettable, but fairly safe. When you finally get level with the Riu Freser at the *Refugi Coma de Vaca* (described on p.178; possibility of a snack when staffed), cross the stream and take the path that leads back along the Freser to Queralbs.

travel details

French trains
Note that the *Train Jaune* (see p.115) also runs a service up the Têt.
Perpignan to Argèles (12 or more daily; 20min); Banyuls (12 or more daily; 40min); Carcassonne (5 daily; 90min); Cerbère (12 or more daily; 50min); Collioure (12 or more daily; 23min), Elne (12 or more daily; 10min); Montpellier (10 daily; 1hr 30min); Narbonne (12 or more daily; 40min); Nîmes (10 daily; 2hr 10min); Salses (12 or more daily; 15min); Toulouse (1 daily; 1hr 40min); and Villefranche-de-Conflent (4–6 daily; 40min).

Quillan to: Carcassonne (3–4 daily; 55min); *NB Most of these services are on SNCF buses.*

Villefranche to: Font-Romeu (3–6 daily; 1hr 20min); Ille-sur-Têt (5–7 daily; 35min); Latour-de-Carol (2–4 daily; 2hr 20min); Mont-Louis (2–4 daily; 1hr); Perpignan (5–7 daily; 45min); and Prades/Molitg (5–7 daily; 20min).

Spanish trains
Figueres to: Barcelona (21 daily; 1hr 45min); Colera (8 daily; 25min); Girona (21 daily; 35min); Port Bou (12 daily; 30min).

Girona to: Barcelona (21 daily; 1hr 20min); Figueres (21 daily; 35min); Llançà (12 daily; 1hr); Port Bou (12 daily; 1hr 15min).

Ribes de Freser to: Núria (9–13 daily in summer; 45min); Queralbs (9–13 daily; 25min).

Ripoll to: Barcelona (8–12 daily; 1hr 45min–2hr 20min); Puigcerdà (6 daily; 1hr 10min; 4–5 continue 7min more to the first French station, Latour-de-Carol).

French buses
Argelès to: Céret (1–4 daily; 1hr); and St-Genis (2 daily; 22min).

Arles-sur-Tech to: Coustouges (1 daily; 40min); and Prats-de-Molló (3–5 daily; 15min).

Axat to: Castelnaudary (1 daily; 1hr 50min); Limoux (1 daily; 50min).

Ax-les-Thermes to: Foix (2–6 daily; 1hr); Pas de la Casa (2 daily; 45min); Tarascon-sur-Ariège (2 daily; 30min).

Caracassone to: Albi (1 daily; 2hr); Axat (1 daily; 1hr 45min); Castelnaudary (4–6 daily; 45min); Castres (8 daily; 1hr 50min); Quillan (4 daily; 1hr 15min).

Comus to: Quillan (2 daily Mon–Fri; 1hr 5min).

La Cabanasse/Mont-Louis to: Puyvalador via Les Angles, Matemale and Formiguères (2 daily in summer and ski season at 10.35am and 6pm, returns mid-afternoon and dawn; 50min; contact SARL Asparre on ☎04.68.04.40.20 to confirm).

L'Hospitalet-près-l'Andorre (SNCF bus) to: Andorra la Vella (2 daily; 1hr 30min–1hr 40min); Pas de la Casa (2 daily; 25–30min).

Latour-de-Carol to: Font-Romeu (4 daily; 50min); Perpignan (2–4 daily; 3hr 5min).

Lavelanet to: Foix (Mon–Sat 4–6 daily; 50min); Mirepoix (2 daily; 40min); Quillan (Mon–Sat 2 daily; 1hr); Toulouse (2–6 daily; 2hr 20min).

Mont-Louis to Formiguères (2–4 daily; 30min).

Perpignan to Argelès (8 or more daily; 30min); Arles-sur-Tech (6–8 daily; 1hr 15min); Amélie-les-Bains (6–8 daily; 1hr); Axat (2 daily; 1hr 40min); Banyuls (3–5 daily; 1hr 10min); Céret (12 daily; 55min); Collioure (4–6 daily; 45min); Elne (Mon–Sat 2–5 daily; 35min); Font-Romeu (1 daily; 2hr 30min); Latour-de-Carol (3 daily; 3hr); Le Perthus (4 or 5 daily; 45min); London (several weekly; 18hr); Mont-Louis (4 daily; 2hr 15min); Narbonne (daily; 1hr 55min); Port-Vendres (3–6 daily; 55min); Prades (3–7 daily; 1hr);

Prats-de-Molló (5 daily; 1hr 40min); Quillan (2–5 daily, 1hr 30min); Saint-Génis (Mon–Sat 4 daily; 45min); Saint-Laurent-de-Cerdans (3 daily; 1hr 45min); Saint-Paul-le-Fenouillet (2–4 daily; 1hr); Salses (Mon–Sat 4 daily; 15min); Tautavel (changing at Estagel: 1–2 daily; 30min; changing at Rivesaltes: 3 daily 40min); Thuir (3–5 daily; 25min); Vernet (4 daily; 1hr 30min); and Villefranche-de-Conflent (7 daily; 1hr 15min).

Quillan to: Axat (2 daily; 20min); Comus (1–2 daily, 65min); Perpignan (2 daily; 1hr 30min); Quérigut (3 weekly in summer; 90min).

Villefranche-de-Conflent to: Casteil (4 daily; 15min); Prades (7 daily; 10min); Sahorre (1–2 daily Mon–Sat; 15min); Vernet-les-Bains (7 daily; 10min).

Spanish buses

Figueres to: Barcelona (3–8 daily; 1hr 30min); Cadaqués (5 daily; 1hr 15min); Castelló d'Empúries (every 30min; 15min); Espolla (1 daily Mon-Sat; 35min); Girona (4–8 daily Mon–Sat, Sun 3; 1hr); Llançà (5 daily Mon–Fri; 20min); Maçanet de Cabrenys via Darnius (1–2 daily Mon–Sat; 45–55min); Olot (2–3 daily; 1hr 30min); Roses (every 30min; 40min); Vilajuïga (1 daily; 50min).

Girona to: Banyoles (13 daily Mon–Sat, 3 on Sun; 30min); Barcelona (6–9 daily Mon–Sat, 3 on Sun; 1hr); Figueres (6–10 daily Mon–Sat, 4 Sun; 50min); Olot via Besalú (11 daily Mon–Sat, 4 Sun; 1hr 15min).

Olot to: Banyoles (Mon–Sat 9–10 daily Mon–Sat, 6 Sun; 50min); Barcelona (7–8 daily Mon–Sat, 4 Sun; 2hr 15min); Besalú (9–10 daily Mon–Sat, 6 on Sun; 30min); Camprodon (1–2 daily; 45min); Figueres (2–3 daily; 1hr); Girona (11 daily Mon–Sat, 4 Sun; 1hr 15min); Ripoll (5 daily; 50min–1hr); Santa Pau (Wed & Sat am, plus 2 Mon, only; 15min); Sant Joan de les Abadesses (2–3 daily; 50min).

Ripoll to: Camprodon (6–8 daily; 45min); Guardiola de Berguedà (1 daily Mon–Fri at 5.25pm; 2hr); La Pobla de Lillet (1 daily Mon–Fri at 5.25pm; 1hr 45min); Olot (5 daily; 50min); Sant Joan de les Abadesses (6–8 daily; 20min).

CHAPTER TWO

ANDORRA AND AROUND

pproaching from the Mediterranean, you begin to see permanently snow-tipped mountains around the principality of Andorra, set in a part of the range containing true wilderness and almost every kind of Pyrenean landscape. On the Spanish side, the best appetizer for high peaks en route to Andorra is the **Parc Natural del Cadí-Moixeró**, featuring that most distinctive Spanish Catalan peak, the cloven **Pedraforca**. In 1906 Pablo Picasso came to Gòsol at the foot of this mountain in search of fresh inspiration, and much of what he found still exists: unspoilt, strangely coloured scenery, golden eagles soaring overhead and herds of isards. The growth of summer holiday communities has been the biggest change in what was once a region of dwindling agricultural villages, but the Cadí remains virtually free of ski development and is still good for spring or autumn hiking and mountain-biking.

La Seu d'Urgell, capital of the Spanish **Alt Urgell** region, just northwest of the Cadí, is one of two main gateways to Andorra, and pivotal to its history. La Seu's bishops controlled the principality with the nobility of Foix in an almost unique feudal power-sharing arrangement that endured, more or less peacefully, for over seven centuries, until Andorra voted for full independence in 1993. There are just two ways of entering **Andorra** by road: along the Valira valley from La Seu d'Urgell, or from the Ariège valley in France. At each frontier, and for a considerable distance beyond, duty-free megastores peddling cut-price consumer goods line streets congested with shoppers' cars. But some of Andorra does remain untrammelled by development, and on foot or skis you can traverse the principality (almost) without touching asphalt or seeing a single shop, experiencing Andorra as it was until the 1950s.

Like Catalonia, the mountain-ringed plateau of **Cerdanya**, southeast of Andorra, was partitioned by the 1659 Treaty of the Pyrenees, a division that left **Llívia** as an island of Spanish territory surrounded by the **Cerdagne**, the French part of this formerly unified territory. **Puigcerdà** on the Spanish side, once capital of the entire district, is now a kilometre or so from the border at Bourg-Madame. To its north, behind the mega-

---

ACCOMMODATION PRICE CODES

Each place to stay in this book has been given a code which corresponds to one of the following price categories.

① Under €13/2200ptas/85F
② €15–24/2500–4000ptas/100–160F
③ €24–32/4000–5400ptas/160–210F
④ €32–40/5400–6600ptas/210–260F
⑤ €40–52/6600–8600ptas/260–340F
⑥ €52–65/8600–10,800ptas/340–430F
⑦ Over €65/10,800ptas/430F

Category ① refers to the price *per person* of a bed; the other categories correspond to the **cheapest available double room in high season**. B&B and HB denote, respectively, when the price includes breakfast, and when it includes half-board. For more details, see p.41.

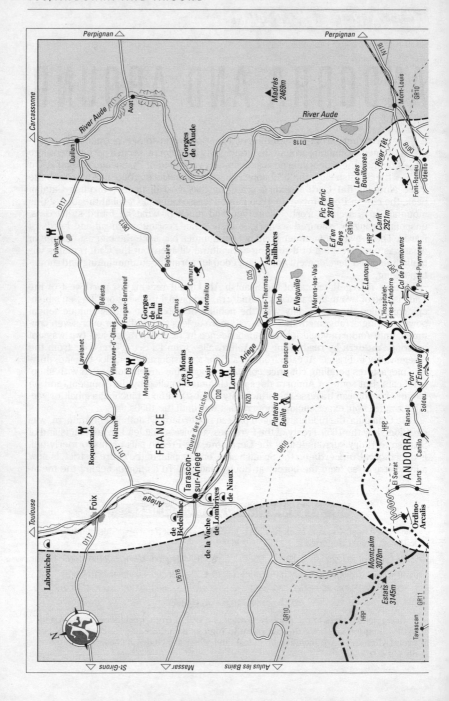

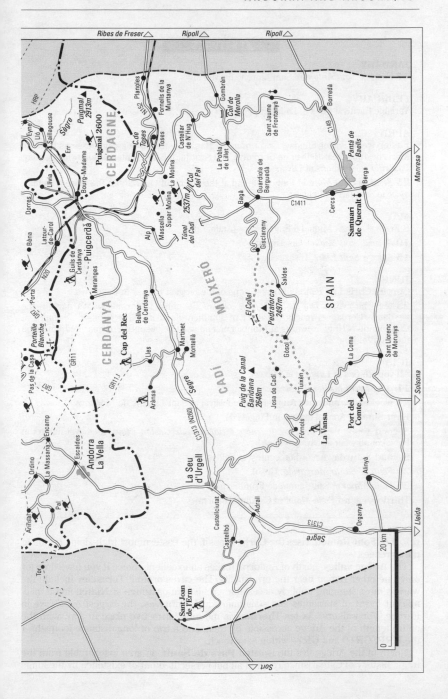

FESTIVALS

JANUARY
17 *Festa de Sant Antoni* in Sant Llorenç de Morunys.

FEBRUARY
Variable Carnival week at La Molina.

APRIL
Easter week Easter Sunday, *La Truitada* at Bagà; Easter Monday, processions to Santa
Maria de Talló, near Bellver de Cerdanya, and Sant Jaume de Frontanyà; following Sunday,
Pascuilla celebrations at Llívia.
25 *Festa de Sant Marc* in Puigcerdà and at the shrine of Queralt; on the closest Sunday,
aplec to Santuari de Falgars.

MAY
8 Festival at Sant Miquel d'Engolasters (Andorra).
10 *Aplec a Sant Miquel*, Gisclareny.
15 *Aplec a Sant Isidre*, Gisclareny.

JUNE
Corpus Christi *La Patum* in Berga – one of the biggest bashes in Catalunya.
23–24 The eve of *Día de Sant Joan*, one of the most important saint's days in the
Cerdanya/Cerdagne, marks the start of summer. *Festa de Sant Joan de Cornudell* at
Castellar de N'Hug; fireworks at Montségur, and solstice events on or near Pedraforca on
the night of June 23.

JULY
All month *Son et Lumière* at Puivert.
11–19 *Mercat Medieval* at Bagà.
All weekends, and into August Music festival at Sant Llorenç de Morunys.
First Sunday Annual festival in Puigcerdà.
Second week Week-long *Les Journées Mediévales de Gaston Fébus*; medieval market at
Foix; country fair at Lavelanet.
Second Saturday Accordion contest at Saldes.
20 *Festa de Santa Margarida*, Gòsol.
25 *Festa Major* at Sant Jaume de Frontanyà.
Third weekend *Festa Major* at Canillo (Andorra).

resort of **Font-Romeu**, rises the **Carlit Massif**, the easternmost high-alpine region in
the Pyrenees.

The **Ariège valley**, north of Andorra, makes an excellent choice if you have time for
only one other region near the principality. The caves around **Tarascon** include the
world's most stunning publicly accessible prehistoric paintings at **Niaux**, and a magnificent forest of stalactites and stalagmites at **Lombrives**, the largest open cave in
Europe. For walkers, **Ax-les-Thermes** is the most attractive place to stay, with the
entire length of the Ariège accessible by train, and a trio of long-distance footpaths –
the **HRP, GR10** and **GR7**– within easy reach.

North of the Ariège lies the isolated **Pays de Sault**, an area inseparable from the
tragic history of Catharism, a religion all but persecuted out of existence by the kings

25–27 *Fiesta Major* at Sant Julià de Lòria (Andorra); also at Sant Jaume de Frontanyà and Bellver de Cerdanya.

AUGUST
All month *Son et Lumière* at Puivert.

1–3 *Festa Major de Sant Esteve*, Bagà.

First weekend *Festa Major* at Andorra la Vella.

12/13 *Son et Lumière* at Puivert.

14–15 Music festival at Pobla de Lillet.

14–17 *Festa Major* with dancing at Gòsol.

15 *Fête* at Font-Romeu.

15–17 *Festa Major* at Encamp and La Maçana (Andorra).

Penultimate Sunday *Festa del Llac* at Puigcerdà, with fireworks, parade and closing ball; sheepdog (*gossos d'atura* in Catalan) trials at Castellar de N'Hug.

Last Sunday Annual fair at La Seu d'Urgell.

Variable Medieval fair at Ax-les-Thermes.

SEPTEMBER
First and second week *Fête* at Foix, with fireworks and torchlit procession.

First Sunday Sardana competition at Berga.

8 *Festa* at Meritxell (Andorra); *Procession de la Vierge* from Font-Romeu to Odeillo; romería from La Pobla de Lillet to Falgars.

16/17 *Festa* at Ordino (Andorra).

Third Sunday Sheepdog trials at Fornells de la Muntanya.

28–29 *Festa Major* at Castellar de N'Hug.

OCTOBER
First Sunday *Festa Major* at Gisclareny; mushroom festival at Berga.

Third Sunday *Foire de La Guinguette* at Bourg-Madame.

31 *Fira de Tots Sants*, Gòsol.

NOVEMBER
1 *Sant Ermengol* celebrations in La Seu d'Urgell.

DECEMBER
4 *Festa de Santa Bàrbara*, Saldes.
24 *La Fia-Faia* torchlit procession at Bagà.

of France and the Catholic Church. At **Montségur** in 1244, the last leading figures of the Cathar sect were besieged by a crusade that ended with the mass execution of more than two hundred members of this community of "pure ones" (see box on pp.242–243).

Public transport in the region is scarce except for routes along the main north–south valleys. Buses from the south run up the corridor from Lleida to La Seu d'Urgell and Andorra, and from Berga to Puigcerdà. The last surviving trans-Pyrenean rail line links Ripoll, Puigcerdà, Ax-les-Thermes and Foix, with a change of trains at the border station of Latour-de-Carol. Exceptional east–west bus services include one between La Seu and Puigcerdà, and another between Quillan and Foix, crossing the Pays de Sault.

THE CADÍ-MOIXERÓ PARK AND AROUND

A little to the west of Ripoll, virtually following the line of the road between **La Pobla de Lillet** and **Castellar de N'Hug**, runs the eastern boundary of the **Parc Natural del Cadí-Moixeró**, an area of more than four hundred square kilometres that extends north to Alt Urgell and the Cerdanya, and west almost as far as the Riu Segre. Too steep for modern agriculture and largely unsuitable for downhill ski development, the greater part of the Cadí-Moixeró massif – essentially a giant block of limestone extending from Ripoll to Adraén in the west – is perfect for hiking and climbing. The area's highest mountain, **Puig de la Canal Baridana**, and the whole **Serra del Cadí** range are completely unexploited, and even the much-visited peak of **Pedraforca** bears only slight marks of development

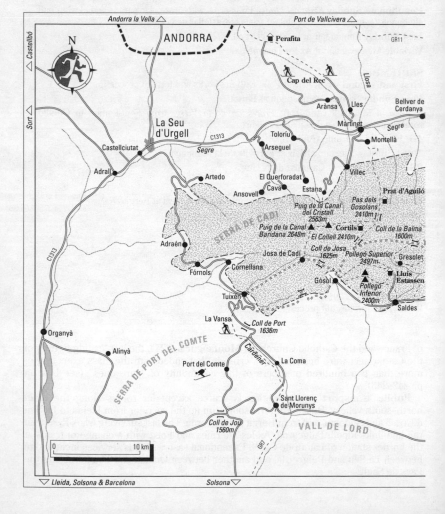

(though many farms and villas in surrounding villages are seasonally occupied by holiday-makers). The boundaries of the actual park are inconspicuously posted with black-on-white "*parc natural*" signs; as a general rule, the park limits begin just outside most of the towns and villages described – there are no entrance booths or other means of controlling access.

Although the designation *parc natural* does not guarantee a great degree of **wildlife** protection, the Cadí-Moixeró now shelters Spain's largest herd of chamois (*isard* in Catalan); hunting restrictions have allowed their number to grow from around fifty to nearly a thousand. Red and roe deer were hunted out, however, and were only reintroduced during the 1980s. Capercaillie breed here, as do the golden eagle and the black woodpecker, symbol of the park. For botanists, a big attraction is the green-petalled *Xatardia scabra*, endemic to the Eastern Pyrenees and common on scree slopes in the park. Also widespread are the deep-blue southern gentian, *Gentiana alpina*; the violet-flowered Ice Age survivor, *Ramonda myconi*; and *Rhododendron ferrugineum*. The lower slopes are heavily forested with dense stands of pine and silver fir.

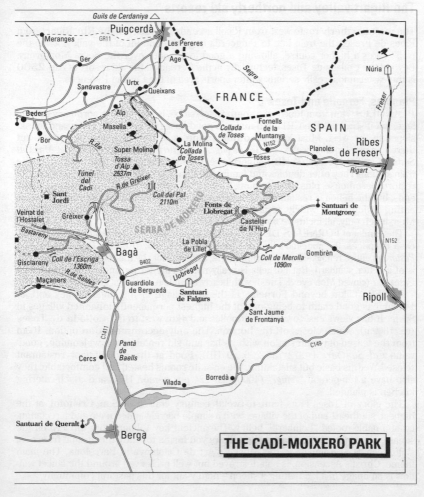

THE CADÍ-MOIXERÓ PARK

The main C1411 from the south – used by buses from Barcelona and Manresa to **Berga** – cuts the park into two unequal portions. The Cadí watershed and half the Moixeró lie to the west of the **Túnel del Cadí**, where the C1411 disappears under the range to emerge near Puigcerdà; the rest of the Moixeró, including Castellar de N'Hug and the ski resorts of **La Molina** and **Masella**, lie to the east.

Approaches from Ripoll

From Ripoll (p.173), two routes skirt the eastern fringes of the *parc natural*: the northerly N152, relatively well served by public transport, passing two popular ski resorts; and the southerly B402 towards the C1411, skimming the edge of the Moixeró region and seeing just one bus a day (more regular services run from Berga).

The Rigart valley and northerly ski resorts

The most **northerly** route west from Ripoll ascends the valley of the **Riu Rigart** from Ribes de Freser; the train line to Puigcerdà hugs the bottom of the valley, while the N152 takes a higher course, allowing a good look south over the Serra Montgrony. Beyond the Collada de Toses, technically in the Cerdanya, the ski resort of **Alp 2500** is the easternmost really serious winter-sports area in the Catalan Pyrenees.

Planoles, Fornells and Toses

PLANOLES, 7km from Ribes on a south-facing slope, is nothing extraordinary as a village, but it straddles the GR11 and makes a good base for the Freser valley and for ski slopes to the west. Most local **accommodation** is of the second-home variety, but there's an outstanding, well-kept *casa de pagès* in the *turisme rural* programme, *Mas Cal Sadurní* (☎972 736 135; ⑤ HB), superbly set on a natural terrace just uphill from the train station. They offer doubles and family-size quads, mostly en suite, in this superbly restored farmhouse, plus an eight-bunk "refuge" for groups. It's packed out most weekends, but the in-house restaurant closes Tuesday and Wednesday, when your best local **eating** option is the widely acclaimed *Restaurant-Casino* behind the church (closed Mon; lunch only, all-inclusive *menú* 1300ptas/€7.80).

The hamlet of **FORNELLS DE LA MUNTANYA**, 8.5km beyond Planoles, has another **casa de pagès**, the none-too-jolly *Cal Mestre* (☎972 736 163; ④ B&B). Their annexe, *Cal Pastor*, an entire renovated self-catering house, also available by the room (4000ptas/€24), is of a better standard. But Fornells is really noteworthy for its single **restaurant**, *Can Casanova* (closed Mon eve & Tues), with hearty mountain cuisine at reasonable prices.

TOSES, 3.5km beyond Fornells, is the last village in the Rigart valley and, at 1450m, has good claim to being one of the highest permanently inhabited villages in Spain. It has views east towards El Ripollès and 4km west to the **Collada de Toses** (ca. 1800m), which closes off the horizon. The only **accommodation** option, 100m from the leased-out train station with its bar and ski rental, is the welcoming, good-value *Cal Santpare* (☎972 736 226; ⑤ HB). Food at the ground-floor restaurant (closed Wed) is basic but sustaining, the en-suite rooms heated and comfortable; they also have a ten-person "*refugi*" (4000ptas/€24 per person HB), and a self-catering kitchen is planned.

The glory of Toses is its tenth-to-twelfth-century church of **San Cristófol**, at the highest, southeast end of the village, with a simple barrel-vaulted nave and a rectangular and gable-roofed "Lombard" belfry. The ancient key (obtain from *Cal Pep* on the square, your other **eating** possibility) allows you inside to study the apsidal **frescoes**, skilful copies of originals in the Museu d'Art de Catalunya in Barcelona. The main theme, Christ's Ascension, is half-destroyed but well preserved around the lancet window is an image of a lad hefting a sheep – highly apt for this pastoral community.

Beyond Toses, road and train enter Cerdanya over and under the Collada de Toses – the railway by the amazing **Cargol tunnel**, where the line executes a full circle to gain altitude. The pass affords excellent views west, the bare rolling mountains of the Montgrony range relieved by swathes of deep green forest.

Skiing Alp 2500 – and Alp village

LA MOLINA, 8km from the pass on the north flank of 2406-metre Puigllançada, ranks as the oldest ski resort in Spain, inaugurated in 1909. From 1922, special Sunday return trains from Barcelona catered to enthusiasts, though for some years the line only ran to Toses, where the intrepid skiers had to proceed through an unfinished rail tunnel by torchlight, then trudge up the slopes to begin their runs – there were no lifts until 1942. Local villagers derived great amusement from the pioneer skiers with their clumsy wooden footwear – "Throw them on the fire and get some benefit from them!" was a typical comment, according to Ernest Mullor, Catalan ski champion of the era. Needless to say, the sport took off, and in 1967 another resort opened at **MASELLA**, 4km west of La Molina, on the slopes of 2537-metre Tosa d'Alp.

Both resorts have Web sites (*www.lamolina.com* and *www.masella.com*), and by Spanish Pyrenean standards the skiing is impressive. The two areas are linked via chair/bubble lifts and runs focused on Tosa d'Alp. Marketed together as **"ALP 2500"**, the largest ski area in the Pyrenees. La Molina is publicly owned by the *generalitat*, and probably better suited for beginners; slightly larger Masella has passed into private hands, and is widely considered the better managed of the two. Certainly it has the edge in scenic appeal, provision of strategic chair lifts and length of runs, including five kilometres of consecutive blue and red runs from Tosa d'Alp summit to Pla de Masella at 1600m, the greatest altitude drop in the range. Despite the northerly orientation and forest cover, both resorts rely heavily on snow canons and may close early in the day during spring.

Getting to the slopes, it's best to have your own car, though during winter one **"Bus Blanc"** departs from the Cerdanya flatlands early morning, with two well-spaced returns in the afternoon. One route serves Ger, Bolvir, Llívia and Puigcerdà; the other begins at Martinet, plying Bellver, Prats, Alp, and other villages. You can forget about local **trains** unless you're happy to shell out for a taxi or imitate the 1920s aficionados – both La Molina's and Alp's train stations are a considerable distance from the action.

With few exceptions, **accommodation** at the foot of the slopes is overpriced, sterile and beset in high season by what Spaniards call *mucho follón* – hassle, noise, congestion; a departure from the norm is *Casa de Pagès Niu dels Falcons* on c/Font Moreu at La Molina (☎972 892 073; open all year; ⑦ HB). Generally, though, you're far better off staying downhill to the north in the villages of the Cerdanya (see pp.217–223). Closest is **ALP**, 6km northwest, where the old quarter up on the hillside is well disguised by *avant*- and *après*-ski facilities, plus vast phalanxes of weekend chalets. Both choices in the centre are slightly snooty and charge accordingly: the *Hostal Roca* at Travessia de la Font 2 (☎ & fax 972 890 011; ⑥ B&B), with updated decor belying its grim exterior, or the smaller but similarly appointed three-star *Hotel Jaume* across the way at c/Central 30 (☎972 890 016, fax 972 144 242; ⑦ B&B). For that sort of money (or much less out of season) you can sample the friendlier *Aero Hotel Cerdanya*, Passeig Agnès Fabra 4, on the northeast edge of town (☎972 890 033, fax 972 890 862; ⑥ B&B), popular with families. The wood-floored rooms have mildly kitsch decor, wall art adorns the common areas, and there's a well-regarded gourmet **restaurant** in the basement, *Ca l'Eudald*.

Gombrèn and La Pobla de Lillet

The **southerly route** from Ripoll aims right at the heart of the Cadí-Moixeró region. Beginning just north of Ripoll, at Campdevànol, this minor road crosses the Riu Freser and heads 9km west to the foothill village of Gombrèn, served by a single weekday 5.25pm bus from Ripoll. Those stranded at **GOMBRÈN** need not worry (other than about sundry hauntings from Comte Arnau – see box p.176) – this village offers a fine spot to **stay**, *Can Xesc* (☎972 730 404; ③ B&B), whose **restaurant** purveys game and pastoral specialities such as mustard-marinated venison, lamb and goat.

About 3km beyond Gombrén, a paved road on the right leads north to the **Santuari de Montgrony**, worth the six-kilometre detour for the secluded setting. Although the resident priest and his cook no longer accommodate visitors, there's a restaurant with *habitacions* adjacent. The track to the left just before the sanctuary leads to a simple, modern **refuge** equipped with a fireplace and running water outside, making this a popular picnic spot in season. With your own transport you can continue another 10km from the *santuari* (12km from the B402 junction) to Castellar de N'Hug (see below), an easier drive than the way up from La Pobla de Lillet.

The main road west continues to the **Coll de Merolla** (1090m) – with some weird rock formations to the southwest and excruciating curves each side of the pass – then drops to **LA POBLA DE LILLET**, 28km from Ripoll. Here two ancient bridges arching over the infant Llobregat river and the old districts on either side make for a pleasant half-hour stroll, but there's little else to see besides a pair of minor Romanesque churches – ruined, monastic Santa Maria and the curious circular Sant Miquel – both 1500m east of town, and both closed indefinitely for restoration. There's a small, well-stocked **Turisme** (daily Easter & June–Sept 10am–2pm & 5–8pm) by the smaller of the bridges. **Accommodation** and **dining** are both overpriced and restricted to the central *Hostal Can Pericas*, c/Furrioles Altes 3 (☎938 236 162; ④), its food only average and the service slow, and the slightly shabbier *Hostal Cerdanya* at Plaça del Fort 5 (☎938 236 083; ③–④).

You'll probably do better in both respects just southwest of La Pobla de Lillet in the **Serra de Catllaràs**, claimed to be the only Spanish habitat of edelweiss (*flor de neu* in Catalan, a common local business name). If you haven't got a 4WD, you can skim the range west on the GR4.2 to Guardiola de Berguedà; the obvious staging point is the rather hideous **Santuari de Falgars (Falgàs)**, where the pilgrims' *hospedaría* houses and feeds all-comers (☎937 441 095; ②) in spartan but clean quarters.

Fonts de Llobregat and Castellar de N'Hug

From La Pobla there's a steady eleven-kilometre ascent northeast towards Castellar de N'Hug, and since you can leave the road only for a short section at the beginning and end, without transport you miss little by hitching – or waiting for the evening **bus** (Mon–Sat) from Berga via La Pobla. Three kilometres out of La Pobla on the left stands a disused cement factory, a flamboyant *modernista* building that looks like a stack of cave dwellings. It was designed by Eduard Ferré and Lluís Homs in 1901 and continued in its original use until the 1970s. Today it houses a transport museum, featuring a selection of old locomotives, train carriages, trams, and cars.

Approaching Castellar, you'll come to the **Fonts de Llobregat**, source of the river that divides Spanish Catalunya in two, entering the sea at Barcelona. Numerous jets of water burst from the rock of a densely wooded ravine, the most powerful forming a broad, photogenic waterfall. Every year hundreds of Catalans come here as if on pilgrimage – summer droughts reduce many of Catalunya's rivers to nothing, so there's great pride in any durable water source, and this one hasn't stopped in living memory, even during the driest year. Coming uphill, the main access is by a signposted turning at about "Km8", leading past the giant *Hostal Les Fonts* to a car park and old water mill, a few minutes' walk from the cascades. You can also get here via a fifteen-minute stepped path from the bottom of Castellar de N'Hug (see below).

Heaped up against the rise of the Serra de Montgrony, **CASTELLAR DE N'HUG** makes a good if slightly touristy base for the Moixeró section of the park, or for Alp 2500 (see p.192); high seasons are September–October, when people hunt mushrooms in surrounding forests, and the ski season of January–February. There's a fair amount of inexpensive **accommodation**: top choices are the friendly *Hostal La*

Muntanya (☎938 257 065; ③) at Plaça Major 4, with excellent, copious dinners and rooms spread over two premises, and the *Pensió Fanxicó* (☎938 257 015; ④) across the way, which also serves meals. One to avoid is the unwelcoming, overpriced *Pensió Pere Miquel*; slightly more luxurious is the *Hostal Alt Llobregat* (☎938 257 074; ⑤), at the southeast edge of the village on the road down towards the Santuari de Montgrony.

North from Castellar, the paved road, sporadically snowploughed in winter, continues over the range to La Molina and the Collada de Toses via the **Coll de la Creueta**. There are paths in this direction as well, but they're not marked, so it's best to ask in the village about the five-hour walks to Toses or Planoles, and to equip yourself with the Editorial Alpina map "Montgrony-Fonts de Llobregat".

Sant Jaume de Frontanyà and beyond

The eleventh-century church at **SANT JAUME DE FRONTANYÀ**, unquestionably the finest Romanesque church in the region, lies just 12km southeast of La Pobla, accessible by a newly paved road which may not yet appear on commercial or tourist office maps. The turning south from the B402, 2km east of La Pobla, is well marked, with only the first kilometre down to the river still unmade.

Built in the shape of a Latin cross with three apses, this Augustinian foundation has an engaging setting at the foot of a naturally terraced cliff. The twelve-sided squinch-supported lantern was unique in Catalunya until the restoration of the monastery at Ripoll. Inside, the church is chill and bare, and evocative in its emptiness (both restaurants have keys – see below).

The surrounding hamlet, all of a dozen stone houses, offers two characterful **restaurants**, *"Hostal" Sant Jaume* and *Fonda Cal Marxandó*; the latter with inexpensive, **rooms** (☎938 239 002; ③) above its beam-ceilinged *menjador*. Despite its tag, *Sant Jaume* has no accommodation but very decent *à la carta* food: Garrotxa beans with sausage, duck in *rattafia* sauce, sweet and drink for under 3000ptas/€18, about 500ptas/€3 less than its rival.

From Sant Jaume the road continues 9km south to nondescript **BORREDÀ** on the C149, where small lumber mills on the outskirts slowly process the lush surrounding forest. If you get stuck here – possible, as just one bus goes each morning to Berga – there's only the *Baix Pirineu* **restaurant** on the main street, with rooms suitable for emergencies, and a few bars. Otherwise, it's another 21km southwest to Berga past the **Pantà de Baells**, a reservoir on the Llobregat, where at low water local boaters claim you can see the cupola and crumbled walls of a submerged monastic church.

Berga and around

From the south, the major public transport approach to the Cadí park is the twice-daily bus from Barcelona to **BERGA**, where the Pyrenees rear up with startling abruptness. The town itself is fairly dull, bearing ample traces of its long history as an industrial centre, but it does have a ruined castle, a well-preserved medieval core and – as capital of Berguedà *comarque* – onward connections to higher settlements in the county, provided by the ATSA bus company at the top of Passeig de la Pau.

Another reason to come to Berga is for the town's **Festa de la Patum** at Corpus Christi, one of the most famous of Catalunya's festivals. For three days in June, huge figures of giants and dwarfs process to hornpipe music along streets packed with red-hatted Catalans intent on a good time. A dragon attacks onlookers in the course of a symbolic battle between good and evil, firecrackers blazing from its mouth, while the climax comes on the Saturday night, with a dance performed by masked men covered in grass.

Not surprisingly, **accommodation** is impossible to find during the festival unless you've booked weeks in advance; at other times you should have few problems. There are eight officially licensed places to stay, most of them reasonably priced: try the small but well-appointed *Hotel Passasserres*, c/La Valldan (☎938 210 645; ④), with sauna, gym and off-street parking; *Pensió Passeig*, Passeig de la Pau 12 (☎938 210 415; ③), run by the electrical appliance store below; or the very central two-star *Hotel Queralt*, Plaça de la Creu 4 (☎938 210 611; ⑤) whose en-suite rooms have all mod cons. There's also a **campsite**, out of town on the C1411 (☎938 211 250; open all year); if you need assistance, the **Turisme** is just behind it (June–Sept daily 9am–1pm & 4–8 pm; Oct–May reduced hours; ☎938 221 500). The best **restaurant** in town is the *Sala* at Passeig de la Pau 27 (closed Sun dinner and Mon) – count on about 5000ptas/€30 for a full gourmet meal (with a rare place of honour for vegetables), less for the *menú*. If your budget won't stretch that far, the *menjador* of the *Hostal Guiu*, Ctra de Queralt, offers regional specialities.

West of Berga: Sant Llorenç de Morunys

Although the scenic drive is magnificent, there's little other than the panoramic **Santuari de Queralt** (4km west of Berga) to stop for along the 32km of winding road to Sant Llorenç de Morunys, which skirts the southern rim of the Pyrenean foothills. Just one **bus** a day covers this route. The eighteenth-century sanctuary, housing a far older image of the Virgin, marks one end of the GR107 trail (see p.76).

The chief appeal of **SANT LLORENÇ DE MORUNYS** lies in its setting near the head of the Vall de Lord, but the ancient city walls enclosing a defensive huddle of houses, and the steep, narrow streets leading to several portals, will reward a half-hour stroll. The eleventh-century monastic **church** has a beguilingly odd interior, one of its two chapels being overwhelmed by Baroque gilt work, the altar by a huge fifteenth-century retable. Until restoration is completed you can't enter the cloisters with their plain-capitalled columns, but must be content to view them through a large window in the church.

Sant Llorenç has an adequate amount of **accommodation** (except perhaps during the ski season), though none is in the old quarter, or particularly inexpensive. If travelling by public transport you should plan on spending the night, as the single daily bus from Berga arrives in the evening. First choice would be the 1997-renovated *Hostal La Catalana*, Plaça del Dr Ferran 1 (☎973 492 125; ④), or the *Hostal Piteus* (☎973 492 340; ③), opposite on the through road, which also has pricier penthouse apartments. Unless both are full, there's little reason to stay at the overpriced, dreary *Pensió Casa Joan* (☎973 492 055; ④) on the road northwest out of town, though it does have a well-regarded restaurant. There's also a summer **campsite**, *Morunys* (☎973 492 213; open July–Sept), 2km north of town, just off the side road to La Pedra hamlet. In the old walled town, a decent independent **restaurant** is *Can Peratà*, on c/Santa Isabel, at the corner of c/San Nicolau.

Onwards from Sant Llorenç

The views are startling in whichever direction you leave Sant Llorenç, though it's best to have a car or bike as there's no public transport. If you hitch, don't accept any partial rides, as traffic to the west especially is sparse.

To the **west** the road climbs 8km to the **Coll de Jou** (1560m), then briefly along a corniche before dropping through a tunnelled gorge to join the C1313, 44km further along, in the Segre river valley near Organyà. Along this paved one-lane road there's little but farming hamlets, each individual house seemingly signposted. The only substantial place en route is **ALINYÀ**, tucked into a Shangri-La valley with a trio of hamlets overhead: La Vall de Mig, L'Alzina (the highest), and Llobera (the lowest), 700m from the main road, with a *casa de pagès* in L'Alzina if you get stranded – *Cal L'Agustí* (☎973 298 157; ②).

A daily bus to Solsona runs along the crests to the **south**, with dizzying ravine views. Alternatively, the GR7 long-distance route goes there too, threading through the Riu Cardener gorge and past the Romanesque church at Olius with its magnificent crypt, before completing a long day at **SOLSONA**. This fine old walled town, rather larger but less spectacularly set than Sant Llorenç, offers inexpensive **accommodation** – most central are *Pensió Sant Roc*, Plaça de Sant Roc 2 (☎973 480 827; ③), and *Pensió Pilar* (☎973 480 156; ②) nearby; there are also transport connections to Barcelona.

To the **north** of Sant Llorenç looms the ski resort of **PORT DEL COMTE**, reached via the village of La Coma, 5km from Sant Llorenç near the sources of the Cardener, or by a more direct road that climbs from the Coll de Jou. There's not much for beginners here – most runs are red-rated – and most lifts are poma-type; despite a respectable top point of almost 2400m, the south and east orientation of most slopes can mean thin snow cover and an early seasonal closure.

Accommodation at the slopes is restricted to a luxury two-star hotel and some apartments. More reasonable options are in **LA COMA**, 11km east and downhill, at the simple *Hostal Cal Nin* (☎973 492 354; ③), in the village centre by the church, or the fancier *Hotel Fonts del Cardener* (☎973 492 377; ⑤), also offering apartments, 1km north of the village on the highway. The latter has an excellent **restaurant** with an emphasis on mushrooms (in season) and local sausages.

The **GR7** heads north from Sant Llorenç via La Coma to the 1636-metre **Coll de Port**, then on to Tuixèn – a day's march – but the marked route is so often track or asphalt rather than path that you'd be best advised to arrange a ride along the paved road. At Tuixèn (see p.199) you're at the very edge of the Cadí park.

North of Berga: Guardiola de Berguedà and Bagà

The towns along the Llobregat and Grèixer valleys **north of Berga** were once centres of a flourishing smuggling trade with Andorra, protected from law-enforcing pursuers by the barrier of the Serra del Cadí. Nowadays the Túnel del Cadí cuts under that mountainous screen, allowing passage for the C1411, and neither of the main towns en route – **Guardiola de Berguedà** and **Bagà** – retains any suggestion of illicit activity. They aren't particularly enticing either, though each has accommodation options suitable for an emergency overnight en route to the Cadí.

Strung out grimly along the old course of the C1411 (a new bypass avoids the town), **GUARDIOLA DE BERGUEDÀ** is on the bus route from Berga to La Pobla de Lillet and just 1500m north of the turning for Saldes and Gòsol (see below). Sole **accommodation** option, *Pensió Guardiola* (☎938 227 048; ②), on the main street at the south end of town, also does meals (basic *menú* 1200ptas/€7.20). There's just one daily bus (5.35pm) to Saldes and Gòsol – note that it doesn't enter town, but turns at the junction 1500m south.

BAGÀ, 5km further north and the second largest town in the *comarque* after Berga, has considerably more going for it in a tiny old quarter with an arcaded *plaça* and several **accommodation** options. Choose between *Hotel La Pineda*, c/Raval 50 (☎938 244 515; ④), at the eastern end of the main shopping street, and the *Hostal Ca L'Amagat* (☎938 244 032; ③), quietly placed in the heart of the old town. On the southeast edge of town, *Hostal Cal Batista* (☎938 244 126; ③) occupies two unexciting modern buildings, but staying here does solve parking problems, plus they've a well-regarded **restaurant** with a nice line in local trout and rabbit *all-i-olli*. A **campsite**, the *Bastareny* (☎938 244 420; open all year), 1km west of town, caters mostly to caravans. Back in the centre, the **park information office** at c/La Vinya 1 (☎938 244 151) doubles as a centre for **certified guides** who offer a range of activities (trekking, snow-shoeing, winter mountaineering) depending on the season.

Continuing north through the five-kilometre **Túnel del Cadí** (no pedestrians or bicycles) brings you into the Cerdanya, for which see p.217. To the west of Bagà runs the GR107, "El Camí de les Bonnes Hommes", which begins in France and is claimed to be the route used by fleeing Cathars (see pp.242–243); locally it links Bagà with Gòsol (see below) via Gisclareny.

The Serra del Cadí

The western part of the Cadí-Moixeró park – the karstic **Serra del Cadí** – offers equipped and experienced hikers three or four days' trekking through wild, lonely areas. A number of tracks and paths cross the range, though the favourite excursion for most visitors remains the ascent of **Pedraforca**. As in other limestone massifs, finding fresh **water** can be problematic, and that – combined with the intense summer heat at this relatively low altitude – means that peak (non-winter) visitor seasons are May to June, and September. The Cadí supports several fairly well-placed, seasonally staffed **refuges**, accessible from a number of foothill villages, which are in turn served poorly or not at all by bus, so you may have to walk or use other means of transport from the larger towns down-valley. Extended explorations of this region require possession of the Editorial Alpina 1:25,000 "Serra del Cadí-Pedraforca" and "Moixeró" **maps** and guide booklets.

From the Llobregat valley north of Berga there are two main ways west into the Cadí. **From Bagà**, a partly paved track follows the Riu Bastareny to the hamlet of Gisclareny. A much busier paved road begins just south of **Guardiola de Berguedà** and leads to Gòsol, via Saldes.

From Bagà: via the Bastareny valley

The fourteen-kilometre vehicle route up the **Bastareny valley** begins at the campsite by the river on the west side of Bagà: from there the road crosses the river, passes through a tunnel, turns to track, then climbs steeply through dense forest to naked white cliffs on the south side of the **Coll de l'Escriga** (1360m). The views over the Saldes valley are superb, the river glinting far below, with range upon range of mountain unfurling south.

GISCLARENY, 3km beyond the pass, is little more than a handful of spread-out farms (total population of 31) and two **campsites**, one of which – *Cal Tesconet* (☎608 493 317 or 937 441 016), 1500m west of the hamlet centre – also operates a **refuge** (24 places; ①). Beyond Gisclareny, the track continues through **Coll de la Balma** (1600m), where it divides left (southwest) in a sharp down-and-up to the village of Saldes (see below) via the lushly forested Gresolet valley, and right (west) in a more level if less interesting trajectory via El Collel. The former route takes about three hours on foot, the latter at least five.

The twisty road up the Bastareny valley can be negotiated on mountain bike or by 4WD; if on foot, you might do better to skip it for the direct Bagà–Gisclareny **path**, shown more or less correctly on the Editorial Alpina "Moixeró" map. From the *Cal Tesconet* refuge (where you'll need to confirm directions) a path drops down into the beeches and silver firs of Gresolet en route to Saldes, two hours shorter – assuming you don't lose the way – than the roundabout track option.

Traverses of the Moixeró

By staying with the Bastareny valley-bottom track rather than going through the Bastareny tunnel, you'll reach a cluster of farms at **VEINAT DE L'HOSTALET**, from where a good trail leads up to the seasonally staffed *Refugi de Sant Jordi* (☎934 120 777 or 933 322 381; 1640m; 44 places; ②), four hours from Bagà. Once over the Coll de Pendis (1800m), just above the refuge, you have to dodge – and briefly use – an unsightly 4WD track, but mostly it's marked path (part of the GR107) for four hours more to Bor in the Segre valley, linked by paved road to Bellver de la Cerdanya. From the refuge you can also ridge-walk east along the Moixeró watershed all the way to Massella, a popular route in winter for cross-country skiers.

From Guardiola: via the Saldes valley

The minor road from just south of **Guardiola to Saldes** and Gòsol is quite a spectacle, with steep drops into the Riera de Saldes giving way to brilliant views of Pedraforca beyond the hamlet of Maçaners (Massanés). **Campsites** and accommodation spaced at intervals along the road attract sufficient cars – mostly Catalan vacationers – in summer almost to guarantee a lift. The *El Berguedà* campsite (☎938 227 432), 3km from the turning off the main road is farmhouse-based; *Cal Susenc* (☎938 258 103), 10km along just outside Maçaners, is fairly basic; the *Repòs del Pedraforca* (☎938 258 044; open all year) 13km from the turning, offers a pool and bungalows; while at the "Km 15" marker, south of the road, the somewhat isolated *Pensió Cal General* (☎938 258 054; ③) makes a feasible base if you have your own vehicle. The municipality of Saldes has for some years now clamped down on rough camping, so those with tents are expected to patronize the sites listed.

Saldes

SALDES, a small village 18km from Guardiola, set dramatically at the foot of Pedraforca, is an ideal starting point for explorations of the peak. Here you'll find two stores with staple provisions suitable for trekking, plus two inexpensive **inns** where reservations are virtually mandatory in season: the *Fonda Carinyena* (☎938 258 025; ③) near the church, and the pricier *Cal Manuel* (☎938 258 041; ④), on Plaça Pedraforca (where cars park) serving meals. Better value is *Cal Xic* (☎938 258 081; ③), a **casa de pagès** 1500m west of the village in Cardina hamlet, at the start of the road up towards Pedraforca. Although it's a modern, somewhat sterile building, the simple, en-suite rooms are heated, clean and cheerful, and asking for a *desayuno salado* gets you ham, sausages, cheese and a *porrón* to wash it all down, rather than the usual sickly continental breakfast.

Beyond Saldes the scenery changes abruptly, first to the black-stained rocks of a lignite mine, then into speckled, deeply eroded gold-and-red rock, then back to lush, extensive pasture and forest. Mining activities have destroyed the old trail between Saldes and Gòsol, leaving walkers no alternative but to hitch or trudge along the road.

Gòsol

The old stone village of **GÒSOL**, 10km beyond Saldes at 1430m, is a more substantial place, spilling invitingly from a castellated hill. Pablo Picasso came here during the summer of 1906 and stayed several weeks in fairly primitive conditions, inspired by the striking countryside; one of the streets off the Plaça Major is named after him. Well established by the ninth century, the original village now lies in ruins, a fifteen-minute walk above the present one; the twelfth-century castle commands sweeping views of the valley, and the less spectacular rear flank of Pedraforca.

Gòsol makes a good alternative base to Saldes for explorations of the entire Cadí; the GR107 goes through here, communicating with the saddle of El Collell to the north (see p.201). There are two **hostals**, both with decent attached restaurants: *Cal Franciscó* (☎ & fax 973 370 075; ③ or ⑤ HB), on the little roundabout as you come into town, or the smaller central *Can Triuet*, Plaça Major 4 (☎973 370 072; ③). There's also a **campsite**, *Cadí de Gòsol* (☎973 370 134; open all year), southwest of the village, reached by dirt road from beside *Cal Francisco*. A handful of **bars** and one other **restaurant** around the main square cater in part to the summer holiday-makers from Barcelona.

West of Gòsol: Josa de Cadí and Tuixèn

To skirt the Cadí by vehicle, keep on the sparsely travelled dirt track – just manageable in an ordinary car – west to Josa de Cadí. This was closed for re-grading in 2000; if it's not finished you'll need to follow another more direct track (17km), of similar rough standard, to Tuixèn. This is signed as the "Camí de Molí" and begins near Gòsol's campsite. The Josa-bound track climbs in two long hairpins to the **Coll de Josa** (1625m), 5km from Gosòl, where there are superb views north, with the summit of Cadí ahead; from here the track drops through Scots pine to the Riu Josa.

JOSA DE CADÍ, 6km beyond the pass on a church-capped hill with one slope plunging to a ravine, is one of the most picturesquely set villages in Catalunya. Despite its remoteness it has become another second-home venue for urban Catalans – the traditional dwellings with windows outlined in chalky blue paint and ancient wooden doors are fast disappearing, replaced by modern conversions. As there's no bar or accommodation here, you'll have to proceed another 8km southwest to **TUIXÈN (TUIXENT)**, one of the more touristically equipped of the Cadí villages. Dominated by the hilltop Romanesque church of Sant Esteve with its square tower, it's an attractive and relatively lively place set at the edge of a gently sloping basin. Tuixèn has an unreliably open **park information office**, just off the main square that doubles as a car park; all **accommodation** stands on or near c/Coll, the short street linking the parking area with the nominal Plaça Major down the hill. Best are *Can Farragetes* (☎973 370 034, *pepfarra@caixamanresa.com*; ⑤ HB) at no. 7, its dining room (and food souvenirs) available to all, and the English-speaking *Hostal Can Custodi*, c/de la Riba 1, corner with Plaça Major (☎973 370 033; ③ or ⑥ HB) with variable en-suite rooms, and the best local **restaurant**, featuring sustaining four-course *menús*. The closest thing to a youth hostel in the Cadí is the *Alberg de Muntanya Can Cortina* (☎973 370 224; ①), opposite *Can Farragetes*, with a lively ground-floor bar, a *menjador* upstairs (3000ptas/€18 HB) and all-inclusive packages of snowshoeing and cross-country skiing at the excellent **LA VANSA** resort a few kilometres south, which has 35km of marked trails between 1660m and 2135m.

South of Tuixèn, a paved road rises a steep 8km to the Coll de Port with its bar-restaurant and the side road for La Vansa, continuing to Sant Llorenç de Morunys (30km). In the opposite direction another road threads through the villages of Cornellana (9km), Fórnols de Cadí (12km) and Adraén (19km), their houses largely renovated as summer homes. **FÓRNOLS** has the best facilities, with a **restaurant** in the village centre and, in the valley below, a **campsite**, *Molí de Fórnols* (☎973 370 001; open all year), next to which is a limited-capacity *casa de pagès* of the same name (☎973 370 021; ③). This northern route is nominally the GR7, which reaches La Seu d'Urgell after a good seven hours' walking. The path, often track or sliced up by the road, is not brilliant and you're best off driving, cycling or hitching this stretch from Tuixèn.

Walks and climbs on Pedraforca

Pedraforca is for Spanish Catalonia what Canigou is to Roussillon: the logo and mascot of the region, and accordingly much loved. The name means "stone pitchfork", supposedly the Devil's, and indeed from afar the mountain does look like an upended goat's hoof. The distinctive two-pronged summit – **Pollegó Superior** (2497m) and **Pollegó Inferior** (2400m) – is divided by a gentler saddle, the **Forcadura** (2350m). In medieval times, local witches' covens met here, and it's still a popular place to camp on the eve of 24 June, *El Dia de Sant Joan*, when some personality from the Catalan "alternative" world generally organizes an after-dark, summer-solstice event either here or down in Saldes.

From behind *Cal Xic*, some 1500m west of Saldes, a partly paved road winds just under 5km to within fifteen minutes' walk of a mountaineers' refuge (the *Refugi Lluís Estassen*, see below), just above the car park and **Mirador de Gresolet**, which looks down into the Gresolet valley. From Saldes a more direct path shortcuts much of this road, but you still face a fair amount of asphalt, so arrange a ride if possible. One kilometre before the *mirador* and the well-signed final trailhead to the refuge, the path from Saldes passes a *zona de acampada libre* with water and tables provided. This impromptu **campsite** is not in fact "free", as someone comes up from Saldes each morning and evening to collect a nominal fee and move along those camped for more than three days.

At 1640m, the **Refugi Lluís Estassen** (☎608 315 312 or 938 220 079; ①), owned by the FEEC, has space for one hundred, and offers hot showers and evening meals (1800ptas/€10.80). Although open all year, the peak seasons are spring and autumn, especially at weekends, when big-wall climbers come to tackle the sheer north face of Pedraforca.

The ascent

Despite appearances, a **walking ascent** of the peak is strenuous but not technically difficult. From the refuge you have a choice of a relatively dull but easy out-and-back walk from the southeast, or a more challenging and exciting loop over the mountain, beginning north of the summit. In either case a dawn start is advisable, or you'll be baked by the summer sun against the bare rock.

For the **simpler approach**, head south forty minutes from the refuge fountain along a narrow but well-trodden path through pine and box, to the base of the giant scree gully leading up to Forcadura. Turning sharply west up this gully, guided by a few red-and-yellow paint splodges, brings you to the saddle in just under two hours from the refuge, after a very slippery, mostly trailless climb. At Forcadura, you'll glimpse Gòsol to the west – and a gentler, distinct trail slithering up the **Canal de Gòsol** (*canal* meaning ravine in local dialect). From Forcadura it's another 25 minutes north up a reasonable, obvious trail to the top of Pollegó Superior, with its assorted Catalan flags, "mailbox" for dedications and the expected views. Return is by the same route, for a total outing of just under five hours.

The **more difficult** circuit starts west from the *Refugi Lluís Estassen* along a trail shaded in the morning, then climbs sharply up to the **Collada de Verdet** (2250m; 2hr), where you meet another path coming up from Gòsol via the **Canal de Verdet**. From this pass you turn south, then east, creeping along the spine of Pedraforca towards Pollegó Superior; a rope and a partner are suggested if you suffer from vertigo, and it will soon be obvious why you can't use this section going downhill. You descend to Forcadura and return to the refuge as in the first itinerary, after a six-hour-plus day.

A south–north traverse of the Cadí

From the south, the peaks of the Cadí appear as a chain of rounded summits separated by shallow saddles, but seen from the north they form a wall of sheer, bare rock, dropping 500m in places. A one-to-two-day **traverse from south to north** takes in all aspects of the Cadí, coming down into the Cerdanya to intercept the Puigcerdà–La Seu d'Urgell road.

For traverses, Gòsol is a slightly better starting point than Saldes; from its centre, take the GR107, which soon dwindles to a path heading northeast through jagged rock teeth to the strategic pass known as **El Collell** (1845m; 2hr 15min), with fine views east over Gresolet and west towards Josa de Cadí. El Collell is also reachable in about an hour from the *Refugi Lluís Estassen*, a rather unexciting if shady track walk. No motorized vehicles are allowed on the mountain slopes north of the pass, though they may continue east.

Stay with the track coming up from the refuge as it curls east towards Gisclareny for another kilometre, then take the zigzagging, obvious path on your left (north), towards the watershed of the Cadí. The ascent to the **Pas dels Gosolans** (2410m; 3hr from El Collell) is not easy and takes longer than expected, owing to the up-and-down, limestone-dell topography and the necessity of clearing the minor Serra Pedragosa.

At the pass – essentially a slight notch in the watershed, well used by smugglers in years past – you're near the roof of the Cadí, with awesome views west along the crest and north across the Segre valley. Plainly visible below, the recently improved *Refugi Cesar Torres* at **Prat d'Aguiló** (☎934 120 777; 2037m; staffed in summer; part always open; ①) is an hour's descent along a steep path negotiating a convenient spur. From the refuge and its spring you should arrange a ride along the 15km of track north via Montellà to Martinet, on the main Puigcerdà–La Seu d'Urgell road, roughly halfway between the two towns.

A more advanced **ridge-walking** option veers west just before the Pas dels Gosolans; two conspicuous paths head to the top of the Cortils canyon, where you'll find a rare spring and a former shepherds' cottage to shelter. You should overnight here before completing a long day west cross-country along most of the Cadí summits, taking in **Puig de la Canal Baridana** (2648m), the highest of the range. Rather than descending the savagely steep namesake *canal*, it's better to backtrack an hour to the **Puig de la Canal del Cristall** (2563m) and use the more gentle ravine there, well provided with springs, to complete the day in the pretty village of **ESTANA** (no amenities other than a single bar-restaurant, camping tolerated nearby). From there you're 10km from the main Segre valley road, where buses run between Puigcerdà and La Seu d'Urgell both ways three times a day.

West of the Cadí: routes to Alt Urgell

Daily buses from Barcelona and Lleida, bound for La Seu d'Urgell, head into the *comarque* of **Alt Urgell** along the C1313 road, which threads through the impressive gorge of Tresponts as it follows the Riu Segre upstream. Exciting as the scenery is, only one spot – **ORGANYÀ** – calls for a brief stop en route. A small, round building on the main road contains both the local **tourist office** (summer Mon–Sat 10am–2pm & 6–9pm, Sun 10am–2pm; winter Mon–Sat 11am–2pm & 5–7pm, Sun 11am–2pm), and what is possibly the oldest document in the Catalan language. Written in the twelfth century, the **Homilies d'Organyà** are annotations to some Latin sermons, discovered in a local presbytery at the beginning of the twentieth century and now displayed in back-lit glass cases. If you get stranded here – and Organyà isn't the most attractive town – there are two similar **hostals** on the bend of the through road almost opposite: *La Cabana* (☎973 383 000; ③), and *Els Tres Ponts* (☎973 383 092; ③), both with **restaurants**.

La Seu d'Urgell and around

Even though it's the capital of Alt Urgell, **LA SEU D'URGELL** (pronounced "*Sodurjey*"), beside the Riu Segre 23km upstream from Organyà, has for years been a rather sleepy place – there's no point in trying to compete with nearby Andorra, the biggest knock-down bazaar in the Pyrenees. But since the 1992 Olympic canoeing events were held nearby, La Seu and its previously neglected medieval core have undergone a mild transformation: there are two or three fancy new hotels, as well as the canoe facilities by the Segre, but as most new development has fallen outside the old quarter, you should still be able to enjoy a fairly relaxed stay before sampling the excesses of Andorra.

The Town

Named after the imposing cathedral (La Seu) at the end of c/Major, the town has always had a dual function as episcopal seat and commercial centre; there's a street farmers' market each Tuesday and Saturday, attracting vendors from throughout the *comarque*. By 820 this was already the seat of a bishopric – there's still an episcopal palace and active seminary here – with all the parishes of Andorra belonging to the counts of Urgell. But in the wake of the Moorish retreat this nobility headed south, and by the early twelfth century La Seu's bishops had acquired these possessions. Ambiguities of jurisdiction eventually led to a conflict between the bishops and the French nobility of Foix, settled in the 1278 Act of Paréatge, which allowed for joint control of Andorra.

The original cathedral and city, on the hill where Castellciutat (see below) now stands, was destroyed in the eighth century by Muslim invaders. The present **Cathedral** (winter Mon–Fri noon–1pm & 4–6pm, Sat–Sun 11am–1pm; summer Mon–Sat 10am–1pm & 4–7pm, Sun 10am–1pm) was consecrated in 839 but completely rebuilt in 1175, and restored several times since. Nonetheless, it retains some graceful interior decoration and fine cloisters with droll capitals; admission to the latter is around the back of the church. The ticket (350ptas/€2.10) also gets you into the adjacent eleventh-century chapel of Sant Miquel and the Museu Diocesano; to see only the cloister and chapel costs 150ptas/€0.90. The **Museu Diocesano** (same hours as Cathedral) merits a visit for a brilliantly coloured tenth-century Mozarabic manuscript with miniatures, the *Beatus*, a commentary on the Apocalypse of Saint John.

Other than these few sights, time is most agreeably spent strolling the dark, cobbled and arcaded streets west of the cathedral, where you'll find many of La Seu's best bars

and restaurants. A strong medieval feel is accentuated by the fine buildings lining c/dels Canonges (parallel to c/Major); the town's fourteenth-century stone corn measures still stand under the arcade on c/Major.

Castellciutat

Comprehensive panoramas of the Segre valley can be enjoyed from the village of **CASTELLCIUTAT**, just 1km southwest of town, and its nearby ruined castle (now a luxury hotel). Follow c/Sant Ermengol across the river and up to the village, which glories in views that La Seu never gets. There's still some farming on the slopes below the tiny stone church, and a *pensió* on the road up to the village and another in the square (see "Accommodation" below) – either makes a nice retreat from La Seu. To continue your walk, follow a path around the base of the castle and cross the main road for the nearby Torre Solsona. The scanty remains of the old fortifications are crumbling away, assisted by quarrying below – take care near the edges. You can vary your route to Castellciutat or back by following the walkways through the very pleasant, post-Olympic riverside **Valira** park, with its modern cloister made from pink stone, near the youth hostel. Salvador Dalí, Pablo Casals, Albert Einstein, Winston Churchill and

Groucho Marx are among the famous twentieth-century characters (mainly men) whose heads decorate the capitals; one reproduces a fragment of Picasso's *Guernica* in 3D, alongside posturing Francoist figures.

Practicalities

The **bus station** is on c/Joan Garriga Massó, just north of the old town; local services include the thrice-daily Alsina Graells buses to Puigcerdà, and much more frequent La Hispano-Andorrana departures to Andorra (for details, see p.207). The **Turisme** (Mon–Sat 10am–2pm & 5–8pm; ☎973 351 511) is in Avda de les Valls d'Andorra, the main road into town from the north; in July and August, there may also be a supplementary office behind the cathedral in the *Ajuntament*, supplying maps and hotel information.

Accommodation

In the wake of the Olympic facelift, very little decent **budget accommodation** remains in La Seu. The standard seems set by *Pensió Palomares*, c/dels Canonges 38–40 (☎973 352 178; ②), a warren of windowless chipboard closets rented out as rooms, tolerable only if you obtain one of the multi-bed front rooms with balcony. Otherwise there's only *La Valira* **youth hostel** (☎973 353 897; closed Sept; ①), at the western end of c/Joaquim Viola la Fuerza beyond the *petanca* court, by the Valira park. The colossal **campsite**, *En Valira* (☎973 351 035; open all year), is 300m northeast of the hostel, at Avda. del Valira 10.

You're probably better off at one of the **hotels** on the main roads through town. Best placed is the *Andría*, Passeig Joan Brudieu 24 (☎973 350 300; ③–⑤), an elegant if externally faded establishment, whose rooms offer all mod cons, and which represents the best value if there are two of you. Less attractive, but friendly and adequate, is the *Pensió Cadí* (☎973 350 150; ⑤) at c/Josep de Zulueta, close to Plaça de Catalunya. Top-of-the-range places include the elegant *Parador* (☎973 352 000; ⑦), converted from a monastery, near the cathedral at c/Sant Domènec 6 with underground parking, and the exclusive *El Castell* (☎973/35 07 04; ⑦), a four-star hotel discreetly incorporated within the castle at Castellciutat. Or consider the village of **Castellciutat** itself: the friendly, family-run *Pensió Fransol* in the central Plaça de l'Arbre (☎973 350 219; ③) is quiet, though without views; by contrast the plusher *Hotel La Glorieta* (☎973 351 045, fax 973 354 261; ⑤), with a pool and restaurant, gets an eyeful of the valley, perched above the river on the road up to the village.

Eating and drinking

Lively **tapas bars** are plentiful in La Seu's old town: try *Bar Eugenio*, c/Major 20, or *Bodega Fabrega*, c/Major 81. For good-value **restaurant** meals, *Cal Pacho*, in a quiet corner on c/la Font (at the southern end of c/Major, then east), has a lunch *menú*, (1000ptas/€6) though *a la carta* (dinner only) will set you back about 2500ptas/€15 for dishes such as cod-stuffed peppers and roast goat, although there has been one serious complaint about slack food and service here. For coffee, cakes and similar, the *Blau Arts Café* on c/dels Estudis makes a good choice.

Outside the old quarter there's somewhat more choice. *Les Tres Portes* at c/Joan Garriga Massó 7 offers a good-value three-course menu (1400ptas/€8.40) in a quaint chalet-style house and summer patio, though again there have been reports of surly service. The *menjador* of the *Hotel Andria* has sharpened up of late and now offers a worthwhile *menú* (1700ptas/€10.20) and local gourmet dishes *a la carta*, featuring own-reared chicken and mushrooms in season. At the snackier end of things, *Restaurant Canigó*, c/Sant Ot 3 (north end of the *passeig*) does mostly pizzas, while east of the main *passeig*, *Bambola Pizzeria-Creperia* at c/Andreu Capella 4, serves tasty pizzas, crêpes and omelettes.

West of La Seu: Castellbó and Sant Joan de l'Erm

Four kilometres south of La Seu the road climbs west along the River Solanell, between cornfields and then over successively more scrubby rises, to the village of **CASTELLBÓ**, 14km from La Seu. This was the seat of Arnau de Castellbó, whose marriage to Arnalda de Caboet was a key event in Andorran history (see below). The only thing to see now is the thirteenth-century church of **Santa Maria**, an example of Romanesque-Gothic transitional style with pointed arches and Romanesque ironwork. The sole indoor **accommodation** here is *Casa de Pagès Molí de Pau* (☎973 351 608; ③), while there's a smallish **campsite**, *Buchaca* (☎973 352 155; May–Oct) with a shop, on the edge of the village.

Beyond Castellbó or Sant Andreu you can climb on to the *Refugi Pla de la Basseta* (☎973 351 343 or 973 352 162; open all year; ③) at **SANT JOAN DE L'ERM**, a superb **cross-country ski** resort with 150km of trails between 1600 and 2150m. Westward progress is by 4WD and mountain-bike tracks, which emerge just below the downhill ski centre of Port-Ainé (see p.258). Those without transport can hitch or take the twice-daily minibus along 47km of paved road west from **ADRALL**, 7km south of La Seu, to Sort in the Noguera Pallaresa. Adrall itself has a clutch of **restaurants** on the through road, more country-style than anything in La Seu – *Can Pere* comes recommended for good food and an entertaining proprietor.

ANDORRA

After seven hundred years of feudalism, modernity finally forced itself upon the **PRINCIPALITY OF ANDORRA**, 450 square kilometres of mountainous land between France and Spain. A referendum held on March 14, 1993 (henceforth a big national holiday) produced an overwhelming vote in favour of a democratic constitution, replacing a system in effect since 1278, when the Spanish bishops of La Seu d'Urgell and the French counts of Foix settled a long-standing quarrel by granting Andorra semi-autonomous status under joint sovereignty. In 1185 the marriage of Arnalda d'Isarn de Caboet and Arnau de Castellbó united the Andorran possessions granted to the families by the bishops of La Seu. Their only daughter Ermensende later married Roger-Bernard II, count of Foix, who claimed sole rights to Andorra when Arnau died without male issue. The bishops of La Seu contested this, claiming that sovereignty reverted to them with the cession of the male line of Castellbó. The consequent strife between the bishops and the house of Foix came to an end with the 1278 Act of Paréatge, through which La Seu d'Urgell and Foix became *co-seigneurs* of Andorra. (Incidentally, the Act also forbade the building of castles in Andorra, which explains their absence here.)

Despite a certain devolution of powers – the counts' sovereignty passed to the French king and later to the French president – the principality largely managed to maintain its independence over the centuries. The Spanish and French *co-seigneurs* appointed regents who took little interest in day-to-day life here. The country was instead run by the *Consell General de les Valls* (General Council of the Valleys), made up of representatives from Andorra's seven valley communes, who ensured that the principality remained well out of the European mainstream – it even managed to stay neutral during the Spanish Civil War and World War II.

It was during these conflicts that Andorra began its meteoric economic rise, as locals first smuggled goods from France into Spain during the Civil War and, a few years later, goods from Spain into German-occupied France. After World War II, this evolved into legitimate duty-free trade in alcohol, tobacco and electronics, coupled with the huge demand for winter skiing. Much of the principality became an unsightly drive-in megastore, with the main road through the country clogged with French and Spanish visitors after cut-price hi-fi and electrical gear, mountain bikes, ski equipment, car parts and a tankful of discount petrol. Seasoned Spain-watcher John Hooper has called Andorra "a kind of cross between Shangri-La and Heathrow Duty-Free", while the Spanish daily broadsheet *El Pais* once dismissed it as a "high-altitude Kuwait".

Ironically, though, this tax-free status contained the seeds of Andorra's belated conversion to democracy. Although the inhabitants enjoyed one of Europe's highest standards of living, twelve million visitors a year began to put a strain on the country: infrastructure was sorely stretched, the valleys were increasingly blighted by speculators' building sites, and the budget deficit grew alarmingly since little entrepreneurial wealth went into the public sector. Spanish entry to the EC in 1986 only exacerbated the situation, reducing the difference in price of imported goods between Spain and Andorra (which now measures about 20 percent, down from thirty-three per cent). However, the damage has long since been done; Andorra's commercial growth has pretty much killed off trade in the nearest French/Spanish towns.

The 1993 referendum was an attempt to come to terms with the economic realities of twentieth-century Europe. Or rather, some of the economic realities, since none of

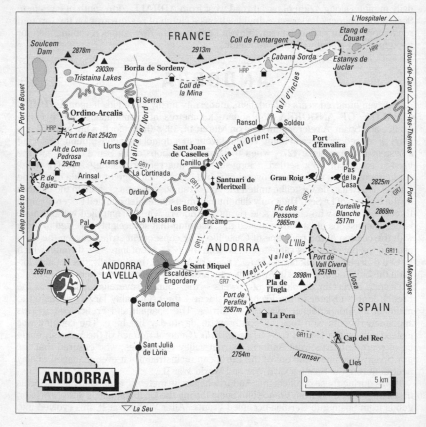

ANDORRA PRACTICALITIES

Getting there
From Spain, there are four daily buses direct from Barcelona (6am, 7am, 2.30pm & 7pm; 4hr 30min), and regular services from **La Seu d'Urgell** which depart at 8am, 9.30am, 12.15pm, 2pm, 3.20pm, 6pm and 7.15pm (Sun 8am, 9.30am, 12.15pm, 2pm, 4.15pm, 7.15pm), taking forty minutes to reach the capital of Andorra la Vella.

From France, buses leave L'Hospitalet on Saturday at 7.35am, 10.30am, 1.15pm, 5pm (additional summer-only service from Ax-les-Thermes at 4.20pm) and 7.45pm, arriving at Pas de la Casa thirty minutes later; on weekdays you may find that only the 7.35am and 7.45pm departures function. From Pas de la Casa the onward bus journey to Andorra la Vella takes one hour ten minutes. Services also leave La Tour de Carol at 10.30am and 1.15pm, taking 45 minutes to Pas de la Casa.

Even if you're **driving** you might as well leave the car behind and take the bus – in high season (summer or winter) the traffic is so bad that the bus isn't much slower, and parking in Andorra la Vella is an ordeal. Drivers are well advised to use the giant car parks provided in the largest towns, or kerbside meters – the traffic police and tow-trucks are both very industrious. On the plus side, petrol is famously cheap – about twelve to fifteen percent less than in Spain, even greater savings compared to France – so fill up before leaving.

Leaving Andorra
Buses **to La Seu d'Urgell** leave from Plaça Guillemó in Andorra la Vella, parallel to the main road. Departures are Monday to Saturday at 8.05am, 9.05am, 11.30am, 1.30pm, 4.05pm, 6pm and 8pm; Sun 9.05am, 11.30am, 1.30pm, 4.05pm and 8.05pm.

To France, La Hispano-Andorrana company (☎376 821 372 or 820 327) runs at least two daily buses from Andorra la Vella to Pas de la Casa (1hr 20min) and L'Hospitalet (1hr 45min), one leaving in the morning and one in the afternoon, with an extra departure in summer and five usually on Saturdays. Towards La Tour de Carol, Autos Pujol Juguet provide two daily services, at 7.30 and 10.30am (2hr 15min).

Getting around
Internal **bus services** are cheap and frequent on the following routes (between about 7.30am and 9pm): Andorra la Vella–Sant Julià de Lòria, Andorra la Vella–Encamp–Canillo, and Andorra la Vella–La Massana–Ordino; buses leave from Plaça Guillemó. Details of the most important long-distance **hiking** routes are given in the text.

Customs
French, Spanish and Andorran police may board buses looking for faces that don't fit, and ask luggage bays to be opened, as a check against illegal immigrants. Inspections of goods when entering are nonexistent, but on leaving, the Spanish police are very interested in just how much their own nationals have acquired – the French at Pas de la Casa seem much less active. As a foreign national you'll be waved through unless you've acquired a van full of consumer durables. Most big busts results from tip-offs, with the authorities going straight for the false bottom in the boot or the engine-compartment stash they've been told to look out for.

Currency, mail and phones
Andorra has no money of its own, so both pesetas and (if you ask) French francs are accepted; prices in shops and restaurants are usually quoted in both currencies, plus euros of late. There's also a shared postal system, with both a French and Spanish post office in Andorra la Vella and Canillo, for example. Andorra has its own phone system and area code – ☎376 – applicable to the whole republic; public phones take *only* Spanish coins. A single mobile network, MobilAnd/STA, provides surprisingly excellent coverage even in the deeper valleys.

Population and language
The **population** of Andorra is currently around sixty-five thousand, of which about twelve thousand are native Andorrans; the rest are mainly French, Spanish and Portuguese, with a smattering of other nationalities. Catalan is the official **language**, but Spanish and, to a slightly lesser extent, French are widely understood.

the parties involved in the negotiations and debate seriously suggested that the solution was to introduce direct taxation: there is still no income tax in Andorra, and barely any indirect tax either. Instead the idea was to transform Andorra into a kind of "offshore" banking centre, to rival the likes of Gibraltar, Lichtenstein and Luxembourg.

Following the referendum, the state's first **constitutional election** was held in December 1993. Only the ten thousand native Andorrans were entitled to vote (out of a total population of sixty thousand) and an eighty percent turnout gave Oscar Ribas Reig, outgoing head of the *Consell General*, the biggest share. His Agrupament Nacional Democratic took eight seats in the new 28-seat parliament – also dubbed the **Consell General** – and formed a coalition with other right-wing parties to usher in the new democratic era. Since then, Andorran citizens (those born here, or who have lived here over 20 years) can vote and join trade unions or political parties, while their government now has the right to run its own foreign policy and establish its own judicial system. The country has also been accepted as a full member of the United Nations and the Council of Europe.

Given all this, it's useful to remember that as recently as 1950 Andorra was virtually cut off from the rest of the world – an archaic region which, romantically, happened also to be a separate country. There are still no planes or trains, but for many visitors that is now the full extent of any attractive quaintness. It can take an hour in bumper-to-bumper traffic to drive the few kilometres from La Seu d'Urgell to Andorra la Vella, the main town. Surprisingly, the main crop here, which you see on either side of the road and in every small available space throughout lower-altitude Andorra, is tobacco. In the higher valleys, large-scale ski resorts have already monopolized the most attractive corners of the state, with further enlargements mooted and a new resort planned for the beautiful Prat Primer upland. This sort of development – coupled with Andorra's historically lax regulations – scarcely benefits wildlife, already hard-pressed by helicopter- and 4WD-equipped gunmen who fire with impunity during officially closed seasons and at protected species.

But it's worth leaving the capital and main developments behind to see some of the scenery that attracted early visitors. Although the highest point (Alt de Coma Pedrosa on the western border) reaches just 2942m, there is still wilderness aplenty here. Scots pine is endemic, and the mountain pines *Pinus uncinata* or *Pinus mugo* thrive at altitudes up to 2200m, or even 2400m on south-facing slopes; moisture-craving silver fir grows on north-facing slopes between 1600 and 2000m. Wild boar, golden eagles and griffon vultures are native to the area, but bears probably aren't any longer – the last confirmed sighting was in 1978.

Through Andorra by road

The main through road – jointly the CG1 from Spain to Andorra la Vella and the CG2 from the latter to the French border – runs 38km north, then east, through the main valley draining Andorra. The CG3 heads northwest to the dead-end, and therefore quieter, Valira del Nord. Whichever way you go, whether by bus or car, it's likely to be a slow business – the hordes of shoppers and skiers are intent on getting from A to B, and rarely leave the traffic queues to go sightseeing.

Andorra la Vella

With its stone church of **Sant Esteve**, fast-flowing river and appealing setting amidst crags and green slopes, the capital **ANDORRA LA VELLA** must have once been an attractive little town. The main street, Avda. Princep Benlloch/Avda. Meritxell, is now a seething mass of tourist restaurants (specializing in six-language menus), tacky discos and brightly lit shops crammed with everything from electricals, perfumes and watches to cars and kitchenware.

There's some respite in the narrow streets of the *barri antic* (old quarter), above the Riu Valira and south of the main street. Besides the church, its sole monument is the **Casa de la Vall** in c/de la Vall (free guided tours Mon–Fri 10am–1pm & 3–7pm). Built in 1580 for the wealthy Busquet family, this solidly built stone house was purchased by the Consell General in 1702; it now houses the Sala de Sessions of Andorra's parliament and the chief courtroom (Tribunal de Corts). Between Sant Esteve and the town hall, Rambla Molines leads to the raised Plaça del Poble, laid out as a spacious pedestrian square with stone benches, sculptures, flower beds, fountains and a covered picnic place; there are cafés, toilets and telephones here too, and the tourist office (see below) is nearby. The church of **Santa Coloma**, over 1km west of the centre in the namesake suburb, merits a look for the oddity of its round tower – nearly all Romanesque churches have square ones.

Practicalities

Buses leave passengers on Avda Princep Benlloch, near the church of Sant Esteve. There are about half a dozen public **car parks** scattered around town, should you bring your own vehicle – count on walking up to a kilometre from any space you happen to find.

Andorra la Vella's **Turisme**, on c/Dr Vilanova (Mon–Sat 10am–1pm & 3–7pm, Sun 10am–1pm; ☎376 820 214), east of the old quarter, has complete lists of local accommodation, restaurants and bus timetables, and also sells a good topographical map of Andorra. It's the main information post for the entire principality, though smaller booths keep similar hours in the more sizeable villages – in particular Ordino, Canillo, Escaldes-Engordanay and Encamp.

There are several reasonable places to **stay**: the friendly, basic *Hostal del Sol*, at Plaça Guillemó 3 (☎376 823 701; ②); the slightly larger *Hotel Les Arcades* (☎376 821 355; ②) in the same square at no. 5; the relatively comfortable *Hotel Florida* (☎376 820 105; ⑤) with balconied rooms nearby at c/La Llacuna 15; the rock-bottom *Residència Baró* (☎376 821 484; ②), at c/Puial 21, just up some steps from the main boulevard; and in the heart of the old quarter, *Hotel Racó d'en Joan*, c/de la Vall 20 (☎376 820 811; ③), which has a ground-floor restaurant.

A better plan, perhaps, is to linger around for something to **eat** before retreating to more attractive surroundings; intense competition fosters low prices, and the town boasts some of the few Asian restaurants in the Pyrenees. Best value in the old quarter is *Minim's*, tucked away in the tiny Placeta de la Consorcia (July–Sept daily 1–3.30pm & 8–11pm; rest of year closed Wed), a small, stylish place with hearty French cuisine (lunch *menú* for 1000ptas/€6, otherwise 1500–2500ptas/€9–15). Other central and characterful places include *Pizzeria Primavera*, c/Dr Nequi 4, near the old quarter; *Restaurant Macary*, c/Mossèn Tremosa 6, just northeast of the Plaça Princep Benlloch; and *Les Arcades* at Plaça Guillemó 5, for filling combo specials and a bargain *menú* (980ptas/40F/€5.90).

There's a fair bit of entertainment, including two **cinemas** (Modern Triplex at Avda. Meritxell 26, Principat at Avda. Meritxell 44) and *Àngel Blau*, a live jazz **club** in c/de la Borda.

Escaldes-Engordany

Andorra la Vella merges seamlessly with **ESCALDES-ENGORDANY**, in effect a northern suburb, its pavements still choked with visitors eager to buy something, or dunk themselves in the hot spa which gave the place its name. The ultramodern thermal baths of **Caldea**, with their landmark glass pyramid and indoor/oudoor lagoons, provide the latest in hydrotherapy and luxury beauty treatments (daily 10am–11pm; minimum 2200ptas/€13.20 for 3hr; ☎376 828 600). Cultural interest is provided by the work of Catalan sculptor Josep Viladomat i Maçanes, 140 of whose pieces are on display at **Salita Parc** in Avda Parc de la Mola (Mon–Sat 5–9pm, Sun 11am–2pm & 5–9pm); his stylistic affinities lie with Miquel Blay and Josep Clarà of Olot (see p.163).

The church of **Sant Miquel d'Engolasters**, one of the most attractive Romanesque churches in the area, stands on a plateau east of Escaldes. The quick way there is to take the road that climbs to the Engolasters reservoir, passing the church after 4km. But if you want to make a day of it, you can follow the **GR7** two hours from the main street in Escaldes to just beyond the hamlet of Ramio, where you follow the marked footpath towards Encamp (see below) for another hour. Sant Miquel's frescoes, like those of many Andorran churches, have been appropriated by the Museu d'Art de Catalunya in Barcelona, but this eleventh-century chapel is still an evocative sight.

There's an abundance of **accommodation** in Escaldes, though most is aimed at the free-spending ski crowd. Exceptions include *Hotel Pont de la Tosca* at Avda. Miquel Mateu 6 (☎376 821 938; ③), *Residència Astòria* at Avda de les Escoles 16 (☎376 820 515; ②), *Residència Roca* at c/Engordany 32 (☎376 820 878; ②), and the slightly more comfortable *Núria* at c/Santa Anna 11 (☎376 821 572; ③). The most reasonable **eating** is found at *Restaurant Bon Profit*, Avda Carlemany 53, and *Pizzeria Roma*, on the same street at no. 95.

The Valira del Nord

For a bit of peace and quiet you can head up the **Valira del Nord** (also known as Valira d'Ordino) from Escaldes, but you'll have to wait until you get past dreary La Massana, 7km northwest, for it to begin.

Arinsal and Pal

The left-hand (northwesterly) fork at La Massana climbs 4km to the popular, mushrooming and quite hideous ski-village of **ARINSAL**, served during winter by three daily buses from Andorra la Vella. Starting in Arinsal's centre, a bubble-lift gets you up to Point 1551 (as does the bus), where there's a chairlift to Point 1950m, base for most of the 23 runs. These tend to be short and sharp except for a number of blue pistes which can be taken in sequence for a long descent from near the resort's top point of 2560m, just this side of the Spanish border.

Much of the **accommodation** is British-package-style, but you could always try one of the more modest establishments within a few paces of the telecabin: the basic *Hostal Poblado* (☎376 835 122; ②); *Hotel Comapedrosa* (☎376 835 123; ③); and *Hotel Micolau* (☎376 835 052; ④). Owing to large numbers of self-catering apartments there are relatively few independent **restaurants** – *Jan*, and *El Rusc* (pricey Basque cuisine, towards La Massana) are about the size of it – but Arinsal is noted for its **nightlife**: *Rocky Mountain* (rock, jazz and blues), or *Surf* (rock and Irish) are both durable clubs going until 3am in ski season.

About 6km south of Arinsal, up yet another side valley, **PAL** is very attractive by Andorran standards, a stone-built village with its fine belfried Romanesque church of Sant Climent but unfortunately no short-term accommodation and just one restaurant. Some 5km further you reach the **Pal ski centre**, 200m lower than Arinsal and thus heavily dependent on snow canons. That said, the skiing is challenging enough with most runs red-rated, though several new blue ones were laid out during 1999 in the Setúria zone; the chairlift from Els Fontanells at 1810m gets you up to the 2358-metre summit of Pic de Cubil and the best pistes. The road carries on 24km out of Els Fontanells to the village of Alins in Spain (see p.260), via the 2300-metre Port de Cabús (road passable only in summer) and the hamlet of Tor.

Ordino to Llorts

Back at La Massana, the right-hand (northeast) fork leads 3km on to **ORDINO**; a quiet, agreeable place where a handful of old stone edifices mingle with new chalets and apartment buildings. The short "high street" threads past the church and most services. One of the seventeenth-century family houses in the middle of the village, with splendid carved wood furniture and patterned pebble floors, is now open as the **Museu-Casa d'Areny-Plandolit** (guided tours 9.30am–1.30pm & 3–6.30pm; 300ptas/€1.80). For delicious cakes and snacks, try the *Granja Patisseria 1930*, opposite the museum; the bar-restaurant *Babi*, next door, has more substantial meals at reasonable prices, while the nearby *Pub Xaloc* provides a semblance of nightlife. Mountain bikes can be rented outside the **tourist office** (☎376 836 963) on the main road, near the church, which also displays the daily weather forecast. The central, inexpensive *Hotel Quim* closed in 2000 – probably permanently – so the next most reasonable option is the *Hotel Santa Barbara* on the *plaça* (☎376 837 100; ⑤ 7000ptas). Just 2km beyond Ordino, there's a pleasant riverside **campsite**, the *Borda d'Ansalonga* (☎376 850 374; closed May & Oct).

You'll have more choice in the little villages of the Valira del Nord proper, along the 8km or so north of Ordino. The landscape becomes more appealing, with fewer tower-cranes and high rises, though even here there are chalet developments and incongruously fancy restaurants overlooking disused pastures. Examples of **accommodation** en route include *Hotel Sucarà* (☎376 850 151; ③) in unspoilt La Cortinada, 2.5km north of Ordino; the *Hotel Arans* (☎376 850 111; ④) 500m beyond in Arans hamlet; and *Hostal Vilaró* (☎376 850 225; ②), slightly isolated just below the village of **LLORTS**, 5km from Ordino. Llorts also offers one of the better rural **restaurants** in Andorra, *L'Era del Jaume* (reservations suggested on ☎376 850 667). They specialize in grills but also do many vegetable-based dishes, such as mushroom *escalivada*; stick to their house wine and *menú* if on a budget, otherwise you're looking at 3000ptas/€18 a head *a la carta* for *minceur* portions.

El Serrat and Ordino-Arcalis

At the head of the valley, 18km from Andorra la Vella (3 daily bus departures), stands **EL SERRAT**, astride the HRP and graced by tumbling waterfalls and horse-riding stables. This also has the last **accommodation** before the ski centre (see below); the fairly basic *Hotel Tristaina* (☎376 850 081; ③) at the top of the village, and the 1999-refurbished *Hostal del Serrat* at the lowest point (☎376 735 735, fax 376 735 740; ⑤), best for après-ski comfort and also with a well-regarded restaurant.

From El Serrat the road climbs steeply to the ski resort of **ORDINO-ARCALIS**, which owing to top points over 2600m and a chilly microclimate retains the best-quality Andorran snow well into April. It's probably the most pleasant place to ski in the principality, with largely Spanish, French and local clientele, plus appealing views north over the Tristaina lakes and border ridge beyond. Ordino-Arcalis is good for intermediate skiers, with five well-placed chair-lifts to the top of mostly blue and red runs ranging from 1km to over 2km in length. Lift passes cost 2950–3700ptas/€17.80–22.30 depending on the day of the week, standard for Andorran resorts except those in the far east.

The Valira del Orient

It's around 33km from Escaldes to the French border at Pas de la Casa along the **Valira del Orient**, a route served as far as Soldeu by hourly buses from the capital. You're unlikely to be tempted to get off anywhere for casual touring, although those with a car or with skiing in mind have several possibilities.

Encamp and Meritxell

ENCAMP, 6km from Escaldes, is the first tolerable place to stay beyond Escaldes. In the centre, among old stone houses and concrete high rises, the modern town hall stands out like a giant video screen. For a pleasant stroll, follow the riverside walkway north along the west bank to the unspoilt village of **Les Bons**, with its tiny twelfth-century Romanesque chapel of **Sant Romà** and the remains of a ruined castle standing above. Recommended **hotels** in Encamp include the *Pere d'Urg* (☎376 831 515; ④), on the riverside at the lower end of town, with a young clientele, and the slightly more upmarket but excellent-value *Hotel Coray* (☎376 831 513, fax 376 831 806; ④), at the top of the hill above the town hall, which is used by the Ramblers' Association as their base for walking holidays (the GR11 passes through here). The only surviving budget option is the *Residència Relax* at c/Bellavista 14 (☎376 834 777; ②). An ambitious funicular, the **Funicamp**, transports skiers up to the runs of El Tarter (see below) from the centre.

Some 3km past Encamp, a small road climbs south to the **Santuari de Meritxell**, the ugly shrine designed by Barcelona Olympics architect Ricardo Bofill to replace a Romanesque building that burned down in 1972. The fire also destroyed the ancient carving known as Our Lady of Meritxell, described by writer Nina Epton as having "the barbaric appeal of a recently converted Christian with her long astonished face and enormous black Byzantine eyes". A replica stands in her place. The local September 8 festival (Birth of the Virgin) is one of the four main national holidays, when most things in Andorra shut down.

Canillo

CANILLO, nearly 6km from Encamp, makes one of the best compromise bases in Andorra: along the main road (and bus route) between Andorra la Vella and the nearby ski resort of Soldeu-El Tarter, but far enough away to retain some dignity and character. Beautifully situated at 1562m, among rocky cliffs and green slopes, it's an excellent base for circular day-hikes. On the eastern fringe of the town, the belfried Romanesque church of **Sant Joan de Caselles** is largely eleventh century, with the porch a fifteenth-century addition; back in the centre of town, a warren of old streets north of the highway leads to **Sant Sadurní**, nearly as ancient. The big recreational attraction is the **Palau de Gel** (daily 10am–11.30pm, though some facilities close at 10pm), with an ice rink, indoor pool, gym, sauna and squash courts. Prices start at 1100ptas/€6.60 for skate rental and an afternoon session on the ice. When the snow level is sufficient, a bubble-lift rises to **El Forn**, an additional domain of the El Tarter ski centre (see below). Incidentally, the direct road to Ordino via the **Coll d'Ordino** is scenic but slow going – allow forty minutes by car for the 19km, with eyefuls of each valley as you ascend and descend.

Hotels line the main through road, c/General, with three inexpensive choices (by Andorran standards): the rock-bottom, slightly shabby *Commerç* (☎376 851 020; ②), which has excellent *table d'hôte* suppers for 2000ptas/€12; and two older, French-style, creaky-floored places just down the street, the friendly partly en-suite *Casa Nostra* (☎376 851 023; ②), with a pleasant bar and restaurant, and *Canigó* opposite (☎376 851 024; ③), better value for big, en-suite rooms at the back, though their diner is poor. For a somewhat higher standard, try the *Hotel Pic Blanc*, at the west, lower end of the street (☎376 851 054; ③). Among several local **campsites**, the tree-shaded *Camping Santa Creu* (☎376 851 462; mid-June to Sept) is recommended, near the centre on the south bank of the river. Among the few independent **restaurants**, best by far is *Molí del Peano* (closed mid-May to mid-June & mid-Oct to mid-Nov) where you can enjoy grilled *conill* (rabbit) *all-i-olli*, goat cheese salad, homemade mousse and a beer or two for less than 2500ptas/€15.

Soldeu-El Tarter

Development at **SOLDEU** village, at the head of the valley 19km from the capital, is surprisingly restrained, especially compared to Pas de la Casa, and considering that the adjacent ski centre is the largest in Andorra. Most of the **hotels** line the boulevard, and while the British package industry tends to get first crack at them, it's worth trying the *Naudi* (☎376 851 148, fax 376 852 022; ⑤), *Bruxelles* (☎376 851 010 fax 376 852 099, closed mid-April to mid-June & Oct–Nov; ③) and *Peretol d'Envalira* (☎ & fax 376 851 264; ④). If these are full, you may have to go 2km east of town to *Residència Supervalira* (☎376 851 082, fax 376 851 062; ④). From **EL TARTER** just below Soldeu – where there's little affordable accommodation – a narrow road heads north up the lovely **Vall d'Incles**. There's an inexpensive though **basic campsite**, *Camping d'Incles* (mid-June to mid-Sept), at the far end of the valley, well placed for the HRP – allow an hour's walk from the main road.

Restaurants and **bars** not affiliated with Soldeu's hotels are limited and Brit-oriented, with après-ski activities winding down from mid-March. *Aspen-Colorado* is the most popular pub, doing Tex-Mex food in season, though try also *Fat Albert's* bar on the upper lane. *L'Esquirol Indien* advertises "mile-high curry" – but at mile-high prices; the same 4000ptas/€24 is better spent across the way at *Hotel Naudi*'s *menjador*, or at the *Cort Popaire* (closed May & Nov) on the upper lane, both serve local cuisine.

Following its enlargement in 1998, the joint **ski centre** of Soldeu-El Tarter ranks as the most extensive in the principality, with ample skiing for all ability levels amongst its 47 runs – it's the best place in Andorra for beginners, a fact appreciated by the British and Spanish families who seem to make up the main clientele. Lift passes are on the pricey side at 4200ptas/146F/€25.30 for a peak day, but chair lifts are numerous, runs well planned, and the views north to the French border ridge magnificent. You're pampered with an initial bubble-lift from the (inexpensive) Soldeu rental centre to **Pla dels Espiolets** (2250m), the novice's area, focus of some very long green runs (Os, Duc, Gall de Bosc) to gain confidence. Gall de Bosc in particular offers a tranquil descent – 8km if you take it all the way from 2560-metre Tossal de la Llosada – through the trees right back into the basement of the bubble-lift building. Intermediate and advanced skiers will find the **Pla Riba Excorxada** zone at 2100m (main restaurant) more suitable, with chair-lifts up to **Tosa dels Espiolets** (ca. 2400m) and **Cap de Clots** (2388m) giving access to more challenging red and blue runs. From Cap, two drag lifts ascend **Tossal de la Llossada**, from where virtually all the runs are accessible, including the newish easterly Solana del Forn area, with its 2600-metre top point and blue/red runs served by two more chairlifts.

Pas de la Casa

Over the **Port d'Envalira** (though a tunnel is being prepared), the road descends steeply down bald hillsides draining into France to the ghastly, high-rise **PAS DE LA CASA**, a combined duty-free bazaar and winter sports station. The best that can be said is that it offers more advanced skiing between points at 2600m and 2050m, and its snow record is good. Runs are linked to those of **Grau Roig**, a relatively tiny place in the next valley, with 27 lifts serving 40 runs (mostly red).

Among Pas de la Casa's expensive **hotels**, *Hotel Residència Casado*, close to the ski slopes at c/Catalunya 23 (☎376 855 219; ⑤), stands out as helpful, clean and good value. Other options slightly further from the ski lifts are *Hotel Olimpic*, c/des Abelletes 6 (☎376 855 322; ⑦), the faded but central *Hotel La Muntanya*, c/Catalunya 12 (☎376 855 318; ③) and *Hotel El Chat*, c/La Solana (☎376 855 361; ⑦ HB), just uphill from the two main chairlifts.

Through Andorra on foot

For a trekkers' traverse of Andorra, the main **traverse routes** are: the **GR7**, which skirts the southeastern mountains; the **GR11**, which traverses quickly between the Perafita area and Alt de Coma Pedrosa, via Encamp, Coll d'Ordino, La Cortinada and Arinsal; and the **HRP**, which keeps to the northern fringes of the principality. Most of the alpine shelters en route are small, unattended and pretty basic. The best **maps** are the Spanish IGN 1:25,000 (sheets 183-I, 183-II, 183-III and 183-IV), the Randonnées Pyrénéennes 1:50,000 "Haute-Ariège-Andorre", and the Editorial Alpina 1:40,000 "Andorra". The eastern half of Andorra is also shown on the French IGN 1:50,000 "Cerdagne-Capcir" sheet, and the IGN 1:50,000 "Fontargente" map. The main tourist office in Andorra la Vella supplies a useful, if rather schematic, free map showing the location and size of all the Andorran mountain refuges.

Southwest from the Porteille Blanche: the GR7

Many walks into and around Andorra follow the old paths of the *paquetaires* (*paqueteros* in Spanish), the smugglers who carried heavy parcels of Andorran tobacco and other contraband across the border, often at night to avoid detection. Porta (see p.226 for access details), at the top of the Carol valley in France, was one of the great smuggling villages in the Pyrenees, on account of its link with Andorra along the Campcardos (Campquerdós) valley, now the route of the **GR7**.

A three-hour climb up the valley from Porta brings you to the **Porteille Blanche** (Portella Blanca; 2517m). The meeting of borders here allowed *paquetaire*'s in trouble to step quickly into France, Andorra or Spain according to who was pursuing them. From here, veer northwest towards **Pic Negre d'Envalira** (2825m), just south of the source of the Ariège; the summit has views into the valley of the Valira del Orient to the northwest. West of Pic Negre, the GR7 descends to the ski station at **GRAU ROIG**, where the only accommodation is the expensive *Hotel Grau Roig* (☎376 855 556; ⑦; closed May). You'll have two less expensive choices at **BORDES D'EN VALIRA**, 3km north, at the *Residència Supervalira* cited on p.213, and *Hotel Austria* (☎376 851 412; ⑥).

Next day you continue via the lake-spangled **Circ dels Pessons** to the **Clots (Ponds) de la Gargantillar**, where there is a refuge at **Estany l'Illa**. The next one – a more logical choice for an overnight – is *Refugi del Riu dels Orris* at **Pla de l'Ingla**, at the head of the beautiful **Madriu** valley. Here you can continue on the GR7 along the valley to Escaldes, or cut through the **Coll de la Maïana** to the west, reaching the Andorra la Vella–La Seu d'Urgell road near Santa Coloma.

West from the Ariège: the GR10/HRP

The routes **west** from the top of the Ariège into the Incles valley are beautiful approaches to the best Andorran landscape. From the train station at **Hospitalet-Près-l'Andorre**, the **HRP** variant initially climbs the Siscar valley, then switches to the Baldarques, going past the **Étang de Pedourrès** to the **Étang de Couart**, where it joins a path from Mérens-les-Vals.

Coming from **Mérens-les-Vals**, you can take the **GR10** southwest up the more inspiring **Mourgouillou valley**. After a little under two hours, the GR climbs west and to the right for a steepish climb of another ninety minutes to the modern, staffed *Refuge de Ruhle* (☎05.61.65.65.01; 2185m; 50 places; June–Sept; ③). For Andorra, go straight on, past the **Étang de Comte**, through the defile and over the chaos of boulders to link up with the HRP at the Étang de Couart. From the lake, amid bleak, rocky terrain, the HRP cuts through the Port de Juclars between the double **Estanys de Juclar** – just inside Andorra, with an emergency, unstaffed *refugi* (2310m, 50 places) – and then down to the head of the **Vall d'Incles**, where you can stay overnight at the campsite.

To avoid going down to Soldeu and the main road along the Valira del Orient, you should continue on the HRP to El Serrat, near the head of the Valira d'Ordino, and finally into France via the **Port de l'Abeille/Abella** or the **Port de Rat**. There are three ways to do this, which more or less parallel each other.

The easiest route is the most southerly, climbing west from the head of the Incles valley, dropping down into the head of the **Ransol valley** and up to the **Coll de la Mina**. A more difficult route passes the small *Refugi Cabana Sorda* (2250m; 8 places) on **Estany de Cabana Sorda**, then runs parallel to the base of the frontier peaks to Coll de la Mina. The hardest and wildest route goes north from Incles through the **Port de Fontargente** to the two Fontargente lakes, then curves west to re-enter Andorra through the **Port de Soulanet/Solaneta**.

Whichever one you choose, you can use the unstaffed **Refugi Borda de Sorteny** towards the end of the trek. From here it's a ten-minute walk to the top of the 4WD track 5km up from El Serrat. Extremists can manage the Incles–El Serrat hike in eight hours; others will take two days.

West from the Cerdanya: the GR11

From Spanish Cerdanya, the logical starting points are the villages of Meranges (see p.219) just south of the GR11, and Lles (see p.217), further west and well inside Lleida province. Either route occupies a fairly leisurely two days; the Meranges-based one is of better quality.

From Meranges, a rough track leads up to the *Refugi de Malniu* (☎938 257 104 or 616 855 535; 2200m; 32 places; ① plus 600ptas/€3.60 parking fee; snowshoe rental open sporadic weekends year-round, Easter break, late June to late Sept). The half-hour walk from the Malniu hut to its namesake lakes is the most popular family outing, but trekkers prefer the 2.5-hour jaunt northwest along the **GR11** to the FEEC-run *Refugi J Folch i Girona* (☎934 120 777; 2400m; same opening periods as Malniu hut), below the cluster of lakes in the Circ d'Engorgs. From the Engorgs area the route heads west into Lleida province, across the Llosa valley and past the crude **Cabana dels Esparvers**, entering Andorra and the Madriu valley via the **Port de Vall Civera** (2519m).

The less challenging route **from Lles** actually starts from the Cap del Rec cross-country ski area (see p.218), 6km north and above the village. From here, **GR11 variant 10** heads west-northwest for 2hr 45min to the scenic lakes and FEEC-managed *refugi* at **La Pera** (☎933 026 416; 2333m; staffed in summer; ①), though this route tangles repeatedly with the 4WD track (closed to cars Nov–May) which takes a roundabout 18km to get there. Beyond La Pera there's a proper trail north, slipping over the **Port de Perafita** (2587m), then down into the eponymous Andorran cirque, before rejoining the main GR11 near the bottom of the Madriu valley. The route then veers north-northeast, skimming above the Engolasters dam, to arrive at Encamp.

West out of Andorra: the HRP and GR11

There are several trails **west out of Andorra** towards the Montcalm-Estats-massif on the Franco-Spanish border; the main ones are the HRP from near El Serrat, initially into France, and the easier GR11 from Encamp directly to Spain.

The classic option begins at the ski station of Ordino-Arcalis, from which a clear trail – part of the HRP – climbs the short distance to **Port de Rat** (2542m) on the French frontier. From there you drop sharply to the track running south from the Soulcem dam, then climb equally steeply on the far side to the **Port de Bouet** (2520m) on the

Spanish border. Descend on the path west until you meet a track at the **Pla de Bouet/Boet** (camping possible); the *Refugi de Vall Ferrera* (☎933 026 416 or 973 624 378; 30 places; June to early Oct; ①) lies a few minutes' walk north. Even with a lift to the trailhead at Ordino-Arcalis, it's a challenging day of about seven walking hours; if you have to hoof it from El Serrat, add two hours more.

The **GR11** from Encamp passes through more developed areas, and has its fair share of roller-coastering, but facilities en route mean you can do without a tent if you make arrangements in advance. Allow just under two hours from Encamp to reach the **Coll d'Ordino** (1980m) on the minor Canillo-Ordino road; if you're starting from Canillo, a non-GR path about 1.5km south of that village also gives access to the pass. Descend west along the Segudet stream valley, then veer northwest away from Ordino through La Cortinada and Arans villages, nearly five hours into the day. You can use the recommended accommodation here (see p.211) if you don't fancy the sharp ascent up to the **Coll de les Cases** (1964m) the same day, with a gentler drop to Arinsal – just over seven hours' walking from Encamp.

From Arinsal you climb west into the valley of **Aigües Juntes**, in the very shadow of 2946-metre Alt de Coma Pedrosa, reaching after a couple of hours the *Refugi de Coma Pedrosa* (☎376 835 093 or 376 327 955; 2260m; June–late Sept; ①), Andorra's only staffed refuge, with sixty places, food and hot showers, five minutes' walk from the attractive Estany de les Truites. From the refuge you climb sharply northeast through the Circ de Coma Pedrosa, past Estany Negre, and then negotiate the **Port de Baiau** (2796m) where snow often remains until July. Once on the Spanish side, you face a steep, scree-laden descent to the lake and simple, unstaffed *Refugi Josep Maria Montfort* (ca. 2500m; 12 places) at the head of the **Baiau valley**, along which the GR11 bears northwest to intersect briefly with the HRP below the Port de Bouet, en route to the *Refugi de Vall Ferrera* (see p.260).

CERDANYA/CERDAGNE

Ringed by mountains, the fertile upland of the **Cerdanya** (Catalan) or **Cerdagne** (French) – about one-fifth of the way west along the Pyrenean watershed – has never quite been able to decide whether it is French or Spanish. The 1659 Treaty of the Pyrenees imposed nominal allegiances, which rather arbitrarily divided a region that considered itself Catalan in language and culture. Yet development of overt French or Spanish national consciousness, and a hardening of the notoriously porous frontier, was a long time coming. The French and Spanish languages didn't come into official use here until the early nineteenth century, following the French Revolution, a border war of 1793–95 and the Napoleonic campaigns. A formal boundary was marked for the first time only after the supplementary Treaty of Bayonne in 1866.

Essentially the basin of a prehistoric lake, once the largest in the Pyrenees, the Cerdanya/Cerdagne's traditional isolation and lack of natural frontiers has lent it an ambiguous identity. It's also inextricably linked with the **Carlit Massif** to the north, which has provided wood, pasturage and water from the very earliest times, and is thus usually considered part of the Cerdagne.

Because of its former military significance, good **roads** have long converged on the region. Mont-Louis, on the eastern fringe of the French Cerdagne, had a road – now the **N116** – in from Villefranche-de-Conflent as early as the seventeenth century, while Napoleon ordered the construction of the original **N20** from the north, terminating at Bourg-Madame. Spanish development lagged behind, but during the 1950s the **C1313** – alias the **N260** – was sealed from La Seu d'Urgell, west of the Spanish Cerdanya, as was the **C1411** from points south, both meeting at **Puigcerdà**, at the geographical centre of the region.

Because of its gentle terrain, the Cerdanya/Cerdagne supported the first – and now last-surviving – trans-Pyrenean **rail line**, between Barcelona and Toulouse via Puigcerdà and Latour-de-Carol. Threatened abolition of the service between Puigcerdà and Ripoll was only averted in 1985 by a massive Cerdan letter-writing campaign to Spanish Premier Felipe Gonzalez, coupled with half-serious threats by local authorities to request renegotiation of the Treaty of the Pyrenees and secession to France.

The Cerdanya

The name **Cerdanya** refers to the Spanish portion of the upper Segre valley (a high plateau which continues on the French side as far as Mont-Louis). To the north it is flanked by mountains rising to the Andorran frontier, dotted with tiny villages high above the Riu Segre, near the top of its tributary streams on sunny shoulders of land. On the southern side, the Cadí mountains form an impressive barrier, with more sleepy settlements tucked away at the base of the range. The frontier at **Puigcerdà** is connected by a six-kilometre road to the anomalous **Llívia**, former capital of the region and now a Spanish enclave in French territory. The Cerdanya remains marginally more rural and traditional than the French side, though it was already a popular summer holiday area for wealthy Barcelonans in the nineteenth century. Since the early 1990s this trend has accelerated, with blocks of holiday flats mushrooming at the edge of, and dwarfing, nearly every village. Skiing, both downhill and cross-country, remains the main impetus for all this construction; but golf, horse-riding, and even gliding and hot-air ballooning grow in popularity, the gently rolling countryside is ideal for such activities.

Martinet – and cross-country skiing resorts

Climbing from La Seu along the C1313/N260, which follows the Riu Segre upstream, the first place you're likely to leave a bus – or halt your transport – is **MARTINET**. The tracks from Estana village and the refuge at Prat d'Aguiló, in the Cadí foothills to the south, also emerge here. The Cadí's north face looks impregnable, but it's actually not that difficult to reverse the hiking directions given on p.201. Martinet is mostly strung uninspiringly along the through road, c/El Segre, but if you need to **stay** there are some good choices: *Fonda Pluvinet* at c/El Segre 13 (☎973 515 075; ③), with a few en-suite rooms, and the quieter, slightly larger *Fonda Miravet*, (☎973 515 016; ③), north of the highway on c/de les Arenes, with views across a little stream. If these are full, there's a *casa de pagès* in the nearby village of **MONTELLÀ**, 2km south and uphill: *Cal Zet* (☎973 515 105; ③). A meal stop in Martinet is positively recommended as both these accommodations have ground-floor **restaurants**; the *Pluvinet*'s (closed Sun eve & Mon) is excellent value at less than 2000ptas/€12 for *trinxat* or *cigrons*, salad, grilled rabbit and a simple sweet, all washed down by palatable house red.

Lles and Cap del Rec

From the western edge of Martinet a narrow paved road climbs steeply north to two villages, each the gateway to their respective cross-country skiing centres. It's 9km, bearing right at the fork just below it, to the somewhat higgledy-piggledy village of **LLES** (pronounced "Yes", officially "Lles de la Cerdanya"; 1471m), a good base for the popular ski centre 6km further on. The most reliable and comfortable **accommodation** and **eating** is at *Ca L'Abel* (☎973 515 048; ④), with newish, tile-floored units – the upstairs ones airy, with high ceilings – and a country-style restaurant adjacent. Otherwise, the *Fonda Domingo* (☎973 515 087; ③) at Travessera 4 near the top of the village also has some views and a pricey restaurant, while the *Hotel Mirador* at the top of the village by Sant Pere church (☎973 515 075; ⑤) seems only to work in peak seasons. The main local *casa de pagès*, *Casa Barber* (☎973 515 236; ③), opposite *Ca L'Abel* in the centre, is for once unattractive.

The **CAP DEL REC** cross-country ski resort at the road's end, exposed to the full glare of the sun at 1940m, has 29km of marked pistes; the *Refugi Eduard Jornet I Esteve* ☎973 293 050; 60 places; ①) here remains open in summer, with a local horse-riding centre and rental mountain bikes providing the means for exploring the myriad local tracks. From the refuge you're also well poised to enter Andorra on a two-day traverse via the Port de Perafita (see p.215).

Aransa

Returning to the fork 1.5km below Lles and then heading 4.5km northwest brings you to **ARÀNSA** (Arànser), much more of a piece architecturally than Lles, compactly set on a spur between two stream valleys, gazing at the Cadí's north wall. Right at the entrance to the village stand your two best **accommodation** choices: *Hostal Pas de la Pera* (☎973 515 001; ④), with a **restaurant**, and a *casa de pagès* opposite, *Cal Mariano* (☎973 515 191; ③), also offering half- or full board. The road continues to the Estanys de la Pera, via the Arànsa **cross-country ski station**, 6km along, with 32km of marked pistes between 1850m and 2150m, enjoying an easterly rather than the southerly orientation of Cap del Rec. There's food but no accommodation up at the station.

Bellver de Cerdanya

The next logical stop east from Martinet, about 8km further, would be **BELLVER DE CERDANYA**, standing on the bank of the trout-laden Segre, 18km west of Puigcerdà on the GR107. With a ruined castle and its sprinkling of old balconied houses, it's an easily accessible and thus "typical" mountain village, made doubly attractive by the Romanesque church of **Santa María de Talló**, a short stroll south of the town. Known locally as the "Cathedral of Cerdanya", this is a rather plain twelfth-century building, but has a few nice decorative touches in the nave and apse, and retains a wooden statue of the Virgin that's as old as the building itself.

Bellver has a **campsite** on its outskirts, *Solana del Segre* (☎973 510 310; open all year), which is quite pleasant by the standards of mammoth, caravan-biased Spanish sites, with tentable plots by the river. The **Turisme** in an old chapel at Plaça Sant Roc 9 (June–Sept Mon–Sat 11am–1pm & 6–8pm, Sun 11am–1pm; otherwise unreliable) can fill you in on other **accommodation** details. Three obvious dreary hostals up on the highway prove unappealing – a much better option is the *Fonda Biayna*, c/Sant Roc 11 (☎973 510 475, fax 973 510 853; ⑤ B&B), an atmospheric, rambling old mansion serving as an inn since 1880. The creaky-leany wood-floored rooms, all with small bathrooms, feature

---

AIRBORNE OVER THE CERDANYA

Beders is easiest reached via Bor, home to Baló Baló (☎619 209 208), one of the area's two **ballooning** outfitters: it's a slightly extravagant undertaking for groups of two to five on one- or two-hour flights. Their competition, Globus del Pirineu (☎972 140 852 or 639 631 264), based at the little airstrip north of Alp, more ambitiously offer long-duration balloon journeys across much of the Pyrenees, plus **flights** in microlights, gliders, and two- to four-person biplanes. These cost 6000ptas/€36 per person for a biplane loop over the Cerdanyan plain; 9600ptas/€58 a head to fly over the Carlit lakes or the Cadí valleys. Glider flights are 14,000ptas/€84 per passenger (max 2); should you wish to pilot a glider yourself, courses start at 240,000ptas/€1440.

antique furnishings and mostly double beds. There's a downstairs bar that is the heart and soul of the village even in low season, and an adjacent *menjador*. Among other restaurants, you could also try *Jou Vell* (closed Thurs & Oct) across the square from the Turisme, or *Mas Marti*, about 3km east in the hamlet of **BEDERS** (open weekends Easter, 24 Dec–6 Jan, and daily late July to late August; ☎973 510 022), which mixes French and local cuisine to good effect for about 3500ptas/€21 per person.

Meranges and Guils Fontanera

From Ger, about halfway between Bellver and Puigcerdà, a narrow road leads 10km northwest to **MERANGES**, past hayfields, hamlets and copses of silver birch and maple. Set at 1540m, the village was once important to the smuggling trade, but is too remote for the second-home complexes that ring neighbouring villages. The only place to **stay** is the prestigious two-star *Hotel Can Borrell* (☎972 880 033, fax 972 880 144; may close mid-Jan to Easter; ⑦), a converted farmhouse which retains rustic decor in its variable-sized rooms, and includes a well-regarded restaurant. The alternative for **dining** is the rather basic but inexpensive *Can Joan* in the village centre, which no longer offers accommodation. Overall, Meranges proves an idyllic place below a pair of lake-filled basins at the foot of **Pic Farinós** and **Puig Pedrós**; for details on visiting these cirques, and traversing west to Andorra on the GR11, see p.215.

Just before arrival in Puigcerdà, another minor road heads northwest to **GUILS DE CERDANYA**, a small village too close to the big town to have many tourist facilities of its own. It is, however, home to the newest and most ambitious **cross-country ski resort** in the Cerdanya, **Guils Fontanera**, with 45km of marked pistes.

Puigcerdà

Although founded by King Alfonso I of Aragón in 1177 as a new capital for then-unified Cerdanya, **PUIGCERDÀ** (pronounced "Poocherda") retains no compelling medieval monuments, partly owing to heavy bombing during the Civil War. The church of Santa Maria no longer exists, a wartime casualty, but its forty-metre-high **bell-tower** still stands in the namesake *plaça*. The east end of town, down the pleasant, tree-lined Passeig Deu d'Abril, escaped more lightly; here, you can see medieval murals in the gloomy parish church of **Sant Domènec**. Dwelling morbidly on the saint's martyrdom, surviving fragments show Dominic's head being cloven in two by a sabre – he's already been run through by a sword thrust – while another monk has a bloody sword through his skull. The renovated thirteenth-century convent next door is now used as a local cultural and youth centre; work continues to restore what's left of the medieval cloisters behind.

The town's greatest attraction is its atmosphere – if you've just arrived from France, the attractive streets and squares, with busy pavement cafés and well-stocked shops, present a marked contrast to moribund Bourg-Madame. Allow at least enough time for a meal or an evening in a bar, though Puigcerdà does not offer much value in budget accommodation. French day-trippers certainly approach it this way, crowding out the bars and eateries during summer. Enjoyable outdoor cafés line the merged squares of Santa María and dels Herois; between drinks, you can explore the old quarter between Plaça de l'Ajuntament and Passeig Deu d'Abril, or amble up to a small lake, five minutes' walk north.

Arrival and accommodation

Puigcerdà is on the main rail line from Barcelona to Latour-de-Carol (normally 6 trains a day in either direction). From the **train station** (outside which buses also stop) in Plaça de l'Estació, wearyingly steep steps lead up to Plaça de l'Ajuntament in the heart of town, with reviving views west over the Cerdanya. At the top of the steps, to the right, stands

the newish **Casa de la Vila**, a replacement for the Gothic original destroyed in the Civil War, with the central **Turisme** alongside at c/Querol 1 (June–mid-Sept daily 9am–2pm & 3–8pm; mid-Sept–May Mon 9am–1pm, Tues–Sat 10am–1pm & 4–7pm; ☎972 880 542), which dispenses useful brochures. However, you're more or less expected to use the giant **regional branch** (summer same hours, mid-Sept–May Mon–Sat 9am–1pm & 4–7pm, Sun 10am–2pm), 1500m southwest of town near the *Puigcerdà Park Hotel* particularly well stocked with leaflets and more convenient with your own transport.

There's no advantage whatsoever in staying at the obvious **accommodation** near the train station, though attrition has recently taken its toll on the number of town-centre establishments (there are good alternatives in the villages around Puigcerdà, see pp.221–222). Acceptable options among the surviving, less expensive places include *Hostal La Muntanya*, c/Coronel Molera 1 (☎972 880 202; ③), close to Plaça Barcelona, fairly quiet and good value; the very central, two-star *Hostal Alfonso*, c/d'Espanya 5 (☎972 880 246; ④), also cheap and friendly; the *Hostal Residència Rita Belvedere* at c/Carmelites 6–8 (☎972 880 356; ③–⑤), offering excellent views and a choice of old-style or more expensive modern rooms. For a mild splurge, there's none better than the garden-set *Hotel del Lago*, Avda. Dr Puiguillém (☎972 881 000 or 972 141 511; ⑦ B&B), just off Plaça Barcelona towards the lake.

None of the three local **campsites** is really appropriate for tenters, but for the record they are the giant *Stel* (☎972 882 361; open all year), with bungalows for rent, 2km out of Puigcerdà on the road to Llívia, just before you cross into France; the shady but caravan-haunted *Pirineus* (☎972 881 062; open all year) 3km northeast of town, beyond the train station, towards Guils; and the *Queixans* (☎972 141 280; open all year) in the eponymous village 5km south, again dominated by caravans but probably the most pleasantly set, and with cabins available.

Eating and drinking

Passing French tourists are responsible for the relatively high prices and bland menus in Puigcerdà, but there are still a number of reasonable places to eat. At the budget end, *Sant Remo* at c/Ramon Cosp 9 is a straightforward if slightly divey bar offering large *menús* at 1100ptas/€6.60 and 1400ptas/€8.40. *La Cantonada* at c/Major 46, beyond the bell-tower, has acceptable though not superlative three-course *menús* with a drink (1300ptas/€7.80), but more attractive surroundings; the *Carmen* nearby on Plaça de Santa Maria, with an upstairs *menjador*, is similar. For a jump in standards in the same area, head for the fancier *La Cachimba* on c/Beates, which serves pizzas as well.

The **bars** with outdoor seating on Plaça dels Herois and the adjoining Plaça de Santa Maria – in particular the adjacent *Kennedy* and *Miami Dos* – are usually busy, okay for a drink and *tapas*, though not very distinguished for full meals. The *Cervesseria Claude* on arcaded Plaça Cabrinetty styles itself as an international beer specialist, and if you're so inclined you can sit indoors or out, tippling your way around the world's breweries.

Finally, Puigcerdà has the only **cinemas** in the Cerdanya, both with first-run programming: the co-managed Avinguda at c/Major 53, and the Cerretà, installed in the old casino on Plaça Barcelona.

Villages around Puigcerdà

You'll find better-value accommodation, and often food, in the hamlets and villages south of Puigcerdà, home to some of the more distinguished members of Girona province's *turisme rural* scheme.

Top billing goes to the superb *Residència Sant Marc*, 1.5km south of town on the road to **Les Pereres** hamlet (☎972 880 007 or 936 322 260; open all year; ⑥ B&B or ⑦ HB). This 150-hectare stud farm is focused on the eponymous *ermita* and 1913-vintage Belle Époque mansion which purveys three-star elegance in old-fashioned but unmusty units (including an attic family suite): antique furniture, wood floors, artistic tiles in the large bathrooms. Though owned by a wealthy Barcelona medical family, it's currently managed by friendly Bolivians who warn of no vacancy between July 15 and September 1 without advance booking.

Equestrian holidays are also offered in unspoilt **AGE**, 2km east of Les Pereres or 3km southeast of Puigcerdà, at *Cal Marrufès/Hípica Age* (☎972 141 174, *www.calmarrufes.com*; open all year; ⑤ B&B). This brand new, tasteful restoration of an old stone-built farm in the village centre recently expanded to include four-person suites (11,800ptas/€70.90) as well as conventional doubles.

If you're not of the horsey disposition, you might prefer sleepy **URTX** 5km south of Puigcerdà, which unlike most Cerdanyan villages has yet to be disfigured by new apartments. Here *Cal Mateu* (☎972 890 495; ④ B&B) is part of a working dairy farm; the good-value en-suite rooms with full-sized bathtubs are bland modern rather than rustic, the breakfast served near the fireplace in the common room is average continental. Self-catering is available, however, and the managing couple are disarmingly friendly; they advise booking far in advance for July–October and Christmas–New Year.

Urtx may have no holiday homes, but it hasn't any other facilities either; closest good **eats** are 1500m downhill inside the semi-converted Queixans RENFE station, where

Several daily **trains** cross the border, northwest to Latour-de-Carol, six minutes away, but only three have instant connections for Toulouse (4hr), and just one does for Paris (12hr). If you're **driving**, you enter France via the adjacent small town of Bourg-Madame (see p.226); it's also a simple matter to walk across to Bourg-Madame, 2km from the centre of Puigcerdà. The border is open 24 hours, year round, and controls are now nonexistent, with the customs/immigration booths typically unstaffed.

L'Estació (closed Wed) offers cheap lunch *menús* as well as *a la carta* at 2000–2500ptas/€12–15 per head. Portions of *escalibada* and *botifarra amb mongetes* aren't huge, but the ingredients are palpably fresh, the presentation exemplary.

Your final Puigcerdà-environs choice is in resolutely rural **SANAVASTRE**, accessible *only* from Alp (not from the main highway to La Seu). At the edge of the village, tucked in a hollow just beyond the airstrip runway, *Can Simó* (☎972 890 240; open all year; ⑤ B&B or ⑥ HB) is another engagingly rustic cow-farm which hasn't been overly restored, though most units are en-suites.

Llívia

The Spanish town of **LLÍVIA**, 6km from Puigcerdà but totally surrounded by French territory, is a curious place indeed. There are several **buses** daily from Puigcerdà (the Alsina Graells coach stops in front of the train station and in Plaça Barcelona), but the ninety-minute walk out isn't too strenuous: bear left at the junction 1km outside town, just before the border at Bourg-Madame, keeping to the main road. From French territory, the turn-off to Llívia is completely unmarked; your only clue is the highway overpass above the *Train Jaune* tracks.

French history books claim that Llívia's anomalous status resulted from an oversight. According to the traditional version of events, in the exchanges that followed the Treaty of the Pyrenees the French delegates insisted on possession of the 33 Cerdan villages between the Ariège and newly acquired Roussillon. The Spanish agreed, then pointed out that Llívia was technically a town not a village, and thus excluded under the terms of the handover. Llívia had in fact been capital of the valley until the foundation of Puigcerdà, and Spain had every intention of retaining it at the negotiations, which were held in Llívia itself.

The Romans were perhaps the first to recognize the strategic value of the site, and named their settlement Julia Livia. The castle was destroyed on the orders of Louis XI in 1479, but there's still a strong medieval feel to the centre of town, not least in the fifteenth-century fortified **church** (June–Sept daily 10am–1pm & 3–7pm; Oct–May Tues–Sun 10am–1pm & 3–6pm), which boasts a curious nail-reinforced door and carved stone floor. Inside is a beautiful gilt altarpiece, delicately carved and painted with cherubs and scenes from the Nativity, and (in the middle side chapel on the left) an unadorned crucifix, the *Cristo de Transición,* a fine example of the Romanesque-Gothic transitional style. Since 1982, an increasingly popular music festival has been held in and around the church on August weekends.

Opposite the church, the unusual **Museu Municipal** (April–Sept Tues–Sat 10am–1pm & 3–7pm, Sun 10am–2pm; Oct–March Tues–Sat 10am–1pm & 3–6pm, Sun 10am–2pm; 200ptas) contains the interior of the oldest pharmacy in Europe, functioning in Llívia from 1594 until 1918. Displays accordingly emphasize apothecarial pots and hand-painted boxes of herbs, as well as local Bronze Age relics, old maps and an eighteenth-century bell mechanism from the church. The entry ticket also gets you into the fifteenth-century **Tour Bernat de So**, adjoining the church and home to the sporadically functioning **Turisme**. The rest of the town is nowhere near as atmospheric as this medieval kernel, though the square kilometres of ski chalets are at least faced in local stone and wood.

Practicalities

Most visitors just stay long enough for a **meal** – not a bad idea given the limited choice of accommodation. In the main Plaça Major at no. 1, there's the attractive *Can Ventura* restaurant (closed Mon eve & Tues), with flower-filled balconies adorning an eighteenth-century building, where Cerdanyan cuisine with the freshest ingredients starts at a mildly extravagant 4000ptas/€24 (no *menú*). *Can Marcel-li*, visible just up the hill at c/Frederic Bernades 7, has a pleasant dining room above the bar serving a *menú* (1600ptas/€9.60). Still further up the slope near the church, *Can Francesc* at c/dels Forns 7–15 has courtyard dining in summer, and good-value fare – a *menú* (1650ptas/€9.90) includes *trinxat*, trout, local yogurt, decent house wine and a coffee.

The few places to **stay** tend to fill quickly and you'll need a reservation during much of the year. Least expensive is *Can Marcel-li* (☎972 146 096; ④), with a few en-suite doubles – ask at the bar. There seems little point in staying at the pair of much more expensive hotels on the busy main road below the old quarter – you'll do much better for the money in the *cases rurals* around Puigcerdà.

The Cerdagne

The **Cerdagne** is the sunniest area in the French Pyrenees; the ripe colours of summer grain and hay on its treeless, rolling hills reinforce this impression. It is bracketed on the west by **Bourg-Madame**, virtually adjacent to Spanish Puigcerdà, and on the east by Mont-Louis at the head of the Têt valley, the plateau's usual point of entry from the French side. To the southeast rises **Puigmal**, one source of the River Sègre, while the northwestern flank is formed by the mountains of the **Carlit Massif**, which provides the pistes for the overrated ski station of **Font-Romeu** but also offers excellent walks.

The *Train Jaune* (see p.115) continues from Mont-Louis as far as **Latour-de-Carol**, from where regular train services run north into the Ariège under the **Col de Puymorens**. The road which snaked over the pass until 1995 now runs through the Tunnel de Puymorens.

Font-Romeu and around

Sprawling at the foot of Roc de la Calme, at the southeast corner of the Carlit Massif, **FONT-ROMEU** (the *Train Jaune* station is Odeillo/Via) is one of the most famous ski resorts in the Pyrenees. Ski brochures make much of its *Cité Préolympique*, without revealing that its main purpose was altitude training for the 1968 Mexico Olympics. Its top station is a mere 2200m, the maximum vertical descent just 500m. Adjacent Superbolquère, now better known as **PYRÉNÉES 2000**, is no higher and of an ugliness exceeded only by other purpose-built French winter resorts. The two linked resorts have forty pistes between them, but drag lifts predominate; the vast majority of the runs are for beginners, and only a handful are north-facing (holding good long-term snow), which is why it has 460 snow-canons (the most in Europe). It does, however, have more than 80km of marked cross-country skiing trails – the second biggest extent in the French Pyrenees.

In summer Font-Romeu keeps its holidaymakers occupied with an Olympic-sized swimming pool and the usual assortment of sporting facilities. Year round there's plenty of nightlife, with several clubs and discos, plus a casino. If that's what you want from your ski resort, Font-Romeu fits the bill perfectly, but if you're looking for a place with a mountain soul, give it a wide berth.

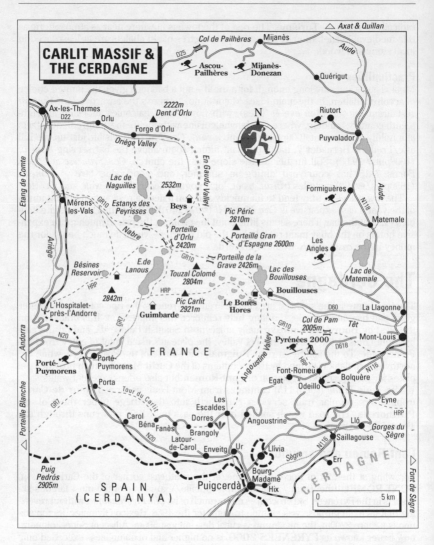

CARLIT MASSIF & THE CERDAGNE

The Ermitage

Font-Romeu is Catalan for "pilgrim's spring" – the legend of the town's foundation tells of a cowherd uncovering a buried figure of the Virgin and a source of clear water, having been led to the spot by a bull. Just a stroll from the main town, off av Emmanuel Brousse, the Virgin has been installed in the barracks-like **Ermitage**, (daily early-July to early-Sept 10am–noon & 3–6pm), a seventeenth-century enlargement of the original fourteenth-century shrine. The Catalan artist Josep Sunyer sculpted the retable in 1707, and five years later created a sumptuous "bedroom" for the Virgin, known as the *camaril*.

On September 8 the Virgin is taken down the hill to **ODEILLO**, returning on Trinity Sunday. Odeillo has the only other "sight" of the immediate area – the **Four Solaire**, or solar power station (daily 10am–12.30pm & 2–6pm, July & Aug 10am–6pm; 30F/€4.60). It no longer functions as a generator, but rather as a museum and PR exercise, with full-moon-powered demonstrations on summer evenings.

Practicalities

From the **train station** it's a fairly steep two-kilometre walk north to Font-Romeu, passing Odeillo about halfway. **Accommodation** in Font-Romeu tends to be expensive, but with eighteen thousand beds you should find something. For a list of holiday apartments ask at the **tourist office** (daily 9am–12.30pm & 2–6.30pm; ☎04.68.30.68.30, *www.font-romeu-station.com*) near the top of av Emmanuel Brousse. In the central area, the *L'Homme des Neiges*, av Emmanuel Brousse (☎04.68.30.07.76; ③), has self-catering facilities instead of a restaurant; the higher rates are for winter. Among hotels, the two-star *Le Regina*, av Emmanuel Brousse (☎04.68.30.03.81, fax 04.68.30.12.00; ⑥), is also open year round, while west of town the *Hôtel Y Sem Bé* (☎04.68.30.00.54, fax 04.68.30.25.42; ⑥) enjoys views over much of the Cerdagne.

Southwest to Latour-de-Carol

Beyond Odeillo, the *Train Jaune* winds its way across the wide open plain to the south side of the Cerdagne to depopulated **SAILLAGOUSE** (1302m), where you can stay at the **youth hostel** (☎04.68.04.71.69; ①), or the *Hôtel Planes*, place de Cerdagne (☎04.68.04.72.08, fax 04.68.04.75.93; ⑤), and **eat** at either the *Planes* or the *Christiana*, also in the village. At the edge of the village you'll also find two **campsites**, *Le Sègre* (☎04.68.04.74.72; open all year) and *Le Cerdan* (☎04.68.04.70.46; closed Nov).

From Saillagouse there's a glorious walk available through the **Gorges du Sègre**. After a couple of kilometres the hiking route passes through the extremely picturesque village of **LLÓ**, where there are no facilities besides the three-star *Auberge Atalaya* (☎04.68.04.70.04, fax 04.68.04.01.29; ⑤), providing expensive accommodation and more affordable high-quality meals, with the first *menu* at 85F/€13. From here an easy track climbs through the gorge to the well-placed but extremely basic and unstaffed *Refuge de la Culasse*, after which the track becomes a path to the **Col de Finestrelles** (2604m), above Núria in Spanish Catalonia (see p.181). From the *col* there are three attractive choices: drop back southwest to the **Font de Sègre**, 400m below the 2795-metre summit of **Pic de Sègre** (it's a day from Lló to the *font* and back); carry on into Spain; or pick up the **HRP** along the crests.

Err and Puigmal 2600

The next *Train Jaune* stop serves **ERR**, a tiny village at the foot of heavily wooded Puigmal – and another place with a "found Virgin" legend. The twelfth-century effigy is housed in the **Chapelle de la Vierge**, considerably enlarged in the eighteenth century. Separated from it by the cemetery is the church of **Saint-Genis**, which an almost indecipherable inscription says is the burial place of Bishop Radulf of Urgell, a close relative of Guifré el Pilos of Ripoll.

The only accommodation option at Err is its *gîte d'étape* (☎04.68.04.74.20; ①). For a quick start to a hike you can call **taxis** here (☎04.68.04.70.18) or in Saillagouse (☎04.68.04.00.46).

Some 7km southeast of Err, on the north slopes of 2913-metre Puigmal, is **PUIGMAL 2600**, one of the smaller of the Cerdagne's ski stations. But the top point is nearly as high as its name implies, and 19 runs, the majority red and black, end most of their descents scenically amongst the pines. There are no snow canons, so check conditions before setting out.

Bourg-Madame and Hix

Skirting Llívia, the *Train Jaune* reaches the border at **BOURG-MADAME**, which in 1815 changed its name from Les Guinguettes d'Hix to honour the wife of the duc d'Angoulême, bearer of the title "Madame Royale". It became an important trading town over the course of the eighteenth century, both as a smuggler's *entrepôt* and legitimate competitor to Puigcerdà. But it hasn't amounted to much since then, and insofar as EU unification reducing the importance of national borders, Bourg-Madame is visibly depressed and fading, its vitality sapped by its more favoured neighbour. There are no **hotels** cheaper than the two-star *Celisol* (☎04.68.04.53.70; ⑤), though you've a choice of three **campsites**, all open year round: *Le Sègre* on route de Toulouse (☎04.68.04.65.87), the *Caravaneige Mas Piques* (☎04.68.04.62.11) and a basic place 4km north, between the Llívia side road and the village of Ur. Simple meals are available at *Snack Bar Le Catalan*, on the train station's access road.

Just to the east, **HIX**, now virtually part of Bourg-Madame, was the summer home of the counts of Cerdagne; its eleventh-century chapel, considered one of the oldest Romanesque structures in the area, has a delicacy which only such early examples display.

Latour-de-Carol/Enveitg

From Bourg-Madame, Puigcerdà is plainly visible on its hill; it's quicker (and cheaper) to get off the *Train Jaune* here and walk across the border. If you stay on board, the line ends fifteen minutes further at the Gare Internationale of **LATOUR-DE-CAROL/ENVEITG**, the interchange for trains south to Barcelona and north for Toulouse. Six well-spaced daily trains (currently 8.19am, 10.40am, 1.11pm, 4.33pm, 6.44pm, 8.34pm) cross the border **into Spain**.

The train station lies between the two villages, though it's actually much closer (700m) to the larger Enveitg – though neither is much bigger than the vast railyards of the international exchange itself. Because this is the main road between Spain and the Ariège, some very tacky **hotels** can get away with charging too much. It's best to stay at Enveitg's *Hôtel Transpyrénéen* (☎04.68.04.81.05, fax 04.68.04.83.75; ⑥), between the Enveitg village centre and the station. You can **camp** at the riverside *Municipal de l'Oratory* in Latour-de-Carol (☎04.68.04.83.70; open all year), or the more expensive *Caravaneige Le Robinson* in Enveitg (☎04.68.04.80.38; open all year).

Northwest to the Col de Puymorens

The long debate over whether or not to tunnel **Col de Puymorens** (1920m), high in the mountains northwest of Latour, was finally decided by the imminent single European market. The new tunnel was completed in 1995 and the faster toll road – like the railway – now disappears under the *col* to reappear in the Ariège (cars 40F/€6.10 one way, 50F/€7.60 return).

Porta

On the way up to the pass you'll see the much-photographed but seldom-visited towers at Carol, all that's left of a castle built to defend the Cerdagne from Foix. Near the top of the climb, 13km from Latour, the village of **PORTA** has a sporadically functioning *gîte d'étape*, *La Pastorale* (☎04.68.04.83.92; ①), which serves the **GR7**. If this is closed, there's only the *Auberge du Campcardos* (☎04.68.04.82.26; ①), whose restaurant staff can be surly and the food overpriced – it's best to **eat** at *Auberge la Cajole*. All these amenities are on the main road, not in the pretty old quarter slightly uphill. Hikers need to come supplied, as there's no store.

Usson château

Santa Maria monastery, Ripoll

Camprodon

MARC S. DUBIN

Nôtre-Dame-de-Pictat chapel, Saint Savin

MARC S. DUBIN

MARC S. DUBIN

The Núria Gorge

Besiberri and Estany Negre, Aigüestortes National Park

Andorra: Port d'en Valira

Montségur village and castle

St-Aventin church, Luchon area

La Seu de Urguell

Refuge Hut, Wallow, Vallée du Marcadau

Porté-Puymorens

The nearby ski station above the village of **PORTÉ-PUYMORENS** – locally referred to as Porté, and thus easily confused with Porta – is probably the best the French Catalan Pyrenees has to offer. While the Col de Puymorens marks the shift from the arid Cerdagne to the damp Ariège, a lot of snow often falls on the Cerdan side and stays there, protected from the worst of the wind. The 17 runs here are fairly evenly distributed amongst all difficulties, with top points at a respectable 2400m and 2500m, and four well-placed chairlifts. There are also 25km of trails for *ski de fond*, a snowboarders' "surf park", and a whole gamut of non-ski leisure facilities (horse-riding, bike trails and fitness). The village itself has a nice valley setting, off the main highway, and horse-riding facilities.

Developers have big plans for **hotels** here; for the moment, there's just the *Hôtel Restaurant du Col* (☎04.68.04.82.06, fax 04.68.04.87.22; ⑥) down in the village, plus two others including the *Michette*, which sells maps. The valley-bottom **campsite** *La Rivière* (☎04.68.04.82.20) is open all year, but you'd have to be a polar bear to stay in winter.

Overall, Porté has a bit more going for it than Porta; the **GR7** east into the Carlit Massif is easy to find at the far end of the village. The path presents the gentlest grade into the Carlit, but it is also the most spoiled western approach, what with overhead cable-cars, various damworks and the generally dull topography. For an alternate trailhead for Carlit, you might consider L'Hospitalet (for the HRP) or Mérens-le-Vals (for the GR10), both slightly north on the Latour–Toulouse rail line (see "The upper Ariège" p.232).

The Carlit Massif

The granite ridges of the lake-spangled **Carlit Massif** occupy a compact area just north of the Cerdanya/Cerdagne, the last truly alpine region of the Pyrenees – east of here, Canigou notwithstanding, only foothills undulate on the horizon. Being easy of access, these mountains are popular; the lakes – even when not dammed – can be a little overly manicured. The massif's upland marshes have been disrupted by EDF dams which manipulate water levels, most notably at Lac des Bouillouses and several other reservoirs. There are still some relatively unspoiled corners however, and ample scope for several days of trekking or scrambling.

The ascent of **Pic Carlit** (2921m) is within the capabilities of any reasonably fit person, especially from Lac des Bouillouses on its eastern slopes. Three major walking routes – the **HRP**, the north–south **GR7** and the trans-Pyrenean **GR10** – as well as marked secondary trails cross the massif, while segments of the GR7 and GR10 comprise sections of the less demanding **Tour du Carlit**. For all of these explorations you'll want the IGN 1:50,000 *Carte de Randonnées no. 7*, "Cerdagne-Capcir"; the IGN TOP 25 no. 2249 ET is also well worth having.

Traverses and alpine loops

The three western **trailhead villages** are Mérens-les-Vals (p.232), L'Hospitalet-près-l'Andorre (p.232) and Porté (above). Each of the suggested routes converge near the centre of the range, close to the focal Porteille d'Orlu.

From Porté, the GR7 leaves the village at the first hairpin, climbing gradually east and then north towards the grey concrete wall of the **Lanous** dam, four hours from Porté – not a particularly aesthetic trip. Just beyond, at the entrance to the Fourats valley, the decrepit, three-person *Refuge de la Guimbarde* (unstaffed) overlooking the reservoir, is only useful in dire emergencies. Most people prefer to camp on the grass below, or get an early enough start from Porté to finish the day at a more exciting spot. The GR7 continues northeast for another ninety minutes above the lakeshore, initially quite steeply, before joining the GR10 which cuts roughly east-west across the top of the lake from the easy pass of Porteille de la Grave.

From Mérens-les-Vals, the GR10 climbs sharply up the **Nabre valley** to reach the staffed **Refuge des Bésines** (☎05.61.05.22.44; 2104m; 50 places; ①), next to the Bésines reservoir in something over five hours; the HRP **from L'Hospitalet-près-l'Andorre** gets you there in roughly half the time. There are no more refuges east of Bésines towards the GR10/GR7 intersection, only a limited number of **campsites** at the north end of Lanous.

From Lanous, the climb up the south grade of the **Porteille d'Orlu** is deceptively easy, but once up top the Carlit reveals its other uncompromising nature in the view north: granite spires, giant boulder falls and drifting cloud. It's vital to keep west here for the grassy route skirting the **Étang de Feury**, avoiding the deadly rocks. At Feury a nameless variant heads west via the **Porteille de Madides** (2.5km) to shortcut the GR10, joining the latter at Courals de la Présasse and allowing rapid descent to Mérens-les-Vals.

Even if the mist doesn't close in, you'll still need about three hours to descend northeast from the Porteille d'Orlu along the often poorly marked GR7 to **Étang d'en Beys** (1980m), a natural lake surrounded by scree, pasture and clumps of rhododendron. Here the useful **refuge** managed by the Orlu municipality(☎05.61.64.24.24; 45 places; June–Sept; ①) is strategically located below the intersection of several traverse routes.

From the lake it's about two hours down to the end of the road tracing the **Oriège valley**, three hours coming uphill, but it's strongly suggested that you elect another way to finish a traverse or circuit. Particularly if you have left a vehicle at Lac des Bouillouses (see below), which lies one day's reasonable march via the Porteille de la Grave, you can return another way. Some twenty minutes below the lake, you part with the GR7 and adopt a cairned and paint-splodged (but unnamed) route which curls around through the **Porteille Gran d'Espagne** (2600m), before descending through a lake-speckled valley enclosed by 2810-metre **Pic Péric** to Bouillouses, all within six hours.

If you're going to finish a traverse in the Oriège valley (see p.233), you might reduce the amount of road-tramping by following yet another anonymous but marked route up to the easy **Couillade de Beys** (2345m), then descend past the easterly **Peyrisse** lake to the **Naguille reservoir**, finally dropping by track to the Forges d'Orlu in about five hours.

Climbing the peak

If you're merely intent on bagging the summit of Pic Carlit, a quick approach can be made from Mont-Louis **on the east** side, up the very narrow but paved D60 road. During peak season, private cars are banned from the 13km of access road up to **Lac des Bouillouses** – you must park near the bottom and take a *navette* most of the way. For purist hikers who don't mind a long slog, the **GR10** out of Bolquère climbs gently through woods to the **Col del Pam** (2005m), where it links with the HRP coming from Font-Romeu; both continue past ski lifts and pistes to Lac des Bouillouses (5hr from either town).

There's plenty of **accommodation** and **food** at the Bouillouses lake, actually a huge reservoir dating from the early 1900s. The CAF-run *Refuge des Bouillouses*, formerly *Combaleran* (☎04.68.04.20.76; 40 places; dorm ①, rooms ⑥ HB) is the cheapest option, east of the dam wall at just under 2000m. Tucked inconspicuously behind this is the smallish, privately managed *Auberge du Carlit* (☎04.68.04.22.23; dorm ①, rooms ③), with *menus* hovering around 100F/€15.30. As in nearly all of the restaurants in this area, regional food dominates the *cartes*, including solid but simple meat dishes, with occasional flourishes, such as *poulet catalan*, served in a thick tomato and mushroom sauce. Just above the west end of the dam at 2050m looms the gigantic *Refuge Le Bones Hores* (☎04.68.04.24.22, fax 04.68.04.13.63; ⑦ HB), popular with families.

Beside *Refuge Le Bones Hores*, where a placard informs fishermen which lakes are legally open, you get on the **HRP**, whose course is scantily marked with faded paint splodges but deeply grooved into the terrain and sometimes cairned. You arc up gently through the woods, between **Étang Noir** and **Étang Vive**, twenty minutes along; the next natural lake, **Dougues**, is just 45 minutes above the dam, and thus a hugely popular outing. The crowds will thin out as you press on past the necklace of smaller lakes – Casteilla, Trébens and Soubirans – under the shadow of **Touzal Colomé** (2804m), and finally up the ridge that leads to the summit from the east. This is a superb climb, the tarns glinting in the sun, the grass green in June but a faded ochre by August, and the scree-strewn pyramid of Carlit overhead. There and back from Lac des Bouillouses is at most six-and-a-half hours, an easy day's walk in good conditions – though rather ominously there are green sheds by most of the lakes to shelter from the foul weather which frequently appears without warning. If you just want to take in the lakes, it's only a three-hour round-trip from the dam to the highest one, Soubirans, at 2320m.

From the west, the ascent of Carlit is a little more difficult, a good four hours one way starting in the vicinity of the derelict *Refuge de la Guimbarde*, close to the Lanous dam (see p.227). Again using HRP cairns and blazes, follow the **Fourats valley** east to its tiny lake and then keep going straight to the summit, or if that looks too formidable, bear away towards the *col* on the south and approach the summit along the line of the ridge, dropping a little way down the eastern slope when the ridge gets too narrow.

The Tour du Carlit

The **Tour du Carlit**, aimed at hikers of medium experience, is meant to take three days, much of it by track through lower altitude zones. If you're coming by regular train, the easiest places to pick up the circuit are at Porta or Porté-Puymorens. If you're on the *Train Jaune*, get off at Béna-Fanès, the stop before Latour-de-Carol, and try to hitch the 6km up to Béna.

From Porta you begin with a short day's walk southeast over the grimly named Col de l'Homme Mort (2300m) to **BÉNA**, a delightful hamlet with an equally wonderful *gîte d'étape* (☎04.68.04.81.64; ①), housed in a restored *mas* or Catalan farmhouse. You could lengthen the day by pressing along the track east, via the hamlets of **Fanès** and **Brangoly**, to the attractive and well-positioned village of **DORRES**, which offers the characterful *Hotel-Restaurant Marty* (☎04.68.30.07.52; ⑤) and a public outdoor hot spring for bathing (daily 8am–9pm, later in summer; 15F/400ptas/€2.40). The second day is less enchanting as you skirt the spa of Les Escaldes to thread north through the Angoustrine valley on dirt track, before linking with the GR10 at **Lac des Bouillouses**. The third day's walking follows the GR10 west over the gentle **Porteille de la Grave** (2426m), alongside the infant River Têt, to intersect the GR7; you then reverse the directions given above under "Traverses and alpine loops" (p.227–228) in a descent to Porté.

THE ARIÈGE AND THE PAYS DE SAULT

Draining north from the Col du Puymorens the **Ariège valley** is one of the most depressed areas of France, with low income levels, high unemployment and an aging population. Coming directly from the Cerdanya, where the disposable incomes of Barcelonans and Gironans have a striking impact on the landscape, a visitor could be mistaken for thinking Spain the wealthier country. Unsurprisingly, perhaps, the

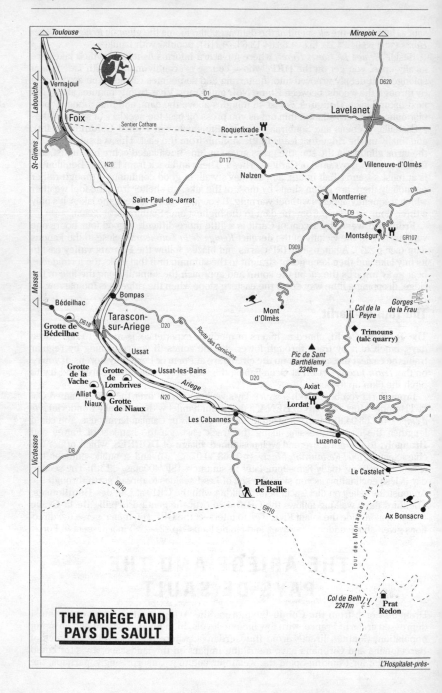

THE ARIÈGE AND
PAYS DE SAULT

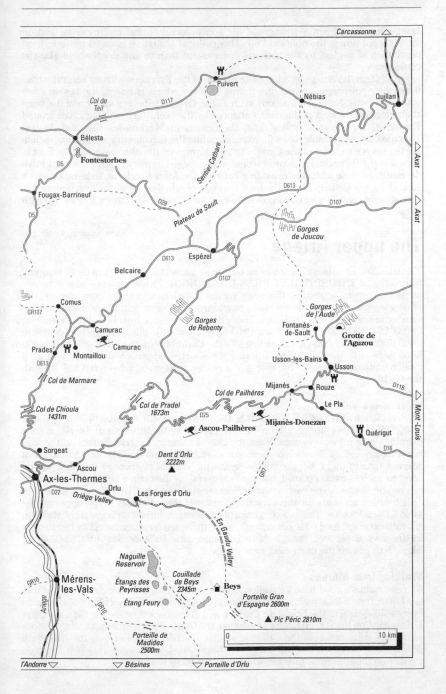

Ariège has long been a stronghold for nonconformists and antiroyalists, and, in more recent times, the political Left. This political affiliation is owed more to local perception of neglect by the national government than to any deeply held Marxist convictions.

For visitors the Ariège is a favourite corner of the Pyrenees with its natural attractions, their patronage sustaining a tourist industry which is one of the region's few going concerns. Natural attractions such as the **Oriège** tributary valley and the bear-sheltering forests west of the river, enhanced by the prehistoric painted caves around **Tarascon**. On the main valley floor, the resorts of **Mérens-les-Vals** and **Ax-les-Thermes** are serviceable bases for excursions into the surrounding mountains, including the severe fastness of the Carlit. Further downriver, the showcase town of **Foix** is almost in the flatlands, but affords access to the gorge-furrowed, Cathar-haunted **Pays de Sault**, an eerie tableland extending between the Ariège and the Aude valley to the east. Here, the Cathars began the local tradition of rebelling against Church and State almost eight centuries ago, antecedents which the modern *Ariègeois* acknowledge with pride.

The upper Ariège

The train line into the valley from the Cerdagne tunnels under the Col de Puymorens to emerge at **L'HOSPITALET-PRÈS-L'ANDORRE**. In the absence of any monumental or natural attraction, this town serves travellers as a route convergence: the HRP goes through here, as do buses to and from Andorra, and trains south into the Cerdagne and north to Toulouse. There are two one-star **hotels** – the *Puymorens* (☎05.61.64.23.03; ④) and *Le Sisca* (☎05.61.64.23.02; ③), plus a municipal campsite (☎05.61.05.20.04; June–Oct). Heading into the Carlit Massif, the **HRP** gets you quickly to grips with the mountains, offering the shortest approach from the west as it climbs unusually gently to the dam and a refuge at Bésines, where you link up with the GR10.

Mérens-les-Vals

The reputation of **MÉRENS-LES-VALS**, 10km further north, rests on the stocky frame of the **Mérenguais horse**, a breed which – partly on the strength of the Niaux cave paintings (see p.236) – is considered the closest thing in western Europe to the wild horse of prehistory. Nowadays there are more specimens outside the mountains of Mérens than in them, but the village remains a place of pilgrimage for horse-lovers. Mérens itself is unexceptional: one part clustered on the main road, the other spread out on the slopes to the east around a Romanesque church. The village straddles the GR10, which accounts for the attractively restored **gîte d'étape** in the upper village (☎05.61.64.32.50; ①). This is a congenial place to base yourself for a few days' walking, serving excellent food – luckily enough, since there are no other hotels or restaurants in the town at present, though there is a **campsite**, *Ville de Bau* (☎05.61.02.85.40; May–Oct), just off the main road, near the river.

Walking from Mérens

Mérens makes a good base for **walks**, short or long. A popular one-day circuit follows the GR10, then a local path southwest up the Mourgouillou valley (where Mérenguais horses still graze) to the **Étang de Couart**, and drops back down to the train station at L'Hospitalet on the HRP. Heading **southeast**, the GR10 offers a more appealing, if more strenuous introduction to the Carlit range than the GR7 from Porté or the HRP from L'Hospitalet, but be warned that both French and translated *topoguides* sketch the route initially on the true right (northeast) bank of the River Nabre.

Ax-les-Thermes and around

Eight kilometres beyond Mérens, at the confluence of the Ariège, Oriège and Lauze rivers, stands **AX-LES-THERMES**. It's an unobjectionable spa resort with little specifically to see owing to numerous disastrous fires in centuries past, but there is a lively Monday market along the river promenade, and it makes the most convenient base for skiing or walking in the Ariège. **Hikes** can be routed in circuits, using the town as a base, and several **ski resorts**, both downhill and cross-country, are scattered in all directions within a convenient distance.

Ax itself dates back at least to Roman times, and the commercial use of its hot springs to the thirteenth century. The smell of sulphur that early twentieth-century travellers complained about has gone, but the ambience of a spa remains. Four *thermes* still exist, all of them part of the central *Hôtel Royal Thermal*. There are more than forty sources, some hotter than 70°C, producing a total volume of water in excess of 600,000 litres per day. If you'd like to experience the waters without paying, you can indulge in the local custom of foot-dangling in the **Bassin des Ladres**, an open bath beside the central place du Breilh, which is the only surviving portion of a thirteenth-century hospital for Crusaders.

Practicalities

The **train station** lies on the northwest side of town, just off the main av Delcassé. You'll pass two-star **hotels** as you walk into the centre, first the *Hôtel de France* (☎05.61.64.20.30, fax 05.61.64.60.97; ⑤) followed by *Les Pyrénées* (☎05.61.64.21.01; ⑤), before arriving at the central place du Breilh, home of the **tourist office** (May–Oct Mon–Sat 9am–noon & 2–7pm Sun 9am–noon & 2–6pm; July & Aug daily 9am–1pm & 2–7pm; Nov Mon–Sat 9am–noon & 2–6pm; Dec–Apr daily 9am–noon & 2–6pm; ☎05.61.64.60.60, *www.vallees-ax.com*) and another old-fashioned two-star hotel, the *La Paix* (☎05.61.64.22.61; ③). Nearby, at Ax Sports (owned by an Englishman), you can replace any lost or worn-out mountaineering and ski gear. Other convenient and quiet accommodation includes the friendly *La Terrasse*, 7 rue Marcaillou (☎05.61.64.20.33; ⑥), which attracts many skiers and has a restaurant; and *Pension Barat-Aliot* near the Hôtel de Ville below place du Marché(☎05.61.64.22.01; ③), also with a restaurant. The municipal **campsite**, *Malazéou* (☎05.61.64.22.21; open all year), is beside the Ariège, 500m from the train station.

Other than the hotel dining rooms and restaurants, **eating** prospects aren't brilliant in Ax, leading many to take advantage of the half-board plans which most of the town's hotels offer. Exceptions include the pizzeria opposite the *Hôtel de France* on the main road, and the *Terminus Bar* near the station. For **snacks** on the hoof, there are numerous cheap *boulangeries* and over-the-counter pizza places in rue de l'Horloge, leading off the place du Marché. More atmospheric venues for a **drink** include the old *Grand Café*, beside *Les Pyrénées*, and *Brasserie Le Club* on place Roussel.

The Oriège valley

Extending east from Ax, the damp, leafy **Oriège valley** allows access to both the Carlit peaks and the **Réserve Nationale d'Orlu**, created south of the road in 1975 to benefit a growing herd of isards as well as roe deer, golden eagles and lammergeiers. Under the shadow of the distinctive Dent d'Orlu, a favourite of technical climbers, the D22 road heads up the valley to **ORLU**, where there's camping at the *Municipal* (☎05.61.64.30.09; open all year) and a popular *gîte d'étape* aimed at walkers, the *Relais Montagnard* (☎05.61.64.61.88; ⑤). A path from **Les Forges d'Orlu** (a place, not a village) further up the valley permits a link-up with the Tour des Montagnes d'Ax (see below), via a climb from near the power station to the dam at **Naguille**.

At a popular picnic area some 12km from Ax, the asphalt ends and all private cars are banned from further progress along a track which climbs south into the *réserve* through the **En Gaudu valley**, meeting the GR7 below the Étang d'en Beys with its refuge. If you prefer to approach the Carlit via the Oriège, it's well worth splashing out for a taxi to the picnic grounds: the walk is tedious and steep, with little chance of a lift in either direction.

Walks near Ax-les-Thermes

With an office next door to the tourist office in Ax, the Bureau des Guides et Accompagnateurs Montagne des Vallées d'Ax (☎05.61.64.31.51; same hours as Ax's tourist office) maintains a list of seventeen brief **walks** around the town, ranging from twenty minutes to seven hours, though most prove rather short and over-generously timed; it also keeps information on all the mountain huts and refuges, climbing courses and weather forecasts. To fill a day properly, take the suggested itinerary to the attractive village of **Sorgeat** and link this hike with other sections.

The five-day, four-night **Tour des Montagnes d'Ax** is most recommended, since it covers a variety of terrain, including parts of the Carlit already described. You can begin at **Le Castelet**, on the main road 5km northwest of Ax, climbing south for a day to hook up with the GR10 at the **Col de Belh** (2247m); nearby is the staffed *Refuge de Rulh* (2185m; 05.61.65.65.01; 50 places). The route then heads east to cross the Ariège valley at Mérens-les-Vals, your second overnight stop. From there you stick with the GR10, and later the GR7, all the way to the *Refuge d'en Beys* (☎05.61.64.24.24; meals available last weekend in May–Sept; ①) – the refuge (see p.228) will be your third night out, after a very long day unless you take the Porteille de Madides shortcut (see p.228), or you could insert an extra overnight stay at the refuge *Les Bésines* (☎05.61.05.22.44; meals available June–Sept & school hols; ①), at the junction of the two trails. From the refuge, you've a shorter day up to the gentle **Couillade de Beys** (2345m), then past the easterly Étang des Peyrisses and the Naguille dam before descending to the Oriège valley floor.

SKIING AROUND AX-LES-THERMES

The nearest ski station to Ax is **AX-BONASCRE**, 8km south up the D820; in winter there are ski-bus services from the town. Bonascre is a hideous knot of black-clad highrises at 1400m, but it's a different matter once you get into the *télécabine* and up to the **Plateau du Saquet** (2040m) with its beginners' area. The snow record is good, there are 70km of pistes (mostly red-rated, some over 3km long) and the top point is 2305m – with the beautiful Andorran frontier peaks as a backdrop.

Three valleys west of Bonascre, the **Plateau de Beille** rivals Font-Romeu in offering some of the best cross-country skiing on the French side. The 60km of pistes range in length from 1–20km, at just under 2000m – which should ensure adequate snow. The plateau is reached by the sixteen-kilometre *Route Forestière* from the village of Les Cabannes, 15km down the main N20 road.

North of Ax there's potentially good cross-country skiing to be had around the **Col de Chioula** (1431m), with 60km of trails; be wary of the low altitude and check conditions before setting out. A pretty drive 13km east of Ax leads to tiny **ASCOU-PAILHÈRES**, which offers just sixteen downhill runs, totalling 20km, and a top point of 2030m. The longest two runs are blue-rated, though the station has a couple of shorter, challenging red and black pistes.

The Route des Corniches

A scenic alternative to the N20 along the floor of the Ariège valley is the **Route des Corniches**, between Ascou and Bompas, which you can access from Ax by taking the serpentine D613 (the Belcaire road) up past Ascou. About halfway along you pass the village of **AXIAT**, which has an appealing Romanesque church and lies a short way south of the extremely unappealing **talc quarry** at **Trimouns**.

This huge, ghastly scar produces around 300,000 tons of talc per season, eight percent of the world's total; so far about thirteen million tons have gone, leaving eleven million to be scoured from the earth. The workers are mainly Spanish, Portuguese and Moroccan, who supplement their income by selling semiprecious stones to tourists (regular tours of the quarry June–Sept). It was by the trail over the Col de la Peyre, just above the quarry, that the four Cathars from Montségur made their escape (see p.243); apparently for aesthetic reasons, this path has not been included on the GR107.

Just below Axiat stands the castle of **LORDAT**. Although it escaped dismantling during the sixteenth-century Wars of Religion – "too big" was the report to the future king, Henri de Navarre – the castle is now comprehensively ruined, but worth a look all the same. The church above has a distinctive squat, square bell-tower, with a double layer of arches on each face. The corniche comes back to the base of the valley at Bompas, 3km north of Tarascon on the road to Foix.

Tarascon-sur-Ariège and its caves

A small, utilitarian mining and metallurgy centre where traffic roars past on the highway, **TARASCON-SUR-ARIÈGE** has nothing to suggest that it's the heart of one of the most fascinating areas in Europe. Any account of the emergence of the human species must include the caves around Tarascon, which together constitute an unequalled display of **prehistoric painting and artefacts**. There are four main sites, all accessible in a single day if you have your own transport.

Yet the town itself is more rewarding than first impressions suggest, and worth an hour's stroll. From the east bank of the Ariège, where riverside cafés provide pleasant vantage points, a narrow pedestrian lane leads up past craft shops and even narrower alleys to the old quarter. Here the church of St-Michel presides over a partly arcaded square, with various surviving bits of the razed medieval walls here and there: the **Tour Saint-Michel**, and the **Porte d'Espagne** with a fountain inside. From the gate, a short hike past walled orchards up to the **Tour du Castella**, now a clocktower, is worthwhile for the views over the five valleys that converge here.

Practicalities

Buses and trains call frequently from nearby Ax-les-Thermes and Foix, on the line from Toulouse to La tour; the **train station** is on the left bank of the Ariège, in the northern half of town. The **tourist office** (July & Aug daily 9am–1pm & 2–6pm; Sept–June Mon–Sat 9am–1pm & 2–6pm; ☎05.61.05.94.94, *pays.de.tarascon@wanadoo.fr*) is inside the multipurpose hall known as the Espace François Mitterand, on av. des Pyrénées in the centre. Quietest and most attractive of the **hotels** is the *Confort* on the riverside quai Armand-Sylvestre (☎ & fax 05.61.05.61.90; ④), with some rooms facing a courtyard where ice cream and light snacks are served. For more comfort, with quieter rooms facing the river, try the *Hostellerie de la Poste*, (☎05.61.05.60.41, fax 05.61.5.70.59, *pays.de.tarascon@wanadoo.fr*; ⑤), 200m north on the main through road. If these are full, in between them is the somewhat noisy *La Bellevue* at 7 place Jean-Jaurès (☎05.61.05.60.45, fax 05.61.05.10.41; ③). There are two **campsites**: *La Bernière*

(☎05.61.05.78.01; open all year), near the junction of the road to Bédeilhac, and the municipal *Pré Lombard* (☎05.61.05.61.94; open all year), upstream from town on the right bank. All the hotels have **restaurants**, with the best food and service at *Hostellerie de la Poste,* which offers a reasonably priced *menu* (95F/€14.50) featuring *auzinat,* a rich hotpot of cabbage, potato, sausage, game and other goodies.

The caves

Painted **prehistoric caves** have been discovered along the northwest coast of Spain, in the Dordogne and in the Pyrenees, of which unquestionably the finest is the **Grotte de Niaux,** 2km southwest of Tarascon. The concentration of caves in the Ariège is due mostly to the amount of limestone in the hillsides, such strata being ideally suited to the millennial work of seeping water that creates caverns. What served as shelters and places of ritual for early humans later came in handy as hideouts for religious dissidents during the Christian era.

Grotte de Niaux

Comparable caves such as Lascaux in the Dordogne and Altamira in Spain are either closed to the public or heavily restricted; access to the **Grotte de Niaux** is by mandatory reservation (☎05.61.05.88.37) for inclusion in a guided group of twenty people (daily: July–early Sept 8.30–11.30am & 1.30–5.15pm; early Sept to end Sept 10–11.30am & 1.30–5.15pm; Oct–June visits at 11am, 3pm & 4.30pm; 60F/€9.20).

The current entrance to Niaux is a tunnel created in 1968 near the low and narrow natural opening under an enormous rock overhang. Using flashlights for illumination, you penetrate 900m (of 4km of galleries) to see some of the famous black outlines of horse and bison, minimally shaded yet capturing every nuance. Studies have shown that these drawings, and those of the ibex and stag in the recess further back, were produced around 10,800 BC with a "crayon" made of bison fat and manganese oxide. A line of footprints left by the artists can be seen in a part of the cave that was opened up in 1970, while their script is represented by dots and bunches of lines on the wall of the main cavity.

NIAUX village itself, between the cave and Tarascon, has a small, private **Musée Pyrénéen** (July & Aug daily 9am–8pm; Sept–June daily 10am–noon & 2–6pm; 35F/€5.30), which displays a splendid collection of tools, furnishings, archival photos and other relics illustrating the vanished traditions of the Ariège. Exhibits also explain local Pyrenean architecture, specifically its use of *lauzes* (stone slabs), *ardoise* (slate) and occasionally *chaume* (thatch) for roofing. About halfway between Niaux and Tarascon, keep your eyes peeled for the picturesque remains of a medieval smelting works by the riverside.

Grotte de la Vache

The **Grotte de la Vache** at Alliat (July & Aug daily 10am–5.30pm; Easter–June & Sept daily except Tues 3–4.30pm; other times ☎05.61.05.95.06; 50F/€7.60) is well worth the couple of kilometres' journey across the valley from Niaux; a path, beginning some 150m before the Niaux museum, slightly shortcuts the road. Excavations over two decades have revealed remains of ten thousand years of habitation from 15,000–12,500 BC to the Bronze Age. Around thirty thousand fragments of flint tools were unearthed here and over six thousand complete tools, mainly for engraving in rock; some pieces are displayed in the cave.

Grotte de Bédeilhac

To reach the **Grotte de Bédeilhac** (Easter–Jun & Sept Mon– 2.15–5pm; mid-Dec to Easter Mon–Sat 2.30–4.30pm & Sun 3pm; July & Aug daily 10am–5.30pm;

CAVE ART

The **painted caves** of the Pyrenees were created by nomadic and seminomadic communities of *Homo sapiens* during the Late Paleolithic period, 10,000 to 35,000 years ago. Almost everything else about them is conjecture.

The big historical names in the evaluation of cave art are the French prehistorians **Abbé Breuil** (1877–1961), **André Leroi-Gourhan** (1911–86) and the latter's colleague **Annette Laming-Emperaire** (1917–1977). Abbé Breuil began his career working on the caves of the Dordogne, but dedicated years of study to the western and central Pyrenees, arriving at the theory that cave art served a **magical function**, to ensure "that the game should be plentiful, that it should increase and that sufficient should be killed". The frequency with which ibex, wild boar, reindeer and bison appear on the walls makes this notion attractive, but there are objections to it, the most obvious being that the animal remains found in the caves show that the commonly depicted species were not the main food supply. Although some animals are marked by symbols that might be arrows, over ninety percent are not. The Late Paleolithic period is also understood to have been a time of plenty, when hunters would have needed no magical assistance.

Leroi-Gourhan's and Laming-Emperaire's main contention is that cave art was arranged in a **specific layout**, much like the decorative schemes of frescoed Christian churches. Their examination of 865 subjects in 62 caves revealed that hands were depicted only at the entrance to caves or in the centre, and that mammoths and bison were confined to the centre. More controversially, they went on to suggest that the arrangement had a sexual polarity, with bison symbolizing the female element, and horses the male. Others have argued that the weak illumination available to the cave-dwellers – grease and a wick perhaps, or wooden torches – would not have allowed them to see the cave decorations as a unity. A problem is also posed by the way successive outlines overlayed each other to the extent that they became indecipherable, even though suitable areas of blank rock were available to either side. Nevertheless, most experts agree that there is some sort of pattern: bison and horses, for example, are thirty times more likely to occur in the central area than are deer.

The most cogent refutation of the above theories appeared in 1996 under the title *Les Chamanes de la Préhistoire* (Éditions Seuil) by Jean Clottes, a French prehistorian and cave-art expert, and David Lewis-Williams, a South African archeologist specializing in the art and beliefs of the Kalahari Bushmen, one of the last surviving hunter-gatherer societies with strong parallels to European Paleolithic culture. They proposed that many of the images were created by **shamans** in a trance or other altered state, and that "the paintings and engravings do not represent real animals that are hunted for food in an actual landscape; rather they are visions drawn from the subterranean world of spirits because of their supernatural powers and ability to help the shamans".

The caves will doubtless continue to stimulate speculation. From the accumulation of rubbish (mostly discarded foodstuffs) on the cave floors – sometimes nearly 4m deep – and from the apparent stylistic development of the paintings, it would seem that habitation in these caves was quite stable, and it is possible that painting was the responsibility of one person within the community. Furthermore, the similarities between decorative work in caves hundreds of kilometres apart indicates that there was interaction between groups all along the range.

A great many decorated caves of the Pyrenees are closed to public viewing; application through a caving organization might gain access to some of these. The most spectacular examples, though, are open to all. After the Tarascon group, the next major Pyrenean cave is **Gargas**, with its vast array of red and black hand prints, many with apparently mutilated fingers (p.318).

Whatever its purposes and origins, Pyrenean cave art offers an extraordinary aesthetic experience, marvellously conjuring shape and movement from the most basic natural materials, and even, in places, exploiting the very contours of the rock. Niaux itself contains an excellent example of such artistic opportunism: one of the bison carved on the clay floor is formed around holes caused by dripping water, which now function as an eye and wound marks.

☎05.61.05.95.06; 50F/€7.60) above the village of Bédeilhac, you have to return to Tarascon and travel 5km along the D618 towards Saurat. This cave, a hollow in the ridge of Soudour, contains examples of every known technique of Paleolithic art, including polychrome painting (now faded to monochrome). The imposing entrance yawns 35m wide by 20m high, making it easy to understand how the Germans managed to adapt the cavern as an aircraft hangar during World War II. Although the art inside is not as immediately powerful as at Niaux, its diversity compensates: low reliefs in mud, paintings of bison, deer and ibex, and stalagmites used to model figures.

In the village below, **beds** are provided at the *Relais d'Étape* (☎05.61.05.15.56; ①) and **meals** (expect to pay 80–100F/€12.20–15.30) at the adjacent *Auberge de la Grotte* (closed Jan & Tues pm) on the through road next to the *mairie* and the post office, with *menus* at 70–190F/€10.70–29.

Lombrives and Fontanet

The **Grotte de Lombrives** (July & Aug daily 10am–7pm; June & Sept daily tours at 10am, 10.45am & 2–5.30pm; Easter–May & Oct–early Nov, weekends & holidays tours at 10am, 10.45am & 2.30pm, plus May Mon–Fri 2–5.30pm; or by appointment, ☎05.61.05.98.40; 40F/€6.10), 3km south of Tarascon along the N20, near Ussat-les-Bains, may disappoint if you've already seen Niaux, Vache and Soudour. Access by underground train gives it the atmosphere of an amusement-park – as do the nocturnal *spéctacles* regularly staged here in July and August. The stalagmite formations are superb, and the sheer size of the complex is impressive. It is, in fact, the largest cavern in western Europe open to tourists, and would take five days' walking to see entirely. Groups of eight or more can arrange three- or five-hour walk-throughs by ringing the number above.

Lombrives was inhabited around 4000 BC, but all the material found here now rests in museums such as that at Foix. Its later history is embellished by legends of the last Cathars walled up inside in 1328, and of 250 soldiers subsequently disappearing without trace, the victims of cave-dwelling bandits. For a specialized visit, you can book on one of the *Visites longue durées caractère spéléologique*, which are run from June to September (same phone number as above).

Qualified cavers can also get permission to visit nearby **Fontanet**, on the north side of the Ariège beyond the village of Ussat. The small but comprehensive inventory includes a polychrome bison, a female figure and human faces.

Labouiche

Some 3km along the Vernajoul road northwest from the centre of Foix (see below) is the subterranean **river-cavern of Labouiche** (April–May & Oct–Nov Mon–Sat 2–5.15pm & Sun 10–11.45am & 2–5.15pm, June–Sept 10–11.15am & 12–5.15pm Sun 10–11.45am & 2–5.15pm, July & Aug Mon–Sat 9.30am–5.30pm Sun 10–11.45am & 2–5.15pm; usually a 15-minute wait; 44F/€6.70), thought to be the longest navigable cave in western Europe. It appears never to have been humanly inhabited, and indeed high water levels in winter completely block access. The amusement-park atmosphere of Lombrives prevails here also: boatloads of a dozen persons each travel 75 minutes in opposite directions along the 1500m of galleries open to the public. Entry is via the natural entrance, or an artificial one bored at the upstream end, by the well-signposted ticket office where you assemble. Highlights are the waterfall at the upstream end of the river and a small chamber full of formations below the artificial entry. These and other curiosities are described by guides who do their best to keep up a witty patter while hauling on the ceiling-mounted cables which are the mode of propulsion.

Foix

FOIX, 16km downstream from Tarascon, is the smallest departmental capital in France, and the most agreeable base in the valley if you don't mind catching a train or bus to get into the mountains. A nonindustrial livelihood based on bureaucracy and tourism has helped preserve its old town of narrow alleys in the triangle between the Ariège and the Arget rivers, where a few of the overhanging houses date from the fourteenth to sixteenth centuries; especially attractive are place Pyrène and place Saint-Vincent with their fountains, though many junctions in the old town sport some sort of water-quirk. All lanes seem to lead eventually to the conspicuously large church of **Saint-Volusien** in the north of the old town, originally Romanesque but almost completely reconstructed after being razed during the Wars of Religion. Its square, along with the Halles des Grains just off cours Gabriel-Fauré, hosts lively Wednesday and Friday **markets**: produce and plants at place Saint-Volusien; meat, cheese, savouries and pastries at the metal-roofed *halles*, which serves as a prime drinking venue other days.

Presiding over everything is the grey hilltop **castle**, not so much a single fortification as three magnificent, dissimilar towers from different eras, dramatic when viewed from any angle. From 1012 the castle on this site was the seat of the counts of Foix,

GASTON FÉBUS

As you travel through the central Pyrenees, you'll inevitably encounter the name of local hero **Gaston Fébus** (or Phébus), count of Foix and viscount of Béarn. Although ultimately frustrated in his plans, he is still celebrated for his struggle towards regional independence and his character, which epitomized the chivalric ideals of the Middle Ages – as well as for his invention of *hypocras*, a spiced-wine drink still enjoyed around Foix. Poet, soldier and provincial aristocrat, Gaston was born in 1331 and died sixty years later, but it is difficult to disentangle the events of the intervening years from the myths – often self-promoted – that sprung up around him. The troubadour poets acknowledged him as a friend and doubtless embellished his deeds in their lyrics, while Jean Froissart – chronicler of the Hundred Years' War – was invited by Fébus to document and popularize his life. Gaston was a poet himself and the author of a book on hunting – an example of the genre of "self-help" books for image-conscious nobles of the era. His surname, Fébus, was his own creation derived from the Occitan for sun and celebrating his long, golden hair. Although an autocratic ruler, who abolished the legislative assemblies of his lands and set himself up as the highest judicial authority, he cultivated a reputation as a fair-minded and dauntless soldier, intending always to lead his men into battle with the cry *Fébus avan* (Fébus at the front).

His ambition was to create an autonomous kingdom of the Pyrenees, adding by conquest the regions of Bigorre and Soule to his inherited domains of Nébouzan (around Saint-Gaudens), Béarn (in the far west) and Foix. This goal was made impossible by the continuing Hundred Years' War, which divided the loyalties of his subjects; Gascony on the west was subject to the English Crown – in particular the Black Prince (in direct control 1362–71), while to the east lay Languedoc, subject to France. In addition, feuding between the leading families of the area kept him occupied; one of his most significant victories came in 1362, when he crushed his arch-enemies, the Armagnacs. In time he lost the appetite to pursue his grand plan, by most accounts after 1380, when it seems Fébus killed his only son on discovering the son's role in a plot to assassinate him.

Thereafter, determined that his enemies should not succeed where he apparently had failed, Fébus dedicated himself to campaigning for a strong, united France, pledging that his lands should be inherited by the Crown of France and not by any of his local enemies. Yet this was not to happen until 1589, with the accession to the Parisian throne of Henri III of Foix-Béarn and Navarre, a descendant of Fébus' fierce rivals, the d'Albrets.

whose association with the Cathar faith led to its being besieged four times by Simon de Montfort, who failed to break the fort's resistance. Count Roger-Bernard II – known as *Le Grand* – was a determined opponent of the anti-Cathar crusade, but perhaps made his most lasting contribution to history by marrying Ermensende of Castellbó early in the thirteenth century, thereby linking the fortunes of Foix and Andorra (see p.205). That dynasty ended illustriously with Henri III of Foix-Béarn and Navarre, who annexed what had become a Pyrenean mini-state to the Crown when he became Henri IV of France. But the biggest name in Foix is that of the fair-haired knight whose features can be seen on postcards all over town – Gaston III, known as Gaston Fébus (see box on p.239).

The best part of a castle visit (daily May–Jun & Sept 9.45am–noon & 2–6pm; July & Aug 9.30am–6.30pm; Oct–April 10.30am–noon & 2–5.30pm; 25F/€3.80) is clambering up worn stairs in the southern and central towers for startling views across the valley. The interior houses the rather listless **Musée d'Ariège** (guided visits only, within hours stated), whose exhibits range from prehistoric to medieval times.

Practicalities

The **train station** sits on the right bank of the Ariège; most **buses** stop on the central cours Gabriel-Fauré, near the Resistance monument. In addition to the mainline train and bus services between Toulouse and the Spanish frontier at Latour-de-Carol, there's a daily **bus** service (not Sun) east via Lavelanet to Quillan on the Aude, and four daily buses west to Saint-Girons in the Couserans. The **tourist office** at 45 cours Gabriel-Fauré (June & Sept Mon–Sat 9am–noon & 2–6pm, Sun 10am–12.30pm; July & Aug Mon–Sat 9am–7pm, Sun 10am–12.30pm & 3–6pm; rest of year Mon–Sat 9am–noon & 2–6pm; Oct–May Mon–Sat 9am–noon & 2–6pm; ☎05.61.65.12.12) can be reached from the train station by walking south along the east bank of the Ariège and then crossing the Pont-Neuf.

Most **accommodation** is in the old town, on the west bank of the Ariège, though little of it is inspiring. If you have the means, the quietest and most comfortable option is the three-star *Hôtel Lons*, on 6 place Duthil, near the Pont Vieux (☎05.61.65.52.44, fax 05.61.02.68.18; ⑥). *La Barbacane*, 1 av de Lerida (☎05.61.65.50.44, fax 04.61.65.50.44; ⑥), and *L'Echauguette*, rue Paul Laffont (☎05.61.2.88.88, fax 05.61.65.29.49; ⑤), occupy the next rank down, though both suffer from traffic noise. The *Eychenne*, 11 rue Nöel-Peyrevidal (☎05.61.65.00.04, fax 05.61.65.56.63; ④) is the only real cheapie, with decent enough rooms but a lively nocturnal bar on the ground floor; across the street at no. 16, the *Auberge Léo Lagrange* (☎05.61.65.09.04; ②) fills the youth hostel niche. The municipal **campsite**, *Lac de Labarre* (☎05.61.65.11.58; May–Oct), is on the N20 towards Toulouse.

The best area for **eating** is rue de la Faurie, the old blacksmiths' bazaar at the centre of the old town, where the best of several establishments is *Des 4 Saisons* at no. 11, serving until 10pm, whose interesting gimmick is to bring to your table a *pierrade* (hot ceramic square), on which you cook fish and meat yourself – they also do a wide range of crêpes. *Le Jeu de L'Oie* (closed Sat noon & Sun in winter) nearby at no. 17 is also worth trying for more traditional fare, while *Auberge Miranda* (closed Mon) at 36 rue Labistour (the continuation of Faurie) is an old-fashioned bar with *plats du jour*. Food at *L'Henri IV* on place Pyrène is nothing extraordinary, but the outdoor seating is a good way to take in the square and the castle. The nearby *Le Petit Creux* at 9 rue Lazéma has a limited but well-executed *menu* which guarantees outdoor-table crowds at lunchtime. At any of these places you can expect to pay 70–90F/€10.70–13.70 for a *menu*.

There is a row of café-restaurants which double as night-time **music-bars** on the west side of the cours Gabriel Fauré, on either side of the old market hall. *Café des Rocher*, *Grand Grosse* and *Le Bon Bouffe* all have decent if unspectacular dinner menus for 65F/€9.90, and stay open for drinking. Later on, you can head to the **disco** *Le*

Crysco Club (Wed–Sat 10pm–3am) at 3 cours Irénée Cros, on the far side of the *pont vieux* over the Ariège.

The Pays de Sault

If you haven't got a car or a bike, the magnificent **Pays de Sault** – the upland area bounded by the Aude, the Ariège and the main road from Quillan to Foix – can be crossed in a few days on foot, making occasional use of the sporadic public transport. A network of **walking itineraries** – the Tour du Pays de Sault, the Tour du Massif de Tabe, the Piémont and the GR107, plus forestry tracks – provide various ways of exploring. The most popular route is the **Sentier Cathare**, which begins at Foix and arrives at Montségur in two stages via Roquefixade (see p.246), then continues to the Mediterranean; it's easy walking much of the year (avoid midwinter and midsummer), with strategically placed accommodation in *gîtes d'étape*.

Regular **bus services** cross the Pays de Sault: one links the train station in Quillan with the one in Foix, via **Puivert** and **Lavelanet**, 10km north of Montségur; the other runs from Quillan via Belcaire and Camurac to **Comus**, 12km southeast, from where Montségur can be reached through the Gorges de la Frau. Because departures are slightly more frequent from the east, the two routes described below approach the area from Quillan.

Much of the Pays de Sault is a spacious agricultural plateau, but it contains more vertiginous terrain, too. At the southeast edge, the dramatic D107 road from Axat to Ax-les-Thermes runs through the **Rebenty** and **Joucou** gorges and over the **Col du Pradel** (1673m), a tough but wonderful cycling route. Further west beyond the heart of the Sault looms the clifftop castle **Montségur**, the greatest stronghold of the Cathars.

The vast highlands are composed primarily of limestone, and thus riddled with caves and ravines such as the spectacular **Gorges de la Frau**. Above ground, its agriculture has changed little since Cathar times; pesticides have yet to infiltrate the region's ecosystem, so the silhouettes of birds of prey are fixtures in the sky.

Neither of the region's downhill **ski stations** is worth much effort. **Les Monts d'Olmes** resort, southwest of Montségur, is focused on a seedy apartment development at the base of twenty runs which, though north-facing, barely reach 2000m elevation. **Camurac**, due north of Ax-les-Thermes along the D613 near Camurac village, is even dinkier and lower (1800m), with the base station consisting of a "village" of decaying institutional chalets for assorted youth groups.

There is good **cross-country skiing** on the plateau, however, with a small rental and tuition operation at **Comus** and especially good terrain at the **Col de Marmare**.

Puivert

Although it's just twenty minutes out of Quillan by vehicle, the countryside around **PUIVERT** feels quite different, a vast upland planted with corn and sunflowers, buzzed by amateur pilots using the small airport near the middle. The village itself offers all amenities, including a **gîte d'étape** just opposite the castle (☎04.68.11.40.70, fax 04.68.11.40.72; ①–②), and the **restaurant** *Dame Blanche*, another establishment with hearty menus around 80F/€12.20. Less than a kilometre south of the village is a small lake with a **campsite** (☎04.68.20.00.58; open all year) and swimming area (daily except Mon), a welcome sight whether you've been cycling, driving or hiking.

The **château**, standing alone like a cardboard cut-out atop a gently rounded hill a kilometre or so east of the village, fell to the anti-Cathar crusade in 1210. More a place of culture than of arms, it was closely associated with the **troubadour** poets, whose

THE CATHARS

The origins of Cathar belief seem to lie in **Manicheism**, a dualistic Middle Eastern doctrine founded on the concept of the material world as an invasion of the world of Light by the powers of Darkness. This first found practical expression in Europe among the Bogomils of the Balkan peninsula during the tenth century, who – following years of persecution – converted to Islam under the Ottomans. By the twelfth century a modified version of this belief system, probably introduced by returning Crusaders, had taken hold in the south of France, especially in the area of Albi where the first disputation between these dualists and the Church authorities took place – hence the alternative name of **Albigeois** (or Albigenses) for the Cathars.

According to Cathar thinking, God reigned over the spiritual world, the creator of the material world was the Devil, and Christ was God's messenger, an apparently physical manifestation of the spiritual world, with whom souls could be united and so be released into immortality. In line with their disdain of the material realm, the most austere believers avoided milk and meat, and considered marriage or procreation evil. These and other Cathar beliefs posed a number of problems for the Church of Rome. Firstly, Cathars denied the doctrine of the Virgin Birth, the mystery of Christ's fully human and fully divine nature, and insisted that the Catholic faithful, in worshipping any Creator of matter, were in fact worshipping the Devil. They were **antimaterialists** by definition – asceticism was seen as the only route to redemption – and thus had no need for sumptuous buildings or trappings favoured by the Church. They were initially **pacifists**, and condemned the Crusades, one of the methods used to increase papal and aristocratic fortunes. Moreover, the austere spirituality of their leaders – the *parfaits* and *parfaites* (lay adherents were known simply as *bons hommes* and *bonnes femmes*) – was a constant rebuke to the dissolute clergy of the Church, while their close contact with the population met the needs of common folk habitually ignored by Catholic institutions. And on top of all this, their conviction that they were exempt from feudal vows of allegiance made them politically attractive to independent-minded petty nobility – and exceedingly dangerous to distant, centralizing powers.

Following the election of **Pope Innocent III** in 1198, some years were spent trying to peacefully convince the heretical clergy of the error of their ways. But it was not until 1208 that Innocent, his patience exhausted, formally declared a crusade and succeeded in convincing the previously reluctant king of France, Philippe Auguste, to provide forces. Ranged against this formidable combination were the *seigneurs* of Languedoc, who had been in constant territorial competition with the bishops of the region, and many of whose subjects had become adherents of Catharism.

The first target was **Raymond VI of Toulouse**, excommunicated by the pope in 1207 for his tacit approval of Catharism (and, nearly as bad in the papal view, employment of Jews). Early the following year Raymond succeeded in persuading the papal legate Pierre de Castelnau to have the excommunication lifted, but on the day after agreement was reached the legate was murdered by a servant of Raymond, providing his enemies with a pretext for military action.

In July 1209 an army led by the archbishop of Narbonne and new legate, **Arnaud Amaury**, invaded Languedoc, with a heavy contingent of English mercenaries in its ranks. Béziers was besieged, taken suprisingly quickly and its entire population – a figure put by some authorities at twenty thousand – massacred for refusing to surrender a score or so Cathars in their midst. When asked how the Catholic citizens were to be distinguished from the heretics, Amaury supposedly replied: "Kill them all, God will recognize His own." Apocryphal utterance or not, this effectively became the motto of a campaign distinguished even by medieval standards for its brutality. After more protracted resistance, Carcassonne fell, eventually to be handed over – as Béziers had been – to the professional Norman crusader **Simon de Montfort**. For a few years Raymond VI played a double game to survive and to have his excommunication definitively revoked, even marching with the crusaders on occasion. But by 1213 the inexorable de Montfort, terrorizing the population with his atrocities, was in control of virtually all of Languedoc, forcing Raymond VI and his son to flee to the English court of

King John, the elder Raymond's brother-in-law. When the two Raymonds returned from exile in 1216, they resumed battle with de Montfort at Toulouse, which their arch-foe was besieging – a campaign that cost him his life in June 1218.

Their success was fairly short-lived; although the younger Raymond, who formally succeeded his father in 1222, managed to regain lost territory and reorganize the Cathar communities therein, a new scorched-earth campaign was unleashed in summer 1226 by the fanatical Parisian king **Louis VIII**. After see-saw battles, Raymond VII sued for peace in 1229; though remaining count of Tolouse, by the terms of the peace treaty he had to submit to public humiliations, the razing of the walls of Toulouse, the loss of his possessions beyond the Rhône, heavy financial indemnities to the Catholic Church, and the marriage of his only daughter to the younger brother of the new Parisian king, the underage Louis IX. Raymond, who died in 1249, was never henceforth able to provide the Cathar community with anything resembling comprehensive protection, and indeed in order to prove his zeal as a "defender of the faith" and stave off repeated attempts at excommunicating him, Raymond denounced heretics and burnt them at the stake of his own accord.

Though the first wave of military crusades had finished, the Cathar heresy was still far from being eradicted, especially in the Pyrenean foothills. In 1233, the new pope Gregory IX authorized the creation of the infamous **Inquisition**, to be supervised by Dominican and Franciscan monks. The Dominican order itself had been founded in 1206 by Domingo de Guzmán, later known to the world as **Saint Dominic**, a proselytizer who came specially from Castille to the Cathar heartland to counter the growing heresy. Leaving violent coercion to others, his preferred strategies were strenuous disputations with Cathar theologians, imitation of their austere habits and the founding of a convent at Prouille to receive Cathar women who recanted their beliefs. But the inquisitors of the late 1230s who fanned out across Languedoc employed the harsher methods for which they became subsequently notorious, and aroused such resistance that at Raymond VII's request, the pope briefly suspended their activities in 1237.

Inquisitorial convictions, imprisonments, stake-burnings and confiscations of the property of aristocratic sympathizers with Catharism resumed in 1240, and the Cathars still at liberty reacted in a manner which sealed their fate. In May 1242, a group of 85 knights from Montségur, led by **Pierre-Roger de Mirepoix**, went to Avignonet and hacked the eleven chief inquisitors to death as they slept. The retaliatory assault on Montségur, by a force of almost ten thousand men, began in May 1243, and continued through the winter – the first time in the Cathar crusades that the fighting was not suspended when the weather turned. On March 2, 1244, de Mirepoix, despairing of relief, agreed terms: the two hundred non-Cathar soldiers within the citadel would be allowed to go unmolested, but after two weeks' truce the Cathars themselves were to abjure their faith or submit to whatever fate their tormenters devised for them. On the night of March 15, in contravention of the terms, four Cathars climbed down the cliffs, escaped over the Col de la Peyre and recovered the Cathar "treasure" from a cave where it had been hidden at Christmas. What happened to it is a mystery, giving rise to legends – especially in German sources – identifying the treasure as the Holy Grail, and the Cathars themselves as the Knights of the Round Table. The next day Montségur surrendered, and the 225 surviving Cathar civilians who refused to abjure their beliefs were burned on a mass pyre, those who could not walk being thrown on with their stretchers.

In effect, Catharism ceased to exist as a significant force in France after the holocaust at Montségur, though two of the four escapees later appeared in Lombardy, where proceeds from the "treasure" would support a refugee Cathar community established there. Quéribus and Puylaurens – the final Cathar fortifications in Roussillon – came under royal control between 1255 and 1258. When Raymond VII's daughter died childless in 1271, all of Languedoc passed to the French Crown. From then on, Catharism persisted mainly as an underground network, with safe houses and escape routes extending across the mountains into Spanish Aragón and Catalonia, where it was more openly practised in the villages there until the Inquisition got to work during the fifteenth century. The last significant figure in Cathar history, Guilhem Bélibaste, was executed in 1321, having been caught returning from Spain to proselytize, and the last Lombard *bons hommes* were rooted out by the Inquisition in 1412, the same year they visited the village of Montaillou.

preoccupation with themes of romance and war was starkly at odds with the asceticism and (initial) pacifism of the Cathars. Indeed most troubadours were unsympathetic to Cathar belief; what united them was the Occitan language, then spoken across southern France. For the troubadours the *langue d'Oc* was simply the natural language of poetry and love; for the Cathars it expressed their defiance of Paris. Little remains of the pre-1210 structure; most of what's visible (daily: April–Sept 8am–7pm; rest of year 10am–5pm; 25F/€3.80) dates from the fourteenth century. Visits concentrate on the various floors of the *donjon*, with stairs all the way to the roof; the chapel features vigil seats at the north and south windows, a wall font and ceiling rib-vaulting culminating in a keystone embossed with images of the Virgin and St George. The highest chamber is dubbed the "musicians' room" after its eight *culs-de-lamps* or torch sockets at the terminus of more rib-vaulting, each sculpted in the form of a figure playing a different period instrument.

Northern approaches to Montségur

From Puivert the road heads west over the Col de Teil, the divide between the Aude and the Ariège, and the Pyrenean watershed: east of it, rivers flow to the Mediterranean, while on the west they empty into the Atlantic. You can walk from Puivert to Montségur along the **Sentier Cathare**, a long but not difficult day of some 25km, mostly through dense fir forests.

Bélesta and Fougax-Barrineuf

A better place to begin the walk, however, is 11km west at **BÉLESTA**, the next stop on the bus route. It's a far more manageable village to use a base for exploring around Montségur than Lavelanet (see below). If you get stranded there's **accommodation** at the somewhat pricey *Le Troubador* (☎05.61.01.60.57; ⑤) on the through road, a cheaper no-name *Café-Hôtel* (③) diagonal from the *mairie* in the main square and **camping** on the east side of the village at *Le Val d'Amour* (June–Sept). Attractions begin almost immediately on the way south: some 1500m out of Bélesta, the route to Montségur passes **Fontestorbes**, an artesian spring (*source intermittente*) under a rock overhang that in summer spurts water for six-minutes evenly separated by 32-minute pauses (in winter the water flows continuously). From the spring you can continue directly to Montségur by walking along various marked GRs (3hr), hitching 13km along the D5 and then the D9, or taking a longer detour via the Gorges de la Frau, 8km south (see below).

The most direct approaches pass through the double village of **FOUGAX-BAR-RINEUF**, 2km southwest, which offers a fine **restaurant**, *Les Cinque Fours* (open May–Sept), occupying an old bone-comb factory (formerly an important local industry, established by Protestants between the sixteenth and eighteenth centuries). The portions aren't huge, but neither are they *minceur*, and the 85F/€13 *menu* is quite adequate as a four-course lunch.

Lavelanet

LAVELANET, 8km west of Bélesta, has little to offer other than onward bus connections, its **tourist office** (July & Aug Mon–Sat 9am–noon & 2–7pm, Sun 9am–noon; Sept–June Mon–Sat 9am–noon & 2–7pm; ☎05.61.01.22.20, fax 05.61.03.06.69, *lavelanet.tourisme@wanadoo.fr*) on the central roundabout and the clean, modern *Camping de Lavelanet* (☎05.61.01.55.54; April–Sept) southwest of the centre. There's no need to get stuck here, and if you do the only **hotels**, the *Parc* (☎05.61.03.04.05, fax 05.61.03.08.66; ⑥), on the road out to Bélesta, and the *Espagne*, on the road to Foix (☎05.61.01.00.78; ③), are hardly enticing.

The southern approach to Montségur via Comus

From Monday to Friday there are two late-afternoon daily buses from Quillan to Comus. If you've read Emmanuel Le Roy Ladurie's *Montaillou* you may want to get off at Camurac, 3km short of Comus, and walk the rest of the way via Montaillou village, subject of the book and a detour which takes about two hours. **CAMURAC**, actually much closer to Ax-les-Thermes (see p.233), offers **accommodation** at the *Auberge du Pays de Sault* (☎04.68.20.32.09; ③) and *Camping les Sapins*. (☎04.68.20.38.11; open all year).

MONTAILLOU subscribed to the Cathar heresy long after the fall of Montségur, until the Inquisition, directed by the bishop of Pamiers, set to work here during the 1320s. The records compiled by the inquisitors were so precise that Le Roy Ladurie was able to re-create every aspect of the villagers' lives, from the minutiae of domestic economics to the details of their sexual habits. Fewer than twenty people live here permanently now, all of them descendants of the Cathars, as you can see by comparing their surnames with those on the headstones in the ancient graveyard.

COMUS isn't much bigger than Montaillou, but does have an excellent **gîte d'étape** (☎04.68.20.33.69; ①) attached to the Centre École Pleine Nature, which specializes in **caving**, the limestone hereabouts being peppered with two hundred known caves. Montségur is 13km away, through the **Gorges de la Frau**. From Comus take the GR107, formerly the GR7B, which drops down as a mule track between fields to a wide gorge that suddenly becomes a defile, where thousand-metre cliffs admit sun only in the early afternoon. The gorge widens again as you meet the dead-end of the D5 coming south from Bélesta and Fougax-Barrineuf. There are two ways of continuing to Montségur: west along the Sentier Cathare, wrapped in tree-shade alongside a stream (turn off at the first farm, 45min along the D5), or on a bridle trail beginning about an hour along the road, offering higher, more open ground. Either way, walking time from Comus is four hours.

Montségur

The ruined castle of **MONTSÉGUR** lives up to the promise of its distant view, its plain stone walls poised emphatically above the straggling, namesake village on a 1207-metre-high *pog* (from the Occitan *puèg*, or "peak"). The original fortifications were built by Guillaume "Short-Nose", duke of Aquitaine. Between 1204 and 1232 it was reconstructed as a bastion of the Cathars under the direction of Guilhabert de Castres, leader of the sect. Drastically eroded into naked vertical faces and gullies, the *pog* would have been a formidable defence. Only on the western side can you walk up to the summit (about 30min) through the *prat dels cremats* where the surviving Cathars were burned to death after the castle fell (a stone memorial pays tribute to them); see p.243.

The beauty of **the site** (open daily but with irregular hours; 25F/€3.80 including admission to the museum; castle only free in Jan) strikes you first since the original walls were reduced by half after the siege, and all internal structures are gone except the simple keep, now open to the sky. Then you begin to wonder how that last Cathar community of five hundred could have held out so long in such a small area. Although some lived in now-vanished houses at the foot of the walls on the north and west faces, the castle itself held a garrison of two hundred, together with the *faydits* – local aristocrats dispossessed by the crusade against Catharism. What's left of it takes no more than a few minutes to view – rather disappointingly, you're no longer allowed to climb up on the walls, merely to traverse the keep to visit the west *donjon*. But it's not so much what you see at Montségur that makes the trip unforgettable, as what your imagination can re-create from its remnants.

Down in the village, 1km below, a one-room **archeological museum** (irregular hours: March–Nov daily; Feb & Dec Tues–Sun; 25F/€3.80, castle entry included) displays artefacts excavated since the 1950s from the original village up beside the walls, from both pre- and post-Cathar periods – mostly food bones, personal effects, tools and surviving fragments of houses.

Practicalities

Despite its small size, tourist numbers at Montségur village have prompted a **tourist office** (July–Sept daily 10am–1pm & 2–6pm; ☎ & fax 05.61.03.03.03, *www.citaenet.com/montsegur*), of prime use for information on the precise route of the GR107; check also the local *topoguide*, which they occasionally stock. If you'd like to stay the night – and the beautiful scenery will certainly encourage you – there are two **hotels**: the old-fashioned *Couquet* (☎05.61.01.10.28; ②), a rambling country *pension* of wood-furnished rooms with washbasins; and the adjacent, en-suite, *Costes* (☎05.61.01.10.24, fax 05.61.03.06.28; ④), just uphill. Both have attached, nourishing and reasonably priced **restaurants**: the *Couquet* represents great value with four large home-made courses for well under 100F/€15.30; the *Costes* is fancier, featuring game and *ariègeois* specialities for well over that figure, while *Le Bufadou* offers a three-course vegetarian *menu* for under 100F/€15.30. The *Costes* manages the nearby **gîte d'étape** (April to mid-Nov; ①), while the closest **campsite** (tents only) is the *Point Acceuil Jeunes* (☎05.61.01.10.27; open all year) at the lower end of the village on the Bélesta side.

Roquefixade

Approximately 8km west of Lavelanet, the village of Nalzen is the best point along the D117 for access to **ROQUEFIXADE**, the westernmost Cathar castle and last stop on the Sentier Cathare before Foix. A two-kilometre side road leads up to the village of Roquefixade, rebuilt after the Cathar crusades as a *bastide*. From the high end of the village it's a twenty-minute climb to the castle (unenclosed, free), which takes its name (originally *roca fissada*) from the vast natural fissures augmenting its defences. Perched at the west end of a long ridge, it's bigger than it appears from below but utterly ruinous; your main reward is the view over the valley below with its clustered villages, and south (weather permitting) to the high Pyrenean ridge.

A *gîte d'étape* (☎05.61.03.01.36 *roquefixade@mail.dotcom.fr*; ①) stands by the base of the path up to the castle, and their outdoor seating is good for a drink after the climb. They only have twelve places, so give them some notice if you wish to **stay**. Alternative accommodation if they're full is the *Relais des Pogs* (☎05.61.01.14.50; ③ B&B), with doubles and dorm space.

travel details

FRANCE

Trains

Foix to: Ax-les-Thermes (6–7 daily; 45min); L'Hospitalet-près-l'Andorre (4 daily; 1hr 10min–1hr 30min); Tarascon-sur-Ariège (6–7 daily; 20min); Toulouse (11 daily; 1hr–1hr 15min). NB SNCF buses often substitute, or supplement, trains in the Ariège valley, especially above Tarascon.

Latour-de-Carol to: Ax-les-Thermes (5 daily; 55min); Bourg-Madame (5 daily; 15min); Foix (4 daily; 1hr 30min–1hr 40min); L'Hospitalet-près-l'Andorre (5 daily; 25min); Mont-Louis (5 daily; 1hr 20min); Puigcerdà (4 daily; 7min); Tarascon-sur-Ariège (4 daily; 1hr 15min–1hr 25min); Toulouse (4 daily; 2hr 30min–2hr 45min); Villefranche-de-Conflent (4 daily; 2hr 25min–2hr 55min).

Buses

Ax-les-Thermes to: Foix (6 daily Mon–Fri, 4 Sat, 2 Sun; 1hr); Pas de la Casa (2 daily; 45min); Tarascon-sur-Ariège (same frequencies; 30min).

Comus to: Quillan (1–2 daily Mon–Sat; 55min).

Foix to: Lavelanet (Mon–Sat 2 daily at 11.30am & 2.35pm, except Wed in school term 1 daily at

2.35pm; 35min); Quillan (Mon–Sat 1 daily at 2.35pm; 2hr); St-Girons (4 daily; 45min).

L'Hospitalet-près-l'Andorre (SNCF bus) to: Andorra la Vella (2 daily; 1hr 30–40min); Pas de la Casa (1 daily; 25–30min).

Latour-de-Carol to: Font-Romeu (4 daily, 2 only on the return journey; 50min).

Lavelanet to: Foix (1–3 daily; 30min); Quillan (Mon–Sat 1 daily at 3.15pm; 45min); Toulouse (6 daily Mon–Sat, 2 Sun; 2hr 30min).

SPAIN
Trains
Puigcerdà to: Barcelona (6 daily; 3hr 15min); Latour-de-Carol (6 daily; 7min); Ripoll (6 daily; 1hr 15min).

Buses
Berga to: Barcelona (4–5 daily; 2hr); Borredà (1 daily Mon–Sat at 1–2pm, returns 7.30–8.30am; 30min); Castellar de N'Hug (1 daily Mon–Sat at 6pm, returns next morning; 1hr 20min); Gòsol via Saldes (1 daily at 5.35pm, returns next morning; 1hr); La Pobla de Lillet (2–4 daily; 1hr); Ripoll (1 daily at 7.15am, returns at 12.30pm; 1hr 20min); Sant Llorenç de Morunys (1 daily Mon–Fri at 5.30pm, returns next morning; 1hr).

Puigcerdà to: Alp (4 daily with Alsina-Graells; 5min); Bagà/Berga (4 daily with Alsina Graells; 35min/1hr); Llívia (4 daily with Alsina Graells, plus 1 on Teisa; 5min); La Molina (at least 1 daily year-round; 30min); La Seu d'Urgell (3 daily with Alsina Graells at 7.30am, 3.10pm & 5.45pm; 1hr).

La Seu d'Urgell to: Andorra la Vella (6–7 daily; 30min); Barcelona (4 daily; 3hr 30min); Lleida (2 daily with Alsina Graells; 2hr 30min); Puigcerdà (3 daily on Alsina Graells at 9.15am, 12.30pm, & 7pm; 1hr).

ANDORRA
Domestic buses
Andorra la Vella to: Arcalis (12 daily in ski season; 45min); Arinsal (3 daily; 30min); El Serrat (2 daily; 30min); Encamp (every 20min 7am–9.30pm; 15min); Ordino (every 30min 7am–9pm; 20min); Pas de la Casa (2 daily; 1hr 30min); Soldeu (hourly 9am–8pm; 45min).

Long-distance buses
Andorra la Vella to: Ax-les-Thermes (2 daily; 2hr 15min–2hr 30min); Barcelona (5 daily; 4hr); L'Hospitalet-près-l'Andorre (2 daily; 1hr 30–40min); La Seu d'Urgell (7 daily Mon–Sat, 5 Sun; 40min); Latour-de-Carol (2 daily; 2hr–2hr 15min); Porté-Puymorens (2 daily; 2hr).

CHAPTER THREE

THE VAL D'ARAN REGION

I solated from Spain and opening towards France, the **Val d'Aran** is something of a curiosity: the frontier here is thrust so far north that both sources of the Garonne, one of southern France's major rivers, lie in Spanish territory. Due to its relatively easy accessibility from both Spain and France, the Val d'Aran makes an obvious jumping-off point into the surrounding mountains. Although heavily developed in most spots for skiers and summer weekenders from Toulouse and Barcelona, the Aran region itself is not lacking in interest.

The popular image of the Pyrenees as two separate mountain chains, overlapping for some 70km at the Val d'Aran, is pervasive and misleading. The definitive geomorphological map of the range, produced in 1973 by the French company Elf-Aquitaine, shows that the watershed is merely distorted here. A significant spur off the main ridge which would ordinarily point south–north is actually deflected east–west, giving the illusion of separate peak lines. In fact, only some low hills to the west in Basque country are tectonically separate from the main body of the Pyrenees.

Between Aran and Andorra, the easternmost of the Pyrenean "three-thousanders", **Montcalm** and **Estats**, rear up over remote valleys on either side of the border. These approaches see few visitors, except along the banks of the mighty **Noguera Pallaresa**, one of the great Pyrenean rivers which flows from just east of Aran south to Lleida. South of Aran, and also accessible from the Noguera Pallaresa valley, spreads the only national park in Catalunya, the **Parc Nacional d'Aigüestortes i Estany de Sant Maurici**, a 15,000-hectare wonderland of crags, tarns and dense forest which delights hikers, alpine skiers and naturalists.

Maladeta – the great massif southwest of Aran, in Alto Aragón – was erroneously translated from the Aragonese *Mala Eta* ("The Highest Point") as "The Accursed" by early French climbers, in reference to the terrifying glaciers which used to dominate this part of the range. Such was the fear induced by their crevasses, that the first successful ascent of **Aneto** – the 3404m roof of the Pyrenees – was not until 1842, by a long and convoluted route avoiding the ice. Owing to global warming, today's glaciers are

ACCOMMODATION PRICE CODES

Each place to stay in this book has been given a code which corresponds to one of the following price categories.

① Under €13/2200ptas/85F   ② €15–24/2500–4000ptas/100–160F
③ €24–32/4000–5400ptas/160–210F   ④ €32–40/5400–6600ptas/210–260F
⑤ €40–52/6600–8600ptas/260–340F   ⑥ €52–65/8600–10,800ptas/340–430F
⑦ Over €65/10,800ptas/430F

Category ① refers to the price *per person* of a bed; the other categories correspond to the **cheapest available double room in high season**. B&B and HB denote, respectively, when the price includes breakfast, and when it includes half-board. For more details, see p.41.

scant vestiges of those that once covered the peaks, and modern maps and equipment further reduce this terrain's power to intimidate.

Immediately west of Maladeta looms the comparatively unsung massif of **Posets**, second highest in the Pyrenees and equally beloved by alpine aficionados. Together these two great mountains form a vast region far easier seen and crossed on foot or skis than by vehicle, so it comes as a welcome surprise to find the populous, comfortable town of **Benasque**, mountaineering capital of eastern Aragón, at the bottom of the Esera valley separating the two mountains. There's no other appreciable settlement until you reach the villages of the **Valle de Chistau**, on Poset's western flank.

If Spain has the region's most spectacular high-mountain scenery, France boasts the finest man-made attractions. Two thousand years of settlement have left their traces at **Saint-Bertrand-de-Comminges**, on the Garonne, and a similar air of antiquity at **Saint-Lizier**, originally founded by the Romans. Further back, the people of the prehistoric Magdalenian culture (15,000–8000 BC) left drawings and sculptures in several caves, including **Mas d'Azil**, between Foix and Saint-Girons, and mysterious, "mutilated" hand outlines at the **Grotte de Gargas** near Saint-Bertrand. Depopulation is severe all over this French region, particularly in the Pays de Couserans region unfolding south from Saint-Girons to the Val d'Aran. The isolation of Pay de Couserans meant that traditional customs, costumes and occupations persisted into the early twentieth century.

The only major signs of development on either side of the frontier are the unsightly **hydroelectric schemes** which have sprung up in almost every canyon. Neither the sites – often still littered with construction debris – nor the procession of pylons marching away from them were conceived with much consideration for aesthetics, wildlife preservation or the wishes of the admittedly dwindling number of local residents.

Public transport is fairly sketchy on the French side, though things tend to improve during the ski season. In Spain, bus services are hardly more frequent, again a consequence of rural depopulation. **Trains** from the south stop at La Pobla de Segur, while in the north there is a foothill rail (or rail-bus) service only on the spur line from Montréjeau to Bagnères-de-Luchon. By contrast the busy main highway between Montréjeau and La Pobla, threading the entire length of Aran and passing close to Aigüestortes, sees a relative abundance of **buses**, as does the road which heads south from Vielha, capital of Aran, for Lleida. Away from this central hub, Benasque in the west has adequate bus services, as does much of the Couserans, with all connections through its regional capital of Saint-Girons.

THE MONTCALM-ESTATS MASSIF AND AROUND

The joint massif of French **Montcalm** (3077m) and border-straddling **Estats** (3143m) – the latter the highest mountain in Catalonia – is so remote from human settlement that until the late 1980s a few bears and lynx were still thought to be living somewhere below the summits. Tucked into a fold of land where the Spanish and French borders meet the westernmost corner of Andorra, this is one of the least-known areas of the Pyrenees – and one of the least accessible. Public transport on both the French and Spanish sides runs no closer than about 20km, from which point it's a good day's walk to the flanks of the mountain.

There are three usual ways into the massif or its foothills: by road from the **Vicdessos valley** in the Ariège; by track, then trail, from the Spanish valleys of Cardós and Ferrera, in turn reached from the larger **Noguera Pallaresa** downstream; or by footpath **from Andorra** (a route covered on pp.215–216). The two **summits** are connected by a ridge walk that crosses the border; to the west a particularly

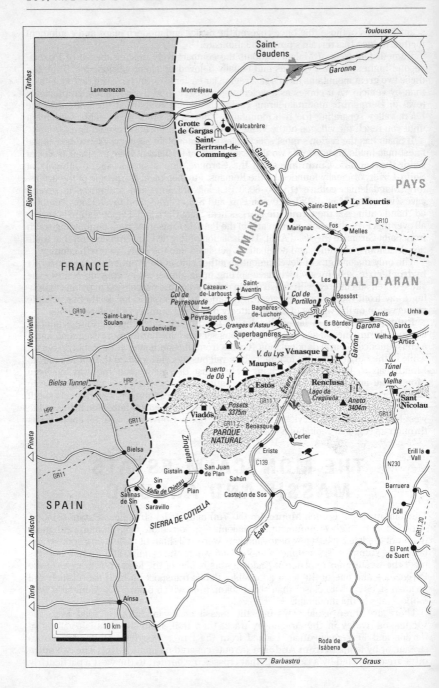

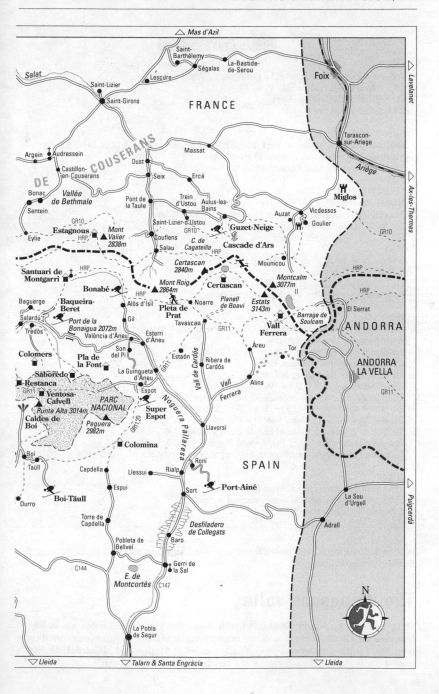

FESTIVALS

JANUARY
7 *Festa Major de Sant Julià* at La Guingueta d'Àneu and Espui.
16 Festival at Gerri de la Sal.
20 Festival at El Pont de Suert.
24 Leather fair at Sort.

FEBRUARY
Variable Shrove Tuesday at Sort, Rialp, Esterri d'Àneu and Pobleta de Bellvcí.
12 *Festa Major de Santa Eulàlia* at Erill la Vall.
14 *Festa Major de Sant Valentí* at Boí.

MARCH/APRIL
Easter Particularly lively festivities at Alins and La Pobla de Segur.
Sunday after Easter *Fira de la Pasqüeta* at Esterri d'Àneu.
28 April Spring fair at Sort.

MAY
3 *Festa de la Santa Creu* at Salardú.
6 Festival at Llavorsí.
First Sunday Festival at Arròs.
First and last Sunday Festival at Gerri de la Sal.

JUNE
Whit Sunday Festival at Mare de Déu de les Ares.
Whit Monday Festival at Arròs.
12 Wool fair at Rialp; sheep-shearing at Llessui.
14 *Romeria de Sant Quirç* at Taüll.
16 *Romeria de Sant Quirç* at Durro.
Third Sunday Festival at Es Bordes.
23 *Feux de la Saint Jean* at Bagnères-de-Luchon.
23–24 Festivals at Arties, Lés, Boí Gil and Saint-Lizier.
28–29 *Festa de Sants Pau i Pere* at Alins and Tor.
30 *Ball de Benás* in honour of San Marcial at Benasque.
Variable *Festival du Chant Pyrénéen* at Bagnères-de-Luchon.
Late June *Raiers*, old-time log-raft festival, at Sort, continues into early July.

JULY
First Sunday *Raiers* at La Pobla de Segur.
First two weeks Classical music festival at Saint-Lizier.
2 Festival at Santuari de Montgarri.

beautiful, challenging and isolated section of the HRP zigzags for two days along the frontier towards Aran.

The Vicdessos valley

Steep-sided, damp-smelling and lined with deciduous forest, the **Vicdessos valley** is typical of the Haute-Ariège: a sunless, uncomfortable place to live in winter. But it does have some intrinsic interest – specifically castles at **Miglos** and **Montréal de Sos** – aside from being the most convenient French corridor to Montcalm.

10 *Festa Major de Sant Cristòfol* at Erill la Vall.
19–20 *Festa Major* at La Guingueta d'Àneu.
24 Festival at Llavorsí.
24–25 *Festa de Sant Jaume* at La Pobla de Segur and Arties.
31 Festival at Gerri de la Sal.
Third weekend *Festa Major dels Rosers* at Taüll; torchlight procession *(faies)* Fri pm, live bands Sat pm, folk dancing Sun noon.
Mid-July to mid-August Music festival at Saint-Lizier.
End July to August Music festival at Saint-Bertrand-de-Comminges.
All month International Canoe Rally on the Noguera Pallaresa.

AUGUST
Early part of the month Music festival at Saint-Lizier.
First Sunday *La Pujada* Catalan-Occitan solidarity festival at the Port de Salau.
1–3 *Festa Major de Sant Feliu* and canoe racing at Sort; *Festa Major* at Barruera.
3 *Festa de Sant Esteve* in Tredòs.
15 Canoe racing at Rialp.
Second weekend *Festa Major* at El Pont de Suert.
10 *Festa Major de Sant Martí* at Torre de Capdella.
15–16 Festivals at several Baixaran villages, including Bossòst.
Third Sunday Flower festival at Bagnères-de-Luchon.
27 *Festa de Sant Llisser* at Alòs d'Isil.
Fourth Sunday *Festa Major* at Capdella.

SEPTEMBER
7–9 Birth of the Virgin observances at Sort, Esterri d'Àneu, Ribera de Cardós, Barruera, Durro, Cóll, Vielha and Es Bòrdes.
22 *Festa Major* at Ermita de Sant Maurici.
Weekend closest to 26 *Festa Major de Sants Cosme i Damià* at Tredòs.
Last Sunday *Festa de Sant Miquel* at Llessuí.

OCTOBER
8 Fair at Vielha.
20 Annual festival at Bossòst.

NOVEMBER
7–9 Grand Autumn Fair at Sort.
23 *Festa de Sant Climent* at Taüll.
30 *Festa de Sant Andreu* at Salardú.

DECEMBER
9 *Festa de Santa Llogaia* at Espot.
24 Festival at La Guingueta d'Àneu.

There are occasional (weekdays in term time, every Friday and alternate Monday otherwise) late afternoon buses from Foix and Tarascon-sur-Ariège up the valley as far as Auzat, which leaves you about 10km short of Mounicou, and the Pinet alpine hut just above it, the usual Montcalm base camp.

Miglos and around

First stop heading up the valley along the D8 could be the ruined fourteenth-century château of **Miglos**, perched atop a rocky outcrop above the valley, a couple of kilometres upstream from Niaux. The medieval locals, resenting taxation by its owner

Guillaume Arnaud d'Arnave, petitioned Gaston Fébus (see p.239) who obliged them by substituting his own taxes. The château was later razed by Cardinal Richelieu, though the towers – best seen from the northerly approach road – remain intact. You can stay at nearby JUNAC (2km downhill on the valley floor) in *chambres d'hôtes* run by a Dutch couple (☎05.61.05.89.88; ③).

If you have your own transport you could detour down the dead-end D24 to SIGUER, where the three-storey, brick-and-timber Maison des Comptes de Foix just off the square (closed for restoration) is a splendid Renaissance hunting lodge used by Gaston Fébus, and another 3km to LERCOUL, a tiny hamlet clinging to the top of a near-vertical cliff. The GR10 passes through both villages as it comes west from Mércns-les-Vals, then continues over the Col de Lercoul to the the village of GOULI-ER, above Vicdessos. Goulier has two gîtes d'étape: *Relais de L'Endron* (☎05.61.03.80.70; ①), on the outskirts, pitched as an activity-coordinating centre with a few rooms as well as a dorm, and the larger, central, welcoming and well-run *Al Cantou* (☎05.61.64.81.84; ①). Both offer half-board for 150–170F/€22.90–25.90 per person, not a bad idea as Goulier village has no shop. The ski-station of Goulier-Neige just uphill was always a bad joke of six short runs, shut for much of each winter owing to a top point of only 2000m; it closed permanently in 1999.

Vicdessos and Auzat

VICDESSOS, 9km beyond Capoulet, and its close neighbour AUZAT are the most southerly outposts of civilization in the valley. Important foundry centres in decades past, neither has much to recommend it now, though Auzat is pleasant enough, with a little stream coursing through between rows of plane trees.

At the nearby Templar château of Montréal de Sos, a medieval mural of the Holy Lance and Grail was discovered in 1890; these days, it's almost invisible. The ruins stand on a mound above the tiny hamlet of Olbier, reached by a footpath from the east bank of the river just past Auzat, or by a track beginning halfway along the road connecting Vicdessos and Goulier. The Templars were responsible for many pilgrims' hospices in the Pyrenees, but became too rich for the liking of the Catholic Church and its allies, who in 1307 accused them of corruption, heresy and sexual depravity, tortured their leaders and finally burnt them to death. The view from the ruins is fabulous, marred only by the aluminium works at Auzat, the last remaining significant source of local employment. In the Middle Ages the inhabitants of Vicdessos who worked in the now-exhausted iron mine at nearby Rancié had the right to sell whatever they extracted to one of the numerous local forges.

Practicalities

Local hotels are limited to the fair-value, one-star *Hivert* in Vicdessos (☎05.61.64.88.17; ②), on the through road, and the overpriced *Hôtel Denjean-La Bonne Auberge* (☎05.61.03.80.99; ③) at the east entrance to Auzat. More attractive are the *chambres d'hotes*, *Les Marmousets*, run by the Pittoni family (☎05.61.64.81.62; ④) in Vicdessos, in the main house and in two chalets. Both hotels have restaurants attached, though the *Denjean*'s is overpriced and mediocre. There is also a campsite in each village: the large *La Bexanelle* at Vicdessos (☎05.61.64.82.22), with cabins, and *La Verniere* at Auzat (☎05.61.64.84.46).

The Maison des Montagnes in Auzat (July & Aug daily 8am–noon & 2–6pm; Sept–June Mon–Fri 8am–noon, Thurs also 2–6pm, Sat 9am–noon; ☎05.61.64.87.53) is quite helpful, with so few passing tourists to attend to. There's also an Office du Tourisme in Vicdessos (☎05.61.64.82.59). Organized local activities are still limited, though you can ride horses at the Centre Equestre in Ournac, 2km south of Auzat (☎05.61.64.84.66), or soar like a bird with a parapente school, Les Aigles du Montcalm (☎05.61.64.87.53; early May–early Oct).

The ascent of Montcalm

Around 10km south of Auzat and 1km past the village of Marc, you'll find an inexpensive but rather poorly maintained *gîte d'étape* (☎05.61.64.87.66; ①) at the tiny hamlet of **MOUNICOU**, situated on both the GR10 and a northerly variant of the HRP. If you've arrived early enough in the day, you might prefer to walk west for two-and-a-half hours uphill to the modern **Refuge de Pinet** (☎05.61.64.80.81; 2224m; 50 places; late June–late Sept; ①). Staying there makes the **ascent of Montcalm** a more manageable five to six hours round-trip, rather than twelve hours from Mounicou. Alternatively, in seven to eight hours you can just trek one-way from Pinet to the *Refugi de Vall Ferrera* (see p.000) in Spain – a beautiful and popular traverse, though you'll need crampons early in the season. The requisite IGN 1:25,000 **map** is TOP 25 2148OT "Montcalm-Estats", though you could probably get by with the Rando Éditions' Carte de Randonnées no. 7, "Haute-Ariège Andorre".

From Marc, follow the side road west towards L'Artigue for about thirty minutes to a car park at road's end, where a clear path waymarked with yellow paint leads to the Pinet refuge, above the Pla de Subra. Montcalm looks formidable from here, its summit looming almost 1000m overhead, the bare rock sunless above the grass and trees. The easy going is all behind you now, and the only emergency campsite is beside the **Étang de Montcalm**. Over scree and rock – with one very steep section – you scramble first to a wide shelf known as the **Tables de Montcalm**, a sort of gangway rising south, then clamber up rocks to the right, finally reaching a relatively easy shoulder of the summit. The walk along the ridge up to Estats takes another forty minutes. To descend, either retrace your steps or reverse the instructions from the Vall Ferrera (see "Approach to Estats from Llavorsí", p.260).

Trekking west of Mounicou

A short distance northwest of the Mounicou *gîte d'étape*, the HRP and the GR10 go their separate ways. The **GR10** runs through Marc (no facilities) and up onto the hillsides above the west bank of the River Vicdessos to the hamlet of Hérout. There it bears northwest, climbing very steeply to the dammed lakes of Escales and Bassiès and up again to Étang d'Alate, from which you descend to the **Port de Saleix** (1794m) and then west through forest to Aulus-les-Bains (p.311) – a total of about eight hours' walking. You can break this sector at the *Refuge des Étangs de Bassiès* (☎05.61.61.89.98; staffed June–Sept, 50 places; 15-place section always open; ①), above the higher, smaller natural lake.

Beyond Marc, the more circuitous **HRP** route goes through L'Artigue, then climbs west-southwest to the **Port de l'Artigue** (2484m; 5hr) on the Spanish frontier. The general line continues northwest, but for the rest of the day good compass work is essential. From the pass you drop to a marshy tarn in the Spanish Aguiló valley, skirting it north and climbing steeply westwards along the stream to the lower of two lakes known as **Estanys d'Aguiló** (*Guiló* on some French maps). Then you continue northwest to the **Port de Colatx/Port de Couillac** (2416m). The first day's goal, the **Étang de la Hillette** (1800m), lies two hours below, magnificently situated above the Cirque de Cagateille (10–12hr from Mounicou). Those without tents can stay in the *Cabane de la Hillette* (15 places) or the *Vieille Cabane de la Hillette* (4 places), until a staffed refuge is built here as planned.

Instead of climbing to the Port de Colatx, you can alternatively follow the Spanish variant of the HRP, which next intersects the French route at the Port de Salau (see p.311); your first shelter is the *Refugi de Certascan* (see p.262). Staying on the French side, beyond La Hillette the HRP grazes the border just below the **Port de Marterat/Materet** (2217m) before veering northwest towards the Col de Crusous

(2300m) on the shoulder of Cap de Ruhous, prelude to a steady descent to Salau (9hr from Hillette).

If you or the weather are not up to this, it's better to opt for the beautiful half-day ramble from Hillette down the **Cirque de Cagateille** (see p.311 for more details), through the woods and along the Cors stream, reaching the D38 and the GR10 at **SAINT-LIZIER-D'USTOU**. Its somewhat basic and seasonal facilities are described on p.311. The downstream hamlet of **TREIN D'USTOU**, 3km away in the Vallée de Ustou, offers the more comfortable *Hotel Restaurant Des Ormeaux* (☎05.61.96.53.22, fax 05.61.66.84.19; ③ B&B), where all rooms have baths. It's open most of the year and thus the most reliable place to eat in the valley, with two choices of *menu*. Next day you can catch the bus to Saint-Girons.

Up the Noguera Pallaresa

The **Noguera Pallaresa**, the most powerful river in the Spanish Pyrenees, was once used to float logs from the upper valley to the sawmills at **La Pobla de Segur**, a job now done by truck. This is the Pyrenean river every rafter wants to tackle, but if you're not of that persuasion, the valley – beautiful and dramatic though it can be – is primarily a way of reaching the mountains to either side, or arriving in the Val d'Aran. To ascend Estats and Montcalm, you leave the Noguera Pallaresa at Llavorsí, heading northeast along the valleys of **Cardós** and **Ferrera**; for Aran, the busier C142 road continues northwest, via the **Vall d'Àneu**, up to the seasonally open **Port de Bonaigua**.

Access from the east

Access to the valley is easiest through La Pobla de Segur, which has public transport connections in every direction. Coming into the Noguera Pallaresa **from the east**, twice-daily minibuses are now available in either direction – you're advised to book seats on the phone numbers in "Travel Details". Otherwise, drive or hitch along the 46-kilometre road from Adrall (near La Seu d'Urgell) to Sort, or take one of a number of mountain-biking or walking routes. The four-wheel-drive track from Sant Joan de l'Erm, beyond Castellbó (west of La Seu), drops into the Noguera Pallaresa between Rialp and Llavorsí, near the Port-Ainé downhill ski resort. There's also a track from Ars, just outside Andorra's extreme southwest corner, coming down to Tirvia near Llavorsí. From inside Andorra there's another track – passable to most cars in summer – from Pal over Port de Cabús, descending into Spain at Tor, at the head of the Tor valley; from there you move into the Vall Ferrera valley at Alins and finally into the Cardós valley, not far from Llavorsí. Yet another possibility is to use the **HRP variant** from El Serrat in the northwest corner of Andorra to Tavascan.

La Pobla de Segur and around

LA POBLA DE SEGUR is a lively enough town if you want to break your journey, but most people only come here for onward connections. As well as buses further north along the Noguera Pallaresa, local services journey west to El Pont de Suert, Boí and Capdella for jumping off into the Aigüestortes region, and to Vielha for the Val d'Aran.

La Pobla is served year-round by a twice-daily Alsina Graells **bus** from Barcelona (departs 7.30am and 2.30pm from Plaça de la Universitat, labelled *Pont de Rei*), and by three daily **trains** from Lleida which terminate here. The bus from Barcelona continues up the Noguera Pallaresa through Sort and Llavorsí, passing the side road for the Cardós and Ferrera valleys, and within 7km of Espot, a major entry point to the Aigüestortes national park (see p.278). From June to mid-November, the morning service continues over the pass into the Val d'Aran. Arriving from Lleida, morning train and bus services should arrive before the bus up the Noguera Pallaresa at 11.35am; there's another service at 6.35pm.

Trains arrive in the new town, from where you walk north up the road, across the bridge to the old town and along the main street to the terminals of the various **bus** companies: Alsina Graells, serving most destinations, is at c/de la Font 8. Should you get stranded, there's just one surviving *hostal*, the bunker-ugly *Torrentet* at Plaça Pedrera 5 (☎973 680 352; ③).

Talarn and Santa Engràcia

If you are stopping overnight, there are far better spots to **stay** and **eat** outside of Tremp, 13km downriver from La Pobla. The large, fortified hill town of **TALARN** 2km northwest of Tremp proves to be an unsung gem, its houses (plus a few ad hoc towers) forming a defensive perimeter, with an old church at the low end of the maze of interior lanes. Just inside from the car-park plaza at c/Soldevila 2, *Casa Lola* shines as a beacon of country cuisine, attracting clientele from near and far; about 3000ptas/€18 will net you wild mushroom salad, *girella* (tasty lamb-and-rice haggis) and a choice from the most extravagant dessert list in the region, with excellent local red wine. Proprietress "Lola" (Glorieta) is a character, giving free *pa amb tomaquet*-making lessons to the unititiated; she also has a few apartments (☎973 650 814; 7300ptas/€44).

Especially with a car, head out from just below Talarn along a narrow but paved ten-kilometre road west to **SANTA ENGRÀCIA**, surely the most spectacularly set village in Catalunya, tumbling off the south flank of a rock monolith. This was the limit of the Cretaceous-era sea, and the entire region is a geologist's paradise of stacked sedimentary rock and exposed fossils. Here Richard and Sandra Loder manage *Casa Guilla* (☎606 333 481 or ☎696 177 257, *www.ctv.es/USERS/casaguilla*; ④ HB; closed Dec–Feb), a restored, rambling farmhouse poised like the prow of a ship at the monolith's east end, with sweeping views. Accommodation is rustically simple – many rooms at this *casa de pagès* are non-en suite – but there's a pool, basement bar, generous continental breakfast and group evening *table d'hôte* meals. The area is a mecca for birders, botanists and geologists alike, so reservations are advised.

Gerri de la Sal and around

From La Pobla de Segur the C147 road threads through the red and steel-grey rocks of the **Desfiladero de Collegats**, an impressive gorge hewn by the Noguera Pallaresa through 300-metre-high cliffs. Unfortunately, since a series of tunnels was blasted through much of the defile, drivers see little of the spectacular valley, though the narrow, abandoned old road is still open to cyclists and pedestrians. The Catalan intelligentsia have been coming to admire the scenery here for over a century, and the portion of the canyon labelled **L'Argenteria**, with its sculpted, papier-mâché-like rockface streaked with rivulets, is said to have inspired Antoní Gaudí's La Pedrera apartment building in Barcelona.

As the canyon opens out, you emerge at the rickety village of **GERRI DE LA SAL** – "de la Sal" because of the local salt-making industry. Salt pans are still in use by the riverside, but more obvious is the Benedictine monastery of **Santa Maria**, founded in 807. The present twelfth-century structure, with its huge and dilapidated bell-wall, faces the village on the far side of a beautiful old bridge. The church interior (200ptas/€1.20) is a three-aisled basilica, with soaring barrel vaulting upheld by four fluted columns; a few recent frescoes are of limited interest. Opening hours are erratic – try hunting for the warden at the little drinks café – but it's worth a look even from the outside, where an arched hay-loft runs along the south side of the building.

If you have a vehicle this is a fine place for a short break, but it's inconvenient for those on public transport. In Gerri itself there's a **restaurant** and bar, but to find

accommodation you must continue 4km north to the tiny village of **BARO**, where there are rooms and food at the *Bar Restaurante Cal Mariano* (☎973 680 550; ②). There's also a large, riverbank **campsite**, the *Pallars Sobirà* (☎973 662 030; open all year), and a supermarket.

West to Pobleta de Bellveí: the Estany de Montcortès
The very minor road from Gerri de la Sal to Pobleta de Bellveí, 17km west, makes a pristine and tranquil run through rolling uplands speckled with picturesque villages. It's ideal for mountain-biking or driving, but don't hitch or walk it: there's little traffic and the initial climb up to Peramea is punishing and unshaded. This road, incidentally, is wrongly shown on the recommended Firestone map – it's not a dead-end, and it's paved all the way. From Bretui, 10km along, you have fine views into the gorge of Cortscastells, a tributary of Collegats, but high point of the route is the idyllic little **Estany de Montcortès** (1021m), just west of the village of the same name. Though reed-fringed, this attractive karstic lake is warm and drops suddenly to thirty-metre depths, so there's no bottom muck to contend with. Several wooden jetties allow access to the deep water, and a swim is just the thing if you're cycling or motoring by. Beyond here lies the sharp, featureless descent to Pobleta de Bellveí in the Vall Fosca (see p.279).

Sort to Port-Aimé

SORT, 30km north of La Pobla, retains an old centre of tall, narrow houses, though it's now hemmed in by apartment buildings. This rapid development is largely due to the reputation of Sort and neighbouring villages as one of the premier river-running spots in Europe. After the spring thaw the area swarms with mostly foreign kayakers, canoeists and rafters, equipped with hi-tech gear. And every year, during late June/early July, the communities of the valley stage the festival of the *Raiers* (Rafters), re-enacting the exploits of the old-time timber pilots who could show the slick new dare-devils a thing or two.

   Because of the upmarket sports clientele it attracts, Sort prices itself outside casual trade, and in any case it's not a place to linger unless you're here for the action (which can be exhilarating; see box opposite). Its main street is almost exclusively devoted to rafting and adventure shops; among these, Rubber River (☎973 620 220, fax 973 620 237, *www.rubber-river.com*) is reputable and recommended. There's nowhere inexpensive to stay or eat, though there is a **tourist office** (summer Mon–Fri 9am–2pm & 5–9pm, Sat 10am–1pm & 5–8pm) on the main street. The bus stops at an obvious shelter on Plaça Catalina Albert, at the north end of town where the two through roads meet. **RIALP**, 3km north, is a marginally more appealing mix of old houses and new boutiques; its bus stop/ticket office is at the bar under the *Hotel Victor* (☎973 620 379; ⑤), the only reasonable if somewhat unexciting place to stay.

Skiing: Port-Ainé
Though still shown on maps, the ski station at Llessui, 16km west of Sort and Rialp, closed some years back. **PORT-AINÉ**, 14km northeast of Rialp, has filled the breach, offering some of the best beginners' and intermediates' skiing in the Catalan Pyrenees on 28 longish runs. First impressions may not be good: the café and restaurant are a bit shabby, rental gear (only at Point 2080) is limited and better sought in Rialp, and the layout of services and lifts is a Heath-Robinsonesque arrangement whereby you must often buy passes at Point 1650 and then go up the main chairlift to Point 2080 in street shoes unless you've shown up with gear. There's an intermediate stop, part-time ticket booth and car park at 1960m. Once the logistics are sorted, the skiing and setting are glorious. From the beginners' runs around Point 2080 there's a short drop to a chair-

lift mounting 2440-metre Pic de l'Orri, start of most runs. These include the aptly named 4300-metre Bella Vista green run along the ridge and through the pines, or the 2300-metre Les Pilones red run to the base of the Pic de l'Orri lift. Pistes' colour-coding is overrated – blues are rather greenish, reds blueish – but the north-facing valley generally enjoys powdery snow, even in spring. A hotel is being built at Point 1960, but until it's ready the closest **accommodation** is a *casa de pagès* (☎973 620 837; ③) in the village of **RONÍ**, 9km downhill on the side road in.

Llavorsí

Probably the most attractive place to stay along this stretch of the valley is **LLAVORSÍ**, 10km above Rialp. Despite extensive renovation, a rash of new bar/restaurants and rafting outfitters on the main road, plus a mammoth power substation across the way, this tight huddle of stone-built houses and slate roofs at the confluence of the Noguera Pallaresa and Cardós rivers still retains some character. There are two good riverside **campsites**, both with pools and bars: the *Aigües Braves* 1km north of town (☎973 622 153; March–Sept), and the smaller *Riberies* east of the centre in the Cardós valley (☎973 622 151; mid-June to mid-Sept), plus ample **accommodation** catering for the river trade. You should reserve in advance in rafting season; try the *Hotel Lamoga* (☎973 622 006; May–Sept only; ④), with a good *menú* for under 2000ptas/€12, and the quieter

---

RAFTING ON THE NOGUERA PALLARESA

The main **rafting season** on the Noguera Pallaresa lasts from April until September, though some organizations, such as Rafting Llavorsí, offer programmes from March to October if snowmelt (and the power company) are amenable. The original rafts for the journey to the sawmills of La Pobla de Segur were logs lashed together ten-wide, controlled by a long, stern-mounted oar.

Today's water-sport versions are reinforced inflatables, up to 6.5m long, and weighing around 100kg. If you sign on for a trip – which guarantees a soaking and as much excitement as any well-balanced person would want – you'll usually share a **boat** with seven others, including your guide/pilot, who sits in the rear. Standard **gear** includes crash helmet, buoyancy jacket (*chaleca*), wet suits (water temperature in April is a bracing 8°C), lightweight paddles, but *not* gloves. You need bare fingers to keep hold of the T-grip at the end of the oar (*remo*), of which you should never let go – even on the calmer stretches a sudden bump could catapult it from your hands and knock your neighbour's teeth out.

Everyone keeps one foot in stirrups, but it's certain that you'll **go overboard** – the more mischievous skippers make sure everyone takes a spill during the first few kilometres of warm-up, so that you lose your fear of the water. When you get pitched in, just "go with the flow", floating on your back feet first with your knees slightly bent to brace for impact against submerged rocks; crewed boats float faster downstream than you, but you'll be thrown a fifteen-metre line if necessary.

Since groups are mostly local, it's worth knowing a few Spanish **commands**: *adelante* (row forward), *atrás* (paddle backward), *alto* (stop rowing), *contrapeso derecho/izquierda* (throw your weight to the right/left, when entering a rapid).

The fourteen-kilometre stretch of river between Llavorsí and Rialp is the easiest and most commonly rafted, while the 18km from Sort to Desfiladero de Collegats is advanced and even more scenic. Daily **departures** are typically at 11am and noon; in the former case you'll be in the water by 11.20am, and clambering into the return shuttle van at Rialp by 12.40pm. **Prices** in the valley for rafting start at about 4500ptas/€27 for a two-hour trip, Llavorsí–Rialp or Sort–Collegats, or 8000ptas for the entire 35-kilometre distance (a full afternoon's outing, packed lunch 2000ptas/€12 extra).

Hostal de Rey, adjacent on the riverfront (☎973 622 011; ③); or the *Hostal Noguera* (☎973 622 012; ③), on the opposite bank, whose restaurant has river-view seating and a reasonable if rather limited *menú*.

Local **sports/adventure operators** include Hípica Llavorsí for horse-riding (☎973 622 252), next to the *Riberies* campsite, and two outfitters offering rafting, canyoning, hydrospeed, mountain-biking and rock-climbing: the bizarrely named Yeti Emotions (☎973 622 201, fax 973 622 260, *www.yetiemotions.com*), 500m south of Llavorsí, on the west bank of the river opposite a road tunnel, the central and friendly Rafting Llavorsí (☎973 622 158, fax 973 622 134, *www.raftingllavorsi.com*).

Approach to Estats from Llavorsí

From Llavorsí, the initially paved road up to the *Refugi de Vall Ferrera* – base for the ascent of Estats and Montcalm – is almost a full day's slog through an underpopulated area of pastures and hayfields, the latter scythed in July; hitch or get a taxi if you're without a vehicle. The first part of the route follows the Cardós valley (see below) from Llavorsí; after about 4km, you turn off east along the **Vall Ferrera** towards **ALINS**, 13.5km from Llavorsí and the valley "capital". At Alins, there's a choice of en-suite **accommodation**: the plush *Hotel Salòria* (☎973 624 341; ④ B&B), offering full savoury breakfasts and balconied rooms, slightly cheaper beds in the co-managed *Fonda Llesuy* across the street (high season only; ③), and the *Hostal Muntanya* (☎973 624 411; ④). If Alins is full or too busy for your taste, *Casa Gabatxó* (☎973 624 322; ③), in Araós 6km downstream back towards Llavorsí, is the most highly regarded of the valley's dozen or so *cases de pagès*, offering half-board.

Another 5km beyond Alins along the main valley lies the tiny village of **ÀREU**, the last settlement before Estats, and on the GR11; it has a small shop, and a pleasant, tent-oriented **campsite**, the *Pica d'Estats* (☎973 624 347; open Easter & late June to mid-Sept), with a pool and a decent restaurant. The most obvious indoor **accommodation** is the rambling *Hotel Vall Ferrera* (☎973 624 343; ④); they also have the main village restaurant, with half-board available. Àreu also offers ample, less expensive lodging in the *casa de pagès* scheme, for example *Casa Gallardó* (☎973 624 344; ③), in the upper quarter. In 1999, a **museum** opened here, a working hydro-powered *serradora* or sawmill (July & Sept Sat & Sun 11am–1pm & 5–7pm, Aug daily same hours except Sun pm; 300ptas/€1.80).

The route up the mountain continues, first via dirt track and then, 3.5km above Àreu, along the marked east-bank trail #17, "Camí Vell del Port de Boet-Pla de Boet", routed in common with the GR11, to just below the **Refugi de Vall Ferrera** (☎973 624 378; 1940m; 30 places; open and staffed June–Sept; ①), nearly four hours from Àreu. Kayakers should note that the stretch of river here, though short (4km), presents some of the best, and least commercialized, white water in the Catalan Pyrenees.

Next day, allow about five hours to get up to **Estats**. Follow the marked path north through the Sottlo valley and past the photogenic lakes of Sottlo and Estats, then up into the Port de Sottlo (2894m); from here a short ridge walk east leads to the summit. Another ridge leads 45 minutes northeast to **Montcalm**, where you can either backtrack or link up with the route from L'Artigue in France.

Other onward routes from the refuge

East of the *Vall Ferrera* refuge, the HRP variant and GR11 lead into Andorra by different sets of passes – described on p.216; the GR11 is easier, not exceeding 2517m elevation en route, at the small unstaffed refuge of Baiau just before the frontier. Northwards, then westwards, you can make the traverse to Tavascan (11hr – see below) initially via the Sottlo lake, where you should bear west over the 2618-metre Coll de Barborte to the **Baborte** lake (5hr from Refugi Vall Ferrera; unlocked 8-person refuge adjacent) and **Planell de Boavi** (9hr), a beautiful but occasionally over-subscribed wilderness camping area among birches and firs. The late-1990s banning of vehicle access to this point did wonders for the local environment, eliminating the former piles of rubbish.

The Vall de Cardós

If you stay with the road up the broader and more developed Vall de Cardós instead of taking a right into the Vall Ferrera, you'll pass through **RIBERA DE CARDÓS** (10km from Llavorsí), a sizeable and attractive village with a twelfth-century, squat-belfried church. For **accommodation**, try the two-star *Hostal Sol i Neu* (☎973 623 137; ⑤; open March–Oct), by the river at the south entry to the village, or the modest *Hostal Cal Quet*, also on the through road (☎973 623 124; ④). There's **camping** at the caravan-oriented, riverside *La Borda del Pubill* (☎973 623 088; April–Oct), with a pool and tennis courts, and *Del Cardós* (☎973 623 112; April–Sept), with similar amenities, north of the village. An adventure centre, Natur Esports (☎973 623 072), operates opposite the *Sol i Neu*, while a giant sawmill injects a bit of industrial reality into the picture.

Tavascan

The road continues past other steeple-crowned hamlets (Ainet de Cardós has another campsite, *Les Contioles*, ☎973 623 156, April–Sept) surrounded by hayfields and grazing sheep to **TAVASCAN**, 20km from Llavorsí, where the single high street is a solid mass of accommodation. This recent gentrification is owed largely to a **nordic ski station** at **Pleta de Prat**, 11km northwest past Noarre hamlet, which has a couple of newish chairlifts and a few token downhill runs. Yet Tavascan is a larger, more traditional village than it appears from the through road, with an old bridge over the Riu Tavascan above the church; the **GR11** slips over this and through lanes of old houses on the west bank.

Among the three **hotels** here, simplest is the friendly, low-key *Marxant* (☎973 623 151, fax 973 623 039, *marxant@autovia.com*; ⑤ HB), something of a trekkers' haven despite its en-suite but plain, well-worn 1970s rooms. Evening meals – typically salad, omelette, rabbit or boar with mushrooms – are more than decent. For more comfort at similar prices, the adjacent *Hotel Llacs del Cardós* (☎973 623 178, fax 973 623 126; ④ or ⑥ HB) is arguably better value, all rooms having balconies; or for a real splurge, there's the co-managed three-star *Hotel Estanys Blaus* opposite (same phone; ⑥), with rear rooms overlooking the river. Sole budget option is the rather ordinary *Pensió Feliu* (☎973 623 163; ③ or ⑤ HB), masquerading as a *casa de pagès*. Also on the high street you'll find the last grocery store before the wilderness. The nearest **campsite**, *Bordes de Graus* (☎973 623 246; April–Oct), lies an inconvenient 5km up towards the ski centre. Another site, *Serra* (☎973 623 117; July–Sept), though roughly the same distance south in Lladorre village, is actually closer to the valley's assorted attractions.

Trekking and walking out of Vall de Cardós

If you're traversing east to west (or vice versa) along the **HRP** (see below), a case can be made for skipping Tavascan altogether – you have to lose and regain a lot of altitude to get there. As noted above, however, the **GR11** goes through Tavascan, and for the less committed hiker forms the partial basis of a six-hour **loop-walk**, dubbed the "Itinerari Panoràmic per l'Alt Cardós", which takes in several villages clinging to the side of the upper valley, using sections of the GR11 plus local PR paths for lateral links. The route is shown on the Editorial Alpina map "Pica d'Estats", and on a placard beside the Hotel Marxant. It heads south from Tavascan to the villages of Aineto and Lleret on the GR11, crosses to the east bank of the valley at Lladorre, then climbs up to Boldís Jussà and Boldís Sobirà to rejoin the GR11 for a northerly descent to Tavascan.

Above Tavascan there's a choice of other tracks: the more easterly, towards Planell de Boavi, is the direct route to Pic de Certascan (2853m); the other northwesterly option, beyond the power station, connects at Noarre with the HRP towards the Val d'Aran. Both lead to delightful wildernesses of long valleys and tarn-spangled cirques up against the border. To a certain extent they can be combined, as the HRP passes the base of Pic de Certascan.

For the **Certascan area**, take a turn-off at the Montalto dam 6km beyond Tavascan on the rough track towards Boavi, at first traversing, then climbing fairly steep up the Sierra Marinera past the western shore of the superb **Estany de Naorte**, with the summit of Estats just visible above the low, rounded hills and sparse pines on the opposite bank. About an hour later (3.5hr from Tavascan) you reach the **Llac de Certascan**, star of many a postcard, and at nearly 100m deep and 1200m long, claimed to be the largest natural lake in the Pyrenees. (With a 4WD vehicle, you can drive to within half an hour of the lake on a track contouring initially far below Naorte. You may soon also be able to use a rehabilitated underground railway, ceded by the power company, to ascend to the lake.) At the south end of the lake stands the *Refugi de Certascan* (☎973 623 230; 2240m; 40 places; staffed mid-June to mid-Sept; 20-place section always open; ③), with hot showers, meals and cooking facilities; from here the **Pic de Certascan** is an easy and enjoyable half-day round-trip ascent.

Since the refuge sits beside the **HRP** it's possible to follow this west for six hours to the hamlet of **Noarre** (no facilities), but it's a tough section with lots of cross-country route-finding, only feasible in good conditions. From Noarre – accessible directly from Tavascan in two hours by the alternative track – or from the next wilderness campsite another hour upstream at **Pleta de l'Arenal**, you can continue west to Salardú in Aran. This involves two or three days' walking on the HRP or one of its variants; the quickest heads due west for Alòs d'Isil, about ten hours away via a necklace of tarns at the base of 2864-metre **Mont Roig**. The only facility en route, about 2hr west of Pleta de l'Arenal, is the unstaffed *Refugi Mont Roig-Enric Pujol* (2290m, 18 places), an ambitious target for a day's trek west from Certascan but well placed for exploring the tarns, as well as the peak.

Alternatively, the Cardós valley is linked to both the Vall Ferrera and the Vall d'Àneu (see below) by the somewhat easier though less dramatic **GR11**, which passes right through Tavascan. From just above Àreu in the Vall Ferrera, the route cuts over Montarenyo ridge via the Coll de Tudela to Boldís and Tavascan, then bears sharply southwest over another 2500-metre spur to La Guingueta d'Àneu via Estaon. The Àreu–Tavascan sector makes for an easy walking day of about six hours; Tavascan–La Guingueta is getting on for nine hours, so many people elect to break the journey roughly halfway at attractive Estaon, in a side valley above Ribera de Cardós, where there's just a single *casa de pagès*, Casa Pau (☎973 623 113; ③).

The Vall d'Àneu

From Llavorsí the road continues upstream along the Noguera Pallaresa, past the turning for Espot (see p.278) and the placid, artificial lake of Pantà de la Torrasa, to **LA GUINGUETA D'ÀNEU** at the head of the reservoir. This is the first of three villages incorporating the name of the local valley, the **Vall d'Àneu**, and consists mostly of a small cluster of roadside **accommodation**. The best options are the budget *Hostal Orteu* (☎973 626 086; ③), whose bar is a local hangout, or the one-star *Hotel Poldo* (☎973 626 080, fax 973 626 385; ⑦ HB). The *Poldo* has a more exciting restaurant, with outdoor seating and spit-grilled meats.

Esterri d'Àneu

ESTERRI D'ÀNEU, 4km further beyond the lake, was transformed quite suddenly in the early 1990s from a sleepy farming community to a chic resort. Parts of town still form as graceful an ensemble as you'll see in the Catalan Pyrenees – the few huddled houses between the road and the river, an arched bridge and slender-towered Sant

Vicenç church – but the new apartment buildings and fancy hotels to the south are another matter. Esterri's growth has stalled of late, linked to any overflow of Super Espot ski clientele, but expansion of the closer Baqueira-Beret resort, lately mooted, to this side of the Port de la Bonaigua could set off another spasm of construction.

Among **accommodation** choices, best value has historically been the delightful *Fonda Agustí* (☎973 626 034; ③), quietly set behind the church in Plaça de l'Església, serving enormous **meals** for well under 2000ptas/€12 in its old-fashioned *menjador*, however it was gutted and overhauled in spring 2000, so expect some changes. *Hostal Costa* at c/ Major 14 (☎973 626 061; ③) is somewhat grim, and the 1750-ptas/€10.50 *menú* poor value; ask for their plusher, second premises *Costa 2* (☎973 626 401; ④) to ensure nocturnal calm and comfort. The closest **campsite**, *La Presalla* (☎973 626 031; April–Sept), renting out chalet-huts, is 1.5km south of the village. From late November to May, the village is also the end of the line for the bus from Barcelona.

The Vall d'Isil

From the centre of Esterri d'Àneu, you can bear north along a narrow but paved road up the **Vall d'Isil**, its atmospheric villages little visited and effectively abandoned, some of them (like roadless Arreu) squatted by "alternative" types from the big city. The highlight, 11km along just before **GIL** (formerly Isil), is the engaging Romanesque church of Sant Joan, with its fine south portal, two Gothic windows retaining some tracery, its apse just about in the river, and pairs of strange carved figures studding the roofline. By the river in the village, *Refugi Casa Sastrés* (☎973 626 522, *www.web.kaos.es/bonabe*; 45 places; ①) is a welcome sight if you've trekked west from Noarre or east from the Mongarri (Montgarry) valley (see p.270). It's in an attractive nineteenth-century building, with a beamed-ceiling diner, though the smallest dorm has six beds. If you want more privacy, there are a few *cases de pagès* locally, such as *Casa Fuster* (☎973 626 196; ③). **ALÒS D'ISIL**, at the end of the paved route, has more hostel-type accommodation outside the village at the *Xalet-Refugi el Fornet* (no phone; 40 places, meals served; ①), geared largely for users of the **Bonabé cross-country ski centre** just 4km north along the dirt track.

València d'Àneu

Three kilometres further up the main road, **VALÈNCIA D'ÀNEU**, with its traditional stone houses and small Romanesque church of Sant Andreu, has been far less developed than Esterri d'Àneu, and should remain pretty rural unless the Baqueira-Beret resort over the hill is extended. València was once much more important than its current sleepiness suggests. An archeological dig on the outskirts has brought to light the remains of a tenth-century **castle**, apparently the power base of local counts who ruled over many of the surrounding valleys. When the volunteers are present in summer, visitors are welcome to look around.

Best choice for **accommodation** here is the exceptionally good-value *Hotel La Morera* (☎973 626 124; ⑤), with enormous balconied rooms, a valley-side pool and wonderful breakfasts. Runners-up are the *habitaciones* above the recommended **restaurant** *La Bonaigua* (☎973 626 110; usually closed Jan 7 to end March & mid-Oct to Nov; ③), which features local game and trout on its affordable *menús*. Another worthwhile spot to eat, in the village centre off the through road, is *Felip*, with a 1350-ptas/€8.10 *menú* or an ample *carta*. Alternative lodging consists of two *cases de pagès*: the well-set *Casa Campaner* (☎973 626 251; ④), near the *Felip*, or *Casa Sala* facing the church (☎973 626 254; ③).

Son del Pi and the Port de la Bonaigua

About 1km beyond València d'Aneu, then 4km south following signs for Estais, is **SON DEL PI** ('Son'), remarkable for its eleventh- to twelfth-century fortified church of **Sants Just i Pastor** (daily 10am–2pm & 5–8pm, hours vary out of season;

100ptas/€0.60). The church has a four-storey Lombard-type belfry with an Aranese pyramidal roof, while a sixteenth-century *retable* and carved stone font (previously a Visigothic sarcophagus) grace the interior. Its most unusual feature is the round tower by the gate, the *Comunidor*, which the local priest used to climb and, sacred Host in hand, cast spells against destructive storms and avalanches. The village is a beauty as well, but the *Bar-Restaurant Casa Masover* opposite the church is shut more often than not, so the only reliable local facility is the **Refugi Pla de la Font**, poised between here and Espot, and accessible by 9km of good dirt track (☎619 930 771 or 973 620 164, *plafont@navegalia.com*; 2016m; 20 places; open mid-June to late Sept plus Dec–May weekends/hols; ①). Although situated in the "peripheral zone" of the Aigüestortes national park (see p.274) this refuge doesn't, however, offer the most convenient approach to the park, being a day's march from either the Mataró or Saborèdo huts.

Beyond València and the turning for Son, the road quits the Noguera Pallaresa and climbs above the quilt of green and brown fields around Esterri. The Riu de la Bonaigua takes over as the roadside stream, lined by forests of silver birch, pine and fir. Views get ever more impressive as you approach the treeline, above which is perched the **restaurant-bar** of *Mare de Déu de les Ares*, next to the eponymous *ermita*. There's a good, varied lunch menu for under 2000ptas/€12, but the place shuts by 7pm; the inn here has ceased operation and the nearest accommodation is the alpine refuge at Mataró (see p.272). Two hairpins above the *ermita*, you'll notice the trailhead for the path up into the Gerber and Mataró valleys (see p.272 for this route) – in season parked cars mark the spot. Near the top of the bleak **Port de la Bonaigua** (2072m; usually closed in winter due to avalanche risk), snow patches persist year round, half-wild horses graze and you get simultaneous panoramas of the valleys you've just left and the Val d'Aran to come.

THE VAL D'ARAN

Though undeniably on the French side of the Pyrenean watershed, the **Val d'Aran** has long been under Spanish sovereignty. This oddity seems even more pronounced when you consider that Andorra, while opening towards Spain, was long semi-autonomous (and opted for full independence in 1993), and that the Cerdanya/Cerdagne, despite a lack of pronounced natural demarcations, is divided between the two countries. However, in June 1990 a special law of the Catalan Generalitat restored a degree of self-rule to the valley.

Cut off from the outside world for centuries, the Val d'Aran has evolved its own language – **Aranès** – which is only spoken (and written, as on the bizarre-seeming road signs) in the valley. It's based on elements of Gascon and Catalan, plus a generous sprinkling of Basque vocabulary. The valley's name, for example, is not Aranés but pure Basque, and "Val" is technically redundant – *aran* means "valley" in Euskera. (From here westwards, Basque place-names are commonly encountered, tide-markers of the former and greater extent of a people now restricted to the west end of the range.) The Aranès **spelling of local place-names** is now exclusively used on local signs and tourist literature (if not yet on internationally published maps), so is given preference in the following account, with the former Castilian or Catalan in parentheses.

Aran has strong historical links to both France and Spain, and was a source of conflict as long ago as 1192, when it passed from the counts of Comminges to the kings of Aragón. In 1808 Napoleon announced its annexation, sending 2500 French troops from nearby Bagnères. Only a thousand reached the Val d'Aran – the rest deserted – but there were enough troops to briefly expel the Spanish. The valley was a stronghold of Republicanism during the Spanish Civil War and a refuge for the defeated afterwards, safe behind passes snowed up half the year. It was invaded once again by Franco's

THE SOURCES OF GARONA/GARONNE

The river draining the Val d'Aran begins life as the **Garona**, then in France becomes the **Garonne**, swinging northeast through Saint-Gaudens and Toulouse, and northwest to the Atlantic at Bordeaux. The river has two commonly accepted sources: the Ruda stream at the east end of the valley, fed by the Saborèdo lakes, and the Joeu, in the west beyond Vielha, up against the French frontier.

Contrary to what was believed until 1931, the **Joeu** doesn't rise in Aran at all, but in the Maladeta-Aneto Massif to the southwest, on the opposite side of the watershed from the Val d'Aran. In that year, the French speleologist Norbert Casteret (see p.316) proved that the Joeu was a resurgence by emptying 55 kilos of dye into the **Forau dels Aigualluts**, the sinkhole for the Aneto glacier's meltwater. In Casteret's own words: "Next day, the Garonne revealed its secret. For twenty-seven hours a million cubic yards of bright green water poured down the Val d'Aran and for over fifty miles into France."

Nationalists in 1944, who took a year or two to completely suppress the Republican resurgence. The isolation of Aran was finally relieved by the boring of the **Túnel de Vielha** in 1948 (using the slave labour of Republican POWs), allowing the N230 road to directly link the valley with the provincial capital of Lleida. At peak periods this tunnel is heavily oversubscribed, and plans are afoot for either the existing tunnel to be doubled or an entirely new one to be bored.

Since Franco's passing, life in the valley has changed dramatically. Your first clues are the high-tension electricity pylons from Llavorsí over the Port de la Bonaigua, and through the dense forest of the Coll du Portillon in the west; heavy traffic through the tunnel to the valley capital of Vielha is another sign of modern development. Scythe-wielding hay-reapers of past summers have been replaced by Massey-Ferguson balers, the hayfields themselves overlooked by holiday chalets that have sprouted at the edge of every village. The increasing number of restaurants and sports shops, and the heavy traffic on the through road in summer and winter, combine to make the Val d'Aran one of the most expensive, overdeveloped and (unless you're skiing) overrated corners of the Spanish Pyrenees.

That said, if you leave the main route in favour of side valleys like the Ruda or the Unhòla, you can recapture something of the region as it used to be. But don't expect superlative wilderness walking: Aran is best viewed as a comfortable overnight stop on Pyrenean traverses, rather than a target in its own right.

Aran's legendary greenness derives not from any extraordinary rainfall but from the streams that drain into it, mostly from lakes in the Aigüestortes country to the south. When the weather *is* wet, black-and-yellow fire salamanders move with unconcerned slowness on damp tracks and paths; before and after the rain, equally brilliant butter-flies, for which the valley is famous, flutter about.

Nautaran

Nautaran, or "High Valley" in Aranés, is the more scenic eastern part of the region, and a good start- or end-point for walks in the Aigüestortes park. Salardú is the largest of a cluster of villages well set near the top of the valley, most within walking distance of each other. From almost any elevated point in Nautaran you'll be treated to full-on views of snowy Maladeta, hovering like a ghost to the west. Sturdy Nautaranese houses are traditionally stone with slate roofs, so there's surprisingly little to distinguish a 400-year-old home from a four-year-old one. Many display dates on the lintels – not of the same vintage as the local **Romanesque churches**, though some date back into the sixteenth century.

Baqueira-Beret

The road descent west from Port de la Bonaigua invariably concentrates minds – and isn't for the acrophobic or those with dodgy brakes, given its hairpins and sharp drop into the Ruda valley. The first place down from the pass is **BAQUEIRA-BERET**, a huge skiing development frequented by French tourists, and by no less than the Spanish royal family. This resort is the primary engine of change in the region, and the road linking the resort core at Baqueira to Point 1700 and the Beret sector was serpentined for maximum access to the ranks of chalet apartments.

The *urbanizació* itself is modern, posey and has little to offer other than four- or five-star hotels, but it's no trouble to stay nearby at Salardú or Tredòs (see below) and show up for some of the best **skiing** in these mountains – with one important qualification, all of the Beret and much of the Baqueira-Bonaigua zones face west or south, and the snow, especially after February, can get mushy early in the day, closing slopes by 3pm. The most reliable, north-facing runs descend to **Orri** (1850m), with its own car park and lifts, and also the link to **Beret** (1850–2516m), most suitable for beginners and weak intermediates, though you'll need your own transport to reach it by road. Beret's development is dwarfed by its grand setting, though you face long slogs from car park to facilities, and between lifts. More advanced skiers can use chairlifts from the hotels and apartments, at Points 1500 and 1700 in Baqueira centre, to get up to the 2500-metre **Cap de Baqueira**, start of numerous, mostly red-rated pistes in open bowls above the trees. The small, south-facing **Bonaigua** sector, immediately below the pass, has just a few intermediate runs and isn't really worth any special effort at present, though it will form the springboard of future resort expansion onto the slopes towards the east.

Lift passes are among the stiffest priced in the Pyrenees, but gear rental is normal for Spain, and you are pampered with lots of chairlifts (15 out of 23) and an interlinked domain of 47 runs (further information at *www.baqueira.es*). Packages for Baqueira-Beret are sold in the UK, typically through Ski Miquel Holidays (see p.6).

Salardú

SALARDÚ, a few kilometres further west, is the notional capital of Nautaran and a logical base for explorations: large enough to offer a reasonable choice of accommodation and food, but small enough to feel pleasantly remote (except during August or peak ski season). With steeply pitched house-roofs clustered around the church, it retains some traditional character, but even here the clock in the octagonal fifteenth-century belfry tolls with an electronic tone instead of a bell (programmed to fall silent between midnight and 7am).

The principal reason to stay is for the opportunity to visit surrounding villages, all centred on beautiful **Romanesque churches**. Salardú's church is the large, thirteenth-century **Sant Andreu**, set in its own pleasant grounds. The usually open doors are flanked by the most elaborate portal in the valley, whose carved column capitals feature birds feeding their young and four eerie little human faces peeping out. Once inside, you can enjoy some fine sixteenth-century fresco patches, restored in 1994, including Christ Enthroned, the Assumption, various saints and smudged panels of the Four Virtues personified.

Practicalities

There's a wooden **Turisme** hut (summer only Mon–Fri 10.30am–1.30pm & 4.30–8pm, Sat 10am–1pm & 4–7pm, Sun 10am–1pm) just off the main road at the turning for Bagergue, near the bus stop. The single village **bank** has normal opening hours, plus an ATM. There is also a **swimming pool** (mid-June to Aug daily 11am–7pm) if you fancy a dip.

Even at the height of the summer you should find a **bed** (though not necessarily a room) in Salardú. Dependable hostels aimed specifically at **hikers** include the *Refugi Rosti*, Plaça Major 1 (☎973 645 308, fax 973 645 814; closed May–June & Oct–Nov; dorms ① B&B, rooms ③ B&B), in a rambling, 300-year-old building on the main square, and *Refugi Juli Soler Santaló* run by the CEC (☎973 645 016; ①), 200m east of the Turisme booth in c/del Port, next to the pool.

For conventional **accommodation**, try the wood-decor **rooms** above the *Bar Montanha* (☎973 644 108; ②–③) at c/Major 8, with breakfast (not included) downstairs, or those at *Residència Aiguamòg* (☎973 645 996; ④) on c/Sant Andreu 12, both pretty central. In addition to these, eight more expensive **hostals** and **hotels** advertise themselves conspicuously; one of the quieter and more reasonable is the two-star *Hotel deth Pais* in cul-de-sac Plaça dera Pica (☎973 645 836, fax 973 644 500; ⑤), whose rather plain rooms have underfloor heating and balconies if south-facing.

Most of the places to stay in Salardú serve good-value **meals**: non-guests can eat excellent *menús* at the highly recommended *Refugi Juli Soler Santaló*, or spend about 3000ptas/€18 *a la carta* at *Aloy*, offshoot of the *Hotel deth Pais*. Alternatives are scarce, especially as the handful of independent village restaurants are overpriced for what you get. While the restaurant at the *Refugi Rosti* is decent enough with a four-course *menú*, its main appeal is the nicest **bar** in town: *Delicatesen*.

Villages around Salardú

UNHA (Unya), 700m up the hill into the Unhòla valley, has a church of the same age as that in Salardú, though you're more likely to be interested in the half-dozen **restaurants**, particularly *Es de Don Juan (Casa Carmela)* and *Casa Restaurante Perez* – the latter the most economical and most consistently open, also offering **accommodation** at *Casa Benito* (☎973 645 752; ③).

BAGERGUE, 2km higher up the road (or reached via the marked GR211 path from Unha and Garòs) remains the most countrified of the Nautaran settlements, and offers yet another handsome church – plus three more **restaurants**. Most famous is *Casa Peru* (reserve on ☎973 645 437), which deserves the plaudits adorning its entrance: an *olha aranesa* (sausage, carrot and potato hotpot) to die for, venison meatballs in wild mushroom sauce, wild-fruit flan with *merengue* plus good house wine for 4500ptas/€27 – far less than the more pretentious places in Salardú or Arties, with courteous service to boot. There's also a recommended place to **stay**, the *Residencia Seixes* (☎973 645 406; ⑤) at the village entrance, with fine views and off-street parking.

Across the river from Salardú, and about twenty minutes' walk upstream along the signposted *Camin Reiau* (King's Road), **TREDÒS** – once the prettiest of the Nautaran villages – has had its old core overwhelmed by a rash of new ski chalets. However it retains a massive twelfth-century church – one of whose murals was removed to the Cloisters Museum in New York – with freestanding belfry. And in the centre is a find: the *Restaurante Saburedo*, where the construction crews for all those apartments **eat**. The food's hearty rather than haute, with four courses (giant salad, onion soup, a meat dish, stewed pears) plus house wine for about 2500ptas/€15. If you're taken with the village, they also have **rooms** (☎973 645 089; ③), as does *Casa Micalot* (☎973 645 326; ②) on the same lane. If money's no object, there are a handful of plusher **hotels** nearby, including the *De Tredòs* on the road to Baquiera Beret (☎973 644 014, fax 973 644 300; ⑦), which can often arrange one-week ski packages, and offers rooms at half their peak rate outside of winter. The *Banhs de Tredòs* (☎973 253 003; ⑦), 8km up the Aiguamotx valley to the south, is a small spa hotel whose handful of large, minimally furnished modern rooms and ordinary country cuisine don't really justify the bumped-up rates.

Arties and Garòs

ARTIES, 3km west and downstream from Salardú, has the usual complement of recent holiday homes, with more under construction. However, if you're driving and/or Salardú is full, Arties has considerable appeal, particularly its high-quality food and lodging (see below), and the old village core straddling the Garona river. There are two **churches**: the ninth-to-fourteenth-century Santa María, with Templar fortifications, and the deconsecrated Sant Joan on the main road, now home to a small **museum** of changing exhibits (Tues–Fri 5–8pm, Sat 10am–1pm & 5–8pm, Sun 10am–1pm; 200ptas). The village is otherwise known for its **hot springs**, long closed but recently sold and undergoing renovation. The *camí* leading past them (marked as the GR211.1) cuts out 3km of the busy main highway, rejoining it at Casarilh village, a boon if you're cycling.

Budget **accommodation** includes, on the through highway, the 1999-refurbished, en-suite *Pensió Montarto* above the *Bar Consul* (☎973 640 803; ④), and the much better and quieter *Pensió Barrie,* alias *Casa Portolá* (☎973 640 828; ③) at c/Mayor 21 in the old quarter, which has three floors of wood-and-tile decor en-suite rooms with bathtubs, the top two storeys very alpine with skylights and dormer windows. For more cash, sample the *Hotel Besiberri* by the stream at c/Deth Fòrt 4 (☎ & fax 973 640 829; closed Nov; ⑤ B&B). Rooms (except for the rambling attic suite, 13,000ptas/€78) are smallish but well-appointed; lovely common areas, Catalan savoury breakfasts and a warm welcome make the place. The slightly larger *Hotel Valarties* at c/Major 3 (☎973 644 364; closed May to mid-June & mid-Oct to Nov; ⑥) has wood-floor rooms, many overlooking an enormous rear garden. A **campsite**, *Era Yerla d'Arties* (☎973 641 602; open all year), just below the village on the main road to Vielha, is considered the best in the valley but as so often is crammed with caravans.

There are about half-a-dozen **restaurants** of a slightly higher standard and better value for money than in Salardú, though many resort to the common local trick of jacking up prices during ski season. New restaurants open each year, but tried-and-tested options include *Montagut* (closed Tues) up on the highway, with attentive service and three *menús* 1500–3100ptas/€9–18.70, the mid-priced one featuring local specialities such as *sopa de ajo* and duck. *Casa Irene,* inside the *Hotel Valarties,* is regarded as one of the most innovative (albeit expensive) restaurants in the valley: budget 5000ptas/€30 for the *menú,* up to 8000ptas/€48 *a la carta.* In the same building as *Montagut,* the friendly South African-run *El Pollo Loco* (Dec–April) offers four *menús* (one vegie) at 1300–2800ptas/€7.80–16.80, with local pâtés, as well as duck, game and chicken, all washed down with natural cider. There's **nightlife** here as well at *Bar La Luna* in the old quarter, which regularly has live music.

The village of **GARÒS**, 3km west, is the lowest-altitude community of Nautaran, completely ringed with new, stone-built holiday cottages. Yet its old core, focused on the twelfth- to fourteenth-century church of San Julian, retains some charm, and offers **accommodation** at the modest *Pensió Garòs* (☎973 640 213; ③), and the luxurious but human-scale *Hotel Vila Garòs* (☎973 641 250; ⑦). There's also a **cake-and-pie** salon, *La Tarteria* (open 9am–1pm & 4–8.30pm), with all fare baked on the premises.

Mijaran and Baixaran

From Nautaran you continue west into **Mijaran** (Mid-Valley) to the major town of **Vielha**, capital of the entire region, and served by two long-distance bus routes: one from Barcelona via La Pobla de Segur (during snow-free seasons only), the other from Lleida via El Pont de Suert, culminating in the 5300-metre **Túnel de Vielha**. You emerge from the tunnel mouth just above the town at the southwest corner of the valley, close to the old but still-used pilgrim's and drover's track descending from the 2442-metre Port de Vielha, which used to guarantee Vielha's isolation. The road (and onward buses) then head north to the French border just 28km away, through **Baixaran**, the lower part of the valley.

Vielha

The ride towards **VIELHA** (Viella) from either direction is more memorable than the town itself, and there's little reason to stay if you have your own transport or can make a bus connection. A sort of mini-Andorra-la-Vella (with few of Andorra's bargains), Vielha has become intensely developed and smartened up since 1990, as evidenced by its numerous supermarkets, boutiques and restaurants. The demise of La Tuca ski centre just to the south hasn't slowed growth; urban density expands each year, such that there is hardly any open space left in the centre, except for a pedestrian walkway along the Garona river. Amongst all this glitz, members of Spain's crack alpine warfare squad are lodged in barracks just east of the centre.

If you have time to kill, pop into the parish church of **Sant Miquèu**, right in the centre on the east bank of the Riu Nere. Its twelfth-century wooden bust, the *Cristo de Mijaran* – probably part of a *Descent from the Cross* – is reckoned the finest specimen of Romanesque art in this part of the Pyrenees. The **Museu deth Val** (Mon–Sat 10am–1pm & 5–8pm, Sun 10am–1pm; 200ptas/€1.20), at c/Major 26, west of the church and across the river, is also worth a look for its coverage of Aranese history and folklore. The only other potential diversion is the mammoth **Palai de Gèu** (Ice Palace) across the Garona, with a swimming pool, ice rink and gymnasium (pool and gym Mon–Fri 8am–noon & 3–10pm, no siesta Tues/Thurs; Sat, Sun & hols 10.30am–2pm & 4.30–9pm; ice rink 5.30–9pm weekdays, 11.30am–1.30pm & 4.30–9pm weekends; 1400ptas/€8.40 admission to all facilities including skate hire).

Practicalities

Buses stop at two marquees opposite each other, just downhill from the major roundabout at the west end of town; schedule information is posted, tickets are bought on the bus. The **Turisme** (June–Sept Mon–Sat 9am–1pm & 4–8pm, Sun 10am–1pm & 4.30–7.30pm; Oct–May shorter opening times vary; ☎976 640 110), offering maps and complete valley accommodation lists, is near the **post office** at c/Sarriulera 6, just off the church square.

As you might expect there's no shortage of **accommodation** in Vielha, but most is aimed at ski clientele, with little of outstanding value. Moving north from the church, you'll find the best of the inexpensive places by turning left along the main street and then right down the lane just across the bridge. Just off to the left at Plaça Sant Orenç 3, there's the *Hostal El Ciervo* (☎973 640 165; ④); the often full *Pensió Puig*, c/Camin Reiau 4 (☎973 640 031; ②); or the tiny en-suite *Pension Casa Vicenta* across the way at no. 3 (☎973 640 819; ④). On the opposite side of the through road, above the museum, *Pensió Monge* (no sign) at Des Clòses 7 (☎973 640 246; ②) is also quiet. For more comfort, go to *Hostal Turrull* at c/Camin Reiau 7 (☎973 640 058; ④), which encourages half-board (5100ptas per person) at its respectable ground-floor restaurant.

The least expensive and most central of Vielha's **restaurants** is *Basteret*, c/Major 6a, with a *menú* for 1800ptas/€10.80, and *Turrull* in the eponymous hostal (*menús* from 1500ptas/€9). With a bit more outlay, try *Eth Hurat* at Passeig dera Llibertat 14, a supper-only crêperie, *a la carta* fare at *Eth Cornèr* on Passeig dera Llibertat 7, or *Casa Turnay* (closed May–June & Oct–Nov; reserve on ☎973 640 292), in the hamlet of Escunhau 2km east, which features Aranese-style game, fish and ornate vegetable dishes.

Baixaran

You can continue from Vielha by bus, car or bike through **ARRÒS** (6km) and **ES BÒRDES** (Era Bordeta; 9km), two places that play a key role in Aranese architecture.

Es Bòrdes supplies the granite for the walls and Arròs the slates for the slightly concave roofs that planners require in Nautaran and Mijaran. Arròs itself, though, is almost in the lower **Baixaran** (Lower Valley) region; its balconied houses around the octagonal bell tower have rendered white walls and red-tiled roofs. There are two big **campsites** at Arròs: the *Artigané* (☎973 640 189; June–Sept) and the *Verneda* (☎973 641 024; June–Sept), plus two smaller ones just past Es Bòrdes. Most indoor accommodation consists of **cases de pagès**, including *Casa Guillamon* (☎973 640 334; ②), *Casa Marium* (☎973 640 341; ②) and *Casa Cucay* (☎973 641 167; ②).

Baixaran is "low" indeed at 800m and fully exposed to the mists which habitually drift up the north slope of the Pyrenees. Its main centre is the large village of **BOSSÒST**, 16km from Vielha, where the houses are strung out along the main road and on both sides of the curving river, alternating with tacky shops. Its twelfth-century **Romanesque** church has a carved tympanum and three apses with raised Lombard brickwork. This being on the direct road between France and the Vielha tunnel, **accommodation** is relatively abundant (4 hotels, 5 pensions) if overpriced and often booked by Spanish tour groups. Apart from the church, there's no real reason to stop (except for petrol, much cheaper than in France). It's only 4km to **LES**, with a spa (open May–Sept) and six less expensive lodgings – *Pensió Europa* (☎973 648 016; ④), with a good **restaurant**, is representative; 9km to the **French border** at Eth Pònt de Rei (Pont de Rei), a place-name only, with no habitation; and 20km to the first significant French town, Saint-Béat.

An alternative road out of Bossòst into France, the C141 from just south of the village, saves a bit of time. It climbs through dense woods to the no-longer-guarded French border at **Coll deth Portilhon** (Coll du Portillon in French), then descends sharply to Bagnères-de-Luchon.

Walking and biking from the Val d'Aran

Numerous tracks and rather fewer footpaths make it possible to walk and mountainbike from the valley in virtually every direction. Editorial Alpina publishes a 1:40,000 "Val d'Aran" map of the whole area, but if you are going to stray outside its coverage you'll need adjacent 1:25,000 sheets as well: "Montgarri" and "Pica d'Estats" if you're going east; "Sant Maurici" plus "Vall de Boí" for the whole of Aigüestortes to the south; "La Ribagorça" together with "Maladeta/Aneto" if you're bound for points west. The French IGN Cartes des Randonnées 1:50,000 series covers the Val d'Aran along with the territory to the north – either the "Couserans-Cap d'Aran" (no. 6) for trans-border treks northeast, or "Luchon" (no. 5) if you want to head northwest.

East to Montgarri and the Vall d'Isil

An easy excursion takes you **east** along the sources of the Noguera Pallaresa, which flows initially northeast before curling south. Make an early start **from Salardú** up the road towards Bagergue, and after 500m cut off onto a wide path that connects to the track between Bagergue and Baqueira. If you're cycling rather than walking, you'll have to pick up the track in Bagergue. In either case, after just under an hour you join the road from Baqueira into the Noguera Pallaresa valley – keep on it, past the first trickle of the river, until the dirt track resumes about an hour later.

You're now on the broad **Plan de Beret**, with grass and cows in the foreground, and a tangle of frontier peaks in the far distance. Four to five walking hours (15km) out of Salardú – half that time on a bike – you come to the twelfth-century **Santuari de Montgarri**, next to which is the *Refugi Amics de Montgarri* (☎973 645 064; 1657m; 50 places; ①), catering for traversers in summer and cross-country skiers in winter.

Although it might seem boring to walk the track, it's an attractive route – popular in summer – with some sweeping views from the plateau, especially beyond Montgarri. Otherwise stay at the refuge or continue for the same distance again to Alòs d'Isil, and then to Gil (see p.263), both with refuges. At Alòs, you're ten hours' very tough walk – no bikes – from Noarre, using cairned cross-country sections of the HRP as often as paths, across wild and sometimes storm-lashed ridges plunging south from Mont Roig. Most people will opt for a paved-road descent for the 12km to Esterri d'Aneu.

North towards France

To head **into France** from the upper Noguera Pallaresa, follow an HRP variant east from Montgarri or north from Alòs through the Port de Salau, or a less-used route over the Coll de la Pala/Col de la Pale (2522m) to the *Refuge des Estagnous* (see p.314), on the west side of **Mont Valier** (2838m). The Salau route is much lower and easier, and both routes are more appropriate for long-haul trekking than biking.

It's also possible to enter France at a more westerly point using the initially dreary, shadeless, rutted track up the **Unhòla valley** from Bagergue, passable in its lower reaches by 4WD and mountain-bike. Beyond some abandoned mines, the landscape and the trail improve before reaching **Estany de Liat** (4–5hr). Here you can link with another section of the HRP, climbing due north from the lake through the **Portillo d'Albi** (2457m) on the frontier, an hour's stiff climb past the tiny Estany d'Albi.

Once through the pass you drop down over scree towards another lake, confusingly known as the Étang d'Albè; from here you head north, contouring along the ridge behind without gaining unnecessary altitude, and northeast to the **Col de la Serre d'Araing**, where you pick up the GR10. After that, simply follow the GR down to the northeast corner of the **Étang d'Araing** reservoir, under the bare pyramid of **Pic de Crabère** (2630m), where there is a **refuge**. This is ten to twelve hours from Salardú and thus provides a welcome respite (see p.314 for full details).

The Étang d'Araing reservoir is about three hours west on foot from Eylie, the road-head to Sentein and Saint-Girons, and lies on the Tour de Biros; the famous Gouffre Martel and Grotte de la Cigalère are both nearby.

South to Aigüestortes

South of Nautaran, two lengths of paved road and a pair of tracks then trails, a track-then-trail, and a narrow path run towards the beautiful Aigüestortes region. Only the latter two approaches provide enticing walking, and are described first.

Via Saborèdo

The approach to Saborèdo begins on the south side of the river at Tredòs as a track, labelled GR211.4, before curling past the edge of Baqueira and along the west bank of the **Riu de Ruda**. Although you can hear traffic descending from Bonaigua to the east, and power lines arc overhead, close at hand there's little other than wide green pasture until you sight the **Circ de Saborèdo** and the jumble of shattered granite peaks along the north edge of the Aigüestortes park. Four hours from Salardú the track dwindles to path, changing banks of the Ruda, and you ascend into the heart of the cirque past a succession of tiny lakes to the **Refugi de Saborèdo** at 2310m, 4hr 30min from Salardú (☎973 253 015; 21 places; staffed late-Feb to early-April & mid-June to Sept; ①). There's no other facility for three hours walking, through the easy **Port de Ratera** (2530m) to the **Refugi-Xalet d'Amitges** (☎973 250 109, *www.rotativo.com/amitges/*; 2380m; 66 places; staffed most of Feb, 2 weeks at Easter, mid-June to end Sept & hols year-round; ①), inside the park by Estany Gran.

Via Gerber

A quicker, though more challenging path to the Amitges refuge takes off from two road-curves 1.5km above *Mare de Déu de les Ares*, the chapel/restaurant 4km southeast of the Port de la Bonaigua. Take the obvious footpath, initially under high-tension cables, south along the **Vall Gerber** to **Estany Gerber**, and next to the Estany de l'Illa with its simple metal *Refugi de Gerber-Mataró* (2460m; 3hr 30min; 16 places, always open). Continue south into the park proper, negotiating the **Coll d'Amitges** (2740m), between Tuc de Saborèdo and Pic d'Amitges, before descending steeply to the Amitges refuge. This will be problematic after a snowy winter, requiring crampons and ice-axe on the north flank, and an early start from the main highway trailhead – count on four hours beyond Mataró.

By using the easier Col de Gerber (2582m) above *Refugi Gerber-Mataró*, you reach the Circ de Saborèdo with its dozen lakes and staffed refuge within five and a half hours of leaving the trailhead, and are thus poised to complete a magnificent and popular **one-day circuit** combining the two approaches detailed above. The main trick, when descending the GR211.4 track along the Ruda stream, is to take a path heading steeply up to the right just before the route changes to the true left bank. This ascending trail returns you to the trailhead below Bonaigua for an eight-to-nine-hour day, with 37 lakes or tarns en route.

Via Aiguamotx

From Tredòs, a partly paved road ascends steeply up the attractive **Vall d'Aiguamotx** (Aiguamoth) towards the exquisite **Circ de Colomers**; walking the steep road is neither attractive nor exquisite, so arrange a ride if possible. The potholed road finishes after about 8km (2hr on foot) at the luxury *Banys/Banhs de Tredòs* hotel, leaving another ninety minutes on dirt track, then path (no cycling) to the **Refugi de Colomers** (☎973 253 008; 2125m; 40 places; staffed Feb/March weekends, Easter weeks, mid-June to late-Sept, major hols otherwise; ①).

The refuge sits by a dam, and there are dozens of natural lakes and tarns in the cirque, set among stands of black pine. An adequate sketch map of two day-hikes – a two-hour circuit waymarked in red and yellow, and a four-hour loop blazed in red – is available from the management. Full-pack treks from Colomers include the five-hour hike south, then west via the **Port de Colomers** (2591m) to the popular *Refugi Ventosa i Calvell* (see p.285). Alternatively, four hours' walk west along the joint HRP/GR11.18 takes you via the easier **Port de Caldes** and the **Port de Collcrestada** (both 2500m) to the *Refugi de la Restanca* (see below). En route you skirt the foot of **Montardo d'Aran** (sometimes Montarto; 2830m) – an easy ascent with fabulous views over Aran.

Via Valarties

The friendly **Refugi de la Restanca** (☎608 036 559, *www.rotativo.com/restanca/*; 2010m; 80 places; staffed weekends most of year, 2 weeks at Easter, & mid-June to late Sept; ①), whose wardens Esther and Albert have been resident since the 1980s, can be reached directly from Arties via a road threading up the **Valarties**. However, there's little chance of hitching it, and the way up on foot, dotted by day-trippers' parked cars and illicitly placed tents, is even less inspiring than the Aiguamotx slog, though shorter. After 5km, asphalt yields to dirt, ending 3km later at the bottom of a short, sharp climb to the *Restanca* refuge near the eastern end of the reservoir dam.

West to Maladeta

The *Restanca* refuge permits the quickest access from the Aran to the **Maladeta** massif, via the refuges and camping spots near the south end of the Túnel de Vielha. You have the choice from Estany de la Restanca of the long and difficult HRP – around **Estany de Mar** and **Estany Tort de Rius** (7hr) – or the GR11, which makes an easy, direct and well-marked traverse past **Estany de Rius** (5hr). The HRP is recommended if you're an experienced, lightly-laden trekker, since Mar is one of the area's most impressive lakes: a small, bare island hunkers in the middle, with a chaos of huge grey boulders on the shore, and the peak of Besiberri Nord looming to the south.

The HRP and GR11 rejoin briefly at the **Refugi Sant Nicolau** (aka *Boca Sud Tunel de Vielha*, or *Er Ospitau de Vielha*), rebuilt on the site of a medieval pilgrims' hospice (☎973 697 052; open year-round except May 1–16, Nov, Dec 24–Jan 7; dorm ① or rooms ⑤ HB). Though virtually on the main highway, it's the only amenity for miles around, and a welcome sight. Hosts Sebas and Juani provide reasonable meals (not Sun pm or Mon Sept 15–June 30), though there's no shop. If you don't stay at the refuge, you may be interested in the unrestricted and sometimes squalid free **campsite** and the large but dilapidated and unstaffed **Refugi de Conangles**, both 1500m south along the well-blazed GR11.

Approaches from the Noguera Ribagorçana

The Noguera Ribagorçana has its source near the tunnel; crossing it you forsake Catalunya for Aragón and face three different approaches to Maladeta and beyond.

The **HRP** takes the classic route west via the Molières valley and the **Coret de Molières** (formerly Coll de Mulleres, 2935m, crampons/ice-axe always necessary) – a gruelling but spectacular traverse, which can be split by overnighting at the simple, metal-shed *Refugi Mulleres* (2360m; 12 places; unstaffed, always open), by a chain of tarns just below the pass. The **Cap deth Hòro/Cap de Tòro** (2969m), a fifteen-minute scramble up the north side of the saddle, gives a magnificent view over Maladeta's northeast glacier – where one branch of the Garona rises – and into the Joeu valley, where the infant river emerges after 4km underground.

The **GR11** continues south from the Conangles campsite/shelter to the head of the **Senet (Basserca) reservoir**, where it crosses the road at Pont de les Salenques and dips into the mouth of the **Salenques valley**, keeping to the south (true right) bank. Fairly well marked at first, the route divides about an hour along.

The inconspicuous right-hand option crosses the stream, then labours northwest through rhododendron-cloaked boulders prior to an exhausting slither up through scree and usually snow to the **Coll de les Salenques** (2807m); camping is possible two-thirds of the way in meadows at the base of the sharpest climb. There's an easier gradient down the other side to the **Plan dels Aigualluts**, one of the best wild campsites in the Pyrenees, also easily accessible from the Coret de Molières.

The waymarked, left-hand bearing is the **official GR11**, which threads through the lake-speckled **Vall d'Anglòs**, then over the easy **Coll de Ballibierna/Collado de Vallhiverna** (2730m), affording spectacular views of Maladeta's southwest face. Passing more lakes on the descent, the GR11 meets the track coming up the **Ball de Ballibierna**, and follows it down to Benasque – again a long day out of Noguera Ribagorçana, best broken with a night out on either side of the pass. There's a tiny, wood-shack, unstaffed refuge at 2220m, beside the easterly Ibón de Anglòs.

Approach via the Joeu valley

The easiest, though nowadays least used, approach to Aragón and the Maladeta region starts from Es Bòrdes, 9km west of Vielha on the main N230 road. From there you walk (or taxi) south down the **Joeu valley** as far as the **Pla de l'Artiga** (8km; 1465m; simple unstaffed refuge) and the resurgence of waters from the Forau dels Aigualluts. From here a path climbs west to the **Pòrt dera Picada/Port de la Picada** (2470m; 3hr from the Pla), through which you descend gently to a range of options: following the Ésera valley in front of you downstream; crossing its head to the Plan dels Aigualluts; or slipping over the nearby Port de Venasque towards Bagnères-de-Luchon. All of these destinations are covered in detail later in this chapter.

THE AIGÜESTORTES-SANT MAURICI REGION

Water is the salient feature of the **Parc Nacional d'Aigüestortes i Estany de Sant Maurici**, a region of flashing streams and waterfalls, nearly 400 lakes reflecting harsh granite peaks, and reed-fringed upland marshes. Rain or snow falls on these mountains – some reaching 3000 metres – almost half the days of the year. The name *Aigüestortes* ("Twisted Waters") has lately acquired something of an unintentional subtext. Local streams have been diverted through enormous galleries into the mountainsides, and the lakes and reservoirs, thus tapped (Sant Maurici among them), intermittently become mud-bowls. The region has been exploited this way since 1914, the Swiss- and German-designed hydroelectric works undertaken to power the rapidly industrializing cities in lowland Catalunya.

The park bounded by the Val d'Aran, the Noguera Pallaresa and the Noguera Ribagorçana was established in 1955 during the hydroelectric schemes' expansion, no conflict being apparent to the Francoist government. Under rules laid down by the International Union for the Conservation of Nature, no hydroelectric exploitation is permitted in such a reserve, but as this is still Catalunya's only fully-fledged national park, the authorities proudly brandish the title despite a continuing lack of international recognition. The arrogance of the bureaucrats of the era is expressed in a 1970s pamphlet published by the Instituto Nacional Para la Conservación de la Naturaleza (ICONA): "Some changes have occurred recently with the construction of hydroelectrical installations which the country needs, and Nature has had to pay her tribute to man, The King."

But attitudes are slowly changing, and park authorities wage constant battle with FECSA-ENHER (the power corporation) in an attempt to limit their depredations. The park's western area increased considerably during 1986 through the cession of lands by the Boí municipality, then again in 1996, when a huge area north of Caldes de Boí was incorporated. Some 140 square kilometres now enjoy full protection, though further expansion is unlikely given the spiralling costs of compensating FECSA-ENHER and other private landowners. It's easy to steer clear of the dams, and recommended **walking routes** keep to the wilder corners as far as possible. There's something for walkers of all abilities here: from the simple mid-altitude track-jaunt across the park east to west, to gruelling climbs over jagged passes requiring snow equipment, by way of several popular trekkers' traverses using the GR11 or its variants. The **Sant Nicolau valley** and its tributaries (in the west) have many glacially formed lakes and cirques, as well as the water-meadows of Aigüestortes. Eastern sector highlights include the Circ de Saborèdo and the Peguera valley around the Josep María Blanc refuge, as well as the Estany de Sant Maurici itself, at the head of the Escrita valley. Just outside the park, in the 27,000-hectare so-called "peripheral zone of protection", are more lake-spangled cirques, particularly towards the Val d'Aran.

Flora and fauna

The most common **trees** in Aigüestortes-Sant Maurici are fir and Scotch pine, and silver birch and beech, especially on north-facing slopes. There's an abundance of **flowers** in spring and early summer, with blooms present until August above 2000m.

Isards are the most conspicuous **mammals**, easily seen in winter when harsh weather drives them downhill, but staying on the high summits in summer. Perhaps the

PARK RULES AND PRACTICALITIES

Park entry
Entry to the park is free, and unrestricted for hikers, but private cars are prohibited except for local shepherds' trucks with special permits. Ordinarily the only means of vehicle access is via the reasonably priced 4WD-taxis from both Espot and Boí; passage is arranged at respective park information offices in Espot and Boí. The closest places you can drive to are 200-vehicle car parks 4km west of Espot, at the east boundary of the park, and at La Farga, north of Boí in the west, by the edge of the peripheral zone.

Accommodation
Accommodation inside the park is limited to five **mountain refuges**, typically staffed at Easter, from mid-June to the end of September, and major *puentes* (long weekends) in autumn. There are five more refuges in equally impressive alpine areas just outside the park boundaries in the peripheral zone. Each refuge has meal service, telephone and/or radio transmitter and bunks (about 1000ptas/€6) for your sleeping bag; FEEC-managed places allow you to cook inside, CEC-managed ones do not. More information is available (in Spanish/Catalan only) at *www.rotativo.com/refugios/* (substituting the name of the hut for "refugios"); the Colomina refuge site is at *www.luthiers.net/colomina/colomc.htm* Camping wild in the park is officially forbidden, and technically restricted within a 27,000-hectare peripheral "protection zone" of varying width – where you're supposed to secure a permit from the nearest village – but as long as you pitch your tent well away from refuges and paths nobody will bother you. There are managed campsites at Taüll in the west, and at Espot to the east. All the approach villages have *cases de pagès*, *hostals* and hotels.

Maps and guides
For extended explorations, you'll want current editions of the Editorial Alpina 1:25,000 "Sant Maurici" and "Montardo/Vall de Boí" **map-booklets**; these are easily available in all gateway villages except Capdella. If you're willing to forego the included pamphlet (text only in Castilian or Catalan), you can buy a two-for-the-price-of-one map-only packet, entitled "Parc Nacional d'Aigüestortes i Estany de Sant Maurici". If you intend to approach from the north, you'll also need the 1:40,000 "Val d'Aran" Alpina, and if you're moving west towards Maladeta, the 1:25,000 "La Ribagorça" makes a good investment. Sketched handouts at the various park information offices generally prove insufficient for route-finding – get a proper commercial map if you intend to leave the most popular paths. The best regional guide is the Editorial Everest volume, *El Parque Nacional de Aigüestortes y Lago San Mauricio*, comprehensive but not yet available in English; *www.catalunya.net/aiguestortes* is also worth a glance for general information.

Weather and route conditions
Be aware of, and prepared for, bad **weather**, which as everywhere in the Pyrenees can arrive rapidly and without warning. In midsummer many rivers are passable which at other times are not, but temperature contrasts between day and night are still very marked. Local climatic patterns in recent years have alternated between daily rain showers throughout July and August, or prolonged drought, with a general trend towards warmer, drier summers. The best time to see the wonderful colour contrasts of the vegetation is autumn or early summer. Many passes, even those mapped with a bona fide trail, will be difficult or impossible after a harsh winter owing to snowpack. If you're doing an unusual traverse, tell the warden of the refuge you'll be leaving, who should be able to give current route pointers and, if there's any cause for concern, phone or radio ahead your estimated time of arrival – and perhaps make you a reservation.

Skiing
In winter, the park is excellent for cross-country (nordic) and high-mountain **skiing**, though there are no marked routes. Many of the refuges open for a week or two around Christmas and Easter, and selected weekends and school holidays in between. There are currently two downhill ski resorts on the fringes of the park – Boí-Taüll in the west and Super Espot in the east – with another planned for the Sallente area above Capdella.

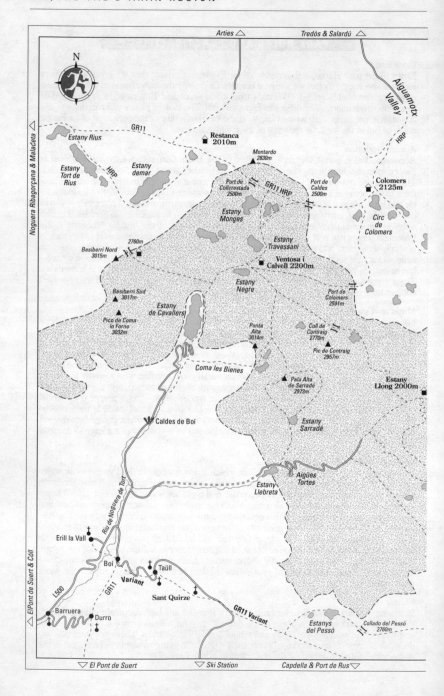

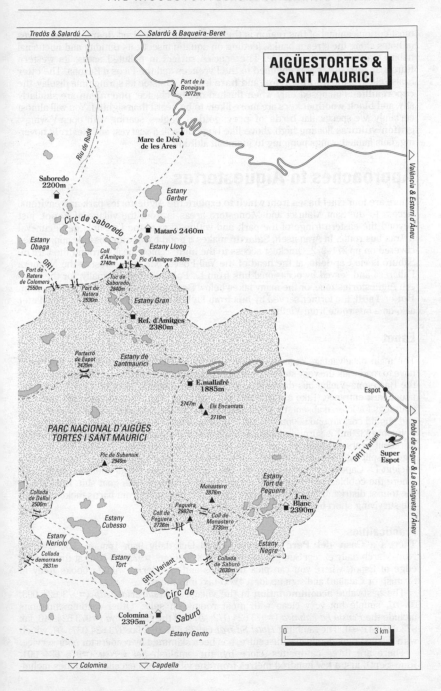

AIGÜESTORTES &
SANT MAURICI

Tredòs & Salardú △   △ Salardú & Baqueira-Beret

Port de la
Bonaigua
2072m

Riu de Ruda

Mare de Déu
de les Ares

Saboredo
2200m

Estany
Gerber

Circ de Saboredo

Estany
Obaga

Mataró 2460m

Estany Llong

Coll
d'Amitges
2740m

Pic d'Amitges 2848m

GR11

Port de
Ratera
de Colomers
2550m

Tuc de
Saboredo
2840m

Port de
Ratera
2530m

Estany Gran

Ref. d'Amitges
2380m

Portarró
de Espot
2420m

Estany de
Santmaurici

E.mallafré
1885m

Espot

2747m ▲ Els Encantats
2710m

PARC NACIONAL D'AIGÜES
TORTES I SANT MAURICI

GR11 Variant

Super
Espot

Pic de Subenuix
2949m

Collada
de Dellui
2500m

Monastero
2878m

Estany
Tort de
Peguera

J.m.
Blanc
2390m

Peguera
2982m

Coll de
Peguera
2726m

Coll de
Monastero
2730m

Estany
Cubesso

Estany
Neriolo

Estany
Tort

Collada
demorrano
2631m

Collada
de Saburó
2630m

Estany
Negre

GR11 Variant

Circ de

Colomina
2395m

Saburó

Estany Gento

0   3 km

▽ Colomina   ▽ Capdella

▷ València & Esterri d'Àneu

▷ Pobla de Segur & La Guingueta d'Àneu

most curious animal of this region is the long-nosed, mole-sized **desman**, which lives in holes along the stream banks, feeding on aquatic insects; its timidity and nocturnal habits make it almost invisible. The species suffers in polluted areas; its western European territory is now confined to the Pyrenees and the Picos d'Europa. The **otter** is also elusive, the **wild boar**, **fox**, and **hare** less so. Outside its spring-time display, the **capercaillie** is glimpsed only when flushed out by chance; **ptarmigan** are similarly shy, and **black woodpeckers** are more likely to be heard than sighted. You will almost certainly see spectacular **birds of prey**: **golden eagles** soaring with open-V wings; **griffon vultures** floating high above like huge tasselled scarves; and **kestrels** hovering, tails fanned, wings pumping to maintain altitude.

Approaches to Aigüestortes

There are four chief **bases** from which to explore the Aigüestortes park and environs. Access to the Sant Maurici and Monestero areas is from the village of **Espot**, just beyond the eastern fringe of the park and within 7km of the La Pobla de Segur–Val d'Aran bus route. In Aran itself, **Salardú** makes a good base, with possible approaches covered on pp.271–272. Quickest access to the high, remote peaks around the Circ de Saburó is via **Capdella**, at the head of the Vall Fosca, one valley west of the Noguera Pallaresa and served by occasional bus from La Pobla de Segur. Finally, for the western Aigüestortes zone, or the many lakes below Besiberri peak, the usual entry is from **Boí** or **Taüll**, the former served by bus from La Pobla via El Pont de Suert – the latter also on a bus route from Vielha.

Espot

The main disadvantage of an approach through **ESPOT** is the probability that you'll have to road-walk the very steep 7km from the turning on the main C147 highway where the Barcelona–Vielha bus drops you, and a similar distance beyond the village to the usual park entrance. Take a **4WD-taxi** if there's one waiting at the turn-off, and save your legs for later; if absent, they will descend to the junction after half an hour at most, and should cost around 600ptas/€3.60 per person for the short run up to the village.

Espot (1320m) is surprisingly unspoiled, despite decades of use as a tourist centre; in recent years a marginal hotel or two has been converted into holiday flats. The village is split into two distinct sections; visitors less often explore the area across the ancient La Capella bridge and beyond the church (Espot Solau, south-facing Espot), where the cobbled streets are still reassuringly splattered with goat shit. But even in the tourist district of Espot Obago (north-facing), hay spills from barns tucked behind the surviving short-term tourist facilities.

Practicalities

There's a **Casa del Parc Nacional** (April–Oct daily 9am–1pm & 3.30–6.45pm, Nov–March daily except Sun pm 9am–2pm & 3.30–6pm; ☎973 624 036) at the eastern edge of Espot, where you can pick up maps and wonderful wildlife books (only in Spanish or Catalan) and sign up for a 4WD-taxi into the park.

The best-value **accommodation** in the village is *Residència Felip* (☎973 624 093; ②–③), simple but very clean with most rooms en suite. Other recommendations include the *Pensió La Palmira* (☎973 624 072; ③) and the *Hotel Roya* (☎973 624 040, fax 973 624 041; ④). The rambling *Hotel Saurat* (☎973 624 162, fax 973 624 037; ⑤), which with the taxi rank dominates the centre, has been slammed by readers for poor service.

There are three **campsites** close by: the smallish *Sol i Neu* (☎973 624 001; June–Sept), just a few hundred metres from the village, has excellent facilities including a swimming pool; *De La Mola* (☎973 624 024; July–Sept), 2km farther down the hill, also has a pool. At the far (upstream) edge of Espot beyond the old bridge, the tiny *Solau* (☎973 624 068) isn't wonderful, but also rents out rooms as *Casa Peret de Peretó* (③), a good fallback if the village centre is full.

Quality **eating** and economical *menús* are both limited; the *menjador* of the *Pensió La Palmira* is an honourable exception. Most of the bars serve sandwiches and *plats combinats*; the pub *La Coveta* provides some semblance of **nightlife**. There are also two well-stocked **supermarkets** and another shop selling maps, camping gas cartridges, and the like.

Super Espot

Around Espot, you can see how development has encroached on the park. Two kilometres above the village, parts of the **SUPER ESPOT** ski centre (info at *www.espotesqui.com*) edge into the peripheral protection zone. Its 31 runs are laid out with two chair lifts from Point 1500 (gear rental and lift tickets) to Point 2000, and further lifts to the tops of mostly intermediate pistes at 2300m, or more advanced runs from 2500m. Despite a northeasterly orientation, its snow record isn't up to most neighbouring resorts; by March many runs may be closed, and the whole place can shut for the day at 3pm.

Into the park

The road divides in the middle of the village. The left side leads up to **Super Espot**; right takes you west into the park. It's 3.5km to its boundary and the designated car park at **Prats de Pierró**, and 7km to the end of the asphalt at **Estany de Sant Maurici**. The GR11 trail avoids most of the road, or the local taxis serve this stretch: they carry eight people, and at 600ptas/€3.60 per passenger provide an inexpensive way to avoid some fairly dull road-walking.

Once at the lake, there is a classic postcard view to the south, dominated by the 2700-metre spires of **Els Encantats** ("The Enchanted Ones"). In legend, these were once two hunters and their dog, who snuck off hunting instead of attending church on the day of the patron saint's festival. Lured heavenward by a spectral stag, the three were turned to stone by a divine lightning bolt. There's a seasonal information post (Easter & July–Sept daily 9.30am–2pm & 4–6.30pm) beside the Sant Maurici dam.

If you're not interested in track-trudging or four-wheel-driving, an enticing trail leads southwest from Espot Obago in just under four hours to the **Refugi Josep Maria Blanc** (☎973 250 108; 2320m; 40 places; open Easter & mid-June to late Sept; ①), inside the park boundary on **Estany Tort de Peguera**. You can then continue another four hours to the Colomina shelter, over the 2630-metre **Collada de Saburó**; the entire way from Espot is a well-travelled, lake-flecked route, marked as the variant GR11.20.

Capdella

The half-dozen villages of the narrow **Vall Fosca** are mostly tucked away, out of sight, up the slopes. There are few tourist facilities as yet along the valley floor (though the road up has been widened and resurfaced), and the bus service from Pobla de Segur outside of the school term has dwindled to three afternoons weekly (Mon, Wed, Fri 5.15). Buses terminate in the lower of the two parts of **CAPDELLA** (30km from Pobla), based around the Central (de Energia), the oldest hydroelectric generator in these mountains. For **accommodation**, *Hostal Leo* (☎973 663 157; ⑥ HB), originally catering to power company workers, is quite elegant. *Hotel Monseny* (☎973 663 079; ⑥ HB), 800m south and officially in Espui village, is newer but equally good value. Since there's no shop or other restaurants in either part of the village, the reasonably priced half-board rates are worthwhile; both only operate from Easter to October, but this may change when the planned ski resort for the area becomes a reality.

Into the park

From Capdella, a half-day trek past the ugly Sallente dam takes you to the wonderful **Refugi Colomina** (☎973 252 000; 2395m; 40 places; open year-round, staffed early Feb, mid-March to mid-April & mid-June to Sept; ③), an old wooden chalet ceded to mountaineers by FECSA-ENHER and set among the alpine lakes of the **Circ de Saburó**, just south of the park boundary in the peripheral zone. You can skip much of the hike by taking the *teléferic* (**cable car**) from the back of the Sallente reservoir to within 45 minutes' walk of the refuge; departures 1 July–30 Sept only, up at 9am and 3pm, down at 1pm and 6pm (600ptas/€3.60 one-way). The immediate surroundings of the refuge have a few two-to-three-hour outings, most notably the circuit of the lakes in the Circ de Saburó, which can be completed in any remaining daylight.

El Pont de Suert

The route into the southwestern area of Aigüestortes begins just past **EL PONT DE SUERT**, a small town 41km northwest of La Pobla de Segur. There's a daily bus in summer from La Pobla de Segur at 9.30am, and two daily services each direction from Vielha and Lleida. All services stop on the main road, opposite an unmissably hideous **modern church**, the most remarkable sight in town. With a baptistry like an upturned egg and a brick belfry resembling the head of Spielberg's ET, it was designed by engineer Eduardo Torroja and architect J. Rodríguez Millares, and erected in 1955 as a bizarre homage to the Romanesque churches further up the valley (see below). The "egg" and the vaulting of the Nissen-hut-like nave are made entirely from curved, prestressed concrete panels, considered a daring technique back then but now looking rather dated.

El Pont de Suert is pleasant enough if you need to spend the night before catching the bus north to Boí (11.15am, June–Sept only), but you shouldn't have to because the morning buses from Vielha, Lleida and La Pobla all connect with the Boí service. The old town, a small maze of arcade streets, compensates for the grim buildings lining the highway, but it's not exactly a tourist hot spot, with only one surviving **accommodation** option in the centre – *Hotel Can Mestre* at Plaça Major 8 (☎973 690 306; ③), which has a pleasant river-view **restaurant**.

North towards Boí

Some 2km northwest of El Pont de Suert, a good side road threads north (right) along the **Vall de Boí**, following the Noguera de Tor towards Caldes de Boí, and passing the side turns for several villages on the way. It's an area crammed with Romanesque churches dating from the twelfth century, when the valleys were more populous and wealthy than any time since. As a happy result, these churches have never been rebuilt, and rank as the finest in Catalunya. All were constructed with astonishing detail and elegance from hand-split chunks of local stone, topped by slates. It's a pity that most of the frescoes are reproductions, the originals having long since been whisked away to the Museu d'Art de Catalunya in Barcelona. Many churches only open for Mass, or guided tours offered by the local tourist office (which also keeps helpful descriptive pamphlets for each church).

Cóll and Barruera

After about 8km there's a turnoff left to the village of **CÓLL** up on the hillside, with the twelfth-century church of **Santa María de l'Assumpció**; its west portal and masonry are particularly fine, but the grounds are usually locked. You're more likely to be here for the family-run *Hotel Casa Peyró* (☎973 297 002; ⑤), whose en-suite rooms are bland Spanish-modern – wood floors, TV, pastel colours – but the ground-floor restaurant is regarded as one of the best in the area. It's not cheap (best take half-board at 11,000ptas/€66) – but the food is worth it, especially the *entrantes*.

BARRUERA, 5km further on and much larger, has several places to **stay**, best value being *Casa Coll* (☎973 694 005 or contact Besiberri Sports on the main road; 3800ptas), an echoing old mansion near the top of c/Major in the old town. The salubrious rooms (one en-suite) are on the top floor, with a kitchen on the ground floor. Alternatives include the *Hotel Farre d'Avall* (☎973 694 029; ⑤) in the village centre, with limited parking, or (in desperation) the noisy *Noray* (☎973 694 021; June–Sept; ④), right on the main road. Barruera supports the main **Turisme** for the entire valley (Mon–Sat 10am–2pm & 5–7pm; ☎973 694 000), right opposite the petrol station. Just opposite the cramped campsite stands Barruera's Romanesque church, the riverside **Sant Feliu**, with its engaging thirteenth-century portal and creaking interior (Tues–Sat 11am–2pm & 4–7pm, Sun noon–2pm & 4–7pm, Mon during Aug only; 100ptas/€0.60).

Durro and Erill La Vall

There is another fine Romanesque church in the village of **DURRO**, 3km away on the hillside to the east, reached by the steep road from Barruera's petrol station. The bell-tower of **La Nativitat de la Mare de Déu** is the tallest in the valley, its raised Lombard-style brickwork contrasting with crude masonry and the stark southern portal. In Durro, certainly the most untouched valley settlement, you can stay at *Can Marquès* in the centre (☎973 694 054; ②) and eat at *Casa Xoquín* which does a reasonable *menú* or *tapas* in the bar. Durro is fairly practical as a staging post, situated on the variant GR11.20 linking El Pont de Suert with Boí, Taüll and the Colomina refuge. Coming from Boí (see below), a well-signed path starts just over the little bridge behind the old district, climbs 45 minutes to a shrine on a saddle, then drops to Durro fifteen minutes later. From the latter, you can make a brief excursion to the twelfth-century *ermita* of Sant Quirze, prominent on the ridge opposite; descend steeply to Barruera on a stake-marked path shortcutting the road; or take a longer day-hike to the Estany de Durro in the hills to the east.

Further on, just before the turn-off for Boí, a 1km side road leads west to **ERILL LA VALL**. Here the twelfth-century church of **Santa Eulàlia** (same hours as Sant Feliu above; 150ptas/€0.90) has an unusual arcaded porch and a six-storey belfry which rivals Sant Climent's in Taüll (see p.283). In high season Erill is relatively quiet, more likely to have a vacancy than Boí or Taüll. Choice **accommodation** includes the 1999-built *Casa Pernallé* (☎973 696 049; ③–④), just before the entrance to the village, with off-street parking and the option of older, cheaper non-en-suite rooms; the *Hostal La Plaça* (☎973 696 026, fax 973 696 128; ④), right opposite the belfry, with comfortable rooms including family suites, and a decent *menjador* (*menú* 2000ptas/€12); and the nearby *Hostal L'Aüt* (☎973 696 048, fax 973 696 126; ⑤), a bit overpriced but with a varied and cheap **restaurant** where three courses and wine *a la carta* will run under 3000ptas/€18.

Erill is also home to the local mountain-guiding centre, Guíes de Muntanya de la Vall de Boí (☎973 696 107), housed in *Bar La Granja*, which organizes trekking, canyoning and rock-climbing expeditions. To start less demanding outings – like the Boí-to-Durro walk noted above – a useful non-GR path links Erill and Boí in half an hour.

Boí

BOÍ stands 1km above the main road, which continues up to Caldes de Boí (see overleaf); buses usually take you into the centre. On arrival, the village may prove something of an anticlimax: a tiny, gatewayed medieval core huddled around a crag, swamped by car parks, modern buildings, old houses defaced with new brick repairs, and overpriced accommodation. Even the twelfth-century church of **Sant Joan** (Tues–Sat 11am–1.30pm & 3.30–6pm; 100ptas/€0.60) has been extensively renovated, the only original parts being the squat belfry and part of the apse; an interior mural (again a copy) depicts the stoning of St Stephen. Like almost every village in the Tor valley, Boí has worthwhile adventure-travel outfits which offer guided hikes, mountain-bike tours and special-interest safaris.

Practicalities

Although Boí is perhaps the least captivating local village, you may need to **stay** here in the course of a visit to the park. Despite being a little out of the way, one good choice is the *Hostal Pascual*, down by the junction and bridge, equidistant from Erill (☎973 696 014; ③), with helpful owners and a decent *menú* in the dining room. In the village itself, the central *Hostal Beneria* (☎973 696 030; ④ B&B) and the *Pensió Pey* (☎973 696 036; ⑤) are more expensive with similar facilities. Less pricey are the clean, modern **rooms** through the stone archway in the old quarter – look for the *habitaciones* sign; these are representative of the five local *cases de pagès* (②).

Eating out, you'll do no better than the *Casa Higinio*, 200m up the road to Taüll, above the village centre. Its wood-fired range produces excellent meat dishes, or try the fine *escudella* (minestrone soup) and trout. A big *menú* accompanied by local wine and coffee (but no dessert) comes to just under 2000ptas/€12 – allow plenty of time for service. Ordering *a la carta* (3300ptas/€19.80) gets you Italian dishes and the full dessert list. None of the other diners attached to the various central *hostals* are anywhere near as good value, though the *Pey* offers *a la carta* for under 3000ptas/€18, served on its popular terrace overlooking the main Plaça del Treio.

At the **Casa del Parc Nacional** (April–Oct daily 9am–1pm & 3.30–6.45pm, Nov–March daily 9am–2pm & 3.30–6pm; ☎973 696 189) on the same *plaça*, you can buy Alpina maps there at a slight markup, or book a 4WD-taxi into the park (see below). The **bank** behind the supermarket has an ATM.

Into the park – and Caldes de Boí

It's 3.5km from Boí to the national park entrance, and another 3.5km to the scenic waterfalls of Aigüestortes, tumbling from water-meadows to feed the reedy Estany Llebreta, where half-wild horses roam. One final kilometre above the falls – passed closely by both road and trail #5, the "Ruta de la Nutria/Llúdriga" (see below) – is another park information booth (Easter & July–Sept daily 9.30am–2pm & 4–6.30pm). There's a map placard beside it with suggested day-hikes and corresponding time estimates. The most popular stroll, about an hour one-way, leads east from the information post to Estany Llong.

Taxis from Boí's village square will take you as far as the booth; as in Espot, passage costs 600ptas/€3.60 one-way, 1200ptas/€7.20 round-trip. Vehicles wait to depart until they're full; last return from Aigüestortes is at 7pm in midsummer. The closest you can get to the park boundary in your own vehicle is the car park at La Farga, or another smaller one 1.5km east, right at the boundary. If you leave your car at either, and arrange to meet a taxi to take you further uphill, at day's end you can follow trail #5 (Ruta de la Nutria, signed as "Aparcament") from the info booth which shortcuts the road by 45 minutes.

Alternatively, you can flag down the one midday bus from the junction of the Boí side road up to the large **spa** complex of **CALDES DE BOÍ** (late June–Sept only), 5.7km upstream. The four-star *Hotel Manantial* here is beyond the reach of most travellers, but the adjacent two-star *Caldas* (☎973 696 230; ④–⑤) is affordable, with half-board rates and every imaginable hydrotherapy available.

Between Caldes de Boí and the high dam at the south end of Estany de Cavallers the former "free" camping area has been shut down, as it falls within the park's peripheral protection zone. The dam itself marks the trailhead for walks towards the beautiful natural lakes northwest of the park, just below the Besiberri and Montarto peaks.

Taüll

TAÜLL – 3km above Boí by road or 2km on a fairly steep, forty-minute section of the GR11.20 – had been a much larger medieval village before an avalanche divided it into two districts; ruined house foundations were found in the empty space between during the 1980s. More recently, it has been massively affected by the ski resort of Boí-Taüll (see below) on the mountainside a few kilometres southeast. There's an enormous holiday complex 1500m beyond the village at Pla de l'Ermita, en route to the ski station, and even in summer Taüll is targeted by tour coaches and family cars in search of panoramic picnic spots. Yet away from the peripheral ski chalets, the old core retains plenty of character, and is certainly preferable to Boí as a base.

Two of the best local Romanesque churches stand in the village, consecrated on successive days in 1123. Of the pair, **Sant Climent de Taüll** (summer 10.30am–2pm & 4–8pm, winter Mon–Sat 10.30am–2pm & 4–7pm, Sun 10.30am–2pm; 150ptas/€0.90) is more immediately impressive by virtue of its famous six-storey belfry and original triple apse. The stark interior, doubling now as a museum of religious artefacts, retains copies of vivid murals showing Christ, saints and apostles, plus scenes from the New Testament and the Apocalypse. The admission ticket entitles you to climb the rickety wooden steps to the top of the bell-tower for sweeping views through delicately arched windows.

At the heart of the upper quarter, **Santa Maria** (daily 10am–8pm; free) is similar in design, though its belfry has only four storeys. After a millennium of subsidence, there's not one right angle remaining in the building, with the tower in particular at an engaging list. The mural (again a reproduction), soberly coloured in reddish brown, yellow and blue, depicts the Adoration of the Virgin and Child by the Three Kings.

Practicalities

Accommodation options, many under the *cases de pagès* programme, include the ensuite *Pensió La Coma* (☎973 696 025; ③) at the village entrance; the *Pensió Sant Climent*, across the lane from *La Coma* (☎973 696 052; ③), with a restaurant; *Casa Plano Minguero* (☎973 696 117; ③), well located in the upper part of the village with its own parking (a problem here); or, highest standard of all, the *Santa Maria* (☎973 696 170, *santamaria@taull.com*), a fine courtyard house with doubles (④–⑦ B&B) and longer-term self-catering units.

Ca de Corral (☎973 696 004 or 973 696 028; ③), run by the *Bar Mallador* (see below), offers rustic rooms without bath on the top floor of an old house well situated in the lower part of the village. Other rooms without bath but with self-catering facilities are at the friendly *Casa Llovet*, Plaça Franch 5 (☎973 696 032; ②), or *Casa Xep* (☎973 696 054; ②), just below Plaça Santa María – ask at the adjacent supermarket. A **campsite** (all year in theory; ☎973 696 082), also with bungalows, spreads attractively on the slope below Sant Climent.

La Coma's **restaurant** is justly popular for its game (wild boar and quail) and good service; a *menú* is available (1600ptas/€9.60), otherwise count on 2200ptas/€13.20 for *a la carta*. *El Caliu*, at the top of Taüll in a modern apartment building, is also well regarded, though its portions tends towards *cuisine minceur*. Last but not least, just beside Sant Climent, *Mallador* (closed May–23 June & 15 Oct–end Nov), run by David and Consell, combines the virtues of being the most popular village **bar** with an excellent **restaurant** (garden seating in summer, upstairs in winter); sample fare (lunch *menú* 1700ptas/€10.20, otherwise affordable *a la carta*) includes creditable *escudella* with meatballs, grilled meat or trout, *trinxat* and strawberries in orange syrup.

Skiing: Boí-Taüll

The ski centre at **Boí-Taüll**, some 11km southeast of Taüll, is the newest in the Catalan Pyrenees (inaugurated in 1990) and the only rival to Baqueira-Beret for really serious skiing with 41 pistes, more than half red-rated, and 16 lifts, mostly drag-type. It's not the best resort for beginners or weak intermediates, as the runs tend to be short and sweet, but advanced skiers can tackle the six-kilometrc off-piste descent of the Vall de Moró, typically an hour to drop the 1000m. Boí-Taüll has the highest lift-top in the range (2750m), start of a four-kilometre advanced run, and the snow quality is good in the glacial bowl facing north to Besiberri and other peaks beyond the Cavallers reservoir. With a 2020-metre bottom point at Pla de Vaques, the centre will probably survive global warming, unlike many other Pyrenean resorts, though early closures are common on spring days. Lift passes and on-site gear rental are pricey; gear can be cheaper to rent in Taüll or Barruera (*www.boitaullresort.es*).

Walking in Aigüestortes

Initial stretches of trail or track into Aigüestortes are detailed in the preceding sections "Approaches to Aigüestortes" and "South to Aigüestortes". Moving deeper into the region, the clearly signposted **GR11** path skims the northern margins of the park, linking Espot with the Túnel de Vielha; variant **GR11.20** connects Espot and the Vall de Boí. There are also numerous waymarked (but unnumbered) linking paths which permit any number of circuits and traverses in the best of the park and peripheral zone. Less exciting, and sometimes overly subscribed because of its ease, is the east–west track crossing the park from Estany de Sant Maurici to the springs of Aigüestortes.

If you want solitude and wilderness, stick to the more difficult south–north trails, which run perpendicular to most hiker traffic. Map, altimeter and compass are essential when departing from more trammelled routes – it's easy to get lost amongst the hundreds of lakes and lookalike granite whalebacks dividing them, especially in cloudy conditions.

Traverses

Three good traverses of the park start from the *Refugi Colomina* (see "Into the park", p.280), in addition to the one to/from Espot via the *Refugi Josep Maria Blanc* (see p.279).

North to Refugi Ernest Mallafré via Monestero valley

Heading north through the often snow-clogged, steep **Coll de Peguera** (2726m) and down the beautiful **Monestero (Monastero) valley**, it's a six-hour hike to the **Refugi Ernest Mallafré**, near the dam and roadhead at Sant Maurici (☎973 250 118; 1885m; 24 places; mid-June to end Sept; ➀). If it's full, you'll need to reserve enough energy and daylight to continue ninety minutes to the more comfortable **Refugi-Xalet d'Amitges** (see p.271). Next day you could leave the park via the gentle **Port de Ratera de Colomers**, finishing this less strenuous leg at the *Refugi de Colomers* (see p.272), where you're well poised to continue along the routes described on p.272.

Northwest to Refugis d'Estany Llong, Ventosa i Calvell and Restanca

A more adventurous route heads northwest from *Refugi Colomina* through the easy trekkers' passes **Collada de Dellui** (2574m) or **Collada de Morrano** (2631m) to the **Refugi d'Estany Llong** (☎629 374 652; 2000m; 36 places; open late Feb, Easter weeks,

June to mid-Oct; ①), beside the lake of that name. If it's full, the nearby, unstaffed *Refugi Centraleta* (8 bunks, fireplace) will be your home for the night. The Dellui route descends through the valley of that name, speckled with natural lakes, additionally (with a slight detour) past the scenic tarns of Corticelles.

On the following day, you climb for three and a half hours to the cirque-bound Estany de Contraig, with two very sharp grades on route. This lies just below the **Coll de Contraix** (2752m) another hour along, with stunning views but requiring snow equipment after a heavy winter. From here you must drop along the horrid north side (self-arrest device always required) to the very popular **Refugi Ventosa i Calvell** (reservations mandatory ☎973 297 090; 2200m; 80 places; open select winter weekends & mid-June to late Oct; ①), 2hr 15min away from the pass beside **Estany Negre**, where again you're near the heart of a lake-rich glacial basin. From here, you can walk an easy four hours to the *Refugi de la Restanca* (p.272) in the peripheral zone, and happily spend any remaining daylight on various hikes around the refuge.

West to Boí

From *Colomina*, it's possible to head west through deserted country along the GR11.20 **to Boí**, a long nine-hour day via one of two passes. The easy **Port de Rus** carries both the variant and the old spa patrons' *camí* from Capdella, but it's more exciting to maintain altitude by the park boundary, via a series of lakes and the inconspicuous **Collado del Pessó** (2760m), testing your cross-country skills.

Sant Maurici to Aigüestortes

If you're not fully committed to alpine trekking, but are in reasonable physical condition, stick to the broad *camí* **between Sant Maurici and Aigüestortes**. Take a 4WD-taxi to/from one or both ends of the fifteen-kilometre traverse, which can be walked in six hours (allow another four hours to Boí if you miss the last taxi). You definitely won't be alone, and will mostly look up to the peaks rather than down from them. The exceptional moments come either side of the **Portarró d'Espot** (2429m), where you can detour for moderate ridge-touring. The main track took its present form early in 1953, when in a pharaonic gesture General Franco commanded that it be widened with hand tools so that his private jeep could pass from one end to the other that summer. Much of the poor labourers' work has since reverted to nature – 4WD vehicles can no longer get through – though most keen walkers regard it as far too easy for serious consideration. Still, if you spread it over two days with an overnight at Estany Llong, there are some excellent day-treks to be enjoyed from the refuge.

Peak ascents

Featured on countless posters, postcards, window-stickers and T-shirts, the double-pinnacle profile of **Els Encantats** is the park's de facto logo. Like the Agulles d'Amitges near the *Amitges* refuge, the pinnacles are a favourite of technical climbers, but experienced mountain walkers equipped with a rope can reach the top of **Grand Encantat** (2747m) in about five hours from the *Ernest Mallafré* refuge, via the gully separating the twin summits.

The second highest peak inside the park, **Pala Alta de Sarradé** (Serrader on some maps; 2973m), is a much easier goal, reached from Boí by the track to the park entrance, then via Estany Sarradé and a gully to the summit – a 4WD taxi cuts it from five to three and a half hours one-way. Its neighbour and highest park summit, **Punta Alta** (3014m), is usually climbed from the Cavallers dam, via a path up the vale and tarns of **Coma les Bienes** and then scrambling. From either of these peaks you can carry on to the *Ventosa i Calvell* refuge.

The third-highest summit, **Pic de Peguera** (2982m), is a nontechnical ascent if tackled from the Coll de Monestero, half an hour to the east; this pass is less than two hours from the *Josep Maria Blanc* hut and three from *Ernest Mallafré*. From the *coll* a cairned route leads southwest to the top in 45 minutes; however the final scramble up (or especially down) a steep, partially blocked couloir can be daunting.

MALADETA AND POSETS

The trough-like **Ésera valley** runs through the heart of the Pyrenees' high mountain wilderness, with Aneto peak (3404m) crowning the **Maladeta** massif to the east, and **Posets** (3375m) looming on the west. Since the creation of the **Parque Natural Posets-Maladeta** in 1994, both ranges have enjoyed some protection from development. **Benasque** is the pivotal point, a small valley-bottom town that lives for alpine tourism but has managed to retain some rural Aragonese character, not least in a vigorous recent campaign to promote renewed use of the **regional language**. Aragonese town names are noted below in parentheses following the Spanish, since this is what you will see on city-limits and road signs; the convention is reversed for place names in the mountains, since on most maps – including Editorial Alpina's – Aragonese now takes precedence.

With the resurgence of regional feeling, efforts have been made throughout under-resourced Alto Aragón to improve the quality of tourist services and information – especially trail guides and maps – to match Catalan standards. The mountain Aragonese feel, with some justice, that the Catalans benefit disproportionately from tourism, and have misrepresented regional history and linguistics. Local advocates point out that Catalunya was long subsumed within the kingdom of Aragón, and that the yellow-and-red Catalan flag is based on the original, horizontal Aragonese version.

Not scaled until 1842, **Aneto** was for a long time visited by mountaineers rather than walkers, not so much for any technical difficulty – though the climb does have vertiginous final moments – as for its inaccessibility. The former approach from France through the Portillón de Benasque was superseded in the 1970s with the extension of the C139 from Benasque to within a short walk of both the Portillón de Benasque, just northwest, and the *Refugio de la Renclusa* (south of the road's end), the standard base for the conquest of Aneto.

The most momentous day at the **Portillón de Benasque/Port de Vénasque** – the historic route across the watershed – was April 1, 1938, when thousands of Spanish Republicans fled from a Nationalist advance that had cut them off in the Ésera cul-de-sac. Many others didn't make it after being trapped in a snowstorm the next day. At the end of World War II, a large number of the surviving Republicans met their deaths when they returned to contest Franco's rule in Spain.

Finishing second seldom impresses, which is perhaps why few tourists know about the marginally lower **Posets**. But the sculpted massif with its paradisal valleys is popular with the Spanish, and has more staffed refuges than any other major Pyrenean peak. If you don't want to bag the 3375-metre summit, a westward traverse or half-circuit is the best and most scenic passage west – otherwise you have to detour way to the south on the bus to Barbastro before heading up the Cinca valley, a route poorly covered by public transport.

The Ésera valley

The **Ésera valley** remains a dead end for cars, and since the area's inclusion in the local *parque natural* further restrictions on private traffic have come into effect (see below). Park status seems to have ended long-mooted plans for a tunnel through the

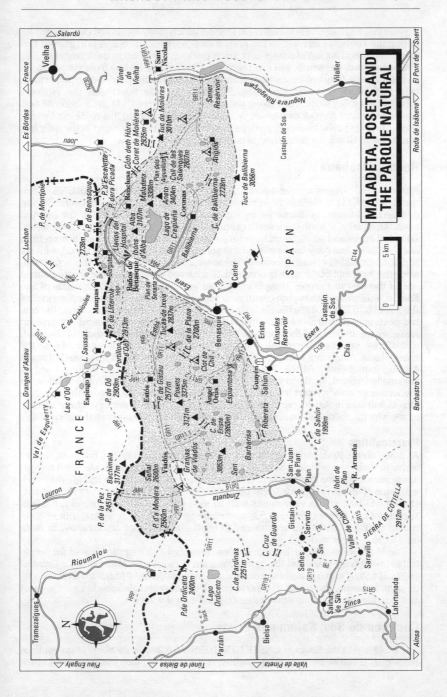

frontier ridge to Bagnères-de-Luchon in France, which many locals had campaigned for during the 1980s. It's an issue on the French side too, where people feel aggrieved that the Alps has had 300km of tunnel built since 1960, versus 17km in the Pyrenees.

Coming from the **south** you can reach the Ésera valley by bus from Barbastro (in turn served by frequent buses from Huesca or Lleida), where twice-daily departures take two hours to reach Benasque. From El Pont de Suert and the Noguera Ribagorçana valley to the **east**, along the lonely 41-kilometre C144 to Castejón de Sos, you're dependent on your own motor vehicle or bicycle; hitching this route can be very slow. The only public transport towards Aragón from El Pont de Suert is the daily bus southwest to Graus, via the cathedral outpost of Roda de Isábena.

Roda de Isábena

Attractive hill villages are ten-a-penny in Aragón, but **RODA DE ISÁBENA**, 32km south of the C144 in the middle of nowhere just above a minor road between El Pont de Suert and Graus, is unique for its superb Romanesque **cathedral** at the heart of town. Originally a tenth-to-eleventh-century monastic church, it has three aisles, Lombard apses and an eighteenth-century octagonal belfry serving as a beacon from afar, but there ends any conformity to the norm. The ornate entrance portal, with six series of capitalled columns inside a Renaissance portico, breaches the south wall, since the west end of the nave is occupied by a carved choir and a fine organ, claimed one of the best in Europe. Mass is celebrated on the purported sarcophagus of San Ramón, squirming with twelfth-century carvings of the Annunciation, the Nativity and the Flight into Egypt. Immediately below the raised altar is a vast triple crypt, the central section with worn column capitals but the northerly one graced by brilliant Romanesque frescoes of the Baptism, Saint Michael weighing the souls of the dead, and Christ in Glory surrounded by the Tetramorph (the four symbols of the Evangelists). Admission is only by guided visit (daily every 45min 11.15am–1.30pm & 4.30–6.45pm; 250ptas/€1.50), though you can see the twelfth-century cloister and its colonnade (eroded like the crypt's) by eating at the excellent restaurant (see below) in the former refectory. Apart from that, there's little else to do but wander the attractive streets and take in 360-degree views from the *mirador* by the refectory, where it's easy to see why the medieval counts of Ribagorça chose Roda as their capital and citadel.

Practicalities

As noted above, Roda can be reached by infrequent public transport, but most visitors arrive in their own vehicle. The place has become a popular Spanish weekend retreat, and **accommodation** booking is necessary year-round. Top choices include the excellent-value *Hospedaría de Roda*, right on the multi-levelled central plaza (☎974 544 554, fax 974 544 500; ③), its view rooms with all mod cons, or the very friendly, English-speaking *Casa Simón* (☎974 544 528 or enquire at *Bar Mesón de Roda*), with en-suite rooms (③ B&B) and 4-bed apartments (6000ptas/€36). Other *casas rurales* in Roda tend to be of lower standard.

The *Mesón de Roda* does decent meals and breakfasts with a ringside seat for people traffic through the plaza. But the best **restaurant** is clearly the *Hospedería La Catedral* (☎974 544 539), with *a la carta* so reasonable (2100–2600ptas/€12.60–15.60) there's little point in having the *menú*. The *carta* has plenty of vegetable-based *entrantes*, meat and game for seconds, homemade desserts and a local wine list.

Castejón de Sos, Sahún and Eriste

The C144 meets the Ésera at **CASTEJÓN DE SOS** (Castilló de Sos), 14km south of Benasque. If you've come up from Barbastro, it's the first place you'll see with much mountain character, at least in the tiny, fortified old quarter north of the highway. The unique local topography has made it a mecca for **parapentists**, with two international competitions here annually. If you want to stay, there's moderately priced **accommodation** on the through road, c/El Real. Top choices include the well-kept, en-suite *Hostal Plaza*, central but quiet at Plaza El Pilar 2 (☎974 553 050, *www.aneto.com/hostalplaza*; ④); the *Hostal Sositana* towards the east end of town on the north side of c/El Real (☎974 553 094; ④), with a bar and *comedor*; the en-suite *Casa Miranda* opposite at no. 60 (☎974 553 222; ③); and further east, the *Hostal Alto Aragón* (☎974 553 023; ④), a characterful *modernista* barracks with a mostly Spanish OAP clientele. There are three dorm-style *albergues* in the area, mostly affiliated with parapente schools; best is the *Pájaro Loco* at c/El Real 48 (☎974 553 516; ①), with six- or eight-bunk rooms instead of the fourteen-to-eighteen berth dorms elsewhere. There's also a campsite at the west edge of town, *Alto Ésera* (☎974 553 456; May–Sept).

Sahún

If you have your own vehicle, the relatively unspoilt hillside village of **SAHÚN** (Saunc), 7km up the valley on the west slope, makes a far more atmospheric base, especially in high season. There are several places to **stay**, including the *Hostal Casa Lacreu* on the Plaza Mayor (☎ & fax 974 551 335; ④), a restored manor house with spotless en-suite rooms, an arcaded bar and cheery, good-value *comedor*. Most accommodation in the village is part of the *casa rural* scheme; of these, *Casa Falisia* at the far south edge of Sahún is mostly without en-suite facilities (☎974 551 340; ②–③), basic and feeling a bit dated. At the north end of town, *Casa Alquesera* (☎974 551 396) offers a high standard for three- and four-place apartments (9000/11,000ptas/€54/66), while the single apartment at *Casa Colás*, next to the church (☎974 551 398) fits six at 10,000ptas/€60 per day and boasts a full kitchen with dishwasher as well as central heating.

Prime outings from Sahún are the **all-day hikes** along locally marked *caminos* 9 and 10. Number 9 heads north past the deconsecrated Guayén (Guayente) monastery (now a private educational foundation), then west along the Aigüeta valley to the Ibón (Lake) de la Ribereta. Number 10 goes south, then west along the Aigüeta de Llisat stream to the scattered *ibones* of Barbarisa. Both are designed for moderately fit walkers, and get a fraction of the patronage of the "classic" walks up-valley (see pp.292–295). These routes can be linked via the 2538-metre Collado de la Ribereta to form a loop, or you can continue northwest from the Barbarisa lakes over the Collado de Barbarisa (2577m) to the Ibón d'el Sen (Sein), and then to San Juan de Plan (see p.301) along another PR route to make an excellent, mid-altitude traverse.

Eriste

ERISTE (Grist), 3km further north and just 4km shy of Benasque, is less immediately appealing than Sahún, especially the modern industrial district abutting the main road. However, quick access to Posets via the Eriste valley makes it a good base if Benasque is full. Eriste is a low-key **water-sports** centre thanks to its position near the Linsoles reservoir; contact Grist-Kayak at the jetty or on ☎974 551 092. Four uninspiring *hostales* with attached restaurants on the main highway seem to survive on Spanish packages. By far the best place to **stay**, at the southwest corner of the old quarter, is Lupe Gea's very kind and homely *Casa Roy* (☎974 55 13 92; ②–③), which offers meals; it's justly popular and requires reservations most of the year.

Benasque and Cerler

Surrounded by hayfields in a wide part of the Ésera valley, **BENASQUE** (Benás) strikes most people as an agreeable place, combining modern amenities with old stone houses, some built as summer homes for the Aragonese nobility in the seventeenth century. The town was once a seat of the counts of Ribagorça, who provided a castle and perimeter walls, both razed during the Napoleonic wars. The surviving old quarter, with its thirteenth-century church of **San Marcial** and fifteenth-century **Torre Juste**, is still homogeneous, atmospheric and large enough to get lost in.

Despite murmurings of despoliation, modern Benasque and its nearby ski annexe of Cerler aren't nearly as obtrusive as the new developments in the Val d'Aran – and, before or after the rigours of Aneto or Posets, you'll welcome the chance to indulge in a little luxury. Benasque seems to attract a younger, less staid clientele than Aran –mostly well-heeled Barcelonans intent on a good time indoors or out – and so has plenty of nightlife as well.

Arrival and information

Buses from Barbastro stop on the main Avda de los Tilos, a little south of the compact old quarter. The **Turismo** (daily 9am–2pm 4–9pm; ☎974 551 289) is found at the southeast corner of the old town, dispensing pamphlets on local walks as well as publicity for local activities outfits. Labelled in Spanish only, and of specialist interest, the **Centro de Visitantes** (mid-June to mid-Sept daily 10am–2pm & 4–8pm; rest of year weekends & holidays same hours, except autumn & winter 10am–2pm & 3–6pm) documents geography, natural history and traditional livelihoods in the park territory. It's an isolated building 500m south of the bus stop on the east side of the Anciles road. Several **banks** have ATMs in Benasque – the only ones you'll see for some distance, trekking east or west – and a **laundry**, Ardilla (no sign out), on the bypass road east of the Torre Juste.

Accommodation

Budget **accommodation** in and around the old town includes: *Casa Bardanca*, c/Las Plazas 6 (☎974 551 360; ②), bathless but pleasant rooms above the *Bar Bardanca*; *Casa Gabás-Pichuán*, on quiet c/El Castillo (☎974 551 275; ③), offering both en-suite rooms and self-catering units; the somewhat shabby *Fonda Barrabés*, c/Mayor 3 (☎974 551 654; ②), run essentially as a mountaineer's *albergue* with a cheap *comedor*; and the slightly run-down *Hostal Salvaguardia* at c/San Marcial 5 (☎974 551 039; ②), a last-resort cheapie despite its prime position by the church.

For more comfort, try the en-suite *Hotel Aragüells* (☎974 551 619, fax 974 551 664; ⑤ B&B) at Avda de los Tilos 1, the main commercial street, or the *Hotel Avenida* next door at no. 3 (☎974 551 126, fax 974 551 515; ⑥), a long-standing mountaineers' hangout, with half-board encouraged. Otherwise the Valero Llanas family own much of the lodging in town, spread over five hotels and *hostales*; consult *www.hoteles-valero.com*, or call in at the conspicuous *Hotel Aneto*, just south of the C139 skirting town on the Anciles road (☎974 551 061, fax 973 551 509; ⑥), which has a pool, tennis courts, gym, sauna and parking. Budget-minded visitors may prefer their nearby *Hostal Valero* (same phone; ③). Less institutional and homier is one of Benasque's three-star hotels, the *San Marsial* at the north end of town on the bypass road (☎ & fax 974 551 616, *www.pirineo.com/hotel.san.marsial*; ⑦).

The closest authorized **campsites** begin 4km upstream along the Ésera valley, conveniently near the GR11 junction: *Aneto* (year-round), *Chuise* and *Ixeia* (June–Sept). Of the three, the *Chuise*, at the mouth of the Estós valley, is the most basic and tent-friendly. The "free camping" area further up at Plan de Senarta, on the boundary of the *parque natural*, is living on borrowed time – it was supposed to have been phased out in 1997; rough camping anywhere near the valley floor is highly frowned upon.

Eating and drinking

Competition means that reasonable *menús* abound at the **bars and restaurants**. Try the *comedores* of the *Bar Bardanca* or the *Bar Sayó* on c/Mayor 13, which includes quails or sardines on its three-course, 1450-ptas/€8.70 *menú*. Snackier options include *Pepe and Company* on c/Mayor, or *La Pizzeria*, just off Plaza Mayor. As a splurge, *La Parilla* on Ctra. Francia (the bypass road), serves nouvelle Aragonese cooking – stuffed vegetables and creative puddings – for 1700ptas/€10.20, *menú* or *a la carta* at 4000ptas/€24 and up. Finally, you can cobble together **breakfast** at durable favourite *Granja Flor de Nieve* at c/Major 17.

Activities and equipment

Everything in Benasque revolves around the great outdoors, evident from the number of people strolling about in brightly coloured Gore-Tex. Three rival **guiding centres** – Casa de la Montaña, Avda. de Los Tilos (☎974 552 094), Equipo Barrabés (☎974 551 056, *www.barrabes.com*) and Compañia de Guías Valle de Benasque (☎974 551 336, *www.guiasbenasque.com*) – organize trekking, technical climbing, alpine skiing, canyoning and rafting expeditions, including both nearby summits in five days. The lower reaches of the rivers in the Estós and Ballibierna valleys offer some of the best **kayaking** in the Spanish Pyrenees, the latter for experts only. You can **horse-ride** with La Cuadra Verde in Anciles, 1.5km south (☎974 551 098, Easter-Sept); rates start from 2000ptas/€12 for two hours. Of the **mountaineering equipment shops**, most conspicuous and one of the biggest in Spain, if not Europe, is Galleria Barrabés, near the corner of the C139 and Avda. de los Tilos: four floors of outdoor gear, with a café on the third floor and a soft-goods annexe across the road. However, do visit Deportes Aigualluts/Casa de la Montaña, with two outlets on Avda de los Tilos, before deciding where to replace worn-out trekking items. Libreria Rodolfoto, across from the *Hotel Aragüells*, has Benasque's best stock of **maps and guidebooks**.

Most useful of the local guidebooks on sale is *Senderos de Pequño Recorrido: Valle de Benasque*, issued by the Aragonese mountain club together with an invaluable map, worthwhile even if you don't read Spanish. If you're unsure about tackling high-mountain walks, then the various local yellow-and-white- or blue-and-white-blazed *pequeño recorrido* (PR) **short-haul paths** make an ideal introduction. The PR itineraries, routed to avoid roads as much as possible, lead to surrounding villages, lower altitude alpine attractions, and also to all three local refuges.

Cerler

CERLER (Sarllé), a small dependency of Benasque reached by a six-kilometre road or the one-hour PR-1 path – worthwhile for the valley views – ranks as the highest (1540m) village in Aragón. It's an attractive enough place, though the old quarter is now engulfed by straggly, low-density modern chalets which come to life in winter courtesy of the adjacent **ski centre** (*www.cerler.com*). This narrowly avoided closure in the early 1990s through massive government investment in lifts and snow canons. A top point of 2630m, second only to Boí-Taüll in the range, and a well-linked system of lifts (half are chairs) has improved this decent intermediate resort, with fourteen red and fifteen blue runs among its 38 pistes. The most reliable action begins at the Llanos del Ampriu (1900m), which has a creditable restaurant (lunch only, July to mid-April).

Reasonable **accommodation** in the old village in summer as well as ski season includes *Hostal Casa Cornel*, c/El Obispo 11 (☎ & fax 974 551 102; ⑤), offering good-standard, en-suite rooms in a stone building facing a courtyard; the en-suite *Casa Llorgodo*, c/La Fuente, above the church plaza (☎974 551 067; ②); or, isolated at the far north end of Cerler, the *Casa Ezequiel* (☎974 551 524; ②). There are also two **bar-restaurantes**: *La Picada*, the hub of village life, and *La Borda del Mastín*, specializing in *carnes a la brasa*. **Horse-riding** is offered by Casa Paulo at the north edge of Cerler (☎974 551 092).

Into the Parque Natural Posets-Maladeta from Benasque

Benasque offers the only road access to the **Parque Natural Posets-Maladeta**, which extends from the Noguera Ribagorçana in the east to the Valle de Chistau in the west. The lowest reaches of the Ésera valley are not included up to the Baños de Benasque, an old spa or *balneario* 10km from Benasque (see below). **Private vehicle traffic** into the park is restricted between July 10 and August 31. The track east into the Ballibierna (Vallhiverna) valley, 6km above Benasque, is closed for entry from 8am to 8pm, and the barrier is lifted for cars exiting only from 10 to 11am and again from 3 to 6pm. The C139 splits some 11.5km north of Benasque; the right-hand option leads after 1500m to a car park at **El Vado**, beyond which entry is again restricted between 8am and 8pm on the dates specified, though exit is always allowed. Guards tend the barriers; the only exceptions are for those continuing about 500m from El Vado to the car park of the Hospital de Benasque (see below). In summer (July 10–Aug 31), there's a **shuttle-bus service** (every 30min 8am–9.30pm, plus a few pre-dawn departures; 300ptas/€1.80) from here to La Besurta, road's end (16km from Benasque) and site of another car park for the *Refugio de la Renclusa* and the Forau dels Aiguallluts. Other routes covered by the same company include Benasque to **La Besurta**, via Plan de Senarta "free camping" area and Baños de Benasque (3–4 daily direct; 600ptas/€3.60 one-way) and Benasque-Senarta-Refugio de Pescadores in the Valle de Ballibierna (3–5 daily; 1200ptas/€7.20), which cuts out a considerable, dull track-section of the GR11. At other times of the year, those without cars wanting a jump-start to excursions might use an **alpine taxi** service: Angel Lledo (☎608 930 450), Daniel Villegas (☎609 448 894), or Manolo Mora (☎974 551 157).

    Camping within the *parque natural* had been forbidden since the park opened; however a law passed in 2000 now permits a one-night tent stay at all points above 2000m – legalizing this previously widespread practice.

The Baños de Benasque and Llanos del Hospital – plus day-hikes

The **Baños de Benasque** (Bañs de Benás), part of the Valero **hotel** empire (☎974 344 000, fax 974 344 249; mid-June to early Oct; ④), presents itself as a contemporary spa with full hydrocure and massage programmes. The premises however, remain resolutely old-fashioned, with a rather funky plunge pool (700ptas/€4.20) downstairs and a popular bar above it, where terrace tables are at a premium on fair days. There's also a **campsite** just downhill at Plan de Bañs, the *Valero* (July to mid-Sept). Its continued existence is clearly an anomaly as it lies well within the park, testimony to the family's local influence.

    From the baths, the best and surprisingly little-frequented outing is the **hike** east up the Ball d'Alba to its cluster of lakes. Start out along the old *camino* northeast towards the Hospital de Benasque; after about ten minutes veer east onto a much fainter side trail which climbs sharply along the bank of the Turonet gully to a saddle at 1975m (50min along). After a brief dip, the ascent continues east-southeast, and within another hour you should arrive at the largest of the three **Ibons d'Alba**, tucked away on the west flank of the Maladeta massif, just below 3107-metre Pico de Alba. Allow about three hours for the round-trip.

    The derelict old pilgrims' hospice of **Hospital de Benasque** (13km from Benasque), a Templar foundation of the twelfth century, was revamped and enlarged to wide acclaim by an activities group as the *Llanos del Hospital* (☎974 552 012, fax 974 551 052, *www.encomix.es/hospital*). It offers fairly pricey **lodging** in three formats: alpine *refugio* with nine-bunk dorms (①), *albergue* with five-to-seven-bunk dorms, ensuite bathrooms and linen provided (3000ptas/€18 per person B&B), or *hostal* (double rooms; ⑤ B&B). It's also the focus of a popular **cross-country skiing** centre, whose routes extend up-valley to La Besurta; in winter you're virtually obliged to take half-board, multi-day "packages". On the ground floor are a convivial **bar** and a highly regarded **restaurant**, with *menús* at three price scales and lots of regional dishes (such as *recau*, a chickpea-and-greens hotpot) available *a la carta*.

The best and most popular summer excursion near *Llanos del Hospital* is the easy **hike** to two small tarns and one sizable lake to the north, the largest bodies of water on the Spanish side of this frontier ridge. The least complicated trailhead, with parking available year-round, is at the abrupt end of the left-hand fork in the C139, below the El Vado car park. The path, shown fairly accurately on the Alpina "Maladeta/Aneto" map, climbs north to cross the Torrente de Gorgutes, then veers briefly east to skim above the two well-hidden **Ibones de la Solana de Gorgutes** (de la Montañeta), the smaller of which is shallow and warm enough to swim. The route then curls west to the **Ibón de Gorgutes**, with the 2367-metre **Puerto de la Glera** just behind, an easy pedestrian route into France. It's a two-and-a-half-hour round trip from the trailhead.

Maladeta climbs and walks

Despite its forbidding appearance from a distance, the **Maladeta Massif** offers scope for day-hikes, traverses and circuits of various levels of difficulty, as well as alpine ascents. The main drawback walking around Maladeta is that there's only one staffed refuge, better positioned for peak-climbers than long-distance trekkers. For any other extended forays you'd do well to have a **tent**. The relevant Editorial Alpina 1:25,000 **map** is "Maladeta/Aneto"; the map of the same scale in the *Senderos de Pequeño Recorrido* booklet unhappily crops half the mountain. For a head-start up the mountain, see opposite for access from Benasque.

The ascent of Aneto

The **ascent of Aneto** typically begins at the **Refugio de la Renclusa** (☎974 552 106 or 689 487 064; 2140m; 150 places; staffed Christmas, Easter, spring weekends Easter–June, daily July–Sept, emergency shelter in winter; ①), located well north of the summit close to the border. The final stop of the summertime shuttle-bus from El Vado at the La Besurta parking area is 45 minutes' hike below *Renclusa*. If you need to walk the whole distance, a forestry track runs most of the way along the east bank of the Ésera, with more path short-cuts on the opposite bank once past *Llanos del Hospital* – the entire way marked as the four-and-a-half-hour **PR-4**.

Unless you're incredibly fit and experienced, plan for a full day to the summit and back with necessary stops, starting before sunrise. Walking equipment must include **crampons**, **ice-axe** and a **rope**. For a winter ascent on **skis**, follow the walking instructions below; it's a 1480-metre climb, possible in about ten hours.

Routes – and their history
There are two basic routes on the northeast face, which can be combined as a circuit. The standard itinerary heads south from the refuge, climbing steeply towards the pass known as **Portillón Inferior** (2742m). Before the top, bear southwest to the next pass along, **Portillón Superior** (2900m), which you should reach in about three hours.

Now you have your first good view of Aneto, with the secondary peak of **Maladeta** (3308m) to your right. The guide Pierre Barrau – who had made the first recorded ascent of Maladeta with Frédéric Parrot on September 29, 1817 – was killed when he fell unroped into a crevasse on the Maladeta glacier in 1824. The death helped to postpone further conquest of Aneto for twenty years. Barrau's body was only recovered when it emerged from the ice over a century later.

A gully descends on the far side of Portillón Superior to a saddle, beyond which ice fields lead to the Aneto glacier. During summer months, a "path" will have been worn across it, a little whiter than the grit-stained glacier each side. It should be perfectly safe but rope up if there is any doubt. You now traverse 2500m south-southeast to the **Collado de Coronas** (3196m; 4hr 30min from the refuge), where a summertime lake forms in the crest below once every five years or so, a brilliant blue on a sunny day.

Climb east beyond the *collado*, possibly with crampons and ice-axe, to the broad jumble of rocks known as the **Puente de Mahoma**. Negotiated on all fours, this represents 50m of sheer terror for the inexperienced, especially if iced up (its name refers to "Mohammed's rope", the Islamic bridge over Hell to Paradise). On the other side of the bridge the **Aneto summit** (3404m) is staked by a large cross and what looks like a small rocket, but turns out to be a Virgin and Child on a metal pedestal. By all means savour your triumph, but don't linger, especially if clouds close in – climbers have been killed by lightning in the mid-afternoon.

The first to stand here, on July 20, 1842, were the Russian Platon de Tchihatcheff, the French count Albert de Franqueville, and their guides, Bernard Ursule, Pierre Redonet, Jean Argarot and Pierre Sanio. However, they did not use the route described, avoiding the formidable northerly glacier by skirting anticlockwise and climbing the smaller Coronas glacier on the south side of the ridge. Today, these pioneers would take the classical modern route, since Aneto's glaciers – like most in the Pyrenees – are half the size they were in the nineteenth century.

To make a **circuit**, descend to Collado de Coronas and then bear right on another path east across the glacier to the Plan dels Aigualluts (below) and the **Forau dels Aigualluts (de Aiguallut)/Trou du Toro** – a pit of grey, splintered rock into which cascading waters of the Aneto glacier disappear before re-emerging in the Joeu valley. Beside a green shed-refuge, upstream from the sinkhole, an initially very faint path leads directly west back to the *Refugio de la Renclusa*.

Walks around Maladeta

If you don't want to stay at the *Renclusa* shelter, or if it's full, wilderness **camping** at the Plan dels Aigualluts is highly recommended. You've reached the 2000-metre camping limit, though if you stay more than one night you're supposed take down your tent during the day. The *plan* is your destination coming west from the Noguera Ribagorçana over either the Coll de Salenques or the Coret de Molières – approaches detailed in "West to Maladeta" on p.272. Using **Plan dels Aigualluts (de Aiguallut)** as a base, you're also well positioned for a few days of rewarding and not too strenuous **day-hikes**; by happy coincidence there are four relatively gentle passes on crests to the northeast, and the paths through them can be combined into circuits. Otherwise, starting **from Benasque**, two other targets for day-hikes are slightly beyond the scope of the local PR excursions in length and effort.

Itineraries around Plan dels Aigualluts

The way up from Plan dels Aigualluts towards the Coret de Molières along the **Valleta de la Escaleta** brings you to the **Còth deth Hòro/Coll de Tòro** (2235m) and, shortly after, the **Còth deth Aranesi/Coll dels Aranesos** (2455m). Both mountains overlook lakes and have sharp but scenic descents – largely cross-country – to the Pla de l'Artiga in the Val d'Aran. You can return to the Aragonese side of the crest via a well-trodden trail up the Pomèro valley, leading to the **Pòrt dera Picada** (formerly Puerto de la Picada; 2477m), where the boundaries of Aragón, Catalunya and France meet.

The **Portillón de Benás/Port de Vénasque** (2445m), the age-old route to Luchon in France, is the next pass west of Picada, an easy three hours' walk by well-trodden paths from either *Refugio de la Renclusa* or Plan dels Aigualluts. Even if you're not bound for France, this notch in the ridge is a worthwhile goal for the opportunity to visit **Tuca de Salbaguarda/Pic de Sauvegarde** (2738m), 45 minutes' climb west of the pass. The views in every direction from the summit are among the best in the Pyrenees, especially south over Maladeta, a giant reef of dark rock striped by patches of snow and ice. Less than an hour north, on the shore of a large lake, is the friendly *Refuge de Vénasque*, well placed for a lunch stop (see p.322 for details).

Itineraries from Benasque

The first, longer hike from Benasque is the steep trek up to **Lago de Cregüeña** (2657m), third largest body of water in the Pyrenees, trapped in a deep cirque southwest of Maladeta. To reach the lake, turn off the PR-4 at the fountain and waterfall of **San Ferrer** (San Farré), about ninety minutes' walk above Benasque (limited parking at trailhead). The path up the Ball de Cregüeña is distinct and cairned; allow at least six hours return (the sign says three-and-a-half hours uphill). Optimistically shown on some tourist office handouts, the route over the 2930-metre pass to the southeast into the Ball de Ballibierna (see below) is a tough exercise for the properly equipped, out of bounds for most casual hikers. The route north from the western tip of the lake over the 2646-metre Brecha d'Alba into the Ball d'Alba is somewhat more feasible, depending on snowpack, and makes possible a day-loop taking in both lake basins.

About half an hour before San Ferrer, at the **Puente de Ballhibierna** by the Paso Nuevo reservoir, you can also leave the PR-4 to explore the **Ball de Ballibierna** (Valle de Vallhiverna), an idyllic tributary forested in black pine, fir and birch, by following the eastbound GR11 – unfortunately forced onto 4WD track here. There's little traffic in high season when access is limited, but still you're best off saving your stamina for the high altitudes by using the seasonal shuttle-bus service (details above) as far as **Puente de Coronas**. Whichever way you arrive, you'll find a permanently open, fourteen-person **refuge** for use if you're traversing rather than day-hiking; camping is theoretically forbidden, as Coronas lies just under the 2000-metre legal limit.

From Puente de Coronas, you can either tackle Aneto via the valley, cirque and glacier of Coronas – final approach of the 1842 pioneers – or, more likely, continue east **along the GR11** into the Anglòs (Angliós) valley on the Noguera Ribagorçana side, via the lakes and **Coll de Ballibierna** (2728m). Even with help from the shuttle bus, it's a long day to the *Refugi Sant Nicolau* at the Vielha tunnel mouth; keep in mind the tiny *cabaña* (see p.273) at the easterly Anglòs lakes two hours below the pass. Otherwise, emergency camping is unlikely to cause a problem given that the country is so rugged and remote.

Posets climbs and walks

From Aneto, the magnificent dark granite mass of **Posets** (3375m), topped by an almost complete circle of low schist ridges, looks like a giant's fort. From the west it seems even more formidable, rising up as a huge freestanding lump, deeply etched by gullies and false trails. An ascent requires ice-axe, crampons and rope, and perhaps a helmet to shield from falling rocks near the summit.

For both day-hikers and long-haul trekkers, Posets is more user-friendly than Maladeta, with three well-sited, staffed refuges, a host of places to camp – though you don't really need to – and options for circuits and traverses of varying length. From Benasque there are two main approaches for climbs and traverses. You're likely to exit the region via the Valle de Chistau to the west, well poised for hikes further into Aragón. The relevant **map** is Editorial Alpina 1:25,000 "Posets"; if you intend walking in or out via the *Viadós* refuge and the Valle de Chistau, take the "Bachimala" sheet too (make sure it's the new edition, out late 2000). At a pinch, the map supplied with *Senderos de Pequeño Recorrido* will do for less rigorous walks, giving the same coverage as the Editorial Alpina.

The approach from Estós

More pastorally attractive and unspoilt than the Ésera, the **Estós valley** curls around Posets to the northeast. Although the track's lower reaches can be driven, private cars are banned except for the 4WD belonging to the warden of the modern three-storey *Refugio de Estós* (☎974 551 483; 1890m; 115 places; self-catering kitchen; staffed all year; ③). However, a number of readers' complaints about curt and unhelpful staff have been received, so it may be preferable to omit the refuge from your overnight plans.

To reach valley and refuge, follow the PR-5 path from Benasque, then a bit of the PR-4, to the medieval **Cuera (San Jaime) bridge** 45 minutes above town, then switch to the GR11 going northwest over the bridge. After another hour or so, the PR-6 peels off from the GR11 and adopts the opposite bank of the valley stream, rejoining it shortly before the *Estós* refuge – though the GR11 track is by no means objectionable. Whichever route you take, count on four hours total from Benasque to the shelter.

The ascent of the peak

The *Estós* refuge marks the start of the easiest and most popular six-hour **ascent of Posets**, whether by foot or ski. Drop down to cross the bridge and follow the path along the stream's right (south) bank. After a couple of kilometres leave the main valley on the path climbing into the Coma de la Paúl, leading to the **Glaciar de la Paúl**, beyond which you reach the **Collado de la Paúl** (3062m). Once on its south side, cross the **Glaciar de Posets** – normally by a clearly trodden path in the ice – to the east face of the summit. A scramble up a narrow gully brings you to the top, known locally as **Llardana**.

The approach from Eriste

The much less frequented **Eriste valley** forges into the alpine heart of Posets from the southeast. Near the top stands the 2000-expanded *Refugio Ángel Orús (Forcau)*, the alternative base camp for a Posets climb (☎974 344 044; 2100m; 95 places; staffed in theory all year). To get there, follow the PR-7 path from Benasque to Eriste village (p.289), then the PR-11 up the narrow wild canyon, cloaked in foothill vegetation thanks to a mild microclimate. After two hours, mostly on track, you come to the bridge and waterfalls of **Espiantosa**, where there's a fair-sized car-park – the five-kilometre track up from Eriste is passable to ordinary cars (or alpine taxis). From here it's ninety minutes' walk on the PR-11 to the refuge, nearly four-and-a-half hours in total from Benasque. If *Refugio Ángel Orús* is full you can **camp** an hour to the north, in or around the simple Cabaña de Llardaneta.

From Espiantosa you could also take a signposted path northeast to the run-down *cabaña* at **Clot de Chil**, well placed for climbing the pointy-headed **Tucas de Ixeia** (2837m), star of many a Benasque postcard, and a favourite launch platform for *parapentistas*.

From the *Ángel Orús* refuge, the best approach to the summit is along the **Ball de Llardaneta**, up the **Canal Fonda** between the outcrops of Tuca Alta and Diente de Llardana at the end of the *canal*, then straight up to the summit – a total of five hours one-way (nine hours return).

Skiing on Posets

A winter ascent of Posets with **skis** is a tougher proposition than Aneto; it's longer and more difficult towards the summit. The easiest approach is to take the summer walking route from the *Estós* refuge, described previously. When you reach the Collado de la Paúl, continue to the summit only if conditions are ideal. The exhilarating ski descent to the *Estós* refuge from the *collado* is your reward for climbing this far at least.

Alternatively, you could make an alpine tour (carrying a heavier load) by skirting the Glaciar de Posets from the pass, instead dropping a little south of east into the Ball d'es Ibóns (see below), to the **Lago de les Alforches** (de las Alforjas, 2250m) – another gorgeous and fairly easy descent. From the lake you have an easy ski south to the *Ángel Orús* refuge. Next day, you move down the Eriste valley to Eriste village and the main C139 road.

Traverses and circuits

The following **traverses and partial circuits** – except for the day-loop out of Viadós – can be combined into a giant loop around the massif, so that with three or four days at your disposal you trek through the best of Posets. Outside peak season – when hut resources are always strained – you can save pack weight by dispensing with food and tent, and relying on the well-spaced refuges.

Traverse via Batisielles

A superb traverse from the vicinity of the *Ángel Orús* refuge to the Estós valley, mostly relying on the variant GR11.2, enters the **Ball d'es Ibóns** northeast of Llardaneta and then, just below the Lago de les Alforches, ascends east to the **Collado de la Plana** (formerly Piana; 2700m). On the other side, a marked but non-GR and essentially cross-country route descends more sharply into the **Ball de Perramó**, with the *ibón* of the same name huddled at the base of the Tucas de Ixeia. The route swings north again to the Escarpinosa lake, where a clearly trodden path leads down to the meadows of **Batisielles** (1900m). The GR11.2 veers north from the pass, taking in the Ibón de l'Aigüeta de Batisielles and the Ibón Grán de Batisielles (camping possible) before dropping to the meadows – a wonderful (if somewhat insect-plagued) place to camp, which you may have to do since the trek from *Ángel Orús* is six to seven hours. Without a tent, you might use the little *cabaña* here, or press on for another ninety minutes along the GR11.2 through meadow and woods to the *Estós* refuge.

The Posets half-circuit

The most popular Posets activity for non-climbers is the **half-circuit** of the massif which follows the main GR11 west, skirting the mountain's north and west flanks. From the *Estós* refuge you continue along the valley, climbing to the **Puerto de Chistau** (2560m; 2hr 15min), before descending the other side to the head of the **Zinqueta de Añes Cruces**. As you amble down this progressively more hospitable valley, you're treated to impressive views of the mountain's forbidding west flank before arriving at **Granjas de Viadós**, a dozen or so scattered barns amongst summer hayfields, and one of the most beautiful spots in the Spanish Pyrenees. You can do the entire walk in five to six hours, with plenty of daylight left for the worthwhile hop up to **Señal de Viadós** (2600m), which has the best possible view east to Posets and west over the Cinqueta valley.

Viadós – and back to Benasque

At Granjas de Viadós, the welcoming **Refugio de Viadós** (or *Biadors*; ☎974 506 163 or 974 506 082; 1760m; 60 places; open Easter and weekends to June 25, thereafter daily to Sept 25; ①) is privately run by Joaquín Cazcarra and family. Señor Cazcarra is partly responsible for the "Bachimala" Editorial Alpina map, providing regular cartographic updates to the publishers. The refuge is accessible by road, meaning that its meals and bunks are cheaper than the Pyrenean norm. The Cazcarra family also run a **camp-**

site, *El Forcallo* (same phone numbers; open Easter & July–Aug), fifteen minutes' walk below at 1580m elevation. Free camping in the meadow beside the refuge, at the *parque natural* boundary, is no longer permitted.

It's possible, and highly recommended, to loop **back to Benasque** by one of two demanding but mostly nontechnical routes, which cut through the much-admired Posets crest. You'll need extra water, crampons and an axe after a severe winter, and rope at one point for the second suggested traverse. From the *Refugio de Viadós*, follow the instructions for the start of the day-loop given next section, climbing up the Bal de Millars to just below and north from the eponymous lake. Here the GR11.2 guides you steeply up a stable slope to a false pass, and then after a slight dip to the true **Collado de Eriste** (2860m), flanked by the peaks La Forqueta (3007m) and Diente Royo (3010m), three hours from the refuge. Great striated bands of tawny orange and purplish serpentine loom above this pedestrian pass over the Posets flank, where you'll have company on a summer's day. From Collado de Eriste, descend east to the vicinity of the Ibón de Llardaneta, then down its valley to the Ángel Orús hut (6hr from Viadós).

Alternatively, you can continue up to the Ibón d'es Millars for a more challenging route. There's no path up from this lake, with only a few cairns guiding you over the rock-girt **Collado de Millares** (2831m), three and a half hours along. The descent southeast calls for more cross-country work through a moonscape of tortured granite before you reach the upper **Bagüeña lake**. Beyond this you turn east, then north through the tricky **Brecha de Llantia** (2842m), where most will require a rope. You then head down the Ball de Forcau, between the spires of Llantia and Forcau, to reach *Refugio Ángel Orús* – a challenging day of seven walking hours. Or you might want to forego the difficult *brecha* and simply follow the Bagüeña valley down to Sahún or Eriste, with a good path once you're below the lower Ibón de Bagüeña (allow eight hours plus).

Lake circuit from Viadós

Of the various day-hikes out of Granjas de Viadós that Don Joaquín recommends, the loop taking in a chaplet of lakes and tarns tucked into Posets' southwest flank is the most beautiful, but (in its trail-less stages) the most arduous. Follow the main GR11 back towards the Puerto de Chistau, then turn right downhill just past the last *granja* or barn towards a plank bridge. A *parque natural* sign points the way, with estimated time-courses to the most popular destinations: "Ibón d'es Millars, 2hr", "Ibón d'es Lerners, 2hr 30min", and so forth. Red-and-white waymarks painted over older lime-green-and-turquoise ones should be visible, as this is now officially the GR11.2 variant. From here, you face a steady climb along the northeast (true right) bank of the *barranco* through pines. At about 2300m, or some 1hr 45min with a daypack, the official GR11.2 goes up left towards the Collado de Eriste. Following the older waymarks, it's just over two hours to the **Ibón d'es Millars** (or *Millás*; 2350m) augmented by a rock dam, with a few turfy patches for a picnic, and where you might want to join the frogs for a swim in August. Continue another half-hour, the path only cairned now, to the **Ibón d'es Leners** (or *Lenés*; 2530m), wedged into even more severe terrain beneath the hulking Bagüenola peaks.

Beyond here there's no more trail, but cairns help you up the 2600-metre ridge dividing Leners from the **Ibón d'es Luceros**, your next goal. As ever, some of the cairns are misleading; don't veer south, but rather north to overlook Luceros, with an enormous barrel-cairn at the lowest point of the descending ridge. There are magnificent views of the frontier peaks before you begin the only safe way down to the lake, using turfy patches in the slope below the barrel cairn. Without getting lost, allow an hour from lake to lake; circle anticlockwise around Luceros to its western shore to find the stream gully feeding the **Ibón de la Solana** (just visible). Descend the right bank of this ravine, keeping to the grassy bits or stable granite, avoiding the cavities created by the alpenrose; it's another hour's attentive downhill trekking "door to door", and at scenic de la Solana there's just enough flat ground at the upstream end for an emergency bivouac.

Exit the lake basin, where forest resumes, via the north bank to a tiny pass – the start of another hour's nasty descent along the right bank of the Barranco de la Solana. There's still no real path, only cairns and hacked-out blazes on pine trees to guide you. At one point you'll have to briefly slither over forested hillside at a forty-five-degree angle. Your target is a vast sloping meadow, the high head at about 1950m, which takes half an hour to cross. At the far end, pick up the resumption of the trail (red paint dots mark it) and broach a little saddle on the shoulder of El Castellazo hill (ca. 1750m). It's another twenty minutes, or just under 2hr from Ibón de la Solana, to the junction with the GR19 and a cheerful sign (appropriately defaced by irate walkers) predicting 1hr 30min uphill to the first lake. Follow the GR19 north another 25min to the refuge, making the **total elapsed time** nearly seven hours. A reverse itinerary is inadvisable – it would be too difficult to find your way uphill to Ibón de la Solana.

Onwards from Posets

From Posets your trekking options are to head north **into France** via several passes of varying difficulty in the border ridge, or continue west and south deeper **into Aragón**.

Into France

If you're walking north from Posets into France, two fairly difficult but spectacular routes lead to the popular **Lac d'Oô** on the GR10 (see p.324). From the *Estós* refuge, ascend north up the **Valle de Gías**, past three tarns and into France via the **Puerto d'Oô** (pronounced "oh"; 2909m). It's an exhausting four-hour climb, much of it through a forbidding boulder field with no real path in the screes for some distance either side of the pass. From here it's another ninety minutes' (easier) trek down to the *Refuge du Portillon* (see below), via the **Lac du Port d'Oô** (shown on many French maps as the *Lac Glacé* after its permanent ice floes).

Alternatively, bear east from the Gías trail about a third of the way up, through the **Collada de Molseret** (2520m), to the frontier pass of **Portillón d'Oô** (2913m; 4hr 30min). The *portillón* is guarded by permanent ice and might require crampons, but the seasonally staffed refuge at **Lac du Portillon** (on the HRP) is just an hour away. The next refuge, *Espingo*, is two hours down-valley via the **Lac Saussat**. An hour below *Espingo* is the Lac de Oô, a favourite picnic spot, not far above the roadhead at **Granges d'Astau**. All these areas are covered in detail under "Walks from Luchon", at the end of this chapter.

Two easier ways into France depart from the *Refugio de Viadós*: up the Zinqueta (Cinqueta) de la Pez to the **Puerto de la Pez** (2451m), opening onto the Louron valley; or through the even easier **Puerto de Ordiceto** (2400m) north of its lake, where a variant of the HRP leads down to the roadhead and hospice in the Rioumajou valley. But neither route can compare to the Oô itineraries; slightly more exciting is a third itinerary, again starting along Zinqueta de la Pez, then veering west up to the **Puerto d'a Madera** (2560m). On its far side you descend along the Couarère stream to the main Rioumajou drainage. All these routes require a full day's walk to reach the next permanent habitation or suitable camping spot.

Into Aragón

From the *Refugio de Viadós*, the main treks west and south into Aragón follow the GR11 or the GR19 Spanish long-distance trails; both begin with a sharp descent to the valley of the **Zinqueta** (Cinqueta) stream.

The GR11 stays with the vehicle track until turning right onto another track at **La Sargueta**, which shortly reaches a junction. Heading up and right puts you on the main GR11 branch to **Lago Ordiceto** (Urdiceto; 2369m) – popular with picnickers despite its unsightly dam – from where another 4WD track descends 11km to the main road at Parzán (see p.400), 5km north of Bielsa. It's best to come here only as a day-walk from *Viadós*, or to enter the French Rioumajou valley. The track in from Viadós has been extended up to the 2000-metre contour, further reducing the appeal of this section of the GR11.

From the ruined **Opital de Chistau**, twenty minutes south of La Sargueta, another 4WD track leads ninety minutes up to the shallow **Collada de Pardinas** (2251m). From there you should contour southwest, without losing unnecessary altitude, to intercept the old *camino* from Gistaín and the Collada de la Cruz de Guardia to Bielsa in the Zinca (Cinca) valley, now waymarked as the GR19.1 and last maintained in 1997. Doubling as the old, mid-altitude shepherd's route west from Viadós, this follows the Cargadué ravine down to the Zinca valley four more hours en route to Bielsa.

The GR19 forest *camino* spares you about an hour of trudging down the main track along the Zinqueta, but it's not brilliant walking so arrange a lift if you can along the main road, either 11km down to the turning for Gistaín or the full 14km to Plan, "capital" of the valley described below.

The Valle de Chistau

Little known except among Spaniards, for whom it's regarded as a famous repository of medieval Aragonese folk culture, the **Valle de Chistau** (Gistau, Xistau), makes a worthwhile rest-stop if you're trekking between Posets and the Ordesa region. Tourism came late to the area, but facilities are multiplying and remain excellent value as there's no local ski industry to drive prices up.

The valley was the focus of national attention in 1985 when many of its bachelors placed a lonely-hearts ad in the press, one of the consequences of Aragonese rural depopulation. Mountain women were (and still are) unwilling to marry those not inclined to relocate to more prosperous towns. The bachelors threw a magnificent three-day *fiesta* to welcome the **caravana de mujeres/"women's caravan"** (as it was dubbed), and a surprising number of the visitors ended up marrying and settling down here.

By car, the valley can be reached during snow-free months from the east, starting at **Chía** in the Ésera valley, via a 26-kilometre, signposted forest track over the 1999-metre Puerto de Saunc/Collado de Sahún. The dirt surface requires first- or second-gear driving most of the way, but the countryside's superb, with views northwest to numerous frontier peaks. The usual approach from the west is along the paved side road beginning at **Salinas de Sin**, home to a keen and well-stocked **Turismo booth** which serves most of the valley (mid-June to mid-Sept daily except Thurs 10am–1pm & 5–8pm; summer ☎974 504 089, winter ☎974 506 001). The road threads past the turn-offs for Saravillo and Sin (see below), and then through a series of dramatic tunnels downstream from the local dam on the Río Zinqueta. Before the tunnels were made, the valley's Shangri-la isolation was instrumental in preserving its culture; bus service remains sparse (see Travel Details).

Plan, San Juan and Gistaín

A trio of villages, linked by a mesh of PR (plus a few GR) trails on the Benasque model, nestles at the head of the valley, and together they offer most of the area's tourist facilities. With no ski centre nearby, the village outskirts are free of the *urbanizaciones* which disfigure so many Spanish Pyrenean communities.

Plan

Boasting a couple of hundred inhabitants, broad streets on a grid plan and imposing architectural detail such as carved lintels and window frames, **PLAN** is the de facto valley "capital". Its main attraction is an eighth- to eleventh-century **church** (usually open), harmoniously blending Visigothic and Romanesque elements. Two side aisles are set off from the main one by arcaded colonnades, all with vaulted ceilings. The nave is slightly asymmetrical to the rear, a consequence of the existing church being built around an older tower.

Plan's **accommodation** includes the one-star *Hotel Mediodía* (☎974 506 006; ④), with easy parking and balconied if blandly modern rooms; bathless rooms at *Casa Ruché* (☎974 506 072; ②) on the bypass road; and studio units at *Casa Mur* (☎974 506 123; ③). **Eating out**, there is the *comedor* of the *Mediodía* and that of *Casa Ruché*, where around 1500ptas/€9 will get decent vegetable *platos primeros*, a grilled main course and house wine; it's a popular local hangout, where the forestry wardens come to lunch. Local amenities include shops, an **ATM** and the Guías del Ball de Chistau (☎974 506 178), offering the usual range of caving, climbing, canyoning and trekking activities.

San Juan de Plan

SAN JUAN DE PLAN (San Chuan de Plan), 2km upstream, is smaller still, but architecturally more interesting, and is also famous for its lively Lenten *Carnaval*. Visitors can enjoy some of the best-value **accommodation and eating** in the valley: *Hostal Casa la Plaza* (☎974 506 052; ②–③), with ingeniously planned, tasteful, wood-decor rooms and an excellent, mountain-style *menú* (1500ptas/€9) downstairs which features *chireta* (like a haggis made with rice and *morcillo*) and a range of sweets. *Casa Sanches* nearby on the same plaza, also with a *comedor*, is a worthy fallback (☎974 506 050; ②), as is the *Hotel Casa Anita* near the church (☎974 506 040; ③), which has meals too. If these are full, there are several simple *habitaciones* nearby, mostly in the *casa rural* scheme – ask around or let yourself be referred. For the budget-minded, there's also the *Albergue El Molín* (☎974 506 208; ①) in San Juan, and another **ATM**.

Gistaín

Well perched on the north flank of the valley, with superb views south to the Cotiella massif, **GISTAÍN** (Chistén) has three prominent **medieval towers** visible from afar. One rises from the church, while the other two were built by feuding families during the seventeenth century. Close up, the village is a little disappointing, with a hotch-potch of half-timbered and modern brick walls, and roofs fashioned from asbestos or tin sheet as often as traditional slate. That said, it's a self-sufficient mountain settle-ment where rural pursuits remain dominant over tourism – no imported fertilizer is used, as there's plenty of animal manure about. The most central **accommodation** is by the church at *Pension Casa Elvira* (☎974 506 078; ②–③), with cheap but sustaining *potajes*, grills and beer by the stein in its ground-floor bar. Gistaín has the biggest con-centration of *casas rurales* in the valley, nearly a dozen in all; the best can be taken up for the entire weekend (or a week) by Spaniards, so it's wise to reserve in advance. Most basic are *Casa Cañau*, on the edge of the village (☎974 506 070; ②), and friend-ly Carolina Bruned's *Casa Zueras* (☎974 506 038; ②), in an old-fashioned but salubri-ous half-timbered house near the village entrance, with huge breakfasts extra. Top standard here is the *Casa Fontamil* up the slope on the eastern outskirts (☎974 506 192; ②–③), with large rooms (including some loft units), great views, common areas, and *table d'hôte* suppers.

West to the Zinca valley

There are buses three times a week to/from the Valle de Chistau, which may not fit into your plans. Heading west, instead of hitching 12km to the main road at Salinas de Sin, it's better to take either the **GR19** track-and-trail from Gistaín via Serveto and Sin, the **GR19.1** to Bielsa from Sin, or the wilder **GR15** along the valley's south slope, easily picked up from Plan.

The GR19 leads high along the north flank of the valley through the quiet village of **SERVETO** (Serbeto; 1hr 30min), where there's a scenic PR around the Peña San Martín down to the valley floor. It also passes through **SIN** (2hr), with its *albergue* that's popular with school groups (☎974 506 212; ①). The GR19.1 then peels northeast through Señés hamlet, north to the Collado de la Cruz de Guardia, finally curling west down to Bielsa as described on p.300. Two hours west from Sin, the now all-trail GR19 leads through dense forest to **SALINAS DE SIN** in the Zinca valley, noteworthy for its previously mentioned tourist booth. Of the two facilities here, the *Caserio San Marcial* (☎974 504 010; ②) – a manor-house built around a twelfth-century *ermita* – is preferable. Open all year, it offers meals and camping (April–Oct). You'll find it uphill on the west side of the highway, just south of the road junction, conveniently near the onward GR19 into the southeasterly sector of the Ordesa national park (see p.405–406). Try to avoid the road-walk to either Bielsa (7km north) or Lafortunada (5km south) by arranging a ride. For coverage of these places, see p.399 and p.404.

From Sin you can descend south via another PR itinerary to **SARAVILLO** (Sarabillo), near the mouth of the valley. There is a large **campsite**, *Los Vivés* (☎974 506 171; Easter & June–Sept), slightly west in the valley floor. One kilometre up the south slope in the village itself there's **accommodation** and **meals** at *Casa Cazcarreta/Pallaruelo* (☎974 506 273; ②) and a newish *albergue*, *Borda Miguela* (☎974 506 218; ①), while Entremon (☎974 506 218) offers **horse-riding**. Saravillo sits on the **GR15** trail, which heads west then south to Lafortunada in just over two pleasant hours, the quality of the route improving after an initial stretch of track.

The Sierra de Cotiella

Saravillo is also one possible starting point for excursions southeast to the two celebrated lakes and *refugio* (longest established in the Spanish Pyrenees) of the evocatively shaped **Sierra de Cotiella**, formerly one of the least visited corners of the Spanish Pyrenees but now rich with marked trails and documentation and well frequented. Editorial Alpina's "Cotiella" map-pamphlet is the most useful aid.

The most common approach to the GR15, from Plan, incorporates the most popular short excursion out of the Valle de Gistau. At the municipal *piscina* across the river from town, take the narrow, rough dirt track marked the PR87 west along the south bank of the river. After 2.2km or about half an hour, take a signposted *camino* heading very steeply south along the banks of the ravine. There's limited parking at the trailhead, and in fact locals discourage you from bringing any vehicle this far. Some 2hr 30min from Plan you'll arrive at the postcard-worthy **Ibón de Plan** (Basa de la Mora), in its own cirque at 1910m. Its other name stems from a charming local legend: if you rise at dawn on Midsummer's Day (June 24) and wash your face in these waters, you'll see a long-lost Moorish princess (*mora* in Castilian) dancing on the surface of the lake.

From the haunted lake, the GR15 heads west from the lake to Saravillo, downhill once past the crude forest hut at Labasar (2hr, or 3hr if coming uphill from Saravillo). Alternatively, southeast from Basa de la Mora, the GR15 effects another two-hour traverse via two moderate passes to the unstaffed but well-equipped *Refugio de Armeña* (1860m; 20 places; open year-round) at the entrance to the Circo de Armeña and twenty minutes from the **Ibón de Armeña**, the massif's other natural lake. Advanced mountaineers can make a clockwise **loop around the massif** over two days, with preferably a dawn start on Day 2: Ibón de Plan – Armeña hut – Circo de Armeña – Cotiella peak (2912m) – various passes south and west of summit – La Ribereta valley – Ibón de Plan.

THE COUSERANS AND THE COMMINGES

North of the Val d'Aran, beyond the frontier, sprawls a neglected corner of France, an isolated realm slashed by eighteen large and small valleys, tilting in every direction. Outside its southeastern corner, where the old spa of **Aulus-les-Bains** sees some entrepreneurial activity, the **Couserans** is an eerily remote landscape of unkempt pastures, abandoned terraces and ruined barns. Most of the local mines – aluminium, tungsten, lead, zinc and, above all, iron – have been worked out, and the small farms bankrupted by competition from mechanized plains agriculture. The population has halved since the 1890s, yet unemployment remains high. Traditionally marginal livelihoods included gold-panning, itinerant peddling and acting as wet-nurses for city families. Nowadays the main rural products are hay, cheese and honey, the latter two on sale everywhere.

Saint-Girons, 44km west of Foix and capital of the Couserans, is not particularly interesting itself, but you'll come here on the way to the adjacent charming old town of **Saint-Lizier**, and for the bus services which make it the hub for all local exploration. Well north of the bus route from Foix to Saint-Girons, **Mas d'Azil** is one of the great prehistoric caves of the Pyrenees, giving its name to an entire epoch – the Azilian.

Heading south into the "Empty Quarter" extending towards the border and the Val d'Aran and furrowed by the River Salat, one has bus connections to Aulus-les-Bains via **Seix**, an important canoeing centre. Buses also run via Castillon-en-Couserans to **Sentein**, near the roadhead for the local stretch of the GR10. The **Vallée de Bethmale**, between Seix and Castillon, is an icon of Pyrenean folklore, its distinctive costume (now rarely displayed) popularized by a number of writers. Here you'll see *Toulousains* who've come to stay in their holiday homes, and walkers bound for **Mont Valier** – an easy, beautiful and popular ascent.

Just to the west, straddling the Garonne, is the slightly more prosperous **Comminges** region. Since 1790, it has fallen into a different administrative *département* (Haute-Garonne), yet the Couserans have always had a deeper connection to it – both areas being Catholic and Gascon-speaking – than with historically Protestant and Languedoc-speaking Ariège, now in the same *département*. There are relatively few tourist facilities and not many man-made "sights" in the southern Couserans and on into the Comminges, the most mountainous part of Haute-Garonne. This changes as soon as you reach the busy road and rail line between **Saint-Gaudens**, functional capital of the Comminges, and **Bagnères-de-Luchon**, an old-fashioned spa now revelling in its modern identity as a ski resort and hikers' centre. Southwest of Saint-Gaudens, the magnificent cathedral at **Saint-Bertrand-de-Comminges** is a highlight, along with the **Grotte de Gargas** and its tracings of truncated prehistoric hands.

Saint-Girons and Saint-Lizier

Well-connected though relatively sleepy **SAINT-GIRONS**, known for its local cigarette-paper industry, will possibly be your first taste of the Couserans. It's a pleasant enough town on the River Salat, with two sets of rapids by the old bridge, reddish-pink marble paving stones, but with little else of note other than nearby Saint-Lizier.

Buses, including those from Foix, Aulus-les-Bains and Boussens, arrive at the **place des Capots** on the left (west) bank. Facing east on the sixteenth-century **Pont-Vieux** over the River Salat, you cross onto the right bank which leads into the old commercial centre. There's a well-stocked **tourist office** inside the **Maison de Couserans** (daily

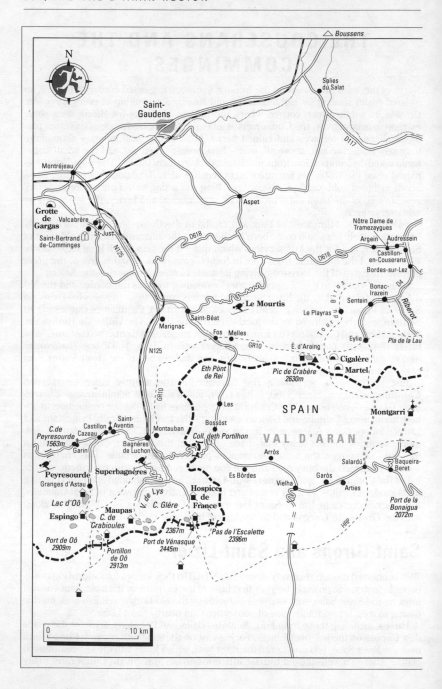

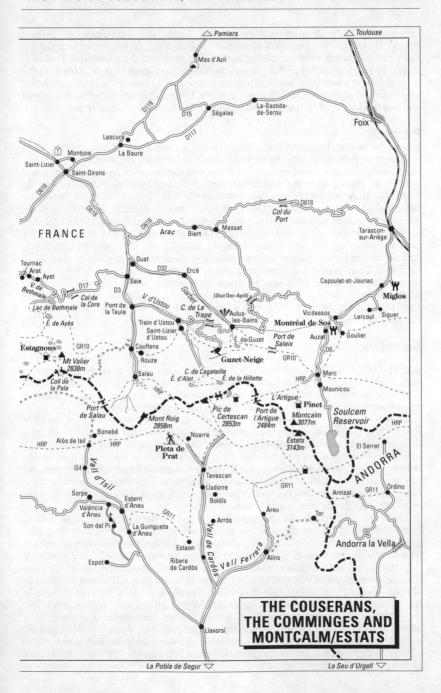

THE COUSERANS,
THE COMMINGES AND
MONTCALM/ESTATS

except Sun: July & Aug 9.30am–6.30pm; Sept–June 9am–noon & 2–6pm; ☎05.61.96.26.60), a few paces left along the river, on Place Alphonse-Sentein. On the right (south), past the little cathedral and also by the river, the **place des Poilus** is ringed by elegantly faded period pieces – including the *Grand Café de l'Union* on the ground floor of a hotel (see below). Between the square and along the river, a gravelled promenade of plane trees, the **Champ de Mars**, hosts a general market on the second and fourth Monday of the month, and a produce market every Saturday morning.

Practicalities

If you want **to stay**, best value is the *Hôtel Mirouze* in the left (west bank) quarter, 300m southwest of Pont-Vieux (☎05.61.66.12.77, fax 05.61.04.81.59; ③), with rear rooms facing a garden, off-street parking and a full range of menus at its creditable restaurant. Otherwise, choose from the central but slightly shabby *Hôtel de l'Union* on rue du Champ de Mars, corner Place de Poilus (☎05.61.66.09.12, fax 05.61.04.81.73; ②–③); the faded *Grand Hôtel de France* at Place de Poilus 4 (☎05.61.66.00.23, fax 05.61.04.84.85; ④), with an acceptable restaurant; or the modern and comfortable two-star *La Clairière*, at the edge of town on the road to Seix (☎05.61.66.66.66, fax 05.34.14.30.32; ④), with a pool and arguably the best gourmet fare in Saint-Girons (90–150F/€13.70–22.90). Apart from the hotels, restaurants are undistinguished, and more seem to shut down each year. There are a few rather dreary places to **eat** in the west bank quarter, as well as the *Bar Galopin*, a good spot to **drink** with outdoor seats opposite the rapids. Alternatively, there's a **campsite** at the Centre de Loisirs du Parc de Paletès (☎05.61.66.06.79), 2km out along av des Évadés, with an excellent terrace restaurant, *La Table de l'Ours*.

Saint-Lizier

SAINT-LIZIER is just five minutes' north of Saint-Girons by bus from the defunct train station on the D117. If you're without transport you may as well stroll the 2km and return via the walled medieval village of Montjoie (3km by a minor road), with its fortified church. From there, it's a 45-minute walk back to Saint-Girons.

An important centre of Christianity since the sixth century, when it traded the Latin *Austria* for the name of its first proselytizing bishop, Saint-Lizier is impressive from a distance with its turreted **episcopal Palace** at the top of the hill and cascades of red-tiled roofs all the way down to the river. Once inside the stone walls – built on fourth-century Gallo-Roman foundations – you'll wander the atmospheric cobbled streets and tiny arcaded alleys flanked by half-timbered houses. As a showcase specimen, Saint-Lizier lacks many conventional tourist facilities, which gives it a curiously lifeless air, especially outside the peak summer season.

The main **Cathédrale de Saint-Lizier** (May–Oct daily 10am–noon & 2–7pm; Nov–April Mon–Sat 10am–noon & 2–6pm; free but admission to pharmacy and treasury only through tourist office) has an octagonal keep-like tower and twelfth-century frescoes faded almost entirely. The highlight is the Romanesque cloister, dating from the same period as the frescoes, with its array of unique sculpted capitals, though these have suffered in recent years compared to those at Ripoll (see p.173) and San Juan de la Peña (see p.425). A second cathedral, **Nôtre-Dame-de-Sède**, within the grounds of the bishop's palace, has closed for long-term renovation, though the palace does house the **Musée Départmentale de l'Ariège** on its first floor (July–Aug daily 10am–12.30pm & 2–6.30pm; April–June & Sept–Oct daily 2–5.30pm, Nov–March weekends & holidays 2–5.30pm; 25F). Its permanent ethnographic collection is devoted to the Vallée du Bethmale and not really worth the admission fee. On rue des Nobles a **cultural centre** hosts expositions and musical events, while the lower cathedral is also used as a performance centre during the summer **music festival** (information on ☎05.61.66.67.89), from early to mid-August.

Saint-Lizier is a minor stop on the Santiago de Compostela route, and the helpful **tourist office** by the lower cathedral (May–Oct Mon–Sat 10am–noon & 2–6pm, Sun 2–6pm; Oct–May Sat & Sun 2–6pm; ☎05.61.96.77.77) will direct bona fide pilgrims to a **hostel**. For non-pilgrims, excellent **accommodation** is available at the 1998-restored *Hotel de la Tour* (☎05.61.66.38.02, fax 05.61.66.38.01, *hotel.de.la.tour@wanadoo.fr*; ③–④) by the river on rue du Pont. The pricier rooms (all with bath) have balconies overlooking the water; its gourmet yet affordable, high-ceiling **restaurant** also takes in the rapids. Best forgo the 55F/€8.40 weekday lunch *menu* in favour of the 105F/€16 (wine extra), which includes *gesiers* salad, salmon in sauce and pear croustade.

East of Saint-Girons: Mas d'Azil

Public transport to the intriguing **Mas d'Azil cave** is poor, though Toulouse offers a direct bus service; four daily buses between Foix and Saint-Girons along the D117 leave you with a fair walk or hitch. The closest bus stop on the D117 is Ségalas, from where it's 12km up-and-down on the pretty D15, past the ruined hilltop château of Saint Barthélémy. Alternatively, you could **rent a bike** in Foix or Saint-Girons, the latter linked directly to the cave by a 25-kilometre road, the D119.

The cave

As you reach the Mas d'Azil, the river and the D119 suddenly disappear into an awesome 65-metre-high opening and the 500-metre-long cavern it has carved over the millennia. The **caves** on the right bank (Easter & June–Sept daily 10am–noon & 2–6pm; April & May Mon–Sat 2–6pm, Sun 10am–noon & 2–6pm; March, Oct & Nov Sun 2–6pm; otherwise by appointment, ☎05.61.69.97.22; 40F/€6.10) can now be toured on a DIY basis, with a loop of paths taking in various artefacts from 30,000 to 8000 BC in several chambers. These include the **Salle Mandment** with its mammoth and bear bones on display, and a rather naff diorama depicting a cave-dwelling family at their hearth. There's also the huge **Salle du Temple**, used as a Christian chapel in the third century and a sanctuary for Cathars and Protestants in more recent times. Despite its size, the cave doesn't quite compare to the painted caves further east in the Ariège, and is the one to miss if time is short.

The **prehistoric finds** exhibited in glass cases at Mas d'Azil include needles, antler harpoons and other tools, engraved bones and decorated stones. There's a superb tiny sculpted head of a neighing horse in the central *vitrine*, and a half-beast half-man embossed in bone, labelled "anthromorphic". Edouard Piette, who discovered these pieces in 1887, was a major player in the controversy over finds in the Spanish Altamira caves, which came to light two years later. While many other prehistorians dismissed Altamira as a forgery on account of the sophistication of its paintings, Piette looked more deeply into the artistry of the specimens, and succeeded in proving their authenticity.

The village and museum

In the centre of the village of **MAS D'AZIL**, 1km beyond the caves, the **Musée de la Préhistoire** (same hours and admission as the cave) has more engravings and tools, including the *faon aux oiseaux* (fawn with birds), a carved antler possibly used as a spear-thrower. The museum also doubles as the local **tourist office**.

The village began life in the late thirteenth century as a **bastide**, one of many fortified settlements built to a grid plan, which were were strategically scattered across southwestern France in the period when Paris began to consolidate its power. Inevitably some of these strongholds fell to the Cathars and later the Huguenots; Mas d'Azil in particular successfully resisted a five-week siege by a 14,000-strong Catholic army in 1625.

If you are thinking of staying overnight – and Mas d'Azil is an attractive little place, if a little slow – there's just one surviving **hotel**: the rambling, old-fashioned *Gardel* (☎05.61.69.90.05, fax 05.61.69.70.27; ②–③) on the main square, with a decent restaurant offering a range of menus (60–150F/€9.15–22.90). Another popular **eating** option, 300m from the square on the road to the cave, is *Le Jardin de Cadettou* (closed Mon all day, Wed & Sun evening, Sat lunchtime), specializing in various *confits* (roasts). There are two riverside **campsites** 1.5km from the centre at Castagnès on the road to Pamiers: the *Terre d'Azil* (☎05.61.69.79.70; mid-June to mid-Sept), usually overrun by youth groups, or the calmer *camping municipal* (☎05.61.69.71.37; same season) on the opposite bank by the bridge. If you have transport and want to stay between Mas d'Azil and Saint-Girons, you might try the British-run *Chambres d'hôte La Baquette* at **LES-CURE** hamlet, near La Baure and the Mas d'Azil junction on the D117 (☎05.61.96.37.67, *www.ariege.com/nature/goldsworthy*; ④ B&B), based in a hilltop farmhouse and geared for nature-watching types.

South of Saint-Girons: the "Empty Quarter"

Every day except Sunday, several buses head **south from Saint-Girons** into the so-called "**Empty Quarter**" between the town and the Spanish frontier; two go southeast to Oust, Seix, Couflens and Aulus-les-Bains (daily during the ski season), and one or two southwest to Castillon-en-Couserans and Sentein. These routes can be used to enter and exit traverses along the **GR10**, which passes through Aulus, Couflens, Seix and Eylie, south of Sentein. The latter two villages are close to the **Tour du Biros**, which skims the flanks of **Mont Valier**, much-loved by climbers and served by both the GR10 and the HRP, as well as a staffed refuge. Between Seix and Aulus, you can detour south at Trein d'Ustou to take in the **Cirque de Cagateille**, second largest in the range after the Cirque de Gavarnie (see p.367), but with a fraction of the crowds. Routes east from Oust towards **Massat** and (eventually) Tarascon are not served by public transport, but under your own steam make an effective corridor between the Ariège and the Couserans. All these places, if a bit depressed and depopulated, have tourist facilities and some interest in the form of ancient churches or rickety houses. Many houses are up for sale at any given moment, though demand from *Toulousains* has ensured that properties are no longer cheap.

Seix, Oust and Massat

SEIX, the county town of the lower Salat valley, forms a congenial jumble of old, galleried houses strewn by the river, culminating in a vine-draped fifteenth-century castle, now closed up and decrepit. The seventeenth-century riverside church has an elaborate *clocher-mur*, illuminated by night, while the old market hall a few paces north sees lively use on the first and third Thursday of the month. Amongst the shops, cafés and bakeries on the west bank are two retailers for hiking maps and outdoor gear. This is also the region's main **canoeing and kayaking** centre, with Passeur de Vagues, 2km south upriver at Base de Moulin (☎05.61.66.84.88), the principal operator on both the Salat and its numerous tributaries.

There's a **tourist office** in a small booth on the Place Champ de Mars on the east bank (summer daily 9am–1pm & 3–7pm; off-season Mon–Sat 9am–1pm; ☎05.61.96.52.90), which sells hiking guides and maps, and has bus timetables – all buses to and from Saint-Girons stop virtually adjacent. Of the two **hotels**, both this side of the river, the *Mont-Valier* on the Ustou road (☎05.61.66.83.68) has some river-view rooms but is currently up for sale. The *Auberge du Haut-Salat* around the corner at Place de l'Allée (☎05.61.66.88.03; ②–④), is a far better bet, not least for **eating**, with gourmet menus (June–Sept) starting at under 100F/€15.30 – the 125F/€19 option pretty much gives you the run of the *à la carte* list. Out of season, they have more basic grub for lunch only, and staying overnight is strictly by arrangement.

Oust

OUST, 2km north back towards Saint-Girons, can also serve as a base. Its one **hotel**, *Hostellerie de la Poste* (☎05.61.66.86.33; ④; closed Nov–Easter), is among the best this side of Aulus, in the same family for five generations, with a pool garden and a well-regarded restaurant. Despite its position at the junction of roads and the rivers Salat and Garbet, the village itself is dead compared to Seix, and turns its back on the Garbet bounding it to the north. Two local **campsites** do take advantage of the riverbanks: *Les Quatre Saisons* (☎05.61.96.55.55; open all year), also with some modern **rooms** (④) on the D32 towards Aulus, and *La Côte* (☎05.61.96.50.53; mid-May to Sept) between Oust and Seix.

Massat

Some 21km north, then east of Oust along the Arac valley and the D618, **MASSAT** does not exactly hum with activity. Its former role as a major market town left a legacy of a large, drafty fifteenth-century church and a **museum-mill** on the river (July–Aug Sat Sun 5–7pm only, otherwise by arrangement on ☎05.61.96.96.66). Massat is one of the doziest places in a generally sleepy region, a hangout for alternative types and those after subalpine pursuits such as **horse-riding** (available at the outskirts and in neighbouring Biert). Among several facilities grouped around the central junction and cathedral, most congenial is the *Hôtel Coutanceau* at 17 rue des Prêtes, the road west (☎05.61.96.15.56; ④). If you find it shut (likely during off-season), the same family runs the *Auberge du Gypaète Barbu* (05.61.04.89.92; ②; closed Jan, Sun pm & Mon off-season) 3km west in pretty **BIERT**, right opposite the church, with several simple menus (70–155F/€10.70–23.60); the pricier features trout stuffed with *cèpes*.

The Vallée de Bethmale

Seix is also the eastern entry, via the D17 over the Col de la Core or the GR10, to the **Vallée de Bethmale**, celebrated in folklore for its vivid, almost Balkan female costumes, and gold-nailed wooden *sabots* (clogs) for both sexes. These have long vanished except for their appearance on a few feast days, for example August 15. What remains is an exceptionally beautiful valley, and exceptionally high depopulation, even by Couserans standards. On the heights there's little specifically to see other than a number of abandoned *granges* or **barns**, traditionally used to store hay but increasingly restored as summer quarters by lowlanders. A little west of the Col de la Core, on both D17 and GR10, the tranquil green **Lac de Bethmale**, ringed by beech trees, is a popular picnic or fishing spot.

In the valley floor, which drains from the *col* northwest towards Bordes-sur-Lez in the Vallée du Biros (see over), huddle six half-empty hamlets. The highest, graced by eighteenth-century architecture, **AYET** offers a friendly, twelve-bunk *gîte d'étape* (☎05.61.02.30.80; open all year; ①), where places must be reserved in summer. If you're without a vehicle, you can take a marked, non-GR trail up to the lake from here. Just downhill on the same path, **TOURNAC** has another *gîte d'étape*, *La Bouche* (☎05.61.04.72.12; 20 places; ①). Adjacent **ARET** has the last **sabot-making workshop** in the valley, open all year for purchases. The curvy-pointed clogs were traditionally exchanged as tokens of betrothal between the newly engaged.

Excursion to the Étang d'Ayès

The Lac de Bethmale marks the start of the most popular excursion from the valley, to the **Étang d'Ayès**, an ideal sampler of mountains hereabouts if you're not committed to full-pack treks. If you're without a car, you'll have to hike the whole distance along the GR10 (2hr 30min one way). With a car, you can avoid much of the climb by driving fifteen minutes along the *piste forestière* marked "Mont Ner/Noir" up to a barred gate and car park. Here a yellow-marked path, the old GR10, toils for forty minutes up to the Col d'Auédole and junction with the new GR10. Turn right here (southeast), and continue another twenty minutes on the GR10 to a sizeable glacial tarn, just above treeline at 1694m, and hemmed in by crags to the south but marvellously open to the north. With such easy access, Étang d'Ayès is understandably a popular picnic and camping spot, just about swimmable on a hot day. The return route is the same, and takes as long owing to a steep grade just above the parking area.

The upper Salat

Upstream and south from Seix, the D3 follows the Salat almost to its source, passing a few hamlets that make tranquil bases and start-points for forays on the GR10 or HRP. **PONT DE LA TAULE**, where the D8 veers up the Vallée d'Ustou (see opposite) 4km south of Seix, is the last spot on the Salat with public transport, and offers the Dutch-run **hotel-restaurant** *Auberge des Deux Rivières* (☎ & fax 05.61.66.83.57; ②–③; closed Nov, Sun Mon low season), where for 120F/€18.30 you can enjoy regional treats at its river-terrace restaurant. Of the rooms, the modern en-suite dormer units may be preferable to the creaky first-floor ones, though the pricier of the latter have shower rooms.

  COUFLENS, 6km up the still-paved but narrowed D3, is a deceptively substantial village along the river, hemmed in by shaggy hillsides. There's no shop here and all tourist facilities are slightly out of town: *Camping Les Bouriès* 1.5km west (six shady

---

THE BEAR TRAINERS

The villages of Oust, Ercé and Aulus-les-Bains were once renowned for their bear-trainers who, driven by poverty, toured the lowlands with their performing beasts. In the 1950s the writer Nina Epton interviewed Jean Doumenc, last of the Pyrenean bear-trainers: "'the best performing bears . . . came from Hungary. We used to go down to the port of Marseilles and buy them there. Our bears could never stand up so straight as they could. They were inclined to be bow-legged and clumsy-looking.

  "When I asked Monsieur Doumenc about the coloured postcards in the bazaar, he chuckled. 'I guess he must have made a packet, that fellow who photographed us in 1899 – yes, that's a photograph of me and my father with the last two bears we ever raised from around these parts. One of them died when it was three years old, but the other one, its twin, lived to a ripe old age. It was my father's last and favourite pet. He took great pains over its training and when it was fully grown they travelled together through every valley in the Pyrenees. In fact, they were never really happy unless they were on the road. The bear followed my father like a dog. But the old man was getting old and his rheumatism was bad. It didn't help, either, to have to sleep out under the stars. . . . Well, one day, we got a telegram at home, sent by a doctor in Pau . . . and the telegram read – "OLD MAN ILL STOP COME AND FETCH BEAST." That meant that I had to go to Pau to collect the bear and then walk all the way back again to Oust with it, while my father stayed in hospital at Pau. It looked so fierce, that bear, nobody would go near it when Father wasn't about. That was my father's last trip and my last trek over the mountains with a bear!'"

sites), or the recommended 18-place **gîte d'étape** (☎05.61.66.95.45; ①), 1km east at Rouze, run by the Assémet family and doubling as a cheese farm.

The highest village, end of the line for most traffic, **SALAU** is even bigger, with various amenities (but no shop) on the single high street. Like Couflens, the place once lived off nearby, long-abandoned tungsten mines. The Knights Hospitallers formerly had a hospice overhead, now crumbled, though the large village church clearly shows their influence. Salau's single **hotel-restaurant** *Auberge des Myrtilles* (☎ & fax 05.61.66.82.58, *myrtilles01@infonie.fr*; ②; closed Nov–Dec 15, restaurant closed Tues) is Dutch-run but jollier than their compatriots in neighbouring Pont de la Taule. The pricier dormered rooms all have showers, while breakfasts (30F/€4.60) are excellent with eggs and yoghurt (45F/€6.90 for the *vaste* gets you *charcuterie* as well). Other meals are à la carte (around 130F/€19.80 with house wine), including the delicious filleted *aiguillettes de canard* and homemade gateaux. If its full, there's also the *Centre de Montagne La Fourque* (☎05.61.66.96.74; ①), a municipally-run *gîte* a few paces downhill.

The HRP skims just above Salau, heading west to the ruined frontier hospice at **Port de Salau**, site of a big solidarity festival (*La Pujada*) between Occitans and Catalans on the first Sunday in August. If you're not interested in a long-haul traverse, the HRP is the partial basis for the **Tour des Montagnes de Salau**, shown on the Carte de Randonnées no. 6 and best spread over two days as it takes in the border peak of Mont Roig (2858m).

The Vallée d'Ustou and the Cirque de Cagateille

From Pont de la Taule, the D8 heads southeast up the sunnier and more generously proportioned **Vallé d'Ustou**, gateway to the Cirque de Cagateille. The main places en route are Trein d'Ustou (see p.256), and **SAINT-LIZIER D'USTOU**, 1km south astride the GR10; the latter offers the tiny, simple *Hotel Marterat* (☎05.61.96.58.75; ②), with restaurant and shop, and a *Camping Municipal* with sixty places and a pool. If neither suits, there's the *Chambres d'Hôte L'Escolau* (☎05.61.96.56.72; ③) at **BIDOUS**, 2km south by road or half an hour's walk on the GR10.

The road ends above the last farms, 7.5km above Trein d'Ustou, at a car park (1000m) with trailheads for the **Étang d'Alet** (3hr one-way, 1900m) and the underrated, forest-girt **Cirque de Cagateille** (35min to its base at 1250m), where several cascades garland the wall during springtime snowmelt. The Cagateille path, sporadically blazed in yellow-and-red but often faint and rough, continues to **Étang de la Hillette** (2hr 30min, 1800m), tucked into a hanging glacial valley above the cirque. A staffed refuge has been proposed for this lake and may be built in the near future. Rather than crossing the frontier to Certascan at the 2416-metre **Port de Couillac**, you can make a satisfying circuit by continuing west to Alet, then down to the car park, on the sporadically maintained paths. It's a seven- to eight-hour walking day, harder and thus less travelled than the nearby Cascade d'Ars loop (see overleaf). If you've arrived without proper maps, a placard at the car park details all walks.

Aulus-les-Bains

Thirty minutes southeast by bus from Seix along the Vallée d'Ustou and over the Col de Latrape, the spa of **AULUS-LES-BAINS** has on a clear day one of the most stunning locations in the Pyrenees. Here at the top of the narrow Vallée de Garbet, dense forests and dramatic peaks rise steeply on either side, while rock walls channel water into numerous lakes and into the River Ars with its waterfalls. If you're driving or cycling, it's much easier to arrive on the D32 threading the Vallée de Garbet, via Ercé.

Aulus itself is a sleepy, faded place with little to do other than enjoy the scenery, though new apartments dwarfing the original houses indicate that bigger plans are afoot. This being a spa town, **hotels** tend to be on the pricey side; the least expensive place is the helpful *gîte d'étape La Presbytère* (☎05.61.96.02.21; 20 places; open all year; ①), 150m downhill from the church, with four- or eight-bunk dorms and secure bike parking. Otherwise, try the one-star *Hôtel de France* (☎05.61.96.00.90, fax 05.61.96.03.29; ②–③; closed mid-Oct to mid-Dec) downstream on the main street passing the *termal*. The **restaurant** here's the epitome of a vanishing breed, with a set *menu de jour* well under 100F/€15.30 (no *à la carte*, wine extra), served amidst wooden pillars, live dogs and a stuffed bestiary. After four hearty courses of duck, offal or trout, they'll have to wheel you out in a barrow. The more comfortable, antique-furnished *Hôtel La Terrasse* (☎05.61.96.00.98, fax 05.61.96.01.42; closed Oct–May; ④–⑤), just upstream from the baths, has a fancier gourmet restaurant (allow 150F/€22.90), with seating on the river-view terrace. If you want the feel of a mountain village rather than a spa, the two-star *Hotel Les Oussaillès* on the main commercial street (☎05.61.96.03.68, fax 05.61.96.03.70; open all year; ⑤) is the place; its modern rooms have TV, phones and full plumbing. The friendly proprietors speak English, and keep a handy binder documenting local walks. The food downstairs at the restaurant (open all year, by arrangement winter weekends), may not be as elaborate as elsewhere but is still good value (*hors d'oeuvres*, trout with carrots and eggplant, *gateaux* for 68F/€10.40), with a wider choice of *ariègoise* specialities and vegetarian plates in peak season. **Camping** is at *Le Couledous* (☎05.61.96.02.26; open all year, also cabins), 500m west between the road to Ercé and the river.

If you'd like to see the surroundings, the **tourist office** (daily: July & Aug 10am–1pm & 2–7pm; Sept–June 10am–noon & 2–6pm; ☎05.61.96.01.79) in allées des Thermes rents out bikes between June and September, and also provides information on canoeing, *parapente* and horse-riding. The Centre Équestre Centaurus (☎05.61.96.02.02) by the river uses the Mérenguais breed of ponies (see p.232). The ornate glass-and-wood, centrally placed **thermal baths** themselves are just the thing to soothe trekkers' aches and pains (early May to early Oct Mon–Sat 8.30am–noon & 3–7pm, Sun 9am–noon & 3–7pm). At busy times, only the afternoon hours may be available for clientele who aren't taking a cure. In an effort to update its image, the spa also offers a wide variety of fitness, yoga and massage programmes.

The Cascade d'Ars and Étang de Guzet

South of Aulus-les-Bains, the famous Cascade d'Ars and the Étang de Guzet are favourite walking destinations, and can easily be combined in a five-hour loop. You are less likely to get lost on an anticlockwise circuit, described as follows: start from the road curve above town, where a sign indicates a non-GR trail for Plan de Souliou and the Étang de Guzet. Climb for one hour through beeches to the junction with the GR10, just past the bracken-covered *plan*, a clearing with great views of ridges surrounding Aulus. It's another half-hour, with firs now on par with the beeches, to the **Étang de Guzet** (1425m), an idyllic clear pool just west below the GR10 via side trails. Most of the climbing is over; the trail proceeds another hour as a corniche route, along the hillside to a meadow and bridge – the **Passerelle d'Ars** (1485m) just above the falls. During the next half an hour the path curls around and under the famous **Cascade d'Ars**, with the best views just before the trail disappears into forest again. The cascades plunge 110m in three stages, the top one long and slender, though during spring melt it is often just one long drop. From the falls it's another ninety minutes back to Aulus, following the river, mostly by path on the left bank, which can get muddy near the bottom. Cross the **Pont de la Mouline** over the Garbet, turn left, then left again when you meet the asphalt, and you're at the edge of town.

Guzet-Neige

A half-hour road journey from Aulus-les-Bains to **GUZET-NEIGE** during winter is worthwhile for the view alone. Located on a high shoulder 13km from Aulus, it looks northwest along the Vallée d'Ustou and (from higher points) south to frontier peaks. Ski-season **buses** (2 daily in the morning, 1 back at about 5pm) climb first into the **Col de la Trape** (1111m), then up to the resort itself at 1380m.

The 34 shortish **runs** are fairly evenly divided into green, blue and red rating, and well linked by 20 **lifts** (mostly "drag" type), making Guzet a fair beginners' or intermediates' resort. However, with a top point of just 2050m on the Pic de Freychet, and given the sunny, westerly orientation of the pistes, Guzet typically operates only from mid-December to mid-March, despite the efforts of numerous snow canons. The three runs descending to Col de la Trape remain shut most seasons. **Accommodation** at Point 1380 comprises two hotels, and a collection of four-person, wood-and-stone chalets, *Le Hameau du Pas du Loup*, rather attractive by the standard of ski resort architecture. Chalets can be reserved on ☎05.61.96.03.21, with weekly rates typically better value than weekend rates (the latter unavailable Christmas/New Year and February school break).

Mont Valier and around

Pyramidal **Mont Valier** (2838m), the most famous mountain of the Couserans, was long mistaken as the highest Pyrenean peak. It's named after a fifth-century bishop, Valerius, who crucifix in hand supposedly made the first ascent. Lying entirely in France, this beacon and mascot of the valleys conceals five lakes in its folds and even a tiny glacier on the north face.

The mines in Mont Valier's foothills may be long defunct, but timber is still a viable enterprise – and if you're driving the narrow roads, beware of slow-moving **lumber trucks**. Another potential "local" industry, far less welcome judging from graffiti, is a superhighway of high-voltage power lines proposed to be installed by EDF (Electricité de France).

Approaches: Castillon and Audressein

Mont Valier is accessible from both the GR10 and the HRP, the former skirting it to the east, north and west, the latter along its south. If you're not following either of these, take a bus or drive from Saint-Girons towards Sentein, along the Vallée du Biros and its River Lez. Some 12km along you'll pass through the old village of **CASTILLON-EN-COUSERANS**, its houses topped by the fortified chapel which is all that Cardinal Richelieu left standing of the château. You'll find the regional **tourist office** in Castillon's disused train station (summer Mon–Sat 9.30am–12.30pm & 2.30–6.30pm, Sun 9.30am–12.30pm; spring/autumn Mon–Sat 10am–noon & 3–6pm, Sun 10am–noon; ☎05.61.96.72.64); the village also hosts a Tuesday street market.

There are no other facilities of note, however, and it's probably better to halt 1km north at **AUDRESSEIN** and its engaging medieval **church of Notre-Dame de Tramezaygues**, built at the confluence of the Lez and the Bourgane, venue for a lively September 8 festival. At other times, its highlight is an unrivalled collection of fourteenth-century **frescoes**, well restored in the late 1980s, adorning the arcade of the west porch (always open). A full explanation of the images is posted in French only. Two pairs of angels in noble period dress play the flute and rebec, and harp and lute; there are ex-voto cartoons of a penitent murderer, a freed prisoner, a recovered invalid, and a curiously bare-arsed youth (presumably saved from harm) falling from a tree. A panel of Saint Jacques du Compstelle confirms this as a minor halt on the pilgrim route to Spain, while another of Saint Jean Baptiste shows him dressed in a bearskin (complete with head), so appropriate for the Ariège.

The village itself has an excellent **hotel-restaurant**: *L'Auberge d'Audressein* (☎05.61.96.11.80; ②–③; closed mid-Nov to mid-Feb), a former forge house at the crossroads near the church. You'll need French to translate the restaurant menu, but rest assured it's all delicious (reputedly the best in the Couserans), and well priced at 115F/€17.50, 149F/€22.70 and 195F/€29.80 for *menus*. The mid-priced option gives you the run of the sweet list, plus a local cheese plate. The rooms are simple but adequate and well furnished, with views to either the mountains or river. If they're full, your nearest comparable fallback lies 4km west at **ARGEIN**: the *Hostellerie de la Terrasse* (☎05.61.96.70.11; closed mid-Nov to mid-Feb; ③), with trout-based *menus* at 70–100F/€10.70–15.30.

Around the Refuge des Estagnous

Most passengers will continue by bus another 4km plus from Castillon to the **Riberot valley** turning on the left. There's a good chance of a lift along the 7km up the Riberot (6km paved) to the parking area and trailhead for the GR10 at **Pla de la Lau** (927m). From here it's four hours' hiking, past the famous **Cascade de Nérech** halfway along, to the **Refuge des Estagnous** (☎05.61.96.76.22; 2240m; 75 places; staffed June to Oct 15, weather permitting May & late Oct to early Nov; part always open; ①).

From Estagnous, the summit is just a couple of hours away next morning, so leave most of your gear at the refuge. You walk southeast on the clear path to **Col du Faustin** (2643m), then northeast by path to the **summit**. The views facing south are terrific – Montcalm and Estats on your left, the Val d'Aran and Aigüestortes in the middle, the Maladeta massif to your right. If you're tempted by what you see, you can trek across the border to the headwaters of the Noguera Pallaresa.

Other standard day-walks from the refuge are to the lakes **Étang Rond** and **Étang Long**, just southwest of Mont Valier, or north over the Col de Pécouch on the shoulder of Valier to follow the longer *Circuit de Trois Lacs*, which takes in the lakes of **Cruzous**, **Arauech** and **Milouga**. A link trail heads north from the top to the GR10, an interesting variant return to the car park.

The Tour du Biros

The popular **Tour du Biros** will occupy four to five days and is clearly marked on the Carte de Randonnées 1:50,000 "Couserans – Cap d'Aran" map.

From the *Estagnous* refuge, you can pick up the Tour by going back down towards Pla de la Lau in the Riberot valley, and taking the GR10 west. After three hours' steep climbing, followed by an equally severe one-hour descent into the Besset forest, you're on the Tour, waymarked in red-and-yellow stripes and for a time accompanying the GR10. There's a well-sited twenty-bunk *gîte d'étape* (☎05.61.96.14.00; ①) at the former mining hamlet of **EYLIE** another four to five hours ahead, at the top of the Vallée de Biros. If you've reached Eylie by car, you'll finally feel you're in the mountains, with barns and rivulets clinging to the steep slopes all around. As a major trailhead, it has ample signposting to various points of hiking interest.

Next day the joint Tour/GR10 climbs past the old lead and zinc mines at Bentaillou, and close by the caves of Gouffre Martel and Cigalère, the latter discovered by Norbert Casteret (see box on p.316). Four hours from Eylie you reach **Étang d'Araing**, with the **Pic de Crabère** (2629m) reflected in its waters and the *Refuge de l'Étang d'Araing* beside it (☎05.61.96.73.73; 1965m; 53 places; staffed mid-June to end Sept, weekends only May to mid-June & Oct; part always open; ①). The remainder of the day can be spent scaling Crabère, a three-hour round-trip.

The Tour now diverges from the GR10, swinging back northeast on a relatively easy half-day through beech forests to the abandoned hamlet of **Le Playras**, where the *gîte d'étape* has closed down. Thus you must carry on from there, along the north flank of the valley, to complete a fairly long walking day at **BONAC-IRAZEIN** (aka Bonac-sur-Lez) on the valley floor. Here, the *Relais Montagnard*, next to the church, serves as a *gîte d'étape* (☎05.61.66.75.57; 24 places; ①), offering good meals, which often include local trout. The final, less frequented leg of the *Tour* heads south from Bonac-Irazein along the east flank of the Orle valley to meet the GR10 again at Besset (unstaffed refuge sleeping five) within six hours.

The main village in these parts, just off the Tour and end of the bus line from Saint-Girons, lies 2km west of Bonac at **SENTEIN**, which features in its central square a curious fortified fifteenth-century church with three towers (originally there were four) and some surviving interior frescoes. It also has a shop, a **tourist office** (summer Mon–Sat 10am–noon & 3–7pm, Sun 11am–1pm & 5–7pm; ☎05.61.96.10.90), a **campsite**, *La Grange*, and the unprepossessing but inexpensive modern **hotel**, *Le Crabère* (☎05.61.96.04.22; ②), on the through road, with a ground-floor restaurant offering two *menus* at under 100F/€15.30.

West: the GR10

Following the **GR10 west** from the Étang d'Araing requires six hours, the last third on asphalt, to **FOS**, a moribund village on the main road between Vielha (in Spain) and Saint-Béat. There's a *gîte d'étape* here (☎05.61.79.87.85; 17 places; ①), a *camping municipal*, and a shop, but no reliable restaurant, nor public transport in any direction. You're probably better off halting 40min east of Fos at **MELLES**, a more attractive village with excellent-value **accommodation** and **meals** at the *Auberge du Crabère* (☎05.61.79.21.99, fax 05.61.79.74.71; ③; closed Wed outside high season). The chef has compiled a book of local recipes, so the food – based on crayfish, wild mushrooms, and other found food – is of high standard.

Skiing: Le Mourtis

About 11km east of Saint-Béat, just above the Col du Menté on the slopes of Tuc de l'Étang (1816m), the little ski station of **LE MOURTIS** struggles to operate most winters. Its 22 short downhill pistes – nearly half green-rated, and without snow canons – are probably on the way out; the 45km of cross-country skiing routes through the forest appear to have a brighter future.

Along the Garonne: into the Comminges

The **Comminges** is an ancient feudal county which, having never had the prestige or power of neighbouring Foix or Bigorre, was absorbed into a unifying France in 1454. Haute-Garonne, the modern successor *département* that approximates the traditional boundaries, is drained by the **Garonne** and its tributary the Pique. The quickest way from the Couserans into the valley of the Garonne is by bus (several daily) from Saint-Girons to **Boussens**, from where more than a dozen daily trains run fifteen minutes west along the river to **Saint-Gaudens**, the first town of any size. This is chiefly of note as a transport hub for visiting the adjacent great attractions, **Saint-Bertrand-de-Comminges** and the **Grotte de Gargas**.

Saint-Gaudens to Valcabrère

Although capital of the Comminges, **SAINT-GAUDENS** is essentially a way-station rather than a place to linger, its commercial and industrial character epitomized by a lively Thursday market – and a cellulose plant, spewing thick yellowish smoke. However, the **Musée du Comminges** (Mon–Sat 9am–noon & 2–6pm), in the Place Mas-St-Pierre by the church, could merit a call for its prehistoric finds, Gallo-Roman ceramics and local history display. Also on this square is one of the town's most pleasant **hotels**, the *Esplanade* (☎05.61.89.15.90; ③). Nearly as central, and of similar calibre, is the two-star *Pedussaut*, 9 av de Boulogne (☎05.61.89.15.70; ③). The **tourist**

NORBERT CASTERET

Norbert Casteret (1897–1987), who lived 4km outside Saint-Gaudens, was almost unique in that he was a professional speleologist, earning his living from his books and from survey work for hydroelectric companies. His first big coup came in 1922 with the penetration of Montespan, a cave on the south bank of the Garonne halfway between Saint-Gaudens and Salies. Casteret's account captures the moment of discovery:

"We entered a gallery which I had neglected to explore on the former occasion, and stopped in amazement before the statue of a bear modelled in clay. Further on lay more of these figures: two felines walking in file, and some horses. The following day we came upon some curious tracks; the cave had undoubtedly been used as a shelter or hiding-place by prehistoric people. We were the first men to enter that chamber since the cave-folk dwelt there several thousand years ago. On the muddy floor there were imprints of their naked feet, and also some stone weapons. The walls had been ornamented with the aid of sharpened flints, and we gazed in wonder upon the fauna of far distant ages: mammoth, reindeer, horses, bison, chamois . . .The clay figures of Montespan . . . date from the beginning of the Magdalenian era, say about 20,000 years ago, and are therefore the oldest known statues in the world."

In 1926, with his wife Elisabeth, Casteret discovered the Grotte Casteret on Mont Perdu/Monte Perdido, the highest known ice cave in the world. Four years later came the discovery of animal engravings at Labastide, west of Saint-Gaudens in the Baronnies. The following year Castaret's dye test – described on p.265 – proved that the Garonne sprang in part from the Aneto glacier, and he also explored the Grotte de la Cigalère, south of Saint-Gaudens. In 1952, as part of a team plumbing the depths of Gouffre Pierre Saint-Martin in the Western Pyrenees, Casteret broke his own cavern-descent mark set two decades previously, at the 303-metre-deep Gouffre Martel near Cigalère. This record of cave exploration in the Pyrenees has no equal, and it's unlikely that anyone will ever surpass his tally of "firsts" in these mountains.

Note: Montespan, Labastide, Cigalère and Pierre Saint-Martin are accessible only to experienced speleologists. For an account of the Grotte Casteret, see p.370.

office is at 2 rue Thiers (☎05.61.94.77.61). A meal stop in Saint-Gaudens is more likely than an overnight stay, in which case head to the **restaurant** attached to the *Pedussaut*, or the carniverous *Restaurant de l'Abattoir*, on bd Leconte-de-Lisle, beyond the station opposite the slaughterhouse (70–120F/€10.70–18.30; closed Sun) with impeccably fresh cuts of meat.

Valcabrère

En route to Luchon, you pass the village of **VALCABRÈRE**, with its rough stone barns and open lofts for hay-drying. To get there without your own transport, take the train from Saint-Gaudens to Montréjeau, transfer to the SNCF bus service (usually 5 daily) south to Luchon and get off after 6km at Labroquère, 500m northeast of Valcabrère, just before the road crosses the Garonne. Standing among cypresses and the village graveyard to the south of Valcabrère, you'll find the jewel-box-like twelfth-century Romanesque church of **Saint-Just** (July–Sept daily 9am–7pm; March–June & Oct–Dec Sat & Sun 10am–noon & 2–6pm; 12F). Saint-Just was built largely of stone from the Roman city Lugdunum Conventarum (see below), founded by Pompey in 72 BC. Beyond the elegantly sculpted north portal, showing Christ borne heavenward by angels, flanked by the four Evangelists clutching their symbols, there's ample evidence of recycled masonry: marble in the altar floor, an inscription dated 347 AD on the wall of the nave and several columns augmenting the six massive stone piers upholding the nave. Between the altar and the triple apse with its blind arches looms a carved Gothic freestanding shrine, with a sarcophagus which presumably once contained the saint's relics. The soaring vaulted ceiling creates splendid acoustics, and Saint-Just is a major music venue for the summer *Festival du Comminges*.

A little further on, protruding from grass at each side of the crossroads, are the foundations of **Lugdunum Conventarum** (currently closed for excavations), a former town of 60,000 and one of the most important in Roman Aquitaine. According to the first-century Jewish historian Josephus, the town was the place of exile for Herod Antipas – who'd executed John the Baptist and received Christ from Pontius Pilate – and his wife Herodias around 39 AD. At its height during the first and second centuries AD, the town survived well into the Christian era despite destructive raids by Vandals and Burgundians in the fifth and sixth centuries.

Taking inspiration from the Romans, Valcabrère supports a posh **restaurant**, *Le Lugdunum* (closed Sun pm, Mon pm & Tues), well southeast of the village, just off the N125. Here, for 175F/€26.70 and up (dessert and drinks extra), you can sample recipes claimed to be favoured by the Caesars themselves, featuring local game and fish (but no tomatoes or lemons, foods unknown in Roman times).

Saint-Bertrand-de-Comminges

This part of the French Pyrenees boasts few monuments, though one of the finest stands at **SAINT-BERTRAND-DE-COMMINGES** – a magnificent cathedral reflecting three distinct eras of architecture. To reach the village from Saint-Gaudens without your own transport, follow directions for Valcabrère outlined above as far as Labroquère, and take the turning west for Saint-Bertrand. It's then a pleasant half-hour walk between fields of grain and hay, with the poplar-lined river to your right and the grey, fortress-like cathedral of Saint-Bertrand commanding the plain ahead. Cars are no longer allowed in the village at peak season between 10am and 7pm, but a *navette* (minibus shuttle) operates from the parking area below, sparing you a ten-minute walk up. At other times, you can drive to the higher car park by the walls.

The Roman city stretched up the hill to where Saint-Bertrand now stands. The lower part was destroyed by the Vandals in 409 AD, and the more protected walled upper part – where a Christian church had since been built – was wrecked in 585 by King Gontran of Burgundy. For five centuries the site lay deserted, until the Gascon aristocrat Bertrand de l'Isle – made bishop of Comminges in 1073 and canonized in 1218 – began to rebuild.

The village and cathedral

The handsome walled and gated village of Saint-Bertrand-de-Comminges, with many half-timbered-and-brick houses dating from the fifteenth and sixteenth centuries, clusters tightly around the **Cathedral** (May–Sept Mon–Sat 9am–7pm, Sun 2–6.30pm; Oct & March–April Mon–Sat 10am–noon & 2–6pm, Sun 2–6pm; Nov–Feb Mon–Sat 10am–noon & 2–5pm, Sun 2–5pm; admission to cloister and choir 20F). Dedicated to the Virgin Mary, not to St Bertrand as one might expect, its white-veined facade and ponderous buttressing seems rather menacing at first. A Romanesque **cloister** with engagingly carved capitals looks south towards the foothills, while the aisleless **interior** forms a showcase of decorative art from three great periods. Bertrand's Romanesque church was enlarged during the late thirteenth century in the Gothic style by the future Clement V (first of the Avignon popes), and the interior was finally remodelled in Renaissance times by another bishop, Jean de Mauléon. In the ambulatory, a fifteenth-century shrine depicts scenes from Bertrand's life, with the church and village visible in the background of the top right panel; the saint's marble tomb, still venerated by pilgrims, is here too. The small area reserved for the laity at the west end has a richly carved oak organ, a pulpit and a spiral stair, but the cathedral's real treasure is the central **choir**, built by *toulousain* journeymen and installed during the decade or so after 1523.

The 66 elaborately carved choir **stalls** are a feast of virtuosity, mingling piety, irony and malicious satire, each the work of a different journeyman. In the misericords and partitions that separate them, the ingenuity and humour of their creators is best seen; each gangway dividing the misericords displays a representation of a cardinal sin. By the middle gangway on the south side, for example, Envy is represented by two monks, faces contorted in anger in a furious tug-of-war over the abbot's baton of office. The arm-rest on the left of the rood-screen entrance depicts the abbot birching a monk, while the bishop's throne has a lovely back panel in marquetry depicting St Bertrand and St John.

Practicalities

Staying in Saint-Bertrand is an attractive proposition, at least outside of peak season. Across the small square in front of the cathedral, the *Hôtel du Comminges* (☎05.61.88.31.43, fax 05.61.94.98.22; ④; closed Nov–March) makes a fine, old-fashioned overnight stay (rooms with shower only) and has a reasonable restaurant (April–Sept). Otherwise there's the modern *Hôtel L'Oppidum* (☎05.61.88.33.50, fax 05.61.95.94.04; ⑤; closed early Jan to late Feb & Wed out of season), behind the cathedral on rue de la Poste. Its en-suite rooms vary engagingly: the first-floor ones clean, whitewashed and almost cave-like, the top-floor ones mansarded and traditional. The ground floor restaurant is excellent, and doubles as a "tea salon" with a British profusion of varieties. The 110F/€16.80 menu may feature spicy *salad de volaille*, roasted lamb shank with braised vegetables, and apple tart (drinks extra). The only unaffiliated **restaurant** of note in the village is *Chez Simone*, west and downhill from the *Hôtel du Comminges*, serving simpler fare (budget 90F/€13.70) on its view terrace. The nearest **campsite** – shady, well laid out and with a few chalets to rent – is *Es Pibous* (☎05.61.94.98.20; May–Sept), north of the road to Saint-Just. In July and August the cathedral and Saint-Just in Valcabrère play host to the musical **Festival du Comminges** (information from festival office in the cathedral square: daily 10.30am–12.30pm & 3–7pm; ☎05.61.95.44.44 or 05.61.88.32.00 in summer, ☎05.61.95.81.25 the rest of the year).

Grotte de Gargas

Easily accessible from Saint-Bertrand, the **Grotte de Gargas** (45-min guided tours only, caves shut 45min before closing time; max group 25 persons; daily July & Aug 9.30am–12.30pm & 2–7pm; Easter–June & Sept 10am–noon & 2–6pm; Oct–Nov & Jan–March 10am–noon & 2–5pm; Dec 10am–noon & 2–4pm; 30F/€4.60; ☎05.62.39.72.39) merits a visit for its mysterious hand prints, which make the presence of their prehistoric creators seem almost immediate.

If you want to walk from Saint-Bertrand (inadvisable, as the road is narrow and heavily travelled), drop down from the upper village onto the road again, turn left (north-west) and keep going for another 6km. You can also walk direct from the station at Montréjeau, heading about 4km southwest via Mazères de Neste.

Although it also has engravings and finger tracings of mammoths, horses, bison and deer, what makes the Gargas cave really special are its **hand outlines**, many of them with half-severed fingers. Castillo in Spanish Cantabria is the only other place where hand images have been found in large numbers; the Castillo cavern has 50 against 231 here, though only a fraction are available for viewing.

Your response to the hands depends whether you regard them as genuine outlines – perhaps created by spraying red and black pigment from a reed – or as free drawings. If they are true outlines, the hands that were placed on the cave walls some 20,000 to 25,000 years ago may have been ritually mutilated, or damaged by leprosy or frostbite. But another theory from French prehistorian André Leroi-Gourhan proposes that the hands are deliberately stylized, representing a code such as that used by South African Bushmen for silent communication when hunting.

The upper Comminges

Upstream from Valcabrère and Saint-Bertrand extends the highest portion of the Comminges. **Bagnères-de-Luchon** – universally referred to as **Luchon** – is a versatile resort at the end of all public transport lines, a staging post for numerous classic walking itineraries and somewhat less rewarding ski runs. There's also a notable collection of Romanesque churches in the vicinity.

Bagnères-de-Luchon

Along with Gavarnie, the spa resort of **BAGNÈRES-DE-LUCHON** – 13km south of Marignac on the River Pique – has long been one of the lodestars for Pyrenean explorers. Luchon re-entered history in the eighteenth century, when Jacques Barrau and Baron Antoine d'Étigny revived the thermal baths built by the Roman emperor Tiberius. Showing a flair for advertising well ahead of their time, they persuaded Louis Richelieu, governor of Gascony and great-nephew of Cardinal Richelieu, to endorse the *thermes* – and the fashionable set from Paris duly descended for the waters and salons. After the peak-climbing expeditions of Ramond de Carbonnières in the late eighteenth and early nineteenth century, Luchon became a base of choice for serious climbers and also attracted numerous Romantic literati.

East of **allée d'Étigny**, the main thoroughfare, Luchon's glory days have left a huge neighbourhood of sumptuous villas, which in some way justify the town's name for itself as "Queen of the Pyrenees". If you venture west of the commercial district, the narrow lanes off the place Rouy with vernacular houses suggest the mountain village Luchon once was. Halfway along the French side of the range, it's the largest and arguably most sophisticated Pyrenean resort, and much the most elegant place this side of Biarritz. There's little of the usual spa-town fustiness, since Luchon has successfully reinvented itself as a versatile resort, attracting all social classes and age groups. Because of the peculiar local topography, the valley here is one of the major French centres for parapente and light aviation. Late in the day everyone gathers at the boisterous pavement cafés under the linden trees along allée d'Étigny, looking up from newspapers, drinks and heated debate to watch aeroplanes and parapentes floating high in the still of sundown.

The Town

Adjacent to the tourist office at 18 allée d'Étigny, Luchon's dusty **museum** (Mon–Sat 9am–noon & 2–6pm, group tour only) has the air of a mad professor's private collection: moth-eaten stuffed birds and animals in glass cases; faded and sometimes signed photographs of famous visitors like Victor Hugo, Bismarck or Marshal Foch; models of the Pyrenees; and a room devoted to the pioneer climbers. Nineteenth-century statues add a few grace notes to the streets and squares of Luchon: there's a concentration in the **Parc de Quinconces** (around the *thermes*), particularly one of Baron d'Étigny, and in the **Parc du Casino**, where Coutheilai's Rodinesque *Baiser à la Source* provides the town's most pleasing image.

The nineteenth-century **thermal baths** (dips for those who haven't been medically referred daily 4–8pm) are once again fashionable, augmented since 1973 by the **Vaporium**, a natural cave sauna.

Practicalities

From the **train station** on av de Toulouse (where **buses** also stop), the way south into town is across the River One and down av Maréchal-Foch, which leads into allée d'Étigny. The **tourist office**, at 18 allée d'Étigny (July & Aug daily 9am–7pm; Sept & Oct daily 9am–1pm & 2–7pm; mid-Dec to March daily 8.30am–7pm; rest of year Mon–Fri 9am–12.30pm & 2–6pm; ☎05.61.79.21.21, *www.luchon.com*, which also covers local skiing), is adjacent to the premises of the Bureau des Guides – the people to see if you want to sign on for organized walks or climbs.

ACCOMMODATION

There's plenty of **accommodation** in Luchon, all heated if open in winter, though for best value you're advised to forsake the obvious establishments on the allée d'Étigny in favour of quieter sidestreets, or the countryside immediately around. If you intend staying for a week or more, note that the tourist office maintains a noticeboard of apartments and rooms to rent. There's no *gîte* or hostel in town, but there are ten **campsites** in the vicinity, including three adjacent ones on av de Vénasque, the continuation of cours de Quinconces. The least cramped and best-amenitied, though caravan-dominated, is *Camping La Lanette* (☎05.61.79.00.38; open most of year), 1.5km east over the Pique (down rue Lamartine) near the village of Montauban-de-Luchon.

L'Auberge de Castelh Vielh, 2.5km south on the D125, en route to Superbagnères (☎ & fax 05.61.79.36.79). Just three en-suite rooms which require reservations, in a lovely forested setting at this fine country restaurant (see below). The *castelh vielh* in question is a nearby hilltop signal tower, originally Celto-Roman but last used during World War II. Open daily April–Oct, weekends only winter. ④.

Hôtel Céleste, 32 rue Lamartine (☎05.61.74.64.84, fax 05.61.79.34.44). Friendly, if somewhat laxly managed, one-star hotel. Rooms are well worn, but the rear annexe, set in a large garden with seating, is blissfully quiet; open all year. ③.

Hôtel Le Chalet, 21 rue Gambetta (☎05.61.79.04.54). No-star cheapie on a pedestrian lane, about as basic as you'd want to be; open April–Oct only. ③.

Hôtel des Deux Nations, 5 rue Victor-Hugo (☎05.61.79.01.71, fax 05.61.79.27.89). Popular (booking essential), well-kept one-star with revamped en-suite rooms, and a busy downstairs restaurant; open all year. ③.

Hôtel Le Jardin des Cascades, above the church in Montauban-de-Luchon, 2km east (☎05.61.79.83.09, fax 05.61.79.79.16). Just a half-dozen peaceful, non-musty, wood-decor rooms in a lovely spot backed by a wild, hilly garden nurtured by the falls. Well-regarded restaurant (see below); both open early April to mid-Oct. ③–④.

Hôtel la Petite Auberge, 15 rue Lamartine (☎05.61.79.02.88, fax 05.61.79.30.03). Installed in a fine Belle Époque manse set well back from the street, this is arguably the best value amongst the one-stars. Ample parking, all rooms en suite, decent restaurant; open all year. ②–④.

Hôtel Portillon, 7 cours des Quinconces (☎05.61.79.02.64, fax 05.61.79.76.21). Affordable slice of faded elegance right opposite the baths; off-street parking. ②–④.

EATING

L'Auberge de Castel-Vielh, see above for location. Converted country house, strong on game and regional dishes including snails and trout, with a creditable wine list. *À la carte* will run 190F/€29 minimum, but *menus* at 100F/€15.25, 160F/€24.40 and 190F/€29 are just fine; the cheapest (drink extra) features a salad with *gesiers* and duck ham, a joint of lamb with vegetables and a *croustade de pomme*.

Le Clos du Silène, 19 cours des Quinconces, ☎05.61.79.12.00. Occupying a grand villa a bit past the old and new baths, this welcoming outfit seats diners in sumptuous interior salons or in the garden during the day. The wine list is steeply priced, and *à la carte* for a light but elegant meal will work out to 170F/€25.90, but the three *menus* at 90F/€13.70, 120F/€18.30 and 150F/€22.90 are interesting enough; the mid-priced one offers various salads, *magret de canard* and assorted homemade desserts. Early lunch, supper until 11pm; closed Tues low season & mid-Nov to mid-Dec; reservations advised.

La Crémaillère, 30 allée d'Étigny. Most of the cafés, bars and snack purveyors along this axis of Luchon life are fairly indistinguishable, but this one does excellent crêpes and buckwheat-flour *galettes* that will do for a light lunch.

Le Jardin des Cascades. Shaded terrace restaurant of the hotel (see above), with creative gourmet food, valley views and good service; there are cheaper midweek lunch *menus*, but normally count on around 210F/€32 per person, plus mandatory reservations.

Le Pailhet, 12 av du Maréchal-Foch, towards the train station. Emphatically non-vegetarian eating revolving around game, duck and regional offal specialities such as *pétéram* (sheep tripe) and *pistache* (a particularly rich *cassoulet*) in portions fit to fell an ox. 135F/€20.60 a head, with drink; closed Mon off-season & Nov 15–Christmas.

ACTIVITIES
Across the Pique, which flows through the heart of town, you'll find the **swimming pool** (daily July & Aug 11am–6.30pm; 16F/€2.50) and **tennis courts** (from 65F/€9.90/hr for the public, when tournaments aren't on). The Centre Équestre (☎05.61.79.06.64) on the north side of the River One provides **horse-riding**, while **kayaks** can be rented at Base d'Antignac (☎05.61.79.19.20), 3km north at Antignac, which also gives lessons and organizes **rafting** expeditions. You can get **airborne** in a biplane or a glider at Aéroclub de Luchon (☎05.61.79.00.48) or learn to parapente from certified instructors at Freddy Sutra (☎06.87.34.20.54) or Soaring, 14 rue Sylvie (☎05.61.79.29.23). If you're not sure what you want to do, Virgule 7 at 4 place du Comminges, off av du Maréchal Foch, offers a bit of everything, including **mountain-bike rental**. For the more sedentary, the **télécabine** is the easy way up the 2666-metre distance to Superbagnères (see p.324), with some superb views en route (April daily 1.30–5pm; May to mid-June & Sept to mid-Oct Sat & Sun 1.30–5pm; mid-June to Aug daily 9.45am–12.15pm & 1.30–6pm; 40F/€6.10 return, 25F/€3.80 one-way). It's frequently used by parapentists as a launch-pad, and is also a popular way for trekkers to cut out a 1200-metre climb on the westbound GR10.

CLIMBING FROM LUCHON IN THE NINETEENTH CENTURY
Charles Packe – barrister, amateur scientist and explorer in the great Victorian tradition – published his famous *Guide to the Pyrenees* in 1862. The book contains this summary of Luchon, his base when climbing Maladeta, and gives an evocative picture of the style of the times:

"Of horses and guides there is an ample supply at Luchon at reasonable charges. Tariffs are fixed at the bathing establishments and at the principal hotels, with the prices for the different courses and by the day. If the excursion is made on horseback, the guide is indispensable to look to the horses; but if the tourist is sufficiently hale and hearty to trust to his own feet, there is scarcely an excursion from Luchon, with the exception of the ascent of the Maladeta, requiring other guide than a good local map and compass . . . .

"Throughout the chain, and especially on the Spanish side, there is a great deficiency of hotel accommodation on the mountains, so that a sleeping bag is almost an indispensable part of his kit to anyone who would see and thoroughly enjoy the grander parts of the Pyrenees . . . . More may be seen in the mountains in four or five days camping out than in three weeks of hotel life with an occasional excursion. Besides the bag, a tin saucepan with a lid, a frying pan and a few spoons ought to be taken. Fresh meat may be provided for two days' consumption; but a good supply of fat bacon stowed in tin boxes is the most useful form of animal food. It always contributes to the meal, whether eaten as rashers or used for frying fish or making soup. This, with bread and wine, tea, coffee, chocolate, sugar, salt and pepper is all that is absolutely necessary, though other little extras will, of course, be added. An extra short, two pairs of socks, towel, pair of espadrilles and perhaps a light overcoat is all that should be taken in the way of clothing. All the eatables should as far as possible be packed in tin boxes, as otherwise the contents . . . are often turned out in a most deplorable plight, especially after a wet night. Each man engaged as porter ought to carry 15 kilogrammes."

Walks from Luchon

There's enough walking **around Luchon** to keep you occupied for a week or so, mostly amongst the frontier peaks and over the border in the Maladeta and Posets massifs. The tourist office sells a booklet of recommended short walks, which is fine as far as it goes – but since waymarking sometimes leaves a bit to be desired, a good IGN map is an essential supplementary purchase.

Southeast towards Maladeta from Hospice de France

If you're at all interested in the history of Pyrenean exploration then you should make the classic approach from Luchon to **Maladeta**, or at least the stretch between **Hospice de France** (1386m) and the **Port de Vénasque** (2445m) on the frontier. The roadhead for Port de Vénasque is 11km southeast of Luchon – if you're car-less, walk or book an excursion at the Bureau des Guides in Luchon. There's ample parking beside the abandoned hospice, built into a wooded hollow by the Knights of St John in the fourteenth century. This has long been scheduled for refurbishment, but until or unless it happens, camping is tolerated in the meadows nearby.

The way up to the pass – appearing U-shaped against the sky at first but culminating in a narrow passage when you actually get to it – lies firstly through a steep stream valley, the grade not deterring a steady procession of dogs and five-year-olds en route. Some two hours along (2hr 30min with a full backpack) you reach the four clear, turquoise tarns known as the **Boums du Port** or **Lacs de Boum**, brimming with trout and the occasional hardy human swimmer. Beside the highest and largest lake stands the CAF *Refuge de Vénasque* (☎05.61.79.26.46; 2249m; June–Oct 15; 15 places; ①), whose genial wardens serve excellent four-course lunches (including homemade dessert) to all comers until late afternoon, as well as supper to overnighters. Suitably fortified, you can now tackle the thirty-to-forty-minute trail-climb to the pass (3hr total to the Port de Vénasque from the Hospice de France), where the entire crestline of Maladeta is literally in your face. If you're continuing that way, the just-visible *Renclusa* refuge is another two and a half hours along well-trodden paths, while the *Llanos del Hospital* refuge-restaurant is just over half as far, on the floor of the Ésera valley (see p.292).

Otherwise you can complete a satisfying circuit by taking the distinct trail labelled as "23" to the left and east, just beyond the Port de Vénasque, leading in Spanish territory 45 minutes to the **Pòrt dera Picada** (2477m). Beyond this you descend gradually for about twenty minutes to the peak and pass of Espelette, with half-wild horses grazing nearby. You can slip north through the frontier again via the "23" trail through the **Pas d'Escalette** (2398m; *Còth de Lunfèrn* on some Spanish maps), but staying close to the border until drawing even with the **Pas de Montjoie**, from where you descend through the woods of the Frêche valley back to the Hospice de France; this completes a seven-hour walking circuit.

Alternatively, you can shorten the day to six hours by plunging down to the **Étangs de Fréche**, the higher one visible from the cement cairn on the frontier ridge a few moments west of the Pas d'Escalette. This route is cairned, though initially there's no path; it's half an hour down to the top tarn at 2200m, and another twenty minutes to the lower, banana-shaped lake (2100m). Here the maintained "24" trail kicks in, taking you back to the Hospice de France after ninety minutes, passing riotous growths of wildflowers on bare slopes near the lakes, with the final stretch through beech and fir.

South of Luchon: the Vallée du Lys and lake circuit

The **Vallée du Lys**, south of Luchon, provides another corridor to serious walking. The road up is initially more impressive than the route to Hospice de France, with the broad glacial valley dominated by the **Cirque de Crabioules** overhead, and the lower slopes dotted with ex-*granges*, now holiday chalets. The asphalt ends after 10km at a giant car-park (1132m) and the **Cascade d'Enfer**, a spectacular waterfall dropping 40m in two stages through a cleft in the cliff, though the effect is spoilt a bit by EDF's adjacent dynamo building and disused *téléphérique*. By the parking area stands the *Auberge-Restaurant Les Délices du Lys*, serving lunch only and, with its under-100F/€15.30 *"menu de passage"* including salad, salmon, dessert and a drink, rather better than you'd expect.

Here also is a large signboard, detailing local **day-hikes** on a myriad of marked and numbered paths. The best can be combined into the suggested seven-hour loop itinerary below, taking in the most spectacular low-alpine lakes and a staffed refuge. First you have a forty-minute stiff climb through fir and beech along trail "40", following a stream up to a slopy meadow at the treeline and the junction right (ignore it) for trail "42" to the Gouffre d'Enfer. At the next junction, 1hr 15min from the car park, turn left towards Lac Vert ("1hr, 2000m") rather than right on "41" to the Refuge de Maupas and Lac Bleu. It's about 1hr 15min (2hr 30min from the car park) to this lake (ignore a left towards the Col de Pinata and Cirque de la Glère), via a glacial basin where springs well up vigorously beyond the Lac des Graués, really just a tiny tarn. **Lac Vert**, multi-lobed and green, is a popular family destination and just about warm enough for swimming – if the anglers' fish-hooks don't snag you.

You can continue fairly easily to Lac Bleu just overhead, but the following route is the only safe one. Proceed along the north shore of Lac Vert, forsaking trail "40" for the ridge at the far end; there's no path, but cross-country progress is initially easy over turf, with no scree. Then you face a sharper climb to link up with the path to **Lac Bleu** just west of its dam, conveniently in sight much of the way (allow 3hr 15min to here). The dam is ugly, but the cirque and bare crags overhead, with streamers of water feeding the lake, are magnificent.

From Lac Bleu, the path goes east around the shoulder of the Pic de Graués, with modest altitude changes, to visit **Lac Charles** and **Lac Célinda** (allow 3hr extra return). In the opposite direction there's a half-hour descent to the junction with the main trail "41", and then 15min climb back up to the **Refuge Maupas** (☎05.61.79.16.07; 2430m; 27 places; staffed June 15–Sept 15; ①), at the top of the *téléphérique*. This hut is a bit elderly, but a welcome site in foul weather; if you time it right you can have lunch here. Incidentally, *Maupas* is a bit of a trekkers' cul-de-sac; traverses exist in theory to the Portillon hut (see below) and the Ball de Remuñe in Spain, but they're advanced undertakings, with axe and crampons required to cross the glacier at the top of the Cirque de Crabioules and the Col de Crabioules (3012m).

From *Maupas*, descend again on the EDF-engineered path, following the rusty funicular pylons, to **Prat Long** (1940m; 1hr below), where neither rough camping in the hummocky terrain nor a crude, Nissen-type hut is likely to appeal. Another 40min along path "41" returns you to trail "40"; when you reach the meadow at the treeline, vary your return by taking the scenic path "42", which passes above the Cascade d'Enfer, then loops around the far side of the valley before dropping to the car park (2hr 45min from *Maupas*).

As noted above, the Vallée du Lys and the Hospice de France areas are linked by a good, half-day path, veering off from trail "40" below Lac des Graués. This threads the Col de Pinata (2152m) and the Col de Sacroux (2034m) en route to the lakeless **Cirque de la Glère** before descending sharply towards the hospice. From the cirque, another path climbs southwest to the easy **Port de la Glère/Puerto de la Glera** (2367m), giving access to Spain at the Ibón de Gorgutes (see p.293).

Southwest to Posets

For **Posets** you take the GR10 steeply south from Luchon up through the Sahage woods to Superbagnères (3hr; see below), then west five hours to the *Refuge Espingo*, situated just south of the GR10, above its namesake lake (see below).

As an alternative you could drive, or take one of the regular daily *navettes* (3 daily, well-spaced, early July–early Sept), to **Granges d'Astau** (1139m), essentially the parking area for **Lac d'Oô**. Here also you'll find the *Auberge d'Astau* (☎05.61.79.35.63; April to mid-Oct), which offers *gîte d'étape* (16 places; ①), inn (③) and restaurant. From the roadhead a crowded section of GR10, initially on broad track, climbs for an hour to the dammed lake (1504m), where the privately run *Refuge Chez Tintin* (☎05.61.79.12.29; May–Oct; ①) perches beyond the west end of the dam, its shoreline tables enjoying views of the superb 300-metre waterfall at the far side of the lake, and Hounts Secs peak to the east. The onward, well-engineered path skims the east shore as it mounts to the Col d'Espingo, where the GR10 bears northeast towards Luchon, but most hikers press on to the *Espingo* refuge just below the pass, exactly an hour above Oô. The hut here (☎05.61.79.20.01; 1967m; 60 places; staffed late May–early Oct; ①) overlooks the beautiful, undammed **Lac d'Espingo**, and the frontier ridge; however, there's no snack bar or drinks service for casual passers-by.

Power lines, and most day-trippers with their toddlers and poodles in tow, tend to stop here; beyond lies serious high-mountain country. The path continues south from the refuge past **Lac Saussat**, whose shores are a popular camping site in season. A short way above, there are two possible routes into Spain, both partly visible from Saussat: directly via the **Port d'Oô** (*Puerto de Oô*), or by an easterly route via the **Lac du Portillon**. The path for the latter, like much of the Oô–Espingo section, is paved with stone slabs, relics of the construction of the Portillon dam in the 1930s.

The *Refuge du Portillon*, an ex-construction workers' hut at the foot of the dam (☎05.61.79.38.15; 2571m; 25 places; staffed June 15–Sept 15; ①), lies on the HRP, two hours from Espingo. On a sunny summer's day the lake appears cobalt blue against the surrounding grey rock and scree, its occasional patches of shoreline grass dotted with saxifrage and gentian. Onward routes into Spain are tricky and require proper equipment and experience on glaciers. The *Llanos del Hospital* hospice or the *Refugio de la Renclusa* on Maladeta lies a full day's trekking east through the **Col de Litérole/Collado de Lliterola** (3049m), while the route to the *Estós* refuge in the Ésera valley slips south through the **Portillon d'Oô**, high above the lake, and then southwest – at first over permanent ice – to join the path descending from the Port d'Oô/Puerto d'Oô. Count on four to five hard-slogging hours, albeit downhill, from either pass to *Estós*.

Skiing around Luchon

Despite relative proximity to the highest mountain in the Pyrenees, Luchon's own ski resort of **SUPERBAGNÈRES** (17km away; regular ski-bus in season, plus the *télécabine*) is too low and exposed to the sun on an east- and west-facing shoulder at around 1800m. Most of the green and blue runs (12 of the 24 pistes) *descend* from here – bad news which snow canons can't really ameliorate. (The Bourg d'Oueil resort, 15km northwest of Luchon at the head of the Oueil valley, was even lower and has ceased operating.) To get to the higher runs you have to ascend from the low point at 1450m, on two long chairlifts (among 14 in total), and even then you only reach 2260m in the north-facing Céciré sector, which offers the most challenging advanced runs. The *Grand Hôtel*, a hulking, Swiss-style edifice, was built half a century before the apartments and ski lifts.

When snow cover at Superbagnères is thin and mushy – all too often the case – keen skiers find better conditions at the resort of **LES AGUDES** and **PEYRESOURDE** ('*Peyragudes*' in tourist-board-speak; *www.peyragudes.com*), which straddles the Col de Peyresourde 15km west of Luchon. Although the top is still only 2400m, the east-, west- and north-facing slopes on each side of the spine from the *col* serve as snow-traps. The development is fairly ugly but the skiing is serious, with 18 lifts and 38 pistes, the latter descending to the two low points at 1600m. With a preponderance of blue and red runs, and a somewhat idiosyncratic lift plan, it's best considered an intermediate-to-advanced centre.

West to the Col de Peyresourde: churches and villages

Along the direct road west from Luchon over the **Col de Peyresourde** (1569m) you can only hitch or drive – there's no bus beyond the turning to Granges d'Astau. Along the way, three **churches** are worth more than a cursory look. The most famous is the twelfth-century **Saint-Aventin**, perched with its namesake village on a very steep slope some 5km from Luchon. Its two Romanesque towers were immaculately renovated in the nineteenth century, and a good deal of **relief decoration** remains on the exterior. Above the south door, the carved tympanum shows Christ in Majesty, borne heavenward in his mandorla by angels, and flanked by the symbols of the Evangelists; on the right is an excellent *Virgin and Child*. The column capitals flanking the door are finely worked as well, depicting the *Washing of the Feet* (left), as well as a bear. The hermit Aventin was the local patron of bears, who would approach him to have thorns removed from their paws. To the right, Aventin is beheaded by the Moors (in 813), and further along on the wall a bullock paws at the ground to reveal the saint's buried body. Inside (key-keeper in the house 100m west, with grey gate), there are more carvings near his tomb showing Aventin helping a bear, and carrying his detached head around, as well as some twelfth-century frescoes.

Two kilometres further on, just above the highway, the parish **church** (usually open daylight hours) of **CAZEAUX-DE-LARBOUST** has a superb, well-preserved series of late fifteenth-century **frescoes** in sombre shades of ochre and red, discovered in the nineteenth century. Opposite the door, a particularly lurid Last Judgement confronts you; also in the vaulting left of the nave are rarely seen panels of St John the Baptist preaching, and (below this) being led to prison. In the apse, just above the altar, to the right of the Nativity are angels giving the glad tidings to the shepherds, one of whom plays bagpipes. Just above this in the conch of the apse, Christ reigns in Glory, while the Virgin, on a crescent-shaped throne, is borne heavenward by more angels. In the vaulting to the right of the nave are Old Testament scenes, including Adam sleeping through the Creation of Eve. After another 2km, the squat and barn-like **Saint-Pé-de-la-Moraine** just west of the village of Garin is a rarity, a pre-Romanesque edifice from the ninth century, cobbled together from Roman masonry.

If you'd like to **stay** locally, try the two-star *Hotel L'Esquérade* in neighbouring **CASTILLON-DE-LARBOUST**, between Cazeaux and Saint-Aventin (☎05.61.79.19.64, fax 05.61.79.26.29; closed Oct–Dec; ④). Half-board is advisable and the excellent restaurant serves game. The hotel also offers weekend or five-day activity packages (kayaking, horse-riding, parapente) in conjunction with local outfitters, as well as ski *forfaits* in winter.

Col de Peyresourde

The **Col de Peyresourde**, hemmed in by steep slopes 5km west of Garin, is often part of the **Tour de France** route, generally the midpoint of a long day's climbing. If you're in the area on the date the pack passes through and you want a good view, be sure to get a place on the roadside a few hours before the expected time of arrival – when the leaders come over the pass, the crowds will be twenty deep. The most ardent devotees of the Tour position themselves under the banner marking the crest of the *col*, armed with sheafs of newspapers – not to fill in the wait reading, but to help the cyclists. As the riders appear, the newspaper is held out so that the cyclists tuck it under their shirts to insulate for the freezing descent, on which the bikes reach speeds of up to 100km per hour. (For more on the Tour, see the feature on pp.348–349).

travel details

Trains

Bagnères-de-Luchon to: Montréjeau (2 daily; 40min).

La Pobla de Segur to: Lleida (3 daily; 2hr 20min).

Montréjeau to: Boussens (14 daily Mon–Sat, 9 on Sun; 25min); Lourdes (10 daily Mon–Sat, 6 Sun; 1hr); Pau (6 daily Mon–Sat, 5 Sun; 1hr 30min); Saint-Gaudens (14 daily Mon–Sat, 10 Sun; 10min); Tarbes (10 daily Mon–Sat, 6 daily Sun; 45min); Toulouse (14 daily Mon–Sat, 9 Sun; 1hr 15min).

Spanish buses

Benasque to: Barbastro (daily 3pm, also Mon–Sat 6.45pm; uphill 11am, plus Mon–Sat 5.30pm; 2hr), with quick connections from Barbastro to Huesca (4–7 daily; 50min) and Lleida (6 daily; 1hr 15min).

Plan to: Aínsa (Mon, Wed, Fri at 6am, returns same day 8.45pm).

La Pobla de Segur to: Barcelona (2 daily; 4hr); Capdella (daily Mon–Fri Oct–May at 5.15pm; 1hr; June–Sept Mon, Wed, Fri only at 5.15pm); Esterri de Àneu (Mon–Sat 1 daily, at 6.20pm; 1hr 10min); Lleida (Mon–Sat 1 daily, at 6.30am; 2hr); El Pont de Suert (1 daily, at 9.30am; 1hr); Vielha via Bonaigua (1 daily early June to mid-Nov, at 11.30am; 3hr).

El Pont de Suert to: Boí (1 daily summer, at 11.15am, returns 2pm; 30min).

Roda de Isábena to: El Pont de Suert (1 daily Mon–Fri at 4.37pm, returns next am at 6.15; 1 hr); Graus (1 daily at 7.18am, returns at 4pm; 40min).

Sort to: La Seu d'Urgell (2 daily by minibus, 7.45am & 5.30pm; returns 10.15am & 7.30pm; 1hr 15min; reserve day before on ☎973 620 733 (am) or %973 620 802 (pm).

Vielha to: French border (Mon–Fri term-time 7 daily, 3 Sat–Sun; vacations Mon–Sat 4 daily, 2 Sat–Sun; 45min); Lleida via Túnel de Vielha (2 daily year-round, at 5.30am & 1.30pm; 3hr); La Pobla de Segur via Salardú and Bonaigua (1 daily, early June to mid-Nov, at 11.40am; 3hr 10min); El Pont de Suert (2 daily, same times as Lleida service; 1hr); Tredòs (Mon–Fri term-time 7 daily, 3 Sat–Sun; vacations Mon–Sat 4 daily, 2 Sat–Sun; 20min).

French buses

Auzat to: Tarascon-sur-Ariège (Mon–Fri in school term, 1 daily at dawn, plus year-round at noon Fri & alternate Mon; 30min).

Bagnères-de-Luchon to: Montréjeau (4 SNCF buses daily; 50min); Saint-Gaudens (1 daily; 1hr 15min); Toulouse (1 daily; 3hr 30min).

Saint-Girons to: Aulus-les-Bains (Mon–Sat 1-3 daily; 1hr 15min); Boussens (Mon–Sat 9 rail coaches daily, 7 on Sun; 45min); Foix (4 daily; 1hr); Massat (4 weekly; 35min); Seix (Mon–Sat 3–4 daily between noon & 7pm; 20min); Sentein (1–2 daily Mon-Sat term-time, 2–3 daily Tues, Thur, Sat otherwise; 45min).

CHAPTER FOUR

AROUND THE NATIONAL PARKS

The allure of the Pyrenees' two largest national parks – the French **Parc National des Pyrénées** and the Spanish **Parque Nacional de Ordesa y Monte Perdido** – remains unmatched by any other part of the range. These contain the landscapes that inspired the gentleman-explorers who pioneered numerous Pyrenean ascents from the late eighteenth century, and it was here that many Romantic poets and painters came to brood. While the exaltation that Ramond de Carbonnières felt standing on the summit of Monte Perdido in 1802 was partly due to his mistaken belief that this was the highest point of the range, he had already explored Aneto – the true high point – without feeling the same delight. So great was the devotion of the eccentric Count Henry Russell that he had caves cut near the summit of Vignemale, highest point of the French Pyrenees, from which he and his guests could watch the changing colours on the frontier peaks. Nobody can walk through the Brèche de Roland, the natural gateway through the wall-like Cirque de Gavarnie, without being profoundly impressed: in one direction you look down over the mighty rock faces of Gavarnie, in the other you gaze out towards the thousand-metre-high walls of the Ordesa canyon.

In the two adjoining high-altitude parks, you will almost certainly see Europe's rarest bird of prey, the **lammergeier**, while **griffon vultures**, **golden eagles**, **isards** and **marmots**, reintroduced in 1948, are also fairly easy to spot. A few lynx and brown bear still survive, but the chances of encountering them are very slim.

The standard approaches to the Gavarnie area **from the north** are along the **Gave de Pau**, the river valley named after **Pau**, the elegant, relatively cosmopolitan capital of the *département* of Pyrénées-Atlantiques. Every summer afternoon, tour buses tear along the narrow roads to the cirque, many of them carrying pilgrims from the Marian

---

ACCOMMODATION PRICE CODES

Each place to stay in this book has been given a code which corresponds to one of the following price categories.

① Under €13/2200ptas/85F
② €15–24/2500–4000ptas/100–160F
③ €24–32/4000–5400ptas/160–210F
④ €32–40/5400–6600ptas/210–260F
⑤ €40–52/6600–8600ptas/260–340F
⑥ €52–65/8600–10,800ptas/340–430F
⑦ Over €65/10,800ptas/430F

Category ① refers to the price *per person* of a bed; the other categories correspond to the **cheapest available double room in high season**. B&B and HB denote, respectively, when the price includes breakfast, and when it includes half-board. For more details, see p.41.

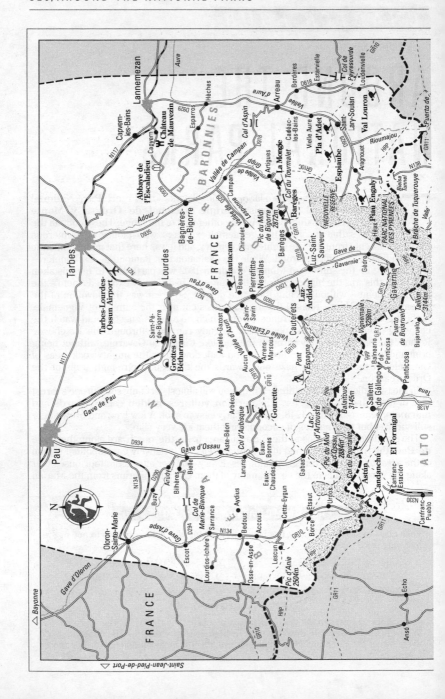

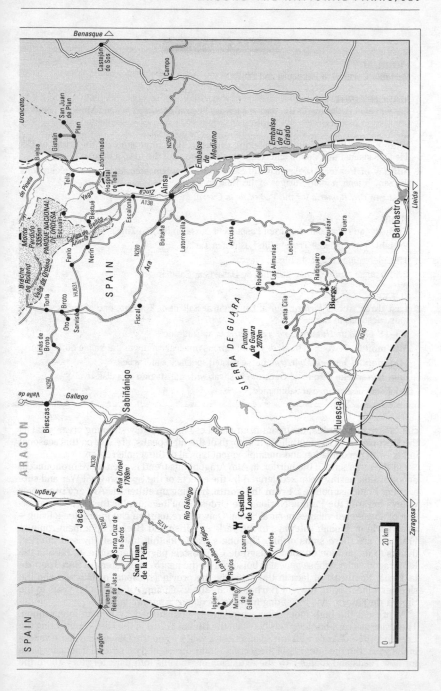

FESTIVALS

FEBRUARY
Variable Carnival at Panticosa and Bielsa.

MARCH/APRIL
Easter Good Friday marks the start of a ten-day Festival of Sacred Art and Music in Lourdes.

MAY
First Friday Processions and folkloric events in Jaca commemorate the battle of Las Tiendas against the Moors, and celebrate the courage of the town's women.
Sunday of Pentecost Pilgrimage of San Indalecio, at San Juan de la Peña. Celebrations for Santa Elena in many villages of the Valle de Tena.
Last Sunday *Romería* for the *Virgen de la Cueva*, Peña Oroel (near Jaca).

JUNE
Early Regatta of tree-trunks from Laspuña to Ainsa on the Río Zinca.
Variable International Travel Film Festival in Tarbes.
13 Celebrations for Santa Elena, Biescas.
25 *Fiesta de Santa Orosía*, at Yebra de Basa, near Sabiñánigo.

JULY
Last three weeks *Pirineos Sur* at Lanuza near Sallent de Gallego, one of the best world music festivals in Europe.
15–18 *Fiesta de Nuestra Señora del Carmen* at Canfranc.
Mid-month, 1 week *Festival de Germ*: various musical events in the Vallée du Louron.
Mid-month, 1 week *Equestria*: horse-related spectacles at Tarbes.
Last two weeks Cirque de Gavarnie Festival, with the staging of a classic play.
25 *Fiesta de Santiago* at Sabiñánigo.

cult centre of **Lourdes**, upstream from Pau. Less immediately stunning areas such as the **Baronnies**, in the foothills to the north of the high peaks, are spared this seasonal influx, with depopulation and unemployment typical of the whole region.

On the other side of the border, in Alto Aragón, this trend is even more pronounced, depopulation having been accelerated by the effects of the Spanish Civil War and subsequent Francoist policies. **From the south**, heading up either the **Ara** or **Zinca** river valleys towards the Parque Nacional de Ordesa, you'll encounter the highest proportion of abandoned villages in rural Spain. Only where tourism can guarantee a living – as at **Torla** or **Fiscal**, gateways to the park, or **Aínsa** and **Bielsa**, on a main route to France – are there signs of life. The one sizeable foothill town of any real interest, thanks to its position on the Santiago de Compostela pilgrimage route, is **Jaca** in the Río Aragón valley, whose appeal is bolstered by the nearby monastery of **San Juan de la Peña**. Southeast of Jaca in the flatlands, the provincial capital of **Huesca** and the sleepier wine-making town of **Barbastro** are the usual jump-off points for visits to the **Sierra de Guara**, also benefiting from protection as a *parque natural*.

At present the high mountains are relatively undisturbed by human intervention. There are no cross-border roads between the **Bielsa** tunnel in the east – connecting the French **Vallée d'Aure** with the Spanish Zinca valley – and the **Ossau** and **Aspe** valleys in the west. But the integrity of the terrain is now threatened on several fronts: by plans for new roads and tunnels, by the extension of ski runs into park territory (both the

Last two weeks to late August *L'Été à Pau*: sport, music and theatre events at various Pau venues.

AUGUST
Early August World music festival at Aínsa.
4 *Virgen Blanca* observances at Candanchú.
First weekend *Festival de la Montagne*, Luz-Saint-Sauveur.
Early August International Folklore Festival of the Pyrenees in Jaca (odd-numbered years) or Oloron (even-numbered years).
5 Fiesta at Sallent de Gállego.
14–15 *Fiestas del Barrio* in Jaca; street markets and parties.
15 and around Celebrations for the Assumption of the Virgin at Panticosa, Oto, Bielsa, Héas and Laruns.
14–17 *Fiesta de San Roque y la Virgen* at Biescas, with a "Big Heads" parade.
Mid-August to mid-September Music festival at Bagnères-de-Bigorre.
31 *Fiesta de San Ramón* at Buesa.

SEPTEMBER
First Sunday Procession at Sarrance.
8 Observance of the Birth of the Virgin at Héas and Sarvisé.
14 *Fiesta de la Santa Cruz* at Sallent de Gállego and Ainsa; also *La Morisma*, a mock Moors-and-Christians battle, held every odd-numbered year in Ainsa's Plaza Mayor.
Third Saturday Pastoral activities festival in Arrens-Marsous.

OCTOBER
First Sunday *Nuestra Señora del Rosario* in Broto.
12 *Fiesta de la Virgen del Pilar*, at Sabiñánigo and Torla.
20 *Fiesta* at Santa Cruz de la Serós.

French and Spanish have built winter resorts at a dozen places along the edges of their parks), and – on the Spanish side – by hydroelectric schemes. On the plus side, the Parque Nacional de Ordesa was expanded in the early 1990s to include the equally spectacular **Cañon de Añisclo** and the head of the glacial **Valle de Pineta**.

THE NORTHERN APPROACHES

The French **Parc National des Pyrénées** (PNP), was a long time coming, meeting such strong local resistance to its establishment in 1967 that it was limited to a thin ribbon of territory along the border. It has real girth only around **Pic du Midi d'Ossau**, between **Cauterets** and **Vignemale**, and where it adjoins the older **Réserve Naturelle de Néouvielle**; in places – for example, near the Col du Somport – it measures barely 1500m across.

The traditional independence of and competition between 87 different mountain *communes* in the Central Pyrenees is the reason why the park isn't as extensive as it should be. Already by medieval times the mountains were carved up between local families, the Catholic Church and a few autonomous valley communities, all grouped together into two huge feudal counties: **Béarn**, created in 820 and not absorbed by the French Crown until 1589, and **Bigorre**, which kept out of Parisian clutches until 1607.

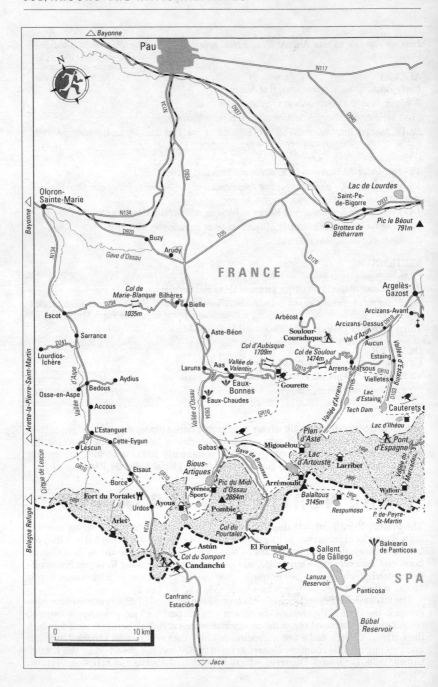

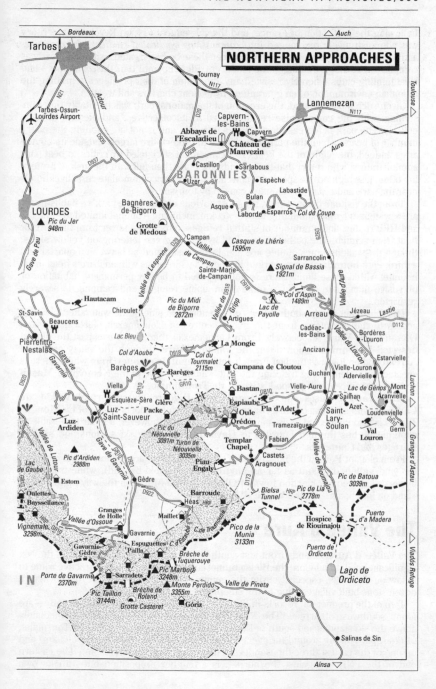

NORTHERN APPROACHES

Following the unification of France, and the subsequent French Revolution, territory was administratively rearranged into *commissions syndicales, syndicats de communes* and *copropriétaires*. However, rivalry between these bodies created a situation nearly as complicated as that prevailing in the feudal era. Right up until 1967 the *communes* – and local hunting clubs – fiercely resisted any abrogation of their privileges regarding the mountain environment, often guaranteed by ancient charters and treaties.

Given such a background, the creation of the national park was inevitably time-consuming, with the compromise result limited in its objectives, and pleasing no one entirely. The park is too easy for vehicles to reach, and is not big enough; the paltry number of bears, which the park is supposed to protect, live largely outside its boundaries. Indeed, the plight of the bears is a convenient stick used by critics to beat park administrators, who retort that their hands are more than full with the task of protecting other, less high-profile species – as well as having to accommodate rural livelihoods near the park and repair the damage caused by tourism.

From the visitor's point of view, the most obvious effects of the park's establishment are a system of **trails** amounting to over 400km, including – but not limited to – the GR and HRP routes, and a number of staffed **refuges**, either taken over from the CAF or built from scratch. The paths are marked by red or green lettering on yellow **signs**, though the walking times quoted are usually overestimated by between a quarter and a third. Park **boundaries** are marked by red-and-white signs with an isard's head in silhouette; within these limits there is not supposed to be any permanent habitation or obtrusive man-made structures other than alpine refuges, and camping is severely restricted.

The four main north–south valleys on the northern side of the watershed give fast access to the mountains from the major centres of Lannemezan, Tarbes, Pau and Oloron-Sainte-Marie respectively. From Lannemezan there are buses past the almost deserted **Baronnies** region down the **Vallée d'Aure**, through the valley capital of **Arreau** and on towards the last French settlement of **Aragnouet**, from where there is spectacular, if demanding trekking into the wildlife reserve of the **Néouvielle Massif** and the magnificent and unspoilt **Cirque de Troumouse**.

From **Tarbes**, buses run to **Bagnères-de-Bigorre** and the rural **Vallée de Campan**, with seasonal onward connections to the winter-sports village of **La Mongie**. Tarbes is also connected by bus and train to **Lourdes**; however, it is far preferable to continue by bus through Lourdes to **Gavarnie**, or to the ski stations and spas of **Barèges** and **Cauterets**.

From elegant **Pau**, in the northwest of this region, there are reliable direct buses up the wild **Vallée d'Ossau** as far as **Laruns** (less reliable beyond), while trains and buses call at the river-junction town of **Oloron-Sainte-Marie** on the way up to **Urdos** – and on into Spain – via the **Vallée d'Aspe**.

The Vallée d'Aure

The **Vallée d'Aure** extends from just south of Lannemezan up to Aragnouet, the last significant habitation before the Bielsa tunnel and the frontier. It's an attractive route to follow on the D929, especially from the county-town of Arreau and beyond, where a dozen stone-built villages cling to the steep, green banks of the valley.

Two of the premier ski resorts in the Pyrenees – **Espiaube** and **Piau-Engaly** – are found southwest of Arreau. The **Réserve Naturelle de Néouvielle**, immediately above the ski stations and south of Pic du Midi du Bigorre and the Col du Tourmalet, offers superb hiking around (or over) the celebrated **Pic de Néouvielle** (3092m) and up one of the easiest three-thousanders, **Turon de Néouvielle** (3035m). The eastern end of the PNP, up against the border, is a tougher proposition but with its own rewards, including a high-mountain approach to the **Cirque de Troumouse**, numbered among the most beautiful spots in the range.

The bus ride along the Vallée d'Aure towards the PNP begins at Lannemezan train station, a major stop on the Pau–Tarbes–Toulouse line. Although the journey provides a geography lesson on glaciation and mountain agriculture – grazing on denuded south-facing slopes, firs on the north-facing hillsides – there's little to justify leaving the bus or your car until Arreau, except for the Romanesque **church of Saint-Ebons**, built to a Greek-cross plan in the village of Sarrancolin, 19km from Lannemezan. Inside you can see the gilded and enamelled copper casket for the saint's relics, and carved choir stalls with typically grotesque faces.

Arreau

ARREAU, 27km from Lannemezan, sits at the confluence of the Louron, Lastie and Aure rivers, a strategic position that first made it capital of the ancient Comté d'Aure under the kings of Aragón. Later it formed the heart of the Pays de Quatre Vallées, finally absorbed by France in 1475. Arreau enjoys an almost rainless microclimate, lying as it does in the shadow of Pic l'Arbizon to the southwest. A small, neat village, its tone is set by the medieval **market** building (Thurs am), the half-timbered houses with their *fleur-de-lys* motifs and flower-boxes (especially the Maison des Lys opposite the market), and shops selling the local speciality *gâteau à la broche*, a spit-cooked cake. On the opposite side of the river from the market, the **Chapelle Saint-Exupère** by the post office merits a look for its flamboyant Gothic nave and eroded Romanesque portal. The town's tenth-century **Château des Nestes** now houses both the **tourist office** (summer Mon–Sat 9.30am–12.30pm & 1.30–7pm, Sun 9.30am–12.30pm; ☎05.62.98.63.15) and a **museum** devoted mostly to the Cagots (see p.347; same hours; 10F/€1.50). If your appetite is whetted for more of the same, the small village of Jézeau, 3km east, can also offer a similarly ancient church surrounded by fine vernacular houses.

Arreau makes an agreeable touring base; places to **stay** include the somewhat noisy *Hôtel de France* on the square by the central crossroads (☎05.62.98.61.12; closed May & Oct 15–Dec 15; ⑥ HB); the central *Hôtel de l'Arbizon* behind the riverside park (☎05.62.98.64.35; ⑦ HB), simple but clean and en-suite, with some of its six rooms having river views; and the much fancier, quieter *Hôtel d'Angleterre* (☎05.62.98.63.30, fax 05.62.98.69.66; closed Oct–Dec, May, & Mon low season; ⑨), off the south end of the main street, which has a peaceful rear garden and private parking. The latter two hotels have good **restaurants**, the *De l'Arbizon*'s with two decent *menus* under 100F/€15.30 and river-esplanade seating; otherwise there's only a riverside *crêperie* opposite the church. The municipal **campsite** (☎05.62.98.65.56; closed Oct) lies just south of the village on the Cadéac road, or there's the *Camping Le Refuge* (☎05.62.98.63.34; open all year) just north of Arreau.

Southeast of Arreau: the Vallée du Louron

The main excursion from Arreau leads into the **Vallée du Louron**, which can also be reached by road from the Col de Peyresourde, or on foot along the GR10 (see below). There's no bus up the valley, which means making your way along the D618 road towards Bagnères-de-Luchon, or picking up the footpath at the hamlet of Lançon, 2km above Arreau on the D618.

The local **tourist office** (Mon–Sat 9am–12.30 & 2–6.30pm, also Sun 9am–12.30pm peak season; ☎05.62.99.92.00), which runs tours to most of the **painted churches** further up the valley, is at Bordères-Louron, another 2km above Lançon, but there's little to see here aside from a Sunday morning riverside market (July–Aug only). The notable concentration of frescoed churches locally is owed to the discovery of the New World, burgeoning Spanish prosperity and consequent new markets for the wool-weavers of the valley; this wealth funded a widespread sixteenth-century mural campaign inside far older churches, part and parcel of the Counter-Reformation.

The first – and one of the best – of the churches is **St-Mercurial** at the village of **VIELLE-LOURON**, containing the saint's tomb and an extraordinary Last Supper with Judas bearing the head of Luther. It's the only one with local key-keepers – a sign points to their house – but hours are limited (Mon–Wed 10–11.30am & 4–6.30pm). The other notable church is **St-Barthélemy**, well up the valley at **MONT**, with secular-historical as well as sacred frescoes in the interior, but it can only be relied on to be open selected late afternoons during August – and even then there's no guarantee; otherwise console yourself with the excellent frescoes in the cemetery chapel. Here St Catherine appears in period dress, and a Last Judgement has some vivid demons, with the Saved beneath the Virgin, Christ and John the Baptist. There's another Last Judgement on the church's exterior south wall, with a classically hairy, horned and clawed Devil seen to the right.

The most convenient **hotel** locally, and a good choice if you're driving, is *Hôtel Les Cimes* (✆ & fax 05.62.99.67.21; ③–④) above **ESTARVIELLE** on the D618, roughly halfway between Mont and Vielle-Louron. This has several balconied, en-suite rooms with valley views and a decent restaurant with some of the heartiest *garbure* around. Otherwise there's just a youth-oriented *gîte,* the *Centre de Montagne* (✆05.62.99.64.12; dorm ①, rooms ②), down by the central church in Estarvielle.

Approach from the east: the GR10

A popular strategy is to walk west from **Granges d'Astau** to the **Vallée de Louron** via the GR10. Initially the way lies along the **Val d'Esquierry**, south of the ski development of Les Agudes-Peyresourde, over the **Pas de Couret (Col) d'Esquierry** (2131m; 2hr 30min) and then briefly along the **Val d'Aube** into the Louron valley before turning north to the hamlet of **GERM**, high up on the east flank of the valley (960m; 2hr 30min from the pass). Most people will call it a day here after five hours of trekking, especially with the incentive to **stay** at the multifunctional *Centre de Montagne Accueil sans Frontière* (✆05.62.99.65.27, fax 05.62.99.63.22; *gîte* ①, chalets ②), with a restaurant, pool and full sports programmes summer and winter; they also do cultural tours of the surroundings, have artist-in-residence programmes and organize the local July events festival.

If they're full – likely if you haven't booked – you'll have to press on downhill to one of two pleasant villages on the southeast shore of the artificial Lac de Génos Loudenvielle (watersports on offer). **LOUDENVIELLE**, 45 minutes by foot from Germ, offers the *Hostellerie des Templiers* (✆05.62.99.68.03, fax 05.62.99.60.94; open school hols only; ④), with sumptuous rooms and a well-regarded restaurant, as well as a campsite, *Pène Blanche* (✆05.62.99.68.85) and an all-important ATM. **ARANVIELLE**, the neighbouring hamlet, is graced by the welcoming, lake-view *Auberge des Isclôts* (✆05.62.99.66.21, fax 05.62.99.66.31; open all year; dorm ①, rooms ④), a restored medieval mountain house, which offers a sporting activities programme, and a *table d'hôte* restaurant. The en-suite "doubles" are cramped, but are fine for one (single rates offered).

From the vicinity of the reservoir, it's 2.5hr further west, mostly on track parallel to the paved road, to the next indoor accommodation. From Loudenvielle the GR10 climbs towards the Col d'Azet (1580m) before dropping to the village of **AZET**, where the best two of three places to **stay** are the well-equipped *La Bergerie* (✆05.62.40.08.98, fax 05.62.40.06.31; dorm ①, rooms ②), and the simpler, "official" *gîte d'étape* (✆05.62.39.41.44; ①). From here you've less than an hour's walk down to the main N129 road at Vielle-Aure, with the comforts and bus connections of Saint-Lary-Soulan (see opposite) 2km to the south.

Skiing and parapente: Val Louron

The local ski station of **VAL LOURON** perches high above the Lac de Génos-Loudenvielle, to the southwest. Although it's across the river from the ski complexes at Peyresourde (see p.324), Val Louron is not nearly so rigorous, with a top point of just 2150m (descending to 1450m) and just three chair lifts, though fourteen of its twenty pistes are red- or blue-rated, making it a respectable intermediate resort. In summer, it's a popular site for **parapente**, with schools based nearby at Génos, Adervielle and Loudenvielle.

South of Arreau: the upper Aure

Continuing up the Aure from Arreau along the D929, after 2km vehicles pass under the rock arch that is the porch of Nôtre-Dame-de-Pène Taillade at **CADÉAC-LES-BAINS**, another possible base. Here there's the two-star *Hôtel Restaurant du Val d'Aure* (✆05.62.98.60.63, fax 05.62.98.68.99, *www.hotel-valdaure.com*; closed mid-Sept to mid-Dec; ⑤, ⑦ HB mid-July to Aug), nicely set in its own park on the riverbank with a pool and tennis courts. The proprietor speaks perfect English and is a certified mountain guide, taking groups on request. In the vaulted, ground-floor billiards rooms is a cold sulphur spring, what remains of a spa established here in Roman times. Their three *menus* (65–125F/€9.90–19.10) feature own-raised trout and meat, but if you want to lunch here, phone ahead as the kitchen closes early otherwise. The budget-minded might prefer *Le Relais de la Neste*, a self-catering *gîte* with en-suite, two-to-six-person rooms (✆05.62.98.62.51; ①) beyond the old bridge east of the through road.

Alternatively, 8km southwest of Cadéac along the D30 side road, **AULON** is an appealing old village at the base of Pic l'Arbizon, where you can **stay** at *Chalet Pyrène*, a pricier-than-usual *gîte d'étape* (✆05.62.39.94.83, fax 05.62.39.94.50; ① dorm, ③ rooms), and **eat** heartily at *Auberge des Aryelets* (may close Nov 15–Dec 15; reserve on ✆05.62.39.95.59), with *menus* at 85–138F/€13–21.

VIELLE-AURE, 9km south of Arreau on the D929 and just before Saint-Lary (see below) – of which it is effectively a suburb – is the last traditional village before the ski-related developments, its older quarter scattered mostly along the west bank. The central **tourist office** (July–Aug daily 10am–12.30pm & 3–7.30pm, closed Sun Sept–June; ✆05.62.39.50.00) sells *topo-guides* for local walks (including the GR10), and can help with **accommodation**. This is mostly *chambres d'hôte*, but there are two comfortable *gîtes*: the *Relais Montagne* (✆05.62.39.42.31; dorm ①, rooms ②) on the west bank of the Neste d'Aure, en route to the large, grassy *Camping Le Lustou* (✆05.62.39.40.64; open all year), 1.5km north at Agos, as well as the *Gîte Mayo* (✆05.62.39.41.36; ②), strictly doubles, up near the attractive church. **Eating** options are pretty much down to *Les Gazaous*, on the campsite road, with four *menus* (69–160F/€10.50–24.40), and *La Millenaire*, serving trout on the west-bank village square.

Saint-Lary-Soulan

SAINT-LARY-SOULAN, 12km south of Arreau, was one of the first Pyrenean resorts to be featured by package-tour operators, its rustic core now enveloped by supposedly compatible modern buildings. The **Office du Tourisme** on rue Principale (daily 9am–7pm, closed lunch low season; ✆05.62.39.50.81) can help with accommodation in *résidences* (apartments by the week). Saint-Lary also has a **Maison du Parc National** (June–Sept & Dec–April Mon–Sat 9am–noon & 2–6.30pm, also Sun July–Aug), providing guides and general information on the local flora and fauna. There are nearly a dozen hotels in Saint-Lary, with more at the pair of ski centres overhead, but these are usually pre-booked for ski packages. **Accommodation** worth trying on spec includes the town's least expensive place, *Pons Le Dahu* on rue de Coudères (✆05.62.39.53.09; ③); the two-star *Aurelia*, north of town on the old road to Vielle-Aure (✆05.62.39.56.90, fax 05.62.39.43.75; ④); and the two-star *La Pergola* at rue Principale 25 (☎05.62.39.40.46, fax 05.62.40.06.55; ⑤), set back from the street and with a well-regarded **restaurant**. As at so many ski resorts, restaurant choices outside the hotels aren't brilliant, though the *Crêperie La Flambée Auroise* at 20 bis rue des Fougères has whole-grain bread and a good range of beers and juices offsetting rather small portions. If you have transport, it's best to head up to the village of **SAILHAN**, 2km northeast, where *Chez Lulu* (closed Mon) offers filling **meals** for under 130F/€19.80 at outdoor tables, while there's a high-quality *gîte* here, *Le Relais du Chemin de l'Empereur* (☎05.62.39.45.83; ①; closed Nov), with some doubles, and half-board rates offered. There's another, cheaper *gîte*, in Saint-Lary proper: *Le Refuge* (☎05.62.39.46.81; open all year; ①). In summer, various outdoor activities on offer include: **parapente** (☎05.62.39.58.75), **rafting** with Adrenaline (☎05.62.40.04.04), **climbing** with the Bureau des Guides (☎05.62.40.02.58) and **horse-riding** at the Centre Equestre de Saint-Lary (☎05.62.39.41.11). Also worth remembering is that Saint-Lary has the last **bank** ATMs before the Spanish frontier.

The Aure ski stations

The adjacent complexes of **PLA D'ADET** and **ESPIAUBE**, just west of Saint-Lary, have a well-linked piste system, with the highest of the thirty lifts (about one-third chair or *télécabine*) reaching 2450m and the 40 runs, facing various directions, divided into eight green, twelve blue, ten red and three black. Pla d'Adet, accessed directly from Saint-Lary village by *téléphérique*, is better suited for beginners and weak intermediates.

PIAU-ENGALY, the last stop on the valley bus route (in winter anyway), 20km above Saint-Lary, is arguably the most futuristic ski resort in Europe, and the newest in the Pyrenees (consult *www.piau-engaly.com*). Some love the futuristic architecture while others hate it, but Piau-Engaly has three undeniable advantages: illuminated night-skiing (7–10pm), an excellent snow record owing to a 2500-metre top height and – for those who have never mastered drag-lifts – 9 chairlifts among 21 lifts in total. The accommodation units are at 1850m, allowing doorstep access to 37 north-facing pistes, which include eight black, eight red and fourteen blue – in short a good intermediate-to-advanced centre.

The Vallée du Rioumajou

Above Saint-Lary, the main river drainage begins to curl west and fray into half a dozen tributaries. The most scenic of these is the **Vallée du Rioumajou**, which joins the Aure just over 3km upstream from Saint-Lary. The hamlet of **TRAMEZAÏGUES** (meaning "between waters") stands dramatically at the river confluence, overlooked by the ruins of an eleventh-century castle-with-church and by steep rock walls that exclude the sun most of the winter. Bears used to live in the dense surrounding forest – thus the local motto, *En Tramezaïgues que cridé: Qu'aouen aoucitet l'ous!* (In Tramezaïgues one shouts: We have killed a bear!). But only after the bears became locally extinct did the Rioumajou valley become a *site classé* (protected area).

A narrow twelve-kilometre road snakes up the valley; about halfway along, the *Auberge de l'Escalette* overlooking a tiny reservoir, does lunch and supper. The pavement ends at "Km8", where the enormous, and enormously popular, Fredançon riverside picnic meadows under the firs seem to attract half of the tourists in the Vallée d'Aure on any summer weekend. The other half continue along the final 4km of very rough track to the renovated **Hospice de Rioumajou** (1560m; aka *Rieumajou*), a traditional halt on one branch of the Santiago pilgrimage trail, and before that a stage of a Roman trade route. It's open in summer for drinks and light snacks from 11am to 6pm, but owing to lack of electricity there's no supper or overnighting. Tenting down in the vast green meadows all around will go unremarked upon, however, and towards dusk you might see shepherds feeding rock salt to their charges.

Aquitaine, Biarritz

Cirque de Gavarnie, main fall

Lourdes

MARC S. DUBIN

MARC S. DUBIN

Pyrenean irises, Cirque de Gavarnie

The Respumoso reservoir

MARC S. DUBIN

Lescun and its cirque

Tour de France on the Col du Tourmalet

Añisclo Gorge, Ordesa National Park

Plaza Mayor, Aínsa

MARC S. DUBIN

Bayonne (Baïona)

MARC S. DUBIN

Boulder farmhouse, Espot

The environs of the hospice are a major crossroads of the **HRP** and its variants: you can continue south across the frontier via the **Port d'Ourdissetou/Puerto de Ordiceto** (2403m; 2hr 30min–3hr) for access to Bielsa in Spain; hike east over the **Port de Madère/Puerto d'a Madera** (2560m) to the refuge at Viadós, or go west via **Pic de Lia** (2778m) and continue along the frontier, eventually reaching the *Refuge de Barroude* (see below) within a day.

Into the Parc National des Pyrénées

The approach to the **Parc National des Pyrénées** from the Vallée d'Aure is a classic alpine walk enlivened at the end by the superb Cirque de Troumouse. Get off the valley bus 13km from Saint-Lary at the stop nearest the Templar chapel (see below), where the side road for Piau-Engaly goes off to the right. From here you take the footpath up the Neste ("River" in local dialect) de la Géla, crossing the boundary of the park almost immediately before joining the **HRP** just north of the *Refuge de Barroude* (2377m; 20 places; staffed July–Sept, part open all year; ①), perched magnificently in a namesake cirque, between two lakes.

It's only a half-day hike up from the chapel, but it's best to spend the night at the refuge, retracing your steps for half an hour next morning to the HRP. This continues northwest on a path around the base of Pic de la Géla (2851m), via the two passes of **Hourquette de Chermentas** (2439m) and the **Hourquette d'Héas** (2608m). Descending from the second *hourquette*, often snowed up early in the summer, you find yourself in the upper reaches of the **Cirque de Troumouse**; follow the Aguila stream steeply down into the Héas valley, reached some five and a half hours out of the *Refuge de Barroude*. From the valley floor the cirque reveals itself in all its glory; for a description see "The Gavarnie region", p.364.

A Templar chapel and the Túnel de Bielsa

Beyond several hamlets which comprise the *commune* of **ARAGNOUET**, just north of the D118, stands an intriguing twelfth-century Templar chapel (usually locked). Its almost windowless and plain exterior gives nothing away, though the jagged perpendicular edge of its tall *clocher-mur* suggests that there was once a large hospice here, at the base of the pedestrian route over 2429-metre Port de Bielsa.

Today most people **cross the frontier** by car, via the three-kilometre **Túnel de Bielsa** (daily: April–Sept 8am–10.30pm; Oct–March 8am–7pm). Such is climate and geography here that a five-minute trip through the tunnel might take you from a damp, misty day on the northern slopes into bright Spanish sunshine, with an attendant change in vegetation from deep green to bare, scorched brown.

The Réserve Naturelle de Néouvielle

France's first protected area, created in 1935, the **Réserve Naturelle de Néouvielle** forms a lake-rich "annexe" at the very eastern tip of the far larger Parc National des Pyrénées. It encloses some of Europe's highest forests of mountain pine, with substantial stands reaching 2400m and isolated specimens even growing at 2600m. This is due to a predominantly southern exposure, unusual for the French Pyrenees, which also encourages a riot of smaller flora. Unfortunately, *réserve* status did nothing for the region's isards, which were hunted out and had to be reintroduced in 1987. However, you should see **marmots** here, and there's a good chance of spotting **golden eagles**, and a slight chance of **lammergeier**.

Néouvielle – *Neoubieh* or *Neu Bielha* in local languages – means "old snow", perhaps a reference to the vestigial glaciers on certain peaks here. It feels similar to the Aigüestortes-Sant Maurici park in Catalunya: day-trippers and dams at the lower elevations, granite walls, tarns and trekkers' passes higher up. And similar rules apply: no camping except in designated areas, and a ban (July–August 9.30am–6pm) on private car passage along the single road into the *réserve*. Between these hours a **navette** operates from the control gate at Lac d'Orédon on the south side of the *réserve* up to the car park at Lac d'Aubert. During the day, car-bound travellers can get as far as Lac d'Orédon by means of a side road, the "**Route des Lacs**", which climbs 14km up from Fabian in the Aure valley, lowest of the Aragnouet hamlets, but as ever in the Pyrenees it's more rewarding to do most of your exploration on foot. **Trails** through the *réserve*, often the GR10 or a variant, are accordingly well signposted. However you arrive, the 1:50,000 IGN Carte de Randonées no. 4 "Bigorre" **map** is invaluable.

Lac d'Orédon loop hike

If you're not keen on full-pack traverse, the following popular three-hour loop, using a small portion of the GR10, gives a good sample of the *réserve*. Starting point is the Touring Club de France-owned *Chalet-Hôtel d'Orédon* (☎05.62.39.63.33; 1900m; 60 places; open & staffed June 15–Sept 15; dorm ①, rooms ③) just above the Orédon dam, with obliging management and excellent food, though sleeping facilities are basic. A bit of road-walking is unavoidable; head 1km up towards Lac d'Aubert, and then bear left onto the trail marked "**Les Laquettes**", three natural, photogenic tarns below the Aubert dam. Also just below Aubert is one of the few legal camping sites in Néouvielle. Next the route swings east past the car park and a defunct refuge overlooking the natural **Lac d'Aumar**. You then pick up the GR10 along a crest, affording fine views over the three southerly reservoirs of Cap de Long, Orédon and Oule, before descending back to the *Chalet-Hôtel d'Orédon* from the **Col d'Estoudou** (2260m) on an unnumbered trail.

Vielle-Aure to Artigues

Without your own transport, the best way to begin a traverse of the Néouvielle country is to take the **GR10** west from Vielle-Aure, climbing past and through the Saint-Lary pistes and then over the Col de Portet (2215m). After about six hours you reach the rustic, unstaffed *Cabane de Bastan*, where you have the choice of the variant **GR10C** towards Artigues or the main Barèges route.

For **Artigues**, hike north from the *cabane* and spend your first night at the lakeside *Refuge du Bastan* (☎05.62.98.48.80; 2250m; 20 places; staffed early June to late Sept, part always open; ①), one hour further, beyond a series of small lakes. Next day, you first climb the scree slopes up to the **Col de Bastanet** (2507m), then descend between several lakes for lunch at the *Refuge de Campana de Cloutou* (☎05.62.91.87.47; 2200m; 25 places; staffed June–Sept, part always open; ①), before tackling a three-hour afternoon stage to Artigues through the wide Garet valley, which culminates in some waterfalls. Minuscule Artigues, on the D918 some 10km northwest of the scenic Col du Tourmalet, has limited facilities (described on p.348).

Bastan to Barèges

For **Barèges**, follow the generally westward trail from the *Cabane de Bastan*, which skims along the eastern, then southern boundaries of the *réserve*, and spend the night at the *Chalet-Hôtel de l'Oule* (☎05.62.98.48.62; 1820m; 26 places; open & staffed mid-Dec to mid-April for Saint-Lary skiers, & early June to mid-Sept; dorm ①, rooms ②), 45 minutes away at the dammed south end of Lac de l'Oule, or at the *Chalet-Hôtel d'Orédon* (see above), just under two hours further. The only problem is that both are easily accessible by the road up from Fabian – the Lac de l'Oule via a dirt track from the **Artigousse** parking area, 6km along – and therefore highly popular. After a night at one of these refuges, follow the GR10 or the "Les Laquettes" trail (see above) into the heart of the *réserve* as far as the adjacent lakes of **Aumar** and **Aubert**, where there's a choice of two onward routes north.

For the first route, you climb along the GR10 to the **Col de Madamète** (2509m), where you leave *réserve* territory, drop to the basic Cabane d'Aygues-Cluses, and then follow the idyllic Aygues-Cluses valley to join the D918 road at the Pont de la Gaubie, seven hours after leaving Orédon.

Alternatively, you can use an equally distinct, signposted but unnumbered trail departing northwest from the Lac d'Aubert, which negotiates the **Horquette d'Aubert** (2498m) before descending past half a dozen medium-sized lakes – the largest, **Dets Coubous** – before rejoining the GR10 half an hour before the Pont de la Gaubie. The time course is the same as for the all-GR10 itinerary.

There's a small snack bar at the bridge catering to walkers; here, you're almost exactly halfway between Barèges and the Col du Tourmalet, about 5km from either. Barèges is discussed in detail on p.361–363.

A Néouvielle circuit

If you have a car to leave at a trailhead, it's recommended that you make a two- or three-day **circuit**, starting from the Lac d'Aubert or the Pont de la Gaubie. Walking instructions for the sectors between the southerly lakes and the D918 are identical to those previously described; what makes a loop possible is a minor trail heading east from the Cabane d'Aygues-Cluses, over the **Horquette Nère** (2465m), and then southeast to the *Refuge du Bastan* (see above) – it's seven to eight hours from Pont de la Gaubie to the refuge.

Traverse via Pic du Néouvielle

It's possible to make a more advanced traverse to Barèges via the summit of **Pic du Néouvielle** (3091m), at the western limit of the *réserve naturelle*. Although the ascent of the peak requires no technical climbing skills, it's long and tough, with crampons and ice-axe mandatory. Allowing for stops, plan on twelve hours to the first attended refuge on the far side, from where Barèges is another three hours further on track.

Follow the clearly marked path from the car park at Lac d'Aubert westwards towards the summit, then swing north to cross the bottom of the ridge known as the Crête de Barris d'Aubert. Once over, the path peters out; ascend west again, keeping the ridge to the left, then gradually bear away northeast towards the **Brèche de Chausenque** (2790m). Before you get to the *brèche*, you swing back southwards into a wide, snow-filled valley, making your way up among huge boulders until a simple chimney takes you onto the final ridge, from which the **summit** is a short walk south (4hr from Lac d'Aubert).

To continue to Barèges, retrace your steps towards the *brèche*, climb through it this time and descend the steep slope on the other side west to the tiny **Lacs Verts**. Swing north along the shelf and gradually descend towards **Lac det Mail**, one of a succession of other lakes below to the left. Pass around its northeast shore then follow the stream down towards **Lac de la Glère** where you reach the *Refuge de la Glère* (☎05.62.92.69.47, fax 05.62.92.65.17, *contact@gite.oasis.com*; 2140m; 70 places; open & staffed weekends & hols March–early June, daily early June–Sept; ①) in about six hours from the summit. From the refuge, Barèges is 10km along a track to the north; the hut warden, Philippe Trey, co-runs the *Gîte L'Oasis* in Barèges (see p.362) and can probably arrange transport down to spare you track-walking. He and his British wife Andrea will also be happy to reserve places in the other five staffed refuges in the area if contacted in advance.

Turon de Néouvielle

In 1787 the astronomer Vidal and the chemist Reboul became the first men to reach the summit of a Pyrenean three-thousander, when they stood on the top of **Turon de Néouvielle** (3035m). Technically it was not a great achievement – it's one of the easiest high peaks in the Pyrenees – but this and the ascent of Pic du Midi d'Ossau in the same year were instrumental in awakening scientific and recreational interest in these mountains.

342/AROUND THE NATIONAL PARKS

For the ascent of Turon (actually just inside the PNP) from *Refuge de la Glère*, take the path south towards the unstaffed *Refuge Packe* and after 1km bear southeast to climb to **Lac de l'Oueil Nègre**. Just beyond, you have a choice. If you leave **Lac det Mail** to your right, you can head south between **Lacs Vert** and **Bleu** and climb the remnants of the **Glacier de Maniportet** to the summit. If you leave Mail to your left, you'll pass **Lacs de l'Estelat** and approach the **Col de Coume Estrète**; the IGN 1:25,000 map no. 275 marks the final approach through the *col*, but you can just as easily leave the *col* to your right and climb to the summit via Lac Glacé. After a heavy winter, crampons, gaiters and ice-axe will be required for the final summit approach. These routes are all of a similar standard and take about ten hours there and back, including stops.

The Baronnies

One of the emptiest areas of the Pyrenees, the **Baronnies** lie between the lower valleys of the Adour and Aure, bounded to the north by the D938 Capvern–Bagnères-de-Bigorre road, and to the south by the D918 linking Sainte-Marie-de-Campan with Arreau. This desertion is owed to a landscape too undulating for modern agriculture, but too low for skiing and too rounded for climbing. For the casual walker and naturalist, however, the Baronnies are perfect: dense forests of beech and pine, lush, little-used pastures and a range of wildlife from desmans to griffon vultures. Monumental interest is lent by the château at Mauvezin and the abbey of Escaladieu, within a few kilometres of each other on the D938.

Public transport into the region is inevitably sparse. From the heart of the Baronnies, it's around 15km to the train station at Capvern, with the stations at Lannemezan and Bagnères-de-Bigorre slightly further. The Minibus des Baronnies company operates out of Lannemezan on Wednesdays and out of Bagnères on Saturdays, while André Pene runs a taxi service (☎05.62.39.01.14) from Esparros, the village at the centre of the region.

Otherwise you'll have to walk, hitch or drive yourself. You can get into the Baronnies from the south by travelling the 13km along the D918 from Arreau to the **Col d'Aspin** (1489m) and then hiking north from the *col* itself, but the route **from the east** is more straightforward. Take a bus from Lannemezan to just north of Hèches in the Aure valley (13km); from the bus stop, stroll 4km uphill along the D26 to the **Col de Coupe** (720m), from where the view west into the Baronnies is all-encompassing: emerald pasture, forest and rolling hills. You can continue on the road to Esparros but it's better to cut off at the pass along the clear and direct horse trail, which takes half an hour.

Esparros and around

ESPARROS was the seat of an ancient *baronnie* of four parishes – hence the name of the region. Like all the villages of the Baronnies, its population has fallen dramatically since the nineteenth century: 844 inhabitants in 1851, under two hundred today. Norbert Casteret discovered the local **Gouffre d'Esparros** in 1938, describing it as a "vast cavern of indescribable magnificence", thanks to walls gleaming with a "hoar-frost" of white aragonite flowers. You can view these crystal formations, as well as a bat colony, on one-hour guided visits (daily school hols, half-hourly departures 10–11.30am & 1.30–5.30pm; otherwise weekends 9.30am–12.30pm & 1.30pm–5.30/6pm; 35F/€5.40; reserve on ☎05.62.39.11.80).

The Baronnies has two official information points: an **Office du Tourisme** in Laborde (☎05.62.39.03.42), 3km west of Esparros, and **La Maison des Baronnies** at Sarlabous, 8km north (summer 9am–noon & 2–5.30pm; ☎05.62.39.05.14).

Most central place to **stay** is *Gîte d'Étape Jean Colomes* at Esparros (☎05.62.39.05.96; open all year; ③), but if you're on your own and would prefer some company, you may find the excellent *Moulin des Baronnies* at Sarlabous (☎ & fax 05.62.39.05.14; all year; ③), also with tenting space, more sociable. There are also a few simple **inns** hereabouts, specializing in regional food: tiny *Le Relais d'Esparros* (☎05.62.39.02.43; closed Wed except July & Aug; ②) at Esparros; *La Ferme de Mamette* (☎05.62.39.18.59; open all year; ④) at Laborde; and the magnificently landscaped *Le Petit Château* (☎05.62.40.90.16, fax 05.62.40.90.18; all year), also at Laborde, with accommodation ranging from a teepee village (①) to comfortable rooms (⑤). Local **campsites** are *Le Randonneur* at Esparros (☎05.62.39.19.34; mid-June to mid-Sept), well laid-out and with a pool, and *Camping à la Ferme* (☎05.62.39.05.26) at Bulan, just over 7km northwest along the D77 from Esparros. If you're in a group and plan to stay for a week or so, the Baronnies has plenty of cottages to rent that can be very good value; ask for a list at **La Maison des Baronnies** in Sarlabous.

Walking: the Tour des Baronnies

Although walking in the Baronnies is not technically difficult, it can present tricky situations. Rainfall is high and mists often dense (some of the valley bottoms are essentially temperate rainforest), and there are vistas devoid of any sign of human habitation, except for the occasional herd of livestock tended by a solitary shepherd and his mangy dog. So you'll need a compass and map, as well as rain gear and possibly waterproof boots.

The **Tour des Baronnies**, marked on the *Carte de Randonnées* 1:50,000 "Luchon" and "Bigorre" maps, is a lopsided figure-of-eight itinerary with its centre at ASQUE, 7km west of Laborde: it takes about four days, generally along tracks. The longer loop leaves Asque – where there's a large, self-catering *gîte d'étape* (☎05.62.39.18.21; open all year; ①) – towards the flat-topped mountain of Casque de Lhéris, then sweeps around towards Uzer, Castillon and Sarlabous; the shorter arc links Asque with Espèche, Esparros and the **Col de Couradabat**. From the *col* it is possible to walk out southwards towards **Col d'Aspin**, via **Signal de Bassia** (1921m) and the **Col de Beyrède**, but this route is unmarked, requiring some navigational skills.

Mauvezin and Escaladieu

Two of the great historical sites of this region, the château of Mauvezin and the abbey of Escaladieu, are situated conveniently close enough to each other to be seen in a single visit. If you're reliant on public transport you'll have to take the train to Capvern (5 daily between Lannemezan and Pau), from where it's a five-kilometre walk to Mauvezin, and thence a further three-kilometre walk to the abbey.

Mauvezin

The **Château** (May–Oct 15 daily 10am–7pm; Oct 15–April daily 1.30–5.30pm; 25F/€3.80) stands on the edge of **MAUVEZIN**, atop a 567-metre-high hill that was first fortified by the Romans. Between the thirteenth and fifteenth centuries it changed hands several times in the wake of protracted hostilities between the English and the French, finally passing after 1373 to Gaston Fébus (see box on p.239).

Built of grey stone, and with a crenellated tower, the square castle is particularly appealing from the outside. Inside, you're left to wander as you please, with the aid of an informative brochure. The now-grassy courtyard was once lined with buildings, the roofs of which funnelled rainwater into the giant cistern, built as an emergency reserve; only once was it drunk dry – during the siege of 1373. On the inside of the cistern it's possible to read the graffito *Dieu seul sera adoré et l'Antéchrist de Rome abisme* ("God alone will be adored and the Antichrist in Rome cast into the abyss"), carved by an imprisoned Huguenot in the sixteenth century.

The current tenant, since 1907, is the Escòla Gaston Fébus, a cultural conservation group that promotes Gascon and Occitan poetry, literature and art, including formal, medieval-themed events in August. The fully restored tower has been turned into a museum, mostly dedicated to the works of the Société Félibrée, a literary organization pledged to revive and preserve the ancient Provençal language. However, the museum is also crammed with various intriguing exhibits: sculptures, paintings, photos and bits of armour. The village itself can offer **snacks** only at the *Auberge du Château*.

The Abbaye de l'Escaladieu

Three kilometres southwest and downhill from Mauvezin in the valley bottom, towards Bagnères-de-Bigorre, you'll find the **Abbaye de l'Escaladieu** (May–Sept daily 10am–1pm & 2–7pm; rest of year daily except Tues 10am–noon & 2–7pm; free), the first Cistercian monastery in the southwest of France. Founded in the middle of the twelfth century, Escaladieu flourished for just a couple of centuries, the monks earning a living by cultivating the Baronnies, a fertile and profitable region before mechanization favoured flat fields. The monastery was burned and plundered by Protestant forces during the Wars of Religion, and early conservationists began restoring the buildings in the seventeenth and eighteenth centuries.

Escaladieu was badly mismanaged and neglected by a private foundation between 1986 and 1993; following a court case and a token pay-out to the previous owner, the *départemental* authorities assumed control of the place in 1997 – plus a bill of 30 million francs for completing its restoration. Meanwhile, the place hosts cinema, seminars, theatre and most accessibly, **concerts**: performances are held sporadically (usually Sun 5pm) from June to September, generally of Baroque music, for which the abbey makes a wonderful setting.

The showpiece of the ongoing restoration is the twelfth-to-thirteenth-century vaulted **chapter house**, opening onto a leafy inner courtyard through the sparse remnants of a cloister, all but two columns of which was shipped to California during the nineteenth century. The rest, by contrast, is typically Cistercian in its plainness, the long, white eastern facade devoid of decoration, and the enormous, echoing abbey church as bare as possible.

There's an unstarred but perfectly tolerable **hotel-restaurant** in **ESCALADIEU** village, the *Auberge de l'Arros* (☎05.62.39.05.05; open all year; ②), which could make a more appealing overnight than anything in Bagnères-de-Bigorre.

Bagnères-de-Bigorre

The revival of thermal resorts was something of a 1980s French fad: Luz-Saint-Sauveur did it, Ax-les-Thermes managed it, and **BAGNÈRES-DE-BIGORRE**, 21km southeast of Tarbes along the D935 in the Adour valley, invested tens of millions of francs in its spa (open March–Nov). Descended from the Roman settlement of Vicus Aquensis, Bagnères reached its apogee with the opening of the *Grands Thermes* in 1823, becoming the "in" place for the likes of George Sand, Giaoacchino Rossini and Gustave Flaubert.

From the 1830s, Bagnères' British community was second in size only to Pau's, many of them having stayed on after the Peninsular War. So foreign-dominated was Pyrenean exploration at this time that of the four founders of the Société Ramond – the mountaineering club established here in 1864 and predating even the Club Alpin Français – two were British: the barrister-explorer Charles Packe and the photographer-inventor Maxwell Lyte. The third was Henry Russell, whose father was Irish, and only Emilien

Frossard was entirely French. The society still publishes a regular bulletin and meets at the town library.

The Town

Beside the long grey *thermes* building stands the ornate **Musée Salies** (May–Nov Tues–Sun 3–6pm except July–Aug daily 3–7pm; 25F/€3.80). An elegant collection, mostly landscapes, hangs on its pink walls, but there are some more surprising artists represented, including John Jongkind, a Dutch precursor of Impressionism, and Francis Picabia, a major figure of the Dada movement. Free exhibitions are often held in the downstairs gallery (same hours). The inevitable spa **casino**, next to the museum, contains what must be one of the world's most lavish cinemas, all columns and chandeliers.

The ticket for the Musée Salies also covers the **Musée du Vieux Moulin**, about ten minutes' walk away across the Adour in rue Hount-Blanque, just over rue Général de Gaulle (Tues–Fri 10am–noon & 3–6pm); it's a typical folk museum, with exhibits of local furniture, agricultural tools and *Bigourdan* crafts, but attractively laid out and well explained.

The main tourist attraction of the area is the **Grottes de Médous** (daily: April–June & Sept–Oct 15 8.30–11.30am & 2–5.30pm; July–Aug 9am–noon & 2–6pm; 34F/€5.20; ☎05.62.91.78.46 for off-season tours), 2km south of the centre on the main road. The twelve-people-minimum-per-tour rule can mean hanging about on a slow day, but it's worth waiting to see the wall known as the *Salle d'Orchidée* (Orchid House), rated by Norbert Casteret as one of the great limestone formations of the Pyrenees. The caves were only discovered in 1948, and thus escaped the vandalism suffered by others during the early part of the century.

Practicalities

The heart of the town lies a five-minute walk south along rue de la République from the disused train station on av de Belgique where only SNCF **buses** from Tarbes stop – though they continue into the centre for a final halt by the fifteenth-century church of Saint-Vincent, within sight of the place Lafayette. Other buses up the Vallée de Campan as far as Payolle (see below) depart from next to the **tourist office** at 3 allée Tournefort (July & Aug Mon–Sat 9am–12.30pm & 2–7pm, Sun 9am–noon & 2–6pm; April–June, Sept & Oct Mon–Sat 8.30–11.30am & 2–5.30pm; ☎05.62.95.50.71, *www.hautebigorre.com*), south of the *place*. From the tourist office it's a short walk northwest to the leafy **allée des Coustous**, the main café street and also home to the post office, west of which is pedestrianized **place de Strasbourg** and the covered market occupying **place Ramond**.

Hotels facing the spa tend to be overpriced and musty, catering for an elderly, rather sedentary clientele. Fans of time warps shouldn't miss *Les Petites Vosges* at 17 bd Carnot near the casino (☎05.62.95.28.31; ②), unchanged since World War II but with showers in the pricier rooms. Nearby, just northwest, stands the inexpensive *Family Pension* at 4 rue Général Menvielle (☎05.62.91.92.22; March–Oct; ②). Otherwise, the quietest area for accommodation lies just north of the *halles* on rue de l'Horloge, named after the clock in the Tour du Jacobins, the last bit of a convent destroyed during the Revolution. Here you'll find the old-fashioned *Hôtel l'Horloge* (☎05.62.91.00.20; March–Nov; ②–③) at no. 3-bis and the slightly more comfortable *Hôtel de Nice* (☎05.62.95.04.65; May–Oct; ②) at no. 17 – plus a **laundry** at no. 7. Noisier, but clean and comfortable, is the two-star *Hotel de la Paix* at 9 rue de la République (☎05.62.95.20.60, fax 05.62.91.09.88; closed early Dec–early Jan; ③–⑥), with a decent attached restaurant. Otherwise, **eateries** – in hotels or out – aren't Bagnères' strong point; among the few independent ones is *Le Bigourdan* (closed Mon) at 14 rue Victor-Hugo, corner rue de l'Horloge, with a great variety of *menus* (from 55F/€40, available lunch only). Right next door at no. 12, the *Crêperie de l'Horloge* also does a range of *plats du jour* for under 50F/€7.60, plus of course crêpes to eat in or take away. At the south end of town, *Au Canard Gourmand* at the corner of rue des Pyrénées and rue Emilien Frossard is also a good traditional-format eatery.

Bagnères has a **music festival** every year, normally from mid-August to mid-September, but a more original musical tradition is the male choir, Chanteurs Montagnards, founded in the 1840s and still performing at most civic functions.

With four to six daily SNCF **buses** from Tarbes, and two to three private ones from Lourdes, Bagnères is easy to get to, but it's harder to move on from – only two buses daily (Transportes Cariane) go south past the Grottes de Médous to Sainte-Marie-de-Campan (see p.348). From July to September this service covers the extra 15km southeast along the D918 to Lac de Payolle (see below); during summer buses go southwest on the D918 only as far as Gripp hamlet, though in winter this line extends all the way to La Mongie.

Upstream from Bagnères

South of Bagnères-de-Bigorre, the valley sides of the Haute-Adour rise steeply into the Baronnies and the **Casque du Lhéris** on the northeast, and towards **Pic du Midi de Bigorre** to the southwest, with the Néouvielle Massif rising ahead to the south. Subsidies, high rainfall and fertile soil keep the thatched farmhouses in business, three crops a year being common, much as they were in the eighteenth century when Tarbes-born politician Bertrand Barère described Haute-Adour as: "The object of admiration by all French people . . . the eye being drawn towards the majestic Pic du Midi which forms the centrepiece of a sublime tableau." Another writer of the time noted "the excellence of its butter and the beauty of its marble".

Away from the main Aure valley and its extension, the **Vallée de Campan**, two tributaries can be explored: the lush **Vallée de Lesponne**, with the much-visited Lac Bleu at its head; and the **Vallée de Gripp**, at the top of which is La Mongie, one of the best Pyrenean ski resorts, and the strategically perched observatory on **Pic du Midi de Bigorre**.

The Vallée de Lesponne

The countryside just north of Barèges, at the head of the **Vallée de Lesponne**, is well worth a day or two. You can take a bus as far as Beaudéan, 5km along the D935, but after that you're dependent on your own resources for the 10km along the D29 side road to its end at **CHIROULET**. This tiny hamlet boasts two decent **hôtel-restaurants**: *L'Isard* (☎05.62.91.72.56; closed Dec–Jan; ③) featuring local dishes and *menus* from 75F/€11.50, and *La Vieille Auberge* (☎05.62.91.71.70; ③). If both are full (just 7 rooms between them), a plush alternative is *Domaine de Ramonjuan* (☎05.62.91.75.75, fax 05.62.91.74.54, *www.perso.infonie.fr/ramonjuan*; ④–⑤), 7km down-valley at Lesponne hamlet, with such luxuries as a gym, sauna and Jacuzzi.

From Chiroulet a popular path rises steeply for nearly three hours to **Lac Bleu** (1950m), set in a peak-ringed cirque. The Col du Tourmalet (see p.350) can be reached by climbing around the eastern side of the 120-metre-deep lake – the path in places cut into the rock – and then heading due east to the **Col d'Aoube** (2389m), from where a faint path continues down to the D918 a short distance from Tourmalet, four hours beyond Lac Bleu.

The Vallée de Campan

Upstream from Beaudéan, the Adour is known locally as the **Vallée de Campan**, whose east flank edges into the Baronnies. Below woods of spruce, pine and beech, the gentle valley's meadows are speckled with farms arrayed in south-facing ranks. The

THE CAGOTS

Numerous towns in the western half of the Pyrenees – Saint-Savin, Luz-Saint-Sauveur, Cauterets and Saint-Jean-Pied-de-Port to name just four – once had sizeable populations of a mysterious people known as **Cagots**, of whom little is known for certain other than that they were persecuted. First mentioned in thirteenth-century manuscripts, Cagots were forbidden to live in the centre of towns, to kiss the Cross, to walk barefoot, to have sexual relations outside the Cagot community or to enter a mill (in case they contaminated the grain). They had to wear a distinguishing symbol on their clothes, variously described as a crow's or a duck's foot, and live in a separate ghetto at the edge of villages. Cagots had their own baptismal fonts – sometimes even their own churches – and were buried in separate graveyards.

There were compensations. Cagots were exempt from feudal duties and taxes, were subject only to ecclesiastical courts and were not expected to bear arms, except for work. Prohibited also from owning land, many therefore became skilled woodworkers in particular, and Gaston Fébus apparently insisted on Cagot carpenters for his fortress at Montaner. But Cagots were excluded from all normal social life, and despite appeals to the pope and the secular authorities, discrimination continued for centuries. The Cagots themselves began agitating for equal rights as early as 1479, but social consciousness lagged behind legal rulings in their favour. It was not until 1789 and the Revolution that their second-class status was officially, and definitely, ended. The measures taken against them sound like those taken against lepers, and indeed one of the many alternative names for the Cagots – *crestianas* – is almost certainly derived from *cristianaria*, the places reserved for "white" lepers – that is, those considered infected but not contagious, and whom modern·medicine would probably recognize as afflicted by some minor skin disease.

So the Cagots may have been lepers or the descendants of lepers, but it also seems plausible that they were racially distinct. Some linguists derive the word Cagot from *can goth* or "dog of the Visigoths", implying a descent from the Visigoths who fled into this area after their defeat by Clovis in 507. Furthermore, the architecture of many Basque country churches – with their low "Cagot windows" through which services could be watched, and proportionally low "Cagot doors" – suggests to some commentators that Cagots were a race of less-than-average stature. It's not even certain that these features had anything to do with the Cagots. The mystery will probably never be solved; the subject was already steeped in confusion by the fourteenth century, when in contemporaneous accounts Cagots were variously described as tall, fair and blue-eyed, or short, dark and Moorish-looking.

individual architecture is unique: house and barn are built as a unit, with the balconied living quarters always to the right as you face the sun. The valley is also known for the local craft tradition of **mounaques** or giant rag dolls; of both genders and variously costumed, these are often propped up on pavements, windowsills or even house gables for summer-long display.

It's indicative of the tenuous nature of tolerance early in the Age of the Enlightenment that when the church of **Saint-Jean-Baptiste** at **CAMPAN** (6km from Bagnères, 1km upstream from the Lesponne turning) was rebuilt after a fire in 1694, a separate Cagot door was inserted at the west end; the Cagot ghetto here was on the right bank of the Adour, in the part known as the *Quartier Charpentier* after their habitual trade. The church's personality is now defined by the ornate white-and-gilt *retable* by the local brothers, the Ferrérers of Asté; the fifteenth-century wooden image of Christ, originally at L'Escaladieu, is a cruder but more moving statement of faith. The village itself, with its slate-roofed houses, is attractive; for **accommodation**, the *Beauséjour* (☎05.62.91.75.30; ③), opposite the colonnaded, sixteenth-century market hall, represents fair value. There's also the *Camping de Layris*, on the northwest side of town, and the main **Tourisme** for the valley (Mon–Sat 9am–noon & 2.30–6/7pm, also Sun 9am–noon peak season; ☎05.62.91.70.36).

At **SAINTE-MARIE-DE-CAMPAN**, another 6km south, there's more **accommodation** at either the *Gîte L'Ardoisière* (☎05.62.91.88.88; closed Nov; dorm ①, rooms ③), with advantageous half-board rates, or the more conventional *Hotel Les Deux Cols* (☎05.62.91.85.60, fax 05.62.91.85.31; closed Oct 15–Dec 15; ②–③), with *menus* at 63–130F/€9.60–19.80. Both cater to cyclists, and are on the main through road (as is the entire town), which as it divides is designated the D918 in either direction.

To the right, this climbs southwest to La Mongie (see below), via Gripp and Artigues. The southeasterly (leftward) fork attains the **Col d'Aspin** – where half-tame horses and cows gambol, causing traffic jams – before dropping into the Vallée d'Aure at Arreau. Just the Campan side of this pass, 25km shy of Arreau, the environs of **Lac de Payolle** offer a respectable 50km of marked cross-country skiing pistes between 1100 and 1450m; during summer, picnickers throng the lakeshore.

Up the Vallée de Gripp: La Mongie, Tourmalet and Pic du Midi

The D918 road to La Mongie from Sainte-Marie-de-Campan rises steadily along the **Gripp valley** to **ARTIGUES**, where there's a reasonable hotel – the *Relais d'Arizes*

THE TOUR DE FRANCE

Every year in July the **Tour de France** passes through the Pyrenees, on its way either to or from the Alps, and most years the riders tackle the savage haul up to the Col du Tourmalet. First incorporated into the route in 1910, it has now been included in almost fifty contests, forming a particularly gruelling (and often wet and freezing) episode in what is invariably one of the toughest days of the three-week race. In 1988, for example, the riders had to cycle through Tourmalet in the course of a 180-kilometre stage that had already climbed the Col de Peyresourde and Col d'Aspin; by 2000 the Pyrenean stage exceeded 200km, and included the the twin *cols* of Aubisque and Soulor.

The Tour brings with it an enormous entourage of back-up teams, advertising people, television crews and journalists, who occupy every hotel room in the vicinity of each day's finishing line. **Accommodation** is not the only problem – actually **seeing the riders** at the crucial points can be tricky, as the race attracts vast crowds even on the mountain-tops. If you want to see the action at any of the major passes, take up your position at least three hours before the bikes are due.

Although a couple of hundred riders start each Tour de France, only a dozen or so have the all-round ability needed to win. In the early stages these star riders generally take it easy, checking out the form of chief rivals and letting themselves be nursed along by their teammates – the so-called *domestiques*. When they reach the mountains, however, the race changes completely. Any rider with pretensions to be wearing the leader's yellow jersey when the Tour finally swings into Paris has to finish each mountain stage near the front, and that requires relentless effort – even a top-class rider can lose fifteen minutes on a bad day in the Pyrenees, and this is a race where the overall winning margin has sometimes been measured in seconds. So by the time the Tour moves out of the Pyrenees the leader board will have resolved itself into a chart of the race favourites.

Within the main race, there's another contest going on in the Pyrenees (and the Alps) – the one for the title "**King of the Mountains**", awarded to the rider who records the best results in the mountain stages. Winning this competition – whose leader wears a white shirt with red polka dots – secures a reputation only marginally less illustrious than the overall winner's. Any rider who takes the polka-dot shirt more than once is assured of quasi-mythical status – the Spanish rider Federico Bahamontes, who won it six times in the 1950s and 1960s, earned himself the reverential nickname "The Eagle of Toledo" for his high-altitude prowess, and Luxembourg's Charly Gaul, winner in 1955 and 1956, became known as "The Angel of the Mountains". The favourites for the yellow jersey of course feature strongly in the "King of the

(☎05.62.91.90.41; ③) – a campsite and not much else. Nevertheless it's a good start- or end-point for hiking in the Réserve Naturelle de Néouvielle (see p.339) and there are short walks to the nearby Cascades de l'Arises and Cascade du Garet.

La Mongie

The ski centre of **LA MONGIE**, 6km above Artigues – together with Barèges on the opposite side of the Col du Tourmalet – constitutes the largest skiing area in the Pyrenees, with 33 pistes totalling 60km on the La Mongie side alone. Once you're away from the unsightly high-rise resort it's beautiful, with a combination of open bowls, runs through trees and some simple but exciting off-piste itineraries. The main development in the middle of the lower pistes – stands at 1800m, with a top point of 2500m. There's only one black run, but it's an eminently suitable place for beginners to intermediates. The blue run from the top lift, the Télésiège de Quatre Termes, to 1800m descends a respectable 3km, while the easy and intermediate runs dropping east from the Espode Béarnais chairlifts are even longer. Of the nine licensed accommodations here, *Chalet La Munia* is the smallest and most characterful (☎ & fax 05.62.91.91.43; open Dec–April & June–Oct; ⑥ HB winter).

Mountains" tussle, but most teams also have a specialist climber who comes to the fore in this part of the race.

A good illustration of this was the reticent Spaniard **Miguel Indurain** ("The Colossus of Roads" or "The Sphinx"), the only rider to have won five consecutive Tours: 1991–95. Yet his mountain stages didn't always show him at his best, and from 1994 to 1997 Frenchman **Richard Virenque** rode off with the "King of the Mountains" jersey. However, scoring is cumulative over the numerous stages, including the important flatlands time-trials, which Indurain usually dominated. After finishing a disappointing eleventh in the 1996 Tour, Indurain announced his retirement in January 1997; it was the end of an era, with no one cyclist then looking set to dominate competition.

Except for Virenque, individual French riders have been almost totally eclipsed, while entrants from countries as diverse as Colombia, Poland and Uzbekistan have captured stages since 1990. **Bjarne Riis** (Denmark) secured the yellow jersey in 1996, while his team-mate **Jan Ullrich** (Germany) powered his way to the title in 1997.

Tainted by lurid **drug scandals**, the "Tour de Farce" (as some newspapers dubbed it) of **1998** cast a long shadow over the sport. France's Festina Watches team, with Virenque as captain, was disqualified when a huge stock of prohibited doping substances was found in their trainer's car. The police and courts were quickly involved, with arrests and prosecutions of various team managers and trainers. After initial protestations of innocence, and allegations that Festina was being made a scapegoat, scores of riders admitted using drugs since at least the 1980s. Eventually seven of the 21 teams were banned, and by the end of the Tour hardly anyone noticed that **Marco Patani** had triumphed, the first Italian victor in 33 years. Besides the potential skewing of results, doctors warned that the most popular doping materials were highly dangerous, implicated in blood clots, heart disease and strokes among racers.

At this nadir of the race's fortunes, the Tour needed a wholesome, against-the-odds saga to restore its image. American **Lance Armstrong**, favoured to do well in both the 1996 Tour and the Atlanta Olympics, had bombed mysteriously in both. A few weeks later, he began coughing up blood and was diagnosed with a cancer that had spread from his testicles to his lungs. Few expected him to live, much less to ever cycle again. But 1999 saw him power through the mountain stages en route to overall victory. In 2000 he repeated this feat, defying gravity in a miserably cold, sodden Pyrenean stage to overtake Pantani, Ullrich, Virenque and the Spaniard Escartín, finishing just a few seconds behind Javier Otxoa, on his way to a second yellow jersey. Thanks to his all-round ability, back-to-back victories and clean-cut character, commentators are now finally able to speculate about a possible successor to Indurain, and the public's faith in the romance of the Tour de France is to some extent restored.

The Col du Tourmalet and the Pic du Midi de Bigorre

The **Col du Tourmalet** (2115m), 4km beyond La Mongie, ranks as the highest drive-able pass in the French Pyrenees, often playing a tormenting role in the Tour de France and almost always closed between late October and the end of April. The name literally means "the bad detour", a title perhaps bestowed by the carriers of the sedan chairs that used to taxi the wealthy between the spas of Bagnères and Barèges by this long, cold road. Wheeled transport first used the *col* in 1788, when the road along the Luz valley was blocked by floods; from the La Mongie side of the pass you can still see the faint trace of the old route. The perennially windy pass itself is dominated by an anatomically correct, lumpy statue of a cyclist, "**Le Géant du Tourmalet**", which commemorates the Tour de France's first passage here in 1910. Opposite stands a stone-clad restaurant which is by far the best of several high-altitude eateries for skiers.

From the *col*, a **toll road** (paved and re-opened in 2001) leads up towards the summit of **Pic du Midi de Bigorre**, stopping at 2720m, a fifteen-minute walk short of the observatory just below the summit (2872m). Bristling with antennae and radio masts, it's a fairly unsightly place, but has the virtue of being an easily accessible high-altitude lookout. On foot it's about two hours from Tourmalet to the top, from where you can see west as far as Balaïtous, south into the Néouvielle country and east as far as Andorra.

Opened in 1880, the **observatory** has been continuously staffed since, even when cut off for months at a time by snow, with all provisions and equipment carted up on the back of man or mule for the first 66 years. Despite the observatory's successful history of lunar observation and its current studies of Mars, Saturn and Jupiter, the future of the establishment hangs in the balance. Although major television and radio antennae have been built here, and a contract to monitor pollution and the ozone layer was awarded late in the 1980s, serious French investment has been switched to even larger installations in Hawaii, Chile and Tenerife.

For years the observatory's resident scientists and technicians resisted plans to develop it as a tourist attraction, maintaining that casual visitors would cramp their style. But by the late 1990s they had bowed to the inevitable, and 2000 saw the opening of a mediocre astronomical museum and restaurant in the grounds. This is currently accessible only by means of a **téléphérique** (daily 9.30am–4.30pm June–Sept only, 130F/€22.90 includes admission to astronomical museum; *www.picdumidi.com*) from La Mongie.

Tarbes

If you're heading towards the Central Pyrenees from the northeast you'll almost certainly pass through **TARBES**, capital of medieval Bigorre and the contemporary, far larger *département* of Hautes-Pyrénées. A medium-sized, suburban sort of place, it will mainly appeal if you have an interest in things military. Destroyed by the Normans, then ruined by the protagonists from both sides in the Wars of Religion, Tarbes retains little evidence of its past. An overall view of the city, best obtained from the Musée Massey tower, gives a general impression of functional and graceless white apartment and office blocks. More inspiring and exceptional architectural efforts include the futuristic National Music School and the Parvis Cultural Centre. Arms manufacture has long been Tarbes' primary industry, but it now employs just eight hundred people compared to sixteen thousand at the end of World War I, with most of the remaining jobs threatened by automation.

The Town

The train station, north of the centre on av Maréchal-Joffre, sits within a few minutes' walk of Tarbes' three main attractions. Off rue Massey sprawls the tranquil **Jardin**

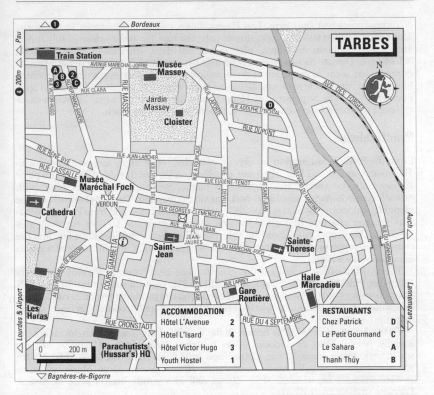

Massey (daily dawn to dusk; free), designed during the nineteenth century by Tarbes-born Placide Massey, who also worked on the gardens at Versailles. This carefully land-scaped botanical collection has its specimens – some local, some as exotic as California sequoias – informatively labelled and discussed in French. Architectural interest is sup-plied by the partially reconstructed Gothic cloister from the abbey of Saint-Sever-de-Rustan, with vivid, if slightly eroded column capitals: swans attacking a bear, and a sword-brandishing angel expelling Adam and Eve from Eden.

The **Musée Massey**, housed in a rather eclectic building in the middle of the *jardin*, will be closed until 2002 while its section on the military hardware and extravagant uniforms of the Hussars regiment, from its fifteenth-century Hungarian origins to today's parachutists, based in Tarbes, is rehoused in a new purpose-built museum in the Foix-Lescun quarter. When the older gallery reopens, it should more generously highlight its other two themes: fine arts and archeology. The arts section groups a miscellany of pleasant pieces spanning the fifteenth to nineteenth centuries, the most attention-grabbing being a Dutch-school *Wild Boar Hunt*. Archeological exhibits include a bronze death mask of unknown date and a Roman votive altar, discovered during excavations at the train station.

Some 300m southwest of the Jardin Massey, at 2 rue de la Victoire, is the **birthplace of Maréchal Foch** (guided tours Mon & Thurs–Sat: May–Sept 9am–noon & 2–6.30pm; Oct–April 9am–noon & 2–5pm; 15F/€2.30), supreme Allied commander on the west-ern front during World War I. A traditional pitched-roof *Bigourdan* town house, it con-tains two floors of photos, medals and other memorabilia from the field marshal's life – including, a little morbidly, the armchair in which he died.

Tarbes' renowned stud farm, **Les Haras**, lies a couple more blocks south on rue Mouhourat (guided visits by appointment only, last tour 1hr before closing; July & Aug Mon–Fri 10am–noon & 2–5pm, plus occasional days otherwise; ☎05.62.56.30.80; 30F/€4.60). Despite its relatively central location, the farm is set in acres of beautiful grounds that seem an extension of the botanical gardens. The immaculately groomed horses have impeccable manners, displayed at exercise drill, usually held at about 3pm. Founded in 1806 by Napoleon, Les Haras is best known for its *cheval Tarbais*, a cavalry breed produced by crossing English, Basque and Arabian stock.

Practicalities

From the SNCF **train station** on avenue Maréchal-Joffre there are connections with Toulouse, Lourdes and Pau. The **gare routière**, on the south side of Tarbes on place au Bois, off rue Larrey, has services to Bagnères-de-Bigorre, Lannemezan (with onward connections to Saint-Lary) and Pau via Soumoulou. **Tarbes-Ossun-Lourdes airport**, 9km southwest of town, has daily, scheduled flights to and from Paris, plus various summer charters (though ski-season services from the UK are currently suspended). The airport bus serves the scheduled flights only, but getting a taxi into the centre is no problem, and the airport has its own train station, with occasional services into the town's station.

The **tourist office** is just off the central place de Verdun at 3 cours Gambetta (Mon–Sat 9am–12.30pm & 2–7pm; ☎05.62.51.30.31). Co-publisher of the helpful IGN 1:50,000 walkers' maps, Randonnées Pyrénéenes has its headquarters at 29 rue Marcel-Lamarque (☎05.62.93.57.57), where French-language publications (as well as the maps) are sold.

Tarbes has some reasonable **hotels** in the vicinity of the train station, including the friendly, helpful *Hôtel de l'Avenue*, 80 av Bertrand-Barère (☎05.62.93.06.36; ③); the small, basic *Victor Hugo*, 52 rue Victor-Hugo (☎05.62.93.36.71, fax 05.62.51.90.27; ②); and the remoter, slightly more comfortable *Hôtel L'Isard*, 70 av Maréchal Joffre (☎05.62.93.06.69, fax 05.62.93.99.55; ③); as well as a **youth hostel** at 88 av Alsace-Lorraine (☎05.62.38.91.20; ①).

When **eating out**, again you can pretty much stay within sight of the station. The restaurant attached to *L'Isard* offers *menus* ranging from subsistence (65F/€9.90 *formule*) to a more interesting gourmet *menu* of the month (100F/€15.30). At 62 rue Bertrand-Barère, *Le Petit Gourmand* is a popular lunch spot, while if you're craving something exotic, *Thanh Thúy* across the street at no. 53 does very passable Vietnamese dishes for well under 100F/€15.30 a head. Other independent eateries include the Moroccan diner *Le Sahara* at 21 rue Victor Hugo, and the old favourite *Chez Patrick*, 6 rue Adolphe-d'Eichtal, corner rue St-Jean, with a regular clientele and a copious *menu* for under 60F/€9.20.

Lourdes and around

LOURDES, just 20km south of Tarbes on the N21, is difficult to avoid if you're touring the French side of the Central Pyrenees, as it sits squarely astride the direct route up to Argelès-Gazost, Cauterets and Luz-Saint-Sauveur. And even if it weren't so pivotal, the town would be an unmissable detour. East of the main street, Lourdes is like many other small, French foothill communities. But the western part, around the *cité religieuse* on the banks of the Gave (River) de Pau, is another world – boarded up in winter, and in summer seething with the pilgrims who constitute its sole reason for existence. The huge crowds attending the Masses and the grotto make an overwhelming spectacle: over six million people come each year to this town of fewer than eighteen thousand inhabitants, and inevitably a substantial fraction disport themselves at a number of low-key attractions in the surrounding countryside.

The cult of Lourdes

The unwitting instigator of the cult of Lourdes was **Bernadette Soubirous**, the fourteen-year-old daughter of a poor local miller. On February 11, 1858 she was collecting firewood near the Grotte de Massabielle when she had a vision of the Virgin Mary, who spoke to her in *Bigourdan* dialect, asking her to return regularly to the cave. During seventeen subsequent visitations, the Virgin revealed her identity (as the "Immaculate Conception") to Bernadette, and commanded the girl to dig at the ground with her hands, thus releasing a spring whose water would supposedly prove to have curative powers. Bernadette's apparition also demanded that she notify the local priests, have a chapel built and organize devotional processions to the spot.

These visions were authenticated by the Church authorities in 1862, and eleven years later the first nationwide pilgrimage took place, organized by the **Assomptionistes**. This was an ultra-conservative Catholic movement founded in 1845 in response to the reigning positivism, republicanism and atheism of the era. Its ranks swelled by press agitation following the short-lived Paris Commune of 1871, the *Assomptionistes* effectively took over the town of Lourdes, dismissing the local clergy and running the pilgrimages as a going concern. Not coincidentally, from its coup dates the proliferation of hotels in Lourdes (more than 350, second most in France after Paris), and shops devoted to the sale of unbelievable (in all senses) religious kitsch:

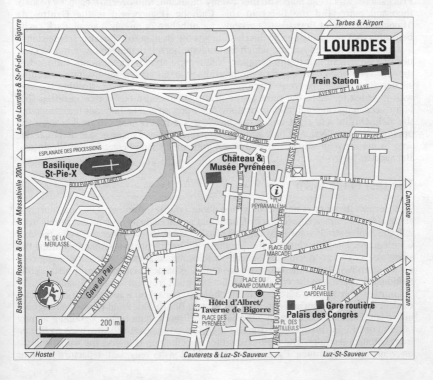

Bernadette and/or the Virgin emblazoned on key rings, candles, candy-bars, thermometers and illuminated plastic grottoes.

With each miraculous cure – of which there were a number, as witnessed by the discarded crutches hanging at the grotto – the pilgrimage to Lourdes gained momentum. Among early rich and famous visitors were Napoléon III and the Empress Eugénie, making the trip on behalf of their sick son. Ironically, the emperor had ordered the closure of the grotto a few years earlier, fearing public disorder. Bernadette herself had been hustled into a convent in 1866, ostensibly for her own safety, where she died thirteen years later.

No matter how cynical you may be about the motives of some who manage the pilgrim business, you cannot fail to be moved by the thousands of pilgrims, many crippled or quite obviously ill, who converge here to give their faith a chance to cure them. You see them everywhere, being wheeled about by *brancardières* – young volunteers, many foreign and not even Catholic, who are each assigned a sick or handicapped pilgrim to push along for the duration of their stay. They're interspersed with legions of nuns, priests and a surprisingly heavy police presence (not least to dispense citations to those parked illegally). What impresses next is the international mix of the crowds: *Malagaches* and *Réunionais*, Africans, Spanish, Italians, Poles, Germans, Dutch and quite a few Anglophones.

The flamboyant, gargantuan double **Basilique du Rosaire et de l'Immaculée Conception**, built between 1871 and 1883 in "Romano-Byzantine" and Gothic styles, was no longer large enough by the centenary of the apparitions; hence the construction of the underground **Basilique Saint-Pie X** dominating the Esplanade des Processions, which can hold a further twenty thousand, with overflow capacity of forty thousand more. But the heart of this Catholic Disneyworld is the **Grotte de Massabielle**, site of Bernadette's visions, for unbelievers merely a small, dark cavity beneath a rock overhang beside the river, below the Basilique du Rosaire. Inside stands a statue of the holy apparition, which Bernadette herself denounced as a mockery of her precise description to the sculptor. Neither the shoddy likeness nor the modest dimensions of the grotto concern the pilgrims who, queuing beside signs demanding silence (in the main obeyed), circumambulate the cave clockwise, stroking the wall with their left hand. To the right of the grotto stand enormous **votive candles** (700 tonnes consumed annually) left to prolong one's prayer, and bathhouses for immersing the sick. On the left, right under the basilica, is a row of taps channelled from the **spring**, for the collection of holy water in containers of every shape, size and material, sold in the souvenir shops and embossed with medallions depicting the Virgin and Bernadette.

The rest of the town

The Bernadette story is not the only one about Lourdes. Another tells how, during a siege of the Muslim-occupied city by Charlemagne, an eagle let drop an enormous trout into the famine-stricken town. Mirat, the Muslim chief, threw it over the walls, tricking Charlemagne into believing that the Muslims still had plenty to eat, and duly lifting the siege. As with all good Christian moral parables, this one ends with Mirat being converted from his Mohammedan ways; he took the name Lorus, which in turn, subtly modified, was given to the city that now bears a giant trout on its coat-of-arms.

Lourdes' only secular attraction is its **château**, poised on a rocky bluff on the east bank of the Gave de Pau and entered from rue du Bourg. Briefly an English stronghold in the late fourteenth century, it later became a French state prison, detaining among others Lord Elgin (he of the Parthenon marbles) on his troubled way back to Britain from Ottoman territory. The main reason for the climb up is to visit the worthwhile, if unevenly labelled **Musée Pyrénéen** (1hr guided visits only, last departure an hour before closure: April–Sept daily 9–11.45am & 1.30–6.45pm; Oct–March daily except Tues 9am–noon & 2–6pm; 30F/€4.60). For the dedicated climber or walker, some of the equipment displays are intriguing, particularly the primitive axes, crampons, ropes and other expedition necessities of the pioneer *Pyrénéistes*. On show, too, are some magnificently detailed maps by Franz Schrader, who first came to the Pyrenees in 1873 on a cartographic mission; he also left paintings and drawings of the high peaks, among them an evocative view of Monte Perdido. Other exhibits include costumes and everyday items of Pyrenean life during recent centuries, plus local flora and fauna, mostly presented in tableau form. The museum has an excellent library (which you can use with permission), containing early edition books such as Charles Packe's *Guide to the Pyrenees*, original documents such as the 99-year lease of Vignemale granted to Henry Russell (see feature on p.371), and hundreds of rare photographs.

Practicalities

The **train station** lies on the far north side of Lourdes, about ten minutes' walk from the centre; there are very frequent services to Tarbes (15min) and Pau (30min). The **gare routière** is in the central place Capdevielle, behind the Palais des Congrès, and there's a not particularly helpful **tourist office** in a glass building on place Peyramale (Easter to mid-Oct Mon–Sat 9am–7pm, Sun 11am–6pm; mid-Oct to Easter Mon–Sat 9am–noon & 2–6pm; ☎05.62.42.77.40). **Tarbes-Ossun-Lourdes International Airport**, some 10km north, has only one regular daily bus service (departs train station 11.30am, meets domestic Paris flight, returns to train station at 1pm), but there are services to Tarbes roughly every hour along the main N21, which pass within a kilometre or so of the airport.

There's an abundance of fairly indistinguishable **accommodation** in Lourdes – some two hundred one- and two-star hotels (most ④–⑤), concentrated in the small central streets close to the castle. Establishment names like *Christ Roi*, *Golgotha* and *Calvaire* give a clue as to the usual clientele; for a slightly upmarket hotel choice, in a "normal" part of town opposite the food *halles*, is the two-star *Hôtel d'Albret* (☎05.62.94.75.00, fax 05.62.94.78.45; ③–⑤), with the co-managed *Taverne de Bigorre* on the ground floor offering a range of *menus* (100F/€15.30 gets you three hearty courses). Most hotels require half-board, so there are few decent independent eateries in town. **Hostel** accommodation is provided by the *Centre Pax Christi*, route de la Forêt (☎05.62.94.00.66, fax 05.62.42.94.44; April to mid-Oct; ①) on the western edge of town. The most central **campsite** is the *Poste* (☎05.62.94.40.35; April to mid-Oct) in rue de Langelle, just south of the train station, though it's reported to be cramped, unhygienic and lacking in hot water.

Excursions around Lourdes

If you want to stay in Lourdes briefly before heading into the mountains, there are a number of **excursions** to be made around the town, albeit expensive and overcrowded ones. For good views with minimum effort, take the *téléphérique* up the 791-metre-high **Pic le Béout** (Easter to mid-Oct daily 9am–noon & 2–6pm), reached from av Francis Lagardère, at the southern end of town. While there, you may like to visit **Gouffre Béout** (same hours), an 82-metre-deep cave discovered, with a number of prehistoric tools inside, by Norbert Casteret in 1938; there's not a lot to see now, and it gets very busy. The other transport-assisted "climb" is up 948-metre **Pic du Jer** (daily Easter–Oct, 9–11.50am & 1.30–6.20pm; 48F/€7.30 return), a funicular ride to another panoramic view; you can walk down, following a well-marked trail.

For a short trip out of town, head 4km west to **Lac de Lourdes**, a pretty though somewhat oversubscribed picnic spot; there are local buses along the main D937 to

Pau. Twelve kilometres further you come to the **Grottes de Bétharram** (March 25–Oct 25 daily 8.30am–noon & 1.30–5.30pm, except Aug daily 9am–6pm; Jan 5–March 25 Mon–Fri tours 2.30 & 4pm only; ☎05.62.41.80.04; 52F/€8), where barges and trains provide rides through 5km of underground galleries. The name of the caves derives from the Bigourdan phrase *Bét Arram*, meaning "beautiful branch": legend has it that the Virgin Mary saved a young girl from drowning here in the Gave de Pau by throwing a branch to her.

Close to the caves are three **accommodation** choices superior to anything available in Lourdes. The *Ferme Campseissillou* (☎05.62.41.80.92; ④), 4km by narrow mountain lane north of **SAINT-PÉ-DE-BIGORRE**, offers four modernized, en-suite rooms in a converted barn. In the centre of Saint-Pé, *Le Grande Cèdre*, 6 rue du Barry (☎05.62.41.82.04, fax 05.62.41.85.89, *www.sdfr.com/grand.cedre*; ⑥) is altogether more sumptuous: a seventeenth-century mansion combining original floors and furnishings with modern bathrooms in its large suites. At the same address, reached via a different door, *La Calèche* (☎05.62.41.82.04, fax 05.62.94.60.50; ④) has even more rustic/antique decor in its varying rooms. Both establishments share a garden, with the monumental cedar of the name, and both offer *table d'hôte* suppers (130F/€19.80 and 100F/€15.30 respectively).

The upper Gave de Pau

The upper **Gave de Pau**, paralleled by the N21, offers a number of potential stops, such as Argelès-Gazost, the abbey-village of Saint-Savin and an aviary of raptors at Beaucens. Both road and river split in the vicinity of these attractions; the most rewarding side trip is from Argelès itself, up the joint **Vallées d'Azun, d'Arrens** and **d'Étaing**.

Argelès-Gazost and around

ARGELÈS-GAZOST, 13km south of Lourdes, is an innocuously dull if rather congested spa that makes a possible base for the lower Gave de Pau. The town itself extends from the valley floor, quite broad here, up to the busy medieval core on a terrace to the west. The **tourist office** (summer Mon–Sat 9am–noon & 2–6.30pm, Sun 9am–noon; closed Sun off season; ☎05.62.97.00.25) is in the principal place de la République (aka Grande-Terrasse), three minutes south of the church. There are a number of old-fashioned but en-suite **hotels** in and around Argelès, most with attached (and good-value) restaurants, including the comfortable *Hostellerie Le Relais*, 25 rue Maréchal-Foch (☎05.62.97.01.27; closed Oct–Jan; ③–⑤), marooned between two car parks but with a peaceful enough back garden; *Le Soleil Levant*, just north of town on the N21, a quiet thermal establishment set back from the road (☎05.62.97.08.68; closed Jan; ④); and perhaps best of all, the *Beau Site* at 10 rue Capitaine-Digoy near the tourist office (☎05.62.97.08.63, fax 05.62.97.06.01; closed Nov; ④), a classic French country inn with the best rooms overlooking an immense, tumbling garden.

Apart from buying mountain equipment from the excellent Lafont Sports in place du Foirail (which doubles as the main parking lot), there's little to do in or near Argelès apart from learning **rafting, kayaking** or **canyoning** at the Pavillon des Sensations (☎05.62.94.52.03), 4km back towards Lourdes at the neat, quiet village of Agos-Vidalos. Nearby **ARCIZANS-AVANT**, 2km southwest by a minor road, can offer the privately run, rather bogus **Château of the Black Prince** (mid-June to mid-Sept daily 10am–noon & 2.30–7pm; April to mid-June & mid-Sept to Oct Sun & public holidays only, same hours), most of it rather later than Edward's time; the château functions mainly as a restaurant, with good-value meals, and has a few **rooms** (☎05.62.97.02.79; ④). Below the church is another hotel, the *Auberge Le Cabaliros* (☎05.62.97.04.31, fax 05.62.97.91.48; closed mid-Oct to mid-Dec; ⑤), with views south over the valley to high peaks from the restaurant's outdoor seats, and a few less expensive rooms under the mansard roof.

Saint-Savin

The twelfth-century **Romanesque abbey** at **SAINT-SAVIN**, 4km south of Argelès-Gazost, is worth visiting partly for its unusual fortifications – the roof was raised in the fourteenth century to accommodate gun slits, the octagonal tower added simultaneously – and for its connection with the persecuted Cagots.

Monastic fortifications in this part of the Pyrenees generally served a double function: aiding enforcement of the *Trêves de Dieu*, the church-imposed truce days between rival *seigneurs*; and acting as a defence against Aragonese raiders. At Saint-Savin defence from irate locals may have become paramount, the abbey having grown rich, unpopular and embroiled in lawsuits stemming from ventures such as the spa at Cauterets. A monastic community existed as far back as the eighth century, and the monks quickly established a virtual mini-state here and in adjacent valleys, along with a reputation for luxury and ungodliness. The contemporary feel of the main church – perhaps the least numinous in the entire range, with little evidence of continued sacred use – seems to reflect this.

There was once a large local Cagot community, and the low opening, now blocked, to the left of the multi-lobed west portal is possibly where they listened to Mass from outside; scholars have concluded that the two granite figures supporting the water stoup in the south transept are Cagots. The organ cabinet (1557) is carved with grotesque faces whose eyes and tongues were designed to move when the instrument was played, said to be the grimacing visages of damned souls unable to endure the sound of heavenly music. St Savin himself, an obscure local seventh-century hermit, is supposedly entombed in the choir. The vaulted chapterhouse north of the church now serves as the entry to a **treasury** (daily summer 10am–noon & 3.30–6.30pm; 12F/€1.80) whose main highlights are various twelfth-century statuettes of the Virgin.

Many visitors prefer the little **chapel of Nôtre-Dame-de-Piétat** (daily unpredictable hours; free), which adorns a hill amongst hay meadows 1km south of the village. Its glory is an elaborately painted ceiling, where birds perch on floral motifs covering every available space of the simple vault; you can examine them at close range from the wooden gallery.

Saint-Savin village has three **hôtel-restaurants**, two of them on the square leading up to the church from the south: the functional *Panoramic* (✆05.62.97.08.22; ③), and *Le Viscos* (✆05.62.97.02.28, fax ✆05.62.97.04.95; closed Mon low season & Dec; ⑤), whose affordable *menus* (120–190F/€18.30–29) feature game, duck or fish; à la carte will run to at least 220F/€33.60 per person. Remoter at the top of the village, peacefully set in its own garden, is the friendly *Les Rochers* (✆05.62.97.09.52, fax 05.62.97.17.78; ④), with easy parking, a rather average restaurant but very high-standard, en-suite rooms (half board encouraged).

Beaucens and around

On the opposite side of the valley to Saint-Savin, there's a chance to see birds of prey in captivity at **Le Donjon des Aigles**, the ruined twelfth-century keep of the château at **BEAUCENS** (Easter–Sept 10am–noon & 2.30–7pm; flying displays July 3.30pm & 5pm, Aug 3pm, 4.30pm & 6pm; 35F/€5.40). You might feel these magnificent raptors shouldn't be kept penned for tourists' entertainment, but seeing them close up – a trained griffon vulture actually "buzzes" the audience – should at least teach people to appreciate them.

To reach the *donjon* by public transport, alight at **PIERREFITTE-NESTALAS**, where SNCF buses veer off for Cauterets (5–7 daily); cross the bridge and walk the well-signposted 2km. Pierrefitte-Nestalas itself, with its belching chemical plant, has little to detain you, except for a small aquarium, **Le Marinarium** (July–Aug only

9.30am–noon & 2–6pm, closed Sun am/Mon am; 35F/€5.40), 50m from the bus stop, incongruously dedicated to tropical fish.

East of Pierrefitte – though the most direct road access is from Argelès – the dinky beginners' ski station of **HAUTACAM** makes an attractive target for a sixteen-kilometre drive, the uplands being a congenial place for red and black kites, sparrowhawks and other birds of prey. The summertime hike east from the nearby Col de Moulata to Lac Bleu (see p.346) is recommended for lovers of solitude, but the downhill skiing in winter isn't particularly – the top point for fourteen pistes is only 1800m and it's open for a month at most, though the 22km of marked nordic tracks could be more worthwhile.

Vallée d'Estaing, Val d'Azun and Vallée d'Arrens

The D918 southwest from Argelès initially follows the Val d'Azun, with a turn-off after 4km south up the D103, which serves the silky green and gentle-sided **Vallée d'Estaing**. There are some good places to **stay** and **eat** along this valley, many aimed at GR10 trekkers: the well-signed *Chez Begué* (☎05.62.96.44.83; ②), just off the road in **ESTAING** village, various **campsites** including *Le Vieux Moulin* (☎05.62.97.43.23) with a pool or the more basic *La Pose* (☎05.62.97.43.10), and a *gîte d'étape* (☎05.62.97.14.37; open all year; ①) at **VIELLETTES** hamlet, with four-to-ten-bed dorms. Last but not least, just below the Lac d'Estaing, the nouvelle-cuisine at *Hôtel Restaurant du Lac* (☎05.62.97.06.25; open May–Oct 15; ③), draws customers from far afield. Unusually for a rural eatery, lunch is provided until 2.30pm; skip the humdrum *menus* (85–165F/€13–25.20) in favour of the *carte* (180F/€27.50) which features crayfish in various guises, goose, duck, decent bread and elaborate desserts, most defying translation. The hotel rooms are old-fashioned, with toilets down the hall, but tasteful. At road's end, the natural **Lac d'Estaing** is rather too popular for its own good with weekenders who rent pedaloes, patronize a pony-ride outfit and pack out a **campsite** at the southerly corner. The lake is also an important **trailhead** for the GR10 (which sticks mostly to road and track on its way over from Arrens-Marsous), leading southeast to the Ilhéou refuge (4hr), and for an unnumbered path going south to the numerous tarns around Pene d'Estradère (2593m) and beyond to the Col de Portet and its lake.

Val d'Azun

The main **Val d'Azun** has two fair-sized villages with facilities and points of interest. At **AUCUN**, 9km above Argelès-Gazost (2 buses daily Mon–Sat), the **Musée Montagnard du Lavédan** (daily during school holidays 5pm tour only; otherwise by appointment on ☎05.62.97.12.03; 20F/€3) has a private collection of traditional Bigourdan agricultural and household items. The uncluttered village church of **Saint-Pierre** is also worth a glance for its apsidal south transept (the oldest, eleventh-century bit), a baptismal font with musicians and hunters carved in relief, the two-level gallery and sixteenth-century *retable*. Aucun is also home to the valley's main **parapente** school, Comme un Oiseau (☎05.62.97.47.63 or 06.82.54.82.26), whose introductory tandem flights run 290–320F/€44–49.

Closest places to stay are 3km up-valley at **ARRENS-MARSOUS**, where the excellent **gîte d'étape**, *La Maison Camélat* (☎05.62.97.40.94, fax 05.62.97.43.01; dorm ①; rooms ②), is run by La Balaguère, one of France's top trekking outfitters (see p.6 in "Basics"); it's a fine, rambling old house just off the central *place*, with a few doubles in the attic and saunas laid on Tuesday and Thursday evenings. None of the more conventional **accommodation** options in and around town are as appealling, with the exception of *Chambres d'Hôte Lucie & Jo Batan*, at the east edge of Arrens (☎05.62.97.12.93; fax 05.62.97.43.88; ④ B&B). In the same area is the better of two local **campsites**, *La Station* (☎05.62.97.00.56; June–Sept). There are just two independent **restaurants**: the somewhat secluded *Le Balaitous*, with ambitious *menus* at 65–149F/€9.90–22.70), and the cheap-and-cheerful *La Renaissance*, with terrace dining on the main through road. The *Maison du Val d'Azun et du Parc National* (daily summer 9am–noon & 2–7pm; ☎05.62.97.49.49) sells farm products and doubles as the **Tourisme**.

From Arrens the D918 snakes west over the beautiful *cols* de Soulour and d'Aubisque into the Ossau valley at Eaux-Bonnes (see p.385); a very minor road also links the village with Estaing village in the Vallée d'Estaing, via the Col des Bordères, a route also followed by the GR10.

Skiing – and the Tour du Val d'Azun

The environs of the Col du Soulour (1474m) are home to the **Soulour-Couraduque** cross-country skiing network, largest in the Pyrenees with 110km of marked trails extending northeast to the Col du Couraduque, at 1350–1600m elevation. For drivers Soulour marks the start of the D126 north, an attractive if initially slow shortcut down to the main road from Saint-Pé-de-Bigorre and Pau. After 9km, you intersect the walkers' **Tour du Val d'Azun** at **ARBÉOST**, clinging prettily to the flanks of the Val d'Ouzoum; there's a *gîte d'étape*, *Petite Jeanne* (☎05.59.71.42.50; ①) by the church. Other *gîtes*, well spaced to the east on the same Tour, are the *Haugarou*, near the Col de Couraduque (☎05.62.97.25.04; ①) and *La Ribère* (☎05.62.97.09.11; ①) at **ARCIZANS-DESSUS**, 3km east of Aucun. The full Tour, which requires at least three days, taking in a mix of open ridge and secluded canyon, is clearly shown on the Carte de Randonées no. 3, "Béarn".

Vallée d'Arrens: into the PNP

The most popular excursions, however, involve the **Vallée d'Arrens**, which extends southwest of Arrens-Marsous, the distance covered by the D105. Some 10km upstream along the road, you reach the Tech dam, with only a primitive camping area as a facility. Neither is there any public transport up the D105, though occasionally the local PNP office arranges shuttles for guided groups. The road ends a few kilometres further at **Plan d'Aste** (1470m), right at the PNP boundary, with limited parking for several trailheads serving the park. The paths link up with the nearby HRP, or go to a trio of refuges, and can be enjoyably combined into short trekking loops of a few days' duration. Trails from either the Tech dam or Plan d'Aste converge on the privately run *Refuge de Migouélou* to the west on its lakeshore (☎05.62.97.44.92; 2278m; June–Sept); it's indicated "2hr 45min" up from Plan d'Aste, though as ever the PNP signboards are pessimistic, and especially with a daypack you'll shave 20min off that. Another path heads south past little Lac de Suyen (20min) to the *Refuge Ledormeur* (1917m; 12 places; unstaffed), "2hr 15min" distant, and to the staffed *Refuge de Larribet* (☎05.62.97.25.39; 2065m; 62 places; June–Sept & weekends April/May; ①), "2hr 45min" away to the southwest. At either hut you're on the HRP as it threads along between the Lac d'Artouste and the Vallée du Marcadau (see p.389 & p.374); the easiest and most obvious hike circuit, using the HRP and link trails, is Plan d'Aste – Migouélou – Artouste – Larribet – Plan d'Aste, which would enjoyably occupy two very long days (best allow three).

Luz-Saint-Sauveur

The double spa-village of **LUZ-SAINT-SAUVEUR**, in two distinct quarters straddling the confluence of the Gavarnie and Bastan rivers, lies 12km south of Pierrefitte-Nestalas. It makes a practical base if you have a car or are content to make day-trips by public transport. For the serious walker, however, it's still a bit too distant from the Gavarnie cirque – the goal of any expedition up this valley – to be ideal, despite a notional situation on the GR10. Skiing is more promising, with the small resort of Luz-Ardidens just to the west, and better ones at Barèges further east. The Gave de Gavarnie, upstream from here as far as Gèdre, also provides some exciting kayaking.

The Town

The oldest, most attractive part of Luz is its upper quarter, whose narrow lanes, hosting a Monday market, radiate from the fortified twelfth-century church of **Saint-André**. Surrounding houses make it difficult to get a good look at the church, a classic of medieval military architecture with its crenellated outer wall, stout, machicolated towers and gun slits just below the roof. These were provided in the twelfth century by the Knights Templar and further modified in the fourteenth by the Knights of St John, who appropriated all of the Templars' strongholds after their suppression. A fine carved Christ in Majesty, flanked by the symbols of the Evangelists, floats on the tympanum over the north portal, and a *clocher-mur* dominates the roofline. The church interior proves disappointing and rather cluttered with three huge confessionals, but in the creaky side chapel there's a free **museum** of sacred artefacts dating back to the twelfth century, including a manuscript on procedures for exorcisms.

The **Saint-Saveur** quarter to the west consists of the startlingly elegant line of *thermes* buildings and slightly pretentious hotels on the left bank of the Gave de Gavarnie. The 21-year-old George Sand visited and was repelled, writing: "The beautiful people strut and preen and talk amongst themselves about their ailments." The spa itself was immaculately redone in 2000, with a kidney-shaped pool and huge windows overlooking the gorge. According to local legend, Napoléon III authorized the superfluous **Pont Napoléon** (built 1861), spanning the canyon, to commemorate his illicit conception at nearby Gavarnie; today, with its 90-metre height, it's a favourite venue for bungy-jumping (*ponting* in French). He also paid for the Chapelle Solférino, south of the fortified church in the main part of the village.

You can cross the river bridge to visit the prominent, thirteenth-to-fourteenth-century **Château Sainte-Marie** (unenclosed, free), just 1km northeast in the adjoining village of Esquièze-Sère. Although the surviving pair of round and square towers don't fulfil their promise as glimpsed from afar, the château provides unrivalled views over the town; it's a popular picnic spot, with a spring, and an occasional venue for concerts.

Practicalities

SNCF buses from Lourdes drop you in place du Huit-Mai, hub of the lower part of the village, beside the helpful **Office du Tourisme** (summer Mon–Sat 9am–7.30pm, Sun 9am–12.30pm; also Sun 4.30–7.30pm peak season; ☎05.62.92.30.30), which can provide lists of long-term apartments for rent. Off place St-Clément, hub of the Monday market, there's a **Maison du Parc National** (summer Mon–Fri 9am–noon & 2–7pm, Sat & Sun 4–7pm; ☎05.62.92.38.38), which organizes outdoor activities, keeps an exhibition of local flora and fauna and hosts films and events certain evenings. Other outfitters include Luz Aventure/Elastic Pacific, for all extreme and not-so-extreme sports (☎05.62.92.33.47).

Among **hotels**, the atmospheric *Templiers*, right opposite the fortified church (☎05.62.92.81.52, fax 05.62.92.93.05; closed May & Oct; ③), is an excellent, quiet choice with a *crêperie* on the ground floor. Alternatives include *Les Cimes* (☎05.62.92.83.03; ③), 80m downhill from the *Templiers* and high-standard enough for certain tour groups, or the imposing *Londres* on the river bank, with private car-park (☎05.62.92.80.09; closed May & Oct; ④), which is fine as long as you don't get a room facing the road. The well-run **gîte d'étape/youth hostel** (☎05.62.92.94.14; open all year; dorm ①, rooms ②), with a few doubles and a good restaurant, and the *Les Cascades* **campsite** above it (☎05.62.92.85.85; closed Oct–Nov) are in the southern neighbourhood, and there's another campsite, *Le Toy* (☎05.62.92.86.85; open Jan–April & June–Sept), right by place du Huit-Mai. Aside from the hotel restaurants, of which the best by far is the *Londres*, independent eateries are limited in quality and quantity; *Bodega La Tasca* on Place-Saint

Clément is only worthwhile as a bar. One bright spot is Ghanaian-run *Resto Taxi-Brousse*, at the start of the Barèges road, where stews and curries form the heart of good-value set *menus* (85F/€13).

If none of this appeals, you might retreat to the hamlet of **VIELLA**, 2km east and above the D918, where you can **stay** at *La Grange au Bois* (☎05.62.92.82.76; fax 05.62.92.95.93; open all year; dorm ①, rooms ②), a *gîte* run by a mountain guide and ski instructor, and **eat** either there or at the *Auberge de Viella*, strong on lamb dishes and *garbure*.

Skiing: Luz-Ardiden

The associated ski development of **LUZ-ARDIDEN**, nearly 1000m higher than Luz itself, is reached by 12km of hairpins on the D12 heading northwest; there are two or three daily *navettes* from the main bus stop in Luz-Saint-Sauveur. Essentially a small, east-facing bowl, the resort musters 19 lifts (including 7 chairs) – to a high point of 2450m – and 33 pistes, almost half of them red-rated; the paltry number and length of the blues and greens mean this isn't a good beginners' resort. The ski *randonnée* is the best thing about the place, with fine ascents of **Pic d'Ardiden** (2988m), and a possible descent to the Cauterets valley. In summer you can also **walk** in a moderate, six-and-a-half-hour day from Luz to Cauterets via Luz-Ardiden on a GR10 variant.

Barèges and around

The two-street village of **BARÈGES** (5–7 summer SNCF buses daily), 8km northeast of Luz-Saint-Sauveur about halfway along the Vallée de Bastan towards the Col du Tourmalet, is the most congenial base in the Gave de Pau, if you're willing to forego instant access to the Cirque de Gavarnie. It pitches itself as an all-in-one sports centre, with opportunities for bike rental (touring and mountain), riding, rafting, squash, walk-

---

PARAPENTE AROUND BARÈGES

There are five permitted **launch sites** for parapente around Barèges, with four more around Luz-Saint-Sauveur; when the weather is bad this side of the Gave de Pau, local outfitters take to the Val d'Auzun. Most of the Barèges sites cluster around the carpark at **Tournaboup meadows** (1450m; 3km east of Barèges), with launchings from the Capet ridge just north (1900–2000m), the Caoubère ridge just east (1900–2000m) and even the Col du Tourmalet itself. One of the busiest **parapente schools** in France operates most days from Tournaboup: Air Aventure Pyrénées (☎05.62.92.91.60 or 06.08.93.62.02; open all year, weather and demand allowing), with English-speaking instructors, in co-operation with Didier Theil (☎05.62.907.93.94 or 06.80.65.85.00). Beginners' *biplace* (tandem) **introductory flights** – *baptêmes de l'air* – typically last about twenty minutes before landing at Tournaboup, though competition-level experts can stay airborne for at least 45 minutes. On a two-seater flight, the instructor sits behind you, and controls the rig, exploiting passive (thermal) lift and creating dynamic lift by changing the air-foil's shape through tugging skilfully on various cord-pulls. Your main task is to run like hell at takeoff when the glider begins to fill, offsetting its tendency to drag you backwards; then you just sit back and enjoy, if you can – some folk never get beyond the guaranteed initial minute of sheer terror. Thermal lift conditions are invariably better later in the day, so higher **rates** are charged for afternoon flights; be warned that it's an expensive sport if you get hooked. Introductory tandem *baptêmes* run 250–300F/€38–46 from Capet or Caoubère, 400F/€60 from Tournalet or for a "long duration" flight. Pupils typically need two-and-a-half days of intensive instruction, both practical and theoretical, before their **initial solo flight**.

ing, snowshoeing, skiing – and, above all, **parapente**. Although this sport is far safer than in the early days of rigid hang-gliders, proper tuition is still a must.

Should you be so unlucky as to break a bone parapenting or skiing, Barèges is not a bad place to do it. It became a fashionable health resort after visits in 1677 by the Duc de Maine, the sickly son of Louis XIV, and the waters were considered particularly efficacious for gunshot wounds – a military hospital was established in 1744, and Napoleon made it one of five military *thermes*. The **military** connection still endures: there's an army R&R facility in the village centre, with a mountain-warfare school for the Armée de Terre just opposite – the Vallée de Bastan's strong similarity to conditions in Bosnia-Herzegovina made it a major training venue for the French contingent during the 1991–95 Yugoslav wars.

Perhaps the spa's most significant guest was the 32-year-old **Ramond de Carbonnières**, whose passion for these mountains can be traced to Barèges, where he came in 1787 as the confidant of the disgraced Cardinal de Rohan. Today the **baths** (May–Oct Mon–Sat unpredictable am hours, & 4–7pm; Christmas–Easter daily 4–8pm) themselves occupy a lovely Palladian building in the centre of Barèges, and have been enthusiastically incorporated into both *après*-trek and après-ski routines. There's little fustiness or Fellini-esque grotesqueness to the place, though you do have to cover or swop your street-shoes and don white bathrobes prior to an attendant shepherding you through. The waters, 38°C and sulphurous, are delivered three ways: 40F/€6.10 for a communal pool plunge, 60F/€9.20 for a private *hydroxeur* tub (basically a Jacuzzi), and 120F/€18.30 for a combination jet-dousing and massage.

Practicalities

Especially if you're traversing the GR10, or are interested in sampling Barèges' sporting opportunities, a top choice for **accommodation** would be the welcoming, Anglo-French-run *Gîte d'Étape l'Oasis*, in a handsome old building just behind the spa (☎05.62.92.69.47, fax 05.62.92.65.17, *andrea@gite-oasis.com*; ①), with showers in the rooms, and sinks in the dorms; it's co-managed with the *Refuge de la Glère* (see p.341). Alternatively, there's *L'Hospitalet* (☎05.62.92.68.08, fax 05.62.92.66.15, *hospitalet.barege@wanadoo.fr*; dorm ①; rooms ③), another high-quality *gîte* at the south upper edge of town, somewhat institutional owing to its past as a military hospital, though it does have a few doubles. Both offer evening meals and reasonable half-board rates, and tend to close Oct 15–Nov 15 and April 15–May 15. Also worth contacting are British expats Peter and Jude at their small en-suite inn *Les Sorbiers* on the main street (☎05.62.92.68.95, fax 05.62.92.83.43, *sorbiers@sudfr.com*; closed Sept 15–Dec 15 & April 1–May 15; ③), with half-board rates available (vegetarian meals). They're mostly geared up for one-week, pre-booked summer hiking and winter skiing holidays, but are happy to take walk-ins space permitting, including them in all activities.

The main through road is lined with a half-dozen gracefully ageing **hotels**, all fairly similar in standard, opening season (May–Oct & Dec 15–March) and price (typically ④). The most modest is *Hôtel de la Poste* (☎05.62.92.68.37, fax 05.62.92.69.58; ③); among the others, *La Montagne Fleurie* (☎05.62.92.68.50, fax 05.62.92.17.53; ④) is engagingly old-fashioned, with a steady repeat clientele. Barèges has just one **campsite**, the high-standard *La Ribère* (☎05.62.92.69.01; closed Oct 15–Dec 15), which you'll pass if arriving from Luz.

Independent **restaurants** in the town itself are limited; best of these by far is friendly *La Rozell*, opposite the ATM and lift-pass vendors, then downstairs: pricey (150F/€22.90) but well-presented *crêpes*, *galletes*, meat and fish dishes, with booking recommended. The closest good choice is the friendly *Auberge du Lienz* (aka *Chez Louisette*; closed early May & Nov), a venerable institution serving hearty *menus* from 135F/€20.60, typically four courses with *garbure*; duck, pigeon, boar or fish as mains;

a cheese platter and a tart. Weather permitting, they set outdoor tables year-round near the end of various ski runs. To get there, head first 2.5km northeast towards Tourmalet, then 1.5km southwest on the paved road up to the wooded Plateau du Lienz.

The central **tourist office** (July–Aug Mon–Sat 9am–12.30pm & 2–7pm, Sun 10am–noon & 4–6pm; rest of year shorter pm hours; ☎05.62.92.16.00) can supply all conceivable accommodation lists and ski-lift plans. There's also an open-air **swimming pool** (daily July–Aug 10am–7pm; 15F/€2.30), **squash courts** (daily 9am–8pm; 25F/€3.80 for 40min) and tennis (daily 9am–8pm; 35F/€5.40 per hour) at the municipally run Hélios recreation centre.

Beyond Barèges the D918 snakes up to the **Col du Tourmalet**, before dropping to La Mongie, Campan and Bagnères-de-Bigorre. At Pont de la Gaubie, 4km from town, is the **Jardin Botanique du Tourmalet** (May–Sept daily 9am–6pm; 25F/€3.80), which has assembled most of the wild flora of the Pyrenees in a single two-hectare site. You can **eat** buckwheat crêpes and light snacks nearby at *Auberge de la Gaubie* (lunch June–Sept only), which flanks the onward trailhead for the GR10.

Walking and snowshoeing from Barèges

The **GR10** passes through Barèges, heading southeast on an interesting traverse through the Réserve Naturelle de Néouvielle to Vielle-Aure. The ascents of **Turon de Néouvielle** and **Pic du Néouvielle** are both challenging expeditions out of Barèges, beginning in earnest at the *Refuge de la Glère*, 10km south of Barèges by track. Both of these climbing routes, which take the better part of twelve hours, are described on pp.341–342 – as is the traverse (in reverse sense). In winter, the valley terrain lends itself to circuits on *raquettes* or **snowshoes**; the best two begin from beside the Gîte L'Hospitalet, and the intermediate station of the Funiculaire de l'Ayré (which starts in the village centre).

Skiing around Barèges

In a snowy year Barèges has some of the best skiing in the Pyrenees, due to its affiliation with La Mongie (joint pass the rule) and some enjoyable off-piste itineraries. It is in fact the second oldest ski resort in France (after Chamonix), and hosted the 1926 Winter Olympics. Barèges had a military-run ski school as early as 1922 and a famous civilian ski club, Société L'Avalanche, whose members have included French champions François Vignole (1929–1935) and Annie Famose (1968 Olympic medallist). The combined resort has 120km of pistes; on its own, Barèges has 60km distributed over 32 runs – 11 green runs, 10 blue, 10 red and 1 black.

From Barèges centre the **Funiculaire de l'Ayré** (closed for repairs 2001) rises to 2020m, but as the village is only at 1250m it is seldom possible to ski all the way back again. Better to take the Télécabine de la Laquette up the next ridge east, using mostly easy runs fed by snow cannons to descend to **Tournaboup** (1450m). Here a 2001-installed six-seat lift whisks you up Caoubère ridge and more pistes dropping to **Super Barèges-Tourmalet** (1750m), where another new high-speed lift gets you to the pass proper, and the link with La Mongie *domaine*. When the snow level is low enough there are some monstrously long runs, even for beginners – in theory you can ski all the way back to the village from the Col du Tourmalet. However, much of the time serious skiing starts at Super Barèges (half-hourly shuttle bus from village, included in lift pass), and the La Mongie side of Tourmalet, sheltered from frequent warm southwest winds, holds snow better.

For a great day on and off piste from there, take the improved Tourmalet chairlift to the pass, and then the La Mongie lifts Coume de Pourteilh and Quatre Termes. The off-piste section begins with a short climb south into the Bassin du Bastan via a narrow gulley; from the top there is an exhilarating descent towards Lac d'Agalops, just below the Hourquette Nére, from where the valley threaded by the summertime GR10 leads back west to Tournaboup.

The Gavarnie region

South of Luz-Saint-Sauveur, the D921 follows the Gave de Gavarnie 20km upstream to its source – the superlative-laden **Cirque de Gavarnie**, a glacial bowl which first sparked touristic interest in the Pyrenees. Its heyday began in the late nineteenth century, after enraptured Romantics like Victor Hugo lauded it in almost self-parodying prose – "It's the most mysterious of buildings, by the most mysterious of architects; it's Nature's Coliseum, it's Gavarnie!" – and hyperbole, estimating its height as "ten miles" and length as "ten leagues". Such publicity drew increasing crowds to the area, reaching a record two million visitors during 1958. Since then, the annual number of visitors has fallen by 75 percent, thanks perhaps to the boom in overseas travel; the cirque and its environs have thus gained a bit of breathing space, while the creation of the national park has been the occasion for tidying up and a proclaimed, though not always effected, improvement of services in **Gavarnie village**.

It's also possible to stay 9km below Gavarnie, in the somewhat calmer village of **Gèdre**. From there you have easy road access to two other cirques: wide and ethereal **Troumouse** and lonely **Estaubé**. Most people head straight for Gavarnie (45min by bus from Luz), but anyone with a couple of days to spare can traverse all three cirques, one of the most extraordinary hiking experiences in the Pyrenees. Alternatively, two of the cirques provide access to the Ordesa region in Spain – via the **Brèche de Roland** from Gavarnie, and the **Brèche de Tuquerouye** from Estaubé. Gavarnie village is also the base camp for approaches to Vignemale peak on the more-used, higher variant of the GR10, which then curves north towards Cauterets. For any such explorations you'll want the 1:50,000 IGN Carte de Randonnées map, no. 4, "Bigorre".

Gèdre and its cirques

Purists can walk south from Luz to Gavarnie in a day along the low-altitude variant of the GR10, but since it's mostly within sight of the D921 road you may as well take the bus (2 daily July–Aug, 3 a week rest of the year, on Mon, Thurs & Sat) at least as far as **GÈDRE** (12km). Almost entirely dependent on nearby electricity-generating installations, Gèdre has no great attraction other than convenience as a base for visiting the nearby Troumouse and Estaubé cirques, but it does hold a place in Pyrenean history as the home of Henri Cazaux and Bernard Guillembet, the guides who in 1837 became the first to climb Vignemale.

There's a central **tourist office** (summer Mon–Sat 9am–noon & 3–7pm, Sun 9am–noon; ☎05.62.92.48.05). If you want to **stay**, choose from among *Pension Les Voyageurs* (☎05.62.92.48.42; closed Oct–Christmas; ③), on the road south towards Gavarnie; *Les Pyrénées* (☎05.62.92.48.51, fax 05.62.92.49.64; open all year; ④) in what passes for the village centre; and the characterful, walnut-wood-furnished *Hôtel La Brèche de Roland* (☎05.62.92.48.54, fax 05.62.92.46.05; closed late April & Oct–Dec; ⑤) also on the through road, with a good, more affordable restaurant. There are a half-dozen campsites of varying standards above and below the village, plus a pair of highly rated **gîtes d'étape** on the outskirts: *Le Saugué* (☎05.62.92.48.73; closed Nov–April; ①), also with camping space, and *L'Escapade* (☎05.69.92.49.37; closed Oct–Nov & April–May; ①). As for independent **restaurants**, *La Grotte* at a bend in the road just above *Hôtel La Brèche* might look and feel like a tourist trap, but it offers an excellent buffet lunch for under 100F/€15.30, serves until 3pm and has outdoor seating with a view of the cascade and grotto of the name in the river just below.

Héas and the Cirque de Troumouse

For the **Cirque de Troumouse**, 15km from Gèdre, take the minor D922 to the east, which starts just south of the village. After 8km you reach the hamlet of **HÉAS**, a collection of farmsteads around a pilgrimage chapel. Until the road was opened in the 1950s – and the HRP was routed through here from Barroude and Gavarnie (see below) – this must have been a lonely spot indeed; it's still one of the highest (1500m) permanently inhabited places in the Pyrenees.

Chambres d'hôtes, camping space and simple meals are available at *La Chaumière*, just below the hamlet (☎05.62.92.48.66; May–Oct; ③), or at the en-suite *Auberge de la Munia*, in Héas proper by the church (☎05.62.92.48.39; April–Nov; ③). Beyond the toll post (23F/€3.50 per car; staffed 9am–5pm), the road climbs steeply in hairpins 4km to the *Auberge de Maillet* (☎05.62.92.48.97; June to mid-Oct; dorm ①, rooms ②), ending 3km later at an enormous car park, still not big enough to accommodate all visitors on a summer's day. Walkers avoid both toll and tarmac by using a clear path up the easterly Touyères ravine starting near the *Snack Bar La Refuge*, by the toll booth.

All around the car park, the desolate, wild cirque stretches 10km from end to end, not high but much bigger than Gavarnie's and, in bad weather, rather intimidating. In better conditions it's a magical spot early or late in the day, when the day-trippers have gone – and even more so in late winter, when you can get in on snowshoes or skis and have it all to yourself.

Beneath the eastern walls of the cirque are scattered a half-dozen glacial tarns, the **Lacs des Aires**; a marked path describes a circuit of them from Héas (2hr up) or the top car park (30min away), snaking through the pastures spangled with wildflowers (ranunculus, gentian and colchicum the most prominent) and divided by rivulets. The air is full of small alpine birds, and the turf, despite national-park status, is grazed by hundreds of cows and sheep as in centuries past. A 2138-metre knoll topped by a nineteenth-century statue of the Virgin, some fifteen minutes' walk northeast of the parking lot, affords the best view possible of the place.

The Cirque d'Estaubé – and hiking to Gavarnie

The relatively small **Cirque d'Estaubé** lies at the head of the next valley west of Troumouse. You can walk there within two hours from the *Auberge de Maillet*, but the easiest way of reaching it involves backtracking 2km from Héas to the mouth of the Estaubé valley, and then climbing the D176 side road up to the **Barrage des Gloriettes**. From there, the cirque is 4km further south along a narrow, cliff-lined glen, remote and little visited except by hikers on the HRP which goes through here, linking Gavarnie and Héas. An ice-choked gulley – approached by an easier side trail from the HRP – leads finally to the **Brèche de Tuquerouye/Brecha de Tucarroya**, at the top of the cirque at its western end (see below for detailed instructions on getting through it).

Continuing west, the **HRP** – just below the cirque and marked by a few cairns – climbs sharply in zigzags to the notch-like **Hourquette d'Alans** (2430m), from where the *Refuge des Espuguettes* can be glimpsed below (see "The Cirque de Gavarnie"); to reach it (under an hour), the path first descends slowly north, then steeply westwards in more zigzags, completing a relatively easy trekking day.

Gavarnie

At first glance **GAVARNIE**, 8km upstream from Gèdre, is nothing but a tacky collection of ramshackle souvenir kiosks, and snack bars, besieged in summer by hordes scarcely less numerous than at Lourdes. A huge, recently bulldozed car park at the entrance to the village (20F/€3) is a reflection of the prevailing commercialization. Once the trippers have departed in their cars or the numerous tour coaches, Gavarnie's pavements roll up promptly at 8pm, having been first cleared of the huge piles of ordure from the horses, donkeys and mules used to carry tourists up for a quick look at the cirque.

Yet almost every house and hotel here has some connection with two centuries of Pyrenean exploration, which goes some way towards justifying the village's nickname, "Chamonix of the Pyrenees". Beside the Romanesque church, last prayer stop for pilgrims along this minor branch of the Santiago route before crossing into Spain, are buried great early climbers such as Jean Arlaud and the Passet family of guides.

Practicalities

The most historic of Gavarnie's seven pricey **hotels**, run by the same family since 1740, is the *Hôtel des Voyageurs* (☎05.62.92.48.01, fax 05.62.92.40.89; closed Oct 15–Dec 15 & Easter–June 15; ③–④), whose "Golden Book" contains the signatures of mountaineers Count Henry Russell, Charles Packe and Francis Swan, as well as those of George Sand, Gustave Flaubert, Victor Hugo and his mistress Juliette Drouet. Rumour has it that Hortense de Beauharnais conceived the future Napoléon III in one of its bedrooms on the night of August 24, 1807 – the father a Gavarnie shepherd. All that said, *Les Voyageurs* seems to have fallen on hard times. Even if you don't stay at the similarly illustrious if overpriced *Grand Hôtel de Vignemale* (☎05.62.92.40.00, fax 05.62.92.40.08; closed Nov–March; ⑦) in the southeast corner of the village, you can still enjoy a drink in its lounge, leaning against the fireplace where, according to his memoirs, Henry Russell would stand in contemplation of Vignemale. More affordable is the small but well-placed *Compostelle* by the church (☎05.62.92.49.43, *compostelle@gavarnie.com*; closed Oct–Christmas; ③), where most rooms face the cirque, and co-proprietor and certified guide Yvan offers day-long hiking excursions to celebrated nearby destinations. Modern, less characterful establishments include *Le Taillon* (☎05.62.92.48.20, fax 05.62.92.41.13; closed Nov 1–Dec 15; ④), with easy parking and hearty breakfasts, and Les Cimes (☎05.62.92.48.13, fax 05.62.92.40.55; closed Nov–Jan; ③), with rooms facing the mountain.

Chambres d'hôtes include *La Chaumière*, 500m from the village centre on the way to the cirque (☎05.62.92.48.08; closed Nov–Christmas; ③), with an attractive breakfast bar overlooking the river; and *Jeanine Fernandes*, on the opposite (northern) outskirts, situated up on a knoll (☎05.62.92.47.41; May–Oct; ③). **Hostel**-type arrangements are provided by *Le Gypaète* (☎05.62.92.40.61; may close Nov; ② HB), a fancy *gîte d'étape* just below the *Hôtel des Voyageurs*, and the CAF refuge *Les Granges de Holle* (☎05.62.92.48.77, fax 05.62.92.41.58; closed Nov; ①), out on the road towards the ski station. This is also a convivial and reasonable place to eat or just share a fireside glass of *eau de vie*. Long-running favourite *La Ruade* closed suddenly in spring 2000 and may not reopen; as of writing the only surviving independent **restaurant** in Gavarnie village is *Le P'tit Toy* (closed Nov 15–Dec 15) on rue de l'Église just behind *Hôtel Taillon*, with panoramic upstairs seating, quick service and two appetizing *menus* below 120F/€18.30.

The closest **campsite** is *La Bergerie* (☎05.62.92.48.41; mid-May to Oct) on the east bank of the river 600m above the village; facilities are exceedingly basic, and the ground sloping, but there are unbeatable views up into the cirque, and a breakfast bar. The other local site, *Le Pain de Sucre* (☎05.62.92.47.55; June–Sept & Christmas–Easter), is marginally more comfortable (hot water, charged extra) but inconvenient, 3.5km north of the village en route for Gèdre.

The Office du Tourisme forms a division of the central **Maison du Parc** (summer Mon–Sat 9.30am–noon & 1.30–6.30pm, Sun 10am–noon & 3–6pm; ☎05.62.92.49.10), which in addition to hiking and wildlife information, plus weather reports, occasionally organizes guided walks. For **snow conditions**, ask the CRS mountain rescue unit opposite *La Bergerie*. There's a Crédit Agricole **ATM** beside the Maison du Parc, and a **post office** nearby.

Skiing: Gavarnie-Gèdre

Although it doesn't compare in size with Barèges-La Mongie, **Gavarnie-Gèdre** rates as one of the great ski *domaines* of the Pyrenees on account of its snow record and wonderful situation. The resort gets its weather from the south, so has plenty of snow when the rest of the French Pyrenees has little or none (though the reverse is also true). Owing to its exposure, it is an especially cold spot, with high winds often stopping the lifts. When you get off the top lift and ski out from behind the concealing summit of 2400-metre Pic des Tentes, you have spellbinding views towards the cirque; from this lift you can also set off on some of the best *ski-randonnées* in the range, including a tour through the Brèche de Roland (see p.368) into the Parque Nacional de Ordesa in Spain.

Otherwise, Gavarnie-Gèdre is a good beginners' and intermediates' downhill resort; five of the seven green runs are longish and descend from the top point, though the five surviving blue runs are less satisfactory. Seven red and two black pistes, out of a total of 21, plus 11 lifts (3 high-speed) round out the tally of facilities (but no ski hire).

The Cirque de Gavarnie

Approaching from the north along the D921, your first, unforgettable sight of the **Cirque de Gavarnie** comes on the road just above Gèdre, from where the Brèche de Roland – the famous gap at the west side – is clearly visible. Close up, the cirque is revealed as one of Europe's most stupendous natural spectacles, scoured by glaciation into an almost perfect semicircle, 1400m from top to bottom and 890m in diameter. Despite appearances the palisades are neither completely vertical nor uniform, actually rising in three stages – a layer of granite sandwiched between two limestone beds – separated by sloping terraces, banked by snow and ice. A main **waterfall** – a straight drop during spring, two separate cataracts later in the year – plus numerous smaller ones, embellish the great wall.

There has long been talk of the Cirque de Gavarnie becoming a World Heritage Site, as it ought to be, but interested parties are pressing for developments, like cable cars, that would make that classification impossible. Between Gavarnie and the cirque (a distance of 4km) the landscape is still relatively unspoiled, meadows stretching out on either side of the stream, dotted with occasional barns.

Visiting the cirque

Ever since Charles Packe wrote in 1867 of "travellers to the cirque who have the indolence and bad taste" to take horses, there has been a tendency to scorn the *muletiers*. But if you do mount up you'll at least be supporting a traditional source of employment, important to most families in a village where lack of work is driving young people away. The *muletiers* jog alongside you for safety, making up to five trips a day. If, as a hiker, you'd rather not share the trail with them – both the crowds and the manure can be overpowering between 9am and 5pm – you can use another, calmer trail along the west bank of the *gave*, below the pilgrim route to the pass.

Either way, on foot it takes nearly an hour to enter the confines of the cirque. The broad, well-trodden "dung trail" climbs first to the *jardin botanique*, where there are more graves of *Pyrénéistes* – Louis Le Bondider and Franz Schrader – and then to the **Plateau de la Prade**, a beautiful area of streams and forest – and now the setting for an open-air summer theatre, used during the annual July festival. Beyond the plateau, another short, steepish climb brings you to the *Hôtel du Cirque et de la Cascade* (1580m; 1hr from Gavarnie) – in the last century a famous meeting place for mountaineers, nowadays a heavily subscribed restaurant with reasonable meals and drinks. It's situated well within the bowl of the cirque, and should you be there during an electric storm (quite probable on summer afternoons) you're unlikely ever to forget the echoes of the thunderclaps.

From the *Hôtel*, where the mule service stops and most clients just mill around, you can hike half an hour up the Oule valley to the **Grande Cascade**, the source of the Gave de Gavarnie (and ultimately the Gave de Pau) and, at 423m, the longest falls in Europe. Above you, the three-banded walls rise to a summit-ridge of nine 3000-metre-plus peaks, curving over 5km between **Astazou** (3017m) in the east and **Le Casque/El Casco** (3006m) in the west. The ridge – the border between Spain and France – is festooned by the shrunken remnants of the glaciers that formed the amphitheatre, some of the last eight square kilometres of glacier remaining in the entire Pyrenees. Inaccessible though it may seem, the cirque is traced by **climbing routes**, and with modern rope technique, more climbers are overcome by heatstroke than are injured in falls. In winter, the ice routes attract contemporary daredevils who jab and stab their way up the frozen waterfalls on twelve-point crampons.

Alternate return route

Rather than retrace your steps, the most pleasant way back to Gavarnie, starting just behind and above the *Hôtel du Cirque*, is via the marked path up to the meadow-set *Refuge de Pailla* (☎05.62.92.48.48; 1760m; 16 places open & staffed July 1–Oct 15; ①), the way up a 45-minute corniche route through fir and black pine, with dripping rock overhangs, grotto-springs and fine views.

Just beyond the Pailla meadow, there's a fork in the path. Left and down leads in sharp zigzags, initially beside a stream, within 45 minutes more to Gavarnie, but most prefer to head right and east a similar time uphill to the popular *Refuge des Espuguettes*, 1hr 30min–2hr from the cirque (☎05.62.92.40.63; 2030m; 60 places; weekends Easter–May & Oct, daily June–Sept; ①), huge, grey and isolated above the tree line. Lupins and crocus are abundant on the way up, and the detour is amply rewarded by sweeping views west along the frontier crest from Marboré to Vignemale and beyond. With a day-pack, allow an hour and a half for the total return to Gavarnie from the refuge; with full kit you should add a third to all the times given this section. From *Espuguettes* you can also continue east in less than a full day to Héas, via the Barrage des Gloriettes (see p.365).

The Brèche de Roland

Every walker in Gavarnie wants to get to, and through, the **Brèche de Roland/Brecha de Roldán** – a curious, nearly vertical gap at the top of the cirque. Tackle it in summer and you'll have company of all ages, nationalities and walking abilities. Such popularity might detract from the experience, but it does have a big advantage – a lone traveller can risk the climb knowing there's no chance of a mishap going unaided. The glaciers guarding the final approach are especially dangerous when there is no snow to cover the treacherous ice, and an ice-axe and crampons will be a big help at any time. If you're able to stay at the *Refuge de la Brèche de Roland* just below the *brèche*, you'll have the opportunity to ascend some peaks flanking it, or visit some famous ice caves just over on the Spanish side. If you do the trip as a day expedition from Gavarnie, count on a minimum of ten hours there and back.

According to legend, the 100m-by-60m gap was hacked out by the dying Roland, nephew of Charlemagne, as he attempted to smash his magic sword Durandal to prevent it falling into the hands of the Muslims. The eleventh-century *Chanson de Roland* describes how:

Count Roland smites upon the marble stone;
I cannot tell you how he hewed and smote;
Yet neither does it break nor splinter,
Though groans the sword,
And rebounds heavenwards.

The battle in which Roland died actually took place nearly 100km to the west near Roncesvalles (see p.466), so the tale is pretty thin, and the startling views from the top need no legend to augment them.

Approaches to the Brèche

There are three **approaches** to the *brèche*, all converging on the *Refuge de la Brèche de Roland*. The lazy way involves driving up to the **Port de Gavarnie/Puerto de Bujaruelo** (Port de Boucharo on some maps), at the end of the road to the ski station (13km); from there a clear path climbs east under the north face of **Taillon/Tallón**, rising gradually until a gully just over an hour along, where it joins a footpath coming directly up from Gavarnie. This trail, which is the next easiest way to the *brèche*, begins by the village's Romanesque church, climbs steadily but manageably on the western flank of the valley, turns into the small plateau of Pouey d'Aspé and, after a time, climbs steeply again in zigzags to join the footpath from the Port de Gavarnie (2hr 45min).

Following either of these approaches, you continue on up through the Col des Sarradets to the **Refuge de la Brèche de Roland** (aka *Refuge des Sarradets*; ☎05.62.92.40.41; 2587m; 57 places; staffed daily May–Sept, weekends Oct, part always open; ③), reached in under an hour from the junction of the paths. Situated in full view of the *brèche* and just 220m below it, the refuge is understandably packed in summer, when an average of ninety walkers a night fight for places.

The third and most challenging route, the **Échelle des Sarradets**, takes between four and five hours from Gavarnie. Having reached the *Hôtel du Cirque* you carry on south a short distance, cross a bridge, then bear southwest on a well-trodden path to the west wall of the lower cirque, below which flourish great banks of Pyrenean irises in midsummer. For the non-climber the next hundred-metre section requires a lot of teeth-gritting and not too much looking down – it's not technically difficult (steps have been cut in places), but it is rather exposed, and you wouldn't want to do it downhill. The final section follows the steep Sarradets valley to the refuge.

From its namesake refuge, the **Brèche de Roland** is about forty minutes' stiff climb away, ending with the glacier crossing. Quite often, on an apparently windless day, you'll be almost bowled over as you step through the rock "doorway" and be sent rushing for something to hold onto, while flocks of calling choughs circle easily and endlessly in the gale. Looking into Spain, a high-altitude scree desert forms the summer foreground, followed by the top of the Ordesa canyon walls and then, receding into the distance, wave after wave of dense blue-green forest, turning pink, red, then purple at sunset. Back into France the summits are barer and more jagged, the light more yellow.

Climbs from the Brèche

To the west of the Brèche de Roland, towards Taillon, the rock rampart is known as **Pic Bazillac** (2975m), which ends at the so-called **Fausse Brèche** with its menhir-like finger of rock. For the ascent of **Taillon** (3144m) continue on the path beyond the Fausse Brèche and climb along the east ridge. This is considered to be one of the easiest three-thousanders in the Pyrenees but the views are no less exciting for that – and proficient climbers can opt for the almost vertical north face.

The **Casque/Casco** (3006m) forms the eastern part of the *brèche* and is climbed with only a little more difficulty than Taillon, by passing through to the Spanish side and following the path that runs hard left, keeping close to the rock wall. A steel cable gives moral and physical support over a difficult section, beyond which you bear left to the slopes that separate Le Casque and **Tour/Torre** (3009m) – next peak of the cirque – and then left again to scramble up to the summit.

The Grotte Casteret

Standing in the *brèche* and looking southeast into Spanish territory, you can see a curious dome-shaped rock about a kilometre away. This is the entrance to **Grotte Casteret**, the most spectacular of a group of 32 ice caves of the Marboré/Monte Perdido Massif, the highest such caverns known in the world. Discovered by Norbert Casteret in 1926, the outer chamber requires no special equipment just to look in. But for the magnificent lower chamber, with the column of ice known as the *Niagara de glace*, you'll need crampons, rope and head lamp. Remember that the formations are delicate and you should do nothing that could break ice off.

It takes a good hour to get to the entrance by one of two routes: either begin as for the Casque/Casco (see above) but then, rather than bearing away left, continue around the boulder- and scree-strewn bowl; or descend into the bowl below the *brèche*, picking your way towards the domed rock and then climbing up again.

South of the Brèche: into Ordesa

Once through the *brèche* you're in the Spanish **Parque Nacional de Ordesa** (see pp.411–412). If you want to explore further – and perhaps make an ascent of **Monte Perdido** – you should head for the *Refugio de Góriz*, two to three hours away to the east-southeast. The terrain is bleak and exposed karst, with no potable water sources, but anyone who can reach the Brèche de Roland can easily get to this shelter. Keeping the bare **Pico del Descargador** (2627m) to your right and the back of the Gavarnie cirque on the left, cross the **Plana de San Ferlús** and follow the valley draining from the **Cuello de Millaris** (2457m). The only difficulty is at the **Circo de Góriz**, just before the refuge, easily negotiated by a path on the north side; if you miss it you'll be confronted by an impassable succession of vertical descents. For walks from the *Refugio de Góriz*, see p.413.

Via the Brèche de Tuquerouye

An alternative access from Gavarnie to the Ordesa lies via the tougher and much less frequented **Brèche de Tuquerouye/Brecha de Tucarroya** (2660m). The first part of the approach partially reverses the itinerary from the **Cirque d'Estaubé** to Gavarnie (described on p.365), climbing from Gavarnie village to the *Refuge des Espuguettes* and the Hourquette d'Alans. Once through the pass, the route drops eastwards in zigzags towards the floor of Estaubé, then – about halfway down – veers south-southeast, more or less along the 2200-metre contour, to the foot of the gully that leads up to the *brèche*. It's a steep ascent – 400m at an eighty-percent grade – for which crampons and axe are invariably essential. Right in the pass itself, sandwiched between the rock walls and looking like a twinned Nissen hut, stands the oldest hut in the Pyrenees, the unstaffed *Refuge de Tuquerouye* (2660m; 12 places), opened – with a lavish banquet – by the Club Alpin Français in 1890. The Gavarnie guide François Bernat-Salles carried a 75-kilo statue of the Virgin up on his back to watch over it. Thoroughly overhauled in 1999 and fitted with a heating stove, kitchen and solar-powered emergency phone, the hut further justifies an overnight stay by its setting and views south to glacier-hung Monte Perdido. If you have a tent or bivvy sac, you could descend on the other side to the camping area around the **Lago de Marboré**, 80m lower in elevation and the first reliable water since the base of the gully.

West of Gavarnie: Vignemale and Russell's caves

Any visit to the **Grottes Russell** and **Vignemale** should begin at the statue of Henry Russell in Gavarnie. The statue – a replacement for one melted down by the Nazis – is beside the main bridge, gazing west up the Ossoue valley towards his beloved Vignemale.

The problem with visiting Vignemale from the east (or any direction, for that matter) is that the approach is long. With a car you can drive on road and track along the Gave d'Ossoue as far as the **Barrage d'Ossoue**, but on foot the GR10 from Gavarnie takes over three hours. It's a wonderful hike, though, first under spectacular cliffs where lammergeier have been nesting since the 1980s, and then across pasture where marmots whistle and isards are a frequent sight. From the simple hut at the dam, the path runs along the eastern shore to a concrete bridge over the Ossoue stream. Beyond the bridge the landscape gets even more interesting, the path zigzagging across a short section of permanent ice at one point in the climb.

About three hours above the lake you reach the dilapidated but aptly named **Grottes Bellevue**, where Russell spent some summers (see box below), with fine views south. Another half-hour's walk brings you to the *Refuge Bayssellance* (☎05.62.92.40.25; 2651m; closed for renovation until 2002; staffed mid-June to Sept; ①), traditional base camp for the **ascent of Vignemale**.

<hr>

HENRY RUSSELL

It's no exaggeration to say that Comte Henri Patrick Marie Russell-Killough – known usually as **Henry Russell** (1834–1909) – was the most original mountaineer of all time. You'll hear or read his name all over the Central Pyrenees, wherever there are mountains worth climbing: a section of the museum at Luchon is dedicated to him, and there are original photographs and letters at the Musée Pyrénéen in Lourdes. God, wrote Russell, is a *présence palpable* in the Pyrenees, and he went to extraordinary lengths to achieve a communion with the spirit of the mountains. One August night in 1880, for instance, he had two guides cover him with scree on the summit of Vignemale, with only his head protruding above the blanket of stone.

Russell was an elegant eccentric who threw great parties and did the full social season in Pau most winters, yet who spoke of Vignemale as his wife and enjoyed nothing more than a seventy-kilometre stroll between Luchon and Bagnères-de-Bigorre. Despite a period of far-flung travel in America, Siberia, Australia and New Zealand, he seemed more than content to come home to Toulouse and explore the nearer wildernesses of the Pyrenees. In 1863, aged 29, he bagged the highest peak of the range, Pic Aneto. In the years that followed he made sixteen first ascents, including a climb of Vignemale in 1869 that was the first winter ascent of a major European peak. The bravery and the flamboyance of the man comes through in his fascinating *Souvenirs d'un Montagnard*: completely impressionist and untechnical, it contrasts strongly with the writings of his friend and fellow *Pyrénéiste*, Charles Packe, who made precise observations on everything from geology to botany.

Vignemale was Russell's greatest obsession. He climbed it 33 times – his last ascent aged 70 – and his passion led him to dig several cave-homes on the peak. In 1882 work began on a set of three caves close to the head of the Ossoue glacier, which soon were joined by two others; a huge party marked their completion, with fine wines and dishes set on damask tablecloths. Within five years the caves had been made uninhabitable by the shifting glacier, so Russell moved lower, carving out the Grottes Bellevue in 1888. The position didn't satisfy him, and in 1893 his seventh and final cave, Paradis, was hollowed out by explosives only 18m below the peak. By this time the commune of Barèges had granted him a 99-year lease on the summit.

Russell spent much time in his mountain homes, sometimes entertaining lavishly – he insisted on guests getting up at dawn in order to witness sunrise, rewarding them with punch at 11am. He tempted people away from the comfort of the established resorts and into the mountains themselves, a relatively new experience for the time. His activities also boosted local commerce, especially for the hotels and guides of Gavarnie, then a poor, pastoral village. It is therefore surprising that, despite his commemorative statue in the village, the caves that Russell constructed are now completely neglected.

Make an early start next morning, dropping back down the path towards the Grottes Bellevue, then cutting off west-southwest just above them to the moraine at the foot of the **Ossoue glacier**, the largest remaining one in the Pyrenees. This is dirty-looking in summer, with huge and thankfully obvious crevasses; the trodden path runs a little right of the centre. You'll need crampons and ice-axe, and you should rope up as a precaution. At the top end of the glacier is another of Russell's summer homes, the **Grotte du Paradis**: just 18m below the summit of **Pique Longue** (3289m), an easy final scramble (4hr in total from the refuge). There are several loftier peaks in Spain, but this is the highest Pyrenean point actually on the frontier.

From the *Refuge Bayssellance* you can continue on the GR10 over the **Hourquette d'Ossoue** (2734m) to the *Refuge des Oulettes* (2hr 30min further; see p.375) and thence to Cauterets.

Cauterets and around

Contrasting sharply with the settlements along the *gaves* de Pau and de Gavarnie, the elegant spa and mountain-sports playground of **CAUTERETS** – 30km south of Lourdes and 10km up the D920 from Pierrefitte-Nestalas – features colonnaded and iron-balconied Neoclassical buildings in its western quarter, especially on bd Latapie Flurin, facing the more traditional part on the east bank of the Gave de Cauterets. A long and narrow village, its surprisingly tall buildings prompted by the lack of flat ground, Cauterets wears a general air of elegance gone to seed; Belle Époque follies lie abandoned or fitted with cinemas, slot machines, bowling alleys and the like. Dozens of *résidences*, apartments and pensions are only available by the week or the month, some with a seemingly permanent contingent of OAPs, though the place in fact attracts all ages and classes, intent on having a good time. All this contrasts markedly with the idyllic alpine setting, and "endorsements" by numerous notables in centuries past.

The town owes its existence to Count Raymond de Bigorre, who in 945 gave a tidy sum to the monks of Saint-Savin, enabling them to establish the baths. National fame came in the sixteenth century when Marguerite d'Angoulême (see "Pau" p.378) became a regular, contented client, reputedly penning her *Heptameron*, the French equivalent of the *Decameron*, while here. In 1807 Louis Napoléon and his wife Hortense stayed for several months after the death of their first son; subsequently George Sand, Gustave Flaubert and Victor Hugo spent time in Cauterets, as did Alfred Tennyson, who with Arthur Hallam arrived in 1830 carrying dispatches for a revolutionary group plotting against the king of Spain. It was at Cauterets, too, that Châteaubriand finally met Léontine de Villeneuve, with whom he had been carrying on a torrid two-year correspondence; when she set eyes on the elderly poet, however, the affair came to an abrupt end. Later, Baudelaire, Debussy and Edward VII of England added their names to the illustrious guest list.

The lush countryside around Cauterets positively haemorrhages with waterfalls and no fewer than eleven **hot springs**, with a million and a half litres of sulphur-laden water claimed to course daily through the two surviving *thermes* of César and Rocher (both open daily except Sun). Rheumatism cures are big, but the chief speciality is ear, nose and throat conditions – brochures are full of pictures of happy clients sticking devices up and down various orifices.

Cauterets' reputation as a winter sports resort is equally well deserved, with nightly discos and all the trappings of package-tour après-ski. As a summer resort it's perennially popular, too, offering ample opportunities for climbing, hiking and tennis. Most of the best walks depart from the massive *parc national* gatehouse at Pont d'Espagne, 6km southwest of the resort: you can explore the valley of the Marcadau further in the same direction all the way to the border and beyond, or fashion an enjoyable loop through the valleys of Gaube and Latour. The same routes are used in winter for cross-country skiing, for which the Cauterets area is perhaps a better bet than downhill activities.

Practicalities

The town is small enough that you should have no trouble finding your way around. **SNCF buses** from Lourdes (4–5 daily) arrive at the *fin-de-siècle* wooden train station at the north edge of the centre; the adjacent **Maison du Parc** (summer daily 9.30am–noon & 3.30–7pm; ☎05.62.92.52.56) has a small wildlife exhibition (10F/€1.50), film shows on Wednesday and Saturday evenings in season and some enthusiastic wardens. The **tourist office** on place Maréchal-Foch (daily: July–Aug 9am–12.30pm & 1.30–7pm; rest of year 9am–12.30pm & 2–6.30pm; ☎05.62.92.50.27, *www.cauterets.com*), sells a useful guide to local short walks, *Cauterets aux Deux Pas*; at the adjacent Bureau des Guides, at 5 place Clémenceau (mid-June to mid-Sept daily 10.30am–12.30pm & 4.30–7.30pm; ☎05.62.92.62.02), you can obtain current information on the condition of mountain paths and climbs, as well as the weather report. Cauterets is also an excellent place to stock up if you're on a long-haul trek; there's a fruit-and-vegetable market, several supermarkets and bakeries, a laundry at rue Richelieu 19, plus several sports-goods shops.

Though many of its thirty-odd **hotels** belong to an era when people took half-board by the month, Cauterets has various affordable short-term places, all pinpointed on a placard at the north end of town. Budget options include *Le Bigorre*, 15 rue de Belfort (☎05.62.92.52.81; ③; closed Nov to mid-Dec & May); *Le Centre et Poste*, 11 rue de Belfort (☎05.62.92.52.69, fax 05.62.92.05.73; ④), and the *Gram* at 4 rue Victor-Hugo, off rue de la Raillère (☎05.62.92.53.01; ③); half-board is encouraged at the latter two hotels. For something more upmarket, all rated two-star, try the *Lion d'Or* at 12 rue Richelieu (☎05.62.92.52.87, fax 05.62.92.03.67; ⑤; closed Oct to mid-Dec); the *César* at 3 rue César on the way up to the namesake baths (☎05.62.92.52.57, fax 05.62.92.08.19; closed May & Oct; ④), with TVs and phones in the rooms; or the *Welcome* at 3 rue Victor-Hugo (☎05.62.92.50.22, fax 05.62.92.02.90; ④). There are two fairly comparable **gîtes d'étape**: the hillside *Beau Soleil* at 25 rue Maréchal-Joffre (☎05.62.92.53.52; closed Nov; dorm ①, rooms ③), with en-suite, two-to-four-bunk rooms, and the less regimented *Le Pas de L'Ours*, 21 rue de la Raillère (☎05.62.92.58.07; fax 05.62.92.06.49; ①), with a "hotel" annexe (④). On the way into Cauterets from the north, there are several **campsites**: *Les Glères* (☎05.62.92.55.34); *Les Bergeronnettes* (☎05.62.92.50.69; June–Sept), quietest by virtue of its position, across the river from *Les Glères*; *Le Peguère* (☎05.62.92.52.28) and *La Prairie* (☎05.62.92.54.28; June–Sept), fairly close to town and shaded.

Eating out, the *Brasserie Le Paris* in place Clemenceau is the prime venue for people-watching, while the friendly *La Brulerie du Gave*, at pedestrianized 7 av de l'Esplanade just east of the river, proffers decent English breakfasts, crêpes, coffee, tea and juice. For more substantial fare, there's unfortunately very little choice outside of the hotel diners; the *Giovanni Pizzeria* at 5 rue de la Raillère and *Casa Bodega Manolo* at no. 11 of the same street, with Spanish-style seafood and a set menu, are about the size of it. You'll probably be happier slightly out of town at *La Ferme Basque* (closed Oct–Nov), 4km west of town on the road to the ski station; the newly managing couple since 1999 have added hearty country fare (black pudding, wild-spinach *garbure*, lamb dishes) to a formerly snack-dominated menu.

Walking around Cauterets

There is magnificent walking around Cauterets, which lies just at the edge of PNP territory extending immediately southwest. The most useful **map** for local treks is the IGN 1:50,000 Carte de Randonnées no. 4, "Bigorre", though if you're not interested in linking up with the Gavarnie area, no. 3, "Béarn", will do. Most worthwhile itineraries depart from the **Pont d'Espagne**, a scenic old stone bridge high over the confluence of the foaming *gaves* du Marcadau and du Gaube (downstream towards Cauterets is some great kayaking), and an important landmark on the historic route across the mountains to Spain. For those with their own car, there are 1500 spaces (25F/€3.80 summer, free for winter skiers) in the **Puntas** car park at the end of the D920, 7km above Cauterets, in front of the giant PNP visitors' centre, straddling the way to the bridge. Except for vans servicing the various refuges beyond, vehicles of any sort are no longer allowed beyond this point. Otherwise six daily *navettes* from Cauterets, up the Val de Jéret (8am–6pm uphill, 9am–7pm downhill), leave you at the centre. Purists can walk there from **La Raillère**, a disused satellite spa building 3km south of Cauterets, along a fine streamside section of the GR10, pressed into double service as a park trail; it's about ninety minutes uphill along this Sentier des Cascades, under fine woods of beech and pine.

Next to the bridge itself, just five minutes from the Puntas car park, stands the *Hôtellerie du Pont* de Espagne (☎05.62.92.54.10, fax 05.62.92.51.72; ③), with perfunctory rooms, and meals served; some fifteen minutes above here, past the base of the *télésiège* to Gaube (see below), the privately run, youth-oriented *Chalet du Clot* (1581m; 45 places; June–April; ☎05.62.92.61.27, fax ☎05.62.92.07.93; ①) on the broad **Plateau du Clot** offers simple meals and overnighting, as well as cross-country skiing on 37km of pistes.

Refuge Wallon and the Pont du Cayan loop walk

From the plateau, signs for the **Vallée du Marcadau** and the *Refuge Wallon* point southwest along the valley, all sparkling streams, meadows and tall pines. At the **Pont du Cayan**, some forty minutes above via either bank of the main stream at the far end of the widest part of the valley, the path climbs left through forest to the **Pont d'Estalaunque**, and then rises more steeply to the rambling, old-fashioned **Refuge Wallon** (☎05.62.92.64.28 or 05.61.85.93.43; 1866m; 116 places; staffed daily early April to early May, June–Oct & winter holidays, plus March weekends; crude annexe always open; ①), which offers a full meal service as well. Although it's barely two hours from the Puntas car park, you gain a real sense of the surrounding mountains, which are ideal for walks and light scrambles of all sorts, rather than technical climbing. Owing to the mild climate, Scots and black pines, some several hundred years old, flourish up to 2000m elevation hereabouts.

If you're returning to Cauterets, rather than retrace your steps you can loop back to **Pont du Cayan** along the alternative marked footpath that heads initially northwest. After an hour, you reach rock-girt **Lac Nère** (2320m), and after twenty minutes further through a chaos of boulders, you arrive at the even more lunar **Lac du Pourtet** (2420m), a sawtooth ridge bounding it on the north. At a small notch on the lake's east shore you turn down and eastwards, passing the three smaller, turf-fringed tarns called the **Lacs de l'Embarrat** (as well as a marked side trail for the Lac d'Ilhéou – see p.376), and just over an hour an a half from the highest lake you should be back at the Pont du Cayan. This circuit does involve a stiff climb, and you should count on six hours' walking time return from the Puntas car park – as opposd to four if you backtrack entirely along the Vallée du Marcadau from *Wallon*. This is, it must be said, one of the more representative – and deservedly popular – day walks you can do around Cauterets; the lakes are all dissimilar, and wildlife surprisingly conspicuous for such a relatively accessible route.

Treks above Refuge Wallon

Above and beyond *Refuge Wallon*, there's a choice of routes in several directions, the most exciting of them along the HRP or its *variante sud*. You can follow the **HRP** west towards the important frontier peak of Balaïtous, using the Lac Nère approach for about 25min, then veering away west-northwest up the Gave de Cambalès, through bare terrain strewn with a dozen lakes, to the **Col de Cambalès** (2706m; 3hr from the refuge). The HRP drops southwest on the other side to the very easy **Port de la Peyre-Saint-Martin/Cuello d'a Piedra de San Martín** (2295m) on the border, then goes north down the Arrens valley to the *Refuge Ledormeur* (see p.359 for details), a six-hour day from the *Refuge Wallon*.

If you have the time and energy, press on for an hour or so to the more comfortable *Refuge de Larribet* (see p.359) – to reach it drop northwards to the junctions of the Arrens and Larribet valleys, then curl back south along the latter. From either refuge you can descend if need be to the village of Arrens-Marsous (see p.358 for details).

The **HRP variante sud** skirts Balaïtous (3146m) to the south on a generally westward course to the next staffed French alpine hut at Arrémoulit – a minimum eight-hour trekking day. It runs initially southwest from the *Refuge Wallon* along the Port du Marcadau stream, then climbs westwards to **Col de la Fache/Cuello da Facha** (2664m); once through this you're in Spain, dropping down to the north shore of the huge **Respumoso** reservoir. There's a relatively new staffed refuge (see p.419) on its north shore, built to serve the Spanish **GR11**, which runs briefly in tandem with the HRP variant here. From Respumoso you head back into France via the **Arriel** lakes and the **Col du Palas/Cuello de Pallas** (2517m) to the *Refuge d'Arrémoulit* (☎05.59.05.31.79; 2305m; 30 places; staffed July–Sept; part always open; ③) between the lakes of the same name, just beyond the southern end of Lac d'Artouste. (For more on Lac d'Artouste and Balaïtous, see p.388.)

To go **south** or **east** from *Refuge Wallon*, take the marked southeasterly HRP trail beginning five minutes below the shelter at a bridge, up the Vallée d'Arratille to the **Col d'Arratille** (2528m; 3–4hr from the refuge). From there you could either continue into the Spanish Ara valley, which drains towards the Ordesa region, or head east for a couple of hours – dropping briefly into the top of the Ara valley and then over the **Col des Mulets/Puerto de los Mulos** (2591m), always on the **HRP** – to the *Refuge des Oulettes* in the head of the Vallée de Gaube. This is a fairly strenuous, but short traverse of five hours, with the route well marked.

Loop via the Gaube and Lutour valleys

The head of the **Vallée du Gaube** is more usually approached directly from the Pont d'Espagne, as part of the deservedly popular, two-to-three-day **loop** back to Cauterets which also takes in the **Vallée de Lutour**. To accomplish it anticlockwise, you first head up the Gave du Gaube for an hour as far as the popular **Lac de Gaube**, with the snack bar *Hôtellerie du Lac de Gaube* at the north end of the lake. If you're heavily laden, a small *télésiège* (daily summer 8.30am–6.30pm up, 9am–7.30pm down; 25F/€3.80 one way, 33F/€5 return) spares you about half the climb. Done as a day-trip, the lake is another "poodle walk" target for the French, though dogs must be kept on a lead and are banned beyond the *hôtellerie*.

From the top of the lift you continue south two hours to the *Refuge des Oulettes* (☎ & fax 05.61.85.85.58, ☎06.13.70.40.00; 2151m; 75 places; staffed daily April & June–Sept, according to weather in winter; part always open; ③), where an overnight stay is recommended so that you may contemplate the gaunt, breathtaking north face of Vignemale at leisure. You'd need an extra day to tackle the peak from here; most casual walkers will continue east steeply over the **Col d'Arraillé** (2583m), which permits passage to the far less crowded Vallée de Lutour, which here forms the boundary of PNP territory.

The next suggested overnight stop is at *Refuge d'Estom* (☎05.62.92.74.86; 1804m; 30 places; staffed June–Sept; ③), perched by its lake; were you to stay here an extra night, you could explore the half-dozen sizeable **Soubiran lakes** hiding under the crags defining the head of Lutour. The main itinerary carries on north along the valley for a very easy half-day back towards Cauterets, joining the Val de Jéret at La Raillère; about an hour before the latter you meet the end of the narrow but paved road in at *La Fruitière*, a popular **hôtel-restaurant** (☎ & fax 05.62.92.52.04; closed Dec & April; ④) renowned for its game, trout and *garbure*. The restaurant's prices are reasonable – two *menus* for under 120F/€18.30 – though quality can vary, and reservations are suggested at weekends.

Traverse to Lac d'Estaing via the GR10

One exception to the pattern of walks arrayed around the Pont d'Espagne is the day-long traverse from Cauterets to **Lac d'Estaing** in the eponymous valley via the Lac d'Ilhéou, following the main **GR10**. Taking the **Téléférique du Lys** from just above bd B. Dulau in Cauterets up to an intermediate station (mid-June to mid-Sept every 30min 9am–12.45pm & 1.45–5.45pm; 33F/€5 one-way) spares you the sharp initial climb, while continuing on the **Télésiège du Grum** (same schedule; 45F/€6.90 for a combined one-way ticket with the Téléférique du Lys) brings you to the Crêtes du Lys, actually 500m higher than the Lac d'Ilhéou, with an hour on foot separating you from the refuge there (see below). For a bit extra you can haul a parapente or mountain bike up too. Without any assistance from mechanical lifts, it will take you the better part of three hours, heading up the Vallée du Cambasque, to draw even with the **Lac d'Ilhéou**, best seen in June when ice floes drift on its calm surface and the surrounding peaks such as Grand Barbat (2813m) are still frosted with snow. The modern, PNP-built *Refuge d'Ilhéou* (☎05.62.92.75.07; 1988m; 50 places; ①) at the northeast end of the lake is staffed all summer and also offers pricey meals and drinks on its outdoor terrace. From here the GR10 bears northwest out of the *parc national*, over the grassy **Col d'Ilhéou** (2242m), dropping down to Lac d'Estaing, with its hotel and campsite, after four more hours.

Skiing around Cauterets

With a selection of circuits from 1300m to 7500m in length, the **Pont d'Espagne** makes an excellent place to hone cross-country skiing skills, and following the route from the bridge into the Marcadau valley constitutes an easy yet spectacular introduction to **ski touring**. The climb to the *Refuge Wallon* (sporadically staffed in winter) totals 369m over a distance of 7km, which should take around three to four hours for beginners; count on half that to descend.

Beyond the refuge, there are possible itineraries into Spain via the **Col de la Fache/Cuello da Faxa** and the **Port du Marcadau/Puerto de Panticosa** into the Panticosa region, or the **Col d'Arratille** into the Ara valley, but these are for experts only, despite their relative ease as summer walking passes. The same goes for the winter ascent of **Vignemale** from the *Refuge des Oulettes*, subject to severe avalanche risk.

As for **downhill** skiing, Cauterets' reputation is perhaps inflated, due partly to a sunny, eastern exposure, but by Pyrenean standards it does have a good snow record. Twenty-five pistes, mostly red- or blue-rated, fill the **Cirque du Lys** to the west, reached by the *téléphérique* described above. A selection of fifteen lifts, one-third of them chairs, continue from 1850m to a top point of 2500m. There are also token downhill facilities above Pont d'Espagne, all of three lifts and five runs.

Pau

Once capital of the medieval viscounty of Béarn, and now of the modern *département* of Pyrénées-Atlantiques, the pleasant, surprisingly cosmopolitan city of **PAU** lies an hour or less by road or rail west of Tarbes. From this major stop on the main east–west

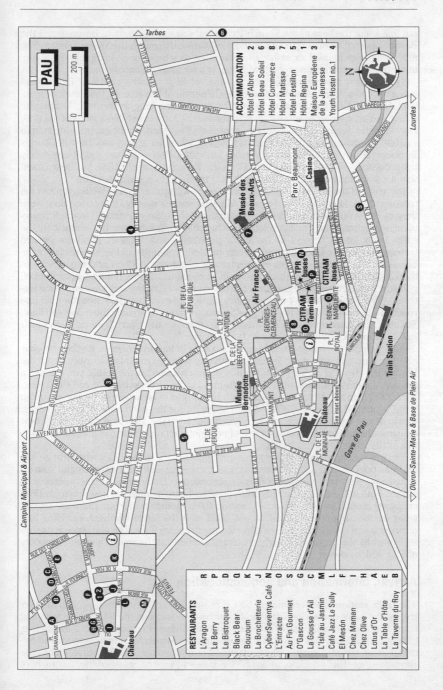

PAU

△ Tarbes   △ ❻

0 ___ 200 m

N

Camping Municipal & Airport ◁

◁ Lourdes

▷ Oloron-Sainte-Marie & Base de Plein Air

ACCOMMODATION

Hôtel d'Albret	2
Hôtel Beau Soleil	6
Hôtel Commerce	8
Hôtel Matisse	7
Hôtel Postillon	5
Hôtel Regina	1
Maison Européene de la Jeunesse	3
Youth Hostel no.1	4

Parc Beaumont

Casino

Musée des Beaux-Arts

Air France

TPR buses

CITRAM Terminal

CITRAM buses

PL. REINE-MARGUERITE

PL. ROYALE

Musée Bernadotte

Château

See inset above

Train Station

Gave de Pau

PL. DE LA MONNAIE

PL. DE VERDUN

AVENUE DE LA RESISTANCE

PL. DE LA LIBÉRATION

PL. DE LA RÉPUBLIQUE

PL. GEORGES CLEMENCEAU

RESTAURANTS

L'Aragon	R
Le Berry	P
Le Bistroquet	D
Black Bear	K
Bouzoum	J
La Brochetterie	N
CyberSeventys Café	O
L'Entracte	S
Au Fin Gourmet	G
O'Gascon	C
La Gousse d'Ail	M
L'Isle au Jasmin	L
Café Jazz Le Sully	F
El Mesón	I
Chez Maman	H
Chez Olive	A
Lotus d'Or	E
La Table d'Hôte	B
La Taverne du Roy	

Château

rail line along the base of the French Pyrenees, you can move on to Bayonne and the Basque country, or directly south to the *parc national* through the Vallée d'Ossau. You may well prefer to use Pau, rather than Lourdes, as a base for heading into the mountains: transportation is no problem and Pau is a far more amenable place.

The city first rose to prominence in 1464, when it became capital of Béarn (and Navarre) under Jean d'Albret and his wife Catherine of Navarre. In 1567, their descendant Henri d'Albret married the sister of the French king François I, Marguerite d'Angoulême, a writer of some gifts who turned the local court into a focus of the arts. Her daughter, Jeanne d'Albret, was by contrast a Protestant philistine, bringing ruin to Pau and its environs during the Wars of Religion, when her armies and those of Charles IX competed in the commission of various atrocities. Peace of a sort was restored only upon the accession of her son Henri IV to the French throne in 1589, but Béarn itself was not formally annexed by Paris until 1620 by Henri IV's son Louis XIII.

Pau entered the historical spotlight once more with the arrival of Wellington and his troops in 1814, following their defeat of Marshal Soult at nearby Orthez. So taken were they by the setting and mild climate that many of the officers returned for their retirement, inaugurating an English colony which would endure for nearly a century. By the early 1860s fifteen percent of the city's population was English, numbers swelled through the tireless (and ultimately wrong-headed) promotion of Pau as especially salubrious for tuberculosis patients, by a certain Dr Alexander Taylor. Enduring legacies of the English include the continuing pursuit of horse-racing, fox-hunting, polo, cricket, golf (the first eighteen-hole course in Europe was here), rugby and a few surviving tearooms. The English weren't the only ones attracted here, though. When the train line reached Pau in 1866, the French intelligentsia followed, among them Victor Hugo, Stendhal and Lamartine, who bestowed an epigram on the place: "*Pau est la plus belle vue de ter, comme Naple est la plus belle vue de mer.*"

Although the city has an altitude of just a couple of hundred metres, it's the only sizeable place on this side of the Pyrenees with any palpable mountain identity. From the **boulevard des Pyrénées** which bounds downtown Pau on the south, you can see a hundred-kilometre stretch of peaks, including Pic du Midi de Bigorre and Pic d'Anie, all identified on a handy *table d'orientation*. In the time of Henry Russell – buried in Pau – the boulevard provided the finest vantage point for the north face of the Pyrenees, overlooking eighty peaks including Vignemale. Now the view is diminished by new construction and a nearly constant veil of pollution, but on a clear day it's still an evocative introduction to the mountains.

Pau's atmosphere (in all senses) changed substantially in the 1950s when a huge natural gas field opened just northwest at Lacq, creating new jobs, suburbs and spin-off industries – plus massive sulphur-dioxide air pollution, lately reduced ninety percent by filtration but still problematic. Gas production and employment are now down, and Pau is casting around for new industries, among them mountain tourism: there are several good outdoor equipment shops, stores filled with the latest climbing, rambling and environmental books, and posters advertising adventure films. The ambience is further enlivened by the presence of eight thousand students at the well-respected University of Pau, which opened in 1972.

Arrival, information and accommodation

The **train station** (and terminal for SNCF buses) lies at the southern edge of the centre, on the bank of the Gave de Pau. Other buses – such as the SALT service to and from Lourdes – use the **gare routière** on rue Michel-Hounau, north of the centre, except for CITRAM and TPR to Tarbes or Lourdes, which have their own shared terminal near place Georges-Clemenceau. Train services are plentiful along the Bayonne–Pau–Toulouse line, as are SNCF buses to Oloron-Sainte-Marie, from where buses up the Ossau and Aspe valleys are less regular. The **airport**, well to the north-east of town (information on ☎05.59.33.33.00) has flights only to Paris; there's a regular shuttle bus to the town centre (☎05.59.02.45.45). Air France, the main carrier serving Pau, has a town office at 10 rue du Maréchal-Foch.

From the train station, a free **funicular** carries you to the bd des Pyrénées on its escarpment, opposite place Royale, at the north end of which is the helpful **tourist office** (July & Aug Mon–Sat 9am–6.30pm, Sun 9am–1pm & 2–6.30pm; Sept–June Mon–Sat 9am–noon & 2–6pm; ☎05.59.27.27.08, fax 05.59.27.03.21). Other sources of information include the local chapter of the Club Alpin Français, at 5 rue René Fournets (Mon–Wed & Fri 5–7pm, Thurs 5–8pm; ☎05.59.27.71.81) and the Librairie des Pyrénées at 14 rue St-Louis, a bookstore stocking a wide range of guides (including this one), maps and general literature on the mountains. Also worth knowing about is a **laundrette** at 6 rue Gambetta (daily 7am–10pm), near the post office.

Accommodation

Reasonable, salubrious **accommodation** is fairly plentiful, scattered pretty evenly around the centre of town; the best hotels are listed below. There are two **youth hostels**: one at 30 rue Michel-Hounau (☎05.59.30.45.77; ①), convenient for the bus terminal, well run and with a canteen, the other at the *Maison Européenne de la Jeunesse*, 18 rue Bourbaki, at the end of rue Montpensier (☎05.59.62.50.50; ①), also with a canteen. There are also a pair of **campsites**, with the *Base de Plein Air* at Gelos (☎05.59.06.57.37; June–Sept), just over the river from the train station, better amenitied and more convenient than the municipal one on bd du Cami-Salié, off av Sallenave towards the autoroute, on the northern edge of town (☎05.59.02.30.49; June–Sept) – take bus #4, "Palais des Sports", to cover the 5km.

HOTELS

Hôtel d'Albret, 11 rue Jeanne-d'Albret (☎05.59.27.81.58). Near the castle; never mind the floral wallpaper – the rooms, most with washbasin only, are big and clean. ②.

Hôtel Beau Soleil, 81 av des Lauriers, over 2km east of the centre in the former British quarter (☎05.59.14.20.10). Looks like the Adams Family's manse from the outside (and a few staff and guests could star in the show), but the rooms, many with full bath, are adequate and clean. Off-street parking makes this a good choice if you're driving. ④.

Hôtel Commerce, 9 rue Maréchal-Joffre (☎05.59.27.24.40, fax 05.59.83.81.74). Comfortable, double-glazed, en-suite (toilet only) rooms at this two-star, plus a decent restaurant (closed Sun) with terrace facing the interior courtyard. ⑤.

Hôtel Matisse, 17 rue Mathieu-Lalanne, opposite Musée des Beaux-Arts (☎05.59.27.73.80). Rooms here are smart enough, and though non-en suite have a fair number of baths in the corridor. ②.

Hôtel Postillon, 10 cours Camou (☎05.59.72.83.00, fax 05.59.72.83.13). Another pricier two-star just behind the place de Verdun car park; all rooms fully en suite, central courtyard garden with fountain. ⑤.

Hôtel Regina, rue Gassion corner rue Maréchal-Joffre (☎05.59.27.29.19, fax 05.59.27.04.62). Even mix of en-suite and bathless rooms at this centrally located, slightly faded two-star; lift to the upper floors. ④.

The Town

Pau possesses no absolutely unmissable sights or museums, so if you choose you can merely stroll about, soaking up the city's relaxed atmosphere without feeling too guilty. The east end of bd des Pyrénées is marked by the twin-towered **Palais Beaumont**, now a convention centre, surrounded by the **Parc Beaumont**, of English inspiration with its lake and waterfall. At the opposite end of the boulevard, the landmark **Château** (exterior grounds free & unenclosed) overlooks the crossing of the Gave de Pau on the vital Bordeaux–Zaragoza route. The first castle here was built by Gaston Fébus as part of his grand strategy to create a unified kingdom of the Pyrenees. More importantly for

France as a whole, Henri III of Foix-Béarn, king of Navarre and later **Henri IV of France**, was born in the castle in 1553.

Pau was an important theatre of the Wars of Religion, provoked here by the virulent Protestantism of Jeanne d'Albret – Henri's mother – whose activities led to equally ruthless reprisals by the Catholic King Charles IX. Later, when Henri became the French king, switching faiths in the process, he found it necessary to accommodate the sensibilities of his Béarnais subjects by announcing that he was giving France to Béarn rather than Béarn to France. Like other Pyrenean regions that became counties and viscounties in feudal times, it retained separatist leanings even after incorporation into France, and today many of the Béarnais still speak Occitan along with French – and Occitan-language street signs are making their appearance here.

At the time of Henri's birth the castle was somewhat neglected, only Gaston Fébus' original brick keep remaining in an otherwise grey monolith. The d'Albrets added some sophisticated touches, like the Renaissance windows and doorways, but the most substantial alterations – including the addition of an arcade and tower close to the entrance – were carried out in the last century, first by Louis-Philippe and then by Napoléon III and Eugénie.

Within the castle, the **Musée National** or Royal Rooms (daily 9.30am–12.15pm & 1.30–5.30pm; 1hr guided visits only; 25F/€3.80) consists essentially of Napoléon III's and Eugénie's apartments, notable mostly for some fabulous eighteenth-century tapestries and Henri IV memorabilia such as the turtle shell that was allegedly his cradle.

Just northwest of the castle, centred on the ravine-bottom chemin du Hédas, is the **quartier du Hédas**, what remains of medieval Pau. At the base of the descending **rue Réné Fournets** is a small square with an ancient fountain and laundry – the only source of water before the Revolution. Today the nearby streets are crammed with numerous places to eat and drink, many of them listed below.

Immediately north of here, at 6 rue Tran, you'll find the mildly interesting **Musée Bernadotte** (Tues–Sun 10am–noon & 2–6pm; 10F/€1.50), birthplace of the man who, having served as a commander under Napoleon, went on to become Charles XIV of Sweden in 1818. As well as pieces of fine traditional Béarnaise furniture, the house contains some valuable works of art collected over his lifetime. At the west end of rue Tran, the arcaded **place Grammont** with its four active fountains is more compelling for most, despite its use as a parking lot.

Pau's final museum, the **Musée des Beaux Arts** (daily except Tues 9am–noon & 2–6pm; 10F/€1.50), lies 500m due east of the quartier du Hédas, on rue Mathieu Lalanne. This houses an eclectic collection of (sometimes deservedly) little-known works from various European schools spanning the fourteenth to twentieth centuries, arranged thematically and chronologically. It's strong on locally born painters such as Eugène Devéria or Victor Galos – two of the few artists to have discovered the Pyrenean landscape – and Alfred de Richemont, with his intimate *The Sacrifice* (two women burning love letters). But the only really world-class items are Rubens' *The Last Judgement* (ground floor) and Degas' famous *The Cotton Exchange* (upstairs), a slice of finely observed Belle-Époque New Orleans.

Eating and drinking

Not too surprisingly for a university town, Pau has a fair quantity of affordable, varied places to eat and drink, concentrated in the pleasant pedestrian lanes around the château (slightly touristy) and the quartier du Hédas (less so).

Restaurants and brasseries

L'Aragon, 18 bd des Pyrénées. An excellent, classic *brasserie*, serving from noon until 3pm, and again 7–11pm; outdoor tables very popular at lunchtime. Seafood choices (including oysters) particularly good, but also meat dishes.

Le Berry, south end rue Gachet, near corner rue Louis Barthou. Popular with a young crowd, who come for the reasonable *brasserie* grub. Arrive early to avoid queueing, but their demi-Chateaubriand with *sauce béarnaise* is worth a wait.

La Brochetterie, 16 rue Henri IV. Good meat grills and fish in a family atmosphere. Prices from 52F/€8 for a *mini-menu* (lunch only) to around 140F/€21.40 à la carte. Open daily until 11pm, except Sat lunchtime.

L'Entracte, rue Saint Louis, opposite the municipal theatre. Offers a range of original salads and other vegetarian plates at indoor/outdoor tables.

Au Fin Gourmet, 24 av Gaston-Lacoste, near the SNCF train station. Several game-oriented *menus* – *foie gras terrine*, pigeon, rabbit – from 95F/€14.50. Closed Sun pm & Mon.

O'Gascon, 13 rue du Château. Currently the most popular and reasonable of the four non-pizzerias on this little *place*; their 140F/€21.40 *menu tradition* – big salad, stuffed quail, free dessert choice – is excellent.

La Gousse d'Ail, 12 chemin du Hédas. Well-prepared traditional French cuisine, pricey aside from two affordable *menus* under 140F/€21.40. Closed Sat lunchtime and Sun; otherwise daily until 10pm.

Lotus d'Or, 1–3 place Grammont. Considered the best Chinese/Vietnamese restaurant in town, with dishes including glazed duck *à l'orange*. Also *menus* 78–105F/€11.90–16. Closed Tues & lunchtime Wed; serves until 11pm.

Chez Maman, 6 rue du Château. A simple but palatable *crêperie/cidrerie*, often with a wait for the outdoor tables facing the castle. Open 11am–midnight.

El Mesón, 40 rue du Maréchal-Joffre. Basque-style *tapas* diner open Mon–Sat, serving until midnight. Closed Mon & Sat lunch, all Sun & Aug.

Chez Olive, 9–11 rue du Château. Despite being in a heavily touristed area, reasonable (100–180F/€15.30–27.50) *menus* with a wide choice of dishes. Closed June, plus Mon lunchtime & Sun.

La Table d'Hôte, 1 chemin du Hédas. An elegant *nouvelle cuisine* restaurant in a bare-brick former warehouse, spotlighting crayfish, quail, sole in Jurançon, and similar. Affordable gourmet *menus* at 118F/€18 and 149F/€22.70, but expect long waits between courses. Closed Sun-Mon.

La Taverne du Roy, 7 rue de la Fontaine, quartier du Hédas. Spanish-influenced cuisine, emphasizing salads and seafood; fair-value *menus* 90–120F/€13.70–18.30, though à la carte a bit over-priced. Serves until 10.30pm; closed Sat lunchtime and all Sun.

Bars, cafés and tea rooms

Le Bistroquet, 20 rue du Hédas. Straight-ahead drinks bar with outdoor tables in summer.

Black Bear, 5 place Reine-Marguerite, off bd des Pyrénées. The local "*Anglais-sportif*" theme pub, offering expensive snacks and morning coffee as well.

Bouzoum, 6 rue Henri IV. Wide-ranging patisserie and tea room; indoor seating only.

CyberSeventys Café, rue Gambetta 7 (*www.CyberSeventys.com*). The only central Internet café.

L'Isle au Jasmin, 28 bd des Pyrénées. Tea (dozens of varieties) and muffins served outside on chaise longues facing the view. Daily except Wed 10am–7pm.

Café Jazz Le Sully, 13 rue Henri IV. A relaxed, mixed-clientele café-bar with drinkers spilling out onto the pedestrian lane.

The Ossau and Aspe valleys

The parallel north–south valleys of the **Ossau** and **Aspe,** both beginning about 20km south-southwest of Pau, are the French Pyrenees at their most *sauvage*, and the region in which the **brown bears** most tenaciously resist extinction: about a half-dozen survive wild on the slopes of the main valleys, in the **Cirque de Lescun**, and in the adjoining Ansó, Echo and Roncal valleys of Spain. Tourism is less developed here because of unreliable snow for skiing, but what havoc tourism has failed to wreak, a major road-widening scheme in the Vallée d'Aspe (see pp.390–391) may accomplish. Even before this, both valleys were major arteries into Spain. Along these main roads – the D934

THE PYRENEAN BROWN BEAR

Local folklore portrays the Pyrenean brown bear – *Ursos arctos* – as a fearsome creature. In fact, unlike the American grizzly or the bears of Siberia, the native Pyrenean species is **small and timid**, its diet largely herbivorous, which means it prefers to stick to forested terrain below 1800m. (A full-grown male can attain 300kg and females 200kg, but average much less.)

The **decline of the bear population** in the Pyrenees has been startlingly rapid. By 1937, when bears had been hunted out of every other corner of France, there were still estimated to be 150–200 in the French Pyrenees. In 1954 numbers were down to about 70; by 1960 they had declined to 40, and today there are just 5 or 6 native bears, concentrated in the Béarn region, almost completely outside of the Parc National de Pyrénées. In early 2000 a wild cub was born, the first in the Ossau and Aspe valleys since the late 1980s.

Majority opinion credits the age-old hostility of pastoral communities to the animals, who do occasionally bag a stray sheep or cow, an act which in the past would lead to instant **bounty-hunting** funded by the aggrieved villagers. (This has been illegal since 1962, and the animal absolutely protected since 1981; today the government pays prompt, ample compensation for such losses.) In Aspe-Ossau, where sheep are milked regularly and closely looked after by shepherds and dogs, just 27 sheep were killed by bears during 2000.

Rural activities such as wood-cutting, berry-picking, bee-keeping and grazing are also blamed for disturbing the animals. In many parts of the Ossau and Aspe valleys such endeavours are severely restricted or banned, much to the villagers' annoyance, though there has been some co-operation; in the 1980s the villagers of Laruns were allotted a large sum to feed the bears by helicopter and refrained from felling certain groves. Until 1993, national policy goals envisioned the setting aside of over a thousand square kilometres of "tranquillity" – meaning off-limits to humans – enabling the bears to survive into this century. RDP governments backed off from this restrictive approach, and tried to provide incentives for local protection ordinances with grants for local economic development.

This conventional wisdom has been lately challenged by certain naturalists, who assert that bears actually thrive in proximity to humans. Their habitat is also not quite as restricted as previously thought – paw-prints have recently been sighted as low as 400m, and a den was detected near a roadworks site at Sarrance (350m), proving tolerance of machinery and human activity. These experts consider **depopulation of the Pyrenees** to be the main culprit in the decline of bear numbers, citing as an example the nearby Ariège, abandoned simultaneously by people and bears alike. Such revisionists maintain that bears and the country-dwellers should be left to sort themselves out by whatever means, barring shotgun massacres – preferably by fencing rogue individuals away from berry-patches and beehives, rather than banning humans from traditional mountain livelihoods. Unfortunately the truth of competing arguments may not be established before the native bears, for whatever reason, disappear.

"Restocking" programmes with "immigrants" have had less than brilliant results. Six Slovenian bears released during 1997–98 near the borders of Aran, Haute-Garonne and the Ariège promptly left the area, shunning prepared feeding sites in favour of sheep-bagging. Nearly eighty dead animals resulted before local shepherds shot the main offender, leaving her two cubs orphaned. Though the Slovenian bears are less afraid of humans and more aggressive, the *ariégois* practice of leaving sheep unsupervised to mature into mutton does not help. It is now proposed to trap the survivors and deport them to a special reserve in the Vallée d'Ossau.

The bear has been exploited as a symbol by various factions in the Vallée d'Aspe. Environmental lobbies opposed to the Tunnel de Somport and road-widening schemes (see pp.390–391) used the presumed fate of the bear as vital ammunition to slow, though ultimately not stop, these projects. Tourist brochures for the Vallée d'Aspe have depicted a cute cub clutching a flower, giving the misleading impression that the beasts are as common and locally loved as in North America's Yellowstone Park. And the same farmers and shepherds who execrate wild bears went dewy-eyed over Jojo, retrieved as an orphaned cub in 1974 and long a tame resident in Borce. In 1993, Jojo died, subsequently replaced by two Slovenian bears rescued from maltreatment at a circus and displayed in Borce's "Clos d'Ors" as a paying tourist attraction – the time has long passed since two suitable Pyrenean bears could be found for such a purpose.

through Ossau, the N134 along the Aspe – the steep, densely forested sides obscure everything other than the valley-bottom rivers and the villages directly on their banks. To see the best of the region, you should get out your large-scale map and walk.

Currently the French train service ceases at **Oloron-Sainte-Marie**, though this may change as part of the controversial developments up the Aspe. Coming from Pau you bypass Oloron completely en route to the Vallée d'Ossau, which has most to offer near the border: the touristic train ride up to **Lac d'Artouste**, tough climbing on **Balaïtous** peak, and easier, classic rambles around the **Pic du Midi d'Ossau**. Highlight of the Vallée d'Aspe, and likely to remain relatively undisturbed by the road-widening project, is the **Cirque de Lescun**: not so grand as Gavarnie's, but infinitely satisfying by virtue of its unexpectedness in a much gentler landscape.

Oloron-Sainte-Marie

The Ossau and the Aspe valleys join at **OLORON-SAINTE-MARIE**, a small town reverberating with the roar of the mingling rivers; it's the traditional centre for the manufacture of the Béarn woollen **beret**, still considered an archetypal item of French male dress. Nowadays, the single surviving factory mixes imported with local wool, and has diversified into fashion hats for both sexes, though they still make berets for most armed forces worldwide. In the town itself, dignified old commercial properties find themselves sandwiched between modern shops and offices. Overall it's a tolerable, if rather sprawling place, older Oloron poised opposite board-flat Sainte-Marie.

Oloron grew from the Roman *Iluro*, founded on a hill just south of the river confluence, where today's Sainte-Croix quarter is located. When barbarian hordes threatened to take the settlement, the inhabitants crossed the Gave d'Ossau to found the Sainte-Marie district, which in later centuries became the episcopal seat, while Sainte-Croix evolved into a commercial and military centre.

The town's two churches are the sole points of interest for the visitor. Hilltop **Sainte-Croix**, one of the oldest Romanesque structures in Béarn, has unusual interior vaulting, created by thirteenth-century Spanish stonemasons in imitation of the Great Mosque at Córdoba; together with six massive piers, it dominates the two-aisled interior, austere in the extreme except for a few ornate capitals near the apse. The Romanesque-Gothic cathedral of **Sainte-Marie** across the Gave d'Aspe boasts an ornately sculpted portal that has escaped damage by religious vandals – even during the Revolution – thanks to the extremely durable Pyrenean marble from which it is constructed. In the upper arch, the elders of the Apocalypse play violins and rebecs, while in the second arch scenes from medieval life – hunting wild boar and fishing for salmon – are represented. Above the left-hand door, the Persecution of the Church is balanced by the Triumph of the Church over the opposite door; the two guards above them recall the sanctioning by the Byzantine emperor Constantine of protection for Christians.

The gallant knight on horseback over the outer column on the right is Gaston IV, count of Béarn, who commissioned the portal on his return from the first Crusade at the beginning of the twelfth century – hence the inclusion of Saracens in chains amongst the sculptures supporting the portal. Inside the church, well away from the main area of worship, stands a Cagot stoup, a stark reminder of the centuries-long persecution and segregation of this mysterious group.

Practicalities

The **train station** lies 200m west of the river confluence; CITRAM **buses** from Pau arrive in place de la Gare out front. The **tourist office** (mid-July to Aug daily 9am–1pm & 2–5.30pm; rest of year Tues–Sat 10am–noon & 1–7pm; ☎05.59.39.98.00) is on the east bank of the Gave d'Ossau in a booth on place de la Résistance, near the nineteenth-century church of Notre-Dame.

It's unlikely that you'll need, or want, to stay the night in Oloron, and in any case most accommodation is noisily situated. That said, there are a few reasonable **hotels**: the two-star *Hôtel de la Paix*, 24 av Sadi-Carnot, between the train station and the river (☎05.59.39.02.63; ③); the two-star *Hôtel Bristol*, rue Carrérot at the corner of rue de la Poste (☎05.59.39.43.78; ④); or, if finances are tight, the faded *De la Poste* (☎05.59.39.60.97; ③), on place de la Résistance. Of higher standard than any of these is the *Château d'Agnos*, 2km south of town via Bidos (☎05.59.36.12.52; ⑥–⑦ B&B), a genuine medieval manor with most period features intact, run as an exceptional inn by a British couple. You can **camp** at the tree-shaded *Camping du Stade* on the D919 heading southwest towards Arette (☎05.59.39.11.26; open all year). Choices of **restaurants** are limited to *Le Biscondau* on rue de la Filature, overlooking the Ossau, with three *menus*; *Le Trinquet* at 3 place des Oustalots, where you can eat for under 100F/€15.30 (closed Sun outside of summer); and that rare thing in France, vegetarian *La Bio Assiette*, at 4 av Charles Moureu, by the cinema (Tues–Sat lunchtime only).

Transport up the valleys

Since the closure (in 1973) of the international rail link through the Aspe valley to Canfranc-Estación in Spain, Oloron-Sainte-Marie has been the end of the line for **trains** from Pau; there are currently up to eight daily services. Five to seven SNCF **buses** run daily south up the Vallée d'Aspe to Urdos (most of them going on to Canfranc in Spain), and four to five daily SNCF services, beginning as a Pau-Buzy train, head from the latter up the Vallée d'Ossau to Laruns, supplemented by three through CITRAM buses from Pau to Gourette, east of Laruns. In July and August only, Monday to Friday, Pic Bus offers a twice-daily service all the way up to the frontier at Col du Pourtalet, via Gabas and the Fabrèges dam, with occasional diversions to the campsite below the Lac de Bious.

Along the lower Ossau

Along the **lower Ossau** between Oloron and Laruns, there are really only two places worth stopping. At **ARUDY**, the **Maison d'Ossau** (July & Aug daily 10am–noon & 3–6pm; Sept–June Mon 10am–noon, Tues, Thurs & Sat 2.30–5pm, Sun 3–6pm; 15F/€2.30), housed in the village church, offers a comprehensive account of the prehistoric Pyrenees and an exhibition of the flora and fauna of the *parc national*. ASTE-BÉON, a few kilometres further up-valley, is home to **La Falaise aux Vautours** (daily June–Aug 10am–1pm & 2–7pm; May & Sept–Oct 2.30–6.30pm; April 10am–1pm & 2–7pm; 39F/€6), a highly worthwhile griffon vulture breeding and viewing centre, where images of vulture families going about their business are transmitted to a giant viewing screen by cameras trained on nests. Telescopes and binoculars are also available for more low-tech viewing, and staff lead walking safaris to pastures where the vultures feed.

If you have your own transport, a more alluring route into the Ossau starts in the Aspe valley at Escot, from where you cut across over the **Col de Marie-Blanque** (1035m) – through thick beech forests and uplands where more vultures wheel overhead – before descending again through pines to the Ossau valley at Bielle, some 7km north of Laruns. Just over a kilometre before Bielle, in **BILHÈRES**, you can pause for a **meal** at *Chez Jean* above the village centre, where various *menus* for under 130F/€19.80 are served on the valley-view terrace. Here, and all along the lower Ossau, the influence of the Atlantic is strong, the fields an Irish green and the forests deciduous. Although it's still some way from the Basque country, many of the villages have a *fronton*, the court used for the Basque game of *pelote*.

Laruns

The best day in **LARUNS**, 15km upstream from Arudy and 4km from Aste-Béon, is unquestionably August 15, the main festival day when young people kitted in traditional red and black – the women wearing multicoloured scarves and the men the local beret – dance to a one-man band of three-holed flute and tambourine. Otherwise it's pretty dull, best kept in mind as the last place to buy provisions before heading up to the PNP. If you need to **stay**, try the dead-central *Hôtel d'Ossau*, place de la Mairie (☎05.59.05.30.14; ③); the *Hôtel de France*, end of rue de la Gare, the street leading east from the *place* to the disused train station (☎05.59.05.33.71; ③), characterful but clean, with a lively bar; or a 28-bunk hostel, the *Chalet-Refuge l'Embaradère*, across the street at 13 av de la Gare (☎05.59.05.41.88; ①), also offering meals until late. Among half a dozen local **campsites**, closest are two down in the Quartier Pon, near the old station: *Pont Lauguère* (☎05.59.05.35.99) and *Ayguebère* (☎05.59.05.38.55), both open all year. One of the few independent **restaurants** in town is *L'Arrégalet*, 37 rue du Bourguet, 250m north of the main *place* (closed Mon noon & Sun), with several *menus* 66–154F/€10.10–23.50 and specialities such as *poule au pot* and the namesake dish – garlic-bread crumbs sautéed in goose grease – washed down with a strictly local wine list. Another, at no. 55 of the same street, is the *Auberge Bellevue*, which manages to secure both saltwater and freshwater fish (*menus* 80–185F/€12.20–28.20). The **Office du Tourisme** (Mon–Sat 9am–noon & 2–6.30pm, Sun 9.30am–12.30pm; ☎05.59.05.31.41), well stocked with literature on the Ossau valley in general, flanks the main place de la Mairie, sharing a building with the local **Bureau des Guides** (daily 2–7pm; ☎05.59.05.33.04).

The Vallée du Valentin

East of Laruns, the D918 heads up the tributary **Vallée du Valentin** to the spa of Eaux-Bonnes (4km) and the ski station of Gourette (10km), last stop (after Laruns) for most CITRAM buses out of Pau, from July to mid-September and again during ski season. **EAUX-BONNES**, yet another Second Empire watering-hole, has been spruced up of late, though the road roars through the Neoclassical central square. You're probably better off staying 1.5km northwest along a dead-end road at **AAS** with its large *Auberge du Chemin de Pleysse* (☎05.59.05.42.04; dorm ①, rooms ②) installed in two old farmhouses, with meals provided. As with a number of spas near ski resorts, the **thermal baths** at Eaux-Bonnes stay open in ski season (daily 5–7.30pm).

By contrast, **GOURETTE** is not much to look at aesthetically – all of a dozen or so concrete high-rises below the aptly named Crêtes Blanches – but its **ski centre** has plenty of interesting red runs from the 2400-metre top point, making Gourette an appealing intermediate resort, though when snow levels are down rank beginners are well served by a clutch of green runs between 1600m and 1350m. The full tally is 27 lifts (7 chairs or *télécabines*) and 30 pistes, supplemented as necessary by dozens of snow canons.

In **summer**, Gourette's position on the GR10 and the Tour de la Vallée d'Ossau hiking routes attracts a walking clientele, who stay in one of two **refuges**: either the *Club Pyrénéa Sport* (staffed July–Aug & Dec 15–April 30; ☎05.59.05.11.35; ①), on the main through road, or the CAF-run *Chalet de Gourette* (staffed July 1–Sept 15 & winter holidays; ☎ 05.59.05.10.56; ①). En route to the Col d'Aubisque, 2km above Gourette, there's a simple **hotel**, the *Crêtes Blanches* (☎05.59.05.10.03; summer only; ②) with shared bathrooms and a *table d'hôte* restaurant, which would be even more appealing to long-distance trekkers if it weren't slightly off the GR10. The closest **campsite** is well below the town, on the road to Eaux-Bonnes.

The Col d'Aubisque and beyond

East of Gourette, the D918 toils up to the **Col d'Aubisque** (1709m, 17km from Laruns), guarded by the Pic de Ger; so does one daily CITRAM bus, dropping you by the summertime café, from where you must find your own way another 18km via the Cirque du Litor and the Col de Souler to Arrens-Marsous. The **GR10** east from Gourette short-cuts most of the road on its six-hour way to Arrens, but there's still too much narrow, dangerous tarmac for it to be a really popular stretch of the long-distance route. East of the pass, the road becomes a dramatic, one-lane corniche route, threading a succession of drippy tunnels; on the bleak moorland outside, shepherds sell ewe cheese amongst the roadside heather. It's best to enjoy the views along the way from your own car, or join the ranks of Tour de France wannabes who make it a point of honour to find the breath for a *bonjour* as they pedal up to the pass.

The upper Ossau

South of busy Laruns, the Gave d'Ossau narrows drastically as the D934 enters its upper reaches at **EAUX-CHAUDES**, a gloomy nineteenth-century spa that makes Eaux-Bonnes seem lively and cheerful by comparison. But there are two reasons to prompt a stop (besides nearby **accommodation** being full in peak season): some excellent **kayaking** in the Gave d'Ossau, subject to EDF water-level manipulations, and the friendly *Chalet-Auberge La Caverne* (☎05.59.05.42.27; dorm ①, rooms ②), where Flemish proprietor Christian promises "discothèque nights" with a professional DJ rig in the cosy bar-restaurant.

Gabas

GABAS, 13km south of Laruns, is a one-street hamlet whose farming livelihood has long since been outstripped by its role as an important gateway to the PNP – accordingly here's yet another **Maison du Parc** summer daily 10am–12.30pm & 1.30–7pm; ☎05.59.05.32.13), with abundant walkers' information.

The best place to **stay and eat** is the *Hôtel Restaurant Chez Vignau* at the north entrance to the hamlet (☎05.59.05.34.06; ③); most rooms at the hotel, east of the road, have showers or baths, and the restaurant across the street, with such delicacies as frog's legs *persillade* and prune pie, is outstanding value, though they serve early even by French standards (7–8.30pm). Honourable runner-up is the cheap and very cheerful *Restaurant du Pic du Midi*, where you get trout dinners and other local specialities for well under 100F/€15.30, watched over by enormous but docile Pyrenean sheepdogs. The slightly overpriced *Hôtel Restaurant Le Biscau* (☎05.59.05.31.37; ④) is a definite second choice in both categories, though most rooms are of a good standard, with full baths. Cramped dormitory accommodation is provided by the CAF **refuge** above the hamlet, serving the GR10 (1035m; 34 places; staffed & open June–Oct & weekends in winter, apart from Nov–Dec 15; ☎05.59.05.33.14; ①); no cooking is allowed, but meals are available.

Around the Pic du Midi d'Ossau

An undisputed Pyrenean classic despite its modest height (2884m), the handsome, double-tipped **Pic du Midi d'Ossau** rears up in magnificent isolation above the Vallée d'Ossau, its distinctive mitten shape recognizable from a great distance. This is one of those summits, like Canigou and Pedraforca in Catalonia, which inspire an affection bordering on reverence; nicknamed "Jean-Pierre" by the locals, it's essentially the logo of high Béarn.

The first recorded ascent of Pic du Midi was by an anonymous shepherd in 1787, who erected a summit cairn which confirmed his success. Today the peak remains a tough scramble at the very least, and is more of a mecca for rock-climbers, but the celebrated Tour du Pic du Midi, designed for walkers to enjoy from all angles, can be completed in a single summer's day. If you want a **map** more detailed than the 1:50,000 Carte de Randonnées no. 3, get hold of the TOP 1:25,000 1547OT, or the PNP 1:25,000 map no. 1 "Aspe Ossau".

Bases

Gabas can be used as a base of activities around the Pic du Midi, but you'll get more immediately to grips with the mountain by heading 4km southwest up the very minor

D231 to the dammed **Lac de Bious-Artigues**, a seasonally crowded picnic spot with desperately inadequate parking. Just beyond there's the cheerful *Cantine de Bious*, excellent for a pre-hike breakfast or post-trek celebration, and the adjacent *Refuge Pyrénéa Sport*, almost due north of the summit (1430m; 45 places; staffed & open daily mid-June to mid-Sept & weekends May to mid-June & early Oct; ☎05.59.05.32.12; ③). If both Gabas' accommodation and this refuge are full – likely in summer if you haven't phoned ahead – your only fallback is the *Camping Bious-Oumettes* (☎05.59.05.38.76; mid-June to mid-Sept), set 1.5km below the dam on grassy terraces, with a shop; this is as high as the occasional bus goes.

A remoter alternative as a local base – though still hugely popular – is the CAF-run *Refuge de Pombie* on the southeastern flank of the mountain (☎05.59.05.31.78; 2031m; 50 places; staffed June 15–Sept 30; part always open; ③), by the Pombie tarn. A well-signposted path, part of the Tour du Pic du Midi (see below) takes you there in about three hours from Bious-Artigues: first head east over the **Col Long de Magnabaigt** (1655m), then south through the **Col de Moundelhs** and **Col de Suzon** (2127m).

The ascent – and the Tour du Pic du Midi

The standard **ascent** begins from the Col de Suzon, a fairly easy climb, but busy in summer and plagued by loose, falling rocks – helmets are recommended. At the *col* you turn west onto a route that leads directly to the mountain; things soon start to get more serious, with movable iron pegs in one section to make the summit more accessible to inexperienced climbers. The proper course is indicated by occasional cairns, and you'll reach the wide summit in about four hours.

You can make the classic, anticlockwise **Tour du Pic du Midi** in seven hours from Lac de Bious-Artigues, beginning by following the **GR10** along the eastern shore. About 1000m beyond the southern tip of the lake, or roughly an hour from *Refuge Pyrénéa Sport*, the trails divide; take the left-hand path, crossing the **Pont de Bious** and entering the *parc national*. Continue upstream on the true right bank, across flat, wet terrain – similar to the *artigues* (meadows) flooded by the Bious-Artigues dam lower down – until a sign reading "Pombie par Peyreget" directs you left (south). It's a steepish, zigzagging climb along a section of the HRP to the tiny **Lac de Peyreget**, reached just under three hours into the day. Next, slip over the **Col de Peyreget** (2322m), between Pic Peyreget (2487m) and the southern spur of Pic du Midi, and then down past the **Lac de Pombie** to the *Refuge de Pombie* just east of it, well placed for a lunch stop some four hours along. From this refuge you return to Bious-Artigues via the good trail through the **Col de Suzon** and **Col de Moundelhs**, reversing the direct *Pombie* access walk described above.

West to the Vallée d'Aspe

To traverse **west** from the Pic du Midi d'Ossau region to the Vallée d'Aspe, start out on the **GR10** as described for the Tour, but don't cross the Pont de Bious; instead, keep right at the fork, following a sign reading "Lac d'Ayous 1.30", and continue climbing westwards, initially through forest, to three successive lakes, each larger than the preceding. You arrive at the PNP-managed *Refuge d'Ayous* (☎05.59.05.37.00; 1960m; 40 places; staffed June 15–Sept 15; part always open; ③), well under two hours' walk from Bious-Artigues. Staying the night here – you'll likely camp by the Lac Gentau below, as the refuge is perennially full – is rewarded by the best available vantage point for experiencing spectacular sunrises over the Pic du Midi, reflected in Lac Gentau.

The GR10 heads west through the **Col d'Ayous**, then curves away northwards through the **Col de la Hourquette de Larry** and then down through the Pacq woods and along the spectacular Chemin de la Mâture to Etsaut in the Aspe valley (3hr; see p.393).

The Tour des Lacs

If you're not confident about tackling the all-day Tour du Pic du Midi, the **Tour des Lacs**, a circuit of about four hours from the Bious-Artigues car park, makes a fine alternative; many consider that it gives better views of "Jean-Pierre". It uses the *Refuge d'Ayous* as a fulcrum and probable lunch halt, and can be combined with the best of the Tour du Pic to make a fine two-day loop, with the Pombie and Ayous refuges (or their environs) as overnight spots.

Begin as for the Tour du Pic at the Pont de Bious, where a sign "Lacs d'Ayous 2.30" hints at what you're about to do, but at the Houn de Peyreget veer southwest, following signs, towards the **Lac Casterau**, then continue northwest over a small pass to the much bigger **Lac Bersau**, and finally north to the refuge, which you should reach two and a half hours along. The downhill return to the car park will take an hour and a half maximum. You should get to the refuge in good time for lunch, as they often run out of dishes in season, and the menu is fairly sparse to begin with.

East or south from Refuge de Pombie

You can trek to or from the *Refuge de Pombie* towards the east or south, without having to return to Gabas or the Lac de Bious-Artigues. Heading **east**, you descend by path along the Pombie stream, changing banks as necessary, until arriving after two hours at **Caillou de Soques** in the Gave de Brousset, on the D934 road 9km north of the frontier, or 7km south of Gabas. From here you can easily continue northeast on the clear **HRP** trail to the Lac d'Artouste (see below), a steep but scenic four-hour climb via the Col d'Arrious, or directly to the *Refuge d'Arrémoulit* from the *col* via the Lac d'Arrious and the somewhat exposed ledge-path called the Passage d'Orteig.

Leaving Pombie towards the **south**, you shun the Col de Peyreget route in favour of another marked trail leading in one hour to the **Col de Soum** (ca. 2100m), from where it's as long again via a heavily used path to a car-parking area 1500m north of the border at **Col du Pourtalet/Puerto de Portalet** (1794m). The trans-border road is now kept snowploughed all winter, to facilitate French patronage of the Spanish ski resort of El Formigal, 8km southeast. If you get stuck here, there's a small, simple **hotel**, the *Col du Pourtalet* (☎05.59.05.32.00; June–Sept; ③), but the nearest proper habitation, with onward bus service, is Sallent de Gállego, below El Formigal.

Around Balaïtous and Lac d'Artouste

Balaïtous, almost directly east of Pic du Midi d'Ossau across the Gave de Brousset, is, at 3145m, the most westerly Pyrenean summit to surpass the magic figure of 3000m, and one of the toughest and remotest. It was first climbed in 1825 by the military surveyors Peytier and Hossard, but they seem not to have divulged their route. Charles Packe, nearly forty years later, had to find his own way up. Balaïtous, he wrote:

> . . . *lies so completely away from the route of the ordinary traveller that the Eaux-Bonnes guides seem quite at a loss as to its exact whereabouts, as a friend who started from Eaux-Bonnes under their guidance found to his cost; for after passing two wretched nights in the mountain cabanes of the shepherds (a lodging which few Englishmen would prefer to the open air) he failed to attain even the foot of the Pic Balaïtous, the object of his search.*

After a failed attempt in 1862, Packe made a second in 1864 with the guide Jean-Pierre Gaspard, and after a week of searching discovered a route to the summit.

The miniature train – and skiing

In Packe's day, of course, there was no *téléphérique* from the giant car park and ski station at the north end of the **Lac de Fabrèges**, 7km southeast of Gabas by a roundabout road (regular summer buses). Neither was there the miniature **tourist train** of bright-red, open carriages running the 10km southeast from the top of the lift on Pic de la Sagette (2031m) to just shy of **Lac d'Artouste**. Built in 1924 to serve a hydroelectric project which raised the lake level 25m, the train was later converted for tourist purposes. Weather permitting, the train normally operates daily from early June until late September; first daily departure from the top of the *téléphérique* is between 9 and 10am depending on the season, but allow a half-hour for the *télécabine* (first departure 8.30–9.30am). Reservations are suggested (☎05.59.05.36.99), and such is the crush at peak season that you may have fixed return time stipulated on your ticket. Fare for the combined lift and subsequent train ride is 69–99F/€10.50–15.10 depending on season and time of day; walkers may be able to negotiate one-ways. It's a fifty-minute trip along the sonorously named Gave de Soussouéou to the end of the line, where the train waits for ninety minutes while passengers walk down to and around the lake before heading back. Some 45 minutes above the south end of Lac d'Artouste, nearly twice that far from the dam, sits the walkers' base camp of *Refuge d'Arrémoulit* (see p.375).

In **winter** the same *télécabine* gives access to the small beginner-to-intermediate downhill **ski centre** – thirteen runs and nine lifts – on the northeast side of Col de la Sagette.

The ascent of Balaïtous

The **ascent of Balaïtous** from *Refuge d'Arrémoulit* takes almost nine hours (return), and as this is very tough country indeed, you should have the TOP 25 1:25,000 1647OT map, or the PNP 1:25,000 map no. 2 "Balaïtous". Ascend east an hour to the **Col du Palas/Cuello de Pallàs** (2517m) on the frontier, descending southeast on the Spanish side to skirt the **Arriel** lakes and the tarn of **Gourg Glacé/Gorg Helada** (a likely lunch stop). Next follow a line of cairns to the primitive Abri Michaud shelter (2698m); the gully above it – full of loose, dangerous rock – leads to the western ridge and then, via more gullies, to the **summit** (3146m). From the top you can appreciate how opposite in character Balaïtous is from Pic du Midi d'Ossau: the latter showcased by a virtual parkland of lakes and grassy turf, your present vantage concealed by savage, lunar crags in every direction, with nothing to soften the landscape.

Traverse east to Refuge de Larribet

The HRP also continues **eastwards** from *Refuge d'Arrémoulit* to *Refuge de Larribet*; this is a short (4–5hr) but strenuous outing, intended for lightly laden trekkers experienced in traversing such terrain cross-country, and assuming passes relatively free of snow.

From the Col du Palas, cross the head of the Spanish Arriel valley to the **Port du/Puerto de Lavedan** (2615m), dropping down on the far side to the tiny **Micoulaou** lakes; from there go northeast with a clearer path past the **Batcrabère** lakes, and finally through the **Brèche de la Garénère** (2189m) to descend on *Refuge de Larribet* (described p.359). If you've been hiking westwards from Gavarnie or Cauterets, simply reverse all of the foregoing directions to move on from the Balaïtous area to the Vallée d'Ossau.

Along the Aspe

The **Vallée d'Aspe** between Oloron-Sainte-Marie and the Col du Somport has long been an important corridor between France and Spain; the Romans had a road through it, the Saracens conducted raids along it, and lately the valley has again become embroiled in controversy over its role in north–south travel (see box overleaf). In 1659, during the Wars of Religion, all the local villages but one suffered the misfortune of being burnt to the ground by Protestant forces; early the next century these settlements were reconstructed simultaneously, and – never having been altered since – now present a pleasingly homogeneous spectacle.

Escot to Cette-Eygun

The upper valley can be said to begin in earnest just south of Escot, 15km from Oloron, where a narrow namesake defile closes in on the road and river. Upstream from the gorge, along the N134, the attractive village of **SARRANCE** has strangely unexploited

THE BATTLE FOR THE VALLÉE D'ASPE

Since 1990 the **Vallée d'Aspe** has been the focus of a bitter battle between advocates and opponents of a road-widening scheme from Oloron-Sainte-Mairie to the Col du Somport, with the supplementary boring of an 8600-metre-long tunnel under the *col*. Such proposals had been debated for years, but received additional impetus upon Spain's accession to the EU in 1986 – and ETA's continuing terrorist campaign, which made a high-speed route to central Spain bypassing Basque lands that much more attractive. The Spanish region of Aragón in particular, smarting over the closure of the rail line between Oloron and Canfranc, embraced the proposal as a remedy for its perceived isolation. In June 1990, the EU granted the first 98 million francs (of an eventual 210 million) towards the project, with a Franco-Spanish agreement, signed the following year, to share more or less equally the remaining 790-million-franc cost.

As originally envisaged, the plan was to facilitate the passage of one thousand heavy trucks daily, by upgrading the N134 between Oloron and the new tunnel to expressway status as part of the trans-European E7. This meant concreting the banks of the Gave d'Aspe, blasting away sections of mountainside and farmland, and placing the tunnel mouth in *parc national* territory. Only token provision for the rail link was made, and there was no consideration of the effects on the various local animal species: eagle owl, capercaillie and lammergeier, as well as the famous brown bear.

Besides the Parisian technocrats, the vast majority of local villagers and politicians favoured the scheme, including the mayor of Lourdios-Ichère, **Jean Lassalle**. In his simultaneous capacity as president of the Parc National des Pyrénées, he had already gained some notoriety for promoting a cross-country ski resort at the Col du Somport, a notion initially quashed by the Paris-based Council of State as illegal and incompatible with the goals of the park – but now reality. Valley residents, meanwhile, saw the project, with its promise of improved communications north and south, as their last chance of rescuing the Aspe from complete stagnation, in particular halting the drift of young people to the cities.

Opposition to the plans crystallized quickly in the form of the **Coordination pour la Sauvegarde Active de la Vallée d'Aspe** (**CSAVA**), based at the *gîte d'étape* in Cette-Eygun and headed by **Eric Pétetin**, who came eventually to be loathed, dismissed as a misguided idealist, or respected – in equal measure – by the inhabitants of the valley. Almost single-handedly, he managed to delay the project for three years.

Already by August 1991, CSAVA and its allies had appealed successfully to the EU to halt funding temporarily, claiming that the Canfranc–Oloron rail line could be reopened to carry both passengers and trucks at a **cost** ten times less than the eventual projected total (one billion francs) for the road works. Next, the anti-development faction raised the spectre of massive **environmental degradation** in the wake of a projected four thousand vehicles in total per day (not just a thousand trucks) through the tunnel by 2010, and also seized on the detail of the tunnel's siting within the PNP.

The French Environment Minister, caught between the ecologists and the numerous *département* officials supporting the tunnel, attempted to placate the former by moving the tunnel mouth 15m out of the PNP, for a total length of over 8km. In August 1992 the prefect of Pau signed the *déclaration d'utilé publique* (**DUP**), or go-ahead decree. But CSAVA had not yet exhausted its legal recourses; in December 1992 an administrative tribunal in Pau found that environmental impact statements had been deficient, nullifying the previ-

associations with Marguerite d'Angoulême, who stayed and wrote here when the weather in Cauterets turned bad. The village surrounds the ancient monastic church of **Nôtre-Dame-de-la-Pierre**, with a fine organ perched in the gallery and a wonderfully rustic cloister. This now houses the **Ecomusée de la Vallée d'Aspe** (daily July–Sept 15 10am–noon & 2–7pm, rest of year Sat, Sun or hols 2–6pm; 25F/€3.80), devoted to valley history, natural and otherwise. The only other tourist amenity is the humble *Restaurant Labay* on the old through road, now traffic-restricted.

---

ous DUP. Rather than appeal against this decision, the government elected to apply for a new DUP, paying careful attention to all the points raised by the ecologists. The government succeeded in July 1993, and the final plan included provisions for bear-crossings and rehabilitation of the abandoned rail line, with work beginning over the winter 1993–1994. With far less opposition, the Spanish had completed the boring from their side, and their approach road – beginning in Zaragoza, bound for Huesca and Jaca – was already of the necessary standard.

CSAVA and its allies hadn't limited themselves to the courts. Throughout 1991 and 1992 they organized escalating campaigns of **civil disobedience**: graffiti, demonstrations, "Sioux" war dances in full tribal regalia around gendarmes designated as "palefaces" (a strategy which earned Pétetin the nickname "l'Indien du Somport"), road obstructions, and – ultimately – extensive vandalism to surveyors' stakes and the tunnel work site. Their ranks were swelled by large numbers of foreign activists, particularly from Belgium and Holland, where the Pyrenees have many avid aficionados. For his pains Pétetin was arrested and detained no less than 35 times, on the final occasion being sentenced to two years' imprisonment.

In the eyes of many *Aspois*, the eco-activists were merely carpetbaggers – as evidenced by the influx of out-of-town agitators during 1992 – who would decamp to the next fashionable cause were the issue decided in their favour, leaving the locals with the consequences. Pétetin was granted a presidential pardon and early release in July 1993 just as the DUP was issued – reflecting the authorities' confidence that work could proceed no matter what new strategies CSAVA devised. The tunnel will open during spring 2001, and civil disobedience in the Vallée de Aspe has taken a new twist. Organized by Greenpeace and the WWF, thousands of activists (including soon-to-be French Environment Minister, Green Party member Dominique Voynet) bought tiny plots of land near Bedous, along the proposed course of the approach highway, to spin out for as long as possible the zoning and compulsory land-purchase process. In any event, the highway won't be finished before 2006 at the earliest, owing in part to the Portalet narrows and difficult rocks at Urdos.

In March 1998, municipalities and interested individuals in France and Spain drew up and signed the **Pacte de Somport**, which endorsed a strategy of accepting the tunnel, but pressing for a dual right of way: a reopened rail line to take passengers and heavy freight, with the roadway (of reduced width) reserved for local traffic and light vehicles. Since the Mont Blanc tunnel disaster, in which juggernaut lorries were implicated, the French government may slowly come around to backing a ban on monster vehicles in the Tunnel du Somport – which would undermine much of the justification for a multi-lane highway. As of writing, rehabilitation of the railway has been approved "in principle", while the French SNCF and CSAVA dropped mutual lawsuits in 1999, with La Goutte d'Eau confirmed in its tenancy of the Cette-Eygun station until the rail line is rehabilitated. Eric Pétetin half-jokingly applied in advance for the job of stationmaster, saying he was best qualified though at present he's not active in CSAVA.

In the end the improvements and their true impact will probably prove anticlimactic, bringing neither the degree of revitalization to the area that its advocates envision – the new road will in fact bypass the Aspe villages – nor quite the environmental damage feared by opponents. However, one enduring legacy of the long campaign against the expressway and tunnel has been to open up decision-making processes to public scrutiny in what is historically an overly secretive and centralized nation.

For a base, you could do far worse than **LOURDIOS-ICHÈRE**, 10km west along the minor D241 over the Col d'Ichère (or by path, part of the Tour de la Vallée d'Aspe, from Sarrance). Here you can choose between *Gîte d'Étape Estivade* (☎05.59.34.46.39, fax 05.59.34.48.04; June–Sept; ①), also with **camping** space, and *Chez Lamothe* (☎05.59.34.41.53; ⑤ HB), which does excellent family-style meals and has just two **rooms**; there's another **restaurant** in the village, the inexpensive *Auberge Bellocq*.

Back in the main valley and 7km south of Sarrance, the first place of any consequence – though still resolutely rural as reflected in its traditional Thursday morning market – is **BEDOUS**. Here you'll find a fine church, an arcaded *mairie* and the miniature, eighteenth-century **Château Lassalle** on the quiet Place de l'Église east of the through road. Also on this *place* is a *crêperie* (May–Sept) and the less institutional of two **gîtes d'étape**, *Le Mandragot* (☎05.59.34.59.33; ①); the other, English-speaking *Le Choucas Blanc* (☎05.59.34.53.71, fax 05.59.34.50.86; dorm ①, rooms ②) is on the through road opposite the main car park, and thus noisier. If you're driving, note that Bedous has the highest petrol pump in the valley – there's nothing else until well into Spain. There's also a quiet **campsite**, open April–Nov. Several **bars** on the through road do snacks and Spanish-style *tapas*, while the lone butcher is recommended for superb picnic pâté.

Villages around Bedous offer further amenities. There's a *gîte* 1500m southwest in **OSSE-EN-ASPE**, *Les Amis de Chaneü* (☎05.59.34.73.23; ①), though the campsite is reportedly small and noisy. About 7km east along the D237, **AYDIUS** offers *La Curette* (☎05.59.34.78.18, fax 05.59.34.50.42; ④), *chambres* and *table d'hôte* in an isolated farmhouse. **ACCOUS**, the valley capital 3km south, has a **tourist office** (☎05.59.34.71.48), the highest supermarket in the valley and the unusually salubrious two-star *Hôtel Le Permayou* (☎05.59.34.72.15, fax 05.59.34.72.68; closed Oct; ④), with fully en-suite rooms and an affordable restaurant (*menus* 70–120F/€10.70–18.30; lunch only Nov–March).

Some 3km beyond Accous at **L'ESTANGUET** hamlet, the *Auberge Cavalière* perches high above the highway (☎05.59.34.72.30, fax 05.59.34.51.97, *www. auberge-cavaliere.com*; ①), specializing in horse-riding, cross-country skiing and walking packages (though walk-ins welcome); the stables are on the premises. Accommodation is either at the *auberge*'s attached hotel (④) or at its *Refuge des Ecuyers Montagnards* further up the hill, accessible by 4WD track. The auberge's restaurant is well regarded, with *menus* 98–165F/€15–25.20 and à la carte.

Just before **CETTE-EYGUN**, 2km southeast from the *Auberge Cavalière* turning, *La Goutte d'Eau* (☎05.59.34.78.83; ①) is an activists' centre housed in the disused train station and managed by CSAVA (see p.390), combined with a *gîte*, restaurant and bar-café. Housekeeping comes a distant second to political activity, but additional accommodation is provided in an old train carriage parked on the overgrown tracks, and there's **camping** space by the river.

Lescun and its cirque

Certainly the highlight of a trip along the Aspe valley is the grey limestone **Cirque de Lescun**, more intimate than Gavarnie's, contrasting sharply with the pastures and dense forest at its foot. Pyramidal, and often marbled with streaks of snow, the toothy peaks forming the cirque – such as the two Billare summits, the Aiguilles de Ansabère and storm-lashed Pic d'Anie (2504m) – rise as a semicircular screen from the quiltwork of fields ingeniously laid out by generations of farmers.

The substantial stone houses of **LESCUN** village, wonderfully placed amidst trickling fountains on a sunny south-facing slope, lend photogenic balance in the foreground. Six steep kilometres along the minor D239 above and west of the valley floor, the village is no longer a going concern; two-thirds of its houses are holiday homes or abandoned altogether, and winter desolation is the rule. This acknowledged, in summer you can buy cheese and milk from one of the few remaining shepherds behind the **post office**, and use Lescun as an excellent base for a walking tour of the cirque. Best **accommodation** is the comfortable, antique-furnished *Hôtel du Pic d'Anie* (☎05.59.34.71.54, fax 05.59.34.53.22; April–Sept; ⑤), which has the village's only **restaurant** with decent, hearty fare, and a basic grocery store on the ground floor. Lescun also has two *gîtes d'étape*: one run by the hotel, just opposite it (①), and the rival *Maison de la Montagne* a bit north (☎05.59.34.79.14; ①), with drinks on the lawn for all-comers, and 4-to-5-bed rooms. There's a medium-sized, grassy, well-equipped and incomparably sited **campsite**, *Le Lauzart* (☎05.59.34.51.77; May–Sept) south of and below the village.

South of Lescun: the head of the Aspe

Once past the Lescun turning, the N134 carries on through Etsaut and passes just below the attractive village of Borce. In the disused train station of **ETSAUT** you'll find the most westerly **Maison du Parc** (daily May to mid-Sept 10am–noon & 1–6pm; ☎05.59.34.88.30), featuring exhibits on the Pyrenean bear. You can **stay** at *Hôtel des Pyrénées* (☎05.59.34.88.62, fax 05.59.34.86.96; ③), quite the heart of the village with the only **restaurant** here; across the road at *La Maison de l'Ours*, a *gîte d'étape* with three-to-six-bed rooms (☎05.59.34.86.38; ②); or at the "official", larger *Gîte Etsaut* (☎05.59.34.88.98, fax 95.59.34.86.91; ①).

BORCE, poised above the valley floor on the west bank, is a medieval showcase, the one place to escape the warfare of 1659 and still graced by sumptuous fifteenth-century mansions. There are three *gîte*-style **accommodations** here: *La Communal*, upstairs from the central bar-*épicerie* (☎05.59.34.86.40; 18 places; ①); the cosier *Gîte Saint-Jacques-de-Compostelle* (☎05.59.34.89.25 or 05.59.34.88.99; ①) at the north outskirts, intended for bona fide pilgrims, with just six beds (including a double room); and *Camping-Gîte du Poey* (☎05.59.34.87.29; open all year), with a *gîte* all year (18 places; ①), just above the village, with great views and meals offered.

Both villages lie on the **GR10**, which en route southeast to Lac d'Ayous negotiates the spectacular **Chemin de la Mâture**, some 3km south. Hacked out of the sheer flank of a ravine, this path is broad enough, but the edge is not for the vertigo-prone; watch out also for ropes across the trail fastened by avid climbers abseiling down the rock face. If you're not up for a point-to-point traverse, you can still experience the *chemin* as a five-hour day loop. At **Pont de Cebers**, 1.5km south, take the GR10 through the ravine, then return to Etsaut via the **Col d'Arras** on local trail no. 34. More ambitiously, over two days, you could vary a return from *Refuge d'Ayous* by using a non-GR trail heading via the **Col d'Ayous** and the unattended *Refuge de Larry*, but this path brings you down to Urdos, not Etsaut.

The grim **Fort du Portalet** (privately owned, no visits) appears atop a sheer cliff west of the N134, directly opposite the Chemin de la Mâture gorge. It acquired some notoriety as a political prison during and after World War II, when the Vichy government here detained Léon Blum, Socialist French premier of the 1930s; later Marshal Pétain himself was held here by the Allies.

Shortly after, **URDOS** is the last village on the French side of the Col du Somport, and arguably worth a special trip for the co-managed *Hôtel des Voyageurs/Hotel Le Somport* (☎05.59.34.88.05, fax 05.59.34.86.74; ③–④), a former post house that's been in the same family for seven generations. The *Voyageurs*' **restaurant** is superb, offering the best value in the valley: the 95F/€14.50 *menu* gets you vegetarian *garbure*, a fish plate such as *brochette de lotte*, a meat/game dish (boned duck breast in green peppercorn sauce), and dessert. There are no longer any shops or petrol pumps, but there is a **bank** (with ATM) and a riverside **campsite** just north.

Beyond Urdos several daily well-spaced SNCF buses continue on through the beech forests and the PNP through the new tunnel under the **Col du Somport**, and beyond to Canfranc, the terminus for trains from Jaca in Aragón. The twisty old road still climbs over the pass itself, accessing the cross-country ski centre of **Somport-Candanchú**, 34km of marked trails (9km on the Spanish side), presumably dodging the numerous ventilation silos for the tunnel.

Walks from Lescun

There are any number of walks for all levels of commitment in the fantastic limestone scenery south and west of Lescun, ranging from day-trips and brief circuits of the upper Aspe to long-haul traverses. Hiking is much the best way to tour the heights of the cirque, since public transport on either side of the border – which these peaks form – is almost nonexistent. Water can be a problem in these rock strata, so top up bottles wherever possible; the best **maps** for the area are the IGN 1:25,000 1547 OT TOP 25, or the PNP 1:25,000 map no. 1, "Aspe Ossau".

West: the GR10, HRP and Pic d'Anie

The **GR10** to Arette-la-Pierre-Saint-Martin is the most northerly route, an easy day's walking of under six hours. It follows a six-kilometre road – no short-cuts possible – for ninety minutes northwest of Lescun as far as the *Refuge de L'Abérouat* (1442m), eye-to-eye with 2300-metre Billare peak; the refuge specializes exclusively in boisterous children's holidays, but offers meals to all-comers. This is as far as cars can go; there's a huge car park for those who've forgone the boring road tramp up. Next, the route – briefly track, then path and cross-country – enters beech forest under the striking organ-pipe formations of **Orgues de Camplong** before emerging above treeline at the basic, five-person Cabane d'Ardinet hut. From here the GR10 climbs to another shepherd's *cabane* – last reliable water for the day, cheese for sale when occupied – at Cap de la Baigt, and then steeply northwards into the **Pas d'Azuns** (1873m; 3hr from Lescun). After dropping into a slight bowl the path climbs again to the **Pas de l'Osque** (1922m), after which the GR10 crosses karst desert en route to Arette-la-Pierre-Saint-Martin (see p.454), two hours due west.

For an **ascent of Pic d'Anie** (*Auñamendi* in Euskera; 2504m), the most westerly summit over 2000m on the French side, head south from Cap de la Baigt, curving under Pic du Soum Couy and up into the **Col des Anies** (2030m). The main HRP carries on westwards from here to Arette-la-Pierre-Saint-Martin; for Pic d'Anie, follow the easy marked path southwards. From the summit (2hr from the *col*; 4hr 30min from Lescun) you can return to Lescun in rather less than four and a half hours, making this a popular day outing from the village.

The best traverse route, though, is the **HRP variante**, which heads for the *Refugio Belagoa* in Spain, where you can pick up a bus. From Lescun you head west on track towards the toe of Petit Billare, reaching an obvious plateau at about 1100m. From here a good trail climbs steeply past a waterfall (fill up) to the **Col d'Anaye** (2052m; 3hr), on the south flank of Pic d'Anie. On the other side of this pass you enter the twisted karst dells of Spain's *Parque Natural Pirenaico*; Belagoa lies two and a half hours further west.

Tour of the border peaks

Using Lescun or Borce as a starting point, you can make a very worthwhile three-day **tour of the border peaks** which satisfactorily covers the terrain south of the preceding itineraries. Beginning in Lescun, head southwest through the Bois de Landrosque, up the *gave* draining from the **Aigulles d'Ansabère**. At the base of the lesser pinnacle (2271m) are some shepherds' huts, near which are some all-important springs and camping spots. But since you're only about three hours out of Lescun, you may wish to continue due south up to the frontier. Cross this via a nameless saddle (2030m) above the tiny **Lac d'Ansabère**, where you're poised to tackle the slight descent to **Ibón de Acherito** (1870m; 5hr from Lescun), just inside Spain and another scenic possibility for water and camping.

From here the topography dictates a wide skirting of the border ridge on its southeast face before crossing back into France via the **Col de Pau/Puerto de Palo** (2017m; 90min from Acherito), just northwest of the similarly low **Pic de Burcq/Pic de Burco**. (From Acherito or the Puerto de Pau it's simple to link up with the Spanish GR11, down in the main valley to the south – see p.448 for a reverse itinerary.)

Back on the French side, now within the final westerly extension of the Parc National des Pyrénées, an increasingly good path, as the HRP, hugs the ridge – except for a diversion north over the **Col de Saoubathou** to avoid **Pic Rouge/Pico Rojo** – to deposit you within five hours from the Ibón de Acherito at the PNP-administered *Refuge d'Arlet* (☎05.59.36.00.99 or 05.59.34.76.88; 2000m; 30 places; staffed July 1–Sept 15; ①), beside the **Lac d'Arlet**.

The most scenic way of returning to the Aspe valley involves heading east along the HRP to the small **La Banasse** cirque with its spring, and then descending north, initially via the **Baralet** valley, and then over the Col de Lagréou to change to the **Belonce** drainage, which leads out of PNP territory on a good if steep path into Borce (5hr from Arlet). If necessary, you can continue northwest along the GR10 to Lescun.

THE SOUTHERN APPROACHES

South of the Spanish **Parque Nacional de Ordesa y Monte Perdido**, in the region of **Alto Aragón**, depopulation is even more pronounced than in the French Pyrenees, as a glance at the map with its sparse villages will confirm. Among towns, only Jaca and the provincial capital Huesca muster over ten thousand inhabitants, while more than four hundred mountain villages languish virtually abandoned – the highest such concentration in Spain – occupied only in summer by older people with flocks to graze, plus a handful of city-dwellers restoring ruins as holiday homes or "alternative" enterprises. This desolation is owed largely to the late General Franco and his policies. Determined to punish the *Alto Aragoneses* for their staunch support of the Republican cause, his regime withheld vital services, ignored the ravages wrought by natural disasters and dammed numerous arable valleys beginning in the 1950s, leaving the villagers little alternative but to migrate to the cities. In the seven thousand square kilometres of Alto Aragón there are now fewer than fifty thousand inhabitants, an average density of seven per square kilometre.

The salient geographical features in the east of this region are impressive valleys or canyons and strange, wedding-cake-like mountains, both eroded from the same banded limestone. The **Valle de Ordesa** – heart of the *parque nacional* and the most popular approach for an ascent of **Monte Perdido**, linchpin of the canyons – was first publicized by the French journalist and adventurer Lucien Briet, who for eight consecutive summers after 1904 traced a route from Gavarnie to Torla. (Some of his photographs can be seen at the Lourdes museum, and a Torla inn has been named in his honour.) Nowadays this landscape needs no advertisement; during holiday periods, the gentle riverside paths of Ordesa and all approach roads from the west or south are packed to the gills, while the gateway villages become increasingly commercialized with each successive year.

Other canyons east or southeast of the Valle de Ordesa, wholly or partly within the park, are no less impressive in their own way but receive far fewer visitors. The absence of public transport to trailheads and limited accommodation here could be both cause and consequence of this neglect, but the extra effort required to visit these other canyons is amply rewarded. Despite having a road through it, the **Valle de Pineta**, draining east from Monte Perdido, discourages casual acquaintance with its heights by

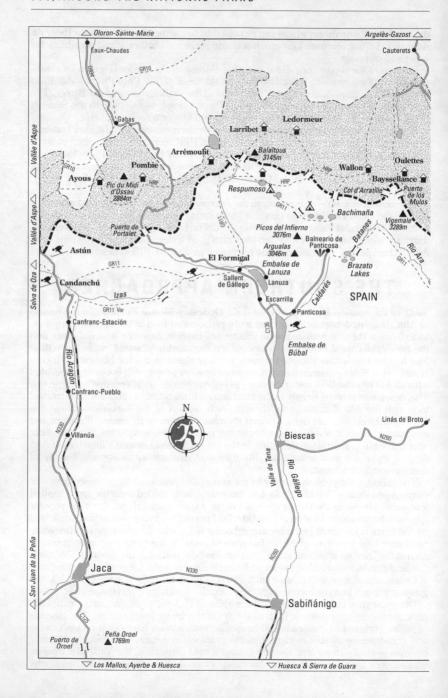

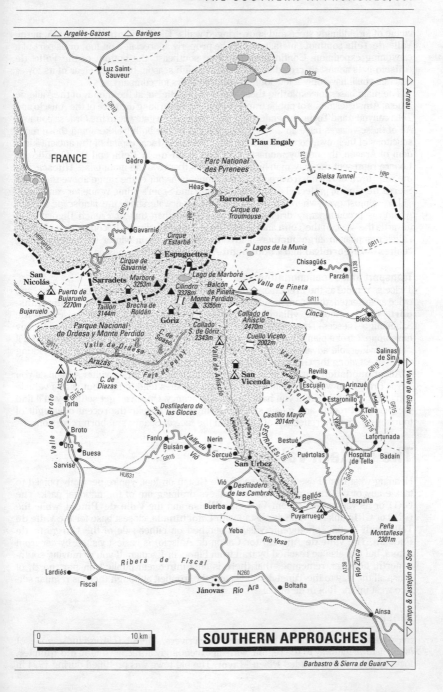

SOUTHERN APPROACHES

virtue of forbiddingly steep and snow-fringed walls. The **Garganta de Escuaín**, in the **Valle de Tella** south of Pineta, can only be properly appreciated on foot or as part of a canyoning expedition. Continuing clockwise southeast, the bottom of the **Valle de Añisclo** gets almost as crowded as Ordesa in high season, but once clear of its lower reaches you'll have only a few long-distance walkers for company.

The main bases for exploring these canyons are **Bielsa**, at the mouth of the Valle de Pineta; **Aínsa**, terminus of public transport and within striking distance of the Añisclo and Tella canyons; and **Torla**, the enduringly popular western gateway to the Ordesa country. All of these villages have an ample range of facilities for both trekkers and those more solicitous of their own comfort. Southwest of the park, **Jaca**, capital of the ancient kingdom of Aragón, the nearby monastery of **San Juan de la Peña** and the **Castillo de Loarre** represent the only man-made attractions that rival the mountains. **Huesca** and the wine town of **Barbastro** are ignored by most in favour of the range above them, the **Sierra de Guara**, protected as a *parque natural* and Spain's prime venue for canyoning.

Like almost everywhere south of the Pyrenean watershed, the landscape of Alto Aragón is predominantly drier and less vegetated than that of French Bigorre, but towards the west, in the **Tena** and **Canfranc** valleys, the climate becomes more humid. Lakes reappear in large numbers above **Panticosa**, and in winter the nearby skiing centres of **El Formigal** and **Candanchú-Astún** do a thriving business.

Transport and accommodation

Twice as remote as the French approaches in terms of distances from major cities, and twice as deserted, the Spanish side has consequently relatively deficient **public transport**. Of the foothill villages described in this section, only those on the Sabiñánigo–Biescas–Torla–Sarvisé axis see more than one daily bus service, and many have none; careful planning is vital if you're to make the necessary connections. You'll gain considerable advantages by renting a car, or bringing your own, or by trekking east-to-west along the GR paths which run perpendicular to most roads.

Accommodation can be a serious problem in peak summer or winter seasons if you haven't reserved well in advance – even the campsites tend to fill – but with a vehicle you can simply drive until you happen upon a vacancy. Once you get settled, you'll find the **prices** of rooms and meals still surprisingly low despite the recent onslaught of tourism – perhaps a reflection of realism in the face of Spain's stubborn recession.

The eastern valleys

Heading west from Posets and the Valle de Gistau on foot, you're perfectly poised to tackle any of the three major easterly valleys draining out of the national park. The GR11 or its variant leads from Viadós to **Bielsa** and the **Valle de Pineta**, while the GR19 or GR15 link the Valle de Gistau with **Lafortunada**, closest base for the **Valle de Tella**, with its tiny, photogenic villages perched on either side of the **Garganta de Escuaín**. The **Valle de Añisclo** (or Cañon de Añisclo) is easiest visited by car from **Aínsa**, but can also be reached by trail from Pineta or Escuaín. If you're moving south-to-north, however, remember that there is only infrequent public transport north of Aínsa all the way to the Túnel de Bielsa and the frontier, although there is regular service west up the Ribera de Fiscal.

Aínsa

Sited above the confluence of the Ara and Zinca rivers, **AÍNSA** (*L'Aínsa* in Aragonese) is the natural gateway to the region, with an exceedingly attractive hilltop **old quarter**, focused on the vast, arcaded **Plaza Mayor**. The old town was prettified during 1994 in an attempt to cash in on some of the cross-border trade pouring down from the Bielsa tunnel, but in fairly good taste, with nowhere near the tackiness associated with Torla; traffic is banned and cars are directed to a car park on the west (200ptas/€1.20). Just off the plaza stands the exceptional Romanesque church of **Santa María**, with a unique triangular cloister dictated by the sloping topography, and an ancient crypt with a forest of magnificently capitalled columns under the apse. For 100ptas/€0.60 you can climb the belfry for splendid views over the river valley, the town, *plaza* and fifteen-to-sixteenth-century **Castillo** to the west. This is under restoration but already acts as venue for the early-August *Festival Internacional de Música*, attracting big names such as Tarika, Clannad and the Afro-Cuban All Stars, as well as lesser-known Spanish acts. If you've time to fill, the **Museo de Oficios y Artes Tradicionales/Museum of Trades and Traditional Arts** (July 1–Sept 15 daily 10am–2pm & 4.30–9.30pm; spring/autumn daily 10am–2pm & 5–8pm; 400ptas/€2.40) is worth a few minutes. It resembles an antique shop, well lit but labelled in Spanish only, highlighting ironwork, carpentry, basketry and so forth.

Practicalities

The only **accommodation** in the old quarter is *Casa del Hospital* (☎974 500 750; ③), a *turismo rural* unit by the church, but there's plenty of choice for **eating** and **drinking** on and near the Plaza Mayor: the *Bodegas del Sobrarbe* (closed Nov–Easter) at no. 2 is the most renowned and expensive (4500ptas/€27 *a la carta*, 2700ptas/€16.20 for dull *menús*), but at the less pricey *Bodegón de Mallacán*, under the arches at no. 6, you can just have coffee. East of the square, you'll find the lively *Bar Restaurante Fes* at Calle Mayor 22, with affordable *menús del día* featuring grilled meat and a more interesting *carta*, and *Bar Restaurante El Portal*, at the easterly Portal del Abajo, with an outdoor terrace but somewhat basic fare.

The unsightly and traffic-plagued **new quarter** below has the **tourist office** (summer daily 9am–2pm & 4.30–8.30pm; ☎974 500 767), as well as Aínsa's **hotels** and **hostales**. Of these, *Hotel Sánchez*, Avda de Sobrarbe 10, the main street (☎974 500 014; ⑤); *Hostal Dos Ríos*, Avda Central 2 (☎974 500 106; ④); and the humble *Hostal Ordesa* (☎974/50 00 09; ②) on the road west are representative. The local **campsite**, *Camping Aínsa* (☎974 500 260; April–Sept), lies 1km east along the C140 towards Campo. Intersport (☎974 500 983) at Avda de Sobarbe 4 comes recommended as an outfitter for **canyoning**, Aguas Blancas next door (☎974 510 008, *www.pireneo.com/aguasblancas*) is one of two local **rafting** and **kayaking** specialists, while the Centro Equestre El Trío at Banastón village 3km southeast offers **horse-riding**. Aínsa is the last stop for the **bus** line plying the C138 road northwest towards Torla, which overlaps partly with the Barbastro-Boltaña line.

Bielsa and Parzán

The surprisingly large town of **BIELSA**, at the entrance to the Pineta valley, hung on as a Republican stronghold long after much of Alto Aragón had been overrun by the Nationalists; when the place finally fell in June 1938, most of it had been bombarded by Franco and finally burnt by the defeated, which explains its somewhat heterogeneous appearance. Today it has become a prime, if slightly tacky, summertime target for more pacific armies of French day-trippers, and could experience another identity change if plans for a nearby downhill ski resort come to fruition. Nonetheless, traces of its identity as a traditional mountain county-town still persist in its old river bridge and porticoed town hall, with magnificently framed first-floor window, on the Plaza Mayor. Walkers heading towards the Valle de Pineta from the Posets Massif are virtually obliged to stop off here, since it's the only place close to the valley with supplies and accommodation. Bielsa is also renowned for its lively **carnival celebrations**; if you've missed it, you can get an idea of some of the rather outrageous costumes from the displays in the **Museo Etnológico** (summer daily 6–9pm, winter Mon–Fri 10am–2pm), housed in the town hall.

Practicalities

At present Bielsa gets sporadic **bus** services **from Aínsa**, three evenings weekly; if driving, you have to use the free car parks at the southern outskirts and walk in the short distance. Coming **from the north**, the Vallée d'Aure bus only reaches Aragnouet-le-Plan; rather than attempting to hitch through the tunnel (no pedestrians allowed in it), a better plan would be to trek southeast from the *Refuge de Barroude* (see p.339) on an HRP variant to **PARZÁN** village, 4km north of Bielsa, also on the GR11. Sleepy Parzán has a small shop on the main highway beside a **bar-restaurante**, plus two **turismos rurales**: *Casa Marión* in an older building (☎974 501 190; ②) and the more modern *Casa Ferrer* (☎974 501 124; ②))

Bielsa, with its **banks** and shops, is a better supply point for trekkers than Parzán. Central **accommodation** here, in rough preference order, includes the welcoming and spotless *Hostal Vidaller* (☎974 501 004; ②–③), just west of the plaza (info in ground-floor shop), with three grades of affordable rooms from basic to parquet-floored "lux"; the *Hostal Marboré* just north of the plaza (☎974/501 111; ③); the *Hostal Pirineos* (☎974 501 015; ③), and the comfortable *Hotel Valle de Pineta* (☎974 501 010; fax 974 501 191; ④) nearby, with rooms overlooking the Zinca valley. Characterful *Bar-Restaurante El Chinchecle*, very near the *Marboré*, has rear-patio seating but is more musical night spot than eatery. For a proper **meal**, try the local-patronized *comedor* of the welcoming *Hostal Pañart*, out on the east side of the A138 (☎ & fax 974 501 116; ③), also endorsed as a lodging.

The Valle de Pineta

A glacial trough scoured into sheer, stepped rock walls, the **Valle de Pineta** extends 15km west-northwest of Bielsa, terminating in the majestic **Circo de Pineta**; just above the *circo* looms **Monte Perdido** (3355m), one of the more celebrated summits in the Pyrenees. The idyllic floor of the valley, where reeds and birches fringe the white, boulder-flecked Río Zinca, broadened in the valley's lower reaches by a dam, contrasts drastically with the awesome cliffs of the Sierra de Espierba to the north and the even more fantastic **Sierra de las Tucas** to the south. At first glance you'll doubt that ascents of either the Circo de Pineta or the Sierra de las Tucas are possible; however, they are attainable, the rewards commensurate with the effort.

Valley **accommodation** is limited to two **campsites** – the reasonably priced and well-equipped *Pineta* at Km 8 of the valley road (☎& fax 974 501 089; April–Sept), and a very basic, inexpensive *acampada libre* in a meadow at "Km 14" – plus the comfortable *Parador Nacional de Monte Perdido* (☎974 501 011; fax 974 501 188; ⑦) at the base of the Circo de Pineta. The *parador* has a bar and lounge room from which more sedentary tourists scan the mountains through a telescope. Hikers might use the newish *Refugio de Pineta*, prosaically set nearby on the left bank of the river (☎974 501 203; 1240m; 73 places; open all year; ①), generally overrun with school groups but serving sustaining meals to all-comers.

Walking out of the Valle de Pineta

The valley's flanking palisades attract legions of technical climbers, but there are a few steep, strenuous walks here, too. The classic hikes – up to the Balcón de Pineta, a shelf 1200m higher than the valley floor at the top of the Circo de Pineta, and the GR11 route climbing a similar height over the Collado de Añisclo – both lead into the northeast corner of the *parque nacional*. For all outings, you'll need the Editorial Alpina 1:40,000 "Ordesa Vignemale Monte Perdido" map.

Lagos de la Munia

Beside the Ermita de Nuestra Señora de Pineta, near the *parador*, an important trail emerges; briefly marked as the GR11 (see below), further along this veers north into the **Río La Larri** stream valley en route to the two lakes (2526m) in the **Circo de la Munia**; allow three hours one way, and a full day to enjoy it.

Balcón de Pineta and beyond

For the **Balcón de Pineta**, take a different path going left (west) just opposite the *parador*, which brings you shortly to a bridge at El Felqueral (1400m) and the foot of the cliffs. A subsequent series of tight zigzags gives progressively more unnerving views, as you climb through loose rock to the *balcón* (2530m; 3hr 45min from *parador*). The ascent is particularly steep in the final stages and shouldn't be attempted early in summer without crampons and ice-axe.

Twenty minutes to the northwest, a one-night tent stay is permitted at **Lago de Marboré** (2595m), which on a sunny day is a welcoming blue against the hard grey rock. But most eyes will be on the mass of Monte Perdido to the south, its savage northeast wall aproned by its huge glacier. Just north of the lake, the frontier pass of **Brecha de Tucarroya/Brèche de Tuquerouye** (2660m), with its historic hut, gives access to the Estaubé cirque and the HRP down to Gavarnie (see p.370). West of the lake, it's a ninety-minute climb through snow fields and across scree to the **Cuello de Astazú/Col d'Astazou** for a magnificent view over the Cirque de Gavarnie.

Finally, you can head south from the lake over the **Cuello del Cilindro** (3074m; 3hr); this is rather more difficult than the three-hundred-metre-lower Brèche de Roland, requiring year-round full snow-climbing gear including rope and, preferably, some prior experience in this sort of terrain. From this pass it takes around three hours more to descend to the *Refugio de Góriz* (see p.413); in theory you could get there in one long July day from the Valle de Pineta, but it's highly advisable to break the journey with an overnight at Lago de Marboré.

The GR11: Parzán to Añisclo

The **GR11** west from Parzán is initially not very exciting: first paved road to **Chisagüés** hamlet, then 4WD track up the valley of the **Río Real** as far as the spring, peak and finally pass of **Petramula** (2160m; 3hr). From the saddle you've fine views of the Valle de Pineta before a steady but not gruelling descent (except in the final moments) to the *ermita* by the *parador* (2hr 30min more).

From the valley floor (ca. 1300m), the GR11 then climbs southwest up what appear to be the impossibly sheer palisades of **Las Fayetas**, through the **Collado de Añisclo** (2453m) and beyond. This is a tough walk, like the Balcón route impossible without crampons and ice-axe until late June, and completely out of bounds in spring because of the danger of avalanches, which have gradually killed most of the trees on these slopes. But during summer it offers marvellous scenery close to hand and a bird's-eye view over the valley.

The start of this gruelling four-hour climb is signposted near the *ermita* beside the *parador*, and again from the track serving the upper primitive campsite. This is the most reliable river crossing; if you try from the refuge downstream, you're in for a mud-wallow and impenetrable riverbank thickets at the very least. Once over on the far side there are no further trail ambiguities until you're up on the *collado*. Beyond this saddle, the main GR11 was rerouted during 1989 in response to walkers' complaints. If inexperienced, or laden with a heavy pack, you should *not* use the variant heading northwest, since this inches perilously for 400m along the sheer face of **Pico de Añisclo** at the 2500m contour, with only a short cable to help you over a particularly nasty stretch always slippery with snowmelt. Instead, descend south for 1hr 45min along the main GR11 to the crude, unattended *Refugio de Cazadores* at the head of the **Añisclo canyon**; there is plenty of turf and water nearby if you prefer or need to camp.

Otherwise, continue west-northwest along the GR11 up the Barranco Arablo (Fon Blanca) – the last reliable water being the vigorous waterfall of **Fon (Fuén) Blanca** at its mouth – where the occasionally scree-laden trail worms its way up along grassy terraces to the **Collado Superior de Góriz** (aka Arrablo; 2343m; 2hr 20min from Fon Blanca). Here you're treated to great views of Monte Perdido, Pico de Añisclo and Sum de Ramond; beyond the *collado* the *Refugio de Góriz* is 40min away, for a total of eight and a half hours' walking from the Valle de Pineta.

The Ribera de Fiscal: the lower Ara valley

The Río Ara is the major tributary of the Zinca from the west, but the lower reaches of its valley are known as the **Ribera de Fiscal** after its most important village. By Aragonese standards the valley bottom is wide and relatively fertile, yet strangely deserted; there are nearly a dozen ghost villages between Fiscal and Aínsa, within sight of the road, sporadically squatted by Spanish anarchists and alternative types who make their views known with banners stretched above the road. Lately there's a more permanent roadside placard above the site of a half-built dam, which would disrupt the flow of the last undammed river in the Spanish Pyrenees, detailing its whole sorry history (see box opposite).

Boltaña

BOLTAÑA, 8km west of Aínsa along the N-260, divides like its near neighbour into two parts: the ugly roadside development on the through highway, and the atmospheric hill quarter. Here the plaza is virtually filled by the sixteenth-century **Colegiata de San Pedro Apostol**, with its rib-vaulted ceiling, sturdy piers and carved choir stalls at the rear. Just downhill in a cul-de-sac, the *Casa Coronel* does just two things in its *bar-restaurante*, but well: chef's salad and garnished grills, served indoors or with mountain views in the courtyard. They also keep a few *turismo rural* **rooms** (☎974 502 154; ②).

Fiscal and Lardiés

FISCAL, 20km upriver from Boltaña, is the next inhabited place, with a genuine country feel: tended kitchen gardens, hay in barns, ambling livestock. Despite falling some distance short of Ordesa it's well worth considering as a base, owing to the tranquillity and high standard of its tourist facilities (including shops and two **banks**, the only ones hereabouts). Signposted 100m before the church, with very jolly, slightly loopy but down-to-earth management by Rony and Anna, *Casa del Arco* (☎ & fax 974 503 042; ③) offers lovely antique- (and textile-) furnished, en-suite rooms in a slate-floored, eighteenth-century mansion. Even higher standard is offered by luxurious *Hostal Casa Cadena*, another restored 1780s farmhouse near the top of the village (☎ & fax 974 503 077, *www.pirineo.com/casacadena*; ④); rooms are modern but unique, with central heating. Downstairs is an equally posh **restaurant**, currently the best in Fiscal; the gourmet *carta* at 5000ptas/€30, strong on fish, meat and Somontano wines, may break budgets but a *menú* (1950ptas/€11.70) of chard with clams, grilled *sepia*, dessert and house wine, is affordable, as are *raciones* at the bar. Families with their own transport might try *Los Tres Albares*, 3km west in the all-but-abandoned hamlet of **LARDIÉS** (☎974 503 006; minimum one-week stay July/Aug/hols), which offers four- and six-person apartments (10,700–12,800ptas/€64.30–76.90). Proprietor Joaquín Puyuelo is a

DAMS IN ALTO ARAGÓN

The reason behind the lower Ara valley's desolation is a proposed but yet-to-be-completed **dam at Jánovas**, at a critical set of narrows 6km west of Boltaña. The process of compulsory expropriation of land and houses to be inundated began in 1959, targeting the residents of Jánovas, Lacort and Lavelilla villages. By today's standards, risible sums were offered as compensation; by 1964 most stubborn holdouts had been evicted by the combined threats of Franco's Guardia Civil and privately hired thugs. Those who sold up had their houses dynamited (thus accounting for the ruinous appearance of the three villages), while "subtler" methods of persuasion such as blocking all water supplies and staving in the door of the Jánovas school with the children still inside were employed *pour encourager les autres*. Just one brave couple – **Emilio and Francisca Garcés** – insisted on staying on in Jánovas, holding out in primitive conditions until 1984, when they too gave up and moved to nearby Campodarbe.

Yet this dam has **never materialized**, beyond an earthen dyke half-obstructing the riverbed, where earth-movers occasionally appear and push mud around. Two binding **deadlines** for interim accomplishment have come and gone, while **Iberduero**, the dam contractor, went bankrupt and re-formed, yet the new company insists it will complete the project in the face of sustained opposition. The dam promoters' strictly legal position is that the valley residents were paid full and **final settlement** in 1960, and having departed (or rather, been made to) should stay out. The displaced and their partisans argue that this took place under conditions of dictatorship, with scarcely realistic compensation; furthermore, that by failing to complete the project by stipulated deadlines, Iberduero and its successor have **voided the original contract** and, upon repurchase of their property (at the original rates, of course), the villagers have a clear case to return unhindered.

The prevailing uncertainty has also caused a wave of nervous abandonment in adjacent Javierre and Ligüerre de Ara, though the consensus is that, despite the hydro-honchos' bluster, the dam won't ever be finished. It would have to be substantially **enlarged** to make it economically viable, and the upstream villages affected have wised up, demanding hefty sums for their land.

Another dam anecdote serves to further illustrate the ruthlessness and collusion of all the establishment organs in Franco's state. One valley west, in the Río Tena basin, **Lanuza** village was forcibly evacuated and token payouts made when most of its lands, and some houses, were submerged by the namesake dam in 1975. Since then, half the original owners – those 5m or more above the mean water line – have **bought back** their old homes and rehabilitated them. But when they went looking for their beloved 700-kilo bronze **church bells** "Elena" and "Quiteria" (patron saints of Lanuza), they had considerable difficulty finding them. The local bishop, wanting no nostalgic rearguard action, had removed them from the belfry and filed the names off. One was eventually recovered in Torla, but the other is still missing.

certified mountain guide, and the region just upstream is ideal for cross-country skiing. Fiscal also has an **albergue** in a Belle Epoque mansion opposite the church, *Saltamontes* (☎974 503 113; ①), as well as two all-year **campsites** just upriver: smallish *El Jabalí Blanco* (☎974 503 074; open all year) with its own pool and a few bungalows, and the giant *Ribera del Ara* (☎974 503 035; open all year), by the municipal pool.

The Valle de Tella

The **Valle de Tella**, through which flows the Río Yaga, opens northwest roughly halfway between Aínsa and Bielsa. Though its praises are little sung in conventional tourist annals, it has long been one of the favourite **canyoning** venues on the flanks of Monte Perdido. At the head of the valley, just inside *parque nacional* territory, plunges the **Garganta de Escuaín**, a series of waterfalls, smooth chutes and pools where, equipped with ropes and wet suits, devotees abseil, slide and swim.

This is great walking country too, especially when the terrain closer to Monte Perdido is snowed up. The **GR15** and **GR19** overlap near Tella village, on the valley's east flank, and a PR itinerary completes a tour of most highlights; the best single base for walkers is Lafortunada, out on the main road below Tella. Scenically, the eight local villages are overshadowed, in all senses, by a landscape dappled by the interaction of soothing vegetation and blindingly bare rock. Green, lush scrub – much of it *boj* (box), made into souvenir utensils – blends into low alpine forest, with two-thousand-metre **Castillo Mayor** presiding on the west, and remoter **Peña Montañesa** (2301m) dominating the skyline to the southeast.

Car access – and canyoning

The top of the valley is easily accessible by ordinary car: paved roads lead to Revilla on the east bank and to the village of Escuaín on the west. The **Revilla turning** leaves the main road at Hospital de Tella, from where it's 8km in total to the end. As the road climbs to the hamlet of Cortalaviña there are wonderful views east to the distinctively tilted lump of Peña Montañesa; then, 2km beyond Cortalaviña, the road divides. The right-hand option climbs to Tella (see below), while the left-hand road continues along a ridge to Revilla, where it ends.

To get into the **Barranco de Consusa** just below Revilla, one of the six main canyoning courses of the area, follow an onward path towards a *mirador* inside the *parque nacional* for ten minutes. The Consusa's course includes a three-hundred-metre-long "staircase" with four thirty-metre chutes and countless smaller drops. It'll take four to six hours to cover the full length of the stream, and at the bottom it's about 45 minutes' walk back to either Revilla or Escuaín.

The **turning for Escuaín** is closer to Aínsa, 9km north on the main A138 to just beyond Escalona, then west along the HU631 towards Añisclo. After 1km on this road, take the paved road on the right (north) signposted to Escuaín (via Belsierre and Puértolas), 15km in total from the A138. Some maps (including the Firestone) mistakenly indicate a nonexistent access road from Hospital de Tella. From Escuaín a track to the northwest (barred to vehicles at the park boundary) affords access to the main canyoning area in the *garganta*.

Lafortunada and Badaín

LAFORTUNADA, on the A138, 17km north of Aínsa and 15km south of Bielsa, isn't the most prepossessing of villages, but it does make the most convenient overnight base for walkers, with a choice of **accommodation**. There's a *turismo rural, Casa Tomas* (☎974 504 019; ③), and *Pensión Casa Sebastian* (☎974 505 120; ②) offers congenial rooms, some with en suite, and filling *menús*, but adjacent *Hotel Badain* (☎974 504 006, fax 974 405 048; *www.rci.es/staragon/hhu/hbadain*; ④) has one of the best restaurants in these valleys, *menú* only (1600ptas/€9.60) but comprising a broad choice of fish or vegetarian dishes. The latter hotel takes its name from the hamlet of **BADAÍN**, 500m southeast, graced by a severe eleventh-century church with a round staircase tacked onto its square belfry, which now houses an **albergue** (☎974 504 075; open all year; ①). The church nave's a bit over-restored, but retains its Gothic stellar vaulting and a finely carved gallery. Both the GR19 and GR15 pass the church: the former on its rather humdrum way along the Río Zinca to Laspuña, the GR15 more excitingly east through the mountains towards Saravillo and the Valle de Gistau (see p.300).

Walking in the Valle de Tella

If you don't have transport, the quickest way into canyon country is along the north-westbound, joint **GR15/19** trail, well signposted 200m north of the church in

Lafortunada. This climbs initially northwest within two hours to the picturesque village of **TELLA**, bigger than it looks from afar and restored for seasonal use. There's a park **information office** (daily July–Oct 9am–2pm & 3–9pm) dispensing glossy brochures, but no other facilities except for an all-important fountain. As well as the imposing Romanesque parish church, there are a clutch of *ermitas* (isolated rural chapels) to which you can detour: oldest are the eleventh-century **Virgen de Fajanillas**, an easy and obvious ten-minute walk west of the village, and **Juanipablo**, fifteen minutes further northwest on an intriguing pinnacle.

Just north of Tella, the GR19 and GR15 part company: the former heads northeast to Salinas, while the GR15 descends to a picnic area and **dolmen**, threads through the hamlet of **ARINZUÉ** and drops to the river at **ESTARONILLO** hamlet (4 summer inhabitants; 1hr 15min from Tella). The final track approach to Estaronillo is often jammed with cars belonging to French rafters, who delight in running the **Garganta de Marval** of the Yaga just downstream.

From Estaronillo you and the GR15 climb another hour and a quarter through thick woods to **ESCUAÍN**, a mostly abandoned settlement taken over in summer by strolling cows and rough campers, usually technically equipped enthusiasts exploring the **Garganta de Escuaín**, which lies just upstream. There's no longer an *albergue* here, but you might pause at the park **information office** (same hours as Tella's) before continuing along paths into the water-sculpted ravine.

From Escuaín a very steep trail drops in twenty minutes to the Río Yaga, then continues on the far bank past a derelict mill, crosses the outflow of the Barranco de Consusa and climbs from the river. Ninety minutes out of Escuaín, five minutes shy of the road up from Tella, be extra observant: here you can veer south on the fairly clear, marked **PR3** trail down to Estaronillo – mistakenly shown on some maps as taking off from the road itself – or north along an overgrown twenty-minute path to **REVILLA**. Even more desolate than Escuaín, with just a few houses modernized as vacation retreats, the hamlet is well camouflaged by the orange and grey cliff immediately behind.

If you opt instead for the PR3 south, you continue past Estaronillo and then along a shelf of land wedged between the Garganta de Marval and Castillo Mayor, finishing after two and a half hours in total at **Hospital de Tella**, 3km west of Lafortunada. It's possible to complete the entire figure-of-eight itinerary of Lafortunada–Tella–Escuaín–Revilla–Estaronillo–Hospital in a single, long summer's day, taking in the best this limestone region has to offer.

Escuaín to Añisclo

Escuaín itself is a good jumping-off point for walking further **into the parque nacional**, specifically the **Valle de Añisclo**. Head northwest, high up on the right (southwest) bank of the Yaga, at first on track (signposted as "Surgencia del Yaga") and then on path, until you reach the **Cuello Viceto** (2002m; 3hr). From here a wide path curves south down into Añisclo, pausing at a shelf on which are the spring and unstaffed refuge of **San Vicenda** (4hr 30min along), adjacent to one of the park's few permitted camping areas.

From San Vicenda the best trail drops north into the bottom of the canyon past **Fuente de Foradiello**, and then crosses the main Añisclo watercourse just downstream from the mouth of the Capradizas ravine. Once on the far bank, you can head north to Fon Blanca and the GR11 (see above), or follow the main Añisclo canyon trail south for three and a half hours to the **Ermita de San Úrbez**, at the very entrance to the Añisclo canyon (see the following section).

More simply, you can also follow the **GR15 southwest** from Escuaín to the *ermita* in about six hours, leaving you enough daylight to reach accommodation in Nerín or Buerba. The trail initially heads west over the **Cuello Ratón** on the shoulder of Castillo

Mayor, and then veers south, mostly on track, to the village of **BESTUÉ**. This has one of the best views southeast in Alto Aragón, with the banded Sestrales ridge on the west separating you from Añisclo; there's also a well-signed, 2000-opened *Albergue Tresserols* in the centre (☎646 809 752; ①), which provides meals and makes a good halt between Lafortunada and Nerín or Buerba (all 4–5hr distant). If you stay overnight, find the time for the half-day trip **up Castillo Mayor** (2014m) on non-GR paths, worth it for guaranteed sightings of lammergeiers and other vultures. Beyond Bestué on the GR15, you're on scenic path again for 2hr 30min to the *ermita*, involving a roller-coaster course over the Sestrales, rewarded by views into Añisclo from the top.

The Valle de Añisclo

The uninhabited **Valle (Cañon) de Añisclo**, forging due south from the Collado de Añisclo and roughly equidistant from Aínsa or Lafortunada, is on a far grander scale than the Valle de Tella and accordingly more visited. It's a beguiling spot, more intimate and wild than its other rival Ordesa; neither is the path running through it, parallel to the Río Vellos (Bellós), a pram-pushing stroll, given its often sharp grades and vertiginous drops from unguarded edges.

If you have transport, you can reach Añisclo on the minor but paved HU631 road heading west from just north of Escalona on the A138. Once past an initially unpromising landscape – where, 2km along, a large **campsite**, *Valle de Añisclo* (☎974 505 096; Easter–Oct 15), below Puyarruego village is noteworthy only for a last chance to swim in the Río Vellos, forbidden further upstream – you enter the *parque nacional* at the dramatic **Desfiladero de las Cambras**, appetizers for the Añisclo canyon. Here the road is confined to a shelf blasted out of the rock wall, too narrow for excursion buses, and designated one-way westbound (eastbound traffic heads to Escalona along a purpose-built detour via Buerba – see opposite). At the west end of the gorge, 12km from the main highway, knots of parked cars announce the mouth of Añisclo just to the north.

The canyon walk
From the parking areas, two broad paths – equally valid, as they form a loop around the confluence of the Vellos and Aso rivers – lead north into the canyon.

The right-hand path crosses a bridge high above the joint streams, then follows a ledge where a cave has been converted into the **Ermita de San Úrbez**. Some fifteen minutes past the *ermita* you change to the west bank and climb to meet the GR15 trail coming east from Nerín on its way to Bestué. Soon you're passing through box thickets and beech woods, with the occasional conifer or yew, the locality all cool, damp and shady except at midday, thanks to the constant misting from the river. Its flashing cascades and tempting green pools glimmer far below you on the right, tantalizingly out of reach, and perhaps just as well, since you're not allowed to bathe. High, sheer walls amplifying the roar of the torrent culminate in the **Sestrales crest** to the east, here interrupted by an uncanny keyhole-shaped cleft.

By now you'll have noticed that progress upstream is not steady – the path roller-coasters constantly, with a particularly notable climb and hairpins away from the river about two hours along, at the top of which you have the best views possible into the lower canyon. The most spectacular section finishes at the grassy expanse of **La Ripareta** (1400m), only about 500m higher than San Úrbez but because of the nature of the trail nearly three hours distant. Here, you're level with the river once more, but camping is not permitted; otherwise it's a good spot for a picnic, or watching the sky for birds of prey.

From La Ripareta there's a choice of onward routes, and whichever you choose you'll have more solitude, since the gradient stiffens and the trails become fainter. About 2km (40min) north you can cross the main river and follow a path up to the authorized bivouac area and shelter at **San Vicenda**. Continuing on the west bank from La Ripareta for about ninety minutes, you'll reach the Fon Blanca cascade at the Barranco Arrablo (see p.402), which funnels the **GR11** west to the *Refugio de Góriz*. In the opposite direction the GR11 leads over the Collado de Añisclo to the Valle de Pineta; you'll want a fairly early start from San Úrbez to finish either of these traverses in a single day (the *Refugio de Góriz* is a more reasonable goal).

West from Añisclo: the Valle de Vió

West from the mouth of the Añisclo canyon, the road follows the **Valle de Vió**, a deserted district particularly hard hit by the exodus to the lowland towns; the half-dozen or so local villages have just a handful of residents, and one place is completely abandoned. But in a reversal of the situation prevailing at the Valle de Tella, the villages with their eleventh-to-thirteenth-century churches are far more interesting than the valley itself, which is sun-scorched and overgrazed to 'barrenness on the north, though still heavily wooded on its south slope.

Vió and Buerba
The namesake village of **VIÓ**, 5km south of the Añisclo gorge car parks, is the one village hereabouts where there are still more tractors than tourists, trundling through the surrounding hayfields. Not so at **BUERBA**, 2km further and the end of the paved road, always packed with canyoners plumbing the secrets of the **Río Yesa** to the south. For non-canyoners, the best outing from here is the two-hour **trail-walk** to Yeba village, crossing the river; the GR15.1, a short *variante* path, links Buerba with the GR15 at San Úrbez.

In terms of **food** and **accommodation**, relaxed en-suite *Casa Marina* (☎698 714 450, *www.integridad-total.com/marina.htm*; all year; ②), first building on right as you enter Buerba with young, English-speaking management and home-cooked vegetarian meals, is homier than the slick and somewhat sterile *Casa Lisa* (☎974 481 181; ③), with variable rooms and meals for guests only (bar open to all).

Nerín
If you're without transport, and only committed to day-walks in Añisclo, you'll have to stay either at Burba or at **NERÍN**, an hour's walk west of the canyon on the GR15, via the forlorn, utterly deserted hamlet of Sercué. By road from San Úrbez (not recommended for pedestrians) it's 5km away. Nerín is blessed with an incomparable setting, gazing east to Peña Montañesa, and a reliable spring, and a little life has returned to what was once a dying hamlet. The 68-bunk *Añisclo Albergue*, with its front garden and ravishing view (☎974 489 010, fax 974 489 008; open all year; ①), serves meals to guests only, sells maps and guides, but requires reservations, as does the more comfortable *Pensión El Turista* (☎974 489 016; ③) with its panoramic *comedor*; otherwise you'll end up **camping** illicitly next to the exceptionally fine Romanesque church. Many of the dozen or so houses in the hamlet have been renovated and sold off as holiday homes, while an ugly new hotel creeps towards completion on the slope below Nerín.

Fanlo
The GR15 carries on west to Fanlo, curling through virtually abandoned, though beautifully sited Buisán (population 4), whose hilltop houses are also being restored for seasonal use. **FANLO**, 6km beyond Nerín by the more direct paved road, and again engagingly sited, is the biggest place hereabouts, with a unique, turreted manor house and an equally photogenic communal laundry just south of it juxtaposed uneasily with forests of cranes engaged in second-home renovation. Despite all this activity, the only short-term **accommodation** is *Casa Nerín Sese*, La Plaza 1 (☎974 489 009; ③), also

offering evening meals and plusher apartments. Otherwise there's just a sandwich-bar (*Las Eras*), unimprovably perched amongst the hilltop grain barns and threshing grounds west of the village.

Just northwest of Fanlo yawns the **Desfiladero de las Gloces**, a good place for a first experience of canyoning, a fact not lost on the French who throng the place. From the high point of the road, west of Las Eras, a path runs north for half an hour through abandoned fields, woods and scrub to the stony riverbed. The first obstacle, a ten-metre chute, presents no problems if you've ever been to a water park, and subsequent drops are easy by comparison. Two to three hours later you emerge a little southwest of Fanlo, though well below the road.

Moving on

West of Fanlo, 12km of steep, potholed, lightly travelled road bring you down to Sarvisé on the N260 road, 4km south of Broto and 6km south of Torla (see below for descriptions of all of these places). Don't try to walk this – the GR15 also emerges on the asphalt an hour out of Fanlo – but instead, either arrange a ride in Fanlo, or use a track, a bit higher than the Desfiladero de las Gloces path, heading northwest within three hours to the **Cuello de Diazas** (2133m), which overlooks the Valle de Ordesa. Once there you've a choice of paths and tracks, either north into the valley or west to Torla, the latter easily reached after another two and a half hours.

The Valle de Ordesa and around

Carved out first by glaciers and later enlarged by the east-flowing Río Arazas, the eight-hundred-metre-deep trough of the superlative **Valle de Ordesa**, in the north of Alto Aragón, deservedly draws hundreds of thousands of visitors a year. It forms the core of the **Parque Nacional de Ordesa y Monte Perdido**, which takes the second part of its name from the imposing limestone massif lying at the centre of park territory.

The two usual road approaches to the *parque nacional*, both served by **public transport**, are via either Sabiñánigo and Biescas (see p.416) to the west, or from Aínsa (p.398) to the southeast, along the N260 following the Río Ara, which has headwaters close to Vignemale and merges with the Zinca some 60km later at Aínsa. Along the first half of its course, before curling east, the Ara flows through the **Valle de Broto**, where villages like **Sarvisé**, **Oto** and **Broto** have been rescued by tourism from the desolation that has befallen most of those further downstream. **Torla**, 45km upstream from Aínsa and 39km northeast of Sabiñánigo, is by far the busiest of these settlements, since it's the closest to the Valle de Ordesa.

North of Torla, beyond the confluence of the Ara and the Arazas, there are just the campsites and refuge at **Bujaruelo**, beyond which is a wilderness not included in the park. Coming from the strategic *Refugio de Góriz* below Monte Perdido, the **GR11** threads through the Ordesa canyon, follows the Ara north almost to its source, then crosses west to Panticosa. Alternatively you can hike **into France** through a number of passes: the Brecha de Roldán (Brèche de Roland) towards Gavarnie, or two others at the top of the Ara into the Cauterets basin.

The Valle de Broto

Travelling upstream from Fiscal (see p.402), the N260 turns north past gradually more forested slopes to reach **SARVISÉ**, lowest village of the **Valle de Broto**, 38km from Aínsa. In high season you could be compelled to stay in Sarvisé, rather than further north, but in consolation **accommodation** here is of a high standard, with heating in winter. In descending order of preference, there's the stone-built, quiet *Casa Puyuelo*

(☎974 486 140; ③), with en-suite rooms, an attic salon, breakfast room and broad front lawn; the *Hotel Casa Frauca* (☎974 486 182, fax 974 486 353; ④) on the main highway, with more rustic, wood-decor en-suite rooms; the *Hotel Viña Olivan*, by itself at the edge of town on the Fanlo road (☎974 486 358; ④); and *Hostal Pirineos* in the village centre (☎974 486 179; ④). *Casa Frauca*'s famous ground-floor **restaurant** (closed Sun low season) deservedly draws crowds from near and far; their *menú* (1875ptas/€11.25) is great value with onion pie, cured pork ribs, dessert and house wine, or allow 3000ptas/€18 *a la carta* for game and seafood.

Perched 4.5km away on the hillside northeast of Sarvisé, beautiful, secluded **BUESA** consists of two *barrios* flanking a wooded vale. This is rustic Aragón as it was until the 1980s, with grilled suppers available at *Bar Merendero Balcón del Pirineo*, and rather basic rooms with self-catering kitchen at *Casa Cleto* up by the church (☎974 486 175; ③) – no palace, but a potential lifesaver in August. Incidentally, between July 1 and August 31, both **buses** from Sabiñánigo call at Sarvisé: the morning one (daily) en route to Aínsa, the evening one (Mon–Sat) turning around here just before 8pm, calling at Broto and Torla then back to Sabiñánigo at 9.30pm.

Broto, Oto and Linás de Broto

By the time **BROTO** itself is reached, 4km north of Sarvisé, you're in the thick of things; the **Turismo booth** (☎974 486 002; summer only Tues–Sun 10am–2pm & 4.30–8.30pm) advise on **accommodation** vacancies in high season. The valley's capital is a noisy, teeming place in summer, its old quarter hemmed by traffic and new construction, a plight symbolized by the collapsed Romanesque bridge just upriver, destroyed during the Civil War. Beside this is the quietest place to stay, and usually one of the last to fill: *Taberna O Puente* (☎974 486 072; ④). Breakfast is served outdoors under what's left of the bridge arch, but other meals here aren't up to much and indeed none of the restaurants in the village is worth singling out. Other accommodation, all on the through road, includes the en-suite *Hostal Español* west of the modern bridge (☎974 486 007; ③), the more comfortable one-star *Hotel Gabarre* at no. 6 (☎974 486 052; ⑤), whose en-suite rooms have balconies, and the less pricey *Hotel Latre* (☎974 486 053; ④) at the west end of town, with parking. Grupo Explora, at c/Santa Cruz 18 downhill from the *Gabarre* (☎974 486 432, *www.grupoexplora.com*), is the most active guides' bureau, specializing in canyoning, caving and especially **rafting** – the stretch of the Río Ara from Puente de los Navarros (see p.415) and Broto is particularly appropriate. Broto also has two **banks** (with ATMs) and the only **auto fuel** between Aínsa, Biescas and Torla.

Alternatively, head for the more attractive village of **OTO**, 1.5km south, which features homogeneous architecture and two notable medieval towers: one on the church, the other on a fifteenth-century baronial mansion. More or less opposite each other in the centre are two surprisingly modern, sterile but spotless **turismos rurales** – *Casa Herrero* (☎974 486 093; ③), above the bar, and *Casa Pueyo* (☎974 486 075; ③), which also manages the large campsite, *Oto* (☎974 486 075; April 1–Oct 15), 500m beyond the village.

LINÁS DE BROTO, a tiny, stone-built hamlet 10km west of Broto on the N260 towards Biescas and Sabiñánigo, would also be a reasonable spot to fetch up, as long as you have a car, with its fine position and clutch of **accommodation** along the through road. This includes the en-suite *Hostal Jal* (☎974 486 106, *hostaljal@wanadoo.es*; ③), often used by Explora (Broto) clients, the co-managed *Hotel Las Nieves* (☎974 486 109; ④) and *Hostal Cazcarro* (③). Without a car, you may prefer to trust to luck in Torla; a well-trodden *camino*, part of the **GR15.2**, leads there in 45 minutes from Broto's ruined bridge.

Torla

The brazenly commercialized village of **TORLA** is the most obvious gateway to the park, which lies just over 8km away by road, and besides Broto or Sarvisé is the only feasible base for anyone without transport. As recently as 1983 the village was the sort of place where *espadrilles* were inadvisable because of the amount of cow dung on the road. But a mushrooming of concrete-block construction on the outskirts since then has obscured the village's profile, though the medieval core remains intact and attractive, despite the conversion of every second building for tourist purposes.

Except in July or August – when even the nearby campsites fill and you must book rooms by phone three weeks in advance – **accommodation** is easy to come by. The reasonable, friendly *Hostal Alto Aragón* (☎974 486 172; ④) and the co-managed *Hotel Ballarín* (☎974 486 155; ⑤) adjacent at c/Capuvita 11 were both remodelled in 1997 and, especially off-season, are a bargain, with views of the village rooftops and TVs in the rooms; the home-style food served at the *Ballarin's comedor* is filling and good value (*menú* 1400ptas/€8.40). Among four fancier hotels, most professionally run is the *Villa de Torla* on the main square (☎974 486 156, fax 974 486 365; ⑤), which though not exactly cosy knows what foreigners want; try for the superior top-floor rooms. It has a pool in the terrace garden, and an excellent restaurant which will outrage animal-lovers with such dishes as *sarrio* (isard) stew. For budget lodgings, with en-suite rooms available, try the two **turismos rurales** on c/Fatás, next to the Turismo: *Casa Laly* (☎974 486 168; ②) and *Casa Borruel* (☎974 486 067, ②). There are also two **albergues**: the cramped, somewhat snooty *L'Atalaya* (☎974 486 022; 21 places; ③) with a downstairs restaurant, or the friendlier, higher-standard *Lucien Briet* (☎974 486 221; 30 places; dorm ①, rooms ②), managed by the *Bar Brecha*, which serves good meals (*menú* 1500ptas/€9) in its upstairs *comedor*. Among **bars**, the *bodega* under *L'Atalaya* vies with the more traditionally Spanish ambience of the bars *La Brecha* and *A'Borda Samper* around the corner, the latter with a particularly good selection of *tapas*.

Finally, there are three **campsites** along the road to Ordesa (all April–Oct): the *Río Ara* by the river (☎974 486 248), 2km from Torla on the east bank; the fancier, gigantic *Ordesa* (☎974 486 146), 3km along the road, intended mainly for cars and camper vans; and the smaller, more basic *San Antón* (☎974 486 063) 3.5km out of town on a terrace above the road.

Rounding off the list of amenities, Torla has both a **bank** (with ATM) and a **post office**, and a **Turismo** just off central Plaza Nueva (☎974 229 804; late June to mid-Sept Mon–Fri 10am–1pm & 6–8pm, Sat & Sun 9.30am–1.30pm & 5–8.30pm). Three stores sell a limited range of provisions suitable for trekking, while La Tienda on the main through lane doubles as the mountain guides' office and supplier of maps and mountaineering gear.

The year-round **bus** to Sabiñánigo, run by La Oscense, leaves Aínsa at 2.30pm, passes Sarvisé and Broto and reaches Torla at around 3.30pm, stopping just shy of the giant car park for the park shuttle bus (see box p.412). In high season there is also the additional service from Sarvisé (Mon–Sat), passing Torla at about 8.15pm on its way to Sabiñánigo.

Into the park from Torla

From Torla the shuttle-bus service rolls 4km northwest by paved road to the boundary of the **Parque Nacional de Ordesa y Monte Perdido**, at the Puente de los Navarros, at which point the road swings east for just over another 4km, where the bus leaves you at the car-parking area (open winter only), well inside the **Valle de Ordesa**. If you're on foot, you should definitely shun the tarmac in favour of the *camino* marked as part of the GR15.2. This begins in Torla next to the *Hostal Bella Vista* (marked as "Ordesa por Senda Peatonal"), crosses the Río Ara on a cement-and-masonry bridge, then turns sharply left (north) to join the Camino de Turieto at the posted park boundary, 45 minutes from Torla. After that, it's an easy and beautiful hike, two hours in total from the village, signposted all the way and taking you high above the river past some voluminous waterfalls. The path, like the road, eventually leads to the car park at **Pradera de Ordesa**, where there are toilets and a restaurant, predictably world-weary but offering a reasonable midday menu. There is no shop, so come prepared with provisions if

THE PARQUE NACIONAL DE ORDESA Y MONDE PERDIDO

The **Parque Nacional de Ordesa y Monte Perdido** was Spain's first protected area, established in 1918 as a reserve of 21 square kilometres to protect the showcase Valle de Ordesa, which lies immediately south of France's Cirque de Gavarnie. In 1982 the *parque nacional* was extended to 156 square kilometres, incorporating half a dozen "three-thousander" summits and the entire Valle de Añisclo, plus the headwaters of the Tella and the Circo de Pineta. This made the Spanish park contiguous with France's *Parc National des Pyrénées*; in the late 1980s the two park administrations signed an agreement for joint policy formulation and management – a sensible strategy given the huge numbers of mountaineers who surge back and forth between the two parks via the Brecha de Roldán (Brèche de Roland; p.368).

Geomorphology
From the Ara river valley in the west to well past the Zinca drainage in the east, the Pyrenees is a great mass of **karstic limestone**, heaved up from the sea floor about fifty million years ago, its beds first tilted and folded, then diligently sculpted by glaciers into a startling backdrop of peaks, cliffs and gorges. The process continues today on a smaller scale as dozens of seasonal waterfalls pour off the *circos* of the Ordesa and Pineta valleys in particular.

Monte Perdido, roughly in the centre of the park, ranks as the highest limestone peak in Europe, and the third highest summit in the Pyrenees. This mountain fills the heads of the four major valleys – **Ordesa**, **Pineta**, **Añisclo** and **Tella** – which drain away from it; a glacier still survives on its forbidding northeast face. Invisible to most visitors' eyes, but no less dramatic on acquaintance, are the hundreds of sinkholes and caves riddling the rock strata here, especially in the karst dells between the French frontier and the *Refugio de Góriz*. Bleak uplands surrounding the Valle de Ordesa on all sides, though parched and cheerless in midsummer, delight alpine skiers during wintertime.

Flora and fauna
Owing to the 2600-metre difference between the highest and lowest points in the park, and the consequent variation in climate, there is a full spectrum of **flora**. Beech, birch and poplar forests thrive in the moist Valle de Ordesa; in the drier Valle de Pineta pine predominates; while at the mouths of the lower, warmer Añisclo and Tella valleys, an almost Mediterranean vegetation of oaks, yew, ash and maple prevails, coexisting at slightly higher elevations with fir and black pine. Above the treeline sprawl vast moors of specially adapted pincushion-type plants, with the genus *Festuca* well represented, but tucked among all of this are nearly 1500 species of small flowering plants, scores of them endemics marooned here by the glaciers and found nowhere else.

Fauna around the *parque nacional* – including golden eagles, lammergeiers, griffon and Egyptian vultures, and isards (*sarrios* in Aragonese) – is much the same as on the French side, with the isards so prolific that at times hunters are allowed to cull the surplus. By contrast the last native **ibex** died in January 2000; introduced specimens failed to survive.

Climate and seasons
Weather in the park is notoriously fickle: during some summers there's not a cloud in the sky for days on end, but at other times there's thunder and hail every afternoon. When venturing out of the valley bottoms, always go prepared. In winter the park lies under one to two metres of snow, which persists in the popular Valle de Ordesa – not to mention higher elevations – until early June. Autumn features the spectacle of turning leaves on the beech and poplar trees, yet the weather remains relatively stable, if cool, and the park is far less crowded. Unless you're equipped with snow gear, the ideal visiting season is June to October.

continues overleaf...

THE PARQUE NACIONAL DE ORDESA Y MONDE PERDIDO contd.

Rules and regulations

Given ever-increasing tourist numbers, the park seems in real danger of being loved to death, so a few of the **rules** are worth elaborating. **Camping is prohibited** within the confines of the park except for a few specified areas: the Balcón de Pineta; at San Vicenda and Fon Blanca in the Valle de Añisclo; beside Escuaín village; and around the *Refugio de Góriz* when it's full. Even at these places, you're must dismount tents and leave them lying flat during the day – if you don't, park employees or the hut warden may do it in your absence. The small **stone huts** marked on most maps are intended for daytime use only, as shelter from storms; the sole staffed **refuge** is the *Refugio de Góriz*, roughly at the centre of park territory. In addition to the expected bans on disturbing plant or animal life, no **fires** are allowed anywhere, even in the emergency hut hearths, and **no washing or swimming** is allowed in the rivers (most of them are too cold to get in anyway except on blazing August afternoons). As at Aigüestortes in Catalunya, there's a **peripheral zone** of varying width to the south and east of the main *parque nacional* where development is controlled but few of the above prohibitions apply – you are allowed to swim, for instance, between Torla and the park boundary.

Motorized vehicles are not admitted beyond the chained gates at various points on the park periphery, and private-car approach from Torla along the paved access road is banned completely during Easter week and from June 1 to October 15 (winter mountaineers, take note). The Pradera de Ordesa car park is closed during those weeks; the only vehicles allowed now are the **shuttle buses** (departs 6, 7, 7.30 & 8am, then 15-minute intervals to 7pm June–Aug; 8am–5pm only Sept–Oct; 375ptas/€2.25 return only) from the fee car park (75ptas/€0.45/hr, 825ptas/€5/day) at the southern outskirts of Torla. A control booth has been erected at the road fork near Puente de los Navarros, to make sure that all private traffic goes north towards Bujaruelo during the restricted periods.

you're intent on trekking or picnicking. About 1km before, housed in the decommissioned *parador* above the approach road, is a **Centro de Visitantes** detailing the geology, flora and fauna of the park.

Walks in the Valle de Ordesa

Most of the walks in the valley begin from the vicinity of **Pradera de Ordesa**, specifically at the **Puente de los Cazadores** a little way upstream. There are dozens of possibilities, encompassing all levels of enthusiasm and expertise: the following examples are just a selection. Be aware that some of the "paths" marked on maps are actually technical climbing routes, and don't underestimate the time and difficulty of the more conventional pedestrian itineraries. Once out of the shady valley floor, the sun can be taxing, and drinking water is usually unavailable en route – take plenty with you, as the various waterfalls are contaminated.

The clearest **maps** of the Valle de Ordesa are the French or Spanish 1:50,000 IGN sheets (which also cover Gavarnie, across the French border), though cheaper ones such as the Editorial Alpina 1:40,000 "Ordesa y Monte Perdido" are perfectly adequate if you're going to stick to the popular, signed paths.

Valley traverse to the Circo de Soaso

This is one of the most popular – certainly in July or August – and rewarding of the short-distance treks. It's not especially difficult: a steep, 7.5-kilometre, three-hour traverse of the entire Valle de Ordesa, along a signposted path from Puente de los Cazadores, to the **Circo de Soaso**, which is also the beginning of the route to the *Refugio de Góriz* (see opposite). From wonderful beech forest the trail climbs past the *mirador* for the **Cascada del Abanico**, 3000m from Pradera de Ordesa, to emerge into the upper valley pasture, with the *circo* at its head and to the left – fanning out over a cliff – the famous **Cola de Caballo** (Horse's Tail) waterfall.

Return via Faja de Pelay

Looking back from the *circo*, you have a clear view of one of the artificial-looking but entirely natural ledges known as *fajas*: a standard feature of banded-limestone terrain, they are formed where a layer of softer calcareous rock has been exploded loose by repeated cycles of freezing and thawing. The ledge running along the south side of the canyon – the **Faja de Pelay** – is negotiated along its entire length by an easy path that can be followed back to the car park. Along the way you get more solitude than is possible in the valley bottom, and an aerial view of the canyon; opposite looms a succession of remote peaks and features – most conspicuously the Brecha de Roldán, and the peaks of Cilindro and Monte Perdido.

The route is almost level at first, then drops gently to the *mirador* and stone shelter at **Calcilarruego**. From there, you descend fiercely along the **Senda de los Cazadores** (the Hunters' Path) by a long series of tight zigzags, finally crossing the Puente de Cazadores to return to the bus stop. The total walk back from the Circo de Soaso is four and a half hours; there's no reliable water source until just before Calcilarruego, so you must carry it the whole way. A good case could be made for doing this loop in reverse: fewer crowds on the way back, and the stiff climb up the Senda de los Cazadores (2hr 30min) in morning shade.

Onward to the Refugio de Góriz

To ascend from the Circo de Soaso to the *Refugio de Góriz*, you have the choice of a gently zigzagging path to the right, or the direct assault up the cliff aided by *clavijas* (pegs and chains). The *clavijas* aren't as bad as they look, but if you've got a heavy pack, or the rocks are wet, the path is much better. Once past this point, follow the marked trail north to the **Refugio de Góriz**, 90min from the *circo* (☎974 341 201; 2200m; 96 places; open all year; reservations advisable; ①), sometimes known as *Delgado Úbeda*, where you can stay cheaply and eat expensively. The refuge, despite its regimentation and famously abrupt staff, is extremely popular and at peak times floor-space, and even food, might run out. When this happens camping is allowed nearby, but often the immediately adjacent area becomes revoltingly unsavoury – budget for extra daylight time to reach some better sites further east, towards the Collado Superior de Góriz (Arrablo).

Ascent of Monte Perdido

The standard expedition from the refuge is the **ascent of Monte Perdido**, which you do more for the views than anything else, since the southwest flank of the mountain – facing the top of the Valle de Ordesa – is the least impressive. It's more of a walk and scramble than a climb, but Monte Perdido can kill, so take advice from the refuge wardens, who have done the climb countless times. First and foremost get an early start, since thunderstorms can break in the afternoon. Follow the path climbing steeply north up the east bank of the **Barranco de Góriz**, where cairns show the way through alternating tracts of grass and boulders. After two tough hours you reach the 3000-metre contour and the small frozen **Lago Helado**, in the shadow of **Cilindro**, Perdido's sister summit.

At the lake you almost double back for the final approach, climbing steeply southeast, often over snow and ice, the grade slackening only a little just before the summit (5hr from the refuge). From the top you can gaze down the Pineta valley to the east; over the Tella and Añisclo canyons to the south; across Lago de Marboré to the Brecha de Tucarroya to the north; and towards distant Vignemale to the west.

Once back down at Lago Helado, you don't have to return to the *Refugio de Góriz*, but can execute a traverse. This implies an extra early start, as you'll not only be climbing

Monte Perdido, but negotiating the Cuello del Cilindro, dropping along the snowfields on the far side to Lago Marboré and – if you don't camp there – descending to the Valle de Pineta via the steep *balcón* trail.

To move on **west** from the *Refugio de Góriz,* trace the north side of the valley past the **Circo de Góriz** to the Brèche de Roland, the Cirque de Gavarnie and the *Refuge de la Brèche de Roland* (see p.369).

To the Cascada de Cotatuero and beyond

A popular side-trip from the valley bottom goes up to the impressive **Cascada de Cotatuero**. Starting from the wayside shrine of Virgen de Ordesa several hundred metres beyond the Puente de los Cazadores, the Cotatuero route takes you steeply but easily through the woods to a vantage point below the waterfall within an hour.

If you have a head for heights, you can continue on from here into France. With the help of more *clavijas,* you climb above the falls (2hr 30min) to reach the Gruta de Casteret and the Brecha de Roldán (4hr from the Puente de los Cazadores), for access to Gavarnie.

Alternatively, you can ford the stream beside the collapsed bridge here and adopt the un-signposted **Senda Canarrellos**, which roller-coasters up to about the 1800-metre contour on its way southeast, across the lips of hanging valleys and under rock over-hangs, to a junction (3hr 30min into the day) with the main valley-bottom track at **Bosque de Haya**. This is just above the **Cascada de la Cueva**, from where the Puente de Cazadores is about an hour downhill. However, the Senda Canarrellos is now unmaintained, with lots of tree-fall and boulder slides, though the path isn't formally closed and shouldn't present problems to experienced hikers. It's certainly the wildest and, after the Faja de Pelay route, the most impressive of the trails in the canyon, and it's a bit easier and quicker if done in reverse from the Bosque de Haya junction (which is still signposted); coming anticlockwise around the flank of Monte Arruebo, you get impressive views of the falls. Going clockwise, allow four and a half hours for this loop; anticlockwise, slightly less.

To the Cascada de Carriata and the Faja de las Flores

Another route signposted from the former car park leads to the **Cascada de Carriata**, pouring out of the **Circo de Salarons**. You head north into the trees, fork left, and begin a steep zigzag up to the falls, which are most impressive in late spring when melt-ed snow keeps them flowing.

If you want to continue into the *circo,* the left-hand route (at a fork on the open moun-tainside ninety minutes above the visitors' centre) ascends via a series of thirteen *clav-ijas,* not nearly as intimidating as those on the Cotatuero route and feasible for any rea-sonably fit walker; once up top you can carry on to the Brecha de Roldán.

The right-hand fork quickly becomes a nail-biting corniche trail along the **Faja de las Flores**. Nowhere wider than a mere 7m, this terrace runs for about 3000m hori-zontally along the 2100-metre contour of the valley's north wall, with an immense drop to the south. If you haven't got a head for heights you'll either have acquired one by the end, or be whimpering on your hands and knees. If you cover the entire distance, you meet up with the ascending path for the Circo de Cotatuero in about ninety minutes; reckon on an hour to descend to the Puente de los Cazadores.

Walks from the upper Ara valley

To reach the **upper Ara valley** on foot from Torla, head up the GR15.2 for just under an hour, as far as the junction with the Camino de Turieto, and then instead of contin-uing east into Ordesa take the **GR11** northwest. This crosses the Arazas at the **Puente de Ereta**, an anticlimactic cement aqueduct with some icy pools beneath it (swimming permitted if you don't fear heart stoppage). Half an hour later the GR11 meets the access road for the *parque nacional* at the **Puente de los Navarros**, and then runs north along the Río Ara: first along the dirt road, and then after the Puente de Santa Elena, as an east-bank trail. About 1km above that bridge, on the road, you'll find *Camping Valle de Bujaruelo* (☎974 486 161; April–Oct 15), where there's a shop for supplies, the highest one in the valley, and a restaurant (reservations usually needed): maybe not worth a detour, but great if you're on trek, where the 1500ptas/€9 *menú* might consist of lentil soup, lamb chops and apple mousse.

Staying instead with the east-bank trail, you'll arrive (1hr 15min from Puente de los Navarros) at the wide riverside meadow of **San Nicolás de Bujaruelo** , graced with the ruined eleventh-century **church** of that name – and some medieval hospice buildings. For decades these housed a private **refugio-restaurant**, purveying simple beds and hearty meals, which shut in 1999; this much-needed facility, along with an adjacent **campsite**, is due to reopen by 2002. From the church, there are a number of possible trekking routes out of the Ara basin, all traced on the Editorial Alpina 1:30,000 "Vignemale Bujaruelo" map. You can, incidentally, proceed no further up-valley by vehicle – there's a locked barrier just past the hospice buildings.

Trekking into France

For the **Gavarnie** basin, take the path that crosses the Ara over a beautiful Romanesque bridge and then zigzags quite steeply east to the frontier at **Puerto de Bujaruelo/Port de Gavarnie** (2270m); at the pass you pick up the HRP trail to the *Refuge de la Brèche de Roland*. Work on the dirt road which the Spanish were slowly bulldozing up to the pass appears to have been halted, the project deemed incompatible with the aims of the two national parks.

For the **Cauterets** area, hike northwest upstream beside the Ara along the **GR11**, but at the point – four hours beyond San Nicolás – where the GR climbs west towards Panticosa, continue instead to the head of the valley, where you pick up the **HRP** west through the **Col d'Arratille**, reaching the *Refuge Wallon* (see p.374) after ten hours. You can also use the **HRP** east through the **Puerto de los Mulos** (2591m) to arrive at the *Refuge des Oulettes* in somewhat less time.

Trekking to Panticosa: the GR11

For **Balneario de Panticosa**, start out as for Cauterets but stay on the GR11. From the Ara valley floor, the route veers west-southwest up the **Barranco de Batanes** to the **Cuello de Brazato** (2578m; 6hr from San Nicolás) before dropping quite sharply to Balneario de Panticosa (see below), for a spectacular if full trekking day of seven and a half hours. The small tarns in the Batanes valley, plus the larger Brazato lakes, make this route a choice strategy for moving west; as part of a day-hike out of Panticosa, it's covered in detail on pp.418–419. In any event don't make the mistake of following the **old GR11** up the Valle de Otal, still marked as a *variante*. This may appear to be easier – the Collado de Tendeñera at the top of Otal is only 2327m – but it's longer and, as the GR marking committee apparently agreed, pretty tedious.

The Valle de Tena and around

The next major north–south valley west of the Ordesa region, the **Valle de Tena**, wins few beauty prizes in the judgement of many travellers. The **Rio Gállego** which waters it, starting near the Puerto de Portalet/Col du Pourtalet and the ski complex of **El Formigal**, has been extensively dammed, with the usual pipelines and high-tension lines in attendance. At **Lanuza** reservoir, many houses in the namesake village stand poignantly half-submerged, as they have since 1975. Recently, though, owners have had some success in reclaiming their properties (see box p.403), and – complete with off-shore floating stage – Lanuza now co-hosts a summer music festival (see below).

Arriving in the crossroads village of Biescas from either Torla or the transport hub of Sabiñánigo (see below), you'll want a sound pretext to head upstream along the C136 road. This is furnished by the westernmost concentration of three-thousand-metre **peaks** and **glacial lakes** in the Spanish Pyrenees, northeast of the Valle de Tena, reached either from **Sallent de Gállego**, near El Formigal, or the side valley of the Río Caldarés, which flows past **Panticosa** village from the agreeable spa of **Balneario de Panticosa**.

Biescas

An hour after leaving Torla, the bus reaches the small town of **BIESCAS**, near the lower end of the Valle de Tena, where the N260 road intersects the C136. If you have any time to spare between connections, have a look at the medieval upper quarter on the east bank of the Gállego, including a church built by the Knights Templar. Biescas comes to life August 14–17, when consecutive festivities in honour of San Roque and La Virgen de la Assunción feature a "Big Heads" procession.

At other times of the year, especially if travelling under your own steam, you might schedule a lunch stop at the **hotel-restaurant** *Casa Ruba*, at c/Esperanza 20 (☎ & fax 974 485 001; closed Oct–Nov; ④) on the east bank of the river. This has been in the same family for three generations, with a lively, authentic bar laying on arguably the best range of *tapas* in the mountains, plus breakfasts. The *comedor* offers *a la carta* supper only, featuring lots of game and fish, though lunch (*menú* only 1800ptas/€10.80) of salad, bean stew, fried *pez espada*, dessert and wine, is a bit dull. Otherwise there's *Hostal la Rambla*, Rambla San Pedro 7 (☎974 485 177; ④), and the *Pensión Las Heras*, an old stone house with shared bathrooms at Agustina de Aragón 35 (☎974 485 027; ③), both in the west-bank quarter. If you take the year-round evening bus service up from Sabiñánigo to Biescas and fail to get a lift onwards, one of these establishments will certainly come in handy – and Biescas is certainly a more appealing place to spend the night than Sabiñánigo. There's also a **tourist office** by the southerly bridge (summer daily 10am–1.30pm & 5–9pm; ☎974 485 002).

Lately, Biescas has become most famous – or notorious – for one of the worst natural disasters ever to befall the Pyrenees. On August 7, 1996, a flash flood swept through the *Las Nieves* campsite south of town, causing 87 deaths. An inquest concluded that *Las Nieves* was fundamentally unsafe, lying within the original, pre-"engineered" course of a tributary of the Tena, at the mouth of a ravine. The new, more central **campsite**, *Edelweiss* (☎974 485 084; Easter & June 15–Sept 15), is hopefully better placed out of the flood plain.

Sabiñánigo – and its museum

Unabashedly industrial **SABIÑÁNIGO**, 14km south of Biescas on the C136 and 18km east of Jaca, persuades few to linger, but almost everybody passes through at some point on their way to or from Ordesa, if only because there's an inevitable change here of buses, or from train to bus. The **train station** lies at the northwest edge of town on the Jaca road, right next to the **bus terminal**.

If you've your own transport, do make an effort to visit the **Museo Ángel Orensanz y Artes de Serrablo** (July–Aug daily 10.30am–1.30pm & 5–9pm; April–June & Sept Tues–Sun 10.30am–1.30pm & 4–7pm; Oct–March Tues–Sat 10.30am–1.30pm & 3.30–6.30pm, Sun 10.30am–1.30pm & 4–7pm; 250ptàs/€1.50), installed in an eighteenth-century farmhouse (plus a modern annexe) at the southern edge of town by Puente Sardás. Justly reckoned the best ethnological museum in Alto Aragón, its displays are themed by room (musical instruments, religious art, wooden tools, etc). There are also fascinating archival photos and the original kitchen, axis of winter life, with its cooking implements and massive chimney hood. What little English labelling there is is eccentric, but two interrelated truths are worth translating. Until the early twentieth century, the eldest son inherited the entire estate in rural Aragón, and alone would marry; his bachelor brothers, the *tiones*, became the family handmen or even itinerant craftsmen, and to them are owed the wealth of displays here. The items on show have been gathered from the 46 deserted villages of the Serrablo, the zone around Sabiñánigo, which in 1910 had a population of 77; its growth during the 1950–70 industrialization depopulated three-quarters of the Serrablo, and by giving them homes in town finally allowed younger brothers to marry.

Should you need to **stay** overnight, Sabiñánigo has a dozen generally overpriced *hostales* and *hoteles*, mostly on the through road, Avda de Serrablo. A reasonable choice, near the transport terminals, is *Hostal Laguarta* (☎974 480 004; ③) at no. 21, above the *Bar Lara*.

Panticosa: skiing, village, spa

Fifteen kilometres upstream from Biescas, buses detour briefly at the far end of the **Embalse de Búbal** for the three-kilometre run northeast to **PANTICOSA** (Pandicosa) village, before continuing to Formigal. With its stucco exteriors and ornate windows on some of the remaining older buildings, Panticosa makes a tolerable (if pricey) base (though hikers might prefer Balneario de Panticosa). The small local **ski complex** has prompted a mushrooming of chalet growth at the village outskirts. With antiquated equipment and a poor natural snow record, the station nearly closed during the early 1990s, but has been rescued (for now) by massive investment in snow canons, new lifts and a new resort building at 1900m. An eight-seat *telecabina* ferries clients from the village (1150m) up to Petrosos (1900m), and from there the Sabocos chairlift – one of six – continues to Valle de Sabocos, focus of the meatier runs, with access to the top point of 2200m. Of 38 pistes, 14 are blue and 15 red, making this a good beginner-intermediate resort (*www.panticosa-loslagos.com*), but a half-dozen runs below Petrosos are seldom usable. In **summer**, the *telecabina* and Sabocos lift take mountain-bikers and walkers to two lakes around the **Valle de Sabocos** (daily 10am–6pm; 1575ptas/€9.50 return).

Accommodation in the village centre is heavily subscribed at peak times; top choices are the one-star *Vicente* up on the road to Balneario de Panticosa (☎974 487 022, fax 974 487 529; ④), offering sweeping views across the valley, and the best value; or the two-star *Escalar* at the village entrance (☎974 487 098, fax 974 487 003; ⑤), with plusher rooms, a pool and off-street parking. The central *Hotel Navarro* (☎974 487 181, fax 974 487 220; ④) on Plaza de la Iglesia has variable rooms – the best up to *Vicente* standards – but eccentric management, noise from poor insulation and feeble hot water; its *comedor* is similarly basic, with a restrictive *menú* (2500ptas/€15). *Sampietro* seems to be the only independent **restaurant**; you can buy trekking provisions in Panticosa, and there are three **banks**, all with ATMs. Pyr Guías Panticosa (☎974 487 409), in a little kiosk on the plaza, is primarily a **canyoning and caving** operator.

Balneario de Panticosa

In July and August there's the option of a noon **bus** from Biescas upstream along the Río Caldarés through the **Garganta del Escalar**, whose walls are so close together that sun seldom penetrates and waterfalls spray the road. **BALNEARIO DE PANTI-COSA**, 10km beyond the village, is another one of those places claiming to be the highest (1636m) permanently inhabited spot in the Pyrenees. This attractive and traditional **spa** is fed by six mineral springs, each sampled for different complaints. The emperor Tiberius supposedly visited Panticosa – the main baths are named in his honour – and there are, in fact, traces of Roman occupation in the vicinity, as well as an imposing Belle Époque casino, more restrained than its opposite numbers on the French side of the range. Most affordable of three surviving **hotels** are the one-star *Continental* (☎974 487 136, fax 974 487 137; ⑤) or the more characterful three-star *Mediodía* (☎974 487 616, *www.hotelmediodia.com*; ⑥), rescued from dereliction. The FAM refuge in the northwest corner of the spa, *Casa de Piedra* (☎974 487 571; 108 places; open all year; ③), sited to serve the GR11 which arrives here from the upper Ara valley, is rather unwelcoming and run for the maximum convenience of the wardens; **meals** must be ordered in advance. The only independent place to eat at Balneario is the **bar** *Casa Belio*, which does *raciones*. The summer-only bus back to Biescas departs at 5.30pm.

Walking from Balneario de Panticosa

You're well poised at Balneario de Panticosa for treks and climbs of all durations and difficulties: either day-hikes up scarcely trodden nearby peaks, the very-long-day traverse to Sallent de Gállego along the GR11 (best broken with an overnight en route), or the equally extended loop east using a GR11 variant. If you're going to attempt any of these routes, the appropriate Editorial Alpina map is the 1:25,000 "Panticosa Formigal", plus the 1:30,000 "Vignemale Bujaruelo" for the easterly loop.

Peak ascents

If you want to polish off an easy three-thousander, try **Pico d'o Argualas** (3046m), the summit immediately to the west – count on eight to nine hours there and back from the spa. Starting from a path marked for the Argualas Reservoir, close to the spa's natural lake, you head northwest first for the **Cuello de Pondiellos** (2809m; 3hr 30min), then for the **Collado de Argualas** (2860m), gaining height by following the crest southwest towards the base of **Pico de Algas** (3021m) and finally tackling a poor footpath to complete the ascent via the west face. From here you have a wonderful view south towards the *sierras* of Telera and Tendeñera, as well as east over Balneario, Pico d'o Brazato and Vignemale.

To tackle the three summits of the **Picos del Infierno** – all of them close to 3100m – repeat the route to Cuello de Pondiellos but then head north towards the saddle that separates the central and eastern peaks, steering a middle course over the easiest terrain. From Pondiellos none of the Infierno peaks are more than ninety minutes away.

Traverse west via the GR11

Access to the **GR11** in Balneario is poorly signposted; from in front of the *Hotel Mediodía*, ascend the broad staircase just east and turn left at the top onto a wide lane, where a few red-and-white double-bars provide confirmation. Some fifteen minutes along, there's a T-junction just above an avalanche weir: right for Brazato ("2 oras"), left for Bachimaña ("1.15"). These timings are brisk – even with a daypack, it's 80 minutes from here to the lower Bachimaña dam, and 35 minutes more to reach another T-junction at the water-meadows at the inflow of the upper **Ibón Bachimaña** (2hr 15 minimum from Balneario). Here you've the option of going north through the Puerto de Panticosa/Port du Marcadau for the *Refuge Wallon*, a short trekking day of about six hours (see p.374). To continue on the GR11 you swing west over gently rising ground to the upper **Ibón Azul** (1hr), where there's good camping.

Next you climb steeply to the double pass of **Cuello d'o Infierno** (2721m) and **Collado de Piedrafita** (2782m), problematic after snowy winters; once through this it's all downhill past the **Ibón de Llena Cantal** (another wonderful campsite) to the **Respumoso (Respomoso) reservoir** (2100m; 3hr from Ibón Azul). This is about as far as you'd comfortably get with a full pack in one day from Balneario; on the north shore stands the *Refugio Respomoso* (☎974 490 203; 2120m; 105 places; open all year; ③). If they're full, or the brusque wardens put you off, there's ample grass for camping on the south shore. The view north to **Balaitus/Balaïtous** and east to the triple pyramids of **Cambales** (2968m), **Petite Fache** (2947m) and **Grande Fache/Gran Facha** (3005m), more than compensates for the ugly concrete dam at the western end of Respumoso. (If you want to climb Balaïtous or head into France on the HRP, see "Around Balaïtous and Lac d'Artouste", p.388.)

To continue on the GR11, drop down the skilfully engineered path west from the lake, following the curving Aguas Limpias stream to Sallent de Gállego village (3hr), the last 45 minutes or so beyond the **Embalse de la Sarra** on asphalt road. If you've made an early start after staying at Respumoso, it's possible and recommended to lengthen this final stage with a side trip north, on a cairned minor trail, to the **Arriel lakes** just below the HRP.

Loop east via Circo de Bramatuero

For this scenic circuit – with none of the potential shuttling problems of arriving in Sallent, if you've left a car at Balneario – begin as for the westerly GR11 traverse. But when you reach the junction at the water-meadows by the upper Bachimaña reservoir, turn right instead of left, following a sign to the lower **Bramatuero dam** ("35" - really 40min), bearing right and slightly down at the next fork to avoid going up to the Puerto de Panticosa and *Wallon*. From the lower to the upper Bramatuero lake (2500m) it's 1hr 15min (4hr 15min from Balneario), on a fair trail through more water-meadows and past natural tarns. Gentians are out in profusion during early summer, with a few black-and-white bar-blazes mixed with cairns as waymarks. At the upper dam, the path fizzles out; cairned isard-traces lead above the north shore to natural **Ibón Letrero** (2540m; 5hr) at the top of the **Circo de Bramatuero**, a fine lunch spot where snow lingers into July.

From Letrero, it's a deceptively easy twenty minutes more up to the **Collado de Letrero** (2680m), with magic views of the Ordesa *fajas* and Vignemale. The 45-minute descent to the upper **Ibón de los Batanes** (2380m) is along a nasty couloir, with a scree slope to negotiate towards the bottom. You've another hour, via the equally scenic lower lake, to the junction with the main GR11 (6hr 45min), avoiding unnecessary altitude loss. Looking north, you glimpse frontier pinnacles comprising the **Circo de Ara**, and probably wisps of cloud in the late afternoon, while at the trail junction (turn west) there's the sound of three mingling streams in spate.

You've 45min up the confusingly named Barranco de Batanes to the first tarn (2350m); marmots shriek all around from boulder piles, and a broad meadow just below is popular with campers. The Alpina map tracing is not precise – the good trail spends as much time on the true right bank as the left. Within 35 minutes more, you attain the **Cuello de Brazato** (2578m), where herds of isards are often seen. If you're overtaken by nightfall, camping is congenial at the natural lake just below the pass, but it's only 1hr 45min more (almost 10hr for the day) to the Balneario. You need stamina, and a long June/July day to accomplish this without spending a night out.

The upper Tena valley

To proceed along the **upper Tena valley** from Panticosa village you can use the once-or-twice-daily onward bus service between Sabiñánigo and Sallent de Gállego. **ESCAR-RILLA**, 500m north of the junction, is the first settlement encountered, much marred by tower-blocks of holiday flats, though with ample facilities. **Accommodation** is available at the *Hostal Sarao* (☎974 487 065, fax 974 487 115; ④), with a popular restaurant, and at the more luxurious *Hotel Ibón Azul* (☎974 487 211, fax 974 487 242; ⑤), both on the main through road. For the economical, there's also an **albergue** (☎974 487 154; ①) and an enormous **campsite**, the *Escarra* (☎974/48 71 28; open all year), west of the highway.

Sallent de Gállego

Once past the **Embalse de Lanuza**, a right turn and another bridge over the Gállego takes you into **SALLENT DE GÁLLEGO** (Sallén de Galligo), a sizeable old village 21km from Biescas, at the confluence of the Gállego and the Aguas Limpias, with a fine bridge across the Gállego and a fortified hilltop church. Sallent plays a dual role as winter sports and summer mountaineering centre, as well as co-hosting the *Pirineos Sur* **festival** the last three weeks in July; this is one of the best world music bashes in Europe, with the likes of Manu Dibango, Khaled, Youssou N'Dour in years past.

Accordingly, **accommodation** is fairly abundant and cheaper than in Escarrilla, pitched largely at French trippers. Working your way from east to west along the single high street of c/de Francia, you encounter *Hostal El Centro* (☎974 488 019, *www.valledetena.com/centro*; ④), whose rear rooms face the stream and the peaks; the less inspiring *Hostal Mediodía* (☎974 488 071; ③); *Hostal Familiar Maximina*, tucked away on a side street at c/La Iglesia 3 (☎ & fax 974/48 84 36, *www.valledetena.com/maximina*; ⑤), with suites for the price, of a standard to attract Spanish packages; *Hostal Faure* (☎974 488 007; ③), in a courtyard off the main road, the budget choice; and last but not least the atmospheric, creaky-floored *Hotel Balaitus* (☎ & fax 974 488 059; ⑤ B&B), with private parking. So travellers may prefer the friendly *Albergue Foratata* near the west end of c/de Francia (☎974 488 112; ①), with a few doubles and an inexpensive canteen on the ground floor. You've a good range of independent **restaurants** at the east end of town, with bilingual French/Castilian menús; *El Rincón de Mariano* is a cheap, reliable and popular locals' choice, with *menús* at 1500ptas/€9, while *Granja Casa Bernet* has a range of imported beers and homemade pastries, plus breakfasts. Sallent also has two **banks** (ATMs) and three shops for trekking supplies. Except for one daily service originating in El Formigal (3.45pm, passes Sallent 4.15pm), Sallent is the usual start-point for downhill **bus** departures (Mon–Fri 7am).

El Formigal

The uphill road from Sallent, with views of pyramidal Peña Foratata on the north, weaves for almost 5km to **EL FORMIGAL**. Neither twee nor chic, it's a more serious ski resort than Panticosa, expanded several times between 1987 and 1997, with further (and controversial) growth planned in the Valle de Izas. Mostly north-facing runs are scattered on a vast, treeless slope across the valley from the chalets, between 1500m and 2200m; as at Panticosa, a *telecabina* gets one up to the hub of the action at 1800m. In total, 22 other lifts (one-third chairs) serve 34 pistes, mostly red-rated – this isn't a great beginners' resort.

Except for the two-star but small, pleasant *Hotel Tirol* at the edge of the *urbanización* (☎974 490 377, *www.arrakis.es/_tirol*; ⑦ HB) with good views, **accommodation** in El Formigal can be extremely expensive for what you get; in high season beds are hard to find anyway, in which case you'll appreciate Sallent and Escarrilla as useful fallbacks.

Jaca and around

The approach to **JACA** (Chaca), 18km west of Sabiñánigo on the N330, takes you through modern, traffic-choked suburbs – an unpromising introduction to this early capital and stronghold of Aragón, and the base from which the kingdom was recaptured from the Muslims. The old centre, however, is a lot more characterful, overlooked by a huge star-shaped citadel and endowed with a **cathedral** that is one of the finest Spanish examples of Romanesque architecture. This and the monastery of **San Juan de la Peña**, 20km southeast, are the major local sights, while in winter the proximity of **Astún-Candanchu**, the most westerly ski resort in the Spanish Pyrenees, provides an added bonus. Rail enthusiasts may be tempted by the train-trip to **Canfranc**, almost at the French border, and a good place to pick up the GR11 trail.

Aftger a spell in the mountains, Jaca's relatively "big town" feel and facilities may well be an equal attraction. It's enlivened by conscripts at the large military academy and civilian students attending a summer university, while boisterous festivals punctuate the spring and summer months.

The Town

Sited at the foot of Peña Oroel, on a broad plain where the Río Aragón suddenly twists westwards into the Canal de Berdún, Jaca is a venerable place, called *Iacca* by the Romans after the Iaccitani tribe who dwelt here. The Muslims occupied Jaca briefly from 715 to 760, when the Christians reconquered the town and held it, save for a brief

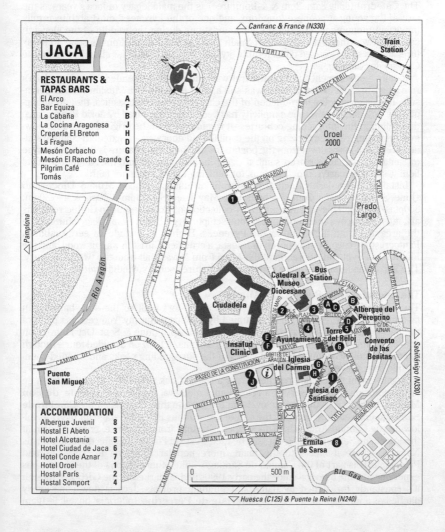

△ Canfranc & France (N330)

JACA

RESTAURANTS & TAPAS BARS

El Arco	A
Bar Equiza	F
La Cabaña	B
La Cocina Aragonesa	J
Crepería El Breton	H
La Fragua	D
Mesón Corbacho	G
Mesón El Rancho Grande	C
Pilgrim Café	E
Tomás	I

Train Station

Oroel 2000

Prado Largo

Catedral & Museo Diocesano

Bus Station

Ciudadela

Albergue del Peregrino

Torre del Reloj

Convento de las Benitas

Insalud Clinic

Ayuntamiento

Iglesia del Carmen

Puente San Miguel

Iglesia de Santiago

Ermita de Sarsa

ACCOMMODATION

Albergue Juvenil	8
Hostal El Abeto	3
Hotel Alcetania	5
Hotel Ciudad de Jaca	6
Hotel Conde Aznar	7
Hotel Oroel	1
Hostal París	2
Hostal Somport	4

0   500 m

Río Gas

▽ Huesca (C125) & Puente la Reina (N240)

spell, from then on. The battle of Las Tiendas (4km west of Jaca), in 795, in which a Moorish army was repulsed mostly by the local women, is still commemorated on the first Friday in May by a mock all-female battle between Christians and Moors.

Within two centuries of these trials an embryonic democracy of sorts had emerged among the Aragonese nobility, who stipulated comprehensive customary rights (*fueros*) – confirmed by King **Sancho Ramírez** in 1077 – limiting the power of the king to issue edicts and levy taxes. Jaca itself reached its zenith during the decades after 1035, when **Ramiro I**, Sancho's father, established the Aragonese court here and began work on the present cathedral.

The Cathedral

The **Catedral** (daily 8am–2pm & 4–9pm; free) is the main legacy of Jaca's years as the seat of the young Aragonese kingdom, and one of the Pyrenees' most architecturally important monuments. Rebuilt on old foundations during the middle of the eleventh century, it was the first cathedral in Spain to adopt the French Romanesque architecture, and, as such, exerted considerably stylistic influence on other churches along the Camino de Santiago.

Ramiro's endowment of the cathedral was undoubtedly intended to confirm Jaca's role as a Christian capital in what was still almost exclusively a Muslim Iberian peninsula. Its design saw the introduction of the classic three-aisled basilica, though unhappily the original Romanesque simplicity has been much obscured by florid Renaissance decoration in the intervening centuries. It retains some of the original sculpture, however, including realistic carving on the capitals and doorway – a sixteenth-century statue of Santiago looks down from the portal. Inside, the main treasure is the silver shrine of Santa Orosía, Jaca's patron saint; a Czech noble, married into the Aragonese royal family, she was martyred by Muslims for refusing to renounce her faith.

Installed in the dark cathedral cloisters is an unusually good **Museo Diocesano** (June–Sept daily 10am–2pm & 4–8pm; Oct–May Tues–Sun 11am–1.30pm & 4–6.30pm; 300ptas/€1.80). This features a superb collection of Romanesque-to-Gothic religious art, mostly frescoes and wooden religious sculpture, gathered from village churches in the area and from higher up in the Pyrenees. Highlights include an eerily modern Pantocrastor fresco from a church in Ruesta, a crucified Christ in walnut wood, and the Flight into Egypt and Adoration of the Magi from Navasa, all from the twelfth century. The Renaissance work is more variable, but features some splendid *retablos*.

The Ciudadela and Puente San Miguel

The **Ciudadela**, a redoubtable sixteenth-century fort built to the star-shaped plan favoured in that era, is still partly occupied by the Spanish army. You can visit parts of the interior (daily: July–Aug 11am–noon & 6–8pm; April–June & Sept–Oct 11am–noon & 5–6pm; Nov–March 11am–noon & 4–5pm; 300ptas/€1.80) on a guided tour – though interest is mostly confined to good views of the surrounding peaks and wooded countryside from the walls.

Northwest of the citadel, reached along a rough track from the end of the Paseo de la Constitución, Jaca preserves a remarkable medieval bridge, the **Puente de San Miguel**. It was across this bridge over the Río Aragón that pilgrims on the **Camino de Santiago** entered Jaca, marking the end of the arduous Pyrenean stage for pilgrims following the Camino Aragonés. This branch, starting from Provence, entered Spain at the Puerto de Somport, and from Jaca headed west via Puente la Reina de Jaca towards Navarra, where it met with the main, more popular route via Roncesvalles and Pamplona. This part of the Camino de Santiago – like other sections of the route – has experienced quite a revival since the early 1990s and is marked as the **GR65.3**, though it's constantly threatened by dams and building projects. Jaca is now consciously pitched as a way-station: there's an **Albergue de Peregrino** (pilgrims' hostel; 9–10am

& 3–10pm) in the medieval hospital on c/Conde Aznar while route maps and pilgrim-age-related souvenirs are widely available.

Practicalities

The **train station** (tickets issued 10am–noon & 5–7pm) is a good 3km north of the cen-tre, so look out for the shuttle bus (75ptas/€0.50) which plies to the **bus station** on Avda Jacetania, around the back of the cathedral. Useful summer bus departures include services to Pamplona (5.30pm Mon–Fri, 11am Fri & Sat, 8pm Sun), Sabiñánigo and Biescas (10.15am & 6.15pm Mon–Sat) and Ansó via Hecho (6.30pm Mon–Sat), as well as even more frequent services to Huesca. Although timetables don't explicitly say so, hardly any buses run on Sundays. **Drivers** will find parking easiest in the roomier southwestern quarter, though beware of metered zones.

The **old town**, where you'll spend most time, divides into a somewhat frowzy north-eastern side – home to all of the budget accommodation, the roughest bars and most of the reasonable restaurants – and the smarter southwestern quarter, abutting Avenida Regimiento de Galicia, with its pavement cafés, restaurants and banks. On the same *avenida* you'll find the helpful **Turismo** (summer Mon–Fri 9am–2pm & 4.30–8pm, Sat 9am–1.30pm & 5–8pm, Sun 10am–1.30pm; winter Mon–Fri 9am–1.30pm & 4.30–7pm, Sat 10am–1pm & 5–7pm; ☎974 360 098), which stocks a range of leaflets on trekking, skiing, mountain-biking, horse-riding, cinema playbills, and festival programmes.

Accommodation

Although at an elevation of only 820m, Jaca counts as a Pyrenean resort and as such fills up in August or during ski season, with prices pushed up year-round by the cross-border trade.

Albergue Juvenil, Avda Perimetral 6 (☎974 360 536). The local youth hostel, in the south of town by the ice rink, has doubles, triples and five-bed rooms. ①.

Hostal El Abeto, c/Bellido 15 (☎974 361 642). Comfortable enough, some rooms en suite, though there may be noise from nearby bars. ③.

Hotel Alcetania, c/Mayor 43–45, but entry from c/Conde Aznar (☎ & fax 974 356 100). Former *hostal* refurbished as a hotel in 1995. ⑤.

Hotel Ciudad de Jaca, c/Siete de Febrero 8 (☎974 364 311, fax 974 364 395). Centrally but quiet-ly located with good en-suite rooms.④.

Hotel Conde Aznar, Paseo de la Constitución 3 (☎974 361 050, fax 974 360 797). An attractive fam-ily-run two-star hotel, with well-renovated rooms and fairly abundant street parking. ⑥.

Hotel Oroel, Avda de Francia 37 (☎974 362 411, fax 974 363 804). Modern hotel with its own pool, and large rooms with kitchens. ⑦.

Hostal París, Plaza de San Pedro 5 (☎974 361 020). Best budget *hostal* in town – clean, spacious rooms with washbasin across from the cathedral. ③.

Hostal Somport, c/Etchegaray 11 (☎974 363 410). Jaca's most affordable en-suite digs, in another renovated old building. ④.

CAMPING

Camping Peña Oroel, 4km east on N330 towards Sabiñánigo (☎974 360 215). Jumbo-sized camp-site, set amid woods, with excellent facilities. Open Easter week and mid-June to mid-Sept.

Camping Victoria, 1500m west on the N240 towards Pamplona (☎974 360 323). An equally shady if cheaper, smaller and rather basic site, near the Río Aragón. Open all year.

Eating and drinking

There's ample choice when it comes to **eating and drinking**, with good places con-centrated in the old town. The entire length of c/Gil Berges, as well as contiguous c/del

Barco and c/de la Puerta Nueva, is home to most of Jaca's rowdier student bars. More sedate pubs and *tapas* bars for an older crowd concentrate on c/Ramiro Primero, a little to the southwest.

El Arco, c/San Nicolás 4. That rare Spanish breed: a vegetarian, no-smoking restaurant. Fresh, filling, international dishes and an inexpensive *menú*. Closed Sun in winter.

La Cabaña, c/del Pez 10. Reasonable *a la carta* meals (2500–3000ptas/€15–18) in unusually cheerful surroundings; also has a few rooms to rent.

La Cocina Aragonesa, c/de Cervantes 4. The round-the-corner restaurant of the *Hotel Conde Aznar*, reckoned the best in town for elaborate, Basque-influenced cooking. Expect to pay 6000–7000ptas/€36–42 (*menú* scarcely less than *a la carta*). Closed Wed.

Mesón Corbacho, c/Ramiro Primero 2. Regional dishes and grills; *menú* (1700-ptas/€10.20) and *a la carta* (4000ptas/€24).

Crepería El Breton, c/Ramiro Primero 10. A passably authentic *crêperie*. Supper only; closed Mon in winter and last half of June.

Bar Equiza, c/Primer Viernes de Mayo. Scruffy pavement tables belie a plush, cavernous interior with famously good *tapas* – especially *gambas*.

La Fragua, c/Gil Berges 4. Generous, reasonably priced grills without any airs or graces. Closed Wed.

Mesón El Rancho Grande, c/del Arco 2. Impressive Aragonese cooking exploits fish, meat and vegetables equally; skip the dull *menú* (1600ptas/€9.60) for *a la carta* (5000ptas/€30).

Pilgrim Café, Avda Primer Viernes de Mayo 7. Inevitably a bit touristy but a fine old Art Deco building with outdoor tables facing the Ciutadela's lawn, and a variety of breakfasts (including bacon and eggs).

Pizzeria Polifemo, c/Dieziocho de Junio 5. Standard pizzeria with a loyal student clientele.

Tomás, c/Ferrenal 8. Hole-in-the-wall, old-fashioned bar with a vast range of *tapas* and *raciones*; one of several such clustered here.

Listings

Adventure activities Trekking, rafting, climbing, skiing, mountain biking (including rental) and other activity expeditions are organized by Jaca Adventura, Avda Francia 1 (☎974 363 521), Mountain Travel on Avda Regimiento Galicia (☎974 355 770) and Alcorce-Pireneos Adventura, opposite the Turismo at Avda Regimiento Galicia 1 (☎974 356 437). These companies have English-speaking staff.

Car rental Don Auto, c/Correos 2 (☎908 833 227). In high season book cars at least a day in advance.

Hospital Besides the main one on c/Rapitan, off the map beyond the train station, there's the very central, public Insalud clinic (see map), good for minor ailments.

Laundry There's a self-service *lavandería* next to the Superpirineos supermarket, on c/Astún.

Trekking maps and gear Maps are available from La Unión bookstore at c/Mayor 34 and at a mountaineering shop, Charli, Avda Regimiento de Galicia 3. There's another outdoor gear shop, Intersport-Piedrafita, at Avda de Francia 4.

Southwest of Jaca: San Juan de la Peña and Santa Cruz de la Serós

San Juan de la Peña, high in the Sierra de la Peña southwest of Jaca, is the best-known monastery in Aragón. In medieval times an important *variante* of the pilgrim route from Jaca to Pamplona passed by, as San Juan reputedly held the Holy Grail – actually a Roman chalice which later found its way to Valencia cathedral. These days, most tourists (and there are many – including school parties) visit for the views and Romanesque cloister.

The most direct **route to the monastery** begins from the Jaca–Pamplona (N240) highway. A side road, 11km west of Jaca, leads south 4km to the village of Santa Cruz de la Serós with its massive Romanesque church, and from here it's a further 7km by road up to San Juan. There is no public transport, although you could take the afternoon Puente la Reina/Pamplona-bound bus from Jaca and walk from there – assuming an overnight in the village. **Renting a mountain bike** would be easier: reckon on an hour's cycling from Jaca to Santa Cruz, then a further hour up the very steep road to San Juan. Returning to Jaca, you can make an enjoyable circuit rather than retracing your tyre-treads: a gradual twelve-kilometre descent east to Bernués, a slight climb to Puerto de Oroel, then a fierce drop to Jaca, 17km from Bernués. This is a very scenic – and car-free – itinerary, but not something to do in reverse.

Santa Cruz de la Serós

The picturesque village of **SANTA CRUZ DE LA SERÓS** is dominated by its thick-set, but nonetheless stylish Romanesque **church** (10am–2.30pm & 3.30–8pm; 150ptas/€0.90); inside, the remarkable stoup incorporates a massive central pillar holding up the vault. The sanctuary was once part of a large Benedictine convent which flourished between the eleventh and sixteenth centuries; indeed *serós* appears to be a corruption of *sorores*, after the nuns who once dwelt here, including (in their old age) the three sisters of King Sancho. There are three places to **eat** and **drink**: a streamside bar with light snacks, the *Casa d'Ojalatero* in the village centre with salubrious if plain fare including good house wine, *trigueros con gambas* and grills (*menús* 1200ptas/€7.20 and 1800ptas/€10.80, *a la carta* 2000–3000ptas/€12–18), and the *Hosteleria Santa Cruz*, with a *menú* (1500ptas/€9) and *a la carta* (4000ptas/€24); they also have high-standard rooms (☎974 361 975; ④), thus far the only **accommodation** here.

From Santa Cruz, walkers can take the old **path** up to San Juan in about an hour. The path is waymarked as GR65.2 and is signposted from near the church (where there is also a map placard). The road takes a more circuitous route of 7km around the mountainside, giving wonderful views of the Pyrenean peaks clearly visible to the north and the distinctive Peña de Oroel to the east.

San Juan de la Peña

SAN JUAN DE LA PEÑA actually comprises two monasteries, 2km apart. Approaching from Santa Cruz, you reach the lower (and older) one first.

Built into a hollow under a cliff from which various springs seep, the **lower monastery** (summer Tues–Sun 10am–2pm & 3.30–8pm; spring/autumn Tues–Sun 10am–1.30pm & 4–6pm; winter Wed–Sun 11am–2.30pm; 400ptas/€2.40) is an unusual and evocative complex, even in its partial state of survival. Entering, you pass first into the **Sala de Concilios**, which once served as the refectory, and the adjacent, double-naved, ninth-century **Mozarabic chapel**, together adapted as the crypt of the main Romanesque **church**, built two centuries later; both retain fragments of Romanesque frescoes. Here, in 1071, Cluniac monks replaced the Mozarabic Mass with the Roman rite – the first such substitution in the Iberian peninsula, made possible by the re-establishment of contact with Rome after centuries of isolation.

Upstairs, alongside the main church, is a **pantheon** of Aragonese and Navarrese nobles; reliefs on the nobles' Gothic tombs show events from the early history of Aragón. Another adjacent pantheon for the kings of Aragón was remodelled in a cold, Neoclassical style during the eighteenth century and later sacked by Napoleon's troops.

The artistic highlight, however, is the twelfth-century Romanesque **cloisters**, at the far end of the complex where the rock overhang has been left open to the sky rather than being completely walled off. Only two of the bays are complete – another is in a fragmentary state – but the surviving capitals are among the greatest examples of Romanesque carving. All depict scenes from the Gospels: *Christ's Entry* into *Jerusalem*, *Meeting Mary Magdalene*, the *Raising of Lazarus*, and the *Deposition* are the most obvious. They were the artistry of an anonymous, idiosyncratic craftsman who left his mark on a number of churches in the region. He is now known as the Master of San Juan de la Peña, his work easily recognizable by the unnaturally large eyes on the figures.

The surrounding cliffs are the nesting grounds of assorted **birds of prey**, and you'll be very unlucky not to see griffon vultures, or the summer-visiting Egyptian vultures. Bonelli's eagles (all year) and short-toed eagles (summer only), identifiable by their habit of soaring with dangling feet, are less frequent sights.

The late-seventeenth-century **upper monastery**, a sizeable complex with a flamboyant Baroque facade, can be seen from the outside only – it now serves as a centre for the study of the old Aragonese kingdom – but it merits the climb east from the older monastery, if only for the views of the Pyrenees from a nearby *mirador*. Facing the monastery is a popular picnic-ground in a huge, forest-enclosed meadow; if you arrive by car, this is where you must **park** – a regular shuttle bus takes you down to the older monastery, in whose vicinity the parking of private **cars** is strictly **banned**.

North of Jaca: Canfranc and Candanchú-Astún

Although it is the Río Aragón which drains south from the Puerto de Somport, its valley – extending directly **north of Jaca** – is known as the **Canfranc**. This is also the name of two settlements along the way: **Canfranc-Pueblo**, 19km out of Jaca on the N330, devastated by fire in 1944 and now mustering just forty inhabitants, and **Canfranc-Estación**, 23km further and (currently) the final stop for northbound trains. Just shy of the frontier, 9km beyond, the double ski resort of **Candanchú-Astún** straddles the approaches to the Puerto de Somport.

Canfranc: Pueblo and Estación

Consistent with its depopulation, tourist facilities in **CANFRANC-PUEBLO** are limited to the *Refugio de Canfranc* (☎974 372 104; 1045m; 100 places; open all year; ①), an **albergue** for pilgrims on the Camino de Santiago, and a single bar for meals and drink. **VILLANÚA**, just 4km south in a wider part of the valley, is more attractive, but offers just a clutch of overpriced hotels and an extremely dour **albergue**, *Refugio Bar Triton* on Plaza Mediodía (☎ & fax 974 378 281, *www.refugiotriton.com*; ①), whose "rules and regulations" cover an entire A4 sheet.

Since the French discontinued their part of the local trans-Pyrenean line, most of the enormous train station at **CANFRANC-ESTACIÓN** – equipped with the second longest platforms in Europe – has become a badly vandalized white elephant where tall weeds grow up through the tracks. It's a sad fate for an elegant spot which saw heads of state attend its inauguration in 1928, and which later served as a location for the film *Doctor Zhivago*. The resumption of rail service north to Oloron is now included in principle as part of the Somport tunnel project (see box pp.390–391), especially since prices at ski resorts on either side of the Pyrenees have attained parity. Spanish undercutting of French resort rates prompted the closure of the line in 1973 after 45 years in operation, though the last straw was the collapse of a bridge on the French side, left unrepaired to this day. A noticeboard at the entrance to the station tells (part of) the whole sad story.

The surrounding village, such as it is, originally sprang up to house those made homeless by the 1944 disaster, and now exists solely to house skiers and catch the passing motorist trade (mostly French), with a few gift shops and hotels. **Accommodation**, all on or just off the through highway, includes the high-quality *Albergue Pepito Grillo* (☎974 373 123; 36 places; open all year; ①), serving the GR11 as well as the Camino de Santiago; the gloomy, one-star *Hotel Ara* (☎974 373 028; ②), and the friendly, quiet, wood-and-stone-built *Hotel Villa Anayet*, at the north end of town at Plaza de Aragón 8 (☎974 373 146; closed mid-April to late June & mid-Sept to mid-Dec; ④). There are also three *casas rurales*, a bit pricier than the norm (③–④), near the *Villa Anayet*, as well as a **campsite** (☎608 731 604; April to mid-Sept), 5km north on the road towards Candanchú. For **meals**, the *comedor* at the *Hotel Villa Anayet* offers by far the best value, with a four-course *menú* costing 1200ptas/€7.20.

Though there's no train, you can travel on **into France** (5 times Mon–Sat, 3 times Sun; 10.30am–4.30/5.20pm), on **SNCF buses**. Coming **from France**, these buses arrive in Canfranc from Oloron with equal frequencies on the days indicated between 9/9.30am and 4pm, with awkward **train** connections for Jaca only at 7.05am and 5.40pm; you're more likely to continue south by much more frequent **municipal bus**, which originates at the ski resorts (see below). Current information is available at the Canfranc **Turismo** (July–Sept Mon–Sat 9am–1pm & 4–8pm, Sun 9am–1pm; Oct–June Wed–Sat 9am–1.30pm & 3.30–6.30pm, Sun 9am–1.30pm; ☎974 373 141), opposite the station.

Walking from Canfranc: the GR11 east and west

The **main GR11** runs **northeast** from between Canfranc and Candanchú via the **Canal Roya** valley, then curls southeast to the attractive, upper **Ibóns de Anayet** (4hr), from where you've fine views of Pic du Midi d'Ossau. From here it's another two hours plus, mostly on 4WD track through the slopes of El Formigal, to Sallent de Gállego, for an easy, six-hour hiking day. For the record, a variant goes east directly from Canfranc along the **Valle de Izas**, the two routes converging at El Formigal, but this is less scenic, and will become even less so if Formigal's expansion into this valley happens.

Heading west from Candanchú itself involves a longer and tougher day's trek hugging the border, enlivened by the **Ibón de Astanés** (2hr), the largest natural lake in these parts. Assuming that the campsite at **Selva de Oza**, near the top of the **Valle de Echo** still hasn't reopened, you'd do better to take the variant via the low Collado de Riguelo and Collado d'o Boxo to the *Refugio de Gabardito*, from where Echo is an easy stage away (see p.445).

Skiing: Candanchú-Astún

Perhaps the best Aragonese ski resort, certainly the most advanced, is **CANDANCHÚ-ASTÚN**, 8km north of Canfranc (5 well-spaced buses daily from Jaca). The unaesthetic but functional complexes – smaller Astún dating from 1975, bigger and higher Candanchú the first established in these mountains – are just 4km apart, and share a lift pass though there's no physical link (yet). Jaca is bidding to host the 2010 Winter Olympics, so expect further improvements to facilities in the coming years.

Both resorts boast extensive north-facing runs in a treeless valley just southeast of the frontier ridge. Given the Atlantic-influenced climate, their top points of 2300–2400m should ensure good snow. **Astún** is particularly well organized and better for intermediates, with 7 blue and 12 red runs among 27 total, with equipment for hire, though chairlifts are sparse. **Candanchú** has 52 pistes of all grades, 31 of them red or black, plus competition-level slalom runs; though only a quarter of 25 lifts are chair, they're well-placed to serve most runs. Off-piste possibilities at both resorts are considerable, with a half-dozen routes recognized and minimally maintained.

Budget **accommodation** in Candanchú, all on the through road Ctra de Francia, can be found at *Pensión Somport*, Ctra de Francia 198 (☎974 373 009; ②), and at two *albergues*: the highly rated *El Águila* (☎974 373 291, *www.infovide.com/elaguila*; 58 places; open ski season & summer; ①), where half-board is encouraged, and *Valle de Aragón* (☎974 373 222; 68 places; all year; ①). The three-star *Hotel Tobazo* (☎ & fax 974 373 125; ⑦), and the mock-Tyrolean two-star *Hotel Candanchú* (☎974 373 025, *www.arrakis.es/hotelcan*; ⑥), reflect the more usual prices for this resort (try for a local "mini-package"), both offering "doorstep" skiing. Astún has just a single, ultra-pricey three-star hotel; with a car, you may prefer to stay in Canfranc (see opposite).

The Romans built the first road through the **Puerto de Somport/Col du Somport** (1632m) itself, below the ski slopes, and the Muslims made grateful use of this handiwork during their northward invasion in 732. The abandoned frontier gate has for company a more venerable relic: the ruins of a twelfth-century pilgrims' hospice built by the rulers of Béarn.

Huesca, Barbastro and the Sierra de Guara

Huesca, one of Aragón's three provincial capitals, lies 56km due south of Sabiñánigo on the broad, fast N330/E7 – or more circuitously, and enjoyably, 76km from Jaca via the A125 southwest through the Puerto de Oroel, and then onto the N240 southeast past the natural wonder of **Los Mallos** and the imposing **Castillo de Loarre**. The rail line out of Sabiñánigo also approximately traces this journey. The next major town east of Huesca is **Barbastro**, smack in the middle of Aragón's most esteemed wine-producing district, just east of the Río Zinca valley, which provides a corridor for the A138 and occasional bus service up to Aínsa or beyond. North of the Huesca-Barbastro road, occupying a huge rectangular territory of roughly 800 square kilometres, looms the low-altitude **Sierra de Guara**, an ever-popular target especially when the higher Pyrenean ranges are still under snow.

Huesca and around

HUESCA is perhaps the least memorable of Aragonese foothill towns, and if you're heading for the mountains you might bypass it altogether, or stay on the train to Jaca. However, to the northeast lies the **Sierra de Guara** with its canyonlands, while northwest of the town, the striking **Los Mallos de Riglos** pinnacles and the castle at **Loarre** present worthy pretexts for breaking a journey towards Jaca.

To call Huesca unmemorable is perhaps unfair, since it has a reasonably well-preserved **old quarter**, tucked into a loop of *paseos* and the Río Isuela. At its core stands a late Gothic **Catedral**, whose unusual facade combines the thirteenth-century portal of an earlier church with a brick Mudéjar gallery, and a pinnacled, Isabelline uppermost section. The great treasure inside is the *retablo* by Damián Forment, a Renaissance masterpiece depicting the Crucifixion and the Deposition.

Next door, the **Museo Diocesano** (summer Mon–Sat 10.30am–1.30pm & 4–7.30pm, winter same but shuts 7pm, closed Sat pm & Sun year-round; 200ptas/€1.20) contains a rather mixed collection, gathered from churches in the countryside. Across the way is a Renaissance **Ayuntamiento**. These apart, there's little to detain you. The liveliest time to visit is during Huesca's big **fiesta** in honour of San Lorenzo, held over the week including August 10.

Practicalities

Finding your way around Huesca shouldn't be a problem. The **train** station is at the south end of c/Zaragoza, a main thoroughfare, and the **bus station** is nearby on c/del Parque. The **Turismo** (July–Sept Mon–Fri 10.30am–1pm & 4–6.30pm, Sat 10am–2pm & 5–8pm, Sun 10am–2pm Oct–June variable opening times; ☎974 292 100), opposite the cathedral in the *Ayuntamiento*, stocks various pamphlets on the Aragonese mountains.

Accommodation can be hard to find, and during summer, when trekkers from all over are passing through, it's worth booking ahead. At the budget end of things, there's the *Pensión Augusto*, c/Aínsa 16, tidy rooms with washbasin above a bar (☎974 220 079; ②); the similar-standard *Pensión Bandrés* at c/Fatás 5 (☎974 224 782; ②), on a pedestrianized street near the bus station; and the en-suite *Hostal El Centro*, c/Sancho Ramírez 3 (☎ & fax 974 226 823; ③), in a grand old building with large, well-renovated rooms, many with balcony. There are more comfortable choices on ultra-central Plaza Lizana, just downhill from the cathedral: the co-managed, adjacent *Hostal Lizana/Lizana 2* (☎974 221 470 or 974 220 776; ④), and the three-star *Hotel Sancho Abarca* at no. 13 (☎974 220 650, fax 974 225 169; ⑦), where most rooms face a quieter side street. The **campsite**, *San Jorge* (☎974 227 416; April–Oct 15), is at the end of c/Ricardo del Arco.

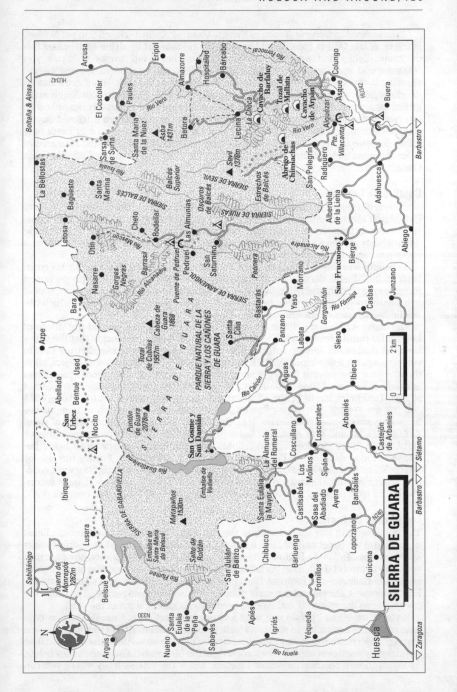

SIERRA DE GUARA

Restaurante Marisquería Navas, c/Vicente Campo Palacio 3 (closed Sun pm & Mon, late June & late Oct) is considered Huesca's top **restaurant** by virtue of delicious fish or game dishes and *artesanal* desserts. The chef's full works will run you 5000ptas/€30, with the pricey wine list extra, all delivered by efficient, liveried waiters shuttling between the front bar and the family *comedor* in the back. But there's also an excellent-value *menú* (2000ptas/€12) – typically seafood appetizer, sourdough rolls, grilled asparagus, *chicharro* fish with spinach and cream sauce, dessert. Its only serious rival is the newer *Restaurante Las Torres* at c/María Auxiliadora 3 (closed Sun & Aug 20–Sept 3), a fancy place purveying *nouvelle* Aragonese cuisine *a la carta* only (allow 5000ptas/€30). For excellent **tapas bars** and **nightlife** head for the *zona* around c/San Lorenzo and c/Padre Huesca, between the Coso Bajo and the Plaza de Santa Clara.

Castillo de Loarre

The eleventh-century **Castillo de Loarre** (April–Sept 10am–1.30pm & 4–7pm; Oct–March 11am–2.30pm; closed Mon & Tues except in August; free) is Aragón's most spectacular fortress. As you approach, the castle at first seems to blend into the hillside but gradually assumes a breathtaking grandeur: superbly compact, it rises dizzily on a rocky outcrop, commanding the landscape for miles around.

Its builder was Sancho Ramírez, king of Navarra, who used it as a base for his resistance to the Muslim occupation. Within the curtain walls a delicately proportioned Romanesque church, with 84 individually carved column capitals. You also have access to a pair of towers, the Torre de la Reina and the taller Torre del Homenaje, which can be climbed by iron rungs cemented into the wall.

The castle stands some 40km northwest of Huesca, and 6km beyond the village of Loarre. By **public transport**, it's an awkward trip and you may decide that the views from the road or rail line are sufficient, as bus timetables in particular do their best to conspire against a day-trip. **LOARRE** village has three daily buses from Huesca, all in the afternoon, but staying the night should cause no distress, since there's more than adequate **accommodation** in both Loarre and **AYERBE**, which has the nearest train station. Top choice has to be the *Hospedaria de Loarre* on Loarre's central plaza (☎974 382 706, fax 974 382 713; ⑤), a restored seventeenth-century mansion with enthusiastic young management; this also has the best **restaurant** around, with a *menú* (2000ptas/€12) and *a la carta* (4000ptas/€24). Failing this, Loarre has one *turismo rural*, while Ayerbe makes a good fallback with three, most characterful being the *Antigua Posada del Pilar* on Plaza Aragón 38 (☎974 380 052; ②). **Eating out**, go for Ayerbe's *Restaurante Floresta*, just at the turning for Loarre, with straightforward country cooking (*menú* 1500ptas/€9) and friendly service. There's also a good, quiet **campsite** on the road between Ayerbe and Loarre: *La Banera* (☎974 380 242; open all year).

Los Mallos de Riglos

The train line from Huesca to Jaca, and the N240 road from Huesca to Puente la Reina de Jaca, give views not only of Loarre but of the fantastic, pink-tinged, cylindrical bluffs known as **Los Mallos de Riglos** – "the ninepins of Riglos". Their majesty, however, may not serve to protect them from partial inundation by a proposed new dam at Biscarrués on the Río Gállego – the Embalse (Reservoir) de la Peña already exists just upstream. For the moment, the pinnacles remain popular with climbers and parapentists, while the river between the reservoir and Ayerbe swarms with rafters much of the year.

If you're travelling by train and want a closer look, get off at **Concilio** station (you have to ask the conductor to stop) and walk along the road to **RIGLOS** village, tucked high up underneath the most impressive stretch of the peaks. Along the way, you'll be rewarded by a series of superb views not only of the Mallos, but also of the valley below. At Riglos there's another (unstaffed) station, below the village, from where you can resume your journey. Alternatively, you can **stay** the night at the 2000-inaugurated rooms above the village *bar-restaurante* run by the welcoming Toni, who's a mine of information on climbing routes up the *mallos*. An 80-bunk rock-climbers' *refugio* at the edge of the village is set to open in 2003. Otherwise, make for **MURILLO DE GÁLLEGO**, out on the highway between Concilio and Riglos, pretty much taken over by rafters and guides in season. They **eat, drink** and listen to music into the small hours at *Bar-Restaurante El Embudo*.

There's another group of Mallos mountains near **Agüero**, a completely isolated village 5km west of the N240 beginning just below Murillo, and easily visible from Riglos. The reward for walking or driving up this side road, in addition to views of the Mallos, is an unspoilt village, and a gorgeous, unfinished Romanesque church, the **Iglesia de Santiago** (12–13th century), with portal carvings by the Master of San Juan de la Peña (see p.425); ask in the village for the key before following the dirt track up.

Barbastro

BARBASTRO, 51km east-southeast of Huesca and straddling the Río Vero before it joins the Zinca, has considerable historic importance. It was here that the union of Aragón and Catalunya was declared in 1137, sealed by the marriage of the daughter of Ramiro of Aragón to Ramón Berenguer IV, count of Barcelona. Although it's now little more than a slightly shabby provincial market town, Barbastro retains an air of dignity in its old quarter. Topping a rise just south of the river, the Gothic **Catedral**, on a site once occupied by a mosque, has a high altar whose construction began under the authority of Damián Forment: when he died in 1540 only part of the alabaster relief had been completed, and the remainder was finished by his pupils. Just northeast, on the Plaza de la Constitución, the **Ayuntamiento**, a restored fifteenth-century edifice designed by the Moorish chief architect to Fernando el Católico, is also worth seeing. Elsewhere, narrow, pedestrianized shopping streets are lined by faded-pastel housing piled up with their backs towards the river, while the central, tree-lined **Paseo del Coso** at the southwest edge of the old quarter is occupied by outdoor tables for many of the town's bars and cafés.

But the foregoing summary is incidental to Barbastro's sole present and future prospects: **wine**, wine and more wine. For the town lies at the centre of the **Somontano**, the most important *denominación de origen* vintage district in Aragón, and indeed one of the most prominent in Spain. This may seem peculiar for a town dominated by the abstemious, militant Catholic movement, Opus Dei, whose main centre is the nearby monastery of Torreciudad, but Opus Dei members are prominent in Spanish industry – including wine-making – raising money to further the faith. Visits can be organized to three of the biggest local wineries – Bodega Pirineos, Viñas del Vero and Enate (details from the Turismo, see below). Both Hemingway and Orwell tippled in Barbastro during the 1920s and 1930s; their favourite watering-hole, at one corner of the *paseo*, was the ground-floor bar of the Fonda San Ramón with its massive oaken barrels. Alas, this closed down in early 2000 when its lease was revoked by the landlord-bank – and a bit of history died with it. There are still, of course, well-stocked bottle shops in Barbastro, one of the best and biggest inside the Turismo.

Practicalities

The **bus station** is at the southwest end of the *paseo*, and offers regular daily departures for Huesca, even more frequent ones to Lleida and two (Mon-Sat) to Benasque. There's a very keen and helpful English-speaking **Turismo** (July & Aug daily 10am–2pm & 5–8.30pm; Sept–June Tues–Sat 10am–2pm & 4.30–8pm; ☎974 308 350) 200m uphill and south from the station, in the **Conjunto de San Julián y Santa Lucía**, a restored thirteenth-century hospice.

Since the demise of the Fonda San Ramón, really appealing budget **accommodation** is scarce; about as basic as you'd want to be is the en-suite *Hostal Goya* (☎974 311 747; ②) at no. 13 c/Argensola, a slightly seedy street just south of the river. More comfort is available at two establishments on c/Corona de Aragón, running parallel to the river at the northeast edge of the old town: *Hostal Roxi* (☎974 311 064; ③), with en-suite rooms, at no. 21, and the *Hotel Clemente* at no. 3 (☎974 310 186; ⑤). With all that wine sloshing about, decent **restaurants** have sprung up to take advantage, making Barbastro worth at least a lunch stop. The most central is just above the Turismo: *Cenador de San Julián* (closed Mon), considered one of the town's best, with a very accessible *menú* (2000ptas/€12). Further afield in the new quarter, within walking distance of the centre via the Avda Pirineos bridge, are three more possibilities (budget 3500ptas/€21): *Flor* at c/Goya 3 and *Cocina Vasca* more or less adjacent, plus *L'Arrabal* two blocks west just off Avda Pirineos itself. Finally, the *Hospedería El Pueyo*, 5km west, has a worthwhile *comedor* within the namesake hilltop monastery, dedicated to Barbastro's patroness, La Virgen del Pueyo.

Sierra de Guara

North of the N-240 road linking Huesca and Barbastro sprawls the **Sierra de Guara**, a thinly inhabited region protected as a *parque natural* since 1990. The sierra is definitely Pyrenean foothills – the highest point is 2078-metre Puntón de Guara – with no dramatic peaks to draw the eye to the horizon, and often distinctly scrubby low-altitude vegetation, enlivened by olive and almond groves. The Guara's allure lies lower down, in its unrivalled array of sculpted gorges, painted prehistoric caves and appealing villages. This is the main venue for **canyoning** in all of Spain, and arguably Europe; it's been known to the French for decades, such that French (and Belgian) cars match or outnumber Spanish ones in the popular centres. They retrace the steps of Belle Époque *pyreneistes* who had first discovered and publicized the canyonlands between 1870 and 1900. French-run, too, are many of the adventure outfitters – there's at least one in every village – though the Spanish are having a go at clawing back some of the trade. **Walking** opportunities are relatively limited, owing to poor trail marking and documentation, and hiking is most prudently confined to the cooler spring or autumn months. July days are best spent in a wetsuit, splashing down a watercourse.

The eastern half of the Guara is more frequented, and covered by the Alpina 1:40,000 **map** *Sierra de Guara II*, a must for touring. Due to massive depopulation, there's **no public transport** anywhere in the region; similarly, the only **petrol** and **bank** (with an ATM) is at Alquézar (see below). **Accommodation** tends to be either pricey, fancy hotels or fairly basic (crowded *albergues* and equally packed campsites), with very little in between.

Alquézar and around

At the far southeastern corner of the range and *parque*, 23km from Barbastro, **ALQUÉZAR** ("Alquezra" in Aragonese) is the Guara's gateway and most developed tourist mecca. Perched on the west bank of the Río Vero, it's a supremely atmospheric ·village, but packed to the gills most weekends and all summer. Arcaded lanes culminate in the eighth-century Moorish **citadel** on a pinnacle dropping to the river; the Christians took it in 1064, and by the start of the next century the **Colegiata de Santa María la Mayor** (guided visits summer daily: 11am–1pm & 4.30–7.30pm; winter 11am–1pm & 4–6pm; 300ptas/€1.80) already existed within the fortifications. Only the cloister, its column-capitals carved with biblical scenes, remains from the Romanesque era; the Gothic-Renaissance church itself dates from the sixteenth and seventeenth centuries. It's crammed with a miscellany of Baroque art, mostly polychrome wood except for an unpainted pine organ, and a masterly thirteenth-century wooden Crucifixion in the side chapel. From near the citadel paths lead down to the river and its **Puente de Villacantal**, one of several ancient bridges in the *sierra*. The only other specific cultural diversion is the **Museo Etnológico Casa Fabián** at c/Baja 16 (daily except Mon & Wed am 11am–2pm & 4–8pm; 200ptas/€1.20), with a working olive press in the cellar.

There's a **Turismo** at the southwest edge of town on c/Arrabal (Easter & July–Sept Tues–Sun 10.30am–1.30pm & 4–9pm, weekends only same hours Oct–June), which sells the recommended Alpina map. **Accommodation** is fairly abundant but still needs advance booking at busy times. Among several *albergues*, two worth noting are *Tintorero* (☎974 318 354; April–Sept; ①) in the heart of town at c/San Gregório 18, and the pricier, smaller *Isuala* at c/San Lucas 16, two streets higher (☎974 318 237; May–Oct; ①). There are also two **campsites** close by: *Alquézar* (☎974 318 300; all year), 1km downhill by the petrol pump, of a slightly higher standard than *Río Vero* (☎974 318 350; April–Oct), down by the river. Representative of six **casas rurales** are the friendly *Casa Jabonero* on c/Pedro Arnal 8 (☎974 318 908; ②), or the en-suite *Casa Espartero* on Plaza Mayor (☎974 318 071; ②). The longer established and more affordable of two **hotels** is the *Villa de Alquézar* on c/Pedro Arnal 12 (☎ & fax 974 318 416, ④), in the heart of the old quarter.

The **bars and restaurants** crowding nearby Plaza Nueva, their tables poised to exploit the view, are generally mediocre, and pricey to boot; you may prefer the *comedor* at the *Bar Villacantal* on Plaza Mayor, with its *menú* at 1700ptas/€10.20. With transport, head west 2.5km to **RADIQUERO**, where the *Monclus* on the bypass road has its own vineyard and winery, or 3km further south from there to **ADAHUESCA**, where *El Puntillo* (☎974 318 168) at c/de la Iglesia 4 operates sporadically. Finally, the village of **BUERA**, 6km southeast across the river, has another lodging/eating possibility in its *Posada de Lalola* (☎974 318 347; ⑤ B&B), with exquisite designer rooms opening onto a garden and respectable *table d'hôte* fare (4000ptas/€24) featuring Enate wines.

North: the road to Lecina

The HU-340 district road from below Alquézar heads northeast 5km to **COLUNGO**, attractive in a low-key way with its arched doorways and massive buttressed church. You can sample the locally made *aguardiente de anís* at A'Olla, opposite the *Hostal Mesón de Colungo* (☎974 318 195; ③), your sole option for **staying** and **eating**, fortunately with helpful and knowledgable staff.

The road continues, in and out of the minor Fornocal gorge, passing two of the four **painted caves** of the Vero valley, which can only be visited on escorted tours (daily Easter week & mid-July to mid-Sept, Sat/Sun only Easter to early July & mid-Sept to early Oct; otherwise make arrangements with the Barbastro Turismo). During peak season, just show up at the signed turn-outs for the **Covacho de Arpán** (10am & 6pm) and **Tozal de Mallata** (12.15 & 4.30pm); for the **Covacho de Barfaluy**, assemble at the Turismo in Lecina (see below) at 10am or 5pm, while 4.30pm visits to the remote **Abrigo de Chimiachas** must always be booked through the Alquézar Turismo, as a long 4WD transfer is involved. The art in Chimiachas and Arpán is classified as *Levantino* or conventional-figural, while that of Mallata and Barfaluy as *esquemático* (stick-figures).

LECINA itself, some 16km from Colungo, has some imposing houses – it was one of the wealthier Guara villages – an enormous oak (thus the name, from *La Encina*) and a sense of height, looking northeast as it does to the main Pyrenean peaks. Moreover, there's a superb place to **stay** and **eat** here: *La Choca* (☎ & fax 974 343 070 or 608 633 636; ④), a restored mansion opposite the church with some of the best food in the Guara (*table d'hôte* for about 2000ptas/€12). There's also a **campsite** down by the river, *Lecina* (☎974 318 386; May–Sept) which doubles as the closest canyoning outfitter, but this is one of the few Guaran areas where **walkers** are actively catered to.

The local municipality has waymarked sixteen **PR trails**, indicated on a sketch map available from the tiny Turismo in Lecina or from *La Choca*. A particularly good outing is the three-hour loop Lecina–Almazorre–Betorz–Lecina, combining three of the most unspoilt paths (#5, 9, 6). It's an hour on #5 from Lecina (760m), mostly through shaded woods on a walled *camino* (but a bit of dreary track), to the bed of the Río Vero (670m) and an old, combined **grain mill and olive press**, used until recently; all the workings are still intact. Allow 15 minutes one-way for the detour up to **Almazorre** village (750m; no facilities), or proceed directly onto trail #9 up a side canyon, first on the left bank, then on the right, though low pines, box and oak to **Betorz** (under 1hr, 970m). This is an attractive, through almost empty, village with a marvellous setting. The descent to Lecina begins with the *camino* starting on the right road verge just past the lowest houses; there's even some cobbling (plus a stretch of track) along the 20 minutes to a **spring**, your only reliable water en route, feeding a round livestock pool in a shady glen. It's an hour in total (not "40min" as posted) along a gentle grade through baby oaks back to Lecina.

CANYONING IN THE SIERRA DE GUARA

There's a **huge variety** of canyons to explore in the Sierra de Guara, from beginners' outings with no special equipment needed, to highly technical chasms visited only by experts holding special permits. Generally you need to know how to swim, and be in reasonable physical condition, since every body part – especially fingers and forearms – will get a workout. Judging from the number of folk hobbling about with arms in slings and bandaged abrasions, canyoning is a moderately dangerous sport. But you shouldn't feel intimidated or excluded: hundreds of people emerge daily in peak season without a scratch, and you frequently see whole families with five-year-olds in tow happily threading the **easier** canyons, such as the Vero near Alquézar, the Peonera just upstream from Bierge and the Barrasil at Rodellar. **Moderate** ravines, with some drops requiring rope or prolonged swims, include Oscuros de Balcés, Estrechos de Balcés and Gorgonchón, all close to Bierge, while **experts-only** absysses above Rodellar include Gorgas Negras, Otín and Mascún Superior, all involving thirty-metre abseilings and strenuous clambering. Organized outings, run daily or by demand April–October, typically **cost** 6000–7000ptas/€36–42 per person, including equipment, with little difference between the simplest and most difficult canyons. Local *albergues* also offer advantageous "packages", such as three days of expeditions and full board for 33,500ptas/€200.

Since all the most popular canyons lie within the **Parque de la Sierra y los Cañones de Guara**, park authorities have stipulated **conditions** of access; many are common sense and spelled out in their leaflet "Normativa Sobre el Descenso de Barrancos" (Rules Concerning the Descent of Ravines). If you go with an outfitter, they'll be well aware of the rules, but for those going solo, an English summary follows. The maximum number of persons per group is 10 in the Vero, Barrasil, Peonera and Balcés ravines; 4 in the Gorgonchón and 8 in all the others. Groups must enter with a minimum **spacing** between them of ten minutes, and entry in summer must be **no later** than 4pm (though Gorgas Negras, Mascún and Peonera via Morrano must be entered by noon, 1pm and 2.30pm respectively). Canyons with permanent water (most of them) require the wearing of a **neoprene suit**, and any descent involving abseiling means mandatory provision with **harness**, **helmet** and adequate **rope**. Certain canyons have restricted access, or are totally off-limits for safety, ecological or archeological reasons. La Choca requires a special permit year-round from the park authorities, as does Otín between March and June; a number of the less used gorges, in particular the Vadiello system, are completely forbidden December–June. You're not to enter the pools of the Canal del Palomo (to protect its rare species). Finally, there are various **general prohibitions** similar to that of the Ordesa park: no fires, rough camping, unnecessary noise, leaving rubbish, molesting flora and fauna, defacing rocks, or introducing motor vehicles onto the many barred 4WD tracks.

Northwest: the road to Rodellar

West from Alquézar and Adahuesca, the next significant village is **BIERGE**, its *ermita* of **San Fructuoso** adorned with frescoes. **Accommodation** is limited to a single *casa rural* in the centre, *Casa Rufas* at c/La Cruz 2 (☎974 318 373; ③) and a welcoming *albergue* at the southwest outskirts, *Casa Barbara* (☎974 318 060; ①), aimed at canyoners who don't mind being packed nine to a dorm, but the food – including own-baked breads and turnovers – is excellent, and served out in the garden; half-board is encouraged (3750ptas/€22.50 per person).

North along the ridgetop HU-341, the scenery gets grander after some 5km, with canyons yawning either side. After 11km you descend through woods to *Expediciones* (☎974 343 008; *www.expediciones.sc.es*; June–Sept), the most pleasant **campsite** of three in the Alcanadre river valley; they're also about the most switched-on canyoning operator. **LAS ALMUNIAS**, 2km further, is the first proper village, offering the *Hostal Casa Tejedor* (☎ & fax 974 343 015; March–Oct; ③) with a restaurant, plus the *Albergue Las Almunias* across the road (☎974 343 218; ①).

RODELLAR, some 4km further and 18km from Bierge at the end of the road, looks achingly photogenic draped along a ridge above the Río Mascún, but the reality close up in peak season is likely to be cars parked nose-to-tail for a kilometre before the village, and overstretched **accommodation**. This comprises *Casa Arilla* (☎974 318 343; ③; April–Oct) and *Casa Regina* (☎974 318 364; ②), while the *Bar-Restaurante Florentino* opposite *Casa Arilla* is the only spot to eat or drink. Two **campsites** – *Mascún* at the edge of the village (☎974 318 367, *www.guara-mascun.com*; April–Oct), and *El Puente* (☎974 318 312; April–Oct), 1500m south by the river and the medieval Pedruel bridge, both act as canyoning guide centres. If you're not interested in plumbing the deep gorges, the most popular activity is the two-and-a-half-hour (one-way) **hike** north to the abandoned hamlet of **Otín**, though path-marking is terrible. It's sobering to reflect that before the current canyoning boom, just two families lived in Rodellar (down from 40 in 1900), plus a few pioneering French canyon-explorers like Pierre Minvielle and Christian Abadie who bought houses here in the 1960s.

travel details

French trains

Pau to: Lourdes (almost hourly 5.30am–midnight; 30min); Oloron-Sainte-Marie (4–6 daily; 35min); Tarbes (almost hourly 5.30am–midnight; 45min).

Tarbes to: Capvern (2 daily (1 may be SNCF bus); 30min); Lannemezan (8 daily Mon–Sat, 6 Sun; 25min); Lourdes (almost hourly 6.30am–10.30pm; 20min).

Spanish trains

Jaca to: Canfranc-Estación (2 daily; 40min); Huesca (2 daily; 2hr); Sabiñánigo (2 daily; 20min); Zaragoza (2 daily; 3hr).

French buses

Bagnères-de-Bigorre to: Campan (3 daily July–Sept, 1 daily in term time; 20min); Lac de Payolle (3 daily July–Sept, 1 daily in term time; 45min); Sainte-Marie-de-Campan (3 daily July–Sept, 1 daily in term time; 35min).

Lannemezan to: Arreau (SNCF or Brunet buses); 7 daily year-round; 25min); Bagnères-de-Bigorre (2 weekly during school term; 50min); St-Lary-Soulan (SNCF buses only; 5 daily year-round; 45min).

Laruns to (all except Pau with Canonge-Pic Bus, July & Aug Mon–Fri only): Bious-Oumette campsite (1 daily; 35min); Col du Pourtalet (2 daily, 1hr 20min); Gabas (2 daily; 25min); Lac de Fabrèges (2 daily Mon–Fri with Canonge-Pic Bus; 55min; 1 daily with SNCF bus, 40min); Pau (2–3 daily on SNCF bus, change to train at Buzy; 1hr 10min).

Lourdes to: Bagnères-de-Bigorre (2 daily during school term, 3 daily in summer; 45min); Barèges (SNCF bus; 6 daily July–Aug, 5 daily Sept–June; 1hr 5min); Cauterets (SNCF bus; 6 daily July–Aug, 5 daily Sept–June; 1hr); Luz-Saint-Sauveur (SNCF bus; 6 daily July–Aug, 5 daily Sept–June; 45min); Pau (4 daily; 1hr 15min); Tarbes (hourly; 30min).

Luz-Saint-Sauveur to: Gavarnie (July–Aug 2 daily with Cars Dubie, 9am & 5.30pm, return 11.40am & 6.30pm; winter 3 weekly, Mon, Thurs & Sat; 40min).

Oloron-Sainte-Marie to (all SNCF buses): Bedous (7 daily Mon–Sat, 4 on Sun; 30min); Cette-Eygun/Lescun junction (7 daily Mon–Sat, 4 on Sun; 45min); Urdos (7 daily Mon–Sat, 4 on Sun; 1hr).

Pau to: Bayonne (run by TPR; 3–4 daily Mon–Sat, 2 on Sun; 2hr); Col d'Aubisque (CITRAM; July to mid-Sept 1 daily; 2hr); Gourette (CITRAM; 3 daily; 1hr 45min); Laruns (CITRAM; 3 daily; 1hr); Lourdes (4 daily; 1hr 15min); Oloron-Sainte-Marie (Mon–Sat 2–3 daily; 45min); Tarbes (6 daily; 1hr).

Tarbes to: Argelès-Gazost (6 daily; 50min); Arrens-Marsous (Mon–Sat 1 daily; 1hr 20min); Bagnères-de-Bigorre (Mon–Sat 8–9 daily, 3 on Sun; 40min); Pierrefitte-Nestalas (6 daily; 1hr); Tarbes-Ossun/Lourdes Airport (1–2 daily; 30–45min).

Spanish buses

Aínsa to: Bielsa (Mon, Wed, Fri only at 8.45pm, returns 6am next day; 40min); Sabiñánigo via Torla (1 daily at 2.30pm; 2hr).

Barbastro to: Boltaña via Aínsa, Mon–Sat year-round at 7.45pm, returns next day 6.45am; July 15–Aug 31 also 11am, returning 3pm (Huesca-Barbastro 10am/6.30pm services link with this); Benasque (daily 11am, plus Mon–Sat 5.30pm; 2hr); Lleida (6 daily; 1hr 15min).

Huesca to: Barbastro (4–7 daily; 50min); Jaca (4–5 daily; 1hr); Lleida (6 daily; 2hr); Loarre (3 daily; 45min); Pamplona (3 daily; 2hr 50min); Sabiñánigo (4–5 Mon–Sat, 3–4 Sun/hols; 55min.

Jaca to: Ansó via Echo (1 daily except Sun at 6.30pm; 1hr 40min); Astún/Candanchú (5 daily; 45min); Biescas (1–2 daily; 50min); Canfranc-Estación (5 daily; 30min); Huesca (4–5 daily; 1hr); Pamplona (1–2 daily; 1hr 35min); Sabiñánigo (2 daily at 10.15am and 6.15pm; 20min).

Sabiñánigo to: Aínsa via Torla (Mon–Sat 1 daily at 11am; 2hr 40min); Biescas (Mon–Sat 2 daily at 11am & 6.30pm; 20 min); Jaca (Mon–Sat 2 daily 8am & 6.30pm, 1 at 5pm on Sun; 15min); Panticosa village (1 daily at 10.45am, also 1 daily Mon–Sat at 6.30pm; July–Aug am service ends at Balneario; 50min); Sarvisé (1 daily at 11am, plus additional service July–Aug Mon–Sat at 6.30pm; 1hr 5min); Torla (1 daily at 11am, plus additional service July–Aug Mon–Sat at 6.30pm; 55min).

Sallent de Gállego to: El Formigal (daily at 11.50am, also regular ski shuttles in winter; 20min); Sabiñánigo (1 daily at 4pm, plus Mon–Sat at 7am; 1hr).

International buses

Jaca to: Lourdes via Canfranc, Pau, Tarbes (Sat at 9.45am, Sun at 5.45pm; 4hr 15min for the entire trip).

Oloron-Sainte-Marie to (SNCF buses): Canfranc via Urdos (Mon–Sat 4 daily, 3 on Sun; 1hr 40min).

CHAPTER FIVE

THE WESTERN PYRENEES

The widespread notion that the Pyrenees begin or end at Pic d'Anie, some 80km from the Atlantic coast, ignores the segment of the range that contains the greatest diversity of wildlife, the densest forest, a seductively green landscape and the most tenaciously retained ethnic identity – that of the Basques. Extreme altitude (and lakes) are the only things the Western Pyrenees lack: there's no peak higher than Pic d'Anie's neighbour Tres Reyes (2444m) between it and the sea, and beyond Pic d'Orhy/Pico de Ori (2017m) the summits diminish markedly.

The **Western Pyrenees** embrace an area more extensive than **Euskal Herria**, the Basques' name for their country on both sides of the frontier. They also include a small pocket of Alto Aragón in the paired **Echo** and **Ansó** valleys, drainages of the same karst country as the **Haute-Soule** in France and **Valle de Belagoa** in Navarra. But geographically the difference between the French and Spanish sides of the border is greater here than anywhere else in the range. In Spain the hills, often alpine in climate, extend far from the frontier, and are often densely clad in trees; the **Irati forest**, for example, dense and extensive in Spain, has been severely reduced by exploitation on its French slopes (where it's also known as 'Iraty'). Much of the French Basque country is strongly reminiscent of the open countryside of Scotland, especially near **Saint-Jean-Pied-de-Port**, its chief inland tourist attraction.

This western region also has the highest concentration of small gateway cities for the mountains. **Bayonne** and **San Sebastián**, near the Atlantic coast below the foothills, gracefully combine roles as commercial *entrepôts*, resorts and administrative centres, with either – along with the dedicated playground of **Biarritz** – proving livelier and more exciting than anything along the Mediterranean coast of the Pyrenees.

Public transport is fairly good on the Spanish side of the Pyrenees but very poor in France except on the coast and along the Nive valley, so the easiest way of tackling the area is from the south. If you're coming from Jaca you can take a bus up into the Echo and Ansó valleys, hike west to the Valle de Roncal valley and then over its head to French attractions, such as the Kakouetta gorges. Returning to Roncal or the Valle

---

ACCOMMODATION PRICE CODES

Each place to stay in this book has been given a code which corresponds to one of the following price categories.

① Under €13/2200ptas/85F	② €15–24/2500–4000ptas/100–160F
③ €24–32/4000–5400ptas/160–210F	④ €32–40/5400–6600ptas/210–260F
⑤ €40–52/6600–8600ptas/260–340F	⑥ €52–65/8600–10,800ptas/340–430F

⑦ Over €65/10,800ptas/430F

Category ① refers to the price *per person* of a bed; the other categories correspond to the **cheapest available double room in high season**. B&B and HB denote, respectively, when the price includes breakfast, and when it includes half-board. For more details, see p.41.

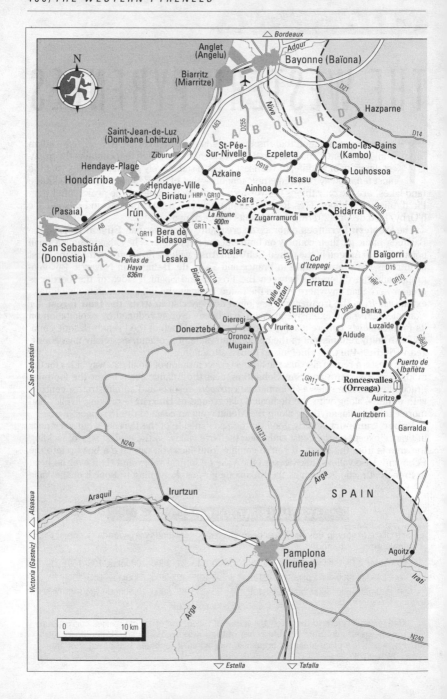

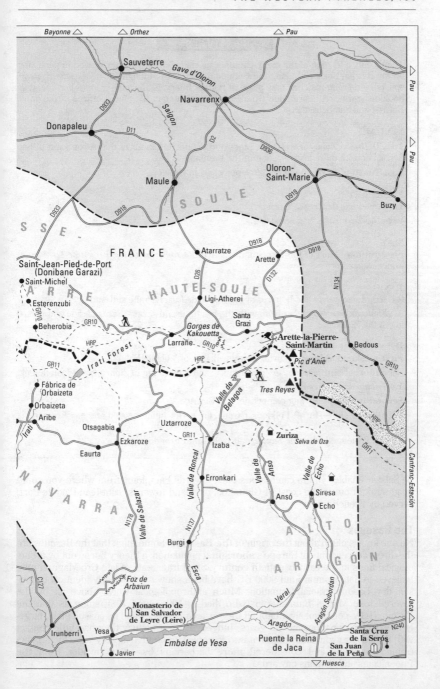

This is only a fraction of the many events, especially during summer, staged in particular on the Basque Coast and along the Camino de Santiago. Bullfights, *force Basque* (Basque sports) and *pelota* matches take place at regular intervals all summer long. For schedule booklets and ticket information where applicable, contact the tourist offices in Bayonne, Biarritz and San Sebastián.

JANUARY
19–20 *Tamborrada* – march with pipes and drums in honour of the patron saint of San Sebastián, with more festive action in the evenings.
Last Tuesday & Wednesday *Pottok* pony sale in Ezpeleta.

FEBRUARY
10 Traditional dancing at Luzaïde.
Variable *Carnival* in San Sebastián.

MAY
First Sunday Start of the three-month season of *romerías* to the *Virgen de Orreaga* at Roncesvalles.

JUNE
24–26 Music, *pelota* and bonfires at Saint-Jean-de-Luz, Larrañe and Auritze.
30 *Fiesta de San Marcial* at Irún, with the five-thousand-strong *Alarde* parade and canoeing in the Bidasoa.

JULY
First weekend Folklore festival, various villages of Valle de Echo.
Second weekend *Fête du Thon*, with music and tuna-eating in Ziburu/Saint-Jean-de-Luz.
13 *Tributo de las Tres Vacas* at Belagoa.
Second full week Surfing competitions at Biarritz.
Third week (Sat–Thurs) Folklore, parade, fireworks, bullfights and *Jazz aux Remparts* at Bayonne.
24–28 Prolonged *Fiesta de Santiago* at Izaba and Elizondo.

de Salazar enables you to catch a bus back towards Pamplona, from where you could head straight out to the coast of Gipuzkoa, or inland towards Saint-Jean-Pied-de-Port, served by French trains.

The Basques

No one knows much about the origin of **the Basques**. Some think that the Basques are the direct descendants of Europe's **aboriginal** population, a theory borne out by archeological finds in the early twentieth century. Skull fragments of late Cro-Magnon man believed to date from around 9000 BC have been shown to be nearly identical to present-day Basque cranial formation. Much anthropological work, above all by the revered Joxe Miguel Barandiaran (who died in 1991, aged 101), suggests that the Basques have continuously inhabited the western Pyrenees and its coastal plain, largely in isolation, for thousands of years. Indeed, in early history they had little contact with the peoples who later migrated into Europe, surrounded as they were by impenetrable mountains and considered mere barbarians by every invader from the Phoenicians and Romans onwards.

25 *Fiesta de Santiago*, at Luzaïde; also one including an *encierro* at Puente la Reina de Jaca.

Variable, last two weeks *International Jazz Festival* at San Sebastián.

August

First Wednesday *Fêtes de Bayonne*, five days of heavy drinking and concerts, plus bull-fights, at Bayonne.

Second week (Sun–Thurs) *Pelota*, street parties, music, dancing and Basque sports at Cambo-les-Bains (Bas Cambo) and at Baïgorri (Saint-Étienne-de-Baïgorry).

15–23 *Semana Grande* – a folk and music festival for *Asunción* at San Sebastián, with fireworks.

13–15 *Pelota*, folklore and dancing at Saint-Jean-Pied-de-Port.

15 *Romería* to the Ermita de Nuestra Señora de las Nieves, near Otsagabia; mock Basque wedding at Baïgorri.

Third weekend *Fêtes de Petit Bayonne*.

September

First ten days *Pelota* championships at Bayonne.

First and second weekends *Trainera* regatta in San Sebastián.

8 *Fiesta de la Virgen de Guadalupe* at Hondarribia; *romería* to the *colegiata* at Roncesvalles; *Fiestas de Bobo* – masqued dancers at Otsagabia.

Second Sunday Start of three-day festival at Sara, with Basque sports, singing and dancing.

Fourth week International Film Festival at San Sebastián.

Last two weeks International Film Festival at Biarritz.

October

Third week *Festival du Théâtre* in Bayonne.

Last weekend Party, then Mass, in honour of red peppers at Ezpeleta.

December

17 *Fiesta de Santo Tomás* – folkloric fun in San Sebastián.

26–27 *Fiesta de San Estéban* at Yesa.

Certainly their **language**, the complex Euskera (often spelled Euskara), is one of the most ancient spoken in Europe, predating the migrations from the east which brought the Indo-European languages some three thousand years ago. It is now considered to be as ancient as the Basque race itself, and to be distantly related – if at all – to certain tongues of the Caucasus. Establishing certainties has been complicated by the fact that, except for one mixed Latin-Basque manuscript of the tenth century, no written examples of Euskera survive from before the fifteenth century. The language has largely been maintained and has also evolved through the oral traditions of *bertsolariak*, or popular poets, specializing in improvised verse, a tradition still alive today. The vocabulary implies a way of life and belief dating back to long before the Christian era, as reflected in terms referring to ancient sites such as dolmens and cromlechs. Further evidence is an extensive Basque mythology relating to *gentiles*, the legendary giants supposedly responsible for building these sites, as well as ancient ways and bridges. Yet crucial though it has been for defining Basque identity, Euskera is nowadays a minority language in the region, spoken – mostly along the coastal strip – by about 500,000 people, roughly twenty percent of the total Basque population in France and Spain.

There are strong dialectal differences in usage, spelling and pronunciation throughout the **seven Basque regions** (four in Spain, three in France). It's worth learning to recognize the Basques' term for themselves – Euskaldunak, sometimes Euskualdunak – and their homeland, referred to as Euskadi or Euzkadi in Spain but more generally as Euskal Herri(a). In Spain, the more or less homogeneous autonomous regions of Gipuzkoa and Bizkaia on the coast account for the bulk of Euskera-speakers; Alaba (Araba) and Navarra (Nafarroa), with a long history of adherence to a unitary Spanish state, experienced – until a recent, conscious revival – a steady decrease in the proportion of Euskera-speakers, to as little as ten percent. The weakening of Euskera's hold was accelerated following the rapid industrialization of Bizkaia and Gipuzkoa during the nineteenth century and the resultant immigration of labour from the rest of Spain, a process deliberately encouraged under Franco (see feature on pp.500–501 for more on Franco's regime and Basque nationalism). By 1975 more than fifty percent of the working class of the coastal Spanish Basque regions came from other parts of the country, whereas in Navarra the proportion of people from elsewhere in Spain was just eighteen percent. During 1990s labour agitation in Gipuzkoa and Bizkaia, an impulse to protect both a rapidly decreasing number of jobs from outsiders and linguistic purity neatly coincided.

BASQUE PLACE-NAMES AND STREET-NAMES

Almost everywhere **in Gipuzkoa**, street and road signs appear in both Basque and Castilian, but the latter is often painted over or "edited" by irate graffiti artists. Recently, many municipalities have officially chosen to prefer the Basque names and this is reflected on new tourist brochures and maps. **In Navarra** – Nafarroa in Euskera – the process is nearly as advanced, to the occasional annoyance of Castilian-speakers, since only about twenty percent of the population here, mostly in the far northwest on the hilly border with Gipuzkoa, speak Euskera. In the three **French Basque regions** of Labourd (Lapurdi), Basse-Navarre (Behea Nafarroa) or Soule (Zuberoa), Basque nationalists have, since the late 1990s, succeeded in implementing bilingual signage for every town and village, though not yet for every street.

This Guide has treated Basque **place-names** variously, according to their international currency and cartographic conventions. Some places, like Hondarribia, Irún, Ainhoa or Lesaka, have no French or Spanish form in current use, and are cited in **Euskera only**. Others, like Biarritz, Saint-Jean-Pied-de-Port, Roncesvalles and San Sebastián, are increasingly known by Euskera names, but given their long-established international reputation, are cited in **French or Spanish first**, with **Euskera in brackets following**. Many smaller villages are losing their Spanish/French versions on road or town-limit signage, and these are cited in the text as **Euskera first, Spanish/French/Euskera variants in brackets following**. International maps have yet to switch over to strictly Euskera tags, except for cases such as Hondarribia and Pasaia (and sometimes Donostia for San Sebastián).

If given an older town plan by a tourist office, beware of the massive campaign of **street renaming** reflected in kerbside signage, especially in **San Sebastián**. Sometimes the difference is slight (Narrika versus Narrica) but just as often the Euskera name is utterly different (c/Nagusia versus c/Mayor). *Kalea*, incidentally, is Euskera for "Street" and follows the proper name.

It is also worth noting a couple of key **letter changes** which may help to decipher initially confusing words on menus and signs. The Castilian *ch* becomes *tx* (*txipirones* as opposed to *chipirones*) or *ts* (Otsagabia rather than Ochagavía), *v* becomes *b* and *y* becomes *i* (*Bizkaia* as opposed to *Vizcaya*). Above all, Euskera features a proliferation of *k*s, as this letter replaces the Castilian *c* and *qu* (*Gipuzkoa* instead of *Guipúzcoa; Okendo*, not *Oquendo*), and as *-ak* forms the plural. In France, Euskera names are often disguised with the French *ç* and final *y*; thus Esterençuby rather than Esterenzubi, Baïgorry rather than Baïgorri, Iraty instead of Irati.

Architecturally, there's a marked difference between the French and Spanish Basque areas. The genuine Basque house – a solid stone structure that often incorporated overhanging upper storeys – is now rare, though some can be seen around Santa Grazi in Haute-Soule, and in a few other settlements. Today the popular image of the Basque house is of a white building with colourful shutters and half-timbering, but this type of house, originally particular to the Labourd region on the French coast, has spread inland comparatively recently, and has been adopted in Spain only along parts of the frontier.

The extended **family** – the word for which, *etxe*, is the same as that for "house" – has always been the basic social unit of Basque life, rather than the village. A farmstead or *baserri* was a multifunctional building housing up to four generations, plopped in the middle of its fields or pastures. A yearning for such a rural idyll probably accounts for the linear, straggled appearance of the smaller Basque hamlets on either side of the border. Property was handed down intact, traditionally from one's paternal aunts, to the oldest son, compelling younger sons to seek their fortunes elsewhere, usually as seamen or emigrants to the Americas.

Basque food is recognized as Spain's finest, and certainly garners respect even in France; the people here are prodigious eaters, whom you'll encounter seated before enormous spreads in reasonably priced roadside eateries on the outskirts of towns throughout the region. You'll also come across traditional Basque food in the form of *tapas* in virtually every bar, freshly cooked and always excellent. The tradition of **gastronomic societies**, unique to the Basque regions, deserves special mention: first founded in the mid-nineteenth century, they came about originally as socializing places for different craftsmen. Controversy has surrounded them because women have traditionally not been allowed to enter (although this is changing); all the cooking is done by men who pay a token membership for the facilities. Members prepare elaborate dishes to perfection as a hobby and it can be said that true Basque cookery has largely retreated to these societies. The so-called *Nueva Cocina Vasca* (New Basque Cookery), heavily influenced by French cuisine, is becoming increasingly evident on menus.

THE KARST COUNTRY AND AROUND

Few landscapes in the Pyrenees have quite the same impact as that immediately to the west of Pic d'Anie. Elsewhere in the range there may be more photogenic glaciers, lakes and wildflowers, but nothing so surreal as the **karst** country around **Tres Reyes**, the highest border mountain of the Basque Pyrenees, and along the Atlantic flank of **Pic d'Anie**, the westernmost peak of Béarn. Their upper slopes have been rain-carved into fantastic shapes and sluiced clean of every particle of soil; yet the heights are waterless, the Atlantic precipitation vanishing instantly through waist-deep fissures and bowl-shaped *dolines*, eroding the limestone underneath into a Swiss cheese of potholes and horizontal caverns. Between the two summits lies a zone of shattered boulders, where occasional stunted black pines erupt.

Yet the lower elevations where water reappears – sometimes weeks later, courtesy of the numerous subterranean rivers – are of an almost tropical lushness, with dense forest and pastures of brilliant green, with which a few red-tiled barns and light-grey, stone-built villages contrast markedly. These are the valleys of **Echo** and **Ansó** in westernmost Alto Aragón, **Roncal** in Navarra, **Sainte-Engrâce** in Haute-Soule and the gorges of **Kakouetta** and **Ehujarré** which open onto the Saint-Engrâce valley.

So far this magnificent landscape is little protected. The French **Parc National des Pyrénées** ends at the border peak of Laraille/Arraya de las Foyas, while the less stringently administered forestry protection zone beyond only guarantees partial preservation of Pic d'Anie and none at all for the Sainte-Engrâce valley. Navarra has conferred *parque natural* status on the **Larra-Belagoa** area at the head of the Valle de Roncal, but

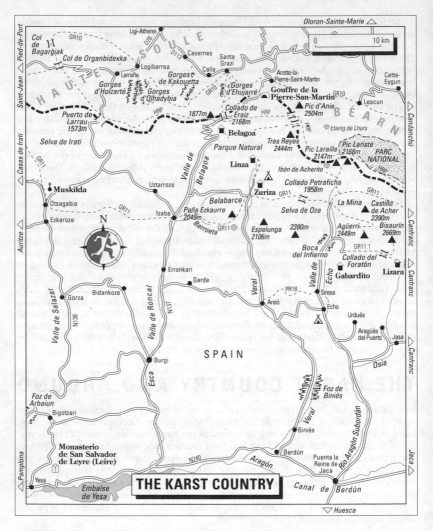

THE KARST COUNTRY

it deserves more – not just to protect the dwindling fauna but to reduce wear and tear on the actual terrain, increasingly popular with Spanish city-dwellers.

The Echo and Ansó valleys

The **Valle de Echo** and **Valle de Ansó**, northwest of Jaca, are the most westerly valleys of Alto Aragón and, in their upper reaches, among the most beautiful, watered respectively by the Aragón Su: ordan and Veral rivers. They intercommunicate over shallow passes between karst summits, with the Haute-Soule region in France to the north and the Valle de Roncal to the west.

The principal villages – Echo (833m) and Ansó (860m) – once lived (and grew wealthy) from sheep-raising. In modern times, timber-cutting has supplanted livestock, but despite a modest altitude on the valley floor, good roads in and their manifest beauty, seasonal or weekend habitation is now the rule for both villages. Echo and Ansó are lonely places in winter, as it's considered too arduous to commute to jobs in the provincial centres. Indeed until quite recently, both villages felt extremely remote all year round, and Echo maintains an Aragonese dialect known as *Cheso*, widely spoken and taught in the school. Another holdover is the presence of the *espantabrujas*, little hoodoo figures perched atop the domed chimneys or over windows; also found in other parts of Alto Aragón, these were believed to repel witches who were in the habit of entering houses through such openings.

These days, Echo and Ansó find themselves squarely on the tourist map, a favourite target for Spanish weekenders. However, in each case the local country shows its best side – and only offers anything in the way of walking – some distance upstream from the villages, though the Valle de Echo makes a more dramatic impression within sight of its village. Developers and planners also have their eyes on the valleys. Now that a long-debated natural-gas pipeline has shifted to the Salazar valley, the big local environmental issue is the proposed enlargement of the Yesa reservoir downstream on the Río Aragon – you'll see (rather bizarrely for English-readers) "YESA NO" graffiti everywhere. In spring 2000 the scheme was given what may be final approval, much to the dismay of local inhabitants (see p.539, in "The Environment").

Access

There is only one daily **bus service** (Mon–Sat), calling first at Echo, then Siresa, and finally to Ansó. This departs **from Jaca** at 6.30pm (summer, may be 1hr earlier winter), reaching Echo at 7.25pm and Ansó 45 minutes later, departing at 6am to return the next day.

If you don't have your own transport, renting a mountain **bike** in Jaca would be a good investment for exploring either valley; reckon on around two and a half hours from Jaca to Echo village, turning off the C134/N240 at Puente la Reina de Jaca, or much the same to Ansó village, turning off at Berdún, 7km west of Puente la Reina de Jaca. The latter side road, not served by bus, is particularly spectacular, passing a privately owned castle at Biniés before threading an unnervingly narrow course through the Foz de Biniés, carved out by the Río Veral.

The **GR65.3.3** – a very minor variant of the Santiago pilgrimage route – also links Berdún and Biniés with Echo, threading over the hills on a variety of surfaces. Trans-Pyrenean trekkers can use the **GR11** to hike into and out of the area, although the trail intersects both valleys considerably above the two villages.

Echo and Siresa

ECHO (formerly *Hecho*, which may still appear on old maps), larger of the two villages, is a splendid old place, though historically less wealthy than Ansó. Arcades ring the main double-plaza, which host the outdoor tables of its two bars, while whitewash outlines the windows and doors on some of the massive houses, the more sumptuous of them built around pebble-mosaic forecourts. Although it seems ancient, Echo in its present form is less than two centuries old; it – and Ansó – were burnt to the ground during the Napoleonic wars. Echo can otherwise lay modest claim to fame in Aragonese history as the seat of an embryonic Aragonese feudal state under Conde Aznar Galíndez in the ninth century, and as the birthplace of the "warrior king" Alfonso I.

An art festival, the Simposio de Escultura y Pintura Moderna, held every summer between 1975 and 1984, left a permanent legacy in an **open-air gallery of sculpture**, on the hillside west of the village. Created by a group of artists led by Pedro Tramullas, the 46 stone or metal pieces are not terribly stunning individually, but their total effect is riveting. The Simposio was initially resisted by most of the locals, who eventually came to terms with it – but now there are insufficient funds for the festival's resumption.

Near the enormous central church, there's a more conventional museum, the **Museo Etnológico** (Easter, July & Aug 11am–2pm & 6–9pm; otherwise contact the *Ayuntamiento*; 150ptas/€0.90), with interesting collections on Pyrenean rural life and folklore.

Practicalities

A **Turismo** in the *Ayuntamiento* (daily June–Sept 10am–2pm & 6–8pm; ☎974 375 329) has information about much of the surrounding area; if it's closed ask upstairs and they may open it for you. In summer, or at weekends, reservations at Echo's **hostales** are virtually mandatory (if your luck runs out, you could try the accommodation around Siresa – see below). The clear first choice, if you can squeeze in around occasional tour groups, is *Casa Blasquico*, barely marked at Plaza Palacio (de la Fuente) 1 (☎974 375 007; ④), next door to the *Bar Surbordan*, its five tastefully converted rooms (including one suite) offering all comforts. Fallbacks, in descending order of preference, are the en-suite *Hostal de la Val* (☎974 375 028; ④), whose front rooms overlook the village; *Casa Chuanet*, rooms with shower or sink above the *Bar Danubio* on Plaza de la Fuente (☎974 375 033; ②); and *Lo Foratón* (☎974 375 247; ③–⑤), comprising a somewhat shabby hostal and a slightly better hotel with en-suite rooms, both at the north end of the village on the road to Siresa. There is also a **campsite**, *Valle de Echo* (☎974 375 361; open all year), just south of the village.

By far the most notable **restaurant** in the village is *Restaurante Gaby* (closed part of Sept, reservations mandatory), on the ground floor of *Casa Blasquico*. Owner-chef Gaby Coarasa was among the first stars of Pyrenean nouvelle cuisine, and the walls of the tiny, six-table *comedor* (seatings at 1.30 & 8.30pm) are lined with awards. The *a la carta* menu has ample choice for vegetarians and fish-eaters – the mushroom crêpe is ace – though these tend to be starters. Game, meat or duck main dishes, any specials, or improbable desserts like fig mousse or wild berry sorbets will bump the bill up, with Dénominación d'Origen wine, to well over 5000ptas/€30 per person. If money's tight, ask about their cheaper *menú* and stick to the adequate house wine. If you can't get in, the *Restaurante Serbal* on the east side of the village is nearly as good, while the friendly *Bar Surbordan* next door to *Restaurante Gaby* will fill you up with superb, inexpensive *raciones* of *pimientos de piquillo*, *longaniza* (sausage) and *chipirones*. The other *hostal comedores* are popular enough but offer far from elegant fare.

Best of several **bars** is the nocturnal *Coco's* (no sign), the closest thing to a Madrid-style nightspot, with occasional live music; *Acher*, *Danubio* and *Batimala* are more conventional village hangouts, while local families and visitors alike drink at all hours outside the *Bar Surbordan*.

Echo has three **banks** (one with an ATM), the only petrol station (no unleaded) in these hills, and an **adventure outfitter**: the local Compañia de Guías (☎974 375 387 or 676 850 843), offering canyoning, rock-climbing, kayaking, snowshoeing and cross-country skiing depending on the season. Also worth contacting is Alto Aragón (☎974 371 267), which offers both summertime treks and winter activities with English-speaking guides. Oddly, Echo has no pool; people just swim in a scooped-out area of the river, east of town.

Siresa

Less than 2km north of Echo stands another beautiful little village, **SIRESA**. Keeping watch over the riverside pastures is a remarkable ninth-century church, **San Pedro** (daily 11am–1pm & 5–8pm; 200ptas/€1.20). A massive structure built to a cruciform, single-apse plan, it was once the core of a monastery and is claimed to be the oldest church in Aragón.

There's a single **hotel** in Siresa, the *Castillo d'Acher* (☎974 375 313; ⑤); this also operates an annexe *pensión* (③), above the village bar, and a reasonable restaurant. If you desire more solitude, the *Hotel Usón* (☎ & fax 974 375 358; March 15–Oct 15; ④), 5km north of Siresa, has enthusiastic young management, ecological design and good Basque-style food accompanied by a superb wine cellar. Rooms are tasteful and colourfully done up but often fill with UK-based trekking groups, so reservations are mandatory. Immediately across the valley, 3km up the side road to the *Gabardito* refuge, *Camping Borda Bisáltico* (☎974 375 098; late June to late Sept & Easter) offers clean facilities, including an *albergue* (①) and simple rooms (②), plus another restaurant.

Walks in the Valle de Echo

Above Siresa, the **Valle de Echo** constitutes a tapestry of pasture and beech forest against a backdrop of towering limestone cliffs and summits, harbingers of the karst country at the border. The most popular **day-walks** east of the valley are the ascents of Bisaurín (2669m), Agüerri (2449m) and Castillo de Acher (2390m), of which the finest is the climb up Agüerri, the summit of the huge bluff that forms the easternmost side of the Boca del Infierno gorge, beginning 7km north of Siresa.

The usual starting point is 12km north of Siresa at **Selva de Oza**, where there's just a pleasant rustic bar, but no functioning campsite. For any outing the best **map** is the Editorial Alpina 1:40,000 "Ansó-Echo", applicable also to all walks discussed up to and including "The Valle de Roncal and the Parque Natural Pirenaico" section, p.451. Walking from Echo, you can avoid dreary road-trudging by taking the GR65.3.3, well signposted as the **Via Romana** some 3km north of Siresa. This "Roman road" (actually early Byzantine) threads through the Boca del Infierno gorge, and continues beyond Selva de Oza to the Puerto de Palo/Col de Pau on the frontier.

Bisaurín and the Osia valley

For **Bisaurín**, make an early start along the variant GR11.1 that climbs east on the southern slopes of the Agüerri valley – it leaves the main valley 6km north of Echo, across the Puente de Santa Ana, and shortcuts the twisty, narrow paved road past *Camping Borda Bisáltico* to run high above the Agüerri stream. About an hour from the valley road, you reach the *Refugio de Gabardito*, 8km in by road (50 places; open all year; ①–②), with a range of en-suite rooms, set on a beautiful grassy clearing near tree-line (1400m). It's managed by Echo's Compañia de Guías (see opposite), who run the popular cross-country skiing centre at the doorstep here, and who are the contacts for reservations year-round. From here the path climbs east to the **Collado del Foratón** (2032m), 2hr 30min from the refuge; then it's a stiff two-hour climb further to the summit, rising steeply to the northeast.

You can also use the approach via the Collado del Foratón as a full-pack traverse, finishing 45 minutes southeast of the pass at the *Refugio Lizara* (1540m), at the top of the **valley of the Río Osia**. This sits in the middle of another major cross-country ski area; in summer you can trek northeast via the Valle de los Sarrios and over **Los Puertos** pass to link up with the main GR11 route at Ibón de Estanes. The GR11.1 continues east from the *Lizara* in under a day to Canfranc.

The Lizara refuge burnt down in 1999, and reconstruction is not scheduled to finish until 2002. For the time being the closest indoor facility lies 12km down-valley in the attractively sleepy village of **ARAGÜÉS DEL PUERTO**, where the *Albergue Lizara* occupies a 1970s built ex-*hostal* (☎974 371 519, *alberguelizara@teleline.es*; dorm ①, rooms ③). You've a choice between en-suite doubles or a place in a nine-bunk dorm; half-board is encouraged, supping at the giant basement *comedor*.

Castillo de Acher and Agüerri

Castillo de Acher and Agüerri can be tackled singly or together in one gruelling day; take plenty of water. Begin along the track that climbs east-southeast from close to the ex-campsite at Selva de Oza; this curves back southwest after crossing the Espata stream and climbs steeply to a simple forest hut (1740m; 2hr), just beyond which the ways divide. The summit of **Castillo de Acher** – from a distance looking exactly like a castle – now lies a little north of east, along a fairly easy path (4–5hr from Selva de Oza).

For **Agüerri**, take the right-hand path just beyond the refuge, climbing east along the **Borreguil de Achert** stream and crossing after about half an hour onto a new path that doubles back on the other side, rising west to a small saddle. Beyond this, the path swings east again, along the **Jardín** stream; at the head of the valley defined by the Collado de Costatiza, climb south for the summit (5hr 30min from Selva de Oza).

Frontier peaks and Ibón de Acherito

North of Selva de Oza, the frontier peaks of **Punta Cristian/Pic Lariste** (2168m) and **Arraya de las Foyas/Laraille** (2147m) make classic targets, with near-identical approaches. Continue on the asphalt road north of the closed campsite, through dense forest, with the Río Aragón Subordan to the left; some 2km above Selva de Oza, before the end of the pavement, you veer left to cross a bridge onto a side track, beyond which the main track follows the eastward curve of the valley. Once over the Barranco Acherito side-stream via another bridge, the track ends at the locale known as **La Mina** (1230m). Here there's just a large signboard-map beside a small car park; cows graze all around, with scattered buildings for the use of the herders, plus a derelict refuge. This is the junction with the GR11, descending from the west and continuing up the main valley; it's also the trailhead for the popular day-outing to both the peaks and the **Ibón de Acherito**, second westernmost lake in the Spanish Pyrenees.

Take the path north along the left (east) bank of the Barranco Las Foyas, switching over to the right bank sooner than indicated on the Editorial Alpina map. In July there are wild irises everywhere, and the occasional Egyptian vulture overhead. After 45 minutes' climbing, guided by red-and-white or single-yellow waymarks, you reach the T-junction with the HRP variant.

Bear right on this, and leave it soon after to head north into the cirque (ca. 1800m; 1hr 30min) under the frontier summits. The routes divide here: Punta Cristian is the summit immediately north, climbed directly in another hour; Arraya looms to the west, reached by a route of similar duration curving to a point just southeast of the summit, then swinging back for the top. From both summits you look down across the idyllic pine forests and fields of the Lescun valley (see p.392) and westwards over the barren karst – an arresting contrast.

To visit **the lake**, bear left along the well-trodden HRP; some ninety minutes out of La Mina, the path grade slackens on a grassy hillside at the base of Arraya, and you get your first eyeful of the limestone cirque to the west. Fifteen minutes further, you round a corner in the landscape and suddenly the Ibón de Acherito is there: one of the most striking in Aragón, with the crests of the frontier peaks as a backdrop and tadpoles in its shallows. Arraya can be climbed equally easy from the lakeshore; allow 45 minutes each way. Camping, while tempting, is more difficult – there's a flat meadow, with a spring, just ten minutes east along the HRP.

To vary the return to La Mina, and include some ridge-walking with views into France, follow the HRP west from the lake along a hogback to a grassy point on the frontier crest at just over 2000m. From here you can glimpse the stagnant pond of **Ibón de Ansabère** at your feet, or gaze over the **Cirque de Lescun**, and to the shattered peaks closing it off on the west. Now descend gently for twenty minutes or so to a rectangular shepherd's shelter, used more from the French side. The obvious continuation along the border ridge would be to the strategic Puerto de Acherito at the top of the cirque, but there is no non-technical way around or over Pic d'Chourique (2084m), which blocks progress. So you must descend, more or less as traced on the Alpina map, steeply cross-country for twenty minutes to the proper trail in the valley bottom, called the **Barranco de Ferrerias**. From the vicinity of an unstaffed, stone-built shelter here, it's about 1hr 20min down to La Mina; the path is unmarked but obvious and gradual.

East or west: the GR11

The GR11 arrives at La Mina from Candanchú to the **east** in a full day's trek along the headwaters of the Río Aragón Subordan, a route enlivened by the large Ibón de Estanes (2hr out), and the squelchy water-meadow of Aguas Tuertas (4hr from Candanchú). Camping is allowed at La Mina – plans to restore and staff the refuge here have never passed the talk stage – and you can have a pleasant river bathe just downstream by the end of the asphalt. But as there are no reliable facilities at Selva de Oza, civilization and its comforts are far away, and you must provision accordingly.

A much easier traverse continues **west** along the same path to Zuriza in the Valle de Ansó (see overleaf). From the upper bridge over the Acherito described above, the GR11 climbs steeply west into the Collado de Petraficha (1958m; 2hr uphill from Selva de Oza), from where it's all downhill along the Petraficha stream, the last forty minutes of the four-hour hiking day on track.

On to Ansó by road or trail

The daily evening bus from Jaca to Echo continues west to Ansó along 12km of narrow, twisting road, climbing over the Sierra de Vedao before dropping into the Valle de Ansó. Final approaches to the valley from the east are guarded by two strangely shaped rocks known locally as "the Monk and the Nun", just above a tunnel.

If you wish to walk there, shun the dangerous road in favour of the very enjoyable **PR18 trail from Siresa to Ansó**, indicated by a sign reading "Fuen d'a Cruz" by the stream below Siresa. This is probably the most useful of the ten or so marked PR trails; a descriptive booklet, published by Prames Ediciones, is now on sale locally.

Starting on the south side of the bridge, the path is initially waymarked by red arrows and purple paint splodges as well as newer PR blazes. Gaining height quickly, you collide with an unmaintained track at a saddle about 45 minutes along; turning onto this, fifteen minutes later you top out at a T-junction in the track system (1180m), where you bear right (north). After another half-hour along the serpentine track, you'll emerge at a pass affording a first view of Ansó village; the track continues north, but you should plunge down left (southwest) on the resurgence of the old *camino*. Passing a ruined farm, continue dropping steeply into the valley running west to the village, zigzagging to meet the stream bed, on whose right bank you should arrive some two hours out of Siresa. Nothing substantial should prevent you from reaching the fountain at the eastern outskirts of Ansó about two and a half hours out of Siresa. With the exception of the initial climb from Siresa, the route is shown more or less correctly on the Editorial Alpina map.

Ansó

Once a more prosperous village than Echo, **ANSÓ** fell upon hard times during the 1950s and 1960s depopulation of rural Aragón. Today, however, there are signs of a small but definite revival, with Jacan or Pamplonan professionals keeping second homes here, plus a growing stream of tourists sampling the village's attractions. It's certainly a congenial weekend base, with a little river beach below for splashing around in the Río Veral. Without having many specific landmarks, the village outshines its setting, whose scrubby pine cover gives no hint of the splendours waiting up-valley. The ancient church is extraordinarily rich inside and houses an interesting ecclesiastical, craft and ethnological **museum** (daily 10.30am–1.30pm & 3.30–8pm; 200ptas/€1.20). In lieu of labelling you're given a plastic-laminated sheet to guide you around the exhibits, which include a video and photographic exhibition of Pyrenean wildlife and rural trades.

Practicalities

Ansó's growing popularity is reflected in several places to stay, somewhat less expensive than in Echo but filling equally quickly in summer. Best is the *Posada Magoria* (☎974 370 049; ④), installed in a 1920s mansion by the church at c/Milagros, with en-suite rooms, views and a garden. The four dormer rooms have double beds, and they serve excellent communal vegetarian meals (preference given to guests). Alternatively, the Peruvian-run *La Posada Veral* at c/Cocorro 6 (☎974 370 119; ③) – inevitably more institutional since it's housed in the former old people's home – has a fairly pricey restaurant. At the north end of town on the bypass road, the modern but cheerful *Hostal Kimboa* (☎974 370 184; ④ B&B), 200m towards Zuriza, is excellent value. Less likely options include the *Hostal Estanes* (☎974 370 146), which was up for sale in 2000, or the eccentrically managed *Hostal Aisa*, on central Plaza Domingo Miral 2 (☎974 370 009; ②), essentially an Aragonese Fawlty Towers crossed with a Victorian orphanage, its clientele and decor unchanged for decades. There's no campsite but tents are tolerated on the grass down by the riverside municipal swimming pool, at the south end of the village.

Besides **restaurants** affiliated with the *hostales* – among which *Kimboa* gets good marks from carnivores – there's only the *Menhir* at the swimming pool. Of the many **bars**, liveliest and friendliest is the spit-and-sawdust *Zuriza* on the main street; the one in the *Posada Veral* occasionally has live gigs. Ansó's two **banks** (one with ATM) complete the list of amenities.

To **leave Ansó** by public transport you catch the 6am bus back through Echo towards Jaca. Going west from Ansó, an eighteen-kilometre minor road past the village of Garde eventually joins the C137, which threads through the Valle de Roncal, in Navarra. There's no bus service in this direction, and it's 21km in total to Roncal village.

Walking in the Valle de Ansó

Other than the path in from Siresa, the lower Ansó valley has little serious trekking potential; to start walking you really must go to Zuriza, 14km north. There's no bus service, and the paved road up-valley makes for tedious trudging, so try to arrange a lift if you don't have transport. The scenery improves as you head upstream, with the Río Veral beside the road, and the steep valley sides covered with pine, later giving way to beech. Dotted around are small stone-built farmhouses, their owners sometimes wearing cloaks of cured but otherwise untreated animal skins. One of these huts has become the *Restaurante Borda Chiquín*, locally popular and the only amenity en route. The mass of **Peña Ezkaurre** (2049m) rises in front, and after 9km you enter the narrow gorge between it and **Espelunga**; there's a chance of seeing rare black vultures here, a species resembling the griffon vulture in outline, but far darker and more solitary.

Eventually the gorge widens onto the luxuriantly green basin of **Zuriza** (1227m), less forested than the Selva de Oza area in Echo. Most obvious amenity is an enormous, somewhat regimented campsite, *Camping Zuriza* (mid-June to early Sept) with an attached *albergue* (☎974 370 196; open all year; dorm ①, rooms ③–④), a general store and a decent restaurant. If these are full – a distinct possibility in summer or winter peak season – you'll find another staffed refuge at **Linza** (Plano de la Casa on many maps), 5km north along the track parallel to the Petrechema stream. Here the friendly, well-run *Refugio de Linza* (☎ & fax 974 370 112; 1320m; 100 places; open all year; ①) rents out cross-country skis to those wishing to follow nearby prepared trails.

Tres Reyes ascent

From Plano de la Casa you can make a day-walk to **Mesa de los Tres Reyes** (*Hiru Erregeen Mahaia* in Euskera), the karst plateau astride the border with France; carry plenty of water, as there's none above the 1900-metre contour. Start by heading a little north of east along the path to the **Collado de Linza** (1906m; 2hr); from this pass the path heads north a short way then resumes its former trajectory, dropping into the shallow Hoya la Solana and then climbing out to the **Collado de Esqueste/Col d'Escoueste** (2114m; 3hr). You're now on the frontier – dramatically delineated by the sharp drop to the French side – amidst unbelievably barren terrain.

Follow the top of the cliffs north, at a suitably respectful distance, into a small *col* that leads to **Tres Reyes summit** (2444m; 4hr); this meeting point of France, Navarra and Aragón is adorned with a bronze statue of St Francis Xavier, the Jesuit evangelist of the Indies. Again there's an amazing contrast between the lush Lescun valley beyond the tarn of Lhurs to the east, and the lunar rock and summits to the north and west, notably the pyramid of Pic d'Anie.

West to Isaba on the GR11

Zuriza straddles the **GR11**, with Selva de Oza an easy day away to the east (see p.447); heading west towards Izaba in the Roncal valley (14km by narrow, paved road), the GR11 was rerouted in the early 1990s. Both new and old westbound itineraries start from the Puerto Navarra, 700m west of Zuriza, at the border between Aragón and Navarra – where the difference in public-works funding between the two autonomous regions is made graphically apparent by the respective states of the asphalt.

The **new path** heads spectacularly, if strenuously, southwest up the flanks of **Peña Ezkaurre/Ezcaurri** (2049m; 2hr 30min), which though not especially high impresses with its profile. Just the other side lies its namesake *ibón*, the westernmost natural tarn in the Spanish Pyrenees. Thereafter, the GR11, now in Navarra, descends west into the **Berroeta valley**, soon becoming a track along the right bank leading to the confluence of the Berroeta and Belabarze streams. From here another track leads west to Izaba, for a six-and-a-half-hour walking day.

The **old itinerary** due west from Puerto Navarra is shadier and more gently graded, but difficult to find owing to inaccuracies in Spanish maps and the complete deterioration of the old waymarking. In theory it traces the length of the pastoral **Valle de Belabarze**, high up on the beech-swathed southern slopes, descending to the valley floor near the point where the namesake stream forsakes the road to flow directly towards Isaba. From Zuriza you'll need four hours to get there by this route, assuming you don't get lost, but if you are hauling a heavy load in the heat, this is preferable to the trans-Eskaurre route.

The Valle de Roncal and the Parque Natural Pirenaico Larra-Belagoa

The **Parque Natural Pirenaico Larra-Belagoa**, which straddles the road connecting Roncal and Arette-la-Pierre-Saint-Martin in France, occupies the head of the **Valle de Belagoa** and harbours landscapes ranging from karst desert to dense forest, by way of lush pastures. Further downstream, the **Valle de Roncal** – next valley west of Ansó – is famous for the delicious, hard, cylindrical *roncalés* cheese, made from sheep's milk and widely available in the two main valley villages of **Erronkari** and **Izaba**.

If you're coming by public transport from the Ansó valley, the easiest way into the area is the daily **bus**, run by La Tafallesa, which originates at 5pm in Pamplona via the Foz de Irbaiun and Burg and follows the course of the Río Esca up the Valle de Roncal. Foresters used to float logs down the Esca by lacing them together into a raft, with three or four such rafts linked and controlled by a pair of huge oars; nowadays the rafts are constructed only for fun.

Erronkari and Izaba

Once beyond the lowland villages of Lumbier and Burgui, the bus climbs slowly to **ERRONKARI** (Roncal), capital of the valley. Here the road crosses to the west bank of the river, where the old quarter (including the arcaded town hall) sits, though much of the east bank is spoilt by blocks of modern flats. The churchyard is worth visiting for the flamboyant mausoleum of the great opera tenor **Julián Gayarre** (1844–90), whose sarcophagus is borne heavenwards by a flight of bronze-sculpted angels. Born into a Roncal shepherd family, Gayarre was regarded by international audiences as the equal of the later Caruso; he died – eerily, from cancer of the vocal cords – just a bit too soon to be captured by the new technology of the grammophone.

Erronkari supports the regional, helpful **Turismo** (summer Mon–Sat 10am–2pm & 4.30–7.30pm, Sun 10am–2pm; ☎948 475 136). **Accommodation** consists of the *Hostal Zaltua* on the through road (☎948 475 008; ②), as well as several *casas rurales*, best of which is *Casa Villa Pepita* (☎948 475 133; ②), which also provides *table d'hôte* meals at very reasonable cost (and pricier en-suite rooms), but you'll have more choice in Izaba.

Izaba

IZABA (Isaba), 7km north of Roncal, is larger and busier; a small, modern district at the south end of the village (with a small **Turismo**, and **bank** with ATM) is easily ignored in favour of its old quarter. This sprawls appealingly around a fortified hilltop church, a massive structure with a rib-vaulted nave and ornate *retablo* and organ inside. Unlike Roncal it's a major year-round touring centre for the Western Pyrenees, regularly descended upon by weekend trippers from nearby cities. Accordingly there's a fair amount of conventional **accommodation**; pick of this, east of the busy through road on narrow c/Mendigatxa, is the sleek and clean *Hostal Lola* (☎ & fax 948 893 012, *hostallola@jet.es*; ⑤), with limited parking (hopeless elsewhere in Izaba) and the best restaurant in town (allow 3500–4000ptas/€21–24 *a la carta*). At the junction of c/Mendigatxa and the high street, the en-suite *Pensión Txiki* (☎948 893 118; ④) perches above the simple, namesake *bar-restaurante* (*menú* at 1500ptas/€9). *Pensión Txabalkua*, west of the through road at c/Izarjentea 16 (☎948 893 083; ③), is probably the quietest option. Izaba has eight *casas rurales* (all ②), though expect to try several places at busy times. Still further down the scale, the *Albergue Oxanea* (☎948 893 153; ①) on c/Bormapéa west of the main street is an unusually salubrious private **youth hostel** which also offers meals. The **campsite**, *Asolaze* (☎948 893 034; open all year), also with bungalows to rent, lies 6km upstream towards the border, at the edge of the *parque natural*.

The Valle de Belagoa

In summer, the evening bus from Pamplona (or an 8am service from Isaba) continues up the valley into the **Parque Natural Pirenaico Larra-Belagoa**. The road enters the park along the Río Belagoa, flanked by forests of beech and silver fir, until the terrain opens out into flat fields and you begin to climb in tight hairpins to the comfortable **Refugio Ángel Olorón de Belagoa** (☎ & fax 948 394 002; 1460m; 140 places; ①), almost at the border but just inside the park. It stands in grand isolation 18km from Izaba, overlooking pastures and the high limestone peaks to the east, with the river gleaming between forested slopes below to the south. The refuge, run by the Club Deportivo Navarra, offers a complete programme of summer and winter sports, so you might make this, rather than Izaba, your base to explore the mountains. The Belagoa hut serves as a staging point on both the GR12 – *El Sendero de Euskal Herria*, which traces the Cantabrian/Mediterranean watershed throughout the Spanish Basque country – and the HRP, while the cross-country skiing pistes of Eskil Zarra literally begin at the door, with links to two other areas up-valley.

Economical **meals** (1500ptas/€9) are provided at the refuge's bar-restaurant, but there's also a self-catering kitchen if you intend to stay several days. Otherwise, at the base of the switchbacks leading up to the refuge, a **traditional inn**, the *Venta de Juan Pito* (May–Oct daily; 1–2pm & 7–8pm outside July & Aug) ranks as one of the most

THE TRIBUTO DE LAS TRES VACAS

Beyond Belagoa the road climbs to the border, crossing close to the frontier cairn which has replaced the original marker of La Pedra de San Martin/Pierre-Saint-Martin. Here, every July 13, the people of the Spanish Valle de Roncal and the French Vallée de Barétous gather to enact the **Tributo de las Tres Vacas**, a ceremony stemming from a 1326 treaty on grazing rights, the oldest of several such agreements or *faceries* still extant. Four representatives of Roncal, dressed in white shirts, black capes and black hats, join hands with four representatives of Barétous *commune*, whose only concession to folklore is sashes in the French national colours. With their hands linked on modern frontier cairn number 262, they chant "Pas aban, pas aban, pas aban" ("Peace above all" in local dialect) while three identical blonde heifers (*las tres vacas*) are handed over to the Roncalese as tribute, securing the right of the French herdsmen to graze cattle in the Spanish valley for another year. Originally such *faceries* and tributes served to prevent violent altercations occasionally provoked by illegal bovine immigrants; these days, though, the cows are discreetly returned to the French afterwards. A huge and disparate crowd (up to 3000) of itinerant food-and-drink vendors, French gendarmes, Spanish forestry wardens, journalists, tourists and locals always turn up, even if it's raining, mainly to take part in the *fiesta* afterwards. If you want to coincide with the ceremony, be sure to arrive by 11am; shortly after noon it's all over, save for the feasting.

pleasant surprises in the Valle de Belagoa, serving hearty meals – including locally concocted milk-based desserts – for under 3000ptas/€18.

Walking in the Parque Natural

The best way of seeing the eastern side of the park – where all the karst formations are – involves taking the **HRP variant** which links the Belagoa refuge with Lescun in France via the Collado de Insolo, also known as the Portillo de Lescun or Col d'Anaye. Don't confuse this pass with the Col des Anies, which is on the north side of Pic d'Anie, well inside French territory (Insolo/d'Anaye is on the frontier, to the south), but you can return via the Col des Anies to make a **circuit**. Take ample water with you, and in deteriorating weather, turn back. Navigating through karst badlands, which form natural mazes, is hopeless when visibility is bad – not to mention the possibility of disappearing down one of the dozens of caves and extremely deep sinkholes which pepper the terrain. Even in the finest weather you should have a compass, the recommended Editorial Alpina map and an update on conditions from the Belagoa refuge wardens.

From the refuge, the path tends slightly south-of-east, first across pasture and then through beech forest, before arriving in the eerily beautiful Larra region, distinguished by bone-white rock and trees stunted by altitude and lack of soil. Yellow paint splodges then guide you through the boulders, until the **Collado de Insolo** (2052m) is reached in about another two and a half hours.

An ascent of Tres Reyes fills another memorable day out from the refuge. The route lies a little south of the HRP, initially close to the cliff-edge of the shelf on which the refuge stands. After climbing over **Lapazarra** (1777m; 1hr 20min), the path heads east through the Collado Larrería. This is again typical Larra scenery, littered with boulders and dotted with bonsai-sized trees in patterns so repetitious that it's easy to get lost. In autumn the landscape is brightened somewhat by the turning foliage of scattered deciduous specimens.

From Larra you continue up to the frontier ridge at the Col d'Ourtets (2182m), next turning south-southeast along it for the **Tres Reyes summit** (3hr 20min). At this altitude the karst seems more like the landscape of Sinai than the Pyrenees, but the views from the top emphasize the paradoxes of the area, where high-mountain desert is fringed by lower pasture and forest – so lush precisely because all the available water percolates down through fissures in the karst, emerging in quantity below the 1500-metre contour.

Pierre-Saint-Martin

Just on the Spanish side of the frontier despite the French name, close to the C137 road, yawns the entrance – now grilled over – of the **Gouffre de la Pierre-Saint-Martin**, among the largest underground caverns in the world. It was discovered by chance in 1950, when, on the last, disconsolate night of an apparently unsuccessful expedition, a stone was thrown into an opening and clattered audibly down into an abyss. In 1953, the year that Everest was conquered, speleologists reached the bottom of this cavern, at 734m the deepest anyone had ever been in a cave system. Norbert Casteret described the pioneering descent:

I came face to face with an atmospheric phenomenon which had often been observed from below during the last few days, and into which I now vanished. It was a patch of fog, a subterranean cloud, which appears at certain hours, on certain days, as a result of peculiar meteorological disturbances. The pothole consists of an immense vertical shaft, followed by a series of colossal chambers through which flows an icy torrent. Naturally, therefore, it possesses its own special climate, with regular changes of temperature, air currents and condensation which sometimes falls as rain or, as today, is suspended in the form of clouds. The narrow opening on the surface alternately sucks in and expels a powerful draught which causes a dull moaning sound, as it were of some great organ.

The vertical entrance shaft of 346m remains the longest known, and its largest chamber, the Sala de la Verna (now desecrated by an EDF tunnel), is an incredible 270m by 230m by 180m. Using higher entrances, subsequent expeditions during 1982 measured a total depth of 1342m and explored an overall length of interconnecting passages exceeding 50km – the second largest cave system in the world after the Jean Bernad cavern of the French Alps.

Arette-la-Pierre-Saint-Martin

Some 10km beyond the *Refugio de Belagoa* and 3km into French territory from the border by road, **ARETTE-LA-PIERRE-SAINT-MARTIN** is a modern **downhill-ski resort**, the westernmost in the entire Pyrenees. Atlantic weather influences generally mean good snow despite a modest top point of only 2153m (descending to 1527m or 1650m). Of the 18 pistes, two-thirds are green- or blue-rated, so Arette-la-Pierre is essentially a beginner-to-intermediate resort. That said, the runs are reasonably long – two of the blue pistes are over 3km – and others were extended in 2000. **Cross-country skiing** is offered in token fashion at **Boucle de Braca**, 1km northeast, and much more substantially at **Issarbe**, 5km northwest. The bleak development consists of a vast number of brutalist-style chalets and flats at Point 1650m.

In **summer** the main thing that counts in Arette-la-Pierre's favour for anyone following the **GR10** between Lescun and Sainte Grazi is the *Refuge Gîte d'Étape Jeandel* (☎ & fax 05.59.66.14.46; 25 places; open all year by arrangement; ①), on a rise at the west edge of the ski pistes. It's a high-quality outfit with one dorm, three- or four-bed rooms mostly pitched at families, hot showers, a fireplace and meal service (May 1–Oct 15) provided by jolly proprietor Jean Hourticq. There's also a self-catering kitchen, and a small stock of trekking groceries for sale, as the *épicerie* in the ski "village" is unreliable – though a single restaurant operates fitfully there in summer. You might schedule an extra night here and use the intervening day to bag Pic d'Anie (*Auñamendi* in Euskera) – a six-hour round trip on sections of the HRP and GR10, making this the easiest French "base camp" for the 2504-metre summit. You're just inside Béarn at Arette-la-Pierre, on the border with the county of Soule.

Gorges of the Haute-Soule

Four gorges, south of the D113/D26 route linking Arette-la-Pierre-Saint-Martin in the east and Larrau in the west, are the principal reason outsiders visit the district of **Haute-Soule** (Zuberoa), easternmost and remotest corner of the French Pays Basque. Here, endless green pastures and beech groves stretch under an open, vulture-haunted sky; there are far more sheep than people, few tourist facilities and no villages to speak of except Larrañe, Ligi-Atherei and (stretching the definition) Santa Grazi.

The superlative-laden **Gorges de Kakouetta** are the best of the managed gorges in the Pyrenees, but if you prefer a completely uncommercialized chasm, the adjacent **Gorges d'Ehujarré** constitute a milder alternative. However, both are somewhat difficult to reach without your own vehicle, as there's no public transport on the French side, and the scattered village of Santa Grazi – at the mouth of Ehujarré – lies four hours' walk northwest of Arette-la-Pierre-Saint-Martin, along the GR10 or its variants. The best way of visiting both on foot is from Belagoa, trekking down the Ehujarré to Santa Grazi and then up alongside the Kakouetta.

The other pair of great gorges, 18km west of Kakouetta by road, are the interconnecting **Holzarté** and **Olhadybia** (Olhadubi), crossed at their junction by a long, terrifying and absolutely unmissable – though very touristed – suspension footbridge. By the serpentining GR10, these lie seven hours west of Santa Grazi, with Larrañe another half hour or so beyond.

A walking tour of the gorges

Head up the C137 road from the refuge at Belagoa for a couple of kilometres until the ridge from the summit of Lakhoura – the 1877-metre peak immediately north of the refuge – subsides at the **Collado de Eraiz**. An HRP variant goes north through this pass onto the Errayzé-Sentolha plateau above the end of the **Gorges d'Ehujarré**, where you quit the HRP and drop into the canyon on another path (see below). Palisades rise as high as 400m above you, but it's not a difficult walk, and this route has been used for decades for the movement of sheep from the Sainte-Engrâce valley onto the pastures around Pic Lakhoura.

Three to four hours from the refuge you emerge at the hamlet of Senta, one of three comprising the *commune* of **SANTA GRAZI** (Sainte-Engrâce, Urdaite). Until 1987 this

---

TRANSHUMANT SHEPHERDS

Like other shepherds in south European or Mediterranean climes, the Basques have always been obliged to take their flocks to the high **mountain pastures** in summer in search of better grazing. They live out on the bare slopes in stone-hut sheepfolds called *cayolars*, with a couple of dogs, milking the ewes twice a day and making cheese, the *fromage de brebis*, whose soft and hard versions are a speciality throughout the pastoral Pyrenees. Trekkers are usually welcome to buy small quantities when passing by such huts. Most of the pastures today are accessible by car, at least at the gentler Basque end of the Pyrenees, so the shepherd's life is not as harsh and isolated as it used to be – though there are still areas in the higher mountains accessible only by mule or *pottok* pony. A measure of the pre-eminence of sheep in the Basque economy is the Basque word for "rich", *aberats* – whose literal meaning is "he who owns large flocks".

was locally characterized as *le bout du monde*, "the end of the world", approachable by road only from the west and arguably the most remote spot in the French Basque country. The extension of the D113 east to Arette-la-Pierre-Saint-Martin was supposed to change that, but despite increasing traffic the Santa Grazi valley has managed to retain its rural somnolence, still surrounded by hay meadows and losing its young to the big cities.

The Santa Grazi hamlets and Ligi-Atherei

SENTA has a combination **inn/gîte d'étape**, the *Auberge Elichalt* (☎05.59.28.61.63; dorm ①, rooms ④), which serves light meals, and has space for a few tents on the rear lawn. It overlooks the church, a strikingly original example of eleventh-century Romanesque architecture, virtually the logo of the Western Pyrenees. It's an engagingly asymmetrical structure, with a sloping-roofed belfry, a lean-to style nave and a graveyard containing some typically Basque disc-crowned headstones, much in evidence as you move further west. The interior offers graphically carved column capitals near the altar, some gaudily painted in the 1880s; look carefully and you'll find the *Adoration of the Magi*, lions devouring Christians, plus Solomon and the Queen of Sheba apparently copulating. Below this stands a rather Hindu-looking statuette of St Catherine, while grimacing owls peer from the base of some columns. Beside the church, a map placard outlines a loop hike – up the east bank of the Ehujarré gorge, then down its bed – for the benefit of day-trippers based here; full details below.

The middle hamlet of **Calla** (alias 'Bourg') lies about 1500m downstream from Senta, but has little to offer passers-by since the *Hôtel Relais de la Pierre-Saint-Martin* shut down and was put up for sale. The northwesternmost settlement is **CASERNES**, 4km beyond Calla, where there's a friendly, well-placed **campsite**, *Camping Ibarra* (☎05.59.28.73.59; Easter–Oct) on the riverbank and the only **food shop** in the valley, opposite the *mairie*. For the time being the closest proper **hotel** is at **LIGI-ATHEREI** (Licq-Athéry), 4km north on the D26, where *Chez Bouchet* (☎05.59.28.61.01; fax 05.59.28.63.85; closed Dec–Jan; ④) also has a decent restaurant, a swimming pool and tenting space on the lawn.

Gorges de Ehujarré loop

This suggested itinerary is indicated schematically on a **map** placard by the church in Senta, with an estimated time-course of six hours, but is also traced with reasonable accuracy on the Carte de Randonées no. 2, "Pays Basque Est". It's suggested you do the loop clockwise, with the climb tackled when fresh, getting you safely down into the gorge by afternoon, when mists tend to obscure the heights. If you have a car, save yourself another half-hour by parking down at the end of the pavement, in the stream valley by the bridge.

The path begins here, marked with green-and-white paint splodges. The initial grade is sharp, and you tangle repeatedly with 4WD tracks, but you've dense shade (and some deerflies) in the **Bois d'Utzia** beech-forest, and trail shortcuts are effective. Some 1hr 45min along, the worst climbing is over as you emerge from the forest at the single, tin-roofed hut of **Cayolars d'Utzipia** (1450m). The waymarked route continues up and right (southwest), curling over the brow of the ridge for great views of the Sainte-Engrâce valley, and allowing a glimpse of the Pic d'Anie hovering above the trees to the southeast. The elevation high point of the day (1600m) is reached about 2hr 45min out, as you cross high moorland with heather and sheep; the frontier appears ahead, while the gorge yawns down on the right.

Some 3hr along, you arrive at the **Cayolars d'Utzigagna**, at the edge of the beech/fir woods; there's no reliable water here, despite what the IGN map says. When you meet a dirt track serving an isolated sheep-farm to the left, turn right (west-south-west); some fifteen minutes later, use a ravine-path shortcut to descend right to the

pastures of Errayze, where herds of *pottok* or Basque ponies often graze. Another quarter hour across the turf should see you to the **Fontaine d'Errayze**, a strong spring at the very top of the gorge – and the only drinkable water en route. A distinct trail appears, initially on the left bank, the torrent disappears into the ravine bed, and beech woods resume. About an hour downhill from the spring, the path crosses to the right bank, where it stays for most of the final hour down to the higher of two tin-roofed barns where you rejoin your uphill route, a few minutes above the end of the asphalt. In many ways this is the most low-key of the four gorges – the dense tree cover and sloping scree means you rarely get an eyeful of the canyon walls – but even in summer you won't pass more than half a dozen people all day.

The Gorges de Kakouetta

The entrance to the **Gorges de Kakouetta** (daily March 15–Nov 15 9am–dusk; 25F/€3.80) yawns between Calla and Casernes. Though Kakouetta lies squarely on the tourist trail, don't be put off – the gorge is genuinely dramatic and, outside high summer, not at all crowded. Its interior is essentially temperate rainforest, the air heavy with mist produced by dozens of seeps and tiny waterfalls, pampering tenacious ferns, moss and other greenery, all of which festoons vertical walls rising up to 300m high and seldom split more than 5m apart. For an organized attraction the going is often hard – sometimes along a boardwalk with a safety cable, sometimes on a narrow, slippery path right in the gorge bottom, with the stream almost lapping over your feet; so come with good boots. The graded path ends about an hour along at a picnic area and cave, next to which pours a twenty-metre waterfall, the accumulated percolation of a winter's precipitation through the karst strata overhead. Unfortunately it is not possible to continue up the gorge and make a circuit back to Belagoa – you'll have to retrace your steps and hike up along its edge on the easterly GR10 sector, making for a very long nine-to-ten-hour day.

Gorges d'Olhadybia, Holzarté and Larrañe

From the entrance of the Kakouetta to the entrance of the Holzarté is about four hours' walk using the newer GR10, traced when the Pont d'Olhadybia (see below) was temporarily washed out. But if possible it's preferable to make a full day of it along the original **GR10**, now rated a *variante*, which leaves the D113 just west of the Kakouetta entrance. From there it climbs gradually southwest into the **Col d'Anhaou** (3hr), and shortly after begins to curve north, almost level, towards the **Gorges d'Olhadybia** (Olhadubi).

Owing to the steepness of the terrain, the GR handles the final approach in a giant S-bend which drops to the head of the gorge at the **Pont d'Olhadybia** (5hr). It then continues above the west bank for another hour to the intimidating Himalayan-style suspension bridge **Passerelle d'Olhadybia**, which crosses the mouth of the Olhadybia to meet the **Gorges d'Holzarté**, swinging over a drop of 180m. Rebuilt in 1920, the bridge was originally constructed before World War I by an Italian miner to facilitate getting out of the woods for lunch hour at Logibarrea. Penetrating the Holzarté is for experts only – it was first achieved in 1933 and has only been done about twenty times since.

Once over the bridge, continue north on the corniche path along the cliff forming the east bank of the joint gorges; it's very sharply graded towards the end, with a safety cable, but within an hour you'll reach the gorge car park at **LOGIBARREA** (Logibar), where there's a good *gîte d'étape* (☎ & fax 05.59.28.61.14; closed Dec–Feb; dorm ①, rooms ②) with reasonable meal service.

If there's no room here, leave the GR and follow the D26 west for 2.5km to the village of **LARRAÑE** (Larrau, Larraine) where the stucco walls and steeply pitched grey-slate roofs of the houses contrast with the green shoulder of land on which they stand, which is slashed by little rivulets and nestled in gardens. The church is nearly as impressive as Santa Grazi's, and despite the modest altitude (630m) there's heavy winter snow here – thus the steep roofs.

Though Larrañe is quiet, almost dead out of season, its two friendly though simple **hotels** are usually busy, for good reason. The rambling, old-fashioned *Hôtel Despouey* (☎05.59.28.60.82; closed Nov 15–Feb 15; ③), the embodiment of *la vielle douze France*, has rooms with shower, the local **shop** on the ground floor, and a bar/breakfast salon but no restaurant. For superb meals, head across "town" to the slightly fancier *Hôtel Restaurant Etchémaïté* (☎05.59.28.61.45, fax 05.59.28.72.71; ④; closed late Jan), whose unusually polished restaurant (closed Sun pm & Mon low season) purveys treats such as guinea-fowl roulade with braised bacon and cabbage, or artichokes stuffed with lamb sausage. Given quality and price (menus 95F/€14.50 and 140F/€21.40), and diners coming up specially from the coast, reservations are usually required. There's also a small **campsite**, *Ixtila* (☎05.59.28.63.09; April to mid-Nov), at the lower, east end of town, and a good bakery.

South of Larrañe, the D26 climbs to the frontier at the **Port/Puerto de Larrau** (1573m), just under **Orhy/Orhi**, the first peak above 2000m as you head east from the Atlantic; on the other side the Spanish C127 drops down to Otsagabia, 33km away (see p.460).

THE IRATI FOREST AND THE VALLE DE SALAZAR

Straddling the frontier between the Port de Larrau on the east and the Puero de Ibañeta on the west, the **Forêt d'Iraty/Selva de Irati** (Iratiko Oihana) is claimed by some to be the largest broadleaf forest on the continent – even if they're mistaken, it's certainly the most extensive in the Pyrenees. The legions of trees, principally beech but interspersed with oak, fir and ancient yew, have long been exploited in boatyards on the nearby Atlantic, as beech especially makes excellent oars. Overcutting was a concern as long as three centuries ago, but only recently has systematic reforestation and controlled logging been implemented – thus much of what you see is actually second-growth forest, if none the less attractive for that. Amazingly, this region does not yet benefit from any official protection.

Beginning from the north, a one-to-two-day traverse samples the best parts of the forest en route to attractive **Otsagabia** village at the head of the **Valle de Salazar** in Spain. From there it's easily followed down towards Pamplona, perhaps pausing en route – easiest with your own transport – to sample the **Foz de Arbaiun** natural reserve and the imposing **Monasterio de San Salvador de Leyre**.

Access to Iraty: The Col de Organbidexka

From the north, the Forêt d'Iraty can be reached conveniently from the **Col d'Organbidexka** (1284m), 10km west of Larrañe along a minor but paved road. During September and October the *col* is the site of amazing bird migrations, well attended by hunters and bird-watchers alike. On the pass itself row upon row of watchers stand by tripod-mounted telescopes, while in the surrounding uplands a line of square hunting hides bristles with shotguns. During this period, millions of woodpigeons, thousands of honey buzzards, kites and cranes, and hundreds of white storks pass over the Pyrenees, the majority over the low western part of the range, mostly through the Organbidexka pass.

The hunters, more often well-heeled city-dwellers in full "battle dress" than locals, are particularly interested in the tasty *palombes* or pigeons, but recent years have seen a drastic reduction in their numbers for reasons not directly linked to the slaughter, such that few days during late October see more than a dozen birds bagged. Occasionally there are altercations between hunters and conservationists, which look set to continue since the EU is not yet disposed to promulgate uniform regulations against the mass slaughter of migratory birds.

At 1327-metre **Col de Bagargiak**, 500m northwest of the shooting-and-watching grounds, you'll find a collection of nine wooden chalets, intended primarily for users of the 44km of cross-country skiing pistes. The same phone, in the **information office** (☎05.59.28.51.29, fax 05.59.28.72.38) at the *col*, takes bookings for a *gîte d'étape* (①) here, while across the car park there's a small shop and inexpensive restaurant which serves forest mushrooms when in season. Some 2km west along the D19, through some of the densest forest, you pass a **campsite** well hidden in the trees near a pond, before emerging temporarily into the open at the **Plateau d'Iraty**, aka the **Plateau des Lacs**. Here there's a small dammed lake, a clutch of snack bars and a "free" camping meadow crammed to capacity with caravans in season. It's better to continue 1km south on the D18 to the more elegant and well-signposted *Chalet Pedro* (☎05.59.28.55.86; closed Nov 15 to Christmas & Tues low season), a local institution offering such delicacies as wild trout, roast pigeon and eel for under 145F/€22.

Without your own transport, the easiest way of reaching Organbidexka/Bagargiak is along the **old GR10** from Larrañe, now a *variante*, taking three and a half hours, mostly tangled with the road. The **new routing** from Logibarrea is more attractive but longer at nearly six hours, a ridge-walk which curls northwest, just above the one-thousand-metre contour, then climbs to 1472m before dropping slightly to the Col de Bagargiak.

Walking in the forest

There's enough walking here to occupy a few days, in particular the **day-hikes** which the information booth at Bagargiak recommends up Pic d'Orhy (5hr return) or the semi-loop ascending Pic des Escaliers to the north, both using well-marked sections of the GR10 or HRP.

But if you're in a hurry, one way to sample all the landscapes of the region is to **traverse** the forest north to south, a two-day itinerary involving a stay at the Casas de Irati on the **GR11**, finishing in Otsagabia at the head of the Valle de Salazar. With an early start, and plenty of stamina, you could make it to Otsagabia in one long day.

From Col Bagargiak follow the GR10 west, shortcutting the D18, as far as the Plateau d'Iraty. Bear south here onto the D18 and keep going for about twenty minutes, ignoring a right turn to Esterenzubi, to *Chalet Pedro*. If you have time to spare, the summit of **Occabé/Okabe** (1456m) is an easy ascent due west along the wide, briefly conjoined GR10/HRP (75min from the plateau). The bare, flat top is decorated by an Iron Age cromlech (circle of low standing stones), possibly linked with contemporary graves discovered adjacent, and gives views all over the forest and the Sierra de Abodi to the south.

Back at *Chalet Pedro*, the paved road continues south for 2.5km and then becomes track. Another diversion is offered by a path to the east, which crosses the **Pont d'Orgaté** and climbs via the Ourdanitzarreta shepherds' shelters to the summit of **Bizkarzé** (1656m; 2hr 30min from the plateau), an even prettier excursion than up Occabé.

Otherwise, keep on the track along the Iratiko Erreka (which later becomes the Spanish Río Irati), crossing the frontier after 1km. An hour after that, you reach the tiny white-painted **Ermita de Nuestra Señora de las Nieves** (where there's a religious procession on the Sunday before Aug 15) and the nearby derelict huts of **Casas de**

Irati (880m). The only "facility" here is an informal camping area serving the GR11/12.

If you spend the night, you'll have sufficient daylight left to stroll a couple of kilometres west along the GR11/GR12 to the Irabia reservoir; despite the power dynamo at the far end, the arrangement of water, mountain and dense forest right down to the shore is eminently satisfying. The main disappointment of the forest is that you see little wildlife, though when the mist licks around the tree-trunks you might mistake it for a *lamin*, the Basque leprechaun that is always blamed when something goes inexplicably wrong.

From Casas de Irati, Otsagabia lies more or less due south. The GR11 climbs steeply over the **Sierra de Abodi** via Harrizabla summit (1496m), with fantastic views over the forest and peaks, then drops more gradually to the village – a minimum four-and-a-half-hour march not to be attempted from the French side without an early start. Moreover, waymarking for the first hour is ambiguous – as on much of the GR11 west of Izaba – so you will certainly lose some time in getting lost. Casas de Irati is also served by a 23-kilometre paved road from Otsagabia, and since the *ermita* is a favourite picnic area there's a slight chance of a lift in peak season.

The Valle de Salazar

The **Valle de Salazar** (Zaraitzu) isn't particularly spectacular but it does possess a gentle beauty, albeit one diminished somewhat by the presence of a gas pipeline, diverted here by local bigwigs from its intended route through the Valle de Echo. The main attractions are at either end: the handsome village of **Otsagabia** near the top, and the natural reserve of **Foz de Arbaiun** and the **Monasterio de San Salvador de Leyre** at the bottom. Of particular interest for anyone emerging from the Selva de Irati is the valley's daily bus service, the quickest way south towards Pamplona.

Otsagabia

With its white plastered walls, stone-framed windows, wrought-iron balconies and pebble-mosaic entry-ways for the grander houses, **OTSAGABIA** (Ochagavía, Otsagi) forms one of the showcases of Pyrenean Navarra. Like Echo and Ansó, it was largely rebuilt after being sacked and burnt by the French in 1794. The river dividing the town is crossed by a series of low bridges, and cobbled streets meander from the streamside esplanades; to the west, on a slight rise, stands a church nearly as massive – but more graceful – than that at Izaba.

On a low hill to the north, the **Ermita de Muskilda** is much older than Nuestra Señora de las Nieves, built in stone with a multi-lobed entrance and a curious square half-timbered tower topped by an overhanging circular roof; every September 8 the festival of the Birth of the Virgin is celebrated by a well-attended *romería* (procession) and followed by dancing in traditional costume.

For conventional **accommodation** on the east bank, the wood-and-antique-decor, riverside *Hostal Urialde* (☎948 890 027; ③–④) represents better value than the *Hostal Auñamendi* on Plaza Gúrpide (☎948 890 189; ⑤), though the latter has a decent **restaurant**. No fewer than thirteen **casas rurales** (mostly ②) offer rooms in traditional stone houses; two worth singling out are the en-suite *Casa Ñavarro* (☎948 890 355; ③) and *Casa Osaba* (☎948 890 011; ②) on the west bank, one of the few buildings to predate the French attack. If you've come from France, three **ATM banks** will be your first sight of Spanish money.

At Otsagabia the minor road from Casas de Irati meets the more important one coming from the Port de Larrau and Izaba. The **GR11** also connects Otsagabia with Izaba via the Sierra de Atuzkarratz, on a mixture of old *camino* and forest track; the grade

GRIFFON VULTURES

Griffon vultures (in Castilian *buitres*, in French *vautours fauve*) occur in several other areas of Spain, but their sole French habitat aside from the Massif Central is the Central and Western Pyrenees, with the greatest concentrations in the Basque country. In the sky they are fairly unmistakeable, with a span of over 2.5m and fawn leading edges to the wings but almost black trailing edges. Exceeding 1m in length, they seem to have almost no head in flight, as the long, pale neck is tucked back.

Griffons live and hunt in colonies of between four and twelve pairs, covering a territory radiating up to 60km from the nest, which is rarely built at an altitude of over 1100m. Nesting time is generally March to May; when they reach maturity the young birds move on to establish a new territory, perhaps within kilometres but possibly as far away as North Africa.

The vultures eat carrion only, especially dead sheep, which are plentiful in the Western Pyrenees. When one of the troupe spots food it descends in spirals, thus attracting the others. The troupe seldom lands immediately but is more likely to keep the carrion under surveillance for one or two days – if the meat is too fresh it will be difficult to penetrate the skin. Once feeding starts a pecking order prevails, the dominant bird keeping the others back with menacing extensions of the neck, wings and claws. Only when satisfied does it give way to a subordinate, who in turn gives way to a bird of lower rank.

Besides the Foz de Arabaiun, other reliable places to see griffon vultures include the **Foz de Burgui** in the Roncal valley, **Cumbre de Arangoiti** near the Puerto de Ibañeta and the **Crête d'Iparla** near Baïgorri.

(except for the final drop to Izaba) is gentle, and the traverse takes under six hours in either direction, but there's no reliable water en route.

The Pamplona-based **bus**, run by La Salacenca, arrives at about 7pm, leaving the village next day at 7am (Mon–Sat); the journey takes 80 minutes. Midpoint of the downhill journey is the Foz de Arbaiun.

Foz de Arbaiun

The only really remarkable portion of the Valle de Salazar comes near its bottom end at the **Foz de Arbaiun** (Arbayún) a six-kilometre limestone gorge carved out by the Río Salazar. Dense vegetation thrives in the shade at the base of four-hundred-metre-high cliffs; higher up, raptor nests are concealed between clumps of bushes. This is the finest place in the entire Pyrenees to see **griffon vultures**, the largest colony of Navarra's several hundred specimens being protected here by a *reserva natural* of 1200 hectares. You can see the gorge from the viewing platform just to the north of the hamlet of Iso; for the intrepid, very steep trails snake down to the river bed.

The Monasterio de San Salvador de Leyre and Yesa

From the north end of the Foz de Arbaiun, 3km above Iso, a narrow road climbs 4km to the hamlet of Bigüezal, from where a track rises to the **Monasterio de San Salvador de Leyre** (Leire), 11km from the gorge. With your own sturdy transport this makes a more exciting approach than the steep side-road up from Yesa on the N240 in the Río Aragón valley.

The monastery (daily 10am–9pm) contrasts vividly with the hermitages back in the mountains, its massive size underlining its former position as both a political and pilgrimage focus of Navarra. After languishing in ruins for over a century, it was restored and reoccupied by Benedictine monks in the 1950s and now basks in an immaculate condition. The leaflet available in English at the porter's lodge sheds useful light on the complicated sculptured facade of the church.

Although the resolutely institutional monastic outbuildings are of sixteenth-to-eighteenth-century vintage, the **church** is largely Romanesque with thirteenth-century Gothic additions, its tall, severe apses and asymmetrical belfry being particularly impressive. Highlights include the **west portal**, carved with images of Christ, the Virgin, St Peter, St John and assorted monsters. Inside, the sturdy little columns of the **crypt** are so short that the capitals are at knee height; they can be illuminated by putting a coin in the slot. Try to catch a service if you can; the Benedictine community here employs the Gregorian chant.

The former pilgrims' hospice adjacent is now run as a two-star **hotel**, the *Hospedería de Leyre* (☎948 884 100, fax 948 884 137; closed Dec–March; ⑤), and although far more expensive than staying in Yesa (see below), it is still a remarkable bargain, providing **meals** as well. Men can stay at the monastery itself for a nominal fee, but anyone wanting to do this should write or phone ahead (☎948 884 011). The monastery is still, as it has long been, an important halt on the Aragonese variant of the Camino de Santiago, today codified as the GR65.3, last encountered at San Juan de la Peña.

A good four-kilometre road drops south from the monastery, down the Sierra de Leyre mountains, to join the N240 in **YESA** (Esa), at the western end of the **Embalse de Yesa**, whose enlargement was recently approved, though it seems that Yesa itself will fall not into the inundated area. Yesa has several **hostales**, the best being *El Jabalí* (☎948 884 042; ④) on the main road, with a pool and restaurant. At least one daily bus links Yesa with both Pamplona and Jaca.

ALONG THE CAMINO DE SANTIAGO

An obvious itinerary from Pamplona entails moving northeast along the principal branch of the **Camino de Santiago** into France, via the fabled **Puerto de Ibañeta**. It's a route easily covered by bus, car, mountain bike or – for purists or pilgrims – on foot along the **GR65** long-distance trail.

Auritze, a village on a wide plain at the foot of the frontier peaks, is an obvious and comfortable staging-point. A short distance north of Burguete, the abbey of **Roncesvalles** has long been a hallowed stop on the pilgrim route to Santiago de Compostela, and occupies a central location in the legend of **Roland**. The famous

THE CAMINO DE SANTIAGO IN NAVARRA

Following the European Parliament's decision to designate the *camino* as Europe's first "cultural itinerary", Navarra has invested considerably in improving facilities along the route. There are now about a dozen pilgrims' refuges in Navarra which bona fide pilgrims can use – to be certified you need to acquire a "passport (40F/€6.10), which can be purchased at any of the official refuges en route. Your "passport" as an accredited pilgrim is then stamped at each subsequent refuge. Most of these have hot showers, some have kitchens and are either free or charge a nominal fee. A few of the hostels may only be open during summer, but regional tourist offices in Navarra can provide up-to-date details.

Although not strictly on the Camino de Santiago, it's worth considering an alternate route northwest from Pamplona to Saint-Jean-Pied-de-Port, initially along the N121. Once over the Cantabrian watershed, beyond which all rivers flow into the Atlantic rather than the Mediterranean, you're in the **Valle de Baztán**, where Elizondo makes a good halting place. From here a minor road heads east via pastoral **Baïgorri** to rejoin the pilgrim route at Saint-Jean.

ambush of Charlemagne's rearguard, supposedly under Roland's command, took place close by – possibly after the Franks emerged from the thick, gloomy beech forest onto the barren expanse of the Puerto de Ibañeta.

This pass notches the main Pyrenean watershed, but an anomalous finger of Spanish territory encompassing **Luzaïde** protrudes north and down halfway to **Saint-Jean-Pied-de-Port**, touristic mecca of the French Pays Basque since its days as a pilgrimage way-station. From here the *chemin* – now paralleled by the modern road and rail line – heads northwest along the valley of the River Nive to the attractive cathedral city of Bayonne, with relatively little to compel a stop before then. In doing so the pilgrim route transects the two westerly historic divisions of the French Basque country, **Basse-Navarre** and **Labourd**.

Auritze

AURITZE (Burguete) is a typically pleasant, one-street Basque Pyrenean settlement, surrounded by fields, cattle barns and wooded ridges on the horizon. Auritze appears to be not much bigger than in Ernest Hemingway's time – he (and his fictional characters Jake and Bill) used to come trout fishing nearby, before or after Pamplona's San Fermín festival.

The GR65, GR11 and GR12 all pass through here on the same right-of-way just outside Burguete to the west, a fact somewhat confused by lingering, faded waymarks for the old GR11 to the east. The new shared GR11 and GR12 trace a very circuitous route north, then east towards Otsagabia for two walking days, with little in the way of facilities or habitation in between. For short day-strolls along streams and through the woods, with Auritze as a base, the rolling countryside immediately east of the village is still your best bet. The relevant Editorial Alpina **map** is "Roncesvalles - Irati".

Practicalities

The best choice amongst three conventional **accommodation** establishments is the *Hostal Burguete* at the north end of the main street (☎948 760 005; ④–⑤), the oldest establishment here: three echoing storeys of huge, spotless, squeaky-wood-floored rooms, most en suite, and with literary cachet to boot. Hemingway stayed here during the early 1920s, and immortalized it in his first novel *Fiesta*; the room he occupied, now #25 (formerly 18), is still preserved much as he described it, save for discreetly placed photos of the great man (including one with his second wife, Martha Gellhorn). The four rooms of the *Hostal Juandeaburre* (☎948 760 078; ③) at the south end of the high street are rather more basic, while directly opposite stands the three-star *Hotel Loizu* (☎948 760 008, fax 948 790 444; ⑥), whose somewhat overpriced, double-glazed rooms, have all the charm of an airport Hilton. Failing these, try one of the *casas rurales* for a more traditional feel: *Casa Loigorri* (☎948 760 016; ②), the characterful and spotless *Casa Loperena* (☎948 760 068; ②), above the **bank** (next-to-last one before the frontier), or the en-suite *Casa Vergara* (☎948 760 044; ③). There's also a **campsite**, *Urrobi* (☎948 760 200; April–Oct), 3km south of the village at **Auritzberri** (Espinal) on the Pamplona road. **Eating** out, the *Loizu* is generally conceded to have the best restaurant in town, with game- and meat-oriented meals for about 3000ptas/€18; otherwise there's little to distinguish the cheaper, sustaining fare at the *Burguete*'s *comedor* from the independent *Txikipolit* across the way.

East of Auritze

The afternoon bus from Pamplona first calls in at Roncesvalles (see below) and then continues 10km east past attractive Garralda to **ARIBE** (Arive), an equally appealing

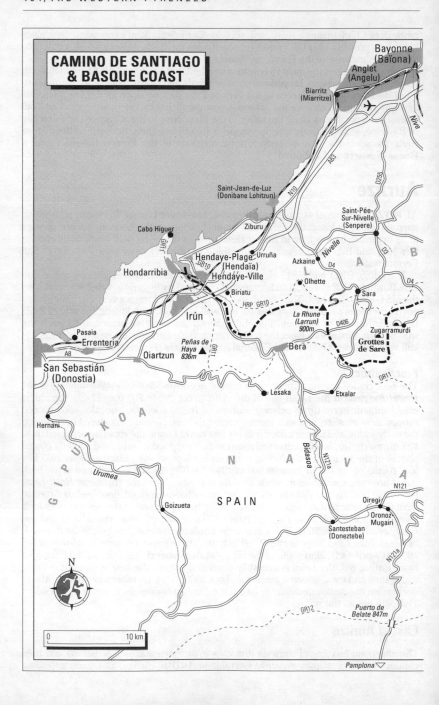

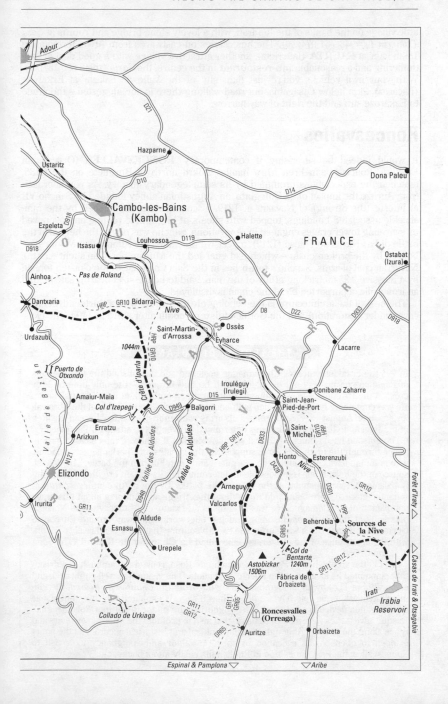

little village on the banks of the Río Irati, with a lovely stone bridge and **rooms** at *Casa Txikirrin I* (☎948 764 074; ③). The bus carries on eastwards from Arive, terminating 18km later at **EAURTA** (Jaurrieta), another attractive village with a good deal of half-timbering and a reasonable **inn-restaurant** in the centre, the *Sario* (☎948 890 187; ③). With your own vehicle, you're just 6km shy of the Valle de Salazar at Ezkaroze (Escaroz), 2km below Otsagabia, but road-walking there is not suggested – the grade to Ezkaroze stiff and the right of way narrow.

Roncesvalles

It would indeed be surprising if contemporary **RONCESVALLES** (Orreaga in Euskera, Roncevaux in French), a hamlet 2.5km north of Burguete on the C135, matched the expectations prompted by its semi-legendary history. As you approach from Auritze the impact of its **Colegiata**, an Augustinian abbey founded by Sancho VII el Fuerte (the Strong) of Navarra in 1219, is considerably diminished by the ramshackle associated buildings, topped with sheets of bright zinc roofing and overawed by swiveling tower cranes engaged in renovations. Sancho was one of the heroes of the battle of Las Navas de Tolosa (1212), a decisive defeat for the Almohadan Moors symbolized by the broken chain – which had guarded the Muslim chieftain's tent – in the Navarran coat-of-arms. Sancho's **tomb** lies in the Sala Capitular of the cloister, topped by a massive 2.25-metre-long effigy of the man, said to be life-size; nearby, safe behind an iron grille, a purported bit of the chain is displayed.

The best of the architecture is the echoing **church** (free, with a thirteenth-century crypt under restoration) and the Gothic **cloister**, rebuilt after a fire in 1400. The clois-

THE LEGEND OF ROLAND

In 778 the Frankish emperor Charlemagne besieged and demolished the fortifications of Pamplona on his way out of Spain, which he had invaded – the only time he ever crossed the Pyrenees – to assist one faction during an outbreak of inter-Moorish strife. He was continuing homeward, laden with booty from various other raids in the Ebro valley, when on August 15, 778, the rear of his army was ambushed somewhere in the area of the Puerto de Ibañeta, by Basques determined to avenge the attack on Pamplona.

The episode hasn't much historical significance, but it achieved international prominence through the myth of Roland, supposedly the greatest of Charlemagne's paladins, who is said to have commanded the rearguard and been killed in the battle. The precise source of the Roland tale is impossible to determine, but its distant origins lie in knightly ballads that were popular at the time of the battle. By the ninth century, *cantilènes* (chanted stories) were being told throughout the Ariège and Andorra about this brave companion of Charlemagne. He was held up as an example of bravery to the Norman battalions at the Battle of Hastings, and the tale worked its way around Europe to Germany and Italy. But it was during the twelfth century that the legend really took off, with the appearance of the mysterious epic called **La Chanson de Roland** (The Song of Roland).

In 1130 the archbishop of Pamplona, Sancho de Rosa, relived the ambush in a dream that pinpointed its location at the Puerto de Ibañeta. The vision was well publicized, and elaborated in 1170 by an anonymous clerk who wrote the *Chanson de Roland*, the ultimate medieval heroic epic. The Catholic Church eagerly exploited the story, not just as a propaganda device against the Infidel – ignoring the minor detail that Roland's final, Basque adversaries were also Christians – but also to promote the sales of souvenirs and relics along the *camino*. Although the geographical and historical accuracy of the poem is open to question, its evocation of chivalric valour adds poignancy to a visit to Roncesvalles; the Penguin edition in English fits easily into a backpack.

ter is visited with the same ticket for a separate, small **museum** (summer daily & weekends all year 10am–2pm & 4–8pm; 300pta/€1.80) at the southwest corner of the monastery building, which contains the expected ecclesiastical reliquaries (one showcasing the mummified fingers of St Marina), processional crucifixes, mitres, croziers and chalices, as well as an exquisite eighteenth-century gold cigarette box from Paris, embossed with a swan confronting a fox – possibly a pilgrim's donation.

Roland's purported martyrdom notwithstanding, the original role of the abbey was as a beacon on the Camino de Santiago; after all, its founding – centuries after the battle – was motivated by the need for a strategically placed pilgrims' hospice a day's journey south of Saint-Jean-Pied-de-Port. Had it really been intended as a memorial to Roland, the *colegiata* would have been sited (rather impractically) up on the Puerto de Ibañeta. The tale of the attack merely provided a general endorsement for the exemplary defenders of Christianity.

In the years immediately following its establishment, the abbey enjoyed a meteoric success, ranking among the most wealthy and powerful in the thirteenth century; it was said that a pilgrim of the era could travel from London to Roncesvalles entirely on lands belonging to the *colegiata*. Today the place is more commonly the destination of numerous local *romerías*, from both the French and Spanish valleys, by virtue of its thirteenth-century image of the *Virgen de Orreaga*, honoured with special fervour on September 8.

Practicalities

Accommodation is fairly abundant, considering that there's no real village here. Non-pilgrims should head for the small *Hostal Casa Sabina*, right next to the monastery (☎948 760 012; ④), or the much larger *La Posada* (☎948 760 225; ⑤), run by the monastery; both serve **meals**. Bona fide **pilgrims** following the Camino de Santiago can use the **hostel** at the monastery (token donation requested). All this seems a mere echo of the medieval hospice here, which for seven centuries listed its services for the (predominantly male) pilgrims as follows: a bath, haircut, shave and mending of shoes or clothes, performed – as various manuscripts attested – "by women solicitous and far from ugly".

The Transpyrenean Camino de Santiago

A better way to get a sense of the Roland legend is to make the half-hour walk up through the beech woods from the back of the abbey to the **Puerto de Ibañeta** (1057m). According to many scholars, you'll be walking through the site where Roland's defeat occurred. On a misty day – and there are many – the pass can seem suitably melancholy. An ugly modern chapel stands on the saddle, on the site of the ancient chapel of San Salvador, whose bell used to guide pilgrims in foggy weather. There are also a couple of small medieval stone monuments to Roland and the vestiges of another built by a doctor from Pamplona in 1934.

Thirty-two years after Charlemagne followed approximately this route, his son, Louis le Débonnaire, avoided a repeat performance of the Basque ambush by forcing the wives and children of local villagers to accompany his troops through the pass. It was also the route taken by Edward the Black Prince to the battleground of Navarrate in 1367; Napoleon's troops retreated this way after the Peninsular War; and the defeated Republicans fled in thousands through the sombre scenery here as the Spanish Civil War drew to a close.

The **Camino de Santiago**, officially marked as the GR65, no longer goes via the Puerto de Ibañeta, but on a more northeasterly bearing from Roncesvalles, avoiding most major roads. It's seven to eight hours to Saint-Jean-Pied-de-Port, much of it on narrow country lanes but occasionally on medieval cobbles, through beautiful countryside.

From the *colegiata*, it's nearly ninety minutes by path through thick beech woods to the **Collada Lepoeder** (1445m), flanked by the rounded summit of Astobizkar (1506m). You descend slightly, past the ruins of the Elizacharre chapel, to cross the border at the **Col de Bentarte/Collado de Betartea pass** (1340m) – which many insist was the more likely place for the ambush (and an extra justification, perhaps, for rerouteing the *camino*). The joint GR11/12 heads east here, parting company with the GR65, which heads north to meet the paved D428 for Saint-Jean after about half an hour, just below **Pic Urdanarré** (1240m). Alternatively, you can walk eastwards on the marked path to the **Urkulu burial tower** (dating from about 1500 BC), and join the same road there, a diversion which cost you an extra hour round-trip.

From the base of Pic Urdanarré, Saint-Jean is about 16km or 4hr away, with the GR65 providing just one or a few short cuts across woods and farmland. Much the best place to break the trek if it looks like you'll be overtaken by darkness – or if you don't fancy the idea of busy Saint-Jean-Pied-de-Port, ninety minutes further – is the tiny French hamlet of **HONTO**, which offers excellent *chambres d'hôte* and hearty evening meals at *Ferme Ithurburia* (☎05.59.37.11.17; ④) – it's a big hit with pilgrims following the Camino de Santiago in summer so phone in advance if possible.

Luzaïde

Alternatively, you can drive from Roncesvalles – beyond which there's no public transport – along the main road into France down the Luzaide valley, a narrow salient of Spanish territory jutting north from the usual frontier ridge. **LUZAÏDE** (Valcarlos), 16km below the Ibañeta pass, is a typical border town full of tatty souvenirs and booze – though the views are better than usual – with the *Hostal Maitena* (☎948 790 210; ③) conveniently situated on the main road should you need to **stay**. On the Frenchward side of the village, the excellent *Casa Etxezuria* (☎948 790 011; ②) has four beautifully furnished rooms offering luxury at a bargain price. There are four other **casas rurales**, however, including the remoter but en-suite *Casa Navarlaz* (☎948 790 042; ③), so you shouldn't be stuck except perhaps in August. Arnegi (Arnéguy), 3km on, is the first French village, right against the border; again it has no public transport links north.

Saint-Jean-Pied-de-Port

SAINT-JEAN-PIED-DE-PORT (Donibane Garazi), 8km from the border on the young River Nive, is a seasonally overrun tourist attraction, its highly photogenic old quarter enveloped in pink sandstone walls and watched over by an imposing fortress. Once capital of Basse-Navarre, Saint-Jean thrived until the sixteenth century on the pilgrimage traffic to Santiago de Compostela, and all over town you'll see the scallop-shell emblem of the shrine. The three main pilgrim routes across France converge some 20km northeast at Ostabat, from where caravans of travellers used to descend on Saint-Jean, singing in reply to the church bells that would ring when a group was spotted on the horizon. From the north, they entered by **Porte de Saint-Jacques** in the town walls and left by **Porte d'Espagne**, heading up to the Puerto de Ibañeta – hence the suffixed Pied-de-Port, meaning "Foot-of-the-Pass".

The oldest neighbourhood lies on the right bank of the River Nive, behind the medieval fortifications, and consists essentially of a single street. This begins as the rue d'Espagne, heading north from Porte d'Espagne, and lined on both sides with souvenir shops and pastel-painted houses, some with carved lintels dating them as far back as the sixteenth century. Crossing the **Vieux-Pont**, which offers the best photo opportunities in town – balconied houses, decked in washing and flowers, handsomely reflected in the placid, trout-filled waters of the Nive – you pass through the well-preserved **Porte Nôtre-Dame** to reach the fourteenth-century, largely Gothic **Nôtre-Dame-du-Bout-du-Pont** on the right. Here the street becomes the cobbled rue de la Citadelle, climbing steeply past the long and narrow **Prison des Evêques** (Bishops' Prison; open daily Easter–Oct mornings and late afternoons; 15F/€2.30), separated by a garden from the episcopal residence. The pilgrimage to Santiago inevitably attracted a few shady characters who preyed on the occasionally gullible genuine pilgrims; when discovered, the con-men were arrested by guards employed by the Church and flung into dungeons such as this. Accordingly you are shown, in addition to a small gallery of knick-knacks, a subterranean earth-floored chamber still complete with chains for restraining the prisoners.

At the top of the rise, above the Porte de Saint-Jacques, looms the classical **citadel**, built in 1628 on the orders of Cardinal Richelieu, and redesigned by Vauban in 1685. It's now a college, but the lower, grassy ramparts have unrestricted access, and are worth the climb up for the sweeping views west and north.

Practicalities

The **tourist office** (Mon–Sat 9am–noon & 2–7pm; daily July–Aug 10.30am–12.30pm & 3–6pm; ☎05.59.37.03.57) is at 14 place du Général-de-Gaulle, a tile-roofed kiosk opposite the *mairie*. The **train station** is ten minutes' walk away at the end of av Renaud, on the northern edge of the centre.

For **pilgrims' and trekkers' accommodation**, there are three possibilities. The basic *Accueil Saint-Jacques* at 39 rue de Citadelle (☎05.59.37.05.09; Easter–Sept; donation) is for bona fide pilgrims only, while *Les Donats* opposite at no. 40 (☎05.59.37.15.64; donation) is less fussy, welcoming *randonneurs* as well. The tiny, helpful *Gîte d'Étape Etchegoin* is at 9 rte d'Uhart, on the Bayonne road (☎05.59.37.12.08; ①). There's a **camping municipal**, the *Plaza Berri* (☎05.59.37.11.19, fax 05.59.37.99.78; June–Sept) on the south bank of the Nive, beside the *frontón*, as well as the site *Arradoy* (☎05.59.37.11.75; March–Sept), north of town on the far side of the rail line.

Less expensive **hotels** include *Les Remparts*, 16 place Floquet (☎05.59.37.13.79, fax 05.59.37.33.44; ④; closed Oct 15–Jan), just before you cross the Nive coming into town on the Bayonne road, not too noisy and with parking spaces nearby (a problem here), or the 1997-renovated *Hôtel Itzalpea*, 5 place du Trinquet (☎05.59.37.03.66, fax 05.59.37.33.18; ③), whose restauarant offers a wide choice of *menus* (average 120F/€18.30). More expensive and comfortable are the *Ramuntcho*, just inside the city walls at 1 rue de France (☎05.59.37.03.91, fax 05.59.37.35.17; ⑤), with a good and reasonably priced restaurant, and the posh *Hôtel Central* on place du Général-de-Gaulle (☎05.59.37.00.22, fax 05.59.37.27.79; closed mid-Dec to mid-Feb; ⑥), offering meals at 100–220F/€15.30–33.60 per head with some river-view rooms (front ones face traffic and the lively **Monday market**) and free parking.

Eating out, there's no better place for a splurge than *Chez Arrambide*, the **restaurant** of the *Hôtel des Pyrénées* at 19 place du Général-de-Gaulle (closed Jan & mid-Nov to mid-Dec), reckoned one of the best in the Pyrenees: count on 400–600F/€61–91.50 for the works, which often include dishes like baby rabbit, duck in Irouléguy wine, roast pigeon with mushroom ravioli and decadent sorbets. Less expensive, but also of high standard, is *Arbillaga* (closed Tues pm, also Weds low season), at 8 rue de l'Église just inside the walls, with *menus* at 85–160F/€12.90–24.40. Otherwise, there are a dozen rather slapdash, fairly indistinguishable pavement *brasseries* and *crêperies* aimed at the not-too-discriminating day-tripper, packed to the gills in season.

The only ways of moving on by public transport are the **train** west to Bayonne or the **bus** west to Baïgorri. You can enquire about **bike rental** at Steunou (☎05.59.37.25.45), next to the tourist office, or at Garazy (☎05.59.37.21.79) for mountain bikes.

Southeast: the upper Nive valley

Heading southeast of Saint-Jean, the D301 road furnishes access to the upper reaches of the **Nive valley**, with its attractive villages and small red- or green-shuttered farmhouses. The GR10 stays well northeast of the river, first paved, then on track and trail along Handiamendi ridge, running roughly parallel to the D301. The road continues almost all the way to the river's source, with a short final approach on foot.

The villages

Sleepy **SAINT-MICHEL**, 4km along the D301, has the excellent *Hôtel Xoko-Goxoa* (☎05.59.37.06.34, fax 05.59.37.34.63; closed Jan–March; ④) on the main through road to prompt a halt. Best are the rear, balconied rooms overlooking hayfields and a stream valley; the restaurant, equally panoramic, is simple but savoury and reasonable (70–140F/€10.70–21.40).

Proceeding 4km further – or three and a half hours from Saint-Jean along the meandering GR10 – brings you to tiny **ESTERENZUBI** (Esterençuby) with its medieval galleried church and ample **accommodation**. Choose between the *Auberge Etchegoyen*, better known as the *Carricaburu* after the managing family (☎05.59.37.09.77; ③), with a streamside restaurant and the lively village bar, or the more institutional *Hôtel Restaurant Andreinia* (☎05.59.37.09.70; fax 05.59.37.36.05; ③), which also keeps a *gîte d'étape* on a nearby knoll.

The valley-floor road continues alongside the Nive, now no more than a mountain stream; there's little cultivation in the progressively deepening valley other than vast hay meadows, scythed and raked in early summer, and equally extensive tracts of bracken fern, prized as animal bedding. En route you pass, after just under 3km, another worthy establishment, the *Hôtel Artzaïn Etchea* (☎05.59.37.11.55, fax 05.59.37.20.16; closed Feb; ④), a modern but well-run place with a popular restaurant (*menus* 65–130F/€9.90–19.80). Some 4km from Esterenzubi the road reaches tiny Béhérobie before climbing to the border and fizzling out. At **BEHEROBIA** (Béhérobie), in the valley bottom beside the infant Nive, one of just a few buildings is the *Hôtel des Sources de la Nive* (☎05.59.37.10.57; ④; closed Jan & Tues low season); its restaurant offers game-dominated *menus* for 80–180F/€12.20–27.50. The hotel is invariably booked out in October – like most of the valley's lodgings – for the wood-pigeon shooting season, but otherwise makes a relaxing hideaway.

The Sources de la Nive

Just before the bridge at Beherobia, a lane keeps up to the left, signposted for the **Sources de la Nive**. With a car, you can drive to the end of the road by a bridge and a few farmhouses, then continue on foot by the dirt track heading left, not the one over the bridge (which carried the old, now-abandoned GR10 from St-Jean – you'll see waymarks covered over with grey paint). The track soon dwindles to trail along the fifteen-minute walk to the springs; water percolates a thousand metres down through karstic hillside to well up as a surging pool feeding rapids. Lost in dense beech woods, it's a magic spot in any weather, with a faint mist often rising from the surface of the water.

East: walking the GR10 or driving

There are just a few other **walking** possibilities in the immediate area, most of them utilizing the **old GR10**; with the waymarks painted over and systematic maintenance suspended, you should probably not attempt them without a 1:25,000 IGN map and an altimeter. The old trail follows a tributary of the Nive southeast, high up the side of the valley to emerge into lush grasslands about an hour out. Another hour should see you at the Col d'Errozaté (1076m), just north of which is Errozaté peak (1345m); if you're traversing rather than dayhiking, it's possible to continue east, via Occabé (see p.459), to the vicinity of *Chalet Pedro* in the Forêt d'Iraty – six to seven hours from Beherobia.

The **new GR10** has been rerouted to head from Esterenzubi to the Forêt d'Iraty via Phagalcette hamlet and Iraukotuturru peak, meeting up with the old route at Occabé. It's nearly six hours to *Chalet Pedro*, (see p.459) the first two hours a rather dull, stiff climb on paved, one-lane road. But once off this onto farm track and path, the scenery is enlivened by wandering herds of healthy-looking horses and ponies, masses of sheep and big sleek caramel cows with bells at their throats on wooden collars marked with their owners' names. There are superb places to camp if you've started late, with views west to the orange and crimson striations of the sunset and the revolving beacon of the Biarritz lighthouse visible in the dark.

Drivers should follow the D301 east out of the Nive valley from the junction near the *Hôtel Artzaïn Etchea*, signposted for the Forêt d'Iraty. This is very steep, narrow and full of tight hairpins, frequent oncoming traffic and the ambling livestock noted above; it's to be avoided at night or in misty conditions, and needs an hour in low gear at the best of times to the junction with the D18 at the Plateau d'Iraty. But there is ample compensation: as you climb higher up the steep spurs and round the heads of labyrinthine gullies, ever more spectacular views open beneath you. You can see way back over the valley of the Nive, St-Jean and the hills beyond. Stands of beech fill the gullies, shadowing the lighter grass whose green is so intense it seems almost theatrical – an effect produced, apparently, by the juxtaposition of outcrops of rock whose purplish hue brings out the cadmium yellow in the grass.

West: Baïgorri and the Vallée des Aldudes

Although **BAÏGORRI** (Saint-Étienne-de-Baïgorry) lies only 11km west of Saint-Jean-Pied-de-Port by the D15, it's a different world, where agriculture rather than tourism is the prime focus of life. Like most other foothill Basque settlements, Baïgorri is divided into quite distinct quarters, more like separate hamlets than a unified village. Market centre of the **Vallée des Aldudes**, it's a prosperous, rather sleek place, its highly profitable farming co-operatives presenting their public face through several sales outlets in town. The strong local **Irouléguy (Irulegi) wines**, the only *appellation* red, white and rosé produced in the Pays Basque, are worth stocking up on; you can taste them at the vintner's outlet 5km east on the D15 (daily 9am–noon & 2–6pm; not Sun in winter). Other local specialities include ham, sheep's-milk cheese and preserved mushrooms.

There are few great sights here: just a hump-backed medieval bridge juxtaposed with the small castle of the Etxauz (Etchaux) quarter, and a seventeenth-century church with an extravagantly gilded Baroque *retable*. The town's Euskera name translates as "beautiful view" and from the outlying quarters, which clamber up pastured and vine-clad hills, you do indeed get a marvellous panorama of the gentle lower slopes of the Pyrenees.

Practicalities

The **tourist office** is opposite the church (Mon–Sat 9am–noon & 2–6pm; July–Aug also Sun 10–12pm & 3–6pm; ☎05.59.37.47.28), and can help with longer stays in local *chambres d'hôtes*. The only budget **accommodation** is the *Gîte d'Étape Mendi* (☎05.59.37.42.39; ①), in the northerly Lespars quarter – closest eating at the *Restaurant Izarra*, offering *menus* from 85F/€12.90 – or the eccentrically run *Hôtel Restaurant Hargain* (☎05.59.37.41.46; ③), in the central Bourg quarter, whose proprietor tends to have vacancies depending on whether she likes your looks or not. You'll have a more predictable reception at *Hôtel Restaurant Maechenea*, 4km north in the hamlet of **Urdos** (☎05.59.37.41.68, fax 05.59.37.46.03; ④), tranquilly set on a stream-bank, or – lightening the wallet considerably – at the professionally run, three-star *Hôtel-Restaurant Arcé* on the west side of the river in Saint-Étienne (☎05.59.37.40.14, fax 05.59.37.40.27; ⑦), with English-speaking management and a more affordably priced **restaurant** with *menus* at 110F/€16.80 and 170F/€26. At the opposite end of the spectrum, the *Mendi* has lawn space for **tents**, while the better-amenitied, riverside *Camping Irouléguy* (☎05.59.37.40.80; open all year) is more central. About the only independent **eatery** in town is the friendly *Bar Chez Oronos*, in Bourg district, where a three-course, daily-changing menu won't top 80F/€12.20 with drink.

Regular SNCF **rail-bus** services connect Saint-Étienne with the train station at Ossès-Saint-Martin-d'Arrossa, 8km northeast along the D948.

The upper Vallée des Aldudes

The villages of the upper **Vallée des Aldudes** are quiet rural spots, beyond the reach of public transport, major hiking routes and most tourism. Although it lies on a fairly major corridor to Pamplona, accommodation and food here is simple and reasonably priced, with rooms likely to fill only in August.

The first village, about 7km south of Saint-Étienne, is **BANKA** (Banka), shoehorned into the steep narrows carved out by the river here. It used to live from mining lead and copper – you can see the ruined works – but now depends on hosting trout fishermen. They stay mostly at the one-star *Hôtel-Restaurant Erreguina*, appealingly set up by the church and a brook (☎ & fax 05.59.37.40.37; ③), with en-suite rooms and offering much the highest standard food or lodging in the valley – and a warm welcome. There are three *menus* under 100F/€15.25 served in the cave-like, beam-ceilinged dining room or out on the lawn, though going à la carte for scarcely more gives a better selection of pigeon, venison and fish both ocean and local. The HRP passes high above Banka, though the link route down from the Col d'Ehunzaroy is poorly marked and unshaded; best to follow tracks if in doubt.

Some 8km further, the valley opens out considerably, with **ALDUDE** (Les Aldudes) plopped in the middle of the fields. The dead-central, somewhat scuffed *Hôtel Restaurant Baillea* (☎05.59.37.57.02, fax 05.59.37.55.01; ②; closed Nov 15–March 1), with equally basic food, is the only facility. Some 4km southeast up a dead-end road, **UREPELE** (Urepel) can offer the equally old-fashioned *Hôtel Restaurant Etchechuria* (☎05.59.37.57.90; ③), with *menus* under 120F/€18.30. For more comfort, follow the main road 1500m towards Spain to **ESNASU** (Esnazu), where there are two establishments, of which the *Hôtel Restaurant Laxague-Menta* (☎05.59.37.57.58; ④) is more reasonable than the other.

Walking around Baïgorri: the Crête d'Iparla

The **GR10** arrives circuitously in Baïgorri from Saint-Jean in about six hours, curling southwest via 1021-metre Monhoa hill, then northeast. It's a rather dull stretch of the trail, with a lot of track sectors.

Not so the continuation west towards Bidarraï, by far the more popular and rewarding outing, which begins near the *gîte* in Lespars district. A sharp, two-and-a-half-hour climb, first through woods and then along a bare ridge, emerges at the **Col de Buztanzelhay** (843m), at the southern end of the **Crête d'Iparla**, which here forms the border. Iparla offers the classic ridge-walk of the French Pays Basque, and indeed one of the best in the entire Pyrenees.

Once up, it's hard to get lost: you simply follow the ridge due north, as close to the eastern face as is prudent. You're virtually guaranteed close-range sightings of griffon vultures and the occasional rare black vulture, though they tend to go to ground after midday when the thermal qualities of the air change. Although the highest point, **Pic d'Iparla** (under 3hr from Buztanzelhay), is only 1044m, it's as impressive a walk as you could hope for, with France precipitously below to the east, and a gentler decline towards a much less developed, almost secret corner of Spain on the west.

You'll need a full eight hours, an hour less with a daypack, to traverse the length of the entire crest to Bidarraï village. You should only attempt it in settled conditions; otherwise you won't get its views or vulture sightings, and every year hikers are struck by lighting or fall off the sheer precipice in mist. It's possible to return to your start-point the same day by public transport, a somewhat easier undertaking if you begin the walk from Bidarraï, a common strategy. Consult current SNCF schedule placards before setting out so that you coincide with one of the afternoon rail-buses back from Baïgorri to the proper train station of Ossès-St-Martin-d'Arrossa, one stop above Pont-Noblia (Bidarraï).

Starting the walk from Bidarraï, begin following the GR10 markers at the *gîte d'étape* and then bear right at each of two subsequent track junctions. The climb is brutal for the first ninety minutes, then slackens at a jagged crag where your spirits will be further lifted by your first glimpse of the vultures – who seem to have lost most fear of humans. Once around the Pic d'Iparla – about 2hr 45min out of Bidarraï with a daypack at a good pace – you descend to the important **Col de Harrieta** (808m) within another hour.

Immediately to the left (east), a communally maintained path, then tractor track, marked with single yellow paint-dashes, descends within ninety minutes to **Urdos** hamlet, your safety bail-out if the weather has turned nasty. From Urdos it's two-and-a-half hours back to Bidarraï, mostly on track and road. Diagonally off to the right or southwest from the *col*, a clear trail leads within five minutes to the **only spring** on Iparla, though even this may run low or dry by August. Straight south along the GR10 should get you to Baïgorri, and the late afternoon rail-bus, within three-and-a-half more hours.

Bidarraï

If you arrive by train at **BIDARRAÏ** (Bidarray), the place seems restricted to a few scattered houses on the riverbank near its medieval, humpbacked Pont Noblia, also the name of the SNCF station on schedules. Hikers arriving on the GR10, whether from Ainhoa on the west or Baïgorri to the south, get a truer picture of the upper village, scattered appealingly on a ridge with superb views; the first building they encounter coming from either direction is *Gîte d'Étape Auñamendi* (☎05.59.37.71.34; ①). Further along, the central place de l'Église is flanked by the 1999-refurbished *Hôtel Restaurant Barberaenea* (☎05.59.37.74.86, fax 05.59.37.77.55; ④), where it's worth enduring often "leisurely" service for the tasty five-course 135F/€20.60 *menu du terroir* (drink extra), typically including *garbure* and cod-stuffed red peppers, served under the plane trees. Down in the riverbank quarter, the better choice of two is the welcoming *Hôtel Restaurant du Pont d'Enfer* (☎05.59.37.70.88, fax 05.59.37.76.60; closed Nov–Easter; ③), better known as *Chez Anny* after the proprietor, with large, non-musty rooms and a restaurant serving on a riverview terrace in summer – among several *menus*, the 128F/€19.50 one is best value. A bit east, equidistant from upper and riverside quarters, lies the *Camping Errekaldia* (☎05.59.37.72.36).

The Valle de Baztán

Due north of Pamplona, the heavily travelled N121a climbs over the **Belate** (Puerto de Velate), on the watershed separating Mediterranean- from Cantabrian-draining rivers. It then descends to **ORONOZ-MUGAIRI**, home to the **Parque Señorío de Bértiz** (daily 10am–2pm & 4–7pm; 200ptas/€1.20), a former private estate now combining the functions of botanical gardens and managed recreational forest. Immediately beyond, at Oieregi, the N121a forks left up the scenic Valle de Bidasoa (see p.496) towards Irún, Hendaye and Hondarribia. Continuing along the right fork and the N121, you enter the **Valle de Baztán** (meaning "Rat's Tail" in Euskera) with its succession of villages, beautiful countryside and cave formations.

Elizondo

The "capital" of this most strongly Basque of Navarran valleys is **ELIZONDO**, seat of a joint municipality composed of fifteen villages. What's visible from the through road leaves a poor impression, but once away from it the town is full of typical Basque Pyrenean architecture, especially alongside the river with its bridge and weir. There are several places to **stay** in and around Elizondo while exploring the beautiful surrounding villages and countryside. One inexpensive option is *Casa Rural Jaén* (☎948 580 487; ②), with six rooms; the unlicensed rooms above the *Restaurante Eskisaroi*, c/Jaime Urrutia 40 (☎948 580 013; ②) make a good second choice. There are also two considerably more expensive places: the three-star *Hotel Baztán* (☎948 580 050, fax 948 452 323; ⑦) on the Pamplona road south of town, an incongruously modern pile complete with garden and pool, and in the town itself, *Hostal Saskaitz*, a mock-traditional structure quietly placed 200m east of the through road at c/María Azpilikueta 10 (☎948 580 488, fax 948 580 615; ⑥).

Restaurants are a bit more reasonable, with again a handful to choose from. In the same family for three generations, the *Txokoto* at c/Braulio Iriarte 25 (west end of the river bridge), has a cosy, water-view *comedor* and a good line in eminently reasonable seafood and meat, though it's closed Wednesday and can be booked out for private functions. The nearby *Eskisaroi* (address as above) can feed you with creative bean dishes, fish fillets, pear tart and assorted drinks (*a la carta* only) for just over 3000pta/€18; it's justly popular, with long waits for tables after 2.30pm. Finally, the *Galarza*, at the very northern town limits by the Río Baztan, is strong on seafood (3000ptas/€18 minimum), though there's also a *menú* (1500ptas/€9), or you could just have a drink under the trees outside.

Three **buses** run daily from both Pamplona and San Sebastián, but there is no public transport to the smaller villages beyond. Elizondo also lies astride the **GR11**, which heads west out of Auritze, then turns north along the border (about 10hr). It's worth getting a dawn start from Auritze and trying to polish off this stretch in a day, as there are no facilities in between. If you have to break the journey, **Puerto de Urkiaga** (912m), about halfway, offers water and the possibility of camping.

Arizkun, Erratzu and Amaiur-Maia

In nearby **ARIZKUN**, beside the minor road to the Izepegui pass on the French border (and beyond to Baïgorri), the seventeenth-century convent of Nuestra Señora de los Angeles flaunts its striking Baroque facade; just beyond the village, there's a typical example of a fortified house (very common in the valley) where Pedro de Ursua, the leader of the Marañones expedition up the Amazon in 1560 in search of El Dorado, was born. You can **stay** in Arizkun at the friendly and well-run *Pensión Etxeberría*, near the west edge of town at c/Txuputo 43 (☎948 453 013; ②), which also serves as a bar, grocery and reasonable if basic restaurant.

Some 4km northeast and the last Spanish village before France on this road, **ERRATZU** is another gem, with a few well-preserved **casas rurales**. *Casa Etxebeltzea* (☎948 453 157; ⑤) is a fourteenth-century seigneurial manor (thus the unusually high price) at the south edge of the medieval core, near a mechanic's. *Casa Kordoa* (☎948 453 222; ③) is also en-suite but more affordable; most economical but without en suite is *Casa Indatxipia* (☎948 453 121; ②).

AMAIUR-MAIA, 6km north of Arizkun but just off the N121, where the last unsuccessful battle to preserve the independence of Navarra took place, is another unspoilt village worth a stop. The gateway to its single street displays the village shield depicting a red bell – most houses still proudly emblazon their door lintels with this coat-of-arms. If you're taken with the place, there are several **casas rurales** here too, including the en-suite *Casa Goiz-Argi* (☎948 453 234; ③) and the *Casa Miguelenea* (☎948 453 224; ②), with pricier en-suite rooms.

Urdazubi and Zugarramurdi

Northwest of Amaiur-Maia, the N121 climbs over the **Puerto de Otxondo** at the top of the Valle de Baztán to the villages of Urdazubi and – reached by side road – Zugarramurdi, both potential stopovers between Pamplona and the French Basque coastal towns of Biarritz and Bayonne.

URDAZUBI (Urdax), ringed by hills and guarded by a tiny castle, has three *hostales* and *pensiones* (but no *casas rurales*); most upmarket and central **accommodation** is the *Hostal Irigoiena* (☎948 599 267, fax ☎948 599 243, *hoirigoienea@jet.es*; ⑥), in a renovated farmhouse. If your budget won't stretch to that, try the more modest *Pensión Beotxea* on the Zugarramurdi road (☎948 599 114; ③), with en-suite rooms, or there's a **campsite**, *Josenea* (☎948 599 011; open all year), out on the main highway. For **eating**, the *Bar Restaurante Indianoa-Baita* opposite the church has reasonable *menús*.

ZUGARRAMURDI, 4km southwest of the border, off the N121, is famous for its **Cueva de las Brujas** (allow 45 minutes for a walking visit) whose highlight is the giant natural arch through which the *regata de infierno* (Hell's stream) flows. The cavern was a major centre for witchcraft in the Middle Ages and consequently the area bore the brunt of persecution at the time of the Inquisition. Underneath the arch, *akelarres* or witches' sabbaths allegedly took place as recently as the seventeenth century; these seem to have survived, in a tame derivative, as the *zikiroyate* rite every August 18, which features a "love-feast" of roast meat held in the grotto. The appealing village makes a good base for excursions into surrounding countryside; one possibility is to walk 3km along the track beyond the caves into France to another set of caves, the **Grottes de Sare** (see p.491). The actual frontier divides the village of Dantxarinea/Dantxaria (the latter just inside France) – a fairly shabby place offering little other than cheap Spanish booze and petrol, best seen from your rear-view mirror.

Zugarramurdi has two **casas rurales** letting rooms short-term, heavily subscribed at weekends: *Casa Sueldeguía* (☎948 599 088; ③) and *Casa Teltxeguia* (☎948 599 167; ③), both in the village centre.

Through Labourd to the coast

Beyond Baïgorri, travelling along the Nive by road or train, you enter **Labourd** (Lapurdi), the westernmost of the three traditional French Basque regions which are now gathered into the *département* of Pyrénées-Atlantiques. The Basque farm- and town houses get even more sumptuous as you approach the coast, and the soft, rolling hills maintain their electric-green livery even in the summer.

The spa of **Cambo-les-Bains** is the biggest place between Saint-Jean-Pied-de-Port and Bayonne; here also, with your own vehicle, you can forsake the Bayonne-bound artery for the westerly D918, which passes through or near such tourist-friendly villages as **Ezpeleta** and **Ainhoa** on its way to Saint-Jean-de-Luz. A bus based in the latter town serves Espelette several times daily in summer.

Itsasu

The small, spread-out village of **ITSASU** (Itxassou), 11km northwest of Baïgorri in a bowl of wooded hills, makes a good introduction to the region, and a great place to hide away (though only one daily train stops here). A quintessentially Basque graveyard of ancient, keyhole-shaped tombstones surrounds the seventeenth-century **church of Saint Fructueux**, 1km south of the centre on the minor D349. Inside you'll find the typical French Basque three-tiered galleries, constructed to deny the Devil mischievous opportunities arising from the mingling of the sexes during Mass: the men sat upstairs, the women down in the nave. Another kilometre southeast along this road (or the rail line), the River Nive loops through a narrow defile at the **Pas-de-Roland**, yet another element in the Roland legend. Merely a hole in a roadside boulder, it's claimed to have been punched out by the hooves of the great knight's horse.

There are a fair number of reputable places to **stay** and **eat** in or around Itsasu. The most central are *Hôtel Arza Mendi* on place du Fronton (☎05.59.29.75.29; ③–④), with attractive, old-fashioned rooms in all sizes and shapes, as well as several variably priced *menus* and English-speaking management; the more formal *Hôtel du Fronton* across the way (☎05.59.29.75.10, fax 05.59.29.23.50; closed Jan 1–Feb 15 & Wed low season; ④), with an outdoor terrace for its excellent, reasonably priced *Restaurant Bonnet*; and the simpler *Hôtel Etchepare*, on the same square (☎05.59.29.75.14, fax 05.59.29.80.59; closed Nov–March; ③), with a decent restaurant. More remote choices include the *Hôtel du Chêne* (☎05.59.29.75.01, fax 05.59.29.27.39; closed Jan–Feb & Mon; ④) and *Hôtel-Restaurant Ondoria* (☎05.59.29.75.39; closed Nov 15–Dec 31 & Mon; ④), both on the road to the Pas de Roland and Laxia hamlet.

Cambo-les-Bains

Ten minutes downstream by train, the spa of **CAMBO-LES-BAINS** (Kambo) ranks as one of the largest towns in the Labourd region. An attractive mixture of town and country, with plentiful shops, bars and hotels encircled by richly rural landscape, it makes an appealing (if somewhat stuffy) place to break the journey. Long a magnet for sufferers of respiratory ailments, the thermal establishment here is the focal point of the ornate houses and hotels that radiate out along the heights above the Nive. The original town of **Bas Cambo**, typically Basque with its square, whitewashed houses and galleried church, lies down in the valley, right beside the river and train station.

The most famous resident was Edmond Rostand, author of *Cyrano de Bergerac*, who from 1903 to 1918 lived in the huge **Villa Arnaga**, a couple of kilometres west of Bas Cambo on the Bayonne road. Today the house is a museum (guided visits April–Sept daily 10am–12.30pm & 2.30–6.30pm; Oct 1–Nov 15 daily 2.30–6.30pm; Feb–March Sat & Sun only 2.30–6.30pm; 30F/€4.60), surrounded by a bizarre formal garden defined by topiary hedges and reflecting pools, with patches of lawn punctuated by blobs, cubes and cones of topiary hedges, and the boundaries lined by limes and blue cedars. Inside, it's very kitsch, with a minstrels' gallery, fake pilasters, allegorical frescoes, chandeliers, numerous portraits and various memorabilia.

The **tourist office** is in the Parc St-Joseph in the upper town centre (mid-July to Aug Mon–Sat 8.30am–noon & 2–6.30pm, Sun 10am–12.30pm; rest of year Mon–Sat till 5.30pm, closed Sun; ☎05.59.29.70.25, fax 05.59.29.90.77). For an overnight **stay**, try the *Auberge de Tante Ursule* in Bas Cambo by the pelota court (☎05.59.29.78.23, fax 05.59.29.28.57; ④; closed Feb 15–March 15 & Tues low season), virtually the only "non-*curiste*" establishment; its excellent **restaurant** offers rich-fare *menus* from 90F/€13.70. The nearest year-round **campsite** is *Ur-Hégia* on route des Sept-Chênes (☎05.59.29.72.03), also in Bas Cambo; *Camping Bixta Eder* is on the other side of town along av d'Espagne (☎05.59.29.94.23; April to mid-Oct).

Ezpeleta

From Cambo it's a five-kilometre trip southwest on the D918 (occasional buses) to **EZPELETA** (Espelette), a somewhat traffic-plagued village of wide-eaved houses, with a church notable for its heavy, square tower, carved doors and painted ceiling. Large red pimentos are the principal crop here, and in summer the streets are garlanded with strings of colourful peppers, hanging in the sun to dry; on the last Sunday in October a special Mass is preceded by a Saturday-night party celebrating the various Basque culinary uses of the pepper. Ezpeleta is primarily a market town, holding a regular Wednesday livestock and general market, and the major event of its social calendar is the annual January fair for trading **pottok** (pronounced *potiok*) ponies. An ancient, stocky breed of Paleolithic origin, apparently little changed from the horses depicted in prehistoric Pyrenean cave paintings, *pottoks* were once exported to work in British mines, but are now reared locally for both riding and meat.

The *Hôtel Euzkadi*, on the through road at the northeast edge of the village (☎05.59.93.91.88, fax 05.59.93.90.19; ⑤), with calmer rear rooms and tennis courts, also has what is reckoned among the best traditional **restaurants** in Labourd – reservations mandatory – and very reasonable for what you get, with three *menus* at 135–175F/€20.50–26.60 (closed Mon all year; Tues in low season; & Nov–Dec). The *Hôtel Chilar* (☎05.59.93.90.01, fax 05.59.93.93.25; ③–④), set back from the same road and thus quieter, has cheaper rooms but its restaurant can't compare.

West to Saint-Jean-de-Luz

The D918 curls west from Ezpeleta via Saint-Pée-sur-Nivelle (Senpere) en route to Saint-Jean, a 25-kilometre distance served occasionally by bus. You might, however, veer south along the D20 to Ainhoa, 8km from Espelette and just 3km shy of the frontier at Dantxaria.

Ainhoa – and the end of the GR10

Yet another showcase village in a region not lacking in them, **AINHOA** gets understandably busy in season, when tourists fill its single street lined with substantial, mainly seventeenth-century houses, whose lintel plaques offer mini-genealogies as well as foundation dates. Take a look at the bulky-towered church with its extravagant Baroque altarpiece of prophets and apostles in niches, framed by Corinthian columns.

Among places to **stay**, *Hôtel Irubea* (☎05.59.29.91.49; ②) has quaint, unheated rooms (there's no longer a *gîte*). For more comfort, try the two-star but still reasonable *Hôtel Oppoca* (☎05.59.29.90.72, fax 05.59.29.81.03; ④–⑤; closed Nov 15–Dec 15 & Mon in low season), with a good restaurant offering four *menus* (90–175F/€13.70–26.70), and the slightly neglected *Ohantzea* (☎05.59.29.90.50; ③–⑤), both on the main street. **Campers** should head for *Camping Harazpy* near the village centre (☎05.59.29.89.38; mid-June to mid-Sept). Alternatively, up on the frontier at otherwise dismal Dantxaria you'll find the small, shady, well-run *Camping Xokoan* (☎05.59.29.90.26, fax 05.59.29.73.82).

Just over the frontier from the campsite stand several little **ventas**, relics of pre-EU times when these rough-and-ready Spanish-run inns, essentially the retail outlets of smugglers, did a roaring trade in the many items – mainly alcohol and canned goods – which were far cheaper in Spain than in France. Today, with price parity approaching for many items, they face an uncertain future.

If you've hiked west six hours from Bidarraï on the **GR10**, Ainhoa is a logical stop. From here towards the Atlantic, the GR meanders over to Sara within three-and-a-half hours, next brings you to the base of La Rhune (see p.491 for both) and finally reaches civilization again at Biriatu, an impossible walking day of nearly eleven hours. Thus it's best to halt six hours from Ainhoa at the isolated *gîte d'étape* at **Olhette** hamlet, *Manttu*

BASQUE SPORTS

The Basque sport of **pelota** (*pelote* in France) is played – and keenly wagered on – all over Spanish Euskadi and the French Pays Basque. Even the smallest village has a *frontón* or *trinquet* (court), and indeed these are found well east into Aragón and Béarn where the sport has also caught on. Over twenty different versions of the game are known throughout the Basque country, including the most famous and spectacular, *cesta punta*, played in a covered court called *jaï alaï* (now widely confused with the name of the game itself). In essence it resembles a high-risk version of squash, the players smashing the ball against the *frontón* either with bare hands or encased in the merest of leather gloves (the *pasaka*), and with a wooden bat (*pala*) or a *chistera*, a narrow wicker-work "claw" that extends the player's forearm. The largest *chisteras* launch the ball at speeds of around 200km an hour, making *pelota* one of the most dangerous games in the world. The *pelotas* themselves are balls of fibre wound tightly around a rubber core, encased in two layers of leather; tedious to make, they are phenomenally expensive and sensitive to extremes of temperature and humidity.

Other unique Basque sports include *palankaris* (tossing an iron bar), *aizkolaritza* (log-chopping), *harri-jasotzea* (stone-lifting), *soka-tira* (tug-of-war) and *segalaritza* (grass-cutting). The finest exponents of the first three are popular local, sometimes international, heroes. The world champion stone-lifter Iñaki Perurena's visit to Japan resulted in the sport being introduced there – he remains the only lifter to surpass the legendary 315-kilo barrier. All form an important part of the many local *fiestas*.

Baïta (☎05.59.54.00.98; ③). Only purists do the final, urbanized stretch through to Hendaye; for detailed reverse walking directions to La Rhune, see p.491.

THE BASQUE COAST

For a region with such a long maritime tradition, the **Basque coast** – *Côte Basque* in French, *Costa Vasca* in Castilian – is surprisingly short and devoid of good natural harbours. It's scarcely more than 120km from the mouth of the River Adour, separating Bayonne and Biarritz from the dunes of the Landes to the north, to the Cantabrian border just past Bilbao in the west. Of that only about 50km – between Bayonne and San Sebastián – can be considered to be Pyrenean shoreline, and only at the mouths of the rivers Nivelle, Bidasoa and Oyarzun is there evidence of past Basque prowess in whaling, navigating and piracy.

The all-enveloping carpet of green vegetation, so unlike the Mediterranean coast, bespeaks a damp, often misty climate, without sharp differences between winter and summer temperature. Yet the sun does shine, just enough in season to attract hordes of holiday-makers, and if you've been up in the hills for any length of time, the sea comes as a very welcome sight. Unfortunately it is often just for looking: frequently dangerous and wave-lashed – to the delight of wet-suited surfers, and the steady employment of lifeguards – and sometimes murky.

This last detail is regrettable, since otherwise the Basque coast has all the ingredients for a perfect vacation: excellent food and drink, seductive scenery, characterful architecture and a handful of not-too-demanding inland side-trips to **Azkaine**, **La Rhune** and **Sara**. The two defining cities of **Bayonne** and **San Sebastián** are the biggest attractions, though the small ports of **Pasaia** and **Saint-Jean-de-Luz**, the historic border town of **Hondarribia** and the period-piece resort of **Biarritz** also have considerable appeal. Once you've sampled the best of the coast, it's possible to return to inland Navarra by the valley of the **Río Bidasoa**, with a trio of handsome villages in its lower reaches.

Bayonne

Although contiguous with the fashionable resort of Biarritz (see p.483), the inland position of **BAYONNE** (Baïona) protected it until the mid-1990s from significant touristic exploitation – which for many makes it a more interesting place to visit. Built astride the confluence of the rivers Adour (navigable) and Nive (less so), 6km from the sea and roughly 60km down the Nive from Saint-Jean, the city has long served as an important commercial port, its future guaranteed by some determined engineering works four hundred years ago to fix the wandering mouth of the Adour. Bayonne is both a Gascon city and the capital of the Pays Basque, but the tall white houses, their shutters and beams picked out in the distinctive brownish-reds and greens of the Basques, betray the major influence.

The place was founded by the Romans as the garrison town of Lapurdum. The name, corrupted to Lapurdi (Euskera) and Labourd (French), was later extended to signify the

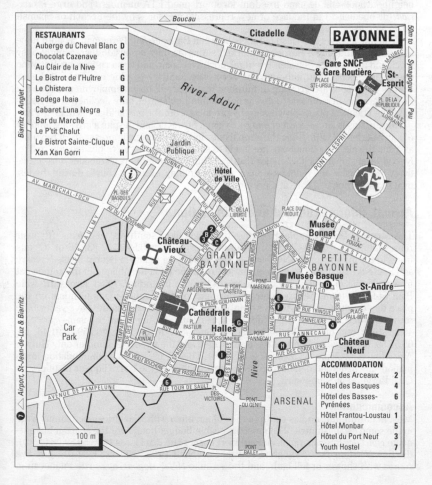

RESTAURANTS

Auberge du Cheval Blanc	D
Chocolat Cazenave	C
Au Clair de la Nive	E
Le Bistrot de l'Huître	G
Le Chistera	B
Bodega Ibaia	K
Cabaret Luna Negra	J
Bar du Marché	I
Le P'tit Chalut	F
Le Bistrot Sainte-Cluque	A
Xan Xan Gorri	H

ACCOMMODATION

Hôtel des Arceaux	2
Hôtel des Basques	4
Hôtel des Basses-Pyrénées	6
Hôtel Frantou-Loustau	1
Hôtel Monbar	5
Hôtel du Port Neuf	3
Youth Hostel	7

entire westernmost French Basque province; the current Euskera-derived name – Bayonne/Baïona – means "good river". For three centuries until 1451, it enjoyed prosperity and relative peace under English domination, until falling to the French in the course of the Hundred Years' War. Some fifty years later, Sephardic Jews fleeing the Iberian Inquisitions arrived, bringing their knowledge of chocolate manufacturing. The city's heyday came during the eighteenth century, based on the dubious underpinnings of armaments manufacture (the word bayonet derives from the place) and a judicious amount of piracy. After the French Revolution, it lost considerable prestige when centralizing zealots in the Parisian regime merged the three traditional French Basque regions into the single modern *département* of Pyrénées-Atlantiques, governed from Pau.

Just as Perpignan became a refuge for Catalans who opposed Franco, so did Bayonne for the Spanish Basques, seeking refuge among their own. For decades the Petit Bayonne quarter was a haven for extreme Basque nationalist practitioners (that is, ETA fugitives), until a late 1980s clampdown by Parisian authorities. Wall posters in the neighbourhood still demand freedom for imprisoned ETA members and urge *insumisoa* (disobedience) in the face of new repressive measures by the French or Spanish governments.

Economically there are also parallels between Bayonne and Perpignan, as both hope to gain from the single European market, sitting as they do beside increasingly busy truck and train routes between Portugal, northern Spain and western Europe. Bayonne needs the business, for although the aerospace industry is a big employer and electronics companies are growing in number, this area still has unemployment above the French average. Traditional footwear and clothing industries have declined severely, as have the chemical plants processing by-products from the gas field at Lacq, near Pau.

None of this is likely to affect you as a visitor, however, and despite a growing amount of tourist-oriented tattiness in the shop fronts, initial favourable impressions of Bayonne as a small-scale, easy-going city are likely to stick. Wherever you're headed you're likely to at least stop in, as it's a major transport hub; you might even consider it as a relatively inexpensive and quiet base for a seaside holiday, except of course during the festival season when beds are at a premium.

Arrival, information and accommodation

The **airport**, Biarritz-Anglet-Bayonne/BAB, lies 6km southwest at Parme (Ryanair reservations on ☎05.59.43.83.93; general airport info ☎05.59.43.83.83; #6 or 'C' bus from/to town). The **gare SNCF** and **gare routière** for points in Béarn, Basse-Navarre and Soule are next door to each other, just off place de la République in the somewhat frowzy district of Saint-Esprit on the north bank of the Adour, 700m across the wide Pont St-Esprit from the city centre. There is, however, another bus terminal on the place des Basques on the Adour's south bank, for destinations in the Nive valley. The **tourist office** is also in place des Basques (July & Aug Mon–Sat 9am–7pm, Sun 10am–1pm; rest of year Mon–Fri 9am–6.30pm, Sat 10am–6pm; ☎05.59.46.01.46, fax 05.59.59.37.55), with a booth at the train station and the airport in summer only (July & Aug Mon–Sat 9.30am–12.30pm & 2–6.30pm). They're useful for accommodation information, city plans and details of guided tours, such as to the Izarra liqueur distillery on Quai Bergeret in Saint-Esprit.

Accommodation

Most **accommodation** lies south of the Adour, often with wide price fluctuations within the same establishment. The most agreeable budget hotels are the spartan but adequate *Hôtel des Basques*, on place Paul-Bert corner rue des Lisses (☎05.59.59.08.02; ②), the tiny *Hôtel du Port Neuf* at 44 rue du Port-Neuf (☎05.59.25.65.83; ③–④), just five rooms with shower or full bath, and the en-suite *Hôtel Monbar*, at 24 rue Pannecau in

Petit Bayonne (☎05.59.59.26.80; ③). The *Hôtel des Arceaux*, below the cathedral at 26 rue Port-Neuf (☎05.59.59.15.53; ②–③), is a distinct fourth choice, loathed by some readers for its saggy beds and paper-thin walls. More comfortable alternatives include the quiet *Hôtel des Basses-Pyrénées* at 14 rue Tour-de-Sault (☎05.59.59.00.29, fax 05.59.59.42.02; ③–⑤; closed Dec 15–Jan 15), a well-converted medieval building with (uniquely in Bayonne) nearby street parking just possible, or the top-end, river-view *Hôtel Frantou-Loustau*, on place de la République (☎05.59.55.08.08, fax 05.59.55.69.36; ⑥), overlooking the river beside Pont St-Esprit; both have more affordable attached restaurants (*menus* from under 100F/€15.20).

Another possibility is the HI **youth hostel** at 19 rte des Vignes in Anglet (see p.487), between Bayonne and Biarritz; take the STAB bus #4 from the Hôtel de Ville, direction "Biarritz-Mairie", which stops right outside. The only **campsite** nearby is relatively luxurious *La Chêneraie* (☎05.59.55.01.31; Easter–Sept), off the N117 Pau road close to the Bayonne-Nord exit from the autoroute, and also on the #4 bus route; take direction "Sainsontan" and get off at Navarre, from where the campsite is a 500-metre walk. Otherwise, try one of the sites at Anglet or Biarritz.

The City

Bayonne is more a wandering town than one offering great sights, but it does have a handful of diversions scattered throughout the three central quarters. You'll spend most of your time south of the Adour, in the quarters of **Grand Bayonne** (in turn on the west bank of the Nive tributary) or **Petit Bayonne** (on the east bank), both still encircled by Vauban's defences. The less monumentally compelling neighbourhood of **Saint-Esprit** spreads out on the Adour's north bank, long home to immigrants of every description.

Grand Bayonne

The twin-towered **Cathédrale Sainte-Marie** (Mon–Sat 10–11.45am & 3–5.45pm, Sun 3.30–5.45pm) on magnolia-shaded place Pasteur at the summit of **Grand Bayonne**, looks best from a distance, with its steeple rising with airy grace above the houses. Up close, the yellowish stone reveals bad weathering, with most of the decorative detail lost to post-Revolutionary vandalism as well. The interior is more impressive, thanks to the height of the nave and some sixteenth-century glass set off by the prevailing gloom. Like other southern French Gothic cathedrals of the period (about 1260) it was based on more famous northern models, in this case Soissons and Reims. On the south side is a fourteenth-century **cloister** (Mon–Sat 9am–5/6pm; 14F/€2.10) with a lawn, cypress trees and beds of begonias: a quiet, secretive spot affording a rather flattering view of the church.

From place Pasteur, rue de la Monnaie and its continuation, rue du Port-Neuf, lead downhill to the main **place de la Liberté**, where you'll find the much-frequented *Café du Théâtre*. The square is flanked by *pâtisseries* and *confiseries* exuding a strong aroma of chocolate, a Bayonne speciality on a par with its famous air-cured hams. Most of it is still made in the Saint-Esprit quarter, but the prestigious retail outlets are Cazenave and Darenatz, arcade shops at nos. 19 and 15 respectively in **rue du Port-Neuf**. South and west of the cathedral, along rue des Faures and the streets above the old walls, or **rue d'Espagne**, the old commercial centre, there's a distinctly Spanish feel, with washing strung at the windows and strains of music drifting from dark interiors.

The Nive Quais and Petit Bayonne

East of the cathedral, the **Nive Quais** are a lively, picturesque and authentic part of town; the *halles* on the Grand Bayonne side host a comprehensive market on Tuesdays, Wednesdays and Saturdays. On the right bank, tall, sixteenth-century houses are reflected appealingly in the placid Nive; one of these, near the end of Pont Marengo, used to contain the excellent Basque ethnographic museum, the **Musée Basque**. When it reopens after "restoration" (really a long-running, arcane political dispute), now scheduled for 2001, the exhibits will probably still illustrate Basque life through the centuries, and include reconstructed farm buildings, house interiors, implements, tools and *makhilak* – innocent-looking walking sticks, often elaborately carved from medlar wood, but with a concealed steel spear tip at one end, used by pilgrims and shepherds for self-protection. There should also be a section on Basque seafaring (Columbus' skipper was Basque, and another Basque, Sebastian de Caro, commanded the first circumnavigation of the world in 1519–22), as well as a wing on the history and stars of *pelota*.

The painting collection of Bayonne's second museum, the **Musée Bonnat** at 5 rue Jacques-Lafitte (Mon, Wed, Thurs, Sat & Sun 10am–noon & 2.30–6.30pm, Fri pm until 8.30pm; 30F/€4.60), plus an annexe at 9 rue Fredéric-Bastiat, provides welcome variation from the usual dross of provincial galleries. Thirteenth- and fourteenth-century Italian art is well represented, as are most periods up to (but not including) Impressionism; highlights include Goya's *Self-Portrait* and *Portrait of Don Francisco de Borja*, Rubens' powerful *Apollo and Daphne* and *The Triumph of Venus*, plus works by Murrillo, El Greco and Ingres. A whole gallery is devoted to high-society portraits by Léon Bonnat (1833–1922), whose personal collection formed the original core of the museum. There are also frequent temporary exhibits of the work of prominent artists, well worth catching.

North of the river: Saint-Esprit

Apart from savouring the wide river skies, there is little reason to venture onto the north bank of the Adour. A deliberately inconspicuous, nineteenth-century **synagogue** at 35 rue Maubec serves as a reminder that Bayonne's Jewish community first settled here in France on arrival from Spain and Portugal during the sixteenth century. Saint-Esprit in effect became their ghetto, since Grand Bayonne was consecrated to the Virgin and off-limits for residence by nonbelievers. The **church of St-Esprit**, opposite the train station, is all that remains of a hostel that once ministered to the sore feet and other ailments of pilgrims on the Chemin de Saint-Jacques – worth a peek inside for an interesting wood sculpture of *The Flight into Egypt*. Just above the station is Vauban's massive **citadelle**; built in 1680 to defend the town against Spanish attack, it actually saw little action until the Napoleonic wars, when its garrison resisted a siege by Wellington for four months in 1813. Don't miss the **Jardin Botanique** inside the castle walls, with its beautiful garden and huge collection of plants labelled in French, Basque and Latin (daily April 15–Oct 15 9am–noon & 2–6 pm; free).

Eating, drinking and entertainment

The best area for **eating and drinking** is along the right-bank (Petit Bayonne) quay of the Nive and in the back streets to either side of the river. Besides the listings below, you'll find other possibilities of varying quality in Petit Bayonne, especially along rue Pannecau, rue des Cordeliers and rue des Tonneliers. For non-European food such as South American, Indian, Tunisian, Chinese – try rue d'Espagne and rue Gosse in Grand Bayonne, or rue Sainte-Catherine in Saint Esprit.

As far as **festivals** go, Bayonne's biggest bash of the year is the *Fêtes de Bayonne*, which starts on the first Wednesday in August and consists of five days and nights of continuous, boozy street parties and entertainment. This finishes with a *corrida* on the following Sunday, and there are three or four more days of bullfighting beginning on August 15. The *Jazz aux Remparts* festival held in mid-July (typically five days of the third week, running from the previous Saturday) has run consistently since 1990, and every October there is a Franco-Spanish theatre festival.

Besides *pelota*, **rugby** is the sport that commands the greatest loyalty in Bayonne, and the town's top-class rugby team has produced many members of the national squad. You might catch a view of them in action by following the Vauban fortifications to the Parc des Sports south of Grand Bayonne, where the solid walls act as grandstands.

Restaurants

Auberge du Cheval Blanc, 68 rue Bourgneuf, Petit Bayonne. Decadent desserts a speciality at this durable gourmets' mecca (it's had Michelin stars in the past); for all that, affordable 125F/€19 weekday lunch menus, though you can easily spend 300F/€45.80. Closed Mon in winter, Sun eve always, one week (variable) in Aug. Book on ☎05.59.59.01.33.

Le Chistera, 42 rue Port-Neuf. *Pelota* decor, as you'd expect with the proprietor, a player in his own right, being the son of a *cesta-punta* champion and trainer. Hearty *bayonnais* specialties based on fish, pork and tripe best ordered off the daily-specials board; count on 85F/€13 *menu* or 100–120F/€15.30–18.30 *à la carte*. Closed random weeks in Feb & May.

Au Clair de la Nive, 28 quai Galuperie, Petit Bayonne. Indoor or outdoor seating on a riverside terrace; 98F/€15 menu, or more interestingly choose two or three courses *à la carte* (120–190F/€18.30–29, pricey drink extra). *Cuisine* – roast anchovies, steamed cod in pepper sauce, delicate desserts – is *minceur* but tasty. Closed Mon noon & Sun.

Le Bistrot de l'Huître, corner of *halles* building, facing Pont Pannecau. Oysters and only oysters, washed down with Jurançon or Irouléguy wine.

Le P'tit Chalut, 24 quai Galuperie. Not as upmarket as its neighbour across the street, but a decent venue for seafood under the arcades; two lunch menus for under 100F/€15.30.

Le Bistrot Ste Cluque, 9 rue Hughes, St-Esprit. The one culinary bright spot across the Adour, and a popular gay hangout. Both indoors and terrace perennially packed for the sake of excellent value, generic French cuisine with a *menu* (70F/€10.70), and *à la carte* (100F/€15.30). Open daily; reservations mandatory on ☎05.59.55.82.43.

Bars and cafés

Cabaret Luna Negra, 7 rue des Augustins. More venue than bar, really, with musical events, cabaret, mime, theatre. Open Thurs–Sat pm only.

Chocolat Cazenave, 19 rue du Port-Neuf. Drink a hot cup of local cocoa under the arcades here; also every conceivable chocolate goodie to take home.

Bodega Ibaia, 49 quai Jauréguiberry. Lively, well-loved bar, reputedly Bayonne's favourite, with a mixed crowd and *plats du jour* for under 50F/€7.60 at midday.

Bar du Marché, 39 rue des Basques. This begins purveying food and drink at 5am to a mix of market sellers and bar-flies on their way home to bed, continuing with economical *plats du jour* at lunchtime. Closed Sat pm & Sun.

Xan Xan Gorri, 9 rue des Cordeliers, Petit Bayonne. Long-running, friendly and popular wine bar, serving *tapas* style food in the evenings; open until 2am.

Biarritz

BIARRITZ (Miarritze), 8km west of Bayonne, makes no secret of its identity as an Atlantic answer to Monte Carlo, and thus a resort that expects a little refinement from its guests. Much of this hotch-potch of giant ocean-liner-style hotels and mock-Gothic châteaux wears a bygone air that appeals to more traditional middle-class visitors, while the town's newer neighbourhoods attract a younger, variably prosperous market.

Biarritz burst into prominence during the mid-nineteenth century when the Spanish-born Empress Eugénie, wife of Napoléon III – whom she met here – brought the entire entourage of the Second Empire to what had been the favourite seaside watering-hole of her childhood. Others soon followed, including Edward VII, who virtually held a second court here, nominating Asquith as prime minister in Biarritz in 1908. After World War I had destroyed the existing European social order, high fashion moguls like

Hermès and Lanvin, film stars like Douglas Fairbanks and Gloria Swanson and various other glitterati replaced the crowned heads and nobility.

Following the next global convulsion, and the rise of the Côte d'Azur during the 1960s, Biarritz went into seemingly terminal decline not unlike that of certain resorts on England's Kent or Devon coast. But since the late 1980s, events have conspired to divert the place from crash-landing on the dust-heap of touristic history. Initially the recovery was slow, spurred by the town's embrace of less elitist pursuits like golf, conferences and even a small cinema festival – but the biggest shot in the arm was Biarritz's transformation into **Europe's biggest surfing mecca**. That all began in 1957, when American screenwriter Pieter Viertel, here for the filming of *The Sun Also Rises*, took to the waves with a board and inspired a group of locals to join him. You still can see many of these white-haired old-timers – *Les Tontons Surfeurs* or "Surf Uncles" as they call themselves – bobbing in the waves with kids their grandsons' age. This international surf-bum fraternity, and more sedentary Parisian yuppies, together fuel a

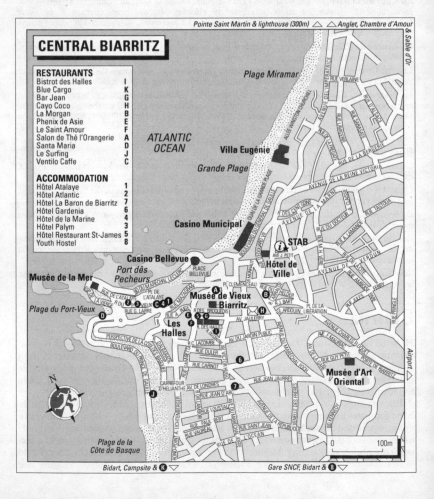

CENTRAL BIARRITZ

RESTAURANTS

Bistrot des Halles	I
Blue Cargo	K
Bar Jean	G
Cayo Coco	H
La Morgan	B
Phenix de Asie	E
Le Saint Amour	F
Salon de Thé l'Orangerie	A
Santa Maria	D
Le Surfing	J
Ventilo Caffe	C

ACCOMMODATION

Hôtel Atalaye	1
Hôtel Atlantic	2
Hôtel La Baron de Biarritz	7
Hôtel Gardenia	6
Hôtel de la Marine	4
Hôtel Palym	3
Hôtel Restaurant St-James	5
Youth Hostel	8

respectable nightlife, existing fairly harmoniously with a population that's one-third retirees. Against all the odds, Biarritz is undeniably chic and trendy once more, new money (or no money) rubbing shoulders with old, and without any Côte d'Azur pretensions.

The Town

Most specific attractions are strung out along the landscaped, clifftop terraces just inland from the promontories and coves around which Biarritz grew. The focus of town is the Art Deco **Casino Municipal**, just behind the Grande Plage, now restored as an exhibit and conference venue. The nearby Bellevue Casino survives as a gambling palace, though its ground-floor slot machines see far more action than the paltry few gaming tables upstairs. Inland, the town forms a suprisingly ordinary and workaday sprawl, with the sole points of interest being the newish **Musée d'Art Oriental** on 1 rue Guy-Petit (Tues 10.30am–7pm, Wed–Fri 10.30am–1pm & 2.30–7/8pm, Sat 10.30am–1pm & 2.30–10/11pm, Sun 2.30–7/8pm; 45F/€6.90), exhibiting the collection of Indian and Tibetan art specialist Michel Postel, and the **Musée du Vieux Biarritz**, installed in a disused Anglican church on rue Broquedis (Tues–Sat 10am–noon & 2.30–6pm; 15F/€2.30), displaying knick-knacks and documents relating to Belle Époque royalty.

Like several spots on the coast hereabouts, Biarritz started life as a whaling centre, a local industry which collapsed late in the eighteenth century, and whose only remnants are a whale-spotting tower near place de l'Atalaye and some memorabilia in the **Musée de la Mer** (daily: July–Aug 9.30am–midnight; rest of year 9.30am–12.30pm & 2–6pm; 45F/€6.90), which sits atop the claw-shaped promontory west of town. Along with exhibitions on local fishing and wildlife, this offers a small aquarium and seal-frolicking section as well, making it – if not exactly a must – at least a good place to take the kids. The promotory ends in the **Rocher de la Vierge**, an offshore rock adorned with a white statue of the Virgin, and linked to the mainland by an iron catwalk built by Eiffel, he of the tower. Around it are scattered other rocky islets where the swell heaves and combs; the scenery figured largely in Eric Rohmer's wonderful film *Le Rayon Vert*. This spot also seems irresistible to lovers, for the seaward view is always obscured by pairs of backs and interlocking arms apparently in thrall to the ocean. Just below is the picturesque **Port des Pêcheurs**, easiest approached by pedestrian lanes zigzagging down through banks of pink and blue hydrangeas. The professional fishermen have now gone, replaced by pleasure boats, but there's a scuba outfitter here and a clutch of pricey seafood restaurants.

The only inland **streets and squares** really conducive to relaxed strolling are those between the Musée de la Mer and the Place Sainte-Eugénie. Both that square and the place de l'Atalaye, high above the Port des Pêcheurs, can muster a number of whimsically **turreted and balconied hotels and villas**. In recent years, any number of these have fallen to the wrecker's ball, but in 1997, under threat of a fifty-acre development proposed to replace the Casino Municipal by Gaullist councillors, the rest of the council resigned, forcing the resignation of the mayor. He was replaced by a centrist acceptable to conservationists, who immediately slapped a preservation order on the town's surviving 230 follies, not coincidentally guaranteeing work for restoration architects and maintenance men for the next generation.

Downhill and south from place Atalaye, you can stroll the length of the characterful if now touristified **rue du Port-Vieux**, which links its namesake beach (see below) with rue Mazagran. At the junction of the latter with the far west end of **place Clemenceau**, one of several central squares, you can nibble a cake or sip a lemon tea at *Miremont's Salon de Thé* – a prissy and frightfully superior place epitomizing old-money Biarritz.

The beaches

The wave-pounded **beaches** either side of the promontory are generously sandy and, according to the fickle weather, either carpeted with a mix of beautiful people and middle-class families tanning themselves cheek by jowl, or abandoned to wet-suited surf fanatics of all descriptions. Served by STAB buses #4, #6 or #9 from Biarritz centre, the strands extend about 5km from the southernmost **Plage de la Milady to Pointe Saint-Martin** in the north. The southerly sections, set apart from one another by smaller headlands, are **Plage Marbella; Côte des Basques**, focus of the annual surf championships; and **Plage du Port-Vieux**, the most sheltered and intimate of the beaches, tucked in the lee of the Rocher de la Vièrge.

But most of the action takes place along the contiguous Grande Plage and Plage Miramar, sweeping northeast from the Port des Pêcheurs. An immaculate sweep of sand, the **Grande Plage** was originally dubbed the "Plage des Fous" after the 1850s practice of taking lunatics to bathe here as a primitive form of thalassotherapy. Picasso later used it as the setting for his *Les Baigneuses*; today it's a highly regimented playground, with separate sections for surfers and bathers, and lifeguards tooting their whistles or paddling out into the water to shoo people out of several danger zones. The **Plage Miramar** just beyond is shadowed by the domes of a Russian Orthodox church dating from 1908, and also overlooked by the former **Villa Eugénie**, a present of Napoléon III to his wife in 1855. Now the luxury *Hôtel du Palais*, it was gutted by fire in 1881 and 1905, so that little remains of the original fabric. Beyond Pointe Saint-Martin and its landmark **lighthouse** (April 15–June Sat–Sun 3–7pm; July–Aug Tues–Sat 10am–noon & 2–7m; 10F/€1.50), built in 1834, begin the even wilder, broader beaches of Anglet (see below).

Practicalities

The **tourist office** abuts the place d'Ixelles (daily: July & Aug 8am–8pm; rest of year 9am–6.45pm; ☎05.59.22.37.10, fax 05.59.24.14.19), in the vicinity of the casino and the *Mairie*. This has information in particular about the various festivals, and Internet access at 50F/€7.60hr. The **gare SNCF** (☎05.59.23.15.69) lies an inconvenient 3km southeast at the end of av Foch/av Kennedy in the *quartier* known as La Négresse (STAB bus #2 or #9 from the central stops). Any other STAB **buses** from Bayonne and Anglet, as well as ATCRB buses from Hendaye and Saint-Jean-de-Luz, also stop near the tourist office and the *mairie*.

Accommodation

Contrary to expectations, there are a handful of affordable **hotels** in town, though obviously for July or August advance reservations are mandatory. **Campers** should try *Biarritz-Camping*, at 28 route d'Harcet, the inland continuation of av de la Plage (☎05.59.23.00.12, fax 05.59.43.74.67; May–Sept), behind Plage de la Milady, to the south of town. The nearest HI **youth hostel** is the 1999-opened one (☎05.59.41.76.00) 2km southwest of the centre on the shore of Lac Mouriscot, just walkable from the *gare SNCF*; otherwise get #2 bus from the centre and look out for the "Bois de Boulogne" stop.

Hôtel Atalaye, 6 rue des Goélands (☎05.59.24.06.76, fax 05.59.22.33.51). Better value perhaps and quieter than its nearby rival on rue Port–Vieux with some parking available on the nearby square, though the management could be jollier. ④.

Hôtel Atlantic, 10 rue du Port-Vieux (☎05.59.24.34.08). Probably overrated as a two-star, but you won't get any closer to the sea at this price, has its own ground-floor bar-restaurant. ④.

Hôtel Le Baron de Biarritz, 13 av Maréchal-Joffre (☎05.59.22.08.22, fax 05.59.22.14.65). Vietnamese-family-run outfit, with gracious service and all rooms with at least a shower. Attached to a Chinese-Vietnamese restaurant which can get lively at weekends with seemingly the entire Vietnamese population of this coast. ④.

Hôtel Gardenia, 19 av Carnot (☎05.59.24.10.46; fax 05.59.2.41.31). Mix of rooms, some with toilet down the hall, being renovated one by one in this old-fashioned but well-cared-for two-star. Closed mid-Nov & mid Jan. ④.

Hôtel de la Marine, corner rue des Goélands and rue du Port-Vieux (☎05.59.24.34.09). Friendly and clean with en-suite rooms; functions as a backpackers' and surfers' cheapie. ③.

Hôtel Palym, 7 rue du Port-Vieux (☎05.59.24.16.56, fax 05.59.24.96.12). Welcoming and offers a variety of rooms, with not a right angle remaining in the building, and the hot water sometimes exhausted on summer evenings; with a ground-floor bar-restaurant. ③.

Hôtel Restaurant St-James, 15 rue Gambetta (☎05.59.24.06.36, fax 05.59.24.87.35). Dead central if potentially noisy, well appointed and under new management as of 2000. ⑤.

Eating and drinking

Finding a reasonable place to **eat** is trickier, but there are some possibilities near the market *halles*, and it's easy to eat well for a price, away from the touristy snack bars on rue du Port-Vieux – and for once in France, until 11pm or so.

Bistrot des Halles, 1 rue du Centre (reservations essential on ☎05.59.24.21.22). Within sight of the *halles*, this is strong on generously portioned, tasty fish dishes, but count on 200F/€30.50 a head plus service, and a stiffly priced wine list.

Blue Cargo,(reservations on ☎05.59.23.54.87). With transport, there's currently no hotter spot, just south of the city limits on the Plage d'Ilbarritz. Here the *beau monde* downs mostly fish and salads on the terrace by an old villa, while the lower tent-bar gets going as a jampacked dance club after midnight. Count on 170F/€26 à la carte, plus drink.

Cayo Coco, 5 rue Jaulerry. Cuban theme bar with free salsa dance lessons.

Bar Jean, 5 rue des Halles. A bullfighting-theme *tapas* spot with dishes 50–60F/€7.60–9.20.

Le Morgan, 4 rue du Helder. A late-night clubbers' repair (open 7pm–dawn), though the cheaper *menus* of plain food are only available until 10pm.

Phenix de Asie, Tiny, decent Chinese hole-in-the-wall, serving continuously and the only spot open for a proper lunch if you've just arrived on the 3pm Ryanair flight.

Le Saint Amour, 26 rue Gambetta. Facing the market, a *lyonnais*-style bistro with a sausage-strong *menu* at 75F/€11.50.

Salon de Thé L'Orangerie, 1 rue Gambetta. Whether you've slept the night before or not, this makes the best start for the day, serving all sorts of hot drinks and a great variety of breakfasts.

Santa Maria, You can tipple from the afternoon into the small hours at this little beach bar over-looking the Plage du Port-Vieux.

Le Surfing, A pilgrimage-site for surfers, behind Plage de Côte des Basques, and run by Robert Rabagny, organizer of the annual Surf Festival. As much shrine-museum, festooned with antique boards, as purveyor of grills and *frites*.

Ventilo Caffe, rue du Port-Vieux. The haunt of Parisian thirtysomethings.

Anglet

Sprawling north and east from Biarritz, amorphous **ANGLET** (pronounced *Anglett*, Angelu in Euskera) occupies most of the triangular territory between the Pointe Saint-Martin, the mouth of the Adour and Bayonne. There is nothing here of note except half a dozen excellent beaches – the most famous being **Chambre d'Amour**, so named after two lovers who were trapped and drowned in their trysting place by the rising tide, and the surfers' mecca of **Sables d'Or**, with boards for rent. As the pair's fate indicates, swimming here is generally dangerous owing to treacherous currents and you should heed the warning signs and lifeguards.

You can catch a #6 or #9 bus here from the central stops in Biarritz, or walk the dis-tance in about thirty minutes, along av de l'Impératrice, av MacCroskey, then second left down to the seaside bd des Plages. Anglet is a good place to stay if you're hostelling, with a spacious, friendly and well-run **youth hostel** in quartier Chiberta at the north end of route des Vignes (☎05.59.58.70.00; ①), which offers a full programme of sporting activities – including, of course, surfing. There is also a **campsite**, the *Camping de la Chambre d'Amour* on route de Bouney (☎05.59.03.71.66; May–Sept), 600m inland from the Plage de l'Océan. For **eating and drinking**, the most notable seaside establishments are the *Havana Café* at Chambre d'Amour, a permanently crowded bar that does *plats du jour* at lunch for under 50F/€7.60, and the nearby *Café Bleu*, more of a proper eatery with a *menu* for 85F/€13. Inland, choose between old warhorse *Udala* at 165 av de l'Adour, for traditional Basque seafood (100F/€15.30 *menu*, 140F/€21.40 à la carte), or relative newcomer *La Fleur de Sel* (closed Sun pm & Wed), 5 av de la Forêt in the Chiberta pine forest, more *nouvelle* but already popular (90F/€13.70 weekday lunch *menu*, 148F/€22.60 otherwise).

Saint-Jean-de-Luz and around

Just fifteen minutes and 20km south of Biarritz by one of the many fast trains, **SAINT-JEAN-DE-LUZ** (Donibane Loitzun – "Saint John of the Marshes" – in Euskera) rates as one of the most popular, though still attractive resorts on the Basque coast, its broad beach staked with striped beach tents all summer long. Saint-Jean has been an active fishing port for centuries, whose tuna, sardine and anchovy catches still find their way onto the menus of countless restaurants around town.

Previously the fishermen were mainly preoccupied with whales and cod; local sailors travelled as far as Newfoundland, which the Basques claim to have discovered one hundred years before Columbus reached America. In the seventeenth century, Dutch and English whalers drove them from their habitual ports in Arctic waters, so the enterprising Basques devised a method of boiling down the blubber on board, enabling the ships – essentially the first factory whalers – to stay at sea much longer. Later, by the provisions of the eighteenth-century Treaty of Utrecht, the local skippers lost their cod-fishing grounds off Newfoundland and only saved themselves from ruin by becoming pirates. The more respectable pursuit of anchovies, tuna and sardines only resumed in the nineteenth century.

The Town

Wrecked by a fire set by invading Spanish in 1558, Saint-Jean has since developed into a solid and pleasant place, its seafaring wealth transmuted into the seventeenth- and eighteenth-century homes of the merchants and shipowners. Apart from wandering the partly pedestrianized streets of the old quarter, you can visit one of these homes, the so-called **Maison Louis XIV** (guided visits Mon–Sat: June–Sept 10.30am–noon & 2.30–5.30pm; July–Aug 10.30am–noon & 2.30–6.30pm; 30F/€4.60). Today beside the Hôtel de Ville, it was actually built for the shipowning Lohobiague family in 1635 but became the temporary residence of the Sun King in 1660 when he came to Saint-Jean for his marriage of political convenience to Maria-Teresa, the Infanta of Castile. (Oddly perhaps, the couple managed to fall in love, and the widowed king years later remarked that her death was "the only annoyance she ever caused me".) The stately interior is authentically Basque, with heavyweight wooden fixtures, some more delicate pieces of furniture and fine examples of tableware and glass. Maria-Teresa lodged in the equally impressive pink Italianate villa known as the **Maison de l'Infante** (June–Sept Tues–Sat 11am–12.30pm & 2.30–6.30pm, Sun & Mon 2.30–6.30pm; 15F/€2.30) overlooking the harbour on the quay of the same name. The corner house on rue Mazarin, nearby, was the Duke of Wellington's HQ during the 1813–14 winter campaign against Marshal Soult.

The royal couple's sumptuous, not to say extravagant, wedding took place in the church of **Saint-Jean-Baptiste** on pedestrianized rue Gambetta. Cardinal Mazarin alone presented the queen with twelve thousand pounds of pearls and diamonds, a gold dinner service and a pair of sumptuous carriages drawn by teams of six horses – all paid for by money made in the service of France. The door through which Louis and Maria-Teresa left the church was permanently sealed immediately afterwards (it's on the right as you enter the existing door). Even without this curiosity, the church deserves a look inside: the largest French Basque church, it has a barn-like nave roofed in wood, lined on three sides with tiers of dark oak galleries reached by wrought-iron staircases. Hanging from the ceiling is an ex-voto model of the Empress Eugénie's paddle-steamer, the *Eagle*, which narrowly escaped running aground near Saint-Jean in 1867.

Practicalities

The **gare SNCF** is on the southern edge of the centre, 500m from the beach, while **buses** arrive at the outdoor terminal at place du Maréchal-Foch, also home to the somewhat harried **tourist office**, behind the Hôtel de Ville (July & Aug 9am–8pm, Sun 10.30am–1pm & 3–7pm; rest of year Mon–Sat 9am–12.30pm & 2–7pm; ☎05.59.26.03.16, *www.saint-jean-de-luz.com*). On Tuesday and Friday there is a **market** in the adjacent boulevard Victor-Hugo. **Bikes** can be rented at Luz Evasion on place Maurice-Ravel or ADO on av Labrouche, as well as at the gare SNCF. **Pelote** matches take place throughout the summer in both St-Jean and Ciboure; ask in the tourist office for details.

Accommodation

Opposite the train station, on and around avenue Verdun, are a few inexpensive (for St-Jean) if uninspiringly located **hotels** – for example the *Hôtel de Verdun*, 13 av de Verdun (☎05.59.26.02.55; ④), with a decent attached restaurant, the *Relais de St-Jacques* (closed Sat pm & Sun), or the en-suite, 1999-redone *Hôtel de Paris*, 1 bd du Comandant-Passicot, on the corner of av Labrouche (☎05.59.85.20.20, fax 05.59.85.20.25; May–Dec; ③). If you want a quieter old-town or sea-view location, you pay accordingly, and half-board is usually obligatory in peak season. About the cheapest of these is the *Hôtel Trinquet Maïtena* at 42 rue du Midi, just east of pedestrianized Gambetta and right next to a *trinquet* (☎05.59.26.05.13, fax 05.59.26.09.90; ④). Next notches up are the English-run *Hôtel Agur*, 96 rue Gambetta (☎05.59.51.91.11, fax 05.59.51.91.21; April–Oct; ⑤), or the *Hôtel Ohartzia* (☎05.59.26.00.06, fax 05.59.26.74.75; ⑥), just inland from the beach, with a huge garden where breakfast is served. A top-end choice overlooking the Grand Plage, the obviously named *Hôtel de la Plage* (☎05.59.51.03.44, fax 05.59.51.03.48; *www.hoteldelaplage.com*; closed Jan–March; ⑦) has its own (fee) car park and ground-floor brasserie. There are numerous **campsites**, all grouped in the *zone des campings* to the left of the N10 between St-Jean and Guéthary.

Eating and drinking

Leading off **place Louis-XIV** – with its cafés, sidewalk artists and free summertime concerts in the bandstand (Tues–Sun 10pm) – rue de la République has numerous, variably touristy **restaurants**. *Le Kaiku*, in a handsome old house at no. 17, has an excellent reputation for fish and seafood but costs upwards of 200F/€30.50 without drink. Less expensive alternatives on the same street include, at no. 19, cheapish and cheerful *La Ruelle*, with seafood menus at 85F/€13 and 145F/€22 (closed Mon), or *L'Alcalde* at no. 22, with mixed platters and seafood specials at 62–105F/€9.50–16. The next street east, rue Tourasse, also has a fair selection, notably *La Vieille Auberge* (closed Weds & Tues lunch), offering six *menus* at 60–140F/€9.15–21.40; and *Le Tourasse*, another classic for seafood and dessert (*menus* at 89F/€13.60 & 165F/€25.20).

There's ample scope elsewhere in St-Jean for good-value eating, especially for seafood. In summer only, *La Grillerie du Port* sets up on the quayside near the tourist office; a sardine- or tuna-based meal will cost 100F/€15.30, though portions are somewhat small. No such problem at the *Buvette de la Halle* (lunch only to 3pm, closed Mon off season) on the corner of the market hall on bd Victor-Hugo, where abundant meals of impeccably fresh crab, oysters and sardines, plus *piperade*, drink and dessert, won't dent the wallet more than 120F/€18.30 each. Nearby, *La Bodega du Marché* at 18 rue Harispe (daily 8am–midnight; closed Sun low season) is an all-purpose spot: stall-holders nursing a glass in the morning, *plats du jour* at noon, *tapas*, beer and maybe music by night.

Across the river: Ziburu, Zokoa, Urrugne

Saint-Jean shares the Nivelle estuary with **ZIBURU** (Ciboure) on its south bank, both *communes* taking maximum advantage of one of the very few sheltered anchorages along the Atlantic coast south of Bordeaux. The harbour is closed off by the village of **ZOKOA** (Socoa) with its little fortress, today home to the local sailing and windsurfing club.

From the Pont Charles de Gaulle linking St-Jean and Ciboure, you look over the dock stacked with nets, blackened lobster traps and other fishing paraphernalia, towards the extremely narrow harbour entrance clogged with grubby tuna boats. In the opposite direction the view inland over small craft beached in the river mud at low tide is dominated by the 900-metre landmark peak of La Rhune (see below).

By comparison to Saint-Jean, Ziburu is calm and untouristy, with two beautiful streets opposite the end of the bridge over from Saint-Jean: the waterfront **quai Maurice-Ravel** (a plaque commemorates the composer's birth at no. 12), and the parallel **rue Pocolette** behind. The latter forms an exquisite terrace of wide-fronted, half-timbered and balconied town houses, many built by seventeenth-century traders who did business with the West Indies and the Orient. Near the south end of rue Pocolette protrudes the octagonal tower of the sixteenth-century church of **Saint-Vincent**, inside which are particularly good examples of a Pays Basque altarpiece and three-tiered gallery, and yet another model-ship ex-voto suspended in the middle.

If Saint-Jean-de-Luz is full, Ziburu makes a possible fallback, with its two **hotels**: *Bakea* on place Camille Julian, opposite Pont Charles de Gaulle (☎05.59.47.34.40; ④), including a moderately priced seafood **restaurant**, and *La Caravelle*, overlooking the sea on bd Pierre Benoit, the westerly continuation of quai Maurice-Ravel (☎05.59.47.18.05, fax 05.59.47.30.43; ⑤).

It is also interesting to visit the **Château d'Urtubie** (daily except Tues April–Oct 2–7pm; 30F/€4.60) at **URRUÑA**, 1500m southwest of Ciboure, which has belonged to the same family since its construction as a fortified château in 1341. It was enlarged and gentrified during the sixteenth and eighteenth centuries, and provided hospitality for the French King Louis XI, as well as for Maréchal Soult and later the Duke of Wellington during the Napoleonic Wars. If you fancy following in their footsteps, it is also a very upmarket *chambres d'hôtes* (☎05.59.54.31.15, fax 05.59.54.62.51; ⑦) with a restaurant offering dinner, including wine and a visit to the château, for 200F/€30.50.

Inland from Saint-Jean: Azkaine, La Rhune and Sara

Heading southwest from Saint-Jean, perhaps on one of the two or three summer weekday buses (on Le Basque Bondissant) towards Sara from the train station, you reach **AZKAINE** (Ascain) after 7km along the D918. Like so many *labourdan* foothill villages, it's doll's-house cute and thus inevitably a target of the overspill from Saint-Jean in season. There are several moderately affordable **hotels** here, in one of which – *De la Rhune* (☎05.59.54.00.04, fax 05.59.54.41.67; ⑤) – Pierre Loti stayed while writing *Ramuntcho* (see below). The most reasonable accommodation is the *Hôtel des*

Chasseurs, place Pierre-Loti by the church (☎05.59.54.00.31; ③), with en-suite rooms and a decent ground-floor restaurant, the public car park behind and green views despite a roadside position.

La Rhune

Conical **La Rhune** (Larrun), straddling the frontier with Spain, is the last skyward thrust of the Pyrenees before they decline into the Atlantic. *The* landmark of Labourd, in spite of its unsightly TV/radio/mobile phone masts, and duly equipped with a rack-and-pinion rail service, it is predictably popular as a vantage point, offering fine vistas way up the Basque coast and east to the rising Pyrenees. To reach La Rhune, you could walk directly from Azkaine in about two and a half hours, or stay on the minor D4 road for 4km more until the **Col de Saint-Ignace**, from where you can ride up on the tourist **rack-and-pinion railway** (daily: July–Sept about every 35min from 8.30am; mid-March to June & Oct to mid-Nov 9am–3pm, according to weather conditions; 40F/€6.10 one-way, 50F/€7.60 return; book on ☎05.59.54.20.26). The 4200-metre journey to the top takes just half an hour, but allow two hours round-trip because of the queues – it's a massively popular outing in high season, with long waits and two snack bars near the base station taking advantage of a captive clientele. Even with a meal to work off, it's a fairly easy, two-hour climb to the top from the *col*.

Sara and its caves

With or without the bus or your own transport, it's worth going on to **SARA** (Sare), a hilltop village ringed by satellite hamlets. This proves to be another perfectly proportioned Basque village, where a ban on central parking enhances enjoyment of the galleried church, *frontón* and tree-shaded streets. Pierre Loti used it, disguised as "Etchezar", for the setting of his 1897 romance *Ramuntcho*. Animal lovers might avoid the place in autumn, when Sara earns its nickname of *l'enfer des palombes* – "woodpigeon hell" – as thousands of the creatures are both shot and trapped in nets strung between trees.

You can either walk on the **GR10** from the intermediate station below the summit of La Rhune in about an hour and a quarter, or drive the 3km of road from St-Ignace in rather less time. If you plan to continue further east, you can make an overnight stop at one of the village's **hotels**: the *Pikassaria*, 1km southwest in Lehenbiscay hamlet (☎05.59.54.21.51, fax 05.59.54.27.40; ④; closed mid-Nov to mid-March); the *Baratchartea* (☎05.59.54.24.48, fax 05.59.47.50.84; ④; closed Jan 1–March 15) in Ihalar hamlet, with a well-regarded **restaurant** serving big-portioned meals at 90–145F/€13.70–22.10; or the three-star, antique-furnished *Arraya* on the village square (☎05.59.54.20.46, fax 05.59.54.27.04; *www.arraya.com*; ⑥–⑦; closed Nov 15–March 31), a former hospice on the St-Jacques pilgrimage route. Even if you only plan to take the bus back to Saint-Jean, it's worth stopping in for a (normally priced) drink at their bar. Alternatively, there are two **campsites** just south of the village: *La Petite Rhune* (☎05.59.54.23.97; April–Sept), opposite the *Hôtel Pikassaria*, and *Telletchea* (☎05.59.54.26.01; July–Aug).

These all lie on the D306 road to the **Grottes de Sare** (daily except Dec 25–Jan 1, typically 9.30am–6pm spring/autumn, 9.30am–8pm July–Aug; 35F/€5.40), occasionally served by the Saint-Jean-based bus. These were inhabited as long as 50,000 years ago, with a small gallery on site displaying finds from the caves.

Hendaye

Running parallel, the D912 road and the **Chemin Piétonnier Littoral** footpath follow the cliffs of the remarkably unspoilt "Corniche Basque" 15km southwest from Saint-Jean-de-Luz to **HENDAYE** (Hendaïa), the road cutting inland a little only at the Pointe

Sainte-Anne. The path goes through the Domaine d'Abbadia, a vast nature reserve around the **Château d'Abbadia** of the nineteenth-century Dublin-born explorer **Antoine d'Abbadie**, on the headland overlooking Hendaye-Plage (guided visits: Mon–Sat June–Sept at 11am, 3, 4 & 5pm; Mon–Fri March–April & May–Oct at 3 & 4pm; 35F/€5.40). After expeditions in Ethiopia and Egypt, d'Abbadie had the château built between 1860 and 1870; the architect was Viollet-le-Duc, and the result is a bizarrre Scottish Gothic folly, with Arabian boudoirs, Ethiopian frescoes, and inscriptions over the doors and lintels inside in Irish, Basque, Arabic and Ethiopian. It is also filled with objects collected by d'Abbadie on his travels. He became president of the Académie des Sciences in 1891, to which he donated the château on his death in 1897.

Arrival in town may prove anticlimactic; neither **Hendaye-Ville** nor the coastal annexe of **Hendaye-Plage** have much intrinsic interest despite a significant past. This includes the long-time residence (and death in 1923) of **Pierre Loti**, author of the locally set *Ramuntcho* as well as assorted orientalist romances. Loti was popular in his time for syrupy, exotic romances, their settings – including Istanbul and Tahiti as well as the Pays Basque – gleaned from a lifetime of far-flung postings in the service of the French navy. You can see his house in rue des Pêcheurs, on the waterfront below bd de Gaulle (no visits, privately owned).

The best **beach**, at Hendaye-Plage, is just west of the promontory, The N10 inland road and rail line continue a couple more kilometres to Hendaye-Ville, which has another well-protected sandy beach fronting the Chingoudy estuary, but a somewhat dull atmosphere.

Hendaye-Ville, served by both the Paris–Bordeaux–Irun and Toulouse-Irún rail lines, lies on the estuary of the River Bidassoa (the French spelling of Bidasoa), with the border running down the middle for about 8km at this point. Just upstream from the town, the tiny wooded island known as **Île des Faisans** or Île de la Conférence is administered jointly by the two countries. It looks insignificant now, but was once used for meetings between their respective monarchs. François I, taken prisoner at the battle of Pavia in 1525, was ransomed here; in 1659 it was the scene of the signature of the **Treaty of the Pyrenees**. The following year it again became the centre of attention when the marriage contracts between Louis XIV and the Spanish Infanta Maria-Teresa were signed here. The great painter Velázquez reputedly died of a chill caught while painting the interior of the negotiations room.

Hendaye almost made history once more on October 23, 1940, when Spanish General Franco met Hitler in the Hendaye train station. Despite the blandishment of a guaranteed Moroccan mini-empire, Franco refused the Fuehrer's invitation to join the war on the Axis side, and Hitler was later overheard saying that he would rather go to the dentist than meet his potential ally again.

Practicalities

Hotel prices are cheaper in Hendaye-Ville, where accommodation clusters around the **gare SNCF** – an exception is *Chez Antoinette*, 1km northeast and away from the tracks (☎05.59.20.08.47; ④). But for that outlay, you can be in more pleasant Hendaye-Plage at the *Hôtel Les Buissonets*, 29 rue des Seringats (☎05.59.20.04.75, fax 05.59.20.79.72; ④–⑥), a converted mansion behind the east end of boulevard de la Mer, with a pool and garden. **Campsites** are mainly grouped around Hendaye-Plage; *Le Moulin*, off the D658 (between the N10 and coastal D912), is one of the cheaper options. In the way of **restaurants**, there's the surprisingly good-value and popular *La Petite Marée*, 2 av des Mimosas (*menus* 58–95F/€8.80–14.50; reservations on ☎05.59.20.77.96), serving seafood until 10.30pm, or for oyster fiends *Le Parc à Huîtres* at 4 rue des Orangers opposite the fishing port (51–69F/€7.80–10.50 the dozen; closed Tues pm, plus Weds low season). For further information, consult the **tourist office** at 12 rue des Aubépines in Hendaye-Plage (July & Aug Mon–Sat 9am–8pm, Sun 10am–1pm; rest of year Mon–Fri 9am–12.30pm & 2–6.30pm, Sat 9am–12.30pm & 2–6pm; ☎05.59.20.00.34, *www.hendaye.com*).

Walking from Hendaye

The **GR10** and **HRP** both start their trans-Pyrenean course beside the former casino at Hendaye-Plage. The first, two-hour stage to Biriatu is dull and gives no sense of the glories that lie ahead: along avenue Général-Leclerc, through Hendaye-Ville on rue des Citronniers, under the rail line, then 50m east on the N10 before following waymarks towards the A63 highway. A cattle track passes underneath and continues to the tiny hilltop village of **BIRIATU** (Biritou), where the walking starts to get interesting. (Those with private transport, or taking a taxi, can start from Biriatu.)

A short, steep section leads to a Basque church with a collection of weather-worn tombstones, next door to the *frontón* and the fifteenth-century *Auberge Hirribarren*, a temporary haven for many Allied soldiers during World War II and now an excellent **restaurant**, with meals at 90–160F/€13.70–24.40 a head (until 9pm; closed Jan, & Mon low season). From here the main footpaths and a number of local variations rise rapidly above the coast to semi-isolation, with only the buzzing power lines (which you soon leave behind) and the occasional long-distance walker or local jogger to disturb the peace. From Biriatu to the *gîte d'étape* at Olhette (see p.477) it's nearly five hours' trek, and from there to Sare via the base of La Rhune, another 2hr 45min – a tent could be handy.

There are a couple of day-hike circuits possible: looping west of the main path at the **Col des Joncs** (500m) and descending along the frontier to follow the Bidassoa back to Biriatu, or circling east by cutting away shortly after the *col*, at frontier stone 11. Both alternatives are well waymarked, and shown clearly on the Randonnées Pyrénéennes 1:50,000 map no. 1, "Pays Basque Ouest-Labourd".

Irún and around

The Spanish Basque coastal province of Gipuzkoa adjoins the French frontier, and its border town, **Irún**, is one of the major road and rail entry points into Spain. The tiny village of Behobia (Béhobie) – an unsightly collection of truck stops, bottle shops and pumps full of cheap petrol – straddles the frontier. There are fast public transport connections to San Sebastián, although if you're travelling more leisurely or with a car, the fishing ports of **Hondarribia** and **Pasaia** are worth a stop. The main C133 road to the south crosses almost immediately into Navarra and leads via the beautiful Valle de Bidasoa to the N121 highway, and then eventually to Pamplona. The **GR11**, traversing northwest from Elizondo, finally finishes its 700-plus-kilometre course from the Catalan Costa Brava, expiring in the Atlantic surf at Cabo Higuer.

Irún

Like most border towns, **IRÚN**'s chief concern is how to make a quick buck from passing travellers, and the main point in its favour is the ease with which you can leave; there are trains to Hendaye in France and to San Sebastián throughout the day, and regular long-distance and international connections. If arriving by train from Paris (or elsewhere in France) at Hendaye, note that it is far quicker to take the local *topo* (mole train, so called because of all the tunnels it goes through) from the separate platform on the right outside Hendaye main station; it runs every thirty minutes to Irún (to the station at Avda de Colón 52) and San Sebastián. Of the town's few attractions, the **Ermita de Santa Elena** (Tues & Thurs 3–5pm, Sat & Sun 10am–noon; free), a museum containing Roman remains discovered here in 1969, is worth a visit.

Practicalities

If you do need to spend the night, there are plenty of bars and places to eat, at prices markedly lower than in France or San Sebastián (which is no place to arrive late at night with nowhere to stay). In the vicinity of Irún's main train station are several small, reasonably priced **hostales** and **restaurants** specializing in good local food. *Pension Bidasoa*, c/Estación 14 (☎943 619 913; ④), and *Bar Pensión los Fronterizos*, c/Estación 7 (☎943 619 205; ⑤), have some of the least expensive rooms; for more comfort try the nearby *Hostal Matxinbenta*, Paseo Colón 21 (☎943 621 384; ④). There are also two reasonable **casas rurales** nearby: the *Mendiola*, Barrio Ventas, Landexte (☎943 629 763; ③), 2km west of town on the N1 road, and *Artzu* (☎ & fax 943 640 530; ③–④), with en-suite rooms available, officially in Hondarribia but actually just northwest of Irún's giant rail-shunting yards. For a modest outlay, the *Asador Baserri* at c/Berrotarán 5 (closed Sun evening and Mon), serves Basque, farm-style meat dishes (2500ptas/€15).

Hondarribia

The fishing port and fortified stronghold of **HONDARRIBIA** north of Irún and looking over the Río Bidasoa to Hendaye, is a far more attractive prospect, though the waterfront itself is disappointingly modern, enlivened with just a few cafés. The town's real appeal lies in main streets running parallel to the front, and the cobbled backstreets further inland; traditional, wood-beamed Basque houses are interspersed with bars offering some of the best seafood and *pintxos* around. In summer, the fine **beaches** just beyond the town are an escape from ultra-crowded Playa de la Concha in San Sebastián.

Hondarribia has a picturesque, walled old town entered via the fifteenth-century **Puerta de Santa María**, carved with the town coat-of-arms and angels paying homage to Our Lady of Guadalupe, who is said to have saved the town in a two-month French siege in 1638. Calle Mayor, leading up to the Plaza de Armas, has further fine examples of wood-beamed houses adorned with wrought-iron balconies and studded doors, some displaying the family coats-of-arms above doorways. At the end of c/Mayor stands the church of **Santa María**, predominantly Gothic though extensively and misguidedly renovated in the seventeenth century. The proxy wedding between Louis XIV and Maria-Teresa which confirmed the 1659 Treaty of the Pyrenees took place here in 1660, six days before the official signing ceremony on the Île des Faisans. The plaza itself is dominated by the **Palacio de Carlos Quinto**, started originally in the tenth century by Sancho el Fuerte of Navarra and subsequently extended by Carlos V in the sixteenth. It is now a luxurious *parador* (see below), and it's worth at least having a drink at the bar inside.

Practicalities

The helpful **Turismo** is on Javier Ugarte 6 (July–Aug Mon–Sat 9am–8pm, Sun 10am–2pm; Sept–June Mon–Fri 9am–1.30pm & 4–6.30pm, Sat 10am–2pm; ☎943 645 458, fax 943 645 466).

There's a fair amount of high-quality, characterful though rather pricey **accommodation** in Hondarribia. Working up the price/comfort ladder, try *Hostal Álvarez Quintero*, c/Beñat Etxepare 2 (☎943 642 299; ④), in the Edificio Miramar near the Turismo, or the *Hostal San Nikolas* on Plaza de Armas 6 (☎943 644 778; ⑤) in the old town. From this pair you've a huge jump up in price for five more plush establishments; pick of these is the three-star *Hotel Obispo*, an old stone manor on Plaza del Obispo (☎943 645 400, fax 943 642 386; ⑦), birthplace of Ricardo de Sandoval, later bishop of Seville and chaplain to Charles V; or, for a honeymoon splurge, the *Parador Nacional El Emperador Carlos Quinto*, Plaza de Armas 14 (☎943 645 500, fax 943 642 153, *pilardemiguel@parador.es*; may close Nov–Feb; ⑧), stunningly located in the town's fortified *palacio*.

The **youth hostel**, *Juan Sebastián Elkano*, is on Carretera Faro (☎943 641 550; ①); fork left beyond c/San Pedro on the way to the beaches for this barracks-like cement building, often packed out in summer with school groups. The closest **campsite**, *Camping Jaiz Kibel* (☎943 641 679; open all year), is 2km out of town along Carretera Guadalupe towards Pasaia Donibane (Pasajes) – but there's no public transport to it.

If you've transport, you'll perhaps get better value at three excellent **casas rurales** just outside of town, though they've been well publicized in various literature and must usually be reserved well in advance. The closest, in Barrio Arkoll-Santiago uphill from the airport, is *Iketxe* (☎ & fax 943 644 391; ⑤), with wood-ceilinged, tile-floor, en-suite rooms meticulously built to traditional standards. Nearby stands *Maidanea* (☎ & fax 943 640 855; ⑤), a well-modernized four-hundred-year-old farmhouse with views to France. More remote, about 3km out of town, is *Arotzenea* in Jaizubia hamlet (☎ & fax 943 642 319; ⑥), a half-timbered farmhouse of equally high standard.

The restaurants and bars along parallel c/Santiago and c/San Pedro, three to four short blocks in from the water, are the best hunting ground for **food** and **drink**, though despite Hondarribia's still-active fishing fleet, seafood isn't particularly cheap. For something special, try the *Hermandad de Pescadores* (Confraternity of Fishermen) on c/Zuloaga 12 (reserve on ☎943 642 738), one of the parallels to the waterfront, once strictly the fishermen's clubhouse but now open to all with a *menú* (1700ptas/€10.25) and *a la carta* (5000ptas/€30). Every July 25, preceded by a brass band and dressed in holiday finest, the confraternity parades into the place, oars aloft, for a ceremonial meal. Otherwise, in the old town, tucked away in a narrow, cobbled alley two streets behind c/Mayor, the *Mamutzar* restaurant serves a good-value *menú*, while next door *tapas* are available in the tiny but lively *Hamlet* bar.

Moving west

Frequent **buses** leave from c/San Pedro to San Sebastián. The stretch of coastline from here as far as the port of Pasaia is particularly rugged and has long been a haven for smugglers. With your own transport you should foresake the busy highway inland in favour of the initially winding minor road towards the chapel of **Nuestra Señora de Guadalupe** (5km), target of a September 8 festival; the road continues climbing more gradually through pine forests to the peak of **Monte Jaizkibel** (543m), with its wonderful views along the Basque coastline. You then descend to Pasai Donibane, a total of 16km.

Pasaia

The one place you might consider stopping for any length of time en route between Irún and San Sebastián is the port of **PASAIA** consisting of three separate settlements built around the sheltered mouth of the Río Oyarzun. Pasai Antxo and Pasai Senpere on the south bank are modern, industrial ports, where cranes steadily pick through heaps of scrap metal. Considered the least problematical on a stretch of coast known for its difficult swells, it was from here that the Marquis de Lafayette, general and statesman, sailed to America to fight for the colonists in the War of Independence.

But well-preserved **PASAI DONIBANE** on the north bank retains its charm; narrow cobbled c/San Juan (Victor Hugo once lived at no. 65, the house built over the tunnel) leads to Plaza de Santiago with its colourful houses. The village is famous for its waterside **fish restaurants**, many of which offer good-value *menús* and even choosing from the evening *cartes* here works out considerably less expensive than those in San Sebastián's old quarter. Two to try are *Casa Camara* at c/San Juan 79, where your prospective meal (stress on shellfish, 3000ptas/€18 and up) is kept in a central tank, or *Ziaboga* at no. 91, with more of an emphasis on fish (from 4500ptas/€27 *a la carta*). A **launch** (*txalupa*) runs throughout the day and evening across the harbour to Pasai Senpere, from where frequent buses run to San Sebastián's Alameda del Boulevard.

Through the Valle de Bidasoa

If you're heading towards Pamplona, you'll pass through the **Valle de Bidasoa** with its succession of beautifully preserved towns; the best of these are Bera, Lesaka and Etxalar, all just over the border in Navarra. At Oieregi, just under halfway to Pamplona, there's the junction left (east) for the Valle de Baztán; continuing right (south) brings you to Pamplona. The main Bidasoa valley road is served by a direct bus route between San Sebastián/Irún and Pamplona.

Bera

The first substantial place beyond the Gipuzkoa/Navarra border, **BERA** (Vera de Bidasoa) offers some of the finest examples of old wood-beamed and traditional stone houses in the region; the brightly painted buildings along c/Altzarte and the main square are particularly attractive. About a hundred metres off the square, just past the old customs house, is the former house (no. 24) of the Basque writer Pío Baroja; at the time of writing this is closed indefinitely. From Bera, Larrun (see p.491), straddling the border is an easy climb.

If you want to **stay**, there's the comfortable *Hostal Euskalduna*, c/Bidasoa 5 (☎948 630 392; ④), with a good restaurant offering a *menú* and local specialities, the *Hostal Zalain* (☎948 631 106; ③), in the Barrio de Zalain just outside town, and a *casa rural*, *Casa Etxebertzea* (☎948 630 272; ③–④), also offering en-suite rooms and bicycle rental.

Lesaka

Some 4km south of Bera along the Bidasoa valley, a right turn leads shortly to **LESAKA**. Despite the large, eyesore factory on the outskirts of town, it's a beautiful place dominated by the hill-top parish church in which the pews bear family names of the local farms and mansions. On the banks of the irrigation channel which flows through town is one of the best remaining examples of a *casa torre* (fortified private house) of a design peculiar to the Basque country, dating back to the days when north-western Navarra was in the hands of a few powerful and constantly feuding families.

Places to stay include the simple *Pensión Tolareta*, Plaza Berria 2 (☎948 637 106; ③), above a clothes shop just off the main square, the *Hostal Ekaitza* at Plaza Berria 13 (☎948 627 547; ⑤), offering en-suite rooms in a converted ancestral home, and the comfortable *Hotel Bereau* (☎948 627 509, fax 948 627 647; ⑤), near the main road.

Etxalar

ETXALAR is a small, bucolic place, 4km off the main road on the way up to a minor border crossing at the Lizarrieta pass, but is perhaps the best-preserved village of the valley, famous for the impressive array of Basque funerary steles in the churchyard. Among numerous **casas rurales** here, mostly houses or apartments rentable only by the week, are two good ones doing rooms with en suite for a short **stay**: the central *Casa Domekenea* (☎948 635 031; ②), and another, *Casa Herri-Gain* (☎948 635 208; ②–③), perched on a steep hill, with fantastic views of the surrounding area. There are also a couple of restaurants and bars near the giant church, so you won't starve or go thirsty.

Walking: the end of the GR11

Heading northwest from Elizondo, the **GR11** finishes its course passing through or very near many of the places above. The penultimate day of a trans-Pyrenean traverse, from **Elizondo to Bera**, is the tougher and more interesting of the two, crossing deserted country to skim the frontier between Etxalar and Sara; count on seven hours to reach Bera. The final half-day is more perfunctory, skirting rather than climbing the

Peñas de Haya, and then unrelentingly urban in character once you enter Irún and Hondarribia. Only at the end is there a bit of drama, as you emerge beyond the beach of Hondarribia onto **Cabo Higuer**, the promontory marking the terminus of both the GR route and the Spanish Pyrenees.

San Sebastián

Capital of Gipuzkoa (Guipúzcoa) autonomous region, and the undisputed queen of the Basque resorts, **SAN SEBASTIÁN** (increasingly known as Donostia) is a picturesque – and expensive – seaside town with good beaches. It has always been among Spain's most fashionable places to escape the heat of the southern summers, and in July and August it's packed. Although San Sebastián tries hard to be chic, it's still too much of a family resort to compete in those terms with the Catalan Mediterranean fleshpots of Roses or Cadaqués. Set around the deep, still bay of La Concha and enclosed by rolling low hills, the town is beautifully situated. The old quarter sits on a promontory between the bay and the Río Urumea which divides the town, its back to the wooded slopes of Monte Urgull, while newer development has spread onto the east bank of the Urumea, around the edge of the bay to the foot of Monte Igeldo and onto the hills overlooking the bay.

Arrival and information

Most **buses** arrive at Plaza Pío XII, fifteen minutes' walk along the river from the centre of town (the ticket office for these companies is around the corner next to the river on Paseo de Bizkaia), but from Pasaia and Astigarraga they arrive on the Alameda del Boulevard, and from Hondarribia on Plaza de Gipuzkoa. RENFE's main-line **Estación del Norte**, for arrivals from Pamplona via Alsasua, is across the Río Urumea on Paseo de Francia, although local lines of the *Eusko Tren* from Hendaia, or Bilbao (Bilbo) via Zarautz and Zumaia (neither line accepts InterRail passes), have their terminus on Plaza Easo at the **Estación de Amara**. The **airport** (internal flights only) is 22km outside the city centre, just outside Hondarribia; an airport bus runs every fifteen minutes into town.

The **municipal Turismo** (June–Sept Mon–Sat 8am–8pm, Sun 10am–1pm; Oct–May 9am–2pm & 3.30–7pm, Sun 10am–1pm; ☎943 481 166) is on c/Reina Regente in the Teatro Victoria Eugenia. For a greater selection of pamphlets there is also the very useful **regional government Turismo** (Mon–Fri 9.30am–1.30pm & 3.30–6.30pm, Sat 9am–1pm & 3.30–6.30pm; July & Aug also open Sun 10am–1.30pm; Oct–May closed Sat pm & Sun; ☎943 426282) at Paseo de los Fueros, just off the main Avenida de la Libertad.

San Sebastián is something of a travel hub for the region. Viajes TIVE, c/Tomás Gros 3 (☎943 276 934), is a youth/student **travel agency** that sells tickets for international buses and discount plane tickets. Another good general travel agency is Viajes Aran, c/Elkano 1 (☎943 429 009). For travel **books and maps** (both local and elsewhere), and books on all things related to the Basque country, head for Graphos on the corner of Alameda del Boulevard and c/Mayor. Also recommended are Bilintx, c/Esterlines 10; Dr Camino, c/Treinta y Uno de Agosto 32–36; Noresta, c/María Lili (☎943 293 520), a travel-book-and-map store that also rents skis and trekking gear; and the library, Koldo Mitxelena, c/Urdaneta 9 (☎943 482 750).

Accommodation

Accommodation, though plentiful, can be pricey and hard to come by in season – if you arrive between mid-July and the end of August, or during the film festival in September, you'll have to start looking early in the day, or book ahead if possible. There is little difference in rates between the cheapest places in the *parte vieja* (old quarter)

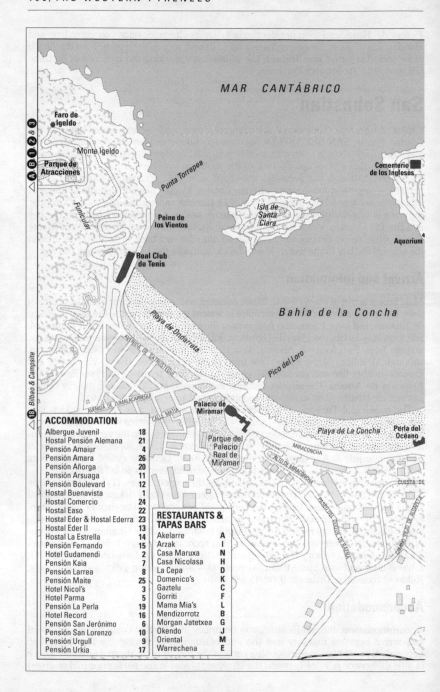

MAR CANTÁBRICO

Faro de Igeldo

◁ⒶⒷ①②&③

Monte Igeldo

Parque de Atracciones

Punta Torrepea

Cementerio de los Ingleses

Funicular

Peine de los Vientos

Isla de Santa Clara

Aquarium

Real Club de Tenis

◁⑱. Bilbao & Campsite

Bahía de la Concha

Playa de Ondarreta

AVENIDA DE SATRUSTEGUI

Pico del Loro

AVENIDA DE ZUMALACARREGUI

CALLE MATIA

Palacio de Miramar

Playa de La Concha

Perla del Océano

MIRACONCHA

Parque del Palacio Real de Miramar

ALTO DE MIRACONCHA

CUESTA DE

PASEO DEL DUQUE DE BAENA

CAMPINO DE DE ANDRETA

ACCOMMODATION

Albergue Juvenil	18
Hostal Pensión Alemana	21
Pensión Amaiur	4
Pensión Amara	26
Pensión Añorga	20
Pensión Arsuaga	11
Pensión Boulevard	12
Hostal Buenavista	1
Hostal Comercio	24
Hostal Easo	22
Hostal Eder & Hostal Ederra	23
Hostal Eder II	13
Hostal La Estrella	14
Pensión Fernando	15
Hotel Gudamendi	2
Pensión Kaia	7
Pensión Larrea	8
Pensión Maite	25
Hotel Nicol's	3
Hotel Parma	5
Pensión La Perla	19
Hotel Record	16
Pensión San Jerónimo	6
Pensión San Lorenzo	10
Pensión Urgull	9
Pensión Urkia	17

RESTAURANTS & TAPAS BARS

Akelarre	A
Arzak	I
Casa Maruxa	N
Casa Nicolasa	H
La Cepa	D
Domenico's	K
Gaztelu	C
Gorriti	F
Mama Mia's	L
Mendizorrotz	B
Morgan Jatetxea	G
Okendo	J
Oriental	M
Warrechena	E

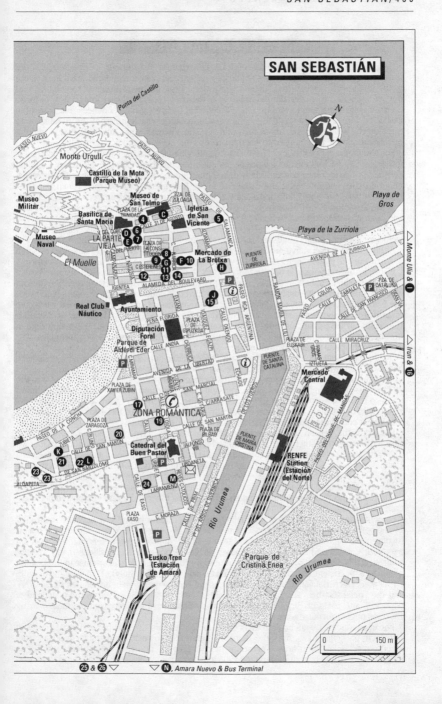

BASQUE NATIONALISM

Despite the high-profile activities of **ETA** (*Euskadi ta Askatasuna* – "Freedom for the Basques"), **Basque nationalism** is not an especially recent phenomenon. Richard Ford wrote in the nineteenth century that "these highlanders, bred on metal-pregnant mountains, and nursed amid storms in a cradle indomitable as themselves, have always known how to forge their iron into arms, and to wield them in defence of their own independence". The Visigoths perceived the *Vascones* as a "dangerous rural population emerging from the mountains to threaten the settled inhabitants of the valleys". The Visigoth king, Recared, unable to completely subdue the region, used to send his troops out here just to keep them fit.

For almost the entire history of both France and Spain, the Basques jealously defended their *fors* or *fueros* – ancient customary privileges guaranteeing them effective autonomy – against constant pressure from Paris and Madrid, and guarded the wealth brought by seafaring skills, mineral riches and industrial enterprise. After the Revolution, in 1790, the French Basques' millennium-old *fors* were abolished as part of the general centralizing strategy of the Jacobins, and the three traditional French Basque regions were lumped together with Béarn in a new administrative *département*. In Spain, it was not until 1876 and the second, final defeat of the Carlists, whom the Basques supported as upholding their own traditionalist values, that the victorious Liberals finally abolished the *fueros* altogether to punish the rebellious Basques.

Although the conservative, traditionalist **Basque National Party** (PNV) emerged in Spain towards the end of the nineteenth century, under the leadership of the frankly racist, extreme-Catholic **Sabino Arana**, it is only in this century that Basque nationalism has become associated with the political Left, mostly in reaction to Franco's regime. Cut off from their Republican allies by predominantly rural Navarra and Alava, whose conservative landowners sided with the Nationalists, the urbanized Basque coastal provinces of Gipuzkoa and Vizkaia were conquered in a vicious campaign that included the infamous German bombing of **Gernika** (Guernica) in 1937. Franco's vengeful boot went in hard, and as many as 21,000 people died in his attempts to tame the Basques after the war. Public use of the language was forbidden, and central control was asserted with the gun.

But Spanish state violence failed signally, succeeding only in nurturing a new resistance based on ETA, which took to the field in 1968. Their terrorist activities have included scores of bombings, with nearly a thousand victims to date; their most spectacular success was the 1973 assassination in Madrid of Franco's right-hand man and probable successor, Admiral Carrero Blanco. Even now the military and the *Guardia Civil* are regarded – and behave – as an army of occupation, and the more radically minded Basques of the *Abertzale* (nationalist) movement continue to support ETA's aims, if not their methods.

Following the **return to democracy**, however, things have changed substantially. The Spanish Basque parliament has been granted a considerable degree of autonomy in its own affairs (it's the only autonomous community allowed to collect its own taxes), and there's a Basque police force, the *ertzaintza* (distinguished by its red berets), much in evidence in the streets. The Basque **language** is flourishing again and is taught in at least half of all primary schools in the coastal regions. The Basque flag (the *ikurriña*, designed by Arana and not particularly ancient) flies everywhere, and street as well as town names are signposted preferentially in Euskera across the land.

Since gaining home rule, Spanish Euskadi has, like Catalunya and Galicia, been controlled by the political Right. When the conservative Partido Popular failed to gain an outright majority of seats in the Madrid parliament in March 1996 elections, they were forced into a coalition pact with Catalan and Basque conservative parties. Among the concessions made was the transfer of 32 convicted ETA terrorists (out of more than 600) to jails in or close to the Basque country, a persistent demand of **Herri Batasuna** (Popular Unity), ETA's political wing. Otherwise, Herri Batasuna has little influence in a Basque parliament dominated by the PNV and the Socialists; their electoral support rarely tops ten percent except in the heartland of Gipuzkoa and parts of Bizkaia. Polls show that while wanting increased autonomy, many Basques oppose forming a breakaway state.

The economic recession no doubt has much to do with this – the former industrial glories of Bizkaia in particular have, since the 1930s, been reduced to rusty, outdated factories and idle steel foundries and shipyards. Terrorism discourages needed new investment, and unemployment is extremely high. In January 1988 a historic pact was signed by all the Basque parties except Herri Batasuna, condemning ETA's tactics while upholding their goals. HB credibility was further dented in 1997 by its organization of street marches in support of ETA, undermining its previous claims to act independently of the terrorists; in subsequent all-party rallies and statements against ETA's activities, HB have always conspicuously abstained.

The Spanish government has periodically offered **amnesties** to activists who publicly renounce ETA's methods – though the few who have done so risk assassination from their former comrades – and until 1989 engaged in secret negotiations with ETA leaders. But Madrid often wielded a big stick while apparently granting concessions. A death squad known by the acronym **GAL**, which liquidated over twenty ETA fellow-travellers between 1983 and 1988 in a clandestine "dirty war", was first thought to consist mainly of certain off-duty members of the Guardia Civil, who considered government anti-terrorist policies to be inadequate. Their operations were even carried out in the French Basque regions, while an extradition treaty with France has also denied gunmen their former safe refuges across the border. But a series of **spectacular trials** in Spain, culminating in 1999, resulted in the exposure of effective Socialist civilian control of the operation – and the convictions of the former PSOE interior minister José Barrionuevo, his deputy Rafael Vera, the governor of Gipuzkoa, and a Guardia Civil general.

In early 1992 the French police arrested the three top-ranking ETA members in one swoop on a house near Biarritz, probably kept by ETA's French counterpart, **Iparreterrak**. Despite the existence of this group, there is no real desire among rank-and-file French Basques for unity with the Spanish community in an independent country, and French sympathy for ETA has largely evaporated since Franco's death and the institution of home rule across the frontier. That said, top ETA members continue to seek refuge in French territory, and periodically the French authorities arrest and either try or extradite these people who are always identified as the core leadership of what is clearly a hydra-headed organization.

Despite all the foregoing, ETA terror has continued, a strategy seen by many as a desperate, last-ditch attempt to force a government return to negotiation; it appears that since 1994 young hardliners, especially from the radical-Left faction **KAS**, including many firebrand women, have seized control from the historic leadership, now mostly in exile in Latin America. Premier Aznar himself narrowly escaped death from a 1996 car bomb detonated by ETA in Madrid, and summer of that year saw numerous small devices – designed more to scare than kill – set off in southeastern coastal resorts popular with Britons. New tactics, such as extorting **"revolutionary taxes"** from Basque-run businesses and kidnapping VIPs for ransom, have emerged since the mid-1990s to fund the estimated $8 million annual ETA "budget". Money can be laundered in a vast network of front businesses, including Basque hotels and restaurants not only in France and Spain but also in the expatriate communities of Mexico, Venezuela and Uruguay.

But each outrage generates increasing revulsion, none more so than when a Partido Popular municipal counsellor, **Miguel Ángel Blanco**, was kidnapped in July 1997 and soon found mortally wounded with two bullets in the neck when ransom demands were ignored. The kidnapping, and funeral, prompted street demonstrations a million strong in the Basque country and across Spain. It was, unfortunately, the first in what have become almost monthly **political assassinations** by ETA, with the exception of a fourteen-month truce which ended in November 1999 after it was deemed not to have produced the desired result in negotiations with Aznar's PP government. Since Ángel Blanco's killing, more than twenty municipal counsellors, MPs, an ex-governor of Gipuzkoa, assorted military personnel, and (in Madrid) a supreme court judge have died at ETA hands, mostly PP members but a few PNV and PSOE personalities as well. It appears the terrorists now consider fair game anybody of any political stripe who disagrees with their agenda, as well as any convenient symbolic targets in the judiciary and armed forces. For the first time in a while, civilian bystanders are also seen as acceptable "collateral damage" by ETA as well. For its part Aznar's government has proclaimed that the bombings and shootings, rather than driving them back to the negotiation table, are having the opposite effect; with a clear majority won in the March 2000 elections, the PP does not have to make concessions to nationalist coalition partners, and clearly intends to pursue a final military solution to the ETA problem. ETA and HB have both been effectively marginalized and the former has become increasingly socially unacceptable on its home turf with every outrage. Even in the face of Aznar's belligerent intransigence, for the moment an overwhelming majority of the Basque population feels that more will be achieved through the available democratic channels than by ETA violence.

and elsewhere, although *hostales* along the Alameda del Boulevard do tend to be slightly pricier. There is often more chance of finding space in the *zona romántica* around c/Easo, c/San Martín, c/Hondarribia and c/San Bartolomé, or on the other side of the river in **Gros**, behind the RENFE station in **Egia**, or in the new part of town, **Amara Nuevo**, on the way to the Anoeta sports complex. Asking in bars in any of the above-mentioned areas about unofficial private rooms can produce a result – although the Turismo strongly recommends sticking to licensed hotels and guesthouses.

The Parte Vieja

Pensión Amaiur, c/Treinta y Uno de Agosto 44, 2° (☎943 429 654). Pleasant, friendly one-star *pensión* with carpeted doubles and a few triples; shared facilities for the seven rooms. ④.

Pensión Arsuaga, c/Narrika 3, 3° (☎943 420 681). One-star with simple, spacious doubles; can be chilly in winter but has its own restaurant and offers good full-board deals. ③.

Hostal La Estrella, Plaza de Sarriegi 1 (☎943 420 997). Attractive old two-star *hostal*, offering a range of old-fashioned but clean rooms overlooking the plaza or Alameda del Boulevard. ⑤.

Pensión Kaia, c/Puerto 12, 2° (☎943 431 342). Pleasant, modern rooms with bath, much cheaper off-season. ⑤.

Pensión Larrea, c/Narrika 21, 1°, corner c/Pescaderia (☎943 422 694). Clean, modern rooms but on a busy street corner, also a bit cramped and noisy. ④.

Hotel Parma, c/General Jauregi Gudalburuaren 11 (☎943 428 893, fax 943 424 082). Nicely located between the *parte vieja* and Paseo Nuevo, this rather characterless modern building offers comfortable rooms with all amenities, the best ones overlooking the sea. ⑦.

Pensión San Jerónimo, c/San Jerónimo 25, 2° (☎943 420 830). Adequate *pensión*, though the rooms are spartan and the hallway and stairs somewhat the worse for wear. ③.

Pensión San Lorenzo, c/San Lorenzo 2, 1° (☎943 425 516). Backpackers' cheapo haven with just six rooms and a self-catering kitchen; generally full, and does not accept advance reservations, so contact them the evening or morning before your intended stay. ②.

Pensión Urgull, c/Esterlines 10, 3° (☎943 430 047). The English-speaking owner won't take reservations far in advance. Just five airy, spotless and tastefully furnished rooms, though there can be nocturnal noise from nearby bars. ③.

Alameda del Boulevard and around

Pensión Boulevard, Alameda del Boulevard 24, 1° (☎943 429 405). Comfortable, modern rooms mostly with washbasins only, plus one en suite. ④.

Hostal Eder II, Alameda del Boulevard 16, 2° (☎943 426 449). Elegant hallway with fine wood panelling leads to spacious rooms, some with bath. ⑤.

Pensión Fernando, Plaza de Gipuzkoa 2, 1° (☎943 425 575). Fair-sized, relatively quiet rooms with washbasin, showers out in the hall at this friendly but slightly over-classified two-star overlooking a leafy square. ④.

Zona Romántica

Hostal Pensión Alemana, c/San Martín 53, 1° (☎943 462 544, fax 943 461 771, *halemana@adegi.es*). Perfectly located just behind La Concha, this 1992-renovated two-star in a fine Belle Époque building offers affordable splendour in large en-suite rooms with all mod cons, off-street parking, and cheerful pastel buffet-breakfast room tucked into a bay-window corner. Reservations mandatory year-round. ⑦.

Pensión Añorga, c/Easo 12, 1° (☎943 467 945). Large, fairly plain *pensión* on two floors, but the rooms are clean and some have bath. ③.

Hostal Comercio, c/Urdaneta 24 (☎943 464 414). Simply furnished *hostal*, offering reasonable rooms with washbasin and fan heaters. ③.

Hostal Easo, c/San Bartolomé 24 (☎943 453 912). Relatively low-priced rooms with washbasin or shower. ④.

Hostal Eder, and **Hostal Ederra**, c/San Bartolomé 33 and 25 (☎943 464 969 & ☎943 426 449). Two *hostales* run by the same management as the *Eder II* in Alameda del Boulevard, with principally their location close to La Concha as a selling point. Open Easter & July–Sept only. ⑤.

Pensión La Perla, c/Inazio Loiola 10 (☎943 428 123). Excellent-value *pensión*, near Buen Pastor cathedral and the food market, offering spotless, recently redone rooms with baths and TV; also advantageous half-board rates. ④.

Pensión Urkia, c/Urbieta 12, 3° (☎943 424 436). Run by Mari, the sister of *La Perla's* owner, this *pensión* has equally good en-suite rooms, though there is some street noise. If full, you may be referred to another relative, *Casa Elisa* (☎943 453 950). ④.

Out of the centre

Pensión Amara, Isabel II 2, 1° (☎943 468 472). Clean, comfortable accommodation in this highly recommended *pensión*. ④.

Hostal Buenavista, Barrio de Igeldo (☎943 210 600). Stone-clad, mock-trad Basque chalet on the main road to Monte Igeldo, featuring sweeping sea views and a good restaurant. Good value for the area. ⑤.

Hotel Gudamendi, Paseo de Gudamendi, Monte Igeldo (☎943 214 000, fax 943 215 108). In a peaceful, park-like cul-de-sac near the top of the mountain, this rambling, slightly neglected, converted hunting lodge scores for its pleasant pool and common areas rather than the functional, tile-floored rooms. Usually has a vacancy because overpriced even for a three-star; better value late Sept to late June. ⑦ B&B.

Pensión Maite, Avda de Madrid 19, 1° B (☎943 470 715). Good, clean rooms with shower and TV; handy for bus station, Astoria cinema and Anoeta football stadium. The owners also run the *Bar Maite* opposite. ④.

Hotel Nicol's, Paseo de Gudamendi, Monte Igeldo (☎943 215 799, fax ☎943 211 724). Just 200m shy of the *Hotel Gudamendi*, this one-star isn't as grand as its neighbour, with less comprehensive views, but more reasonable and with a well-regarded restaurant on site; much cheaper Oct–June. ⑦.

Hotel Record, Calzada Vieja de Ategorrieta 35 (☎943 271 255, fax 943 278 521). At the far end of Gros and a pleasant alternative to the bustle of the Parte Vieja and the Zona Romántica; well connected by bus or a fifteen-minute walk from the centre, with plenty of parking. All rooms with shower or bath (though the cheapest lack toilet); the larger have terraces. ⑥.

Camping and youth hostel

Igeldo, Paseo Padre Orkolaga 69, Barrio de Igeldo (☎943 214 502). San Sebastián's campsite is excellent, although it's a long way from the centre on the landward side of Monte Igeldo, reached by bus #16 from the Alameda del Boulevard. Open all year.

Albergue Juvenil, Paseo de Igeldo (☎943 310 268, fax 943 214 090). San Sebastián's youth hostel, known as *La Sirena*, is just a few minutes' walk from the end of Ondarreta beach; otherwise take bus #5 or #16 to reach it. Toilet/shower in every room, open all year. ①.

The Town

A fire destroyed most of the **Parte Vieja** (Old Quarter) in 1813, but its narrow streets were renovated so expertly that you would never guess the comparative modernity of most buildings. The medieval defensive wall was demolished later in the century to make way for expansion of the new town; Alameda del Boulevard marks its former course. The cramped and lively streets of the Parte Vieja remain the focus of interest, where crowds congregate in the evenings to wander among the many small bars and shops, or sample the shellfish from the street traders down by the fishing harbour.

The *parte vieja* contains San Sebastián's chief sights: the elaborate Baroque facade of the eighteenth-century church of **Santa María**, and the more elegantly restrained sixteenth-century Gothic church of **San Vicente** (somewhat confusingly, on Plaza de la Trinidad). The centre of the old quarter is **La Plaza de la Constitución** (known by the locals simply as *La Consti*) – the numbers on the balconies of the apartments around the square refer to the days when it was used as a bullring. Situated just off c/Treinta y Uno de Agosto (the only street to survive the great fire of August 31, 1813), behind San Vicente, is the excellent **Museo de San Telmo**, which was closed for renovation during 2000. When it reopens, its displays – around the cloisters of a former convent – will probably still include a fine Basque ethnographic exhibition on the first floor and the largest collection of keyhole-shaped funerary steles in the Spanish Basque country. There should continue to be regular exhibitions of work by modern Basque painters and the convent chapel is decorated with a series of frescoes by José Sert, depicting scenes from Basque life. In the same square as the side entrance to the museum is the oldest surviving gastronomic society in the city, the **Artesana**.

Behind the plaza rises **Monte Urgull**, crisscrossed by winding paths through the park here (daily 7am until 1hr after sunset). From the mammoth figure of Christ on its summit, a 45-minute climb, there are great views out to sea and back across the bay to the town; also up here stand the dilapidated remains of the castle. On the way down you can stop at the **Aquarium** (mid-May to mid-Sept daily 10am–8pm; mid-Sept to mid-May Tues–Sun 10am–1.30pm & 4–7.30pm; 1100ptas/€6.60) on the harbour; it contains the skeleton of a whale caught in the nineteenth century and an extensive history of Basque navigation, although not many fish. Close by, at Paseo de Muelle 24, is the **Museo Naval** (mid-June to mid-Sept Tues–Sat 10am–1.30pm & 5–8.30pm, Sun 11am–2pm; mid-Sept to mid-June Tues–Sat 10am–1.30pm & 4–7.30pm, Sun 11am–2pm), with video facilities and exhibits tracing the tradition and history of Basque fishing.

Still better views across the bay can be had from the top of **Monte Igeldo**: take the #16 bus marked *Igeldo* from the Boulevard, or walk round the bay to its base near the tennis club, from where a **funicular** (daily summer 10am–8pm, winter 11am–6pm; every 15min; 170ptas/€1 round-trip) will carry you to the summit.

Beaches

There are **four beaches** in San Sebastián: Playa de la Concha, Playa de Ondarreta, Playa de la Zurriola and Playa de Gros. **La Concha** is the most central and the most celebrated, a wide crescent of yellow sand stretching round the bay from the town. Despite the almost impenetrable mass of flesh here all summer long, this is the best (if most regimented) of the beaches, enlivened by sellers of peeled prawns and cold Cokes and with great swimming out to the diving platforms moored in the bay; buoy lines discourage you from venturing beyond into the pleasure-boat anchorage. Out in La Concha bay is a small island, **Isla de Santa Clara**, which makes a good picnic spot; a boat leaves from the port every half-hour in the summer (daily 10am–8pm; 250ptas/€1.50 round-trip).

La Concha and **Ondarreta** are the best beaches for swimming – the latter is a continuation of the same strand beyond the rocky outcrop which supports the **Palacio de Miramar**, once a summer home of Spain's royal family. Set back from Ondarreta beach are large villas, some of the most expensive properties in Spain, and mostly owned by wealthy families from Madrid who vacation here. This area used to be known as La Diplomática for this reason and has a reputation for being more staid than the central area, although the lively district of **El Antiguo** with its many bars is only a few minutes' walk beyond.

Far less crowded, and popular with surfers, **Playa de la Zurriola** and the adjacent **Playa de Gros** were regraded and fitted with breakwaters during the 1990s to shield them from dangerous currents and river pollution. The elegant promenade, however, has more recently been blighted by the construction of a huge concrete cube containing restaurants, shops, an auditorium for concerts and an art gallery. One of the best views of the whole town and bay may be had by climbing up the steps to the sidrería (see box p.506) on the side of **Monte Ulia** from the far end of the beach. This walk can easily be extended for about 5km along the coast to the lighthouse overlooking the entrance to Pasaia harbour.

Eating, drinking and entertainment

If you're in the mood for a gastronomic treat, San Sebastián has some of the best **restaurants and tapas bars** in Spain (note that most are closed Sunday evening and

Monday), mostly in the *parte vieja* but a few in the *zona romántica*. Inclusion of a phone number in the listings below means reservations are suggested most of the year. Prices tend to reflect the popularity of the old quarter, especially in the waterside restaurants, but lunchtime *menús del día* are generally good value, and the *pintxos* and *raciones* set out in all but the fanciest bars are a great way to eat cheaply in the evenings. For those on a budget, the **Mercado de la Bretxa** is conveniently situated in the centre of the *parte vieja* on c/San Juan.

Restaurants and tapas bars

Akelarre, Paseo de Padre Orkolaga 56 (☎943 212 052). In Barrio Igeldo well beyond the terminus for the #16 bus, this is reckoned one of the city's top restaurants, with wonderful sea views. Put on your best rags, join the other Porsches and BMWs in the big car park and be prepared to spend 9000ptas/€54 each.

Arzak, Alto de Miracruz 21, Monte Ulia (☎943 278 465). A shrine of Basque cuisine, with three Michelin rosettes and a superb *menú* for around 8000ptas/€48.

La Cepa, c/Treinta y Uno de Agosto 7. Inexpensive *raciones* served amidst decor of bullfighting kitsch and dangling hams; also a pricier *comedor*. Closed Wed.

Domenico's, c/Zubieta 3. Smart but affordable (3000–4000ptas/€18–24) Italian restaurant with an emphasis on the pasta; very popular in season, with only about 50 seats, so reservations mandatory on ☎943 471 537.

Gaztelu, c/31 de Agosto 22. Fine choice in the *parte vieja* where you can choose from a selection of reasonably priced *raciones*; if you sit in their *comedor*, allow about 3500ptas/€21.

Gorriti, c/San Juan, corner c/Fernando Calbetón. One of the best counter-top collections of *tapas* and *pintxos*, in a town not short of such.

Mama Mia's, c/San Bartolomé 18, corner c/Triunfo. Good, relatively inexpensive Italian restaurant serving vegetarian dishes and pizzas; allow about 3000ptas/€18 for a meal.

Casa Maruxa, Paseo de Bizkaia 14, Amara. Specializes in food from Galicia and attracts the crowd on their way to the Astoria cinema complex just around the corner.

Mendizorrotz, Barrio Igeldo, at the hamlet's central plaza two stops from end of #16 bus line. Brief but superbly executed *carta*, with specialities like *pimientos de padrón* (grilled green peppers) and *puding de txangurro* (spider-crab mousse); budget 3500–4000ptas/€21–24 including local cider and dessert in the tiny *comedor*, or have the special cheap *menú* (Mon–Fri) at the bar tables. Reserve *comedor* tables on ☎943 212 023.

Morgan Jatetxea, c/Narrika 7. Purveys the French-influenced "new Basque" school of cookery, especially the lighter, tasty starters. It's quite normal to order two of these instead of the heartier main courses.

Casa Nicolasa, c/Aldamar 4, 1° (☎943 421 762). Classic – and expensive – Basque cookery; there's a 7000-peseta/€42 *menú*, while *a la carta* isn't much more.

Okendo, c/Okendo 8. A decor of cinema-festival posters, youngish crowd and an appetizing *menú* (1350ptas/€8) make this an appealing target; *a la carta* gives you access to delicacies like crab cannelloni.

Oriental, c/Reyes Católicos 6. Best of several local Chinese restaurants in terms of quality of food, price and extremely friendly atmosphere; eat in or take away.

Warrechena, c/Nagusia (ex-Mayor), corner c/Puerto. A fairly busy place to go when you're down to your last *duro*/euro; basic fare served up in what are essentially tarted-up London fish-and-chip-shop surroundings.

Nightlife

In the evenings, you'll find no shortage of action, with **clubs** and **music bars** everywhere. The two main nuclei are the *parte vieja*, especially lively **c/Fermín Calbetón** where virtually every address is a bar, and the area around the intersection of **c/Reyes Católicos and c/Larramendi**, where a large number of the city's more expensive music pubs are located. For **jazz**, try *BeBop* on Paseo de Salamanca, *Etxekalte* or *Altxerri*, all on the edge of the *parte vieja*. Once the pubs close, usually by about 3.30am, the night continues at the *Komplot*, a techno-disco on c/Pedro Egaña.

SIDRERÍAS

If you're in San Sebastián between late January and early May, a visit to one of the many sidrerías (*sagardotegiak* in Basque, "**cider houses**") in the area around **Astigarraga**, about 6km from town, is a must – take the red Hernani-bound bus from the Alameda del Boulevard or a taxi for about 1000ptas/€6.

Cider production is one of the oldest traditions in the Basque country – until the Civil War and the subsequent move towards industrialization, practically every farmhouse in Gipuzkoa and to a lesser extent the other provinces produced cider, which was a valuable commodity used for barter. Barter remained the main form of exchange in rural communities here until comparatively recently, and the farms were effectively open houses where local people socialized – the *bertsolariak* tradition of oral poetry originated in these places – and drank cider.

Since the 1980s, cider houses are again flourishing, and for 1500–3000ptas/€9–18 you can feast on enormous steaks, grilled fish and codfish omelette accompanied by local cheese and walnuts, drink unlimited quantities of cider and in general enjoy the raucous atmosphere. Of the fifty or so *sidrerías*, some of the most accessible include *Petritegi* and *Gartziategi*, just a few kilometres out of town, while many of the more rustic (authentic) ones, such as *Sarasola* and *Oiarbide*, are on the so-called *ruta de las sidrerías* (cider trail) beyond Astigarraga. Check in the Turismo for a full list with phone numbers.

Festivals

Throughout the summer there are consecutive **fiestas**, many involving Basque sports including the annual rowing (*trainera*) races between the villages along the coast, which culminate in a final regatta on September 9. The **Jazz Festival**, at different locations throughout the town for five days during the latter half of July, invariably attracts top performers as well as hordes of people on their way home from the fiesta in Pamplona. The week preceding August 15, known as **Semana Grande** (*Aste Nagusia* in Euskera), sees numerous concerts, special events and fireworks laid on. There is also the one-week **Film Festival** in the second half of September, plus frequent theatrical and musical performances throughout the year at both the Teatro Victoria Eugenia and the Teatro Principal. The Turismo produces a monthly guide to what's on.

Listings

Bike rental You can rent mountain bikes from Comet, Avda de la Libertad 6 (☎943 426 637).

Car rental Atesa, Amezketa 7 (☎943 463 013); Avis, c/Triunfo 2 (☎943 461 527); Hertz, c/Zubieta 5 (☎943 461 084); and Europcar, RENFE station, Paseo de Francia (☎943 322 304).

Post office The *Correos* is at c/Urdaneta, just south of the cathedral (Mon–Fri 8am–9pm, Sat 9am–2pm).

Swimming pools The sports centre in Anoeta, Polideportivo de Anoeta (☎943 458 797), has an open-air pool, track, tennis courts and a gym. There's another pool, Termas La Perla, at Paseo de la Concha (☎943 458 856), which also has a gym and sauna.

---

travel details

Spanish trains
San Sebastián to: Bilbao (9 daily; 2hr 30min–3hr); Hendaye, France (every 30min 7am–10pm; 35min); Irún (every 30min 5am–11pm; 30min).

French trains
Bayonne to: Biarritz (13 daily; 10–15min); Hendaye (13 daily; 35min); Irún (4–5 daily; 45min); Lourdes (5–7 daily; 1hr 45min); Pau (5–7 daily; 1hr

15min); Saint-Jean-de-Luz (13 daily; 30min); Tarbes (5–7 daily; 2hr).

Saint-Jean-Pied-de-Port to: Bayonne (4–5 daily; 1hr); Bidarraï (Pont-Noblia, 4–5 daily; 20min); Cambo-les-Bains (4–5 daily; 45min); Itsasu (1 daily; 30min).

Spanish buses
Ansó/Echo to: Jaca (Mon–Sat 1 daily at 6am; 1hr 40min).

Pamplona to: Auritze (Mon–Sat 1 daily; 1hr 30min); Elizondo (Mon–Fri 3 daily, Sat & Sun 1 daily; 2hr); Irún (3 daily; 2hr); Izaba (Mon–Fri 1 daily; 2hr); Jaca (Mon–Sat 1 daily year-round, additional departure in summer; 2hr 30min); Eaurta (Mon–Sat 1 daily; 2hr 30min); Otsagabia (Mon–Sat 1 daily; 2hr); Roncesvalles (Mon–Sat 1 daily; 1hr 35min); Yesa (Mon–Sat 1 daily; 1hr).

San Sebastián to: Elizondo (3 daily; 2hr); Hondarribia (every 20 min; 30min); Lesaka (2 daily; 1hr 15min); Pamplona (6 daily; 1–3hr/*autovía*-normal road); Bera (2 daily; 1hr).

French buses (including SNCF coaches)
Bayonne to: Biarritz (every 10–20 mins on STAB urban buses; 15–20min); Cambo-les-Bains (several daily; 40min); Hendaye Ville & Plage (3–7 daily by inland route; 70–90min); San Sebastián (1 daily Mon–Sat on ATCRB; 1hr 45min); St-Jean-de-Luz (6–14 daily on ATCRB; 40min).

Baïgorri to: Ossès-St-Martin-d'Arossa rail junction (3–6 daily; 10min).

Biarritz to: Hendaye-Plage & -Ville (5–7 daily by coastal corniche road; 30min).

Saint-Jean-de-Luz to: Cambo-les-Bains (2–3 daily in summer; 45min); Ezpeleta (2–3 daily in summer; 35min); Hendaye (9–16 daily by coast or inland route; 30min); Sara (2–3 daily in summer; 25min).

PART THREE

THE

CONTEXTS

HISTORY

The history of the Pyrenees inevitably draws on that of both France and Spain, although through the ages the border region has often found itself well out of the social and political mainstream. The following summary highlights the salient events and trends which directly impinged on the mountains and their people.

PREHISTORIC HABITATION

The history of the Pyrenees begins with a man who died aged twenty some 455,000 years ago near the present-day village of Tautavel in the Fenouillèdes foothills. Excavated from the floor of a limestone cave in 1971, the bones of "Tautavel Man" rank as some of the earliest human remains found anywhere in Europe. However, the trail then grows cold until late Paleolithic times (35,000–10,000 BC), the era of the paintings left by cave-dwelling hunter-gatherers in various parts of the Pyrenees. The most spectacular discoveries date from the end of the Paleolithic era – known as the Magdalenian period – and include the painted caves of Niaux and Bédeilhac in France. At around 5000 BC dolmens appear, either stone burial chambers or – as recently conjectured – seasonal shelters for shepherds, found throughout most of the Pyrenees. No habitations from this period have been discovered, but it can be assumed that perishable huts of some sort were erected, and farming had certainly begun by this time.

EARLY INVASIONS

Before the start of the **Bronze Age** (around 2000 BC), Pyrenean people – as elsewhere in Europe – began to move into fortified villages, and from then until the thirteenth century AD, when the Muslims were effectively driven out of Spain, the area experienced a succession of **invasions**. First, around 1000 BC, came a mix of Celtic and Germanic peoples. The **Celtic** "urnfield people" settled in Catalonia, and later mingled with the Iberians from the south to become the **Celto-Iberians**. The mysterious **Vascones**, whose origins remain unclear, probably occupied what is now the Basque country at around the same time.

Later, by 550 BC, the **Greeks** established a trading post at Roses, on the Catalan coast. During the third century BC the **Carthaginians** occupied Catalonia, principally in the Spanish part, from where their most famous commander, Hannibal, crossed the Pyrenees in 214 BC on his way to Italy. But after the Second Punic War (218–201 BC) the Carthaginians were expelled from the peninsula by the **Romans**, who despite strong resistance from the Celto-Iberian tribes – and never-complete dominance of the Vascones – succeeded in making the Pyrenees, as well as Iberia and Gaul to either side, an integral part of their empire. Although a political backwater, the Pyrenean foothills were endowed by the Romans with a network of roads, bridges, villas and garrison towns.

Roman rule soon began to be eclipsed – a process not completed for several centuries – with raids by **Franks** and **Suevi** (Swabians), who overran the Pyrenees between 262 and 276 AD. Two centuries later followed new invasions of **Alans** and **Vandals**, eventually superseded by the fifth-century incursions of the **Visigoths** from Gaul, former Romanized allies of Rome who had been pushed out of France by the Franks under King Clovis. The Visigoths established a capital first at Toulouse and then another at Barcelona in 531 AD. By the end of the sixth century, the Visigothic kingdom extended from the Pyrenees to include most of modern Spain and half of modern France, although the Basque region retained its independence. Apparent strength and unity were spurious, however: the Visigothic monarchy was elected, leading to constant factional strife; adherence by many to the Arian heresy forfeited the kingdom support from the Byzantines; and the bulk of the population lived in a state of virtual serfdom.

THE "MOORS" AND THE RECONQUEST

With the Visigothic state in terminal decline, the **Moorish** (or more properly, Muslim North African) **conquest of Spain** was – in contrast to Rome's protracted campaigns – startlingly rapid. In 711, less than a century after Mohammed had left Mecca, governor of Tangier Tariq the Berber led a force of seven thousand across the Straits of Gibraltar and defeated the Visigothic army of King Roderic. Little effective resistance was mounted elsewhere, and within ten years these Berber clans controlled most of the peninsula, including the foothills of the Pyrenees. By the standards of its time, Muslim administration was remarkably tolerant: virtual autonomy was conceded to remoter communities in return for regular payment of tribute, while Jews and Christians were allowed to continue in their faith, those who did not convert being called **Mozarabs**.

The Muslims called the area they controlled **al-Andalus**, whose borders expanded and contracted over the next eight centuries. Their authority soon stretched beyond the Pyrenees, a progress only halted at Poitiers in 732 by the Frank, **Charles Martel** – so named because he crushed the invaders like a *marteau* (hammer). A scion of the Merovingian dynasty which then dominated what is now modern France, he drove the Muslims south out of Aquitaine, a fight continued by his son Pepin, and his more famous grandson **Charlemagne** (768–814), whose empire at its height effectively included the southern slopes of the Pyrenees as well as the northern, most of modern Catalonia and much of Navarra. But Charlemagne endured setbacks, most notably the massacre of his rearguard near Navarran **Roncesvalles** in 778. No reliable account of this event exists, but it seems he had crossed the Pyrenees to assist a Catalan Muslim faction opposed to the Umayyad emir of Córdoba. His putative ally defeated, Charlemagne contented himself with raiding and sacking most of the important towns of the Ebro valley, slighting their fortifications for good measure. By demolishing the walls of Pamplona as well, he antagonized its Basque inhabitants; as his army retreated over the Pyrenees, the Pamplonans retaliated by wiping out his rearguard.

After Roncesvalles, Charlemagne switched his attention to the Mediterranean side of the Pyrenees in an attempt to defend his empire against the Moors. He took Girona in 785, and his son Louis le Débonnaire directed the successful siege of Barcelona in 801. Continued Frankish military success meant that any influence the Muslims had wielded in the Pyrenees waned long before the turning point for the whole peninsula, the battle of **Las Navas de Tolosa** in 1212, won by the united Christian kings of León, Castile, Aragón and Navarra.

To secure recaptured territory, castles were built in strategic places south of the Pyrenean crestline from Barcelona to the hills of western Aragón. A vassal who held a castle in fief for his lord was variously known as a *castellanus, castlá* or *catlá*, from which is possibly derived the name **Catalonia** – or, in Catalan, Catalunya. To the west, the Navarran capital of Pamplona and the Aragonese early-medieval capital of Jaca remained important strategic towns, and from the ninth century onwards were astride, or just to one side, of the two main pilgrim routes to the shrine of Santiago de Compostela in Galicia. Protected by the castles and made wealthy by the patronage of kings and pilgrims, **monasteries** flourished throughout the Pyrenees. Benedictine monks established themselves in Roussillon, Catalunya, Aragón and the Comminges, beginning in the tenth century and taking advantage of lands and funds granted by the local Pyrenean leaders to build on a grand scale. Thus there are numerous surviving **Romanesque churches** across the range, the cathedral at Jaca being one of the finest examples.

Although Islamic influence lingered in Spain until as late as the sixteenth century, when the last **mudéjars** – Moors living under Christian rule – were expelled from Andalucía, there is a continuing debate as to whether or not any remained on the north side of the Pyrenees. Partisans in favour point to apparent versions of the word "Moor" in the names of mountains and places – Moreau, Serre Mourène and Pouey-Morou, for example. But these are more easily explained as variations on the old French word *moreau*, meaning brown. If they colonized any of the high ground, it could only have been briefly: by 920 Jaca was out of Muslim hands for the last time, Huesca was reconquered in 1096, and Barbastro returned to Christian rule in 1100.

EARLY NATION-BUILDING

Charlemagne's grandsons divided his empire between themselves after 843, and it was only a matter of time before the Frankish empire fell apart. In the face of destabilizing attacks by Normans and Norsemen during the ninth century, the **Carolingian kings** were forced to delegate more power and autonomy to provincial governors, whose lands already had acquired strong identities of their own. With the death of the last Carolingian in 987, **Hugues Capet** was elected king of what was left of the empire, founding a dynasty of Paris-based rulers that lasted until 1328.

The **Capetians** were initially no more than first among (un)equals, surrounded by nominal vassals who were often more powerful than the king. In feudal France, such provincial *seigneurs* spent their time fighting each other, occasionally besieging each other's castles but more usually destroying crops, stealing cattle and burning villages. Things got so out of hand that the bishops introduced *La Trêve de Dieu* (God's Truce), which banned fighting from Wednesday evening until Monday morning – but they fortified their own monastic churches as a precaution, examples being at Saint-Savin and Luz near Lourdes.

The situation began to change when **Eleanor**, daughter of the powerful William VIII, duke of Aquitaine, married the future Louis VII, thus bringing that duchy under Parisian control. But Eleanor divorced him and immediately – in 1152 – remarried Henry of Normandy, who shortly became Henry II of England. Thus the English gained control of a huge chunk of what would become modern France, with the vast **Angevin empire** stretching from the Channel to the Pyrenees. The most notorious British personality was **Edward the Black Prince**, whose harsh tactics – thus the epithet – provoked revolts in Bigorre late in the fourteenth century.

At the same time, Catalunya and Aragón were also active in "French" territory. In 1137 the betrothal of Count Ramon Berenguer IV of Catalunya to Petronella, the two-year-old daughter of King Ramiro II of Aragón, united the two kingdoms. His son Alfonso I added Roussillon and much of southern France to his territories, and fancied himself as the "Emperor of the Pyrenees".

Philippe Auguste (1180–1223) began to reverse the Angevin gains, undermining English rule by exploiting the bitter relations between Henry II and his sons, one of whom was Richard the Lionheart. By the end of his reign, the Capetian royal lands were for the first time greater than those of any other French lord, a process assisted by the support given to the pope's crusade against the **Cathars**, which began in 1209. The Cathars – also known as the Albigensians – were a heretical religious group who had rapidly gained support in Languedoc and the Eastern Pyrenees. By convention, the lands and other property of defeated heretics went to the victors, which explains the enthusiasm of Paris for the venture.

First Béziers fell to the papal crusade, then Carcassonne. In 1213 Pedro (Pere) II, son of Alfonso I and king of Aragón and Catalonia, intervened on the Cathar side, but was killed besieging the papal general Simon de Montfort at Muret. His defeat signalled the end of Catalan aspirations north of the Pyrenees: had he won, Languedoc might be Spanish today. The outcome of the crusade was the virtual extinction of Catharism and the strengthening of French influence in the Pyrenean foothills. Much of the property of Raymond VII, defeated count of Toulouse, was forfeited to the Crown, and the walls of Toulouse and many other fortified places were razed. Indirectly, the success of the crusade also spelt the end of patronage for the **troubadour poets**, with whom the local nobility had been associated, and consequently the decline of the *langue d'oc*, the southern French language that they had championed. From this period also date the first **bastides**, some three hundred fortified new towns scattered across the Pyrenean foothills by the victors, built to a grid plan around proportioned central squares.

With the death of Pedro, **Jaume I of Aragón**, nicknamed "the Conqueror" (1208–76) succeeded to the throne at the age of five. The 63 years of his reign were a period of concerted expansion for the joint kingdom of Aragón and Catalunya: he drove the Muslims from Mallorca in 1229, took Menorca in 1231 and Ibiza in 1235, and reached Valencia in 1238. Realizing that the Catalan future lay to the south and east, he was less determined north of the Pyrenees and in 1258 signed the **Treaty of Corbeil**, by which he renounced all territorial rights in France (except Montpellier, the Cerdagne and Roussillon), in return for King Louis of France's renunciation of claims on Catalunya.

FROM THE HUNDRED YEARS' WAR TO THE WARS OF RELIGION

The northern part of the Angevin empire was lost by King John in 1204, and from then on the Capetians steadily chipped away at English rule in Aquitaine. When the Capetian male line expired in 1328, the French throne went to Philippe VI of Valois, nephew of Philippe the Fair, but this succession was quickly disputed by Edward III of England, Philippe the Fair's grandson. Thus began the **Hundred Years' War** (1338–1453), with Paris aiming to take Aquitaine and Gascony – which included much of the western Pyrenees – and the English attempting to recover what John had lost.

Against this background **Gaston Fébus**, count of Foix, disputed with the powerful house of Armagnac for the part of Gascony known as Bigorre. Fébus' defeat of the Armagnacs at the **Battle of Launac** in 1362 was the first step towards the creation of a small **kingdom of the Pyrenees**, and at its zenith the area ruled by Fébus included Foix, Bigorre, Béarn and Soule. However, he died without an heir in 1391, and the chance of an independent northern Pyrenees went with him.

Roussillon was taken from an increasingly united Spain by Louis XI of France in 1463, but Perpignan revolted against the French a decade later. Although the city was recaptured in 1474 after a harsh siege followed by brutal repression, Charles VIII – who succeeded Louis in 1483 – decided there were richer pickings to be had in Italy and handed Roussillon back to Spain in 1493.

Despite coming out on top in the Hundred Years' War, France was eventually forced by the Spanish to relinquish most of its interest in the Pyrenean-straddling kingdom of **Navarra/Navarre**, which it had held since the early thirteenth-century election of Theobald (Thibaut), count of Champagne, as king of Navarre. Later Navarre passed first to the Fébus clan of Foix, and then early in the sixteenth century to the French house of Albret, which was shortly to embrace Protestantism. All of Navarra was conquered by Fernando of Aragón in 1512, though the region of Basse-Navarre north of the watershed was returned to the French in the person of Henri II d'Albret in 1530, who ruled – as did his descendants – from Pau.

His daughter, the militantly Calvinist **Jeanne d'Albret**, created an important secondary the-

---

PYRENEAN LIFE IN THE MIDDLE AGES

Before the Black Death struck the Pyrenees in the mid-fourteenth century, the **population** in the mountains was greater than it is today, with a well-developed social structure. Each village had its minor aristocracy acting as military agents for the local count, plus a bailiff to collect rents and dues, and settle small disputes. However, there was little of the rigid class distinction of major towns in Spain and France, and aristocrats, clergy and villagers met on fairly equal terms.

There were no taverns, so socializing was limited to the fireside, the village square and Sunday Mass. Though knowledge of religious teaching was rudimentary, the **Church** was an enormously significant force for social cohesion, and all people were highly God-fearing. The local priest was accepted as one of the villagers, but the distant bishop was despised as the one who imposed unjust tithes – though outright opposition to these was a recipe for trouble with the **Inquisition**. The poorest houses, and even the shepherds' summer huts, were repositories of ancestral superstition, maintained through years of continuous habitation by the same families, who would keep fingernail clippings and locks of hair as household talismans.

It was an introverted society. Most people married within the village and spent their entire lives there, except for visits to the nearest **market** town to buy or sell produce. Money was little used: villagers survived on their own farm produce and craft, by bartering and swapping favours. Only the shepherds moved freely, sometimes over surprisingly long distances: it was not uncommon to winter the flock in the very south of Catalonia, but to spend the summers in the lush upland pastures of the Ariège.

Little is known about the general **health** of people in the Pyrenees in the late Middle Ages, but all social classes were certainly infested with parasites such as lice. Bathing was unheard of, except for medical reasons at one of the spas. The lot of **women** was correspondingly harsh. Treated as chattel, they were married off for social gain and could expect frequent beatings. Apart from the inevitability of regular childbearing, a woman's duties included fetching water and kindling, tending the fire and the garden, cooking, weeding the fields and harvesting.

atre in the **Wars of Religion** racking France at this time, defeating the Catholic troops of Charles IX at nearby Navarrenx. Like the Cathars before them, the Protestants were especially strong in the south of France, but also claimed a considerable number of adherents in the west. Jeanne's more easy-going son, Henri III of Béarn and Navarre, put himself in line for the French Crown by marrying Marguerite of Valois in 1572. Accordingly when he acceded to the throne of France in 1589 as **Henri IV**, his inheritance of Foix-Béarn and Basse-Navarre was incorporated into France, and the Pyrenean boundary of southwestern France was thus finalized. But as a Protestant, Henri was unacceptable in the Catholic north, and it was only after four years of fighting against the ultra-Catholic league led by the Guise family, and his own eventual conversion to Catholicism ("Paris is worth a Mass", he is reputed to have said) that he could truly claim to be king of all France.

Henri set about reconstructing the country and attempting to accommodate the religious factions that had been at war since 1562. By the 1598 **Edict of Nantes** the Huguenots – as the Protestants were also called – were accorded freedom of worship in specified places, the right to education and public office on the same basis as Catholics, their own courts and the retention of certain fortresses as a guarantee against renewed attack. But Henri's assassination in 1610 ended royal protection for the growing numbers of Protestants in the French Pyrenees. The new King Louis XIII's agent **Cardinal Richelieu**, having crushed the Protestant strongholds of La Rochelle and Montpellier, then set about razing various Pyrenean fortresses such as Miglos in the Ariège.

FRANCO-SPANISH WAR AND THE TREATY OF THE PYRENEES

In 1635 an ascendant France and a greatly weakened Spain were again at war, and by 1640 the Catalans had taken advantage of this state of affairs to declare themselves an **independent republic**, under the presumed protection of Louis XIII. Their marching song, *Els Segadors* (The Reapers), was later to become the Catalan national anthem. Louis annexed Roussillon from the Spanish Crown and came personally to supervise the siege of Perpignan, which fell on September 9, 1642. The inhabi-

tants were grateful, and looked forward to an independent Catalonia, but this was never to be: Barcelona fell to Spanish forces in 1652 and Catalonia was effectively split in two. In July 1654, the French besieged Villefranche-de-Conflent, which capitulated after eight days, and in October the key Cerdanyan town of Puigcerdà also fell to France. The French razed the walls of Villefranche in 1656 fearing that the Spanish might retake the city, which was somewhat rash, since the town soon became theirs by the **Treaty of the Pyrenees**. This, negotiated by the respective foreign ministers of France and Spain on a neutral island in the River Bidasoa near Bayonne in 1659, provided for permanent French control of Roussillon and part of the Cerdagne. The Spanish paid a heavy price when the details were thrashed out the following year at Llívia, ancient capital of the Cerdanya/Cerdagne. They lost Perpignan – then one of the most important towns in Europe – and the fortified port of Collioure. Puigcerdà and Llívia remained Spanish, but the surrounding territory became French, leaving Llívia as an enclave. As for the Catalans, they forever lost the prospect of a united, independent country.

With **Louis XIV,** the *Roi Soleil* or "Sun King", reigning alone after the death of Cardinal Mazarin in 1661, **Sébastien le Prestre de Vauban** began fortifying dozens of towns for the king along the north slopes of the Pyrenees, his most famous work being **Mont-Louis** in the Cerdagne. Even Vauban, however, was to fall out of favour for his criticism of Louis' war-mongering and wealth-amassing, financed by taxation from which aristocrats and clergy were exempt.

Although the boundary envisioned by the treaty was not formally delineated until the mid-nineteenth century, it has long been one of the most stable and peaceful in Europe. For the Pyrenean population, especially in the upland of Cerdanya/Cerdagne, the treaty's terms conferred dubious benefits: age-old local customs were superseded by centralizing states; the power of the Church – whose dioceses frequently overlapped the new boundaries – was severely challenged; and smuggling was an inevitable consequence of the zealously re-energized customs services. For the first time many Pyreneans, especially on the French side, became liable to conscription and thus saw parts of the wider world, often settling far away in the lowlands – the beginning of the massive mountain depopulation that continues to this day. Not only the Catalans but the Basques at the opposite end of the range suffered progressive erosion of the fors/fueros, ancient charters which had guaranteed some degree of home rule.

WAR OF THE SPANISH SUCCESSION

With the death of the Habsburg King Charles II of Spain in 1700, the throne was offered to the grandson of Louis XIV, Philippe d'Anjou, provided he renounce his rights to the throne of France. Louis XIV's acceptance of the deal, which put a Bourbon on the throne of Spain and gave him indirect control there, guaranteed war with Habsburg Austria, whose Archduke Charles had already been named as successor. England too was drawn into the conflict, fearing a combined French-Spanish power. The **War of the Spanish Succession** lasted thirteen years from 1701, with Holland, Portugal and Denmark on the side of Austria and England, arrayed against France, Spain and Bavaria. Peace was eventually achieved by the treaties of **Utrecht** (1713) and **Rastatt** (1714), with Philippe remaining as **King Felipe V** of Spain, but his realm was divested of all territory in Belgium, Luxembourg, Italy and Sardinia, with Gibraltar and Menorca being ceded to England. In revenge for its support of the Austrian claimant, Felipe V suppressed what little remained of Catalunya's autonomy. The war effort had effectively bankrupted the French, and Louis XIV, his sun well and truly set, died in 1715.

THE FRENCH REVOLUTION AND THE PENINSULAR WAR

On the evening of July 28, 1789, a group of strangers arrived in the Roussillonais town of Prades, sounded the alarm bell and forced the doors of the salt store, instrument of the hated gabelle (salt tax). The **French Revolution** had reached the eastern Pyrenees, and within a few days all the crown agents and tax-gatherers had been beaten up and ejected from Roussillon. But the euphoria was short-lived. After the solidarity of the anti-tax riots, the Revolution degenerated into a settling of old personal scores, of village against village; peasants went armed just to tend their vines. People soon realized that they had swapped a

despised but distant monarchy for a system of government that would far more effectively pervade every aspect of their lives, not least in the suppression of the traditional regions such as Bigorre and Béarn and their replacement with new, gerrymandered départements designed to sever all old loyalties.

Land reform, with its abolition of feudal dues and tithes, was popular on the plains but less significant in the mountains where there was already a complex system of communal grazing rights. There was no support for the war with the royalist empires of Prussia and Austria who were determined to crush the Revolution, and men became fugitives rather than be conscripted, turning instead to smuggling. The **Terror** of 1792–95 claimed few Pyrenean lives, but when it did peasants suffered disproportionately. In Tarbes, for example, six people who had been overheard to criticize the new regime were guillotined: one naval officer, one priest and four peasants.

THE PENINSULAR WAR

Soon after becoming emperor of France in 1804, **Napoleon** saw an opportunity to take over Spain. The Spanish fleet was defeated at the Battle of Trafalgar in 1805, precipitating the abdication of Carlos IV. In April 1808 Napoleon summoned the disgraced Spanish royal family to Bayonne, deported Carlos IV and his wife to Italy and imprisoned their sons Fernando and Carlos in France. Napoleon then installed his own brother, Joseph Bonaparte, as king of Spain. Among Spanish intellectuals, opposition was initially muted by the hope that French rule would serve as a liberalizing force, but optimism quickly evaporated, and Britain and Portugal joined Spain against France in the **Peninsular War** (1808–14). Napoleon organized hospitals for his troops at Bagnères-de-Bigorre, Cauterets, Barèges and Capvern, a move that led to the revitalization of these spa towns. The emperor also planned various civil engineering projects in the Pyrenees to support his troops in Spain, including roads across passes above Marcadau and Gavarnie, but his army was forced back before anything came of them. His men retreated along the famous pilgrim route via Roncesvalles and were pursued eastwards along the Pyrenees by **Wellington**. Wellington's armies were rapturously received by a people sick of Napoleonic bellicosity –

scoring extra points by paying for supplies rather than just requisitioning them – and many of his officers returned after the war to settle at Pau.

SEEDS OF THE SPANISH CIVIL WAR

Between 1810 and 1813 a *Cortes* or Spanish parliament attempted to found a liberal regime, envisioning ministers answerable to it in the framework of a constitutional monarchy. But Fernando VII, upon being restored to the throne in 1814, immediately abolished this embryonic parliament and remained an implacable opponent of any liberalization, presiding at the same time over the loss of most of Spain's colonies in South America. Upon his death in 1833 the crown was claimed both by his daughter Isabella II (a child under the regency of her mother), and by his brother Carlos, backed by the Church, the conservatives and the Basques. The **First Carlist War** (1833–39) ended with victory for the relative liberals supporting Isabella, who came of age in 1843. Her reign was a long record of scandal, political crisis and constitutional compromise, until liberal army generals forced Isabella to abdicate in 1868. The experimental **First Republic** (1873–75) failed, and following the **Second Carlist War** the throne went to Isabella's son Alfonso XII.

Thereafter, attempts to balance monarchism with parliamentary government were only partly successful. Working-class **political movements** such as the Socialist Workers' Party were developing rapidly the socialist trade union, the UGT, formed in 1888, took hold in the industrialized Basque country, while the anarchists' rival union, the CNT, was especially well represented in Catalunya. The loss of Cuba, Puerto Rico and the Philippines to the USA in 1898, and the "Tragic Week" of rioting in Barcelona in 1909 – following a call-up of army reserves to fight in Morocco – represented significant blows to national morale.

During World War I Spain was neutral but inward turbulence continued, and in 1923 **General Primo de Rivera** overthrew the government to establish a dictatorship. After his death in 1930, the success of antimonarchist parties in the municipal elections of 1931 led to the abdication of the king and the foundation of the **Second Republic**.

Catalunya declared itself an independent republic two days after the municipal elections on April 14, 1931, but had to settle for a statute of limited autonomy granted by Madrid the following year. A relatively dynamic region, it had long felt itself exploited by the rest of Spain. Meanwhile the Madrid government was too paralysed by the expectations of left-wingers and the potential of right-wing reaction to accomplish anything substantial in the way of agrarian or tax reform. Additionally, all the various brews of extreme political ideology that had been fermenting in Spain over the course of the previous century were ready to explode. Anarchism, communism and socialism all derived some impetus from the Russian Revolution, while at the other end of the spectrum were the **Falangists** – a black-shirted fascist youth group founded in 1923 by José Antonio Primo de Rivera, son of the dictator.

The **army** was divided between the anti-monarchists, monarchists who supported the Bourbon dynasty and monarchists who supported the Carlist line – whose power base was conservative Navarra. But they were sufficiently united in their opposition to left-wing government, and though General José Sanjurjo's 1934 coup attempt failed, it spawned the infamous **Spanish Military Union**, whose members included General Manuel Goded, General Emilio Mola and **General Francisco Franco**, all openly talking of another rebellion should the Catholic right fail to win the coming election. When the left-wing *Frente Popular* (Popular Front) won the election of February 1936 by a tiny majority, the stage was set.

EVENTS IN FRANCE 1810–1938

Following the end of Napoleonic rule, France endured over half a century of turbulence despite nominal restoration of the monarchy in 1815. There were reversals of revolutionary tenets under a series of reactionary kings or self-styled emperors, alternating with growing popular discontent and periods of liberal retrenchment, all taking place against a backdrop of growth in industrial and economic power.

The trauma of defeat in the 1870 Franco-Prussian War resulted in the definitive declaration of a **republic**, and indirectly in the growing influence of the political Left; the Spanish UGT had a near-exact counterpart in the French CGT, which eschewed political organization in favour of "direct action". As in Spain, the various socialist and communist parties found it difficult to co-operate, even amidst the opportunity presented by the aftermath of World War I, whose 25 percent casualty rate among the French ranks and massive devastation on French soil had dealt the old social order a huge blow. The scale of the demographic decimation can be gauged by the memorial cenotaphs in every French Pyrenean village, with their long lists of the dead – often far more numerous than the current local male population.

The Catholic right, whose *Action Française* shock troops dated from the early years of the century, mirrored the analogous groupings in Spain. Faced by the growing threat of both Nazism across the Rhine and homegrown fascist activism, the French Left papered over its internal differences and – in the same year as the Spanish Popular Front victory – won a rather more convincing mandate in the Parisian Chamber of Deputies. "Encouraged" by a wave of spontaneous sit-ins and wildcat strikes celebrating the poll triumph, the first **Front Populaire** government of 1936–37, headed by **Léon Blum**, nearly succeeded in ratifying the sorts of reforms – nationalization of key industries, 40-hour week, collective bargaining – which the Spaniards were only able to contemplate. But within a year these measures had been stymied by a corollary proposal on currency exchange control. Similarly blunted by "reasons of state" (for which read "fear of the English and the Germans") were Blum's ineffectual attempts, despite his evident personal sympathy with the Spanish *Frente Popular*, to intervene openly in the Civil War – or even just supply armaments to the Republicans – until the fall of his second government in 1938.

THE SPANISH CIVIL WAR

On July 17, 1936, the military garrison in Morocco rebelled under the leadership of Franco, the agreed signal for revolt throughout Spain. Sanjurjo, by now in exile in Portugal, was the Military Union's choice for provisional head of state but was killed when his plane crashed between Portugal and Burgos. Another Franco rival, Goded, was captured by Republican loyalists in Barcelona and shot, leaving the way open for Franco to be proclaimed commander of the rebels – and "Head of State" – in October 1936.

The Nationalists, as the rebels styled themselves, had expected a short campaign but the **Spanish Civil War** (1936–39) turned out to be long and bloody. In the Pyrenees, only Navarra immediately came out in favour of the Nationalists, who had convinced the heirs of the Carlists to allow themselves to be absorbed into Franco's Falange. Gipuzkoa and Bizkaia, which had recently benefited from a home rule statute similar to Catalunya's, remained devoutly Republican as did Catalunya and Aragón, where the mountain villages were particularly attracted by anarchism, an ideology that shared their traditional values of equality and personal liberty. Whatever their precise stripe, Republicans were overwhelmingly secular and virulently anticlerical, and the opening months of the war saw numerous instances of churches or monasteries sacked, with priests and nuns murdered or raped.

Although the Nationalists initially had little popular support, they gradually swept the country by a mixture of audacity and deliberate terror, backed by a flood of arms and men from Nazi Germany and Italy. The Republicans were less effectively supplied by Russia, and very sporadically by France, and reinforced by the socialist International Brigade. An international arms embargo and declaration of nonintervention was universally and selectively winked at by interested parties. Nominally a civil war, the Spanish conflict was really the opening act of World War II, and the first "modern" campaign: Italian and German airmen demonstrated the efficacy of terror bombings on civilian targets, and radio saw service as a propaganda weapon.

In the north, their foothold in Navarra allowed the Nationalists to attack both east and west. The Basque country was overwhelmed by the end of 1937, paving the way for a major Nationalist offensive into Aragón during March 1938. As the Nationalists advanced eastwards, **Republican** soldiers, marooned in the valleys of Alto Aragón and Catalunya, fled north across the high passes into France, joined or preceded by their families, and others fearful of a Falangist victory. Many Republicans believed, or perhaps deluded themselves, that theirs was a tactical withdrawal, and hoped to be saved by a pan-European war in the wake of Hitler's provocations in Czechoslovakia. But by the beginning of 1939 it was all over, and the majority now arrived quite openly at ordinary road frontier crossings like Le Perthus, sometimes in columns of thousands. The Republican parliament held its last meeting at Figueres on February 1, 1939.

WORLD WAR II

Ironically, the outbreak of **World War II** soon led to a refugee movement in the opposite direction. With the capitulation of France in spring 1940, small numbers began making their way over the Pyrenees, intent on reaching England via neutral Spain, in response to de Gaulle's June 1940 radio appeal to join the Free French forces. There was also a weekly movement from France into Spain of Swiss gold ingots, two truckloads at a minimum, as payment for humanitarian food aid to occupied Europe from America.

The Germans were initially content to leave the south of France, including the Pyrenees, under the control of the collaborationist **Vichy** government, but the Allied landings in North Africa in November 1942, only briefly opposed by Vichy troops in Morocco and Algeria, left them vulnerable to attack from across the Mediterranean. Hitler immediately ordered the formal occupation of the south, prompting a new wave of escapes over Pyrenean passes.

ESCAPEES AND ESCAPE ROUTES

These later refugees fell into four categories: **Allied personnel**, mainly airmen who had been shot down; **évadé(e)s**, who had escaped prison or internment in France (though the word *évadé(e)s* tends to be applied to all escapees); **réfractaires**, French people who were in trouble with the Vichy or German authorities for falling foul of Occupation rules; and, of course, **Jews.**

Their guides were known as **passeurs** in French, **pasadores** in Castilian. Some of these knew the old contraband trails from lengthy experience, but the majority were ordinary people, working in hotels and cafés and perhaps smuggling occasionally for a little extra money. Another contingent was made up of Spanish Republicans who, having fled from the frying pan into the fire, lived in hiding along the border, especially around the Cerdanya/Cerdagne. Some clergy were involved, as well as a few shepherds, a handful of mountaineering guides, and even a scattering of officials such as mayors and customs officers. Altogether, three thousand French (including two hundred women) were active in the Pyrenean escape routes, and five hundred Spaniards.

Until the **German occupation** of the French Pyrenees on November 11, 1942, it was left to the French themselves to patrol the frontier, a task entrusted to no more than eight hundred customs officers, policemen and support staff, and these were easily circumvented by well-established methods. Fugitives and their guides, for example, could take the Sunday afternoon train to Latour-de-Carol, stroll up to the frontier to mingle with the local Spanish and French who by custom gathered there to chat, and then just drift away onto the Spanish side. In Vichy Marseille, the American and Mexican consulates simply provided escapees with visas and put them on the train to Spain via Cerbère and Port Bou.

However, from the end of 1942 the frontier was patrolled by over a thousand military police, backed by mobile units that doubled their number. In addition, there were about a hundred Nazi agents working covertly in the region, assisted by French volunteer forces and informers motivated by money, anti-Semitism or both. Though the Germans were mostly older men considered unsuitable for the rigours of a combat front, these frontier guards were nevertheless formidable – tough Bavarian or Austrian mountaineers, well trained and well equipped, using reconnaissance aircraft to track their quarry. The Spanish had about eight hundred border guards and police on their side, and additionally 30,000 troops were also stationed not more than 30km south of the frontier.

The **escape organization** that developed to counter this intensified border security was run like a business, and an occasionally ruthless one. Known by the codename **MAURICE**, it had an annual income of more than 16,000,000 francs for transport, false documents, food, the hiring of a guide and other expenses. Much of the money was raised by loans from sympathizers, for whom coded messages were broadcast on the BBC to acknowledge the receipt of funds and confirm later repayment. The cost of each crossing depended on the negotiating skill of the organizer and the difficulties of the route involved: if transport had to be arranged to the start of a crossing, the cost shot up astronomically as fuel was difficult to obtain. As particularly "hot" items, Jews had to pay – or be paid for – at many times the normal going rate to be guided out of the country, whether individually or in a group. Those who demurred, and attempted to flee via the normal daily rail link between Oloron and Canfranc, were liable to be returned by the Spanish authorities or sent to an internment camp (see below).

M.R.D. Foot, in his *SOE in France*, described the methods of the covert escape chain: "The security measures taken . . . for the bodies passing down the line are very strict. They change hands as many times as possible, and each courier acts as a cut-out, not knowing where the bodies come from or where they are going. The bodies are kept in a park or other public place until nightfall, when they are taken to the house where they are to sleep. They are not told the address of the house, however, and seldom have any idea where they are, or which courier is in charge of them. Safe houses and contacts are changed every three months, regardless of whether they are blown or not."

In the early days of the war the consequences of arrest on the French side were not too harsh: imprisonment, a fine or perhaps "volunteering" for the Vichy Foreign Legion. Later, the penalties became more severe: about 1000 escapees died in concentration camps in France or elsewhere, as did 150 of the 500 *passeurs* who were caught. Arrival in Spain did not mean the end of danger; Spain might have been neutral but it was a pro-fascist country, and no official could be trusted. Anyone captured on the Spanish side would be sent to one of the local **internment camps**, where conditions were so bad as sometimes to be fatal – and approximately one out of seven escapees ended up in internment. Despite these hazards, about 35,000 people succeeded in escaping into Spain, including approximately 5000 Jews, 2000 Belgians, 500 Dutch, 800 Poles and around 1000 members of the Resistance.

THE PYRENEES AFTER THE WARS

Although the Spanish Civil War had left more than half a million dead, destroyed a quarter of a million houses and sent a third of a million Spaniards into exile in France and Latin America, Franco was in no mood for reconciliation. He set up **war tribunals** which sentenced thousands of Republicans to death and interned nearly two million others in concentration camps until "order" had been restored. The Falange was the only permitted political organization, and censorship was rigidly enforced.

By the end of World War II, during which Spain was too weak to be anything but neutral, Franco was the last remaining fascist head of state in Europe, and had in fact sanctioned more judicial deaths than any other ruler in Spanish history. Spain remained politically and economically isolated into the early 1950s, despite diplomatic recognition of Franco's regime by most of Europe. With the economy at a standstill, Pyrenean villagers began to drift down to the towns in a usually fruitless search for work, accelerating the **depopulation** of the mountains. Mismanagement of the economy was so blatant that by 1953 the country was exporting less than it had twenty years earlier. The traditional livelihood of **smuggling** across the Pyrenees mushroomed into a major enterprise, but even this was dwarfed by the corruption of army officers and customs officials who imported luxury goods on false documents, an illicit trade that was equal to half the official imports.

Franco's otherwise probable overthrow was only averted in 1953 by the acceptance of **American aid**, on condition that he provided land for American air bases. The economy was revitalized not only by US loans, but remittances from tourism and Spaniards working in northern Europe, resulting in a growth rate during most of the 1960s second only to Japan's. Such investment, however, merely brought forward the death of traditional Pyrenean agriculture, as the **mechanization of farming** on the plains marginalized mountain life even further. A Spain of increasing urbanization and lowland agriculture required massive amounts of water and power, supplied by a burgeoning number of dams in Catalunya and Aragón; their flooding of Pyrenean pastoral valleys, combined with the punitive neglect of Madrid in failing to provide the most basic services to the overwhelmingly pro-Republican mountaineers, pretty well finished off any hope of subsistence in various parts of the Pyrenees.

Meanwhile in **France**, with **Charles de Gaulle** emerging as the undisputed leader of the Free French government-in-exile, the Allies had little choice but to co-operate with him; as of D-Day and the subsequent liberation, an uneasy coalition of Right and Left, the *Conseil National de la Résistance*, emerged as the basis of a provisional government for the demoralized, bankrupt nation. By 1947, thanks to the Cold War and the Marshall Plan, the Left – as well as (temporarily) de Gaulle – had been excluded from what became the Fourth Republic, though not before a new constitution had been agreed upon, providing for women's suffrage, the nationalization of key industries, trade union rights and the rudiments of a welfare state.

In the French Pyrenees themselves, hundreds of communities had been destroyed by the German burning of villages in reprisal for supporting the Resistance. Thousands of villagers who had been driven out decided to remain in the valley towns after the war, and even today villages are still abandoned entirely or in part – though this changed somewhat after 1968 (see below).

If thoroughgoing political reform had been thwarted, France during the 1950s transformed itself from a primarily agricultural country to a modern industrial giant, its growth rate often rivalling that of West Germany, with whom it established in 1957 the European Coal and Steel Community, predecessor to the Common Market/EC/EU. Although the country, like Spain, was a member of NATO, much of France's military resources soon became embroiled in the **Algerian colonial rebellion**, which coming on the heels of the 1954 catastrophic defeat at Dien Bien Phu in Indochina proved to be an eight-year experience nearly as traumatic as the German occupation. By 1958, hard-line rightists among the army and the so-called **pieds noirs** – a million civilian settlers in Algeria virulently opposed to its possible independence – threatened to take on both loyal army units and the native rebels. De Gaulle returned from political limbo, dissolving the Fourth Republic and demanding extraordinary powers to settle the Algerian mess. For his pains, as president of the Fifth Republic, de Gaulle provoked an even more serious military revolt in 1961, with the **OAS** – a rogue army faction intent on preventing any settlement – mounting several attempts on his life. But Algerian independence was finally granted in 1962, prompting a flood of refugees – mostly *pieds noirs*, Jews and Arabs who had fought for the central government – into France. The *pied noirs* in particular, many of them settling in the south of France, would later lend considerable support to a resurgence in assorted racist and fascist activities, including the *Front National* of the 1990s.

CRACKS IN THE OLD ORDER

De Gaulle's style in diplomacy was idiosyncratic, to put it mildly; by the mid-Sixties he had ruffled numerous feathers abroad by blocking British entry to the Common Market, rebuking the US for its policy in Vietnam, calling for a "free Québec", withdrawing from the central command structure of NATO and refusing to sign any nuclear test-ban treaties. Even at home he was far from universally popular, and not just among the rightist fringe; a young challenger on the Left, **François Mitterrand**, nearly upset him in the 1965 presidential elections.

Yet despite these rumblings of discontent, the events of **May 1968** took everyone by surprise. What started as a provincial student protest against the paternalistic education system quickly escalated into a broad spectrum of agitation by both blue-collar and white-collar workers as well as academics, culminating in a protracted general strike. *Autogestion* – workers' self-management – was the dominant slogan; rather than specific demands for reform, there was general sentiment that all French institutions were too hierarchical and elitist. De Gaulle dropped out of sight for two weeks, consulting with army commanders; upon his return, he dissolved parliament and, to quell the "revolution", demanded a fresh electoral mandate from the frightened silent majority – who complied.

Although the protesters could point to few specific gains except in education, the events of 1968 changed French society in subtler ways over the next two decades; there was a perceptible lessening in formality and authoritarianism, and various domestic alternative movements (such as the Green Party) can trace their start to the "days of May". Numerous self-employed professionals who felt themselves thwarted by the return to normality in the main power centres **fled south**, as had generations of dissidents before them, to the shelter of the Cévennes and the Pyrenees, forming the advance guard of the **nouveaux ruraux** (new rurals) who would slowly repopulate the abandoned villages and eventually set up tourism-related enterprises.

Spain's increasing prosperity as the 1960s proceeded merely underlined the intellectual and financial bankruptcy of Franco's regime, and its inability to cope with popular demands. Higher incomes, the need for contemporary education and skills, plus a creeping invasion of outside culture made the anachronism of the Falange starkly clear. Franco's only reaction was an attempt to withdraw what few traces of increased liberalism had emerged, and his last years mirrored the repression of the early 1940s. Basque nationalists, whose 1973 assassination of Admiral Carrero Blanco effectively destroyed Franco's last hope of a like-minded successor, were singled out for particularly harsh treatment. When Franco finally died in November of that year, few expected much of his second-choice heir as head of state, the Bourbon prince **Juan Carlos**, cynically nicknamed *El Breve* (The Brief) for the anticipated duration of his reign.

In the event, and much to his credit, over the next seven years the new Spanish king oversaw a cautious, gradual but steady progress towards "democracy without adjectives", the demand of street activists in the late 1970s. The first **free elections of 1977** returned a coalition government, with the extreme Left and Right marginalized. Recognizing that his own future depended on the maintenance of the fledgling democracy, Juan Carlos declined to support the **attempted coup** of February 1981 by disaffected elements of the *Guardia Civil* and the army; its collapse, and attendant further discreditation of those nostalgic for the old order, set the stage for the landmark elections of October 1982.

Meanwhile, **in France**, the 1970s had been dominated by the two presidential terms of the centre-rightist **Valéry Giscard d'Estaing**, who defeated Mitterrand in 1974 and 1978. Despite a series of embarrassing scandals and the defection of Giscard's prime minister Jacques Chirac to form his own party, the Left seemed incapable of presenting a united front for the 1978 polls in particular. As in Spain of the late 1970s, few would have predicted the decisive result of the French elections of May 1981.

THE SOCIALIST GOVERNMENTS

In May 1981, Parisians gathered spontaneously at the Place de Bastille to celebrate the victory of Mitterrand's Socialists, the first left-of-centre triumph in France since the 1930s. Just over a year later, Felipe González's PSOE – the Spanish Socialists – also came to power with massive support, an even more dramatic reversal considering the nearness of the Falangist past. Despite enjoying substantial goodwill at the outset, both movements subsequently foundered on domestic and international realities, amidst increasingly acrimonious accusations of unprincipled

betrayals of campaign promises and party manifestos. As a result, the French Socialists lost power between 1986 and 1989, and again between 1993 and 1997, while their Spanish counterparts only just squeaked back into office in 1993 before being eased out in 1997.

The presence of four Communist ministers in the first post-1981 French cabinet reflected the inital commitment to an aggressively leftist agenda; by 1984, in the face of capital flight and bureaucratic foot-dragging, Mitterrand was compelled to back down as a centrist cabinet worked under Prime Minister **Laurent Fabius**. 1986 saw the return of the Right under **Jacques Chirac**'s Gaullists, an uneasy arrangement under a sitting Socialist president – because parliamentary and presidential elections were then out of sync in France – referred to as **cohabitation**. Chirac's monetarist fumblings and flirtations with **Jean-Marie Le Pen**'s overtly racist *Front National* resulted in a centre-left parliamentary coalition returning by a bare margin in 1989, under Social-Democrat prime minister **Michel Rocard**. Though some of Chirac's privatization programmes were stalled, the unpopularity of Rocard's own austerity measures resulted in **Édith Cresson** replacing him in 1991. Her abrasiveness and numerous gaffes prompted her sacking in 1992 in favour of **Pierre Bérégovoy**, a confidant of Mitterrand's. All these comings and goings virtually guaranteed a landslide coalition victory of the RPR and the UDF, the two conservative parties, in 1993; two months later, Bérégovoy – accused of accepting a private loan from a dubious character – shot himself, leaving no explanatory note.

This thumbnail summary of French elections and regimes to the early 1990s gives just a hint of the malaise which gripped the French scene. Scandal had been a near-constant feature of public life since 1981; equally disappointing was the Socialists' failure to change traditional militarism, all-pervasive secrecy, and environmental-unfriendliness in one of the most centralized states in the world. In the Pyrenees especially, despite lip service to ecological considerations, mega-projects such as the Somport tunnel were usually only slowed or modified rather than halted.

Spain by contrast enjoyed a certain amount of stability throughout the 1980s; the PSOE was convincingly re-elected in 1986, and only began to falter visibly in 1989 as the recession started to bite. Yet there was a similar pattern of compromise on core issues, which often made the PSOE government seem indistinguishable from Britain's contemporaneous Conservative government or from Germany under Chancellor Kohl. **Felipe González** had entered office in 1982 partly on an anti-NATO platform, but campaigned for continued membership in the hard-fought 1986 referendum on the issue, which went narrowly in favour. Control of inflation, supposedly in deference to EC-stipulated goals, had a higher priority than employment, and loss-making state-owned industries were drastically overhauled, and many privatized. **Anti-labour measures** such as cuts in already meagre unemployment benefits, a pay freeze for civil servants and a differential minimum-wage law for under-25s resulted in general strikes co-ordinated by the PSOE's own trade union, the powerful UGT (resurrected after the Franco years).

By the early 1990s, it became increasingly obvious that prolonged time in office had made the PSOE not just corrupt but complacent, with only the lack of compelling alternatives to "Felipe" (as the prime minister was universally called) and the enduring suspicion of the Right combining to maintain the status quo. The PSOE barely survived a strong 1993 challenge by the centre-right Partido Popular (PP) under its uncharismatic chief **José María Aznar**, and continued to govern only by dint of support from the Catalan nationalist party, having fallen short of an outright majority. As in France, spectacular scandals regularly punctuated the news, eroding the PSOE's position still further. Most damaging of these was the discovery of **GAL** (Grupo Antiterrorista de Liberación), a semi-autonomous antiterrorist unit which had been waging a "dirty war" throughout the 1980s, kidnapping and/or assassinating suspected ETA members and fellow-travellers. The press and an independent judiciary – both interfered with repeatedly by the PSOE government – exposed police participation in these acts and a clear chain of command extending up to the highest echelons of the PSOE.

FRANCE: THE RIGHT IN POWER – AND OUT AGAIN

The first major crisis for Prime Minister **Edouard Balladur**'s centre-right government in early 1994 was the violent reaction to his pro-

posal of reduced wages for young people. A similar response by Air France workers, farmers and fishermen to further monetarist measures caused Balladur to back down, losing him the respect of his natural constituency. Political violence in the south of France and corruption scandals continued unabated, adding – along with stubbornly high unemployment – to the support for fringe parties on the Left and Right (especially the racist *Front National*).

Meanwhile **Mitterrand**, terminally ill with prostate cancer, clung to office until mid-1995 despite various assaults on his reputation – specifically revelations about his war record as an official in the Vichy regime before he belatedly joined the Resistance. Yet when he **died** in January 1996, after fourteen years as head of state, he was mourned as a man of culture and vision, a tenacious political operator and a committed European.

The **May 1995 presidential elections** saw the Socialist Lionel Jospin pitted against a rightist field split between Balladur, Chirac, Le Pen (who scored 15.5 percent) and the anti-European Philippe de Villiers, a French equivalent to James Goldsmith. In a run-off, **Jacques Chirac** narrowly edged Jospin by mouthing comforting noises about unemployment and social exclusion.

One of Chirac's first decisions was the **abolition of conscription**, in favour of supposedly more efficient professional armed forces. The decree provoked impassioned response from left-wing parties, for whom conscription represented social levelling and the revolutionary spirit expressed in the words of the national anthem: "Aux Armes, Citoyens . . . ". Another Chirac move was to delay signing the Nuclear Non-Proliferation Treaty until France had carried out a new series of **nuclear tests** in the South Pacific. These provoked almost universal condemnation, boycotts of French goods, attacks on French embassy buildings in Australia and New Zealand, plus full-scale riots in Tahiti. The French navy captured Greenpeace's *Rainbow Warrior II*, almost ten years to the day after French secret service agents had sunk *Rainbow Warrior* in Auckland harbour.

On the domestic front, Chirac's new prime minister was **Alain Juppé**, a clever but clinical technocrat. It was left to him to fulfil election pledges of job creation and maintenance of pensions or welfare benefits with promised tax cuts, a continued strong franc and a reduction of the budget deficit with an eye to European monetary union. Juppé also promised to clean up corruption but ironically became immediately involved in an uproar concerning his own subsidized luxury flat in Paris. This and other scandals irritated voters, who had previously accepted nest-feathering as a perk of power but now, hard-pressed by austerity programmes, took a dim view of double standards.

The last straw came in autumn 1995, when Chirac announced that fiscal rectitude would have to take precedence over social comfort, and Juppé proposed changes in social security and "downsizing" of the rail network. The response was an all-but-general **strike** in November and December, when five million public-sector workers took to the streets with considerable support from becalmed private-sector commuters – the strongest show of protest in France since May 1968. Amazingly, Juppé survived this storm, abandoning some proposals and postponing others. A new tax to pay off the social security deficit was imposed, and cuts in the health service proceeded; the economically depressed Pyrenean regions, always net beneficiaries of every sort of public welfare programme from crèches to SNCF buses, were starkly affected by every policy wobble.

The UDF-RPR coalition stumbled through 1996, fulfilling predictions by Mitterrand and Giscard d'Estaing that Chirac's opportunism and impetuousness would make him and his government a laughing stock within months of assuming power. Although Chirac and Juppé enjoyed a four-hundred-seat parliamentary majority, valid until spring 1998, hanging on to the bitter end was not Chirac's cup of tea. Incredibly, in April 1997 he called **snap elections** for late May, perhaps hoping for a smaller but less fractious majority – and an end to future potential *cohabitation* by making the start of the next parliamentary and presidential terms coincide in 2002.

In the event Chirac totally miscalculated the public mood and the Socialists' ability to attract potential coalition partners, while his arrogant ploy to strengthen the presidency backfired spectacularly over two rounds of voting. **Jospin** and his allies, the Communists, the Greens and the anti-Maastricht Citizens' Movement, swept back to power in June on a programme featuring a proposed 35-hour week, minimum wage hikes, an emergency youth employment programme

and a more humane policy on immigration and naturalization. Thirty-eight Communists, seven Greens and more than a hundred women took seats. The *cohabitation* Chirac had gone to such lengths to avoid had come to pass a year earlier than it otherwise would have.

SPAIN: THE RIGHT FINALLY BACK IN POWER

Despite the ongoing woes of the PSOE, the Spanish **elections of late 1996** yielded yet another **hung parliament**, though this time Aznar's PP had a bare plurality of fifteen seats over the PSOE. Denied the "absolute majority" he had believed to be his throughout the campaign, Aznar had to do a **coalition** deal with the Catalan, Basque and Canary Island nationalist parties (whom he had described as "greedy parasites" on the hustings) to get a parliamentary majority. In return for their support, these regional parties – including those in the Eastern Pyrenees – expected continued, often disproportionate benefits to their regions.

González, for his part, seemed not to have drawn the proper conclusion from the result: "A couple more weeks of campaigning and we would have won" was his off-the-cuff reaction, as he dismissed the idea of retirement. The close finish initially denied the PSOE a period of urgently needed self-reflection that a crushing defeat and a quick change of leadership would have permitted. But early in 1998, languishing in public opinion and with the PSOE still in turmoil, **"Felipe"** finally **resigned** the leadership of the party he had dominated for 23 years.

The reasons for Aznar's failure to win an outright majority in 1996 were equally significant. At the last moment, memories of the long and repressive Franco era unnerved many voters wary of losing hard-won decentralization and the PSOE-established social benefits system – a vital lifeline in many poorer regions, including the Pyrenees. The electoral weight of Andalucía, González's power base, fulfilled its traditional role of offsetting the conservative North by supplying many of the discredited PSOE's surviving MPs.

During his first term as prime minister, Aznar gradually moved his party towards the centre, sidelining PP hardliners in the hope of gaining the electorate's confidence and a working majority not dependent on alliances with the regional nationalists. He frequently declared his admiration for the ideas of British Prime

Minister Tony Blair; apparently, one of the notions to be emulated was **keeping a tight rein on the news media**.

The PSOE replaced González with **José Borrell**, a former transport minister in González's government, but not his preferred choice of successor. González hovered constantly in the background, making it impossible for Borrell to stamp his own mark on the party. In 1999, when a financial scandal erupted, involving Borrell's performance as minister, he resigned and was replaced by the party hierarchy's – and González's – original nominee, **Joaquín Almunia**. With a general election now on the horizon and the PSOE still trailing in the polls, Almunia fashioned an electoral pact with the ex-Communist Izquierda Unida (United Left), thinking that their combined votes could overturn a likely Aznar victory.

The outcome of the March 2000 **general election** was a stunning **triumph for Aznar** and the PP, who took 183 of the 350 parliamentary seats with a ten-percent plurality; for the first time since the death of Franco the Right were in power with a clear majority.

Naturally, the results were a disaster for the Left: the electorate had apparently been unconvinced by the "shotgun marriage" between the PSOE and the IU (bitter enemies since the Civil War), which smacked more of an opportunistic patchwork than a government-in-waiting. Moreover, large numbers of voters seemed unwilling to risk the indisputable economic gains of Aznar's period in office, while many of the Left's traditional supporters didn't bother to vote at all. On election night, when the scale of the PSOE/IU defeat became clear, Joaquín Almunia **resigned** from the leadership of the PSOE, which clung to just 125 seats. At the party convention which followed, the old guard and its candidates were swept aside when delegates elected a relative unknown, **José Luis Rodríguez Zapatero**, a member of the moderate-socialist "Nueva Vía" (New Way) faction with PSOE. The party clearly hopes that a young (born 1961), new leader will bring them back to power. The problem is that, given how similar he is to Aznar (both are rather wooden technocrats from central Spain), not enough voters may see the point in swapping one for the other.

In hindsight, a defeat for the Left always appeared likely, if only because the lacklustre Aznar had kept the economy on course with a **growth rate** among the best in Europe. Unemployment, though still the highest in the EU, has fallen to below 20 percent for the first time since 1988, while new jobs are being created faster than in any other European economy. The PP seems intent on continuing as the PSOE had begun: withdrawing subsidies from ailing industries such as shipbuilding, accelerating privatization of former state-owned industries, reducing corporate taxes and "liberalizing" labour laws. However, after years in opposition spent rooting out sleaze in the PSOE government, the PP has also become vulnerable to charges of cronyism and **corruption**.

When he announced the day after the election that despite his majority he would seek to make a governing **alliance** with the regional parties (excepting the troublesome Basques), Aznar was apparently respecting the delicate consensus which has maintained stability in the post-Franco period. This approach may have won over many voters who appeared unconvinced by warnings from the Left during the 2000 election campaign that, once in power with an overall majority, the PP's social-democratic mask would come off and wholesale dismantling of the social welfare systems would follow, together with attacks on the trade unions. An acknowledgement of the PSOE's prior role in modernizing Spain, coupled with a declaration that the PP is now a party of the "reforming centre", suggests that Aznar intends to ply a stable course during his second term.

FRANCE: THE SECOND COHABITATION

Jospin's victory inevitably raised unrealistic expectations of how much a left-of-centre government could accomplish, with its room for manoeuvring severely limited by Brussels and economic globalization. But to its credit, the new government quickly adopted a consensual style of government, with decisions reached only after debate and monitoring of public opinion, markedly in contrast to Juppé's high-handed, from-the-top-down style. By so doing it was able to propose a 15-billion franc **increase in taxation** for social programmes, borne equally by corporations and individuals, without seriously denting its popularity.

Jospin's **poll ratings** remained high through 1999, despite increased friction with Chirac (both men intend to contest the presidency in

2002), dissension in the Left coalition's own ranks and some predictable back-pedalling on campaign stances. By spring 1999, despite his execrating the practice on the hustings, Jospin had surpassed all former French prime minsters in **privatizations** of major state enterprises, selling off over $20 billion worth; unlike in other countries, though, it was made sure that small shareholders would benefit. In the March 1999 **Euro-elections**, the Greens did surprisingly well, surpassing the Communists as France's second party of the "Left". Accordingly, at the Greens' party conference in September 1999 there were murmurings that, with their strong position, they should press for more action from Jospin on such issues as the future of nuclear power, a 35-hour work-week, GM foods and regional languages, or consider pulling out of

BASQUE AND CATALAN NATIONALISM: A COMPARISON

Although the **Basque and Catalan separatist movements** share certain concerns – resistance to exploitation from central governments, and the preservation of a distinctive language and culture – they also differ markedly. In Catalunya, demands for autonomy haven't acquired the same dimension as in much of the Basque country; the notion of an independent Catalan nation has very few adherents aside from the extremists of the *Terra Lliure* group. Whereas the Catalan complaint is of a relatively successful province milked by the rest of Spain, and therefore draws support from all social classes, the Basque protest remains fundamentally motivated by fears over non-Basque immigrant labour and is predominantly lower-middle-class and working-class in character. Finally, there are sharp political differences within the Basque provinces: urbanized, industrialized Bizkaia and Gipuzkoa are Basque-nationalist, but more rural Navarra and Araba are conservative and Spanish-loyalist, while the French Basque areas see themselves as separate from both their Spanish counterparts and the rest of France.

Tension between Madrid and the Spanish Basques first arose in the eighteenth century, with the abrogation of the region's *fueros*, the age-old charters guaranteeing a measure of self-government. The situation worsened considerably after Franco's victory in the Civil War, when the October 1936 statute of autonomy granted by the Republicans to Gipuzkoa and Bizkaia was rescinded, the Basque language banned outside the home and "politically unreliable" teachers dismissed. The Catholic Church's opposition to supposedly atheistic socialism had made it pro-Falangist during the war, but the reality of Franco's victory prompted a gradual change. From the 1950s onwards, the Church encouraged part-time Basque schools or *Ikastolas*, and by the end of the Franco era there were 33,000 pupils enrolled in them.

The nature and prevalence of Euskera is an index of the distinctness – and precariousness – of Basque culture. While a Catalan-speaker stands a chance of being understood in the rest of Spain and even in France, someone speaking only the archaic Basque language cannot communicate with outsiders. A poll in 1970 (before Franco died) highlighted the relative strengths between the two principal minority languages of the Pyrenees: 90 percent of Catalan housewives were found to understand Catalan, 77 percent to speak it, 62 percent to read it and 38 percent to write it; for the Basque country the figures were 50 percent, 46 percent, 25 percent and 11 percent respectively.

The failure of the **Basque National Party** (PNV or *Partido Nacionalista Vasco*), founded in the late nineteenth century, to gain lasting political autonomy for the coastal Basque provinces, followed by the Francoist repression, led to the emergence by the early 1950s of ETA (*Euskad Ta Azkatasurra* – "Basque Homeland and Freedom"). Originally a middle-class student movement whose methods included – and still embrace – bank robberies, kidnappings for ransom, protection rackets and assassinations, it eventually split into two factions: the violent *ETA-Militar* and the *ETA-Politico-Militar*, the latter being socialists first and Basque nationalists second. Although full-time ETA membership has never exceeded one thousand, its methods provoked widespread reprisals, including mass arrests, torture and show trials as at Burgos in 1970, which backfired internationally, and closer to home caused Catalan intellectuals to stage a sympathy sit-in at the monastery of Montserrat. Meanwhile, there was little violence in Catalunya itself and no counterpart of ETA: a 1963 petition against language restrictions, or a pointed rendition of the traditional anthem "Els Segadors" in Franco's presence, was more typical of the Catalan approach.

Following the restoration of democratic process by referendum in 1976, the free elections of the following year gave **Pacte Democratico per Catalunya** – an alliance of pro-Catalan parties – ten seats in the lower house of the Spanish parliament; among the Basques, the reconstituted PNV won eight seats and a new left-wing nationalist party, **Euskadi Eskerra**, won one. The PNV and *Euskadi Eskerra* remain theoret-

the government (where their member **Dominique Voynet** was minister of environment).

The long-promised 35-hour work-week, designed to reduce the still-stubborn unemployment rate, was finally implemented in February 2000, and initially pleased nobody. Public unions threatened to strike, freelancers demanded the right to work as much as they liked, and owners warned that it would make French industry uncompetitive. In April, Jospin carried out a radical cabinet reshuffle, replacing old friends and non-Socialist personalities with a "traditional" Socialist line-up. In August the cabinet became still less diverse when Interior Minister **Jean-Pierre Chevènement**, sole representative in the government of the pro-sovereignty Citizens' Movement, resigned, sup-

ically committed to independence but seek change by constitutional means – in contrast to **Herri Batasuna** (United People), linked to *ETA-Militar*. In the 1980 elections, HB won eleven seats in the Basque regional parliament, in 1984 eleven again and in 1986 thirteen, but in all cases the deputies refused to take up their seats, leaving the PNV in control. Subsequently, the PNV divided: Carlos Garaikoetxea, the first Basque premier, decamped with half his regional deputies to form the centralist *Eusko Alkartasuna* (EA), leaving the PNV to the decentralist José Antonio Ardanza.

Although Catalunya's experiences earlier this century paralleled those of the Basque country – the granting of a statute of autonomy by the Republicans, followed by severe cultural repression after 1939 – relations with Madrid are currently more cordial. Catalunya is now effectively run day-to-day by its **Generalitat**, the regional government, which controls education, health, social security, tourism, commerce, agriculture and cultural matters. Curiously, in light of the Republican past, centre-right regional parliaments have been consistently returned by Catalunyan voters since 1978; they are apparently seen as better able to look after Catalan business interests, and – by participating in the coalition governments of 1993 and 1996 – to extract fiscal concessions from Madrid.

For many Basques the wounds of large-scale immigration, exploitation by a non-Basque elite and denial of significant independence still fester. Yet alone thus far among Spain's autonomous regions, the Basque provinces have the right to collect and disburse all of their own revenues, and the *Guardia Civil* has been replaced by a home guard, the *Ertzainza*.

Continuing **ETA outrages**, apparently designed to provoke centralist repression which will convince waverers to support the extreme solution of independence, garner less and less approval, and would seem to be a desperate rearguard action by a fringe group that perceives its support to be waning. The kidnapping and eventual murder of PP municipal councillor Miguel Ángel Blanco in July 1997 – his release had been contingent on the PP relocating six hundred ETA prisoners to Basque-province jails – sparked an unprecedented wave of anti-ETA street demonstrations across the country; many more recent killings have been met with equally vehement and well-attended public denunciations. Nonviolent Basque local parties have moved to oust HB mayors in certain ETA strongholds, in conjunction with Madrid's efforts to break up the front-business networks (often hotels and restaurants) which finance ETA. But PP-inspired calls during 1997 to "socially isolate" HB in the Basque country, for example by boycotting its supporters' shops, have been denounced, somewhat hyperbolically, as reminiscent of early Nazism.

ETA was much slower to take root in the overwhelmingly rural **French Basque regions**, where – except in Bayonne – an urban proletariat is almost nonexistent. Grievances here have more to do with a perceived Parisian policy of relegating the Pays Basque to "Third World" status, promoting only tourist-related industries at the expense of others. As for cultural identity, the 61 teachers in the *ikastolak* or Basque-language primary schools around Bayonne were finally recognized as state employees in November 1989. Since signing the European Charter on Regional and Minority Languages in May 1999, Paris must acknowledge the existence of **regional languages** such as Euskera (and Catalan, Breton, or Occitan), and allow them to be read, spoken, taught and broadcast. But according to a French Supreme Court decision the same year, the government is not obliged to accord them any official status for legal or administrative procedures – ie, no title deeds, weddings or trial transcripts in minority languages – and formal ratification is pending. The chances of a separate Pays-Basque *département*, with its capital at Bayonne, being hived off from Pyrénées-Atlantiques any time soon would appear to be similarly remote, though such a proposal is now in the public arena, much to the dismay of prominent figures who balefully predict the "balkanization of France" and "the dislocation of French identity".

posedly because he disagreed with Jospin's handling of negotiations with Corsican separatists – but more likely to prepare a bid for the 2002 presidential race.

Despite Jospin's government having pulled France out of a long recession and spurred renewed economic growth, and despite the 35-hour work-week proving wildly popular and effective with almost everyone by late 2000, its **re-election** in 2002 is by no means certain. One of the consequences of the decline in the extreme Right has been a reinvigoration of the traditional Right. However, the UDF and RPR are still each beset by scandals, and French patience with the arrogance and corruption of the traditional elite, most of them schooled at the École Nationale d'Administration, is now thin to the point of transparency. Future cohabitations, at least, will be far less likely: by the terms of a recent referendum, France's presidential term, formerly seven years, will be brought into step with the five-year parliamentary term as of the 2002 elections.

THE CONTEMPORARY OUTLOOK

Despite ongoing political turmoil **in France** since the 1980s and frequent (often self-inflicted) damage to the country's international reputation, the **French economy** remains sounder – with a current unemployment rate of nine percent and falling – and the standard of living higher than in Spain.

The overriding contemporary issues in France are the interrelated ones of **racism**, general xenophobia, remorse (or lack thereof) for the fate of its **Jews** during World War II and **immigration control**. The main exploiter of these concerns has been the quasi-fascist **Front National** under its foot-in-mouth leader **Jean-Marie Le Pen**, which, although it has long since lost its parliamentary seats through some creative gerrymandering, has captured four municipalities in Provence since 1995. Until the late 1990s it consistently polled about fifteen percent nationwide (on one occasion thirty percent around Perpignan), but it is now showing signs of being a spent force – at least until the next economic downturn. Personal rivalry between Le Pen and his protégé **Bruno Mégret** led to the FN splitting into two separate parties on January 24, 1999, and in the Euro-elections soon after the parties combined barely got nine percent of the vote.

Other politicians of various stripes have seen fit to jump on the nativist bandwagon at critical times, for example in the wake of the Algerian terrorist incidents which punctuated 1996. Charles Pasqua, Balladur's minister of the interior, considerably tightened up procedures for granting right of residence, let alone citizenship, to immigrants or their descendants, and introduced random street identity checks. Under Juppé, matters worsened when police evicted hundreds of unsuccessful Malian asylum-seekers from the Paris church where they had sought refuge. In a welcome gesture which reduced tension, Jospin's government almost immediately regularized the position of the Malian church-occupiers, and in a one-off amnesty granted residence to thousands of other illegals who had been working and paying taxes in France for years. While the extreme Right considers Jews, in particular those of North African descent, no better than Muslims, in September 1997 French Catholic bishops formally apologized for the Church's complicity in the 1942 rounding-up of local Jews.

But no single event improved the racial climate in France, if only perhaps temporarily, as much as the French football team's unexpected **triumph in the 1998 World Cup**, which France hosted. Of the 22 squad members, half of them were of foreign descent, including two born overseas, despite Le Pen's calls for immigrants to be excluded from the team. Hero of the hour was **Zinedine "Zizou" Zidane**, from Marseilles but the grandson of settlers from Algeria, who scored two of the goals in the team's 3-0 win over favoured Brazil. The wild celebrations across France, with blacks, whites and *beurs* (French-born of North African descent) embracing in the streets just two days before Bastille Day, were a revelation in a country which had just published a survey showing its populace to have among the most racist attitudes in Europe. For once, the odious Le Pen had nothing to say other than mumbling he'd always meant that France could be "composed of different races and colours", provided they were patriotic. President Chirac had early on come out as a high-profile supporter of the team and its composition, praising the "tricolour and multicolour" victory and warning the conventional Right to cease its extended flirtation with National Front policies. But as the warm glow of the victory faded, glaring details re-emerged, such as the absence of any MPs of North African descent, the lack of

Arabs or Africans in high-visibility media positions, or the fact that the official racism phone hotline (opened May 2000) receives 500 substantiated cases of discrimination daily.

Spain's voice is now listened to with respect in international circles, and its cities are conceded to be some of the art and entertainment beacons of Europe. But too often there has been lavish spending on high-profile, prestige projects – such as high-speed rail links and the Sevilla Expo – while sustained, incremental investment in the country's infrastructure and human resources is neglected. For example, following France's lead, conscription in Spain is to be phased out by 2002, leaving a professional army – and a 125,000-man annual shortfall in staffing for the numerous charities which used to rely on a steady stream of conscientious-objector volunteers, in the absence of funds for salaried positions.

In accordance with the constitution of 1978, there has been an appreciable **devolution of powers** to the seventeen autonomous regions or **autonomías** into which Spain is divided. Each has its own president, parliament and civil service – an enormously expensive duplication of functions. Variable statutes of autonomy have been granted to Catalunya, Aragón, Navarra and Gipuzkoa, which between them include the entire Spanish Pyrenees. However, Madrid has reserved too many powers – most notably tax collection, followed by proportional disbursement – for the system to have yet approached true federalism, though Catalunya's Generalitat has extracted from the central government the concession of collecting, and spending, thirty percent of its own budget. Elsewhere, especially in Aragón where the regionalist Partido Aragonés (and ample graffiti in the local language) are much in evidence, the political authority has been present for local Pyrenean initiatives, but funds have often proved to be insufficient. Another obvious downside to decentralization is the tendency of *autonomías*, when they do get cash, to subsidize one-off payments to buy votes, rather than fund economic development. Balancing peripheral self-determination with fiscal responsibility is the task confronting Madrid governments of any complexion, and one that goes against the grain of the national impulse to live for the moment and let tomorrow take care of itself.

The stubbornly high Spanish **unemployment** rate – still well into double figures even in the most prosperous regions – means that petty crime is a stable feature of life, even in isolated areas. Catalunya, especially Girona province, is markedly better off for work; many of the young people you'll see in seasonal jobs at Catalan Pyrenean resorts are migrants from distant provinces, working with little in the way of employment contracts or security.

Mountain agriculture has long since ceased to be profitable on either slope of the Pyrenees, so the ancient terraces are crumbling back into wilderness. Repopulation is therefore left to the *nouveaux ruraux/neo-rurales* in search of alternative lifestyles, and to people renovating second homes. France in particular offers a range of grants for permanent mountain-dwellers, but **full-time Pyrenean residence** remains a precarious undertaking. The advent of solar-power panels (especially on the Spanish side) and mobile telephony does mean that business and residence can now be conducted in previously abandoned, non-viable spots, which conventional state utilities have always refused to supply.

While Spain is no longer as starry-eyed about the **EU** as it was in 1990, a significant majority of Spaniards still strongly back European integration and see their participation at the launch of the **euro** and its replacement of the peseta in 2002 as a landmark in Spain's move into the European mainstream. Most citizens are also acutely aware of the benefits accruing to the country from huge EU "convergence" grants for important infrastructure projects, as well as subsidies to the pivotal farming sector under the Common Agricultural Policy. The **single European market** has had a discernible impact on towns like Perpignan and Bayonne (as well as Jaca and Girona), which handle or service much of the freight and transit personnel moving north and south. The effect of EU money is highly visible in the Pyrenees, where it funds civil engineering projects otherwise beyond the means of the autonomous regions. Much of this development is highly unsympathetic to the environment, with the Pyrenees at risk of transformation into a cluster of tame theme parks linked by motorways, where genuine indigenous culture and wildlife have been destroyed. That said, commercial exploitation is still far below the level prevailing in the Alps, even as the Pyrenees have "arrived" as a popular overseas-tourist destination since the mid-1990s.

WILDLIFE

There is plenty of wildlife to observe in the Pyrenees, despite the effects of hunting and environmental damage (see "The Environment", p.536). The range is especially rewarding for bird-spotters, with a variety of magnificent resident indigenous species, and enormous numbers of migrating birds to be seen flying over the western Col d'Organbidexka and, in the east near Canigou, the Col d'Eyne.

The round-up below picks out the major animal species that you might encounter (as well as the declining species that you probably won't), and details some of the more interesting types of Pyrenean flora. However, it is only a general guide to occurrence and habitat. For something more specific, see the list of recommended wildlife titles on p.545.

BIRDS

The **lammergeier** or bearded vulture (*gypaète barbu* in French; *quebrantahuesos* in Castilian) was persecuted almost out of existence by herdsmen fearing for their livestock, but lately has made a slight recovery. It is easily identified by the wonderful pinkish-gold breast of the adult, a long wedge-shaped tail, narrow wings and enormous size – weighing up to 6kg, with a wingspan of almost 3m. Still rare enough to be a thrill when spotted, lammergeiers can most reliably be seen in several places: at Gavarnie, in the Aspe/Ossau region, in the Valle de Ordesa and in their principal strongholds of the Echo, Ansó and Roncal valleys northwest of Jaca.

The lammergeier's diet consists mainly of bone marrow, which it exposes by dropping bones onto a rocky surface from a height of 30–50m (hence the Castilian name, meaning "breaks-bones"). To locate its meal, the solitary lammergeier often works in conjunction with a flock of **griffon vultures** (*vautour fauve* in French; *buitre común* in Spanish), which are similar in size, but lack the wedge-shaped tail and streamlining, and have a distinctive white head and neck, as well as black wing-tips. Only when the griffons have finished stripping the flesh from the carcass does the lammergeier move in. Flocks of griffon vultures patrol much of the Pyrenees, especially in the Basque country and the Aspe/Ossau valleys.

Occasionally, the rare **black vulture** is seen in the Western Pyrenees, particularly in the Valle de Echo or over the Iparla ridge, either with griffons or on its own. This bird can be distinguished from the griffon by its longer and more rounded tail, its much darker plumage and a black area around the eye.

Unlike the above species, the **Egyptian vulture** (*percnoptère* in French; *acantilados alimoche* in Castilian) is found in the Pyrenees only during the breeding season, when it can be seen in the Aspe, Ossau and Soule valleys or around the Ordesa region. The smallest of the vultures – with a wingspan of about 150cm – the Egyptian has white plumage and black wingtips. Nicknamed *Marie-Blanque* or *La Dame Blanche* in the French valleys, its arrival in the April skies announces the start of spring.

The **golden eagle** (*aigle royal* in French; *aguila real* in Castilian) is glimpsed everywhere in the high mountains, each breeding pair having a territory of between 90 and 130 square kilometres. You can identify juveniles by the white patches on the wing underside, but for adult birds over five years old, identification is more by size (around 80cm from beak to tail, with a wingspan of 3m) and the open V-shape of its upturned wings as it soars. Whereas the golden eagle and the scarcer Bonelli's eagle – dark on top, paler underneath, with a dark, striped tail – are seen all year round, the **booted eagle** and the **short-toed eagle** settle here only during the summer breeding season. The booted is the smallest of the European eagles, with a wingspan of up to 120cm. It has a long, narrow tail and is either pale with an almost white front and white-flecked head, or uniformly mahogany-coloured with slender white stripes along the front of the wings. The short-toed eagle is often almost pure white with darker banding all round the wings, and has a head that seems disproportionately large. A unique characteristic is its habit of hovering motionless over its intended prey, commonly snakes, with its legs dangling freely.

The acrobatic kites are perhaps the most entertaining birds to watch. The **red kite** (*milan royal* in French; *milano* in Castilian) has a deeply forked tail, and continuously twists in the air as it manoeuvres over carrion. The **black kite** (*milan noir* in French; *milano negro* in Castilian) is darker than the red kite, its tail shorter and straighter-edged, and its wingspan smaller at around 115cm. It is most often seen circling over municipal rubbish dumps, unconcerned by the comings and goings of the trucks. The autumn migration to the Pyrenees greatly supplements the summertime population.

The turkey-like **capercaillie** (*grand tétras* in French; *urogallo* in Castilian), hunted and harassed to extinction in the French Alps, survives in small numbers in the Pyrenees, protected – though not entirely effectively – in the national parks and in Andorra. Despite its size it is a very elusive bird, but you might see one breaking noisily from cover, or witness the late-winter mating display of the cock, when it throws back its green-ringed neck, and dances and sings. The hen is duller, mostly brown flecked with white, and with smaller bright red "eyebrows" than the male.

Since it is also seldom seen in flight, except when flushed out of hiding, the **ptarmigan** (*lagopède alpin* in French; *perdiz blanca* in Castilian) is also difficult to spot. It's found in pairs around the central Pyrenees during summer, and in winter in flocks, when the birds are almost totally snow-camouflage white, except for a black tail and red "eyebrows".

Several smaller but distinctive birds of high altitude are the playful and acrobatic **alpine chough**, a slim crow with a curved yellow beak, sometimes seen with its red-beaked cousin, the **common chough**; the **snow finch**, like a large sparrow, but noticeably black and white in flight; and the **wall-creeper**, red, grey and black, with a thin curved beak and usually found on or near cliffs. Lower down, the **white-backed woodpecker** has

its only western European home in the woodlands of the Pyrenees.

MAMMALS

The most agile and conspicuous wild mammal of the high mountains is the **isard** or **Pyrenean chamois** (*rebeco* or *camuza* in Castilian; *sarrio* in Aragonese), a member of the antelope family and a close relative of the larger Alpine chamois. Living among the peaks in summer and descending in the winter, they are numerous in the Parc National des Pyrénées and the contiguous Parque Nacional de Ordesa y Monte Perdido. Individuals around Port d'Espagne, near Cauterets, as well as in Ordesa are uncharacteristically tame because of their contact with tourists. Gavarnie, the Sierra del Cadí, Canigou and Aigüestortes are other good places to see them. A few individuals do manage to survive at high altitudes during the snowy months, so you should brace for the surprise value of isards darting across ski runs, or the path of your lift.

The **mouflon** (*muflón* in Castilian), which resembles a very large and sturdy sheep with curling black horns, is a recently reintroduced species. Bones found near Perpignan show that they inhabited the region thousands of years ago, but Corsica, Sardinia and Cyprus were this sheep's only modern natural strongholds. Mouflon are now doing well in the Carlit massif and on Pic Pibeste, near Lourdes, where the arid, Mediterranean-like microclimate allows them to thrive.

The dark-bristled **wild boar** (*sanglier* in French; *jabalí* in Castilian) is nocturnal, and nomadic when under hunting-season pressure, covering up to 40km between dusk and dawn. You may see it at its mud-bath, to which the beast returns regularly, but are more likely to notice signs of its presence than the animal itself. Large areas of disturbed earth are often indicative that a wild boar has been rooting around with its tusks, especially in woodland where it forages for beech nuts and acorns. Boar are much disliked locally, owing to their habit of damaging fields; they have become a prolific pest since the 1990s owing to mild winters and overzealous reintroduction programmes by hunting clubs.

Red deer and the much smaller, slim-horned **roe deer** live in the central Pyrenees, both favouring calcareous zones where open pasture meets forest and the necessary combination of food and cover is provided. Dawn and dusk are the best times to view deer, when feeding activity is most intense; they are elusive animals, though, and local advice will usually be needed to find them. On the Spanish side, however, hunting reserves set aside for them have proven too small for exploding populations; hungry animals have wandered out of the limited areas, resulting in numerous traffic accidents and demands from hunters to be allowed to cull the surplus. Numerous deer migrating south from central France have attracted a following of **wolves** – animals not known in the Pyrenees in living memory – to within 70km of the range, and they should arrive within the next few years.

Throughout much of the high Pyrenees you will hear, though probably not see, the **marmot** (*marmotte* in French; *marmota* in Castilian), a now-common dweller above the tree line that once disappeared from the Pyrenees after centuries of hunting, mostly for dog food but partly for its fur. This robust rodent – reaching a length of 75cm – was reintroduced to the French Central Pyrenees during the 1960s and 1970s, and has now spread to both sides of the range. The shrill alarm shriek emitted by "sentry" individuals sends the colony scurrying to its extensive tunnel system, which is generally dug on warm, south-facing scree slopes at around 2000m – a habitat where its fawn-grey fur makes the marmot almost invisible. Despite their cuddly appearance and anthropomorphic habit of standing on two legs, marmots can be fierce, fighting to the death over territorial disputes.

The Pyrenean **wildcat** (*chat sauvage* in French; *gato montés* in Castilian) is genetically much the same as that found in other parts of Europe; it looks like a domestic tabby, only much larger, with a distinctively thick tail. Pyrenean wildcats prefer south-facing forests well below alpine habitats, where their preferred prey of fieldmice and voles is abundant; they dislike snow, and descend as necessary in winter. Wildcats are protected on both sides of the Pyrenees, and are actually increasing in numbers and expanding their range, but are shy and seldom seen.

Wildcats shouldn't be confused with the **genet**, which inhabits lower altitudes up to about 1000m. Neither a member of the weasel family nor a feline, these curious creatures have a cat-like head, a leopard-spotted body and an outsize ringed tail. They're an introduced species, having been brought as pets from North Africa by the Moors – and subsequently escaping into the wild. Opportunist carnivores, they will eat anything from frogs to rabbits.

Stoats are another small, sinuous carnivore of the weasel family which prey on small rodents and rabbits. In their reddish-brown summer fur with a black-tipped tail they are fairly conspicuous, but in winter they change colour to white to camouflage themselves in the snow, at which time they are called **ermines**. A larger relative is the **pine marten** (*martre* in French; *marta garduña* in Castilian), which remains a warm brown colour all year round, and is found up to the tree line in the Pyrenees in coniferous and mixed woodland. The **red squirrel** (*ardilla roja* in Castilian; *écureuil rouge* in French) favours much the same habitat and – not subject to competition from greys as in Britain – remains relatively abundant.

ENDANGERED SPECIES

The Pyrenean **ibex** (*bouquetin* in French; *cabra montés* in Castilian, *bucardo* in Aragonese), a stocky species of wild goat, is effectively extinct. Until 1999 the slopes of the Valle de Ordesa supported the range's single troupe, but conservation-programme blunders, a harsh winter or two, inbreeding and bad luck doomed it; the last individual died in January 2000, struck by a falling tree. However cells from the fresh corpse were quickly rescued, and it's now planned to clone new specimens, with the less hardy Gredo ibex serving as surrogate mothers. Some thousand of the latter survive, though they are a distinct subspecies of those formerly native in the Pyrenees. Hunting has been the principal cause of Pyrenean ibex's demise, their distinctive ribbed horns a much-esteemed trophy during the nineteenth century.

The small, unaggressive Pyrenean subspecies of **brown bear** (*ours* in French; *oso pardo* in Spanish) is nearly as close to extinction. No one knows precisely how many native bears remain in the Pyrenees but the top figure is only around seven. Bears are most likely to survive in an area straddling the border around the Aspe, Ossau and Roncal valleys; there may still be some in the border area between Luchon and Benasque; while those few remaining in the Couserans are scheduled to be transferred to the Vallée d'Aspe. Experience with other species shows that so small a population seldom retains sufficient genetic diversity to reproduce successfully. Effectively, therefore, the brown bear of the Pyrenees is finished as a distinct subspecies, though there might still be time to cross the remaining specimens with stock from other European brown bear populations; Slovenia was the source of a few individuals introduced into the Couserans in 1997. For a lengthier discussion of bears, see the box on p.382.

The only other large carnivore of the area is the rare **lynx** (same in French; *pardelo* in Castilian), which like the bear has been widely persecuted. Out of a total French/Spanish population of some six hundred, just a few dozen remain in the western French Pyrenees, but these are vulnerable to loss of habitat through deforestation. Wildcats (see above) are sometimes mistaken for them.

Few have heard of the **desman** (same in French; *almizclera* or *desmán* in Castilian), yet this trunk-nosed, aquatic, mole-like mammal is one of the great curiosities of the Pyrenees. All attempts to study the creature have failed, since in captivity specimens die almost immediately, and it is extremely scarce in the wild. Needing undisturbed and unpolluted streams to survive, the desman has been sighted in the Baronnies, in the Aspe and the streams of the Eastern Pyrenees, which are the cleanest in the range; the parks and reserves south of the watershed are promising too, especially Aigüestortes and Roncal's Parque Natural Pirenaico.

AMPHIBIANS, REPTILES AND BUTTERFLIES

The slow-moving **fire salamander** (*salamandre jaune et noire* in French; *salamandra común* in Spanish) is like a soft-skinned lizard, with brilliant yellow-and-black markings that warn potential predators of its toxic skin secretions. They are primarily nocturnal, and usually only seen by day in damp weather, when heavy rain can lure them out onto paths and roads. The smaller, camouflaged Pyrenean **brook salamander** is endemic to the mountains, and found in cold lakes and streams.

A true reptile, the **Iberian rock lizard** can be found, unlike most of its sun-loving relatives, at surprisingly high altitudes in the Pyrenees. Several snakes occur in the area, none of them

poisonous except the **asp viper**. Like most snakes, this species, with a dark wavy or zigzag pattern along the spine, only bites if under threat of attack and needs merely to be left alone.

Numerous **butterflies** (French *papillon*; Castilian *mariposa*) make a home in the Pyrenees, even to quite high altitudes, with July and August being the best months; the Val d'Aran is one of the best locales for them. Apollo butterflies are white, with distinctive red or yellow eyespots on the wings, whereas the humbler clouded apollo could be mistaken for a small cabbage white. The endemic Gavarnie blue is a rather disappointing shade of grey, but the slightly more widespread Eros blue can equal the colour of the gentians it feeds among. Ringlets are a group of medium-sized brown butterflies, with wings marked by black eyespots. They are difficult to distinguish, even for experts, but two species and seven subspecies are endemic to the Pyrenees.

FLORA

Pyrenean high-altitude flora resembles that of the Alps in many ways, but with the warmer average temperatures, the treeline of the Pyrenees can be much higher in a few favoured positions, reaching 2600m on southern slopes of the Néouvielle massif, or 2100m in the Marcadau valley. The highest-altitude **trees** are Pyrenean mountain pines (either *Pinus uncinata* or *Pinus mugo*, and hybrids), with distinctive hooked tips to the cone scales – thus the French name of *pin crochet*. Black pines (*Pinus nigra*, ssp *salzmanii*) are the next most tolerant of alpine conditions, occurring up to about 2100m; lower down, in roughly descending order of occurrence, Scots pine, beech, silver fir, birch and poplar form dense forests, with some of the finest being in the Ordesa National Park. Lower still (below about 1000m) grow maple, hornbeam, sweet chestnut and various deciduous oaks. To the east, near the Mediterranean coast, appear groves of umbrella-shaped stone pine, whose edible seeds are gathered as pine nuts.

Because of the rainfall disparity between some of the dry Spanish slopes and the much wetter French slopes, the vegetation in one country is often very different to that at a similar altitude on the opposite side of the border. The underlying igneous and metamorphic rocks are hard and slow-weathering, but often overlaid with more plant-friendly limestone. The range's altitude has made the mountains an effective barrier, preventing the spread of many lower-altitude Spanish species northwards into France, and vice versa. June and July are the best months for finding wildflowers in bloom, but a few species begin as early as May, while others carry on into August, with a few exceptional autumn flowers.

More than 3300 species of **plants** are recorded for the Pyrenees, about 180 of them endemic – found growing wild nowhere else. The two unspectacular and very similar species of **Pyrenean yam**, with tiny green flowers, a swollen starchy root and tropical relatives, are ancient relics of a warmer climate. Both are confined to the Pyrenees, with the rarer one living only in the Noguera Ribagorçana gorge. A much more attractive relict from the Tertiary period is the **ramonda**, named after Ramond de Carbonnières, the doyen of Pyrenean exploration in the late eighteenth century. Although not rare, it is endemic to limestone slopes in northeastern Spain and the Pyrenees. Resembling its distant relative, the African violet, it has fleshy wrinkled leaves and, in summer, small purple flowers with a central yellow cone of stamens.

Other endemics are more flamboyant. The long-leaved **butterwort**, clinging spectacularly to the cliffs at Gavarnie, has "flypaper" leaves that trap and digest insects; the large purple **storksbill** sports bright, almost garish flowers. The ashy and western **cranesbills** have far more subtle shades of soft pink on their trumpet-shaped flowers; more delicate still are the little **horned pansies**, with fragrant violet blooms. The rare **silvery vetch** has spikes of pea flowers that are white with thread-like violet veining; the Pyrenean and Aragonese **columbines** have long-spurred flowers of a wonderful blue, while their relative, the Pyrenean **adonis** or pheasant's eye produces huge golden bowl-shaped flowers over feathery foliage in early summer. The higher areas of the Pyrenees are home to tussocky **fescue** grasses (genus *Festuca*), many species of which are endemic to these mountains. South-facing slopes in Alto Aragón turn yellow with **broom** during early summer.

Several **primroses** in subtle shades of lilac to red can be found in rocky or marshy places, but their small, compact and more delicate relatives the **rock jasmines** are mostly restricted to high-altitude cliffs and screes; *Androsace ciliata* and *A. cylindrica* are two of the rarest, confined to the central areas around Gavarnie and Monte Perdido. The **Pyrenean snowbell** has deeply fringed violet flowers and favours damp, shady conditions in the west of the range.

Growing mostly above the treeline, though sometimes in shady woodland, are many species of **saxifrage**, five of them endemic to the Pyrenees. Their flowers are usually small, numerous and starry, coloured white or pinkish in loose sprays. The endemic **water saxifrage** grows in mountain bogs and along streams up to about 2500m, its white flowers appearing in midsummer; the cliff-dwelling **Pyrenean saxifrage** has a large rosette of lime-encrusted leaves, which eventually produces a tall red-stemmed spike of flowers before dying. The **paniculate** (or livelong) **saxifrage** is similar to the Pyrenean but has a smaller, more ragged rosette, with yellow and white flowers only at the top. The most spectacular of this group, the **purple saxifrage**, has large, stemless flowers over carpets of tiny leaves, and grows on the highest peaks.

Succulent **stonecrops** (*Sedum* spp.), with yellow, white or pink flowers, and frequently red leaves, grow in dry, open places, often where there is little soil. The equally fleshy, but neatly rosetted, **houseleeks** produce occasional spikes of reddish flowers, and are capable of growing at altitudes of nearly 3000m. A smaller, pale pink flowered species of houseleek is endemic to the Sierra del Cadí.

Globularias are dwarf shrubs, with spherical tufted heads of blue or purple flowers and a long flowering period of May to August. There are numerous types of **daisy**, some with large flowers, like the endemic purple **Pyrenean aster**, and the even larger shasta daisy – the latter now widely cultivated elsewhere as a garden plant. The huge **cardoon knapweed** brandishes spectacular purple thistle heads, up to 7cm across, in late-summer meadows; parts of this plant, a close relative of the artichoke, are edible and sometimes appear stewed in restaurants.

Members of the heather family cover large areas, and add colour to the slopes all through the summer. **Bilberries** (April–July), **bearberries** (June–Sept) and **cowberries** all have greenish-white or pinkish, often bell-shaped flowers, followed by edible berries. The prostrate, mat-forming creeping **azalea** (May–July) produces tiny pink flowers, but its bigger cousin the **wild rhododendron** (May–Aug) or alpenrose has clusters of conspicuous red flowers. Various species of **heather** itself provide colour from May to October.

The higher alpine meadows are home to some gorgeous members of the lily family, such as the chocolate or deep purple bells of the **Pyrenean fritillary**; the large white trumpets of **Saint Bruno's lily**; the yellow **Turk's-cap lily**, which prefers cliffs or rockpiles; the **dogstooth violet**, which takes its name from the white oval bulb, not the magenta blossom; and *Brimeura*, a small amethyst **hyacinth**. Belonging to the same family, but crocus-like in shades of pink and white, are *Bulbocodium*, *Colchicum* and pink-purple *Merendera*, most of these autumn-blooming. The **true crocuses** appear both in early summer amongst receding snow-patches, and in autumn as the season cools. During spring, half a dozen small members of the **daffodil family** appear, usually in damp meadows and often in great quantity; the rush-leaved narcissus, rock narcissus and lesser wild daffodil are among the more common. **Buttercups** are also well represented, for example the glacier crowfoot *(Ranunculus glacialis)*, conspicuous as shiny white or pink flowers on high-altitude glacial moraines or screes, to 3000m and beyond. They are followed, in summer, by the deep, purplish-blue, so-called "English" **iris** (*Iris latifolia*, ex-*xiphioides*), which despite its name is more or less confined in the wild to the Pyrenees, forming spectacular, early-summer clusters on treeless slopes between 1600m and 2000m elevation. This species is the parent of many cultivated forms in northern Europe, and shouldn't be confused with the more widespread, lower-altitude Spanish iris (*Iris xiphium*).

Twelve types of **gentian** are recorded for the Pyrenees, at elevations over 1500m, but they can sometimes be tricky to identify. Most species are small and delicate, with starry or trumpet-shaped flowers of a piercing blue that can mirror the sky or mountain tarns, but the more robust yellow gentians can attain a metre in height. The most common are the large, deep-blue trumpet gentians, *Gentiana acaulis* (ex-*kochiana*) and closely related species. Another legendary alpine dweller which may grow with them is the **edelweiss**, though the fuzzy whitish flowers can be disappointing up close and lack the gentian's charisma.

Numerous **bellflowers** occur, including a number endemic to the Pyrenees. The taller ones grow in open or woodland areas, but the real gems grow nestled into crevices of the limestone, or running delicate stems through the debris of scree slopes. With them, but in contrasting shades of purplish-red through to pale pink, are **wild carnations** and **pinks** (*Dianthus* spp), which often have powerful fragrances according to the kind of soil or rock rooted in; the fringed pink, thriving up to 2000m, is one of the most attractive.

A number of alpine or central European **orchids** grow in woodland and meadows on the French side, while lower areas on the Spanish side and at the hotter eastern and western ends of the range, are home to more Mediterranean species. *Epipactis parviflora* and *Dactylorhiza caramulensis* are two specialities of the area, but the endangered **lady's slipper** still survives in a few places in the east.

During late summer and autumn local people harvest the abundant **wild fungi**. Robust ceps, crinkly yellow chanterelles and saffron milkcaps are favourites, but most in demand are the brown honeycombed morels of springtime, scarce but almost worth their weight in gold when gathered and dried. You will see favourite picking grounds jealously signposted against nonresidents on the Spanish side (*Cota de Setas – Prohibido Coger Hongos sín Autorización*/Mushroom Reserve – Forbidden to Pick Fungi without a Permit).

THE ENVIRONMENT

Human populations may be lower in most of the Pyrenees than they were a century ago, but the landscape is nonetheless threatened, and since the early 1980s French and Spanish conservationists have turned considerable attention to the region. Concerns are numerous: the potential extinction of endangered species, massacres of migrating birds, the death from pollution of thousands of hectares of trees, and (most pressing) obstruction of waterways and inundation of valleys by hydroelectric schemes. Their arguments might not be changing developmental priorities yet, but environmental protests get a hearing these days, and occasionally succeed in stopping or altering destructive projects. At ground level, the standard of rural tidiness has improved, especially on the Spanish side of the range: dumpster or recycling bins are ubiquitous and well used, and public education campaigns on environmental matters seem slowly to be having an effect.

However, there are still formidable obstacles to be overcome, not least the mind-set of governmental officials in Spain, from regional levels all the way to the top. Whatever its economic wizardry and new-found centrist positioning, the PP government is set to continue as one of the most environmentally unfriendly in western Europe; vice-president Álvarez Cascos set its tone in 1997 when he proclaimed that environmental considerations were the concern of a few smelly hippies, and that any opposition to developmental projects should be ignored or brushed aside. Rubbush collection notwithstanding, there is no powerful Spanish Green party as in France, and environmental awareness remains embryonic in Spain, which like many other recently developed countries remains in thrall to high-prestige projects such as high-speed trains, dams and motorways.

NATURAL RESERVES

Among the qualifications for national park status, as defined by the International Union for the Conservation of Nature and Natural Resources (IUCN), are that there should be no hunting and no exploitation other than that consistent with the "natural" way of life of mountain people, such as grazing or wild-food gathering. So far there are just three **national parks in the Pyrenees**, and only two of those actually meet the IUCN criteria – the Parc National des Pyrénées in France and the adjoining Parque Nacional de Ordesa y Monte Perdido in Spain. The Parc Nacional d'Aigüestortes i Sant Maurici in Catalunya is not officially recognized by the IUCN because of its numerous hydroelectric installations, which are a source of constant friction with conservationists.

Other areas of the Pyrenees are administered under less stringent conservation schemes. In Spain there are the *parques naturales* of Cadí-Moixeró, Maladeta-Posets, the Sierra y Cañones de Guara, the Garrotxa and Larra-Belagoa; France has various *réserves naturelles*, including that of Néouvielle – but these do not entirely protect wildlife from hunting.

HUNTING

Hunting in the Pyrenees is **controlled** in a number of ways besides the outright ban in the national parks. Various private reserves keep the numbers of hunters down by charging high fees; permits are limited by auction or the drawing of lots; certain animals are designated as protected species; the number of hunting days is restricted; and voluntary management plans have been implemented by (French more than Spanish) hunting associations.

In some instances these restraints have been effective. There are around fifteen thousand **isards** on the French side of the range and probably a similar number on the Spanish, a reasonably healthy situation that leads hunters to insist that further kill limits are unnecessary. However, permitted hunting has taken a heavy toll of this species in places: the Néouvielle region's population, for example, had to be restocked after being depleted. Herds have territories of just a few square kilometres, so those within the protected areas are fairly safe; the animals at risk – solitary old males, youngsters rejected by their mothers and mature males driven off by rivals – are those that stray outside the protected reserves.

But the hunters' main interest is in **smaller game animals**, and for these species the situation is far from satisfactory. For instance, there is no explicit protection for capercaillie in the management plans of many hunting associations, even where it is on the verge of local extinction.

Even if an animal is classified as a protected species, it isn't necessarily safe. The twenty-five thousand annual pigeon-hunters often illegally kill other species, such as vultures and kestrels, in the same barrages of shot. Since the late 1990s the migratory pigeon population has crashed dramatically owing to conditions in the species' summer or winter quarters, but their previous slaughter at strategic Pyrenean passes certainly didn't help. The one avian bright spot is a steady increase in lammergeier populations in the Western Pyrenees, thanks to EU-funded conservation projects and growing awareness amongst country people that these raptors feed only on already-dead livestock.

In any event, the power of the hunting lobby – at least in France – cannot be underestimated. Their **political party**, Hunting, Fishing, Nature and Traditions (CPNT in French), caused a major upset in the March 1999 Euro-elections by equalling the 6.8 percent tally of the Communists – in some *départements* they got over a quarter of the vote – and sending several Euro MPs to Brussels.

SKI DEVELOPMENT

Given the relatively poor snow record of the Pyrenees, **ski development** here has lagged far behind that of the Alps, especially on the Spanish side of the range. A recent EU report has advised, in light of **global warming** being a confirmed phenomenon, that no new downhill developments should plan to have a base point of under 2000m elevation. At present, most lie at 1600–1850m, and many French stations have a *top* lift point of under 2000m. Already on the Spanish side, the 1990s saw Llessui and La Tuca close down owing to various combinations of financial mismanagement and unco-operative climate, and others such as Panticosa and Cerler narrowly escaped **bankruptcy** through massive investment in snow-canons and new lifts. However, all the snow-canons in the world will not make a difference if average winter temperatures remain too high. In France, most ski stations are publicly owned and run at a loss, kept going as the major local employer and spur to the mountain economy. But while many French Pyrenean winter-sports centres have hitherto got away with lower siting owing to severe Atlantic weather, a half-dozen minor

resorts – including Hautacam, Le Mourtis, Mijanès-Donezan and Guzet-Neige – now spend most of each winter inoperative, and are clearly on the way out (indeed Goulier-Neige and Bourg d'Oeuil closed permanently in 1999).

Expanding the network of **cross-country** ski destinations has not yet proven sufficiently attractive to planners or investors. Though a lower-profit game, it's also lower-risk and lower-impact – if warm winters force them to fold, there's no hardware left littering the slopes, and no scarred mountainsides where pistes used to be.

Existing downhill stations frantic over recent poor winters are, in accordance with the above-cited report, looking to the **highest slopes** of the range to alleviate their problems – one rejected expansion plan at Candanchú actually hoped to blast away part of the Pico d'Aspe to lengthen its ski runs. Worse, other resorts hope to drain natural lakes to feed new snow-canons. An as-yet unapproved French scheme – to link the *domaine* of La Mongie with that of Saint-Lary-Soulan – demands exemption from the ban on development in the Parc National des Pyrénées and the Réserve Naturelle de Néouvielle, and on the Spanish side none of the various plans or completed projects has been subject to an environmental impact study.

However, despite global warming making any further investment in downhill ski infrastructure extremely risky, and local surveys showing that the number of skiers is not set to grow significantly, funds continue to pour in. On the Spanish side, Formigal and Astún-Candanchú are to be united into one "macro"-station via the Valle de Izas, in preparation for Aragón's bid for the **2010 Winter Olympics**; it failed to host the 1998 competition. The main potential beneficiaries of such plans are developers who have constructed hundreds of apartments around Jaca since the 1980s; if Aragón's latest Olympic bid is successful (the verdict's due in 2003), expect another wave of building. In fact, proposals for new ski centres are a means, not an end, for speculators wishing to justify yet more of the **urbanizaciones** (chalet complexes) which blight nearly every alpine village on the Spanish side that doesn't fall within the protection zone of a national park; the Cerdanya and the Val d'Aran in particular have been almost completely disfigured. Once the blocks of flats are up and sold, developers couldn't care less whether the adjacent ski resort is viable in the long term.

Such projects have repercussions beyond the obvious visual disturbance, sewage pollution, increase in traffic densities and disruption of natural habitats. There is growing awareness, for example, that the clearance of forests for the construction of pistes and resorts can lead to a higher incidence of **avalanches**, with devastating effects on hitherto protected settlements.

FORESTS

In 1989 research institutes at Toulouse and Lannemezan in France and Vitoria in Spain reported that 21 percent of Pyrenean trees were sick, with the worst-affected forest being the silver firs of the Luchon valley. Several causes have been identified, including repeated dry periods, late frosts and errors of forestry management, but **acid rain** emerges as a major culprit, with the gas field at Lacq, near Pau, particularly singled out. A filtration system at Lacq has drastically cut the release of sulphur into the air, but emissions remain high here and in the industrial conglomerations of Catalunya, Aragón and the Basque country. Andorra's main power station launches 324 tonnes of sulphur into the air each day, while the factories of western Euskadi produce 490 tonnes – more than twice as much as the whole city of London. On the north flank of the Pyrenees 79 percent of forest environments register a pH factor of between 4 and 5 (pH7 is neutral), which ranks with the level in the Vosges, long considered the worst-affected area of France.

Forest **fires** have so far had less impact along the Pyrenees than in Provence, but throughout the range, fires have begun to break out progressively earlier in the year, yet another symptom of global warming. Many are deliberately set by shepherds attempting to clear fresh grazing land; in one incident in February 2000, four Spanish mountaineers were burnt to death while hiking the French GR10 near Esterenzubi when such a blaze was driven into their path by sudden winds. In the Albères, on the Mediterranean side of the range, there has been talk of planting more cork oak, a species highly resistant to fire. Improved husbandry of vineyards and olive groves through the clearance of undergrowth and the construction of firebreaks has given some protection to vegetation in the vulnerable Alt Empordà region, behind Catalunya's Mediterranean coast, but the nearby Cap de Creus promontory in Catalunya seems to burn with depressing regularity every few years.

Destructive **logging practices**, especially in the Spanish Valle de Ansó, are responsible for massive erosion and habitat depletion. Instead of sustainable, selective extraction using mules or horses along existing tracks and paths, clear-cutting and haulage with heavy machinery are the rule. Compounded by the absence of systematic replanting programmes, such methods are still leaving behind ever-worsening erosion scars, plus the prospect of floods and altered rainfall patterns.

HYDROELECTRIC POWER – AND NEW DAMS

Although **hydroelectric power** is in principle more acceptable than fossil-fuelled or nuclear alternatives, and can be almost benign environmentally, neither Spain nor France has devoted much effort to make it so in the Pyrenees. Valleys have been scoured and flooded in an entirely unaesthetic way, with almost no money spent on landscaping or tidying up. Construction has often occurred with no thought given to the impact on wildlife – the Laparan dam project near Ax-les-Thermes, for example, helped hasten the local extinction of the bear. Tunnel-sized feed pipes have been routed through once-wooded areas, and substations send out their rhythmic roar day and night even in the remotest locations. High-tension pylons are strung across otherwise empty sky, while left-over construction and maintenance materials, including rusty, aerial cable cars, deface the most unexpected places. Virtually no major river is untouched, and multilingual warning notices advise you to keep away from the banks downstream from dams in case the power company instigates sudden changes in water level.

The pace of hydroelectric development on the French side, which hit its stride between the world wars, has now slowed down considerably as France enjoys a kilowatt surplus (often sold abroad). The latest north-to-south scheme envisions a 400,000 volt line – the high-tension **autopiste/autopista** – through the Couserans to Graus in Aragón; the route is as yet undecided – it's distinctly unpopular on both sides of the border, if graffiti is any indication – but it may cross over the already sullied Parc Nacional de Aigüestortes, or even skim the boundaries of the Ordesa park.

The Spaniards were latecomers to the hydrogame: while the very first dams appeared in the hills of Catalunya at the turn of the century, most

Spanish projects were commissioned after World War II, and proposals for **new dams** are still on the drawing boards for depopulated Alto Aragón and Navarra – with the bulk of accumulated water to be sent, in all cases, down to farms and towns in the flatlands, or even as far away as the giant plantations of Andalucía, by means of giant **trasvases** or pipelines. Under Franco, dams served a dual purpose: as prestige projects which proved that the country was "developing", and as a convenient way to clear the hills of potentially independent-minded folk. While paying token homage to rural-dwellers as the repositories of ur-folkloric values, authoritarian regimes have always distrusted them as unlikely to fit in well with their social engineering schemes. In democratic Spain, there has been a subtle shift: projects approved under Franco remain valid, and Pyrenean dwellers are expected to sacrifice their homes and livelihoods for the benefit of the millions in the thirsty cities down the hills. But they are not going quietly – those affected are considerably more sophisticated than the villagers who were terrorized into leaving Jánovas in 1960 (see box p.403). Encouraged by the success of anti-dam movements in India and Turkey, locals have mounted vigorous, if not always successful **campaigns against hydro-projects** in their own country.

Besides dams on the Río Ara at Jánovas, Santaliestra on the Río Ésera and the Río Gállego at Biscarrués (see p.430), the most controversial projects at present are the enlargement of the existing Embalse de Yesa on the Río Aragón, and the completion of an extremely high dam at Itoiz on the Río Irati.

The original **Yesa reservoir**, built in 1960, caused the abandonment of three villages with 1500 people and inundated 2500 hectares of arable land – with token or no compensation. The dam's enlargement to triple the reservoir's capacity will destroy three more villages, displace 400 inhabitants, and inundate a large number of Roman and early Christian monuments in the Canal de Berdún (including 22km of the original Camino de Santiago). The extra water will go to irrigate fields near Bardenas, and address an alleged shortfall of drinking water for Zaragoza. Opponents of enlargement charge that Zaragoza loses nearly half its mains water to leaks at present, doesn't bill for roughly the same fraction, and hasn't adequately explored the option of obtaining potable water from the Ebro, its own river. Moreover, the Bardenas irrigation zone is apparently not authorized to expand more than eight percent anyway, and the current water-delivery systems are obsolete and inefficient. Following months of street demos in major Aragonese towns, the "anti" faction saw the government approve the new Yesa project in spring 2000; their only recourse, should opponents choose to pursue it, is to appeal the matter to the European Court in Strasbourg.

The **Itoiz dam** has had an even stormier history. The project, which foresaw the construction of a 135-metre-high dam on the Río Irati downstream from Auritze and Aribe, was first conceived in Franco's last years as a way of irrigating farms on the plains near Pamplona. In 1985, when plans were revived, locals first mobilized to oppose the reservoir, citing among other issues the inundation of three villages upstream, and the ecological value of the Itoiz valley with its two nature reserves and bird protection zone, sheltering rare bearded vultures. By 1992, the Navarran government had dismissed these arguments and began to build. The environmental activists went to the Spanish supreme court – and won. The judges ruled that nature reserves could not be flooded, and ordered a reduction in dam height from 135m to 25m – which would completely undermine the project's economic viability. The Navarran parliament responded in 1995 by dissolving the nature reserves and ordering that construction resume. At this point, faced with the limits of the local justice system, a direct-action group called **Solidarios con Itoiz** (ScI) formed. With members of the press invited to watch, in spring 1996 eight members of ScI overpowered a security guard at the dam site and severed critical cables with power-grinders, delaying further construction for a year. For their pains, the ecosaboteurs got a thorough beating from the *Guardia Civil* who came to arrest them, and a draconian five-year sentence at their subsequent trial. The ScI 8 intend to serve their time, but before going inside they conducted a tour of Europe during late 1999 to publicize their cause, beginning with a press conference at the European Parliament and culminating in attention-getting stunts such as scaling London's Millennium Wheel, Berlin's Brandenburg Gate and even the Dome of St Peter's at the Vatican. In early 2000 the last Spanish legal obstacle to the high dam was removed by its proponents, and as with the Yesa project only the Strasbourg court remains as an option for ScI.

BOOKS

This list is a sample of general and specific books that will enrich a visit to the range. Not all are concerned exclusively with the Pyrenees, but certain titles that deal with the whole of France and Spain have been chosen because they contain much that is relevant to the mountains and their cultures. For all books in print, publishing details are given in the form "UK publisher; US publisher", where they differ; if books are published in one country only, this follows the publisher's name; "o/p" means out of print – consult a library or specialist secondhand book-dealer.

GENERAL ACCOUNTS & TRAVEL

Alain Bourneton *Rivages Pyrénéens* (Éditions Milan, Toulouse, France). Expensive but beautifully photographed tour around a thousand Pyrenean lakes. Covering geography, wildlife and legends, it makes a wonderful souvenir.

Alastair Boyd *The Essence of Catalonia* (André Deutsch; o/p). Part history, part guide, this is strong on the art and architecture of the obvious towns and monuments, but weaker on the Pyrenean mountain side of things.

Norbert Casteret *The Descent of Pierre Saint-Martin* (Dent, UK; o/p). English translation of Casteret's *Trente Ans sous Terre*, dealing with the exploration of what was then the world's deepest known cave system. Other translations of books by Casteret, the greatest of Pyrenean speleologists, include *Ten Years Under the Earth* (Mendip; Cave Books, Missouri), *Cave Men New and Old* (Dent, UK; o/p) and *The Darkness Under the Earth* (Dent, UK; o/p).

Eleanor Elsner *Romance of the Basque Country and the Pyrenees* (Herbert Jenkins; Dodd, Mead & Co; o/p). Published in 1927, but still a treasure for its old photographs and anecdotes.

Nina Epton *The Valley of Pyrene* (Cassell, UK; o/p). Record of a tour through the Ariège in the 1950s, with copious anecdotes and reflections. Encounters with luminaries – including Dalí – give added depth to the account.

Norman Lewis *Voices of the Old Sea* (Picador, UK). Set between 1948 and 1950, this blend of novel and social record movingly charts the lives of two remote Costa Brava villages and the breakdown of the old ways with the arrival of tourism.

Rose Macaulay *The Fabled Shore* (Oxford UP; o/p). The Spanish coast as it was in 1949 (read it and weep), travelled and described from Catalunya to the Portuguese Algarve.

Edwin Mullins *The Pilgrimage to Santiago* (Signal Books, UK). While just a brief section of the medieval pilgrims' route from Paris to the shrine of St James (Santiago) passes through the Pyrenees, this is by far the best history of the Santiago legend and the pilgrimage it sparked. Mullins points out churches along the way, giving incisive accounts of their social and architectural background.

Henry Myhill *The Spanish Pyrenees* (Faber & Faber; Transatlantic; o/p). The Spanish side as it was in the early Sixties; excellent for its historical speculation and human anecdotes, less commendable for an obvious pro-Francoist bias.

John Sturrock *The French Pyrenees* (Faber & Faber; o/p). Another detailed historical travelogue, but one in which the author rarely gets out of his car. Sturrock starts at the west coast and works east, stopping abruptly at borders with the exception of a detour to Roncesvalles.

HISTORY, SOCIETY AND POLITICS

Raymond Carr *Modern Spain, 1875–1980* (Oxford UP). One of the best concise narratives.

Alfred Cobban *A History of Modern France* (3 vols: 1715–99, 1799–1871 & 1871–1962; Penguin; Viking). Complete and very readable account of the main political, economic and social strands in French history from Louis XIV's death to the middle of the de Gaulle era.

Roger Collins *The Arab Conquest of Spain, 710–797* (Basil Blackwell, UK). Controversial study which documents the "Moorish" invasion and the significant influence that the conquered Visigoths had on early Muslim rule. For a broader overview of the same subject, see also his *Early Medieval Spain, 400–1000* (Macmillan, UK).

John A. Crow *Spain: The Root and the Flower* (University of California Press, UK & US). Cultural and social history from Roman Spain to the present.

Natalie Zemon Davis *The Return of Martin Guerre* (Harvard University Press). A man presents himself as a woman's long-lost husband, and persuades many that he is who he claims to be, despite his extremely tenuous resemblance to the missing spouse. A perplexing and titillating hoax which actually occurred in the Pyrenean village of Artigat during the sixteenth century; even better than the movie or the musical.

J.H. Elliot *Imperial Spain 1469–1716* (Penguin). Best introduction to the centuries immediately after unification – academically respected and a gripping tale.

Jonathan Fenby *France on the Brink* (Arcade, US). Somewhat alarmist diagnosis of France's current woes, putting the blame squarely on its complacent, greedy ruling class.

Christopher Hibbert *The French Revolution* (Penguin; Morrow; o/p). Good, concise popular history of the period and salient events.

John Hooper *The New Spaniards* (Penguin). A 1995 update of a perceptive 1987 portrait of post-Franco Spain and the new generation by the *Guardian*'s long-time Madrid correspondent. Though the revision is also ageing fast, still the best one-volume introduction to contemporary Spain.

Peter Sahlins *Boundaries: The Making of France and Spain in the Pyrenees* (University of California Press). Using the partition of the Cerdanya/Cerdagne as a model, this explores the process of instilling French and Spanish national identities in a formerly unified area of the Catalan Pyrenees; academic and groaning with charts and tables, but has its readable moments.

Alexander Worth *France 1940–55* (Beacon Press, US; o/p). Excellent and emotionally engaging portrayal of the most taboo period in French history: the Occupation, followed by the early Cold War and colonial-struggle years in which the same political tensions and heart-searchings were at work.

THE CATHARS

In its anti-centralist, anticlerical essentials, the Cathar issue still fascinates the French. The publication of material on the Cathar era is something of a major industry in the Pyrenean provinces in particular, with two Toulouse publishers – Éditions Privat and Éditions Loubatières – specializing in it. The following are just some of the titles currently available in French and English.

Catherine Bibollet and Michel Roquebert *Ombre et Lumière en Pays Cathare* (Éditions Privat). Attractive coffee-table effort, available also in an English edition.

Anne Brenon *Petit précis de catharisme* (Éditions Loubatières). Short summary of the sect's beliefs, drawn from a course given at the University of Montpellier. Her *Le vrai visage due catharisme* (Éditions Loubatières) discusses its flourishing in the Occitan-speaking areas and the details of its suppression.

Jean Duvernoy *Histoire et Religion des Cathars* (2 vols, Éditions Privat). Over forty years, Duvernoy completed the original translation from Latin of the Inquisition's records, which made Le Roy Ladurie's work possible; this is his own history. Vol. 1 analyses the records; Vol. 2, more interestingly, tallies all the medieval sects, from Asia Minor to Britain, allied with Catharism.

Emmanuel Le Roy Ladurie *Montaillou* (Penguin; Vintage). Life in a Cathar village in the Pays de Sault, as recorded by the Inquisition in the fourteenth century, and stored away until the 1970s in the Vatican archives. Hard going in places but a fascinating insight.

Zoé Oldenbourg *Massacre at Montségur* (Phoenix, UK). English translation of the standard (1961) history of the Cathar crusades. Vivid and partisan (as in extremely sympathetic to the Cathars), stressing the connection between the suppression of the heresy and that of Languedoc separatism. Good appendices give some insight into Cathar beliefs – and the Church's horror of them.

Michel Roquebert *L'Epopée Cathare* (4 vols, Éditions Privat). Exhaustive but readable history, 31 years in the making, drawing on nearly everything known about the sect. His more focused *Montségur, Les Cendres de la Liberté* (Éditions Privat) may be more accessible.

Steven Runciman *The Medieval Manichee* (Cambridge UP, UK & US). Classic account of the evolution of the dualist heresy from the Bogomils and Paulicians up to the Cathars.

Jonathan Sumption *The Albigensian Crusade* (Faber & Faber). Lively, somewhat revisionist history of the crusade in which the Cathars are made out to be nearly as contemptible as their adversaries, who are given more depth than usual. Good on the cultural clash between the dour Normans, who largely staffed and directed the campaign, and the anarchistic Languedocians – as well as the extensive Aragonese involvement in the wars.

SPANISH CIVIL WAR

Gerald Brenan *The Spanish Labyrinth: An Account of the Social and Political Background of the Spanish Civil War* (Cambridge UP). As the subtitle says: not a straight history of the war, but one of the best nonacademic studies on Spanish rural society of the time.

Ronald Fraser *Blood of Spain* (Pimlico; Pantheon). Subtitled *The Experience of Civil War*, this oral history of 1936–39 gives a voice to the people who fought in and lived through the war. As a record of ordinary lives in extraordinary times, more immediately accessible than conventional histories.

George Orwell *Homage to Catalonia* (Penguin; Harvest Books). Journalist Orwell cut his teeth on this – if not his most celebrated book, certainly his best reportage. A forthright account of battles on the Aragón front, followed by Orwell's injury and disillusionment with the factional fighting among the Republican forces.

Paul Preston *Franco* (Fontana; HarperCollins). Penetrating, monumental biography of Franco and his regime, demonstrating how he won the Civil War, how he survived in power so long, and what his ultimate significance was. Preston's more recent *Concise History of the Spanish Civil War* (Fontana, UK) is a compelling introduction to the subject, and more digestible than Hugh Thomas' tome.

Hugh Thomas *The Spanish Civil War* (Penguin; Touchstone). Massive, exhaustive political study of the period, and still the best single telling of the convoluted story.

WORLD WAR II: FRENCH OCCUPATION AND RESISTANCE

Marc Bloch *Strange Defeat* (W.W. Norton). Moving personal study of the reasons for France's defeat and subsequent caving-in to Nazism. Found among the papers of this Sorbonne historian and Resistance member after his death at the hands of the Gestapo in 1942.

Philippe Burin *Living with Defeat* (Arnold, UK). Excellent French account of the Occupation that focuses in particular on the experiences of ordinary people.

Emilienne Eychenne *Les Pyrénées de la Liberté* (Editions France-Empire, France). History of World War II escapes over the Pyrenees into Spain, by a historian who has made this her special subject. She has also written other titles dealing with specific segments of the range.

H.R. Kedward *In Search of the Maquis: Rural Resistance in South France 1942–44* (Oxford UP). Slightly dry, but full of fascinating detail about the brave and often mortal struggle of the countless ordinary people in the region who fought to drive the Germans from their country.

Ian Ousby *Occupation: The Ordeal of France 1940–1944* (Pimlico; Random House). Somewhat revisionist 1997 account which shows how relatively late resistance was, how widespread collaboration was, and why. Good mix of salient events and how it felt to live through these times.

Paul Webster *Pétain's Crime: The Full Story of French Collaboration in the Holocaust* (Papermac; Ivan Dee). The fascinating and alarming story of the Vichy regime's more than willing collaboration with the deportations of Jews and the bravery of those, especially the communist resistance in occupied France, who attempted to prevent it.

ETHNOGRAPHY, NATIONALISM AND FOLKLORE

Claude Bailhé *Autrefois les Pyrénées* (Éditions Milan, Toulouse, France). The French Pyrenees as they were from the latter half of the nineteenth century until World War I, in early photos. Organized by topic (mountaineering, family life, local industries) with intelligent text.

Roger Collins *The Basques* (Basil Blackwell, UK; o/p). Except for a section on the *fueros*, this is disappointingly dull but there's little currently available that's any better.

Daniele Conversi *The Basques, the Catalans and Spain* (Christopher Hurst; University of Nevada Press). Scholarly exploration of the differing evolutions of Basque and Catalan nationalism.

Antoine Lebègue *Lieux Insolites et Secrets des Pyrénées* (Éditions Sud Ouest, Bordeaux, France). Inexpensive miscellany of legends, odd rites and semi-mythic personalities, organized by region. Sketchy (quite literally, with reproductions of old engravings) but fun.

Severino Pallaruelo *Pastores del Pireneo* (Spanish Ministry of Culture; o/p). A thorough – though rather specialist – research into the arts and popular traditions of Pyrenean mountain people, with good photographs.

ART AND ARCHITECTURE

Jean Clottes and David Lewis-Williams *Les Chamanes de la Préhistoire* (Éditions Seuil, France). Revisionist view of the Ariège cave paintings, declaring that designated shamans rendered the art from their visions; see box on p.237.

Kenneth J. Conant *Carolingian and Romanesque Architecture, 800–1200* (Yale UP). Fastidious, scholarly treatment of the subject, with excellent material on the French side of the St-Jacques (Santiago) pilgrim route.

John Golding *Cubism: A History and an Analysis 1907–1914* (Faber & Faber; Harvard University Press). The standard work on the years of purist Cubism – essential reading to get the most out of a trip to Céret.

Bertrand Lorquin *Aristide Maillol* (Skira-Thames & Hudson). Short and surprisingly reticent monograph on the sculptor by the curator of the Paris Maillol museum – and the son of Maillol's last model, Dina Vierny.

Meyer Schapiro *Romanesque Art* (Thames & Hudson; George Braziller). An excellent illustrated survey of Spanish Romanesque art and architecture – and its Visigothic and Mozarabic predecessors.

Ann Sieveking *The Cave Artists* (Thames & Hudson; o/p). Comprehensive introduction to

late-Paleolithic cave painting, with explanations of the theories on meaning and layout; two chapters devoted to the Pyrenees.

Sarah Whitfield *Fauvism* (Thames & Hudson). Although its reproductions can't do justice to the vibrant colours of Matisse and the artists in his orbit, this serves well as an introduction to the preoccupations of the Fauves.

LITERATURE

Victor Català (pseudonym of Caterina Albert i Paradís) *Solitude* (Readers International). This tragic tale of a woman's life and sexual passions in a mountain village is regarded as the most important pre-Civil War Catalan novel.

Pierre Loti *Ramuntcho* (in French). Cloyingly tragic romance, a sort of early, high-class Mills & Boon-type affair, set in the French Basque country.

The Song of Roland (Penguin). The most famous French epic, translated by Glyn Burgess. Written around the end of the eleventh century, this mini-saga conjures up the whole legend of Roland and the famous ambush near Roncesvalles in the Basque Pyrenees.

Colm Toibin *The South* (Picador, UK; o/p). Toibin's wonderful first novel follows a woman fleeing her boring, middle-class family in Ireland for a lover and new life in the Spanish Pyrenees.

SPECIFIC GUIDES

The Confraternity of Saint James publishes two *Pilgrim Guides to the Roads through France to Santiago de Compostela*, which are more useful and current than the Cicerone guide. Volume 1, *The Camino Francés*, despite the name, covers the stretch from Saint-Jean to Pamplona; volume 4, *Arles to Puenta la Reina*, goes via Jaca. Both have good route and facilities details, but no maps. In case of difficulty purchasing, contact them directly at 1 Talbot Yard, Borough High Street, London SE1 1YP (☎020/7404 4500).

GR11, Senderos de Gran Recorrido/Senda Pirenaica (PRAMES, Zaragoza, Spain). In Castilian. Comes in two packagings: the complete range, covered in a two-ring binder – you extract sections and carry them about in the provided case – or paperbound in three separate volumes: *Andorra/Catalunya, Aragón, Navarra/Gipuzkoa*. Invaluable, and updated regularly (current pages available for the binder edition), though as ever some of the timings are way out.

Paul Lucia *Through the Spanish Pyrenees, GR11: A Long-Distance Footpath* (Cicerone, UK). Now in its second edition, with accurate time-courses, altitude profiles and lists of available facilities, but poor maps and coverage of variants.

Pierre Merlin *Guide des Raids à Skis* (Denoël, France). Guide, in French only, to the Pyrenean traverse on skis.

Pierre Minvielle *Randonnées en Aragon* (Diffusion Randonnées Pyrénéennes, France). A well-illustrated pocket-sized walking guide devoted to one of most spectacular walking areas of the Pyrenees.

Jean-Paul Pontroué and Fernando Biargue *Au coeur des Sierras du Haut Aragón* (Editions J-C Bihet, Pau, France). French-language guide to the canyons, best on Ordesa area walks and canyoning but also with sketchy summaries of the Valle de Gistau, Echo/Ansó and Panticosa/Sallent. Also by the same authors, *Canyons et Barrancos du Haut Aragón* and *Parc National d'Ordesa et du Mont Perdu* (Randonnées Pyrénéennes, France), though currently out of print, are much better than Biargue's later solo effort *Parque Nacional de Ordesa y Monte Perdido, 100 Itinerarios* (self-published).

Por los Valles de Ansó, Echo y Aragües (PRAMES, Zaragoza, Spain). Everything you would want to know (in Castilian) about the valleys and their settlements, plus tips for walking, rock-climbing and canyoning.

Alison Raju *The Way of St James: A Walker's Guide* (Cicerone; Hunter). Covers the pilgrim route only from the Puerto de Ibañeta to Pamplona and beyond; some useful route maps, updated 1998.

Kev Reynolds *Walks and Climbs in the Pyrenees* (Cicerone; Hunter). Now in its third edition, this is the standard English-language guide for trekkers and scramblers, covering the most spectacular parts of the range. His *Classic Walks in the Pyrenees* (Oxford Illustrated Press, UK; o/p) is a bit more clearly presented for route-planning, if rather purple in the prose.

Patrick Santal *White Water Pyrenees* (Rivers Publishing; Menasha Ridge Press). All you possibly need to know about every worthwhile (and

a few not so worthwhile – they tell you) rafting and kayaking river in the range, in this English translation of a brand-new (2000) French guide. Meticulous ratings, diagrams, instructions and outfitter contacts in what's clearly a labour of love.

Douglas Streatfeild-James *Trekking in the Pyrenees* (Trailblazer, UK). The best and most current (1997) English-language guide to the GR10 and its variants, also including choice bits of the Camino de Santiago, the Parque de Ordesa and the Aigüestortes/Sant Maurici area. Easy-to-use sketch maps, but some complaints about inconsistent time courses and out-of-date facilities recommendations.

Sua Edizioak is a Bilbao-based mountaineering publisher with several guides (unfortunately in Castilian and Euskera only) pertaining to the Pyrenees. These include *GR11, Pirineo Vasco*, a *topoguía* describing the trail from Zuriza to Hondarribia; *La Alta Ruta de los Pirineos en Bici*, for mountain-biking close to the HRP; *El Camino de Santiago en Bici*, rather less strenuous touring-bike itineraries along the pilgrim route; and *Rutas y Paseos por Belagoa*, selected excursions in the *parque natural* at the head of the Roncal valley.

Georges Véron *Pyrenees High Level Route* (West Col Publications, UK). English translation of the standard mountaineer's traverse of the Pyrenees (original published by Gastons), by the Frenchman who knows the range better than anyone.

Rafael Vidáller Tricas *Guía del Valle de Benasque* (Editorial Pirineos, Huesca, Spain). More rigorous than the Aragonese government's and mountain club's co-published PR booklet (see p.291); this one grades the progressively more difficult walks.

Derek Walker *Rock Climbs in the Pyrenees* (Cicerone; Hunter). The first English guide for climbers; serious stuff, including Pic du Midi d'Ossau and the palisades of the Valle de Ordesa.

WILDLIFE FIELD GUIDES

Most of the following titles are best mail-ordered through specialist dealers; a good one in the UK is Summerfield Books, Main Street, Brough, near Kirkby Stephen, Cumbria CA17 4AX (☎017683/41577, *www.summerfield-books.com*).

Note that the system of Linnaean classification is in a constant state of flux in the case of small flora, where entire families have been suppressed in recent years, and various species have been renamed or even assigned to a different genus. So while you may find photos of the live specimens in front of you, you can't always expect to have a currently correct identification.

Marjorie Blamey and Christopher Grey-Wilson *The Alpine Flowers of Britain and Europe* (HarperCollins, UK). Comprehensive field guide, with coloured drawings; recent and taxonomically current.

John A. Burton *Field Guide to the Mammals of Britain and Europe* (Kingfisher, UK). A bargain: well illustrated and thorough.

John A. Burton, E. N. Arnold and D. W. Ovenden *Field Guide to the Reptiles and Amphibians of Britain and Europe* (HarperCollins; Stephen Green Press). For all those alpine newts, lizards and frogs.

Lance Chilton *Plant List for the Pyrenees* (Marengo Publications, UK). Slim but dense pamphlet, cataloguing every tree and plant known to occur in the range, whether as a native or introduced species. Best to order direct from Marengo at: 17 Bernard Crescent, Hunstanton, Norfolk PE36 6ER (☎01485/532710, *marengo@supanet.com*).

Corbet and Ovenden *Collins Guide to the Mammals of Europe* (Collins; Stephen Green Press). The best of several field guides to warm furries.

Jacquie Crozier *A Birdwatching Guide to the Pyrenees* (Arlequin, UK). Illustrated and mapped guidelet, detailing 18 regions in Spain, France and Andorra; includes practical directions and checklist.

Pierre Delforge *Orchids of Britain and Europe* (HarperCollins, UK). The best and most up-to-date guide, though beware small inaccuracies in the translation from the French.

Heinzel, Fitter and Parslow Collins *Guide to the Birds of Britain and Europe* (Collins; Stephen Green Press). One of the best general guides to the subject.

Lionel Higgins and Norman Riley *Field Guide to the Butterflies of Britain and Europe* (HarperCollins; Stephen Green Press). Not specific to the Pyrenees, but an excellent start.

Oleg Polunin and B. E. Smythies *Flowers of South-West Europe* (Oxford UP). Covers all of Spain, Portugal and southwest France, including the Pyrenees; taxonomy is old despite 1997 printing, but still unsurpassed for its introductions, plates, line drawings and keys.

A.W. Taylor *Wildflowers of the Pyrenees* (Chatto & Windus, UK; Clarke, Irwin & Co, Toronto; o/p). Rare and somewhat elderly (1971), this slim volume is the only guide specifically dedicated to the range. Easy to use, but far from comprehensive.

LANGUAGE

One of the characteristics of the Pyrenees is the number of regional languages – linguists recognize Catalan, Aranés, Aragonese, Occitan and Euskera – and the strong dialects which seemingly exist in every French valley. There will be little opportunity to learn any of these on a short visit, though a smattering of French and Castilian Spanish should serve you adequately for most purposes.

FRENCH

French is far from an easy language, despite the number of words and structures it shares with English, but the bare essentials are not difficult to master, and they make all the difference. Even just saying "Bonjour Monsieur/ Madame" when you enter a shop will usually get you a smile and helpful service. People working in tourist offices, hotels and so forth almost always speak better English than you do French, and so tend to reply in it when you're struggling to stammer out something in French – be grateful, not insulted.

Differentiating words is the initial problem in understanding spoken French, as it's very hard to get people to slow down – if all else fails, get them to write what they've said, as you are bound to recognize more words that way. Even outside the Basque and Catalan areas, there are districts where the language of daily life is a strong dialect of French or, in places, something more like a different species. Don't be dismayed – though you'll probably never understand an overheard conversation, any attempt to make yourself understood in school-book French will meet with a sympathetic response and a fairly comprehensible reply.

CASTILIAN SPANISH

Although Spain, like France, has its regional dialects and six recognized written languages, **Castilian** Spanish – the language of the central *meseta* – is understood over most of the peninsula. Once you get into it, Castilian is the easiest language there is, and you'll be helped everywhere by people who are eager to try and understand even the most faltering attempt. English is spoken, but only in the main tourist areas to any extent, and wherever you are you'll get a far better reception if you at least try communicating with Spaniards in their own tongue. Being understood, of course, is only half the problem – and getting the gist of the reply, often rattled out at a furious pace, may prove more difficult.

FRENCH LEARNING MATERIALS

Rough Guide French Phrasebook (Rough Guides). Mini dictionary-style phrasebook with both English–French and French–English sections, along with cultural tips for tricky situations, and a comprehensive menu-master.

French and English Slang Dictionary (Harrap/Prentice Hall); **Dictionary of Modern Colloquial French** (Routledge). Both volumes will be a bit bulky to carry in the mountains, but they're the key to all you ever wanted to understand. The **Collins Gem** (HarperCollins, UK) is a far more compact dictionary, cheap and adequate for beginner's needs.

Breakthrough French (Pan Macmillan, UK; book and 2 cassettes). Excellent teach-yourself course.

Verbaid (Verbaid, Hawk House, Heath Lane, Farnham, Surrey GU9 0PR). CD-size laminated paper "verb wheel" giving you the tense and conjugation endings for the regular verbs.

A Vous La France; France Extra; France-Parler (BBC Publications, UK; EMC Publishing, US; each course a book and 2 cassettes). BBC radio courses, running from beginners' to fairly advanced levels.

A BRIEF GUIDE TO SPEAKING FRENCH

PRONUNCIATION

One easy rule to remember is that **consonants** at the ends of words are usually silent. *Pas plus tard* (not later) is thus pronounced "pa-plu-tarr". But when the following word begins with a vowel, you run the two together: *pas après* (not after) becomes "pazapray".

Vowels are the hardest sounds to get right. Roughly:

a	as in t**a**r
e	as in g**e**t
é	between g**e**t and g**a**te
è	between g**e**t and g**u**t
eu	like the **u** in h**u**rt
i	as in mach**i**ne
o	as in h**o**t
ô, au	as in **o**ver
ou	as in f**oo**d
u	as in a pursed-lip version of **u**se

More awkward are the **combinations** in/im, en/em, an/am, on/om, un/um at the ends of words, or followed by consonants other than n or m. Again, roughly:

in/im	like the **an** in **an**xious
an/am, en/em	like the **don** in **Don**caster when said with a nasal accent
on/om	like the **don** in **Don**caster said by someone with a heavy cold
un/um	like the **u** in **u**nderstand

Consonants are much as in English, except that: ch is always "sh", ç is "s", c is "s" before i or e only, but always hard at the end of a word, h is silent, th is the same as t, ll is like the y in yes, w is "v", and r is growled (or rolled).

GENDER

French nouns are divided into masculine and feminine. This causes difficulties with adjectives, whose endings generally have to change to agree with the gender of the nouns they qualify. If you know some grammar, you will know what to do. If not, stick to the masculine form, which is the simplest – it's what we have done in the glossary, except for adjectives of nationality which have the feminine final 'e' or 'ne' in brackets.

BASICS

Today	*Aujourd'hui*	At midday	*À midi*	Less	*Moins*
Yesterday	*Hier*	Man	*Un homme*	A little	*Un peu*
Tomorrow	*Demain*	Woman	*Une femme*	A lot	*Beaucoup*
In the morning	*Le matin*	Here	*Ici*	Cheap	*Bon marché*
In the afternoon	*L'après-midi*	There	*Là*	Expensive	*Cher*
In the evening	*Le soir*	This one	*Ceci*	Good	*Bon*
Now	*Maintenant*	That one	*Cela*	Bad	*Mauvais*
Later	*Plus tard*	Open	*Ouvert*	Hot	*Chaud*
At one o'clock	*À une heure*	Closed	*Fermé*	Cold	*Froid*
At three o'clock	*À trois heures*	Big	*Grand*	With	*Avec*
At ten-thirty	*À dix heures et demie*	Small	*Petit*	Without	*Sans*
		More	*Plus*		

TALKING TO PEOPLE

When addressing people you should always use *Monsieur* for a man, *Madame* for a woman, *Mademoiselle* for a girl. Plain *bonjour* by itself is not enough. This isn't as formal as it seems, and it has its uses when you've forgotten someone's name or want to attract someone's attention.

Excuse me	*Pardon, excusez-moi*	I'm English	*Je suis anglais[e]*
Do you speak English?	*Parlez-vous anglais?*	Irish	*irlandais[e]*
How do you say it in French?	*Comment ça se dit en français?*	Scottish	*écossais[e]*
		Welsh/American	*gallois[e]/américain[e]*
What's your name?	*Comment vous appelez-vous?*	Australian	*australien[ne]*
My name is . . .	*Je m'appelle . . .*	Canadian	*canadien[ne]*

continues overleaf...

TALKING TO PEOPLE contd.

a New Zealander	*néo-zélandais[e]*	How are you?	*Comment allez-vous?/Ça va?*
Yes	*Oui*	Fine, thanks	*Très bien, merci*
No	*Non*	I don't know	*Je ne sais pas*
I understand	*Je comprends*	Let's go	*Allons-y*
I don't understand	*Je ne comprends pas*	See you tomorrow	*À demain*
(I'm) sorry	*(Je suis) désolé[e]*	See you soon	*À bientôt*
I'll be right with you	*J'arrive*	Sorry	*Pardon/Je m'excuse*
Please speak slower	*S'il vous plaît, parlez moins vite*	Leave me alone (aggressive)	*Fichez-moi la paix!*
OK/agreed	*D'accord*	Please help me	*Aidez-moi, s'il vous plaît*
Please	*S'il vous plaît*		
Thank you	*Merci*	Where?	*Où?*
Hello	*Bonjour*	How?	*Comment?*
Goodbye	*Au revoir*	When?	*Quand?*
Good morning/ afternoon	*Bonjour*	How many/how much?	*Combien?*
		Why?	*Pourquoi?*
Good evening	*Bonsoir*	At what time?	*À quelle heure?*
Good night	*Bonne nuit*	What is.../ which is...?	*Quel est...?*

GETTING ABOUT

Bus	*Autobus, bus, car*	Where are you going?	*Où allez-vouz?*
Bus station	*Gare (routière)*	I'm going to . . .	*Je vais à . . .*
Bus stop	*Arrêt*	I want to get off at . . .	*Je voudrais descendre à...*
Car	*Voiture*	The road to . . .	*La route pour . . .*
Train/taxi/ferry	*Train/taxi/ferry*	The path to . . .	*Le sentier pour . . .*
Boat	*Bâteau*	Beware! Field set with animal traps	*Attention! Piégé*
Plane	*Avion*		
Railway station	*Gare (SNCF)*	Near	*Près/pas loin*
Platform	*Quai*	Far	*Loin*
What time does it leave?	*À quelle heure part-il?*	Left	*À gauche*
		Right	*À droite*
What time does it arrive?	*À quelle heure arrive-t-il?*	Straight on	*Tout droit*
		On the other side of	*À l'autre côté de*
A ticket to . . .	*Un billet pour . . .*	On the corner of	*À l'angle de*
Single ticket	*Aller simple*	Next to	*À côté de*
Return ticket	*Aller retour*	Behind	*Derrière*
Validate your ticket	*Compostez votre billet*	In front of	*Devant*
Valid for . . .	*Valable pour . . .*	Before	*Avant*
Ticket office	*Vente de billets*	After	*Après*
How many kilometres?	*Combien de kilomètres?*	Under	*Sous*
How many hours?	*Combien d'heures?*	To cross	*Traverser*
Hitchhiking	*Autostop*	Bridge	*Pont*
On foot	*À pied*		

ACCOMMODATION

A room for one/two people	*Une chambre pour une/deux personnes*	Can I see it?	*Puis-je la voir?*
		A room on the courtyard	*Une chambre sur la cour*
A double bed	*Un lit double*		
A room with a shower	*Une chambre avec douche*	A room over the street	*Une chambre sur la rue*
A room with a bath	*Une chambre avec salle de bain*	First floor	*Premier étage*
		Second floor	*Deuxième étage*
For one/two/three nights	*Pour une/deux/trois nuits*	With a view	*Avec vue*
		Key	*Clef*

To iron	*Repasser*	I would like breakfast	*Je voudrais prendre le petit déjeuner*
Do laundry	*Faire la lessive*	I don't want breakfast	*Je ne veux pas le petit déjeuner*
Sheets	*Draps*		
Blankets	*Couvertures*		
Quiet	*Calme*	Can we camp here?	*On peut camper ici?*
Noisy	*Bruyant*	Campsite	*Un camping/terrain de camping*
Hot water	*Eau chaude*		
Cold water	*Eau froide*	Tent	*Une tente*
Is breakfast included?	*Est-ce que le petit déjeuner est compris?*	Tent space	*Un emplacement*
		Youth hostel	*Auberge de jeunesse*

CARS

To park the car	*Garer la voiture*	Inflate the tyres	*Gonfler les pneus*
Car park	*Un parking*	Oil	*Huile*
No parking	*Défense de stationer/ stationnement interdit*	Battery	*Batterie*
		The battery is dead	*La batterie est morte*
Service station	*Garage*	Spark plugs	*Bougies*
Petrol station	*Poste d'essence*	To break down	*Tomber en panne*
Fuel	*Essence*	Traffic lights	*Feux*
To fill it up	*Faire le plein*	Insurance	*Assurance*
Petrol can	*Bidon*		

NUMBERS

1	*un*	15	*quinze*	80	*quatre-vingts*
2	*deux*	16	*seize*	90	*quatre-vingt-dix*
3	*trois*	17	*dix-sept*	95	*quatre-vingt-quinze*
4	*quatre*	18	*dix-huit*	100	*cent*
5	*cinq*	19	*dix-neuf*	101	*cent et un*
6	*six*	20	*vingt*	200	*deux cent*
7	*sept*	21	*vingt et un*	300	*trois cent*
8	*huit*	22	*vingt-deux*	500	*cinq cent*
9	*neuf*	30	*trente*	1000	*mille*
10	*dix*	40	*quarante*	2000	*deux mille*
11	*onze*	50	*cinquante*	5000	*cinq mille*
12	*douze*	60	*soixante*	first	*première*
13	*treize*	70	*soixante-dix*	second	*deuxième*
14	*quatorze*	75	*soixante-quinze*	third	*troisième*

DAYS AND DATES

January	*janvier*	Monday	*lundi*	
February	*février*	Tuesday	*mardi*	
March	*mars*	Wednesday	*mercredi*	
April	*avril*	Thursday	*jeudi*	
May	*mai*	Friday	*vendredi*	
June	*juin*	Saturday	*samedi*	
July	*juillet*			
August	*août*	August 1	*Le premier août*	
September	*septembre*	March 2	*Le deux mars*	
October	*octobre*	July 14	*Le quatorze juillet*	
November	*novembre*	November 23	*Le vingt-trois novembre*	
December	*décembre*	1998	*dix-neuf-cent-quatre-vingt-dix-huit*	
Sunday	*dimanche*	2003	*deux-mille-et-trois*	

A BRIEF GUIDE TO SPEAKING SPANISH

PRONUNCIATION

The rules of **pronunciation** are pretty straightforward and, once you get to know them, strictly observed. Unless there's an accent, words ending in d, l, r and z are **stressed** on the last syllable, all others on the second to last. All **vowels** are pure and short.

A	as in f**a**ther	**N**	is as in English unless it has a tilde (accent) over it (**Ñ**), when it becomes NY: *mañana* sounds like "manyana"
E	as in g**e**t		
I	as in pol**i**ce		
O	as in r**o**le	**QU**	is pronounced like an English K
U	as in r**u**le	**R**	is rolled, RR doubly so
C	is a theta before E and I, hard otherwise: *cerca* is pronounced "thairka"	**V**	sounds like B, *vino* becoming "beano"
G	works the same way, a guttural "H" sound (like the *ch* in loch) before E or I, a hard G elsewhere – *gigante* becomes "higante"	**X**	has an S sound before consonants, n o r - mal X before vowels. More common in Basque, Gallego or Catalan words, where it's "sh" or "zh"
H	always silent		
J	the same sound as a guttural G: *jamón* is pronounced "hamon"	**Z**	is the same as a soft C, so *cerveza* becomes "thairvaitha". Catalan does not lisp c or z before i or e
LL	sounds like an English Y: *tortilla* is pronounced "torteeya"		

GENDER

Spanish nouns are divided into masculine and feminine. This causes difficulties with adjectives, whose endings generally have to change to agree with the gender of the nouns they qualify. If you know some grammar, you will know what to do. If not, stick to the masculine form, which is the simplest – it's what we have done in the glossary.

BASICS

Yes	*Sí*	Now	*Ahora*	Small	*Pequeño*
No	*No*	Later	*Más tarde*	More	*Más*
OK	*Vale*	Open	*Abierto*	Less	*Menos*
Please	*Por favor*	Closed	*Cerrado*	A lot	*Mucho*
Thank You	*Gracias*	With	*Con*	A little bit	*Un poco*
Here	*Aquí*	Without	*Sin*	Today	*Hoy*
There	*Allí*	Good	*Buen(o)*	Tomorrow	*Mañana*
This	*Este*	Bad	*Mal(o)*	Yesterday	*Ayer*
That	*Eso*	Big	*Gran(de)*		

TALKING TO PEOPLE

Hello	*Hola*	I (don't) understand	*(No) entiendo*
Goodbye	*Adiós*	Do you speak English?	*¿Habla (usted) inglés?*
Good morning	*Buenos días*	I don't speak Spanish	*No hablo castellano*
Good afternoon/ evening	*Buenas tardes*	My name is . . .	*Me llamo . . .*
		What's your name?	*¿Cómo se llama usted?*
Good night	*Buenas noches*	I want . . .	*Quiero . . .*
See you later	*Hasta luego*	I'd like . . .	*Querría . . .*
Sorry	*Lo siento/disculpeme*	Do you know . . . ?	*¿Sabe . . . ?*
Excuse me	*Con permiso/perdón*	I don't know	*No sé*
How are you?	*¿Cómo está (usted)?*	There is (is there)?	*(¿)Hay (?)*
You're welcome	*De nada*	Give me . . .	*Deme . . .*

(one like that)	*(un tal)*	What's that?	*¿Qué es eso?*
How much?	*¿Cuánto?*	What's this called in	*¿Cómo se llama este en*
Do you have . . . ?	*¿Tiene . . . ?*	Spanish?	*español?*
. . . the time . . .	*la hora*	When?	*¿Cuando?*
What is there to eat?	*¿Qué hay para comer?*	Where?	*¿Donde?*

GETTING ABOUT

How do I get to . . . ?	*¿Cómo se va a . . . ?*	. . . the post office . . .	*el correo (la oficina de*
Left, right, straight	*Izquierda, derecha, derecho*		*correos)*
ahead		. . . the toilet . . .	*los aseos/el retrete*
Old inter-village track	*Camino*	Where does the bus	*¿De dónde sale*
Trail	*Sendero, senda*	to . . . leave from?	*el autobús para . . . ?*
Forest road	*Pista forestal*	Is this the train for Jaca?	*¿Es este el tren para Jaca?*
Where is . . . ?	*¿Dónde esta . . . ?*	I'd like a (single/	*Querría un billete*
. . . the bus station . . .	*la estación de autobuses*	return) ticket to . . .	*(sencillo/de ida y vuelta)*
. . . the train station . . .	*la estación de*		*para . . .*
	ferrocarriles	What time does it	*¿A qué hora sale*
. . . the nearest bank . . .	*el banco mas cercano*	leave (arrive at . . .)?	*(llega en . . .)?*

ACCOMMODATION

Do you have . . . ?	*¿Tiene . . . ?*	It's fine, how much is it?	*Está bien, ¿cuanto es?*
. . . a room . . .	*una habitación*	It's too expensive	*Es demasiado (caro)*
. . . with two beds/	*con dos camas/*	Don't you have	*¿No tiene algo más*
double bed . . .	*cama matrimonial*	anything cheaper?	*barato?*
It's for one person	*Es para una persona*	Can one . . . ? . . .	*¿Se puede . . . ?*
(two people)	*(dos personas)*	camp (near) here?	*acampar aquí (cerca)?*
. . . for one night	*. . . para una noche*	Is there a hostel/	*¿Hay una albergue/*
(one week)	*(una semana)*	fonda/hostal nearby?	*fonda/hostal aquí cerca?*

NUMBERS

1	*un/uno/una*	14	*catorce*	80	*ochenta*
2	*dos*	15	*quince*	90	*noventa*
3	*tres*	16	*diez y seis* or *dieciséis*	100	*cien(to)*
4	*cuatro*	17	*diez y siete* or *diecisiete*	101	*ciento uno*
5	*cinco*	18	*diez y ocho* or *dieciocho*	200	*doscient(os)/(as)*
6	*seis*	19	*diez y nueve* or *diecinueve*	500	*quinient(os)/(as)*
7	*siete*	20	*veinte*	700	*setecient(os)/(as)*
8	*ocho*	21	*veintiuno*	1000	*mil*
9	*nueve*	30	*treinta*	2000	*dos mil*
10	*diez*	40	*cuarenta*	first	*primer(o)/(a)*
11	*once*	50	*cincuenta*	second	*segund(o)/(a)*
12	*doce*	60	*sesenta*	third	*tercer(o)/(a)*
13	*trece*	70	*setenta*		

DAYS AND DATES

January	*Enero*	September	*Se(p)tiembre*	Friday	*Viernes*
February	*Febrero*	October	*Octubre*	Saturday	*Sábado*
March	*Marzo*	November	*Noviembre*	Sunday	*Domingo*
April	*Abril*	December	*Diciembre*	1998	*mil novecientos*
May	*Mayo*	Monday	*Lunes*		*noventa y ocho*
June	*Junio*	Tuesday	*Martes*	2003	*dos mil tres*
July	*Julio*	Wednesday	*Miércoles*		
August	*Agosto*	Thursday	*Jueves*		

CATALAN PRONUNCIATION

IG or **TG**	sound like "tch" in scratch; thus *Contraig* is pronounced "contraytch", *Mitg* sounds like "meetch"	**L.L**	pronounced as two separate "l"s
		L-L	pronounced as two separate "l"s
		NY	replaces the Castilian Ñ
Ç	is like S; *plaça* is pronounced "plassa"	**T**	can sound like D, as in the words *viatge* (pronounced "veeadzheh") or *dotze* (pronounced "dodzeh")
C	followed by E or I is a soft S-sound, not a TH as in Castilian	**UI**	is same as U – the I is silent; thus "maduixa" sounds like "madusha", "puig" like "pootch"
G	followed by E or I is like the "zh" in Zhivago; otherwise hard		
J	is soft as in French, unlike the Castilian *jota*	**X**	is like CH when initial, SH when medial, but as in English for certain loan-words like *excursionista*
LL	as in Castilian, even when final, which case doesn't exist in Castilian – thus "Ripoll" sounds like "ripoy"	**Y**	in the final syllable is virtually silent: thus "Morunys" sounds like *morunsh*, "Montgrony" like *montgron'*

The boxes above/opposite/overpage contain lists of a few useful words and phrases that will enable you generally to get what you want. Anyone travelling for any length of time, however, would be well advised to invest in a decent dictionary or phrasebook. A cursory glance at a Spanish **dictionary** might be perplexing – bear in mind that until 1994 CH, LL and Ñ counted as separate letters, and in older dictionaries will still be found after the C, L and N words respectively.

EUSKERA AND CATALAN

After French and Castilian, the two most prevalent languages of the Pyrenees are Euskera and Catalan. There are no written records of

Euskera, the Basque tongue, before the Middle Ages, even though it had been spoken for at least a thousand years by then. Its origins are contentious: some scholars propose that it can be traced to a language spoken on the Iberian peninsula before the Roman occupation, while others maintain that it bears a familial resemblance to certain Caucasian languages, such as Georgian. There are currently about half a million Euskera-speakers in Spain and France, at the western end of the Pyrenees.

Catalan, a Romance language evolved from medieval Provençal, survived centralist campaigns either favouring Castilian or actively suppressing *Català* (as it calls itself), from the fif-

CASTILIAN AND CATALAN LEARNING MATERIALS

Spanish Rough Guide Phrasebook (Rough Guides). Mini dictionary-style phrasebook, with Castilian–English and English–Castilian sections, cultural tips and menu-masters.

España Viva and Dígame (BBC). Decent tape-only series to get you started in a hurry.

Breakthrough Spanish (Pan Macmillan, UK). The best teach-yourself course comprising a book and 2 cassettes.

Collins Gem Spanish Dictionary (HarperCollins, UK). Compact, cheap and good enough for most beginner's queries.

Teach Yourself Catalan (Hodder & Stoughton, UK; David Mackay, US). A not very ambitious primer, presented in English.

Catalan Grammar (Dolphin Book Company). Exactly as it says.

Parla Català (Pia, Spain). The only available English–Catalan phrasebook.

Digui Digui (Generalitat de Catalunya). The best total-immersion course if you're serious about learning Catalan, comprising a series of books and tapes. In Britain, it's most easily available at Grant & Cutler, 55 Great Marlborough St, London W1 (☎020/7734 2012).

MOUNTAIN TERMINOLOGY

EASTERN AND CENTRAL PYRENEES

Agua/aigue/aygue	Water	Gorg	Tarn
Aigüeta	Small stream	Grange/granja/ grangera	Barn
Artigue/artiga	Pasture, meadow		
Bal/ball/bat/batch/ val/vall	Valley	Grau	Pass
		Hont/hount	Source of a river
Barrage	Dam	Hourquette/ forqueta/horcado	Steep pass
Borde/borda	Isolated cottage		
Boum	Deep lake	Ibón	Tarn, small lake
Brèche	Gap in a ridge-line	Mas/masia	Farm
Caillaouas	Rocky	Né/ner/nère	Black
Camí	Inter-village drovers' track	Neste	River (Bigorre)
Campana	Pointed rock	Noguera	River (Catalunya)
Can, cal	Isolated lowland farmhouse	Obaga/ ubago/ umbría	North-facing slope
Cap	Highest point on a ridge; also means coastal cape, or the rear/back side of something		
		Oule/oulette	Small "bowl" in terrain
		Pántano/Pantà	Reservoir
		Passerelle/passarella	Suspension bridge, catwalk
Cirque/circ/cirro	Alpine amphitheatre	Peña/Peyre	Prominent rock outcrop
Clot	A depression or narrow valley	Port/porteille/puerto	Pass (implies long use as a trade or pilgrimage route)
Col/coll/collado/ coret/cuello	A pass or saddle		
		Prat/prado/pradère	Meadow
Corral	Enclosure for animals	Pic/puig	Peak
Cortal	Shepherd's hut	Pujol/puy/puyo/ pouey	High point
Coma/Coume	Bare incline between trees		
Desfiladero/ garganta/ congost(o)//foz	Gorge	Raillère/ralhère	Avalanche gallery
		Ribera/ribèra	Riverbank or river valley
		Río/riu	River
Embalse	Reservoir	Salhèt	Riverbank
Eras/Eres	rain barns, usually by a threshing cirque	Salto	Waterfall, cascade
		Seilh	Glacier
Estanyet/estanyol	Small lake, pond	Serre/serra	Serrated, tooth-like ridge
Estibe/estive	High pasture	Soula/solana/ soulane	South-facing slope
Étang/estany/llac	Lake		
Faja/faxa/feixa	Natural terrace in limestone	Soum/turon/turoun	Rounded summit
Farge /fragua	Forge	Tartera/tartère	Scree slope
Font/fount/fuente	Source of a river	Tozal/tuc/tuca	Peak
Gave	River (Béarn)	Veinat	District, neighbourhood

BASQUE PYRENEES

Aran	Valley	Erreka	River	Kayolar/cayolar	Pastoral hut
Ardi	Sheep	Etche/etxe	House	Larra/larria	Moor, pasture
Arri	Stone	Etchola/etxda	Hut	Lepo	Pass
Artz	Bear	Gain/gagna	Summit	Orri/orry	Pastoral hut
Artzain	Shepherd	Gorri	Red	Mendi	Mountain
Beltz	Black	Goyen/gora	High	Oyhan	Forest
Bide	Route	Handi	Big	Portilloua	Pass
Celhay/selhai	Plateau	Harri	Stone	Tchipi/txipi/ttipi/ tiki	Small
Chara	Wood	Hegi	Hill		
Chipi	Small	Ibar	Valley	Ur	Water
Churi/chouri/txuri	White	Ichouri/itxurri	Slope		
Çuby/Zubi	Bridge	Ithourri	River source		

teenth to the twentieth century. Although the teaching, printing and broadcasting of Catalan was prohibited under Franco, it is again a flourishing language, spoken by between three and four million people around the eastern part of the range. Since the early 1990s, all signposting in Catalunya (as well as rural restaurant menus) has been solely in Catalan, the official language.

To the outsider, **written** Catalan is a far easier language to comprehend than Euskera – with a knowledge of both high-school Castilian and French you can get the gist of most tourist pamphlets or trekking booklets in *Català*. **Spoken** *Català*, with its harsh sound and strong dialects, is much harder to follow. The **sounds of letters** in Catalan are often completely different from those of Castilian; the most important points of divergence are summarized in the box (see p.552), enabling you to at least pronounce place-names accurately. Though the Catalans in particular are always delighted if you make some attempt to use their language,

all Basques and Catalans understand and speak Castilian or French as the case may be, if sometimes grudgingly. Thus the basic French and Spanish vocabularies given in this section should be sufficient to make yourself understood as you travel through either end of the Pyrenees.

However, a few **local terms** can be useful for interpreting maps and signs in the Basque and Catalan regions (as well as those French valleys with strong dialects), so a comprehensive "Mountain Terminology" section appears below. Be aware, also, when travelling with internationally published maps that these usually lag well behind nationalistically motivated **name-changing campaigns** in every region of the Pyrenees, but particularly in Aragón and the Basque country. Often the local-vernacular name is proudly displayed on an official highways-division sign, but equally often Castilian or French signs have been suitably "edited" with spray paint.

GLOSSARY

APLEC (Catalan) A pilgrimage to a rural shrine.

APSE Often multiple, semicircular or polygonal terminations at the east end of a church.

AYUNTAMIENTO In Spain, the town hall; *ajuntament* in Catalan.

BAROQUE Late-Renaissance period of art and architecture, distinguished by extreme ornateness.

BARRIO (Castilian) Suburb or quarter.

BASTIDE One of the grid-plan fortified towns established in southern France during the thirteenth century.

CAMINO DE SANTIAGO/CHEMIN DE SAINT-JACQUES The medieval pilgrim's route to the shrine of St James at Santiago de Compostela in northwest Spain, with several branches crossing the Pyrenees west of Luchon.

CARRER Catalan for 'street'.

CATALONIA The geographical and cultural homeland of the Catalan people, disregarding the frontier established between France and Spain in 1659.

CATALUNYA The autonomous region of Spain comprising the provinces of (from northwest to southeast) Lleida, Girona, Barcelona and Tarragona.

CATHARISM Heretical religion of the thirteenth century, with strongholds in the Ariège and Pays de Sault.

CESTA PUNTA The most spectacular, high-speed version of *pelota/pelote*, played by teams of two; sometimes called jaï alaï.

CLAVIJAS A fixed peg-and-chain for hauling yourself up rock faces.

CLOCHER-MUR A triangular bell wall, either freestanding or at one end of the church, often topped with decorative detail and often attributed to the Knights Templar.

CLOISTER Colonnaded walled courtyard, usually Romanesque and square, adjoining a monastic church on its south side.

COLEGIATA (Castilian) Large parish church, not quite ranking with a cathedral.

COMARCA/COMARQUE (Castilian/Catalan). Equivalent to an English county.

COMEDOR Formal dining room of a hotel, or at the rear of a *bar/restaurante*.

COMMUNE Smallest administrative division of the French Pyrenees.

CORREOS/CORREUS (Castilian/Catalan) Post office.

DÉPARTEMENT One of the French administrative provinces created after the Revolution of 1789, replacing the traditional feudal duchies.

DOLMEN Neolithic stone monument, consisting of two or more upright slabs and a capping stone, thought to be either tombs or – from their frequent position on ridgelines – shepherds' shelters.

ERMITA/ERMITAGE (Spain/France). A wayside chapel, usually (but not always) out in the country.

FORFAIT/FORFET (French/Catalan) A daily or multi-day ski-resort pass.

FRESCO A wall painting made more durable by being applied to wet plaster.

FRONTÓN The playing court for *pelota/pelote*, found in most villages of the Basque country.

GENERALITAT The governing authority of Spanish Catalunya.

GOTHIC Architectural style prevalent from the twelfth until the sixteenth century, distinguished by pointed arches and rib-vaulting.

HALLE(S) In France, a covered produce market.

HOSPICE/HOSPITAL/HÔPITAU Medieval travellers' hostel built by religious or chivalric orders, often at the foot of strategic passes.

HÔTEL DE VILLE The town hall of a larger town in France.

ISARD French or Catalan for the Pyrenean chamois or izard, ubiquitous at higher elevations; known as *rebeco* in Castilian, *sarrio* in Aragonese.

MAIRIE The municipal office of a village in France.

MAJESTAT Carved medieval wooden image of a fully dressed Christ, formerly common in Catalunya; most examples were destroyed during the Republican church-sackings of 1936.

MAQUISARD A French resistance fighter of World War II; derived from *maquis*, the dense Mediterranean scrub-forest where they preferred to hide.

MENJADOR Catalan for *comedor*.

MIRADOR A viewing point or platform intended for trekkers or motorists in the mountains.

MODERNISME/MODERNISTA (noun/adjective) Catalan version of Art Nouveau, prevalent between 1890 and 1920, relying heavily on stylized or grotesque forms from the natural world.

MOZARABIC Pertaining to the religion, art/architecture or culture of Mozarabs, medieval Spanish Christians living under Muslim rule.

MUDÉJAR Pertaining to the religion, art/architecture or culture of medieval Spanish Muslims living under Christian rule.

NAVE Main body of a church.

NAVETTE In France, a shuttle bus.

PARADOR Luxury hotel in Spain, often installed in a minor historical monument.

PASADOR/PASSEUR (Castilian/French) Person who during World War II guided refugees and Allied servicemen over the Pyrenees from occupied France into neutral Spain.

PELOTA/PELOTE (Castilian/French) A court ballgame similar to fives/handball, originating in the Basque country, and played in several versions.

PETANCA/PÉTANQUE (Catalan/French). A game, similar to English bowls, where two teams of one to three persons each compete to pitch heavy balls as close as possible to a *cochonnet* or wooden marker jack 6–10m distant. From the Provençal *pied tanqués* or "feet together", after the small circle within which bowlers must stand as they pitch.

PLAÇA Catalan spelling of plaza.

(LA) POSTE (French) The post office.

RETABLE/RETABLO   (French/Castilian). Intricately carved altarpiece.

ROMANESQUE Unadorned, squat architectural style prevalent from the eighth to the thirteenth century; characterized by rounded arches and naively sculpted column capitals.

ROMERÍA In Spain, a religious procession to a rural shrine, often with a venerated image in tow.

SALLE CAPITULAIRE (French) Chapterhouse off a Romanesque cloister, often with fine rib-vaulting.

SANTUARI(O) (Catalan/Castilian) Remote religious shrine, larger and more exalted than an *ermita* – may have permanent staff.

TRANSEPT Transverse arms of a church, perpendicular to the nave.

TRINQUET Smaller version of a *frontón*.

TYMPANUM The vertical, half-circular space above a Romanesque church portal, often decorated with a relief of Christ in Majesty.

URBANIZACIÓ(N) (Catalan/Castilian) Can be any new apartment development, but in this guide refers to a ski-chalet complex surrounding any Spanish Pyrenean village.

VARIANT(E) An alternate routeing of the long-distance trails GR10, GR11 and HRP.

ACRONYMS

ARP *Alto Ruta Pirenaico* in Castilian; see HRP below.

CAF *Club Alpin Français*, the French Alpine Club, administering many staffed refuges.

CEC *Centre Excursionista de Catalunya*, rival to the FEEC (see below).

EDF *Électricité de France*; national power corporation responsible for all dams and dynamos in the Pyrenees.

ENHER Spanish power company active across the Pyrenees.

FAM *Federación Aragonesa de Montañismo*, the Aragonese alpine club and refuge-managing entity.

FECSA Catalan power company restricted to the Catalan Pyrenees.

FEEC *Federació de Entitats Excursionistes de Catalunya*, important alpine club and refuge operator in Catalunya.

FNM *Federación Navarra de Montaña*.

GR *Gran recorrido* (Castilian), *grande randonnée* (French), long-distance trekking trails for which you must have overnighting/mountaineering gear.

HRP *Haute Randonnée Pyrénéenne*, strenuous, longitudinal traverse of the range, sticking close to the watershed.

ICONA *Instituto Nacional Para la Conservación de la Naturaleza*, the Spanish natural resources administrator, responsible for certain picnic grounds, unrestricted campsites and unstaffed shelters.

PNP *Parc National des Pyrénées*, administering most staffed mountain refuges within its area.

PR *Pequeño recorrido* (Castilian), *petite randon-née* (French), resort-based walking itineraries which take a day or less, without special experience or equipment.

RENFE *Red Nacional de Ferrocarriles*, the Spanish state rail corporation.

SNCF *Société Nationale des Chemins de Fer*, the French state rail corporation.

INDEX

Stay in touch with us!

ROUGHNEWS is Rough Guides' free newsletter. In three issues a year we give you news, travel issues, music reviews, readers' letters and the latest dispatches from authors on the road.

I would like to receive ROUGHNEWS: please put me on your free mailing list.

NAME . . . .

ADDRESS . . . .

Please clip or photocopy and send to: Rough Guides, 62–70 Shorts Gardens, London WC2H 9AH, England or Rough Guides, 375 Hudson Street, New York, NY 10014, USA.

IF KNOWLEDGE IS POWER,
THIS ROUGH GUIDE IS A POCKET-SIZED
BATTERING RAM

THE MILLION-COPY BESTSELLER

THE ROUGH GUIDE TO

The
Internet

Angus J. Kennedy

2001 EDITION · FOR PCs AND MACS

£6.00
US$9.95

Written in plain English, with no hint of jargon, the Rough Guide to the Internet will make you an Internet guru in the shortest possible time. It cuts through the hype and makes all others look like nerdy textbooks

AT ALL BOOKSTORES · DISTRIBUTED BY PENGUIN

www.roughguides.com

Check out our Web site for unrivalled travel information on the Internet.
Plan ahead by accessing the full text of our major titles, make travel reservations and keep up to date with the latest news in the Traveller's Journal or by subscribing to our free newsletter ROUGHNEWS · packed with stories from Rough Guide writers.

ROUGH GUIDES: Travel

Alaska
Amsterdam
Andalucia
Argentina
Australia
Austria

Bali & Lombok
Barcelona
Belgium &
  Luxembourg
Belize
Berlin
Brazil
Britain
Brittany &
  Normandy
Bulgaria
California
Canada
Central America
Chile
China
Corsica
Costa Rica
Crete
Croatia
Cuba
Cyprus
Czech & Slovak
  Republics

Dodecanese &
  the East Aegean
Devon &
  Cornwall
Dominican
  Republic
Dordogne & the
  Lot
Ecuador
Egypt
England
Europe
Florida
France
French Hotels &
  Restaurants
  1999
Germany
Goa
Greece
Greek Islands
Guatemala
Hawaii
Holland
Hong Kong &
  Macau
Hungary

Iceland
India
Indonesia
Ionian Islands
Ireland

Israel & the
  Palestinian
  Territories
Italy
Jamaica
Japan
Jordan
Kenya
Lake District
Languedoc &
  Roussillon
Laos
London
Los Angeles
Malaysia,
  Singapore &
  Brunei
Mallorca &
  Menorca
Maya World
Mexico
Morocco
Moscow
Nepal
New England
New York
New Zealand
Norway
Pacific
  Northwest
Paris
Peru
Poland
Portugal
Prague
Provence & the
  Côte d'Azur
The Pyrenees
Romania
St Petersburg
San Francisco

Sardinia
Scandinavia
Scotland
Scottish
  highlands and
  Islands
Sicily
Singapore
South Africa
South India
Southeast Asia
Southwest USA
Spain
Sweden
Switzerland
Syria

Thailand
Trinidad &
  Tobago
Tunisia
Turkey
Tuscany &
  Umbria
USA
Venice
Vienna
Vietnam
Wales
Washington DC
West Africa
Zimbabwe &
  Botswana

AVAILABLE AT ALL GOOD BOOKSHOPS

ROUGH GUIDES: Mini Guides, Travel Specials and Phrasebooks

MINI GUIDES

Antigua
Bangkok
Barbados
Beijing
Big Island of Hawaii
Boston
Brussels
Budapest
Cape Town
Copenhagen
Dublin
Edinburgh

Florence
Honolulu
Ibiza & Formentera
Jerusalem
Las Vegas
Lisbon
London Restaurants
Madeira
Madrid
Malta & Gozo
Maui
Melbourne
Menorca

Montreal
New Orleans

Paris
Rome
Seattle
St Lucia
Sydney
Tenerife
Tokyo
Toronto
Vancouver

TRAVEL SPECIALS

First-Time Asia
First-Time Europe
Women Travel

PHRASEBOOKS

Czech
Dutch
Egyptian Arabic
European
French
German
Greek

Hindi & Urdu
Hungarian
Indonesian
Italian
Japanese
Mandarin
 Chinese
Mexican
 Spanish
Polish
Portuguese
Russian
Spanish
Swahili
Thai
Turkish
Vietnamese

AVAILABLE AT ALL GOOD BOOKSHOPS

ROUGH GUIDES Mini Guides
Travel Specials and Phrasebooks

AVAILABLE AT ALL GOOD BOOKSHOPS

Trans*HIRE*

WorldWide Ltd.

The **A**uckland to **Z**urich of Leisure Car Rental!

Booking car rental <u>before</u> you travel can save you money and problems locally, so take advantage of our fast, friendly service, providing car rental in over 2,000 locations in 30 countries throughout Europe, South Africa, U.S.A, Canada, New Zealand and Australia.

Tel: 0044 + (0)1923 834 910
Tel: 0044 + (0)1923 834 919

41-43 Green Lane. Northwood MIDDX HA6 3AE,UK

TRANSHIRE is a member of Travel industry partner scheme

HOLIDAYS
in the Spanish
PYRENEES

Friendly and informal small group & independent
holidays in the best of the Spanish Pyrenees

- Walking & trekking
- Guided or independent
  holidays
- Cross country skiing
  & snow shoeing
- Hotel Breaks

altoaragon@ctv.es
31 Heathside, Esher, Surrey, KT10 9TD.

Brochures & Enquiries Tel/Fax 01869 337339

Les Sorbiers

Barèges/Hautes-Pyrénées

A warm welcome in a magnificent
mountain setting
Meat and vegetarian cuisine

<u>Summer</u>

Superb walking in the National Park, wildlife tours,
mountain-biking, Tour de France
Free route guides, optional daily programme
of guided activities

<u>Winter</u>

Largest Pyrenean ski area with 125kms piste,
just 200m from lifts
Snowshoe walking, cross-country, ski-touring

**BORDERLINE HOLIDAYS
LES SORBIERS
65120 BAREGES FRANCE**
Tel. : +33 562 926 895 Fax: +33 562 928 343
e-mail: sorbiers@sudfr.com www.borderlinehols.com

Contact Peter or Jude

NORTH SOUTH TRAVEL
Great discounts

North South Travel is a small travel agent offering excellent personal service. Like other air ticket retailers, we offer discount fares worldwide. But unlike others, all available profits contribute to grassroots projects in the South through the NST Development Trust Registered Charity No. 1040656.

For **quotes** or queries, contact Brenda Skinner or Bridget Christopher, Tel/Fax 01245 608 291. Recent **donations** made from the NST Development Trust include support to Djoliba Trust, providing micro-credit to onion growers in the Dogon country in Mali; assistance to displaced people and rural communities in eastern Congo; a grant to Wells For India, which works for clean water in Rajasthan; support to the charity Children of the Andes, working for poverty relief in Colombia; and a grant to the Omari Project which works with drug-dependent young people in Watamu, Kenya.

Great difference

Email brenda@nstravel.demon.co.uk
Website www.nstravel.demon.co.uk

ATOL 75401

North South Travel, Moulsham Mill, Parkway, Chelmsford, Essex, CM2 7PX, UK

Will you have enough stories to tell your grandchildren?

©2000 Yahoo! Inc.

Yahoo! Travel

Do You YAHOO!?